T0253697

Lecture Notes in Computer Science 10784

Commenced Publication in 1973
Founding and Former Series Editors:
Gerhard Goos, Juris Hartmanis, and Jan van Leeuwen

More information about this series at http://www.springer.com/series/7407

Kevin Sim · Paul Kaufmann et al. (Eds.)

Applications of Evolutionary Computation

21st International Conference, EvoApplications 2018
Parma, Italy, April 4–6, 2018
Proceedings

 Springer

Editors

see next page

ISSN 0302-9743   ISSN 1611-3349   (electronic)
Lecture Notes in Computer Science
ISBN 978-3-319-77537-1   ISBN 978-3-319-77538-8   (eBook)
https://doi.org/10.1007/978-3-319-77538-8

Library of Congress Control Number: 2018935897

LNCS Sublibrary: SL1 – Theoretical Computer Science and General Issues

Printed on acid-free paper

This Springer imprint is published by the registered company Springer International Publishing AG
part of Springer Nature
The registered company address is: Gewerbestrasse 11, 6330 Cham, Switzerland

Volume Editors

Kevin Sim (ORCID)
Edinburgh Napier University
UK
k.sim@napier.ac.uk

Paul Kaufmann (ORCID)
Mainz University
Germany
paul.kaufmann@gmail.com

Gerd Ascheid
RWTH Aachen University
Germany
gerd.ascheid@ice.rwth-aachen.de

Jaume Bacardit
Newcastle University
UK
jaume.bacardit@newcastle.ac.uk

Stefano Cagnoni
University of Parma
Italy
cagnoni@ce.unipr.it

Carlos Cotta
Universidad de Málaga
Spain
ccottap@lcc.uma.es

Fabio D'Andreagiovanni
CNRS, UTC - Sorbonne University
France
d.andreagiovanni@hds.utc.fr

Federico Divina
Universidad Pablo de Olavide Sevilla
Spain
fdivina@upo.es

Anna I. Esparcia-Alcázar
Universitat Politècnica de València
Spain
esparcia@upv.es

Francisco Fernández de Vega
University of Extremadura
Spain
fcofdez@unex.es

Kyrre Glette
University of Oslo
Norway
kyrrehg@ifi.uio.no

J. Ignacio Hidalgo
Universidad Complutense de Madrid
Spain
hidalgo@ucm.es

Julien Hubert
Vrije Universiteit Amsterdam
Netherlands
jghubert@gmail.com

Giovanni Iacca
RWTH Aachen University
Germany
giovanni.iacca@gmail.com

Oliver Kramer
University of Oldenburg
Germany
oliver.kramer@uni-oldenburg.de

Michalis Mavrovouniotis
Nottingham Trent University
UK
michalis.mavrovouniotis@ntu.ac.uk

Antonio M. Mora García
Universidad Internacional de La Rioja
Spain
antoniomiguel.mora@unir.net

Trung Thanh Nguyen
Liverpool John Moores University
UK
T.T.Nguyen@ljmu.ac.uk

Robert Schaefer
AGH University of Science
and Technology
Poland
schaefer@agh.edu.pl

Sara Silva
Faculdade de Ciências, Universidade
de Lisboa
Portugal
sara@fc.ul.pt

Alberto Tonda
INRA
France
alberto.tonda@grignon.inra.fr

Neil Urquhart
Edinburgh Napier University
UK
n.urquhart@napier.ac.uk

Mengjie Zhang
Victoria University of Wellington
New Zealand
mengjie.zhang@ecs.vuw.ac.nz

Preface

This volume contains the proceedings of EvoApplications 2018, the International Conference on the Applications of Evolutionary Computation. The event was held in Parma, Italy, during April 4–6.

EvoAPPS, as it is familiarly called, is part of Evo*, the leading event on bio-inspired computation in Europe. EvoAPPS aimed to show the applications of the research, ranging from proofs of concept to industrial case studies. At the same time, under the Evo* umbrella, EuroGP focused on the technique of genetic programming, EvoCOP targeted evolutionary computation in combinatorial optimization, and EvoMUSART was dedicated to evolved and bio-inspired music, sound, art and design. The proceedings for all of these co-located events are available in the LNCS series.

This edition combines research from 14 different domains: business analytics and finance (EvoBAFIN track); computational biology (EvoBIO track); communication networks and other parallel and distributed systems (EvoCOMNET track); complex systems (EvoCOMPLEX track); energy-related optimization (EvoENERGY track); games and multi-agent systems (EvoGAMES track); image analysis, signal processing, and pattern recognition (EvoIASP track); real-world industrial and commercial environments (EvoINDUSTRY track); knowledge incorporation in evolutionary computation (EvoKNOW track); continuous parameter optimization (EvoNUM track); parallel architectures and distributed infrastructures (EvoPAR track); evolutionary robotics (EvoROBOT track); nature-inspired algorithms in software engineering and testing (EvoSET track); and stochastic and dynamic environments (EvoSTOC track).

This year we received 84 high-quality submissions, most of them well suited to fit in more than one track. We selected 36 papers for full oral presentation, while a further 23 works were presented as posters. All contributions, regardless of the presentation format, appear as full papers in this volume (LNCS 10784).

Many people contributed to this edition: We express our gratitude to the authors for submitting their works, and to the members of the Program Committees for devoting such a big effort to review papers pressed by our tight schedule.

The papers were submitted, reviewed, and selected through the MyReview conference management system, and we are grateful to Marc Schoenauer (Inria, Saclay-Île-de-France, France) for providing, hosting, and managing the platform.

We would also like to thank the local organizing team led by Stefano Cagnoni and Monica Mordonini from the University of Parma, Italy, for providing such an enticing venue and arranging an array of additional activities for delegates.

We would like to acknowledge Pablo García Sánchez (University of Cádiz, Spain) for his continued support in maintaining the Evo* website and handling publicity.

We credit the invited keynote speakers, Una-May O'Reilly (MIT Computer Science and Artificial Intelligence Laboratory, USA) and Penousal Machado (Computational Design and Visualization Lab at the University of Coimbra, Portugal), for their fascinating and inspiring presentations.

We are grateful to the support provided by SPECIES, the Society for the Promotion of Evolutionary Computation in Europe and Its Surroundings, and its individual members (Marc Schoenauer, President; Anna I. Esparcia-Alcázar, Secretary and Vice-President; Wolfgang Banzhaf, Treasurer) for the coordination and financial administration.

And last but not least, we express our continued appreciation to Jennifer Willies for her ongoing support and expertise as one of the founding organizers of Evo* and also to Anna I Esparcia-Alcázar, from Universitat Politècnica de València, Spain, whose considerable efforts in managing and coordinating Evo* helped to build our unique, vibrant, and friendly atmosphere.

February 2018

Kevin Sim
Paul Kaufmann
Gerd Ascheid
Jaume Bacardit
Stefano Cagnoni
Carlos Cotta
Fabio D'Andreagiovanni
Federico Divina
Anna I. Esparcia-Alcázar
Francisco Fernández de Vega
Kyrre Glette
Julien Hubert
J. Ignacio Hidalgo

Giovanni Iacca
Michael Kampouridis
Oliver Kramer
Michalis Mavrovouniotis
Antonio M. Mora García
Trung Thanh Nguyen
Fernando Otero
Robert Schaefer
Sara Silva
Alberto Tonda
Neil Urquhart
Mengjie Zhang

Organization

EvoApplications Coordinator

Kevin Sim   Edinburgh Napier University, UK

EvoApplications Publication Chair

Paul Kaufmann   Mainz University, Germany

Local Chairs

Stefano Cagnoni   University of Parma, Italy
Monica Mordonini   University of Parma, Italy

Publicity Chair

Pablo García Sánchez   University of Cádiz, Spain

EvoBAFIN Chairs

Michael Kampouridis   University of Kent, UK
Fernando Otero   University of Kent, UK

EvoBIO Chairs

Federico Divina   Universidad Pablo de Olavide, Seville, Spain
Jaume Bacardit   Newcastle University, UK

EvoCOMNET Chairs

Fabio D'Andreagiovanni   CNRS, UTC - Sorbonne University, France
Giovanni Iacca   RWTH Aachen University, Germany

EvoCOMPLEX Chairs

Carlos Cotta   Universidad de Málaga, Spain
Robert Schaefer   AGH University of Science and Technology, Poland

EvoENERGY Chairs

Paul Kaufmann   Mainz University, Germany
Oliver Kramer   University of Oldenburg, Germany

EvoGAMES Chairs

Antonio M. Mora García	Universidad Internacional de La Rioja, Spain
Alberto Tonda	INRA, France

EvoIASP Chairs

Stefano Cagnoni	University of Parma, Italy
Mengjie Zhang	Victoria University of Wellington, New Zealand

EvoINDUSTRY Chairs

Kevin Sim	Edinburgh Napier University, UK
Neil Urquhart	Edinburgh Napier University, UK

EvoKNOW Chairs

Giovanni Iacca	RWTH Aachen University, Germany
Gerd Ascheid	RWTH Aachen University, Germany

EvoNUM Chair

Anna I. Esparcia-Alcázar	Universitat Politècnica de València, Spain

EvoPAR Chairs

Francisco Fernández de Vega	University of Extremadura, Spain
J. Ignacio Hidalgo	Universidad Complutense de Madrid, Spain

EvoROBOT Chairs

Kyrre Glette	University of Oslo, Norway
Julien Hubert	Vrije Universiteit Amsterdam, The Netherlands

EvoSET Chairs

Anna I. Esparcia-Alcázar	Universitat Politècnica de València, Spain
Sara Silva	Faculdade de Ciências, Universidade de Lisboa, Portugal

EvoSTOC Chairs

Michalis Mavrovouniotis   Nottingham Trent University, UK
Trung Thanh Nguyen   Liverpool John Moores University, UK

Program Committees

Bahriye Basturk Akay	Erciyes University, Turkey [EvoINDUSTRY]
Jhon Amaya	UNET, Venezuela [EvoCOMPLEX]
Jacopo Aleotti	University of Parma, Italy [EvoIASP]
Michele Amoretti	University of Parma, Italy [EvoIASP]
Anca Andreica	Universitatea Babeş-Bolyai, Romania [EvoCOMPLEX]
Jarosław Arabas	Warsaw University of Technology, Poland [EvoKNOW]
Antonio Fernández Ares	Universidad de Granada, Spain [EvoGAMES]
Ignacio Arnaldo	PatternEx, USA [EvoPAR]
María Arsuaga-Ríos	CERN [EvoINDUSTRY]
Jason Atkin	University of Nottingham, UK [EvoINDUSTRY]
Joshua Auerbach	Champlain College, USA [EvoROBOT]
Lucia Ballerini	University of Edinburgh, UK [EvoIASP]
Tiago Baptista	Universidade de Coimbra, Portugal [EvoCOMPLEX]
Thomas Bauschert	Technical University Chemnitz, Germany [EvoCOMNET]
Vitoantonio Bevilacqua	Politecnico di Bari, Italy [EvoIASP]
Hans-Georg Beyer	Vorarlberg University of Applied Sciences, Austria [EvoNUM]
Leonardo Bocchi	University of Florence, Italy [EvoIASP]
János Botzheim	Tokyo Metropolitan University, Japan [EvoKNOW]
Juergen Branke	University of Warwick, UK [EvoSTOC]
Nicolas Bredeche	Institut des Systèmes Intelligents et de Robotique, France [EvoROBOT]
Jörg Bremer	University of Oldenburg, Germany [EvoENERGY]
Cédric Buche	ENIB, France [EvoGAMES]
Doina Bucur	University of Twente, The Netherlands [EvoCOMNET, EvoKNOW]
Aleksander Byrski	AGH University of Science and Technology, Poland [EvoCOMPLEX]
Raúl Lara Cabrera	Universidad Autónoma de Madrid, Spain [EvoGAMES]
David Camacho	Universidad Autónoma de Madrid, Spain [EvoGAMES]
Fabio Caraffini	De Montfort University, UK [EvoKNOW]
Hui Cheng	Liverpool John Moores University, UK [EvoSTOC]
Luca Chiaraviglio	University of Rome Tor Vergata, Italy [EvoCOMNET]
Francisco Chicano	Universidad de Málaga, Spain [EvoSET]

Anders Christensen	University Institute of Lisbon, ISCTE-IUL, Portugal [EvoROBOT]
Antonio Della Cioppa	University of Salerno, Italy [EvoIASP]
Myra Cohen	University of Nebraska, USA [EvoSET]
José Manuel Colmenar	Universidad Rey Juan Carlos, Spain [EvoPAR]
Stefano Coniglio	University of Southampton, UK [EvoCOMNET]
Ernesto Costa	University of Coimbra, Portugal [EvoSTOC]
Sam Cramer	University of Kent, UK [EvoBAFIN]
Antonio Córdoba	Universidad de Sevilla, Spain [EvoCOMPLEX]
Anthony Clark	Michigan State University, USA [EvoROBOT]
Christian Darabos	University of Pennsylvania, USA [EvoBIO]
Stephane Doncieux	Institut des Systèmes Intelligents et de Robotique, France [EvoROBOT]
Bernabé Dorronsoro	Universidad de Cádiz, Spain [EvoCOMPLEX]
Jitesh Dundas	Indian Institute of Technology, India [EvoBIO]
Marc Ebner	Ernst Moritz Arndt University, Greifswald, Germany [EvoIASP]
Aniko Ekart	Aston University, UK [EvoINDUSTRY]
Kai Olav Ellefsen	University of Oslo, Norway [EvoROBOT]
Andries P. Engelbrecht	University of Pretoria, South Africa [EvoSTOC]
Şima Etaner-Uyar	Istanbul Technical University, Turkey [EvoNUM]
Ivanoe De Falco	ICAR - CNR, Italy [EvoIASP]
Thomas Farrenkopf	Technische Hochschule Mittelhessen, Germany [EvoINDUSTRY]
Carlos Fernandes	University of Lisbon, Portugal [EvoCOMPLEX]
Gianluigui Folino	ICAR-CNR, Italy [EvoPAR]
Francesco Fontanella	University of Cassino, Italy [EvoIASP]
Gordon Fraser	University of Sheffield, UK [EvoSET]
Alex Freitas	University of Kent, UK [EvoBIO]
Mario Garza	Liverpool John Moores University, UK [EvoSTOC]
Gregory Gay	University of South Carolina, USA [EvoSET]
Mario Giacobini	Universitá di Torino, Italy [EvoBIO]
Raffaele Giancarlo	Università degli Studi di Palermo, Italy [EvoBIO]
Rosalba Giugno	University of Verona, Italy [EvoBIO]
Michael Guckert	Technische Hochschule Mittelhessen, Germany [EvoINDUSTRY]
Evert Haasdijk	VU University Amsterdam, The Netherlands [EvoROBOT]
Ahmed Hallawa	RWTH Aachen University, Germany [EvoKNOW]
Heiko Hamann	University of Lübeck, Germany [EvoROBOT]
Jin-Kao Hao	University of Angers, France [EvoBIO]
Emma Hart	Edinburgh Napier University, UK [EvoINDUSTRY]
Jacqueline Heinerman	VU University Amsterdam, The Netherlands [EvoROBOT]
Daniel Hernández	Instituto Tecnológico Nacional, Mexico [EvoPAR]

Malcom Heywood	Dalhousie University, Canada [EvoBAFIN]
Ronald Hochreiter	WU Vienna University of Economics and Business, Austria [EvoBAFIN]
Rolf Hoffmann	Technical University Darmstadt, Germany [EvoCOMNET]
Ting Hu	Memorial University, Canada [EvoBIO]
Joost Huizinga	University of Wyoming, USA [EvoROBOT]
Andreas Kassler	Karlstad University, Sweden [EvoCOMNET]
Shayan Kavakeb	AECOM, UK [EvoSTOC]
Graham Kendall	University of Nottingham, UK [EvoINDUSTRY]
Mario Koeppen	Kyushu Institute of Technology, Japan [EvoIASP]
Wacław Kuś	Silesian University of Technology, Poland [EvoCOMPLEX]
Fergal Lane	University of Limerick, Ireland [EvoKNOW]
William B. Langdon	University College London, UK [EvoNUM, EvoPAR]
Juan Luis Jiménez Laredo	Université du Havre, France [EvoCOMPLEX, EvoPAR]
Antonio Fernández Leiva	Universidad de Málaga, Spain [EvoGAMES]
Charly Lersteau	Liverpool John Moores University, UK [EvoSTOC]
Changhe Li	China University of Geosciences, China [EvoSTOC]
Antonios Liapis	University of Malta, Malta [EvoGAMES]
Federico Liberatore	Universidad Carlos III, Spain [EvoGAMES]
Piotr Lipinski	University of Wroclaw, Poland [EvoBAFIN]
Francisco Luna	Universidad de Málaga, Spain [EvoPAR]
Evelyne Lutton	INRA, France [EvoIASP]
Chenjie Ma	Fraunhofer Institute for Wind Energy and Energy System Technology, Germany [EvoENERGY]
Tobias Mahlmann	Lund University, Sweden [EvoGAMES]
Carlo Mannino	Sintef, Norway [EvoCOMNET]
Elena Marchiori	Radboud Universiteit van Nijmegen, The Netherlands [EvoBIO]
Ingo Mauser	Karlsruhe Institute of Technology, Germany [EvoENERGY]
Michalis Mavrovouniotis	Nottingham Trent University, UK [EvoSTOC]
Michael Mayo	University of Waikato, New Zealand [EvoBAFIN]
Vinícius Veloso de Melo	UNIFESP-SJC, Brazil [EvoKNOW]
Tim Menzies	University of Nebraska, USA [EvoSET]
Juan Julián Merelo	Universidad de Granada, Spain [EvoGAMES, EvoCOMPLEX, EvoNUM]
Martin Middendorf	University of Leipzig, Germany [EvoENERGY]
Wiem Mkaouer	University of Michigan, USA [EvoSET]
Maizura Mokhtar	Heriot-Watt University, UK [EvoENERGY]
Jean-Marc Montanier	Softbank Robotics Europe, France [EvoROBOT]
Roberto Montemanni	IDSIA, Switzerland [EvoCOMNET]
Jared Moore	Grand Valley State University, USA [EvoROBOT]
Vincent Moulton	University of East Anglia, UK [EvoBIO]

Jean-Baptiste Mouret	Inria Larsen Team, France [EvoROBOT]
Nysret Musliu	Vienna University of Technology, Austria [EvoINDUSTRY]
Enrico Natalizio	UTC - Sorbonne University, France [EvoCOMNET]
Boris Naujoks	TH Cologne University of Applied Sciences, Germany [EvoNUM]
Antonio Nebro	Universidad de Málaga, Spain [EvoCOMPLEX]
Ferrante Neri	De Montfort University, UK [EvoNUM, EvoIASP, EvoKNOW, EvoSTOC]
Geoff Nitschke	University of Cape Town, South Africa [EvoROBOT]
Rafael Nogueras	Universidad de Málaga, Spain [EvoCOMPLEX]
Stefano Nolfi	Institute of Cognitive Sciences and Technologies, Italy [EvoROBOT]
Gustavo Olague	CICESE, México [EvoPAR]
Carlotta Orsenigo	Politecnico di Milano, Italy [EvoBIO]
Ender Ozcan	University of Nottingham, UK [EvoINDUSTRY]
Ben Paechter	Edinburgh Napier University, UK [EvoINDUSTRY]
Peter Palensky	Technical University of Delft, The Netherlands [EvoENERGY]
Antonio González Pardo	Universidad Autónoma de Madrid, Spain [EvoGAMES]
Anna Paszyńska	Jagiellonian University, Poland [EvoCOMPLEX]
Riccardo Pecori	eCampus University, Italy [EvoCOMNET]
David Pelta	University of Granada, Spain [EvoSTOC]
Raffaele Perego	ISTI-CNR, Italy [EvoPAR]
Sanja Petrovic	University of Nottingham, UK [EvoINDUSTRY]
Nelishia Pillay	University of KwaZulu-Natal, South Africa [EvoINDUSTRY]
Clara Pizzuti	ICAR-CNR, Italy [EvoBIO]
Mihai Polceanu	ENIB, France [EvoGAMES]
Riccardo Poli	University of Essex, UK [EvoIASP]
Arkadiusz Poteralski	Silesian University of Technology, Poland [EvoCOMPLEX]
Simon Powers	Edinburgh Napier University, UK [EvoINDUSTRY]
Petr Pošík	Czech Technical University in Prague, Czech Republic [EvoNUM]
Mike Preuss	University of Münster, Germany [EvoGAMES, EvoNUM]
Mauricio Resende	Amazon, USA [EvoCOMNET]
Jose Carlos Ribeiro	Politechnique Institute of Leiria, Portugal [EvoPAR]
Hendrik Richter	Leipzig University of Applied Sciences, Germany [EvoSTOC]
Florentino Fernández Riverola	Universidad de Vigo, Spain [EvoBIO]
Simona Rombo	Università degli Studi di Palermo, Italy [EvoBIO]

Claudio Rossi   Universidad Politecnica de Madrid, Spain
                               [EvoROBOT]
Guenter Rudolph   University of Dortmund, Germany [EvoNUM]
Mohammed Salem   University of Mascara, Algeria [EvoGAMES]
Pablo Mesejo Santiago   University of Granada, Spain [EvoIASP]
Pablo García Sánchez   Universidad de Cádiz, Spain [EvoGAMES]
Sanem Sariel   Istanbul Technical University, Turkey
                               [EvoINDUSTRY]
Thomas Schmickl   University of Graz, Austria [EvoROBOT]
Sevil Sen   Hacettepe University, Turkey [EvoCOMNET]
Chien-Chung Shen   University of Delaware, USA [EvoCOMNET]
Anabela Simões   Institute Polytechnic of Coimbra, Portugal [EvoSTOC]
Moshe Sipper   Ben-Gurion University, Israel [EvoGAMES]
Stephen Smith   University of York, UK [EvoIASP]
Maciej Smołka   AGH University of Science and Technology, Poland
                               [EvoCOMPLEX]
Andy Song   RMIT, Australia [EvoIASP]
Andreas Steyven   Edinburgh Napier University, UK [General]
Giovanni Squillero   Politecnico di Torino, Italy [EvoGAMES, EvoIASP]
Jose Santos Reyes   Universidad de A Coruña, Spain [EvoBIO]
Ke Tang   University of Science and Technology of China, China
                               [EvoNUM]
Andrea Tettamanzi   University of Nice Sophia Antipolis/I3S, France
                               [EvoBAFIN]
Renato Tinós   Universidade de São Paulo, Brazil [EvoSTOC]
Julian Togelius   New York University, USA [EvoGAMES]
Krzysztof Trojanowski   Cardinal Stefan Wyszyński University in Warsaw,
                               Poland [EvoSTOC]
Wojciech Turek   AGH University of Science and Technology, Poland
                               [EvoCOMPLEX]
Ryan Urbanowicz   University of Pennsylvania, USA [EvoBIO]
Andrea Valsecchi   University of Granada, Spain [EvoIASP]
Leonardo Vanneschi   Universidade Nova de Lisboa, Portugal [EvoIASP]
Sebastien Varrete   Université du Luxemburg, Luxemburg [EvoPAR]
Nadarajen Veerapen   University of Stirling, UK [EvoINDUSTRY]
Francisco Goméz Vela   Pablo de Olavide University, Spain [EvoBIO]
José Manuel Velasco   Universidad Complutense de Madrid, Spain [EvoPAR]
Marco Villani   University of Modena and Reggio Emilia, Italy
                               [EvoCOMNET]
Rafael Villanueva   Universitat Politecnica de Valencia, Spain [EvoPAR]
Tanja Vos   Open University, The Netherlands [EvoSET]
Jaroslaw Was   AGH University of Science and Technology, Poland
                               [EvoCOMNET]
Simon Wells   Edinburgh Napier University, UK [EvoINDUSTRY]
David White   University College London, UK [EvoSET]

Bing Xue   University of Wellington, New Zeland [EvoBIO,
                               EvoIASP]
Anil Yaman   Technical University of Eindhoven, The Netherlands
                               [EvoKNOW]
Shengxiang Yang   De Monfort University, UK [EvoINDUSTRY,
                               EvoSTOC]
Georgios Yannakakis   University of Malta, Malta [EvoGAMES]
Danial Yazdani   Liverpool John Moores University, UK [EvoSTOC]
Aleš Zamuda   University of Maribor, Slovenia [EvoKNOW]
Nur Zincir-Heywood   Dalhousie University, Canada [EvoCOMNET]

Contents

EvoCOMPLEX

EvoENERGY

EvoGAMES

EvoIASP

EvoINDUSTRY

EvoKNOW

EvoSTOC

General

EvoBAFIN

Multi-objective Cooperative Coevolutionary Algorithm with Dynamic Species-Size Strategy

Karoon Suksonghong[1(✉)] and Kittipong Boonlong[2]

[1] Faculty of Management and Tourism, Burapha University, Saen Suk, Thailand
karoon@buu.ac.th
[2] Faculty of Engineering, Burapha University, Saen Suk, Thailand
kittipong@buu.ac.th

Abstract. Although numbers of heuristic algorithms are successfully developed for solving portfolio optimization problems, this is not for all cases of the large-scale ones. A large-scale portfolio optimization involves dealing with the large search space and dense variance-covariance matrix associated with the problem. This paper proposed a new multi-objective algorithm for solving a large-scale optimization problem based upon the notion of cooperative coevolutionary algorithms (CCA). The new problem decomposition scheme was designed by allowing the species-size to be dynamically adjusted as the runs progress. This scheme enhances capability of traditional CCA in dealing with non-separable optimization problem. The collaborator selection method was modified to allow the proposed CCA to perform in a multi-objective (MO) optimization framework. Additionally, the proposed algorithm, named as "DMOCCA", was implemented for solving large-scale portfolio optimization problem with cardinality constraint using the real-world data set having scale up to 2196 dimensions. Moreover, its performances were benchmarked with those of the SPEA-II and MOPSO.

Keywords: Cardinality · Cooperative coevolutionary
Dynamic problem decomposition · Large-scale optimization
Portfolio selection

1 Introduction

Intuitively, one plausible way to handle a large domain problem is to employ a divide-and-conquer strategy. The cooperative coevolutionary algorithm (CCA) proposed by Potter and De Jong [1] offers a convincing framework for decomposing and solving a large-scale problem at the same time. CCA is able to focus the search on relevant areas while simultaneously making adaptive changes between interacting and evolving activities. Basically, CCA involves the use of multiple species to represent a complete solution. By decomposing a full solution vector into multiple species, the search space in which algorithm has to explore is significantly reduced. For instance, in the case that a solution is encoded into a binary chromosome of length 100, the number of possible solutions is $1.27 \times 10^{30} = 2^{100}$. On the other hand, by dividing a full solution into 20 species and each species is represented by a 5-bit binary string, the

© Springer International Publishing AG, part of Springer Nature 2018
K. Sim and P. Kaufmann (Eds.): EvoApplications 2018, LNCS 10784, pp. 3–17, 2018.
https://doi.org/10.1007/978-3-319-77538-8_1

number of possible solutions is reduced to only $20 \times 2^5 = 640$ which allows an algorithm to discover the optimal solutions faster and more efficient.

Potter and De Jong [1] applied this framework for solving the optimization problems having decision variables up to 30. The experimented results revealed that CCA outperformed the conventional GA on the separable problems; however, it performed worse on the non-separable problems. Subsequently, Liu et al. [2] developed the fast evolutionary programming (FEP) and integrated it with CCA. The resulting algorithm was successfully implemented for solving the optimization functions having decision variables up to 1,000. They reported that, however, the proposed algorithm was trapped in the local optima when dealing with non-separable functions. It is clear that the interdependency among variables raises difficulties in CCA execution.

It is argued that effectiveness of CCA depends heavily on problem decomposition method [3, 4]. In the past decade, several works proposed new problem decomposition strategies to address interdependency issues. For example, Van den Bergh and Engelbrecht [3], who integrated CCA with particle swarm optimization (PSO) algorithms, decomposed n decision variables into K species. Each species contains s individuals, i.e. $n = K \times s$. Therefore, each species represents s variables rather than one variable as the case of the original CCA. However, the members in each species were not altered as iterations progress. Shi et al. [4] proposed the cooperative coevolutionary differential evolution (CCDE) with splitting-in-half decomposition strategy. In their work, the problem was divided into two subcomponents and evolution of these subcomponents was performed separately. Similarly, the members of these two subcomponents were not changed throughout the algorithm runs. The common underlying idea of these two strategies is to increase the number of variables in each species, i.e. species-size, by expecting that the interacting variables will be placed within the same species. However, these two static decomposition strategies require *a priori* knowledge about the structure of the problem at hand and perform poorly when the problem size is very large [5, 6].

Instead of using static decomposition strategy, the species-size and the species member that can be dynamically adjusted during run time using rules pre-specified by algorithm settings could be useful for alleviating problems mentioned earlier. Yang et al. [5] proposed a new dynamic decomposition strategy, the so-called "*random grouping*", based on probability assignment and integrated this idea with CCDE for solving non-separable problem with 1,000 variables. This decomposition method allows group size, i.e. species-size, to be varied throughout the course of optimization. They demonstrated that the more often the grouping size is adjusted, the higher the probability the interacting variables will be placed within the same group In the time since this remarkable decomposition strategy was published, the superiorities of dynamic decomposition CCA for solving non-separable functions were widely reported [7–9].

In this paper, we developed multi-objective CCA (MOCCA) for solving a large-scale optimization problem. To enhance the capability of the proposed MOCCA, a new problem decomposition scheme based upon dynamic species-size strategy and the dynamic process were developed. Concurrently, collaborator selection scheme was designed in order to allow CCA to perform in multi-objective framework. Then, the proposed MOCCA, denoted by "DMOCCA", was tested for solving the large-scale cardinality constraint mean-variance portfolio optimization problem (CCMVPOP) with problem size up to 2196 variables. Lastly, its performance was benchmarked with that of the SPEA-II [10] and MOPSO [11].

This paper is organized as follows. The detailed developments of the MOCCA with dynamic species-size strategy are described in Sect. 2. Section 3 discusses and formulates the portfolio optimization problem. The experimented results are reported in Sect. 4 and conclusion is given in Sect. 5.

2 Multi-objective CCA with Dynamic Problem Decomposition

Although the prominent ability of CCA to divide the problem into smaller search space and to increase the influences of the evolutionary operators on these smaller subcomponents is widely recognized, CCA with static decomposition strategy is inapplicable for solving a non-separable problem. With the presence of interrelation between variables, the use of dynamic decomposition strategy that allows CCA to adjust species-size and species member during the algorithm runs could be the efficient way to handle this type of problem [8]. Li and Yao [9] demonstrated that by changing species-size frequently (the so-called "*grouping size*" in their work), the probability that two interacting variables will be placed into the same subcomponent significantly increases.

In the literature, two dynamic problem decomposition schemes based upon dynamic species-size strategy were proposed. Firstly, in Yang et al. [7], a set of potential species-size is subjectively identified. Then, at the beginning of generation, species-size is randomly selected from this potential set based upon probabilities. The higher probability will be rewarded to a species-size having better past performance. Thus, species-size that works well is more likely to be used in the next generation. Secondly, Li and Yao [9] adjusted species-size by comparing the fitness values before and after each generation run. If the fitness value is greater than the previous run, the next generation run will be executed using the same species-size. In contrast, if fitness value turns worse, species-size will be changed by randomly choosing a new specie-size from pre-determined set of species-size. The common idea of these two schemes is to allow species-size that performs well to be used for the next generation run. The criterion for changing species-size is straightforward since the term "*better*" or "*worse*" can be objectively compared by scalar value. In the other words, the existing dynamic problem decomposition strategies were designed for solving SOOP.

2.1 Dynamic Species-Size

Our proposed dynamic species-size method allows CCA to handle both SOOP and MOOP. According to our method, a set of dynamic species-size (SS) is firstly identified. This set is generated by a geometric series which the first term is 1 and common ratio is 2, i.e. $\{1, 2, 4, 8, 16,...\}$. Thus, a set of number of species (NS) is the result of division where numerator is number of variable (N) and denominator is species-size, i.e. $NS = N/SS$. The algorithm starts by randomly selecting a species-size from SS. Then variables assignment is conducted in chronological sequence from the first species to the last species. This implies that variables will be selected and allocated to the first species until it is fully filled. Then, allocation process moves on to the second species and so forth. It should be noted that number of variables assigned to the last species may not equal to that of other previous species if fraction from the division of N/SS exists. The managing rule for this case is that if the remainder is equal or greater than half of species-size; all residual variables will be allocated to the next species, otherwise they will be combined with the previous species.

For example, a set of number of species (NS) for a problem having 100 variables is defined as $NS = 100 \div \{1, 2, 4, 8, 16, 32, 64\} = \{100, 50, 25, 13, 6, 3, 1\}$. Considering the case that the chosen SS is 8, thus NS is 12.5. By allocating 8 variables to each of the first 12 species, the remaining variables are 4 which equal to half of species-size. Therefore, algorithm assigns them to the 13th species. In contrast, if the selected SS is 16, the computed NS is 6.25. By appointing 16 variables to each of the first 6 species, the remainder is 4 which is smaller than half of species-size. Therefore, algorithm combines them with the 6th species. The aim of the proposed procedure described above is to provide the diversity of species-size ranging from largest to smallest size. Although a set of SS is still needed to be supplied, it is identified based on simple rule and does not require sophisticated setting from user. It can be thought of that CCA that adopts the largest species-size from SS is analogous to the traditional multi-objective optimization algorithms whose solutions are represented by only one species containing all decision variables. Whereas, the classical CCA adopts the smallest species-size, i.e. $SS = 1$.

2.2   Dynamic Process

The proposed DMOCCA begins by randomly selecting a species-size from SS. The selection without replacement is employed in this scheme to ensure that all species-sizes are chosen for execution. For dynamic mechanism, the selected species-size will be used in the next iterations if solutions obtained from the current iteration are better than those of the previous iteration. Otherwise, species-size will be adjusted. The comparison of solutions between iterations for MOOP is different from that for SOOP since there is no the best solution to a MOOP. Instead, a set of non-dominated solutions is obtained in each algorithm run. In this paper, we employed "convergence detection" as a method for comparing the solution sets of current and previous iteration and as a trigger criterion for adjusting of species-size. The convergence detection process can be described as follows.

Given $\mathbf{A}_i$ and $\mathbf{A}_{i-1}$ are non-dominated solution sets of the current iteration and previous iteration, respectively. The condition for solutions convergence is proposed as:

$$C(\mathbf{A}_i, \mathbf{A}_{i-1}) \leq C(\mathbf{A}_{i-1}, \mathbf{A}_i) \tag{1}$$

where $C(\mathbf{A}_i, \mathbf{A}_{i-1})$ is coverage ratio of solution set $\mathbf{A}_i$ over solution set $\mathbf{A}_{i-1}$ while $C(\mathbf{A}_{i-1}, \mathbf{A}_i)$ is the reverse value of $C(\mathbf{A}_i, \mathbf{A}_{i-1})$. The solution coverage, C, which is used for comparing any two sets of solutions, is mathematically expressed as:

$$C(\mathbf{A}_i, \mathbf{A}_{i-1}) = \frac{|\{a_{i-1} \in \mathbf{A}_{i-1}; \exists a_i \in \mathbf{A}_i : a_i \prec a_{i-1}\}|}{|\mathbf{A}_{i-1}|} \tag{2}$$

where $a_i \prec a_{i-1}$ means that solution a_i covers, i.e. dominates solution a_{i-1} and $C(\mathbf{A}_i, \mathbf{A}_{i-1}) \in [0, 1]$. In the case that $C(\mathbf{A}_i, \mathbf{A}_{i-1}) = 1$, all solutions in set $\mathbf{A}_{i-1}$ are dominated by solutions in set $\mathbf{A}_i$. In contrast, $C(\mathbf{A}_i, \mathbf{A}_{i-1}) = 0$ represents the situation that none of solutions in set $\mathbf{A}_{i-1}$ are covered by those of set $\mathbf{A}_i$. From this sense, $C(\mathbf{A}_i, \mathbf{A}_{i-1}) > C(\mathbf{A}_{i-1}, \mathbf{A}_i)$ implies that solutions set of the current iteration is better than that of the previous iteration. Whereas, $C(\mathbf{A}_i, \mathbf{A}_{i-1}) \leq C(\mathbf{A}_{i-1}, \mathbf{A}_i)$ indicates solutions convergence condition that activates algorithm to change species-size.

2.3   Collaborator Selection Method

According to CCA framework, the fitness of individuals of the considered species can be evaluated after combining them with individuals of the other species, the so-called "collaborator". In practice, it is widely recognized that collaborator selection method is crucial for CCA performance. As illustrated in Fig. 1(a), the classical CCA which is usually applied for SOOP selects collaborators from the current best individual. Therefore, all individuals of the evaluated species are cooperated with the similar set of collaborators. In this paper, the new collaborator selection scheme based upon elitism strategy is presented and its procedure is demonstrated in Fig. 1(b). For example, considering a problem having four variables and species-size equals one. At the end of iteration, algorithm obtains a set of non-dominated solutions and keeps them in archive. In the case that species 1 containing variable x_1 is evaluated, algorithm chooses collaborators from the current archive and combines them with the evaluated species with random ordering. We found that this proposed method enhances search ability since it increases probability of exploring to new searching area that eventually helps avoid trapping within the local optima.

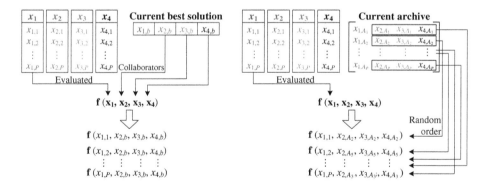

(a) Collaborator selection method for single-objective optimization problem

(b) New collaborator selection scheme for multi-objective optimization problem

Fig. 1. Collaborator selection schemes

2.4   DMOCCA Main Algorithm

In this section, procedure of the DMOCCA is illustrated in Fig. 2 and described below.

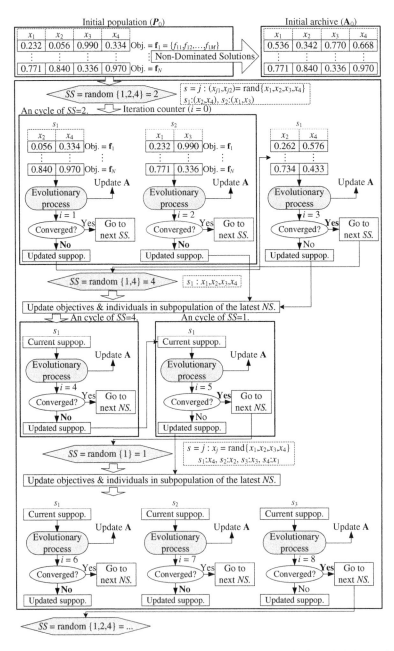

Fig. 2. Execution diagram of the DMOCCA to CCMVPOP with four decision variables

Step 1 Generate an initial population $\mathbf{P}_0$ and an initial empty archive $\mathbf{A}_0$.

Step 2 Evaluate the objectives of an individual in $\mathbf{P}_0$.

Step 3 Select and copy non-dominated solutions in $\mathbf{P}_0$ into archive $\mathbf{A}_0$. Truncate [12] $\mathbf{A}_0$ if the number of the non-dominated solutions is higher than the setting archive size Q.

Step 4 Define a set of species-size as $SS = \{1, 2, 4...\}$ and compute its corresponding set of number of species (NS).

Step 5 Select randomly without replacement the implemented species-size from SS.

Step 6 Randomize decision variables to fill in the first species until full-sized. Then, filling the remainder variables in the second species and so on.

Step 7 Decompose initial population $\mathbf{P}_0$ into NS species whose subpopulation are $B_1, B_2, ..., B_{NS}$. The objective values of an individual j^{th} in each of subpopulations $B_1, B_2, ..., B_{NS}$ are inherited from those of its antecedent, i.e. the solution j^{th} in $\mathbf{P}_0$.

Step 8 Start the iteration counter by setting: $t = 1$.

Step 9 Start the species counter, whose values are 1 to NS, to identify the evaluated species by setting: $s = 1$.

Step 10 Select parent subpopulation ($\mathbf{R}_{t,s}$) from $B_{t,s}$ based on the binary selection method.

Step 11 Apply crossover and mutation process on $\mathbf{R}_{t,s}$ to form child subpopulation ($\mathbf{C}_{t,s}$).

Step 12 Evaluate objective values of an individual in $\mathbf{C}_{t,s}$ by combining it with the selected collaborators from the current archive ($\mathbf{A}_t$) based upon the collaborator selection method.

Step 13 Combine solutions obtained from previous process with those from $\mathbf{A}_t$. Update archive by selecting non-dominated solutions from the combined set into $\mathbf{A}_{t+1}$. Apply truncation operator if the number of non-dominated solutions is not fit with predetermined archive size (Q).

Step 14 Merge subpopulation $B_{t,s}$ and $\mathbf{C}_{t,s}$ to form merged subpopulation $\mathbf{M}_{t,s}$.

Step 15 Perform the environmental selection using *rank assignment method* [13] on $\mathbf{M}_{t,s}$ to update subpopulation $B_{t,s}$.

Step 16 Increase the iteration counter by one ($t + 1$).

Step 17 If $t + 1$ meet the termination condition ruled out by the predetermined maximum number of iteration, finish the search and report the final archival individuals as the output solutions set.

Step 18 Compare $\mathbf{A}_{t+1}$ and $\mathbf{A}_t$ based upon the convergence detection method. If the convergence is not detected, continue to the next step, otherwise species-sized will be adjusted by going to step 5. In the case that SS is currently an empty set, reinitialize set SS before performing step 5.

Step 19 Increase the species counter by one ($s + 1$). If $s + 1 > NS$, resetting species counter and go back to step 9, otherwise go back to step 10.

3 Formulation of CCMVPOP

We considered portfolio selection process with a single holding period where N securities are available as investment opportunities. At the beginning of the holding period, an investor determines the proportion of initial investment that will be allocated to any available securities. Given that $\mathbf{x}$, which represents a portfolio solution, is a $N \times 1$ vector of investment allocation proportion to N securities. Let vector $\mathbf{R}$ with size $N \times 1$ represent the expected returns of N securities. Matrix $\mathbf{\Lambda}$ is a non-singular $N \times N$ variance-covariance matrix. According to Markowitz [14], investors whose utility can be approximated by the first two moments of return distribution aim to maximize the expected returns and minimize the portfolio variance simultaneously. Suppose that the expected return and variance of a portfolio are denoted by $R_p(\mathbf{x})$ and $V_p(\mathbf{x})$, respectively. Two objectives of the mean-variance model can be expressed as follows:

$$\text{Maximize } R_p(\mathbf{x}) = \mathbf{x}^{\mathrm{T}} \mathbf{R} = \sum_{i=1}^{N} x_i R_i \tag{4}$$

$$\text{Minimize } V_p(\mathbf{x}) = \mathbf{x}^{\mathrm{T}} \mathbf{\Lambda} \mathbf{x} = \sum_{i=1}^{N} x_i x_j \sigma_{i,j} \tag{5}$$

where $\mathbf{x}^{\mathrm{T}}$ is the transpose of vector $\mathbf{x}$ and x_i is the proportion of investment allocated to security i. R_i is the expected return of security i. $\sigma_{i,j}$ is covariance between securities i and j which quantifies the correlation between two assets. These associations among securities cause interdependency among decision variable. The cardinality constraint mean-variance portfolio optimization problem (CCMVPOP) can be formulated as follows:

Prob. 1 $\min_{\mathbf{x}} F(\mathbf{x}) = \left[-R_p(\mathbf{x}),\ V_p(\mathbf{x}),\ K_{x_i > 0}(\mathbf{x}) \right]$

Subject to $\sum_{i=1}^{N} x_i = 1$
$x_i \geq 0$
$l_i \leq x_i \leq u_i$

where $K_{x_i > 0}(\mathbf{x})$ is the minimum criterion that represents the number of assets having positive weight in a portfolio solution, i.e. cardinality. This objective can be expressed mathematically as $K_{x_i > 0}(\mathbf{x}) = \sum_{i=1}^{N} 1_{x_i > 0}$. The first constraint is applied to make sure that all investment is fully allocated to available securities. The second constraint implies that the short selling is not allowed. For the third constraint, l_i and u_i are the lower and upper bound of investment proportion of x_i. Thus, by optimizing $F(\mathbf{x})$ in **Prob. 1,** the Pareto solutions of CCMVPOP can be obtained within a single of algorithm run.

4 Computational Experiments

4.1 Data

To demonstrate the proposed algorithm, the benchmark data sets were quoted from http://w3.uniroma1.it/Tardella/datasets.html which is publicly available. These data sets contain the historical weekly data of stocks listed in the EuroStoxx50 (Europe), FTSE100 (UK), MIBTEL (Italy), S&P500 (USA), and NASDAQ (USA) capital market indices during March 2003 and March 2007. This database also provides the series of expected return vectors, variance-covariance matrices, as well as the theoretical true Pareto front for given values of cardinality constrains. In this paper, the FTSE 100, S&P500 and NASDAQ index containing 79, 476 and 2196 stocks, respectively, were selected to represent a normal-scale and large-scale problem.

4.2 Parameter Setting

The experimented algorithms were executed for solving the CCMVPOP, formulated earlier as **Prob. 1**, within the multi-objective optimization framework. Solutions to the problem were encoded into real-value chromosome with the length of 79, 476 and 2196 as the number of stock included in FTSE100, S&P500 and NASDAQ index, respectively. The parameter setting for the DMOCCA and SPEA-II can be described as follow. The simulated binary crossover (SBX) [15] which adapts the one-point crossover on binary strings for the real number encoded chromosomes was employed. The crossover probability is set as 1 to allow the crossover operator to be performed on all parent individuals. The Variable-Wise Polynomial mutation [15] is used to transform an offspring individual into a new individual to maintain the diversity of individuals in a population and to prevent premature convergence of solutions. The mutation probability is equal one over the chromosome length for SPEA-II and equal one over the species-size for DMOCCA. This setting makes sure that, in average, there is one bit on a solution will be mutated. The parameter setting for the MOPSO is referred to [11]. The population and archive sizes are both equal to 200, while the number of generations is 10000. Next, 30 repeated runs were set for suitable statistical comparisons.

4.3 Computational Results

This study utilized two performance comparison methods, namely, the average distance to the true efficient frontier (M_1) [16] and the Hypervolume (HV) [17]. M_1 is measured by firstly computing the shortest distance between a solution i and the true efficient frontier which is the Euclidean distance of the solution i to its nearest solution j on the true efficient frontier. M_1 is the average of distance of all individuals in a solutions set. Therefore, M_1 is a measure of the closeness of solutions to the true efficient frontier. Meanwhile, the hypervolume, which is a maximum criterion, measures not only the closeness to the true efficient frontier but also the diversity of solutions. The HV refers to area (two objectives), volume (three objectives) or hypervolume (four or more objectives) between a given reference point on the efficient frontier and the evaluated solution.

Table 1. Mean and standard deviation (Std. Dev.) of M_1

Algorithm	Test problem					
	FTSE100 ($N = 79$)		S&P500 ($N = 476$)		NASDAQ ($N = 2196$)	
	Mean	Std. Dev.	Mean	Std. Dev.	Mean	Std. Dev.
SPEA-II	0.030684	0.006038	0.051614	0.008785	0.065479	0.008230
MOPSO	0.049679	0.009856	0.062821	0.015550	0.161872	0.044951
DMOCCA	0.013657	0.006121	0.020170	0.010486	0.026009	0.015305

Table 2. Mean and standard deviation (Std. Dev.) of HV

Algorithm	Test problem					
	FTSE100 ($N = 79$)		S&P500 ($N = 476$)		NASDAQ ($N = 2196$)	
	Mean	Std. Dev.	Mean	Std. Dev.	Mean	Std. Dev.
SPEA-II	0.021214	0.000276	0.001819	0.000015	0.011261	0.000128
MOPSO	0.020630	0.000230	0.001687	0.000167	0.009379	0.000852
DMOCCA	0.022594	0.000675	0.001981	0.000193	0.012081	0.000153

Table 3. Runtime (Second); Personal computer: Intel Core i5 M450 2.4 GHz, Ram of 4 GB

Algorithm	FTSE100 ($N = 79$)		S&P500 ($N = 476$)		NASDAQ ($N = 2196$)	
	Algorithm time	Objective calculation	Algorithm time	Objective calculation	Algorithm time	Objective calculation
SPEA-II	1,019.19	24.85	1,109.29	99.96	1,512.69	480.19
MOPSO	646.53	22.06	759.17	96.49	1,394.72	479.09
DMOCCA	335.84	31.96	442.56	134.98	927.36	666.56

Tables 1 and 2 report the means and standard deviations of the M_1 and HV, respectively, for the SPEA-II, MOPSO and DMOCCA with three test problems. The statistics were computed from 2×10^6 solutions generated for each run. According to the M_1 criterion, the smaller the value of M_1, the shorter the distance between the evaluated solution and the true Pareto front. Table 1 shows that, DMOCCA performs significantly better than SPEA-II and MOPSO. This implies that the solutions obtained from MOCCA are located closer to the true Pareto front compared to those from SPEA-II and MOPSO. HV is a maximum criterion whose values represent the level of diversity of the solutions. In Table 2, the higher value of HV indicates that the solutions are well distributed along the true Pareto front, whereas a lower HV denotes that the solutions are clustered in some particular areas. It is revealed from Table 2 that DMOCCA outperforms the other two algorithms. Table 3 shows runtime of all experimented algorithms for three test problems. It is evidenced that DMOCCA is faster than SPEA-II and MOPSO, regardless of test problem. As claimed earlier, DMOCCA was designed for handling a large-scale problem. It is clear from the results that the superiority of DMOCCA is strengthened when problem dimensionality increases.

According to the MVCCPO problem formulated as **Prob. 1**, cardinality constraint is treated as an objective to be optimized. Therefore, the optimal solutions provided by the algorithm can be graphically visualized as Pareto surface in three-dimensional chart, i.e. mean-variance-cardinality diagram. To illustrate the optimal solutions for different values of cardinality (K), the optimal solutions can be sorted in ascending order of K values. In the other words, the efficient frontier for given values of cardinality is the cross-section of the Pareto surface along the cardinality axis. The optimal solutions of S&P500 and NASDAQ test problem generated by SPEA-II, MOPSO and DMOCCA are plotted together with the true Pareto front[1] with different values of cardinality and displayed in Figs. 3 and 4, respectively.

It is revealed from Figs. 3 and 4 that the optimal solutions obtained from DMOCCA are better than those generated by SPEA-II and MOPSO since they are not only closely approximated, but also extensively distributed along the true efficient frontier for both cardinality values. It can be visualized from Fig. 4 that solutions provided by SPEA-II are trapped at some points resulting an unevenly distribution of the solutions along the true efficient frontier.

4.4   Effects of Implementing the Dynamic Species-Size Strategy

The superiorities of our DMOCCA over the SPEA-II and MOPSO may be mainly attributed to an implementation of the proposed dynamic species-size strategy. The proposed DMOCCA has ability of combining and balancing the tasks of exploring new search space and focusing on a specific neighboring area. It is acknowledged that the prominent feature of the classical CCA is the ability to decompose a large search space into multiple smaller search spaces. This ability increases probability of exploring the new searching area that helps obtaining the solutions that not only spread along, but also close to the efficient frontier. However, this ability dramatically decreases for the case of non-separable problem. On the other hand, SPEA-II and MOPSO clearly have nothing to worry about the interrelation between variables since all decision variables are placed into a single chromosome. Nevertheless, having a large search space, the solution always prematurely converges after algorithm run started which forces algorithm to focus on searching the neighboring area rather than exploring the new searching area. As a result, solutions provided by SPEA-II and MOPSO are easily trapped into the local optima when dealing with large-scale problem.

To support this argument, Fig. 5 illustrates speed of convergence of M_1 and HV criterion values for NASDAQ test problem. In general, the better algorithm is the one whose performance values converge at a lower number of generations. Although, the results show that the solutions of SPEA-II and MOPSO achieved convergence faster than those of DMOCCA, these criteria values remain stable at the worse level compared to those of DMOCCA. These results support our argument articulated earlier that

---

[1] It should be noted that the data source employed provides the true Pareto front for given values of cardinality. However, these values are restricted for only $K = 2, 3, 4$, and 5. To conserve space, only results of $K = 2$ and $K = 5$ are reported.

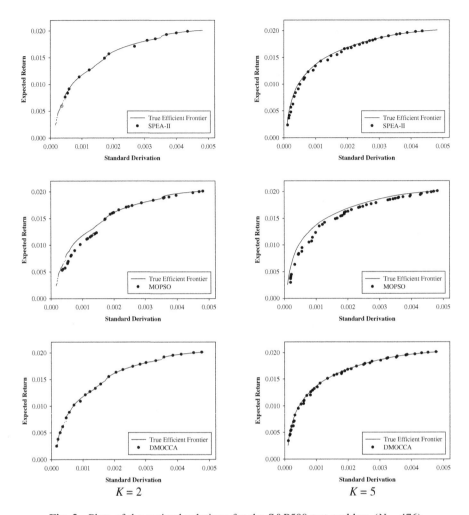

Fig. 3. Plots of the optimal solutions for the S&P500 test problem ($N = 476$).

classical algorithms always prematurely converges and is trapped at the local optima when dealing with large-scale problem.

The proposed DMOCCA is equipped with the additional ability to adjust species-size as iterations progress. For instance, it may start with small species-size to explore the new searching area until solution convergence is found, then increases species-size to focus at some particular neighboring areas for obtaining the fitter solutions. This dynamic process effectively manages searching space to be explored and efficiently handles interrelation among variable simultaneously. The dynamic process for NASDAQ test problem, exhibited in the left panel of Fig. 6, reveals that the use of convergence detection works well since adjusting process is clearly presented and all species-sizes were employed before the new loop was started. It is noticeable that the species-size that performs greatly will be used for numbers of iterations before

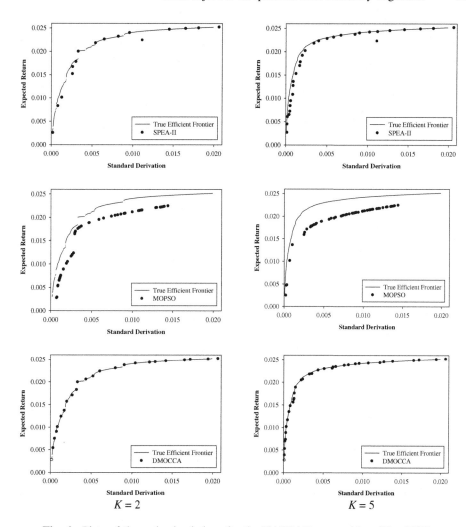

Fig. 4. Plots of the optimal solutions for the NASDAQ test problem ($N = 2196$).

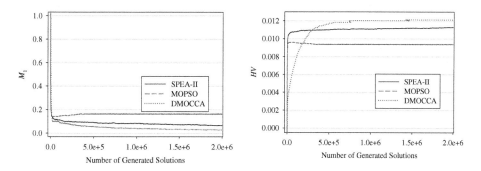

Fig. 5. Mean HV versus number of generated solutions

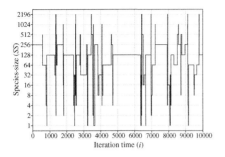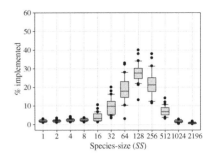

Fig. 6. Adapting process throughout the run (left) and effects of dynamic species-size (right)

switching to the other species-size whenever solution convergence is detected. The right panel of Fig. 6 shows that DMOCCA performed an average of 27% of total iteration by using species-size of 128 followed by 256, 64 and 32, respectively. Meanwhile, the species-size of one that similar to standard CCA was rarely used.

5   Conclusions

The proposed algorithm, DMOCCA, is able to adjust the species-size as iterations progress. The dynamic process was designed by imposing a decision making rule on the algorithm for adjusting species-size based upon the convergence detection method. Additionally, the proposed DMOCCA can be efficiently implemented for both SOOP and MOOP. The experimental results reveal that, regardless of performance comparison criteria and test problems, our proposed DMOCCA outperformed SPEA-II and MOPSO. The proposed decomposition strategy helps prevent algorithm from prematurely converging and trapping at the local optima. While, the developed dynamic process effectively manages searching space to be explored and efficiently handles interrelation among variable simultaneously. Ultimately, it is clearly evidenced that the optimal solutions obtained from DMOCCA excellently approximated the true Pareto front.

References

1. Potter, M.A., De Jong, K.A.: A cooperative coevolutionary approach to function optimization. In: Davidor, Y., Schwefel, H.-P., Männer, R. (eds.) PPSN 1994. LNCS, vol. 866, pp. 249–257. Springer, Heidelberg (1994). https://doi.org/10.1007/3-540-58484-6_269
2. Liu, Y., Yao, X., Zhao, Q., Higuchi, T.: Scaling up fast evolutionary programming with cooperative coevolution. In: Proceedings of the 2001 Congress on Evolutionary Computation (IEEE Cat. No.01TH8546), vol. 1102, pp. 1101–1108 (2001)
3. van den Bergh, F., Engelbrecht, A.P.: A cooperative approach to particle swarm optimization. IEEE Trans. Evol. Comput. **8**, 225–239 (2004)
4. Shi, Y., Teng, H., Li, Z.: Cooperative co-evolutionary differential evolution for function optimization. In: Wang, L., Chen, K., Ong, Y.S. (eds.) ICNC 2005. LNCS, vol. 3611, pp. 1080–1088. Springer, Heidelberg (2005). https://doi.org/10.1007/11539117_147

5. Yang, Z., Tang, K., Yao, X.: Large scale evolutionary optimization using cooperative coevolution. Inf. Sci. **178**, 2985–2999 (2008)
6. Iorio, A.W., Li, X.: A cooperative coevolutionary multiobjective algorithm using non-dominated sorting. In: Deb, K. (ed.) GECCO 2004. LNCS, vol. 3102, pp. 537–548. Springer, Heidelberg (2004). https://doi.org/10.1007/978-3-540-24854-5_56
7. Yang, Z., Tang, K., Yao, X.: Multilevel cooperative coevolution for large scale optimization. In: IEEE Congress on Evolutionary Computation, 2008, CEC 2008, (IEEE World Congress on Computational Intelligence), pp. 1663–1670 (2008)
8. Omidvar, M.N., Li, X., Yang, Z., Yao, X.: Cooperative co-evolution for large scale optimization through more frequent random grouping. In: IEEE Congress on Evolutionary Computation, pp. 1–8 (2010)
9. Li, X., Yao, X.: Cooperatively coevolving particle swarms for large scale optimization. IEEE Trans. Evol. Comput. **16**, 210–224 (2012)
10. Zitzler, E., Laumanns, M., Thiele, L.: SPEA-II: Improving the Strength Pareto Evolutionary Algorithm. Computer Engineering and Networks Laboratory (TIK), Swiss Federal Institute of Technology (ETH), Zurich, Switzerland (2002)
11. Coello, C.A.C., Pulido, G.T., Lechuga, M.S.: Handling multiple objectives with particle swarm optimization. IEEE Trans. Evol. Comput. **8**, 256–279 (2004)
12. Deb, K., et al.: A fast and elitist multiobjective genetic algorithm: NSGA-II. IEEE Trans. Evol. Comput. **6**(2), 182–197 (2002)
13. Fonseca, C.M., Fleming, P.J.: Genetic algorithms for multi-objective optimization: Formulation, discussion and generalization. In: ICGA, pp. 416–423 (1993)
14. Markowitz, H.: Portfolio selection. J. Finan. **7**, 77–91 (1952)
15. Deb, K., Beyer, H.-G.: Self-adaptive genetic algorithms with simulated binary crossover. Evol. Comput. **9**, 197–221 (2001)
16. Zitzler, E., Deb, K., Thiele, L.: Comparison of multiobjective evolutionary algorithms: empirical results. Evol. Comput. **8**, 173–195 (2000)
17. Zitzler, E., Thiele, L.: Multiobjective evolutionary algorithms: a comparative case study and the strength Pareto approach. IEEE Evol. Comput. **3**, 257–271 (1999)

EvoBIO

Task Classification Using Topological Graph Features for Functional M/EEG Brain Connectomics

Javier Del Ser[1,2,3(✉)] , Eneko Osaba[1] , and Miren Nekane Bilbao[2]

[1] TECNALIA. OPTIMA Unit, 48160 Derio, Spain
{javier.delser,eneko.osaba}@tecnalia.com
[2] University of the Basque Country UPV/EHU, 48013 Bilbao, Spain
{javier.delser,nekane.bilbao}@ehu.eus
[3] Basque Center for Applied Mathematics (BCAM), 48009 Bilbao, Spain
jdelser@bcamath.org

Abstract. In the last few years the research community has striven to achieve a thorough understanding of the brain activity when the subject under analysis undertakes both mechanical tasks and purely mental exercises. One of the most avant-garde approaches in this regard is the discovery of connectivity patterns among different parts of the human brain unveiled by very diverse sources of information (e.g. magneto- or electro-encephalography – M/EEG, functional and structural Magnetic Resonance Imaging – fMRI and sMRI, or positron emission tomography – PET), coining the so-called brain connectomics discipline. Surprisingly, even though contributions related to the brain connectome abound in the literature, far too little attention has been paid to the exploitation of such complex spatial-temporal patterns to classify the task performed by the subject while brain signals are being registered. This manuscript covers this research niche by elaborating on the extraction of topological features from the graph modeling the brain connectivity under different tasks. By resorting to public information from the Human Connectome Project, the work will show that a selected subset of topological predictors from M/EEG connectomes suffices for accurately predicting (with average accuracy scores of up to 95%) the task performed by the subject at hand, further insights given on their predictive power when the M/EEG connectivity is inferred over different frequency bands.

Keywords: Human connectome · M/EEG · Graph theory
Task classification

1 Introduction

Understanding the brain has been one of the most challenging paradigms faced by the human being over history, from ancient studies dealing with post-mortem methods to less invasive approaches fueled by the advent and evolution of

K. Sim and P. Kaufmann (Eds.): EvoApplications 2018, LNCS 10784, pp. 21–32, 2018.
https://doi.org/10.1007/978-3-319-77538-8_2

sensing techniques. Not in vain the so-called *neuroscience* discipline has been widely acknowledged as one of the most gravitational scientific branches of the entire research community, involving an ever-growing spectrum of technologies such as neuroimaging, biochemistry, neural computation, optogenetics, massive data analysis and spatio-temporal pattern visualization, among many others [1]. Achievements by virtue of this technology portfolio are foreseen to unleash novel insights on how brain reacts against emotions, gets stimulated when undertaking tasks of different nature, or degrades under distinct mental illnesses. Therefore, huge research efforts are being currently invested by worldwide funding agencies to support novel approaches, methods and techniques aimed at acquiring a deeper knowledge and confronting the challenges in this vibrant field [2,3].

In this context, this paper focuses its scope on the adoption of elements, techniques and tools from Computational Intelligence and Data Mining to exploit the immensity of data produced by brain observational experiments of growing coverage, resolution, sensitivity and comprehensiveness. Among other data-intensive brain studies, one of the neuroscience areas where the research activity has been particularly notable in the last few years is the study of the so-called human *connectome*, which refers to a thorough map of how different structural parts of the brain connect to each other under diverse circumstances [4,5]. When conceived as a network, parts that are tightly wired in the connectome representation become a constituent element of an functional circuit that represents the emerging state and dynamics of the brain under the task developed by the subject. Connectomics have hitherto shown a paramount potential for manifold medical and clinical applications in psychopathology, traumatic injury assessment, brain degeneration (e.g. Alzheimer disease) or aging [6].

Despite its obvious relevance and the upsurge of related research in the last decade, the application of graph theory and tools (e.g. community structure analysis, centrality indices and other metrics alike) to brain connectomics is still under debate [7,8]. Several contributions have elaborated on the use of graph kernels in an attempt at accommodating the large variability of the human connectome among subjects for a given function [9,10], whereas recent studies have instead focused on classifying brain connectomes by representing them with graph embedding, a mapping of a given graph to a certain n-dimensional real space mostly put to practice using MRI data [11,12]. Surprisingly, the literature is scarce in what relates to the use of topological properties of the inferred connectome graph to extract functional brain patterns, even though several advantages can be intuitively expected therefrom: (1) a better resilience of the discovered pattern against the renowned small-world connectome variability among subjects; (2) a higher ease of computation (as opposed to graph kernels), since many of such properties are highly parallelizable; (3) the straightforward use of machine learning methods, as graphs are transformed in feature vectors.

This manuscript aims at covering this research niche by presenting a study on the potential of topological properties of brain connectivity graphs for predicting the task performed by the subject at hand. In particular this work evinces that a tailored selection of graph properties quantifying different structural and connectivity aspects of the network is enough to predict the task with high accuracy.

The study is buttressed by an intensive benchmark to select among a variety of machine learning models to predict a multi-task dataset of real M/EEG traces retrieved from the public Human Connectome Project database (*500 Subjects Plus MEG2* data release [13]). The obtained results (accuracy scores of up to 95%) certainly encourage further research aimed at extrapolating these findings to brain connectomes extracted from other sensors.

The rest of the manuscript is structured as follows: Sect. 2 poses the model selection problem whereas Sect. 3 delves into the processing flow utilized in this study, with emphasis on the considered classification models and graph features. Experimental results are analyzed in Sect. 4 and finally, Sect. 5 concludes the paper and outlines future research.

2 Model Selection as an Optimization Problem

As shown in Fig. 1, we consider a cohort of N subjects, each undertaking a subset $\mathcal{T}_n \subseteq \mathcal{T}^\top$ of tasks from an overall set $\mathcal{T}^\top \doteq \{\tau_1, \ldots, \tau_\Upsilon\}$, with Υ denoting the number of tasks. While undertaking such tasks, the brain activity of every subject can be registered by different sensors and techniques. In this work we specifically focus on M/EEG signals, which are registered by electrodes capable of sensing the magnetic or electric field furnished by naturally produced electrical currents in the brain. Such signals are usually represented as time series captured by electrodes deployed on the scalp of the subject, usually arranged over its surface in a regular lattice. Let $\mathcal{S}$ denote the set of such sensors (whose cardinality $S \doteq |\mathcal{S}|$ is assumed to be constant among subjects), so that $x_s^{n,\tau}(t)$ denotes the time series corresponding to subject $n \in \mathcal{N}$, task $\tau \in \mathcal{T}_n$ and electrode $s \in \mathcal{S}$.

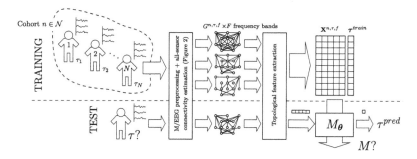

Fig. 1. Schematic diagram of the connectome extraction process that lies at the core the problem tackled in this paper. The design goal is to build a supervised learning model capable of predicting the performed task τ by using topological properties of the recorded M/EEG connectome.

By measuring the magnitude of temporal dependence between signals via techniques as the one described in the next section, it is possible to infer the causality between the signals $x_s^{n,\tau}(t)$ and $x_{s'}^{n,\tau}(t)$ captured by different sensors $s \in \mathcal{S}$ and $s' \in \mathcal{S} - \{s\}$ for a given subject n and task τ. When analyzed for every pair

(s, s'), the causal relationships found for (n, τ) can be modeled as an undirected, weighted graph $G^{n,\tau} = (\mathcal{S}, \mathcal{E}^{n,\tau})$, where $\mathcal{S}$ denotes the set of vertices or nodes representing each electrode, and $\mathcal{E}^{n,\tau} = \{(s, s') : s, s' \in \mathcal{S}\}$ stands for the set of links or edges interconnecting every pair of electrodes. Each vertex $(s, s') \in \mathcal{E}^{n,\tau}$ is associated with a weight $w^{n,\tau}(s, s') \in \mathbb{R}$, computed by connectivity estimators as the one later explained in Sect. 3. This weight represents the degree of causality between the time series registered by sensors s and s'. It is important to note that connectivity analysis can be also performed over different frequency bands $\mathcal{F} = \{f_1, \ldots, f_F\}$ (also referred to as *channels*), so that the notation used hereafter embraces this possibility by including superscript f in all variables that can be computed per every frequency $f \in \mathcal{F}$, e.g. $w^{n,\tau,f}(s, s')$.

The ultimate design goal tackled in this work is to select a predictive model $M_{\boldsymbol{\theta}}$ (with $\boldsymbol{\theta}$ denoting the hyper-parameters of the model) in order to predict the task performed by a subject based on his/her brain connectivity patterns. We are interested in models leading to an optimal generalization performance when fitted to any given supervised set of examples. In other words, an emphasis is placed on decoupling the estimation of the generalization capability from the specific set of training examples under use, so that the selection of the model $M_{\boldsymbol{\theta}}$ becomes unbiased with respect to its configuration $\boldsymbol{\theta}$ tuned optimally for a given training dataset. This uncoupling can be accomplished by using a pair of nested cross-validation loops, so that model tuning and fitting is performed in the first inner loop, while generalization is estimated in the outer loop. By repeating this process over Z permutations of the dataset to remove any further bias due to train-test partitioning, a more realistic estimation of the average generalization performance can be obtained for any model $M_{\boldsymbol{\theta}}$ than other overly optimistic techniques. This dual cross-validation strategy is known in the literature as *nested cross-validation* [14,15].

Mathematically, this design criterion can be formulated by defining a set of possible models $\mathcal{M} \doteq \{M_{\boldsymbol{\theta}_1}^1, \ldots, M_{\boldsymbol{\theta}_M}^M\}$, where M denotes the number of possible model choices and $\boldsymbol{\theta}_m$ the vector of hyper-parameters for model $m \in \{1, \ldots, M\}$. Once tuned and trained over a set of supervised examples $(\boldsymbol{G}^{tr,f}, \boldsymbol{\tau}^{tr})$ (tr: training, with $\boldsymbol{G}^{tr,f}$ standing for the vector of connectivity graphs for the frequency band under study and $\boldsymbol{\tau}^{tr}$ their associated task labels), the performance of model $M_{\boldsymbol{\theta}_m}^m \in \mathcal{M}$ can be measured by means of several scores for multiclass classification, from the standard accuracy score to other approaches better suited to imbalanced datasets, e.g. the so-called Cohen's Kappa Coefficient [16]. Disregarding the specifically chosen measure, the score can be denoted as $\Psi(\boldsymbol{\tau}^{test,pred}, \boldsymbol{\tau}^{test,true})$, where $\boldsymbol{\tau}^{pred} \doteq M_{\boldsymbol{\theta}_m}^m(\boldsymbol{G}^{test,f})$ denotes the vector of tasks predicted by the model for a vector of test connectomes $\boldsymbol{G}^{test,f}$, and $\boldsymbol{\tau}^{test,true}$ their true task labels. Without loss of generality and to ease further derivations, this score will be assumed to be higher the better the model is for the prediction of the task at hand. This being said, the design problem can be mathematically formulated as the choice of the index of the optimal model $m^{opt} \in \{1, \ldots, M\}$ from a portfolio of M possible models, under the following criterion:

$$m^{opt} = \operatorname*{arg\,max}_{m \in \{1,\dots,M\}} \frac{1}{Z} \sum_{z=1}^{Z} \left(\frac{1}{K} \sum_{k=1}^{K} \Psi(\boldsymbol{\tau}_{z,k}^{test,pred}, \boldsymbol{\tau}_{z,k}^{test,true}) \right) \tag{1}$$

where, by extending the previous notation,

$$\boldsymbol{\tau}_{z,k}^{test,pred} = M_{\boldsymbol{\theta}_{m,z,k}^{opt}}^{m} (\boldsymbol{G}_{z,k}^{test,f}) \tag{2}$$

stands for the predicted task labels for the test dataset $\boldsymbol{G}_{z,k}^{test,f}$ corresponding to partition $k \in \{1,\dots,K\}$ and repetition $z \in \{1,\dots,Z\}$. For each (z,k) the hyper-parameters $\boldsymbol{\theta}_{m,z,k}^{m}$ of the model are tuned by cross-validating with K' folds over

$$\boldsymbol{G}_{z,k}^{train,f} \doteq \{\boldsymbol{G}^{f}, \boldsymbol{\tau}\} - \{\boldsymbol{G}_{z,k}^{test,f}, \boldsymbol{\tau}_{z,k}^{test,true}\}, \tag{3}$$

yielding an optimal vector of hyper-parameter values $\boldsymbol{\theta}_{z,k}^{opt}$. As anticipated earlier, this process allows inferring an estimation of the generalized performance of model $M_{\boldsymbol{\theta}}$ unbiased with respect to the optimal configuration for the training dataset at hand.

Before proceeding with the model portfolio addressed in this paper, it must be noted that a thorough design process should also span the search over the space of possible *features* that could be engineered over the extracted connectivity graphs. However, the space of possible features that can be inferred from a graph is huge, and traversing it would demand huge computational resources. Instead of undertaking this complex search, a set of topological indicators computed over such graphs will be shown to suffice for predicting the task performed by the subject with high accuracy.

3   Models and Methods

As concluded above, the design problem posed in the previous section can be tackled in practice by using very different supervised learning models and graph feature construction techniques. Beyond graph transformation techniques such as graph embedding [17], in this manuscript we postulate that global topological features excel at capturing the brain connectivity patterns that permit to discriminate the task that the subject is performing. In essence, we propose to transform every connectivity graph $G^{n,\tau,f}$ into a set of P predictor variables $\{X_p^{n,\tau,f}\}_{p=1}^{P}$ that capture different connectivity and structural aspects of the brain connectome captured for user n, task τ and frequency band f. By properly defining such predictors, the subsequent predictive model $M_{\boldsymbol{\theta}}$ should be able to discern between tasks by inferring the pattern among $\{X_p^{n,\tau,f}\}_{p=1}^{P}$ and the task τ of any given test subject.

Before delving into the details of such topological properties, we proceed with an overview of the complete processing flow, which is schematically depicted in Fig. 2. Once signals have been recorded for every sensor during the session for subject $n\mathcal{N}$ and sensor $s \in \mathcal{S}$, a preprocessing stage removes artifacts, noise and extracts the epochs based on the stimuli channels utilized during the session. Thereafter connectivity among any sensor pair is estimated, which can be accomplished by several methods [18]. In this paper we will resort to the so-called Phase Lag Index (PLI), which is based on the asymmetry of the distribution of phase differences between two given signals [19]. This method is widely acknowledged to be efficient for multi-channel M/EEG connectivity estimation, due to the instantaneous nature of volume conduction, which ultimately makes a difference in phase directly linked to the existence of spatial interdependency of activity between signals. Mathematically $PLI(s, s')$ falls in the range $\mathbb{R}[0, 1]$, where 0 indicates no relationship between signals and 1 denotes a perfect phase coupling at a phase difference different from the trivial case $0 \bmod \pi$. For simplicity, we compute the unsigned version of PLI so that the produced sensor-to-sensor connectome can be modeled as an weighted, undirected graph with weights $w^{n,\tau,f}(s, s') = PLI(s, s')$.

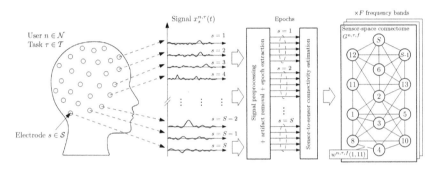

Fig. 2. Processing flow to extract the connectome $G^{n,\tau,f}$ from M/EEG signals $\{x_s^{n,\tau,f}(t)\}_{s=1}^S$ corresponding to subject n and task τ.

Once the graph $G^{n,\tau,f}$ has been built for any sensor pair (s, s'), several topological features $\mathbf{X}^{n,\tau,f} \doteq \{X_i^{n,\tau,f}\}_{i=1}^{10}$ are extracted from their network representations to capture global connectivity patterns that discriminate among tasks:

- *Average effective eccentricity* $(X_1^{n,\tau,f})$, which is defined as the average value of the maximum length of the shortest path from any node in $G^{n,\tau,f}$ so that the node can reach at least 90% of the other nodes in the graph.
- *Effective diameter* $(X_2^{n,\tau,f})$, which stands for the maximum value of the effective eccentricity over all nodes in the graph.
- *Effective radius* $(X_3^{n,\tau,f})$, which is the minimum value of the effective eccentricity computed over all nodes in the graph.
- *Effective eccentricity dispersion* $(X_4^{n,\tau,f})$ which, similarly to the previous features, returns the standard deviation of the effective eccentricity over the nodes of the graph.
- *Spectral radius* $(X_5^{n,\tau,f})$, i.e. the largest magnitude eigenvalue of the weighted adjacency matrix relating each node pair in the graph.
- *Second largest eigenvalue* $(X_6^{n,\tau,f})$, namely, the value of the second largest eigenvalue of the aforementioned adjacency matrix.

- *Energy* $(X_7^{n,\tau,f})$, equal to the squared sum of eigenvalues of the adjacency matrix.
- *Average clustering coefficient* $(X_8^{n,\tau,f})$, which yields the average of the local clustering coefficients of all the vertices of the network, where the local clustering coefficient is defined as the geometric average of the subgraph edge weights.
- *Average node degree* $(X_9^{n,\tau,f})$, given by the average of the sum of edge weights adjacent to every node in the network.
- *Average eigenvector centrality* $(X_{10}^{n,\tau,f})$, which averages a structural measure of the importance of every node computed as a function of the centralities of its neighbors.

The rationale behind the selection of these topological features is to capture structural and connectivity information about M/EEG co-activation patterns of brain regions so as to help the subsequent classifier M_θ discriminate among different tasks. Several studies have revealed varying levels of activity among neuronal populations during different cognitive tasks (see e.g. [20,21] and references therein). As will be proven experimentally, the selected feature set permits to effectively extract and quantify such activity levels, specially when the connectivity graphs from which such features are computed result from signal processing analysis performed at high frequency bands.

4   Experiments and Results

The performance of the proposed feature set is assessed by using real experimental data collected as the so-called *500 Subjects Plus MEG2* release of the well-known Human Connectome Project [13,22]. The 500 Subjects Release includes behavioral and MRI data from more than 500 healthy adult participants, from which 67 subjects were scanned in resting-state MEG (rMEG) and task MEG (tMEG), giving rise to a set $\mathcal{T}^\top$ of four tasks labeled as $\{rest, working\_mem, story\_math, task\_motor\}$. The protocol followed to implement standardized experiments for each task are described in [23, pages 45 to 62]. Signals utilized to extract the sensor-to-sensor connectivity graphs have been processed previously through a series of pipelines aimed at removing artifacts, cleaning the raw data and estimating power spectrum levels at the sensor level, all required for estimating the all-sensor connectivity via PLI. Connectivity graphs are computed therefrom over different frequency bands $\mathcal{F}$ following the conventions for M/EEG analysis: DELTA (1–4 Hz), THETA (4–8 Hz), ALPHA$_1$ (8–10 Hz), ALPHA$_2$ (10–13 Hz), BETA (13–32 Hz) and GAMMA (32–100 Hz). An additional case (AVERAGE) spanning the entire frequency range between 1 and 100 Hz is also included in the experiments.

The experiments discussed in what follows consider a benchmark of $M = 7$ well-known supervised learning models $\{M_{\theta_i}^i\}_{i=1}^7$: a Gaussian Naive Bayes classifier (GNB), a CART Decision Tree (DT), a k Nearest Neighbors classifier (kNN), a Gradient Boosting Classifier (GBC), a Random Forest Classifier (RFC), a Multi-Layer Perceptron (MLP) and a Support Vector Machine (SVM). Parameters θ_i have been tuned for each model in the portfolio by searching over a fine-grained grid of values for each parameter, which is efficiently performed by an evolutionary wrapper with crossover probability $P_c = 0.5$, mutation probability $P_m = 0.1$, a population size of 20 individuals and 50 generations run for every model. In all cases a nested cross-validation with $Z = 20$ repetitions has been used to estimate the generalization capability of the evaluated models, with $K = K' = 4$ splits for both inner and outer cross-validation loops as per Expression (1) to (3). In this regard, scores will be provided in terms of accuracy and Cohen's Kappa Coefficient, the latter for avoiding any interpretative bias due to the slight class imbalance present in the dataset. Features of training examples are transformed to their standard score prior to model learning, whereas validation and test instances were also standardized but using statistics computed over the training subset.

The discussion starts by inspecting the results in Table 1, where $mean\pm std$ values for the accuracy and the Kappa Coefficient are shown for all models under choice and the different frequency bands considered in the study. Bold scores correspond to those models performing best (in terms of accuracy – first cell row – or Kappa Coefficient – second cell row) for every frequency band (column) in the table, where the statistical equivalence of any two given models has been decided by performing a Wilcoxon rank sum test with significance level equal to 5% over their obtained scores. A close look at this table suggests that MLP and SVM outperform the rest of models in the benchmark over all frequency bands in terms of both performance scores, with SVM dominating in isolation over the THETA and AVERAGE bands. Interestingly, scores are especially good when computed over the GAMMA band (up to a Kappa Coefficient equal to 95% for both SVM and MLP), which shed light on the predictive capability of the proposed topological properties extracted from the M/EEG connectivity graph of every subject. This promising result must be gauged jointly with the particularities of the dataset at hand, in which every subject is represented by one single example. Therefore, these reported cross-validated scores are in fact a quantitative measure of the generalization capability of every model when processing new *subjects* rather than *examples*.

The discussion follows by analyzing the relative contribution of each proposed feature to the predicted task. Among other approaches for measuring the feature importance (e.g. ReliefF [24] or Boruta [25]), this work embraces the so-called Mean Decrease in Impurity (MDI), which in essence computes the relative importance of every feature as the sum of the Gini Impurity over the number of splits of all trees of a RFC model implemented on the feature, proportionally to the number of samples it splits [26]. While this strategy is known to misinterpretation when dealing with strongly correlated features, it does help to assess whether there is any predictor that does not contribute at all to the predicted target. Nevertheless, when constructing the RFC classifier the search for the best split in any node of its compounding tree learners is done over a randomly selected feature subset with size 4, so that this effect is minimized

Table 1. Accuracy scores (first cell row) and Cohen's Kappa Coefficient (second cell row) obtained over different frequency bands (mean ± std).

Model	Bands $\mathcal{F}$						
	AVERAGE	DELTA	THETA	ALPHA$_1$	ALPHA$_2$	BETA	GAMMA
GNB	0.60 ± 0.01	0.76 ± 0.01	0.45 ± 0.02	0.36 ± 0.01	0.45 ± 0.03	0.61 ± 0.02	0.78 ± 0.01
	0.46 ± 0.02	0.68 ± 0.01	0.26 ± 0.02	0.12 ± 0.02	0.27 ± 0.04	0.49 ± 0.02	0.70 ± 0.01
DT	0.67 ± 0.02	0.82 ± 0.02	0.70 ± 0.02	0.70 ± 0.03	0.65 ± 0.03	0.78 ± 0.02	0.83 ± 0.02
	0.54 ± 0.03	0.76 ± 0.02	0.59 ± 0.03	0.59 ± 0.03	0.54 ± 0.03	0.70 ± 0.03	0.77 ± 0.03
kNN	0.70 ± 0.02	0.79 ± 0.02	0.71 ± 0.02	0.72 ± 0.03	0.60 ± 0.02	0.77 ± 0.02	0.81 ± 0.03
	0.59 ± 0.02	0.71 ± 0.02	0.61 ± 0.02	0.63 ± 0.02	0.49 ± 0.02	0.69 ± 0.02	0.75 ± 0.02
GBC	0.72 ± 0.02	$\mathbf{0.85 \pm 0.02}$	0.75 ± 0.02	0.72 ± 0.02	0.70 ± 0.03	0.81 ± 0.02	0.86 ± 0.02
	0.61 ± 0.03	0.79 ± 0.03	0.66 ± 0.02	0.61 ± 0.03	0.60 ± 0.02	0.75 ± 0.02	0.81 ± 0.02
RFC	0.73 ± 0.01	$\mathbf{0.86 \pm 0.01}$	0.78 ± 0.02	0.75 ± 0.02	0.71 ± 0.02	0.82 ± 0.01	0.85 ± 0.02
	0.63 ± 0.02	$\mathbf{0.82 \pm 0.02}$	0.71 ± 0.03	0.66 ± 0.03	0.61 ± 0.02	0.76 ± 0.02	0.81 ± 0.02
MLP	0.79 ± 0.02	$\mathbf{0.86 \pm 0.01}$	0.79 ± 0.01	$\mathbf{0.78 \pm 0.01}$	$\mathbf{0.77 \pm 0.02}$	0.84 ± 0.01	$\mathbf{0.95 \pm 0.01}$
	0.71 ± 0.02	$\mathbf{0.80 \pm 0.02}$	0.74 ± 0.02	$\mathbf{0.72 \pm 0.03}$	$\mathbf{0.69 \pm 0.02}$	0.82 ± 0.02	0.94 ± 0.02
SVM	$\mathbf{0.81 \pm 0.01}$	$\mathbf{0.86 \pm 0.01}$	$\mathbf{0.81 \pm 0.01}$	$\mathbf{0.78 \pm 0.01}$	0.76 ± 0.02	$\mathbf{0.86 \pm 0.01}$	$\mathbf{0.95 \pm 0.01}$
	$\mathbf{0.75 \pm 0.02}$	$\mathbf{0.81 \pm 0.02}$	$\mathbf{0.76 \pm 0.02}$	$\mathbf{0.71 \pm 0.02}$	$\mathbf{0.68 \pm 0.03}$	$\mathbf{0.82 \pm 0.02}$	$\mathbf{0.94 \pm 0.01}$

(yet not removed in its entirety). This being said, Fig. 3 depicts the obtained feature importances averaged over the Z repetitions of the nested cross-validation loop; it is clear from this plot that those properties related to effective eccentricity ($X_i^{n,\tau,f}$ for $i \in \{1, 2, 3, 4\}$) are relevant for low frequencies, whereas for the GAMMA band features $X_5^{n,\tau,f}$, $X_6^{n,\tau,f}$, $X_7^{n,\tau,f}$ and $X_9^{n,\tau,f}$ compile most of the importance for predicting the task, which might advert that differences among graphs over the GAMMA band could rely on the degree of connectivity and the uniformity of the weights over all graphs.

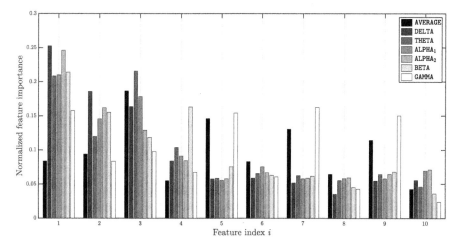

Fig. 3. Average predictive importances of the utilized topological features over the frequency bands considered in the study.

Finally, we end the discussion by exploring the distribution of misclassified samples in this multi-class problem. Figures 4a and b shows the confusion matrix corresponding to two different (model, band) combinations: (SVM, AVERAGE) and (RFC, GAMMA). It is straightforward to note that most of the prediction error lies beneath the lack of full separability between *task_motor* and *story_math*. In particular a better predictability of the *task_motor* task is noted in the GAMMA band, which goes in line with previous studies in brain connectomics reporting higher signal oscillations in upper bands (BETA and GAMMA) when the task involves the motor system [27]. Indeed, most of the predictive improvement between both plotted cases resides in a better discrimination of *task_motor* (65.7% versus 75.8%) when considering higher frequencies, which is in agreement with the latter statement.

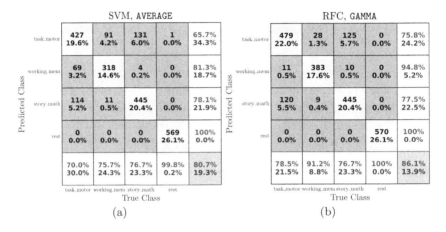

Fig. 4. Confusion matrices corresponding to (a) the SVM model for the AVERAGE case; and (b) the RFC model for the GAMMA band. It can be observed that most misclassified examples belong to *task_motor* and *story_math* classes, as opposed to *working_mem* and *rest* tasks, which can be discriminated much more reliably.

5   Conclusions and Future Research Lines

This manuscript has elaborated on the design of topological graph features for predicting the task developed by a subject based on the sensor-to-sensor connectivity graph inferred from the M/EEG signals captured while the task is performed. The proposed group of predictors represent several measures of structural connectivity of the graph modeling the relationships found between pair of sensors, measures that are postulated to suffice for accurately determining the task performed by the individual. Experiments aimed at validating this hypothesis for different supervised learning models have been discussed over real MEG experimental data made public by the Human Connectome Project. Results are convincing, specially in high-frequency bands where motor processing tasks occur to be more discriminable (with Cohen's Kappa Coefficient scores of up to 95% in the GAMMA band). This unprecedented use of graph classifiers to get insights on the role of different frequency bands in human brain connectomics is promising, and unleashes many interesting research directions towards leveraging the sensor-level information embedded in recorded brain data.

In this regard, we plan to explore other feature extraction approaches suited to deal with connectomics, such as graph embedding or evolutionary feature transformation techniques. Strategies for fusing decisions made over different frequency bands will be also investigated, along with the extrapolation of this study to multi-source connectomes, such as those inferred from MRI scans. Alternative methods to interpret the relevance and interplay between predictors will be also examined, such as partial dependency plots and other schemes alike.

Acknowledgments. This work has been supported by the Spanish Ministerio de Economía y Competitividad (MINECO) under the RETOS COLABORACION research programme, through its funded CELEXITA project (Connectome-basEd knowLedge EXtraction for dIagnosis and Therapy evaluAtion, ref. RTC–2016–5334–1).

References

1. Kandel, E.R., Schwartz, J.H., Jessell, T.M., Siegelbaum, S.A., Hudspeth, A.J., et al.: Principles of Neural Science, vol. 4. McGraw-hill, New York (2000)
2. Schacter, D.L., Addis, D.R.: The cognitive neuroscience of constructive memory: remembering the past and imagining the future. Philos. Trans. R. Soc. B: Biol. Sci. **362**(1481), 773–786 (2007)
3. Markram, H.: Seven challenges for neuroscience. Funct. Neurol. **28**(3), 145 (2013)
4. Sporns, O., Tononi, G., Kötter, R.: The human connectome: a structural description of the human brain. PLoS Comput. Biol. **1**(4), e42 (2005)
5. Zuo, X.N., He, Y., Betzel, R.F., Colcombe, S., Sporns, O., Milham, M.P.: Human connectomics across the life span. Trends Cogn. Sci. **21**(1), 32–45 (2017)
6. Yap, P.T., Wu, G., Shen, D.: Human brain connectomics: networks, techniques, and applications [life sciences]. IEEE Sig. Process. Mag. **27**(4), 131–134 (2010)
7. Sporns, O.: Contributions and challenges for network models in cognitive neuroscience. Nat. Neurosci. **17**(5), 652–660 (2014)
8. Fornito, A., Zalesky, A., Breakspear, M.: Graph analysis of the human connectome: promise, progress, and pitfalls. Neuroimage **80**, 426–444 (2013)
9. Vega-Pons, S., Avesani, P.: Brain decoding via graph kernels. In: International Workshop on Pattern Recognition in Neuroimaging (PRNI), 2013, pp. 136–139. IEEE (2013)
10. Takerkart, S., Auzias, G., Thirion, B., Schön, D., Ralaivola, L.: Graph-based intersubject classification of local fMRI patterns. In: Wang, F., Shen, D., Yan, P., Suzuki, K. (eds.) MLMI 2012. LNCS, vol. 7588, pp. 184–192. Springer, Heidelberg (2012). https://doi.org/10.1007/978-3-642-35428-1_23
11. Richiardi, J., Achard, S., Bunke, H., Van De Ville, D.: Machine learning with brain graphs: predictive modeling approaches for functional imaging in systems neuroscience. IEEE Sig. Process. Mag. **30**(3), 58–70 (2013)

12. Richiardi, J., Ng, B.: Recent advances in supervised learning for brain graph classification. In: Global Conference on Signal and Information Processing (GlobalSIP), 2013 IEEE, pp. 907–910. IEEE (2013)
13. Hodge, M.R., Horton, W., Brown, T., Herrick, R., Olsen, T., Hileman, M.E., McKay, M., Archie, K.A., Cler, E., Harms, M.P., et al.: Connectomedb – sharing human brain connectivity data. Neuroimage **124**, 1102–1107 (2016)
14. Stone, M.: Cross-validatory choice and assessment of statistical predictions. J. Roy. Stat. Soc. Ser. B (Methodological) **36**, 111–147 (1974)
15. Varma, S., Simon, R.: Bias in error estimation when using cross-validation for model selection. BMC Bioinf. **7**(1), 91 (2006)
16. Cohen, J.: A coefficient of agreement for nominal scales. Educ. Psychol. Measur. **20**(1), 37–46 (1960)
17. Yan, S., Xu, D., Zhang, B., Zhang, H.J., Yang, Q., Lin, S.: Graph embedding and extensions: a general framework for dimensionality reduction. IEEE Trans. Patt. Anal. Mach. Intell. **29**(1), 40–51 (2007)
18. Lang, E.W., Tomé, A.M., Keck, I.R., Górriz-Sáez, J., Puntonet, C.G.: Brain connectivity analysis: a short survey. Comput. Intell. Neurosci. **2012**, 8 (2012)
19. Stam, C.J., Nolte, G., Daffertshofer, A.: Phase lag index: assessment of functional connectivity from multi channel EEG and MEG with diminished bias from common sources. Hum. Brain Mapp. **28**(11), 1178–1193 (2007)
20. Stanley, G.B.: Reading and writing the neural code. Nat. Neurosci. **16**(3), 259–263 (2013)
21. Rubinov, M., Sporns, O., van Leeuwen, C., Breakspear, M.: Symbiotic relationship between brain structure and dynamics. BMC Neurosci. **10**(1), 55 (2009)
22. Larson-Prior, L.J., Oostenveld, R., Della Penna, S., Michalareas, G., Prior, F., Babajani-Feremi, A., Schoffelen, J.M., Marzetti, L., de Pasquale, F., Di Pompeo, F., et al.: Adding dynamics to the human connectome project with MEG. Neuroimage **80**, 190–201 (2013)
23. Human Connectome Project: WU-Minn HCP 500 Subjects + MEG2 Data Release: Reference Manual (2014). https://www.humanconnectome.org/storage/app/media/documentation/s500/hcps500meg2releasereferencemanual.pdf. Accessed Oct 2017
24. Kira, K., Rendell, L.A.: The feature selection problem: traditional methods and a new algorithm. AAAI **2**, 129–134 (1992)
25. Kursa, M.B., Rudnicki, W.R., et al.: Feature selection with the boruta package. J. Stat. Softw. **36**(i11), 1–13 (2010)
26. Breiman, L.: Random forests. Mach. Learn. **45**(1), 5–32 (2001)
27. Waldert, S., Preissl, H., Demandt, E., Braun, C., Birbaumer, N., Aertsen, A., Mehring, C.: Hand movement direction decoded from MEG and EEG. J. Neurosci. **28**(4), 1000–1008 (2008)

Feature Selection for Detecting Gene-Gene Interactions in Genome-Wide Association Studies

Faramarz Dorani and Ting Hu$^{(\boxtimes)}$

Department of Computer Science, Memorial University,
St. John's, NL A1B 3X5, Canada
{faramarz.dorani,ting.hu}@mun.ca

Abstract. Disease association studies aim at finding the genetic variations underlying complex human diseases in order to better understand the etiology of the disease and to provide better diagnoses, treatment, and even prevention. The non-linear interactions among multiple genetic factors play an important role in finding those genetic variations, but have not always been taken fully into account. This is due to the fact that searching combinations of interacting genetic factors becomes inhibitive as its complexity grows exponentially with the size of data. It is especially challenging for genome-wide association studies (GWAS) where typically more than a million single-nucleotide polymorphisms (SNPs) are under consideration. Dimensionality reduction is thus needed to allow us to investigate only a subset of genetic attributes that most likely have interaction effects. In this article, we conduct a comprehensive study by examining six widely used feature selection methods in machine learning for filtering interacting SNPs rather than the ones with strong individual main effects. Those six feature selection methods include chi-square, logistic regression, odds ratio, and three Relief-based algorithms. By applying all six feature selection methods to both a simulated and a real GWAS datasets, we report that Relief-based methods perform the best in filtering SNPs associated with a disease in terms of strong interaction effects.

Keywords: Feature selection · Relief algorithms · Information gain
Gene-gene interactions · Genome-wide association studies

1 Introduction

The fundamental task of genetic association studies is to detect genetic variations that contribute to a disease status. In genome-wide association studies (GWAS), partial or all of the human genome is genotyped for discovering the associations between genetic factors and a disease or a phenotypic trait [1]. GWAS first began as a consequent of the HapMap Project [2] in 2005 aiming at discovering new treatments for common human diseases such as cancers. GWAS investigate the

© Springer International Publishing AG, part of Springer Nature 2018
K. Sim and P. Kaufmann (Eds.): EvoApplications 2018, LNCS 10784, pp. 33–46, 2018.
https://doi.org/10.1007/978-3-319-77538-8_3

genetic variations in two phenotypically distinguished populations, healthy and diseased, to find the variants that can explain the disease. There are two types of genetic variation: single nucleotide polymorphism (SNP) and copy number variation (CNV). In GWAS the genetic variants under consideration are SNPs, the most common type of variation among people. SNPs occur within a person's DNA in almost every 300 nucleotides, meaning that there are around ten million SNPs in the whole human genome. A SNP generally refers to a base-pair (or locus) in the DNA sequence which has a variation higher than 1% in a population [3]. Variations represent different alleles at a bi-allelic locus. In GWAS, genome data of a group of healthy individuals (i.e., controls) and diseased individuals (i.e., cases) are collected and genotyped, which usually contain more than one million SNPs and thus are regarded as *high dimensional* data.

It is a challenging task to analyze high dimensional SNP data for GWAS. The number of variables, i.e., SNPs, brings an extensive computational burden for informatics methods [4,5]. Moreover, in the studies of common human diseases, it has been accepted that the non-additive effects of multiple interacting genetic variables play an important role explaining the risk of a disease [6,7]. The traditional one-gene-at-a time strategies likely overlook important interacting genes that have moderate individual effects. Therefore, powerful data mining and machine learning methods are needed in order to examine multiple variables at a time and to search for gene-gene interactions that contribute to a disease. A GWAS dataset with a million variables can be prohibitive for the application of any machine learning algorithms for detecting gene-gene interactions, since enumerating all possible combinations of variables is impossible. In addition, many of those variables can be redundant or irrelevant for the disease under consideration. Thus the selection of a subset of relevant and potential variables to be included in the subsequent analysis, i.e., *feature selection*, is usually needed [4].

Feature selection is frequently used as a pre-processing step in machine learning when the original data contain noisy or irrelevant features that could compromise the prediction power of learning algorithms [8]. Feature selection methods choose only a subset of the most important features, and thus reduce the dimensionality of the data, speed up the learning process, simplify the learned model, and improve the prediction performance [9,10].

Feature selection involves two main objectives, i.e., to maximize the prediction accuracy and to minimize the number of features. There are two general approaches for selecting features for predictive models: filter and wrapper. The key difference between these two is that in filter approaches the learning algorithm has no influence in selecting features. That is, features are selected based on a filtering criterion independent of the learning model. Both filter and wrapper approaches have wide applications. Filter approaches have the advantage of high speed while wrapper approaches generally can achieve better prediction accuracies [11]. Of those two, filter approaches are often used in bioinformatics studies given the fact that they can easily scale to very high-dimensional data, that they are computationally simple and fast, and that they are independent of the classification algorithm [12].

There have been studies investigating the performance of feature selection methods on high dimensional datasets in bioinformatics. Hua et al. [13] evaluated the performance of several filter and wrapper feature selection methods on both synthetic and real gene-expression microarrays data with around 20,000 features (genes) and 180 samples. Shah and Kusiak [14] used a genetic algorithm (GA) to search for the best subset of SNPs in a dataset with 172 SNPs. The feature subset was then evaluated by a baseline classifier to compare with using the whole feature set. Wu et al. [15] proposed an SNP selection and classification approach based on random forest (RF) for GWAS. Their stratified random forest (SRF) method was tested on Parkinson and Alzheimer's case-control data and was shown to outperform other methods including the original RF and support vector machines (SVM) in terms of test-error and run time. Brown et al. [16] proposed a framework of using mutual information for feature selection. Their objective was to select the smallest feature subset that has the highest mutual information with the phenotypic outcome.

However, most existing studies used the classification accuracy as the indicator for feature selection performance. The contribution of a feature to a phenotypic outcome could be its individual main effect or its interacting effect combined with other features. Using the overall classification accuracy was not able to distinguish the interaction effects of multiple variables and the individual main effects.

In our study, we focus on searching for features (SNPs) that have strong associations with the disease outcome in terms of gene-gene interactions. This differentiates our work from many existing studies that mostly focus on SNPs with high main-effects. We apply information gain to quantify the pair-wise synergy of SNPs and use that to evaluate various feature selection methods in order to identify the ones that can find subsets of SNPs with high synergistic effects on the disease status. We investigate six most popular filter algorithms, and test them on both simulated and real GWAS datasets. Our findings can be helpful for the recommendation of feature selection methods for detecting gene-gene interactions in GWAS.

2 Methods

In this section, we first discuss the data that will be used in this study, which include a simulated and a real population-based GWAS datasets. Then we introduce the information gain measure that will be employed as the quantification of the synergistic interaction effect of pairs of SNPs. Last, we present the six feature selection algorithms that will be investigated and compared.

2.1 Datasets

GWAS collect DNA sequencing data from two phenotypically distinguished populations, namely the diseased cases and healthy controls. A few thousand to a million of SNPs are usually genotyped for each sample. Each SNP can be regarded as a bi-allelic variable, i.e., it has two different variations, with the common allele among a population called the *reference* and the other called *variant*. Given the fact that human chromosomes are paired, three categorical values are usually used to code for each SNP, i.e., 0 for homozygous reference, 1 for heterozygous variant, and 2 for homozygous variant.

For this study, we use a simulated genetic association dataset generated by the genetic architecture model emulator for testing and evaluating software (GAMETES) [17,18]. GAMETES is a fast algorithm for generating simulation data of complex genetic models. Particularly, in addition to additive models, GAMETES is specialized for generating pure interaction models, i.e., interacting features without the existence of any main effects. Each n-locus model is generated deterministically, based on a set of random parameters and specified values of heritability, minor allele frequencies, and population disease prevalence. Since we focus on pairwise SNP interactions, we use GAMETES to generate a population of 500 samples with half being cases and half being controls. The dataset has 1000 SNPs, where 15 pairs are two-locus interacting models with a minor allele frequency of 0.2 and another 970 are random SNPs. We set the heritability to 0.2 and population prevalence to 0.5.

In addition, we use a real GWAS dataset collected for a case-control study on colorectal cancer (CRC) from the Colorectal Transdisciplinary (CORECT) consortium [19]. The dataset has over two million genetic variants of 1152 individuals of which 656 are CRC cases and 496 are healthy controls. Quality control [20] is first conducted to remove low-quality samples and sub-standard SNPs from the dataset. Then we remove redundant SNPs that are in linkage disequilibrium (LD). After quality control and LD pruning steps, 186,251 SNPs and 944 samples pass various filters. In this remaining population, 472 samples are cases and 472 are controls. The minimum and maximum minor allele frequency (MAF) of the SNPs are 0.04737 and 0.5 respectively.

2.2   Quantification of Pairwise Interactions Using Information Gain

Information theoretic measures such as entropy and mutual information [21] quantify the uncertainty of single random variables and the dependence of two variables, and have seen increasing applications in genetic association studies [22–25]. In such a context, the *entropy* $H(C)$ of the disease class C measures the unpredictability of the disease, and the conditional entropy $H(C|A)$ measures the uncertainly of C given the knowledge of SNP A. Subtracting $H(C|A)$ from $H(C)$ gives the *mutual information* of A and C, and is the reduction in the uncertainty of the class C due to the knowledge about SNP A's genotype, defined as

$$I(A;C) = H(C) - H(C|A). \tag{1}$$

Mutual information $I(A;C)$ essentially captures the main effect of SNP A on the disease status C.

When two SNPs, A and B, are considered, mutual information $I(A, B; C)$ measures how much the disease status C can be explained by combining both A and B. The *information gain $IG(A; B; C)$*, calculated as

$$IG(A; B; C) = I(A, B; C) - I(A; C) - I(B; C), \qquad (2)$$

is the information gained about the class C from the genotypes of SNPs A and B considered together minus that from each of these SNPs considered separately. In brief, $IG(A; B; C)$ measures the amount of synergetic influence SNPs A and B have on class C. Thus, information gain IG can be used to evaluate the pairwise interaction effect between two SNPs in association with the disease.

2.3   Feature Selection Algorithms

We choose six most widely used feature selection algorithms in our comparative study, and investigate their performance on searching variables that contribute to the disease in terms of gene-gene interactions. These six feature selection algorithms include three uni-variate approaches, chi-square, logistic regression, and odds ratio, and three Relief-based algorithms, ReliefF, TuRF, and SURF. They will be applied to both simulated and real GWAS datasets and provide rankings of all the SNPs in the data.

Chi-square: The chi-square (χ^2) test of independence [26] is commonly used in human genetics and genetic epidemiology [4] for categorical data. A χ^2 test estimates how likely different alleles of a SNP can differentiate the disease status. It is a very efficient filtering method for assessing the independent effect of individual SNPs on disease susceptibility.

Logistic regression: Logistic regression measures the relationship between the categorical outcome and multiple independent variables by estimating probabilities using a logistic function. A linear relationship between variables and the categorical outcome is usually assumed, and a coefficient is estimated for each variable when such a linear relationship is trained to best predict the outcome. The variable coefficient can then be used as a quantification of the importance of each variable.

Odds-ratio: Odds ratio (OR) is the most commonly used statistic in case-control studies. It measures the association between an exposure (e.g., health characteristic) and an outcome (e.g., disease status). The OR represents the odds that a disease status will occur given a particular exposure, compared to the odds of the outcome occurring in the absence of that exposure [27].

ReliefF: Relief is able to detect complex attribute dependencies even in the absence of main effects [28]. It estimates the quality of attributes using a nearest-neighbor algorithm. While Relief uses, for each individual, a single nearest neighbor in each class, ReliefF, a variant of Relief, uses multiple, usually 10, nearest neighbors, and thus is more robust when a dataset contains noise [29,30]. The basic idea of Relief-based algorithms is to draw instances at random, compute their nearest neighbors, and adjust a feature weighting vector to give more

Table 1. Ranks of the 30 known interacting SNPs by feature selection algorithms.

	Logit	χ^2	OR	ReliefF	TuRF	SURF
Mean	549.16	548.30	444.10	202.63	**166.96**	233.16
SD	277.99	267.18	287.04	201.74	259.74	212.13
Median	617.50	536.50	346.50	130.00	**21.50**	183.50

weights to features that discriminate the instance from its neighbors of different classes. Comparing to uni-variate feature selection algorithms, ReliefF is able to capture attribute interactions because it selects nearest neighbors using the entire vector of values across all attributes [4,30].

Tuned ReliefF (TuRF): It is an extension of ReliefF specifically for large-scale genetics data [31]. This method systematically and iteratively removes attributes that have low-quality estimates so that the remaining attributes can be re-estimated more accurately. It improves the estimation of weights in noisy data but does not fundamentally change the underlying ReliefF algorithm. It is useful when data contain a large number of non-relevant SNPs. It is also more computationally intense because of the iterative process of removing attributes.

Spatially Uniform ReliefF (SURF): SURF is also an extension of the ReliefF algorithm [32]. It incorporates the spatial information when assesses neighbors. Instead of using a fixed number of neighbors as the threshold in ReliefF, SURF uses a fixed distance threshold for choosing neighbors. It is reported to be able to improve the sensitivity detecting small interaction effects.

3 Results

3.1 Feature Selection Algorithms on the Simulated Data

First, we apply all six feature selection algorithms to the simulated dataset that contains 30 known SNPs with pairwise interactions and 970 random SNPs. The chi-square, odd-ratio, ReliefF, TuRF, and SURF algorithms are implemented using the multifactor dimensionality reduction (MDR) software with default parameter settings [33]. Logistic regression is implemented using the Python *scikit-learn* package [34].

Each algorithm yields a ranking of all 1000 SNPs. Table 1 shows the statistics of the ranks of those 30 known SNPs by each feature selection algorithm. We see that TuRF has both the highest mean and median ranks among all the methods, and the differences are significant. ReliefF performs the second best, followed by SURF.

Figure 1 shows the recall-at-k for all six feature selection algorithms. The y-axis shows the fraction of those 30 known SNPs detected by the top k SNPs ranked by each feature selection algorithm. We can see that for all values of k, TuRF has the highest recalls. In addition, all three Relief-based algorithms outperform the other methods.

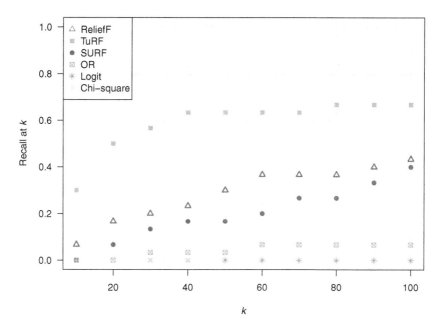

Fig. 1. Diagram of recall-at-k for six feature selection algorithms applied to the simulated dataset. Recall-at-k is the fraction of the 30 known interacting SNPs detected by the top k ranked SNPs using each feature selection algorithm.

Figure 2 shows the distributions of the ranks of those 30 known interacting SNPs using different feature selection algorithms. The x-axis is the rank of SNPs and the y-axis is the density. Again, TuRF has the highest density around high ranks, meaning that it produces the highest ranks for those 30 known SNPs. SURF and ReliefF also have better ranking performance comparing to the other three methods. Odds-ratio, logistic regression, and chi-square have flat distributions across the entire rank range, which indicates their inability to identify those 30 interacting SNPs.

3.2   Feature Selection Algorithms on the CRC Data

We then compare the performance of those six feature selection algorithms using the CRC GWAS dataset. The CRC GWAS dataset is processed using PLINK software [35]. PLINK can conduct some fundamental association tests by comparing allele frequencies of SNPs between cases and controls. We use the command `--assoc` to compute chi-square and odds-ratio scores for each SNP, and the command `--logistic` for logistic regression analysis. Again, we used the MDR software [33] to implement ReliefF, TuRF, and SURF algorithms.

Each feature selection algorithm generates a ranking of all the 186,251 SNPs in the dataset. For detecting gene-gene interactions, exhaustive enumeration of all possible combinations of SNPs is usually considered. Even for pairwise

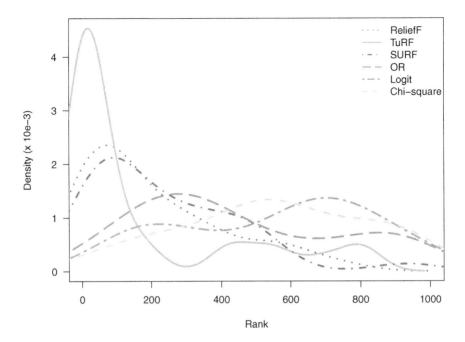

Fig. 2. Density of the ranks of the 30 known interaction SNPs using different feature selection algorithms on the simulated dataset.

interactions, the total number of possible pairs $\binom{n}{2}$ grows fast with the number of SNPs n. Therefore, we can only consider a moderate subset of SNPs for interaction analysis, and we use the rankings estimated using feature selection algorithms to filter those potentially more important SNPs. We choose the subset of the top 10,000 SNPs by each feature selection algorithm. Then, for the six subsets of filtered 10,000 SNPs, we evaluate their pairwise interactions separately using the information gain (IG) measure.

Table 2. Statistics of the information gain values of all $\binom{10,000}{2}$ SNP pairs filtered by each feature selection algorithm ($\times 10^{-3}$).

	Logit	χ^2	OR	ReliefF	TuRF	SURF
Max	27.4	27.6	27.4	**30.2**	28.9	28.2
Min	−4	−5.1	−4	−3.2	−2.9	−5.7
Mean	2.760	3.047	2.776	3.190	**3.191**	3.056
SD	2.117	2.221	2.120	2.243	2.251	2.224
Median	2.3	2.6	2.3	2.7	2.7	2.6

Table 2 shows the maximum, minimum, mean, standard deviation, and median values of the information gain calculated using all $\binom{10,000}{2}$ pairs of the

10,000 SNPs filtered by the six feature selection algorithms. As we can see, ReliefF finds the SNP pair with the highest interaction strength, and TuRF has the best overall distribution.

Figure 3 shows the distribution of the interaction strength of all $\binom{10,000}{2}$ pairs of SNPs selected by each feature selection algorithm. We see that the distributions of ReliefF and TuRF have overall more SNP pairs with higher IG values. The distributions of SURF and chi-square are comparable, and logistic regression and odds ratio have the lowest overall IG values.

The significance of the IG value of each pair of SNPs can be assessed using permutation testing. For each permutation, we randomly shuffle the case/control labels of all the samples in the data in order to remove the association between the genotypes of SNPs and the disease status. Repeating such a permutation multiple times generates a null distribution of what can be observed by chance. For each permuted dataset, we compute the IG value of each pair of SNPs. In this study, we perform a 100-fold permutation test. The significance level (p-value) of the IG of each SNP pair can be assessed by comparing the IG value of the pair calculated using the real dataset to the IG values calculated using the 100 permuted datasets (see Algorithm 1).

Algorithm 1. Permutation testing algorithm

1: **procedure** COMPUTEPVALUE
2:     $D \leftarrow$ *original dataset*
3:     $n \leftarrow$ *number of permutations*
4:     $m \leftarrow$ *number of SNP pairs*
5:     $C \leftarrow$ *counter for each SNP pair*
6:     $i \leftarrow 1$
7:     **while** $i < n$ **do**
8:         *Generate a random permutation D' of the original dataset D*
9:         $j \leftarrow 1$
10:        **while** $j < m$ **do**
11:            *calculate $IG_j^{D'}$ for the j-th SNP pair*
12:            *increase C_j by 1 if $IG_j^{D'}$ is greater than the real observed IG_j^D*
13:            $j \leftarrow j + 1$
14:        $i \leftarrow i + 1$
15:    *compute the significance level p_k for each SNP pair k as $\frac{C_k}{n}$*

We apply permutation testing to all six subsets of $\binom{10,000}{2}$ pairs of SNPs selected by each feature selection algorithm, such that their significance level p-values can be assessed. Figure 4 shows the number of SNP pairs that pass two different p-value thresholds, 0.01 and 0.05. TuRF has more SNP pairs with significant interaction strength using both thresholds. All three Relief-based algorithms have higher numbers of significant SNP pairs than the other three methods. Logistic regression and odds ratio find the least numbers of significant interacting SNP pairs.

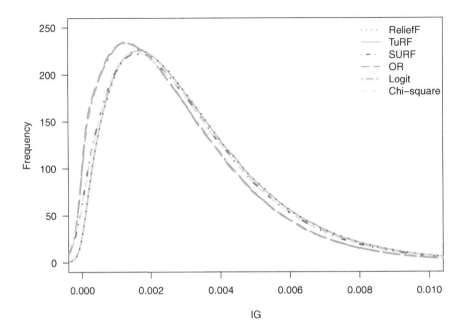

Fig. 3. Distribution of the information gain (IG) values of all pairs of filtered 10,000 SNPs by each feature selection algorithm.

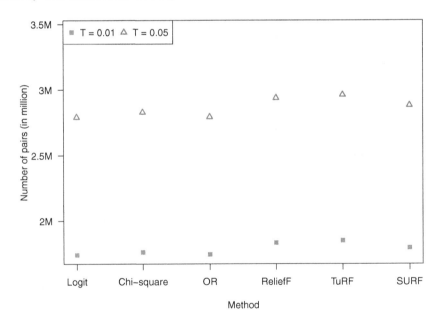

Fig. 4. The number of SNP pairs with significant interaction strengths using p-value cutoff T. Red triangles show the results using cutoff $p \leq 0.01$, and blue squares show the results with cutoff $p \leq 0.05$. (Color figure online)

4   Discussion

The goal of genome-wide association studies (GWAS) is to identify genetic markers that can explain complex human diseases. Most existing analyses for GWAS look at one gene at a time due to the limitation of analytical methodologies and computational resources. Such a strategy very likely overlook potentially important genetic attributes that have low main effects but contribute to a disease outcome through multifactorial interactions. Detecting such non-additive gene-gene interactions help us better understand the underlying genetic background of common diseases and better develop new strategies to treat, diagnose, and prevent them.

Detecting gene-gene interactions for GWAS imposes computational challenges since enumerating combinations of genetic attributes becomes inhibitive when up to a million variables are under consideration. Thus, feature selection becomes a necessity for the task.

In this study, we investigated the performance of six widely used feature selection algorithms for detecting potentially interacting single nucleotide polymorphisms (SNPs) for GWAS. We used both a simulated and real genetic datasets. We adopted information gain as a measure for quantifying pairwise interaction strength of SNPs in order to evaluate the filtering performance of those six feature selection algorithms. Among the investigated feature selection methods, three are single variable feature scoring methods. That is, they only consider individual main effects of SNP on the disease status. Three other methods are extensions of the Relief algorithm which is a multivariate feature selection algorithm.

For the simulated dataset, we generated a population-based dataset with 1000 SNPs including 15 pairs of interacting SNPs and 970 random ones. We applied all six feature selection algorithms to rank those 1000 SNPs and look into the recall-at-k of detecting those 30 known interacting SNPs. The TuRF algorithm has the highest recall-at-k for all k values, followed by ReliefF and SURF. All three Relief-based algorithms perform better than odds ratio, logistic regression, and chi-square.

We also tested the feature selection algorithms using a real GWAS dataset on colorectal cancer (CRC). We used information gain to quantify pairwise interaction strength of SNPs in order to evaluate the filtering performance of the feature selection algorithms. We chose 10,000 top-ranked SNPs by each feature selection algorithm and applied information gain measure and permutation testing to compute the interaction strengths and their significance levels of all pairs of SNPs. We found that TuRF again was able to filter more significant interacting SNPs than the rest of the feature selection algorithms. All three Relief-based algorithms outperformed the other three methods.

TuRF and ReliefF had comparable performance on the application to the real CRC dataset. By looking at their top 10,000 SNPs, we saw that only 1474 were overlapped. That is, only 14% of their top 10K SNPs are the same. This is interesting that they seemed to be able to find different sets of interacting SNPs.

There is no general rule for selecting the best feature selection method in machine learning studies. The decision mostly depends on the data and research question of the investigation. For the purpose of detecting gene-gene interactions, Relief-based methods were shown to have better performance than the common univariate methods. Gene-gene interactions can be very challenging to detect by univariate methods since interacting genetic factors may not show significant individual main effects. By evaluating sample similarity using all genetic attributes, Relief-base algorithms are able to capture the non-addition interaction effects among multiple attributes, and are recommended for detecting gene-gene interactions for GWAS.

In future studies, we expect to explore more sophisticated feature selection algorithms, especially wrapper and embedded methods, and test their utilities in genetic association and bioinformatics studies.

Acknowledgments. This research was supported by Newfoundland and Labrador Research and Development Corporation (RDC) Ignite Grant 5404.1942.101 and the Natural Science and Engineering Research Council (NSERC) of Canada Discovery Grant RGPIN-2016-04699 to TH.

References

1. Wellcome Trust Case Control Consortium, et al.: Genome-wide association study of 14,000 cases of seven common diseases and 3,000 shared controls. Nature **447**(7145), 661 (2007)
2. Gibbs, R.A., Belmont, J.W., Hardenbol, P., Willis, T.D., Yu, F., Yang, H., Ch'ang, L.Y., Huang, W., Liu, B., Shen, Y., et al.: The international HapMap project. Nature **426**(6968), 789–796 (2003)
3. The 1000 Genomes Project Consortium, et al.: A map of human genome variation from population scale sequencing. Nature **467**(7319), 1061 (2010)
4. Moore, J.H., Asselbergs, F.W., Williams, S.M.: Bioinformatics challenges for genome-wide association studies. Bioinformatics **26**(4), 445–455 (2010)
5. Hu, T., Andrew, A.S., Karagas, M.R., Moore, J.H.: Statistical epistasis networks reduce the computational complexity of searching three-locus genetic models. Proc. Pac. Symp. Biocomput. **18**, 397–408 (2013)
6. Cordell, H.J.: Epistasis: what it means, what it doesn't mean, and statistical methods to detect it in humans. Hum. Mol. Genet. **11**(20), 2463–2468 (2002)
7. Hu, T., Chen, Y., Kiralis, J.W., Moore, J.H.: ViSEN: methodology and software for visualization of statistical epistasis networks. Genet. Epidemiol. **37**, 283–285 (2013)
8. Yu, L., Liu, H.: Feature selection for high-dimensional data: a fast correlation-based filter solution. ICML **3**, 856–863 (2003)
9. Dash, M., Liu, H.: Feature selection for classification. Intell. Data Anal. **1**(1–4), 131–156 (1997)
10. Guyon, I., Elisseeff, A.: An introduction to variable and feature selection. J. Mach. Learn. Res. **3**(Mar), 1157–1182 (2003)
11. Freitas, A.A.: Data Mining and Knowledge Discovery with Evolutionary Algorithms. Springer Science & Business Media, Heidelberg (2013)

12. Saeys, Y., Inza, I., Larrañaga, P.: A review of feature selection techniques in bioinformatics. Bioinformatics **23**(19), 2507–2517 (2007)
13. Hua, J., Tembe, W.D., Dougherty, E.R.: Performance of feature-selection methods in the classification of high-dimension data. Pattern Recogn. **42**(3), 409–424 (2009)
14. Shah, S.C., Kusiak, A.: Data mining and genetic algorithm based gene/SNP selection. Artif. Intell. Med. **31**(3), 183–196 (2004)
15. Wu, Q., Ye, Y., Liu, Y., Ng, M.K.: SNP selection and classification of genome-wide SNP data using stratified sampling random forests. IEEE Trans. Nanobiosci. **11**(3), 216–227 (2012)
16. Brown, G., Pocock, A., Zhao, M.J., Luján, M.: Conditional likelihood maximisation: a unifying framework for information theoretic feature selection. J. Mach. Learn. Res. **13**(Jan), 27–66 (2012)
17. Urbanowicz, R.J., Kiralis, J.W., Fisher, J.M., Moore, J.H.: Predicting the difficulty of pure, strict, epistatic models: metrics for simulated model selection. BioData Min. **5**, 15 (2012)
18. Urbanowicz, R.J., Kiralis, J., Sinnott-Armstrong, N.A., Heberling, T., Fisher, J.M., Moore, J.H.: Gametes: a fast, direct algorithm for generating pure, strict, epistatic models with random architectures. BioData Min. **5**(1), 16 (2012)
19. Schumacher, F.R., Schmit, S.L., Jiao, S., Edlund, C.K., Wang, H., Zhang, B., Hsu, L., Huang, S.C., Fischer, C.P., et al.: Genome-wide association study of colorectal cancer identifies six new susceptibility loci. Nature Commun. **6**, 7138 (2015)
20. Anderson, C.A., Pettersson, F.H., Clarke, G.M., Cardon, L.R., Morris, A.P., Zondervan, K.T.: Data quality control in genetic case-control association studies. Nat. Protoc. **5**(9), 1564–1573 (2010)
21. Cover, T.M., Thomas, J.A.: Elements of Information Theory, 2nd edn. Wiley, Hoboken (2006)
22. Hu, T., Sinnott-Armstrong, N.A., Kiralis, J.W., Andrew, A.S., Karagas, M.R., Moore, J.H.: Characterizing genetic interactions in human disease association studies using statistical epistasis networks. BMC Bioinform. **12**, 364 (2011)
23. Fan, R., Zhong, M., Wang, S., Zhang, Y., Andrew, A., Karagas, M., Chen, H., Amos, C.I., Xiong, M., Moore, J.H.: Entropy-based information gain approaches to detect and to characterize gene-gene and gene-environment interactions/correlations of complex diseases. Genet. Epidemiol. **35**(7), 706–721 (2011)
24. Li, H., Lee, Y., Chen, J.L., Rebman, E., Li, J., Lussier, Y.A.: Complex-disease networks of trait-associated single-nucleotide polymorphisms (SNPs) unveiled by information theory. J. Am. Med. Inform. Assoc. **19**, 295–305 (2012)
25. Hu, T., Chen, Y., Kiralis, J.W., Collins, R.L., Wejse, C., Sirugo, G., Williams, S.M., Moore, J.H.: An information-gain approach to detecting three-way epistatic interactions in genetic association studies. J. Am. Med. Inform. Assoc. **20**(4), 630–636 (2013)
26. Yates, F.: Contingency tables involving small numbers and the $\chi 2$ test. Suppl. J. Roy. Stat. Soc. **1**(2), 217–235 (1934)
27. Szumilas, M.: Explaining odds ratios. J. Can. Acad. Child Adolesc. Psychiatry **19**(3), 227 (2010)
28. Kira, K., Rendell, L.A.: A practical approach to feature selection. In: Proceedings of the Ninth International Workshop on Machine Learning, pp. 249–256 (1992)
29. Kononenko, I.: Estimating attributes: analysis and extensions of RELIEF. In: Bergadano, F., De Raedt, L. (eds.) ECML 1994. LNCS, vol. 784, pp. 171–182. Springer, Heidelberg (1994). https://doi.org/10.1007/3-540-57868-4_57
30. Robnik-Šikonja, M., Kononenko, I.: Theoretical and empirical analysis of relieff and rrelieff. Mach. Learn. **53**(1–2), 23–69 (2003)

31. Moore, J.H., White, B.C.: Tuning ReliefF for genome-wide genetic analysis. In: Marchiori, E., Moore, J.H., Rajapakse, J.C. (eds.) EvoBIO 2007. LNCS, vol. 4447, pp. 166–175. Springer, Heidelberg (2007). https://doi.org/10.1007/978-3-540-71783-6_16

32. Greene, C.S., Penrod, N.M., Kiralis, J., Moore, J.H.: Spatially uniform relieff (SURF) for computationally-efficient filtering of gene-gene interactions. BioData Min. 2(1), 5 (2009)

33. Ritchie, M.D., Hahn, L.W., Roodi, N., Bailey, L.R., Dupont, W.D., Parl, F.F., Moore, J.H.: Multifactor-dimensionality reduction reveals high-order interactions among estrogen-metabolism genes in sporadic breast cancer. Am. J. Hum. Genet. 69(1), 138–147 (2001)

34. Pedregosa, F., Varoquaux, G., Gramfort, A., Michel, V., Thirion, B., Grisel, O., Blondel, M., Prettenhofer, P., Weiss, R., Dubourg, V., Vanderplas, J., Passos, A., Cournapeau, D., Brucher, M., Perrot, M., Duchesnay, E.: Scikit-learn: machine learning in Python. J. Mach. Learn. Res. 12, 2825–2830 (2011)

35. Purcell, S., Neale, B., Todd-Brown, K., Thomas, L., Ferreira, M.A., Bender, D., Maller, J., Sklar, P., De Bakker, P.I., Daly, M.J., et al.: Plink: a tool set for whole-genome association and population-based linkage analyses. Am. J. Hum. Genet. 81(3), 559–575 (2007)

Fitness Functions Evaluation for Segmentation of Lymphoma Histological Images Using Genetic Algorithm

Thaína A. A. Tosta[1(✉)], Paulo Rogério de Faria[2], Leandro Alves Neves[3], and Marcelo Zanchetta do Nascimento[1,4]

[1] Center of Mathematics, Computing and Cognition, Federal University of ABC, Santo André, Brazil
tosta.thaina@gmail.com
[2] Department of Histology and Morphology, Institute of Biomedical Science, Federal University of Uberlândia, Uberlândia, Brazil
[3] Department of Computer Science and Statistics, São Paulo State University, São José do Rio Preto, Brazil
[4] Faculty of Computer Science, Federal University of Uberlândia, Uberlândia, Brazil

Abstract. For disease monitoring, grade definition and treatments orientation, specialists analyze tissue samples to identify structures of different types of cancer. However, manual analysis is a complex task due to its subjectivity. To help specialists in the identification of regions of interest, segmentation methods are used on histological images obtained by the digitization of tissue samples. Besides, features extracted from these specific regions allow for more objective diagnoses by using classification techniques. In this paper, fitness functions are analyzed for unsupervised segmentation and classification of chronic lymphocytic leukemia and follicular lymphoma images by the identification of their neoplastic cellular nuclei through the genetic algorithm. Qualitative and quantitative analyses allowed the definition of the Rényi entropy as the most adequate for this application. Images classification has reached results of 98.14% through accuracy metric by using this fitness function.

Keywords: Nuclear segmentation · Lymphoma histological images
Genetic algorithm · Fitness function evaluation

1 Introduction

Lymphomas are cancers that develop in the cellular components called lymphocytes [1]. Their subtypes are divided into Hodgkin's lymphoma (HL) and non-Hodgkin's lymphoma (NHL), which is responsible for 85% of lymphoma cases [2]. The wide variety of NHL subtypes makes their classification and segmentation complex tasks and a challenge for images analysis.

K. Sim and P. Kaufmann (Eds.): EvoApplications 2018, LNCS 10784, pp. 47–62, 2018.
https://doi.org/10.1007/978-3-319-77538-8_4

NHL diagnoses are performed by pathologists who analyze tissue samples stained with hematoxylin-eosin (H&E) [1]. The digitization of these samples allows the application of computational methods that aid specialists in their clinical decisions. Segmentation methods are applied to identify regions of interest (ROIs) that indicate the NHL incidence. The segmentation application allows the extraction of highly specific features from ROIs, which can improve the classification performance [1]. Using these features, classification techniques can aid in diagnoses definition [3].

There are two classes of the NHL that are investigated in literature and addressed by this work: chronic lymphocytic leukemia (CLL) and follicular lymphoma (FL). CLL is a different manifestation type of small lymphocytic lymphoma. It is the most frequent case of leukemia in western countries, with an incidence of 30%. FL is the second most common type of B-cells lymphoma in the classification defined by the world health organization [4].

Some studies propose the segmentation of histological images of these lesions. [5,6] presented segmentation methods of lymphocytes on blood images of CLL with 100× magnification. Both works were evaluated with ROIs localized in the center of the images. In [5], the authors also considered an uniform illumination condition and [6] presented limitations for overlapping cells segmentation.

For FL images, there are many works proposed due to its high incidence rate [4], such as [7–9]. Segmentation of these images is divided into the identification of centroblasts and follicular regions, with some limitations addressed by this work. [9] presented limitations due to the merging of different identified ROIs. This is a common condition, as indicated by [5,8–10]. Moreover, studies as [7,11–13] presented methods that employed images stained with IHC and H&E for FL segmentation. Thus, these methods require these two types of images for application.

Due to empirical definition of threshold values, [14–17] become not sufficiently robust for application on different images. In the studies of [3,9], the authors indicated limitations for processing low magnification images and low quality images resulting from the tissue sample preparation. Using private images datasets, the correlated works can present poor performance when applied on public images that have great variations of contrast and illumination. Thus, it is important to use public images to demonstrate the robustness of new proposals [18].

Thresholding is a major method for efficient segmentation of different histological structures [19]. The optimization method of genetic algorithm (GA) is a powerful technique to define the best threshold values due to its efficiency in complex combinatorial problems. Besides, GA explores its search space in a parallel way with no local convergence of its result [20]. Using this technique, it is possible to efficiently explore the parameters used for the definition of threshold values.

The information used by the GA method in its search for the best solution is the fitness function [21]. This function is responsible for the evaluation of the individuals, playing an essential role in the algorithm by defining the best solutions through its maximization. Since this function defines the algorithm execution, explore different fitness functions is necessary so the best threshold values of segmentation can be obtained.

This paper presents an algorithm to aid specialists in diagnoses of CLL and FL using segmentation and classification steps. Neoplastic nuclei were segmented through the evaluation of the metrics of Fisher information and the entropies of Rényi, Shannon and Tsallis as GA fitness function for quantifying extracted information. Intensity and texture features were classified by the support vector machine (SVM) method to obtain objective diagnoses. The main contribution of this study is the evaluation of these different quantitative metrics to best associate the image intensity levels to the neoplastic nuclei of CLL and FL histological images. Besides, the evaluation of the proposed method was performed on images from a public domain that are characterized by color variations found in clinical practices.

2   Materials and Methods

This section describes the used image dataset, the proposed algorithm, the analyzed fitness functions and the quantitative evaluation metrics.

2.1   Images Dataset

The used lymphoma cases were digitized with a Zeiss Axioscope microscope with white light, objective lens of $20\times$ and a CCD AxioCam MR5 color camera. All images were obtained under the same configuration of the used equipment for digitization of histological samples stained with H&E. The resulting images are represented by the RGB color model with 24 bits of quantization, available for download at [22].

The public images used for validation of the proposed method compose a set of 12 and 62 images of CLL and FL, respectively. In both classes, each case has almost 2,000 cells, a quantity close to other studies dedicated to segmentation of histological and cytological images [12,23].

2.2   Proposed Algorithm

Figure 1 illustrates the methodological sequence used for development of the proposed method. This work used the MATLAB® language for implementation of the proposed method.

In the preprocessing step, the R channel from RGB color model was extracted for having the greatest contrast difference in relation to the image background [24]. The histogram equalization technique was applied to deal with variations of contrast and illumination. This method allows the redistribution of image intensity levels, leading to a histogram with an uniform distribution. Thus, the images are now characterized by a greater contrast [25]. Subsequently, the Gaussian filter was used for small noise removal and image smoothing. This method consists of a convolution process with a mask characterized by

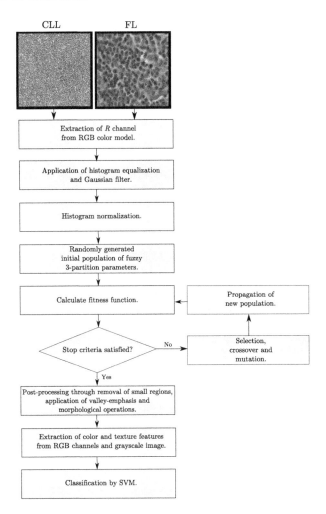

Fig. 1. The methodological sequence used by the proposed algorithm for segmentation and classification of CLL and FL images.

its elements distribution defined by a 2-dimensional Gaussian function [25]. For its application, the mask size was assigned to 3×3 pixels and the σ variable was given by the value 2, which were empirically defined. The results of the channel extraction and application of histogram equalization and Gaussian filter are illustrated by Fig. 2(b) and (c), respectively.

Following, a thresholding method based on a fuzzy 3-partition technique [26] segmented the neoplastic nuclear regions. For this purpose, the S and Z functions, represented by Eqs. 1 and 2, define a membership degree of each intensity level (k) to the investigated structures: neoplastic nuclei, cytoplasm and background.

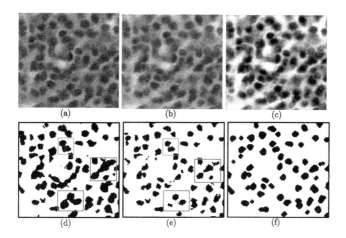

Fig. 2. Example of application of preprocessing, segmentation and post-processing steps on a subimage of *sj-05-5389-R1_012* case from FL class: (a) original image, (b) R channel from the previous image, (c) resulting image of preprocessing, (d) resulting image of segmentation using GA and Shannon entropy, with more than one nucleus identified as one object indicated by red rectangles, (e) result of valley-emphasis application with indication of corrected regions, and (f) result of morphological operations of dilation and opening.

In this case, it is necessary to compute two threshold values to separate these three regions of the images. So, two pairs of these functions were calculated.

$$
S(k, u, v, w) = \begin{cases}
1, & k \leq u \\
1 - \dfrac{(k - u)^2}{(w - u) \cdot (v - u)}, & u < k \leq v \\
\dfrac{(k - w)^2}{(w - u) \cdot (w - v)}, & v < k \leq w \\
0, & k > w
\end{cases}
\tag{1}
$$

$$
Z(k, u, v, w) = 1 - S(k, u, v, w). \tag{2}
$$

These functions allow the assignment of pixels to three fuzzy sets, defined by Eqs. 3, 4 and 5, that correspond to membership degrees to neoplastic nuclei, cytoplasm and image background, respectively.

$$
M_n(k) = S(k, u_1, v_1, w_1), \tag{3}
$$

$$
M_c(k) = \begin{cases}
Z(k, u_1, v_1, w_1), & k \leq w_1, \\
S(k, u_2, v_2, w_2), & k > w_1,
\end{cases}
\tag{4}
$$

$$
M_b(k) = Z(k, u_2, v_2, w_2), \tag{5}
$$

where, u_1, v_1, w_1, u_2, v_2 and w_2 $(0 \leq u_1 < v_1 < w_1 < u_2 < v_2 < w_2 \leq 255)$ are parameters that determine the membership degrees distribution. The threshold values (t_1 and t_2) are defined by the intersection points of M_n and M_c, and M_c and M_b.

The GA algorithm was used to assign intensity values to u_1, v_1, w_1, u_2, v_2 and w_2 with an initial random generation of 60 possible solutions coded by six values using the preprocessed image normalized histogram. Each individual was evaluated by a fitness function. The Fisher Information metric (FIM), defined by [27], was one of the evaluated GA fitness functions (H):

$$H(u_1, v_1, w_1, u_2, v_2, w_2) = w_n \cdot I_n + w_c \cdot I_c + w_b \cdot I_b, \tag{6}$$

$$I_n = \frac{1}{w_n} \sum_{i=1}^{t_1} \frac{(P_{i+1} - P_i)^2}{P_i}, \tag{7}$$

$$I_c = \frac{1}{w_c} \sum_{i=t_1+1}^{t_2} \frac{(P_{i+1} - P_i)^2}{P_i},$$

$$I_b = \frac{1}{w_b} \sum_{i=t_2+1}^{255} \frac{(P_{i+1} - P_i)^2}{P_i},$$

where, w_i represents the probabilities of intensity levels of the investigated structures (neoplastic nuclei, cytoplasm and background):

$$w_n = \sum_{i=0}^{t_1} P_i, \qquad w_c = \sum_{i=t_1+1}^{t_2} P_i, \qquad w_b = \sum_{i=t_2+1}^{255} P_i, \tag{8}$$

where, P_i is the probability of the intensity level i, i.e. the number of pixels with intensity i divided by the total number of pixels in the image.

The Rényi entropy metric (REM) was also used, as expressed by [28]:

$$H(u_1, v_1, w_1, u_2, v_2, w_2) = \frac{1}{1-\alpha} \left[\ln \sum_{i=0}^{t_1} \left(\frac{P_i}{P_n} \right)^\alpha \right]$$

$$+ \frac{1}{1-\alpha} \left[\ln \sum_{i=t_1+1}^{t_2} \left(\frac{P_i}{P_c} \right)^\alpha \right] \tag{9}$$

$$+ \frac{1}{1-\alpha} \left[\ln \sum_{i=t_2+1}^{255} \left(\frac{P_i}{P_b} \right)^\alpha \right],$$

with the empirical assignment of 2 to α and the probabilities P_n, P_c and P_b representing the probabilities of each investigated structure:

$$P_j = \sum_{k=0}^{255} h(k) \cdot M_j(k), \tag{10}$$

where, $j = \{n, c, b\}$, $M_j(k)$ corresponds to the fuzzy sets defined by Eqs. 3, 4 and 5 and h($\cdot$) represents the image normalized histogram.

The Shannon entropy metric (SEM) [29] also evaluated the values of u_1, v_1, w_1, u_2, v_2 and w_2, defined by:

$$H(u_1, v_1, w_1, u_2, v_2, w_2) = -P_n \cdot \log(P_n) - P_c \cdot \log(P_c) - P_b \cdot \log(P_b). \tag{11}$$

The Tsallis entropy metric (TEM) was also used, defined by Eqs. 12 and 13 [30]:

$$
\begin{aligned}
H(u_1, v_1, w_1, u_2, v_2, w_2) = S_q^n &+ S_q^c + S_q^b \\
&+ (1 - q) \cdot (S_q^n \cdot S_q^c + S_q^n \cdot S_q^b + S_q^c \cdot S_q^b) \\
&+ (1 - q)^2 \cdot S_q^n \cdot S_q^c \cdot S_q^b, \quad (12)
\end{aligned}
$$

$$S_q^j = \frac{1 - \sum_{i=lb}^{ub}(P_i^j)^q}{q - 1}, \tag{13}$$

where, the constant q was empirically assigned to 10 and it represents an index that denotes the degree of nonextensivity. P_i^j represents the normalization of the probabilities of each investigated structure ($j = \{n, c, b\}$) defined by the intensity values between its lower bound (lb) and upper bound (ub):

$$P^n = \frac{P_1, ..., P_{t_1}}{w_n}, \qquad P^c = \frac{P_{t_1+1}, ..., P_{t_2}}{w_c}, \qquad P^b = \frac{P_{t_2+1}, ..., P_{255}}{w_b}. \tag{14}$$

Then, the GA used an elistim process in which only 30% of the individuals that have reached the best results of the fitness function were preserved in subsequent iterations. For the population to have 60 individuals again, the crossover step was applied selecting individuals for combination through a crossover probability of 0.65. The crossover point, that defines the combination point between two individuals, was randomly obtained in the interval [1, 6], corresponding to the parameters of the fuzzy 3-partition technique. The populational diversity was then guaranteed by the mutation step. This process randomly changes some parameters of the individuals through the definition of a mutation probability equal to 0.01.

The termination condition of the GA method was based on the approach of [31]. In this method, if the average of intensity levels of each identified structure was the same over two consecutive iterations, the algorithm execution is interrupted. The segmentation result is exemplified by Fig. 2(d), where it is noticeable some limitations.

To refine the segmentation results, a post-processing step was necessary. Initially, segmented regions with areas smaller than 10 pixels were removed due to their correspondence to false positive regions. The segmentation was not able to individually identify some neoplastic nuclei. These regions, highlighted by red rectangles in Fig. 2(d), were characterized by inter-nuclear regions with intensity levels brighter than the ROIs. Thus, the valley-emphasis method [32] was locally applied on segmented regions with areas bigger than 80 pixels, an indicative condition of representation of more than one segmented nucleus as one object. This method defined as its threshold value (T) the valley regions of the preprocessed image histogram to identify neoplastic nuclei and inter-nuclear regions. Its application is based on Eq. 15:

$$T = max\{(1 - p_t) \cdot (\omega_1(t)\mu_1^2(t) + \omega_2(t)\mu_2^2(t))\}, \tag{15}$$

where, ω corresponds to the probability of neoplastic nuclei and inter-nuclear regions and μ represents the average of the intensity levels of these regions. The result of this application is presented in Fig. 2(e), where regions in red rectangles can be compared with their correspondences in the segmentation result.

Finally, the morphological operations of opening and dilation were applied. The opening allows to increase space between objects, smooth contours and remove small noises, meanwhile, the dilation increases the objects areas and fills small holes [25]. The structuring elements of opening and dilation operations, in this study, had disk and square distributions, respectively, with their parameters assigned to the value 2. The result of these operations is illustrated in Fig. 2(f), where it is possible to note a better representation of nuclear contours and their internal regions.

Using the segmented regions, intensity features (mean, median, standard deviation, kurtosis, skewness, variance, 1-norm, 2-norm and entropy) were extracted from the R, G and B channels and grayscale images, as explored in [33]. Measures of median, standard deviation, entropy and energy were also extracted from the diagonal, horizontal and vertical sub-bands of Daubechies4 wavelet, which has a perfect reconstruction compared to other wavelet types [34], composing a texture descriptor of the image [35]. The classification step was performed through the SVM method with the radial basis function and the cross-validation method with 10 folds.

2.3 Evaluation Metrics

The images manually segmented by a pathologist were used to evaluate the results. It was possible to obtain the measures of accuracy (Ac), sensitivity (Se) and specificity (Sp) by analyzing the pixels identified by both segmentations. These pixels were divided into four possible classes: true positive (T_P), corresponding to correct identifications, true negative (T_N) that represents the pixels correctly undetected, false positive (F_P) that presents the amount of incorrectly detected pixels, and false negative (F_N) that denotes incorrectly undetected pixels [36]. These metrics are expressed by:

$$Ac = \frac{T_P + T_N}{T_P + T_N + F_P + F_N}, \tag{16}$$

$$Se = \frac{T_P}{T_P + F_N}, \qquad Sp = \frac{T_N}{T_N + F_P}. \tag{17}$$

These metrics were also used for classification evaluation. High values of Eqs. 16 and 17 represent better results of segmentation and classification. For classification evaluation, the metric of concordance probability (Cp), defined by the product between the sensitivity and specificity, was also used for expressing the area of a rectangle associated with the receiver operating characteristic curve [37,38]. In this way, the higher the rectangle area, the better the classification.

3   Results and Discussion

Figures 3 and 4 exemplify the results of CLL and FL images segmentation, respectively, where yellow arrows were used to indicate some false negative regions and green arrows for some false positive identifications. Application of the Fisher information (Figs. 3(c) and 4(c)) and the entropy of Tsallis (Figs. 3(f) and 4(f)) presented an expressive amount of false negative regions, mainly in the CLL lesion. Due to their similar amounts of false positive and false negative regions identified and the fewer number of over or under segmentation regions, the results achieved with the Rényi and Shannon entropies are the most adequate.

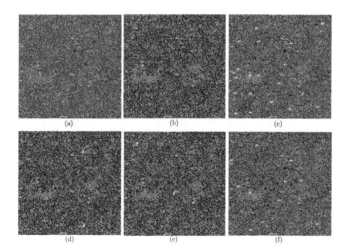

Fig. 3. Application of the proposed method on a subimage of *sj-03-852-R2_012* case from CLL: original image (a), manually segmented image (b), segmentation result using the Fisher information (c) and the entropies of Rényi (d), Shannon (e) and Tsallis (f).

The accuracy, sensitivity and specificity results of segmentation are presented by Table 1 by the metrics of mean and standard deviation of five executions of the proposed segmentation algorithm. For both lesions, the best results of accuracy and specificity were obtained by the Tsallis entropy. However, this function has reached the worst results of sensitivity. In comparison to the best

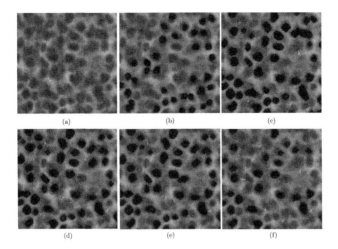

Fig. 4. Application of the proposed method on a subimage of *sj-05-5389-R1_012* case from FL class: original image (a), manually segmented image (b), segmentation result using the Fisher information (c) and the entropies of Rényi (d), Shannon (e) and Tsallis (f).

Table 1. Mean and standard deviation results of five executions of CLL and FL segmentations using the fitness functions of FIM, REM, SEM and TEM through accuracy (%), sensitivity (%) and specificity (%) metrics.

Fitness functions	CLL segmentation			FL segmentation		
	Ac	Se	Sp	Ac	Se	Sp
FIM	79.42	**45.22**	87.97	81.82	**55.55**	85.64
	(0.26)	**(1.08)**	(0.58)	(0.30)	**(0.96)**	(0.46)
REM	80.42	42.48	88.15	82.39	54.35	85.31
	(0.14)	(1.04)	(0.60)	(0.25)	(1,93)	(2.38)
SEM	80.55	43.00	88.10	82.78	53.24	86.97
	(0.22)	(0.79)	(0.19)	(0.26)	(0.78)	(0.32)
TEM	**82.82**	17.34	**95.79**	**86.72**	22.68	**95.57**
	(0.33)	(1.27)	**(0.43)**	**(0.09)**	(0.92)	**(0.17)**

results of this metric, differences of 27.88% and 32.87% were obtained for the CLL and FL lesions, respectively. Despite its good sensitivity results, the Fisher information had a poor performance in the proposed segmentation, as illustrated by the Figs. 3 and 4. The analysis of the obtained results points out the good performance of Rényi entropy. In comparison with the best results of accuracy, sensitivity and specificity, this function has obtained differences of 2.40%, 2.74% and 7.64% for CLL segmentation and 4.33%, 1.20% and 10.26% for the FL lesion. Through this analysis, it is possible to define the Rényi entropy as the most adequate fitness function for the proposed algorithm.

The Wilcoxon rank sum test was performed with a significance level of 5% for evaluation of the color and texture features obtained by the different fitness functions used in the segmentation step. The null hypothesis is that the features from CLL and FL segmented nuclei compose samples from continuous distributions with equal medians. As it can be seen on Fig. 5, all investigated functions have presented a number of relevant features higher than 50%.

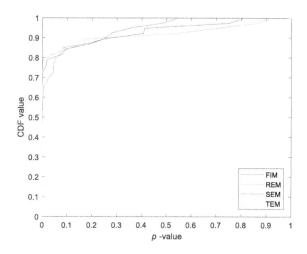

Fig. 5. Wilcoxon rank sum test for CLL×FL classification using GA segmentation with Fisher information and entropies of Rényi, Shannon and Tsallis.

The nuclear segmentation methods for H&E images of [39,40] were used for comparison with the proposed segmentation technique. The segmentations proposed by these studies do not use any search method, like the GA. The study of [39] presented a segmentation method of cellular nuclei with the extraction of the R channel from RGB color model and the application of the Gaussian filter and the morphological operations of erosion and dilation in the preprocessing step. In the segmentation, this proposal used the radial symmetry transform and the Otsu thresholding to reduce the over-segmentation of the watershed algorithm applied. The post-processing was composed of the removal of false positive regions by morphological operations. [40] initially used a deconvolution method for application of the opening reconstruction on the hematoxylin channel obtained. The segmentation of cellular nuclei was performed by a multilevel thresholding based on the Otsu method. Finally, the morphological operations of opening and hole filling were applied in addition to the removal of false positive regions by its area.

As illustrated by Fig. 6, the results of [39] are not satisfactory for this application. For the CLL segmentation, this technique has reached 77.07%, 21.01% and 88.10% of accuracy, sensitivity and specificity, respectively. In the FL segmentation, the results of accuracy, sensitivity and specificity of [39] were

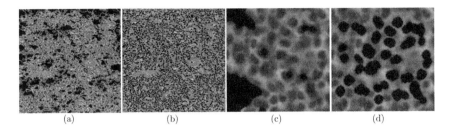

Fig. 6. Segmentation results of [39](a)(c) and [40](b)(d) applied to CLL and FL images.

79.38%, 25.66% and 86.78%, respectively. [40] obtained better results but with more false positive regions, as indicated by its specificity, with values of 72.57% and 75.30% for CLL and FL images, respectively. In combination with sensitivity of 70.39% for CLL and 69.95% for FL, lower accuracy values were obtained: 71.97% and 74.56% for CLL and FL, respectively.

Table 2 presents the quantitative results of CLL×FL classification. Among the evaluated fitness functions, the Rényi entropy has reached the best results in the metrics of accuracy and specificity. The worst results were reached by the Fisher information and intermediate results were obtained by the entropies of Shannon and Tsallis. Through the concordance probability metric, it is noticeable the relevant performance of the Rényi entropy applied in the segmentation, which allowed to obtain the most discriminant features between CLL and FL neoplastic nuclei.

Table 2. Results of CLL×FL classification using the fitness functions of FIM, REM, SEM and TEM through accuracy (%), sensitivity (%) and specificity (%) metrics computed by the 10-fold cross-validation, and the concordance probability.

Fitness functions	Classification			
	Ac	Se	Sp	Cp
FIM	90.54	**100.00**	41.67	0.4167
REM	**98.14**	99.33	**83.33**	**0.8277**
SEM	91.89	**100.00**	50.00	0.5000
TEM	93.24	**100.00**	58.33	0.5833

Table 3 presents the classification results of T_P, F_P, T_N and F_N, with a high rate of true positive samples identified by the analyzed fitness functions. Considering false positive and false negative rates, the Rényi and Tsallis entropies have reached the highest values of these metrics, respectively. This indicates that the regions identified by these entropies contribute to misclassification, demanding a detection step to remove false positive and false negative regions segmented.

Table 3. Confusion matrix of the proposed classification computed by the 10-fold cross-validation using different GA fitness functions for neoplastic nuclei segmentation.

Folds	FIM				REM				SEM				TEM			
	T_P	F_P	T_N	F_N	T_P	F_P	T_N	F_N	T_P	F_P	T_N	F_N	T_P	F_P	T_N	$F_\mathbf{N}$
Fold 1	6	1	0	0	6	1	0	0	7	1	0	0	7	0	0	1
Fold 2	12	1	0	1	12	1	0	1	13	1	0	1	13	1	0	1
Fold 3	18	1	0	2	18	2	0	1	19	1	0	2	19	1	0	2
Fold 4	24	1	0	3	25	2	0	2	25	2	0	2	25	2	0	2
Fold 5	30	1	0	4	31	4	0	2	32	2	0	3	31	4	0	2
Fold 6	37	2	0	4	37	6	0	2	38	3	0	3	37	4	0	3
Fold 7	43	3	0	4	44	6	0	3	44	4	0	4	43	4	0	4
Fold 8	49	4	0	4	50	7	0	3	50	5	0	5	49	4	0	5
Fold 9	56	5	0	5	56	8	0	3	56	5	0	6	56	5	0	6
Fold 10	62	7	0	5	62	8	0	4	62	6	0	6	62	5	0	7

4   Conclusion

To define diagnoses of different types of cancer, the identification of indicative regions of these diseases in histological images is an essential task. When manually performed by pathologists, this task becomes time-consuming and subjective. In order to obtain objective diagnoses, segmentation and classification techniques are able to aid specialists.

In this study, an unsupervised segmentation algorithm of neoplastic nuclei of CLL and FL was presented with an evaluation of different GA fitness functions. Experimental results defined the Rényi entropy as the most adequate for this application. In comparison to Fisher information and the entropies of Shannon and Tsallis, the Rényi entropy was the one that best quantitatively evaluated the membership degrees of the intensity levels, which allowed to obtain the most adequate threshold values for the segmentation of CLL and FL neoplastic nuclei. Through intensity and texture features extracted from the segmented regions, it was possible to classify the images using the SVM method. With 98.14% of accuracy in the images classification, the proposed algorithm indicates the importance of the segmentation step for definition of diagnoses of CLL and FL.

A limitation of the proposed method was the false positive and false negative regions identified in the segmentation. Thus, in future works, additional features to the intensity information used in the segmentation will be explored to correctly identify the ROIs of CLL and FL images.

Acknowledgments. T.A.A.T. and M.Z.N. thank to CAPES (1575210) and FAPEMIG (TEC - APQ-02885-15 project) for financial support.

References

1. Orlov, N.V., Chen, W.W., Eckley, D.M., Macura, T.J., Shamir, L., Jaffe, E.S., Goldberg, I.G.: Automatic classification of lymphoma images with transform-based global features. IEEE Trans. Inf. Technol. Biomed. **14**(4), 1003–1013 (2010)
2. Lowry, L., Linch, D.: Non-Hodgkin's lymphoma (2013)
3. Belkacem-Boussaid, K., Samsi, S., Lozanski, G., Gurcan, M.N.: Automatic detection of follicular regions in H&E images using iterative shape index. Comput. Med. Imaging Graph. **35**(7), 592–602 (2011)
4. Canellos, G.P., Lister, T.A., Young, B.: The Lymphomas, 2nd edn. Saunders Elsevier, Philadelphia (2006)
5. Mohammed, E.A., Far, B.H., Naugler, C., Mohamed, M.M.A.: Chronic lymphocytic leukemia cell segmentation from microscopic blood images using watershed algorithm and optimal thresholding. In: 26th Annual IEEE Canadian Conference on Electrical and Computer Engineering (CCECE), pp. 1–5. IEEE (2013)
6. Mohammed, E.A., Far, B.H., Naugler, C., Mohamed, M.M.A.: Application of support vector machine and k-means clustering algorithms for robust chronic lymphocytic leukemia color cell segmentation. In: 15th International Conference on e-Health Networking, Applications and Services. IEEE (2013)
7. Sertel, O., Kong, J., Lozanski, G., Catalyurek, U., Saltz, J.H., Gurcan, M.N.: Computerized microscopic image analysis of follicular lymphoma. In: Medical Imaging, vol. 6915. International Society for Optics and Photonics (2008)
8. Kong, H., Belkacem-Boussaid, K., Gurcan, M.: Cell nuclei segmentation for histopathological image analysis. In: SPIE Medical Imaging, p. 79622R. International Society for Optics and Photonics (2011)
9. Belkacem-Boussaid, K., Prescott, J., Lozanski, G., Gurcan, M.N.: Segmentation of follicular regions on H&E slides using a matching filter and active contour model. In: SPIE Medical Imaging. International Society for Optics and Photonics (2010)
10. Oztan, B., Kong, H., Gurcan, M.N., Yener, B.: Follicular lymphoma grading using cell-graphs and multi-scale feature analysis. In: SPIE Medical Imaging, vol. 8315 (2012)
11. Oger, M., Belhomme, P., Gurcan, M.N.: A general framework for the segmentation of follicular lymphoma virtual slides. Comput. Med. Imaging Graph. **36**(6), 442–451 (2012)
12. Dimitropoulos, K., Barmpoutis, P., Koletsa, T., Kostopoulos, I., Grammalidis, N.: Automated detection and classification of nuclei in pax5 and h&e-stained tissue sections of follicular lymphoma. Signal Image Video Process. 1–9 (2016)
13. Dimitropoulos, K., Barmpoutis, P., Koletsa, T., Kostopoulos, I., Grammalidis, N.: Classification of nuclei in follicular lyphoma tissue sections using different stains and bayesian networks. In: Kyriacou, E., Christofides, S., Pattichis, C.S. (eds.) XIV Mediterranean Conference on Medical and Biological Engineering and Computing 2016. IP, vol. 57, pp. 234–238. Springer, Cham (2016). https://doi.org/10.1007/978-3-319-32703-7_47
14. Dimitropoulos, K., Michail, E., Koletsa, T., Kostopoulos, I., Grammalidis, N.: Using adaptive neuro-fuzzy inference systems for the detection of centroblasts in microscopic images of follicular lymphoma. Signal Image Video Process. **8**(1), 33–40 (2014)
15. Luo, Y., Celenk, M., Bejai, P.: Discrimination of malignant lymphomas and leukemia using radon transform based-higher order spectra. In: Medical Imaging, pp. 61445K-1–61445K-10. International Society for Optics and Photonics (2006)

16. Sertel, O., Kong, J., Lozanski, G., Catalyurek, U., Saltz, J.H., Gurcan, M.N.: Histopathological image analysis using model-based intermediate representations and color texture: follicular lymphoma grading. J. Signal Process. Syst. **55**(1–3), 169–183 (2009)

17. Sertel, O., Kong, J., Lozanski, G., Shana'ah, A., Catalyurek, U., Saltz, J., Gurcan, M.: Texture classification using nonlinear color quantization: application to histopathological image analysis. In: IEEE International Conference on Acoustics, Speech and Signal Processing (ICASSP), pp. 597–600. IEEE (2008)

18. McCann, M.T., Ozolek, J.A., Castro, C.A., Parvin, B., Kovacevic, J.: Automated histology analysis: opportunities for signal processing. Signal Process. Mag. **32**(1), 78–87 (2015)

19. Oswal, V., Belle, A., Diegelmann, R., Najarian, K.: An entropy-based automated cell nuclei segmentation and quantification: application in analysis of wound healing process. Comput. Math. Meth. Med. **2013**, 1–10 (2013)

20. Tang, L., Tian, L., Steward, B.L.: Color image segmentation with genetic algorithm for in-field weed sensing. Trans. ASAE **43**(4), 1019 (2000)

21. Maulik, U.: Medical image segmentation using genetic algorithms. IEEE Trans. Inf. Technol. Biomed. **13**(2), 166–173 (2009)

22. Shamir, L., Orlov, N., Eckley, D.M., Macura, T.J., Goldberg, I.G.: IICBU 2008: a proposed benchmark suite for biological image analysis. Med. Biol. Eng. Comput. **46**(9), 943–947 (2008)

23. Wang, P., Hu, X., Li, Y., Liu, Q., Zhu, X.: Automatic cell nuclei segmentation and classification of breast cancer histopathology images. Sig. Process. **122**, 1–13 (2016)

24. Zorman, M., Kokol, P., Lenic, M., Rosa, J.L.S., Sigut, J.F., Alayon, S.: Symbol-based machine learning approach for supervised segmentation of follicular lymphoma images. In: 20th IEEE International Symposium on Computer-Based Medical Systems (CBMS), pp. 115–120. IEEE (2007)

25. Gonzalez, R.C., Woods, R.E.: Processamento de Imagens Digitais. Edgard Blucher, São Paulo (2000)

26. Yin, S., Zhao, X., Wang, W., Gong, M.: Efficient multilevel image segmentation through fuzzy entropy maximization and graph cut optimization. Pattern Recogn. **47**(9), 2894–2907 (2014)

27. Abo-Eleneen, Z., Abdel-Azim, G.: A novel algorithm for image thresholding using non-parametric fisher information. In: International Electronic Conference on Entropy and Its Applications, vol. 1, p. 15. Multidisciplinary Digital Publishing Institute (2014)

28. Sarkar, S., Das, S., Chaudhuri, S.S.: Hyper-spectral image segmentation using rényi entropy based multi-level thresholding aided with differential evolution. Expert Syst. Appl. **50**, 120–129 (2016)

29. Shannon, C.E.: A mathematical theory of communication. ACM SIGMOBILE Mob. Comput. Commun. Rev. **5**(1), 3–55 (2001)

30. Zhang, Y., Wu, L.: Optimal multi-level thresholding based on maximum tsallis entropy via an artificial bee colony approach. Entropy **13**(4), 841–859 (2011)

31. Hammouche, K., Diaf, M., Siarry, P.: A multilevel automatic thresholding method based on a genetic algorithm for a fast image segmentation. Comput. Vis. Image Underst. **109**(2), 163–175 (2008)

32. Ng, H.: Automatic thresholding for defect detection. Pattern Recogn. Lett. **27**(14), 1644–1649 (2006)

33. Dong, F., Irshad, H., Oh, E., Lerwill, M.F., Brachtel, E.F., Jones, N.C., Knoblauch, N.W., Montaser-Kouhsari, L., Johnson, N.B., Rao, L.K., et al.: Computational pathology to discriminate benign from malignant intraductal proliferations of the breast. PLoS ONE **9**(12), e114885 (2014)

34. Abbas, Q.: Segmentation of differential structures on computed tomography images for diagnosis lung-related diseases. Biomed. Signal Process. Control **33**, 325–334 (2017)

35. Semler, L., Dettori, L., Furst, J.: Wavelet-based texture classification of tissues in computed tomography. In: IEEE Symposium on Computer-Based Medical Systems, pp. 265–270. IEEE (2005)

36. Chang, V., Saavedra, J.M., Castañeda, V., Sarabia, L., Hitschfeld, N., Härtel, S.: Gold-standard and improved framework for sperm head segmentation. Comput. Methods Programs Biomed. **117**(2), 225–237 (2014)

37. Unal, I.: Defining an optimal cut-point value in ROC analysis: an alternative approach. Comput. Math. Meth. Med. **2017**, 1–14 (2017)

38. Liu, X.: Classification accuracy and cut point selection. Stat. Med. **31**(23), 2676–2686 (2012)

39. Vahadane, A., Sethi, A.: Towards generalized nuclear segmentation in histological images. In: International Conference Bioinformatics and Bioengineering, pp. 1–4. IEEE (2013)

40. Phoulady, H.A., Goldgof, D.B., Hall, L.O., Mouton, P.R.: Nucleus segmentation in histology images with hierarchical multilevel thresholding. In: SPIE Medical Imaging, p. 979111. International Society for Optics and Photonics (2016)

Mutual Information Iterated Local Search: A Wrapper-Filter Hybrid for Feature Selection in Brain Computer Interfaces

Jason Adair$^{(\boxtimes)}$ ⓘD, Alexander E. I. Brownlee ⓘD, and Gabriela Ochoa ⓘD

Computing Science and Mathematics, University of Stirling, Stirling, UK
{jason.adair,alexander.brownlee,gabriela.ochoa}@stir.ac.uk

Abstract. Brain Computer Interfaces provide a very challenging classification task due to small numbers of instances, large numbers of features, non-stationary problems, and low signal-to-noise ratios. Feature selection (FS) is a promising solution to help mitigate these effects. Wrapper FS methods are typically found to outperform filter FS methods, but reliance on cross-validation accuracies can be misleading due to overfitting. This paper proposes a filter-wrapper hybrid based on Iterated Local Search and Mutual Information, and shows that it can provide more reliable solutions, where the solutions are more able to generalise to unseen data. This study further contributes comparisons over multiple datasets, something that has been uncommon in the literature.

Keywords: Brain Computer Interface · Mutual information
Evolutionary search · Iterated Local Search

1 Introduction

Brain Computer Interfaces (BCI) allow neurological signals to be decoded to enable the control of external devices. The most common mode of recording signals for use in such devices is electroencephalography (EEG). This involves the placement of electrodes on the scalp of a user, to record the electrical activity within the underlying brain region. With these signals, practitioners can analyse the working state of the patient's brain to detect seizure triggers, sleep patterns, or even allow the control of external devices — a life-altering application for people in need of prosthetic limbs, or with muscle-degenerative disorders.

EEG-based devices are safer, more accessible, and more cost-effective than invasive techniques, but they do come with substantial caveats: enough energy must be produced by the brain region to pass through three centimetres of bone and soft tissue. This requires at least $6\,\mathrm{cm}^2$ of neural material to be active, greatly reducing the spatial resolution of the signal. The problem is further compounded by multiple sources of noise: eye movements, muscle contractions, and cardiac rhythms. Pre-processing the data by band pass filtering, and using a technique

© Springer International Publishing AG, part of Springer Nature 2018
K. Sim and P. Kaufmann (Eds.): EvoApplications 2018, LNCS 10784, pp. 63–77, 2018.
https://doi.org/10.1007/978-3-319-77538-8_5

known as *Feature Extraction* can help emphasize characteristics in the data that are useful for constructing effective, predictive BCI models. However, as BCI datasets typically consist of a large number of variables, with few instances, it is prudent to reduce the feature set to avoid overfitting, decrease training times, and remove noisy or redundant features.

Filter methods rank features according to a statistical measure, which creates generalised models, but fail to exploit the nature of the machine learning algorithm intended for use. Wrapper methods use the classifier as a 'black-box' evaluation of feature subsets, achieving high classification accuracies, but are prone to over-fitting on training sets. We propose a hybrid of both categories of feature selection algorithms: filters and wrappers. This hybridisation is defined here as *Minimal Redundancy Maximal Relevance Iterated Local Search (MRMR-ILS)*; a metaheuristic known as Iterated Local Search that utilises a mutual information measure to guide the perturbation operator, while allowing a normal wrapper-based local search heuristic.

The aim of this study is to provide a new hybrid-heuristic that is capable of finding small feature subsets that generalise more effectively than typical wrapper approaches, and are more accurate than those found by filter approaches. Specifically, the contributions of this study are:

1. A new filter-wrapper hybrid combining Iterated Local Search with the Minimum Redundancy Maximal Relevance mutual information measure.
2. Results based on three different datasets, originating from three different motor-imagery based problems.
3. Analysis of interactive effects between mutual information measures, error rates obtained from training sets, and the predictive accuracy on unseen data.

This paper is structured in the following manner: a general background to BCI based feature selection is given in Sect. 2, with interest to mutual information, wrapper methods, and their hybrids. This is followed by our proposed algorithm in Sect. 3 and the methodology used to evaluate it in Sect. 4. We then present our results and discussion in Sect. 5, and conclusion in Sect. 6.

2   Background

Extra-cranial BCI recordings are notoriously noisy; while we are only interested in the energy generated from the neurons that correspond to the task at hand, the signals also contain unrelated neural processes, muscle movements, and other sources of information that can negatively impact the performance of our classifiers. This can render data recorded from some frequencies, or even entire channels, redundant to our needs. Selecting the data to retain, and what to disregard, is a non-trivial task. However, obtaining near optimal feature subsets reduces the dimensionality of the data, decreases the training and prediction time costs, creates simpler models, and increases the predictive accuracy [1]. Feature Selection algorithms can be divided into three groups: Filter, Embedded, and Wrapper methods.

2.1   Filters

Filter based methods rank variables according to a criterion, independently of the classifier. Examples of these performance measures include the Pearson correlation coefficient [2], Fisher score [3], and measures based in Information Theory [4]. The advantages of such techniques tend to be that they are typically less computationally expensive, simpler to implement, and resulting feature subsets are more generalisable as they are not tied to a specific classifier [5]. That being said, they lack the ability to exploit specific characteristics of the machine learning algorithms intended for use, and therefore rarely obtain the highest classification accuracies.

The following concept definitions explain the mutual information aspects of the algorithm presented by this paper.

Entropy is an integral concept within Information Theory, defining the uncertainty of a variable. A key measurement of this is Shannon's entropy [6]:

$$H(X) = -\sum_x p(x) \log p(x). \tag{1}$$

Entropy is calculated by the summation of all the probability distributions ($p(x)$) of values (x) of the set X, multiplied by the natural log of those probability distributions.

Mutual Information is the unique information shared between two variables. Using entropy, it is possible to quantify the conveyable information from a variable, however, what is often of interest, is how much variables 'overlap' in what they have recorded. This is especially useful when we want to consider how effective one variable is at predicting another; higher shared information suggests that they are measuring a similar source of information:

$$I(X:Y) = H(X) - H(X|Y) = H(X) + H(Y) - H(X,Y). \tag{2}$$

To do this, we consider how much information is conveyed by each variable as individuals, in comparison with how much information is conveyed when they are paired.

Maximum Relevance Minimal Redundancy. Mutual Information can detect even non-linear interactions between variables, but it is limited due to it being a univariate approach. This is a source of weakness in applications such as feature selection, as we frequently find multivariate interactions between variables and their labels. To solve this, Peng et al. [7] proposed the minimal-redundancy-maximal-relevance approach. It seeks to address two conditions; maximisation of selected features *Relevance*, and minimisation of their *Redundancy*:

$$maxD(S,c), D = \frac{1}{|S|} \sum_{x_i \in S} I(x_i; c). \tag{3}$$

where $I(x_i; c)$ is the mutual information between each selected feature (x_i) in the subset (S) and the class (c).

$$minR(S), D = \frac{1}{|S|^2} \sum_{x_i, x_j \in S} I(x_i; x_j). \tag{4}$$

where $I(x_i; x_j)$ is the mutual information between each pair of selected features within the selected subset (S).

$$max\Phi(D, R), Phi = D - R. \tag{5}$$

MRMR seeks to maximise the distance between the Relevance (D) and Redundancy (R).

2.2 Wrappers

Wrapper methods select feature subsets by utilising the classifier as a 'black box' fitness function. By iteratively evaluating feature subsets using the machine learning algorithm to make predictions on the training set, models created from the selected subset can be tested on their validity. The simplest, and one of the most common forms of this in feature selection is *Sequential Forward Selection* (SFS). Every feature is used to train a model, and then used to make predictions on the available instances. The one with the highest predictive accuracy is selected as the first feature in the subset. Each following feature is found by appending the existing subset, and evaluating it as before [8]. Simple heuristics such as SFS are successful, but rarely provide state-of-the-art results due to their inability to detect feature interactions; when a feature is added, no consideration is given to previously selected features and their counter-dependencies. More complex heuristics such as Genetic Algorithms [9], Particle Swarm Optimisation [10], and Ant Colony Optimisation have been widely used in Brain Computer Interface feature selection with great success [11].

2.3 Hybrid Approaches

A relatively uncommon approach in BCI is the combination of filters and wrappers in hybrid methods. A common form of this is a two-stage approach: a filter method is first applied to remove the most redundant features, before a wrapper is applied to the remaining features. A variation of this is seen in Gan [12], where *Sequential Forward Floating Search (SFFS)* was combined with *MRMR* by using the mutual information approach to select a set of candidate features for addition and removal at each phase. This reduced the computational training cost of utilising the classifier across all the candidate features. *Ant Colony Optimisation* was combined with *Differential Evolution* in Khushaba *et al.* [13]. This technique used a mutual information evaluation function as the Selection Measure in ACO, and evaluated each of the ants using a Linear Discriminate classifier.

In other feature selection fields, hybridised approaches involving mutual information are somewhat more prevalent. Mutual information was used to reduce the search space in advance of running a *Genetic Algorithm* in Tan, Zhang, and Bourgeois [14] and *Particle Swarm Optimisation* in Ali and Shahzad [15]. It has also been successfully used within memetic algorithms as a local search method to refine the solutions found by PSO in Particle Swarm Optimisation Backwards Elimination (PSOBE) [16] and in Genetic Algorithms [17]. A common observation however, is that mutual information is almost always used as a local search operator in these cases, and to our knowledge, has not been used in the explorative phase of a metaheuristic prior to this paper.

3   Proposed Method

Here we introduce the existing Iterated Local Search (ILS) algorithm, followed by our contribution, the MRMR-ILS.

3.1   Iterated Local Search

Iterated Local Search is an iterative search based algorithm that has demonstrated interesting results across a variety of domains [18], but with almost no application to the BCI domain. The ILS used in this paper consists of a layered search; a local search, in the form of a hillclimber, and a diversification mechanism, in the form of a strong mutation, known as a perturbation. A solution is either randomly generated or provided to the algorithm. A hillclimber is then used to search the local space; a candidate solution is created by performing a single point mutation on the current solution. This is achieved by randomly choosing one of the selected features in the current solution, and replacing it with an unselected feature. This is then evaluated by performing 10-fold cross-validation using the training set and obtaining the average prediction error rates on each of the folds.

Cross-validation is a technique used to assess algorithm performance when using limited quantities of data. K-Fold cross-validation is commonly used within the machine learning community to evaluate the performance of models. To do this, training data is subdivided into K sets. $K-1$ sets are used to train a classifier, and is then used to predict the labels of the 'left out' set and its error rate is measured. This is then performed on all K sets, and the average error rate returned.

3.2   Minimal Redundancy Maximal Relevance-Iterated Local Search

In the Mutual Information-based Iterated Local Search (*MRMR-ILS*) algorithm proposed by this paper, the stochastic perturbation stage of the ILS is replaced by an information-measure based selection process. Instead of randomly selecting features for replacement, features are selected for retention based on the information they share with each other, and the label. The mRMR score for each feature is calculated and those that score most highly, that is, those that have the highest relevance with the label, and lowest information overlap with other features within the selected solution, are retained. The remaining features are randomly replaced with unselected features.

4   Methodology

The experimental methodology is presented in the following order; dataset descriptions, feature extraction method, solution size, classification algorithms used, fitness function, search algorithm parametres, and benchmark methods for comparison.

4.1   Datasets

The datasets provided by the Berlin Brain Computer Interface Competitions have been some of the most prevalent in literature over the past few years. Two of these datasets were used in this paper; Berlin BCI competition II, datasets III and IV[1]. Both of these datasets have proven popular in literature due to their challenging, but well-defined, nature. The third dataset was acquired by the RIKEN Centre of Advanced Intelligence Project[2]. It does not appear as frequently in literature as the BCI competitions, but was chosen as diversity is essential to foster amongst the state-of-the-art benchmarks. The following section will describe the paradigms used in each dataset, the conditions of their recording, and any pre-processing steps required before feature extraction.

Dataset A - Berlin BCI Competition II Datasets III
Over a set of 280 9-s trails, a participant was asked to imagine left and right hand movements to control an on-screen cursor. Three electrodes were placed on the participants scalp, and a blank screen displayed. The first two seconds were a resting phase, followed by an auditory signal and cross being displayed in the centre of the screen to focus the participant's attention. On the fourth second, the cross became an arrow, signifying the motor-imagery (left or right hand movements) that the participant was required to imagine. Three electrodes placed at C3, C4, and Cz, and sampled at 128 Hz. The signal was then bandpass filtered between 0.5 and 30 Hz. The first 140 instances were assigned as 'training data', and the remaining 140 as 'testing data'.

Dataset B - Berlin BCI Competition II Datasets IV
A set of 28 EEG electrodes were used to record a single subject during a self-paced finger movement task. The participant was asked to sit at a computer with their hands in a typical position at the keyboard. The participant was then allowed to press keys at a rate of one per second, in a self-determined order. In total, 416 instances were collected; 316 of which were designated as training, and

---

[1] http://www.bbci.de/competition/ii/#datasets.
[2] http://www.bsp.brain.riken.jp/~qibin/homepage/Datasets.html.

100 were provided, unlabelled, as testing data. This results in 416 instances of 500 ms, stopping 130 ms before the key-press, each labelled with either 'right' or 'left' hand. The sampling was performed at 1000 Hz, band-pass filtered between 0.05 and 200 Hz, before being down sampled to 100 Hz. The electrodes were arranged according to the international 10/20-system.

Dataset C - Riken - Subject A

Sessions one and two from Subject A were taken from the RIKEN EEG Datasets homepage. A subject was asked to sit in a chair and pay attention to a blank screen. After 2 s, an arrow pointing left or right appeared and, for the following three seconds, the user imagined the corresponding left or right hand movements. The recording was obtained via six channels, sampled at a rate of 256 Hz, which was then band-pass filtered between 2 and 30 Hz. In total, 264 instances were recorded: session one was selected as the training dataset with 130 trials, with the remaining 134 trials from session two serving as the testing data.

4.2   Features

Power Spectral Densities were selected in the following experiments as they preserve spatial and frequency dimensionality, and by epoching the data, some temporal resolution is preserved. This type of feature can provide practical insight into the problem: allowing understanding as to where the key regions of interest are in terms of which electrodes and frequencies provides the richest information.

4.3   Solution Size

As noted by Chandrashekar and Sahin [19], there are no ideal methods to choose the size of the subset for selection. For this reason, we selected a solution size for the *Iterated Local Search (ILS)* and *Minimal Reduncancy Maximal Relevance-Iterated Local Search (MRMR-ILS)* for Berlin BCI Competition II Dataset III based on Rejer [9]. As there is no background literature that utilises Power Spectral Densities in this way, to the authors' knowledge, for Berlin BCI Competition II Dataset IV, and RIKEN Subject A, preliminary exploration was required.

4.4   Classifiers

The key aim of BCI paradigms is simply to produce an effective model to classify some aspect of neural recordings. The creation of such a model relies heavily on which machine learning algorithm that was chosen. In this paper, we evaluate two such algorithms:

- *K-Nearest-Neighbours (KNN)*, while commonly used in other fields, have been largely neglected within the BCI literature due to their known sensitivity to the 'Curse of Dimensionality' [20]. They were selected for use in this paper for exploration, and to support our deliberate selection of small feature subsets.
- *Support Vector Machines (SVM)* are commonly used in BCI literature, and often obtain the best accuracies. This is thought to be due to their ability to handle larger feature sets, and their resistance to overfitting [21].

Fitness Function. The fitness of a proposed feature subset was evaluated using k-fold cross-validation of the training data. $K = 10$ was selected due to preliminary experimentation revealing a noisy fitness function, originating mainly from the randomly chosen splits in cross-validation. While 10-folds creates an expensive fitness function, it is required in such datasets where we find high-dimensionality, with low number of samples and poor signal-to-noise ratios [22].

Search Algorithm Parametres. Each algorithm was run 25 times, with 100,000 evaluations of the classifier set as the termination criteria. In each run, there were 100 perturbation 'kicks', and local searches were limited to 1000 evaluation first-improvement hillclimbers.

Benchmark Methods
Filters - Two mutual information filter methods were evaluated using a greedy forward-search to select the feature subset size, as used in Lan *et al.* [23]. Mutual Information Feature Selection (*MIFS*), relies on selecting features that increase the selected subsets mutual information with the class label. *MRMR* seeks to maximise the selected subsets mutual information with the class label (relevance), while minimising the mutual information between features (redundancy).

Wrappers - Two wrapper approaches were selected for comparison: *Sequential Forward Search*, a greedy algorithm that selects the next best feature as evaluated by the classifier; and *Iterated Local Search*, a two layer search involving perturbations and local searches. SFS is a very popular technique, and is often used as an exploratory measure in feature selection. ILS has been used in a wide variety of different search areas, but is almost unheard of within BCI.

Embedded - Least Absolute Shrinkage and Selection Operator (LASSO) (or L1 regularisation) performs feature selection by reducing the sum of the absolute values of the model parametres below an upper bound. It does this by shrinking the coefficients of the features, often to zero, effectively deselecting them. It can provide two feature subsets: Sparse, and Mean Squared Error (MSE). This method provides relatively poor cross-validation error rates on the training set, but tend to be reasonably more generalisable.

5   Results and Discussion

Tables 1 and 2 present results obtained using the KNN and SVM classifiers respectively. The list of measures are: the number of features selected by each algorithm (Selected f); the average final solutions' fitnesses (cross-validation error rate on training data; *CVE*); and their accuracy on the unseen, testing data. The datasets were labeled: *A* - Berlin BCI Competition II Dataset III; *B* - Berlin BCI Competition II Dataset IV; *C* - Subject A from the Riken dataset.

When using a KNN classifier, we see in Table 1 that the MRMR-ILS finds solutions with the lowest cross-validation error rates on two datasets: A (10.56%)

Table 1. Results of each feature selection algorithm while using the KNN Classifier. Number of selected features, cross-validation error rates, and accuracy is shown for Datasets A, B and C. Figures in bold denote the highest performing algorithm for each measure.

Dataset	Algorithm	Selected f	CVE	Accuracy
A	**MIFS**	20	0.410476	0.6
	MRMR	43	0.329524	0.728571
	LASSO (Sparse)	8	0.2186	0.7143
	LASSO (MSE)	29	0.1993	0.7143
	SFS	14	0.1357	0.7357
	ILS	**6**	0.1110	**0.7918**
	MRMR ILS	**6**	**0.1057**	0.7896
B	**MIFS**	10	0.483861	0.56
	MRMR	34	0.475422	0.52
	LASSO (Sparse)	11	0.4269	0.5500
	LASSO (MSE)	13	0.4222	0.5500
	SFS	15	0.2816	0.6200
	ILS	**6**	0.2716	0.6164
	MRMR ILS	**6**	**0.2707**	**0.6464**
C	**MIFS**	6	0.517179	0.619403
	MRMR	30	0.477179	0.522388
	LASSO (Sparse)	4	0.2408	0.6045
	LASSO (MSE)	15	0.2615	0.5672
	SFS	14	**0.1385**	0.5896
	ILS	4	0.1539	0.5997
	MRMR ILS	4	0.1492	**0.6085**

and B (27.07%). On dataset C, it achieved the second lowest (14.92%), falling only just behind the SFS (13.85%). In all three cases, the MRMR ILS outperformed the unguided ILS. These cross validation error rates reflected the algorithms' performance on unseen data by achieving the highest accuracy on datasets B (64.64%) and C (60.85%), with the second highest accuracy on dataset A (78.96%).

In Table 2, the SVM classifer produces results with a similar pattern as using the KNN, with the MRMR ILS achieving the lowest cross-validation error rates in dataset A and C (8.843% and 7.72% respectively), and falling behind the ILS by just 0.17% on dataset B. Classification accuracies on unseen datasets in this case are slightly more nuanced; the MRMR-ILS achieved the highest accuracy on dataset B (69.48%). In datasets A and C, it achieved the second highest accuracies (84.23% and 65.67%) to ILS and the MSE LASSO solutions (84.23% and 65.67%) respectively.

Table 2. Results of each feature selection algorithm while using the SVM Classifier. Number of selected features, cross-validation error rates, and accuracy is shown for Datasets A, B and C. Figures in bold denote the highest performing algorithm for each measure.

Dataset	Algorithm	Selected f	CVE	Accuracy
A	**MIFS**	20	0.374048	0.607143
	MRMR	43	0.258095	0.792857
	LASSO (Sparse)	8	0.1493	0.7929
	LASSO (MSE)	29	0.1757	0.7929
	SFS	8	0.0857	0.8071
	ILS	**6**	0.0846	**0.8423**
	MRMR ILS	**6**	**0.0843**	0.8269
B	**MIFS**	10	0.415295	0.52
	MRMR	34	0.399684	0.58
	LASSO (Sparse)	11	0.3095	0.6700
	LASSO (MSE)	13	0.3168	0.6200
	SFS	**9**	0.2532	0.6200
	ILS	12	**0.2422**	0.6836
	MRMR ILS	12	0.2439	**0.6948**
C	**MIFS**	6	0.407692	0.537313
	MRMR	30	0.28	0.567164
	LASSO (Sparse)	4	0.2377	0.6045
	LASSO (MSE)	15	0.1508	**0.6567**
	SFS	17	0.1000	0.5970
	ILS	15	0.0735	0.6197
	MRMR ILS	15	**0.0772**	0.6391

The graphs in Figs. 1a, 2a, and 3a show the average incumbent solution fitness based on the cross-validation error rates over each iteration of the ILS and MRMR-ILS algorithms. In a post-hoc analysis, we extracted these incumbent solutions and evaluated their predictive accuracy on the testing data, plotted in Figs. 1b, 2b, and 3b. We can see that the relationship between the MRMR-ILS fitness function, and the performance on unseen data is much stronger than that observed in the ILS. In order to find a real-world feature subset for BCI applications, it is imperative that the estimated accuracy provided by the fitness function in our algorithms correlates as closely as possible to accuracy rates obtained from new, unseen data. We further explore this in Table 3, in which the Pearson's correlation coefficient is calculated for the cross-validation error rates and accuracies of the incumbent solutions. In five of the six test cases, there is a substantially higher correlation between the predicted accuracy (CVE rate) and the accuracy on the unseen data in the MRMR ILS than that of the

ILS. The most notable examples of this is the use of KNN in dataset A, and the use of SVM in dataset C, where the correlations seen within the solutions of the ILS have weak negative correlations (-0.1464 and -0.3787), which is heavily contrasted against the strong negative correlations in those of the MRMR ILS (-0.8954 and -0.7203) (Figs. 4, 5 and 6).

Table 3. Correlations between Cross Validation Error Rates and Accuracy of Solution during ILS and MRMR-ILS Search. Figures in bold denote the highest performing algorithm for each measure.

Classifier	Dataset	Algorithm	
		ILS	**MRMR ILS**
KNN	**A**	-0.1464	$-\mathbf{0.8954}$
	B	-0.7598	$-\mathbf{0.8871}$
	C	-0.9224	$-\mathbf{0.9686}$
SVM	**A**	$-\mathbf{0.9370}$	-0.9100
	B	-0.8348	$-\mathbf{0.8619}$
	C	-0.3787	$-\mathbf{0.7203}$

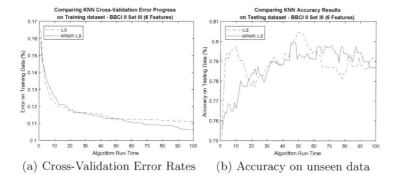

(a) Cross-Validation Error Rates   (b) Accuracy on unseen data

Fig. 1. Comparison between ILS and MRMR-ILS over each iteration of the algorithms for the KNN classifier on dataset A - BCI Competition II dataset III

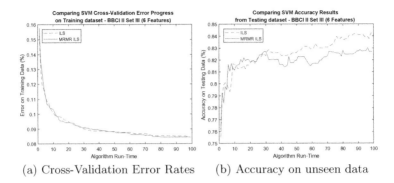

(a) Cross-Validation Error Rates   (b) Accuracy on unseen data

Fig. 2. Comparison between ILS and MRMR-ILS over each iteration of the algorithms for the SVM classifier on dataset A - BCI Competition II dataset III

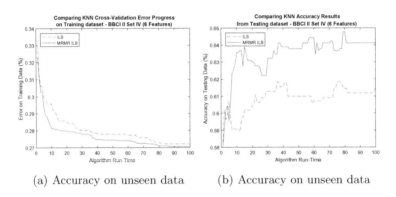

(a) Accuracy on unseen data   (b) Accuracy on unseen data

Fig. 3. Comparison between ILS and MRMR-ILS over each iteration of the algorithms for the KNN classifier on dataset B - BCI Competition II dataset IV

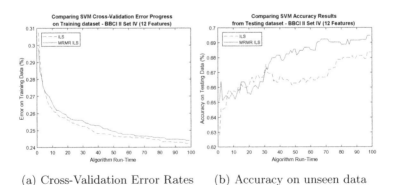

(a) Cross-Validation Error Rates   (b) Accuracy on unseen data

Fig. 4. Comparison between ILS and MRMR-ILS over each iteration of the algorithms for the SVM classifier on dataset B - BCI Competition II dataset IV

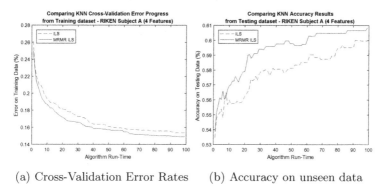

(a) Cross-Validation Error Rates   (b) Accuracy on unseen data

Fig. 5. Comparison between ILS and MRMR-ILS over each iteration of the algorithms for the KNN classifier on dataset C - RIKEN Subject A

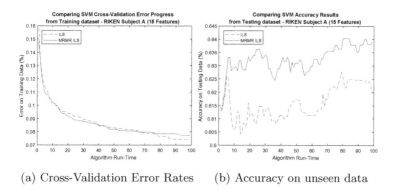

(a) Cross-Validation Error Rates   (b) Accuracy on unseen data

Fig. 6. Comparison between ILS and MRMR-ILS over each iteration of the algorithms for the SVM classifier on C - RIKEN Subject A

6   Conclusion

This paper proposed MRMR-ILS; a hybrid Filter-Wrapper method involving mutual information for feature selection. Evaluations over three datasets using KNN and SVM classifiers demonstrated that feature subsets found by our method were typically of higher quality, with lower error rates on training sets and higher accuracy on testing data, than those found by the compared traditional methods. What is of additional interest, is the quality of the solutions found during the search process of the MRMR-ILS in comparison to those of the ILS. Relying solely on the cross-validation error rates allowed feature subsets to be discovered that were highly effective for creating models that represent the training data but, when tested on unseen data, their performance was unpredictable. When MRMR was incorporated into the algorithm, the search was partially constrained to areas in the search space rich in mutual information. This resulted in models that generalised to unseen data in a much more consistent manner. Further experimentation should seek to compare the MRMR-ILS with other mutual information based hybrid methods from the wider feature selection literature, and investigate the relationship between mutual information, cross-validation error rates, and predictive accuracy on unseen data.

Acknowledgements. Work funded by UK EPSRC grant EP/J017515 (DAASE).

References

1. Xue, B., Zhang, M., Browne, W.N., Yao, X.: A survey on evolutionary computation approaches to feature selection. IEEE Trans. Evol. Comput. **20**(4), 606–626 (2016). https://doi.org/10.1109/TEVC.2015.2504420
2. Vega, R., Sajed, T., Mathewson, K.W., Khare, K., Pilarski, P.M., Greiner, R., Sanchez-Ante, G., Antelis, J.M.: Assessment of feature selection and classification methods for recognizing motor imagery tasks from electroencephalographic signals. Artif. Intell. Res. **1**, 37–51 (2016). https://doi.org/10.5430/air.v6n1p37
3. Cabrera, A.F., Farina, D., Dremstrup, K.: Comparison of feature selection and classification methods for a brain-computer interface driven by non-motor imagery. Med. Biol. Eng. Compu. **48**(2), 123–132 (2010). https://doi.org/10.1007/s11517-009-0569-2
4. Ang, K.K., Chin, Z.Y., Wang, C., Guan, C., Zhang, H.: Filter bank common spatial pattern algorithm on BCI competition IV datasets 2a and 2b. Front. Neurosci. **6**, 1–9 (2012). https://doi.org/10.3389/fnins.2012.00039
5. Alotaiby, T., El-Samie, F.E.A., Alshebeili, S.A., Ahmad, I.: A review of channel selection algorithms for EEG signal processing. EURASIP J. Adv. Signal Process. **2015**(1), 66 (2015). https://doi.org/10.1186/s13634-015-0251-9
6. Shannon, C.E.: A mathematical theory of communication. Bell Syst. Tech. J. **27**, 379–423 (1948). https://doi.org/10.1145/584091.584093. (July 1928)
7. Peng, H., Long, F., Ding, C.: Feature selection based on mutual information: criteria of max-dependency, max-relevance, and min-redundancy. IEEE Trans. Pattern Anal. Mach. Intell. **27**(8), 1226–1238 (2005). https://doi.org/10.1109/TPAMI.2005.159
8. Ciaccio, E.J., Dunn, S.M., Akay, M.: Biosignal pattern recognition and interpretation systems: Part 2 of 4: methods for feature extraction and selection. IEEE Eng. Med. Biol. Mag. **12**, 106–113 (1993). https://doi.org/10.1109/51.248173
9. Rejer, I.: Genetic algorithm with aggressive mutation for feature selection in BCI feature space. Pattern Anal. Appl. **18**(3), 485–492 (2014). https://doi.org/10.1007/s10044-014-0425-3
10. Wei, Q., Wang, Y.: Binary multi-objective particle swarm optimization for channel selection in motor imagery based brain-computer interfaces. In: 2011 4th International Conference on Biomedical Engineering and Informatics (BME I), pp. 667–670 (2011). https://doi.org/10.3233/BME-151451
11. Atyabi, A., Luerssen, M., Fitzgibbon, S.P., Powers, D.M.W.: Use of evolutionary algorithm-based methods in EEG based BCI systems. In: Swarm Intelligence for Electric and Electronic Engineering, pp. 326–344 (2012). https://doi.org/10.4018/978-1-4666-2666-9.ch016
12. Gan, J.Q., Hasan, B.A.S., Tsui, C.S.L.: A filter-dominating hybrid sequential forward floating search method for feature subset selection in high-dimensional space. Int. J. Mach. Learn. Cybern. **5**(3), 413–423 (2014). https://doi.org/10.1007/s13042-012-0139-z

13. Khushaba, R.N., Al-Ani, A., AlSukker, A., Al-Jumaily, A.: A combined ant colony and differential evolution feature selection algorithm. In: Dorigo, M., Birattari, M., Blum, C., Clerc, M., Stützle, T., Winfield, A.F.T. (eds.) ANTS 2008. LNCS, vol. 5217, pp. 1–12. Springer, Heidelberg (2008). https://doi.org/10.1007/978-3-540-87527-7_1

14. Tan, F., Fu, X., Zhang, Y., Bourgeois, A.G.: A genetic algorithm-based method for feature subset selection. Soft. Comput. **12**(2), 111–120 (2008). https://doi.org/10.1007/s00500-007-0193-8

15. Ali, S.I., Shahzad, W.: A feature subset selection method based on symmetric uncertainty and Ant Colony Optimization. In: 2012 International Conference on Emerging Technologies, pp. 1–6 (2012). https://doi.org/10.1109/ICET.2012.6375420

16. Nguyen, H.B., Xue, B., Liu, I., Zhang, M.: Filter based backward elimination in wrapper based PSO for feature selection in classification. In: Proceedings of the 2014 IEEE Congress on Evolutionary Computation, CEC 2014, pp. 3111–3118 (2014). https://doi.org/10.1109/CEC.2014.6900657

17. Zhu, Z., Jia, S., Ji, Z.: Towards a memetic feature selection paradigm. IEEE Comput. Intell. Mag. **5**(2), 41–53 (2010). https://doi.org/10.1109/MCI.2010.936311

18. Lourenco, H.R., Martin, O.C., Stutzle, T.: Iterated local search: framework and applications. In: Gendreau, M., Potvin, J.Y. (eds.) Handbook of Metaheuristics. International Series in Operations Research & Management Science, vol. 146, pp. 363–397. Springer, Boston (2010). https://doi.org/10.1007/978-1-4419-1665-5_12

19. Chandrashekar, G., Sahin, F.: A survey on feature selection methods. Comput. Electr. Eng. **40**(1), 16–28 (2014). https://doi.org/10.1016/j.compeleceng.2013.11.024

20. Lotte, F., Congedo, M., Anatole, L., Lotte, F., Congedo, M., Anatole, L.: A Review of Classification Algorithms for EEG-based BCI (2007). https://doi.org/10.1088/1741-2560/4/2/R01

21. Ramos, A.C., Vellasco, M.: Feature selection methods applied to motor imagery task classification. In: 2016 IEEE Latin American Conference on Computational Intelligence (LA-CCI) (2016). https://doi.org/10.1109/LA-CCI.2016.7885731, ISBN 9781509051052

22. Kohavi, R.: A study of cross-validation and bootstrap for accuracy estimation and model selection. In: International Joint Conference on Articial Intelligence (IJCAI), vol. 5, pp. 1–7 (1995). https://doi.org/10.1067/mod.2000.109031, ISBN 1-55860-363-8

23. Lan, T., Erdogmus, D., Adami, A., Pavel, M., Mathan, S.: Salient EEG channel selection in brain computer interfaces by mutual information maximization. In: Conference proceedings Annual International Conference of the IEEE Engineering in Medicine and Biology Society, vol. 7, pp. 7064–7067. IEEE Engineering in Medicine and Biology Society (2005). https://doi.org/10.1109/IEMBS.2005.1616133

Automatic Segmentation of Neurons in 3D Samples of Human Brain Cortex

G. Mazzamuto[1]([✉]), I. Costantini[1], M. Neri[2], M. Roffilli[2],
L. Silvestri[1,3], and F. S. Pavone[1,3,4]

[1] European Laboratory for Non-Linear Spectroscopy (LENS),
Via Nello Carrara, 1, 50019 Sesto Fiorentino (FI), Italy
mazzamuto@lens.unifi.it
[2] Bioretics Srl, Corte Zavattini, 21, 47522 Cesena (FC), Italy
[3] National Institute of Optics, National Research Council (INO-CNR),
Via Nello Carrara, 1, 50019 Sesto Fiorentino (FI), Italy
[4] Department of Physics and Astronomy, University of Florence,
Via G. Sansone, 1, 50019 Sesto Fiorentino (FI), Italy

Abstract. Quantitative analysis of brain cytoarchitecture requires effective and efficient segmentation of the raw images. This task is highly demanding from an algorithmic point of view, because of the inherent variations of contrast and intensity in the different areas of the specimen, and of the very large size of the datasets to be processed. Here, we report a machine vision approach based on Convolutional Neural Networks (CNN) for the near real-time segmentation of neurons in three-dimensional images with high specificity and sensitivity. This instrument, together with high-throughput sample preparation and imaging, can lay the basis for a quantitative revolution in neuroanatomical studies.

Keywords: Segmentation · Brain images · Convolutional neural network

1 Introduction

A full reconstruction of the cellular and molecular architecture of the human brain cortex is one of the "holy grails" of contemporary neuroscience. From a technological perspective, the production of such a map is highly challenging for at least three reasons: (a) the intact brain tissue must be properly labeled with specific probes for different cell types; (b) a macroscopic specimen must be imaged with micrometric resolution in a reasonable time; and (c) imaging data must be analyzed in an automatic fashion to extract quantitative information about the sample.

In the last years, considerable progress has been made in the field of tissue preparation, with the revival of century-old clearing methods [1] and the development of tissue transformation technologies capable of efficient and specific staining of the sample [2, 3]. In addition, on the imaging side, the renaissance of light-sheet microscopy has provided a

---

G. Mazzamuto and I. Costantini—Contributed equally to this work.

© Springer International Publishing AG, part of Springer Nature 2018
K. Sim and P. Kaufmann (Eds.): EvoApplications 2018, LNCS 10784, pp. 78–85, 2018.
https://doi.org/10.1007/978-3-319-77538-8_6

valuable method for the three-dimensional scan of intact tissue blocks with micrometric resolution, and with a volume throughput as high as 10 mm^3/min [4, 5].

These technical advancements open unprecedented opportunities for the study of complex organs, but also pose exceptional challenges in extracting semantic information form the collection of pixels produced by the microscope, with datasets ranging from tens of GigaBytes to tens of TeraBytes in size. Indeed, image segmentation is a well-known challenging problem in computer science, aimed at labeling each pixel of an image from a limited number of given options. Pixel labels are then exploited in order to extract a semantic picture of the scene where interesting objects are found and precisely located. The definition of "objects" depends on the type of query we ask at the semantic level of abstraction. Commonly, objects are represented by collections of touching pixels that share the same visual appearance or, in other words, that belong to the same visual pattern.

In the simplest setup, segmentation requires to split background pixels (or not-interesting objects) from foreground ones (or target objects). Even in this very simple formulation, the segmentation process is an ill-posed problem given that, especially in natural images, there is a lack of formal definition regarding the labeling of pixels that belong to transient areas where background becomes foreground and vice-versa. Nonetheless, many algorithms available in the literature are able to capture key visual proprieties of foreground objects thus providing a good split. Many of them make use of color or geometric appearance models in order to propagate labels iteratively from seed points to neighbor pixels. More recent approaches under the umbrella of semantic segmentation try to label the entire scene directly, integrating the intermediate neighbor collection step into an Artificial Neural Network architecture [6].

Here, we present a framework for segmentation of neurons in 3D images of human brain cortex, working at the level of local visual pattern (i.e. texture) rather than of single pixels, and relying on deep convolutional neural network architectures. This application is remarkably novel in the field of microscopic analysis of human brain samples, where image segmentation has been addressed using shallow rather than deep architectures [7].

2   Materials and Methods

2.1   Sample Collection and Preparation

The human brain sample used in this paper was obtained from the Institute of Neuroscience and Medicine, Research Centre Jülich, Germany, within a collaboration of the European Union's H2020 research and innovation programme under grant agreements No. 720270 (Human Brain Project). The sample was obtained after informed consent, according to the guidelines of the Human Research Ethics Committee of the institute. Upon collection, the sample was placed in neutral buffered (pH 7.2–7.4) formalin (Diapath, Martinengo, Italy) and stored at room temperature until the clearing process.

The fixed sample was processed following the protocol published by Costantini et al. [2]. Briefly, the sample was embedded in a poly-acrylamide hydrogel, and lipids were washed away by incubation in a clearing solution of sodium dodecyl sulfate.

After clearing, the sample was manually cut into a piece of approximately $1.2 \times 2.5 \times 0.4$ mm^3 using a vibratome. To perform the immunostaining, the processed sample was incubated at room temperature (RT) for 2 days with the primary antibody NeuN (ABN78 Merk S.p.A) at a dilution of 1:400 in PBST0.1 solution, followed by washing at RT for 1 day in PBST0.1 solution. The tissue was then incubated with the Alexa Fluor 594 conjugated secondary antibody (ab150080 Abcam) at a dilution of 1:200 at RT for 2 days in PBST0.1 solution, followed by washing at RT for 1 day in PBST0.1 solution. During the last incubation, the sample was stained also with DAPI (LifeTechnologies, CA, D1306) for nuclei labeling (dilution, 1:20000).

After staining, the sample was optically cleared with serial incubations in 10 ml of 20% and 47% (vol/vol) 2, 2'-thiodiethanol in 0.01 M PBS (TDE/PBS) for 10 min at 37 °C while gently shaking before imaging with two-photon fluorescence microscopy (TPFM) in two color channels.

2.2 Imaging: Two-Photon Fluorescence Microscopy

A mode-locked Ti:Sapphire laser (Chameleon, 120 fs pulse width, 90 MHz repetition rate, Coherent, CA) was coupled into a custom-made scanning system based on a pair of galvanometric mirrors (VM500+, Cambridge Technologies, MA). The laser is focused onto the specimen by a tunable 25× objective lens (LD LCI Plan-apochromat 25x/0.8 IMM Corr Dic M27, Zeiss, Germany). The system is equipped with a motorized xy stage for axial displacement of the sample (U-780.DOS, PILine Stage System 100×75 mm for Inverted Microscope from Olympus with controller and Joystick, Physik Instrumente, Germany) and with a closed-loop piezoelectric stage for the displacement of the objective along the z axis (ND72Z2LAQ PIFOC objective scanning system, 2 mm travel range, Physik Instrumente, Germany). The fluorescence signals are collected by two photomultiplier modules (H7422, Hamamatsu Photonics, NJ). The instrument is controlled by custom software, written in LabView (National Instruments, TX).

2.3 Image Stitching

The Two-Photon Fluorescence Microscopy (TPFM) setup described above produces a mosaic of overlapping 3D stacks, one for each position of the stage. In order to recreate the imaged volume, the acquired stacks need to be fused together. We perform this delicate step using a software tool for image stitching that was developed in house from scratch. The tool is written in Python and is able to cope well with multichannel images such as those produced by the TPFM. It is also capable of processing TB-sized datasets or large volumes as big as 10^{12} voxels such as those produced when imaging large specimens or whole organs through a Light-Sheet Fluorescence Microscope, for which the software was initially developed. The stitching is performed in two steps. Initially, pairwise alignment is determined by evaluating the cross correlation between adjacent stacks. The final position of each stack in the reconstructed volume is determined by applying a global optimization algorithm. Finally, the full imaged volume is reconstructed in a 3D TIFF file, where overlapping tiles are meld together. The sample shown in Fig. 2 resulted in a final RGB image of $2496 \times 4667 \times 205 \approx 2.4 \; 10^9$ pixels and a file size of roughly 7GiB. For much larger datasets, where reconstructing the full volume in a single file is impractical, the stitching software provides a public API that can be used to query an arbitrary region of interest within the fused volume. This is also a convenient way to pass portions of the reconstructed volume to subsequent analysis steps in the processing pipeline.

2.4 Pattern-Level Segmentation by CNN

In this work, by following an original idea of the so-called "likelihood image" by [8], we propose an alternative approach, novel to this application field, that lies between the pixel-based and the fully semantic level (i.e. working on the whole image). In our setup, the segmentation procedure is formulated as a standard multi-class supervised classification task of visual patterns followed by a step of probabilistic blob detection [9]. In the following, each slice of the z-stack is considered an independent image and processed separately. Subsequent reconstruction of the 2.5D volume is performed via computer graphics algorithms. In a second setup, not presented in this work, we are processing close slices of the z-stack concurrently with the same classifier.

A standard 3-layered Convolutional Neural Network classifier is then adopted in order to classify independently each single pixel of each image. Hidden layer convolutions make use of (32, 64, 64) kernels of respectively ($5 \times 5, 3 \times 3, 3 \times 3$) size with ReLU activation function all followed by a 2×2 max pooling. Finally, two fully connected layers of 128 neurons with ReLU forward the information to the 2-neuron softmax output layer. The whole network then performs an information compression from $64 \times 64 \times 1$ pixel to a 2-class probabilistic value. The classification is indeed performed on a very large but fixed-in-size surrounding area (i.e. 64×64 pixels) centered on the pixel. In doing so, we ask the classifier to recognize the local visual pattern (i.e. the texture) to which the pixel belongs. The classifier was previously trained on a dataset of the same type of patches collected from a small set of images manually annotated by a human biologist (see Table 1 for details). In order to increase the number of samples, patches have been virtually data augmented by standard geometric and colour transformations [10]. Taking care of common padding issues at the borders, the trained CNN is applied on each pixel of the image, producing labels and their associated probabilities. Indeed, remarkably, the multi-class CNN does not return a hard label but, for each admissible label, the probability of that label being the correct one. Values achieved for each label are rearranged spatially into the so-called heatmap, that is a new image of the same size of the original one where the value of each pixel represents the probability that the corresponding pixel in the original belongs to the given object (see Fig. 1). A contour finding algorithm [11] is then applied to all the heatmaps at the same time in order to locate objects. Being the heatmap a

Table 1. Numerical facts about the dataset used for training the CNN.

	Quantity	Generated by
Images	**29**	Biologist
Annotated neurons	**941**	Biologist
103×103 patches	**321'542**	Automatic patch extraction
Virtual 64×64 patches	**~69'632'000**	Automatic data augmentation

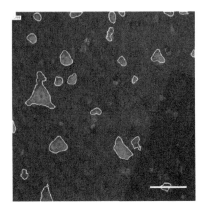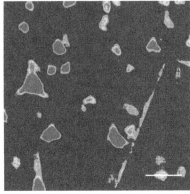

Fig. 1. Left: result of segmentation (solid yellow lines) overlaid on top of the original image. Right: heatmap for the object class "neuron". Only the red channel of the source 24 bit RGB image was used for segmentation. In the heatmap, pseudocolors represent the probability for each pixel to be the center of a 64 × 64 patch containing the visual pattern of a neuron. Visually, pixels ranging from yellow to red have more than 50% probability to be a neuron pattern, and thus have been selected. Note how the bleached area (the darker squared area in the bottom right corner) is correctly identified as background. Scale bar = 50 μm. (Color figure online)

probabilistic intermediate representation, it is possible to set the desired confidence value for accepting or rejecting objects in the contour finder.

3   Results

We randomly selected a small set of 4 annotated images and used them for evaluation purposes. These images were not used for training or validation, but were from the same physical specimen. Performance measure has been assessed on two levels of abstraction: pattern level and object level. The 4 test images count for 104 objects of class "neuron" manually annotated by an expert biologist. From these blobs we extracted 8'893 patches of size 64 × 64 representing a visual pattern of neuron and also 108'071 patches of background patterns. Background consists of areas of the image that do not overlap with target objects.

The trained CNN was asked to classify those 116'964 patches achieving an accuracy of 0.970, a sensitivity of 0.874 and a specificity of 0.977. Table 2 shows detailed information on the statistical evaluation via confusion matrix.

Table 2. Confusion matrix of the trained CNN at pattern-level in absolute (top) and normalized (bottom) values.

	Background	Foreground
Background	**105'636** **(0.977)**	**2'435** **(0.023)**
Foreground	**1'123** **(0.126)**	**7'770** **(0.874)**

We then performed a visual evaluation of the recognized objects by adopting a criteria of Intersection over Union (IoU): we considered a neuron correctly segmented if the boundary drawn by the algorithm covers more than 85% but no more than 115% of the corresponding annotated one. By following this policy, we found 88 neurons correctly segmented with 12 false positive blobs, resulting in 0.846 of sensitivity.

The CNN was then applied to perform segmentation of neurons across the entire dataset, consisting of about 2.4×10^9 pixels (Fig. 2). Notably, as the processing time for a 1024×1024 image is of about 100 ms on a standard Linux workstation running the Aliquis[TM] framework [12], and equipped with Intel Core i7-7700, 32 GB RAM, and NVIDIA GPU GTX1080, large datasets can be efficiently handled at a throughput comparable to the acquisition rate. The Aliquis[TM] framework is available free-of-charge for research purposes.

Fig. 2. Effective segmentation of large areas, also in the presence of large luminosity variation. Stitched and fused version of the original source images (up) and result of segmentation (down). Only the red channel of the source 24 bit RGB image, used for the segmentation, is shown. A total of 769 neurons were found in the image above. Scale bar = 200 μm. (Color figure online)

4 Discussion and Conclusion

The combination of the various techniques used in this work shows that it is possible to study the three-dimensional organization of neurons in large specimens of human brain samples obtaining quantitative information about the localization, shape, and position of the cells. In particular, we described a pattern-level segmentation with CNN which can effectively and efficiently process large-scale 3D microscopy datasets, regardless of the great variability in contrast and in structure of the raw images. Remarkably, images are processed – on a standard computer – in a time comparable to the acquisition time, opening the possibility to perform real-time analysis.

The current method affords a sensitivity of about 85% with few false positive signals per-image at the blob level, and even higher at the patch level. We anticipate that these values can become even higher when using concurrent segmentation of the adjacent slices in the z-stack, and by using a higher number of examples in the training phase.

The result shown here refers only to a binary classification (neuron/non neuron). However, as the segmentation methods inherently support multiple classification, it will be possible, with sufficient training, to discriminate different neuronal classes based on shape (e.g. pyramidal vs non-pyramidal cells) as our preliminary results suggest.

In conclusion, we have shown a proof-of-principle segmentation of 3D large microscopic images of the human brain cortex, highlighting the different spatial distribution of cells along the entire cortical thickness. Being able to provide not only cell position [13], but also cell shape, the method described here opens new exciting possibilities for the quantitative histological analysis of biological tissues, both in healthy and diseased samples, for both research and diagnostic purposes.

Acknowledgements. We thank Prof. Katrin Amunts from the Institute of Neuroscience and Medicine, Research Centre Jülich, Germany, for providing human brain samples used in this study. This project received funding from the European Union's H2020 research and innovation programme under grant agreements No. 720270 (Human Brain Project) and 654148 (Laserlab-Europe), and from the EU programme H2020 EXCELLENT SCIENCE - European Research Council (ERC) under grant agreement n. 692943 (BrainBIT). The project is also supported by the Italian Ministry for Education, University, and Research in the framework of the Flagship Project NanoMAX and of Eurobioimaging Italian Nodes (ESFRI research infrastructure), and by "Ente Cassa di Risparmio di Firenze" (private foundation).

References

1. Spalteholz, W.: Über das durchsichtigmachen von menschlichen und tierischen präpareten und seine theoretischen bedingungen, n.p. (1914)
2. Costantini, I., Ghobril, J.P., Di Giovanna, A.P., Mascaro, A.L.A., Silvestri, L., Mullenbroich, M.C., Onofri, L., Conti, V., Vanzi, F., Sacconi, L., Guerrini, R., Markram, H., Iannello, G., Pavone, F.S.: A versatile clearing agent for multi-modal brain imaging. Sci. Rep. **5**, 9808 (2015)

3. Silvestri, L., Costantini, I., Sacconi, L., Pavone, F.S.: Clearing of fixed tissue: a review from a microscopist's perspective. J. Biomed. Opt. **21**, 081205 (2016)
4. Dodt, H.U., Leischner, U., Schierloh, A., Jahrling, N., Mauch, C.P., Deininger, K., Deussing, J.M., Eder, M., Zieglgansberger, W., Becker, K.: Ultramicroscopy: three-dimensional visualization of neuronal networks in the whole mouse brain. Nature Meth. **4**, 331–336 (2007)
5. Silvestri, L., Bria, A., Sacconi, L., Iannello, G., Pavone, F.S.: Confocal light sheet microscopy: micron-scale neuroanatomy of the entire mouse brain. Opt. Express **20**, 20582–20598 (2012)
6. Garcia-Garcia, A., Orts-Escolano, S., Oprea, S., Villena-Martinez, V., Garcia-Rodriguez, J.: A Review on Deep Learning Techniques Applied to Semantic Segmentation. arXiv preprint arXiv:1704.06857 (2017)
7. Alegro, M., Theofilas, P., Nguy, A., Castruita, P.A., Seeley, W., Heinsen, H., Ushizima, D. M., Grinberg, L.T.: Automating cell detection and classification in human brain fluorescent microscopy images using dictionary learning and sparse coding. J. Neurosci. Meth. **282**, 20–33 (2017)
8. Roffilli, M.: Advanced machine learning techniques for digital mammography. Technical report, Department of Computer Science University of Bologna, Italy (2006)
9. Lindeberg, T.: Detecting salient blob-like image structures and their scales with a scale-space primal sketch - a method for focus-of-attention. Int. J. Comput. Vision **11**, 283–318 (1993)
10. Krizhevsky, A., Sutskever, I., Hinton, G.E.: Imagenet classification with deep convolutional neural networks. In: Advances in neural information processing systems, pp. 1097–1105 (2012)
11. Maple, C.: Geometric design and space planning using the marching squares and marching cube algorithms. In: Proceedings of 2003 International Conference on Geometric Modeling and Graphics, 2003, pp. 90–95. IEEE (2003)
12. Bioretics srl: The Aliquis^{TM} framework. http://www.bioretics.com/aliquis. Accessed on 4 Nov 2017
13. Frasconi, P., Silvestri, L., Soda, P., Cortini, R., Pavone, F.S., Iannello, G.: Large-scale automated identification of mouse brain cells in confocal light sheet microscopy images. Bioinformatics **30**, i587–i593 (2014)

Analysis of Relevance and Redundance on Topoisomerase 2b (TOP2B) Binding Sites: A Feature Selection Approach

Pedro Manuel Martínez García[1], Miguel García Torres[2],
Federico Divina[2](✉), Francisco Antonio Gómez Vela[2],
and Felipe Cortés-Ledesma[1]

[1] Andalusian Molecular Biology and Regenerative Medicine Centre, Seville, Spain
{pedro.martinez,felipe.cortes}@cabimer.es
[2] Computer Science, Universidad Pablo de Olavide, Seville, Spain
{mgarciat,fdivina,fgomez}@upo.es

Abstract. Topoisomerases are proteins that regulate the topology of DNA by introducing transient breaks to relax supercoiling. In this paper we focus our attention on Topoisomerases 2 (TOP2), which generate double-strand DNA breaks that, if inefficiently repaired, can seriously compromise genomic stability. It is then important to gain insights on the molecular processes involved in TOP2-DNA binding. In order to do this, we collected genomic and epigenomic information from publicly available high-throughput sequencing projects and systematically quantified them within experimentally measured TOP2 binding sites. We then applied feature selection techniques in order to both increase the performance of classification and to gain insight on the particular properties that can be of biological relevance. Results obtained allowed us to identify a core set of predictive chromatin features that faithfully explain TOP2 binding.

Keywords: Feature selection · Classification · Binding sites
Topoisomerase 2b · Double-strand DNA breaks

1 Introduction

Type 2 topoisomerases (TOP2) relax supercoiled DNA by carrying out decatenation and unknotting to solve DNA topological problems [1]. Aberrant activity of TOP2 often causes double-strand DNA breaks [2], whose inefficient repair can seriously compromise genomic stability, which in turn leads to the potential formation of oncogenic mutations [3].

Mammalian genomes harbour two TOP2 genes, TOP2A and TOP2B. While TOP2A is mainly expressed in proliferating cells, where it is required for chromosome segregation, TOP2B is essential for transcription in post-mitotic cells [4]. The functions of the latter, though, are much less well known. Recent data from chromatin immunoprecipitation followed by DNA sequencing (ChIP-seq) have shed light to the specificities of TOP2B binding at the genome wide level. It

K. Sim and P. Kaufmann (Eds.): EvoApplications 2018, LNCS 10784, pp. 86–101, 2018.
https://doi.org/10.1007/978-3-319-77538-8_7

seems clear that TOP2B binding events are enriched in promoters or proximal to them [5]. TOP2B also associates with DNase I hypersensitivity sites, as well as with epigenetic marks of active transcription and enhancers [5]. Novel findings point to TOP2B activity as an important player in the chromosome loop extrusion model [6]. Accordingly, a considerable number of TOP2B binding sites follow a model in which TOP2B and the cohesin complex component RAD21 are spatially organized around the architectural protein CTCF, all of them hallmarking the base of loop domains [5].

Regarding sequence preferences, current data suggest that TOP2B does not have a specific DNA binding motif [5], which in principle agrees with the fact that topoisomerases act wherever topological problems originate. However, TOP2B associates with DNA regions that are actively bound by sequence-specific transcription factors [5], and whether topological problems can preferentially occur at sites with specific sequence properties is an open question.

In summary, previous studies have highlighted the association between TOP2B and several chromatin features, mainly by either studying genome wide correlations or proportions of overlapping binding sites. However, none of them have devoted to explore the ability of such features to predict TOP2B localization using machine learning, and in particular feature selection techniques. This is of particular interest, since it allows for the ranking of variables, which can provide information on which repertoire of features are relevant for TOP2B binding. In this regard, feature selection methods can be really helpful in finding redundancies and determining a minimum set of informative variables. In this work, we made use of a feature selection approach to comprehensively study the predictive power of a wide set of chromatin features to identify TOP2B sites. To faithfully profile such chromatin landscape, we included experimental information from high-throughput sequencing experiments that involve histone modifications, transcription factors, chromatin arquitecture, gene expression, open chromatin factors and DNA methylation. In addition to this, we also incorporated information of DNA sequence and DNA shape patterns. Our machine learning approach on such combination of chromatin features, unprecedentedly tested together to predict topoisomerase localization, may allow us to determine the chromatin code that defines TOP2B binding.

Classically, feature selection is defined as the process that seeks the minimal size of relevant features such that the classification error is optimized. In order to identify the optimal subset of relevant features, different criteria have been proposed to evaluate the goodness of feature subsets. Feature subset selection strategies are essentially divided into wrapper, filter and embedded methods [7]. In the wrapper approach the quality of feature subsets for classification is defined with respect to the induction algorithms. The learner is used as a black box to score the subsets. Filter approaches assess each subset according to intrinsic properties of the data and are independent of the learner. Finally, the embedded methods cannot separate the learning and the feature selection and, so, the search for an optimal subset of features is done during the induction of the classifier. The main advantage of wrappers is that they include the interaction between feature subset and model selection. However, they have a higher risk of overfitting than filters and are computationally expensive. The filter methods, in contrast, are computationally fast, so that they easily scale to high-dimensional datasets. They ignore the interaction with the classifier, which may lead to worse classification performance. Finally embedded approach are far less computationally intensive than wrappers and combine the interaction with the classification model. In this paper we will focus on the use of filter methods.

Recent works have studied the association between specific DNA locations, such as transcription factor binding sites or replication origins, and several chromatin features by using machine learning approaches. Some of these studies include the use of Support Vector Machine [8], random forest and multiple linear regression [9] and lasso in [10].

In this work we tackle the identification of topoisomerase binding sites from a machine learning perspective. First we study the performance of two widely used learning algorithms -Support Vector Machine [11] and Naive Bayes [12]-. Then, we apply three feature selection algorithms to find a subset of highly predictive power features. For such purpose, we compare two evolutionary strategies -Scatter Search [13] and Genetic Algorithm [14]- with the popular heuristic Fast Correlation Based Filter [15]. Results show the importance of applying a feature selection approach to analyse the relevance and redundance of features to a high dimensional biological dataset.

The rest of the paper is organised as follow. In Sect. 2 we first provide a description of the data used in this paper, and then we provide details about the particular feature selection mechanisms used. Results are described in Sect. 3, and are discussed in Sect. 4. Finally, in Sect. 5 we draw the main conclusions and identify possible future developments.

2   Materials and Methods

2.1   Data

Identification of TOP2B Binding Sites

To date, few high resolution genome wide profiles of TOP2B binding have been performed [5,6]. Among them, we have chosen the one published in Uusküla-Reimand et al. (2016) to build up our model due to two main reasons. First, it represents the best quality genome wide ChIP-seq experiment on TOP2B that is available to date, both in terms of number of replicates generated and sequencing depth. Second, it was conducted in mouse liver cells, which represents an ideal TOP2B-expressing tissue (non-dividing), with abundant genomic datasets available.

For the computation of TOP2B binding sites (peaks), we first merged the reads of biological replicates and corresponding input samples. Then we mapped them to the mouse genome (mm9) using Bowtie 1.2 [16] with option "-m 1" so that reads that map only once to the genome were retained. Peaks were called with MACS2 [17] with option "-q 0.01" and only peaks showing a fold change greater than 5 were kept. Adjacent peaks (less than 700 bp apart) were combined and the resulting whole set of peaks were resized to 300 bp. Finally, peaks overlapping with non-mappable regions or regions of the ENCODE blacklist (https://sites.google.com/site/anshulkundaje/projects/blacklists) were discarded. The final set comprised 13, 131 TOP2B peaks, which were equally distributed through the mouse chromosomes. To get an equal number of observations for each class (TOP2B binding/not binding), 13, 131 random regions of 300 bp length were also generated so that they had the same distribution across chromosomes. Again, non-mappable regions and regions of the ENCODE blacklist were discarded. To make sure they had low TOP2B binding intensity, genomic regions enriched in TOP2B/INPUT signal were also discarded. Finally, in order to avoid sequence composition biases, random regions were selected so that their sequence had the same GC content distribution as that of TOP2B peaks.

Table 1. High throughput sequencing experiments included in the TOP2B binding model.

Experiment	Target	Biological feature	Database	Identifier
DNase-seq	-	Open chromatin	ENCODE	ENCSR000CNI
MNase-seq	-	Open chromatin	GEO	GSM717558
RNA-seq	-	Expression	ENCODE	ENCSR000CLO
ChIP-seq	POLR2A	Pol2 binding	ENCODE	ENCSR000CBR
ChIP-seq	CBP	Transcription factor	ArrayExpress	E-MTAB-941
ChIP-seq	CEBPA	Transcription factor	ArrayExpress	E-MTAB-941
ChIP-seq	FOXA1	Transcription factor	ArrayExpress	E-MTAB-941
ChIP-seq	FOXA2	Transcription factor	ArrayExpress	E-MTAB-941
ChIP-seq	GABPA	Transcription factor	ArrayExpress	E-MTAB-941
ChIP-seq	HNF1A	Transcription factor	ArrayExpress	E-MTAB-941
ChIP-seq	HNF4A	Transcription factor	ArrayExpress	E-MTAB-941
ChIP-seq	HNF6A	Transcription factor	ArrayExpress	E-MTAB-941
ChIP-seq	P300	Transcription factor	ArrayExpress	E-MTAB-941
ChIP-seq	YY1	Transcription factor	ArrayExpress	E-MTAB-941
ChIP-seq	RAD21	Chromatin arquitecture	ArrayExpress	E-MTAB-3587
ChIP-seq	STAG1	Chromatin arquitecture	ArrayExpress	E-MTAB-941
ChIP-seq	STAG2	Chromatin arquitecture	ArrayExpress	E-MTAB-941
ChIP-seq	CTCF	Chromatin arquitecture	ENCODE	ENCSR000CBU
ChIP-seq	H3K27ac	Histone modification	ENCODE	ENCSR000CDH
ChIP-seq	H3K27me3	Histone modification	ENCODE	ENCSR000CEN
ChIP-seq	H3K36me3	Histone modification	ENCODE	E-MTAB-3587
ChIP-seq	H3K4me1	Histone modification	ENCODE	ENCSR000CAO
ChIP-seq	H3K4me3	Histone modification	ENCODE	E-MTAB-3587
ChIP-seq	H3K79me2	Histone modification	ENCODE	ENCSR000CEP
ChIP-seq	H3K9ac	Histone modification	ENCODE	ENCSR000CEQ
WGBS	-	CpG methylation	GEO	GSM1051157

Collection and Quantification of High-Throughput Sequencing Data

We collected experimental data on mouse liver cells that could be incorporated into the TOP2B binding model. We inspected both the literature as well as the ENCODE database and selected the 26 high throughput sequencing experiments shown in Table 1, which were categorized according to their biological function. For the quantification of ChIP-seq experiments within TOP2B peaks we used the scoring approach of [18]. For each peak, reads aligning within its genomic coordinates were first considered, normalized to the size of the corresponding sequencing library and scaled to the size of the smaller library (among test and input). Then, they were added 1 as a pseudocount and the ratio of test versus input signal was calculated before being log transformed. RNA-seq, DNase-seq and MNase-seq were scored as the number of reads aligning within TOP2B-binding sites divided by the library size.

Besides high throughput sequencing data, we also included sequence and DNA shape information in order to evaluate their contribution to TOP2B binding. Recently, the inclusion of sequence-dependent DNA shape features to models based on DNA sequence alone has been shown to improve the prediction of transcription factor binding sites [19]. In such studies nucleotides are represented by 4 features to encode 1-mers, 16 features to encode 2-mers, 64 features to encode 3-mers, and 8 features to encode DNA shape. Therefore, we made use of DNAshapeR [20] to produce DNA sequence and DNA shape vectors, which were added to the above 26 high throughput sequencing features, resulting in the $26,262 \times 27,451$ matrix of Fig. 1. However, in this paper, due to computational limitations, we randomly selected 1000 rows, equally distributed among positive (TOP2B binding) and negative examples (TOP2B not binding). However such subset is a significant subset and will allow to draw biologically valid conclusions, since it is guaranteed that all the samples display both the same distribution through the mouse chromosomes and the same GC content as those of the original set.

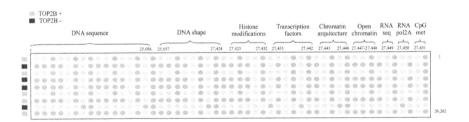

Fig. 1. Final data matrix for the modeling of TOP2B binding.

2.2 Classification

In Machine Learning, classification is the problem of learning a function that identifies the category to which a new observation belongs to. Formally, let $\mathcal{E}$

be a set of n examples characterized by the pair $(\mathbf{x}_i, y_i)$, so that each $\mathbf{x}_i \in \mathcal{X}$ is an instance described by a vector of d features $\mathcal{X} = (X_1, \ldots, X_d)$, and $y_i \in \mathcal{Y}$ is the known class label of $\mathbf{x}_i$. The classification problem consist in inducing a function $\mathcal{C} : \mathbf{X} \rightarrow \mathcal{Y}$, called classifier, that maps a vector $\mathbf{X}$ to a given class label in $\mathcal{Y}$. In this work we use two popular classifiers: Support Vector Machine (SVM) and Naive Bayes (NB). We have chosen these methods since they represent algorithms which are very different (almost opposite extremes) in terms of simplicity with SVM being more complex. Moreover both SVM and NB are very popular classifiers.

Support Vector Machine. [11] (SVM) is a discriminative classifier based on the concept of decision hyperplanes that define decision boundaries. It finds the hyperplane that optimally separates the data into two categories by solving an optimization problem. Such hyperplane, called optimal hyperplane, is the one that maximizes the margin between classes. In case of non-separable data, it optimizes a weighted combination of the misclassification rate and the distance of the decision boundary to any sample vector. Those points that define the decision boundary are called support vectors. When the decision boundary is not a linear function, SVM uses a kernel function for mapping the original feature space to some higher-dimensional feature space where the data set is separable. In our experiments we used a linear kernel, for simplicity reasons.

Naive Bayes. [12] (NB) is a probabilistic classifier based on Bayes' theorem. It is the simplest form of Bayesian network, which is a probabilistic graphical model that represents the features and their conditional dependencies as a directed acyclic graph (DAG). In such DAG a node represents a feature and the edges represent conditional dependencies between two features. However, since NB assumes that the predictor variables are conditionally independent given the value of the class, building the classifier consists in learning the set of conditional probability tables (CPTs) with respect the class. Despite its simplicity, it has been observed that its classification accuracy may be high on datasets where there are strong dependencies among features.

2.3   Feature Selection

Given a set of examples $\mathcal{E}$, as defined in the previous section, the aim of feature selection is to find the subset of features $S \subseteq \mathcal{X}$ with which a classifier $\mathcal{C}$ achieves the lowest error rate.

In general, not all the features hold the same information about the class label, and, depending on this, features are divided into irrelevants and relevants. A feature is considered irrelevant if it provides no information about the class while it is relevant if it embodies information about the class concept. Therefore, removing irrelevant features may improve the predictive model as well as the speed of the learning algorithm. In order to find a subset of *good* features for the classification, we define a quality measure $J(.)$ so that the associated optimization problem consists of finding the subset of features S that optimises $J(S)$. In order to find the optimal subset of features for minimizing the error rate it may not be necessary to select all relevant features, but only the subset with the most predictive power. Furthermore, such subset of features may not be unique due to redundance.

Redundance can be defined in terms of feature correlation so that two features are redundant if their values are correlated. In order to establish whether or not two features a redundant, the Symmetrical Uncertainty (SU) [21] can be used. SU is an entropy based measure, which was proposed as non-linear correlation in [15]. It is defined as follows:

$$SU(X,Y) = 2 \left[\frac{IG(X|Y)}{H(X) + H(Y)} \right],$$

where

$$H(X) = -\sum_i P(x_i) \log_2(P(x_i)),$$

represents the entropy and measures the uncertainty about the values of X,

$$H(X|Y) = -\sum_j P(y_j) \sum_i P(x_i|y_j) \log_2(P(x_i|y_j)),$$

is the conditional entropy and measures the uncertainty about the value of X given the value of Y, and

$$IG(X|Y) = H(X) - H(X|Y)$$

is the Information Gain (IG) and measures the reduction in uncertainty about the value of X given the value of Y. A drawback of IG is that it is biased in favor of variables with more values. SU overcomes this effect by normalizing by individual entropies. Normalization ensures that the values have the same scale, are comparable and have the same effect. SU takes values in $[0,1]$, so that a value of 0 indicates that X and Y are independent, while a value of 1 would indicate complete dependency.

The identification of redundant features can be defined in terms of the concept of Markov blanket introduced by Holler and Sahami in [22]. Such concept is defined as follows

Definition 1 (Markov blanket). *Given a feature X_i, $M_i \subset \mathcal{X}$ ($X_i \notin M_i$) is said to be a Markov blanket for X_i iff*

$$P(\mathcal{X} - M_i - \{X_i\}, \mathcal{Y}|X_i, M_i) = \\ P(\mathcal{X} - M_i - \{X_i\}, \mathcal{Y}|M_i). \tag{1}$$

Therefore, a set of features M is a blanket for a feature X_i if X_i is conditionally independent of $\mathcal{X} - M - \{X_i\}$. If so, then X_i is also conditionally independent of $\mathcal{Y}$. Such condition is stronger than the conditional independence between X_i and $\mathcal{Y}$ given M. It requires that M subsume not only the information that X_i

has about $\mathcal{Y}$ but also about all of the other features. Therefore, given a subset $S \subseteq \mathcal{X}$, a feature $X_i \in S$ can be removed from S if we find a Markov blanket M for X_i within S. In this case we can say that X_i is a redundant feature of S and so removing it from the subset will not affect to the predictive power of the classification model.

In [15] the authors define heuristically the approximate Markov blankets (AMb) by using SU correlation measure between features to analyze feature redundancy.

Definition 2 (Approximate Markov blanket). *Given two features X_i and X_j ($i \neq j$) so that $SU(X_j, \mathcal{Y}) \geq SU(X_i, \mathcal{Y})$, then X_j forms an approximate Markov blanket for X_i iff $SU(X_i, X_j) \geq SU(X_i, \mathcal{Y})$.*

This definition is based on pairwise comparison and assumes that a feature X_j with larger values of SU with the class contains more information about the class than a feature X_i with smaller value.

The approximate Markov blanket is computed by comparing the correlation between the features X_i and X_j, and the SU value of X_i and the class. If the correlation between such features is larger, then X_j forms an approximate Markov blanket.

In the same work, authors also introduce the concept of predominant feature to guarantee that only redundant features will be removed, so that no information will be lost.

Definition 3. *Given a set of features S, a relevant feature is a predominant feature iff it does not have any AMb in S.*

SU is a pairwise measure and, so, it is not possible to evaluate the interaction between a feature and a subset of features. A possible approach to do so is subsuming the contribution of pairwise interactions. The Correlation based Feature Selection (CFS) measure [21] uses this approach. It assigns higher values to feature subsets that contains features highly correlated with the class, yet uncorrelated with each other. CFS is defined as follows:

$$J(S) := \frac{m \cdot \overline{SU}(S, Y)}{\sqrt{m + m(m-1) \cdot \overline{SU}(S, S)}},$$

where m is the size of the subset S and

$$\overline{SU}(S, Y) = \frac{1}{m} \cdot \sum_{X_i \in S} SU(X_i, Y),$$

and

$$\overline{SU}(S, S) = \frac{2}{m(m-1)} \cdot \sum_{X_i \in S} \sum_{\substack{X_j \in S \\ X_i \neq X_j}} SU(X_i, X_j).$$

In this work we compare the performance of three feature selection strategies, that make use of the above concepts for selecting features. Two are based on evolutionary computation, namely Scatter Search (SS) [23] and the Genetic Algorithm (GA) [24]. The third is a heuristic called Fast Correlation Based Filter (FCBF) [15].

Scatter Search. [13,25] (SS) is an evolutionary population-based metaheuristic that was introduced in [23]. The method starts with a population of solutions from which a moderate-sized set, called *reference set* (*RefSet*), is selected to evolve. In order to explore regions of the search space with features associated with good solutions and to be able to escape from local optima, the evolution is based on intensification and diversification strategies.

The solutions of the *RefSet* are combined to generate new ones and then a local search is applied to the resulting solutions. The *RefSet* is then updated to incorporate solutions taking into account quality and diversity. These steps are repeated until a stopping criterion is met.

Unlike other evolutionary strategies, such as genetic algorithms, the combination of solutions is guided and the subset f solutions that are evolved is smaller in size to usual populations. For more details regarding the implementation of such method, we refer the reader to [26]. Following the recommendations of the authors, the population size was set to 50; the *RefSet* to 10 and the maximum number of iterations to 5. In this work SS uses CFS to evaluate feature subsets.

Genetic Algorithm. [14] (GA) is an evolutionary population-based strategy that uses techniques inspired by evolutionary biology such as inheritance, mutation, selection, and crossover. GAs has been widely applied to many optimization problems, e.g. [27,28], including feature subset selection.

Each individual of the population represents a candidate solution, the standard solution is based in bit strings, where each bit is called a gene.

A GA starts by generating (usually randomly) an initial population of individuals from which, a subset of promising individuals are selected to generate new ones using genetic operators such as crossover and mutation. The purpose of crossover is to recombine parents to generate new offsprings. Mutation produces some small changes on a single individual and introduces diversity in the population. The process continues across several generations until a stopping criterion is reached. In this paper, we used the simple GA implemented in Weka [29]. The parameters were set as follows. The population size of 50, and a total number of generations of 50. The crossover probability was set to 0.9, while the mutation probability to 0.01. Finally we also considered elitism so that the best solution of the previous generation will be considered in the next population. GA uses, as fitness function, CFS.

Fast Correlation Based Filter. [15] (FCBF) is a heuristic strategy that consists of two stages: obtaining the subset of relevant features and selecting the predominant features from it. In a practical sense, a feature X is relevant if $SU(X,Y)$ exceeds a predefined minimum threshold δ. Moreover, a relevant feature X_i is predominant if there is no other relevant feature X_j, $j \neq i$, such that X_j is an approximate Markov blanket for X_i.

Figure 2 shows the pseudocode of the FCBF. As we can see, the algorithm starts by calculating $SU(X_i, \mathcal{Y})$ for each feature in order to estimate its relevance. A feature X_i is considered irrelevant if $SU(X_i, \mathcal{Y}) \leq \delta$, where δ is a threshold set to 0 in our experiments, which means that only features that are totally irrelevant are removed. In order to detect a subset of predominant features, the remaining features are ordered in descending order according to the $SU(X_i, \mathcal{Y})$ value. Then a backward search is performed in the ordered list S'_{list} to remove redundant features. The first feature from S'_{list} is a predominant feature since it has no AMb. Note that a predominant feature X_j can be used to filter out other features for which X_j forms an AMb. Therefore a feature X_i is removed from S'_{list} if X_j forms a Markov blanket for it. The process is repeated until no predominant features are found.

Procedure *Fast Correlation Based Filter*
begin
1:   **for** $i = 1$ to d **do**
3:       calculate SU_{ic} for X_i;
4:       **if** $(SU_{ic} > \delta)$
5:           append X_i to S'_{list};
6:   **end**;
7:   order S'_{list} in descending SU_{ic} value;
8:   $X_j = \text{getFirstElement}(S'_{list})$;
9:   **do begin**;
10:       $X_i = \text{getNextElement}(S'_{list}, X_j)$;
11:       **if**$(X_i <> NULL)$
12:           **do begin**;
13:               **if**$(SU_{ij} \geq SU_{ic})$;
14:                   remove X_i from S'_{list};
15:               $X_i = \text{getNextElement}(S'_{list}, X_j)$;
16:           **end until** $(X_i == NULL)$;
17:       $X_j = \text{getNextElement}(S'_{list}, F_j)$;
18: **end until** $(X_j == NULL)$;
19: $S_{best} = S'_{list}$;
end

Fig. 2. Pseudocode of the FCBF method.

3   Experimental Results

This section presents the experiments performed and an analysis of the results obtained on the datasets under study. In order to assess models quality and compare such models, we used k-fold cross-validation method for estimating generalization error.

In k-fold cross-validation the data is splitted into k equally sized subsets or folds. Then, k iterations are performed so that each time a different fold is held-out for validation while remaining $k - 1$ folds are used for learning purpose.

Finally the performance measures are averaged over the runs. In general, lower values of k produce more pessimistic estimates and higher values more optimistical results. However, although the *true* generalization error is not usually known, k-fold cross-validation is a suitable estimator for model comparison purposes. In the experiments performed, k was set to 10, following the recommendations of Kohavi [30].

3.1   Baseline Classification Results

Before presenting the results obtained by the feature selection algorithms, we apply classification using the different feature groups described in Sect. 2.1. This may help in understanding the predictive power of the different groups. Table 2 shows the accuracy achieved with NB and SVM. The first column refers to the feature type. Then, the number of features is presented followed by the accuracy obtained by NB and SVM respectively, with the corresponding standard deviations.

Table 2. Accuracy of NB and SVM classifiers.

Data	#Feats	NB	SVM
DNA sequence	25056	55.30 ± 4.90	53.80 ± 6.36
DNA shape	2368	53.50 ± 3.27	49.30 ± 2.67
Histone modifications	8	77.80 ± 4.61	82.00 ± 3.65
Transcription factors	10	74.30 ± 3.92	78.90 ± 4.01
Chromatin architecture	4	88.70 ± 2.75	92.20 ± 3.08
Open chromatin	2	75.50 ± 3.03	54.50 ± 9.63
RNA seq	1	50.30 ± 1.25	50.20 ± 0.42
RNA pol2A	1	56.80 ± 4.42	53.90 ± 4.68
CpG methylation	1	60.00 ± 5.40	67.00 ± 5.14
all features	27451	79.90 ± 5.02	94.80 ± 1.87

In general, the behaviour of both classifiers is similar except in the Open Chromatin data and the full one. In the former case NB outperforms SVM, which produces a model with no predictive power. In the latter case SVM induces a better model than NB. Moreover, this model is the one with the highest predictive power in this experiment.

When using the other feature groups, both classifiers achieve better performance on Histone modification, Transcription factors, Chromatin architecture, specially in the last on with SVM. In all these cases, SVM outperforms NB. Finally, the models obtained from DNA sequence and Shape, RNA sequence and pol2A and CpG Methylation have no predictive power or a very poor one.

3.2 Feature Selection

In this section we study the results of applying feature selection algorithms to the full dataset. Table 3 presents the results achieved. The first column presents the feature selection algorithm used, the second column the averaged size of the feature subset of the best solution found. Then, the accuracy of NB and SVM respectively. Each result is presented with its corresponding standard deviation.

Table 3. Results of the feature selection. The first column indicate the algorithm used, the second the average number of features obtained, followed by the accuracies obtained by NB and SVM when the selected features are used

Algorithm	$\mid S\mid$	NB	SVM
SS	3.00 ± 0.00	93.90 ± 2.33	94.40 ± 2.59
GA	17416.20 ± 2720.92	84.00 ± 3.50	95.40 ± 2.17
FCBF	53.20 ± 3.77	94.30 ± 1.49	94.30 ± 1.83

The accuracy achieved with NB and SVM are very similar for Scatter Search and FCBF. However, SS is the strategy that reduces the most. Moreover, it found the same feature subset on all runs. In contrast, GA is the strategy that performs worst with NB while results with SVM are similar with the other strategies. A possible reason for this poor performance could be that this strategy requires more generation and/or a larger population size to find better solutions.

4   Feature Analysis

4.1 Baseline Classification

Models trained with all variables enabled accurate predictions for SVM (94.8%) and a more modest performance for NB (79.9%), indicating that chromatin feature information can systematically separate TOP2B binding sites from the rest of the genome.

When using subsets of features based on biological functions, divergent classification performances were obtained. Models trained with features associated with chromosome architecture achieved significant prediction accuracies (88.7% and 92.3%). These results are in line with previous findings of TOP2B associating with chromosome loop anchors [5,6]. Such remarkable predictive power contrasts with that of RNA-seq, which was not found to be informative (50%). Interestingly, a model trained only with Pol 2 binding information exhibited similarly low prediction accuracy (56.8% and 53.9%). This surprising result does not imply, though, that transcription associated features do not have prediction ability at all; on the contrary, histone modifications features, many of which mark transcriptional activity, achieved accurate classifications (77.8% and 82%). In this line, transcription factors alone were also found to exhibit moderately high prediction accuracies (74.3% and 78.9%).

DNase I hypersensitivity sites are known to highly correlate with TOP2B binding [5]. Strikingly, a SVM classifier trained only with open chromatin features showed no predictive power (54.5%). Such low accuracy was outperformed by the NB algorithm (75.5%), which seems to more reliable reflect the preference of TOP2B to bind accessible DNA. In any case, none of these classifiers produced remarkable classification performances when trained with open chromatin features, which contrasts with those obtained using future selection algorithms (see next section).

DNA sequence and (sequence-dependent) DNA shape classifiers deserve special attention. We need to keep in mind that, in order to control for sequence composition biases, we generated a set of random regions with the same CG content distribution as that of TOP2B binding sites. With this restriction, we aimed to make sure that the potential predictive power of DNA sequence and/or DNA shape was not affected by the fact that TOP2B sites are GC-rich. Neither SVM nor NB algorithms exhibited any predictive ability when trained with DNA sequence or DNA shape, suggesting that these features are not relevant for TOP2B binding. We need to be cautious, though, interpreting this result. First, GC rich regions tend to display DNA shape features such as decreased helix twist, high propeller twist and minor groove width, which may be more prompt to be bound by TOP2B (and we might be missing this by controlling for CG). Second, the nucleotide resolution of the experimental data (ChIP-seq) leads to the estimation of broad binding sites that are likely to contain superfluous sequence information, which in turn could be disturbing the identification of patterns that are really informative.

Controlling for GC content allows for a more reliable measure of CpG methylation, a well known epigenetic mark in vertebrates [31]. Since CG rich regions tend to be unmethylated [32], it would be interesting to observe significant differences in CpG methylation between TOP2B binding sites and random regions (with similar GC). Such is indeed the case, with TOP2B regions displaying decreased CpG methylation (data not shown). This result agrees with unmethylated CG rich promoters being more expressed than methylated ones [32]. In any case, models trained with this mark show modest prediction accuracies (60% and 67%), suggesting a poor informative ability to identify TOP2B binding.

4.2   Feature Selection

The use of scatter search allowed for quite accurate prediction outcomes for both NB and SVM (93.9% and 94.4%, respectively). This is of particular interest, since only 3 variables were needed to achieve such remarkable performance: DNase-seq and the architectural proteins RAD21 and STAG2. It is worth noting that CTCF, another well known protein whose role in chromatin organization has been widely described [33,34] and displays a high degree of colocalization with TOP2B [5], was not selected by the scatter search approach. These results were confirmed when using the FCBF algorithm, which systematically selected

RAD21 and STAG2 (as well as DNAse-seq) and discarded CTCF in every CV iteration. This is in agreement with previous findings of TOP2B interacting with CTCF almost exclusively in the presence of the cohesin complex [5]. In this regard, STAG1 and STAG2 genes code for different cohesin subunits that form two clearly differentiated populations of cohesin variants (cohesin-SA1 and cohesin-SA2), both of them harbouring RAD21. Our results highlight STAG2 and RAD21 as highly positive predictors of TOP2B binding, while STAG1 and CTCF are systematically rejected by both the scatter search and the FCBF algorithm, probably indicating that they provide redundant information. Taken together, our feature selection analysis support a model in which accessible chromatin and co-localization with the cohesin complex predominantly define TOP2B binding.

5   Conclusions and Future Works

In this work we have tackled the problem of associating TOP2B with several chromatin features from a supervised learning approach. For such purpose we have applied the NB and SVM algorithms.

Results presented in this work are promising since in some data types the predictive power is high and the classifierapplied are simple. NB assumes that the predictor variables are conditionally independent and SVM uses a linear kernel. Therefore more complex classification algorithms may yield better performance.

We have also applied feature selection techniques to analyze the relevance of the different features collected and remove redundance. In this case we have applied the heuristic FCBF and the evolutionary techniques SS and GA. Feature selection had very little effect on the predictive performance of SVM, whilst Naïve Bayes's predictive performance was in general substantially improved by the use of feature selection. This was probably caused by the removal of redundant features, which is know to have a negative effect on Naïve Bayes. However a further study on redundancy is needed in order to confirm this.

Although evolutionary algorithms are slower than heuristics, they may find smaller subsets of features with high discriminative power. As a future development, in order to speed up the search, we can perform a two step feature selection approach so that we can filter feature by using FCBF and then, apply the evolutionary strategy.

From a biological perspective, our study helped us to identify a core set of chromatin features that define TOP2B binding. Of course, the use of more complex algorithms and their application to a whole set of TOP2B binding sites of several cell lines will be needed in order to validate and strengthen our results.

Acknowledgements. This research was partly funded by the Ministry of Economy and the European Regional Development Fund under grant TIN2015-64776-C3-2-R (MINECO/FEDER).

References

1. Pommier, Y., Sun, Y., Shar-yin, N.H., Nitiss, J.L.: Roles of eukaryotic topoi-somerases in transcription, replication and genomic stability. Nature Rev. Mol. Cell Biol. **17**(11), 703–721 (2016). http://www.nature.com/doifinder/10.1038/nrm.2016.111
2. Deweese, J.E., Osheroff, N.: The DNA cleavage reaction of topoisomerase II: wolf in sheep's clothing. Nucleic Acids Res. **37**(3), 738–748 (2009)
3. Jackson, S.P., Bartek, J.: The DNA-damage response in human biology and disease. Nature **461**(7267), 1071–1078 (2010)
4. Sng, J.H., Heaton, V.J., Bell, M., Maini, P., Austin, C.A., Fisher, L.: Molecular cloning and characterization of the human topoisomerase IIα and IIβ genes: evidence for isoform evolution through gene duplication. Biochimica et Biophysica Acta (BBA) - Gene Struct. Expr. **144**(3), 395–406 (1999)
5. Uusküla-Reimand, L., Hou, H., Samavarchi-Tehrani, P., Rudan, M.V., Liang, M., Medina-Rivera, A., Mohammed, H., Schmidt, D., Schwalie, P., Young, E.J., Reimand, J., Hadjur, S., Gingras, A.C., Wilson, M.D.: Topoisomerase II beta inter-acts with cohesin and CTCF at topological domain borders. Genome Biol. **17**(1), 1–22 (2016). https://doi.org/10.1186/s13059-016-1043-8
6. Canela, A., Maman, Y., Jung, S., Wong, N., Callen, E., Day, A., Kieffer-Kwon, K.R., Pekowska, A., Zhang, H., Rao, S.S., Huang, S.C., Mckinnon, P.J., Aplan, P.D., Pommier, Y., Aiden, E.L., Casellas, R., Nussenzweig, A.: Genome organiza-tion drives chromosome fragility. Cell **170**(3), 507–521 (2017)
7. Guyon, I., Elisseeff, A.: An introduction to variable and feature selection. J. Mach. Learn. Res. **3**, 1157–1182 (2003)
8. Arvey, A., Agius, P., Noble, W.S., Leslie, C.: Sequence and chromatin determinants of cell-type-specific transcription factor binding. Genome Res. **22**(9), 1723–1734 (2012)
9. Liu, L., Jin, G., Zhou, X.: Modeling the relationship of epigenetic modifications to transcription factor binding. Nucleic Acids Res. **43**(8), 3873–3885 (2015)
10. Comoglio, F., Schlumpf, T., Schmid, V., Rohs, R., Beisel, C., Paro, R.: High-resolution profiling of drosophila replication start sites reveals a DNA shape and chromatin signature of metazoan origins. Cell Reports **11**(5), 821–834 (2015)
11. Vapnik, V.: Statistical Learning Theory. John Wiley and Sons, New York (1998)
12. John, G.H., Langley, P.: Estimating continuous distributions in Bayesian classi-fiers. In: Eleventh Conference on Uncertainty in Artificial Intelligence, pp. 338–345. Morgan Kaufmann, San Mateo (1995)
13. Laguna, M., Martí, R.: Scatter Search: Methodology and Implementations in C. Kluwer Academic Press, Norwell (2003)
14. Holland, J.H.: Adaptation in Natural and Artificial Systems: An Introductory Analysis with Applications to Biology, Control and Artificial Intelligence. University of Michigan Press, Ann Arbo (1975)
15. Yu, L., Liu, H.: Efficient feature selection via analysis of relevance and redundancy. J. Mach. Learn. Res. **5**, 1205–1224 (2004)
16. Langmead, B., Trapnell, C., Pop, M., Salzberg, S.: Ultrafast and memory-efficient alignment of short DNA sequences to the human genome. Genome Biol. **10**(3), R25 (2009). https://genomebiology.biomedcentral.com/articles/10.1186/gb-2009-10-3-r25

17. Zhang, Y., Liu, T., Meyer, C.A., Eeckhoute, J., Johnson, D.S., Bernstein, B.E., Nussbaum, C., Myers, R.M., Brown, M., Li, W., Liu, X.S.: Model-based analysis of ChIP-Seq (MACS). Genome Biol. **9**(9), 137 (2008). http://genomebiology.biomedcentral.com/articles/10.1186/gb-2008-9-9-r137
18. Comoglio, F., Paro, R.: Combinatorial modeling of chromatin features quantitatively predicts DNA replication timing in Drosophila. PLoS Comput. Biol. **10**(1), e1003419 (2014)
19. Mathelier, A., Xin, B., Chiu, T.P., Yang, L., Rohs, R., Wasserman, W.W.: DNA shape features improve transcription factor binding site predictions in vivo. Cell Syst. **3**(3), 278–286 (2016)
20. Chiu, T.P., Comoglio, F., Zhou, T., Yang, L., Paro, R., Rohs, R.: Dnashaper: an r/bioconductor package for DNA shape prediction and feature encoding. Bioinformatics **32**(8), 1211–1213 (2016)
21. Hall, M.A.: Correlation-based Feature Subset Selection for Machine Learning. Ph.D. thesis, University of Waikato, Hamilton, New Zealand (1999)
22. Koller, D., Sahami, M.: Toward optimal feature selection. In: Proceedings of the Thirteenth International Conference on Machine Learning, pp. 284–292 (1996)
23. Glover, F.: Heuristics for integer programming using surrogate constraints. Decis. Sci. **8**, 156–166 (1977)
24. Goldberg, D.E.: Genetics Algorithms in Search, Optimization and Machine Learning. Addison Wesley, Reading (1989)
25. da Silva, C.G.: Time series forecasting with a non-linear model and the scatter search meta-heuristic. Inf. Sci. **178**(16), 3288–3299 (2008). Including Special Issue: Recent advances in granular computing, Fifth International Conference on Machine Learning and Cybernetics
26. García-López, F.C., García-Torres, M., Melián-Batista, B., Moreno-Pérez, J.A., Moreno-Vega, J.M.: Solving the feature selection problem by a parallel scatter search. Eur. J. Oper. Res. **169**(2), 477–489 (2006)
27. Kaya, I.: A genetic algorithm approach to determine the sample size for attribute control charts. Inf. Sci. **179**(10), 1552–1566 (2009). Including Special Issue on Artificial Imune Systems
28. Cheng, C.H., Chen, T.L., Wei, L.Y.: A hybrid model based on rough sets theory and genetic algorithms for stock price forecasting. Inf. Sci. **180**(9), 1610–1629 (2010)
29. Witten, I.H., Frank, E., Hall, M.A., Pal, C.: Data Mining: Practical Machine Learning Tools and Techniques, 4th edn. Morgan Kaufmann Publishers Inc., San Francisco (2017)
30. Kohavi, R.: A study of cross-validation and bootstrap for accuracy estimation and model selection. In: Proceedings of the 14th International Joint Conference on Artificial Intelligence - Vol. 2, IJCAI 1995 pp. 1137–1143. Morgan Kaufmann Publishers Inc., San Francisco (1995)
31. Jones, P.A.: Functions of DNA methylation: islands, start sites, gene bodies and beyond. Nature Rev. Genet. **13**(7), 484–492 (2012). http://www.nature.com/doifinder/10.1038/nrg3230
32. Vinson, C., Chatterjee, R.: CG methylation. Epigenomics **4**(6), 655–663 (2012). http://www.futuremedicine.com/doi/abs/10.2217/epi.12.55?url_ver=Z39.88-2003 &rfr_id=ori:rid:crossref.org&rfr_dat=cr_pub=pubmed&
33. Ong, C.T., Corces, V.G.: CTCF: an architectural protein bridging genome topology and function. Nature Rev. Genet. **15**(4), 234–246 (2014)
34. Ghirlando, R., Felsenfeld, G.: CTCF: making the right connections. Genes Dev. **30**(8), 881–891 (2016)

EvoCOMNET

Multimodal Transportation Network Design Using Physarum Polycephalum-Inspired Multi-agent Computation Methods

Rishi Vanukuru[✉] and Nagendra R. Velaga

Transportation Systems Engineering, Department of Civil Engineering,
Indian Institute of Technology (IIT) Bombay, Mumbai 400076, India
rishi.vanukuru@gmail.com

Abstract. In this paper, a new approach towards P. Polycephalum inspired computational efforts is proposed, with specific application to the problem of Multimodal transportation network design for planned cities of the future. Working with a multi-agent model of the Physarum Polycephalum, parallels are drawn between agent properties and mode characteristics, and agents are allowed to dynamically change from one mode to another. A mechanism to compare the performance of resultant multimodal networks against single mode networks involving the same component modes is demonstrated. The observations point to the potential applicability of the new approach in city planning and design.

Keywords: Physarum Polycephalum · Multimodal transportation
Network design · City planning

1 Introduction

The need to design efficient and resilient transportation networks has over the years led to the development of a large number of novel possibilities with regards to solutions that create near-optimal networks. To that end a variety of natural phenomena, such as ant colony behaviour [1,2] and human blood flow patterns [3] have been studied to see if insights can be gained from the way networks are created, sustained, and reorganised in these natural systems. More recently, the True Slime Mould, Physarum Polycephalum, has been at the centre of multidisciplinary scientific research that seeks to move towards more unconventional forms of computing that hope to utilise the simplicity of natural frameworks to model emergent systems in a better way, and achieve more efficient computation on the whole. The behaviour of P. Polycephalum is of special interest to the field of Transportation Network planning, as the foraging behaviour it displays during and after its growth phase results in the formation of routes and networks that satisfy both the aims of efficiency and resilience. This behaviour has inspired research into creating computational models based on P. Polycephalum, using

© Springer International Publishing AG, part of Springer Nature 2018
K. Sim and P. Kaufmann (Eds.): EvoApplications 2018, LNCS 10784, pp. 105–116, 2018.
https://doi.org/10.1007/978-3-319-77538-8_8

a number of approaches, some of which are Cellular Automata-based modelling and Multi-agent Modelling.

The main thrust of this paper involves the application of one of these approaches - Multi-agent Physarum modelling - to solve the problem of multimodal networks. This is inspired by two main causes for concern with respect to transportation network design -

1. The nature of most big cities in today's world is a consequence of their urbanisation taking place in multiple well-defined stages. This has led to the creation of extremely heterogeneous transportation systems. Coupled with the increasing population and number of vehicles across the globe, we are currently in a position where a large majority of people are forced to utilise multiple modes of transport to commute on a daily basis, and where these multimodal networks are plagued by a variety of problems ranging from poor quality and overcrowding to excessively large transfer times between nodes.
2. Looking to the future while keeping current trajectories of population growth in mind, finding solutions to these problems of multimodal transport is of crucial importance. Such a network would influence the creation of the city as a whole, and once implemented, allow for a sustainable transportation system that would increase the welfare of the masses living in the city. The idea of creating Planned Cities has been in existence since the late 19th century, and has had mixed results in terms of success and impact thus far. However, with space becoming more and more valuable, and with the ever-increasing pressure that a growing population places on each square kilometer of land, the need for planning cities well into the future cannot be understated.

This is especially relevant when applied to countries developing at a rapid pace, like India [4,5]. As a country it has seen a great number of such planned cities flourish over the last few decades, the prime example of which is the city of Navi Mumbai, known today to be one of the largest planned cities in India and the world. Many plans to build cities are currently underway, in order to cater to the country's growing population as well as a significant portion of the current rural population that is making a shift towards cities in search for modern amenities. Perhaps the biggest and most recent of such endeavours is the creation of the city of Amaravati, the proposed capital of the Indian state of Andhra Pradesh.

As we build cities for the future and rework the cities of today to make them better places to live in, ensuring that the transportation network is efficient and robust is of paramount importance. Through this paper, the authors propose a new approach to solving such network problems using Physarum based multi-agent modelling, demonstrate possible ways by which the solutions obtained could be evaluated, and discuss the potential for further research and refinement of the model moving forward. The rest of the paper is divided as follows. Section 2 provides a brief review of literature and research work related to Physarum computing and modelling. The formulation of the proposed extension to the model, its results, and potential mechanisms for validation are detailed in

Sects. 3 and 4. In conclusion, the shortcomings of this work are discussed, along with future research directions in the area of computational network design.

2 Previous Work

As a natural system, the Physarum Polycephalum has demonstrated a remarkable ability to perform computational feats. This is especially significant given the mould's lack of a nervous system, or any overarching complex structure. Over the last few years, significant research efforts have been directed towards the applications of Physarum based computing [6–9] - its formulation [10,11], demonstrations of its ability to solve complex mathematical problems [12] and studies on its evolution and emergent behaviour [13,14]. Applications to areas such as the Traffic Network Equilibrium Assignment Problem [15], approximating real-world road networks and recolonisation problems [16,17], and Shape Representation in response to environmental stimuli [18] have been explored to a large extent. A multi-agent model of the Physarum Polycephalum is presented in [19]. The multimodal transportation problem is one that has been discussed a great deal over the years, and some research efforts regarding the same include [20–22].

One aspect that does not seem to have been touched upon in the Physarum based research reviewed for the purpose of this paper, however, is the nature of the agents in the model, and the possibilities afforded by allowing these agents to change dynamically in response to certain cues, either geometric or environmental. This is the primary direction that we go on to look into in the sections that follow.

3 Research Methodology

3.1 Model Background

The Physarum model implemented in this paper is based on the multi-agent simulation approach in [19]. Here, a number of simple agents follow a set of rules that outline motive, growth, and movement on a representation of a real substrate that is modelled using a diffusion-based matrix. Each agent has a limited ability to sense its environment (by means of the sensors FL, F, and FR), and interacts with surrounding agents by means of depositing quantities of chemoattractant that diffuse over the substrate. For the model used, the parameters that define the agent's field of perception are the Sensor Angle and Sensor Offset, while those that characterise its physical response to stimuli are its Speed and Rotation Angle. Figure 1 presents a simplistic version of such an agent, indicating the relative positioning of the sensors with respect to the agent center.

Once initialized at random locations within a given geometry and with random values for initial parameters, these agents begin their operations, eventually leading to complex forms of emergent behaviour. At every iteration, the agents

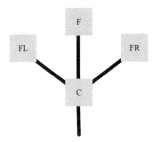

Fig. 1. Simple agent schematic (based on [19])

sense their surroundings, turn by an amount defined by the characteristic rotation angle towards the direction with the strongest chemical trail concentration, and attempt to move in said direction. The success or failure of this attempt is what determines the amount of chemoattractant deposited in turn by the agents themselves. Further, the substrate itself diffuses the trail values that it contains, hence imparting temporal variability independent of the motion of the agents, much like the manner observed during similar real-world experiments. Over multiple iterations on a given geometry with specific locations of nodes that constantly deposit the chemoattractant, distinct paths are developed that resemble those obtained through established mathematical network design and assignment solutions.

The parameters mentioned earlier, namely sensor angle, sensor offset, rotation angle and agent speed, can vary between certain limits to ensure that the desired emergent behaviour is produced by the simulation. These Physarum based models have been used to create efficient and resilient transportation network designs in the past.

Fig. 2 presents the progression of a simulation at specified cycle times for a nodal network based on the train stations in the city of Tokyo. Below these snapshots are illustrations of the actual train network, the Minimum Spanning Tree based on the network nodes, and a sample modified minimum spanning tree network with more links to improve resilience [15]. As can be seen, the Physarum network at various points shows characteristics and links that are quite similar to the established networks, an indication of how as a framework, the model seems to be sound.

3.2   The Multimodal Physarum Model

The Authors propose an alternative approach to the use of such models (as in [19]) when applied to problems in Transportation Network Design, and more specifically, to the Multi-Modal Network design problem. Each agent within the model has a common set of characteristics, and communicates with agents via chemical trails, eventually finding routes that can be used as solutions to problems on network design. Building upon this, parallels are drawn between the four parameters stated above - Sensor Angle, Sensor Offset, Rotation Angle,

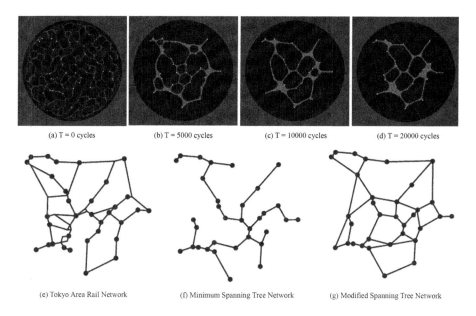

(a) T = 0 cycles   (b) T = 5000 cycles   (c) T = 10000 cycles   (d) T = 20000 cycles

(e) Tokyo Area Rail Network   (f) Minimum Spanning Tree Network   (g) Modified Spanning Tree Network

Fig. 2. Processing model comparison (from [15])

and Speed - and the real world characteristics of various modes of transport. For a given mode, a certain set of parameters would define its properties to the best extent, and by allowing an agent to morph between one mode type to another within a given topography, a continuous, multi-modal network can be obtained.

In this paper, the authors have chosen to focus on two modes of public transportation - Bus Rapid Transit Systems (BRTS) and Monorail networks. Assigning a standard set of values for the four agent parameters to the BRTS mode, hypothetical values for the same parameters are then associated with Monorail mode. This association is informed by the physical relationships between vehicle and agent as mentioned earlier. Here, the authors draw parallels between the speed of the agent and the speed of the mode, the sensor offset of the agent and the awareness along path of the mode, sensor angle and the angular window of focus, and between the rotation angle of the agent and how constrained a vehicle would be to the path of that mode. Comparing the two modes qualitatively, it can be seen that Monorail systems have higher average vehicular speeds than buses, are usually more constrained to their path over a longer distance, and have lower maneuverability. As opposed to buses, Monorail systems need to be aware of objects farther away along their current trajectory due to an increased stopping time, and usually do not need to factor in stimuli that are much outside a small angular window centred around their tracks. The parameters assigned to the BRTS mode are scaled in accordance with these guiding principles to determine and generate a sample set of Monorail agent parameters.

Further, a predefined nodal arrangement was used as an environment to test the two agent types and their mutual interactions. This arrangement consists of six sources, two intermediate stations, and four destinations. The models were made to run within the environment, and three main test cases were observed based on the nature of the network population - Only BRTS agents throughout, only Monorail agents throughout, and BRTS agents till the intermediate stations with Monorail agents for the remaining route area till the destination. The simulations were halted when a steady state network pattern had been formed by the agents in all three cases. The test geometry and resultant networks after simulation are presented in Fig. 3. A clear variation in the networks formed in the three cases can be seen, indicating that agent characteristics play an important role in determining the nature of the route mapped out by the simulation. Further, these networks are non-trivial ones, in the sense that on repeated trials using the same initial conditions, the steady state pattern remains the same for each case. A thorough study on the relationship between the agent parameters and real transport mode behaviour would be needed before commenting on how close these networks approximate their real-world counterparts. However, for the purposes of this paper, the three model geometries obtained were considered and further studied.

4   Model Evaluation

The network diagrams obtained for the three cases are implemented and analysed using Anylogic agent based simulation software. The model is created in Anylogic 8.1.0, with [23] being an example of its use in transportation-based research. A simple demonstration of the logic used to generate idealistic traffic flows for the BRTS network is presented in Fig. 4. Two main test scenarios are considered. In both cases the networks obtained from the previous model are used to create further simulations in a road network setting. First, the average travel time for vehicles and the network performance at nodes is qualitatively analysed, after which the network is placed in a real world context and its behaviour is gauged using certain ideal conditions of flow. These approaches are intended as indications towards possible future research into the analysis of similarly obtained networks.

4.1   Basic Network Performance Analysis

In this step, all three networks were recreated within Anylogic, and agents native to the software were modified to represent BRTS and Monorail agents. These agents were then deployed in the network and studied, by creating intersection speed/density maps and recording the times spent by the vehicles within the network. Samples of the resultant data representations obtained are shown in Figs. 5 and 6. The nodal analysis (Fig. 5) depicted is for all three scenarios; however, the plot of Transit Time in network versus Cycle time is for the specific case of the BRTS agent network (Fig. 6).

For the nodal analysis (Fig. 5), the colours of red and green are assigned to specific values of low and high speeds respectively, and intermediate speeds are

(a) BRTS Agents - Steady State Network

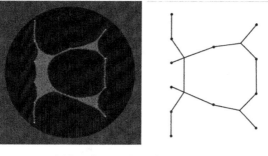

(b) Monorail Agents - Steady State Network

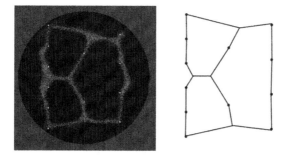

(c) Mixed Agents - Steady State Network

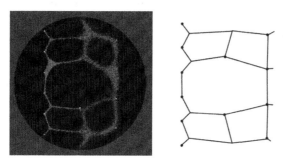

Fig. 3. Model results

represented by shades between the colours. From this initial level analysis of the results obtained, it was observed that the mixed network allowed the junctions to function with more ease in terms of traffic density at the node, and that jam conditions were more prominently seen in the single-mode networks. The vehicular input volumes were generated by idealised sources with a constant rate of arrival.

In the Transit time graph for the BRTS network (Fig. 6), the horizontal axis represents time in model time units, and the vertical axis represents the Transit Time per agent as a fraction of the model time. The discretization of

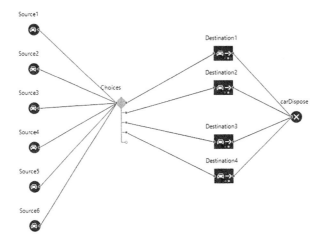

Fig. 4. BRTS model flow diagram

the Transit Time graph is a consequence of the ideal nature of the vehicular volumes generated - there are only a finite number of possibilities as no element of randomness or continuity has been introduced to a significant effect. This points towards further work involving the refinement of these test cases and deployment in more realistic scenarios. However, on comparing the values of BRTS Transit Time with those obtained in the remaining two cases of Monorail and Mixed BRTS with Monorail, it was seen that the performance of the Mixed network was in fact better than the initial single-mode networks. While further work would involve going about these forms of analysis with more mathematical rigour and in a variety of contexts, these preliminary indications serve to highlight the applicability of the Physarum multi-agent model to transportation problems, with specific emphasis on the improvements obtained upon the introduction of agents that are allowed to change their characteristics in response to geometric and geographic cues.

4.2   Implementation in Real-World Context

To demonstrate a possible application of the networks generated via the Physarum Model, the characteristic network for the combined BRTS and Monorail case was considered and the routes were marked via a GIS interface onto the map of the proposed planned city of Amaravati in Andhra Pradesh, India. Given how the city is yet to be built in entirety, the transportation networks have a large degree of flexibility without pre-existing barriers to paths, and hence this provides a good basis to test new networks like the ones obtained from the Physarum models earlier. Fully developed versions of these models could even be used as design tools for Policy makers as they go about the planning and construction of cities.

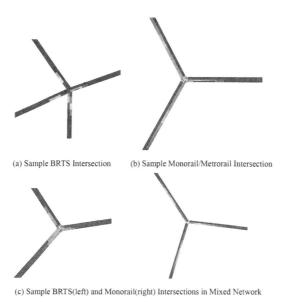

(a) Sample BRTS Intersection   (b) Sample Monorail/Metrorail Intersection

(c) Sample BRTS(left) and Monorail(right) Intersections in Mixed Network

Fig. 5. Intersection speed maps (Color figure online)

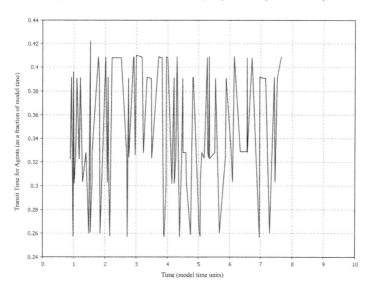

Fig. 6. Transit time graph for BRTS Network

The same nodal configuration as the previous examples of the BRTS and Monorail networks have been used. The network was defined using native tools that allowed the routes obtained via the Processing model to be replicated as roads within the simulation software. The roads were then assigned a certain

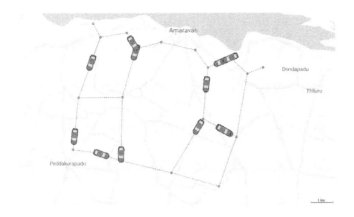

Fig. 7. Real-world network visualisation

sense of direction, and the number of lanes on which vehicles are allowed to travel was specified. The route choice logic was defined as a simple probabilistic model wherein at each junction the vehicle is equally likely to move along the possible paths that would take it towards the destination. These relatively ideal test conditions were established, and the simulation was allowed to run. Figure 7 presents the simulation at a certain instant of time. Here the vehicle modes are represented by generic car icons.

Such an analysis allows us to visualise the impact of these proposed networks in a more tangible manner, and also allows to take insights from the actual geography of the proposed area of implementation and factor those into the Physarum model. An example of this could be to use illumination parameters (a deterrent to the Physarum agents) to indicate water bodies, valleys and the like as demonstrated in [10,11,16]. Such simulation packages offer robust testing frameworks for the networks obtained through the Physarum model, with emphasis on the system's functioning amidst a number of constraints modelled on real life. At this stage, given the nature of the networks used and the work yet to be done with regards to the calibration of the agent characteristics with real-world transport mode behaviours, as well as the development of more rigorous testing and validation mechanisms, the immediate results obtained from these simulations serve more as an indication of the potential use of these networks, and demonstrate how a Multimodal Physarum model is different from its single mode counterparts.

5   Conclusions and Future Research

In this paper, an extension to existing Physarum based computational models was proposed, and implemented within the Processing Framework. Test cases for two different public transport modes were formulated, and networks relating to their individual and combined behaviours were generated via this Physarum model. Finally, the resultant network routes were visualised using the Anylogic software package, both in an ideal network context as well as a demonstration of one network placed in a real geographical region. From all of this, indicators of the potential validity and applicability of the proposed model were obtained, as well as directions for further research and the issues that will have to be addressed through the same. Firstly, the relationship between agent parameters in the model and real-world transport mode behaviour would need to be rigorously analysed for multiple test cases and networks to prove that a true correlation exists between the mode and the agent. Once these links are established, the agents would have to be deployed on a number of synthetic networks and the performance of the multimodal network will need to be gauged against those with a single mode of transport. After this step, the multimodal networks will have to be tested against networks obtained through other bio-inspired algorithms, conventional route assignment techniques, as well as real-world situations to finally understand the validity and usefulness of the approach as a potential design tool for planning transportation networks for cities of the future. Further research will be directed with significant focus on two major aspects -

1. Working to establish a defined link between agent parameters within the model and the real-world behaviour of the various transportation modes
2. Creating an interface to allow for the Processing model to be used as a tool for network design.

References

1. Adamatzky, A., Holland, O.: Reaction-diffusion and ant-based load balancing of communication networks. Kybernetes **31**(5), 667–681 (2002)
2. Luyet, L., Varone, S., Zufferey, N.: An ant algorithm for the steiner tree problem in graphs. In: Giacobini, M. (ed.) EvoWorkshops 2007. LNCS, vol. 4448, pp. 42–51. Springer, Heidelberg (2007). https://doi.org/10.1007/978-3-540-71805-5_5
3. Ambrosi, D., Bussolino, F., Preziosi, L.: A review of vasculogenesis models. Comput. Math. Meth. Med. **6**(1), 1–19 (2005)
4. Registrar. General and Census Commissioner, India: Census of India 2001 (2001)
5. Gill, K.K.: Population Growth Family Size and Economic Development. Deep & Deep Publications, New Delhi (1995)
6. Tero, A., Yumiki, K., Kobayashi, R., Saigusa, T., Nakagaki, T.: Flow-network adaptation in physarum amoebae. Theory Biosci. **127**(2), 89–94 (2008)
7. Nakagaki, T., Kobayashi, R., Nishiura, Y., Ueda, T.: Obtaining multiple separate food sources: behavioural intelligence in the physarum plasmodium. Proc. Roy. Soc. Lond. B: Biol. Sci. **271**(1554), 2305–2310 (2004)
8. Tero, A., Kobayashi, R., Nakagaki, T.: A mathematical model for adaptive transport network in path finding by true slime mold. J. Theor. Biol. **244**(4), 553–564 (2007)
9. De Lacy Costello, B., Adamatzky, A.: Routing physarum "Signals" with Chemicals. In: Adamatzky, A. (ed.) Advances in Physarum Machines. ECC, vol. 21, pp. 165–193. Springer, Cham (2016). https://doi.org/10.1007/978-3-319-26662-6_9
10. Jones, J.: Influences on the formation and evolution of physarum polycephalum inspired emergent transport networks. Nat. Comput. **10**(4), 1345–1369 (2011)

11. Tero, A., Takagi, S., Saigusa, T., Ito, K., Bebber, D.P., Fricker, M.D., Yumiki, K., Kobayashi, R., Nakagaki, T.: Rules for biologically inspired adaptive network design. Science **327**(5964), 439–442 (2010)
12. Caleffi, M., Akyildiz, I.F., Paura, L.: On the solution of the steiner tree np-hard problem via physarum bionetwork. IEEE/ACM Trans. Netw. **23**(4), 1092–1106 (2015)
13. Tsompanas, M.A.I., Sirakoulis, G.C., Adamatzky, A.I.: Evolving transport networks with cellular automata models inspired by slime mould. IEEE Trans. Cybern. **45**(9), 1887–1899 (2015)
14. Jones, J.: The emergence and dynamical evolution of complex transport networks from simple low-level behaviours. arXiv preprint arXiv:1503.06579 (2015)
15. Zhang, X., Mahadevan, S.: A bio-inspired approach to traffic network equilibrium assignment problem. IEEE Trans. Cybern. **PP**(99), 1–12 (2017)
16. Adamatzky, A.I.: Route 20, autobahn 7, and slime mold: approximating the longest roads in USA and germany with slime mold on 3-D terrains. IEEE Trans. Cybern. **44**(1), 126–136 (2014)
17. Adamatzky, A., Martinez, G.J.: Recolonisation of USA: slime mould on 3D terrains. In: Adamatzky, A. (ed.) Advances in Physarum Machines. ECC, vol. 21, pp. 337–348. Springer, Cham (2016). https://doi.org/10.1007/978-3-319-26662-6_17
18. Jones, J., Mayne, R., Adamatzky, A.: Representation of shape mediated by environmental stimuli in physarum polycephalum and a multi-agent model. Int. J. Parallel Emerg. Distrib. Syst. **32**(2), 166–184 (2017)
19. Jones, J.: From Pattern Formation to Material Computation. ECC, vol. 15. Springer, Cham (2015). https://doi.org/10.1007/978-3-319-16823-4
20. Fojtík, D., Ivan, I., Horák, J.: Database of public transport connections its creation and use. In: 2011 12th International Carpathian Control Conference (ICCC), pp. 115–119. IEEE (2011)
21. Zhao, Y., Lu, J., Qiu, H.: Applicability of multi-modal public transport system based on accessibility analysis. Int. J. Comput. Commun. Eng. **4**(3), 211 (2015)
22. Krygsman, S., Dijst, M., Arentze, T.: Multimodal public transport: an analysis of travel time elements and the interconnectivity ratio. Transp. Policy **11**(3), 265–275 (2004)
23. Merkuryeva, G., Bolshakovs, V.: Vehicle schedule simulation with anylogic. In: 2010 12th International Conference on Computer Modelling and Simulation (UKSim), pp. 169–174. IEEE (2010)

Improving Multi-objective Evolutionary Influence Maximization in Social Networks

Doina Bucur[1], Giovanni Iacca[2], Andrea Marcelli[3], Giovanni Squillero[3], and Alberto Tonda[4(✉)]

[1] EEMCS, University of Twente, Zilverling, 2027, 7500 AE Enschede,
The Netherlands
doina.bucur@gmail.com
[2] Integrated Signal Processing Systems, RWTH Aachen University,
52056 Aachen, Germany
giovanni.iacca@gmail.com
[3] DAUIN, Politecnico di Torino, Corso Duca degli Abruzzi 24, 10129 Torino, Italy
{andrea.marcelli,giovanni.squillero}@polito.it
[4] INRA, UMR 782 GMPA,
Avenue Lucien Brétignières, 78850 Thiverval-Grignon, France
alberto.tonda@inra.fr

Abstract. In the context of social networks, maximizing influence means contacting the largest possible number of nodes starting from a set of seed nodes, and assuming a model for influence propagation. The real-world applications of influence maximization are of uttermost importance, and range from social studies to marketing campaigns. Building on a previous work on multi-objective evolutionary influence maximization, we propose improvements that not only speed up the optimization process considerably, but also deliver higher-quality results. State-of-the-art heuristics are run for different sizes of the seed sets, and the results are then used to initialize the population of a multi-objective evolutionary algorithm. The proposed approach is tested on three publicly available real-world networks, where we show that the evolutionary algorithm is able to improve upon the solutions found by the heuristics, while also converging faster than an evolutionary algorithm started from scratch.

Keywords: Influence maximization · Social network
Multi-objective evolutionary algorithms · Seeding

1 Introduction

Social networks (SNs) are graphs that model a generic society and the internal flows of ideas. Nodes represent the actors, usually individuals, and edges their capability to transmit information. While the high-level structure is quite simple, a sharp definition of the rules that control the passage of information, together

K. Sim and P. Kaufmann (Eds.): EvoApplications 2018, LNCS 10784, pp. 117–124, 2018.
https://doi.org/10.1007/978-3-319-77538-8_9

with the amount of data willfully provided by users, enable the creation of very precise models. The situation has been plainly acknowledged by scholars for years, and recently reached popular recognition [1–3].

In the simplest SN model, a directed edge $a \rightarrow b$ denotes that b is exposed to a and may be influenced by it. The rule used for determining whether the information is actually transmitted is called the *propagation model*. Scholars of social sciences studied a number of *probabilistic propagation models*: the edge $a \rightarrow b$ signifies that there is a given probability p for node a to influence node b. Common models include using fixed probabilities, probabilities inversely proportional to the number of edges directed to b, or other topological features [4].

Given the set of *seeds* nodes, that is, network nodes who broadcast a specific information, and a propagation model, the eventual set of influenced nodes $\mathcal{I}$ may be computed. Indeed, one of the most studied problem in SNs is "influence maximization" and consists in determining the optimal set of seed nodes for maximizing the final influence. Such a problem was initially formulated in [5], and it was later proven NP-hard for most propagation models [4].

As with many other NP-hard problem, evolutionary algorithms (EAs) where used to explore the vast search space of all possible subsets of nodes [6]. More recently, a multi-objective EA (MOEA), was used to maximize the influence $\mathcal{I}$ while concurrently minimizing the size of the seed set [7], providing users the necessary data to trade off between *budget* (the number of nodes that need to be influenced) and *effect* (the final influence over the whole network). This paper progresses on the same research line, showing how significant improvements can be attained by carefully initializing the initial population. The results obtained on three different social network graphs are compared against five state-of-the-art heuristics, and clearly demonstrate the efficacy of the proposed methodology.

The rest of the paper is organized as follows: Sect. 2 introduce the background and survey the related works; Sect. 3 details the proposed approach, while Sect. 4 reports an extensive experimental evaluation; finally, Sect. 5 concludes the paper.

2   Background and Related Work

In this section we first describe the models available in the literature for simulating the influence propagation, and the general formulation of the influence maximization problem; then, we briefly survey the existing methods for solving this problem, based on either ad hoc heuristics or computational intelligence algorithms.

2.1   Models for Influence Propagation and Problem Formulation

As most influence propagation models are stochastic, an approximate estimation of the global influence can be obtained empirically, by simulating the propagation process a given number of times: this approach, however, can be computationally expensive, especially when included in an optimization framework.

Furthermore, as the propagation of a message from a node to another may be modeled as a discrete event, propagation models are also time-discrete.

As the receptiveness of users to incoming messages from the network differs, several models have been proposed: the most popular belong to the "Cascade" family [4], which views influence as being transmitted through the network in a tree-like fashion, where the seed nodes are the roots. In this work, we will use in particular the Independent Cascade (IC) model, whose pseudocode is given in Algorithm 1. IC was first studied in the marketing domain, modeling the effects that word-of-mouth communication has upon macro-level marketing [8]. Each newly "activated" node n will succeed in activating each inactive neighbor m with a fixed probability p, which is a global property of the system, equal for all edges $n \rightarrow m$ in G.

Algorithm 1. The **Cascade** family of propagation models. G is the network graph, S the set of "seed" nodes, and $p(n \rightarrow m)$ the probability that information will reach across a graph edge $n \rightarrow m$.

```
 1: procedure CASCADE(G, S, p)
 2:     A ← S                    ▷ A: the set of active nodes after the propagation ended
 3:     B ← S                    ▷ B: the set of nodes activated in the last time slot
 4:     while B not empty do
 5:         C ← ∅
 6:         for each n ∈ B do
 7:             for each direct neighbor m of n, where m ∉ A, do
 8:                 with probability p(n → m), add m to C
 9:             end for
10:         end for
11:         B ← C
12:         A ← A ∪ B
13:     end while
14:     return the size of A
15: end procedure
```

In the classical problem of influence maximization, the goal is to optimize the seed set S given a budget $k = |S|$ so that its eventual influence over the whole network is maximal. The influence of a seed set **I** is measured as the size of the set $\mathcal{I}$ of active nodes, obtained by the propagation model. Independently from the influence propagation model used, the problem has been proven to be NP-hard [4], and approximating the optimal solution by a factor better than $1 - \frac{1}{e}$ (roughly 63% approximation) is also NP-hard [4].

2.2   Existing Solutions for Influence Maximization

Several heuristics have been presented to find good solutions to the influence maximization problem. *High degree* (HIGHDEG) is a greedy heuristic that simply adds nodes n to A in order of decreasing out-degree [4]. *Single discount* (SDISC) is a refinement of HIGHDEG proposed by Chen et al. [9], using the idea that if a node n is already active and also there exists an edge $m \rightarrow n$, then, when considering whether to add node m to A, this edge should not be counted towards the out-degree of m. Other popular techniques include DISTANCE, that greedily adds to the set S nodes in order to increase average distance to other nodes in the network, following the intuition that being able to reach other nodes quickly translates into higher influence; *Generalized degree discount* (GDD) [10], a refinement of SDISC, which considers not only the direct neighbours of a node candidate to being a seed, but also nodes one level deeper in the graph; and *Cost-Effective Lazy Forward selection* (CELF), a greedy hill-climbing algorithm [11]. Several metaheuristics and optimization algorithms have also been applied to the problem, ranging from simulated annealing [12] to genetic algorithms [6]. In [7], a Multi-Objective Evolutionary Algorithm (MOEA) [13] was proposed for influence maximization, where the two considered objectives were (i) maximizing the influence of a seed set and (ii) minimizing the number of nodes in the seed set. Intuitively, this produced a Pareto front of candidate solutions, each one a different compromise. While the proposed methodology was shown to outperform both HIGHDEG and SDISC for all values of the budget k (number of seed nodes) on the considered case studies, the main drawback was the computational time required to reach satisfying solutions: millions of individual evaluations were necessary, each one consisting of multiple runs of an influence spread model. This observation provided the motivation for the present work, where we try to reduce the time consumption needed for the MOEA to converge in order to make the method applicable also in contexts with limited computing resources.

3   Proposed Approach

To improve upon the work presented in [7] and overcome the aforementioned limitations due to the method time consumption, we introduce here a seeding mechanism. In particular, we show that by seeding the initial population of the MOEA with the results of computationally cheap heuristics, the number of individual evaluations required to reach satisfying solutions drops dramatically.

Another important difference with respect to the MOEA used in [7] concerns the algorithmic implementation: while that work was based on a C++ open source customizable evolutionary tool [14], here we use *inspyred*[1], a Python open source framework for creating biologically-inspired computational intelligence algorithms, including evolutionary computation, swarm intelligence, and immunocomputing. *inspyred* provides easy-to-modify canonical versions of several bio-inspired algorithms, among which the MOEA NSGA-II [15], that we use in the experiments presented in this paper.

Individual representation and evolutionary operators were custom-designed for this specific application: for the problem at hand, a candidate solution is a set of nodes of variable size, consisting of a subset of the set of nodes in the

---

[1] http://pythonhosted.org/inspyred/.

original network. Individuals are thus unordered sequences of unique integer node identifiers, representing the seeds of influence in the network.

As for the evolutionary operators, we used three problem-specific mutations (add, remove or replace one node in a set), and one crossover operator with a check that removes inconsistencies from the resulting individuals, ensuring that a specific node appears only once in each individual. The operators are always applied with uniform probability, while the parent individuals are selected through a tournament selection of size 2.

Finally, the fitness value of a candidate solution is a probabilistic metric of the number of nodes that are likely to be reached, starting from a given set of seeds of influence—according to the IC model of influence propagation (described in Sect. 2). Given the stochastic nature of both propagation models, the fitness estimation is empirical, and itself a stochastic process: repeated simulations of the network propagation model yield an extent to which the network is reached, and the final fitness value is the average of these fitness samples.

4   Experimental Evaluation

4.1   Benchmarks

In order to assess the proposed improvements for influence maximization, we selected three case studies among social network graphs available in the Network Repository[2] and SNAP[3] databases. Two of the selected social networks, **ego-Facebook** and **ca-GrQc** were also considered in [7], while **soc-ePinions1** was not considered in the previous study. The selected benchmarks, with their respective features, are reported in Table 1.

Table 1. Main features of the case studies considered for the experimental evaluation of the proposed MOEA approach.

Name	ego-Facebook	ca-GrQc	soc-ePinions1
Nodes	4,039	5,242	75,879
Edges	88,234	14,496	508,837
Type of graph	Undirected	Undirected	Directed
Nodes in largest WCC	4,039	4,158	75,877
Nodes in largest SCC	4,039	4,158	32,223
Average clustering coefficient	0.6055	0.5296	0.1378
Diameter	8	17	14

---

[2] http://networkrepository.com/.
[3] https://snap.stanford.edu/index.html.

4.2   Experimental Results

In all the experiments, we consider the IC propagation model. The MOEA configuration used here is: $\mu = 2000$, $\lambda = 2000$, tournament selection of size $\tau = 2$, influence propagation model IC with $p = 0.05$, stop condition 500 generations.

Figures 1, 2 and 3 show the results for the social networks **ego-Facebook**, **ca-GrQc** and **soc-ePinions1**, respectively. Considering the first two networks, we observed that with respect to [7] the improved algorithm is able to find solutions that outperform the heuristic already during the first few generations, with less than 10,000 evaluations (compared to the almost 1,000,000 that were necessary to outperform both HIGHDEG and SDISC in the previous study). A similar trend was observed also on the third network, **soc-ePinions1**, for which we could not even run two of the heuristics, CELF and DISTANCE, due to their excessive time complexity (approximately one data point in ten hours).

In summary, while the seeding procedure requires running the heuristic once, the computational cost is roughly equivalent to just one generation of the MOEA.

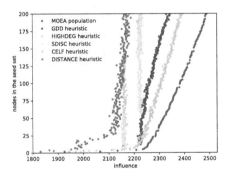

Fig. 1. Experimental results for the benchmark graph ego-Facebook. The MOEA in this experiment was seeded with the results of the GDD heuristic, and the evolution was able to outperform even the effective CELF.

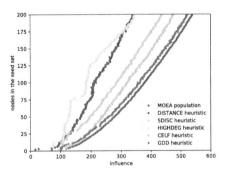

Fig. 2. Experimental results for the benchmark graph ca-GrQc. In this case, GDD was already the most performing heuristic of the group, but the MOEA seeded with the initial results was able to eventually find improvements over the initial approximation.

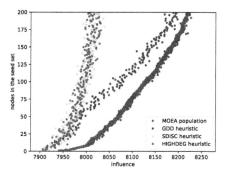

Fig. 3. Experimental results for the benchmark graph soc-ePinions1. The MOEA in this experiment was seeded with the results of the GDD heuristic. DISTANCE and CELF could not be run on this network due to their excessive time complexity.

Furthermore, the proposed methodology is able to outperform even more refined heuristics which were not considered in [7], such as CELF. Finally, the new configuration also solved previously experienced issues with populating the higher part of the Pareto front (see [7] for more details).

5 Conclusions

In this paper, we introduced an improvement over a previously proposed multi-objective evolutionary approach for influence maximization in social networks.

A MOEA is tasked with finding the set of k seed nodes that, given a model of influence propagation, maximize the nodes reached in the network. As minimizing the value of k is also given as an optimization objective, the MOEA is able to find a Pareto front of compromises between number of seed nodes in the set and global influence in the graph. While the main weak point of the previously proposed approach was the time required to reach good solutions, in this paper we show how initializing the first generation properly leads to faster convergence on better Pareto fronts. The approach has been tested on three real-world social networks, and proved to be able to overcome also the state-of-the-art heuristics.

In future works, we aim to progress on this research line by combining the seeding mechanism proposed here with a surrogate model approach, in order to speed up even further the computations and make the method applicable also on larger networks.

Acknowledgments. This article is based upon work from COST Action CA15140 'Improving Applicability of Nature-Inspired Optimisation by Joining Theory and Practice (ImAppNIO)' supported by the COST Agency.

References

1. Hersh, E.D.: Hacking the Electorate: How Campaigns Perceive Voters. Cambridge University Press, Cambridge (2015)
2. Kreiss, D.: Prototype Politics: Technology-intensive Campaigning and the Data of Democracy. Oxford University Press, Oxford (2016)
3. Grassegger, H., Krogerus, M.: The data that turned the world upside down. Luettu **28** (2017). Luettavissa: http://motherboard.vice.com/read/big-data-cambridge-analytica-brexit-trump
4. Kempe, D., Kleinberg, J., Tardos, É.: Maximizing the spread of influence through a social network. Theory Comput. **11**(4), 105–147 (2015)
5. Richardson, M., Agrawal, R., Domingos, P.: Trust management for the semantic web. In: Fensel, D., Sycara, K., Mylopoulos, J. (eds.) ISWC 2003. LNCS, vol. 2870, pp. 351–368. Springer, Heidelberg (2003). https://doi.org/10.1007/978-3-540-39718-2_23
6. Bucur, D., Iacca, G.: Influence maximization in social networks with genetic algorithms. In: Squillero, G., Burelli, P. (eds.) EvoApplications 2016. LNCS, vol. 9597, pp. 379–392. Springer, Cham (2016). https://doi.org/10.1007/978-3-319-31204-0_25
7. Bucur, D., Iacca, G., Marcelli, A., Squillero, G., Tonda, A.: Multi-objective evolutionary algorithms for influence maximization in social networks. In: Squillero, G., Sim, K. (eds.) EvoApplications 2017. LNCS, vol. 10199, pp. 221–233. Springer, Cham (2017). https://doi.org/10.1007/978-3-319-55849-3_15
8. Goldenberg, J., Libai, B., Muller, E.: Talk of the network: a complex systems look at the underlying process of word-of-mouth. Mark. Lett. **12**(3), 211–223 (2001)
9. Chen, W., Wang, Y., Yang, S.: Efficient influence maximization in social networks. In: Proceedings of the 15th ACM SIGKDD International Conference on Knowledge Discovery and Data Mining, KDD 2009, pp. 199–208. ACM, New York (2009)
10. Wang, X., Zhang, X., Zhao, C., Yi, D.: Maximizing the spread of influence via generalized degree discount. In: PloS one (2016)
11. Leskovec, J., Krause, A., Guestrin, C., Faloutsos, C., VanBriesen, J., Glance, N.: Cost-effective outbreak detection in networks. In: ACM SIGKDD International Conference on Knowledge Discovery and Data Mining (KDD), pp. 420–429, August 2007
12. Jiang, Q., Song, G., Cong, G., Wang, Y., Si, W., Xie, K.: Simulated annealing based influence maximization in social networks. In: Burgard, W., Roth, D. (eds.) AAAI. AAAI Press (2011)
13. Coello, C.A.C., Van Veldhuizen, D.A., Lamont, G.B.: Evolutionary Algorithms for Solving Multi-objective Problems, vol. 242. Springer, New York (2002). https://doi.org/10.1007/978-0-387-36797-2
14. Squillero, G.: MicroGP - an evolutionary assembly program generator. Genet. Program. Evolvable Mach. **6**(3), 247–263 (2005)
15. Deb, K., Pratap, A., Agarwal, S., Meyarivan, T.: A fast and elitist multiobjective genetic algorithm: NSGA-II. IEEE Trans. Evol. Comput. **6**(2), 182–197 (2002)

Social Relevance Index for Studying Communities in a Facebook Group of Patients

Laura Sani[1], Gianfranco Lombardo[1], Riccardo Pecori[1,2(✉)] [iD],
Paolo Fornacciari[1], Monica Mordonini[1], and Stefano Cagnoni[1]

[1] Dip. di Ingegneria e Architettura, Università di Parma, Parma, PR, Italy
riccardo.pecori@unipr.it
[2] SMARTEST Research Centre, Università eCAMPUS, Novedrate, CO, Italy

Abstract. Identifying Relevant Sets, i.e., variable subsets that exhibit a coordinated behavior, in complex systems is a very relevant research topic. Systems that exhibit complex dynamics are, for example, social networks, which are characterized by complex and dynamic relationships among users. A challenging topic within this context regards the identification of communities or subsets of users, both within the whole network and within specific groups. We applied the Relevance Index method, which has been shown to be effective in many situations, to the study of communities of users in the Facebook group of the Italian association of patients affected by Hidradenitis Suppurativa. Since the need for computing the Relevance Index for each possible variable subset of users makes the exhaustive computation unfeasible, we resorted to the help of an efficient niching evolutionary metaheuristic, hybridized with local searches. The communities detected through the aforementioned method have been studied to search similarities in terms of number of posts, sentiments, number of contacts, roles, behaviors, etc. The results demonstrate that it is possible to detect such subsets of users in the particular Facebook group we analyzed.

Keywords: Complex systems · Relevant sets · Social network
Community detection · Evolutionary metaheuristic

1 Introduction

The analysis of complex systems is related to the study of collective behaviors and emerging properties of systems whose components are usually known well. Measuring the complexity of a composite system is a challenging task: dozens of measures of complexity have been proposed, several of which are based on information theory [1]. Even more challenging is identifying clusters of highly interacting subsystems only by looking at how their state evolves over time. The temporal behavior of a complex system can be studied by analyzing its dynamical structures, i.e., subsets of variables whose elements interact tightly with one another, as well as by identifying higher-level interactions that occur between such sets.

© Springer International Publishing AG, part of Springer Nature 2018
K. Sim and P. Kaufmann (Eds.): EvoApplications 2018, LNCS 10784, pp. 125–140, 2018.
https://doi.org/10.1007/978-3-319-77538-8_10

Villani et al. [2] introduced a method to identify relevant structures in complex systems, based on a dataset including samples of the system status at different times. The method is based onto a metric named Relevance Index (RI) that quantifies how much the behavior of these relevant structures deviates from the behavior of a reference (homogeneous) system, in which the variables have, individually, the same distribution as in the observed dataset, but are homogeneously correlated.

Systems composed by many physically connected parts that exhibit complex dynamics include, for example, telecommunication networks such as the Internet, sensor networks, distributed peer-to-peer networks [3,4], transportation networks [5], social network [6] and other abstract network systems.

The identification of a community structure in these networks could mirror the detection of the aforementioned highly interacting subsystems in complex systems. A community structure can be described as the gathering of nodes of the network into groups, which exhibit a higher density of edges within their members than with other groups. The edges, or links, may change over time and may refer to a different semantics according to the particular scenario behind the network. In a social network the nodes represent users (or better, user accounts) and the edges the connections between users that convey information, thoughts, news over time. These connections vary over time, as they can be established, removed and then established again, and can be of different types, according to the nature of the particular social network, since a connected user can be a friend, a relative, a colleague, a sport teammate, etc.

In this paper we report the results we obtained by applying the RI technique, implemented through an evolutionary algorithm named HyReSS, to a closed group of Facebook users, and we compare its performances against an exhaustive search. The group is made of 612 users but we focused on the most active ones, i.e., those ones that, on average, posted at least 2 posts per year (32 users). This choice was made in order to analyze only significant data, and it is not due to a limitation of the proposed method, since it has been proven to scale with the dimension of the system under consideration, as shown in [7]. The group belongs to the Italian association of patients affected by Hidradenitis Suppurativa and has been studied from the point of view of time and of sentiment. More precisely, the dynamic communities detected in the group by the RI method, based on the sentiment expressed in the posts during a certain period of time, are found to be correlated with the degree of the users, that is, the number of friend connections within the Facebook group itself.

The rest of the paper is structured as follows: in Sect. 2 we summarize the origins and previous applications of the RI as well as past and recent usage of genetic algorithms to analyze complex networks; in Sect. 3 we describe the most significant theoretical steps underlying RI computation; in Sect. 4 we describe in detail the evolutionary algorithm used in the paper in combination with the RI; in Sect. 5 we assess the results obtained applying the proposed method to the Facebook group we took into consideration and, finally, in Sect. 6, we draw some conclusions.

2 Related Works

Previous works have already documented the use of information-theoretical measures for studying complexity and criticality. On the one hand, concepts such as complexity, self-organization, emergence, adaptation and evolution are interpreted [1] and measured [8] in terms of entropies and mutual information. On the other hand, in [9] Fisher information is used to identify the critical state in the Ising model, while in [10] information theory concepts are applied to the critical states of two traffic light control methods.

However, none of the existing methods has all the following desirable properties:

- ability to identify groups of variables that change in time in a coordinated fashion;
- ability to identify critical states;
- direct applicability to data, with no need to resort to models;
- robustness against sampling effort and system size.

The Relevance Index (RI) method, which is based on Shannon's entropy, appears to be a step forward in the right direction [11]. The RI is an extension of the Cluster Index (CI) introduced by Edelman and Tononi in 1994 and 1998 [12,13] to detect functional groups of brain regions, assuming system fluctuations around a steady state. With respect to the CI, the RI can be applied to a broad range of non-stationary dynamical systems, including abstract models of gene-regulatory networks and simulated chemical systems [2], biological [11] and social [14] systems.

The identification of the network structure and of communities in different types of network systems has gained great interest during the years, whatever the type of the considered network system: the Internet, particular social networks such as Facebook, LinkedIn, Google+, etc., citation networks, e-mail networks, and the like [15]. These networks can be considered either static or dynamic complex systems and different methods have been devised to study their structures accordingly. In this work, we focus onto community detection in a particular dynamic network complex system, i.e., a social network. The different nodes it is composed of are users, while links or edges among the nodes represent social relationships, such as friendship, co-working, following, and they may vary and evolve during time, causing the system to show a dynamical behavior.

Researchers have tried for years to employ genetic algorithms to tackle the problem of communities detection in complex networks: in [16], the authors proposed a scalable genetic method based onto the network modularity metric, demonstrating its effectiveness in a Karate club and in a College Football scenario. However, the work is based onto the *a-priori* knowledge of the number of edges connecting nodes in the network, and is characterized by an *ad-hoc* crossover phase as well as the initial assignment of a node to a random community.

The contribution in [17] presents GA-Net, a method to detect communities in social networks using a genetic algorithm, where the variation operators are tailored to take into consideration only the actual correlations among the nodes. The fitness function is called community score and is based onto the locus-based adjacency representation, which requires the *a-priori* knowledge of the adjacency matrix of the nodes of the network.

More recently, in [18] the authors have employed an extended compact genetic algorithm to identify communities in complex networks. The method seems to address effectively the complex nonlinear optimization problem and the epistasis in the representation of chromosomes, both for benchmark and real-world networks, resulting more efficient and stable than other genetic algorithm-based solutions while, at the same time, requiring less time to reach convergence. However, it uses the modularity metric as a fitness function, and a marginal product model, which is quite complex, even if built through clusters based on mutual information, to model the probability distribution of the individuals.

In [19], the authors propose a novel generational genetic algorithm to solve the communities detection problem. The method is shown to outperform other genetic algorithms in terms of accuracy in finding communities; however, it is based onto the modularity metric and on *ad-hoc* initialization methods and search operators. Moreover, differently from our technique, it employs normalized mutual information only in the end of the process, to evaluate the performances of the algorithms studied, and it provides a range of available solutions, i.e., a lowest and highest number of possible communities to be detected.

The application of genetic and evolutionary algorithms to complex social networks is not limited only to communities detection. For example, recently, the authors of [20] tried to maximize the influence of certain nodes, while, at the same time, minimizing their number. This was done by means of a particular Multi-Objective Evolutionary Algorithm, which outperformed two other state-of-art heuristics, and according to two different influence propagation models. Such a technique was effective in two complex network scenarios, namely ego-Facebook and ca-GrQc; however, it requires prior knowledge of the probabilities of influence propagation.

On the contrary, the solution we propose, thanks to the RI, does not require any *a-priori* knowledge on the structure of the social network, and allows one to dynamically study communities it detects from different points of view, such as sentiments, degrees, etc., without the need to modify invasively crossover and mutation operations. To the best of our knowledge, this is the first work that applies the RI method in combination with a genetic algorithm with the aim of identifying and studying, in a dynamical way, subsets of users in a social network.

3   The Relevance Index Approach

The RI can be used to study data from a wide range of dynamical system classes, with the purpose of identifying sets of variables that behave in a somehow coordinated way, i.e., the variables belonging to the set are integrated with each other, much more than with the other variables not belonging to the set. These subsets can be used to describe the whole system organization, thus they are named Relevant Subsets (RSs).

The computation of the RI, which is an information theoretical measure based on Shannon's Entropy [21], is usually based on observational data, and probabilities are estimated as the relative frequencies of the values observed for each variable. The theoretical definition of the RI is summarized in the following.

Let us consider a system composed of n random variables $X_1, X_2, ..., X_n$ (e.g., agents, chemicals, genes, artificial entities, social network users, etc.) and suppose that S_k is a subset composed of k elements, with $k < n$. The RI(S_k) is defined as:

$$RI(S_k) = \frac{I(S_k)}{MI(S_k; U \backslash S_k)}, \tag{1}$$

where I is the integration (multi-information), which measures the mutual dependence among the k elements in S_k, and MI is the mutual information, which measures the mutual dependence between subset S_k and the remaining part of the system $U \backslash S_k$.

The integration is defined as:

$$I(S_k) = \sum_{s \in S_k} H(s) - H(S_k) \tag{2}$$

where $H(.)$ is Shannon's entropy both for a single variable and a set of variables, according to the specific notation.

On the other hand, the mutual information $MI(S_k; U \backslash S_k)$ is defined as follows:

$$MI(S_k; U \backslash S_k) = H(S_k) + H(U \backslash S_k) - H(S_k, U \backslash S_k) \tag{3}$$

Trivially, the RI is not defined if $MI(S_k; U \backslash S_k) = 0$. However, a vanishing MI is a sign of separation of the subset under exam from the rest of the system, and therefore the subset needs to be studied separately.

We observe that the RI scales with the subset size, therefore a normalization method is required to compare RI values of subsets of different size. Moreover, the statistical significance of RI differences should be assessed by means of an appropriate test. For these reasons, a statistical significance index is introduced:

$$T_c(S_k) = \frac{RI(S_k) - \langle RI_h \rangle}{\sigma(RI_h)} = \frac{\nu RI - \nu \langle RI_h \rangle}{\nu \sigma(RI_h)} \tag{4}$$

where $\langle RI_h \rangle$ and $\sigma(RI_h)$ are, respectively, the average and the standard deviation of the RI of a sample of subsets of size k extracted from a reference homogeneous system U_h, and $\nu = \langle MI_h \rangle / \langle I_h \rangle$ is its normalization constant. Following our previous works [7, 22], we use as reference homogeneous system a system composed of the same number of variables and observations as the system under analysis, the values of each variable being randomly chosen from the distribution of all its possible values.

A post-processing sieving algorithm [23] can be used to select the most relevant sets, reducing the list of Candidate Relevant Sets (CRSs) to the most representative ones. The sieving algorithm is based on the criterion by which, if CRS

C_1 is a proper subset of CRS C_2 and ranks higher than CRS C_2, then CRS C_1 should be considered more relevant than CRS C_2. Therefore, the algorithm keeps only those CRSs that are not included in or do not include any other CRS with higher T_c: this "sieving" action stops when no more eliminations are possible and the remaining groups of variables are the proper RSs. This procedure can also be extended to the identification of hierarchical relations among RSs: this topic is the subject of ongoing work.

4   HyReSS: Hybrid Relevant Set Search

HyReSS is a hybrid metaheuristic for searching relevant subsets within dynamical systems. This kind of search corresponds to an optimization problem (T_c index maximization). HyReSS is used to counteract the complexity of an exhaustive RS search, which increases exponentially with the system size.

The proposed metaheuristic hybridizes a basic genetic algorithm with local search strategies that are driven by statistics, computed at runtime, on the results that the algorithm is obtaining.

HyReSS does not search a single CRS, but the N_{best} highest-T_c CRSs. The evolutionary search is therefore enhanced by a niching technique that maintains population diversity, exploring many peaks in parallel.

The genetic algorithm is first run to draw the search towards the basins of attraction of the main local maxima in the search space. Then, the regions identified during the evolutionary process are explored more finely and extensively by a series of local searches, to improve the results.

The method is composed by five main cascaded steps:

1. Genetic algorithm;
2. Variable relevance-based local search;
3. Variable frequency-based local search;
4. CRS cardinality-based local search;
5. Merging.

The T_c index computation, which is the most computation-intensive module within the algorithm, is parallelized for large blocks of CRSs through a CUDA[1] kernel, which fits the computational needs of this problem particularly well [22]. The T_c index has been computed in parallel in all the five steps of the algorithm.

4.1   Genetic Algorithm

The genetic algorithm is based on the Deterministic Crowding (DC) algorithm. DC does not require any *a priori* setting of problem-related parameters, such as the similarity radius, and has low complexity, since it scales as $O(n)$ with the dimension of the search space.

Each individual corresponds to one CRS and is represented as a binary string of size N, where N is the number of variables that describe the system. Each bit

---

[1] https://developer.nvidia.com.

is set to 1 if the corresponding variable is included in the CRS, otherwise it is set to 0. The fitness function to be maximized corresponds directly to the T_c. As specified above, the fitness (T_c) values of large blocks of individuals are computed in parallel.

The best individuals found during the run are stored in a list ("best-CRS memory") along with their fitness values. At the end of the run, the best-CRS memory should contain all CRSs in the set $\mathcal{B}$ of the N_{best} highest-T_c CRSs.

The initial population, of size p, aims to represent a sample that is as representative as possible of the whole search space, avoiding repetitions. For this reason, the initial population is obtained by generating random individuals according to a pre-set distribution of the cardinality of the CRSs (pairs, triplets, etc.).

In the evolutionary process, p children are generated from $p/2$ random pairs of individuals through single-point crossover. After crossover, each child possibly replaces the most similar parent of lower fitness. The similarity between two individuals is computed as the Hamming distance between the binary strings that represent the corresponding CRSs. To maintain genetic diversity, a parent is replaced only if the child is not already present in the population.

The implemented algorithm is elitist, since a child is inserted in the new population only if its fitness is better (higher) than the fitness of the parent it substitutes. Therefore, the overall fitness of the population increases monotonically with the algorithm iterations.

The evolutionary process is iterated until the population is no more able to evolve, *i.e.*, the new generation remains equal to the previous one. When that happens, new random parents are generated up to α_p times to create new variants of the CRSs.

Mutation is implemented as bit flips and applied with low probability (P_{mut}) after each mating.

For this phase, the termination condition is reached when the number of evaluations of the fitness function exceeds a threshold α_f or when the new generation has remained equal to the previous one for α_p times.

After the end of the evolutionary algorithm, the N_{best} highest-T_c individuals (CRSs) are selected for the subsequent phases, in a cascaded process.

4.2   Variable Relevance-Based Local Search

This phase is driven by a relevance coefficient RC_i, computed in the previous phase while running the genetic algorithm.

Within each iteration of the genetic algorithm, RC_i is computed for each variable i of the system under examination. RC_i is high if the variable i is frequently included in high-fitness CRSs.

A fitness threshold τ is set at the end of each iteration t of the GA to separate high-fitness CRSs from low-fitness ones, on the basis of a percentile β of the whole fitness range computed up to that point.

$$\tau(t) = minFitness + (maxFitness - minFitness) * \beta \tag{5}$$

For each variable i, a presence coefficient (PC_i) and an absence coefficient (AC_i) are defined as the sum of the fitness values of the CRSs having fitness greater than τ, in which the variable has been present or absent, respectively. The values of these coefficients are cumulated over the generations and normalized with respect to the number of generations in which the corresponding CRSs have been included.

Based on these two coefficients, the ratio $R_{ap,i} = AC_i/PC_i$ is computed. The variable i is classified as relevant if PC_i is greater than a threshold (the γ_{th} percentile of the full range of PC_i values) and $R_{ap,i}$ is lower than a certain threshold δ.

The local search procedure performs a recombination of the most relevant variables with other, randomly chosen, ones.

At first, all possible subsets (simple combinations) of the most relevant variables are computed, excluding the subsets of cardinality 0 and 1, which are not relevant in the system analysis. Then, for each possible cardinality, the highest-fitness individual is selected. New CRSs are generated from the selected individuals, by forcing the presence/absence of relevant/irrelevant variables, respectively, and by randomly adding other variables into the CRSs. Every newly generated individual is evaluated and replaces the lowest-fitness individual in the best-CRS memory if its fitness is higher than the lowest one.

At the end of this phase a local search is performed in the neighborhood of the best individual of the best-CRS memory, which is updated in case new high-T_c individuals are found.

4.3   Variable Frequency-Based Search

The same procedure as in the previous phase, based on a different criterion, is used to generate new individuals and to explore the neighborhood of the best one.

This step starts by computing the frequency with which each variable has been included in the CRSs evaluated in the previous phases. This value is then used to identify two classes of variables:

- variables with much lower frequency than the average;
- variables with much higher frequency than the average.

Variables of the first kind may have been previously "neglected", thus it may be worth verifying whether they are able to generate high-fitness individuals. Variables of the latter kind are likely to have been selected very frequently in the evolutionary process because they actually have a significant relevance, thus it may be worth exploring more finely those regions of the search space.

For these reasons, the same procedure which, in the previous phase, has been used to generate new individuals and to explore the neighborhood of the best ones, is repeated, starting from the variables included in the two classes.

4.4   CRS Cardinality-Based Search

During the previous phases, HyReSS analyzes each individual, counting the number of variables composing the corresponding CRS. The number of occurrences of CRSs of each possible cardinality (2, ..., N-1) is recorded.

Then, these values are normalized according to the a priori probability of occurrence of such groups, given by the corresponding binomial coefficient $\binom{N}{c}$, where N is the total number of variables and c the cardinality of the group. These normalized values indicate the percentage of individuals analyzed for each cardinality, compared to the total number of possible groups of that size.

Finally, new CRSs are generated using a procedure driven by the normalized values, such that cardinalities having lower values have higher probability of occurring and are possibly stored into the best-CRS memory according to their fitness.

4.5   Merging

In this phase, a limited pool of variables is selected by considering all variables which are included in the highest-fitness CRSs stored in the best-CRS memory.

A size θ for the pool is set; then, the best individuals are progressively OR-ed bitwise, in decreasing order of fitness, starting from the best two CRSs. The termination condition is reached when the result of the bitwise OR contains θ bits set to 1 or all the CRSs have been processed.

A final exhaustive search is performed over all the possible CRSs that contain the selected variables, updating the best-CRS memory accordingly.

5   Experimental Results

In order to use the Relevance Index method to study a Facebook group composed by patients affected by Hidradenitis Suppurativa, we used the labeled data obtained in [24]. In that work, an automatic emotion detection and a social network analysis technique have been used to analyze the emotional states of each member of the group. In particular, the sentiments have been obtained using a manually annotated training set and a seven-output hierarchical classifier system [25] based on Parrots emotion categorization [26] (3 positive: joy, love, surprise, 3 negative: fear, anger, sadness and 1 neutral: objective). In [24], the authors have estimated how these emotions are correlated with their own degree in the social network (the number of mutual connections in the group).

5.1   Dataset Description

Our datasets have been obtained using the information about the group members who published at least 15 posts between 2010 and 2016. This choice has allowed us to reduce the number of users taken into consideration from 612 to 32 and to study the most active members of the community. Each observation (sample) of the system represents a specific month within the period of interest. In particular, we focused onto two different case studies, based on two kinds of values:

1. Post-based value. This feature is set to 1 if the user has posted during the considered month, otherwise it is set to 0.
2. Sentiment-based value. This feature describes 4 different cases for each user in the considered month: no posts, positive sentiment, negative sentiment, neutral sentiment. The sentiment polarity has been obtained by looking at the overall emotion expressed by the user (counting his positive, negative and neutral emotions).

5.2 HyReSS Performances

The datasets have been analyzed using both exhaustive search and HyReSS. Given the stochastic nature of HyReSS, 10 independent runs of the algorithm were executed to asses its performance. The results have been evaluated both in terms of quality and of speed-up with respect to the exhaustive search.

The quality of the results has been evaluated by comparing the list of highest-T_c subsets produced by HyReSS with the results of the exhaustive search. To let results be comparable, we relied on the same homogeneous system to compute the T_c values in both approaches.

The two algorithms have been compared also in terms of efficiency (execution time). It is to be noticed that the methods relied on the same GPU implementation of the fitness function, which means that the differences observed depend only on the efficiency and complexity of the algorithms and not on their implementation.

Tests were run on a Linux PC equipped with a 1.6 GHz Intel I7 CPU, 6 GB of RAM and a GeForce GTX 680 GPU by NVIDIA. The parameters regulating the behavior of HyReSS have been set as reported in Table 1.

Table 1. HyReSS parameter settings. The parameters are defined in Sect. 4.

Dataset	P_{mut}	p	α_f	α_p	β	γ	δ	θ
Post-based	0.1	25600	256000	3	0.75	0.75	0.3	15
Sentiment-based	0.1	25600	256000	3	0.75	0.75	0.3	15

Results are summarized in Table 2 and discussed in the following.

The results obtained by HyReSS and by the exhaustive search are almost identical. Only occasionally at most one out of the top 50 sets, usually more than enough to understand the main dynamics of the systems we took into consideration, was not detected by HyReSS.

The speedup of HyReSS algorithm is due to a number of fitness evaluations that is much lower than the number of fitness evaluations of the exhaustive search (both algorithms are based on the same parallel code for the RI computation).

Table 2. Summary of HyReSS performances and comparison with the exhaustive search (ES). HyReSS execution time is expressed as the average and the standard deviation of the execution times measured over 10 runs. The speedup of HyReSS algorithm is related with the execution of a number of fitness evaluations which is much lower than the number of fitness evaluations of the exhaustive search.

Dataset	N. Variables	N. Samples	Time[s] (ES)	Time[s] (HyReSS)	Speedup
Post-based	32	84	1007.78	30.85 ± 0.61	32.67
Sentiment-based	32	84	1272.85	35.48 ± 0.55	35.88

5.3   Social Network Results

This section presents the highest-T_c RSs identified using the post-based and the sentiment-based datasets described in Sect. 5.1. They have been identified by HyReSS and they are the same found by the exhaustive search.

Table 3 shows the users composing the highest-T_c subsets, together with their user-degree, which is defined as the number of Facebook friends in the considered Facebook group. As one can notice the sentiment-based subset is composed, on average, by users with a higher degree compared with the post-based subset. For the sake of completeness, in Fig. 1 we show the overall distribution of users according to their degree.

Table 3. The highest-T_c RSs identified on the post-based (left) and sentiment-based (right) datasets.

Highest-T_c RS (post-based)	
User	**Degree**
User 1A	120
User 2A	5
User 3A	0
User 4A	5
User 5A	8
User 6A	0
User 7A	13
User 8A	6
User 9A	0
User 10A	0
User 11A	0

Highest-T_c RS (sentiment-based)	
User	**Degree**
User 1B	42
User 2B	120
User 3B	38
User 4B	1
User 5B	31
User 6B	19
User 7B	1
User 8B	31
User 9B	23
User 10B	16
User 11B	3
User 12B	0
User 13B	9
User 14B	10
User 15B	5
User 16B	1

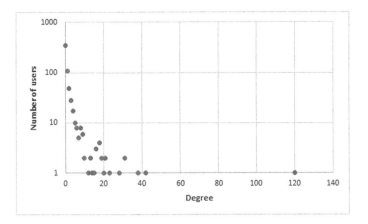

Fig. 1. Graph representing the distribution of node degrees in a logarithmic scale.

The bidirectional graphs in Fig. 2 represent all the 612 users of the Facebook group. Each node of a graph represents a user and each edge represents a friendship relationship between two users.

In order to better appreciate the results, the size of each node has been made proportional to the node degree.

The red nodes in the left graph represent the highest-T_c RS identified by using the post-based dataset, while the blue nodes in the right graph represent the highest-T_c subset identified by using the sentiment-based dataset. The two communities represented in the figure are the most representative in terms of T_c; other detected communities are simply subsets of these main communities and are not represented.

The sentiment-based analysis provides additional information with respect to the post-based one. In particular, it provides not only a timeline information about users' posts, but also an emotional information about the feeling expressed in the posts.

It is important to notice that the sentiment-based subset is composed by users with higher degree. This result may represent an evidence of the influence of the group on the feelings expressed by users. Patients who developed many relationships with other users in the Facebook group express a similar dynamical behavior in terms of feelings, e.g., from negative posts to positive posts and vice versa.

This result can be better appreciated in Fig. 3, which shows the portions of the graphs corresponding to the 32 users who posted at least 15 times in the considered period. The figure shows that almost all users in the sentiment-based subset are the ones with the highest degree in the represented connected component.

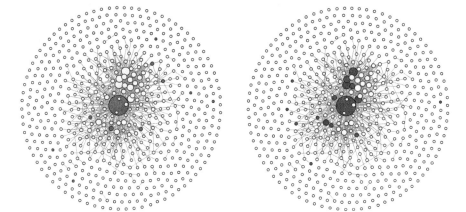

Fig. 2. Graphs representing all 612 users of the Facebook group with the post-based community (red nodes, on the left) and the sentiment-based community (blue nodes, on the right). The size of each node is proportional to its degree, and each edge represents a friendship relationship. (Color figure online)

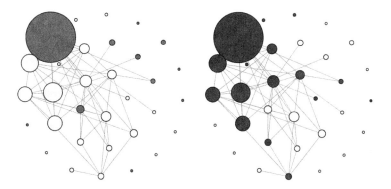

Fig. 3. Graphs representing the 32 users who posted at least 15 times in the considered period with the post-based community (red nodes, on the left) and the sentiment-based community (blue nodes, on the right). The size of each node is proportional to its degree, and each edge represents a friendship relationship. (Color figure online)

6 Conclusion

The search for hidden relationships between variables in complex systems is a computationally heavy task. HyReSS is an ad-hoc hybrid metaheuristic which extracts such relationships as quickly and precisely as possible, using the Relevance Index method to find the candidate Relevant Subsets of variables that describe a dynamical system.

The GAs' capacity of providing a good tradeoff between convergence speed and exploration has been combined with local searches, which refine and extend results, when correctly seeded. The metaheuristic is based on the Deterministic Crowding algorithm, which guarantees that a large number of local maxima are taken into consideration in the early stages of HyReSS. The subsequent local searches refine the results more systematically to restrict the search only to those CRSs that are most likely to have high fitness values.

The performance of HyReSS in searching relevant sets has been analyzed in two case studies (post-based and sentiment-based) obtained from a real social network: the closed Facebook group of users belonging to the Italian association of patients affected by Hidradenitis Suppurativa.

HyReSS results have been compared with those obtained by an exhaustive search based on the same parallel code for computing the RI, evaluating both its quality and the obtained speed-up. HyReSS provided the same results as the exhaustive search, performing much fewer fitness evaluations in a significantly shorter time. The efficiency and the precision of the algorithm will allow us to extend our research on the detection of candidate RSs to complex systems of much larger sizes than previously possible, for which an exhaustive search is not feasible on a standard computer due to the exponential increase of its complexity with the system size.

The application of the RI method to the Facebook group identified interesting communities. In particular, the emotional information highlighted a subset of users who developed many friendship connections with other users in the Facebook group.

Thanks to HyReSS scalability, we will extend the analysis to larger-sized social networks, in order to unveil their hidden structures. Moreover, we will compare the proposed method with other algorithms for community detection in dynamic graphs.

References

1. Prokopenko, M., Boschetti, F., Ryan, A.J.: An information-theoretic primer on complexity, self-organization, and emergence. Complexity **15**(1), 11–28 (2009)
2. Villani, M., Filisetti, A., Benedettini, S., Roli, A., Lane, D., Serra, R.: The detection of intermediate-level emergent structures and patterns. In: Miglino, O., et al. (eds.) Advances in Artificial Life, ECAL 2013, pp. 372–378. The MIT Press (2013). http://mitpress.mit.edu/books/advances-artificial-life-ecal-2013
3. Pecori, R.: A comparison analysis of trust-adaptive approaches to deliver signed public keys in P2P systems. In: 2015 7th International Conference on New Technologies, Mobility and Security (NTMS), pp. 1–5, July 2015
4. Pecori, R., Veltri, L.: 3AKEP: triple-authenticated key exchange protocol for peer-to-peer VoIP applications. Comput. Commun. **85**, 28–40 (2016)
5. Canale, S., Giorgio, A.D., Lisi, F., Panfili, M., Celsi, L.R., Suraci, V., Priscoli, F.D.: A future internet oriented user centric extended intelligent transportation system. In: 2016 24th Mediterranean Conference on Control and Automation (MED), pp. 1133–1139, June 2016
6. Fornacciari, P., Mordonini, M., Tomaiuolo, M.: Social network and sentiment analysis on twitter: towards a combined approach. In: KDWeb (2015)

7. Sani, L., et al.: Efficient search of relevant structures in complex systems. In: Adorni, G., Cagnoni, S., Gori, M., Maratea, M. (eds.) AI*IA 2016. LNCS (LNAI), vol. 10037, pp. 35–48. Springer, Cham (2016). https://doi.org/10.1007/978-3-319-49130-1_4

8. Gershenson, C., Fernandez, N.: Complexity and information: measuring emergence, self-organization, and homeostasis at multiple scales. Complex. **18**(2), 29–44 (2012)

9. Prokopenko, M., Lizier, J.T., Obst, O., Wang, X.R.: Relating fisher information to order parameters. Phys. Rev. E **84**, 041116 (2011). https://link.aps.org/doi/10.1103/PhysRevE.84.041116

10. Zubillaga, D., Cruz, G., Aguilar, L.D., Zapotécatl, J., Fernández, N., Aguilar, J., Rosenblueth, D.A., Gershenson, C.: Measuring the complexity of self-organizing traffic lights. Entropy **16**(5), 2384–2407 (2014). http://www.mdpi.com/1099-4300/16/5/2384

11. Villani, M., Roli, A., Filisetti, A., Fiorucci, M., Poli, I., Serra, R.: The search for candidate relevant subsets of variables in complex systems. Artif. Life **21**(4), 412–431 (2015)

12. Tononi, G., Sporns, O., Edelman, G.M.: A measure for brain complexity: relating functional segregation and integration in the nervous system. Proc. Natl. Acad. Sci. **91**(11), 5033–5037 (1994)

13. Tononi, G., McIntosh, A., Russel, D., Edelman, G.: Functional clustering: identifying strongly interactive brain regions in neuroimaging data. Neuroimage **7**, 133–149 (1998)

14. Filisetti, A., Villani, M., Roli, A., Fiorucci, M., Poli, I., Serra, R.: On some properties of information theoretical measures for the study of complex systems. In: Pizzuti, C., Spezzano, G. (eds.) WIVACE 2014. CCIS, vol. 445, pp. 140–150. Springer, Cham (2014). https://doi.org/10.1007/978-3-319-12745-3_12

15. Scott, J.: Social Network Analysis. Sage Publications (2017)

16. Tasgin, M., Herdagdelen, A., Bingol, H.: Community detection in complex networks using genetic algorithms. arXiv preprint arXiv:0711.0491 (2007)

17. Pizzuti, C.: GA-Net: a genetic algorithm for community detection in social networks. In: Rudolph, G., Jansen, T., Beume, N., Lucas, S., Poloni, C. (eds.) PPSN 2008. LNCS, vol. 5199, pp. 1081–1090. Springer, Heidelberg (2008). https://doi.org/10.1007/978-3-540-87700-4_107

18. Li, J., Song, Y.: Community detection in complex networks using extended compact genetic algorithm. Soft Comput. **17**(6), 925–937 (2013)

19. Guerrero, M., Montoya, F.G., Baos, R., Alcayde, A., Gil, C.: Adaptive community detection in complex networks using genetic algorithms. Neurocomputing **266**(Suppl. C), 101–113 (2017)

20. Bucur, D., Iacca, G., Marcelli, A., Squillero, G., Tonda, A.: Multi-objective evolutionary algorithms for influence maximization in social networks. In: Squillero, G., Sim, K. (eds.) EvoApplications 2017. LNCS, vol. 10199, pp. 221–233. Springer, Cham (2017). https://doi.org/10.1007/978-3-319-55849-3_15

21. Cover, T., Thomas, A.: Elements of Information Theory, 2nd edn. Wiley-Interscience, New York (2006)

22. Vicari, E., et al.: GPU-based parallel search of relevant variable sets in complex systems. In: Rossi, F., Piotto, S., Concilio, S. (eds.) WIVACE 2016. CCIS, vol. 708, pp. 14–25. Springer, Cham (2017). https://doi.org/10.1007/978-3-319-57711-1_2

23. Filisetti, A., Villani, M., Roli, A., Fiorucci, M., Serra, R.: Exploring the organisation of complex systems through the dynamical interactions among their relevant subsets. In: Andrews, P. et al. (ed.) Proceedings of the European Conference on Artificial Life 2015, ECAL 2015, pp. 286–293. The MIT Press (2015)

24. Lombardo, G., Ferrari, A., Fornacciari, P., Mordonini, M., Sani, L., Tomaiuolo, M.: Dynamics of emotions and relations in a facebook group of patients with hidradenitis suppurativa. In: Guidi, B., Ricci, L., Calafate, C.T., Gaggi, O., Marquez-Barja, J. (eds.) GOODTECHS 2017. LNICST, vol. 233, pp. 269–278. Springer, Cham (2018). https://doi.org/10.1007/978-3-319-76111-4_27

25. Angiani, G., Cagnoni, S., Chuzhikova, N., Fornacciari, P., Mordonini, M., Tomaiuolo, M.: Flat and hierarchical classifiers for detecting emotion in tweets. In: Adorni, G., Cagnoni, S., Gori, M., Maratea, M. (eds.) AI*IA 2016. LNCS (LNAI), vol. 10037, pp. 51–64. Springer, Cham (2016). https://doi.org/10.1007/978-3-319-49130-1_5

26. Parrott, W.G.: Emotions in Social Psychology: Essential Readings. Psychology Press, New York (2001)

A Fast Metaheuristic for the Design of DVB-T2 Networks

Fabio D'Andreagiovanni[1,2,3](✉) and Antonella Nardin[4]

[1] French National Center for Scientific Research (CNRS), Paris, France
[2] Sorbonne Universités, Paris, France
[3] Université de Technologie de Compiègne, CNRS, Heudiasyc, Compiègne, France
d.andreagiovanni@hds.utc.fr
[4] Universitá degli Studi Roma Tre, Via Ostiense 169, 00154 Roma, Italy
nardin.an@gmail.com

Abstract. In order to better exploit scarce radio spectrum resources, the second generation of the Digital Video Broadcasting - Terrestrial standard (DVB-T2) has been developed and is under adoption in many countries, especially in Europe, for providing digital television services. The switch from the first to the second generation of DVB-T will require new operators to design their new networks and old operators to reconfigure their existing networks to better adapt to the features and opportunities of the new services. In this work, we propose an optimization model and a fast metaheuristic for the design of DVB-T2 networks. The metaheuristic is based on combining a probabilistic variable fixing procedure with an exact large neighborhood search and is developed to tackle the unsatisfying performance of state-of-the-art optimization solvers when adopted to solve realistic instances. Computational tests on realistic instances show that our metaheuristic can find solutions of much better quality than those identified by a state-of-the-art optimization solver.

Keywords: Telecommunications · DVB · Network design
Mixed integer linear programming · Tight linear relaxations
MIP heuristics

1 Introduction

In recent times, digital telecommunications services provided through high-performance mobile networks and high-speed cable-based internet networks have become an essential part of our fast-moving everyday life and new technological paradigms like *cloud* and *5G* are going to offer even more performing

This work has been partially carried out in the framework of the Labex MS2T program. Labex MS2T is supported by the French Government, through the program "Investments for the future", managed by the French National Agency for Research (Reference ANR-11-IDEX-0004-02).

K. Sim and P. Kaufmann (Eds.): EvoApplications 2018, LNCS 10784, pp. 141–155, 2018.
https://doi.org/10.1007/978-3-319-77538-8_11

connectivity experiences (see e.g., [1–3]). Notwithstanding the great expansion and diffusion of such new telecommunications services, the "dear old" television broadcasting services still constitute an extremely important telecommunication service that can easily reach the vast majority of the population and represents a crucial voice in the telecom agenda of national governments.

Thanks to the switch from analogue to digital television technology, the television market has known an increased competition between broadcasters that has stimulated the enlargement of programme variety and led to an increased quality of services and interactivity. Among the available digital television standards, the DVB-T (Digital Video Broadcasting – Terrestrial) [4] is the most widespread standard in the world and since its introduction in 1995 has been adopted in more than half of all world countries. Due to the need for better exploiting the scarce radio spectrum resources and provide services of higher quality, since 2006 the DVB Project has undertaken research projects to develop a 2nd-generation DVB, which is commonly called DVB-T2 [5]. DVB-T2 was standardized by the European Telecommunications Standardisations Institute (ETSI) in 2009. In Europe, since its first introduction in UK in 2010, it has been adopted by several European broadcasters. The full upgrade from DVB to DVB-T2 will take place in major European countries like Germany and Italy in the next few years.

A crucial benefit granted by the DVB-T2 is the increase in system capacity: for the same usage of spectrum, DVB-T2 provides an increase of capacity of at least 30% with respect to DVB-T, allowing the market entry of new broadcasters or the launch of new innovative services. On the other hand, adopting and implementing the new standard will translate into new costs for the broadcasters and users, which will need new broadcasting equipment and receiving devices.

Given the need for new DVB-T2 operators to design their new networks and for old DVB operators to reconfigure their existing networks to better adapt to the features and opportunities of the new services, we study here the question of developing an optimization model and algorithm for the design of DVB-T2 network. Specifically our contributions are:

1. We present a mixed integer linear programming problem for modelling fundamental decisions that must be taken in a DVB-T2 design problem (essentially, configure the network transmitters so to maximize the number of users covered with services) and discuss a way to strengthen the mathematical model through the insertion of additional valid inequalities. The model is based on signal-to-interference quantities recommended to be used for coverage evaluation by international regulatory bodies;

2. In order to fast solve the resulting challenging optimization problem, we propose a metaheuristic based on combining a probabilistic variable fixing procedure with an exact large neighborhood search. Our metaheuristic constitutes a solution approach that places itself in between exact (i.e., guaranteeing convergence to an optimum) but slow optimization approaches for DVB (e.g., [6–8]) and fast (bio-inspired) heuristics (e.g., [9–11]) which cannot provide guarantees about the quality of the produced solution: the metaheuristic indeed runs fast but also exploits the valuable information associated with

the linear relaxation of a strengthened formulation of the problem, using it to guide a variable fixing procedure (this allows to derive a so-called *optimality gap* that can measure the quality of the produced solution);
3. Computational experiments based on realistic DVB instances, showing that our metaheurisitc can produce solutions of much higher quality than a state-of-the-art optimization solver.

The remainder of this paper is organized as follows: in Sect. 2, we introduce an optimization model for DVB-T2 network design; in Sect. 3, we present a new metaheuristic to fast solve the design problem; in Sect. 4, we present our hybrid metaheuristic and computational results. Finally, in Sect. 5, we derive conclusions.

2   An Optimization Model for DVB-T2 Network Design

For modelling purposes, we can essentially describe a DVB-T2 network as a set S of *DVB Stations (DSs)* that provide a broadcasting television service to a set of customers located in a territory of interest. Following the recommendations of major international and national regulatory bodies in the field of telecommunications (e.g., [12,13]), we discretize the territory into a raster of small elementary squared areas of identical size: the point at the center of each area is called *testpoint (TP)* and is assumed to be representative of all the points inside the elementary area. We denote by T the set of all testpoints in the territory.

Each DS is characterized by a location (its geographical coordinates) and a number of radio-electrical parameters (e.g., power emission, antenna diagram, frequency channel). The *DVB-T2 Network Design Problem* (DND) consists in choosing the location and setting the parameters of the DSs in order to maximize an objective function that typically represents the total number of people in testpoints covered with service.

As it is common in wireless network design problems, the optimization does not aim at optimizing all the parameters of the DSs, but just focuses on a subset of them. In the vast majority of studies, the two critical design decisions that are included in the optimization models are: (1) setting the power emissions of the transmitters providing the wireless telecommunication service (in our case the DSs); (2) assigning testpoints covered with service to a deployed transmitter. These are indeed two critical decisions that must be taken by a network administrator, as indicated in several real studies (e.g., in DVB [6–8,14], 5G [15–17], in FTTx [18], in UMTS [19,20], in WiMAX [21,22], in WLANs [23,24] and in other wireless network design problems such as [8,25–30]).

We now proceed to discuss how service coverage is assessed, focusing on a generic TP $t \in T$: when t is covered with service (or shortly, *served*), the service is provided by one single DS $\sigma \in S$, which acts as *server* of t. All the remaining DSs, i.e. all $s \in S \backslash \{\sigma\}$, act as interferers for t, reducing the quality of wireless service obtained from the server σ. More formally, if we denote the power emission of a DS $s \in S$ by $p_s > 0$, a TP $t \in T$ is served by $\sigma \in S$ when the ratio of the *received* service power and the sum of the *received* interfering powers (so-called *signal-to-interference ratio* - *SIR*) is above a threshold $\delta > 0$ [31,32]:

$$SIR_{t\sigma}(p) = \frac{a_{t\sigma} \cdot p_\sigma}{N + \sum_{s \in S \setminus \{\sigma\}} a_{ts} \cdot p_s} \geq \delta. \tag{1}$$

Here, the value of δ depends upon the desired quality of service and $N > 0$ is the noise of the system. The *received* power that t gets from any DS $s \in S$ is expressed as the product of the power p_s emitted by s and a factor $a_{ts} \in [0, 1]$ that is commonly called *fading coefficient* and expresses the power reduction that a wireless signal undergoes when propagating from s to t [32].

The inequality (1) can be easily transformed into the following linear inequality, commonly called *SIR inequality*:

$$a_{t\sigma} \cdot p_\sigma - \delta \sum_{s \in S \setminus \{\sigma\}} a_{ts} \cdot p_s \geq \delta \cdot N. \tag{2}$$

Since assessing service coverage constitutes a crucial issue when designing any kind of wireless network, the SIR inequalities are at the basis of most mathematical optimization models adopted for wireless network design (see e.g., [22,29]. In order to model the two fundamentals decisions exposed above, namely setting the power emissions of DSs and assigning served TPs to activated DSs, two kind of decision variables are introduced:

- a continuous *power variable* $p_s \in [0, P^{\max}]$ that represents the power emission of each DS $s \in S$;
- a binary *service assignment variable* $x_{ts} \in \{0, 1\}$, $\forall t \in T, s \in S$, which is set equal to 1 if TP $t \in T$ is served by DSs $s \in S$ and equal to 0 otherwise.

Through these two kind of decision variables the problem of designing a DVB-T2 network can be cast as the following Mixed Integer Linear Programming problem (DVB-MILP):

$$\max \sum_{t \in T} \sum_{s \in S} r_t \cdot x_{ts} \qquad\qquad \text{(DVB} - \text{MILP)}$$

$$a_{t\sigma} \cdot p_\sigma - \delta \sum_{s \in S \setminus \{\sigma\}} a_{ts} \cdot p_s + M \cdot (1 - x_{t\sigma}) \geq \delta \cdot N \qquad t \in T, \sigma \in S \quad (3)$$

$$\sum_{s \in S} x_{ts} \leq 1 \qquad\qquad t \in T \qquad (4)$$

$$0 \leq p_s \leq P^{\max} \qquad\qquad s \in S$$

$$x_{ts} \in \{0, 1\} \qquad\qquad t \in T, s \in S.$$

The objective function pursues the maximization of the number of users covered with service (for each TP $t \in T$, $r_t > 0$ is the number of users located in t). Constraint (3) constitutes a slightly modified version of the SIR inequality (2) and it is called *SIR constraint*: it includes a sufficiently large value M (so-called, *big-M coefficient*) multiplied by $(1 - x_{t\sigma})$ in order to activate/deactivate the constraint: if $x_{t\sigma} = 1$, then TP t is served by DS and the corresponding SIR inequality must be satisfied; if instead $x_{ts\sigma} = 0$, then the big-M coefficient "activates" and makes the constraint satisfied for any valorization of the power variables, thus actually making it redundant. Finally, constraints (4) impose that each TP must be served by at most one DSs.

2.1   Strengthening the Formulation DVB-MILP

The formulation DVB-MILP represents a very natural way for modelling the problem of designing a DVB network. However, it is known that the presence of the big-M coefficients combined with the presence of the fading coefficients, which may vary in a very wide range thus causing numerical instabilities, may reduce the effectiveness of commercial state-of-the-art MILP solvers, as discussed in [7,8,22,26,33].

With the aim of reducing these computational issues, we adopt a strengthening method proposed in [7,22]. The method is based on considering a discretization of the continuous power emissions of DSs, which follows the practice of networking professionals. To this end, the continuous power variable p_s of each DS $s \in S$ is replaced by a non-negative integer power variable $\bar{p}_b \in \mathcal{P} = \{P_1, \ldots, P_{|\mathcal{P}|}\}$, with $P_1 = 0$ (*switched-off value*), $P_{|\mathcal{P}|} = P_{\max}$ and $P_l > P_{l-1} > 0$, for $l = 2, \ldots, |\mathcal{P}|$. This integer variable can be expressed as the linear combination of the power values P_l and suitable binary variables: specifically, for each $s \in S$ a binary power variable z_{sl} is introduced and is equal to 1 if s emits at power P_l and 0 otherwise. Denoting by L the set of feasible power levels, formally we have:

$$\bar{p}_s = \sum_{l \in L} P_l z_{sl}$$

Such linear combination must be accompanied by the *generalized upper bound (GUB)* constraints:

$$\sum_{l \in L} z_{sl} \leq 1,$$

expressing that each DS may emit at a single power level.

Using what introduced above, we can define the following SIR constraints based on binary variables, which replaces their continuous form (3):

$$a_{t\sigma} \cdot \left(\sum_{l \in L} P_l z_{\sigma l} \right) - \delta \sum_{s \in S \setminus \{\sigma\}} a_{ts} \cdot \left(\sum_{l \in L} P_l z_{sl} \right) + M \cdot (1 - x_{t\sigma}) \geq \delta \cdot N t \in T, \sigma \in S$$

$$(5)$$

We denote by DVB-01 the resulting model based on binary power variables.

In order to operate the strengthening, we exploit the presence of the GUB constraints to replace the SIR constraints (5) including the binary power variables with a set of *GUB cover inequalities*. For an exhaustive introduction to the concept of cover inequalities and to their GUB version, we refer to [34,35]. We concisely recall here the main theoretical results about the well-known general *cover inequalities*: a *knapsack constraint* $\sum_{j \in J} a_j x_j \leq b$ with a_j, $b \in \mathbb{R}_+$ and $x_j \in \{0,1\}$, $\forall j \in J$, can be replaced by its cover inequalities $\sum_{j \in C} x_j \leq |C| - 1$, where C is a *cover*. A cover is a subset $C \subseteq J$ such that the summation of the coefficients a_j with $j \in C$ violates the knapsack constraint, i.e. $\sum_{j \in C} a_j > b$. The cover inequalities thus identify combinations of binary variables x_j that cannot be activated at the same time (we can activate at most $|C| - 1$ variables in each cover C). The GUB cover inequalities represent a stronger version of the simple cover inequalities, which are defined by exploiting the presence of GUB constraints $\sum_{j \in K \subseteq J} x_j \leq 1$, which allows to set to 1 at most one variable in K.

Proceeding as in [7], we can define the general form of the GUB cover inequalities (GCIs) needed to replace the binary SIR constraint (5):

$$x_{t\sigma} + \sum_{l=1}^{\lambda} z_{\sigma l} + \sum_{i=1}^{|\Gamma|} \sum_{l=q_i}^{|L|} z_{sl} \leq |\Gamma| + 1, \tag{6}$$

with $t \in T$, $\lambda \in L$, $\Gamma \subseteq S \backslash \{\sigma\}$, $(q_1, \ldots, q_{|\Gamma|}) \in L^I(t, \sigma, \lambda, \Gamma)$, with $L^I(t, \sigma, \lambda, \Gamma) \subseteq L^{|\Gamma|}$ representing the subset of interfering levels of DSs in Γ that deny the service coverage of t provided by the server σ, emitting with power level λ. Intuitively, for given TP, server DS and subset of interfering DSs, a GCI is defined by fixing the power of the server DS and defining a power setting of the interfering DSs that deny the coverage of the considered TP.

By replacing the SIR constraints (5) with the GCIs (6) in the model DVB-01, we obtain *Power-Indexed* model (DVB-PI) that has the big advantage of eliminating the big-M and fading coefficients, thus greatly strengthening and stabilizing the formulation [7]. On the other hand, DVB-PI presents an exponential number of constraints that should be generated dynamically as in a typical *cutting plane* method [34]: initially, the model just contains a subset of GCIs (6) and then additional required GCIs are added by solving an auxiliary separation problem (see [7] for a detailed discussion about the separation of GCIs for Power-Indexed formulations).

In the metaheuristic that we propose in the next section to solve the DVB network design problem, we limit our attention to the following subset of GCIs:

$$x_{t\sigma} + \sum_{l=1}^{\lambda} z_{\sigma l} + \sum_{l=q}^{|L|} z_{sl} \leq 2, \tag{7}$$

which are defined by considering a relaxed version of the SIR constraints (5) obtained by breaking the SIR constraints containing multiple interfering DSs into multiple single-interferer SIR constraints. Such single-interferer relaxation comes from the observation that in real-world networks it is common to find one interfering DS that is much stronger than all the other interefering DS and thus service coverage just depends on the power emitted by it (see [7,22]). The GCIs (7) of the relaxed SIR constraints can be added to DVB-MILP in order to strengthen it.

3 A Metaheuristic for DVB-T2 Network Design

DVB-MILP, as a mixed integer linear programming problem, can be solved in principle by adopting a commercial optimization solver, such as IBM ILOG CPLEX [36]. Nevertheless, even instances of DVB-MILP of moderate size may result very challenging to be optimally solved even by a state-of-the-art solver like CPLEX. This is especially due to the presence of the fading and big-M coefficients in the SIR constraints.

In order to overcome such unsatisfying performance of commercial solvers, we propose to adopt a metaheuristic that first executes a *probabilistic fixing procedure*, guided by the solution of suitable linear relaxations of the design problem, and then executes an MILP heuristic, based on an *exact very large neighborhood search*. The probabilistic fixing is partially inspired by the algorithm ANTS (*Approximate Nondeterministic Tree Search*) [37] an improved ant colony algorithm that aims at exploiting the information about bounds available for the specific optimization problem. In particular, we follow the principle of using suitable linear relaxations of the problem at hand, instead of generic bounds, that has been originally proposed in the works [38–40] and extended in further works such as [41].

Ant Colony Optimization (ACO) is a metaheuristic inspired by the behaviour of ants, which has been initially proposed in [42] and then been object of uncountable further studies and applications (e.g., [37,43–47] - see also [48,49] for an overview). The essential pseudocode of an ACO algorithm (ACO-alg) is presented in Algorithm 1.

Algorithm 1. General ACO Algorithm (ACO-alg)

1: **while** an arrest condition is *not* satisfied **do**
2:     ant-based solution construction
3:     pheromone trail update
4: **end while**
5: local search

In an ACO, a number of *ants* are defined and each ant iteratively builds a feasible solution until an arrest condition, such as a time limit, is met. At every iteration, the ant is in a *state* that corresponds to a *partial solution* for the optimization problem and can execute a *move* to further complete the partial solution. The move consists of fixing the value of a decision variable that is still not fixed and such variable is probabilistically chosen, using a formula that mixes an *a-priori* and an *a-posteriori* measure of fixing attractiveness. The a-priori attractiveness measure is called *pheromone trail value* in an ACO-alg context and is updated at the end of the construction phase: the updates aim at penalizing variable fixing of bad quality and rewarding good quality fixing. When the arrest condition is reached, it is common to execute a local search in order to bring the current best solution to a locally optimal solution.

In this work, we emphasize that we do not propose an ACO-alg, but we propose a metaheuristic that can be in some sense seen as a stronger and improved version of the ANTS algorithm, based on the principles formalized in the works [38–40], which heavily exploit the valuable information coming from suitable linear relaxations of the problem. Specifically, in our case, the a-priori measure is given by a strengthened linear relaxation of the problem (we use the model DVB-01 strengthened by adding the inequalities (7)), while the a-posteriori measure is given by the linear relaxation of DVB-MILP including the partial fixing of power variables. The essential structure of our algorithm can be thus stated as in Algorithm 2.

Algorithm 2. General metaheuristic (META)

1: **while** a time limit is not reached **do**
2:      linear relaxation-based probabilistic variable fixing
3:      variable fixing measures update
4: **end while**
5: MILP improvement heuristic

We now describe in detail the new metaheuristic for DVB-T2 network design.

3.1   Feasible Solution Construction

Before describing how the solution construction work, we make some preliminary considerations. The model DVB-01 employs 2 types of variables: (1) binary power variables z_{bl}; (2) binary service assignment variables x_{ts}. Once that the power variables are fixed, it is easy to check which SIR constraints (5) are satisfied and thus which service assignment variables x_{ts} can be set to 1 contributing to increase the value of the objective function. As a consequence, in the solution construction phase we can just limit the attention to power variables and we introduce the concepts of power state.

Definition 1. *Power state (PS): A* power state *represents the activation of a subset of DSs on some power level* $l \in L$ *and excludes that the same DS is activated on two power levels. Formally:* $PS \subseteq S \times L : \nexists (s_1, l_1), (s_2, l_2) \in PS : s_1 = s_2$.

We say that a power state PS is *complete* when it specifies the power configuration of every DS in S (i.e., $|PS| = |S|$). Otherwise the PS is said *partial* and such that $|PS| < |S|$. Furthermore, for a given power state PS, we denote by $S(PS)$ the subset of DSs whose power is fixed in PS (we call such DSs *configured*), i.e. $S(PS) = \{s \in S : \exists (s, l) \in PS\}$.

In order to reach a complete power state, a sequence of partial power states is defined. Specifically, the execution of a move brings from a partial power state PS_i to a new partial power state PS_j such that:

$$PS_j = PS_i \cup \{(s, l)\} \quad \text{with } (s, l) \in S \times L : s \notin S(PS_i).$$

We remark that, by definition of power state, the added couple (s, l) may not contain a DS whose power is already fixed in a previous power state. Every move adds one new element to the partial solution. Once that the construction phase ends, the value of the decision variables z_{sl} is completely specified and, as previously explained, we can deduce the value of the variables x, therefore defining a complete feasible solution (x, z) for the model DVB-01.

Given a *partial*, the probability π_{sl} of operating an additional move/fixing $(s, l) \notin PS$ is established through the formula [37,39,40]:

$$\pi_{sl} = \frac{\alpha \, \tau_{sl} + (1 - \alpha) \, \eta_{sl}}{\sum_{(\sigma\lambda) \notin PS} \alpha \, \tau_{\sigma\lambda} + (1 - \alpha) \, \eta_{\sigma\lambda}} , \tag{8}$$

which combines the a-priori attractiveness measure τ_{sl} with the a-posteriori attractiveness measure η_{sl} through a coefficient $\alpha \in [0, 1]$. In our case, τ_{sl} is given by the optimal value of the linear relaxation DVB-01 including the strengthening inequalities (7), while η_{sl} is the value of the linear relaxation of DVB-MILP with included the variable fixing associated with the current partial power state.

At the end of a solution construction phase, we update the a-priori measures τ on the basis of the quality of fixing, adopting a formula proposed in [18] partially based on that originally proposed in ANTS [37]. To define the formula, we first introduce the concept of *optimality gap* (*OGap*): given a feasible solution of value V and a lower bound B that is available on the optimal value V^* of the problem (note that it must hold $B \leq V^* \leq V$): the *OGap* allows to evaluate the quality of the feasible solution and is defined as $OGap(V, B) = (V - B)/V$. The a-priori attractiveness measure that we use is:

$$\tau_{sl}(h) = \tau_{sl}(h - 1) + \sum_{\text{SOL}=1}^{\Sigma} \Delta\tau_{sl}^{\text{SOL}}$$

$$\text{with } \Delta\tau_{sl}^{\text{SOL}} = \tau_{sl}(0) \cdot \left(\frac{OGap(\bar{V}, L) - OGap(V_{\text{SOL}}, B)}{OGap(\bar{V}, B)} \right) \tag{9}$$

where $\tau_{sl}(h)$ is the a-priori attractiveness of fixing (s, l) at fixing iteration h, B is a lower bound for the optimal value of the problem (in our case we use as lower bound the strengthened formulation DVB-01 with included the inequalities (7)), V_{SOL} is the value of the SOL-th feasible solution built in the last construction cycle and $\bar{V}$ is the (moving) average of the values of the Σ solutions produced in the previous construction phase. $\Delta\tau_{sl}^{\text{SOL}}$ is the reward/penalization factor for a fixing and depends upon the initialization value $\tau_{sl}(0)$ of τ (in our case, based upon the linear relaxation of DVB-01), combined with the relative variation in the optimality gap that V_{SOL} implies with respect to $\bar{V}$.

3.2   MILP Improvement Heuristic

Given a feasible solution defined in the construction phase, we operate a search for better solutions by adopting an MILP heuristic that executes a very large neighborhood search *exactly*, by formulating the search as a mixed integer linear programming problem that is solved through an MILP solver [49]. More formally, given a feasible solution $(\bar{x}, \bar{z})$ to the problem DVB-01, we define the neighborhood by allowing to switch the binary value of at most $U > 0$ power variables $\bar{z}$ and allowing all the other variables to vary freely. Expressing such condition can be done by introducing the following hamming distance constraint to DVB-01:

$$\sum_{(s,l):\bar{z}_{sl}=0} z_{sl} + \sum_{(s,l):\bar{z}_{sl}=1} (1 - z_{sl}) \leq U$$

The modified problem is then solved through an MILP solver like CPLEX, running with a time limit.

3.3 The Complete Algorithm

The complete algorithm for solving the model DVB-01 is presented in Algorithm 3. We base the algorithm on the execution of two nested loops: the outer loop runs until a global time limit is reached and contains an inner loop inside which has the task of building Σ feasible solutions. In more detail, the first task of the algorithm is to solve the linear relaxation of DVB-01 strengthened by (7) for the possible fixings of the power variables z_{sl}, obtaining the corresponding optimal value and using it to initialize the a-priori measure of attractiveness $\tau_{sl}(0)$. This is followed by the definition of a solution (x^*, z^*) that represents the best solution found during the execution of the algorithm. Each run of the inner loop is aimed at deriving a complete power state that is then used as basis to check which SIR constraints are satisfied. At the end of the inner loop, the a-priori measures τ are updated according to formula (9), considering the quality of the produced solutions, and the global best solution (x^*, z^*) is updated, if necessary. After having reached the global time limit, the MILP improvement heuristic is executed with the aim of improving the best solution found (x^*, z^*).

4   Computational Tests

We tested the performance of our metaheuristic on 20 instances that refer to realistic DVB regional networks potentially deployable in Italy. The network represented in an instance is constituted by a set of DVB stations that broadcast the same telecommunication service in a synchronized way using the same frequency in a given territory. Each station can emit at a power that lies in the range $[-40, 26]$ dBkW. The experiments were performed on a 2.70 GHz Windows machine equipped with 8 GB of RAM and adopting IBM ILOG CPLEX 12.5 as MIP solver. The code implementing the optimization model and the solution algorithm was written in C/C++ and interacts with CPLEX through Concert Technology.

A global time limit of 3600 seconds was adopted for solving each instance. In the case of the metaheuristic, the available time budget is distributed in this way: the construction phase loop is associated with a time limit of 3000 s, whereas

---

Algorithm 3. - Metaheuristic for DVB-01

1: compute the linear relaxation of DVB-01 for all $z_{sl} = 1$ and initialize the values $\tau_{sl}(0)$ with the corresponding optimal values
2: let (x^*, z^*) be the best feasible solution found
3: **while** a global time limit is not reached **do**
4:     let (x^B, z^B) be the best solution found in the inner loop
5:     **for** $SOL := 1$ to Σ **do**
6:         build a complete power state PS
7:         check the SIR constraints satisfied by PS
8:         derive a feasible solution $(\bar{x}, \bar{z})$
9:         **if** the coverage granted by $(\bar{x}, \bar{z})$ is better than that of (x^B, z^B) **then**
10:             update the best solution found $(x^B, z^B) := (\bar{x}, \bar{z})$
11:         **end if**
12:     **end for**
13:     update τ according to (9)
14:     **if** the coverage granted by (x^B, z^B) is better than that of (x^*, z^*) **then**
15:         update the best solution found $(x^*, z^*) := (x^B, z^B)$
16:     **end if**
17: **end while**
18: run the MILP improvement heuristic for (x^*, z^*)
19: return (x^*, z^*)

---

the MILP-based improvement phase is associated with a time limit of 600 s. For the metaheuristic parameter setting, we impose $\alpha = 0.5$ (i.e., we balance the a-priori and a-posteriori attractiveness measure) and $\Sigma = 5$. The results of the computational tests are presented in Table 1, where: ID identifies the instance; *COV-CPLEX%*, *COV-Meta% (best)* and *COV-Meta% (avg)* are the percentage of population covered by the best solution found by CPLEX, by the best solution found by the metaheuristic and by the metaheuris-tic on average within the time limit, respectively; $\Delta COV\%$ *(best)* and $\Delta COV\%(avg)$ are the percentage increase in population coverage that the metaheuristic grants with respect to CPLEX in the best case and on average, respectively.

Concerning the results of the computational tests, it is clear that in all cases the coverage granted by CPLEX is sensibly lower than that granted by the meta-heuristic on average, lying in the range between 52 and 75% (in contrast, the metaheuristic offers a coverage between 56 and 86%). The better performance of the metaheuristic is more evident when looking at the best solutions found, which offer a percentage coverage between 63 and almost 89%. The percentage increase in coverage is equal to 15.1% on average and, for the best cases, increases to the very remarkable value of 21.8%. The performance of the meta-heuristic is particularly good in the case of instances like I11 and I16, which almost reach the remarkable coverage of 90%. We note that the improvement in the value of solutions that we get are very significative, since in region-wide network instances improving a solution even by a small percentage can lead to an additional coverage of population of the order of thousands of people, thus being practically very attractive for the planning of television service broadcasters.

Table 1. Experimental results

ID	COV-CPLEX%	COV-Meta% (avg)	ΔCOV% (avg)	COV-Meta% (best)	ΔCOV% (best)
I1	53.3	61.0	14.5	63.2	18.6
I2	62.9	74.3	18.16	77.1	22.7
I3	57.4	69.3	20.8	73.5	28.2
I4	71.6	81.1	13.2	85.2	19.0
I5	66.5	78.6	18.2	83.8	26.1
I6	51.1	61.0	19.3	63.7	24.8
I7	54.1	60.4	11.6	63.2	19.5
I8	63.8	67.4	5.6	64.6	13.4
I9	68.2	79.3	16.3	72.3	20.3
I10	66.0	78.7	19.2	82.0	29.0
I11	74.4	83.0	11.5	85.1	17.8
I12	52.0	56.3	8.2	87.6	15.6
I13	60.6	69.0	13.8	60.1	19.4
I14	59.4	68.6	15.5	72.3	20.2
I15	56.8	70,3	23.7	71.3	27.8
I16	74.7	85.5	14.4	72.5	18.4
I17	67.3	80.2	19.2	88.4	27.0
I18	63.5	71.5	12.6	85.4	23.5
I19	64.8	75.6	16.6	82.1	26.8
I20	58.0	63.6	9.7	67.8	16.9

5   Conclusion and Future Work

In this paper, we have derived an optimization model for the design of digital television broadcasting networks adopting the second generation of DVB-T standard, i.e. the DVB-T2. Since even a state-of-the-art optimization solver may have difficulties in finding good quality solutions for real-sized instances, due to the presence of complicating wireless coverage signal-to-interference constraints, we have proposed a metaheuristic that combines a probabilistic variable fixing procedure with an exact large neighborhood search formulated as a Mixed Integer Linear Programming problem. Computational tests on realistic instances show that the metaheuristic is able to identify solutions that guarantee a much larger service coverage than those identified by a state-of-the-art optimization solver.

As future work, we plan to further strengthen the performance of the solution algorithm by considering the integration with other heuristic (specifically, cutting plane methods exploiting conflicts between variables, similarly to [50], and sequential heuristics as in [51])). Furthermore, we plan to consider variants of the problem including multiple objectives, taking into account trade-off between user coverage and power consumption, in a way similar to [52]. Last but not least, we plan to address the uncertainty of signal propagation and system capacity, by adopting Multiband Robust Optimization [25,53] and robust cutting plane methods [54].

References

1. Shojafar, M., Javanmardi, S., Abolfazli, S., Cordeschi, N.: Fuge: a joint meta-heuristic approach to cloud job scheduling algorithm using fuzzy theory and a genetic method. Cluster Comput. **18**(2), 829–844 (2015)
2. Shojafar, M., Chiaraviglio, L., Blefari-Melazzi, N., Salsano, S.: P5G: A bio-inspired algorithm for the superfluid management of 5G Networks. In: Proceedings of IEEE GLOBECOM 2017, pp. 1–6. IEEE (2017)
3. Tsai, C.W., Cho, H.H., Shih, T.K., Pan, J.S., Rodrigues, J.J.P.C.: Metaheuristics for the deployment of 5G. IEEE Wirel. Commun. **22**(6), 40–46 (2015)
4. DVB Project: DVB-T. https://www.dvb.org/standards/dvb-t
5. DVB Project: DVB-T2. https://www.dvb.org/standards/dvb-t2
6. D'Andreagiovanni, F., Mannino, C., Sassano, A.: Negative cycle separation in wire-less network design. In: Pahl, J., Reiners, T., Voß, S. (eds.) INOC 2011. LNCS, vol. 6701, pp. 51–56. Springer, Heidelberg (2011). https://doi.org/10.1007/978-3-642-21527-8_7
7. D'Andreagiovanni, F., Mannino, C., Sassano, A.: GUB covers and power-indexed formulations for wireless network design. Manage. Sci. **59**, 142–156 (2013)
8. Mannino, C., Rossi, F., Smriglio, S.: The network packing problem in terrestrial broadcasting. Oper. Res. **54**, 611–626 (2006)
9. Anedda, M., Morgade, J., Murroni, M., Angueira, P., Arrinda, A., Prez, J.R., Basterrechea, J.: Heuristic optimization of DVB-T/H SFN coverage using PSO and SA algorithms. In: 2011 IEEE International Symposium on Broadband Multimedia Systems and Broadcasting (BMSB), pp. 1–5 (2011)
10. Koutitas, G.: Green network planning of single frequency networks. IEEE Trans. Broadcast. **56**, 541–550 (2010)
11. Lanza, M., Gutierrez, A., Perez, J., Morgade, J., Domingo, M., Valle, L., Angueira, P., Basterrechea, J.: Coverage optimization and power reduction in SFN using simulated annealing. IEEE Trans. Broadcast. **60**, 474–485 (2014)
12. Italian Authority for Telecommunications (AGCOM). Specifications for a DVB-T planning software tool (in Italian). http://www.agcom.it/Default.aspx?message=downloaddocument&DocID=3365
13. Chester 1997 Multilateral Coordination Agreement. Technical criteria, coor-dination principles and procedures for the introduction of terrestrial digi-tal video broadcasting (1997). http://www.archive.ero.dk/132D67A4-8815-48CB-B482-903844887DE3?frames=no&5
14. Martinez, G., Sanchez, J., Barquero, D., Cardona, N.: Optimization of the digital terrestrial television transmission mode of DVB-T2 in Colombia. IEEE Lat. Am. Trans. **13**(7), 2144–2151 (2015)
15. Kang, M., Chung, Y.: An efficient energy saving scheme for base stations in 5G networks with separated data and control planes using particle swarm optimization. Energies **10**, 1417 (2017)
16. Marotta, A., D'Andreagiovanni, F., Kassler, A., Zola, E.: On the energy cost of robustness for green virtual network function placement in 5G virtualized infras-tructures. Comput. Netw. **125**, 64–75 (2017)

17. Marotta, A., Zola, E., D'Andreagiovanni, F., Kassler, A.: A fast robust approach for green virtual network functions deployment. J. Netw. Comput. Appl. **95**, 42–53 (2017)
18. D'Andreagiovanni, F., Mett, F., Nardin, A., Pulaj, J.: Integrating LP-guided variable fixing with MIP heuristics in the robust design of hybrid wired-wireless FTTx access networks. Appl. Soft Comput. **61**, 1074–1087 (2017)
19. Amaldi, E., Capone, A., Malucelli, F., Signori, F.: UMTS radio planning: optimizing base station configuration. In: Proceedings IEEE 56th Vehicular Technology Conference, vol. 2, pp. 768–772 (2002)
20. Amaldi, E., Belotti, P., Capone, A., Malucelli, F.: Optimizing base station location and configuration in UMTS networks. Ann. Oper. Res. **146**, 135–151 (2006)
21. Andrews, J., Ghosh, A., Muhamed, R.: Fundamentals of WiMAX. Prentice Hall, Upper Saddle River (2007)
22. D'Andreagiovanni, F.: Pure 0–1 programming approaches to wireless network design. 4OR-Q. J. Oper. Res. (2012)
23. D'Andreagiovanni, F., Garroppo, R., Scutell, M.: Power savings with data rate guarantee in dense WLANs. In: 2017 International Conference on Selected Topics in Mobile and Wireless Networking (MoWNet) (2017)
24. Gendron, B., Scutellà, M., Garroppo, R., Nencioni, G., Tavanti, L.: A branch-and-benders-cut method for nonlinear power design in green wireless local area networks. Eur. J. Oper. Res. **255**, 151–162 (2016)
25. Büsing, C., D'Andreagiovanni, F.: New results about multi-band uncertainty in robust optimization. In: Klasing, R. (ed.) SEA 2012. LNCS, vol. 7276, pp. 63–74. Springer, Heidelberg (2012). https://doi.org/10.1007/978-3-642-30850-5_7
26. Capone, A., Chen, L., Gualandi, S., Yuan, D.: A new computational approach for maximum link activation in wireless networks under the SINR model. IEEE Trans. Wirel. Commun. **10**, 1368–1372 (2011)
27. D'Andreagiovanni, F.: Revisiting wireless network jamming by SIR-based considerations and multiband robust optimization. Optim. Lett. **9**, 1495–1510 (2015)
28. Kalvenes, J., Kennington, J., Olinick, E.: Base station location and service assignments in W-CDMA networks. INFORMS J. Comput. **18**, 366–376 (2006)
29. Kennington, J., Olinick, E., Rajan, D.: Wireless Network Design: Optimization Models and Solution Procedures. Springer, Heidelberg (2010). https://doi.org/10.1007/978-1-4419-6111-2
30. Resende, M., Pardalos, P.: Handbook of Optimization in Telecommunications. Springer, Heidelberg (2006). https://doi.org/10.1007/978-0-387-30165-5
31. Ligeti, A., Zander, J.: Minimal cost coverage planning for single frequency networks. IEEE Trans. Broadcast. **45**(1), 78–87 (1999)
32. Rappaport, T.: Wireless Communications: Principles and Practices. Prentice Hall, Upper Saddle River (2001)
33. D'Andreagiovanni, F., Gleixner, A.M.: Towards an accurate solution of wireless network design problems. In: Cerulli, R., Fujishige, S., Mahjoub, A.R. (eds.) ISCO 2016. LNCS, vol. 9849, pp. 135–147. Springer, Cham (2016). https://doi.org/10.1007/978-3-319-45587-7_12
34. Nehmauser, G., Wolsey, L.: Integer and Combinatorial Optimization. John Wiley & Sons, Hoboken (1988)
35. Wolsey, L.: Valid inequalities for 0–1 knapsacks and mips with generalised upper bound constraints. Discrete Appl. Math. **29**(2–3), 251–261 (1990)
36. IBM ILOG CPLEX. http://www-01.ibm.com/software
37. Maniezzo, V.: Exact and approximate nondeterministic tree-search procedures for the quadratic assignment problem. INFORMS J. Comput. **11**, 358–369 (1999)

38. D'Andreagiovanni, F., Krolikowski, J., Pulaj, J.: A hybrid primal heuristic for robust multiperiod network design. In: Esparcia-Alcázar, A.I., Mora, A.M. (eds.) EvoApplications 2014. LNCS, vol. 8602, pp. 15–26. Springer, Heidelberg (2014). https://doi.org/10.1007/978-3-662-45523-4_2
39. D'Andreagiovanni, F., Krolikowski, J., Pulaj, J.: A fast hybrid primal heuristic for multiband robust capacitated network design with multiple time periods. Appl. Soft Comput. **26**, 497–507 (2015)
40. D'Andreagiovanni, F., Nardin, A.: Towards the fast and robust optimal design of wireless body area networks. Appl. Soft Comput. **37**, 971–982 (2015)
41. D'Andreagiovanni, F., Nardin, A., Natalizio, E.: A fast ILP-based heuristic for the robust design of body wireless sensor networks. In: Squillero, G., Sim, K. (eds.) EvoApplications 2017. LNCS, vol. 10199, pp. 234–250. Springer, Cham (2017). https://doi.org/10.1007/978-3-319-55849-3_16
42. Dorigo, M., Maniezzo, V., Colorni, A.: Ant system: Optimization by a colony of cooperating agents. IEEE Trans. Syst. Man Cybern. B **26**, 29–41 (1996)
43. Dorigo, M., Di Caro, G., Gambardella, L.: Ant algorithms for discrete optimization. Artif. Life **5**, 137–172 (1999)
44. Gambardella, L.M., Montemanni, R., Weyland, D.: Coupling ant colony systems with strong local searches. Eur. J. Oper. Res. **220**, 831–843 (2012)
45. Olivas, F., Valdez, F., Castillo, O., Gonzalez, C.I., Martinez, G., Melin, P.: Ant colony optimization with dynamic parameter adaptation based on interval type-2 fuzzy logic systems. Appl. Soft Comput. **53**, 74–87 (2017)
46. Perez-Carabaza, S., Besada-Portas, E., Lopez-Orozco, J.A., de la Cruz, J.M.: Ant colony optimization for multi-UAV minimum time search in uncertain domains. Appl. Soft Comput. **62**, 789–806 (2018)
47. Sun, Y., Dong, W., Chen, Y.: An improved routing algorithm based on ant colony optimization in wireless sensor networks. IEEE Commun. Lett. **21**(6), 1317–1320 (2017)
48. Blum, C.: Ant colony optimization: introduction and recent trends. Phys. Life Rev. **2**, 353–373 (2005)
49. Blum, C., Puchinger, J., Raidl, G., Roli, A.: Hybrid metaheuristics in combinatorial optimization: a survey. Appl. Soft. Comput. **11**, 41354151 (2011)
50. Bley, A., D'Andreagiovanni, F., Karch, D.: WDM fiber replacement scheduling. Electron. Notes Discrete Math. **41**, 189–196 (2013)
51. Dely, P., D'Andreagiovanni, F., Kassler, A.: Fair optimization of mesh-connected WLAN hotspots. Wirel. Commun. Mob. Comput. **15**, 924–946 (2015)
52. Zakrzewska, A., D'Andreagiovanni, F., Ruepp, S., Berger, M.: Biobjective optimization of radio access technology selection and resource allocation in heterogeneous wireless networks. In: 11th International Symposium on Modeling & Optimization in Mobile, Ad Hoc & Wireless Networks (WiOpt), 2013, pp. 652–658. IEEE (2013)
53. Bauschert, T., Büsing, C., D'Andreagiovanni, F., Koster, A.M.C.A., Kutschka, M., Steglich, U.: Network planning under demand uncertainty with robust optimization. IEEE Commun. Mag. **52**, 178–185 (2014)
54. D'Andreagiovanni, F., Nace, D., Pioro, M., Poss, M., Shehaj, M., Tomaszewski, A.: On robust FSO network dimensioning. In: 2017 9th International Workshop on Resilient Networks Design and Modeling (RNDM), pp. 1–8 (2017)

EvoCOMPLEX

A Genetic Algorithm for Community Detection in Attributed Graphs

Clara Pizzuti$^{(\boxtimes)}$ and Annalisa Socievole

Institute for High Performance Computing and Networking (ICAR),
National Research Council of Italy (CNR), via P. Bucci 7/11C,
87036 Rende, CS, Italy
{clara.pizzuti,annalisa.socievole}@icar.cnr.it

Abstract. A genetic algorithm for detecting a community structure in attributed graphs is proposed. The method optimizes a fitness function that combines node similarity and structural connectivity. The communities obtained by the method are composed by nodes having both similar attributes and high link density. Experiments on synthetic networks and a comparison with five state-of-the-art methods show that the genetic approach is very competitive and obtains network divisions more accurate than those obtained by the considered methods.

Keywords: Attributed networks · Community detection
Genetic Algorithms · Complex networks

1 Introduction

Complex networks constitute one of the main formalisms to model and study relationships of real-world systems. Networks have been mainly studied at the level of interactions among nodes, i.e. with respect to their structure. However, nodes are often endowed with a set of characteristics [1] such as work, gender, hobbies, age, and race. In online social networks, for example, people publish data regarding their personal profile, thus providing important information for analyzing relationships and properties of the social systems they participate. *Attributed graphs* extend network models by enriching nodes and/or edges with a set of features that measure the characteristics of the actors and/or the strength or type of links. As pointed out in [2], when attributes are related to nodes, attributed graphs are referred to as *node-attributed graphs*, while when related to edges, they are called *edge-attributed graph*. In this paper, we deal only with node-attributed graphs.

Because of the wealth of data available on social networks, the simultaneous analysis of the topological structure and the characteristics of the objects composing a network has received, in the last years, the interest of researchers for finding communities in complex networks. In fact, it has been observed that in real-world social systems there exists a correlation between attribute values

K. Sim and P. Kaufmann (Eds.): EvoApplications 2018, LNCS 10784, pp. 159–170, 2018.
https://doi.org/10.1007/978-3-319-77538-8_12

and connectivity [3], and that the *homophily* effect, for which individuals are more likely to create relationships with others having similar attribute values, and the *social influence* effect, for which people tend to modify their behavior to be akin to their friends, often co-occur. Thus, the utilization of the information coming from both attributes and links can be beneficial to methods for community detection to obtain groups of nodes not only densely connected, but also having similar characteristics.

In the last year, several methods for detecting communities in attributed graphs have been proposed. A recent survey of Bothorel et al. [2] gives a detailed description of the most recent state-of-the-art algorithms. Approaches to find communities in attributed graphs, according to Bothorel et al. [2], can be classified into different categories, depending on the strategy adopted. One category uses a function to compute the similarity between couples of nodes, and then reduces the network to a weighted graph. At this point any community detection method for weighted graphs can be used. Neville et al. [4], for instance, define a similarity measure that computes the number of attribute values two nodes have in common. They compare three existing graph-partitioning techniques and show that a spectral clustering approach outperforms the others. The main drawback of these methods is that the number of groups to obtain must be given as input parameter. Cruz et al. [5] obtain the node similarity by grouping nodes with a self-organizing map [6] that takes into account the similarity between the features. The Louvain method [7] is then used to find the communities of the weighted graph. Another category of approaches combines structural and attribute similarity, and applies clustering methods to nodes with the combined similarity. Combe et al. [8] define a distance measure between two nodes as the sum of the attribute distance, computed for the features with any measure such as the Euclidean or the cosine distance, and a structural distance given by the shortest path between such nodes. A hierarchical agglomerative clustering is then applied on the computed distance matrix. The *unified distance measure* proposed by Papadopoulos et al. [9], extensively described in the next, follows the same principle. The authors formalize the problem as an optimization fuzzy clustering problem with an objective function that assigns different weights to edges and attributes, computed iteratively with the gradient descent technique during the clustering process. Dang and Viennet [10] extend the modularity concept [11] to include the similarity between node attributes. Zhou et al. [12] builds an attribute augmented graph by adding to the initial graph new vertices representing the attributes. Elhadi and Agam [13] propose an algorithm that uses either the structure data, or the attribute data depending on the type of graph, and then executes the *Louvain* method in the former case, and the *k-means* in the latter case.

In this paper, we propose a method for clustering attributed graphs, named @NetGA, based on *Genetic Algorithms (GAs)*, that optimizes a fitness function derived from the *unified distance measure* of Papadopoulos et al. [9], combining node similarity and structural connectivity. The communities obtained by the method are composed by nodes having both similar attributes and high link density. Experiments on synthetic networks and a comparison with five state-of-the-art methods show that the genetic approach is very competitive and obtains network divisions more accurate than those obtained by the considered methods. The paper is organized as follows. In the next section we give preliminary definitions. In Sect. 3 the fitness function is introduced and the algorithm @NetGA is described in detail. Section 4 describes the synthetic networks used for evaluating the methods, the algorithms with which @NetGA has been compared, the evaluation measures adopted to perform the comparison, and the results obtained by all the methods. Section 5, finally, concludes the paper and discusses future developments.

2   Problem Definition

In this section we give the definition of attributed graph and the community detection problem for these kind of graphs.

Definition. An *attributed graph* is a 4-tuple $G = (V, E, A, F)$ where $V = \{v_1, v_2, ..., v_N\}$ is a set of N vertices, $E \subseteq V \times V$ is a set of M edges, $A = \{\alpha_1, \alpha_2, ..., \alpha_A\}$ is the set of numerical and categorical attributes (features), and $F = \{a_1, a_2, ..., a_A\}$ is a set of functions. Each node $v \in V$ is characterized by a vector of feature values, obtained by the functions $a_\alpha : V \to D_\alpha, 1 \le \alpha \le A$, with D_α the domain of attribute α.

The objective of community detection in attributed graphs is to find a partition $\mathcal{C} = \{C_1, \ldots, C_k\}$ of the nodes of V such that

- intra-cluster density is high and inter-cluster density is low, and
- nodes belonging to the same community are similar, while nodes of different communities are quite dissimilar.

3   @NetGA Description

The *GA* method we propose minimizes a fitness function based on the *unified distance measure*, introduced by Papadopoulos et al. [9], that takes into account both the graph structure and the attributes. We first recall the definition of this distance measure and then we define our fitness function. Given an attributed graph $G(V, E, A, F)$, the *similar connectivity* measures how dissimilar two vertices are with respect to all their outgoing edges as:

$$SC(i,j) = \frac{1}{N} \sum_{k=1}^{N} [w(i,k) - w(j,k)]^2 \tag{1}$$

where

$$w(i,j) = \begin{cases} 1 & if \ (i = j) \ or \ (i,j) \in E \\ 0 & otherwise \end{cases} \tag{2}$$

The *attribute distance* between two nodes measures their dissimilarity with respect to their attribute values. It is computed as:

$$AD(i,j) = \sum_{\alpha \in A} W_\alpha \cdot \delta_\alpha(i,j), \quad \sum_{\alpha \in A} W_\alpha = 1 \qquad (3)$$

where W_α is a weight corresponding to the importance of attribute α, and $\delta_\alpha(i,j)$ is the attribute distance between nodes i and j for attribute α. For numerical attributes scaled in the interval $[0, 1]$, $\delta_\alpha(i,j) = [a_\alpha(i) - a_\alpha(j)]^2$, while, for the categorical attributes

$$\delta_\alpha(i,j) = \begin{cases} 1 & if \quad a_\alpha(i) = a_\alpha(j) \\ 0 & otherwise \end{cases}. \qquad (4)$$

The *unified distance measure (udm)* balances with appropriates weights the structural and attribute properties by combining *attribute distance* (AD) and *similar connectivity* (SC) between two nodes i and j as follows

$$d(i,j) = W_{attr} \cdot AD(i,j) + W_{links} \cdot SC(i,j) \qquad (5)$$

where W_{attr} and W_{links} are weights representing the importance of attributes and edges, respectively.

Given a network division $\mathcal{C} = \{C_1, \ldots, C_k\}$, we define the *clustering unified distance measure* $cudm(\mathcal{C})$ of the solution $\mathcal{C}$ by computing for each $C_i \in \mathcal{C}$, $1 \le i \le k$, the *udm* of pairs of nodes belonging to C_i, and then averaging the results with respect to the number k of obtained communities:

$$cudm(\mathcal{C}) = \frac{1}{k} \sum_{C \in \mathcal{C}} \sum_{\{i,j\} \in C \ i \neq j} d(i,j) \qquad (6)$$

where k is the number of communities of the solution $\mathcal{C}$, i and j are nodes of a community $C \in \mathcal{C}$ and $d(i,j)$ is the *unified distance measure* between nodes i and j.

The @NetGA method, thus, minimizes the *cumd* measure to obtain a community division that takes into account both the similarity of node features, as well the connections shared by pairs of nodes inside the network structure. Together with the *cumd* as fitness function, @NetGA uses the locus-based adjacency representation [14], uniform crossover and neighbor-based mutation. In the locus-based representation, an individual of the population is represented through a vector of n genes assuming values in the range $\{1, \ldots, n\}$. A value j assigned to the ith gene means that there is a link between the nodes i and j. A decoding step identifies the connected components of the graph corresponding to the network division in communities. Uniform crossover generates a random binary vector of length N, then an offspring is obtained by selecting from the first parent the genes where the value is 0, and from the second parent the genes where the value is 1. Finally, the neighbor-based mutation operator randomly changes the value j of a i-th gene with one of its neighbors.

@NetGA receives in input the graph $G = (V, E, A, F)$, the weighting factors W_{attr} and W_{links} to assign a score to attributes and links, respectively, an importance weight to each attribute W_α, and performs the following steps:

1. run the Genetic Algorithm on G for a number of iterations by using *cumd* as fitness function to minimize, uniform crossover and neighbor mutation as variation operators;
2. obtain the partition $\mathcal{C} = \{C_1, \ldots, C_k\}$ corresponding to the solution with the lowest fitness value $cumd(\mathcal{C})$;
3. merge two communities if the number of inter-cluster connections is higher than the number of intra-cluster connections.

In the next section, we execute @NetGA on a number of synthetic networks and compare it with other state-of-the-art methods.

4   Experimental Evaluation

To validate the effectiveness of @NetGA, we performed several simulations on synthetic networks and compared the results with those obtained by other five methods. The algorithm has been implemented in Matlab 2015b by using the Global Optimization Toolbox. Since finding a balanced weight for attributes and links is not our aim, differently from Papadopoluos et al. [9], for each simulation, we fixed equal weight to attributes and links, thus setting $W_{attr} = W_{links} = 0.5$, and also $W_\alpha = 1/\mathcal{A}, \forall \alpha$. In the following, we describe the synthetic datasets used, the contestant algorithms, the evaluation measures employed to assess the quality of the methods, and the results obtained.

4.1   Datasets

We generated a set of synthetic datasets using the *LFR-EA* benchmark proposed by Elhadi and Agam [13], which is an extension of the *LFR* benchmark by Lancichinetti *et al.* [15].

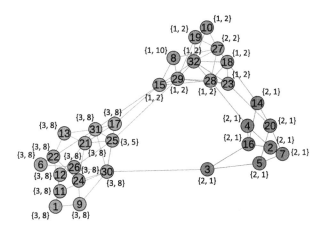

Fig. 1. Network structure and ground truth for the LFR-EA-32 dataset with $\mu = 0.1$ and $\nu = 0.1$: the 32 nodes are partitioned into 3 distinct communities.

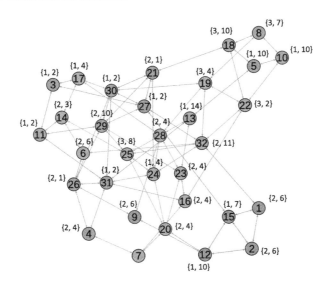

Fig. 2. Network structure and ground truth for the LFR-EA-32 dataset with $\mu = 0.3$ and $\nu = 0.5$: the 32 nodes are partitioned into 4 distinct communities.

The generator uses two parameters μ and ν, both ranging in the interval [0.1, 0.9], to control the structure and the attribute values, respectively. μ is called *mixing parameter* and determines the rate of intra- and inter-communities connections. Low values of μ give a clear community structure where intra-cluster links are much more than inter-cluster links. Analogously for ν, called *attribute noise*, low values generate similar features of nodes belonging to the same community. Besides ν, the number of attributes and the size of the domain D_α of each attribute α must be specified. The combination of μ and ν values produces graphs with a clear to ambiguous structure and/or attributes. To better understand the kind of networks that can be generated, Figs. 1 and 2 show two examples of synthetic networks with 32 nodes. The network of Fig. 1 has both clear structure and attributes ($\mu = 0.1$ and $\nu = 0.1$), while the network of Fig. 2 has a less clear structure and attributes with medium similarity ($\mu = 0.3$ and $\nu = 0.5$).

The parameters used to generate the *LFR-EA* datasets are shown in the Table 1. We created networks with 1000 nodes (LFR-EA-1000) by setting 2 numerical attributes for each node. All the nodes in a community, in particular, share the same attribute domain values. The attribute's domain cluster assignment is set to random selection without replacing, in order to cover all the domain values across the different communities. We generated ten different instances of the combination of μ and ν parameters reported in Table 1, and executed @NetGA by fixing the population size to 300 individuals, the number of generations to 200, a mutation rate of 0.4, and a crossover fraction of 0.8. These genetic parameters have been selected with a trial-and-error procedure and choosing the values giving the best performance of the algorithm.

Table 1. LFR-EA-1000 parameters setting.

Parameter	Value
Number of nodes (N)	1000
Average degree (k)	25
Maximum degree ($maxk$)	40
Exponent for the degree distribution ($t1$)	2
Mixing parameter (μ)	$[0.1; \ldots; 0.9]$
Exponent for the community size distribution ($t2$)	1
Minimum for the community sizes ($minc$)	60
Maximum for the community sizes ($maxc$)	100
Number of overlapping nodes (on)	0
Number of memberships of the overlapping nodes (om)	0
Number of attributes (T)	2
Attribute's domain cluster assignment ($ainf$)	1
Attribute # 1 domain size	3
Attribute # 1 noise	$[0.1; 0.5; 0.9]$
Attribute # 2 domain size	15
Attribute # 2 noise	$[0.1; 0.5; 0.9]$

4.2   Algorithms in Comparison

We compared @NetGA to five types of algorithms: (1) structure-only, i.e. a classical community detection method that does not consider the attributes, (2) attribute-only, i.e. a method that uses only node similarity, (3) composite, i.e. that builds an attribute augmented graph, (4) ensemble, i.e. that combines different clustering results, and (5) selection, i.e. that decides which method to use depending on the graph. In the following, we briefly summarize these algorithms.

- **Louvain** [7] (structure-only) aims at optimizing the modularity [11] of a partition using a greedy technique. First, the method searches small communities locally optimizing modularity. Then, each community found is considered a node and modularity-based community detection is applied again until a hierarchy of high-modularity communities is obtained.
- **k-means** [16] (attribute-only) is considered one of the most famous clustering algorithms. Data points are randomly assigned to a number k of clusters. Then, the centroid of each cluster is computed and every data point is assigned to its closest centroid. These steps are repeated until there are not assignments of data points to clusters, and a stopping criterion is reached.
- **SA-Cluster** [12] (composite) builds an attribute augmented graph by adding to the initial graph new vertices representing the attributes. An edge between a graph vertex and an attribute vertex is present if the graph vertex has that

attribute and the edge weight between them reflects the importance of that attribute. The method uses the neighborhood random walk model on the attributed augmented graph to compute a unified distance measure between vertices (i.e., combination of structural closeness and attribute similarity).

- **CSPA** [13] (ensemble) is a modified version of the *Cluster-based Similarity Partitioning Algorithm* of Strehl and Gosh [17] that combines *Louvain* and the *k-means* cluster labels through a cluster ensemble. A cluster ensemble solves the clustering problem in two steps. In the first step, a data set is taken as input and an ensemble of clustering solutions is generated as output. In the second step, the cluster ensemble is taken as input and these solutions are combined to produce a single clustering as the final output. *CSPA* uses binary similarity matrices for representing the similarity between objects in the same cluster. Through these similarity matrices, *CSPA* establishes a pairwise similarity measures and realizes a combined clustering.
- **Selection** [13] (selection), instead of combining the structure and the attribute data, this method makes the choice to use either the structure data, or the attribute data depending on the type of graph (clear or ambiguous structure). It detects the boundaries between clear and ambiguous graph structure content and applies the structure-only method of *Louvain* when the graph has a clear structure, while the *k-means* attribute-only method when the graph has an ambiguous structure.

4.3   Evaluation Measures

To assess the quality of the solutions, we use the following evaluation measures.

- **Normalized Mutual Information (NMI)**. The normalized mutual information $NMI(A, B)$ [18] of two divisions A and B of a network is defined as follows. Let C be the confusion matrix whose element C_{ij} is the number of nodes of community i of the partition A that are also in the community j of the partition B.

$$NMI(A, B) = \frac{-2 \sum_{i=1}^{c_A} \sum_{j=1}^{c_B} C_{ij} log(C_{ij} n / C_{i.} C_{.j})}{\sum_{i=1}^{c_A} C_{i.} log(C_{i.}/n) + \sum_{j=1}^{c_B} C_{.j} log(C_{.j}/n)} \tag{7}$$

where c_A (c_B) is the number of groups in the partition A (B), $C_{i.}$ ($C_{.j}$) is the sum of the elements of C in row i (column j), and n is the number of nodes. If $A = B$, $NMI(A, B) = 1$. If A and B are completely different, $NMI(A, B) = 0$.
- **Cumulative NMI (CNMI)**. $CNMI$ [13] is a modified NMI measure allowing the integration of NMI values over different settings of structure mixing parameter μ and attribute noise ν:

$$CNMI = \frac{\sum^{\mu} \sum^{\nu} NMI}{S} \tag{8}$$

where S is the number of samples of the network graphs considered.

4.4   Results

Figure 3 shows the results obtained by @NetGA and the methods described in the previous section for the experiments conducted on the LFR-EA-1000 datasets. Each subplot refers to a value of the mixing parameter μ ranging from 0.1 to 0.9, with three degrees of attribute noise (0.1: low, 0.5: medium, 0.9: high) reported on the x-axis and the corresponding NMI values on the y-axis.

The *Louvain* algorithm, being a structure-only method, obtains rather stable values of the NMI, independently from the ν values. For $0.1 \leq \mu \leq 0.4$, the network graph has a clear structure and the method is able to correctly identify the underlying communities. As the mixing parameter increases, the NMI value sensibly decreases, especially for $0.7 \leq \mu \leq 0.9$. For these mixing parameter values, the normalized mutual information is below 0.2.

The NMI values returned by the *k-means* method, since using only the attributes, are not influenced from the network structure. It is able to find communities with an NMI value medium-high only when the graph attributes are clear. Differently from Louvain, the *k-means* method is not able to match the ground-truth with good NMI values. The highest value of 0.75 is reached only when the attribute noise is 0.1.

SA-Cluster performs the worse in our settings. Even if it uses both structure and attributes, it is not able to correctly identify the communities. The NMI values it obtains are between 0.5 and 0.6 for $\mu = 0.1$ and all the three ν values. It reduces below 0.2 for $\mu \geq 0.5$.

CSPA, combining *Louvain* and *k-means* through cluster ensemble, performs better than SA-Cluster. However, the low NMI values of *k-means* in medium-high attribute noise situations influence the high NMI *Louvain* values in situations of low mixing parameter. Thus, the resulting NMI value of *CSPA* sensibly decreases with the ensemble.

The *Selection* method, being driven by both attributes and structure, performs better than the previous methods. It obtains an NMI value equal to 1 for $0.1 \leq \mu \leq 0.5$ for all the attribute noise settings. When the structure of the graph becomes less clear $(0.7 \leq \mu \leq 0.9)$, it is able to properly find the boundary between clear and ambiguous graph structure content. By exploiting the attribute-based clustering through *k-means*, *Selection* obtains an NMI value around 0.75 when $\nu = 0.1$. However, for $\nu = 0.5$ and $\nu = 0.9$ these values drastically decrease below 0.3 and 0.2, respectively.

@NetGA is able to achieve very high NMI values for all the mixing parameter values. In particular, for high μ values, @NetGA outperforms all the other algorithms for all the attribute noise values considered. Moreover, as Table 2 shows, @NetGA achieves the highest $CNMI$ value, obtained by averaging the NMI values for all the attributes and structure settings, compared to the other methods considered. @NetGA, for this cumulative metric, reaches 0.98, while the *Selection* method, which is the best performing method when compared to the other attribute and structure based contestant methods, achieves only 0.77. As such, @NetGA is able to better exploit both the attributes and the structure of the graph on all the settings considered.

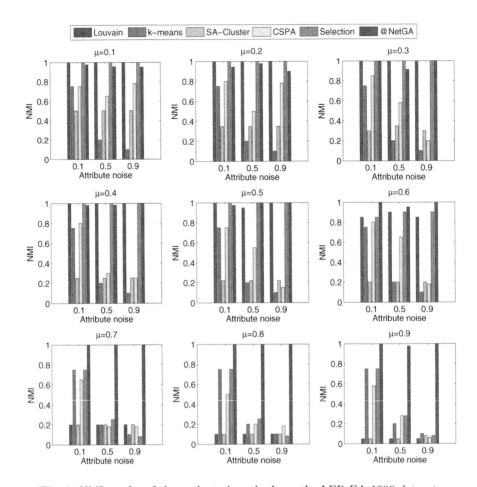

Fig. 3. NMI results of the evaluated methods on the LFR-EA-1000 datasets.

Table 2. Cumulative NMI of the methods on the LFR-EA-1000 datasets.

Method	CNMI
Louvain	0.69
k-means	0.35
SA-Cluster	0.24
CSPA	0.49
Selection	0.77
@NetGA	0.98

5   Conclusion

Genetic Algorithms, in the last years, showed to be a valid approach for the detection of community structure in complex networks. The method we proposed for attributed graphs confirms their ability also in this kind of networks, where nodes are characterized by a set of features. This additional information can be very important, combined with the topological structure, to detect relevant communities that share common characteristics. A comparison with other five methods, finding communities with different strategies, on synthetic networks has highlighted the capability of the genetic approach to obtain more accurate divisions. Future work aims at experimenting the method on real-world attributed networks.

References

1. Wasserman, S., Faust, K.: Social Network Analysis: Methods and Applications, vol. 8. Cambridge University Press, Cambridge (1994)
2. Bothorel, C., Cruz, J.D., Magnani, M., Micenkova, B.: Clustering attributed graphs: models, measures and methods. Netw. Sci. **3**(03), 408–444 (2015)
3. La Fond, T., Neville, J.: Randomization tests for distinguishing social influence and homophily effects. In: Proceedings of the 19th International Conference on World Wide Web, WWW 2010, pp. 601–610 (2010)
4. Neville, J., Adler, M., Jensen, D.: Clustering relational data using attribute and link information. In: Proceedings of the Text Mining and Link Analysis Workshop, 18th International Joint Conference on Artificial Intelligence, pp. 9–15 (2003)
5. Cruz, J.D., Bothorel, C., Poulet, F.: Semantic clustering of social networks using points of view. In: CORIA, pp. 175–182 (2011)
6. Kohonen, T., Schroeder, M.R., Huang, T.S. (eds.): Self-Organizing Maps, 3rd edn. Springer-Verlag, New York Inc., Secaucus (2001)
7. Blondel, V.D., Guillaume, J.L., Lambiotte, R., Lefebvre, E.: Fast unfolding of communities in large networks. J. Stat. Mech. Theory Exp. **2008**(10), P10008 (2008)
8. Combe, D., Largeron, C., Egyed-Zsigmond, E., Géry, M.: Combining relations and text in scientific network clustering. In: 2012 IEEE/ACM International Conference on Advances in Social Networks Analysis and Mining (ASONAM), pp. 1248–1253. IEEE (2012)
9. Papadopoulos, A., Pallis, G., Dikaiakos, M.D.: Weighted clustering of attributed multi-graphs. Computing **99**(9), 813–840 (2017)
10. Dang, T., Viennet, E.: Community detection based on structural and attribute similarities. In: International Conference on Digital Society (ICDS), pp. 7–12 (2012)
11. Newman, M.E., Girvan, M.: Finding and evaluating community structure in networks. Phys. Rev. E **69**(2), 026113 (2004)
12. Zhou, Y., Cheng, H., Yu, J.X.: Graph clustering based on structural/attribute similarities. Proc. VLDB Endow. **2**(1), 718–729 (2009)
13. Elhadi, H., Agam, G.: Structure and attributes community detection: comparative analysis of composite, ensemble and selection methods. In: Proceedings of the 7th Workshop on Social Network Mining and Analysis, p. 10. ACM (2013)

14. Park, Y., Song, M.: A genetic algorithm for clustering problems. In: Proceedings of the Third Annual Conference on Genetic Programming, vol. 1998, pp. 568–575 (1998)
15. Lancichinetti, A., Fortunato, S., Radicchi, F.: Benchmark graphs for testing community detection algorithms. Phys. Rev. E **78**(4), 046110 (2008)
16. Hartigan, J.A., Wong, M.A.: Algorithm as 136: a k-means clustering algorithm. J. Roy. Stat. Soc. Ser. C (Appl. Stat.) **28**(1), 100–108 (1979)
17. Strehl, A., Ghosh, J.: Cluster ensembles-a knowledge reuse framework for combining multiple partitions. J. Mach. Learn. Res. **3**, 583–617 (2002)
18. Danon, L., Diaz-Guilera, A., Duch, J., Arenas, A.: Comparing community structure identification. J. Stat. Mech. Theory Exp. **2005**(09), P09008 (2005)

Maximizing the Effect of Local Disturbance in the Dynamics of Opinion Formation

Long Him Cheung, Ka Wai Cheung, and Kwok Yip Szeto$^{(\boxtimes)}$ ⓘ

Department of Physics, Hong Kong University of Science and Technology,
Clear Water Bay, Hong Kong
phszeto@ust.hk

Abstract. The dynamics of opinion formation process in a social network is of great interest for many non-equilibrium systems, such as election, competition of market share in advertising etc. By introducing local disturbance in the social network, such as the implantation of an agent, we can use numerical simulation to measure the effect of this agent on the result of the election, which has a deadline. By extending the statistical physics of damage spreading in spin models on lattice to social network, we investigate the effect of one agent on a two-party election on the time to dominance as a function of the given time to the deadline of the election. We find that certain rewiring mechanism of the social network will enhance the speed to dominance by the party that implant the agent. Using genetic algorithm, we also find good methods of rewiring that can greatly increase the efficiency of the agent. Our model is an Ising model defined on a Watts-Strogatz network. We perform Monte Carlo simulations on the effect of interaction and use a genetic algorithm with a mutation matrix to find the best way of rewiring to amplify the effect of the agent in influencing the result of the election. We also discuss the general topological feature of an optimal rewiring condition in maximizing the effect of the local disturbance in opinion formation.

Keywords: Opinion formation · Multi-agent system · Social network
Election · Genetic algorithm

1 Introduction

Complex networks have been applied to model various systems including the Internet [1], social networks [2], logistics [3], ecosystems [4], and neurosystems [5]. One important aspect of research in network science is the dynamics of information spreading, such as damage spreading in a network, epidemic outbreak [6], power blackout [7], and traffic jam [8]. In this paper, the effect of a spy in an opinion formation process is analyzed by a damage spreading model [9, 10]. Opinion formation is of great interest nowadays, not just in the context of voting dynamics, but also in marketing. The key issue in an opinion formation process is the time scale to dominance by a party, in the case of an election, or by a brand, in the case of market share. In these processes, the existence of a certain deadline implies that the analysis of the time scale to dominance is of critical importance. This problem of time scale in a physical system is extremely difficult to deal with as the system is never at the

© Springer International Publishing AG, part of Springer Nature 2018
K. Sim and P. Kaufmann (Eds.): EvoApplications 2018, LNCS 10784, pp. 171–184, 2018.
https://doi.org/10.1007/978-3-319-77538-8_13

equilibrium state. For example, in an election, it is meaningless to discuss the equilibrium property of the system as the deadline is never at time infinity. One way to investigate the non-equilibrium dynamics is by numerical simulation. In this paper, the issue of opinion formation in the context of local disturbance is addressed [11, 12]. In a voting process, the local disturbance is to introduce a spy in the opponent's camp and see how much faster the spy's party can win, say, by simple majority. To investigate the problem, a numerical simulation of a damage spreading model on a social network is performed. One may question about the topological features of the node where a spy is to be put to achieve maximum effect in shortening the time to dominance; but even when certain topological features are earmarked, there are generally more than one candidate node with these desired features. Furthermore, one may also like to know the way that a spy can exert maximum influence on his neighbors in favor of his party. In order to formulate this problem with some resemblance to a real social network, a possible rewiring mechanism is considered as a way to achieve faster dominance by the spy's party. Again, there are many possibilities to rewire a link in a network; the complexity of choosing a suitable node, and the subsequent actions such as rewiring, far exceeds the capacity of an exhaustive search. To overcome this difficulty, genetic algorithm is considered since it is effective in addressing problems with a large solution space across various fields, such as control system [13] and finance [14]. Consequently, we will use genetic algorithm to search for the rewiring mechanism that is used by the spy to enhance the efficiency of winning an election.

Our problem addresses the situation of an election involving two parties, the red and the blue party. Initially, there are equal number (N) of voters in favor of each party. The individuals can interact with his neighbor in the social network, which is a Watts-Strogatz network with 2N nodes in our problem. The voter can change his mind through interactions with neighbors or simply due to random noise. After a certain time, a party win the election if it has reached a certain level of dominance. Under a fair competition, it is expected the chance of winning for both party should be the same. Now, an individual in the red party is chosen to be a devoted blue party member at time zero to study how this conversion reduces the time to dominance by the blue party. One basic assumption for this agent (or so-called spy) is that he remains in favor of the blue party throughout the whole election. Therefore, the spy agent should affect his red neighbors more effectively than an ordinary blue party voter. With the existence of this spy, it is expected that the blue party has a higher chance to win. The probability of winning by the blue party with initially $N + 1$ voters compared to the red party with initially $N - 1$ voters will be a function of time to the deadline of the election.

2   Model

To model the on-spy election problem, we use a Ising model defined on an undirected Watts-Strogatz (WS) network [15]. In recent years, social network has revealed the existence of small-world properties, such as short average path and high average clustering coefficient [16]. WS network is an artificial random network which exhibits small world properties and is a common candidate for modelling a social network [17–19]. There are different models for describing an opinion formation process, such as

Ising model [17–19] and Voter model [20]. In this paper, an Ising model is used as it is a physical model with interpretations that can provide insights on a damage spreading problem. Since the election only involves two parties, Ising model is an appropriate model as it has two-state spins that can describe the party choice of the voters. The links between nodes describe the interaction between voters in the network [17–19]. The interaction is modeled by the standard Ising Hamiltonian:

$$H = - \sum_{<i,j>} J \, s_i s_j$$

where J represents the interaction strength, s represents the spin of the node (or party choice of the voter, with s = +1 for the red party and s = −1 for the blue party) and <i, j> denotes that node i and j are neighbors. We assume that voters interact favorably if they support the same party and interact unfavorably if they support different parties. In terms of Hamiltonian, individuals should favor a lower energy state and it can thus be concluded that J > 0. With an interaction strength greater than zero, this corresponds to ferromagnetic interaction in magnetism. For simplicity, in the following discussion, we set J = 2. To ensure fair competition between parties, two identical WS networks with N = 50 nodes are constructed as the model for the social network of voters. In the following discussion, we construct the WS network with a rewiring probability p = 0.3 and number of layer L = 3. Initially, one of the WS networks has all nodes with spin +1 (red), while the other has all nodes with spin −1 (blue). To connect the two isolated networks, the nodes in each network are labeled with index (i = 1,...,N) and the nodes with same index in the two networks are linked. To introduce local disturbance in the red party, we randomly choose a node with +1 spin and flipped it permanently as a −1 spin. This "spy" implanted by the blue party thus create a local disturbance in the red party. The blue party has now N + 1 voters with one forever-loyal spy, while the red party has N − 1 voters. With this initial setup, Monte Carlo Simulation is performed at the critical temperature T_c of the Ising model to evaluate the time step needed for the blue party to reach a dominance with 56% (which is our measure of winning). For each Monte Carlo step, a node i is randomly chosen and the probability for the chosen node to flip is given by:

$$\min \left[1, \exp \left(-\frac{\Delta E_i}{k_B T} \right) \right]$$

where ΔE_i is the change in energy if the spin of node i is flipped. Here, we choose 56% as a reference for dominance. We perform Monte Carlo simulation at the critical temperature so that the influences between voters and neighbors are at the highest sensitivity. For temperatures much lower than the critical temperature, the voters cannot influence their neighbors much. This will lead to an extremely long time for any party to reach 56% dominance. For temperatures much higher than the critical temperature, the voters will be confused by the thermal noise and change their mind without much influence from their neighbor, which also again leads to an extremely long time for dominance.

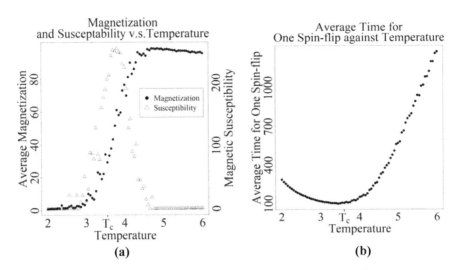

Fig. 1. (a) The relationship between average Magnetization, magnetic susceptibility and Temperature. (b) The relationship between average time step for spin-flip and Temperature.

In order to determine the critical temperature for the coupled network with 100 nodes, we perform numerical experiments without spies by iterating with different temperature and measuring the average magnetization, the magnetic susceptibility, and the average time for one spin-flip. These three ways of determining the critical temperature provide consistent results. As shown in Fig. 1, all three methods result in the same critical temperature $T_c \approx 3.5$. The dependence of the critical temperature on the network parameters N, p, L is also investigated with the magnetic susceptibility method. We also repeat the simulation for different sets of parameters and obtain Fig. 2, where we observe that the critical temperature has a positive correlation with both N and L and a negative correlation with p.

In order to make the best use of the spy, one can consider different ways to increase the influence of spy to his neighbors. A method is to rewire an existing link (i, j) to a new link (m, n) which otherwise does not exist; with such method, the key issue is to identify the candidates for the existing link and new link such that the rewiring process increases the performance of the spy. A rewiring can either boost or hinder the effectiveness of the spy depending on the choice of rewiring, and we can use an exhaustive search to find the best rewiring condition. However, since there are $O(N^3)$ possibility to rewire a WS network with N nodes, the time complexity of searching the best rewiring will be of order $O(N^3)$. If we use genetic algorithm to search for a good rewiring candidate, the time complexity will be of order $O(GN_p)$, where G is the number of generations for genetic algorithm and N_p the number of chromosomes in a population. This will usually be faster than using exhaustive search, suggesting that genetic algorithm would be more suitable to be used, especially for a large N. In more complex spy-rewiring problems such as choosing more than one spy with multiple rewiring, the time complexity of exhaustive search would be $O(N^{(s+3r)})$, where s is the number of spies and r the number of rewiring. Furthermore, the time to introduce a spy

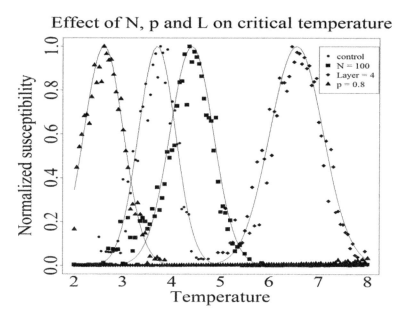

Fig. 2. The relationship between the size of network N, the rewiring probability p, and the number of layer L to the critical Temperature. (circle dot: the control data with N = 50, $p = 0.3$, and L = 3; square: N = 100, $p = 0.3$, and L = 3; diamond: N = 50, $p = 0.3$, and L = 4; triangle: N = 50, $p = 0.4$, and L = 3)

or a rewiring is not limited to t = 0, so if spies and the rewiring are allowed to be introduced at any time during the election, the efficiency of exhaustive search would be even worse. This complex search problem for the choice of rewiring is addressed with the method of adaptive genetic algorithm in the form of MOGA, which stands for Mutation Only Genetic Algorithm, as distinct from the other usage of this acronym for multi-objective genetic algorithm. With MOGA, every spy and rewiring condition are stored in the chromosome and thus the time complexity remains of order $O(GN_p)$.

3   Genetic Algorithm

Genetic Algorithm simulates the evolution of species under the principle of survival of the fittest. Through the evolution of data-encoding chromosomes according to a fitness function with the evolutionary pressure due to competitions among the population, chromosomes with higher fitness emerge with time. There are different ways to implement the idea of "Survival of the fittest" into genetic algorithm, but the one used in this paper is based on Mutation Only Genetic Algorithm (MOGA) [18]. The reason of using MOGA instead of simple genetic algorithm (SGA) is that MOGA performs better than SGA in many cases investigated [21–25]. In ordinary SGA, a population of R binary-coded chromosomes with L digits each is considered. The population at time t can be described by a R × L matrix A(t), with entries $A_{ij}(t)$ representing the value of the *j*-th locus of the *i*-th chromosome ($i \in [1,R], j \in [1,L]$). The convention is to order the rows of A by the fitness f(t) in descending order, such that $f_i(t) \geq f_k(t)$ for i $\leq$ k. In SGA, the population is divided into three groups: survivors, offsprings, and random. The evolution of $A(t)$ to $A(t+1)$ is determined by r_1 and r_2 which denote the survival ratio and offspring ratio respectively. The fittest R_1 (= r_1R) chromosomes in $A(t)$ are copied and passed to $A(t+1)$ as survivors, R_2 (= r_2R) offspring are produced from the survivors by genetic operators such as mutation and crossover. The remaining R_3 (= R–R_1–R_2) chromosomes are generated randomly to maintain diversity in the population. Unlike SGA, MOGA makes use of the ranking of chromosome and the locus statistics to compute the R × L mutation matrix M(t) with entries M_{ij}(t) = $a_i(t)b_j(t)$, where $a_i(t)$ and $b_j(t)$ are called the row mutation probability and column mutation probability respectively with definition:

$$a_i(t) = \frac{i-1}{R-1}, b_j(t) = \frac{1 - |p_{j0} - 0.5| - |p_{j1} - 0.5|}{\sum_{j'=1}^{N} b_{j'}} \text{ with } p_{jX} = \frac{\sum_{i=1}^{R} \left((R+1-i) \times \delta_{ij}(X)\right)}{\sum_{k=1}^{R} k} \quad (1)$$

where p_{jX} is the probability of changing locus j to X (0 or 1): Here $\delta_{ij}(X) = 1$ if the *j*-th locus of the *i*-th chromosome is equal to X, or otherwise $\delta_{ij}(X) = 0$. There are two ways to perform MOGA: one can first select the chromosomes and then the locus to be mutated, which is known as Mutation Only Genetic Algorithm by Row (MOGAR); alternatively, one can first decide the locus and then the chromosome to be mutated, which is known as Mutation Only Genetic Algorithm by Column (MOGAC). For MOGAR, a random number x is generated on [0,1] for every row i. If $x < a_i(t)$, mutation is performed on the K = $a_i(t)$ × L loci of the *i*-th chromosome with the maximal column mutation probability $b_j(t)$. For MOGAC, the operation is similar except that we take the transpose of $A(t)$ every time before determining which loci to be mutated. Even though MOGAR and MOGAC have similar operations, the two algorithms have different performances. MOGAR demonstrates a bias towards "exploration", which means it explores a larger solution space, but it has a problem of slow convergence. On the other hand, MOGAC demonstrates a bias towards "exploitation", which means it exploits the solution space around the fit chromosomes, but has a drawback of early convergence [21]. To take benefit from both MOGAR and MOGAC, in this paper, an algorithm namely Mutation Only Genetic Algorithm with Switching (MOGAS) is used. For MOGAS, the algorithm switch between MOGAR and MOGAC alternatively; the switching occurs when MOGAR or MOGAC cannot search for a better solution for τ generations. In the following subsections, the stages of MOGAS are presented.

Chromosome Representation: In this paper, MOGAS is applied to optimize the rewiring condition. For each rewiring, an existing link is deleted, and a non-existing link is created. To describe this mechanism of link rearrangement, a chromosome thus should consist of four genes, with the first two genes corresponding to the two ends of the deleted link and the latter two genes the two ends of newly created link. For each gene, four binary digits are taken to represent the common topology characteristic of the nodes [26, 27].

Gene: A gene is defined by four parameters: Degree, Local Clustering coefficient, Spin, and Second neighbor dominance (this order is used in the following discussion), where

1. Degree equals to 1 for nodes with degree greater than the average degree and 0 otherwise.
2. Local Clustering coefficient equals 1 for nodes with clustering coefficient greater than average and 0 otherwise.
3. Spin refers to the spin carried by the node, with 1 for +1 spin and 0 for −1 spin.
4. Second neighbor dominance = spin of node $\times \sum$ (spin of second nearest neighbor), with 1 for positive, meaning its second neighbors are dominated by same spin type, and 0 for negative.

Since a chromosome consists of four genes and each gene carries four binary bits, a chromosome contains sixteen binary bits.

Initialization: The population A(0) is initialized with R = 10 and L = 16. The row mutation probability $a_i(0)$ and the column mutation probability $b_j(0)$ are thereby calculated, giving us the whole mutation matrix M(0). A graph with two identical WS networks is generated and a +1 spin node is randomly chosen to be flipped permanently as a spy.

Evaluation: For every chromosome, the average time step for spin −1 to dominate in the rewired graph is a measure for the fitness, and a chromosome with a shorter time to dominance is fitter. The chromosome provides the prescription for rewiring the initial graph. A node, namely node 1, is chosen according to gene 1; then a neighboring node, namely node 2, is chosen according to gene 2, and the link between node 1 and node 2 is deleted. If there is no neighbor of node 1 which matches the criteria for gene 2, then the chromosome will be considered to have worst fitness. A new link is formed by choosing node 3 and node 4 from gene 3 and gene 4 using the same principle, except that node 4 should not be a neighbor of node 3 originally. A Monte Carlo Simulation is performed to evaluate the average time step needed for spin −1 to dominate in the rewired graph and thereby the fitness of every chromosome. The chromosomes are then sorted in descending order of fitness. Figure 3 shows the flow chart for this link rearrangement process and the fitness evaluation of the chromosome.

Reproduction: With sorted population A(t), the mutation probability $a_i(t)$, $b_j(t)$ and mutation matrix M(t) are calculated and updated. MOGAS is then performed to obtain A(t + 1).

Evolution: G generations of Evaluation and Reproduction are performed to obtain the fittest chromosome, which carries the information for the optimized rewiring condition. (Figure 4 shows a flow chart of the algorithm).

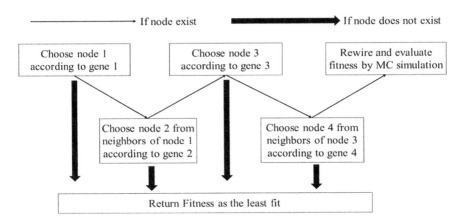

Fig. 3. Flow chart of rewiring and fitness evaluation

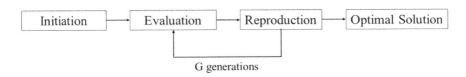

Fig. 4. Flow chart of executing the algorithm with G generations

4   Result

We carry out the test for five trials, each with the same graph and same spy, but with initial population of chromosome generated randomly every time. In every trial, MOGAS has performed for 250 generations, and the best chromosome for the 5 trials are tabulated in Table 1.

Table 1. The best chromosome after 250 GA generation for five trials.

	Gene 1	Gene 2	Gene 3	Gene 4
Trial 1	0010	0010	1000	0000
Trial 2	0010	0010	0101	1100
Trial 3	0010	0010	0101	0000
Trial 4	0011	0110	0101	0000
Trial 5	0010	1010	0001	0010

From the distribution of time to dominance, we obtain the mean, standard deviation and skewness, as well as the speed of winning, which is the reciprocal of the time to dominance. Table 2 tabulates the statistics of performance with and without GA respectively.

Table 2. Statistics of performance with and without GA respectively

	Average time	SD of time	Average speed	SD of speed	Sharpe ratio of speed	Skewness
Trial 1	452.2	361.7	0.004015	0.003823	1.050	1.993
Trial 2	483.3	393.3	0.003847	0.003682	1.045	1.935
Trial 3	485.9	396.6	0.003854	0.003774	1.021	1.962
Trial 4	550.8	452.4	0.003414	0.003317	1.029	1.977
Trial 5	**414.1**	**330.3**	**0.004312**	**0.003972**	**1.086**	**2.016**
no GA	672.1	565.5	0.002928	0.003001	0.976	2.000

Another measure to determine a best solution is to use the Sharpe ratio of speed to measure time to dominance. Since election is a one-time activity, we should not only consider the ensemble average of the MC simulation, but also the performance of the individual MC simulation. In a particular MC simulation, if a solution has both a high average speed to dominance and a large standard deviation, then there is a high risk of a low speed to dominance if we only consider only one incident using such solution. Therefore, the Sharpe ratio that incorporates both the average and the standard deviation of speed is another suitable measure to evaluate the chance of winning under certain rewiring.

To understand the effect of each locus value and its corresponding topological difference in the rewiring choice, we focus our investigation on the chromosome from trial 1: each time only one locus of the chromosome is flipped and the other loci unchanged. Table 3 shows the performance of the original chromosome and each of the locus-flipped chromosome.

Table 3. Performance of the original chromosome and the locus-flipped chromosome

Locus changed	Average time	SD of time	Average speed	SD of speed	Sharpe ratio of speed	Skewness
15	**358.8**	**272.4**	**0.004701**	**0.004106**	**1.14491**	**1.995**
Original	**452.2**	**361.7**	**0.004015**	**0.003823**	**1.050222**	**1.993**
6	452.5	362.1	0.003980	0.003739	1.064456	1.994
9	458.9	354.4	0.003800	0.003444	1.103368	1.900
12	484.1	394.5	0.003835	0.003663	1.046956	1.979
14	485.5	398.6	0.003883	0.003813	1.018358	1.969
13	485.7	395.3	0.003843	0.003811	1.008397	1.939
10	488.0	385.0	0.003688	0.003492	1.056128	1.916
16	490.1	389.1	0.003682	0.003488	1.055619	1.961
11	497.4	409.4	0.003794	0.003763	1.008238	1.978
4	521.3	417.4	0.003525	0.003389	1.04013	1.910
8	522.8	419.1	0.003516	0.003381	1.039929	1.916
2	554.6	447.4	0.003338	0.003199	1.043451	1.909
7	633.1	516.5	0.002992	0.002968	1.008086	1.886
3	686.7	571.8	0.002873	0.002991	0.960548	1.912
5	740.3	624.0	0.002714	0.002896	0.937155	1.955
1	**748.8**	**636.6**	**0.002696**	**0.002863**	**0.94167**	**1.929**

The distribution of time to dominance of 5000 trials of Monte Carlo Simulation for rewiring with GA and without GA are shown in Fig. 5. We plot the ratio between the respective probabilities of winning with and without GA as a function of deadline in Fig. 5(c). We see that the effect of using GA for rewiring becomes less significant if the election has a later deadline. In Fig. 5(c) it can be clearly seen that the resulting best chromosomes lead to a beneficial rewiring that increases the probability of winning before a given deadline of election. Figure 5(d) shows a log-log plot of the above ratio against deadline, which reveals a power law relation between the ratio and the deadline, with an exponent of -0.2309. In Fig. 5(c) and (d), it can be seen that the ratio between the respective probabilities of winning with and without GA decreases exponentially as

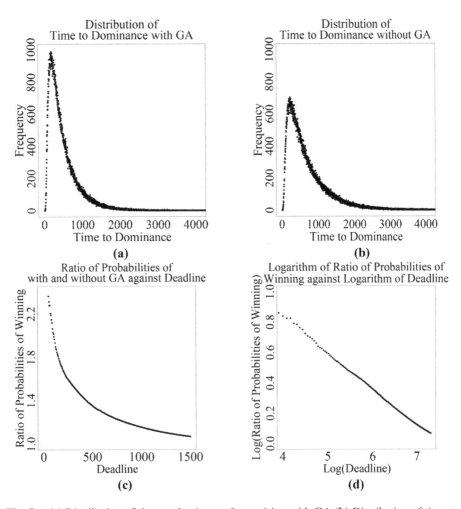

Fig. 5.   (a) Distribution of time to dominance for rewiring with GA **(b)** Distribution of time to dominance for rewiring without GA **(c)** The ratio of probability of winning with and without the use of GA against deadline. **(d)** Logarithm of ratio of probability of winning against logarithm of deadline.

the deadline increases. At a given time step, the system has $\sim 2N$ number of possible states to evolve into. A system evolving for τ number of time steps should have state multiplicity of order $O((2N)^{\tau})$. Since the entropy of a system is proportional to the logarithm of multiplicity, the entropy of our system should be proportional to number of time steps passed. Therefore, as the system undergoes more time steps, the entropy increases linearly, and the randomness starts to cancel out the positive effect of rewiring. From this argument, we can conclude that the effect of rewiring at t = 0 is only significant for an election with a short deadline. Otherwise, entropy builds up in a long election and this cancels the effect of rewiring. Figure 5(c) reveals that the above ratio has a power law relation with the deadline. The power law with time may be a consequence of the spy and rewiring having a long memory. This opens up the question of having multiple spies and rewiring at different times in the election, as the effect of the previous spy and rewiring may still have an effect on the new spies or new rewiring. Therefore, the complexity of having multiple spies and multiple rewiring at different times would be much greater, and the result should be significantly different from the case where we introduce the spy and rewiring only at the beginning of the election.

In Table 2, the best chromosome is from trial 5 with the lowest average time and highest average speed to dominance. As we translate the chromosome into node information, it is observed that the link deleted connects a node having "low degree, low clustering coefficient, spin +1 and second neighbors dominated by opposite spin (i.e. −1 spins)" with a node having "high degree, low clustering coefficient, spin +1 and second neighbors dominated by opposite spin node (i.e. −1 spins)". Meanwhile, the link created has one end being a node having "low degree, high clustering coefficient, spin −1, and second neighbors dominated by same spin (i.e. −1 spins)" and a node having "low degree, low clustering coefficient, spin +1, second neighbors dominated by opposite spin (i.e. −1 spins)".

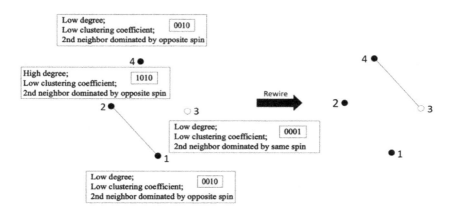

Fig. 6. Illustration of Rewiring Based on Chromosome of Trial 5. Black disk denotes spin +1 and empty circle denotes spin −1.

We illustrate the scenario of trial 5 in Fig. 6. We can provide a heuristic under-standing of the effectiveness of trial 5 for link rearrangement. The nodes of spin +1 chosen for the link deletion have low clustering coefficients and second neighbors dominated by spin −1 node (node 1 and 2 in Fig. 6). This describes the situation that these two nodes are surrounded by a cluster of spin −1 nodes. When we remove the link between the chosen nodes, they lose a neighbor with same opinion, and they become more vulnerable to flipping due to the effect of a surrounding cluster of nodes with the opposite opinion. On the other hand, the newly created link has two nodes (node 3 and 4). The one with spin +1 (node 4) is originally surrounded by a cluster of spin −1 nodes, as it is newly linked to node 3, which has spin −1 and backed up by a spin −1 cluster, which makes node 4 much more likely to be flipped to spin −1 after the rewiring. If node 4 is flipped during the election, both nodes 3 and 4 have spin −1 and connected to a spin −1 cluster, which creates a strong spin −1 cluster with node 3-node 4. Thus, the members of this cluster are unlikely to be flipped and can effectively protect their spin −1 neighbors while affecting their spin +1 neighbors. In Table 2, trial 5 gives the greatest Sharpe ratio of speed. Therefore, no matter which criteria we choose to determine the best solution, trial 5's solution remains the best among all trials. On top of this, one should expect that as we swap Gene 1 with Gene 2 or Gene 3 with Gene 4, the chromosome should still describe the same rewiring condition, because the sequence describing the two ends of a link does not matter in the description of the link. Hence, the fittest chromosome after a fixed number of generation needs not converge to the same sequence of genes, as long as they describe the same combination for gene 1-gene 2 and gene 3-gene 4.

Finally, we would like to discuss the advantage of using MOGAS in this problem of maximizing the effect of spy on voting dynamics. The critical process in determining the speed of our search on good rewiring condition is the Monte Carlo Simulation in each fitness evaluation. If exhaustive searches are applied, since the number of existing and non-existing links in a 3 layer WS network is 350 and 4600 respectively, 1610000 (=350 * 4600) Monte Carlo simulations are needed to evaluate all rewiring possibili-ties. However, we used MOGAS to search for the optimized solution, in which 10 (=N_p) Monte Carlo simulation are performed in each generation and we have 250 (=G) generation. Thus, a total of 2500(=Np * G) Monte Carlo Simulation is performed. Therefore, in this case, MOGAS provide a 99.84% efficiency boost in searching the optimized solution compared to exhaustive search. From the good per-formance in the speed to dominance in the results of using MOGAS, we see that G = 250 is sufficient. For a larger network, which means a larger N, we expect a larger G is needed. The optimal value of G, or a suitable stopping criterion for MOGAS for general N would be out of the scope of our study. Currently, we only study the one-spy and rewiring problem in a WS network. Different types of artificial networks, such as Erdos-Renyi Network, as well as real network, can also be used for analyzing the one-spy rewiring problem, and one should observe if the result is different across different types of network. We will investigate the scaling behavior of the one-spy problem in opinion formation for networks of different sizes in a separate paper.

5   Conclusion

In this paper, Mutation Only Genetic Algorithm with Switching (MOGAS) is applied for optimizing the rewiring condition for a one-spy election problem in a combined WS network with size 2N = 100, rewiring probability $p = 0.3$, and number of layers L = 3. Our algorithm uses of both MOGAR and MOGAC with a switching criterion related to the fitness evolution and the fittest chromosome after G = 250 generations are tabulated as Table 1. The numerical result suggests an effective rewiring at the beginning can boost the performance of the spy. Furthermore, the effect of rewiring is important only when the deadline is close. Our model of local disturbance on the dynamics of opinion formation is not only applicable in boosting the performance of a spy in an election, but also in hindering the damage spreading over the community. For example, we can minimize the damage spreading by the same model with a fitness such that a longer time to dominance corresponds to a fitter chromosome. We can also apply our method of analysis to similar problems such as maximizing the effect of advertising agent in the competition of market share by two brands of mobile phone or the prevention of virus spreading in social network.

Acknowledgement.   Cheung Long Him acknowledges the support of the Hong Kong University of Science and Technology through the Undergraduate Research Opportunity Program (HKUST-UROP).

References

1. Calvert, K.L., Doar, M.B., Zegura, E.W.: Modeling internet topology. Commun. Mag. IEEE **35**(6), 160–163 (1997)
2. Scott, J.: Social Network Analysis. Sage, London (2012)
3. Rieser, M., Nagel, K.: Network breakdown 'at the edge of chaos' in multi-agent traffic simulations. Eur. Phys. J. B **63**(3), 321–327 (2008)
4. Dunne, J.A., Williams, R.J., Martinez, N.D.: Food-web structure and network theory: the role of connectance and size. Proc. Natl. Acad. Sci. **99**(20), 12917–12922 (2002)
5. Rubinov, M., Sporns, O.: Complex network measures of brain connectivity: uses and interpretations. Neuroimage **52**(3), 1059–1069 (2010)
6. Cai, W., Chen, L., Ghanbarnejad, F., Grassberger, P.: Avalanche outbreaks emerging in cooperative contagions. Nat. Phys. **11**(11), 936–940 (2015)
7. Arianos, S., Bompard, E., Carbone, A., Xue, F.: Power grid vulnerability: a complex network approach. CHAOS: Interdisc. J. Nonlinear Sci. **19**, 013119 (2009)
8. Zhao, L., Lai, Y.-C., Park, K., Ye, N.: Onset of traffic congestion in complex networks. Phys. Rev. E (2005). https://doi.org/10.1103/physreve.71.026125
9. Hinrichsen, H., Domany, E.: Damage spreading in the Ising model. Phys. Rev. E **56**, 94–98 (1997)
10. Svenson, P., Johnston, D.A.: Damage spreading in small world Ising models. Phys. Rev. E. **65** (2002)
11. Guo, Z., Szeto, K.: Survivor statistics and damage spreading on social network with power-law degree distributions. Physica A Stat. Mech. Appl. **374**, 471–477 (2007)
12. Guo, Z.Z., Szeto, K.Y.: Damage spreading in two-dimensional trivalent cellular structures with competing Glauber and Kawasaki dynamics. Phys. Rev. E (2005). https://doi.org/10.1103/physreve.71.066115

13. Xia, C., Guo, P., Shi, T., Wang, M.: Speed control of brushless DC motor using genetic algorithm based fuzzy controller. In: Proceedings of the 2004 International Conference on Intelligent Mechatronics and Automation, Chengdu, China, 3rd edn. A Treatise on Electricity and Magnetism, pp. 68–73 (2004)
14. Sefiane, S., Benbouziane, M.: Portfolio selection using genetic algorithm. J. Appl. Financ. Banking 2, 143 (2012)
15. Watts, D.J., Strogatz, S.H.: Collective dynamics of 'small-world' networks. Nature 393, 440–442 (1998)
16. Li, P.-P., Zheng, D.-F., Hui, P.M.: Dynamics of opinion formation in a small-world network. Phys. Rev. E (2006). https://doi.org/10.1103/physreve.73.056128
17. Grabowski, A., Kosiński, R.: Ising-based model of opinion formation in a complex network of interpersonal interactions. Phys. A Stat. Mech. Appl. 361, 651–664 (2006)
18. Herrero, C.P.: Ising model in small-world networks. Phys. Rev. E (2002). https://doi.org/10.1103/physreve.65.066110
19. Pękalski, A.: Ising model on a small world network. Phys. Rev. E (2001). https://doi.org/10.1103/physreve.64.057104
20. Kimura, M., Saito, K., Ohara, K., Motoda, H.: Opinion formation by voter model with temporal decay dynamics. In: Flach, P.A., De Bie, T., Cristianini, N. (eds.) ECML PKDD 2012. LNCS (LNAI), vol. 7524, pp. 565–580. Springer, Heidelberg (2012). https://doi.org/10.1007/978-3-642-33486-3_36
21. Szeto, K.Y., Zhang, J.: Adaptive genetic algorithm and quasi-parallel genetic algorithm: application to knapsack problem. In: Lirkov, I., Margenov, S., Waśniewski, J. (eds.) LSSC 2005. LNCS, vol. 3743, pp. 189–196. Springer, Heidelberg (2006). https://doi.org/10.1007/11666806_20
22. Shiu, K.L., Szeto, K.Y.: Self-adaptive mutation only genetic algorithm: an application on the optimization of airport capacity utilization. In: Fyfe, C., Kim, D., Lee, S.-Y., Yin, H. (eds.) IDEAL 2008. LNCS, vol. 5326, pp. 428–435. Springer, Heidelberg (2008). https://doi.org/10.1007/978-3-540-88906-9_54
23. Chen, C., Wang, G., Szeto, K.Y.: Markov chains genetic algorithms for airport scheduling. Comput. Intell. (2010). https://doi.org/10.1142/9789814324700_0138
24. Wang, G., Wu, D., Chen, W., Szeto, K.Y.: Importance of information exchange in quasi-parallel genetic algorithms. In: Proceedings of the 13th Annual Conference Companion on Genetic and Evolutionary Computation - GECCO 11 (2011). https://doi.org/10.1145/2001858.2001931
25. Law, N.L., Szeto, K.Y.: Adaptive genetic algorithms with mutation and crossover matrices. In: Proceeding of the 12th International Joint Conference on Artificial Intelligence (IJCAI2007), Hyderabad, India, 6–12 January 2007, vol. II, pp. 2330–2333. Theme: AI and Its Benefits to Society (2007)
26. Albert, R.C.A., Barabási, A.-L.: Statistical mechanics of complex networks. Rev. Mod. Phys. 74, 47–97 (2002)
27. Hu, J.X., Thomas, C.E., Brunak, S.: Network biology concepts in complex disease comorbidities. Nat. Rev. Genet. 17, 615–629 (2016)

Accelerating the Computation of Solutions in Resource Allocation Problems Using an Evolutionary Approach and Multiagent Reinforcement Learning

Ana L. C. Bazzan$^{(\boxtimes)}$ (iD)

PPGC/UFRGS: C.P. 15064, 91501-970, Porto Alegre, RS, Brazil
bazzan@inf.ufrgs.br

Abstract. In systems composed by a high number of highly coupled components, aligning the optimum of the system with the optimum of those individual components can be conflicting, especially in situations in which resources are scarce. In order to deal with this, many authors have proposed forms of biasing the optimization process. However, mostly, this works for cooperative scenarios. When resources are scarce, the components compete for them, thus those solutions are not necessarily appropriate. In this paper a new approach is proposed, in which there is a synergy between: (i) a global optimization process in which the system authority employs metaheuristics, and (ii) reinforcement learning processes that run at each component or agent. Both the agents and the system authority exchange solutions that are incorporated by the other party. The contributions are twofold: we propose a general scheme for such synergy and show its benefits in scenarios related to congestion games.

Keywords: Multiagent systems · Reinforcement learning
Metaheuristics

1 Introduction

In systems composed by a high number of coupled components in which resources are scarce, there is a conflict between the desired performance of the system as a whole and the performance that each individual component of the system can achieve. For an illustrating example, take congestion games: while a central authority is interested in optimizing a measure over the collective (e.g., *average travel time*), the individual components (e.g., drivers), are interested in optimizing their own individual travel times. This frequently leads to conflicts and sub-optimal solutions. The same is true for many other problems that deal with assignment of scarce resources among rational agents: this can be done either

© Springer International Publishing AG, part of Springer Nature 2018
K. Sim and P. Kaufmann (Eds.): EvoApplications 2018, LNCS 10784, pp. 185–201, 2018.
https://doi.org/10.1007/978-3-319-77538-8_14

by each agent (thus in a non-coordinated, selfish way), or by a central authority (but then it is not clear whether the computed solution will be adopted by the agents since some of them are better off deviating to solutions they compute selfishly). Therefore, there is a need for approaches that combine centralized computation of solutions with others that depend on autonomous individuals performing experimentation at local level, thus constituting a cross-fertilization of the optimization and multiagent systems (MASs) areas.

In the context of optimization and MAS, the literature reports some works that deal with such combination. Bazzan and Chira [1] have proposed a hybrid approach between a genetic algorithm (GA) and the popular algorithm for reinforcement learning (RL), Q-learning (QL) to tackle assignment of scarce resources to each agent. In [1], individual agents send their solutions to a central authority, which uses a GA, while each agent uses QL to learn to select a resource (a route in a traffic network). Although [1] has shown the value of QL providing solutions to a GA, the situation in which both the central authority and the agents can benefit from sharing solutions was not explored.

In the present paper, a novel approach is proposed, in which not only the central authority benefits but also the individual agents. We argue that our approach addresses systems in which, besides a central authority, there are individual agents competing for resources. This contrasts with the case in [1], which assumes that either the system is cooperative, or it takes only a perspective of a central authority that controls the system and is interested in optimizing its overall performance. This was also the aim of the multiobjective approach proposed in [2]. Similarly, in [3], the authors deal with co-evolution of teams of agents that must cooperate to achieve some system objective. This approach though deals with cooperative system. We discuss other works in Sect. 3.

To summarize, our approach is based on a two-way exchange of solutions between metaheuristics and MARL. Moreover, our MARL is able to deal with thousands of agents learning to use scarce resources. As shown in the next sections, this task is far from solved in the MASs literature because convergence guarantees do not hold when more than one agent is learning simultaneously. The more agents there are, the more difficult it gets. Our approach thus can be employed in all kinds of problems dealing with scarce resources such as congestion games, in which the selfish choices of individual driver-agents lead to a system wide poor performance. Assuming that there is some sort of central authority that aims at regulating the system or at incentivizing individuals to take certain actions, our approach shows that an exchange of information can benefit the authority (thus the performance of the overall system), as well as the performance of individual agents.

The next two sections briefly introduce MARL and related works. The general description of our approach follows in Sect. 4. Section 5 then shows the use of this approach in a particular problem related to congestion games; the experiments conducted in such scenarios are discussed in Sect. 6. We then give the main concluding remarks and discuss future work.

2   Multiagent Reinforcement Learning

A single agent RL problem can be modeled as a Markov Decision Processes (MDP), which is described by a set of states, $\mathcal{S}$, a set of actions, $\mathcal{K}$, a reward function $R(s, k) \rightarrow \mathbb{R}$ and a probabilistic state transition function $T(s, k, s') \rightarrow [0, 1]$. An experience tuple $\langle s, k, s', r \rangle$ denotes the fact that the agent was in state s, performed action k and ended up in s' with reward r. Given an MDP, the goal is to calculate the optimal policy π^*, which is a mapping from states to actions such that the discounted future reward is maximized. As discussed in Sect. 5, one possible RL algorithm to be used at agent level is QL, which works by estimating state–action values, the Q-values. These are numerical estimators of quality for a given pair of state and action. More precisely, a Q-value $Q(s, k)$ represents the maximum discounted sum of future rewards an agent can expect to receive if it starts in state s, chooses action k and then continues to follow an optimal policy. The update rule for the Q-values $\langle s, k, s', r \rangle$ is shown in Eq. 1, where α is the learning rate and γ is the discount for future rewards.

$$Q(s, k) \leftarrow Q(s, k) + \alpha \ (r + \gamma \, max_{k'} \, Q(s', k') - Q(s, k)) \tag{1}$$

In the single agent case, if all pairs state-action are visited during the learning process, then QL is guaranteed to converge to the correct Q-values with probability one [10]. When the Q-values have nearly converged to their optimal values, the action with the highest Q-value for the current state can be selected. During the learning process itself, some kind of action selection policy has to consider the trade-off between exploitation versus exploration (as discussed later, we employ the ε-greedy policy).

In case there is more than one agent acting and learning in the environment, a common representation for this extension of the previously introduced MDP is a stochastic game (SG), also known as Markov game or multiagent MDPs (MMDP). An n-agent SG is a tuple $(\mathcal{A}, \mathcal{S}, \mathcal{K}, R, T)$ where:

$\mathcal{A} = A^1, ..., A^i, ..., A^n$ is the set of agents
$\mathcal{S} = \times S^i$ is the discrete state space (set of joint states)
$\mathcal{K} = \times K^i$ is the discrete action space (set of joint actions)
R^i is the reward function (R determines the payoff for agent A^i as $r^i : S^1 \times K^1 \times \ldots \times S^n \times K^n \rightarrow \mathbb{R}$)
T is the transition probability (set of probability distributions over the state space $\mathcal{S}$).

If all agents keep mappings of their joint actions, then each agent needs to maintain tables whose sizes are exponential in the number of agents: $|S^1| \times \ldots \times |S^n| \times |K^1| \times \ldots \times |K^n|$. Thus, in multiagent RL (MARL) an issue is the exponential increase in the space of joint states and joint actions. MARL is thus fundamentally different from single agent RL. In the former, many complications arise due to the presence of a high number of agents. Complicating issues arise firstly due to the fact that while one agent is trying to model the environment (other agents included), the others are doing the same and potentially changing the environment they share. This yields an environment that is inherently non-stationary. Therefore, at least in the general case, convergence guarantees, as previously known from single agent RL (e.g., QL), no longer hold.

A second issue in MARL is the fact that aligning the optimum of the system (from the perspective of a central authority) and the optimum of each agent in a MAS is even more complicated when there is a high number of agents interacting.

In this paper we assume that the performance at agent level can be levered by external information to some extent, and, conversely, that the system in which agents act is able to benefit from observing agents policies.

3   Related Work

Here works discussing forms of combination of evolutionary and MASs approaches are discussed. These are grouped into two major fronts: the second explicitly deals with some sort of metaheuristic approach, combining it with RL or not (as discussed ahead). We start with the first group, in which meta-heuristics are not used; rather the focus is on biasing the exploration that is part of the learning by the agents.

Hines and Larson [5] use repeated games where agents can follow the advice of a mediator that makes suggestions to the agents related to what actions to take. A different form of biased exploration was proposed in [13], in order to speed up the convergence of MARL. Hierarchically superior agents keep abstract states of lower-level agents. This view is used to generate rules or suggestions, passed down to these agents. The authors argue that the learning process can be coordinated using some kind of organizational control for biasing the exploration.

Now, we discuss a second group of works that are relevant to our technique, i.e., those that use some sort of metaheuristic. This group also includes [1–3], already discussed in Sect. 1.

Wolpert et al. [11] used RL and simulated annealing to minimize the loss of communication of satellites data. In their case, the utility of the agent is set to the system utility, rather than the individual utilities, as we propose here.

Lima Jr. et al. [7] used QL as exploration/exploitation strategy for the meta-heuristics GRASP and GA. They applied this approach to solve the traveling salesman problem, thus a single agent problem.

D'Acierno et al. [4] applied ant colony optimization to the traffic assignment problem. However, the pheromone information has to be known to all agents.

4   Methods: General Scheme

The approach's main idea is that combining solutions between learning agents and a central authority that represents the system as a whole (and thus aims at optimizing its performance) is beneficial. To illustrate this idea, Fig. 1 depicts these two components, showing their interaction. In the bottom of the figure we show a collective formed by n autonomous agents. Each agent A^i has a local observation of the environment and has autonomy to select an action $k \in K^i$ that

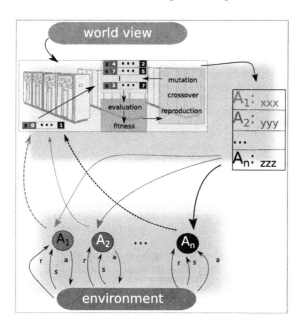

Fig. 1. General Scheme: interaction between central authority/PBM and reinforcement learners

maximizes its own reward r when in state $s \in S^i$. We remind that learning is non-coordinated, i.e., states, actions, and rewards of other agents are not observed by A^i and thus are not explicitly considered in A^i's learning process. Given such limited observation and the selfish behavior of the agents, each will learn an action that is not necessarily optimal from the collective point of view. In fact, it rarely is. On the other hand, the central authority (top of the figure) has a more global view of the world and aims at optimizing the system as a whole, i.e., it computes a solution that maximizes the utility over all agents and, periodically, sends such solution to the agents. Figure 1 also shows that each agent informs the central authority about its choice, i.e., an action (computed using RL). The authority then assembles all choices/actions into a global candidate solution and replaces the worst existing solution in the population with this new one.

Regarding the general functioning of the proposed approach, as mentioned, the learning task by the agents is based on RL. We remark that although QL was previously mentioned, in fact any RL method could be used. The same goes for the method used by the central authority: any population-based metaheuristic can be used (for illustration, in the next section we use a GA).

In short, our approach is based on biasing solutions that are computed both at agent level as well as at central authority level. In the former case, the learning task at agents level is biased by a solution coming from the central authority. This is not an unreasonable assumption (see, e.g., scenarios in Zhang et al., as well as works that are based on reward shaping). In the opposite direction, the

---

Algorithm 1. Algorithm's general scheme

```
// agents:
input  : A: set of n agents
input  : Kⁱ: set of actions for agent Aⁱ ∈ A
input  : specific parameters of the RL method
// environment:
input  : fᵢ: a function that assigns reward to Aⁱ ∈ A (depends on other agents actions)
// central authority:
input  : f_c: a function that gives the objective to be optimized at global level
input  : PBM: a population-based metaheuristic
input  : Δ: frequency of interaction PBM → RL
input  : |POP|, g: population size, number of generations
input  : other specific parameters of PBM
output : one element in ×Kⁱ ∈ K: set of actions, where kᵢ ∈ Kⁱ is an action for agent Aⁱ
```

1 $\tau = 0$
2 Generate initial population with $|\mathcal{POP}|$ individuals; each is a list of size n
3 **while** $\tau < g$ **do**
4      $CS \leftarrow \emptyset$
    // RL: <action selection/reward/value update> carried out:
5   **if** $\tau > 0$ *and* $\tau \% \Delta = 0$ **then**
        // interaction $PBM \rightarrow RL$ happens:
6   **for** $A^i \in \mathcal{A}$ **do**
            // PBM recommends to A^i an action that is globally efficient; A^i tries it
            $(PBM \rightarrow RL)$:
7              $k_i \leftarrow \mathcal{BS}[A^i]$
    else
        // no interaction $PBM \rightarrow RL$
8   **for** $A^i \in \mathcal{A}$ **do**
            // some form of action selection (e.g. ε-greedy):
9              $k_i \leftarrow$ action_selection(A^i)
10   **for** $A^i \in \mathcal{A}$ **do**
        // assignment of reward and update of action value
11   **for** $A^i \in \mathcal{A}$ **do**
        // $RL \rightarrow PBM$ solution is formed:
12   CS.append(k_i)
    // PBM: reproduction and other operations:
13   Evaluate individuals in $\mathcal{POP}$ using f_c
14   Replace worst solution in $\mathcal{POP}$ by CS
15   Evolve population
16     $\mathcal{BS} \leftarrow PBM$.best_solution

---

solutions to be evolved by the central authority are biased by a solution that is assembled using the agents' learned actions.

The idea underlying this approach is as in Algorithm 1. The input is: a set of $\mathcal{A}$ agents; each with a set of actions K^i; a (domain dependent) description of the environment (f_i, a function that gives agent A^i its reward depending on the actions of other agents, f_c, a function that gives the objective to be optimized at global level); a RL method (with its parameters' values); a population based metaheuristic – PBM – (with its parameters' values); and Δ, the frequency with which solutions are exchanged. The output is an element of $\times K^i \in \mathcal{K}$, i.e., a set of actions, where $k_i \in K^i$ is an action for A^i.

Algorithm 2. General algorithm instantiated to the case of GA and QL

```
// agents:
input : A: set of agents
input : Kⁱ: set of actions for agent Aⁱ ∈ A
input : α, γ, ε₀, δ: learning and discount rate, initial exploration rate and its decay
        rate
// environment:
input : fᵢ: a function that assigns reward to Aⁱ ∈ A (depends on other agents actions)
// central authority:
input : f_c: a function that gives the objective to be optimized at global level
input : PBM: GA
input : Δ: frequency of interaction GA → QL
input : |POP|, g: population size, number of generations
input : m, c, e: mutation and crossover probabilities; elite size
output: one element in Kⁱ ∈ K: set of actions, where kᵢ ∈ Kⁱ is an action for agent Aⁱ
```

$\tau = 0; \varepsilon = \varepsilon_0$

2   Generate GA's initial population with $|POP|$ individuals; each is list of size n

3   **while** $\tau < g$ **do**

4      $CS \leftarrow \emptyset$

5   **if** $\tau > 0$ *and* $\tau \% \Delta = 0$ **then**

6   **for** $A^i \in \mathcal{A}$ **do**

         // GA recommends to A^i an action that is globally efficient; A^i
           tries it $(GA \rightarrow QL)$:

7          $k_i \leftarrow BS[A^i]$

     else

8   **for** $A^i \in \mathcal{A}$ **do**

9   k_i is selected using ε-greedy mechanism

10   **for** $A^i \in \mathcal{A}$ **do**

       // assignment of reward and update of Q value:

11        $r_i \leftarrow f_i(.)$

12        $Q_i(k_i) \leftarrow (1 - \alpha) * Q_i(k_i) + \alpha * r_i$

13      $\varepsilon \leftarrow \varepsilon * \delta$

14   **for** $A^i \in \mathcal{A}$ **do**

       // $QL \rightarrow GA$ solution is formed:

15   CS.append(k_i)

     // GA: reproduction and other operations:

16   Evaluate individuals in POP using f_c

17   Replace GA worst solution by CS

18   Evolve population

19      $BS \leftarrow$ GA.best_solution

Given such input, Algorithm 1 works roughly as follows (in the next section, we instantiate it for a concrete congestion game and give more details): an initial population of solutions is generated (for the metaheuristic), where an individual in this population is a list of size n containing an action for each A^i. In each learning episode[1] (for the RL), either agents learn by interacting with the

---

[1] A learning episode for the RL coincides with a generation for the metaheuristic.

environment (lines 8–9), or agents select an action that is recommended by the central authority (lines 6–7; this is the PBM→RL part). In both cases, the agents observe their rewards, update the value of their actions (line 10), and each informs its action to the central authority (this the RL→PBM part, line 12). This assembles a candidate solution that replaces its worst solution in the population (line 13). Then reproduction, crossover and mutation happens (lines 14–15) and the best solution is selected (line 16), which will eventually be recommended to the agents (line 7). This loop is repeated until some criteria is reached.

5   Methods: Specific Problem

5.1   Instantiation to a Congestion Game

The aforementioned method is now instantiated to a particular scenario dealing with a congestion game in traffic assignment, where resources (routes usage) are scarce.

At this stage, we pause for a brief explanation about how the traffic assignment problem is solved. In the literature, two ways for this are to compute the user equilibrium (UE), and the system optimum (SO) [9]. The UE is achieved by assuming that each user performs adaptive route choices until the user perceives that all routes between its origin and destination (an OD pair) have minimum costs. This means that the UE is computed *individually*. On the other hand, the assignment that leads to the SO is computed by an optimization procedure, which is based, for instance, on the minimization of the travel time *over all* users. To see the difference between SO and UE, we use the known Braess paradox: the addition of an edge may *increase* the total travel time. Consider the network in Fig. 3, where each edge e has a cost function, and where f_e is the flow using e. For a total flow of 4200 agents, without the extra edge v_1w_1 (red one), 2100 use route sv_1t and 2100 sw_1t; thus the individual travel time is $10 + 5$. Here the SO coincides with the UE because no agent can do better than this time. With the addition of v_1w_1 (which costs zero), each agent tries to use route sv_1w_1t because it is the cheapest from a selfish point of view. The UE here corresponds to a (higher) travel time of $10 + 0 + 10$ when everyone follows this rational choice.

For not so simple networks, under the general approach presented in Sect. 4, the SO is computed by the central authority using a metaheuristic, while the UE is reached when each agent, individually, performs experimentation in order to learn to select its least travel time using RL.

We remark also that while there are ways to compute these solutions exactly, this is only possible for very simple cases (e.g., a few edges connecting few OD pairs). In general, it is not possible to solve the equilibrium flows algebraically. Additionally, some problems have objective functions that cannot be solved by quadratic programming thus preventing the use of solvers such as cplex. This justifies the use of metaheuristics and learning to find the SO and the UE respectively. One issue here is that the computation of the SO by means of metaheuristics generally leads to local minima. Similarly, the convergence of the QL cannot be guaranteed in a MARL problem, as already mentioned. Both these issues are related to the fact that edges in the network have travel times that depend on the number of agents using them, thus potentially each choice affects the travel times of many other agents. Thus the optimization process is not trivial.

Our approach aims at solving these issues by means of a synergy between the central authority (computing routes for each driver) and the learning processes by the agents/drivers, as shown in Fig. 2: the central authority uses GA to compute the SO and informs agents which actions are recommended in order to achieve the SO (this is the GA → QL part); these agents periodically follow it, but mostly they learn to select their own actions (routes) by means of QL, and then inform the central about these actions (this is the QL → GA part). The pseudo-code is as Algorithm 2. Henceforth we refer to it as GA↔QL. The input was mostly already explained in the previous section. The values of the parameters in Eq. 1, as well as for the GA must be input. The output is a route for each agent.

We now explain how the GA and the QL work; first separately and then their combination, for this specific domain.

The part that refers to the computation of the SO uses a GA with elitism. Each chromosome of the population of solutions is a list indicating one route to be recommended to each agent. Thus the length of the chromosome that represents each solution is n, and each position can take an integer value between 0 and $|K|-1$, where $|K|$ is the number of routes. Henceforth, with some abuse of notation, we use $|K| = k$. A chromosome is, for instance, <370664 ...01>, where each digit from 0 to 7 (for $k = 8$) represents the k-th route. These routes are computed using the algorithm proposed by Yen [12], which outputs k shortest routes. The fitness of a GA solution is given by the *average travel time over all agents* when each select its specific route given in the chromosome (we discuss the exact formulation – Eq. 3 – after discussing how travel times are computed). Then, given a population containing $|POP|$ chromosomes, the GA evolves the population so that the average travel time is minimized. We use crossover pairing with probability c and a mutation probability m as input to the *pyevolve* package (http://pyevolve.sourceforge.net/).

A remark on scalability: At first glance, it seems that this method does not scale well with the number of agents, especially if k is large. Two, complementary, solutions for this are: (i) keep k low; in fact, k is typically not more than a couple of routes (either because there are indeed not many significantly different routes in real-world networks, or because drivers do not know them and/or do not know their costs with accuracy); (ii) the number of agents to be put in the chromosome can be reduced by grouping them (e.g., a number of agents that have origins and destinations in the same districts of the network, and/or similar driving patterns can be grouped so that a route will be assigned for the group). These two measures greatly limit the size of the chromosome.

Now, turning to the QL, in our formulation the reward that appears in Eq. 1 is the *agent's own* travel time, not the average travel time. The available actions are the selection of one among k shortest routes (again, using, e.g., [12]). Due

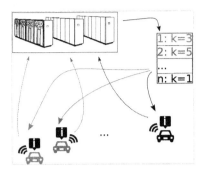

Fig. 2. Central authority computing the SO using a GA and driver agents learning to select routes using QL.

to this formulation of the problem it is necessary to represent just one state (in our case, the OD pair of the agent). Therefore, Eq. 1 can be simplified, without the need of using a discount rate.

For action selection (line 9 in Algorithm 2) we use the ε-greedy method: with probability $1 - \varepsilon$, the action that has the highest Q-value is selected, while, with probability ε, an action is selected randomly. We follow the strategy of setting a high value for ε (ε_0, line 1) at episode $\tau = 0$, and multiply it by a decay rate δ at each further episode (line 13).

Finally, as for combining GA and the QL, when assembling the population of solutions that takes part in the selection process of the GA, our approach replaces the worst solution in the GA pool (line 19) by one that is assembled by concatenating the actions taken (and informed) by the agents in the specific episode (line 15). The agents receive recommendations from the GA with frequency Δ and try them (lines 5–7).

5.2   Traffic Networks

In order to illustrate the use of the approach, some traffic assignment scenarios are discussed. One of them allows not only a partial comparison with results in [1], but also the assessment of the approach in an instance with thousands of agents competing for resources, a known difficult task. Another reason is that these scenarios make sense since it is difficult to optimize both from the global point of view (the cost function in one of these scenarios is non-linear), as well as from the point of view of the user (finding the UE in such scenarios is not trivial).

Traffic networks can be represented as a graph $G = (V, E)$, where V is the set of vertices, and E is a set of directed edges. The travel time to cross each edge $l_e \in E$ is t_e. A route or path p is defined by a sequence of connected vertices $(v_0, v_1, v_2, ...)$. The cost of each p is the sum of the costs of all edges l_e that connect these vertices.

Apart from the Braess paradox already mentioned, another network was used in [1] (Fig. 4). In this (referred as OW), the set $\mathcal{A}$ contains $n = 1700$ agents. There

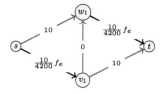

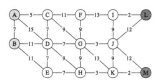

Fig. 3. Braess paradox

Fig. 4. OW network

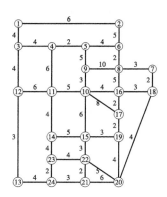

Fig. 5. SF network

are two origins (nodes A and B) and two destinations (nodes L and M), thus four OD pairs. The travel time for each edge is $t_e(f_e) = t_e^f + 0.02 \cdot f_e$, where f_e is the total flow in e and t_e^f is the free-flow travel time of e (t_e^f's are shown in Fig. 4). Thus, the travel time in each edge is increased by 0.02 for each agent using it.

The third—Sioux Falls (henceforth SF)—traffic network (Fig. 5) is a more realistic one: not only the number of agents is very large ($n = 360600$), but also it has 528 OD pairs. Therefore the number of actions is very large as, in each of the 528 origins, agents may select among k routes. We follow the original description of [6], in which the travel time for each edge is given as in Eq. 2, where f_e and t_e^f are as aforementioned, and c_e is its nominal capacity; we use $a = 0.15$ and $b = 4$ as in [6].

$$t_e(f_e) = t_e^f \left(1 + a \left(f_e/c_e\right)^b\right) \tag{2}$$

Previous experiments have shown that there is no less than 100 agents per route. Hence, as explained in Sect. 4, agents are grouped in groups of 100, thus reducing the length of the chromosome to 3606. A position in the chromosome represents a solution to be recommended to 100 agents in the same group.

The fitness function f_c that is one input for Algorithm 2 is the average (over all agents) of the travel time incurred when each agent selects the route indicated by its respective position in the chromosome. This can now be formulated as in Eq. 3, where t_e is as given before for each network.

$$f_c = \frac{\sum_{A^i \in A} \sum_{e \in p} t_e}{n} \tag{3}$$

Finally, the reward of each agent is given by $f_i = -\sum_{e \in p} t_e$, i.e., it is the negative of the travel time an agent experiences when crossing edges that belong to route p.

6   Results

Computational experiments were done using the three mentioned networks. For each, extensive tests were performed to determine the best values for k (number of shortest routes to be selected by (QL) or for (GA) each agent), m (mutation rate), c (crossover) and other parameters. For the OW network (Fig. 4), we have followed the suggested values in [1,2], in order to reproduce possible experiments, and also concluded that $k = 8$ is a good compromise. Thus, for the OW, we used $k = 8$, $c = 0.2$, and $m = 0.001$. Still regarding the GA: population size is 100 with elitism (the 5 best solutions were transferred to the next generation without change). For the remaining individuals in the population, selection (roulette-wheel method) and reproduction, crossover, and mutation are performed.

For the SF network (Fig. 5), $c = 0.2$ is also a good choice; the value of m was varied. Regarding the k, the GA alone cannot reach the SO, no matter the value of k. Hence we set $k = 4$ since this best option for the QL.

Regarding the values for the QL parameters, for the OW network we used $\alpha = 0.5$ (following [1]). We set $\varepsilon = \varepsilon_0 = 1.0$ and $\delta = 0.99$, so that ε is multiplied by δ at each episode. For the SF network, experiments have shown that $\alpha = 0.5$ also works well if enough time is given to agents to learn, thus we also set $\delta = 0.99$. Columns 1–9 in Table 1 summarize the networks characteristics as well as the values of the main parameters used ($c = 0.2$, $e = 5$, $|POP| = 100$, and $g = 1000$ remain unchanged).

Table 1. Overview three networks: characteristics (columns 2–5); parameters values (6–9). Results: SO and UE known from literature (10–11); average travel time (and std. dev.) for GA alone (column 12), for QL alone (13), and for GA under the GA↔QL approach (last column)

| | | | OD | | | GA | QL | | Literature | | Results (avg. travel time) | | |
| | | | | | | | | | | | | Our Approach | |
Net.	$|V|$	$|E|$	pairs	$n = |\mathcal{A}|$	k	m	α	δ	SO	UE	GA	QL	GA/GA↔QL
OW	24	24	4	1700	8	0.001	0.5	0.99	66.93	67.16	68.75 (.14)	67.17 (.1)	66.97 (.01)
SF	24	76	528	3606 (x100)	4	{0.01,0.001}	0.5	0.99	19.95	20.74	53.2 (1.13)	21.0 (.03)	20.83 (.02)
Braess	4	5	1	4200	3	0.01	0.5	0.99	15	20	15 (.001)	16.9 (.66)	15.02 (0.01)

We now discuss the results, for each network, in three situations: when only GA is used to compute an approximation for the SO; when only QL is used (this approximates the UE); both GA and QL exchange solutions (GA↔QL; see Algorithm 2). The latter requires setting the value of an extra parameter: Δ, which is the frequency with which the GA recommends solutions to the agents. In the experiments $\Delta = 10$ was used.

The GA↔QL produces two distinct traffic assignments: one is produced by the GA and one by the QL. Thus, plots shown ahead in fact depict 4 curves. Each point in the curve is the average travel time over n agents, in each episode/generation—we remark that a generation (GA) coincides with an episode (QL). In all cases, 30 repetitions of the experiments using the same values for the parameters were performed. To render these plots clearer we do not show the standard deviation but give them in Table 1.

6.1   Network: OW

The average travel time over the $n = 1700$ agents is shown in Fig. 6. It can be seen that the use of GA alone does not lead to convergence to the SO (no matter the value of k and m, as also stated in [1,2]), which is 66.93 in this case. As for the UE, the average travel time under UE is known to be 67.1573. Agents using QL are able to reach 67.17 (see red curve for QL in Fig. 6) around episode 700.

GA↔QL here helps basically the GA, which, by receiving input from the actions taken by the agents using QL, is able to escape the local minima and reach the SO (compare black and blue curves in Fig. 6). However, the agents themselves also benefit. As mentioned in Sect. 5.1 reaching the UE is not necessarily the best agents can, collectively speaking, do. When agents receive recommendation from the GA, they try these and update the Q-values of such route choices. Some agents may eventually learn to select routes that are aligned with the SO, which, we remind, have travel times that are lower than those obtained in the UE. For some agents, the update of the Q-values after using routes recommended by the GA seems not to fully compensate for results of selfish route choices. Indeed, some agents are better off deviating; this causes the oscillations that are seen in the curve named QL under GA↔QL in Fig. 6.

6.2   Network: SF

This network is more challenging for both the GA and the QL, as it has more options for the agents (more OD pairs, more edges), as well as more agents (see Table 1). From the literature, we know that approximations for the SO and UE correspond to average travel times of 19.95 [8] and 20.74 respectively.

The same procedure applied to the OW network, but using parameter values as in Table 1 has generated results depicted in Fig. 7. This figure has an inset plot showing the first 100 generations/episodes for more details. Again, we see that the GA alone cannot converge to the SO, no matter the value of k (the plot has two illustrative cases: $m = \{0.01, 0.001\}$). QL has proved efficient to approximate the UE: agents were able to reach an average travel time of 21, thus very close to the value of 20.74.

Again, the GA was able to benefit most from GA↔QL: the input from agents reporting their action selections led the GA to converge to a value close to 20.8, thus much closer to the SO of 19.95. The GA↔QL also led agents to experiment routes that led them to slight improvements in travel times, as it was also the case for the OW.

Network: OW

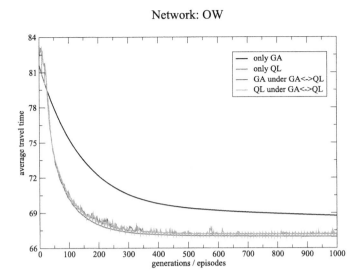

Fig. 6. OW: Average travel time along generations ($k = 8$, $m = 0.001$, $c = 0.2$) (Color figure online)

Network: SF

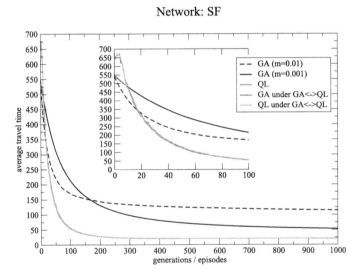

Fig. 7. SF: Average travel time along generations ($k = 8$, $m = \{0.001, 0.01\}$, $c = 0.2$)

6.3   Network: Braess Paradox

This network is simple and the SO (15) and UE (20) are known. However, it has the issue of the paradox, which changes the panorama of the use of GA↔QL. Now, finding the SO is simpler due to the few options (only one OD pair, just 3 routes to be selected). Indeed, the GA comes close to the SO after nearly 500

Network: Braess

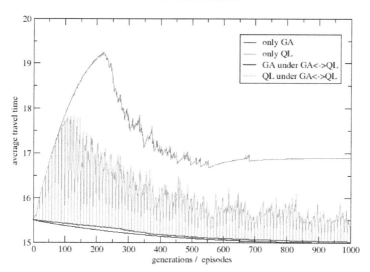

Fig. 8. Braess paradox: Average travel time along generations ($k = 3$, $m = 0.001$, $c = 0.2$)

generations and, by 900 generations it reaches it (Fig. 8). However, the agents have a much harder time here trying to achieve the UE, because although route sv_1w_1t can be cheap when few use it, this changes completely when lots of agents select it. Thus the learning task is much noisier and harder. This can be seen in Fig. 8, for the QL curve: up to time 200, agents are still exploring, thus by chance, only a subset select route sv_1w_1t. Hence, the value of this action selection is high. When agents start to exploit more than explore, this obviously changes: a more greedy selection of sv_1w_1t reduces the value of this action for every agent. Then, a part of these agents change to one of the other two options (thus the oscillations). Eventually, they settle to choices that are not as bad as the UE, but not as good as the SO. The use of GA↔QL here thus benefits the agents because the GA, having reached the SO, recommends solutions to these agents, leading them to better route choices. These choices however are not stable; agents exploiting route sv_1w_1t are still better off trying this route.

6.4   Discussion

Columns 12–14 in Table 1 show an overview of the results of our approach. For each network, it shows the average travel time (over 30 repetitions) once convergence was achieved around generation/episode 1000. Two remarks here. First, while the SO and UE in the OW and Braess networks can be computed using solvers and manually respectively, this is not the case in the majority of the traffic networks, as mentioned before. Therefore heuristic methods must be used. Second, QL can be efficient to find the UE (see lines 1 and 2 in Table 1) but the aim is not to assign routes related to the UE but rather with the SO. Obviously, when these two are close (again, lines 1 and 2), QL has an apparent advantage but this is an artifact of those two networks that have SO close to UE. To compute an approximation for the SO we used a GA, while the UE is approximated by QL. If used alone, these are not always effective or efficient. As shown, the SO is not achieved using GA alone, especially for the SF network. Here the GA↔QL is more effective when compared to the GA alone. As for the UE, QL alone is not always able to reach it. In the Braess network, the GA↔QL not only helps agents to learn to align their actions with the global objective, but also slightly accelerates the convergence regarding the pure QL.

7   Conclusions and Future Work

The alignment of the system optimum with the optimum for each agent in a complex system has received attention in the literature. Issues are not only computing these optima in the first place, but also finding ways to try to align them as much as possible. While this is possible in cooperative systems, the same task turns more difficult in systems in which the agents compete for scarce resources.

In this paper we address the issue of computation of those optima by means of metaheuristics and also reinforcement learning, and combine these in order to bias these processes either to reach some target state (e.g., align the optimum for the system and for the users as much as possible), as well as to accelerate the convergence of the metaheuristics and the learning. We describe the general scheme for this synergy, as well as instantiate it for a particular problem related to how to assign routes to agents in a traffic network. Our results show that this synergy is able to find solutions that are better than other methods, and that this is done faster. Future work relates to testing different frequency of interactions $PBM \rightarrow RL$, as well as simulating the learning process of heterogeneous agents, as for instance those associated with different learning paces and/or adherence to route recommendation.

Acknowledgments. Ana Bazzan is partially supported by CNPq (grant 311558/ 2013-5).

References

1. Bazzan, A.L.C., Chira, C.: Hybrid evolutionary and reinforcement learning approach to accelerate traffic assignment (extended abstract). In: Bordini, R., Elkind, E., Weiss, G., Yolum, P. (eds.) IFAAMAS Proceedings of the 14th International Conference on Autonomous Agents and Multiagent Systems (AAMAS 2015), pp. 1723–1724, May 2015. http://www.aamas2015.com/en/AAMAS_2015_USB/ aamas/p1723.pdf

2. Chira, C., Bazzan, A.L.C., Rossetti, R.J.F.: Multi-objective evolutionary traffic assignment. In: Proceedings of the 18th IEEE Annual Conference on Intelligent Transport Systems (ITSC 2015), pp. 1177–1182. IEEE, September 2015. https://doi.org/10.1109/ITSC.2015.194
3. Colby, M., Tumer, K.: Shaping fitness functions for coevolving cooperative multi-agent systems. In: Proceedings of the Eleventh International Joint Conference on Autonomous Agents and Multiagent Systems, Valencia, Spain, pp. 425–432, June 2012
4. D'Acierno, L., Montella, B., De Lucia, F.: A stochastic traffic assignment algorithm based on ant colony optimisation. In: Dorigo, M., Gambardella, L.M., Birattari, M., Martinoli, A., Poli, R., Stützle, T. (eds.) ANTS 2006. LNCS, vol. 4150, pp. 25–36. Springer, Heidelberg (2006). https://doi.org/10.1007/11839088_3
5. Hines, G., Larson, K.: Learning when to take advice: a statistical test for achieving a correlated equilibrium. In: McAllester, D.A., Myllymki, P. (eds.) UAI, pp. 274–281. AUAI Press (2008)
6. LeBlanc, L.J., Morlok, E.K., Pierskalla, W.P.: An efficient approach to solving the road network equilibrium traffic assignment problem. Transp. Res. **9**(5), 309–318 (1975)
7. de Lima Jr., F., Neto, A., de Melo, J.: Hybrid Metaheuristics Using Reinforcement Learning Applied to Salesman Traveling Problem. INTECH Open Access Publisher (2010)
8. Stefanello, F., Buriol, L., Hirsch, M., Pardalos, P., Querido, T., Resende, M., Ritt, M.: On the minimization of traffic congestion in road networks with tolls. Ann. Oper. Res. **249**, 1–21 (2015)
9. Wardrop, J.G.: Some theoretical aspects of road traffic research. Proc. Inst. Civ. Eng. Part II **1**(36), 325–362 (1952)
10. Watkins, C.J.C.H., Dayan, P.: Q-learning. Mach. Learn. **8**(3), 279–292 (1992)
11. Wolpert, D.H., Sill, J., Tumer, K.: Reinforcement learning in distributed domains: beyond team games. In: International Joint Conferences on Artificial Intelligence (IJCAI), pp. 819–824 (2001)
12. Yen, J.Y.: Finding the k shortest loopless paths in a network. Manag. Sci. **17**(11), 712–716 (1971). https://doi.org/10.1287/mnsc.17.11.712
13. Zhang, C., Abdallah, S., Lesser, V.: Integrating organizational control into multi-agent learning. In: ao Sichman, J.S., Decker, K.S., Sierra, C., Castelfranchi, C. (eds.) Proceedings of the 8th International Conference on Autonomous Agents and Multiagent Systems (AAMAS), Budapest, Hungary, pp. 757–764 (2009). http://mas.cs.umass.edu/paper/465

EvoENERGY

Achieving Optimized Decisions
on Battery Operating Strategies
in Smart Buildings

Jan Müller$^{(\boxtimes)}$ ⓘ, Mischa Ahrens, Ingo Mauser ⓘ, and Hartmut Schmeck

Karlsruhe Institute of Technology – Institute AIFB, 76128 Karlsruhe, Germany
{jan.mueller,ahrens,mauser,schmeck}@kit.edu

Abstract. Battery energy storage systems are a key to the utilization of renewable energies, allowing for short-term storage of electricity and balancing of energy generation and consumption. However, the optimal operation of these systems is still an area of research. This paper presents operating strategies and their optimization with respect to total operational energy costs in buildings that are equipped with automated building energy management systems. The presented approach uses an evolutionary algorithm to set the parameters of the battery system controller for a rolling horizon. The combination of scheduling and control is chosen to aim at robustness against deviations of local loads from predictions. Scenarios comprising different electricity tariffs and the optimization of three operating strategies are simulated and evaluated. The results show that the operating strategies and their optimization lead to significantly different results, reflecting their ability to cope with uncertainty of future consumption and generation.

Keywords: Energy management · Smart building
Evolutionary algorithm · Battery energy management system

1 Introduction

One of the main measures to fight climate change is the transition from fossil to intermittent renewable energy sources (RES), such as wind power and solar radiation, leading to more distributed electricity generation. Not only photovoltaics (PV) but also small combined heat and power plants (microCHPs) increase the power feed-in to distribution grids. In some cases, the distributed generation (DG) is already leading to voltage and overload problems in distribution grids [1], since both generation and consumption are volatile and not synchronized. There are three fundamental mechanisms for the balancing of generation and consumption. Firstly, the generation may follow the consumption, as it has traditionally been the case but is unfavorable in case of RES. Secondly, consumption may follow generation, which is called demand side management (DSM) and includes direct load control and shifting of operating times [2].

© Springer International Publishing AG, part of Springer Nature 2018
K. Sim and P. Kaufmann (Eds.): EvoApplications 2018, LNCS 10784, pp. 205–221, 2018.
https://doi.org/10.1007/978-3-319-77538-8_15

Finally, the imbalance may be tackled by battery energy storage systems (BESS), which enable to utilize surplus generation and potentially reduce problems in distribution grids. However, the impact of BESSs on distribution grids depends largely on their operating strategy [1].

This paper proposes an algorithm that dynamically chooses and parameterizes operating strategies for BESSs by means of an optimization. The general goal is to minimize the energy costs in scenarios with multiple energy sources and carriers and in the presence of time-variable energy tariffs. The optimization of the operating strategies considers a receding horizon of 24 h and is triggered periodically or whenever a relevant event occurs. This dynamic optimization enables the continuous adaptation of the operating strategies to current events or changing conditions, such as requested ancillary services or changes of weather, energy tariffs, and grid states. The operating strategies are closed-loop controllers allow for a fast reaction in the operation of the system, i. e., they enable to account for variations in electricity generation and consumption without running an optimization. However, the horizon of 24 h in the regular optimization allows for the consideration of predicted future events.

Section 2 provides an overview of related work on BESSs and energy management in buildings. In Sect. 3, the general smart residential building scenario, the models and methods, the used BEMS, and the concrete experimental setups are described in detail. Section 4 outlines the approach to dynamically optimized battery operating strategies. Section 5 presents and discusses the results of the experiments. The conclusion and an outlook are provided in Sect. 6.

2   Related Work

Commonly, BESSs are controlled by a static closed-loop controller using the net grid exchange power at the grid connection point. For instance, in [3], this type of controller is used to maximize the self-consumption. The performance of such a closed-loop controller in combination with deferrable appliances and a scheduled microCHP is evaluated by Mauser *et al.* [2]. In [4], two different operating strategies are evaluated. Although these strategies are similar to those in this paper, they remain static and do not adapt dynamically to new situations. In other cases, the operation strategy depends on a given time-variable price [5]. Finally, simple controllers are used to dimension BESSs and to assess their economic benefit and impact on grids [6,7].

Other approaches use an optimization method to set the (dis-)charging power values, i. e., a power profile, of BESSs for a given horizon. In [8], the (dis-)charging power profile is optimized by an evolutionary algorithm (EA). Similarly, the authors of [9] compare an optimization approach using perfect prediction of future loads to three simple rule-based controllers. In [10], the authors use a dynamic programming approach, which leads to good results in simulations, but lacks the consideration of uncertainty and deviations of predicted loads.

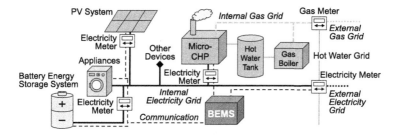

Fig. 1. Overview of the energy system of the evaluation scenario.

Recently, an increasing number of approaches combines closed-loop controllers with scheduling. Usually, they propose a two-tier architecture: The first tier consists of a closed-loop controller, which controls the BESS in *near real-time*, and the second tier consists of a rolling horizon optimization, which creates an additional schedule that is taken into account by the first-tier controller to deviate from the usual behavior. In general, this includes two types of schedules: firstly, a temporal override of the original behavior and, secondly, new parameters that alter the original controller. The naming, definition, and purpose of these control parameters vary in the literature. The approach presented in [11] introduces a vector of binary decision variables defining the operation mode of the tier-one controller. The authors of [12] focus on the peak reduction by a BESS and introduce decision variables that correspond to the energy that is provided by the BESS in a specific time step and may be used for peak reduction. In [13], the optimization of the operating strategy of a BESS is presented, but uses only limits on the battery (dis-)charging power parameters.

This paper extends these approaches by new operating strategies and an algorithm that is capable of choosing from given operating strategies and parameterizing them to adapt to specific scenarios. In addition, approaches to handle uncertainties in predictions are presented.

3 Scenario and Setup: Smart Residential Building

This paper considers a residential building scenario that consists of a single household (see Fig. 1), which is equipped with deferrable home appliances, a PV system, a microCHP, a condensing gas boiler, a hot water storage tank, and a BESS comprising lithium-ion cells and an inverter. To simulate and optimize the building, we use the simulation and evaluation framework of the *Organic Smart Home* (OSH)[1] [2,14]. It provides a simulation of smart residential buildings and allows for evaluations in real buildings. The source code as well as all models used in this paper are published on GitHub[2].

---

[1] http://www.organicsmarthome.org, https://github.com/organicsmarthome.
[2] https://github.com/organicsmarthome/OSHv4_BESS_fork.

3.1 Building Model and Battery Energy Storage System Model

An overview of the technical data of the exemplary scenario, which is depicted in Fig. 1, is given in Table 1. The residential building is simulated using a resolution of $\Delta t = 1\,\mathrm{s}$. The starting times and selected programs of the five major appliances are determined randomly using probability measures based on statistical data and recorded consumption profiles [14]. The residual electrical load is simulated using the German standard load profile of households (H0) [15]. Feed-in by the PV system is modeled using a PV profile that has been recorded using a resolution of one minute in [anonymous city] in 2013 and is scaled to match the selected size of the PV system. The model of the microCHP is based on the one given in [2], which has been reduced to a more reasonable size for households. The thermal space heating and domestic hot water (DHW) demands of 2000 kWh and 700 kWh per person, respectively, are simulated using a randomized heating demand profile and a simulation of the DHW consumption that is based on the VDI Guideline 6002 [14].

We use a time-of-use (TOU) electricity tariff [16] that is scaled to an average price of 30 cent/kWh. Three different PV feed-in tariffs are modeled (see Fig. 2a): a constant feed-in compensation of 10 cent/kWh (FT-1), a realistic time-variable feed-in tariff (FT-2), which is created by multiplying the TOU electricity tariff by –1 and performing a linear shift of 21 cent/kWh to obtain the inverted dynamics at an average compensation of 11.4 cent/kWh, and an artificial

Table 1. Evaluation scenario: smart residential building (4-person household)

Electricity consumption	4500 kWh/a
Appliances (simulated)	Dishwasher, washing machine, dryer, hob, oven
Baseload	Standard load profile H0
Heating demand	2000 kWh/(person · a)
DHW demand	700 kWh/(person · a)
PV system	4.5 kW$_{\mathrm{peak}}$, 4500 kWh/a
Inverter (battery)	4 kW, variable non-linear efficiency
Charger (battery)	4 kW, efficiency 92%
Battery	7 kWh, variable non-linear efficiency, $U_{\mathrm{EoC}} = 4.1\,\mathrm{V}$, $P_{\mathrm{Ch}}^{\max} = P_{\mathrm{Disch}}^{\max} = 3.5\,\mathrm{kW}$
microCHP	0.9 kW$_{\mathrm{el}}$, 2 kW$_{\mathrm{th}}$, 3.3 kW$_{\mathrm{gas}}$
Condensing gas boiler	15 kW$_{\mathrm{th}}$, 15 kW$_{\mathrm{gas}}$
Hot water storage tank	3250 L, $\approx$80 kWh, $T_{\min} = 57\,^{\circ}\mathrm{C}$, $T_{\max} = 78\,^{\circ}\mathrm{C}$
Electricity tariff	Time-of-use, see Fig. 2a
PV feed-in tariff	Time-variable, see Fig. 2a
CHP feed-in tariff	9 cent/kWh
CHP self-consumption compensation	5 cent/kWh

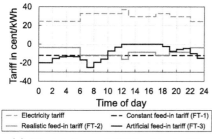

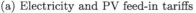

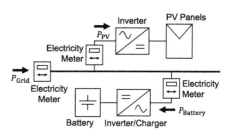

(a) Electricity and PV feed-in tariffs

(b) Overview of the PV system and the battery energy storage system (arrows indicate algebraic signs of power flows)

Fig. 2. Overview of tariffs and the PV-battery system

electricity tariff (FT-3), which is based on an extreme day at the intra-day market at the *European Power Exchange* in September 2015. Feed-in and self-consumption of electricity generated by the microCHP are remunerated using a flat feed-in tariff of 9 cent/kWh and compensation of 5 cent/kWh, respectively.

The battery is connected via an inverter and a charger to the electricity grid of the building (see Fig. 2b), forming the BESS. To model the charging process of a battery accurately, several characteristic parameters and dependencies have to be considered. The typical constant-current constant-voltage charging of a lithium-ion battery has been modeled using the data given in [17, p. 26.53]. The battery charging and discharging efficiencies are assumed to be 96.5% each.

Based on data sheets of commercially available chargers, the efficiency of the charger is set to 92.0% [18]. An inverter model having a non-linear inverter efficiency that depends on the part-load ratio has been developed using the technical specification of a commercially available inverter [19].

3.2 Building Energy Management System

This section summarizes information on the BEMS relevant for this paper. More details about the BEMS are given in [14].

Optimization Objective. Let $X = (x_1, \ldots, x_D)$ be a potential schedule for the D devices in a building that are optimized by the BEMS. Each x_i defines the control sequence or parameters for a certain device i, such as the starting time of an appliance, the operating times of the microCHP, and the parameters of the operating strategy of the BESS (see [2] for a more detailed description). The goal of the optimization is to minimize the total electricity costs $f(X)$ in cent. Equation 1 shows how this is influenced by the electricity price $c_{\mathrm{Con},\tau}$, the feed-in compensations for the PV system $c_{\mathrm{PV,FI},\tau}$ as well as for the microCHP $c_{\mathrm{CHP,FI},\tau}$, and the compensation for self-consumed energy that is generated by the microCHP $c_{\mathrm{CHP,SC},\tau}$, the electricity obtained from the grid $E_{\mathrm{Con},\tau}(X)$, the electricity fed-in to the grid by

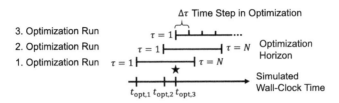

Fig. 3. Overview of the different time scales in the detailed building simulation (simulated wall-clock time) and the building simulation in the optimization

the PV system $E_{\text{PV,FI},\tau}(X)$ as well as the microCHP $E_{\text{CHP,FI},\tau}(X)$, and the self-consumed energy generated by the microCHP $E_{\text{CHP,SC},\tau}(X)$ at the time step τ of N total steps in the optimization horizon:

$$\begin{aligned} f(X) = \sum_{\tau=1}^{N} (&c_{\text{Con},\tau} \cdot E_{\text{Con},\tau}(X) \\ &+ c_{\text{PV,FI},\tau} \cdot E_{\text{PV,FI},\tau}(X) + c_{\text{CHP,FI},\tau} \cdot E_{\text{CHP,FI},\tau}(X) \\ &+ c_{\text{CHP,SC},\tau} \cdot E_{\text{CHP,SC},\tau}(X)). \end{aligned} \qquad (1)$$

Predictions. To take future loads of the devices and systems into account, they are predicted using appropriate methods. Instead of perfect predictions, we use methods that use historical values and probabilities to predict local loads. The consumption of the appliances is predicted using their individual average load profile. As soon as a device is programmed or started, this average demand is replaced with the actual load profile. The baseload is predicted using a scaled H0 profile [15]. The prediction of the PV generation is the average load profile of the antecedent 14 days of any given day, leading to a root mean square percentage error of $\text{RMSPE} = 0.140$ and a coefficient of determination of $\text{R}^2 = 0.655$ compared to a perfect prediction, i. e., the actual generation. The predicted thermal demands are the average thermal load profiles of the heating and DHW systems.

Optimization Algorithm and Horizon. The OSH uses an EA to schedule the operation of all controllable devices for the subsequent optimization horizon. More precisely, the EA is the *genericGeneticAlgorithm* of the *jMetal* framework [20], using binary tournament selection, two-point-crossover, bit-flip-mutation with an elitist (μ,λ)-strategy and a rank-based survivor selection, and a population size of 100. The stopping criteria are, firstly, a maximum of 80,000 evaluations, i. e., 800 generations, or, secondly, an improvement of the total costs in comparison to the previous 20 generations that is lower than $5 \cdot 10^{-15}$ cent [14]. Nevertheless, it is important to note that the presented approach is independent of the specific optimization algorithm that is used by the BEMS.

    The performance of the schedules is evaluated using a simulation of the building energy system with a resolution of $\Delta\tau = 60\,\text{s}$. The simulation uses discrete time steps of the rolling optimization horizon, beginning from the time of the current optimization run and is visualized in Fig. 3: At $t_{\text{opt},1}$ of the *simulated wall-clock time*, the first rolling horizon optimization is performed. At $t_{\text{opt},2}$, the next regular optimization run is performed, because $t_{\text{opt},2} - t_{\text{opt},1}$ is greater than the maximum time between two optimization runs. At $t_{\text{opt},3}$, a relevant

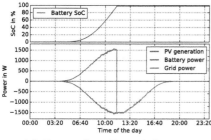 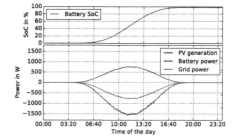

(a) *Power-flow Control Strategy*

(b) *Net-Power-proportional Power-flow Control Strategy* with $\beta = 0.5$

Fig. 4. Exemplary power flows and battery state of charge (SoC) for two different battery charging strategies in a simplified scenario comprising the BESS and the PV system only

event or deviation occurs, e. g., a deviation between the predicted and measured SoC values, triggering the third optimization run. Each optimization run uses an optimization horizon that consists of the N simulated time steps $\tau = 1$ to $\tau = N$, having a length of $\Delta\tau$. The length of the horizon is 24 h ($N = 1440$).

4   Battery System Controller: Approach and Optimization

In case of an optimized operating strategy of the BESS, every schedule X comprises at least one vector $\boldsymbol{\beta}$ consisting of the time-dependent settings β_τ of the BESS operating strategy for all time steps τ.

To allow for a real-time adaption of the battery (dis-)charging power, a closed-loop controller has been implemented, which calculates the power of the battery. The controller uses the following parameters to determine the battery charging power $P_{\text{Battery},\tau}$ in the time step t: the control parameter β_t, the power to the grid $P_{\text{Grid},\tau-1}$, the battery (dis-)charging power $P_{\text{Battery},\tau-1}$, and the battery state of charge $E_{\text{SoC},\tau-1}$ of the previous time step $\tau-1$. Hence, the charging power is given by:

$$P_{\text{Battery},\tau+1} = (-P_{\text{Grid},\tau} + P_{\text{Battery},\tau}) \cdot \beta_\tau, \ \forall \tau \in \{1, \ldots, N\}. \qquad (2)$$

The controller may be used to perform several operating strategies, each designed to achieve a specific goal. The operating strategies differ in the selection of the control parameter β_t. Two examples are depicted in Fig. 4.

4.1   Non-optimized and Optimized Operating Strategies

In case of the non-optimized operating strategies, all β_τ of the vector $\boldsymbol{\beta}$ have the same value: the parameter of the operating strategy is fixed and does not depend on the time. The *Power-flow Control Strategy* (O-1, see Fig. 4a) selects the battery charging power $P_{\text{Battery},\tau}$ for a time step τ based on Eq. 2. This strategy maximizes the self-consumption of the local energy system and is realized by setting the control parameter $\beta_\tau = 1$ at all time steps.

The *Net-Power-proportional Power-flow Control Strategy* (O-2, see Fig. 4b) targets on achieving a proportional reduction of the electricity feed-in as well as the consumption. This can be used to extend the time in which the battery is charged and thus help to reduce the maximum feed-in power. The strategy is realized by setting $\beta_\tau = \beta$ for all τ in $\{1, \ldots, N\}$ with $0 \leq \beta \leq 1$.

The controller reacts on the current state of the local energy system at every time step. However, it does not incorporate knowledge about future behavior of the energy system. This paper integrates the adaption of the parameters of the closed-loop controller into a BEMS and its optimization functionality. The integration allows for the selection of parameters that are suitable for the predicted future behavior. Hence, in case of the following optimized operating strategies, the values of all β_t of the vector $\boldsymbol{\beta}$ are determined by the optimization and thus the parameters of the operating strategy may be changing over time.

The *Optimized Net-power-proportional Power-flow Control Strategy* (O-3) defines all β_t using the optimization of the BEMS, subject to $0 \leq \beta_\tau \leq 1$ for all τ in $\{1, \ldots, N\}$. In so doing, the charging power of the BESS utilizing the PV generation may be limited in the morning and thus delayed or the discharge may be limited, saving the stored electrical energy for the future.

The *Optimized Power-flow Reduction with Fixed Set Point Strategy* (O-4) extends O-1 by introducing optimized power limits for the power P_{Grid} at the grid connection point. This strategy aims at complying with these limits and thus O-4 is equivalent to the introduction of a band of intended minimal and maximal grid exchange power, i. e., a peak reduction instead of a targeted grid exchange power of $0\,\text{W}$. Although O-4 is already implemented in the BEMS and shows the versatility of the presented approach of an optimized decision on the battery operating strategy, this strategy is not yet evaluated in this paper.

4.2   Integration into the Optimization

The main idea of the optimized BESS operation is to select the future settings β_τ of a control parameter β dynamically by the optimization of the BEMS. Therefore, additional decision variables are added to the optimization problem.

Since a rolling horizon approach is used, each decision variable reflects a control parameter for the N time steps of the optimization horizon starting at time step t_{opt}, i. e., the time step the optimization is started in (see Fig. 3). Thus, in every optimization run, the vector $\boldsymbol{\beta} = (\beta_1, \ldots, \beta_N)^\intercal$ is optimized.

Although the temporal resolution of the optimization is already lower than that of the simulated wall-clock time, most likely, it is not necessary to use N different values β_τ, i. e., a value for each time step of the optimization. To limit the number of decision variables, we reduce the granularity of each control parameter by introducing a vector $\boldsymbol{\gamma} = (\gamma_1, \ldots, \gamma_G)^\intercal$, which is optimized. Each component of the control parameter $\boldsymbol{\beta}$ is then defined by:

$$\beta_\tau = \gamma_{\left\lfloor \frac{\tau \cdot G}{N} \right\rfloor} . \tag{3}$$

As an EA is used for optimization, more precisely a genetic algorithm, the control parameters are mapped to bit strings. In the current implementation, each value of a parameter is mapped to a gray-encoded bit string of four bits. Hence, the domain of the original parameter is reduced to a solution space having a lower resolution. In preliminary evaluations, this encoding has shown to provide good results for the parameters that are used in the battery controller. However, a more detailed study of the effects of different resolutions and of real-valued parameters in the EA will be part of future work.

4.3 Handling of Uncertainty in Predictions

First evaluations of the operating strategy O-3 showed that its performance in the optimization depends heavily on the quality of the predictions. In case of a low prediction quality, the simple operating strategy O-1 may perform better than the more sophisticated combination of optimization and closed-loop control in O-3. This is caused by the deviation of the actual local consumption and generation from the prediction, leading to situations that would require a different parameter setting: Schedules that are optimal with respect to the predictions are not necessarily optimal with respect to the actual local consumption and generation. To account for this problem and to enforce schedules which perform reasonably well with the actual local consumption and generation, the following additional improvements to the approach presented above have been developed and are evaluated separately in Sect. 5.

In addition to the selection of a net-power proportional factor, the optimization selects whether to consider the β_τ in a time step τ or simply use 1. Therefore, we introduce L additional binary decision variables $\boldsymbol{\lambda} = (\lambda_1, \ldots, \lambda_L)^\mathsf{T}$.

$$P_{\text{Battery},\tau} = (-P_{\text{Grid},\tau-1} + P_{\text{Battery},\tau-1}) \cdot (\lambda_{\left\lfloor \frac{\tau}{\Delta\tau_\lambda} \right\rfloor} + (1 - \lambda_{\left\lfloor \frac{\tau}{\Delta\tau_\lambda} \right\rfloor}) \cdot \gamma_{\left\lfloor \frac{\tau}{\Delta\tau_\gamma} \right\rfloor}) \quad (4)$$

To support the finding of good solutions that work with imperfect predictions, terminal costs are added to the objective function $f(X)$ (see Eq. 1). The costs are negative and thus do not penalize but reward the electrical energy in the BESS at the end of the optimization horizon $E_{\text{SoC},N}$ by multiplying it with the average electricity tariff in the subsequent N time steps:

$$f_{\text{Ext}}(X) = f(X) - E_{\text{SoC},N} \cdot \frac{1}{N} \sum_{\tau=N+1}^{2N} c_{\text{Con},\tau} . \quad (5)$$

In so doing, the extended objective function $f_{\text{Ext}}(X)$ considers the value of the energy stored in the battery at the end of the optimization horizon.

5 Results and Discussion

Several experiments have been defined to evaluate the operating strategies described in Sect. 4. They differ in the usage of the microCHP, i. e., either none or a scheduled microCHP is used, and the feed-in tariff, i.e., either the FT-1, FT-2, or FT-3 tariff is used. Every experiment is performed ten times using different random seeds for the EA. In every experiment, a building with the devices defined in Sect. 3 is simulated using the first 28 days of July. The operating strategy O-1 is compared to O-3. As there are no power limits regarded by this paper, the evaluation of operating strategies O-2 and O-4 are not part of this particular paper. All experiments are performed with $\Delta\tau_\gamma = 1\,\mathrm{h}$. In case of additional decision variables, $\Delta\tau_\lambda$ is set to $1\,\mathrm{h}$, $8\,\mathrm{h}$, $12\,\mathrm{h}$, or $24\,\mathrm{h}$. Furthermore, the additional penalty costs (PC) as well as the usage of the appliance load prediction (LP) are evaluated to determine their particular impact.

5.1   Exemplary Optimized Day

The lower part of Fig. 5 shows the PV feed-in tariff in cent/kWh (magenta line) and the local electricity consumption (blue line), PV generation (red line), and power of the BESS (cyan line) resulting in the grid exchange power (green line) in W of one exemplary day in July using the operating strategy O-3. The upper part visualizes the SoC (cyan dashed line) of the BESS in Wh. The simulation results show an adaption of the local consumption (blue line): The operation of the washing machine is deferred to about 10:30, i.e., the time of a high predicted generation by the PV system and a comparatively low electricity tariff. The operation of the dishwasher is deferred to the time after the price peak of the electricity tariff between 12:00 and 13:00. The operation of the tumble dryer is deferred to the late evening, i.e., the nightly low-price period of the electricity tariff. The parameters of the BESS operating strategy have been adapted by the BEMS in a way leading to a charging with a $\beta = 1$ until 06:00 and a reduced charging in the time before noon (cyan line). In the time of the operation of

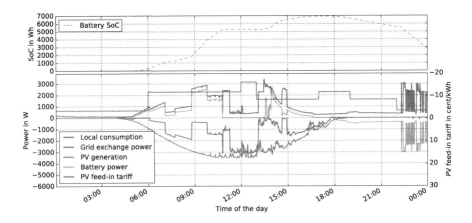

Fig. 5. Electrical loads and the state of charge (SoC) of the battery in the simulation of one day in July. The *Power-proportional Power-flow Control Strategy* is used. (O-3 LP DP $\Delta t_\lambda = 24\,\mathrm{h}$, without microCHP, realistic feed-in tariff) (Color figure online)

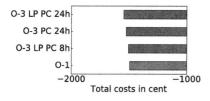

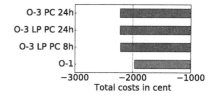

(a) Three best combinations plus O-1 with FT-1, without the microCHP

(b) Three best combinations plus O-1 with FT-2, without the microCHP

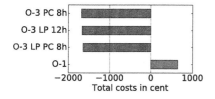

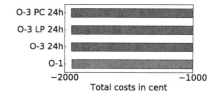

(c) Three best combinations plus O-1 with FT-3, without the microCHP

(d) Three best combinations plus O-1 with FT-1 and the scheduled microCHP

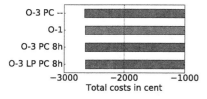

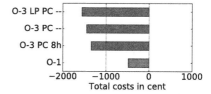

(e) Three best combinations plus O-1 with FT-2 and the scheduled microCHP

(f) Three best combinations plus O-1 with FT-3 and the scheduled microCHP

Fig. 6. Simulation results

the dishwasher and during the feed-in tariff peak from 12:00 till 13:00 (magenta line), the battery charging is interrupted and then continued in the afternoon to still achieve a fully charged battery at sunset (cyan dashed line). Although the electricity tariff is low during the night, the last run of the optimization decides to use a value $\beta = 1$ for the time of the operation of the tumble dryer, most probably because the SoC of the BESS is still sufficiently high until the period of PV generation the next day. The resulting grid exchange power (green line) shows the expected minimization of total costs by charging the battery at times of a comparatively low PV feed-in tariff, i. e., in the morning and in the afternoon, and feeding power back to the grid at times of high feed-in compensations.

5.2   Discussion of the Results

This section discusses the results of the simulation which are given in Figs. 6a–f and Figs. 7, 8, 9, 10, 11 and 12. The performance of O-1 depends on the tariff.

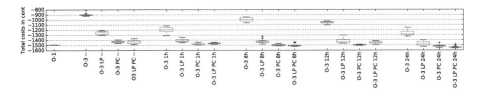

Fig. 7. Results for the experiments with constant feed-in tariff (FT-1) and without the microCHP.

In the case of FT-1, O-1 leads to comparably good results and only few of the operating strategies lead to better results. In contrast, in case of the feed-in tariffs FT-2 and FT-3, there are significantly better strategies than the simple strategy O-1. This is caused by the fact that FT-1 provides no incentive for changing the time of battery charging. Furthermore, in this case, O-1 profits from the fact that it does not rely on predictions and thus does not suffer from uncertainty, i.e., deviations from predictions. In FT-2 and FT-3, there is an incentive to adapt the charging process. In particular, the operating strategies that rely on schedules, i.e., variants of O-3, and use the predictions ("LP") are most beneficial. They result in a better operation of the BESS, because they are able to exploit the changes of the tariffs and the achieved benefit is larger than the possible change for the worse induced by the uncertainty.

When comparing experiments using the same $\Delta\tau_\lambda$, the results show that the load prediction and the additional penalty costs lead to better results in experiments without microCHP, whereas in the experiments with a scheduled microCHP the results are similar to the experiments without load prediction and penalty costs. The first observation can be explained by the fact that the additional load prediction and penalty costs incentivize finding schedules that lead to a non-empty battery at the end of the optimization horizon, assuming that the remaining energy may provide some benefit in the time after the optimization horizon. In fact, this turns out to be beneficial.

The explanation of the second observation is not as self-evident as the first one. In case of a scheduled microCHP, the PV feed-in tariff has to be compared to the CHP feed-in tariff: the feed-in tariff for the microCHP is mostly lower during times of noteworthy PV generation. Only in FT-3 and in the afternoon, the PV feed-in tariff is lower than the feed-in tariff for the microCHP. As a result

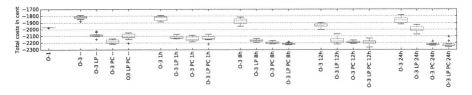

Fig. 8. Results for the experiments with the realistic feed-in tariff (FT-2) and without the microCHP.

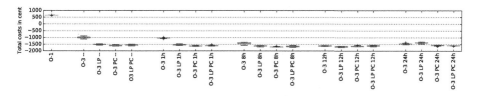

Fig. 9. Results for the experiments with the artificial feed-in tariff (FT-3) and without the microCHP.

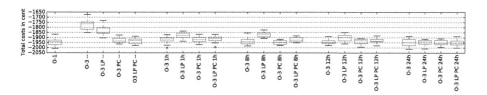

Fig. 10. Results for the experiments with the constant feed-in tariff (FT-1) and scheduled microCHP.

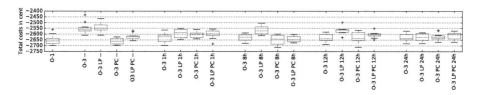

Fig. 11. Results for the experiments with the realistic feed-in tariff (FT-2) and scheduled microCHP.

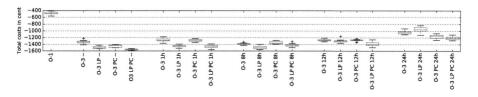

Fig. 12. Results for the experiments with the artificial feed-in tariff (FT-3) and scheduled microCHP.

of this, the battery is charged using the electricity generated by the microCHP and not by the PV system. The compensation for the self-consumption supports this behavior and leads to an at least partially charged battery at the end of the optimization horizon. In fact, the battery is often even still nearly fully charged when the PV system starts generating electricity in the morning. This effect is comparable to the effect of the additional load prediction and penalty costs. Only in case of FT-3, the dependence of the total costs on the additional load prediction and penalty costs indicates that the incentive by the PV feed-in tariff is large enough to have an impact on the optimization results.

Although there is an effect of the additional decision variables, it is relatively low and the impact on the total costs varies across the scenarios. In scenarios with FT-1 and FT-2, i.e., scenarios with a smaller variation in the feed-in tariff, experiments with a higher $\Delta\tau_\lambda$ tend to perform better. In contrast, in the experiments using FT-3, the opposite is the case. Therefore, the value of $\Delta\tau_\lambda$ has to be selected by the user to be suitable for the given scenario. Even though the positive effect of the additional decision variables is mainly caused by the chosen heuristic approach towards optimization in this paper, it may also be useful in other (meta-)heuristic approaches.

In summary, the results show that for the constant feed-in tariff, the unoptimized approach O-1 performs competitively to O-3, which uses the scheduling of control parameters. The performance of O-3 surpasses that of O-1 in case of the more dynamic feed-in tariffs FT-2 and FT-3. The differing results of scenarios with and without microCHP as well as the varying effect of the length of the additional decision variables supports the conclusion that parameters of operating strategies have to be selected based on the local scenario and current situation.

Currently, the optimization algorithm in the BEMS does not consider the uncertainty of the predictions. To achieve more robust solutions, the algorithm may be replaced by an optimization algorithm for the optimization under uncertainty, as described in [21]. The results of the experiments depend heavily on the performance of the used energy forecasting methods, i.e., the prediction of generation by the PV system and the microCHP as well as the consumption within the building [5]. Therefore, the results will have to be verified using other energy forecasting methods, such as those presented in [22–24].

6   Conclusion and Outlook

In this paper, an approach to the optimized decision on battery operating strategies in smart buildings is presented, evaluated, and compared to a simple closed-loop controller. The results show that the performance of the optimized decision on battery operating strategies depends heavily on the prediction of the local loads as well as the electricity tariff and the feed-in compensations.

In particular in scenarios that benefit from the temporal deferral of the charging process and the adaption of the charging power, e.g., scenarios with an extremely dynamic feed-in tariff, a closed-loop controller is outperformed by the optimized decision on battery operating strategies. Other scenarios that are likely to benefit from the presented approach include strict load limitations, i. e., power limits at the grid connection point, load-variable electricity tariffs, measures of DSM, or the provision of some sort of ancillary service to the grid. In future energy systems, such scenarios are likely to become more relevant than today.

Furthermore, the results show that integrating a microCHP in addition to a PV system has a severe impact on the performance and has to be considered when selecting the operating strategy of a BESS. This includes seasonal changes and variations of the used parameters, because the usage of a microCHP is subject to heating demands. Therefore, the usage of automated BEMSs adapting the strategies that are used by the BESS controller promises to provide benefits.

As a next step, further battery operating strategies will be added to the approach and evaluated. This includes in particular strategies that target on the compliance with local load limits, such as the *Optimized Power-flow Control with Fixed Set Point Strategy*. To tackle the common and important problem of the valuation of any kind of energy that is stored in a storage system at the end of an optimization horizon, the calculation of the additional penalty costs will be improved. It is planned to respect the uncertainties of the prediction of the local generation and consumption directly in the optimization by using an optimization algorithm suited for the optimization under uncertainty.

The optimization of the operating strategies may also be applied to other devices, such as electrical insert heating elements and heat pumps that are able to adapt their power setting and convert electricity to hot water or electric vehicles that support flexible charging. These devices may also be used in scenarios that comprise BESSs and thus compete for locally generated electricity or mutually utilize temporally cheap electricity from the grid.

To evaluate the application of the presented approach towards flexible battery operating strategies in a real building and validate the results, we are currently working on an evaluation in one of our smart building laboratories.

References

1. Moshövel, J., Kairies, K.P., Magnor, D., Leuthold, M., Bost, M., Gährs, S., Szczechowicz, E., Cramer, M., Sauer, D.U.: Analysis of the maximal possible grid relief from PV-peak-power impacts by using storage systems for increased self-consumption. Appl. Energy **137**, 567–575 (2015)
2. Mauser, I., Müller, J., Allerding, F., Schmeck, H.: Adaptive building energy management with multiple commodities and flexible evolutionary optimization. Renewable Energy **87**(P2), 911–921 (2016)
3. Castillo-Cagigal, M., Caamaño-Martín, E., Matallanas, E., Masa-Bote, D., Gutiérrez, A., Monasterio-Huelin, F., Jiménez-Leube, J.: PV self-consumption optimization with storage and active DSM for the residential sector. Sol. Energy **85**(9), 2338–2348 (2011)
4. Zeh, A., Witzmann, R.: Operational strategies for battery storage systems in low-voltage distribution grids to limit the feed-in power of roof-mounted solar power systems. Energy Procedia **46**, 114–123 (2014)

5. Kazhamiaka, F., Rosenberg, C., Keshav, S.: Practical strategies for storage operation in energy systems: design and evaluation. IEEE Trans. Sustain. Energ. **7**(4), 1602–1610 (2016)
6. Von Appen, J., Braslavsky, J.H., Ward, J.K., Braun, M.: Sizing and grid impact of PV battery systems - a comparative analysis for Australia and Germany. In: 2015 International Symposium on Smart Electric Distribution Systems and Technologies (2015)
7. Uhrig, M., Koenig, S., Suriyah, M.R., Leibfried, T.: Lithium-based vs. vanadium redox flow batteries - a comparison for home storage systems. Energy Procedia **99**, 35–43 (2016). 10th International Renewable Energy Storage Conference, IRES 2016, 15–17 March 2016, Dsseldorf, Germany
8. Soares, A., Gomes, A., Antunes, C.H., Oliveira, C.: A customized evolutionary algorithm for multi-objective management of residential energy resources. IEEE Trans. Ind. Inform. **PP**(99), 1 (2016)
9. Meunier, J., Knittel, D., Collet, P., Sturtzer, G.: Simulation of real-time multi-objective optimization for a photovoltaic system with grid connection. In: IECON 2016, pp. 7101–7106 (2016)
10. Toersche, H.A., Hurink, J.L., Konsman, M.J.: Energy management with TRIANA on FPAI. In: 2015 IEEE Eindhoven PowerTech, pp. 1–6, June 2015
11. Clastres, C., Pham, T.H., Wurtz, F., Bacha, S.: Ancillary services and optimal household energy management with photovoltaic production. Energy **35**(1), 55–64 (2010)
12. Wang, Y., Lin, X., Pedram, M.: Adaptive control for energy storage systems in households with photovoltaic modules. IEEE Trans. Smart Grid **5**(2), 992–1001 (2014)
13. Müller, J., März, M., Mauser, I., Schmeck, H.: Optimization of operation and control strategies for battery energy storage systems by evolutionary algorithms. In: Squillero, G., Burelli, P. (eds.) EvoApplications 2016. LNCS, vol. 9597, pp. 507–522. Springer, Cham (2016). https://doi.org/10.1007/978-3-319-31204-0_33
14. Mauser, I.: Multi-modal Building Energy Management. Ph.D. thesis, Karlsruhe Institute of Technology (KIT), Karlsruhe, Germany (2017)
15. VDEW Verband der Elektrizitätswirtschaft: Repräsentative VDEW-Lastprofile, VDEW-Materialien M-28/99 (1999)
16. Liebe, A., Schmitt, S., Wissner, M.: Quantitative auswirkungen variabler stromtarife auf die stromkosten von haushalten. WIK Wissenschaftliches Institut fr Infrastruktur und Kommunikationsdienste GmbH Bericht (2015)
17. Reddy, T.B.H., Linden, D.B. (eds.): Lindens Handbook of Batteries, 4th edn., McGraw-Hill, New York (2011). Previous ed.: published as Handbook of Batteries. McGraw-Hill, New York (2002)
18. Elcon: User Manual and Spec Sheet for the Elcon PFC5000 Charger (2017). http://www.elconchargers.com/f/PFC5000.pdf. Accessed 16 Jan 2017
19. Fronius: Technical data Fronius Energy Package, November 2016. https://www.fronius.com/cps/rde/xbcr/SID-F7812949-5B8F237D/fronius_international/SE_DS_Fronius_Symo_Hybrid_EN_386411_snapshot.pdf. Accessed 14 Dec 2016
20. Durillo, J.J., Nebro, A.J.: jMetal: a java framework for multi-objective optimization. Adv. Eng. Softw. **42**(10), 760–771 (2011)
21. Jin, Y., Branke, J.: Evolutionary optimization in uncertain environments-a survey. IEEE Trans. Evol. Comput. **9**(3), 303–317 (2005)
22. Antonanzas, J., Osorio, N., Escobar, R., Urraca, R., de Pison, F.M., Antonanzas-Torres, F.: Review of photovoltaic power forecasting. Solar Energ. **136**, 78–111 (2016)

23. González Ordiano, J.Á., Doneit, W., Waczowicz, S., Gröll, L., Mikut, R., Hagenmeyer, V.: Nearest-neighbor based non-parametric probabilistic forecasting with applications in photovoltaic systems. In: Hoffmann, F. (ed.) 26th Workshop Computational Intelligence, pp. 9–30. KIT Scientific Publishing, Karlsruhe (2016)
24. Schachter, J., Mancarella, P.: A short-term load forecasting model for demand response applications. In: 2014 11th International Conference on the European Energy Market (EEM), pp. 1–5 (2014)

Phase-Space Sampling of Energy Ensembles with CMA-ES

Jörg Bremer[✉] and Sebastian Lehnhoff

University of Oldenburg, 26129 Oldenburg, Germany
{joerg.bremer,sebastian.lehnhoff}@uni-oldenburg.de

Abstract. Smart grid control demands delegation of liabilities to distributed, small energy resources. Resource independent algorithm design demands abstraction from individual capabilities for integration into a general optimization model. For predictive scheduling with high penetration of renewable energy resources, agent approaches have shown good performance especially when using classifier-based decoders for modeling flexibilities. Such decoder-based methods currently are not able to cope with ensembles of individually acting energy resources. Aggregating training sets that are randomly sampled from phase-spaces of single units results in folded distributions with unfavorable properties for training a decoder. Nevertheless, for integrating e. g. a hotel, a small business, or similar with an ensemble of co-generation, heat pump, solar power, or controllable consumers a combined training set is needed. Thus, we improved the training process. We present an approach using evolution strategies for sampling ensembles that moves new instances to better positions according to spread and coverage of the feasible region. As a test case we use CMA-ES and present preliminary results demonstrating the applicability of the proposed approach.

Keywords: CMA-ES · Smart grid · Flexibility modeling
Folded distributions

1 Introduction

Virtual power plants (VPP) are seen as a promising organizational structure for bundling small and distributed energy resources to bundle their flexibility and potential for responsible control tasks in the future smart grid [1]. The general optimization problem to be solved for scheduling in a VPP is known as predictive scheduling (day-ahead based on predicted conditions) as approach to the unit commitment problem [2]. Under given constraints, operation modes have to be chosen for each unit such that the joint operation meets some desired load profile for a given planning horizon.

Agent-based approaches as an appropriate means for controlling the likewise distributed energy resources (DER) have been widely discussed [3]. In most

© Springer International Publishing AG, part of Springer Nature 2018
K. Sim and P. Kaufmann (Eds.): EvoApplications 2018, LNCS 10784, pp. 222–230, 2018.
https://doi.org/10.1007/978-3-319-77538-8_16

agent-based control approaches, an agent has to decide at some stage on a feasible schedule for its energy resource. Depending on the type of DER, different constraints restrict possible operations. The information about individual local feasibility of schedules has to be modeled appropriately in order to allow unit independent algorithm design. For this purpose, meta-models of constrained spaces of operable schedules have been shown indispensable as a means for independently modeling constraints and feasible regions of flexibility. Each energy unit has its own individual flexibility – i. e. the set of schedules that might be operated without violating any technical operational constraint – based on the capabilities of the unit, operation conditions (weather, etc.), cost restrictions and so forth. Modeling flexibility independent of specific energy units demands a means for meta-modeling that allows model independent access to feasibility information. In [4] a support vector based model has been introduced that captures individual feasible regions from training sets of operable example schedules. Systematic solution repair using these models has been introduced in [5]. Agents can derive a so called support vector decoder automatically from the surrogate model and use it for systematically generating feasible instances from the unit's phase space without domain knowledge on the situational operations of the controlled DER. First a training set of feasible schedules is generated using a situationally parametrized simulation model of the energy unit. Then, the flexibility model is derived from the training set. During the succeeding load planning phase, decoders allow using a space mapping approach for constraint-handling.

In decentralized and self-organized algorithms, usually each agent is assigned to exactly one energy unit and locally decides on feasible schedules for the represented unit. But, as soon as an agent has to represent a local ensemble of energy units instead of a single device, a problem arises because flexibilities have to be aggregated [6]. Generating a single decoder for handling all constraints and feasible operations of the whole ensemble is hardly possible due to statistical problems when combining training sets from individually sampled flexibility models. Due to the folded densities only a very small portion from the interior of the feasible region (the dense region) is captured by the machine learning process. But, a combined training set is needed for model and decoder. As a workaround, [6] proposed to treat the ensembles as individual sub-VPPs in a bi-level approach. We propose a different approach that tackles the problem already during the sampling phase.

To address the problem of sampling, we propose generating the ensemble sample guided by an evolution strategy that generates the instances in a way that minimizes folding of the distributions. After a recap of phase space sampling and an analysis of the folding problem, we present an approach that uses a covariance matrix adaption evolution strategy (CMA-ES) for generating instances of the training set. We conclude with first results showing the applicability and an outlook on further research directions.

2   Scheduling and Flexibility Modeling

In general, distributed control schemes based on multi-agent systems are considered advantageous for large-scale problems due to the large number of DER that take over control tasks from large-scale central power plants [3,7,8]. As a use case, we consider predictive scheduling, where the goal is to select exactly one schedule $\boldsymbol{p}_i$ (each element denoting mean power in the respective time interval) for each DER U_i from a search space $\mathcal{F}_i$ of feasible schedules specific to the possible operations and technical constraints of unit U_i and with respect to a future planning horizon, such that a global objective is met by the sum of individual contributions. A basic formulation of the scheduling problem is given by [5,7]

$$\delta \left(\sum_{i=1}^{m} \boldsymbol{p}_i, \boldsymbol{\zeta} \right) \to \min; \text{ s.t. } \boldsymbol{p}_i \in \mathcal{F}_i \ \forall U_i \in \mathcal{U}. \tag{1}$$

In Eq. (1) δ denotes an (in general) arbitrary distance measure for evaluating the difference between the aggregated schedule of the group and the desired target schedule $\boldsymbol{\zeta}$. Solving this problem without unit independent constraint handling leads to specific implementations that are not suitable for handling changes in VPP composition or unit setup and thus leads to enlarged integration cost for new units.

Flexibility modeling can be seen as the task of modeling constraints for energy units. With the help of decoders, Eq. (1) can be extended to

$$\delta \left(\sum_{i=1}^{m} \gamma_i(\boldsymbol{p}_i), \boldsymbol{\zeta} \right) \to \min \ \text{(constraint-free formulation)}, \tag{2}$$

Here, γ denotes a decoder function $\gamma : \mathbb{R}^d \to \mathbb{R}^d$; $\gamma(\boldsymbol{x}) \mapsto \boldsymbol{x}^*$ with

- $\boldsymbol{x}^*$ is operable by the respective energy unit without violating any constraint,
- the distance $\|\boldsymbol{x} - \boldsymbol{x}^*\|$ is small and small depends on the problem at hand and often denotes the smallest distance of $\boldsymbol{x}$ to the feasible region.

In [5] a decoder approach based on support vector data description has been proposed which has rendered useful in several smart grid use cases [9]. To train the support vector decoder, a training set of feasible schedules is generated by sampling the phase space of feasible operation states of the energy unit with the help of a simulation model. With this training set a one-class support vector classifier is trained and from this classifier a decoder is derived.

3   Phase Space Sampling

For generating a training set of feasible schedules, [10] developed a method that samples the phase space of a single DER. Sometimes the technical equipment of a single unit in a VPP consists of more than just a single generator (or prosumer or controllable load). Nevertheless, the owner as operator is still represented by a single controlling agent when embedded into a decentralized agent-based control scheme inside a VPP. In this case that agent has to handle the ensemble of energy units as a single unit and negotiate to the other agents with the aggregated flexibility [6].

An agent that controls an ensemble of DER needs a flexibility model and a decoder that cover the aggregated feasible region. A model that covers the joint operation of an ensemble is often not available. Using the training sets of individual energy units and randomly combining them by adding up exactly one from each training set to joint schedules in order to gain a training set for the joint behavior is not targeted. The problem is that all source trainings sets are independent random samples and thus the aggregated training set exhibits a density (of operable power levels) that results from folding the source distributions. Figure 1(a) shows an example. Uniformly distributed values for levels of power as in the case of an co-generation plant with sufficient buffer capacity fold up – in case of ensembles – to an multi-modal Irvin-Hall-distribution [11] with similarities to a sharp normal distribution. The more individual training sets (and thus energy units in the ensemble) are folded the more leptokurtic the pdf gets. This leads to an aggregated training setwith a very high density in the middle of the feasible region. At the outskirts the sample is extremely sparse. Thus, instances from the outer parts are neglected as outliers from a machine learning approach that tries to learn a model for the region.

Hence, a decoder trained from such a skewed training set reproduces only a very small, inner portion of the feasible region. In this way, most of the flexibility that an ensemble could bring in into a virtual power plant control is neglected. This can also be seen in Fig. 1(b). The rather small grey boxes represent the data (power levels for different time intervals) that actually should spread over the area denoted by the outer whiskers. Only the small inner part is going to be captured in a model.

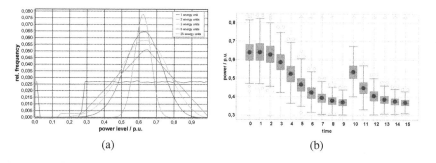

(a)   (b)

Fig. 1. Left: Probability density of folded distributions of operable power levels for co-generation plants. Right: Probability distribution of power levels at different time intervals of an ensemble of 10 micro CHP units. The training set exhibits a concentration in the inner part of the whole flexibility (grey boxes denoting 3/4 of the samples) making it highly imbalanced.

4   CMA-ES for Optimized Sampling

The naïve way of sampling the aggregated phase space of an ensemble would be to generate a random schedule for each energy resource and add up all these schedules. To overcome the problem we want to generate new instances for the training set not completely random but in a way that minimizes folding. An individual training set for each DER in the ensemble can easily be generated. We derive a decoder for each DER and produce a new instance $x^* = \arg\min E(x)$ that minimizes a deviation E from an even distribution. For evaluating a new instance in the sample we need an objective that measures spread *and* size of the captured region. For a first approach we go with a linear combination of two indicators. We start by defining $X = x_1, \ldots, x_n$ as a set of n aggregated ensemble schedules that are already in the training set. Now we define

$$h(X \cup x) = \sum_{i=1}^{d-1} h\left(\frac{\{x\}_{i,j}}{\{x\}_{(i+1),j}} \right). \tag{3}$$

Function $h(X \cup x)$ denotes a concave hull [12] around the training set X and the new instance x. As the calculation of high-dimensional concave hulls quickly grows intractable, we approximate by summing up over a set of 2-dimensional concave hulls around neighboring cross-sections through the d-dimensional schedules in the training set. Maximizing the area of the concave hull $A(h)$ ensures that the flexibility is captured also at the outskirts of the feasible region. In order to spread samples equally across this maximized area, the second indicator comes into play. Let $x_{j,1} \leq x_{j,2} \leq \cdots \leq x_{j,m}$ be the sorted values of the jth elements of X and let $x^{\delta} = x_{i,2} - x_{i,1}, x_{i,3} - x_{i,2}, \ldots, x_{i,n} - x_{i,m-1}$ be the series of successive differences, P_i: pmf. Now we define the variance

$$\sigma_{\delta}^2 = \sum_{i=1}^{m-1} P_i \left(x_i^{\delta} - \frac{1}{n} \sum_{j \geq 1}^{n-1} x_j^{\delta} \right)^2 \tag{4}$$

to measure the spread of differences of the vectors in the training set. Minimizing this spread ensures equalizing the spread across the feasible region. With these two indicators we can now define our objective that minimizes unfavorable folding when a new instance is added to the already sampled training set X:

$$E(X \cup x) = w \cdot \sigma_{\delta}^2 + \frac{1-w}{A(h)} \rightarrow \min \tag{5}$$

as a weighted mixture of both criteria, which is to be optimized with respect to feasibility of individual constraints ensured by using individual decoders. We used CMA-ES due to its known capability to manage with less objective evaluations [13].

CMA-ES is a well-known evolution strategy for black box problems. New solution candidates are sampled from a multi variate normal distribution $\mathcal{N}(0, C)$ with covariance matrix C which is adapted in a way that maximizes the occurrence of improving steps according to previously seen distributions for good steps. Sampling is weighted by a selection of solutions of the parent generation. In a way, a second order model of the objective function is exploited for structure information. A comprehensive introduction can for example be found in [13]. In order to ensure feasibility of the aggregated schedules, a decoder for each unit in the ensemble is integrated into CMA-ES after [6]. In each iteration g of CMA-ES a multivariate distribution is sampled to generate a new offspring solution population:

$$x_k^{(g+1)} \sim m^{(g)} + \sigma^{(g)} \mathcal{N}(0, C^{(g)}), \ k = 1, \ldots, \lambda. \tag{6}$$

$C^{(g)} \in \mathbb{R}^{n \times n}$ defines the covariance matrix of the search distribution at generation (iteration) g with overall standard deviation $\sigma^{(g)}$ which can also be interpreted in terms of an adaptive step size. The mean of the multivariate distribution is denoted by $m^{(g)}$, $\lambda \geq 2$ denotes the population size. The new mean $m^{(g+1)}$ for generating the sample of the next generation in CMA-ES is calculated as weighted average

$$m^{(g+1)} = \sum_{i=1}^{\mu} w_i x_{i:\lambda}^{(g+1)}, \ \sum w_i = 0, \ w_i > 0, \tag{7}$$

of the best (in terms of objective function evaluation) individuals form the current sample $x_i^{(g)}, \ldots, x_\lambda^{(g)}$. In order to introduce the decoder into CMA-ES, ranking is done with the help of the decoder mapping Γ: $f(\Gamma_1(x_{1:\lambda}^{(g)})), \ldots, f(\Gamma_\lambda(x_{\lambda:\lambda}^{(g)}))$, $\lambda \geq \mu$, to define $x_{i:\lambda}^{(g)}$ as the ith ranked best individual. A solution candidate is the concatenation of schedules $x = p_1 p_2 \ldots p_m = (p_{11}, p_{12}, \ldots, p_{1d}, p_{21}, \ldots, p_{2d}, \ldots, p_{md})$ with $p_1, \ldots, p_m$ denoting schedules for the units in the ensemble. Thus, the decoder Γ is defined as the concatenation of individual decoders for individual schedule parts: $\Gamma(x)$: $\gamma_1(p_1)\gamma_2(p_2) \ldots \gamma_m(p_m)$. The covariance matrix is updated as usual, but based on the decoder based ranking:

$$C_\mu^{(g+1)} = \sum_{i=1}^{\mu} w_i \left(x_{i:\lambda}^{(g+1)} - m^{(g)} \right) \left(x_{i:\lambda}^{(g+1)} - m^{(g)} \right)^\top. \tag{8}$$

CMA-ES has a set of parameters that can be tweaked to some degree for a problem specific adaption. Nevertheless, default values applicable for a wide range of problems are available. We have chosen to set these values after [13] for our experiments.

5   Results

For evaluating the feasibility of the proposed sampling approach we used a model of co-generation plants that has been tested and used in several projects [7,9]. To simulate and sample an ensemble of different co-generation plants we instantiated differently parameterized models. The models were used to generate training samples (schedules of a single resource) and to derive a decoder for each plant [5,10]. These decoders where used twice: for generating an aggregated training set of combined instances for the ensemble by simply adding up random schedules from each plant. A second training set was generated using the optimization approach described in the previous section.

Table 1. Comparison of classifiers derived from naïve and optimized training sets for ensembles of 5 units and 8-dimensional schedules.

Indicator	Combined instances	Optimized sample
Fallout	0.0094 ± 0.0080	0.0731 ± 0.0131
Precision	0.8982 ± 0.0959	0.9263 ± 0.0102
Negative prediction value	0.5296 ± 0.0269	0.9490 ± 0.0130
Recall	0.0956 ± 0.0744	0.9479 ± 0.0152
Miss rate	0.9044 ± 0.0744	0.0521 ± 0.0152
Specificity	0.9906 ± 0.0080	0.9269 ± 0.0131
Correct classification rate	0.5484 ± 0.0378	0.9374 ± 0.0080

Table 2. Comparison of classifiers derived from naïve and optimized training sets for ensembles of 10 units and 8-dimensional schedules.

Indicator	Combined instances	Optimzed sample
Fallout	0.0045 ± 0.0051	0.0433 ± 0.0320
Precision	0.9888 ± 0.0109	0.9564 ± 0.0338
Negative prediction value	0.5972 ± 0.0870	0.9771 ± 0.0110
Recall	0.2574 ± 0.2402	0.9772 ± 0.0111
Miss rate	0.7426 ± 0.2402	0.0228 ± 0.0111
Specificity	0.9955 ± 0.0051	0.9567 ± 0.0320
Correct classification rate	0.6383 ± 0.1142	0.9666 ± 0.0194

From both training sets a decoder for the whole ensemble was generated. The support vector classifiers that found the basis of the decoder where compared using standard indicators for classifier evaluation. The performance was measured using new, unseen schedules generated by the simulation models. Tables 1, 2 and 3 show the results for different ensemble sizes. Up to now, we succeeded with schedules up to around 8 dimensions. For larger schedules the results quickly degrade as the problem becomes too high-dimensional. But, for the test cases the optimized training set yields a classifier that always outperforms the one derived from naïve aggregated training sets.

The specificity denotes the rate of correctly classified infeasible schedules. It is immediately clear that the original training set performs better here, because

Table 3. Comparison of classifiers derived from naïve and optimized training sets for ensembles of 20 units and 8-dimensional schedules.

Indicator	Combined instances	Optimzed sample
Fallout	0.0084 ± 0.0085	0.0403 ± 0.0297
Precision	0.8738 ± 0.0118	0.9571 ± 0.0331
Negative prediction value	0.6192 ± 0.1206	0.9940 ± 0.0024
Recall	0.3037 ± 0.2853	0.9937 ± 0.0025
Miss rate	0.6963 ± 0.2853	0.0063 ± 0.0025
Specificity	0.9916 ± 0.0085	0.9597 ± 0.0297
Correct classification rate	0.6581 ± 0.1336	0.9756 ± 0.0167

it seriously underestimates the feasible region. For all other indicators the optimized set performs better. Especially, the overall correct classification rate and the miss rate that denotes the share of feasible schedules that are falsely classified infeasible demonstrate the increase in modeled flexibility with the optimized set. Classifiers generated from the optimized training set encode a larger flexibility. From these results it can be concluded that also a derived decoder performs better and generates schedules with a larger variety.

6   Conclusion

Modeling flexibility by using machine learning approaches and automatically deriving decoders for constraint handling and domain knowledge independent implementation of (distributed) optimization methods has proven a useful tool in managing the future smart grid. So far, these models can only be applied to single energy units, because distributions of power levels in the training sets of single units fold up when aggregating them to ensemble training sets. Thus, such training set render useless for appropriately deriving a model for the joint flexibility of a group of energy units. With our approach we went one step towards integrating also households, hotels, small businesses, schools or similar with an ensemble of co-generation, heat pump, solar power, and controllable consumers into predictive scheduling for providing energy services in future smart grid architectures without a need for an (expensive) individual link of each single device in the ensemble. So far we tested CMA-ES. Future work will additionally address higher dimensionality and different Optimization approaches as well as different indicators for evaluating the distribution of the training set inside the phase space of the energy unit.

References

1. Awerbuch, S., Preston, A.M. (eds.): The Virtual Utility: Accounting, Technology and Competitive Aspects of the Emerging Industry, Topics in Regulatory Economics and Policy, vol. 26. Kluwer Academic Publishers, New York (1997)
2. Padhy, N.: Unit commitment - a bibliographical survey. IEEE Trans. Power Syst. **19**(2), 1196–1205 (2004)
3. Nieße, A., Lehnhoff, S., Trschel, M., Uslar, M., Wissing, C., Appelrath, H.J., Sonnenschein, M.: Market-based self-organized provision of active power and ancillary services: an agent-based approach for smart distribution grids. In: 2012 Complexity in Engineering (COMPENG), pp. 1–5 (2012)
4. Bremer, J., Rapp, B., Sonnenschein, M.: Encoding distributed search spaces for virtual power plants. In: IEEE Symposium Series on Computational Intelligence 2011 (SSCI 2011), Paris, France (2011)
5. Bremer, J., Sonnenschein, M.: Constraint-handling for optimization with support vector surrogate models - a novel decoder approach. In: Filipe, J., Fred, A. (eds.) ICAART 2013 - Proceedings of the 5th International Conference on Agents and Artificial Intelligence, vol. 2, pp. 91–105. SciTePress, Barcelona (2013)
6. Bremer, J., Lehnhoff, S.: Hybrid multi-ensemble scheduling. In: Squillero, G., Sim, K. (eds.) EvoApplications 2017. LNCS, vol. 10199, pp. 342–358. Springer, Cham (2017). https://doi.org/10.1007/978-3-319-55849-3_23
7. Hinrichs, C., Bremer, J., Sonnenschein, M.: Distributed hybrid constraint handling in large scale virtual power plants. In: IEEE PES Conference on Innovative Smart Grid Technologies Europe (ISGT Europe 2013). IEEE Power Energy Society (2013)
8. McArthur, S., Davidson, E., Catterson, V., Dimeas, A., Hatziargyriou, N., Ponci, F., Funabashi, T.: Multi-agent systems for power engineering applications - part I. IEEE Trans. Power Syst. **22**(4), 1743–1752 (2007)
9. Sonnenschein, M., Lünsdorf, O., Bremer, J., Tröschel, M.: Decentralized control of units in smart grids for the support of renewable energy supply. Environ. Impact Assess. Rev. **52**, 40–52 (2014)
10. Bremer, J., Sonnenschein, M.: Sampling the search space of energy resources for self-organized, agent-based planning of active power provision. In: Page, B., Fleischer, A.G., Göbel, J., Wohlgemuth, V. (eds.) EnviroInfo 2013, pp. 214–222. Shaker (2013)
11. Hall, P.: The distribution of means for samples of size n drawn from a population in which the variate takes values between 0 and 1, all such values being equally probable. Biometrika **19**(3/4), 240–245 (1927)
12. Duckham, M., Kulik, L., Worboys, M., Galton, A.: Efficient generation of simple polygons for characterizing the shape of a set of points in the plane. Patt. Recogn. **41**(10), 3224–3236 (2008). http://www.sciencedirect.com/science/article/pii/S0031320308001180
13. Hansen, N.: The CMA Evolution Strategy: A Tutorial. Technical report, Inria Research Centre Saclay (2011). www.lri.fr/~hansen/cmatutorial.pdf

Many-Objective Optimization of Mission and Hybrid Electric Power System of an Unmanned Aircraft

Teresa Donateo$^{(\boxtimes)}$ 🆔, Claudia Lucia De Pascalis,
and Antonio Ficarella

Department of Engineering for Innovation, University of Salento, Lecce, Italy
teresa.donateo@unisalento.it

Abstract. This work aims at comparing different many-objective techniques for the optimization of mission and parallel hybrid electric power system for aircraft. In particular, this work considers, as input of the optimization, the specification of the flight mission, the size of the main components and the energy management strategy for a Medium Altitude Long Endurance Unmanned Aerial Vehicle (MALE-UAV). The goals of the optimization are maximization of electric endurance, minimization of overall fuel consumption, improvement of take-off performance and minimization of the additional volume of the hybrid electric solution with respect to the initial conventional power system. The optimization methods considered in this study are those included in the Mod-eFRONTIER optimization environment: NSGA-II, MOGA-II, MOSA (Multi Objective Simulated Annealing algorithm) and Evolutionary Strategy of type $(\mu/\rho + \lambda)$-ES. Initially, appropriate metrics are used to compare the proposed methods in a simplified problem with only two objective functions. Then a complete optimization is performed, in order to underline the degradation of the proposed optimization methods as the size of the problem increases and to define the best method according to the number of objective functions.

Keywords: Many-objective optimization · Evolutionary algorithms
Hybrid electric aircraft · Performance metrics

1 Introduction

Thanks to the superior energy density of hydrocarbon fuels, internal combustion engines, in particular gas turbines, are the favorite technology in the aircraft propulsion field. However, engines have a lower efficiency and power-to-weight ratio when compared to electric motors. Hence, hybrid-electric propulsion systems have been proposed to take advantage of the synergy between engines and motors and to improve the overall fuel economy.

Since the late 1990s, a series of theoretical, experimental and commercial activities have focused on electric and hybrid electric power systems, initially only for secondary power (more-electric aircraft) but recently also for propulsion. A good review can be found in [1] however, the literature in this field is getting richer and richer in the recent years. Electric aircraft uses a battery-motor system to move the propellers instead of a

© Springer International Publishing AG, part of Springer Nature 2018
K. Sim and P. Kaufmann (Eds.): EvoApplications 2018, LNCS 10784, pp. 231–246, 2018.
https://doi.org/10.1007/978-3-319-77538-8_17

conventional thermal engine. Because of the limited energy density of batteries with respect to fossil fuel, the range of this kind of aircraft is quite low but so it is also its environmental impact. Hybrid electric aircraft exploits the advantages of both energy sources and converters. When the power request is very high, typically takeoff and first climb, the engine is helped by the battery through the electric machine that works as a motor. When the power request is low, i.e. in descent, the excess power of the engine can be used to charge the battery by using the electric machine as a generator. Some parts of the flight can also be performed in electric mode. The choice among the different operating mode is the so-called energy management strategy.

The design of a hybrid electric power system requires a complex optimization procedure because its performance will strongly depend on both the size of the components and the energy management strategy. The problem is particularly critical in the aircraft field because of the strong constraints in terms of weight and volume and of the necessity of adapting the flight specifications (altitude and speed) to the performance of the propulsion system. In the present investigation, the problem is addressed by linking an in-house code for the simulation of hybrid electric power systems with a commercial many-objective optimization software, namely Esteco ModeFRONTIER.

Real-world engineering design problems often involve the satisfaction of multiple performance indexes and, contemporarily, the respect of some constraints on the design variables. Automotive and aerospace, in particular, provide many examples of design challenges involving a large number of objectives (or goals) like that considered in this investigation.

When the functions to be optimized are more than one, a problem is named "multi-objective", if they are more than three, it is called "many-objective optimization" [2–5]. In the study of Li et al. [3], a survey of many-objective evolution algorithms (MaOEAs) is conducted. They are categorized into seven classes: relaxed dominance based, diversity-based, aggregation-based, indicator-based, reference set based, preference-based, and dimensionality reduction approaches.

In the industrial design, the role of multi- and many- objective optimization is more and more relevant, because the increasing computing power of modern computers provides designers with the ability of building complex parametric models that can be used to realize automatic optimization procedures. However, commercial optimization tools are often used without a deep knowledge of their behavior and in particular of their loss of performance when increasing the complexity of the problem [2].

Multi-objective optimization methods can be classified in aggregating methods (classical approach, with weighted or utility functions) and non-aggregating methods (classification of the population based on Pareto dominance). The concept of Pareto dominance or Pareto-optimal solution (2,3) is based on the identification of non-dominated solutions.

$$f_t\left(\bar{x}_j\right) \leq f_t(\bar{x}_i) \,\forall t = 1, \cdots, k \,\forall j = 1, \cdots, m \neq i \qquad (1)$$

$$f_t\left(\bar{x}_j\right) \leq f_t(\bar{x}_i) \; for \; at \; least \; one \; t \,\forall j \qquad (2)$$

The set of all non-dominated solutions is called Pareto-front and is the final aim of any multi-objective optimization. Theoretically, a Pareto-front can contain a potentially infinite number of optimal solutions. The task of a multi-objective optimizer is to provide to the decision-maker a trade-off surface as near as possible to the real one. The set of solutions generated by the optimizer is an approximation set and is characterized by different qualities: proximity or convergence, diversity and pertinence [4].

Convergence refers to finding a set of solutions that lie on or close to the true Pareto-optimal front. Diversity refers to finding a set of solutions that are diverse enough to represent the entire range of the Pareto-optimal front. Diversity is important because the approximation set should contain a good distribution of solutions, in terms of both extent and uniformity. Pertinence means that this set should only contain solutions in the decision maker's (DM) region of interest (ROI). In practice, and especially as the number of objectives increases, the DM is interested only in a sub-region of objective space. Thus, there is little benefit in defining trade-off regions that lie outside the ROI. Focusing on pertinent areas of the search space helps to improve optimizer efficiency and reduces unnecessary information that the DM would otherwise have to consider.

The performance of optimization methods with respect to the quality of the Pareto front for multi- and many-objective optimization is usually tested over mathematical problems [5]. In the present investigation, on the contrary, four different methods are compared with reference to a real-world engineering problem in the aircraft field. As already explained, the algorithms already implemented in the ModeFRONTIER environment were considered without changing their parameters. This commercial software was chosen because it is very user-friendly. Moreover, it allows a clear representation of the overall results of the optimization and an easy choice of the final configuration. On the other hand, as any other commercial software, it does not perform measurements of the performance of the optimization algorithm. In this work, the comparison of four optimization methods will be accomplished with the help of several performance metrics retrieved in literature and applied to the results of the Mode-FRONTIER software after appropriate handlings.

1.1 Evolutionary Methods

The term evolutionary algorithm (EA) indicates a class of stochastic optimization methods that simulate the process of natural evolution. Based on the concepts of individuals, population, generation, selection and variation, natural evolution is simulated by an iterative computation process that is usually ended when a predefined maximum number of generations is reached. Other stop conditions, e.g., stagnation in the population or existence of an individual with sufficient quality, can be used to end the optimization.

Here follows a short description of the optimization methods implemented in modeFRONTIER and compared in the present investigation. NSGA-II is a fast and elitist multi-objective evolutionary algorithm. Its main features are: a fast non-dominated sorting procedure, the implementation of elitism, a parameter-less diversity preservation mechanism, a modified definition of dominance used to solve constrained multi-objective problems and the possibility to handle both continuous ("real-coded") and discrete ("binary-coded") design variables [7]. MOGA-II is an multi-objective genetic algorithm that uses a smart multi-search elitism. This elitism operator is able to preserve excellent solutions without bringing premature convergence to local-optimal frontiers [7]. Evolution strategies are characterized by the following four properties: selection of individuals for recombination is unbiased, selection is a deterministic process, mutation operators are parameterized and therefore they can change their properties during optimization and individuals consist of decision parameters as well as strategy parameters. The standard notation of these methods is $(\mu/\rho +, \lambda)$-ES; where λ is the number of off-springs generated by ρ parents at each step, μ parents are overall involved at each step [8]. MOSA is based on the well-known work of Kirkpatrick et al. (1983) [9] about Simulated Annealing (SA). In contrast with the original SA which is a single objective optimization method, MOSA is a genuine multi-objective optimization algorithm.

Despite their simplicity, EAs have proven themselves as a general, robust and powerful search mechanism for single and multi-objective optimizations also thanks to their ability to capture multiple Pareto-optimal solutions in a single simulation run. For this reason, they are extensively used in engineering applications.

However, EMOAs scalability to many-objective problems is critical. In particular, a deterioration of the search ability of Pareto dominance based EMO algorithms such as NSGA-II, an exponential increase in the number of solutions required for approximating the entire Pareto-front and a difficulty of the visualization of solutions are reported in literature. In the study of Ishibuchi et al. [6] the above mentioned difficulties are reviewed and demonstrated. In the present investigation, they will be addressed with reference to real world optimization problems.

2   The Optimization Problem

In this study, the optimization of both the hybrid electric power system for a Medium Altitude Long Endurance Unmanned Aerial Vehicle (MALE-UAV) similar to the General Atomics Predator RQ-1 and its mission specification is considered.

The UAV has an aspect ratio (b^2/S) equal to 19.1 and a wing load $W_0/S = 818.1 \text{ N/m}^2$ (where b is the wing span, S the wing area and W_0 the takeoff weight). The aircraft is modelled with an in-house simulation software named PLA.N.E.S. [10]. The time histories of speed (V) and altitude (z) are used to perform, at any time step, the balance of the forces acting on the aircraft in the lift (L) and drag (D) directions. The thrust obtained from balance of forces is used to calculate the thrust power (THP) to be generated by the propeller that is connected to a planetary gear box. The gear box is used to perform the power-split between the engine and the electric machine.

As in all hybrid power systems, two energy sources are used. At any time step, a supervisory controller has to decide among the following operational modes:

1. Thermal, the engine produces all the power required by the propeller ($m = 1$);
2. Electric, the propeller shaft power is generated by the motor using the battery as only energy source ($m = 2$);
3. Charging, the engine generates the power to move the propeller and to charge the battery while the electric motor works as a generator ($m = 3$);
4. Power-split, both the engine and the motor generate mechanical power that is delivered to the propeller ($m = 4$).

Where m is a design parameter to be optimized during flight, (see Sect. 2.1).

In the present investigation, the following rule-base strategy is used. Mode 1 is used when the batteries' State of the Charge (SOC) is below a limit (SOCmin) and the engine is not able to charge the batteries. Mode 2 is used when the SOC is above the SOCmin and the electric drive is able to sustain the flight without the usage of the engine. In the case of modes 3 and 4, there is a further degree of freedom in the amount of power to be generated by the engine. The outputs of the supervisory control strategy are the current to/from the electrochemical storage system speed and torque of the engine. The electric power is assumed to be negative when the battery is in charge. The battery state of charge is allowed to vary between 20% and 90% to optimize the battery life [11]. The gearbox is modelled as a simple mechanical power split device with a mass of 20 kg and a efficiency of 0.9. In addition, the propeller is modeled as a black box with the following values of efficiency: 0.65, 0.7 and 0.8 at takeoff, climb/descent and cruise, respectively. The mass of the propeller is also assumed constant for all the designs.

Scaling methods are considered for the most critical components of the hybrid power system, namely the engine, the motor and the battery. The scalable models used for the engine and the battery are described in [12].

2.1   Inputs of the Optimization

The UAV mission optimization is run starting from a typical mission profile of Predator RQ-1 shown in Fig. 1.

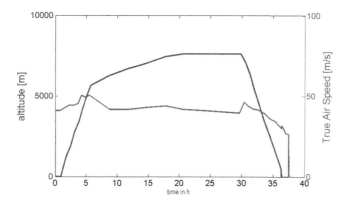

Fig. 1. A typical mission profile of Predator RQ-1

In particular, an in-house code was written to build a mission profile with the same phases of the real one, starting from inputs of Table 1. These inputs will be optimized together with some parameters concerning the design and the control of the hybrid electric power system, which are listed in Table 2.

The UAV flight mission is composed by these phases: take-off, two phases of climb characterized by different rates of climb, cruise, loiter, descent and landing. The starting

Table 1. Design parameters related to the UAV mission

Description	Unit	Min	Max	Step
Cruise speed	m/s	41.0	61.0	0.5
Cruise altitude	m	4900	6900	100
Loiter speed	m/s	37.0	57.0	0.5
Loiter altitude	m	6950	7450	25
Altitude of rate of climb switch	m	2300	3300	25
Rate of climb of the first part of the climb	m/s	0.224	0.424	0.05
Rate of climb of the second part of the climb	m/s	0.224	0.424	0.05
Rate of descent	m/s	0.144	0.344	0.01
Climb energy mode	–	1	4	1

Table 2. Design parameters concerning the sizing and the energy management

Parameters	Unit	Min	Max	Step
Nominal Engine power	kW	40	160	2
Battery elements in series		50	100	1
Battery nominal capacity (C)	Ah	20	150	2
Battery typology		3	5	1
Discharge current	C	0.5	20	0.1
Recharge current	C	0.1	1	0.01

values of the mission parameters for the optimization are obtained by the real mission of Fig. 1. The mission requirements are represented by the cruise range (926 km) and the loiter endurance (24 h).

2.2 Optimization Methods and Goals

The proposed optimization methods (NSGA-II, MOGA-II, MOSA and Evolutionary Strategy) are applied to two optimization problems, which differentiate for:

- the number of objective functions: two for simplified optimizations (multi-objective) and four for complete optimizations (many-objective), with the same aim of optimizing the hybrid electric power system of Predator RQ-1 UAV and its mission;
- the number of total design evaluated: 2500 for simplified optimizations, 10000 for complete optimizations.

In the complete optimization, the objective functions are electric endurance, overall fuel consumption, additional volume and take-off field length. In the simplified optimization, only electric endurance and overall fuel consumption are considered. Objective functions are scaled with respect to reference values of a baseline non-hybrid power system and modified so that all of them had to be maximize.

Evolution strategy method has: $\mu = 50$ $\rho = 2$ and $\lambda = 5$ in the simplified optimizations, $\mu = 100$ $\rho = 2$ and $\lambda = 10$ in the simplified optimizations.

3   Performance Analysis

Over the years, various performance indexes have been proposed in literature for multi- and many-objective optimizations. In this study, the first three metrics suggested by Riquelme et al. [13] are used to compare the different methods:

- *hypervolume* (or *S-metric*): based on the estimation of the hypervolume dominated by the approximated Pareto-front set and bounded by the reference point (percentage);
- *generational distance (GD)*: indicates how far approximated Pareto-front is from the real one;
- *inverted generational distance (IGD)*: similar to GD, it calculates the minimum distance by using real Pareto-front as reference instead of the approximation set.

In addition, the following parameters are also considered [14, 15]:

- *average distance (Davg)* between neighboring vectors of Pareto-front;
- *distance variance (Var)* between neighboring vectors of Pareto-front;
- number of *non-dominated solutions* or Pareto-optimal solutions *(NNS);*
- percentage of solutions of Pareto-front A dominated by Pareto-front B, *C(A,B);*
- *maximum sum of the objective values (MaxSum)*: for each generation G, the maximum sum of the objective values is calculated as follows:

$$MaxSum(G) = max \sum_{i=1}^{K} f_i(x) \quad with\, x \in G$$

where K is the number of objective functions, this measure evaluates convergence of solutions toward the Pareto-front around its center region;

- *sum of the maximum objective values (SumMax)*: the sum of the maximum objective value of each objective is calculated in each generation, *G,* as follows:

$$SumMax(G) = \sum_{i=1}^{K} maxf_i(x) \quad with\ x \in G$$

it evaluates convergence of solutions toward the Pareto-front around its K edges;

- *sum of the ranges of the objective values (Range)*: the sum of the range of objective values for each objective is calculated in each generation G as follows.

$$Range(G) = \sum_{i=1}^{K} [max\{f_i(x)\} - min\{f_i(x)\}] \quad with\ x \in G$$

this measure evaluates diversity of solutions in the objective space.

3.1   Results of the Simplified Problem

The simplified optimization is run by using the above-mentioned optimization methods with the same starting population (or Design of Experiment, DOE) for each of them. Optimizations are deliberately performed with standard set of parameters proposed by modeFRONTIER guide for each method, except for Evolutionary Strategy. In fact, the latter needs particular settings in order to obtain a number of total evaluated design equal to that of the other methods.

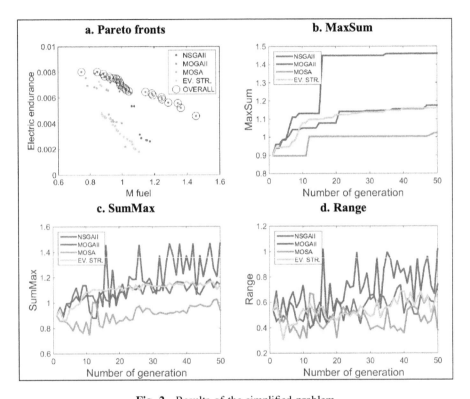

Fig. 2. Results of the simplified problem

Figure 2 compares the Pareto fronts found with the different methods, while Tables 3 and 4 shows the values of the proposed metrics. In particular, Fig. 2a shows the comparison of Pareto fronts from a qualitative point of view. The overall best Pareto-front shown this figure is obtained by merging the Pareto-optimal solutions found by all methods. In the simplified case, it corresponds in part to NSGA-II's Pareto-front and in part to MOGA-II's Pareto-front. Note that:

– NSGA-II is the best method in terms of number of Pareto-optimal solutions non-dominated by fronts of the other methods; it also is characterized by a good definition;

Table 3. Absolute metrics (simplified problem)

Parameter	MOGA-II	NSGA-II	MOSA	EV. STR.
n_NNS	16	25	14	29
Davg	0.0253	0.0082	0.0102	0.0062
Var	7.8287e-04	6.0694e-05	5.1337e-05	3.2478e-05
GD	0.0024	0.0060	0.0101	0.0122
IGD	0	0	0.0031	0.0032
hv	≈0.9190	≈0.7460	≈0.6410	≈0.5920

Table 4. Relative metrics (simplified problem)

C(A,B)	B				
A	MOGA-II	NSGA-II	MOSA	EV. STR.	OVERALL
MOGA-II	–	37.5%	0%	0%	37.5%
NSGA-II	32%	–	0%	0%	32%
MOSA	100%	100%	–	29%	100%
EV. STR.	100%	100%	55%	–	100%

- Although MOGA-II is dominated by NSGA-II in the first part of the graph and has a lower definition, it is able to explore regions where other methods fail;
- Results of MOSA and Evolutionary Strategy are dominated by the Pareto-fronts of both NSGA-II and MOGA-II;
- Evolutionary Strategy is the best method both in terms of number of non-dominated solutions and in terms of distance between them in the first part of the graph. In fact, the distance is lower and more regular then that of the other methods. This indicates a better Pareto-front definition and distribution compared to the other methods (see also the best values of indexes n_NNS, Davg and Var in Table 4).

In Table 3 the best method for each metric is highlighted in grey. Note that MOGA-II is characterized by the minimum values of GD and IGD. This means that its approximation set is the closest to the overall best Pareto-front. Moreover, it has the best value of hypervolume (hv), so Pareto-optimal solutions from MOGA-II cover the largest region in the space of solutions. As already pointed out, Evolutionary Strategy is characterized by the best values of n_NNS, Var and Davg, which indicate a better definition of Pareto-front.

Table 4 shows a comparison of the Pareto-fronts in terms of percentage of Pareto-front A dominated by Pareto-front B. It is possible to observe that NSGA-II has the lowest percentage of dominated solutions. This is probably because its Pareto-front dominates the other methods in a part of the graph of Fig. 2a (in fact, MOGA-II has this characteristic too), but also because NSGA-II has a higher number of non-dominated solutions compared to MOGA-II thanks to its better definition.

Figure 2b, c and d respectively show comparison of MaxSum, SumMax and Range of the different methods. Figure 2b shows that MOSA converges faster than the other methods and Evolutionary Strategy is characterized by the slowest convergence. But MOGAII first and then NSGA-II move to and reach higher values.

Figure 2c shows a gradual improvement of SumMax parameter during the execution of all methods, this suggests a difficulty in finding a set of non-dominated solutions that covers the entire real Pareto-front within a small number of generations; however, the steepest positive trend (so the best) is that of MOGA-II. Figure 2d shows that MOGA-II is characterized by the best capability of exploring the space of solutions, this is also confirmed by Fig. 2a, as above stated. Finally, MOGA-II finds the highest percentage of real and feasible design. From this point of view, NSGA-II is second, Evolutionary Strategy third and MOSA the worst.

According to these considerations, MOGA-II can be said to be the best method for the optimization problem with only two objective functions.

3.2   Results of the Complete Problem (Many-Objective Optimization)

A complete optimization is run by using the same optimization methods used for the simplified problem, with same initial population. Like in the simplified case, optimizations with NSGA-II, MOGA-II, MOSA and Evolutionary Strategy are deliberately performed with the values of parameters proposed by ModeFRONTIER manual, except for Evolutionary Strategy. By using these settings, Evolutionary Strategy evaluates 12753 designs, but only the first 10000 are considered in order to compare methods over the same number of evaluations.

Figures 3 and 4 show the qualitative comparison of the methods. Again, the overall best Pareto-front is approximated by individuating the Pareto-optimal solutions of the set consisting of the designs evaluated by all the methods.

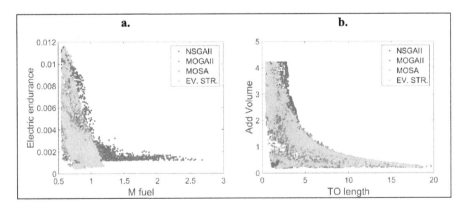

Fig. 3. Pareto fronts (complete problem)

In Fig. 3a and b compares the Pareto fronts by representing the objective functions in pairs. It is possible to observe that NSGA-II is able to explore regions that other

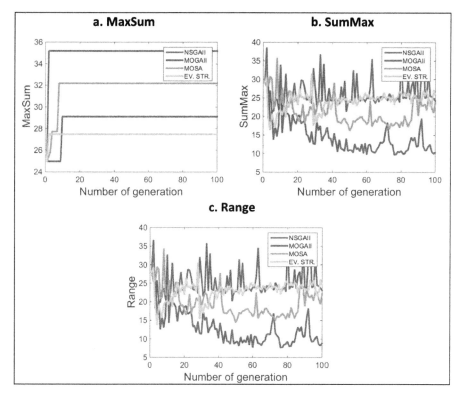

Fig. 4. Results of the complete problem

methods do not reach. Evolutionary Strategy is the best in terms of non-dominated solutions and distance, but also MOGA-II and NSGA-II are characterized by a good definition of the Pareto front. MOSA is again the worst. These considerations are confirmed by the values of parameters n_NNS and Davg in Table 5.

Table 5. Absolute metrics (complete problem)

Parameter	MOGA-II	NSGA-II	MOSA	EV. STR.
n_NNS	3946	4204	1668	4871
Davg	0.0411	0.0413	0.0586	0.0405
Var	0.0051	0.0013	0.0022	7.6688e-04
GD	0.0270	0.0444	0.0288	0.0243
IGD	0	1.5701e-16	0	8.6736e-19
hv	≈0.4230	≈0.4640	≈0.4190	≈0.4050

Evolutionary Strategy is characterized by the minimum value of GD, a value of IGD very close to the best ($8.6736e-19 \approx 0$), the best values of n_NNS, a value of Davg close to the best and the best value of Var. It is the approximation set closest to the overall best Pareto-front. Moreover, it has a good definition and the best distribution. NSGA-II is characterized by the maximum value of hypervolume (hv), i.e. its Pareto-optimal solutions cover a larger region of the space of solutions (see Table 5, where the best method for each metric is again highlighted in grey).

Table 6 shows a comparison of the methods in terms of percentage of solutions of Pareto-front A dominated by Pareto-front B. It is possible to observe that NSGA-II has the lowest percentage of dominated solutions when compared to the others.

Table 6. Relative metrics (complete problem)

C(A,B)	B				
A	MOGA-II	NSGA-II	MOSA	EV. STR.	OVERALL
MOGA-II	–	38%	7%	6%	28%
NSGA-II	4%	–	5%	15%	18%
MOSA	27%	32%	–	35.6%	50.1%
EV. STR.	24.8%	35.4%	8.1%	–	35.6%

Figure 4a, b and c report the trends of MaxSum, SumMax and Range for the different methods. NSGA-II and Evolutionary Strategy converge faster than the other methods and NSGA-II reaches the highest values of all indexes. Figure 4b shows an almost flat trend for NSGA-II and Evolutionary Strategy and a decreasing tendency for MOGA-II and MOSA. This suggests a difficulty in finding a set of non-dominated solutions that covers the entire real Pareto-front within a small number of generations. However, in terms of SumMax, NSGA-II and Evolutionary Strategy perform better thanks to their non-negative trends. Figure 4c shows that NSGA-II is characterized by the best capability of exploring the space of solutions as confirmed also by the analysis of Fig. 3a.

Finally, NSGA-II finds the smallest percentage of errors and an acceptable percentage of unfeasible designs. On the contrary, MOSA shows a high number of errors, but less unfeasible solutions. MOGA-II seems to be the best in terms of real and feasible designs found in the optimization.

Thus, the best methods for the optimization problem with four objective functions seem to be NSGA-II and Evolutionary Strategy. The first shows also a better relative coverage (see Table 6); therefore, it should be preferred in this kind of applications.

4   Discussion of the Results

A comparison between simplified and complete optimizations is done in order to study how the behavior of the different methods changes as the number of objective functions increases.

Since the simplified optimizations evaluated 2500 total design, while the complete optimizations evaluated 10000 total designs, only the first 2500 evaluated designs of the latter are considered in this analysis. Moreover, the Pareto-fronts are first analyzed with reference to the two objective functions of the simplified problem (Fig. 5). The other two objectives are shown in Fig. 6.

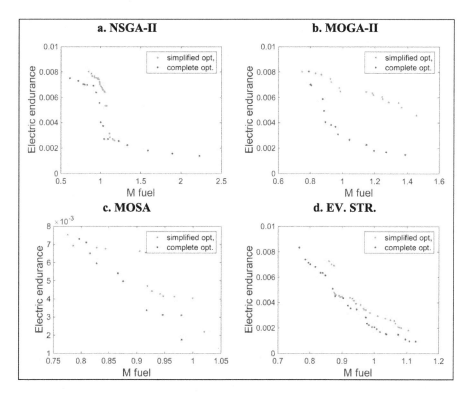

Fig. 5. Simplified versus complete optimization problems about electric endurance and fuel consumption

Note that a better definition of the Pareto front for the first two functions is obtained in the simplified problem. This is an obvious result because in the complete problem it is necessary to find a compromise between more conflicting objectives. In fact, the results related to the other two functions are very poor in the simplified problem because they are not included in the optimization process (Fig. 6).

The percentages of Pareto-optimal solutions of the complete optimization dominated by those from the simplified problem are: 93.3% for MOGA-II, 72.2% for NSGA-II, 80.0% for MOSA and 85.71% for Evolutionary Strategy. However, Fig. 5a confirms the good performance of NSGA-II in a many-objective optimization. In fact, the complete optimization with NSGA-II explores a region of the solutions space that is not found in the simplified optimization. This also implies that not all Pareto-optimal solutions of the complete problem are dominated by those of the simplified case. On the other hand, Fig. 5d shows a similar behavior of Evolutionary Strategy in the two cases.

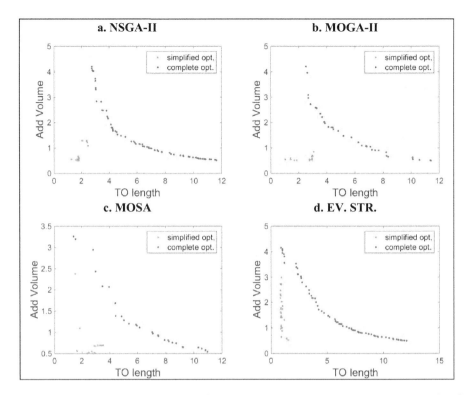

Fig. 6. Simplified versus complete optimization problems about additional volume and take-off length

Comparison in terms of MaxSum, SumMax and Range, still referred to electric endurance and fuel consumption, shows that in the complete optimization NSGA-II converge slower, but moves to higher values. Moreover, NSGA-II is able to cover a wider region of the overall best Pareto-front in the complete optimization, in fact the trend of SumMax is still gradual but is steeper than that of the simplified optimization, and has better capabilities of exploration in the complete optimization. It is possible to observe the same for Evolution Strategy, while this is not true for MOGA-II. MOSA converges faster in the complete optimization, but it shows worse search capability, so it probably converges to local optimal solutions.

In modeFrontier, both NSGA-II and Evolution Strategy use non-dominated/ crowding distance sorting techniques [7], MOGA-II uses a multi-search elitism that combines random selection and directional crossover [16], while search method of MOSA is based on random perturbations of the points [17]. So, probably, as the number of objective functions increases, the crowding distance sorting technique allows a better search than the other methods.

A general worsening of the other parameters is found in the complete optimization, except for the parameter of hypervolume. Since hypervolume is critical in this kind of applications, the SMS-EMOA algorithm [18] will be considered as further investigation. Unlike modeFRONTIER codes, SMS-EMOA is written as an open source code.

Therefore, it will be possible to better understand its mechanisms (for example, the handling of unfeasible designs) and to introduce opportune changes.

Note that this work refers to a state-of-the-art real-world engineering problem. A similar problem is addressed in [19] where the authors use the same optimization environment in an optimization problem with four goals.

5 Conclusions

The present work compares the behaviors of different optimization methods in the multi- and many- objective optimization of a parallel hybrid electric power systems for aircraft. In particular, NSGA-II, MOGA-II, MOSA and Evolutionary Strategy $(\mu/\rho + \lambda)$-ES methods have been applied to two optimization problems differentiating for the number of total individuals analyzed and for the number of objective functions: two for the simplified optimization (multi-objective) and four for the complete one (many-objective). Both qualitative analyses of the Pareto fronts and quantitative performance indexes are used for the comparison.

In this preliminary work, the authors deliberately considered only evolutionary methods (EAs) available in the ModeFrontier platform and the default values of each of their parameters, in order to test quality of solutions that can be obtained from a commercial software by non-specialized users.

The results of this investigation show that MOGA-II is the best in the multi-objective optimizations with only two objective functions, while NSGA-II performs very well in the many-objective optimization. However, Evolution Strategy shows interesting results in terms of definition and distribution of the Pareto-front in both cases. On the other hand, the only non-evolutionary algorithm considered in the investigation (i.e. MOSA) gives always the worst Pareto front. In addition, a general worsening of the behavior of the optimization methods was found when shifting from the multi- to the many-objective optimization. Optimization methods specifically developed for many-objective problems will be considered as further investigation.

This work refers to a specific state-of-the-art real-world engineering problem. Future works will include other EAs that will be tested both on benchmark problems and on other real-world engineering problems in the aeronautical and space fields.

References

1. Pornet, C., Isikveren, A.T.: Conceptual design of hybrid-electric transport aircraft. Prog. Aerosp. Sci. **79**, 114–135 (2015)
2. Gimelli, A., Muccillo, M., Sannino, R.: Multivariable and multiobjective optimization for cogeneration plants. Part A: methodology. In: La Termotecnica, pp. 55–58 (2015)
3. Li, B., Li, J., Tang, K., Yao, X.: Many-objective evolutionary algorithms: a survey. ACM Comput. Surv. **48**(1), Article No. 13 (2015)
4. Fleming, P.J., Purshouse, R.C., Lygoe, R.J.: Many-objective optimization: an engineering design perspective. In: Coello Coello, C.A., Hernández Aguirre, A., Zitzler, E. (eds.) EMO 2005. LNCS, vol. 3410, pp. 14–32. Springer, Heidelberg (2005). https://doi.org/10.1007/978-3-540-31880-4_2

5. Zitzler, E., Knowles, J., Thiele, L.: Quality assessment of pareto set approximations. In: Branke, J., Deb, K., Miettinen, K., Słowiński, R. (eds.) Multiobjective Optimization. LNCS, vol. 5252, pp. 373–404. Springer, Heidelberg (2008). https://doi.org/10.1007/978-3-540-88908-3_14

6. Ishibuchi, H., Tsukamato, N., Nojima, Y.: Evolutionary many objective optimization: a short review. In: Proceedings of 2008 IEEE Congress on Evolutionary Computation, Hong Kong, 1–6 June 2008, pp. 2424–2431 (2008)

7. ModeFRONTIER 2014, Update 1, Version Number 4.6.1 b20150227, User Manual (2014)

8. Beyer, H.-G., Schwefel, H.-P.: Evolution strategies a comprehensive introduction. Nat. Comput. 1, 3–52 (2002)

9. Kirkpatrick, S., Gelatt Jr., D., Vecchi, M.P.: Optimization by simulated annealing. Science 220(4598), 671–680 (1983)

10. Donateo, T., Ficarella, A., Spedicato, L.: Development and validation of a software tool for complex aircraft powertrains. Adv. Eng. Softw. 96, 1–13 (2016). https://doi.org/10.1016/j.advengsoft.2016.01.001

11. Lam, L.L., Darling, R.B.: Determining the optimal discharge strategy for a lithium-ion battery using a physics-based model. J. Power Sources 276, 195–202 (2015)

12. Donateo, T., Ficarella, A.: Designing a hybrid electric powertrain for an unmanned aircraft with a commercial optimization software. SAE Int. J. Aerosp. 10, 1–12 (2017)

13. Riquelme, N., Lücken, C.V., Baran, B.: Performance metrics in multi-objective optimization. In: Computing Conference (CLEI), Latin American (2015)

14. Donateo, T., De Risi, A., Laforgia, D.: Choosing an evolutionary algorithm to optimize diesel engines. In: TCN CAE 2005, University of Lecce, Department of Engineering for Innovation, Lecce, Italy (2011)

15. Lee, S., von Allmen, P., Fink, W., Petropoulos, A.E., Terrile, R.J.: Comparison of multi-objective genetic algorithms in optimizing Q-law low-thrust orbit transfers. In: GECCO 2005, 25–29 June 2005, Washington, DC, USA (2005)

16. Rigoni, E., Poles, S.: NBI and MOGA-II, two complementary algorithms for multi-objective optimizations. In: 04461 - Practical Approaches to Multi-Objective Optimization (2005)

17. Rigoni, E.: MOSA Multi Objective Simulated Annealing. Technical report 2003-003, ESTECO (2003)

18. Beume, N., Naujoks, B., Emmerich, M.: SMS-EMOA: Multiobjective selection based on dominated hypervolume. Eur. J. Oper. Res. 181, 1653–1669 (2007)

19. Aksugur, M., Inalhan, G.: Design, build and flight testing of a VTOL tailsitter unmanned aerial vehicle with hybrid propulsion system. In: Ankara International Aerospace Conference, Ankara, Turkey (2011)

Evolving Controllers for Electric Vehicle Charging

Martin Pilát(✉)

Faculty of Mathematics and Physics, Charles University,
Malostranské náměstí 25, 118 00 Prague, Czech Republic
Martin.Pilat@mff.cuni.cz

Abstract. We describe an algorithm to design controllers for the charging of electric vehicles. The controller is represented as a neural network, whose weights are set by an evolutionary algorithm in order to minimize the changes in the overall electrical consumption. The presented algorithm provides de-centralized controllers that also respect the privacy of the owner of electric vehicles, i.e. the controller does not share the information about charging with any third party. The presented controllers also require only a very small amount of memory and computational resources and are thus suitable for implementation in embedded systems.

Keywords: Electric vehicle charging · Evolutionary algorithm
Neural network

1 Introduction

The rising number of electric vehicles brings the problem of their charging. In a typical scenario, the users of the vehicles use them during the day and charge them at night. However, the charging can place significant load on the electrical grid and increase the electricity consumption at some parts of the day. For example, most people commuting for work come home at a similar time in the afternoon. In case they start charging the cars immediately, the charging can create significant peaks. Therefore, it is important to use a more clever charging plan. Ideally, the charging of the electric vehicles is performed at night in the valleys of electricity consumption and it helps to equalize the consumption during the day.

In this paper, we assume owners of electric vehicles charge their cars at home using a charging station, which can decide on the speed of charging (the charging current). Once the car is connected to the charger, the owner additionally specifies the time, when the car needs to be fully charged. Typically, the owner comes home one day and sets the time they want to leave the next day. We aim to create a control algorithm that fulfills all the charging requirements (i.e. all the cars are charged by the set time), and additionally aims to equalize the electricity consumption during the day.

© Springer International Publishing AG, part of Springer Nature 2018
K. Sim and P. Kaufmann (Eds.): EvoApplications 2018, LNCS 10784, pp. 247–255, 2018.
https://doi.org/10.1007/978-3-319-77538-8_18

While there is an optimal charging protocol for this problem [1], it requires two-way communication between the car and the electrical grid – the grid provides control signal to the cars which, based on this signal, compute the new charging profile by solving an optimization problem. There are also other centralized and de-centralized algorithms for the charging of electric vehicles, but in all of these, some information on the presence of the electric vehicle is shared with a third party. For example, in the decentralized method proposed by Ma *et al.* [2], the utility company and the electric vehicles exchange their predictions of the consumption and the charging requests in an iterative algorithm in order to come up with optimal charging strategy for all the vehicles. This reveals the presence of the electric vehicles to the utilities company. The privacy is even worse for the centralized strategies, like the one developed by Clement *et al.* [3], where a central node receives the information about the time, when the car needs to be charged and the optimization problem is solved centrally.

We consider the privacy of the owners the main priority. In an ideal case, the fact that a car is connected to a charger and the requested time of full charge are not shared among the owners and neither with another independent party. We also aim to minimize the changes in the power consumption during the day which coincidently also minimized the losses in the grid. However, the objective function in our approach can be easily replaced by another one. In this paper, we present the first preliminary result we obtained in this work.

2   Evolution of Controllers

We assume a controller is a function $C(o_t, h_t, \rho, \Sigma, \theta)$, where o_t and h_t are respectively the current overall electricity consumption of the grid and of the household owning the controller, ρ is the current charging request consisting of the required charge r and the ending time of the charging, θ are internal parameters of the controller and Σ is the internal state of the controller. The controller returns the charging current for the next step and the new internal state.

We consider controllers that consist of three modules – the input module, the control module and the output module. The input module $\iota(o_t, h_t, \rho, \Sigma_\iota)$ receives the raw information from the grid and household (o_t, h_t – the overall and household electricity consumption), together with the charging request ρ from the user and transforms this information into inputs σ of the control module. It also changes its internal state. The control module $\Gamma(\sigma, \theta)$ uses these inputs to provide a raw output γ, that is processed by the output module. The output module $\omega(\gamma, r, \Sigma_\omega)$ maps the output of the control module into charging current and ensures that it fulfills all the requirements (i.e. that it does not exceed the maximum allowed charging current and that it is large enough to charge the car in time). The overall controller can thus be expressed as $C(o_t, h_t, \rho, \theta, (\Sigma_\iota, \Sigma_\omega)) = \omega(\Gamma(\iota(o_t, h_t, \rho, \Sigma_\iota), \theta), \rho, \Sigma_\omega)$.

The internal state of the input module ι consists of the history of household and overall consumptions in the last 24 h. Therefore in each call, ι adds a single number to each of the two vectors and removes the oldest one (if the stored history is already longer than 24 h). In case the charging request is empty (i.e. charging is not required), the whole controller returns 0 immediately and the other modules are not executed (the state of the output module is also reset in such a case). Otherwise, the module computes several features that are used by the control module, namely:

- the percentage of the original charging request that is not (yet) fulfilled,
- the percentage of time steps remaining from the charging request,
- the change in the overall consumption and household consumption in the last time step, in the last hour, and in the last 3 h (6 features in total),
- the current household and overall consumption as the percentage of the average over last 24 h (2 features in total),
- a ratio expressing where the current household and overall consumption lies compared to the minimum and maximum over the last 24 h computed as $\frac{current-min}{max-min}$ (2 features in total), and
- the minimum required charging speed and the constant charging speed required to fulfill the request as a percentage of the maximum possible charging speed.

The control module $\Gamma(\boldsymbol{\sigma}, \theta)$, where $\theta = (\boldsymbol{W}_1, \boldsymbol{W}_2, \boldsymbol{b}_1, \boldsymbol{b}_2)$, is encoded as a two layer neural network $n(\boldsymbol{\sigma}) = \mathrm{sigm}(\mathrm{ReLU}(\boldsymbol{\sigma} \cdot \boldsymbol{W}_1 + \boldsymbol{b}_1) \cdot \boldsymbol{W}_2 + \boldsymbol{b}_2)$, where $\boldsymbol{W}_1$ and $\boldsymbol{W}_2$ represent the weight matrices and $\boldsymbol{b}_1$ and $\boldsymbol{b}_2$ represent the biases of the network, $\mathrm{sigm}(x) = \frac{1}{1+e^{-x}}$ is the sigmoid function, and $\mathrm{ReLU}(x) = \max(0, x)$ is the linear rectifier function. Both sigm and ReLU are applied coordinate-wise.

Finally, the output module uses only a single number as its internal state Σ_ω– the charging current in the previous step and has a single parameter α. The output module first multiplies the output of the control module by the maximum possible charging current (obtained from the request) to get the current raw charging current R, and then works as a low-pass filter and at the same time ensures the current is high enough to charge the car in time, i.e. it computes the new charging current (and its new internal state) as $\Sigma_\omega \leftarrow \max(\alpha \Sigma_\omega + (1 - \alpha)R, m)$, where m is the minimum required charging current.

We assume each household has its own controller and that all the controllers use the same internal parameters θ. In order to set these parameters, we assume we have historical information on the baseline consumption of each household (b_t^h the consumption of the household h in every time-step t without the consumption used for the charging of EV) and the past charging requests of the household in the form $\rho^h = \{(t_s, t_e, \mathrm{MC}_h, r)\}$, where t_s is the starting time of the request, t_e is the ending time of the request (when the car needs to be charged), MC_h is the maximum charging current and r is the required charge in kWh. We can then simulate the working of the controller on this historical data. We start by defining the set of active requests at the start of simulation at time t_0 as $A = \{\rho^h | t_s < t_0 \le t_e\}$. Let A^h is the active request for household h if it exists and $\emptyset$ otherwise. In a single step of the simulation, the following happens:

1. the controller in each household is called to obtain the new household consumptions and new internal states of the controllers

$$(c_t^h, \Sigma_t^h) = C(b_t^h + c_{t-1}^h, c_{t-1}, A_t^h, \Sigma_{t-1}^h, \theta)$$

where c_{t-1} is the sum of household consumptions at time $t - 1$, i.e. $c_t = \sum_h c_t^h + b_t^h$,

2. the set of active requests A_t is updated to include new requests $A_n^t = \{\rho^h | t - 1 < t_s \le t\}$, remove expired requests $A_e^t = \{\rho^h | t - 1 < t_e \le t\}$, and update the rest of the requests to reflect the charging in the past time step.

Let $\mathrm{sim}(H, \theta)$, where H represents the historical data and θ are the internal parameters of the controller, is the function that performs the simulation above and returns the sequence of the overall consumptions c_t. Then the internal parameters θ can be set by solving an optimization problem in the form $\min_\theta o(\mathrm{sim}(H, \theta))$, where o represents an objective about the consumptions. As the goal is to equalize the changes in the consumption, we chose to use the standard deviation of the consumptions as the objective. More specifically, $o(\mathrm{sim}(H, \theta)) = \mathrm{std}\{\sum_h b_t^h + c_t^h | 1 \le t \le N\}$, where b_t^h and c_t^h is the baseline consumption and the charging consumption of the household h, and N is the number of simulation steps. The objective defined above minimizes the differences from the constant consumption (the average of the consumption). Another common objective could be the minimization of peaks, however, this one provides more information to the optimization algorithm. The optimization problem can be solved using any optimization algorithm, however, we use the CMA-ES algorithm [4] as it is considered one of the best optimizers for similar problems.

In this work, we are interested in two types of controllers, the one described above will be called NN-14 as it is based on neural network with 14 inputs (as defined by the input module). Such a controller does not need to share the charging request with anyone and its only external input is the overall consumption of the whole grid (we assume the household consumption is measured locally). The NN-14 controller requires one-way communication with a central node that provides the information on the overall grid consumption. We also compare the performance of the NN-14 controller to a more limited NN-9 controller, which does not have access to the information about the consumption of the whole grid. Such a controller does not require any external communication as all the inputs can be computed using only the charging request and the measurement of the household consumption. The inputs for this controller are the same as those for the NN-14 one without those needing the overall consumption.

The controllers respect the privacy of the owners – neither the charging requests, nor the fact that a car is charging are shared. This information is only needed during the training of the controller and we consider the historical information less sensitive than the current one. The controllers are also fast and require very little memory. The internal state consists of roughly 200 floating point numbers (we used time step of 15 min), and the parameters θ are also small (with 5 neurons in the hidden layer, there are roughly 100 parameters). Therefore less than 1 kB of memory is required for the operation of the controllers. The computation in each time-step consists of the computation of the average of the historical values, simple computations of the inputs for the control module, the computation of the control module itself (multiplication of a vector by a matrix), and the computation of the output module. Overall these are at most thousands of simple arithmetic operations. The simplicity of the controllers make them ideal for implementation on simple embedded systems.

3   Experiments

In order to evaluate the performance of the proposed algorithms, we designed a simple experiment. To this end, we first need to obtain data on electricity consumption and define realistic charging requests. Then, we use a part of the data to train the controllers and the rest can be used for testing. Here, we first describe how we obtained the data, then we discuss the settings for the experiment and some baseline control algorithms and, finally, the results.

The data for the simulation combine information from two data sources. The electricity consumption is based on the data from the Dataport database (http://dataport.cloud), which contains detailed measurements on the electricity consumption of several hundred houses in the United States. We specifically chose the data on households in Texas that own an electric vehicle and we downloaded the information on the consumption of the whole household and of the vehicle charging in the first three months of 2015 with 15 min resolution. We obtained information on 74 households. The Dataport data does not contain any information on the times when the cars are available for charging. Therefore, we used the data from the National Household Transportation Survey (NHTS) [5], that contain information on travels in the US. From this database, we selected travels performed by cars in January to March in Texas. We only consider the first time in a day a car leaves the house and the last time it comes back. We consider the car to be unavailable for charging between these times. We obtained more than 3,000 individual travels that contain the information on the start and end of the travel and the day of the week.

The information from these two datasets can be used to generate charging requests in the following way:

1. For each household h from the Dataport database and for each day d between January 1, 2015 and March 31, 2015 choose a random travel (time of departure dep_d and arrival arr_d) from the NHTS database such that the day of the week in the NHTS database corresponds to the day of the week of the request, thus obtaining a database of travels in the form $\langle h, d, \text{dep}_d, \text{arr}_d \rangle$.
2. For each household h from the Dataport database set the maximum charging speed MC_h to the maximum consumption used for charging in the dataset.
3. For each household in the Dataport database h and each day d generate a charging request in the form $\langle h, d, \text{MC}_h, \text{arr}_d, \text{dep}_{d+1}, \text{req}_d \rangle$, where MC_h is the maximum charging speed for household h, arr_d is the time of arrival (from the travels database created in Step 1) on day d, dep_{d+1} is the time of departure on day $d+1$, and req_d is the electricty used for charging the car between dep_d and dep_{d+1}.
4. Remove any requests where the total charge req_d is zero.

The steps above ensure that the charging requests are somewhat realistic. The times of departure and arrival are given by the NHTS data and represent actual departures and arrivals of cars in similar months of the year and geographically close to the Dataport data. The required charge is computed from the Dataport data and represent actual charge that was required for charging. We compute the required charge as the amount of charging done between the departures of day d and departure on day $d + 1$. This ensures that the total amount of charge required corresponds to the charge used in the Dataport data.

For the evolution of weights of the controller we first fixed the topology of the neural network: it uses 5 neurons in the hidden layer and one output neuron. As we already discussed, the number of input neurons depends on the setting – the NN-14 uses 14 input neurons, while NN-9 uses 9 input neurons. We used the ReLU activation function in the hidden layer and the logistic sigmoid as the activation in the output layer.

The initial weights in the network are set to $0.1 \cdot \mathcal{N}(0, 1)$. The weights are tuned using the well known CMA-ES algorithm. The population size is given as per the recommendation in CMA-ES, which leads to 17 individuals for the NN-14 network and 16 individuals for the NN-9 one. The evolution is run for 250 generations. During the evolution, the data from two weeks in January 2015 are used (starting on January 3, at 4 p.m. in order to reduce any effects caused by the ending holidays). During the evolution, the low-pass filter uses $\alpha = 0.0$ and is thus not used. After the evolution, the parameter for the low-pass filter was set to $\alpha = 0.25$ after tuning of the trained controllers using data from January 20th to January 27th. There are only small differences for values lower than 0.5, but the values around 0.25 seem to give slightly improved results.

The evolved controller is compared to four simple baseline controllers. The Min and Max controllers use respectively the minimum or maximum charging speed such that the car is charged in time. The Const controller charges the car with a constant speed for the whole time and the Rand controller chooses a random charging speed for each time step.

Table 1. The comparison of the controllers. The tables shows the average objective value, as well as statistics on the power consumption over three weeks in March 2015 – minimum, maximum and 2.5-th and 97.5-th percentiles. For the evolved controllers and for the random controller it also shows the standard deviations of these values.

Planner	Objective	Min	2.5-th	97.5-th	Max
NN-9	$16.639^{\pm 0.420}$	$49.416^{\pm 0.792}$	$59.817^{\pm 0.929}$	$124.058^{\pm 0.719}$	$151.016^{\pm 1.307}$
NN-14	$14.693^{\pm 0.398}$	$47.088^{\pm 2.674}$	$58.841^{\pm 0.863}$	$119.566^{\pm 1.086}$	$141.592^{\pm 1.262}$
Rand	$31.330^{\pm 0.044}$	$35.137^{\pm 0.581}$	$41.115^{\pm 0.117}$	$154.324^{\pm 0.877}$	$190.555^{\pm 7.229}$
Max	34.720	32.919	38.035	161.692	194.111
Const	19.451	49.812	58.442	133.924	155.238
Min	24.780	35.383	42.437	141.031	169.649

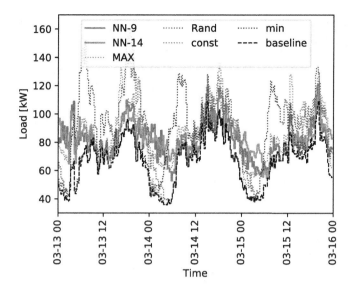

Fig. 1. The electricity consumption for the different controllers during three full days in March. The black dashed line shows the baseline consumption without EV charging.

The results of the experiments are shown in Table 1. It shows the statistics on the electricity consumption of the whole grid in case the controllers were used to control the charging of vehicles in three weeks in March 2015 (starting on March 9). The training of the controllers was repeated five times, and the table shows the average results for the five evolved controllers (the random controller was also tested five times). The numbers in the index show the standard deviation of these numbers. The "objective" column shows the values of the objective, i.e. the standard deviation of the electricity consumption over the three weeks. The "min" and "max" columns show the minimum and maximum consumption, and the "2.5-th" and "97.5-th" columns show the 2.5-th and 97.5-th percentile of the consumption. The percentiles were included as the min and max values are often strongly affected by random effects or drops/peaks in the baseline consumption.

The results indicate that the NN-9 and NN-14 have the best objective value followed by the Const controller. The other controllers are much worse than these three. Mostly because the Min and Max controllers perform most of the charging in the morning or afternoon peaks and do not fill the valleys in the electricity consumption. The Const controller on the other hand charges the cars slowly, and while some of the charging happens during the peaks, it generally charges slower in these times than the Min or Max controllers.

The other values in the table are practically more interesting than the objective. We can see that both the NN controllers and the Const controller have very similar minimum (and 2.5-th percentile) values for the consumption. These are reached in cases where there are not enough charging requests to fill the valleys. However, both the NN controllers are much better than the Const controller in the peaks of the consumption. The NN controllers are generally able to avoid both the morning and afternoon peaks and charge the cars while the baseline consumption is lower. Overall, the Const controller kept the consumption between 58 and 133 kW, while the NN-9 controller kept it between 59 and 124 kW, and the NN-14 controller between 59 and 119 kW for most of the time.

The behavior of the controllers is also graphically shown in Fig. 1 which shows the electricity consumption for three days in March. It shows the NN controllers are able to fill the valleys while avoiding increasing the peaks. The NN-14 controller seems to better avoid the peaks and provide smoother consumption in general, however, the difference between the NN-9 and NN-14 controllers is not very large. This shows that even without the information on the consumption of the whole grid, it is possible to create interesting controllers. The missing communication with the grid can be important, as the NN-9 controllers can be employed in individual households without the need to change the rest of the infrastructure.

4   Conclusions and Future Work

We presented a simple approach to creating controllers for the charging of electric vehicles in smart grids. The controllers are based on an internal neural network trained using the CMA-ES evolution strategy in order to minimize the variance in the electricity consumption. We have demonstrated that the evolved controllers are able to react to the changes in the consumption and change the charging speeds accordingly. The controllers do not share the charging requests or the fact that a car is connected to the grid with any third party and thus ensure the privacy of the owners. The controllers are also extremely fast and memory-efficient, thus, they can be implemented cheaply.

The controllers can definitely be improved. We plan to use recurrent neural networks which may implicitly predict the consumption and are generally more suitable for problems regarding time-series. The features the models use can also be extended – features encoding the day of the week or the time of the day might help to improve the quality of the network.

Acknowledgments. This work was supported by Czech Science Foundation project no. 17-10090Y.

References

1. Gan, L., Topcu, U., Low, S.H.: Optimal decentralized protocol for electric vehicle charging. IEEE Trans. Power Syst. **28**(2), 940–951 (2013). https://doi.org/10.1109/CDC.2011.6161220
2. Ma, Z., Callaway, D.S., Hiskens, I.A.: Decentralized charging control of large populations of plug-in electric vehicles. IEEE Trans. Control Syst. Technol. **21**(1), 67–78 (2013). https://doi.org/10.1109/TCST.2011.2174059

3. Clement, K., Haesen, E., Driesen, J.: Coordinated charging of multiple plug-in hybrid electric vehicles in residential distribution grids. In: 2009 IEEE/PES Power Systems Conference and Exposition, pp. 1–7 (2009). https://doi.org/10.1109/PSCE.2009.4839973
4. Hansen, N., Ostermeier, A.: Completely derandomized self-adaptation in evolution strategies. Evol. Comput. **9**(2), 159–195 (2001). https://doi.org/10.1162/106365601750190398
5. U.S. Department of Transportation, Federal Highway Administration: 2009 National Household Travel Survey (2009). http://nhts.ornl.gov

Network Coordinated Evolution: Modeling and Control of Distributed Systems Through On-line Genetic PID-Control Optimization Search

Holm Smidt[✉], Matsu Thornton, and Reza Ghorbani

University of Hawai'i at Mānoa, Honolulu, HI 96822, USA
{hsmidt,matsut,rezag}@hawaii.edu

Abstract. The evolution of the modern power grid has evident challenges as increasing renewable distributed energy resources are outpacing grid adaptation. With increasing availability and access to real-time sensors and actuators for equipment, distributed control and optimization mechanisms are coming within technical and economic reach. Applying these now feasible mechanisms to known and existing technologies in-place brings rise to new opportunities for the integration of distributed energy resources. This work demonstrated the use of evolutionary computation in finding optimal control parameters of refrigeration systems whose dynamics are unknown and difficult to estimate. By networking evolutionary processes through administrative layers in the form of cyber-physical graph database models, controllers can be deployed at scale and then configured through genetic search algorithms and network interfaces. The premise and direction of this work focuses on leveraging relational information inferred from the graph database to improve the efficiency of the evolutionary process.

Keywords: Network coordinated evolution
On-line evolutionary learning · Genetic algorithm · PID control tuning
Graph database

1 Introduction

The modern power grid is evolving. Driven by societal and political interests, and fueled by environmental considerations, the integration of renewable distributed energy resources (DERs) has been steadily rising in recent years [1, 2]. However, as we begin to take action to integrate greater proportions of renewable generation resources into the power grid, we begin to see several problems arise. Many grids are still built with the old architecture in mind. When we consider the total demand in terms of power and energy supplied by the modern power grid, we are faced with the fact that the amount of renewable DERs currently integrated into the grid are far below the capacity to deliver the amount of power

© Springer International Publishing AG, part of Springer Nature 2018
K. Sim and P. Kaufmann (Eds.): EvoApplications 2018, LNCS 10784, pp. 256–271, 2018.
https://doi.org/10.1007/978-3-319-77538-8_19

and energy required by today's standards. We add the additional complication that renewable DERs are of course restricted to the whims of nature in general and will be able to produce energy relative to the current environmental conditions. This is in stark contrast to the conventional generator which is able to be adjusted at the turn of a steam governor or other mechanism.

Simultaneously, the state of affairs of what is technologically and economically feasible at large scale is changing for the better. In the past, real time access to sensors and controls for equipment has been prohibitively expensive. Historical device data from aggregates of devices were generally not available and optimization is often on a one to one basis. With the advent of affordable network connected devices and controllers, and large capacity for data storage and processing, we are now able to implement more powerful control strategies for coordinated optimization that can transform long-known and well-established technologies into viable economic solutions for improving system efficiencies and reducing energy demand on the grid.

With these problems and technological advances in mind and the increase in renewable DERs outpacing grid adaptation, new methods need to be considered for optimized control strategies for these technologies. This work considers the use of evolutionary computational methods in order to re-purpose existing technologies to address current challenges. In particular, we consider the integration of renewable DERs that come in the form of Internet-of-Things (IoT) assets and how we might be able to leverage advances in data analysis through graph theory, on-line learning, and evolutionary processes for decentralized control tuning. A framework for applying an on-line genetic search algorithm is proposed to investigate the efficacy of genetic search algorithms for optimal control parameter tuning of dynamical systems, and to test the framework's utility in facilitating a parallelized, networked and distributed controller tuning method.

2   Problem Description

This work investigated the use case of a (hybrid solar) mini-split variable speed air conditioning unit for walk-in cooling and refrigeration. Conventional walk-in cooling and refrigeration systems are integral to extending the longevity of perishable products; yet, their operations are prone to energy inefficiencies. Leveraging the advent of affordable network connected control devices, the IoT controller shown in Fig. 1 (left) can be added to a conventional mini-split system (right) to control the air conditioner system beyond its default temperature operating range by outputting a 0–5 v 8-bit pulse-width-modulated (PWM) signal that replaces the mini-split system's thermometer feedback signal and thereby governs the system's behavior. That is, applying a higher voltage would appear to the system's internal controls as if the room temperature is high, which would then cause the compressor to work harder, and vice versa.

Regulating the cooling system's temperature then becomes a closed loop control problem for a system of unknown internal dynamics (the air conditioner unit) and considerable control lag (due to unknown internal controls and temperature signal filtering). Proportional, integral, derivative (PID) control is a

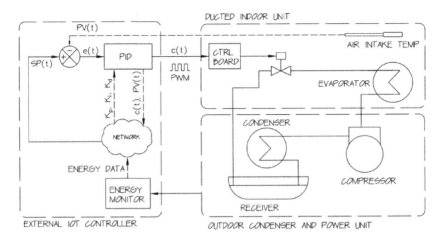

Fig. 1. System model of a hybrid solar mini-split air conditioning unit (right) and external IoT controller (left).

fundamental control mechanism for feedback control systems and widely used in the industry, especially in heating, ventilation, and air conditioning (HVAC) applications [3,4]. A PID controller was thus the natural choice for this use case application.

Given a dynamic system with setpoint $SP(t)$ and process variable $PV(t)$ that tracks the currently sensed position, PID-control aims at tracking and minimizing the error $e(t) = SP(t) - PV(t)$ by applying a control signal, $c(t)$, that would steer the PV(t) to the SP(t) [3]. PID control is a combination of proportional response, automatic-reset response, and pre-act response, and can be expressed as

$$c(t) = K_p e(t) + K_i \int_0^t e(\tau)d\tau + K_d \frac{de(t)}{dt} \tag{1}$$

where K_p is the proportional gain, K_i is the integral (automatic reset) gain, and K_d is the derivative (pre-act) gain. As shown on the left side of Fig. 1, in the proposed application, the PID controller is implemented on the external IoT control unit. The SP is set by the user of the refrigeration unit through a web interface based on the unit's use case application. The PV is measured by the IoT controller and then reported with control variable—computed based on (1) and latest PID gains—and measured energy usage to the administration layer (further described in Sect. 3.2). Unlike many embedded devices with predefined and static control gains, PID gains of the IoT controller can and need to be set over the network as the same set of gains showed to perform significantly different in different system installations.

In [3], Ziegler and Nichols describe the role of each gain in (1) and how controllers can be tuned prior to their installation, known as the Ziegler-Nichols method. However, when controlling systems of unknown dynamics, with non-linearities, or with delays, all situations where conventional tuning methods are hard to apply, literature shows that evolutionary approaches such as genetic algorithms [4], particle swarm optimization [5,6], and differential evolution [7,8] are viable alternatives to conventional tuning methods.

[4–8] and references therein provide a detailed literature review of existing PID tuning approaches that use evolutionary computation as means for finding good PID control gains. Computer simulation results are used to validate proposed methods; yet, the application of these methods on dynamical systems rather than dynamical models demands more testing. The vast web of knowledge on evolutionary computation methods in the literature shows the tremendous reach that evolutionary computation has and the potential application opportunities there can be for it when applied to use case scenarios where conventional control remains a daunting task. The proposed work is not trying to add to the vast pool of evolutionary computation methods for PID tuning, but to draw from it and investigate the challenges that arise during implementation on a testbed systems. The problem then becomes the development of a framework that can facilitate evolutionary learning on an individual controller level, the integration of the controller and the physical system, as well as the integration of the controller with other controllers in the same control domain to utilize distributed knowledge in cyber-physical systems; an on-line learning method is proposed and its inherent challenges in the case of distributed HVAC control for walk-in cooling applications investigated. This work is particularly concerned with using the proposed framework to see if network coordinated genetic search can be an effective means for PID controls tuning in IoT energy applications.

3 Network Coordinated Evolution

3.1 On-line Genetic Search Algorithm

A genetic search algorithm is applied to find optimal control parameters that would control the system of interest with desired control behaviors, in this application, that is minimal error and energy consumption. The genotype population is expressed as a group of m possible solutions, genes, that each consist of the three continuous, real-valued control gains, K_p, K_i, and K_d. Genetic operators of recombination, mutation and selection define the dynamics of the evolutionary process through probabilistic transition rules between generations [4,9]. The likelihood of survival for a gene is determined by its objective function, which is assessed based on the phenotypic behavior of the system, i.e. how well the PV tracks the SP. To apply the genetic search algorithm to the control parameters of the distributed IoT controller for the hybrid solar mini-split air conditioner, each gene's objective function has to be assessed on the actual system to record the system response for evaluation purposes. Figure 1 summarizes the proposed genetic search algorithm. The objective of the search is to find the gene with parameters K_p, K_i, and K_d that optimally control the system, that is, tracking error and energy consumption are minimized. In addition, each learning agent (IoT controller), shall leverage the distributed knowledge in the network of deployed controllers to make better initial guesses when starting the evolutionary process and periodically push its own parameters (knowledge) to the network for others to use. Section 3.2 elaborates on the integration of a graph databases during the genetic search.

The input to the genetic search is an initial pool of m genes, that are queried from a graph database based on the type of control application and control environment. Each generation of the evolutionary process is composed of a parent population and an offspring population obtained through recombination and mutation. The next generation's parent population is then selected through tournament selection among parents and offspring to keep a fixed population size of m genes. To evaluate a population's objective function, the process shown in Fig. 3 is applied, which entails the sequential updating of system setpoints, and observing of process variables and energy data for objective function computation for each cooling process,

$$J(K_p, K_i, K_d) = \omega_1 E + \omega_2 Err \tag{2}$$

where ω_1 and ω_2 are configurable weights, E is the consumed energy during the cooling process, Err is the equally weighted linear combination of the integral

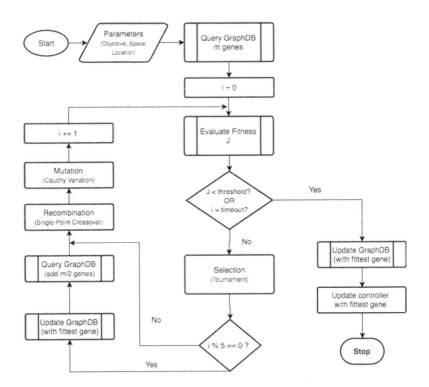

Fig. 2. Flowchart of the evolutionary optimization process with graph database integration.

absolute error, IAE, the integrated time absolute error, $ITAE$, and the integral squared error, ISE. According to [4–6], these are commonly employed metrics for PID control performance evaluation. For the cooling interval of duration $t_2 - t_1$, each of the error functions can be expressed as follows.

$$IAE = \int_{t_1}^{t2} | e(t) | \, dt \tag{3}$$

$$ITAE = \int_{t_1}^{t2} | te(t) | \, dt \tag{4}$$

$$ISE = \int_{t_1}^{t2} e(t)^2 dt \tag{5}$$

A gene's fitness is hence assessed as a combination of energy consumption and control error, where the configurable weights w_1 and w_2 determine preference towards energy efficiency over control performance. Finding the optimal control parameters is then equivalent to minimizing objective function J of a gene.

During the evaluation process, the IoT controller is tasked to control the system in a predefined sequence of positions (SP's); that is for example, one may first let the system passively reach a maximum position T_{max}, and then actively drive the system to a desired SP, and then to a minimal position T_{min} with a time interval Δt between the two positions. The objective function is then evaluated for each cooling cycle and ultimately averaged over all cooling cycles in the control sequence. (Due to the lack of an active heating functionality of the IoT controller, the heating cycle is not considered for computing J.) Single cooling-phase cycles were also employed, in which case there would only be one cooling cycle per gene per fitness evaluation. In cases where the temperature may not surpass some threshold, e.g. because the cooling unit is in operation, one may also just evaluate genes on their ability to maintain the system at a constant temperature.

Given long time intervals for cooling cycles, the system behavior ought to be monitored to filter out genes early whose creations have low potential for producing selective advantages under further variation. That is, if genes indicate high overshoot early for example, they are being assigned a high J value and the fitness loop is interrupted midway to evaluate the next gene.

3.2 Graph Database

To truly realize the proposed application of network coordinated genetic search and leverage the distributed knowledge in the cyber-phsyical network, an administration layer needs to be in place that can be directly integrated with the prescribed evolutionary process. That is, as shown in Fig. 2, the genetic search algorithm shall be able to easily query parameters used by similar IoT controllers and publish its own fittest gene for others to use. Given the highly cyber-physical nature of such an information system, prior work involving the use of graph databases for distributed IoT asset management in cyber-physical

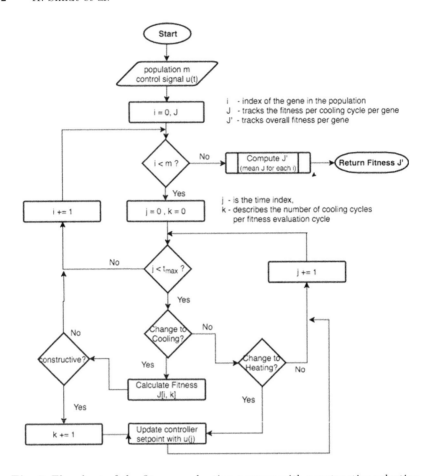

Fig. 3. Flowchart of the fitness evaluation process with constructive selection.

systems (see [10]) was applied here. [10] shows that by implementing IoT admin-istration shells [11] in the form of node and relationship properties in a neo4j graph database [12], one can leverage inherent connections in the cyber-physical system for real-time analytics and asset management, and describes a software architecture for communicating between actors in the cyber-physical model (e.g. devices and humans) and updating the system status in the graph database.

In the sample application, one would describe purely physical components, e.g. a mini-split air conditioner, as nodes with descriptive properties, e.g. cooling capacity, brand and model, power rating, etc., and then describe their connectiv-ity using relationships, e.g. the air conditioner cools a standard decommissioned $33.3\,\mathrm{m}^3$ shipping container and is controlled by an IoT controller. The IoT con-troller, also modeled as a node in the graph, bridges the gap between the physi-cal and the cyber-side of the system. Using this graph-based modeling approach leads to an information system that can act as the system administration layer and enable IoT controllers to quickly search for other devices with the same connections and governing parameters.

Figure 4 shows a small subgraph for illustration of the modeling concept for this system. Two people, Sally and John, own various cooling spaces (yellow nodes) for various cooling applications (red nodes) and thus require some form of cooling apparatus (blue nodes). The IoT controller (green node) can then be described in the graph through its neighbors: an air conditioner (1 node away) being directly controlled by the IoT controller, a space for cooling applications (2 nodes away) with certain volume and ambient temperature, as well as the object being cooled (3 nodes away) with its optimal temperature setpoint. Consider the following simplified example, John's $33.3\,\mathrm{m}^3$ container (shown in yellow) is to be used for refrigeration of produce with a desired setpoint of 54 °F. A new refrigeration mini-split air conditioner is to be installed with an IoT controller. This new controller would need to find its optimal control gains by applying the aforementioned genetic search algorithm, starting with querying the graph database for initial PID control gains. Given that Sally has the same type of container with the same product in it, its IoT controller would be a good choice to pull the gains as an initial gene. The new IoT controller could also query Sally's second container based on the container size, or John's wine cellar with a similar setpoint of 55 °F.

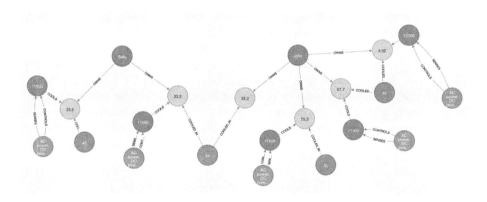

Fig. 4. Graph representation of the modeled cyber-physical system with nodes pertinent to the optimal control parameters. (Color figure online)

In the following Cypher query, neo4j's native query language, such control parameter search is illustrated. The query finds other controllers that control the same type of object and returns the control parameter and SP of matched controllers. Recall that objects are three edges (relationships) away from an IoT controller vertex (node), which is indicated by the three square brackets between the i:CU and o1:Object. Note that in Cypher's asci-art syntax, square brackets indicate relationships and parentheses indicate nodes.

```
MATCH (i1:CU {mac: 'b827ebe0f622'}) - [c1:CONTROLS] - () - [] - () -
[] - (o1:Object) - [] - () - [] - () - [c:CONTROLS] - (i:CU)
RETURN c.kp, c.ki, c.kd, c.sp
```

Besides querying control parameters for the initial parent population from the graph database, Fig. 2 shows that genes are queried periodically during the tuning process to replace genes with low objective function, and that the IoT controller publishes its own fittest parameters as well. The graph database thus provides information on the current state of the system at any time.

4   Implementation

4.1   Genetic Search Implementation

Figure 2 and Sect. 3.1 describe the genetic search algorithm that was implemented using real number encoding and population sizes between 3–6. Given the small sample population size, tournament selection with fixed population size was applied as the contracting evolutionary operator. Single-point crossover with recombination rates between 0–30% was applied when generating the offspring population. The variational mutation operator was chosen as a random sample from the Cauchy distribution with a mutation rate of 35–50%. Table 1 summarized the genetic search parameters. The high mutation rate and fat-tailed distribution were selected based on the small population and gene sizes, as well as the wide PID operator search space (see Table 2).

The slow dynamics (oscillation periods of about 4 min) of the system with the added lag between control signal and system response require a slow controller with slow settling times, which is also expressed in the PID parameter range (Table 2). Parameter ranges were estimated using the Ziegler-Nichols method [3], which suggests higher pre-act control response to prevent undesirable overshoot as the system cannot be actively controlled in the opposite direction (i.e. cooling can only be opposed using passive heat transfer, in other words by turning off the compressor of the air conditioner).

Table 1. Parameters for the genetic search algorithm.

Parameter	Type/Value
Search space	K_p, K_i, K_d
Encoding	Real number
Population size	3–6
Selection	Truncation
Mutation	Cauchy distribution
Mutation rate	0.3–0.5
Recombination	Single point crossover
Recombination rate	0.0–0.3

Table 2. PID parameter range.

Parameter	K_p	K_i	K_d
Lower limit	0	0	100
Upper limit	60	5	800

4.2   Testbed Realization

The efficacy of this approach was tested with three LEZETi hybrid solar air conditioner systems with added IoT controllers of which one was running the genetic search algorithm. One of the test locations was a small-sized farm, shown in Fig. 5, and entailed the cooling of two $33.3\,\text{m}^3$ containers with two IoT controllers, shown in Fig. 6, each controlling a LEZETi air conditioner unit. The cooling setpoint was kept at $54\,°\text{F}$. The other location was an indoor cooling application of a small office room, emulating a cold storage or wine cellar with temperature setpoints between 48–$54\,°\text{F}$ and a volume of $75.3\,\text{m}^3$. While one device was running the genetic search with control inputs shown in Table 3, the idle IoT installations ran with fixed gains and reported their settings to the graph database. A simulated graph model, as shown in Fig. 4, was used to provide additional reference points for the genetic search algorithm (Fig. 2).

Fig. 5. Testbed with hybrid solar mini-split air-conditioner connected. Outdoor condenser and power unit are mounted on the side of the container.

Fig. 6. IoT controller installed for temperature regulation and power monitoring.

The IoT controller consisted of a power acquisition component capable of individually monitoring the DC solar power and AC grid power, a temperature

Table 3. Control signal inputs

Setpoint sequence [°F]	Interval
[70, 54, 48]	15 min
[65, 53]	20 min

logger for temperature acquisition and process variable feedback, and the PID controller interfacing with the mini-split air conditioner system. The IoT controller communicated via MQTT protocol, a pub/sub protocol, such that the server side application (see [10]) can process telemetry data from the device for storage in a relational data store, updating the graph database, and visual display in a front-end application. In the opposite direction, the server side application allows sending of updates to the IoT controller (utilizing the MQTT pub/sub broker), including PID gains and setpoint, over the network. The genetic search algorithm can thus be run on a server or on the device itself as the system response is recorded in near real-time in a relational data store. Figure 7 summarized the system infrastructure. With message brokers, relational and graph data store, and API service on a cloud-server, multiple units can be tracked, controlled, and used for EV testing.

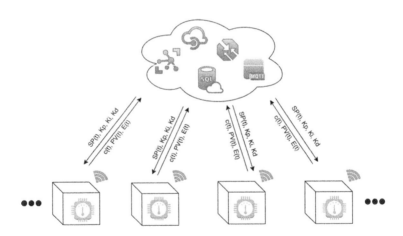

Fig. 7. System framework with services running on a centralized server that publishes and subscribes to IoT control topics. Graph and relational databases, message broker, message gateway, and API endpoint are used for the network coordinated evolutionary process involving IoT control devices.

The aforementioned implementation allowed for the GA script to be executed on the IoT controller or on a proxy server as SP and PID gains can be updated over the network, and historical data (PV) queried from a database. For a limited number of devices and pilot testing, testing is simplified if the GA is executed on a centralized proxy server; however, if scaled to considerably more devices, direct implementation on the IoT controller is recommended.

5   Results

The objectives were to develop a framework capable of facilitating network coordinated evolutionary processes, and to test the utility of the network coordinated tuning method for overcoming challenges inherent to running evolutionary processes on physical hardware devices. The genetic search algorithm was tested on one of the three deployed IoT controllers, which showed that the system framework is capable of facilitating evolutionary learning. Control parameters, genes, were updated on a deployed IoT controller by running the GA on a proxy system, a cloud Linux server, that would send API calls to the information systems that would then send out signals to the IoT controller with an overall response time of less than 3 s. Retrieval of time-series data from the centralized database for objective function evaluation was also achieved. In addition, visual analytics dashboards were developed and used for real-time tracking of the evolutionary process, as shown in Fig. 8. The dashboard implementation allowed the user to track if the GA script is running as desired and illustrates the efficacy of the overall framework.

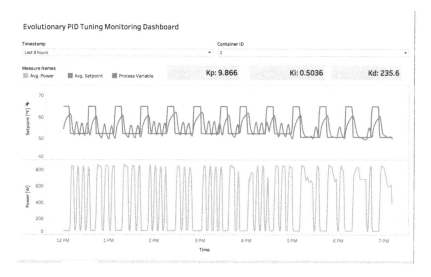

Fig. 8. Monitoring dashboard with live connection to the relational database with system response data. *SP* and *PV* (control input and system output) were shown in the upper graph and average power consumption in the lower graph. The latest control parameters are displayed above the graphs. Time and container (i.e. learning agent) may be filtered using the drop-down menus on the top. The GA shown here consisted of six genes with a mutation rate of 35%, recombination rate of 25% and tournament selection.

In order to evaluate the utility of the genetic search algorithm, a base-line experiment with a single learning agent was performed before investigating distributed evolutionary processes with multiple agents learning together. The developed genetic search algorithm was thus first tested on a single agent with-out graph database connection, and a snapshot of generation five in the process was shown in Fig. 9. In this scenario, the input signal was given as $[70, 54, 48]\,°F$ and pre-filtering was applied when settling time or overshoot were too high dur-ing the first cooling cycle. The comparison of the parent and offspring genes in this population of three genes detailed the effects of mutation and pre-filtering. The gene 1 parent met the criteria for pre-filtering during the first of the two cooling cycles such that it was assigned a very poor J-value. The offspring of this gene after mutation (50% mutation rate) continued to meet the pre-selection criteria. Parent and offspring of gene 2 on the other hand performed better and were evaluated for both cooling cycles. Lastly, the mutation operation in gene 3 significantly improved its behavior as the offspring was not weeded out in the pre-filtering process unlike its parent. Recall that heating occurs in a passive process and is not considered in the objective function evaluation; consequently, as shown, the given time interval did not allow for the system to reach the maximum temperature of $70\,°F$.

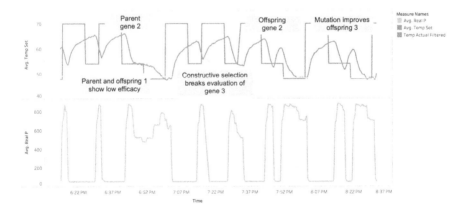

Fig. 9. Comparison of parent and offspring population in an early generation (genera-tion 5) illustrates the concepts of mutation and constructive selection during the fitness evaluation process. In this GA, the population size was 3, the mutation rate was 50%, recombination was not applied, and fitness proportional selection was used.

Following initial observations on the performance of the genetic algorithm on a single agent, recombination was introduced as a second variational operator so that mutation rates could be lowered. In addition, the graph database usage was introduced using a graph database with predefined control parameters. The new design was tested on a population size of six genes with a mutation and recombination rate of 35% and 40% respectively and only a single cooling phase

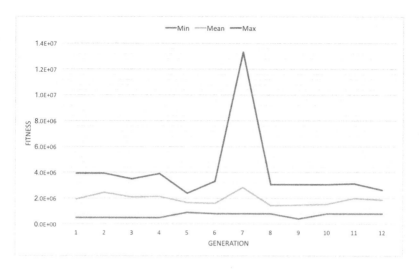

Fig. 10. Maximum, minimum, and average fitness of the parent and offspring population after mutation (before selection) for a process with a population size of six genes, mutation and recombination rates of 35 and 40% respectively, and tournament selection.

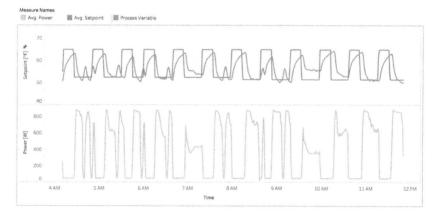

Fig. 11. Process observations for the last generation of the 12 generation process with a population size of six genes, mutation and recombination rates of 35 and 40% respectively, and tournament selection.

per fitness evaluation per gene. The maximum number of generations was limited to 12, which resulted in a runtime of 51 h. Figure 10 compared the minimum, maximum, and mean fitness of the combined parent and offspring population of each generation.

The comparison showed that within the limited time frame, the best solution (minimum fitness) could not be improved compared to the initial input.

In addition, one notices that the jump in maximum and thus mean fitness in generation 7 occurred after the graph database had been queried. This showed that the control parameters stored in the graph database (randomly chosen at this point) were not constructive for this process. It further showed however that querying new genes throughout the evolutionary process can change the dynamics of the process by introducing variation beyond the mutation and recombination operators. One could further observe that the same gene, the fittest gene, performed differently in two different generations as shown by the increase in fitness of the best-performing gene. This observation can be attributed to the fact that the lower temperature bound, the desired temperature, was varied between generations to avoid bias towards single temperature SPs and that environmental conditions may vary between execution runs. As shown by the process output shown in Fig. 11 for the last generation (parent and offspring) for this GA process, the process did not converge in 12 generations, as expected. Nonetheless, although not optimal, some candidates showed promising behaviors.

6   Conclusion

The proposed framework illustrated that evolutionary computation can be applied to dynamical systems and not just models. By testing possible solutions on the actual dynamical system and observing its response, genetic search algorithms were able to evaluate candidate solutions' objective functions and then apply evolutionary mechanism of mutation, recombination and selection to evolve better control parameters.

It was further shown that the implementation of genetic search algorithms can be applied to a collection of distributed dynamical systems, such as hybrid solar mini-split air-conditioning units, to then search for optimal control parameters in a network coordinated approach, which entails the use of a centralized graph database that models the cyber-physical system and connects physically disconnected systems in their virtual abstractions. Experimental efforts did not provide conclusive evidence for a converging genetic search algorithm with optimal PID control parameters; however, it successfully illustrated a method for deploying network coordinated genetics search algorithms in IoT energy applications. The lack of convergence was attributed to the fact that only limited devices and IoT controllers were available at the time of testing.

As pointed out in Sect. 2, much of the literature used simulations to evolve optimal PID control parameters. Using simulations, researchers were able to run their genetic search for hundreds of generations. A distributed approach would thus require considerably more devices to converge in less generations. In addition, approximate system models shall be simulated and added to the network to contribute to the learning process. While these may only be results based on approximate models, they would possibly be superior to the randomly generated ones that were currently used and that caused the spike in generation seven of Fig. 10.

Initial genetic search implementations showed efficacy of control devices and the effect of the different evolutionary mechanisms in the learning process.

As additional systems are currently being installed, more work is needed to evaluate the intricacies and performances at larger scale. Continued and prolonged execution will provide the needed data to perform statistical analysis on the stability and convergence of the genetic algorithm.

Acknowledgements and Remarks. The authors would like to thank GreenPath Technologies Inc. for providing their LEZETi air conditioner units and laboratory space for testing and Kahuku Farms for allowing implementation on their farm refrigeration units. H.S. also thanks Dr. Lee Altenberg for the great introduction to the field of evolutionary computation in his ICS674 course at the University of Hawai'i at Mānoa that motivated the use of evolutionary computation for distributed parameter tuning.

References

1. Amin, S.M.: Smart grid: overview, issues and opportunities. Advances and challenges in sensing, modeling, simulation, optimization and control. Eur. J. Control **17**(September), 547–567 (2011)
2. Lehnhoff, S., Nieße, A.: Recent trends in energy informatics research. it - Inf. Technol. **59**(1), 1–3 (2017). http://www.degruyter.com/view/j/itit.2017.59.issue-1/itit-2016-0058/itit-2016-0058.xml
3. Ziegler, J., Nichols, N.: Optimum settings for automatic controllers. Transa. ASME **64**, 759–768 (1942)
4. Jayachitra, A., Vinodha, R.: Genetic algorithm based PID controller tuning approach for continuous stirred tank reactor. Adv. Arti. Intell. **2014**, 1–8 (2014)
5. Menhas, M.I., Wang, L., Fei, M.R., Ma, C.X.: Coordinated controller tuning of a boiler turbine unit with new binary particle swarm optimization algorithm. Int. J. Autom. Comput. **8**(2), 185–192 (2011)
6. Zhangjun, Z.K.: A particle swarm optimization approach for optimal design of PID controller for temperature control in HVAC. In: 2011 Third International Conference on Measuring Technology and Mechatronics Automation, vol. 1(2), pp. 230–233 (2011)
7. Zhang, X., Zhang, X.: Shift based adaptive differential evolution for PID controller designs using swarm intelligence algorithm. Cluster Comput. **20**(1), 291–299 (2017)
8. Zhao, S.Z., Qu, B.Y., Suganthan, P.N., Willjuice Iruthayarajan, M., Baskar, S.: Multi-objective robust PID controller tuning using multi-objective differential evolution. In: 11th International Conference on Control, Automation, Robotics and Vision, ICARCV, 1 December 2010, pp. 2398–2403 (2010)
9. De Jong, K.: Evolutionary Computation: A Unified Approach (2006). http://mitpress.mit.edu/0262041944
10. Smidt, H., Thornton, M., Ghorbani, R.: Smart application development for IoT asset management using graph database modeling and high-availability web services. In: 51st Hawaii International Conference on System Sciences (2018)
11. Hübner, I.: RAMI 4.0 und die Industrie-4.0-Komponente. Open Automation, pp. 24–29 (2015)
12. Neo4j, the world's leading graph database. https://neo4j.com

EvoGAMES

Piecemeal Evolution of a First Person Shooter Level

Antonios Liapis[(✉)]

Institute of Digital Games, University of Malta, Msida, Malta
antonios.liapis@um.edu.mt
http://antoniosliapis.com/

Abstract. This paper describes an iterative process for generating multi-story shooter game levels by means of interlocking rooms evolved individually. The process is highly controllable by a human designer who can specify the entrances to this room as well as its size, its distribution of game objects and its architectural patterns. The small size of each room allows for computationally fast evaluations of several level qualities, but these rooms can be combined into a much larger shooter game level. Each room has two floors and is generated iteratively, with two stages of evolution and two stages of constructive post-processing. Experiments in generating an arena-based level for two teams spawning in different rooms demonstrate that the placement and allocation of entrances on each floor have a strong effect on the patterns of the final level.

Keywords: Procedural content generation · Level design
First person shooter · Constrained optimization · Iterative refining

1 Introduction

While procedural content generation (PCG) has a history of almost four decades in the game industry, it remains a niche —almost mystical— topic for many game development teams. Especially for the PCG research community, communication and collaboration with industry experts and game designers has been sparse. Highlights of academic PCG taking the commercial route usually have the researcher lead the game development cycle; notable examples include *Galactic Arms Race* [1], *Petalz* [2], *Sure Footing* [3], *Unexplored* by Joris Dormans (Ludomotion 2017) and *Darwin's Demons* [4].

Admittedly, a factor for the skepticism of the game industry towards PCG research is the often poor communication between the academic and the game developer community. However, a more tangible factor is that PCG research often builds monolithic generative systems for a specific game; most often, such games are either simplifications of outdated games, such as *Super Mario Bros* (Nintendo 1985), or games designed explicitly for the research problem at hand, such as GVGAI level generation [5]. Even when the generated artefacts could be —under circumstances or after post-processing— applicable to a broader genre

ⓒ Springer International Publishing AG, part of Springer Nature 2018
K. Sim and P. Kaufmann (Eds.): EvoApplications 2018, LNCS 10784, pp. 275–291, 2018.
https://doi.org/10.1007/978-3-319-77538-8_20

of games, developers are skeptical because they do not see a way to control the generative processes [6]. Being able to both understand (e.g. through visual inspection) and control the outcomes of the generative process is an important reason why commercial generators are often based on *templates*. Indicatively, dungeons in *Diablo III* (Blizzard 2012) consist of large hand-authored 'jigsaw pieces'[1] stitched together by a simple generator that chooses which piece attaches to which, then populates each piece with monsters and treasure. A similar process is followed by *Spelunky* (Mossmouth 2012), where every level is split into 16 'segments' with randomized connections; the layout of each 'segment' is selected from a set of templates and is then randomized somewhat and populated with treasures and monsters [7]. In contrast, academic PCG rarely focuses on modularity for two reasons: (a) often complicated algorithms are included which can not be compartmentalized; (b) in search-based PCG [8] or constraint-based PCG [9], content must usually be in its final form in order to assess its quality (in order to improve it or to test all constraints, respectively).

Providing different degrees of control to human designers has also been a topic of research within PCG, of course. Generators such as those by Doran and Parberry [10] give a multitude of parameters (many of them not entirely intuitive) for the user to tweak. The shader generators of Howlett, Colton and Browne [11] allow the user to specify the target color which evolution will try to match. The editor for *Refraction* allows the designer to specify how each generated level must be solved [12]. *Danesh* [6] allows users to view the generative space and explore more intuitively how the different parameters impact the quality of the results. Generators working alongside designers, e.g. in mixed-initiative design [13], also offer a large degree of control to the designer but are unable to create new content for players during runtime. The academic PCG approach closest to the commercially popular template-based generation is based on grammars [14], where one generator first creates the mission graph —a high-level representation of the final level— and then replaces the high-level nodes of that graph with level architecture which in most cases is based on human-made 'jigsaw pieces'. As an example, in the commercial game *Dwarf Quest* (Wild Card 2013) the mission can be generated from editable grammars describing the allowed sequence of generative commands [15] or evolved towards a designer-chosen fitness function [16]; then the mission is converted into a *Dwarf Quest* level consisting of pre-made rooms mapped to the description of the node (e.g. a boss room will have a specific room layout, monsters and treasures within it).

Inspired by template-based commercial generators, this paper presents a generative algorithm for first person shooter (FPS) games which allows many degrees of control and outputs *rooms* which can then be combined like jigsaw pieces as desired by game designers (or while the game is played) to create the full map. The generator creates rooms with two floors because many level patterns popular in FPS games, such as a gallery or a sniping position [17], require the presence of areas above and below them. The generative process is iterative, first evolving

---

[1] Interior jigsaw pieces is a term used by a Blizzard employee on the Blizzard forums under the nickname Bashiok.

a draft of the ground floor's architecture, then creating a draft of the top floor's architecture which is then evolved along with the placement of game objects. A two-step evolutionary process has been shown to be beneficial when evolving levels with two floors [18,19]. Both evolutionary steps use a constrained optimization algorithm to ensure that the final content is playable; the criteria for what is playable, the room's size and the game items within it are controlled by the designer before evolution begins. More importantly, the designer specifies the number and placement of entrances to the room, which cannot be changed by the evolutionary process. Where entrances are placed affects how different rooms connect to each other, but also affects the patterns favored by the generated content as entrances are considered in the fitness functions of the evolutionary iterations; this will be evaluated in experiments of this paper.

Unlike many other search-based PCG projects in academia, the generative processes in this paper are iterative, modular and parameterizable. While artificial evolution is the core generative method, it takes place in iterations interspersed with post-processing steps which can significantly affect the look and feel of the final level. Moreover, the evolutionary steps themselves integrate several constraints which are not strictly based on playability but rather on the look and feel of the level. These additions were made at the request of game designers and with specific gameplay concerns in mind, during the collaboration with Luiz Kruel and his game development team[2]. The room-based generation which allows for modular re-combination of different pieces (generated or human-authored) was found preferable to level designers than a monolithic level generation algorithm. Controlling the room size and entrance placement was similarly vital in order to integrate procedural generation to the team's design process. Dead-end removal in post-processing steps was deemed essential because dead-ends disrupt the run-and-gun FPS gameplay by forcing players to become "trapped" and vulnerable to an ambush. Finally, constraints on open air tiles and walls in each evolutionary step allows designers further control over the patterns they would prefer in the generated level. This parameterized design space gives sufficient control to designers in order to control the look and play patterns that are produced by the generator.

2   Background Work on Map Sketches

The notion of a *map sketch* originates from *Sentient Sketchbook* [20], and encompasses all low-resolution representations of game levels which contain the minimal number of tile types needed to describe the intended gameplay. For example, in real-time strategy games the core necessary tile types are impassable terrain, players' bases, resource-rich locations around the map, and empty passable tiles. For the shooter genre, the core tile types could be the players' (or teams') spawn locations, weapon pickups, and possibly also health pickups if the game does

---

[2] A talk by Luiz Kruel at the 2017 Game Development Conference (GDC) highlighted the generative pipeline followed in this paper, focusing on the transformation of the top-level views of this approach into 3D levels.

not feature regenerating health [21]. Since the low-resolution sketch is composed of a few tiles of even fewer types, it can be evolved using a direct encoding [8] with genetic operators changing each tile individually, e.g. changing from one tile type to another or swapping adjacent tiles.

Map sketches are general level descriptors as they can be translated (or represented) at a post-processing *detailing* step into a high-resolution game level in 2D or 3D [21]. A number of general evaluations of game level patterns [21] have been designed with map sketches in mind, focusing on the patterns of *exploration*, *balance* (or symmetry) and *strategic resource control* introduced by Bjork and Holopainen [22]. These evaluations are straightforward to compute via pathfinding (for resource control) and flood fill (for exploration) algorithms, and are lightweight in the small map sizes of sketches. This paper iteratively evolves FPS rooms towards improving exploration and safe area evaluations: the former captures the effort taken to reach one or more tiles starting from another tile, while the latter counts the number of tiles (of any type) which are much closer to one tile than to all other tiles of the same type. Balance for exploration and safe area assesses whether some tiles are easier to find than others or some tiles have far more safe tiles around them than others, respectively. Details of the calculation of these fitness dimensions are provided by [21].

3   Methodology

The levels generated by the algorithm are composed of two floors, one placed on top of the other. Players can move from the ground floor to the top floor through *jump pads*, which lead to *jump landings* on the top floor right above them. Players can move from the top floor to the ground floor through the same jump landing holes, but also through open air tiles which do not have a floor and allow players to jump down to adjacent tiles on the ground floor. Since the levels are intended for team-based deathmatch gameplay, tiles where each team starts from are included (spawn points). Moreover, the level contains weapon pickup tiles which allow players passing through them to gain more powerful weapons (and replenish their ammo). Both floors can contain wall tiles which block line of sight and movement through them. As with all map sketches, these few tile types (in addition to entrance tiles which have no gameplay effect but are vital for connecting rooms together) constitute the minimal components[3] that facilitate FPS gameplay in levels with more than one floor.

The principle behind the entire generative pipeline presented in this paper is iterative design, summarized in Fig. 1. As shown in Fig. 1a, each level is split into rooms which are evolved separately, one at a time. When evolving each room, the iterative process becomes obvious (see Fig. 1b): note that each step for individual room generation is automated and does not require designer intervention. First, evolution produces a draft of the ground floor, laying out impassable tiles, jump

---

[3] Unlike [21], health pickups are not included following discussions with game designers who did not consider them necessary; health pickups they easily be placed in a constructive fashion post-generation or omitted due to re-generating health.

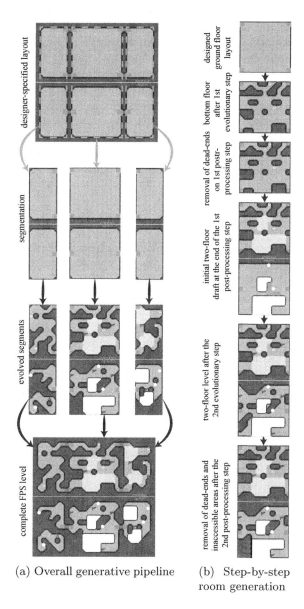

(a) Overall generative pipeline   (b) Step-by-step
                                        room generation

Fig. 1. Overall generative pipeline for partitioning and combining rooms (Fig. 1a); the designer specifies how the rooms are sized and where their entrances (in magenta) are placed, and the iterative generation results in two-floor rooms which can be combined into the final shooter level. Each room is generated through a step-wise process shown in Fig. 1b, where an evolved ground floor which after post-processing generates a first draft of the top floor; then both floors are evolved and finalized through a second post-processing step. (Color figure online)

pads and entrances. The fittest ground floor draft is used as a basis for creating the two-floor level; initially, the only tiles of this draft top floor are open air tiles, jump landings and empty tiles (which are specified by the patterns of the floor under them) and the entrances (which are specified by the user). After this process, all tiles specified by the above two-step drafting process are "frozen": evolution can not change pre-existing walls, jump pads/landings or open air tiles during subsequent stages, although it can change empty tiles normally. The second stage of evolution populates both floors with weapons and spawn points and may also add walls on either floor. The fittest two-floor level is then post-processed to remove unused corridors and jump pads/landings. Once this process is complete for each individual room, the final rooms are connected together as desired by the designer to form the final FPS game level.

3.1   Evolving the Ground Floor

The first stage of generation is the evolution of a first draft of the ground floor, the structure of which will form a draft for the top floor. In this stage only the ground floor is evolved: the genotype stores only half of all tiles in the room. Evolution starts from an initial population containing the designer-specified number of jump pads and a number of wall tiles equal to 10% of all tiles randomly placed in the room, as well as the entrances placed where the designer has requested them; entrance tiles will not be changed or moved by evolution. Evolution uses mutation alone to (a) transform an unoccupied passable tile into a wall or vice versa (25% chance), or (b) swap any tile with an adjacent one (5% chance). Following the literature [21], between 5% to 20% of all tiles can be mutated in this way per individual. In order to ensure that evolving levels satisfy certain playability constraints, evolution in carried out in two separate populations using the feasible-infeasible two-population genetic algorithm (FI-2pop GA) paradigm [23]. Each population contains only individuals which satisfy all playability constraints (the *feasible* population) or individuals which fail them (the *infeasible* population); offspring of feasible individuals may be infeasible in which case they migrate to the infeasible population, and vice versa. Both populations evolve to maximize or minimize a fitness value, using fitness-proportionate roulette-wheel selection and minimal elitism: the best individual in each population is copied unchanged to the population of the next generation.

The feasible population evolves to maximize a sum of three equally weighted fitnesses formulated in [21]: (a) exploration from any entrance or jump pad to any other entrance or jump pad, (b) balance of exploration from any entrance to any entrance, (c) balance of exploration from any entrance to any jump pad. On the one hand, exploration rewards all entrances and jump pads which are far away, but the two balance metrics distinguish between entrances (which may be closer together due to designer specifications) and jump pads; the two jump pads should be equally hard to reach from all entrances, but that does not need to be comparable to the exploration effort between two entrances. The calculation of exploration is shown graphically in Fig. 2.

Meanwhile, the infeasible population contains individuals which fail one or more of these constraints: (a) all entrances and jump pads must be connected

(a) Exploration from TLE to BRE.   (b) Exploration from BRE to TLE.   (c) Exploration from TLE to top JP.   (d) Exploration from top JP to TLE.

Fig. 2. Fitness calculation of the first evolutionary step: exploration between entrances (top left as TLE and bottom right as BRE). Exploration effort from TLE to BRE is almost as high as from BRE to TLE (i.e. two fewer tiles covered). On the other hand, from TLE the nearest jump pad (JP) is easily found, while starting from that JP the exploration required to find TLE is much higher, and the two efforts are not balanced.

via passable paths, (b) jump pads are not placed under entrance tiles on the top floor, (c) entrances or jump pads are at least two tiles away from any entrance or jump pad, (d) the number of walls does not exceed 30% of the floor's tiles and (e) the number of tiles that have all their neighbors passable does not exceed 10% of the floor's tiles. Some of these constraints are self-evident; all entrances and jump pads must be connected so that a player can use them but also so that the exploration metric can be calculated. Other constraints are based on designer feedback, so that maps are not overwhelmed by walls and maze-like corridors but also not leading to overwhelming open air sections in the top floor (discussed in Sect. 3.2). The infeasible population evolves to minimize an infeasible fitness function proportionate to the distance to feasibility, which is a sum of features that violate constraints (e.g. the number of disconnected entrances and jump pads or the number of game elements closer than two tiles to each other).

3.2 Creating the Top Floor from the Ground Floor

Once the first evolutionary step is complete, the fittest individual in the final population becomes the basis for the first draft of the top floor. Before this happens, however, a constructive algorithm removes corridors leading nowhere (i.e. dead-ends); this level pattern was found undesirable for the FPS genre as players could easily be ambushed, or must backtrack their steps which is not desirable for the run-and-gun aesthetic of such games. This step iteratively replaces unoccupied dead-ends with a wall (red circles in Fig. 1b). A *dead-end* is a tile with only one connection (on the navigation mesh) to adjacent passable tiles. Dead-ends with jump pads or entrances are not removed as they still allow movement to the top floor or to the next room respectively.

Once dead-ends are removed, the top floor is initialized with entrances (as specified by the designer), jump landings (on the same locations as their jump pad counterparts on the ground floor), passable platforms and open air tiles. Open air tiles represent areas of the top floor which have no solid flooring, allowing the player to aim at opponents on the ground floor or jump down to it. In order to maintain some structural integrity with the ground floor, only large

 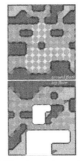 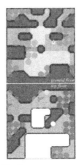

(a) Exploration effort   (b) Exploration effort   (c) Safe areas around
from ground floor.   from top floor.   weapons & entrances.

Fig. 3. Exploration effort from the bottom right (BRE) entrance on the ground floor to the left (LE) entrance of the top floor (Fig. 3a) which requires use of jump pads. Compare with the exploration effort from LE which uses the open air sections to jump down and quickly find BRE (Fig. 3b). The other fitness when evolving both floors is the number of safe tiles to an entrance, weapon, or spawnpoint (Fig. 3c). Two weapons on the top floor have safe tiles on both floors: the weapon with blue safe tiles (due to open-air tiles); the weapon with yellow safe tiles (due to the nearby jump landing). (Color figure online)

areas in the ground floor have open air sections above them. This is calculated based on the navigation mesh by finding tiles on the ground floor which are fully connected, i.e. all their neighbors are passable tiles. If there is a fully connected tile in the ground floor (yellow circles in Fig. 1b), then the top floor tile above it and its immediate neighbors become open air tiles with one exception: if any open-air tile inserted in this way is adjacent to an entrance or jump landing, then it is replaced by a passable platform instead (such exempt tiles appear as cyan circles in Fig. 1b). This exception ensures that jump landings and entrances always have a platform around them for the player to land on or survey the level.

All rooms with two floors have a special navigation mesh which provides connections across floors. Two-way connections are created between jump pads and jump landing tiles, which is the only way that a path from the ground floor to the top floor can be computed. The system also creates one-way connections between platforms on the top floor and passable tiles on the ground floor which are over open air tiles adjacent to these platforms. The navigation mesh assumes that players can not jump more than a tile's worth of distance, and thus can not jump over an open air tile to another platform on the top floor.

3.3 Evolving both Floors

Once the layout of the top floor is created, both floors go through another evolutionary step which adds walls, weapon pickups and the teams' spawn points in the room. Using the same FI-2pop GA and parameters (including the mutation operators and probabilities), evolution starts by randomly allocating in both floors the weapons and spawn points. The number of weapons and spawn points are the same in all evolving levels, and are specified by the designer. Unlike the previous evolutionary stage, no additional wall tiles are placed in the initial population but are added via mutation (which changes passable tiles to walls). This mutation can add walls on either floor in theory; however, most of the level structure of the ground floor is "frozen", so walls seem to be added almost exclusively to the top floor. Elements evolved (and post-processed) from the previous steps are "frozen", which allows for the room to be refined in steps, adding new elements (e.g. weapons) but respecting designs finalized in past steps.

Evolution is carried out in a feasible and an infeasible population as described in Sect. 3.1. The feasible population attempts to maximize a sum of these equally weighted fitnesses: (a) exploration from any entrance, spawn point or jump pad/landing and (b) the balance thereof, (c) the number of safe tiles around weapons, spawn points and entrances and (d) the balance thereof. Any passable tile is safe for e.g. a weapon if the tile's distance to this weapon is half or less of the distance to the next closest weapon, spawn point or entrance. Formulations and parameters of these metrics are found in [21]. The constraints for feasible individuals are: (a) all entrances, jump pads/landings, weapons and spawn points must be reachable via a passable path (including jumps through open air tiles), (b) the number of total walls does not exceed 30% of the total room's tiles.

3.4 Post-processing to Create the Final Room

Once evolution of two-floor rooms is complete, the fittest feasible individual is chosen as the final result. Several post-processing steps are applied before it is presented to the designer. Dead-ends are again iteratively filled with wall tiles unless they are occupied by entrances, jump pads/landings, weapons or spawn points; the process continues until no more walls can be placed. After this step, jump pads or landings which are surrounded only by wall tiles or open air tiles are removed along with their corresponding tile on the other floor. This step is necessary in case the jump pad leads nowhere, especially after dead-end removal. After this step, inaccessible areas on both floors are filled with wall tiles; this is achieved via flood-fill algorithms originating from the jump pad tiles (for the ground floor) or the jump landings (for the top floor). All tiles removed in this fashion are shown as red circles in Fig. 1b.

4 Experiments

Five example layouts for FPS levels will be tested in this paper, to evaluate the impact that entrance placement has on the evolved rooms. For the sake of simplicity, three rooms are evolved per level: a large square *arena* of 11 by 11 tiles, and two rooms of 6 by 11 tiles acting as *bases* —each hosting a team's spawn point. The three rooms are horizontally aligned and are simply joined together side-by-side in the end, as in Fig. 1a. Experiments in this paper test five configurations of entrances for each of these rooms (entrances are mirrored between adjacent rooms). The arena can have two entrances to each base either on the

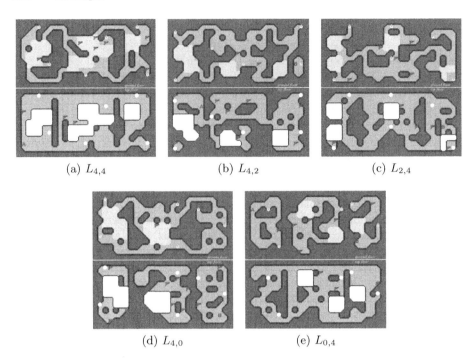

(a) $L_{4,4}$ (b) $L_{4,2}$ (c) $L_{2,4}$

(d) $L_{4,0}$ (e) $L_{0,4}$

Fig. 4. Sample evolved levels for different layouts.

top or on the ground floor, four entrances (two per floor), and combinations of three entrances. In all cases, each base has one spawn point tile and two weapon tiles while the arena has six weapon tiles; all rooms have two jump pads and two landing tiles. From this point forward, the different layouts are identified as $L_{i,j}$ where i and j is the number of entrances on the ground floor and on the top floor respectively: $L_{4,2}$ has four entrances on the ground floor and two entrances on the top floor (see Fig. 1a). In the visualization of Fig. 4, spawn points are shown as A and B in the left and right base respectively; open air tiles are shown as white and passable tiles and platforms in light gray.

In this experiment, 100 evolutionary runs are used to create the total of 15 rooms (3 per layout). Each evolutionary step is performed on a population of 100 individuals evolving for 20 generations. Indicative results of evolved levels for the different layouts are shown in Fig. 4. Each of the sample levels has a fair number of open-air tiles, although not always in every room (e.g. in the right base of Fig. 4d or the left base of Fig. 4e). Except for Fig. 4a, the top floor has passages that are almost as winding as the ground floor. Except for Fig. 4c, it seems that both spawn points are often found on the floor with the fewest entrances. The general patterns of evolved levels for different layouts in terms of tile placement and winding passageways will be explored in Sects. 4.1 and 4.2. Meanwhile, it is interesting to note some properties of the specific levels of Fig. 4. Walls and open air tiles tend to create 'islands' on the top floor which can not be accessed from other parts of the top floor without traversing the ground floor and ascending again through a jump pad. Examples include parts similar to sniper positions which allow players to aim at opponents on the floor below via adjacent open air tiles (e.g. left base in Fig. 4e, or left and right base in Fig. 4c). In other cases, such as the left base in Fig. 4b, these islands are surrounded by walls and act more as a fortified position for a defending player: opponents can only attack through the singular jump pad; defending the spot is easy but leaving it again is almost impossible. This pattern of a locked-in 'island' accessible only via jump pad can also be found on the ground floor, for instance in the right base of Fig. 4b. Another interesting pattern is found in Fig. 4a, where open air tiles in the central arena partition the floor into two equally-sized platforms (only accessible via a narrow passage surrounded by walls on the left of the arena); in this case, the ground floor is a shortcut via the jump pads near each platform.

4.1   Comparing Level Structures

Table 1 shows the number of tiles in each level (i.e. the three rooms joined together) and how they are distributed between the two floors. Results are collected from 100 independent evolutionary runs per layout. Obviously the number of weapons and spawn points is always the same in every layout (10 and 2 respectively); the number of entrances depends on the layout but does not differ among runs using the same layout. Since the last post-processing step removes jump pads/landings leading nowhere, the number of jump pads is on average less than what was specified by the designer (6), but not by much. In 75% of runs (across all layouts) the number of jump pads was indeed 6; this number is not affected by layout much. The layout does affect the number of wall tiles and open air tiles: despite constraints, there is sufficient leeway for important differences. There are certain patterns worth noting: layouts with few entrances on the ground floor ($L_{2,4}$, $L_{0,4}$) have fewer open air tiles than other layouts. Layouts with more entrances on the ground floor ($L_{4,2}$, $L_{4,0}$) have more wall tiles than other layouts. Interestingly, $L_{4,0}$ has far more wall tiles than all others but also far more open air tiles, likely due to the second post-processing step filling unreachable areas (due to lack of entrances) with walls on the top floor.

A much clearer picture is gleaned from the ratios of tiles per floor. Table 1 summarizes this, as the ratio of tiles of one type on the ground floor over the total number of tiles of that type. Due to the five layouts chosen, the entrance ratio on the ground floor is unique for each layout (bold in Table 1). Using this as the primary characteristic to compare effects of the layout, we observe statistically significant Pearson correlations ($p < 0.05$) with all other tile ratios shown in Table 1. Specifically, there are very strong negative correlations between entrance ratio and wall ratio ($\rho = -0.941$), weapon ratio ($\rho = -0.959$), spawn point ratio ($\rho = -0.906$) and game element ratio, i.e. weapons and spawn points combined ($\rho = -0.953$). Finally, there is a significantly positive correlation between entrance ratio and total open air tiles in the level ($\rho = 0.988$); a strong correlation with the number of total wall tiles ($\rho = 0.755$) is however not significant due the small set of 5 layouts tested. Even with the few layouts tested in this

Table 1. Average number of tiles, tile ratios and metrics for the different tested layouts. Results are averaged from 100 generated levels, along with the 95% confidence interval. The game elements metric encompasses weapon and spawn point tiles.

Layouts	$L_{4,4}$	$L_{4,2}$	$L_{2,4}$	$L_{4,0}$	$L_{0,4}$
Wall tiles	326 ± 3	349 ± 2	334 ± 3	364 ± 3	335 ± 3
Open air tiles	41 ± 2	41 ± 2	36 ± 2	47 ± 3	30 ± 3
Jump pad tiles	5.8 ± 0.1	5.7 ± 0.1	5.8 ± 0.1	5.8 ± 0.1	5.8 ± 0.1
Ratio of tiles on the ground floor					
Entrances	**0.50**	**0.67**	**0.34**	**1.00**	**0.00**
Walls	0.48 ± 0.00	0.45 ± 0.00	0.49 ± 0.00	0.43 ± 0.01	0.50 ± 0.00
Weapons	0.48 ± 0.03	0.39 ± 0.03	0.55 ± 0.02	0.38 ± 0.03	0.64 ± 0.02
Spawn Points	0.15 ± 0.05	0.11 ± 0.04	0.36 ± 0.07	0.08 ± 0.04	0.76 ± 0.06
Game Elements	0.43 ± 0.02	0.34 ± 0.03	0.51 ± 0.02	0.33 ± 0.03	0.66 ± 0.02
Level patterns and fitnesses					
Spawn distance	31.8 ± 0.9	34.8 ± 1.0	35.4 ± 1.3	43.4 ± 1.4	39.4 ± 1.7
Spawn exploration	0.92 ± 0.011	0.94 ± 0.008	0.93 ± 0.01	0.94 ± 0.008	0.91 ± 0.014
Spawn explor. balance	0.95 ± 0.009	0.94 ± 0.010	0.93 ± 0.01	0.95 ± 0.008	0.93 ± 0.013
Weapon area	0.33 ± 0.010	0.35 ± 0.012	0.36 ± 0.012	0.38 ± 0.016	0.41 ± 0.012
Weapon area balance	0.57 ± 0.013	0.58 ± 0.014	0.58 ± 0.012	0.56 ± 0.017	0.59 ± 0.012

paper, there are clear trends which are common-sensical given the fitnesses used for feasible individuals in both evolutionary stages. For the first stage, when there are few or no entrances on the ground floor, exploration focuses only on placing jump pads as far apart as possible. This is easier than trying to improve exploration of e.g. 6 tiles (4 entrances and 2 jump pads in the arena), so the room does not need many walls to create winding passageways. In the second stage, exploration favors spawn points as far away from jump pads/landings and entrances as possible; tile safety favors weapons far away from entrances and spawn points. When entrances are only on the top floor ($L_{0,4}$) then obviously the most distant spots for weapons or spawn points are on the ground floor. Since weapons must also be far away from each other, on the other hand, it is often the case that a few weapons are on the floor with more entrances while most weapons are on the floor with fewer entrances.

4.2   Comparing Level Patterns

While ultimately a playtest with human players must test the playability of each level, some gameplay qualities can be estimated based on the distance and exploration effort between the two teams' spawn points as well as how spaced apart weapons are. Distance between spawn points is calculated on the shortest path; exploration between spawn points, safe areas around weapons (and their balance) are calculated through the same formulas as for evolution (except no other tiles are considered), and the whole level is assessed rather than each room.

Table 1 shows the average fitness scores and metrics of 100 generated levels per layout. The high value for spawn point exploration (and its balance) indicates that players of both teams will explore most of the level to find the opponents' spawn point, regardless of layout. Exploration for $L_{4,0}$ and $L_{4,2}$ has almost identical scores, which are significantly higher than those of $L_{0,4}$ and $L_{4,4}$. After a few minutes of playtime, however, players will have identified the other team's spawning area so the more pertinent metric is the distance between spawn points: the lowest distance is for $L_{4,4}$ and the highest for $L_{4,0}$ (both findings are statistically significant). The other layout without entrances on one floor ($L_{0,4}$) has significantly higher spawn point distances than all other layouts except $L_{4,0}$. There are therefore some similarities between the patterns shown from spawn point exploration and their distance: the few entrances of $L_{4,0}$ lead to longer paths that are more complex to follow, while the many entrances of $L_{4,4}$ provide shortcuts to opposing players and makes spawn points easier to find. While neither distance nor exploration effort of spawn points is explicitly targeted by evolution (since no room has more than one spawn point), when rooms are combined these desirable patterns emerge as each room rewards exploration between entrances (and one spawn point, in the case of base rooms).

On the other hand, roughly 40% of tiles in the levels are much closer to one weapon than to others but not all weapons have similar number of safe tiles around them. This admittedly points to a sub-optimal level pattern, as some weapon locations may be more easily reachable and thus preferred to others. It is not surprising however that any algorithm struggles to balance the placement of so many weapon pickups. Moreover, the rooms are not equal: the arena has double the size and triple the number of weapons of each base. Weapons in bases have far more safe tiles than those in arenas, which explains the imbalance of this metric. Here, splitting the level into rooms is detrimental as the algorithm has no way of knowing how other rooms place weapons. There is no easy way of alleviating that fact except by having weapons proportionate to each room's area, yet this would remove much of the benefit of ad-hoc controllability of each room by the designer. Regarding differences between layouts, the only significant difference worth noting is for $L_{4,4}$ which has the lowest weapon area score than all other layouts, likely due to the fact that the arena has to optimize the safe areas around 8 entrances and 6 weapons versus fewer entrances of other layouts.

5   Discussion

The modular way in which the level is built out of components offers substantial control to the designer. While experiments focused on a small subset of possible level layouts, there are endless possibilities for how custom-defined rooms can be combined together. For example, the current rooms can be combined to form four-floor shooter levels, by placing $L_{4,4}$ bases on either side of a stacked set of $L_{0,4}$ (top) and $L_{4,0}$ (bottom) arena. The current two-floor rooms can also be combined with single-floor rooms evolved in a variant of the second evolutionary and post-processing step, to create two-story levels with an internal courtyard, for instance. Finally, the designer can combine evolved rooms with human-authored ones, such as a manually designed corridor or gallery to connect two arenas. The ability to specify rooms of any size, any connectivity and however many game objects within it, as well as the ability to combine rooms in many ways with other generated or human-authored rooms affords an exceptionally large design space for both designer and algorithm to explore. While the connectivity between rooms, and the properties of the rooms themselves, are currently controlled by human designers, an extension of the current system could allow another generator to produce the high-level layouts (i.e. room sizes and how they connect to each other) in a similar fashion as [24].

While the different entrance setups can affect the patterns that emerge, all tested layouts seem to achieve high-quality results with diverse pathways connecting one team's spawn area to the other and weapons which generally are not clumped together. Further experimenting with layouts, room sizes, and the many controllable parameters of the generator (maximum ratio of walls or open air tiles, number of weapons and spawn points) could allow designers to find the perfect setup for parts of a shooter level (e.g. a "bunker" or a "sniper's nest" room). The relatively large number of parameters in the generative system are admittedly kept constant for the most part in the experiments of this paper; the values chosen however came from experimentation and designer feedback by Luiz Kruel. The system proved quite sensitive to constraints on minimum wall ratio and maximum open air ratio, which affected discovery of any feasible results.

The work presented here is intended for use in a commercial game, leading to specific design decisions, post-processing steps, fitness functions and constraints. While this system outputs 2D maps, converting them into 3D is relatively easy with *Houdini*, an engine developed by SideFX; the 3D output of the two-floor levels of this paper for use in the *Unreal Engine 4* (Epic Games 2014) was shown in the GDC 2017 talk by Luiz Kruel. The generative system is a specialized version of the general generative framework of [21], since the included game objects and navigational patterns are both biased by and biasing the design options for such a game. For instance, the tile-based representation complicates the addition of larger structures which span multiple tiles (e.g. staircases): jump pads/landings are convenient for the generator but may limit designers. On the other hand, the team-based gameplay of the intended game guides the sparse use of spawn points and the fitness functions that assess them, which favor 'hiding' them away from entrances to prevent enemy camping. In a free-for-all deathmatch game, the generator would likely benefit from more spawn points which could be evaluated differently: see [18,25] for examples. Finally, dead-end removal was requested by FPS level designers: the post-processing steps provided an easy fix to this problem, but at the cost of the resulting room being at times much different than what is being evolved (and evaluated). A different representation, for instance based on rooms as in [26], could make removing deadends and placing larger structures more straightforward.

6   Conclusion

This paper described a multi-step process for generating rooms of a shooter game which can be specified *a priori* and re-combined *a posteriori* by a human designer. Generated two-floor levels allow for level patterns such as sniping positions and shooting galleries to emerge as a byproduct of multiple evolutionary steps which target the core qualities of each room: exploration effort from different locations of the room and dispersal of game items within it. Experiments tested several room layouts, combining them into a simple arena-based shooter level for two teams, and showed that the placement of entrances affects how game items are allocated on each floor, and thus indirectly which floor will be visited more frequently by human players. However, different layouts do not severely impact the general qualities of the generated levels (e.g. the effort of reaching opponents' bases). As the game is developped, these hypotheses must be tested with human players competing in 3D levels generated from different layouts.

Acknowledgements. This project has received funding from the European Union's Horizon 2020 research and innovation programme under grant agreement No 693150. The generator was the result of a collaboration with Luiz Kruel, who provided valuable feedback on level patterns and designer constraints for using the system.

References

1. Hastings, E.J., Guha, R.K., Stanley, K.O.: Automatic content generation in the galactic arms race video game. IEEE Trans. Comput. Intell. AI Games **1**(4), 245–263 (2009)
2. Risi, S., Lehman, J., D'Ambrosio, D.B., Hall, R., Stanley, K.O.: Combining search-based procedural content generation and social gaming in the Petalz video game. In: Proceedings of the Artificial Intelligence and Interactive Digital Entertainment Conference (2012)
3. Dewsbury, N., Nunn, A., Syrett, M., Tatum, J., Thompson, T.: Scalable level generation for 2d platforming games. In: Proceedings of the FDG Workshop on Procedural Content Generation (2016)
4. Soule, T., Heck, S., Haynes, T.E., Wood, N., Robison, B.D.: Darwin's demons: does evolution improve the game? In: Squillero, G., Sim, K. (eds.) EvoApplications 2017. LNCS, vol. 10199, pp. 435–451. Springer, Cham (2017). https://doi.org/10.1007/978-3-319-55849-3_29
5. Khalifa, A., Perez-Liebana, D., Lucas, S., Togelius, J.: General video game level generation. In: Proceedings of the Genetic and Evolutionary Computation Conference (2016)
6. Cook, M., Gow, J., Colton, S.: Danesh: helping bridge the gap between procedural generators and their output. In: Proceedings of the FDG Workshop on Procedural Content Generation (2016)

7. Shaker, N., Liapis, A., Togelius, J., Lopes, R., Bidarra, R.: Constructive generation methods for dungeons and levels. In: Shaker, N., Togelius, J., Nelson, M.J. (eds.) Procedural Content Generation in Games. CSCS, pp. 31–55. Springer, Cham (2016). https://doi.org/10.1007/978-3-319-42716-4_3

8. Togelius, J., Yannakakis, G.N., Stanley, K.O., Browne, C.: Search-based procedural content generation: a taxonomy and survey. IEEE Trans. Comput. Intell. AI Games **3**(3), 172–186 (2011)

9. Smith, A.M., Mateas, M.: Answer set programming for procedural content generation: a design space approach. IEEE Trans. Comput. Intell. AI Games **3**(3), 187–200 (2011)

10. Doran, J., Parberry, I.: Controlled procedural terrain generation using software agents. IEEE Trans. Comput. Intell. AI Games **2**(2), 111–119 (2010)

11. Howlett, A., Colton, S., Browne, C.: Evolving pixel shaders for the prototype video game subversion. In: Proceedings of AISB 2010 (2010)

12. Smith, A.M., Butler, E., Popovic, Z.: Quantifying over play: constraining undesirable solutions in puzzle design. In: Proceedings of the International Conference on the Foundations of Digital Games (2013)

13. Yannakakis, G.N., Liapis, A., Alexopoulos, C.: Mixed-initiative co-creativity. In: Proceedings of the 9th Conference on the Foundations of Digital Games (2014)

14. Dormans, J., Bakkes, S.C.J.: Generating missions and spaces for adaptable play experiences. IEEE Trans. Comput. Intell. AI Games **3**(3), 216–228 (2011). Special Issue on Procedural Content Generation

15. van der Linden, R., Lopes, R., Bidarra, R.: Designing procedurally generated levels. In: Proceedings of the AIIDE Workshop on Artificial Intelligence in the Game Design Process (2013)

16. Karavolos, D., Liapis, A., Yannakakis, G.N.: Evolving missions to create game spaces. In: Proceedings of the IEEE Conference on Computational Intelligence and Games (CIG) (2016)

17. Hullet, K., Whitehead, J.: Design patterns in FPS levels. In: Proceedings of the Foundations of Digital Games Conference (2010)

18. Cachia, W., Liapis, A., Yannakakis, G.N.: Multi-level evolution of shooter levels. In: Proceedings of the AAAI Artificial Intelligence for Interactive Digital Entertainment Conference (2015)

19. Liapis, A., Yannakakis, G.N.: Refining the paradigm of sketching in AI-based level design. In: Proceedings of the AAAI Artificial Intelligence for Interactive Digital Entertainment Conference (2015)

20. Liapis, A., Yannakakis, G.N., Togelius, J.: Sentient sketchbook: computer-aided game level authoring. In: Proceedings of the 8th Conference on the Foundations of Digital Games. pp. 213–220 (2013)

21. Liapis, A., Yannakakis, G.N., Togelius, J.: Towards a generic method of evaluating game levels. In: Proceedings of the AAAI Artificial Intelligence for Interactive Digital Entertainment Conference (2013)

22. Bjork, S., Holopainen, J.: Patterns in Game Design. Charles River Media, Rockland (2004)

23. Kimbrough, S.O., Koehler, G.J., Lu, M., Wood, D.H.: On a feasible-infeasible two-population (FI-2Pop) genetic algorithm for constrained optimization: distance tracing and no free lunch. Eur. J. Oper. Res. **190**(2), 310–327 (2008)

24. Liapis, A.: Multi-segment evolution of dungeon game levels. In: Proceedings of the Genetic and Evolutionary Computation Conference (2017)
25. Cardamone, L., Yannakakis, G.N., Togelius, J., Lanzi, P.L.: Evolving interesting maps for a first person shooter. In: Di Chio, C., et al. (eds.) EvoApplications 2011. LNCS, vol. 6624, pp. 63–72. Springer, Heidelberg (2011). https://doi.org/10.1007/978-3-642-20525-5_7
26. Lopes, P., Liapis, A., Yannakakis, G.N.: Targeting horror via level and soundscape generation. In: Proceedings of the AAAI Artificial Intelligence for Interactive Digital Entertainment Conference (2015)

Online-Trained Fitness Approximators
for Real-World Game Balancing

Mihail Morosan$^{(\boxtimes)}$ and Riccardo Poli

University of Essex, Colchester, UK
{mmoros,rpoli}@essex.ac.uk

Abstract. Recent work has shown that genetic algorithms are a good choice for use in game design, particularly for finding improved versions of a game's parameters to better fit a designer's requirements. A significant issue with this approach to game optimisation is the very long time it can take to evaluate fitness, since this requires running the target game many times. In this work we test the use of several different fitness approximators, all used in a similar manner, to greatly reduce the number of times a game has to be played for the purpose of fitness evaluation. The approximators use data generated online by the genetic algorithm to train an underlying model. When the model is ready, it is invoked to provide an estimate of the fitness of each newly created individual. If this is worse than a given threshold, it is taken to be the fitness of the individual. Otherwise, the original fitness function is invoked. We assess this approach on two video games *Ms PacMan* and *TORCS*. Results are positive and move us one step closer to the goal of a games balancing tool usable in industry.

Keywords: Genetic algorithm · Neural network · PacMan · TORCS
Approximator · Balancing

1 Introduction

1.1 Motivation

Our previous work in the area of game balance involved the use of genetic algorithms (GA) to change several parameters in a video game to eventually achieve a set that fulfils a designer's stated requirements [1]. This was done by playing the new variation of the game a number of times with one or more artificial agents, collecting metrics about that agent's performance, then assigning the parameter set a fitness based on the aforementioned designer metrics.

The performance of evolutionary algorithms is directly dependent on how quickly the fitness evaluation can be done. In the case of video games fitness

M. Morosan—This work is supported by the EPSRC Centre for Doctoral Training in Intelligent Games & Game Intelligence (IGGI) [EP/L015846/1].

K. Sim and P. Kaufmann (Eds.): EvoApplications 2018, LNCS 10784, pp. 292–307, 2018.
https://doi.org/10.1007/978-3-319-77538-8_21

measures tend to require simulating tens or hundreds of games for a single individual. Each of these evaluations can take seconds, or even minutes. As a result, evaluating a large population typically takes a long time.

However game developers want quick suggestions, as their time is valuable, and often limited. As our goal is to create AI-driven tools that can be successfully used by the games industry, having the fastest versions possible is critical.

As mentioned previously, running a game once can be computationally costly. However, to get an accurate representation of several metrics in a game with stochastic elements one must run it multiple times. Also, regardless of the presence of random variables, the search space can be vast, requiring much computation to explore the fitness landscape.

For the task of balancing games, when utilising computationally cheap agents, such as a trained neural network, a finite state machine or a random agent, the speed of evaluating a game variation is mostly dependant on how quickly simulations of the game mechanics can be done by the developer or researcher. However, expensive agents, such as those utilising Monte-Carlo Tree Search, can take anywhere between several seconds or even minutes to complete even a single game. This is due to a common practice with such agents where they utilise as much as possible of a given maximum time limit they have, such as 40 ms per frame in games attempting to run at 25 frames per second [2]. This results in code that needs to run in real time instead of being able to be sped up during simulation, which results in very long simulation times. When using these agents, the game mechanics are not the most demanding aspect of the entire simulation.

This work revolves around utilising machine learning based approximators to quickly estimate the fitness of an individual and to decide whether it should be evaluated or not. This work focuses on designing and comparing 3 different approximators: a simple feed-forward neural network, C45 decision trees and the K nearest neighbours algorithm. Our aim is to find ways to accelerate the generation of valuable suggestions for the game balancing task mentioned previously, with minimal cost to their accuracy.

We apply our optimisations to the algorithms described in our previous work [1] by attempting to balance two games: *Ms PacMan*, similarly to their approach, and *TORCS*, a racing simulator. This will be done by evolving changes to various game parameters in each game, then testing the desirability of those changes by collecting the results after play and comparing them to a given set of optimal values.

1.2   Previous Work

Fitness approximation, which this work is helping improve, is an ongoing research area being actively explored [3,4]. Many GA tasks are bottlenecked by expensive fitness evaluations and greatly benefit from accurate estimations.

Genetic algorithms and neural networks have often been paired to great success. Quite often, GAs have been used to evolve the parameters or structure of neural networks [5,6]. Our work is, arguably, the opposite, as we use neural networks to, at times, replace the evaluation of individuals in the GA.

Utilising neural networks to simulate the actual fitness evaluation is also not something new. It was applied by Johanson and Poli [7] in their evolution of music using genetic programming. Their need for neural network predictions came from the very expensive task of having humans evaluate each individual personally, with no accurate automated method available and a lot of subjectivity involved.

Later work had researchers employ neural networks to estimate the fitness of entire clusters of individuals [8]. The clusters were generated by machine learning techniques, particularly the k-nearest-neighbour algorithm. Their approach is tested on several synthetic experiments, but no real-world scenarios.

A lot of work has been previously done by researchers on methods to approximate fitness functions during GA runs [9], or even use GA runs to generate new approximation models to then be used in subsequent runs [10]. These optimisations are applied differently than the solution we propose in this paper.

Recently, researchers studying techniques to treat cancer made use of neural networks as a surrogate model for fitness evaluations in their goal to optimise Intensity Modulated Radiotherapy Treatment beam angles [11]. The genetic algorithm they employ, with the help of the neural network, proves to be successful in finding better solutions compared to traditional methods used in practice. Their implementation uses a pre-trained neural network as a surrogate model. This requires expert knowledge and data on the subject, something not all game developers have access to.

1.3   Structure

The paper is structured as follows.

In Sects. 2.1 and 2.2, we present the methodology of our experiments by introducing the two games: *Ms PacMan* and *TORCS*. This is followed by Sect. 2.3, where we give descriptions of the genetic algorithm employed, of the structure of the neural network and of the machine learning algorithms used as approximators. Section 2.4 describes the integration between the GA and the approximators in depth, followed by technical details about each one of the three machine learning algorithms used. The experiments themselves are described in Sect. 2.8.

Section 3 presents the findings of the experiments described.

Finally, the results are discussed and future research directions are presented in Sect. 4.

2   Methodology

2.1   Ms Pacman

Ms PacMan is a single-player game played on a 2-dimensional board, where the player controls the "PacMan" and has the goal of collecting as many points as possible while navigating a maze-like map. There are 4 ghosts opposing the player.

The ghosts follow predictable strategies, but their movements can be random at times, making for an unpredictable game every time it is played. This means deterministic AI agents will not always achieve the same score in consecutive games.

To automate the control of the "PacMan", we used a rules-based system based on work done by Thompson *et al.* [12], with modifications by Shelton [13].

The metrics chosen to assess the fitness of modified versions of the game were the average score achieved by the aforementioned agent, as well as how many of said scores were above a given value. These are sensible analytics to look at, from a designer standpoint, as they can represent play performance fairly well. The average score is an immediate value one can assess an agent's performance by. The ratio of scores above a given value allows the designer to control, to a small extent, the distribution of scores, as it is equal to the complementary cumulative distribution function.

The fitness evaluation is expensive due to the fact that one must play many games per individual to calculate this win-rate. In the *Ms PacMan* experiment using the scripted AI, we ran 100 games for each individual.

For *Ms PacMan*, the elements of the game that are adjustable are the speeds at which each of the characters moves, with two different values available for the ghosts: when chasing the PacMan and when being chased by the PacMan. Displacements from the default values to these game parameters are what the GA evolves.

As a result, there are 9 parameters being evolved: the PacMan's speed, the chasing speed of each of the 4 ghosts, and the fleeing speed of each of the 4 ghosts. For these experiments, for each of the 9 parameters, only values between -3 and 5 were accepted, as values outside these ranges would result in massive changes to the game.

Formally, the fitness function can be written as:

$$Fitness = Avg_S + R_S + \Delta_P \tag{1}$$

$$Avg_S = |Mean(S) - DS| \times C_A \tag{2}$$

$$R_S = \begin{cases} 0 & \text{if } Ratio \geq DR \\ (DR - Ratio) \times C_R & \text{otherwise} \end{cases} \tag{3}$$

$$Ratio = \frac{1}{n} \times \sum_i \delta(S_i \geq TS) \tag{4}$$

$$\Delta_P = C_\Delta \times \sum_i |\Delta_i| \tag{5}$$

There are three major objectives in the fitness evaluation: the average score fitness, the score ratio fitness and the parameter fitness. After running a number of games using the modified parameters, the resulting scores give us an *average score fitness* (Avg_S) and a *score ratio fitness* (R_S).

The *average score fitness* is the absolute value of the difference between the achieved mean score and the desired mean score. The *score ratio fitness* requires that at least a given proportion of the scores are greater than, or equal, to a given value. The *parameter fitness* (Δ_P) is proportional to the sum of the absolute values of the parameters, representing how far the solution is from the default game parameters.

In the *score fitness* component Avg_S, S is the array of scores achieved by the individual, $Mean(S)$ is the average of those scores, and DS is the desired average score to be achieved. In the component R_S, n is the number of scores in the array S, S_i is the ith element in the array S, TS is the score considered as a threshold for the comparison, and DR is the desired ratio of scores that should be above TS. In the *parameter fitness* component Δ_P, Δ_i = difference between the original ith parameter and the evolved ith parameter, $C_{\Delta i}$ = parameter difference weight for the ith parameter. C_A, C_R and C_Δ are the values that the game designer can change to give each fitness component a different importance.

For these experiments, $DS = 1600$, representing a desired average score of 1600, $DR = 0.5$ $C_A = 1$, $TS = 1600$, $DR = 0.5$, meaning at least half the scores should be above 1600, $C_R = 5000$ and all values in C_Δ were set to 100. The values for C_A, C_R and C_Δ give the three objectives similar relevance.

With *Ms PacMan* we do not expect any run to achieve a fitness of 0, as that would mean the default version of the game fits the requirements perfectly (as that would result in a parameter fitness of 0). Running the game with unchanged parameters results in a fitness value of 2175.6.

2.2   TORCS

TORCS is an open source racing game simulator [14]. It is extremely configurable, with almost every element of the game being modifiable without recompiling the source code. Another interesting element is its lack of stochastic elements. Unless the driver has random decisions, a race with the same car on the same track will yield the same lap performances every time.

Many elements of the game could be considered for changes, from the layout of the tracks, to the technical specifications of the cars, to way artificial agents drive in the game. For this study we decided to look at changing the performance of a single vehicle in the game, the *car1-ow1*.

After discussing this with an experienced engineer from the racing industry, the elements of the car chosen for tweaking were: the total mass of the car (P_M), the drag coefficient (P_D), the clutch inertia value (P_C), the steering speed (P_S), the steering lock (P_L), the rear differential ratio (P_R), the maximum pressure applicable by the breaking system (P_B), the front anti-roll bar spring value (P_{A1}), and the rear anti-roll bar spring value (P_{A2}). Displacements from the default values to these car parameters are what the GA evolves. These elements, as well as the ranges the displacements could take, can be seen in Table 1.

The car was driven by one of the game's default driver agents, *berniw*. To collect performance metrics, the car was driven on 3 different tracks, one for each distinct type available in the game (dirt, oval and road). The values gathered were the lap times achieved on each one. As an example of a real world scenario, a designer could seek to balance the car itself, with the goal to improve the car's performance on the road track, decrease its performance on the oval track,

Table 1. Parameters chosen, their ranges and fitness weights

	Description	Min change	Max change	$C_{\Delta i}$
P_M	Car Mass	$-300\,$kg	$300\,$kg	0.5
P_D	Drag Coefficient	-0.15	0.15	1000
P_C	Clutch Inertia	$-0.05\ kg.m^2$	$0.05\ kg.m^2$	3000
P_L	Steering Lock	$-15°$	$20°$	7.5
P_S	Steering Speed	$-300°/s$	$0°/s$	0.5
P_R	Rear Differential Ratio	-5	5	30
P_B	Brake Pressure	$-19000\,$kPa	$19000\,$kPa	0.005
P_{A1}	Front Anti-Roll Bar Spring	$0\,$lbs/in	$5000\,$lbs/in	0.025
P_{A2}	Rear Anti-Roll Bar Spring	$0\,$lbs/in	$5000\,$lbs/in	0.025

but maintain its performance on the dirt track. The performance of the original version of the car, as well as the desired new values, can be seen in Table 2.

There are four major objectives in the fitness evaluation: the road track time fitness (T_{Road}), the oval track time fitness (T_{Oval}), the dirt track time fitness (T_{Dirt}) and the parameter fitness (Δ_P). The *parameter fitness* (Δ_P) is a weighted sum of the absolute values of the parameters, representing how far the solution is from the default game parameters.

Formally, the fitness function can be written as:

$$Fitness \quad = T_{Road} + T_{Oval} + T_{Dirt} + \Delta_P \tag{6}$$
$$T_{Road} = |Time_{Road} - DTime_{Road}| \times C_{Road} \tag{7}$$
$$T_{Oval} = |Time_{Oval} - DTime_{Oval}| \times C_{Oval} \tag{8}$$
$$T_{Dirt} \quad = |Time_{Dirt} - DTime_{Dirt}| \times C_{Dirt} \tag{9}$$
$$\Delta_P \qquad = \sum_i |\Delta_i| \times C_{\Delta i} \tag{10}$$

In the T_{Road}, T_{Oval} and T_{Dirt} components, $Time$ represents the achieved time by the modified car on the respective track, $DTime$ represents the desired time for that track, and C represents the weight for that track. In the *parameter fitness* component Δ_P, Δ_i = difference between the original ith parameter and the evolved ith parameter, $C_{\Delta i}$ = parameter difference weight for the ith parameter. C_{Road}, C_{Oval}, C_{Dirt} and $C_{\Delta i}$ are the values that the game designer can change to give each fitness component a different importance.

Table 2. Times achieved by the unchanged car on each track, alongside desired times

Track	Original time	Desired time
Road	78.33 s	70.00 s
Oval	26.95 s	32.00 s
Dirt	63.93 s	64.00 s

For these experiments, each $DTime$ was given the values from Table 2, C_{Road}, C_{Oval}, C_{Dirt} were set to 70, while all $C_{\Delta i}$ were set to the values in Table 1. The latter were chosen so that all of the parameter fitness sub-objectives have similar importance. This results in all four main objectives having similar relevance to the final fitness score.

Running the game with unchanged parameters results in a fitness value of 941.5.

2.3   Genetic Algorithm

Each individual was represented by a vector of values representing the displacements to the various parameters described for each game. These values could be anywhere between the ranges described in the respective sections.

The evolutionary algorithm employed is a variant of a generational GA with two-point crossover [15] (applied with a rate of 30%), a specialised mutation operator (applied with a per-individual rate of 30%) and elitism (applied to the top 20% of the population). The final 20% of the each generation is randomly sampled from the search space through reinitialisation [16].

The mutation operator was applied with a (per allele) mutation rate of 0.5 (meaning that on average 50% of the elements of an individual would be mutated). At each application of the operator the allele is replaced with a new random value between the accepted range.

Due to the significant computational load required by the fitness function in these experiments, the population size was 100 for each experiment. All experiments used tournament selection, with a tournament size of 6. Experiments ran until 2000 evaluations of the fitness function were used. This represents the budget available. For each experiment, 20 runs were completed.

2.4   Approximator Integration

At the end of each GA generation, all the individuals that were evaluated by running the games instead of approximation, and, as a result, have accurate fitnesses, are passed to the approximator. These individuals are stored in the approximator's data set, for use during model generation.

Whenever a new individual is added to the data set, if there are more individuals than a given maximum (N_{Max}) in it, the oldest one is removed. The data set acts as a queue with a maximum capacity.

During a generation, after the population goes through elitism, crossover and mutation, the new population, that now has individuals that have not been evaluated yet and do not have a fitness value, is passed to the approximator.

Using 80% of the data set described earlier, the approximator generates or trains its model of the fitness landscape, mapping the parameters to either the fitness objectives or a fitness class (more details on the fitness class in Sect. 2.6). The model generation is only done if there is a minimum number of individuals in the data set (N_{Min}). For all the experiments in this paper, both N_{Min} and N_{Max} are set to 200.

```
function  GA_Generation(population , approximator):
    approximator.updateExamples(population)
    approximator.learnModelFromExamples()

    median <- medianFitness(population)

    population.elitism()
    population.crossover()
    population.mutation()
    population.reinitialisation()

    if approximator.accuracy >= 0.75 then:
        foreach individual in population:
            f <- approximator.predict(individual)
            if f >= median then:
                individual.fitness <- f

    population.evaluateIndividualsWithoutFitness()
```

Fig. 1. Pseudo-code for the integration of an approximator in a GA run

The remaining 20% of the data set is used to validate the approximator's model, resulting in an accuracy value. This accuracy is computed using the root mean square error. Should the accuracy be above a given threshold (75% for these experiments), it is allowed to predict the fitness values of each new individual. Otherwise, the approximator does not get used at all for that generation.

When applied to an individual, the approximator receives that individual's parameter vector and is expected to return a prediction on the fitness. Should the approximator predict a fitness class, the expected return value is one that is mapped from that class and will be covered in a later section. If the predicted fitness is worse than the median of the previous generation's fitnesses, it is accepted and no time consuming evaluation is done for that individual.[1]

However, if the predicted fitness is better than the median of the previous generation's fitnesses, a normal evaluation of that individual is done regardless. The reason we evaluate these individuals is to better assess incremental changes to already good individuals and to, potentially, further improve on the generation's average fitness. Pseudo-code presenting the integration of an approximator into the normal run of a GA is presented in Fig. 1.

Because the approximator is only considered during evaluation, it does not interfere with any other GA optimisations that an experiment designer would want to implement.

---

[1] For the purpose of these experiments, we evaluate each individual regardless of it having been predicted or not, but do not replace an approximator's prediction with the actual simulation results. Instead, we use this evaluation to calculate the number of false negatives generated by the system.

It is also worth mentioning that any individuals whose fitness was predicted are not added to the approximator's data set.

For these experiments we implemented 3 different approximators: a neural network (NN), a C4.5 decision tree classifier (C4.5), and a k-nearest neighbours (k-NN) classifier. These are described in the next three sub-sections.

2.5   Neural Network

The neural network employed for these experiments is a feed-forward neural network with a single hidden layer, using the sigmoid activation function. The training is done via backpropagation [17]. This is a simple, yet powerful and fast, neural network that, while rarely the best option for every task, is a safe choice for many situations [18–20].

Choosing the network's topology is important when using neural networks [21]. The number of input neurons is equal to the number of parameters the GA is evolving. The number of output neurons is equal to how many fitness objectives are being tracked, which, for *Ms PacMan* is 11, while for *TORCS* is 12. This is due to the fact that minimising each parameter is considered an independent objective due to the architecture of our GA. For these experiments, the number of hidden layers and hidden layer neurons was chosen arbitrarily to be 1 and 20 respectively.

When training the neural network with the data described in the previous section, some manipulation has to be done. The inputs and outputs are normalized to be within the 0 to 1 range. Given a known range of values the inputs could have, defined as $Range_{Min}$ and $Range_{Max}$ (The values for the relevant parameters in both experiments can be found in Sect. 3.1 and Table 1), normalisation is done as defined in Eq. 11.

$$Normalise(Val) = (Val - Range_{Min})/(Range_{Max} - Range_{Min}) \qquad (11)$$

Outputs are maintained in a different manner, as only the minimum values are known beforehand ($Range_{Min} = 0$). The maximum values are tracked by comparing the values stored to the ones received from the GA every generation. Should there be output values higher than the ones on record, they are replaced with the new values. While not a perfect solution, this allows the algorithm to adapt to various tasks without prior knowledge.

2.6   C4.5 Decision Trees

C4.5 decision trees [22] is a classification algorithm often used in machine learning due to its transparency. It analyses the already classified training data and builds an effective decision tree.

Because this is a classification algorithm, we had to be able to assign classes to various fitnesses, regardless of the game being optimised.

Table 3. The mapping of fitness values to classifier classes

Fitness class	Fitness min	Fitness max
Class 0	0	FirstQuartile(Fitnesses)-1
Class 1	FirstQuartile(Fitnesses)	Median(Fitnesses)-1
Class 2	Median(Fitnesses)	ThirdQuartile(Fitnesses)-1
Class 3	ThirdQuartile(Fitnesses)	Infinity

The sum of all fitness objectives is taken, which represents the final fitness of an individual, then compared to the first quartile, median, and third quartile of the previous generation's fitness values. Depending on where it lands on this axis, a fitness class from 0 to 3 is assigned to that individual. This mapping can be seen in Table 3.

Once the data set has all the fitnesses mapped to fitness classes, the C4.5 model can be generated using the training set, then validated on the validation set. The model is generated anew every generation, as the relevant statistics used to map the fitness to a class change over time.

Validation is done by using the model to predict the class of individuals in the validation set, then comparing the result to the actual class of that individual. The accuracy value is, just as with the neural network approximator, calculated by using the root mean square error.

Should the resulting model have a high enough accuracy (over 75%), it is then used to predict that generation's unevaluated individuals as described in Sect. 2.4. However, the prediction is a class instead of a fitness value. As a result, a second mapping, from fitness class to fitness value, has to be done. For simplicity, for each class except class 3, the fitness value assigned is the highest value it would be allowed to have (Fitness Max in Table 3). For individuals classified as class 3, they receive a fitness value equal to $ThirdQuartile(Fitnesses) + 1$.

It would have been possible to only have 2 classes: individuals worse than the median and individuals better than the median. However, we decided to have 4 classes to offer slightly more granularity to the algorithm.

2.7 K-Nearest Neighbours

The k-nearest neighbours algorithm [23] is a non-parametric method commonly applied for classification and regression. The reason behind choosing it for this task is due to the likelihood of similar solutions belonging to the same fitness class.

Apart from the model being generated and used for classification, everything is done in the exact same way as with the C4.5 algorithm. Mapping the fitness values of the data set to the classes (see Table 3) and then back to fitness values, as well as calculating the validation error, are done identically.

For these experiments, the value of k was chosen to be 3, while the number of classes we used to split fitnesses in was the same (4).

Table 4. Average run times for each experiment

Experiment	Average run time
Ms PacMan Base	15 s/run
Ms PacMan C45	17 s/run
Ms PacMan Neural Network	19 s/run
Ms PacMan KNN	17 s/run
TORCS Base	5 m 40 s/run
TORCS C45	5 m 42 s/run
TORCS Neural Network	5 m 46 s/run
TORCS KNN	5 m 42 s/run

2.8 Experiments

For both games we ran 20 GA runs without an approximator, and then the same number of runs with each of the 3 approximators described previously. All runs were paired, such that the ith run of each experiment had the same random seed and starting populations.

From each experiment we collected several metrics:

– average fitness per generation
– best fitness per generation
– fitness evaluations done per generation, as this value can be less than the population size when using the approximator
– false negatives generated by the approximator. These are instances where the approximator assigned an individual a fitness worse than the median, however the real result would have been better than the median (and should have been evaluated instead of keeping the prediction).

3 Results

3.1 PacMan

These algorithms for fitness approximation are for eventual use in industry and, as a result, can have various use cases. Some might benefit from better results faster, while others will be willing to wait a long time for more accurate results.

To better assess the quality, we kept track of the best fitnesses achieved at every time point, by every run. Snapshots were taken every 20 evaluations, comparing the best fitnesses for each run with, and without, the relevant approximator. This allowed for a significance to be calculated, using the two sample Wilcoxon Signed Ranked test, with the null hypothesis that the approximator yielded worse results, for each of those snapshots.

The final result is a graph of statistical significance over total evaluations. An example can be seen in Fig. 2, where both the relationship between best fitness

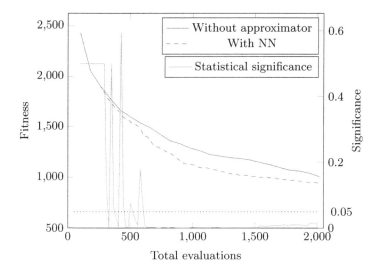

Fig. 2. Average best fitness values achieved after a given number of evaluations by the GAs without and with the neural network approximator, in the *Ms PacMan* experiment. Significance of difference between the paired results is also plotted. Lower values are better

and total evaluations used can be seen, as well as the aforementioned statistical significance at every time point.

We tracked the percentage of time that the best fitness with the approximator is statistically different ($p < 0.05$ with the Wilcoxon Signed Rank Test) from the best fitness without it for the period 0 to 2000 evaluations. The results can be seen in Table 5.

The neural network approximator had a slow start, with the first 600 iterations not showing any significant improvement. However, past that number of evaluations, using it proved significantly better, with fitness values being 9 to 12% better than without at almost every data point. This can be seen in Fig. 2.

Table 5. In the *Ms PacMan* experiments: percentage of time that using the approximator resulted in significantly better results; the average number of predictions generated by the approximator each run and the average percentage of which were false negatives; the average number of individuals observed during the runs

Approximator	% Significant	Predictions	False negatives	Individuals/Run
None				2000.0
C45	70%	1699.3	12.9%	3699.3
Neural network	80%	1298.5	4.3%	3298.5
KNN	71%	796.9	7.2%	2796.9

Table 6. In the *TORCS* experiments: percentage of time that using the approximator resulted in significantly better results; the average number of predictions generated by the approximator each run and the average percentage of which were false negatives; the average number of individuals observed during the runs

Approximator	% Significant	Predictions	False negatives	Individuals/Run
None				2000.0
C45	42%	1963.3	7.6%	3963.3
Neural network	0%	0.0	0.0%	2000.0
KNN	39%	492.9	22.5%	2492.9

The C4.5 decision trees behaved quite differently. Significantly better results appeared much earlier, after only 280 evaluations. However, results eventually converged with the ones that did not use an approximator after 1700 evaluations. This marks this algorithm as great for achieving good results fast, at least for this task.

Using the k-nearest neighbour algorithm as the approximator had similar results to the neural network, with no better results in the first 500 iterations, but accelerated results past that point. Past 1000 iterations, every single data point presented results that were better when using this approximator.

3.2 TORCS

The data collection was done in a very similar manner as done with the *Ms Pac-Man* experiments. Results, however, painted a very different picture.

Looking at the table of results (Table 6), it is clear to see that while C4.5 decision trees and KNN managed to have good results again, the neural network did not provide any improvement to the number of individuals explored. The reason behind this is the fact it never managed to achieve the minimum accuracy required after training.

It is important to note, however, that despite the fact the neural networks were unable to learn the relationships behind the various parameters, they did not negatively impact the quality of results. The two fitness over time graphs are also identical. The total runtime is also virtually identical, even though the version using the approximator has an extra layer of machine learning code to run. This is due to the fact that the network takes very little to train compared to even evaluating a single individual. Runtimes can be seen in Table 4.

Results for the successful C4.5 approximator can be seen in Fig. 3. Again, similarly to the *Ms PacMan* experiment, results accelerate towards good values in the early stages, then converge towards the end.

The lower number of points at which results were significant can be attributed to the fact that the search plateaus around 1000 evaluations, making the algorithms with and without the approximators to converge.

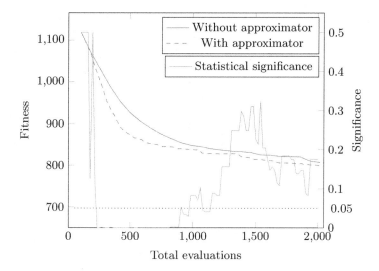

Fig. 3. Average best fitness values achieved after a given number of evaluations by the GAs without and with the C45 decision tree approximator, in the *TORCS* experiment. Significance of difference between the paired results is also plotted. Lower values are better

4 Discussion and Conclusion

Our goal is to create tools and techniques that are usable by industry. For this we need good accuracy, but also much greater speed and scalability. This method of combining GAs and other machine learning algorithms brings significant benefits in these respects.

By using an approximator to predict the fitness of individuals in a GA population, then evaluating only the predicted best, we have managed to allow the GA to explore more individuals in the same amount of time. This has proven highly effective, regardless of algorithm, for *Ms PacMan*, with only one algorithm having difficulties in *TORCS*. Results are promising and optimisations to our methodology should bring further speed improvements.

It is valuable to note how there is no single best approximator. While the neural network was very efficient in the *Ms PacMan* experiment, it failed to bring improvements in the *TORCS* experiment. Meanwhile, both k-nearest neighbours and C4.5 decision trees were able to be very valuable for both tasks.

Given the very small impact on overall performance, with high potential upside and minimal downside, it is very fair to say that our approximators are valuable in speeding up game balance suggestions, as well as other similar areas.

The speed increase could be higher if the approximators would be reused between runs. It is something worth looking into in future research, as those outside academia that would benefit from this would likely want to run multiple runs as quickly as possible and reusing data can be extremely valuable.

One area that we are interested in further assessing is how the training data the predictor uses is managed. While it is purely rolling at this point, it can result in approximators that overfit areas of the landscape and fail to correctly predict individuals of interest. An idea worth following is curated lists, where the data is split in categories, each category accepting and removing entries based on given requirements. These requirements could have one category keep the best fitnesses ever generated by the GA, with another storing the worst fitnesses.

Should the approximator represent an accurate simulation of the fitness landscape, the designer would be left with a model capable of reasonably predicting the fitness of other, custom parameter sets. This approximator would be another tool available to the designer to assess any changes they would want to apply to their games before they go through the much more expensive task of doing AI-driven plays or, even more costly, human player driven plays. Assessing the possibility of this becoming a reality is work we will be attempting in the future.

On the topic of fitness classification, we made use of 4 classes. It would be interesting to explore how more (or fewer) classes would influence the quality of the algorithm.

Overall, this is an optimisation that can benefit the creation of tools for use in games design, while also having potential for use outside the digital entertainment sector.

Acknowledgements. We would like to thank Charlie Bokor for his valuable advice on the inner workings of cars, to better aid us in designing the *TORCS* experiment.

References

1. Morosan, M., Poli, R.: Automated game balancing in Ms PacMan and StarCraft using evolutionary algorithms. In: Squillero, G., Sim, K. (eds.) EvoApplications 2017. LNCS, vol. 10199, pp. 377–392. Springer, Cham (2017). https://doi.org/10.1007/978-3-319-55849-3_25
2. Pepels, T., Winands, M.H.M., Lanctot, M.: Real-time monte carlo tree search in Ms Pac-Man. IEEE Trans. Comput. Intell. AI Games **6**(3), 245–257 (2014). http://ieeexplore.ieee.org/document/6731713/
3. Jin, Y.: A comprehensive survey of fitness approximation in evolutionary computation. Soft Comput. **9**(1), 3–12 (2005)
4. Bhattacharya, M.: Evolutionary approaches to expensive optimisation. Comput. Soc. **2**(3), 53–59 (2013)
5. Liu, Y., Yao, X.: Evolutionary design of artificial neural networks with different nodes. In: Proceedings of IEEE International Conference on Evolutionary Computation, pp. 670–675. IEEE (1996). http://ieeexplore.ieee.org/document/542681/
6. Schaffer, J., Whitley, D., Eshelman, L.: Combinations of genetic algorithms and neural networks: a survey of the state of the art. In: Proceedings of International Workshop on Combinations of Genetic Algorithms and Neural Networks, COGANN 1992, pp. 1–37. IEEE Computer Society Press (1992). http://ieeexplore.ieee.org/document/273950/
7. Johanson, B., Poli, R.: GP-Music: an interactive genetic programming system for music generation with automated fitness raters. Technical report (1998)

8. Jin, Y., Sendhoff, B.: Reducing fitness evaluations using clustering techniques and neural network ensembles. In: Deb, K. (ed.) GECCO 2004. LNCS, vol. 3102, pp. 688–699. Springer, Heidelberg (2004). https://doi.org/10.1007/978-3-540-24854-5_71

9. Deb, K., Sinha, A., Korhonen, P.J., Wallenius, J.: An interactive evolutionary multiobjective optimization method based on progressively approximated value functions. IEEE Trans. Evol. Comput. **14**(5), 723–739 (2010). http://ieeexplore.ieee.org/document/5585740/

10. Nain, P.K.S., Deb, K.: A multi-objective optimization procedure with successive approximate models. http://www.iitk.ac.in/kangal

11. Dias, J., Rocha, H., Ferreira, B., Lopes, M.D.C.: A genetic algorithm with neural network fitness function evaluation for IMRT beam angle optimization. Cent. Eur. J. Oper. Res. **22**(3), 431–455 (2014)

12. Thompson, T., McMillan, L., Levine, J., Andrew, A.: An evaluation of the benefits of look-ahead in pac-man. In: IEEE Symposium Computational Intelligence and Games, pp. 310–315. IEEE (2008)

13. Shelton, L.: Implementation of high-level strategy formulating AI in Ms pac-man. Technical report (2013). http://lucshelton.com/assets/Uploads/Dissertation-Main-Copy.pdf

14. Wymann, B.: TORCS. http://torcs.sourceforge.net/

15. Goldberg, D.E.: Genetic Algorithms in Search, Optimization and Machine Learning., 1st edn. Addison-Wesley Longman Publishing Co. Inc., Boston (1989)

16. Cobb, H.G., Grefenstette, J.J.: Genetic algorithms for tracking changing environments. In: Proceedings of the 5th International Conference on Genetic Algorithms, pp. 523–530 (1993). http://dl.acm.org/citation.cfm?id=657576

17. Hecht-Nielsen, R.: Theory of the backpropagation neural network. In: International Joint Conference on Neural Networks, pp. 593–605. IEEE (1989). http://ieeexplore.ieee.org/document/118638/

18. Hornik, K., Stinchcombe, M., White, H.: Multilayer feedforward networks are universal approximators. Neural Netw. **2**(5), 359–366 (1989)

19. Demuth, H.B., Beale, M.H., De Jess, O., Hagan, M.T.: Neural Network Design, 2nd edn. USA (2014)

20. Vora, K., Yagnik, S., Scholar, M.: A survey on backpropagation algorithms for feedforward neural networks (2015)

21. Lawrence, S., Giles, C.L., Tsoi, A.C.: What size neural network gives optimal generalization ? Convergence properties of backpropagation. Networks (UMIACS-TR-96-22 and CS-TR-3617), pp. 1–37 (1996)

22. Quinlan, J.R.: C4. 5: Programming for Machine Learning. Morgan Kauffmann, San Mateo (1993)

23. Altman, N.S.: An introduction to kernel and nearest-neighbor nonparametric regression. Am. Stat. **46**(3), 175–185 (1992)

Recomposing the Pokémon Color Palette

Antonios Liapis[(✉)]

Institute of Digital Games, University of Malta, Msida, Malta
antonios.liapis@um.edu.mt
http://antoniosliapis.com/

Abstract. In digital games, the visual representation of game assets such as avatars or game levels can hint at their purpose, in-game use and strengths. In the Pokémon games, this is particularly prevalent with the namesake creatures' type and the colors in their sprites. To win these games, players choose Pokémon of the right type to counter their opponents' strengths; this makes the visual identification of type important. In this paper, computational intelligence methods are used to learn a mapping between a Pokémon's type and its in-game sprite, colors and shape. This mapping can be useful for a designer attempting to create new Pokémon of certain types. In this paper, instead, evolutionary algorithms are used to create new Pokémon sprites by using existing color information but recombining it into a new palette. Results show that evolution can be applied to Pokémon sprites on a local or global scale, to exert different degrees of designer control and to achieve different goals.

Keywords: Pokémon · Procedural content generation
Game aesthetics · Decision trees · AI-assisted game design

1 Introduction

As a practice, both game design and artificial intelligence (AI) tend to treat digital games as *systems* which, while not as strictly mathematical as game theory [1], prioritize the discovery of winning strategies. For game design, such winning strategies must ideally be varied to avoid a "shortcut" to victory; for AI aiming at efficient game playing, the task revolves around discovering such winning strategies [2] (and even exploiting shortcuts). For similar reasons, research in procedural content generation in games largely targets creating playable, balanced content [3]; at best, the player's experience is accounted for via computational models [4] which are again based on interactions with the system (such as jumps or enemy hits). However, an important part of play goes beyond the game's mechanics (or their combination) but expands into the aesthetic experience [5] of exploring a vast and colorful world, getting involved in the backstories of non-player characters and listening to the audioscapes formed by the soundtrack and environmental sounds based on the player's location.

It is therefore important that elements other than the game's mechanics or the game levels' architecture are considered, both from the game design and

© Springer International Publishing AG, part of Springer Nature 2018
K. Sim and P. Kaufmann (Eds.): EvoApplications 2018, LNCS 10784, pp. 308–324, 2018.
https://doi.org/10.1007/978-3-319-77538-8_22

from the AI perspective. For game design, adding visual cues in a vast open world via e.g. landmarks can help player navigation by directing them towards important areas [6]. Similarly, rendering a weapon or an enemy in a way that makes their mode of interaction or challenge level recognizable by mere visual inspection makes for an intuitive player interaction. For AI, building models of player experience based on audiovisual stimuli can complement player modeling based on in-game events [7]. For procedural generation, identifying patterns of visual appeal or associations between a shape or color and its in-game purpose allows us to generate visual depictions of content in an informed way.

This paper describes how a mapping between visual representation and in-game identity can be learned from simple image information, and then used to drive the generation of new game visuals. Identity in games is particularly important, especially concerning player avatars; the mapping between an avatar's visual identity and user-provided game statistics or narrative has been explored in [8]. In this paper, we instead focus on non-player characters, i.e. on the pet creatures of the Pokémon series; moreover, we learn the design principles and rules behind the choice of colors to identify and represent specific elements (e.g. fire, water) or other Pokémon types (e.g. fighting, psychic). There are many goals and directions for this research: on the one hand, the learned models can inform game designers on the principles behind artists' renderings and guide them to create new Pokémon; on the other hand, the learned model can be used to predict the type of unseen Pokémon sprites. Taking advantage of the latter, this paper shows how evolution can create new Pokémon sprites by changing the color mapping of existing ones. This can be used to assist designers or to automate the design of recolored Pokémon with new types, similar to *Alolan* Pokémon or more generally *shiny* Pokémon in existing games. As demonstrated in Sect. 5, this can be applied to change the type of a single Pokémon to a designer-defined one, to change the type of a set of Pokémon of the same type to any other, or to balance the instances of each Pokémon type. However, far more applications for the learned model of visual identity are discussed in Sect. 6.

2   Related Work

While not prevalent in AI for games, creating computational models of visual identity is a core direction of computer vision for tasks such as object detection [9] and image recognition [10]. Just as computer vision tasks try to answer "what are the essential visual clues of a chair?", this research attempts to answer "what are the essential visual clues of a fire Pokémon?". Computer vision models have also been used for generation of new visual artifacts that match real-world knowledge, such as alphabets based on Optical Character Recognition accuracy [11] or 3D models based on the confidence of a deep learned image recognition system [12]. In games, computer vision has been applied to recombine facial features of 2D avatars in a way that makes them recognizable as faces of celebrities [13].

While the design of computer games hinges on a number of creative facets [14], research in AI and content generation focuses heavily on the more "measurable" rule and level design tasks. For generating in-game visuals, evaluation often relies on human feedback via interactive evolution [15,16], or an inferred [17] or stated [18] objective of the designer. Human expertise can also be used indirectly, however, to learn and replicate patterns of e.g. level design from high-quality human designs [19] or, as in this study, to learn the rules behind visual associations inserted by a game's designers and exploit them to generate new content (via their color recombinations) which still retain their human-provided form (via the sprite's shape and brightness information).

Table 1. Types of Pokémon and the number of instances of this type in the database (including dual types).

Water (141)	Normal (116)	Flying (113)	Grass (109)	Psychic (100)	Bug (83)
Ground (75)	Fire (72)	Poison (69)	Rock (67)	Fighting (63)	Dark (60)
Electric (60)	Dragon (59)	Steel (58)	Ghost (55)	Fairy (53)	Ice (43)

3   Processing the Pokémon Dataset

Pokémon are fantastical creatures featuring in the Pokémon game series by Nintendo from 1996 to 2016. The games revolve around capturing and using Pokémon in combat against other Pokémon. Each Pokémon has one or two *types* (e.g. fire Pokémon or grass–poison Pokémon), which affects their moves (which also have a type) in combat. Moves that cause damage have their damage amplified depending on its type and the type of the enemy Pokémon: e.g. a fire move deals double damage to ice Pokémon, but half damage to fire Pokémon. A Pokémon's type thus affects both its defenses (versus moves of different types) and its offenses (its available moves and their types).

3.1   The Dataset

The Pokémon dataset was collected from the Pokémon Database[1] which contains statistics and sprites of every Pokémon from all seven generations of the Pokémon game series. While Pokémon statistics include numerical data such as health, attack, defense etc., the Pokémon's type is very important as choosing the right

Fig. 1. Pokémon sprites which capture extremes of saturation, sprite size, color etc.

---

[1] https://pokemondb.net/pokedex/all.

Pokémon to counter another Pokémon's type is the key to victory. Each Pokémon also has a low-resolution sprite for its visual representation (examples in Fig. 1).

The main focus of this paper is to identify the relationship between the visual depiction of different Pokémon, especially regarding their color, and their type(s). The dataset contains 908 Pokémon entries, including evolved forms and alternate forms. The dataset includes 18 types of Pokémon shown in Table 1; out of those, Water, Fire and Grass are considered the three basic elemental types. Table 1 includes the number of instances of each type in the database; since 488 Pokémon have dual types, the total instances of type are 1396. Water Pokémon are by far the most common; ghost, fairy and ice Pokémon are far fewer.

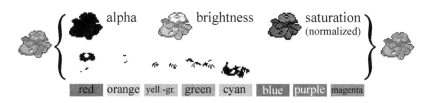

Fig. 2. Breakdown of the base sprite (far leftt) into alpha, brightness, saturation, and color channels for the 8-color encoding. The channel information can be used to reconstruct the sprite (far right) with some color accuracy loss. (Color figure online)

3.2   Decomposing Pokémon Sprites

Each Pokémon sprite is 40 pixels wide and 30 pixels tall: the actual Pokémon is much smaller (leaving the rest of the canvas transparent). For the purposes of this paper, the image is split into constituent parts (channels) which can be used to reconstruct it. In the Hue, Saturation, Brightness (HSB) image format, the three channels describe the type of color of each pixel, how vibrant the color is, and how bright or dark it is, respectively; an additional Alpha channel describes whether the pixel is transparent. The HSB format is followed here, with some important modifications. Each image is split into the alpha channel (black pixels for opaque color and white pixels for empty areas), the brightness channel (i.e. a grayscale version of the image) and the saturation channel which is multiplied, in this case, by the brightness channel since dark pixels (low brightness) are not perceived as saturated by the human eye regardless of saturation score. Saturation in this paper always refers to this normalized saturation channel which also performed well in [8]. The hue channel is problematic as it is a wheel: high and low hue scores are both red-tinted. This paper splits hue into value ranges (colors) and stores them as black and white images representing presence or absence of that color. Therefore, all red or almost-red pixels are black in the red color channel, blue or almost-blue pixels are black in the blue color channel etc. (see Fig. 2). To avoid noise due to black or white pixels being stored in a random color channel, sprite's pixels with less than 5% in their normalized saturation value (i.e. low saturation, low brightness, or both) are omitted from all color channels.

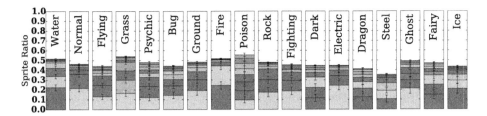

Fig. 3. Color ratios per Pokémon type. Error bars display the 95% confidence interval of the average ratios shown. (Color figure online)

These channels are then processed to derive visual metrics for each Pokémon sprite. This paper uses only the color ratios as a metric, calculated as the ratio of black pixels in a color channel (see Fig. 2) over the Pokémon's total number of pixels (i.e. black pixels in the alpha channel). Since the sprite contains black pixels (e.g. as outline) or white, the sum of color ratios is usually far below 100%.

3.3 Analysis of Pokémon Sprite Metrics

Pokémon sprites are very diverse in terms of sprite size, brightness as well as saturation; sprite sizes range from 92 to 585 pixels (with an average of 209). Out of those pixels, 48% are occupied by any color on average. For this analysis, the color channels considered are set to 8 (see Fig. 2). Across all sprites, the most prominent color is orange (average ratio of 15%), red (11%) and blue (10%).

Looking at specific types of Pokémon, Fig. 3 shows the distribution of colors in their sprites (sorted by coverage ratio). Most Pokémon types have a large ratio of orange pixels, but there are obvious differences among different types of Pokémon. Fire Pokémon have a high ratio of red and orange pixels and little else, while poison Pokémon have a much fairer distribution of colors. Water and ice Pokémon have the highest coverage in blue pixels, while only poison and ghost Pokémon have a substantial presence of purple colors. Grass Pokémon have more coverage in green or yellow-green colors than other types; steel Pokémon have the least coverage in any color. It is expected that most of these patterns can be learned by the classifiers discussed below.

4 Building a Classifier for Pokémon Types

In order to understand how color reflects a Pokémon's type, a machine learning approach is used to predict unseen Pokémon such as those evolved in Sect. 5. Each Pokémon belongs to one or two types, so the learning task is one of *multi-label classification* since types are not mutually exclusive. In this paper, decision trees are used to classify Pokémon types, based on their image properties (i.e. image metrics) described in Sect. 3.2. Decision trees were chosen as they are among the few algorithms that handle multi-label classification tasks out-of-the-box, but also due to the fact that they are human interpretable and can be

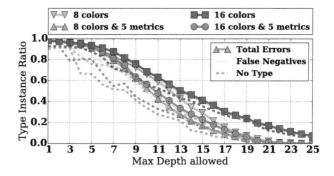

Fig. 4. Sensitivity of the decision tree classification task for different maximum tree depths and inputs. Type errors are normalized to the 1396 instances of type and Pokémon with no type are normalized to the 908 Pokémon in the dataset.

visualized. As a white box model, a decision tree allows a designer to understand the rules that make a Pokémon visually reminiscent of its type. The inputs of the decision tree are exclusively the sprite's image metrics, i.e. the different color ratios and, optionally, the sprite size, average and standard deviation of brightness, average and standard deviation of saturation. The output is an array of 18 integers each representing membership in a type (outputs can be 0 or 1).

All 908 data points are used to build the decision tree based on the ground truth of the Pokémons' types. Since decision trees may suffer from over-fitting, it is worthwhile to perform a sensitivity analysis regarding the maximum depth of the tree. The larger and more complex the decision tree, the more likely it is that niche rules were added that do not generalize to unseen Pokémon sprites. It should be noted that for all intents and purposes all Pokémon from the games will technically be "seen" by the classifier; however, as we intend to create new sprites based on recoloring methods of Sect. 5, its ability to generalize remains important. Moreover, alternative inputs could also be considered such as more color channels or including the 5 non-color metrics. The sensitivity analysis below will explore the impact of all those parameters. The core performance metric is of course the accuracy of the classifier, i.e. the sum of false positives (i.e. the classifier predicts that the Pokémon belongs to a type, but in truth it does not) and false negatives (i.e. the classifier fails to predict one of the Pokémon's types). Due to the nature of the dataset and the purposes of this study, an important secondary performance metric is the number of Pokémon which have no type whatsoever (i.e. 0 in all the classifier's outputs); Pokémon that can not be classified (not even mis-classified) are problematic for the purposes of evolving a new color palette, as the overall number of Pokémon essentially becomes smaller.

Figure 4 shows how accuracy and the number of Pokémon without types change as the depth of the decision tree increases. Using only color information (either 8 or 16 color channels) needs larger trees for accurate classification despite the fact that the metrics are fewer. Including the 5 other image metrics described above helps with classification tasks, and using only 8 colors seems beneficial as errors and Pokémon without a type drop more abruptly in larger trees. While the number of errors is fairly low for the 13 feature input set after a depth of 15 and for the 8 colors after a depth of 17, the number of Pokémon without a type is a concern. Erring on the side of caution, the ratio of Pokémon without a type drops to 0.5% at depth 20 for the 13 feature set and at depth 22 for the 8 colors; their misclassificiation ratio is 2% and 0.6% respectively. While the 13 feature set is beneficial as it takes into account information missing from the color channels (including white and black pixes or how saturated the colors are), over 58% of its decision nodes test those 5 non-color features. When evolving a color palette in Sect. 5, the system can only control the colors (and not e.g. the size of the sprite) which causes some Pokémon with specific sizes or brightness values to never be able to change their type. For that reason, and despite somewhat lower accuracies, the decision tree using 8 colors as input (and a depth of 22) is used in the remaining experiments of this paper.

5   Evolving the Pokémon Pallette

The classifier of Pokémon types based on their color ratio can be used to analyze existing Pokémon and could be useful to designers as a white-box model. However, in this study it serves an ulterior goal of classifying unseen procedurally generated Pokémon sprites. In this paper, the generative process revolves around the recoloring of existing Pokémon sprites from the database of 908 sprites, achieving new color combinations without changing the sprite's outline or the Pokémon's physiology. This design choice was taken not only to test how much can be achieved with a simple representation, but primarily to ensure that recognizable and high-quality Pokémon can be produced. Moreover, the impact of color on people's perception has been studied extensively in advertising or psychology but rarely in game design (and even less so in procedural content generation); therefore evaluating how generated color palettes can be used to strengthen human assumptions on the meaning of color is particularly relevant.

As described in Sect. 3.2 and Fig. 2, each Pokémon sprite is split into different image channels. These images can be recombined to create a sprite almost identical to the original. As color channels are binary and the sprite is colored based on the midpoint of the hue range, some errors in the colors of reconstructed sprites may occur; with 8 colors, however, obvious miscolorations are rare and only in some Pokémon. This method of reconstructing a Pokémon sprite from its alpha, brightness, saturation and color channels will be used to re-color existing Pokémon sprites via the process explained in Fig. 5. The top row shows the 8 color channels (which are binary as per Fig. 2) and the color palette mapped to them: those are colored with the appropriate hue as shown in Fig. 5 and combined with the brightness and saturation channels to reconstruct the Pokémon on the top right. However, if these same color channels are mapped to different hues as shown in the bottom row, when recombined they will create a very differently colored Pokémon which remains recognizable due to the alpha, brightness and saturation channels.

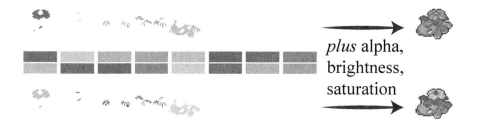

Fig. 5. Recoloring process with a re-shuffled color palette (bottom).

In order to generate new color palettes, the original 8 colors are taken and swapped randomly. As we avoid having two channels map to the same color in this study, the possible permutations of 8 colors is $40,320$; searching this space exhaustively would be cumbersome. Instead, evolution is used to stochastically search the space of color combinations for ones that satisfy the designer's objectives. These objectives will be discussed in the next subsections. Regardless of objective, the evolutionary process is the same: an initial population of random permutations of the colors' original order evolves via mutation alone to increase an objective score. Crossover is not used as it could lead to multiple channels with the same color, i.e. mostly monochrome sprites. Mutation can (a) create a new permutation (ignoring the previous genetic encoding), (b) reverse the order in the gene, (c) swap a random color with another random color in the palette's order, (d) swap a random color with its adjacent in the palette, (e) shift all colors to the left (red to magenta etc.) or (f) right (green to cyan etc.). One of these mutations is applied to each individual, and each mutation has an equal chance of being chosen. In the order they are presented, mutations range from disruptive to minor changes; their combination should be sufficient to drive evolution towards more promising solutions without risking genetic drift. Evolution follows a μ, λ evolutionary strategy [20] with 50% elitism: in each generation the fittest half of the population is copied without mutation, and these elites are also chosen (at random) to produce offspring via mutation. The least fit 50% of the individuals are replaced by the mutated offspring of the most fit 50%. This is a somewhat aggressive evolutionary strategy (as it lacks the stochasticity of roulette wheel selection and its elitism ratio is high), which is why mutations that can introduce new genes are desirable to avoid premature convergence.

In the following subsections, a number of experiments will cover different objectives of recoloring Pokémon sprites, from local changes to sweeping changes on the entire dataset. All objective functions in the following experiments must be maximized during evolution, and there are criteria for early stopping if the desired value (which is known in advance in all the listed cases) is reached. Finally, in order to avoid creating color combinations that can not be handled by the classifier, all fitness scores are reduced by the penalty function P of Eq. (1) which deters more Pokémon of no type than in the original dataset, as well as

Pokémon which are predicted to have more than two types.

$$P = C_e min(0, E - E_{orig}) + C_{mt} \sum_{i \in S} \left(\sum_{t \in T} p_t(i) - 2 \right) \qquad (1)$$

where T is the set of all 18 types; $p_t(i)$ is the predicted value (0 or 1) for type t of the decision tree using the evolving pallette of i as input; E is the current number of Pokémon with no type and E_{orig} is the number of Pokémon with no type before recoloring for the same dataset S; C_e and C_{mt} are constants (in this paper $C_e = C_{mt} = 10$).

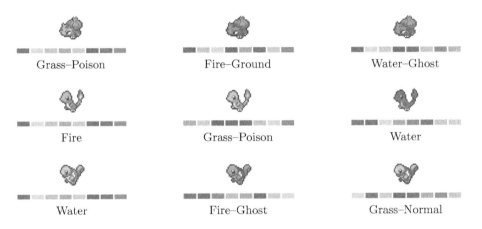

Fig. 6. Evolving a pallette for changing one Pokémon's types. In the first row, Bulbasaur (1st) is evolved to gain the fire type (2nd) and the water type (3rd). In the second row, Charmander (1st) is evolved to gain the grass type (2nd) and the water type (3rd). In the third row, Squirtle (1st) is evolved to gain the fire type (2nd) and the grass type (3rd).

5.1   Customizing a Single Pokémon

The simplest use of a generative color palette is to change a single Pokémon sprite to a desired new type. This is obviously a local change which only affects the Pokémon sprite in question, but can be used to create a broad range of Pokémon (especially considering dual types) from a single sprite. The decision tree is used to classify the recolored Pokémon sprite based on the evolving color palette; its fitness, as shown in Eq. (2), is proportional to the misclassifications from its original type(s) and its correct classifications of the desired type(s).

$$f_1 = \frac{1}{|D|} \sum_{t \in D} p_t(i) - \frac{1}{|O|} \sum_{t \in O} p_t(i) - P \qquad (2)$$

Table 2. Ratio of Pokémon retaining their original type at the end of evolution which attempts to remove the type from a subset of the database. In the "Replaced by" row, the table includes the most popular type among the recolored Pokémon of that subset. Results are averaged from 10 independent runs.

Type	Water	Normal	Flying	Grass	Psychic	Bug	Ground	Fire	Poison
Remaining	0.07%	0%	0.8%	0%	2%	0%	0%	0%	2.03%
Replaced by	Grass	Psychic	Psychic	Ice	Grass	Fairy	Psychic	Poison	Psychic
Type	Rock	Fighting	Dark	Electric	Dragon	Steel	Ghost	Fairy	Ice
Remaining	0%	0%	0%	0%	1.19%	2.41%	0%	0%	0%
Replaced by	Grass	Psychic	Dragon	Steel	Fairy	Dragon	Grass	Ground	Fairy

where O and D are the set of types of the original Pokémon i and the desired Pokémon i respectively. P and all other notations are covered by Eq. (1).

As a demonstration, the three basic elemental types (water, fire and grass) will be used to recolor the starter Pokémon of the first generation of games. The three starter Pokémon shown in Fig. 6 are widely recognizable: the grass-poison Pokémon is Bulbasaur, the fire Pokémon is Charmander and the water Pokémon is Squirtle. Evolution will recolor them so that they no longer belong to their original types but instead belong to one of the other elements of that triangle. Results in Fig. 6 are chosen among 10 evolutionary runs for each objective, with 20 individuals evolving for 50 generations (although evolution terminated prematurely in all runs). Evolution evidently took advantage of the learned pattern that water Pokémon tend to be blue, fire Pokémon tend to be red and grass Pokémon tend to be green (see Fig. 3). The second type of the recolored sprites is more insteresting, as purples in the recolored fire Squirtle and the water Bulbasaur give them the ghost type. Although this is a simple task that could likely be solved by random swaps and/or a hill climber, evolution easily found these results which is promising for the more challenging tasks of Sects. 5.2 and 5.3.

5.2   Removing a Pokémon Type

As shown in Sect. 5.1, it is possible to recolor a single Pokémon in a way that it is not recognized as belonging to its original type. Taking this approach one step further, an entire category of Pokémon sprites can be recolored in order to change their type. In the experiments of this section, we focus on a set of Pokémon grouped by type and attempt to recolor them in a way that removes that specific type. Contrary to the previous approach, evolution now operates on a larger scale as it needs to find a pallette that works on a large set of Pokémon; however, the goal of evolution is only to make these sprites not be identifiable as Pokémon of their original type but does not include a designer-specified target type. This allows more freedom for initially compatible Pokémon (in type, if not strictly visually) to adopt different appearances and types. The system extracts a set S_t of all Pokémon belonging to type t (including dual type Pokémon with t as one of their types) and attempts to maximize the fitness of Eq. (3).

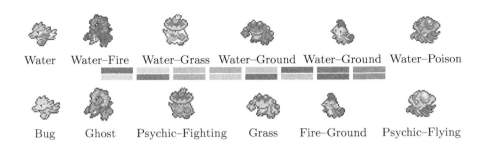

Fig. 7. A sample of water Pokémon's which, after evolution, have been converted to a diverse set of types excluding water. (Color figure online)

$$f_2 = -\frac{1}{|S_t|} \sum_{i \in S_t} p_t(i) - P \tag{3}$$

where i the Pokémon in set S_t which belonged, originally, to the same type t; P and other notations are covered by Eq. (1).

Table 2 shows how removing the type of specific sets of Pokémon is handled by the evolutionary system in terms of both the fitness (i.e. the ratio of Pokémon that retain their type) and the most popular type that replaces it. All results are averaged from 10 independent evolutionary runs, collected after evolution is carried out on 20 individuals for 50 generations. Most evolutionary runs succeed in completely removing the chosen type, and only fire and dragon types had one Pokémon of that type remaining even in their most successful run. The easiest types to eradicate are ghost and ice, which are fully removed in less than 3 generations on average. Looking at the most popular types found in the recolored Pokémon of different subsets, the psychic type is surprisingly popular and the water type surprisingly absent as a prevalent replacement. As will be discussed below, this is likely because psychic Pokémon often feature cyan or purple hues (see Fig. 3) which are rarely shared by other Pokémon. The simplest way to remove a Pokémon's original type is thus to recolor it in such rare hues.

Among the most successful attempts at changing the type of an entire set of Pokémon is shown in Fig. 7. The shown evolved color pallette managed to remove the water type from all 141 water Pokémon; water was the most popular type based on Table 1. While none of the recolored Pokémon were classified as belonging to the water type, all other types are represented. The most popular type among recolored Pokémon is grass (28%) and flying (25%) and the least popular is fairy and poison (1% of each). The examples of Fig. 7 shows that blue sprites became yellow-green and orange sprites became purple; generally, colors originally adjacent now have stark contrasts. Since many water Pokémon were initially blue, it makes sense that more grass Pokémon are predicted with the evolved mapping of blue to green (see Fig. 3).

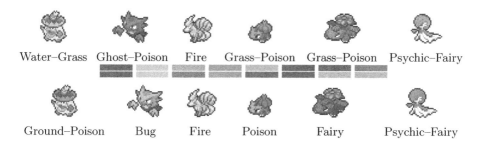

| Water–Grass | Ghost–Poison | Fire | Grass–Poison | Grass–Poison | Psychic–Fairy |

| Ground–Poison | Bug | Fire | Poison | Fairy | Psychic–Fairy |

Fig. 8. Sample sprites evolved to balance the ratio of Pokémon types. (Color figure online)

5.3 Balancing the Number of Pokémon Per Type

The most ambitious application of the proposed approach is to apply the recoloring rules globally, to the entire database. There are many reasons for doing so, including those motivating evolution in the previous sections. For instance, evolution can recolor the entire database to minimize the number of Pokémon of a specific type, as in Sect. 5.2 (e.g. if a designer decides to eradicate one specific type from the lore) or to create as many Pokémon of a specific designer-defined type (or combination of types) as in Sect. 5.1. In order to show another application of the proposed approach, this section instead attempts to create recoloring rules which minimize the discrepancy between the number of Pokémon of each type. As seen in Table 1, some types are present in more Pokémon than others (the number of water Pokémon is triple that of ice Pokémon). Using the entire dataset of 908 sprites, evolution attempts to maximize f_3 of Eq. (4), which is the standard deviation of the number of Pokémon per predicted type.

$$f_3 = -\sqrt{\sum_{t \in T}(N_t - \bar{N})} - P \qquad (4)$$

where $N_t = \sum_{i \in S} p_t(i)$, i.e. the number of Pokémon predicted to belong to type t; $\bar{N}$ is the average of all N_t for $t \in T$; T is the set of all 18 types and S is the set of all 908 Pokémon. P is formulated in Eq. (1).

Results are collected from 10 runs where 20 individuals evolved for 50 generations. Optimization was generally consistent, but this section analyses in depth the fittest result among those runs. The fittest color pallete is shown in Fig. 8: it maintains the original color of primary, popular colors (red, orange, green, blue) while altering the rest. Therefore, many of the Pokémon sprites do not change color or type, e.g. the fire Pokémon of Fig. 8. Unlike results in Fig. 7, evolution here follows a more conservative recoloring strategy.

Since many of the colors remain the same after evolution, it should not be surprising that the color ratios of different types largely stay the same. Figure 9 shows the color ratios for different Pokémon types (as predicted by the classifier) with the evolved palette. General patterns remain the same: water

Pokémon tend to be blue, fire Pokémon tend to be red, grass Pokémon tend to be green, and all Pokémon have a fairly high ratio in orange. There are notable differences too: magenta is much more prevalent (it has the highest ratio for poison Pokémon now), while cyan is rarer in water and ice Pokémon compared to Fig. 3.

The distribution of predicted types with the new palette is shown in Table 3, sorted by popularity. Notable changes from Table 1 is the drop of water and grass Pokémon by over 20 instances (slightly less for dragon and fire). At the same time, most other types of Pokémon increase, especially fairy and ghost Pokémon. This shouldn't be surprising, as the more prevalent magenta and purple colors were quite prevalent in the original fairy and ghost Pokémon respectively, based on Fig. 3. While the distribution of types is still not entirely balanced, there are more types with values closer together by reducing the number of some popular types (water, grass) and increasing that of less popular ones (ghost, fairy). The deviation of instances among the types was 27 in the original dataset; with the evolved palette it is 22. This is admittedly not a large improvement, but it is likely the limit of what can be achieved with a simple color swap and without introducing more Pokémon that are classified as having no type.

Observing the sample Pokémon of Fig. 8 shows some trends of the evolved color mapping. For many sprites, due to colors such as yellow and red remaining the same, their appearance and type was retained (e.g. the fire Pokémon); even when recolored, some sprites retained their type e.g. the psychic–fairy Pokémon. On the other hand, even small changes in color can result in changes of types as in the water–grass Pokémon which gains two completely new types due to a change in the color of the "hat" and limbs. Of interest are the two grass–poison

Table 3. Predicted types in the recolored sprites that maximize f_3.

Normal (120)	Water (116)	Flying (110)	Psychic (105)	Bug (88)	Fairy (87)
Grass (81)	Rock (78)	Poison (70)	Ground (69)	Electric (69)	Ghost (68)
Fire (66)	Dark (61)	Fighting (59)	Steel (56)	Dragon (49)	Ice (42)

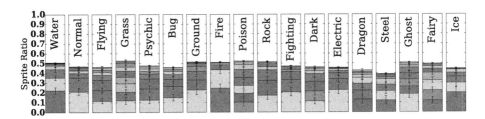

Fig. 9. Color ratios per Pokémon type of the evolved set that maximizes f_3. Error bars represent the 95% confidence interval of the displayed average ratio (per type). (Color figure online)

Pokémon which, while one is an evolution of the other, when recolored gain different colors (one is originally more cyan than the other) and different types.

6 Discussion

The purpose of experiments in this paper was to explore and demonstrate how the proposed evolutionary system can be used to create new Pokémon by recombining their color palettes. As a small sample of the possible use cases of this approach, the recolored palette can change the type of a Pokémon to a desired type, for local changes, remove a type from all Pokémon of that type, and find a new color palette for all Pokémon to change the distribution of their types. Results show that all of these are largely successful: in most cases evolution is able to perform its goal (find all desired types, remove all instances of a type from a subset of the database) although for the more challenging task of global palette swaps, it seems that it requires that certain colors retain their original hues and consequently many of the Pokémon retain their original type.

The decision tree classifier showed that at sufficient depth it can be accurate in its predictions. Moreover, as a white-box system it can be a useful design tool, especially if some of its rules are converted into natural language: e.g. "if sprites are large and their red color is higher than average...". There is a concern regarding the number of instances which could not be classified (i.e. Pokémon without a type) which led to adopting a large tree that perhaps overfits to the data. Experiments on evolving a color palette used a tree with only decision nodes based on color ratios; this was less accurate overall to a model which includes information on brightness, sprite size and saturation. Preliminary experiments using those additional features during evolution were problematic as some Pokémon would not change their type due to metrics beyond the control of evolution (e.g. small Pokémon were overfitted to always be bug types). While using additional metrics is valuable as a design tool and for designer feedback, when used for automated generation via recoloring it underperforms.

Admittedly, both the motivation and the evaluation of this paper was based on designer intuition and the desire to only partially automate the design process. For instance, there is no parameter tuning reported in the results, and parameters such as mutation and population size are not argued for. The purpose of experiments was to demonstrate rather than benchmark the potential of the algorithm; while many more experiments with different fitness functions, population sizes etc. were performed, only a handful are reported to give more of a "taste" of potential applications. For instance, experiments with penalty functions which reward fewer Pokémon with no predicted type showed that this reward dominated the fitness in the more challenging tasks of Sect. 5.3. Using crossover resulted in many colors in the original sprite mapped to the same color in the recolored version, reducing the visual appeal while also not reaching higher fitnesses than mutation alone. In terms of reporting, there are not many baselines that could be considered for such a task (apart from exhaustive search); significance testing in an approach aiming at recoloring Pokémon in interesting ways seems exorbitant, considering that most evolutionary runs ended prematurely as they reached the stated objective. As a final note, the use of existing color channels, and their recoloration in a one-to-one mapping was a design decision in order to increase the quality of resulting sprites. Changes in saturation values or brightness channels is also possible, provided there is some constraint that deters the creation of "pure noise"; in that case, computer vision approaches such as deep learning would be more suitable than the numerical representation of the image used here as input to the classifier.

Finally, Pokémon generation could have more dimensions than their sprites and type mapping. Pokémon statistics such as hit points and attack could be classified, along with their type, based on image metrics; this could allow a more fine-grained sprite generator to create Pokémon for specific strategies (e.g. a "Wall" Pokémon with high hit points and high defense). Moreover, the moves of the Pokémon could be mapped to their sprite's appearance and type (and possibly stats). Consistency of Pokémon types in their evolved forms, or in higher resolution versions could also be considered. More niche computational models such as a name generator learned from current Pokémon names could also potentially be used to give names to the newly generated Pokémon sprites to match their new types. There are many straightforward as well as intricate ways in which this initial study can be expanded.

7   Conclusion

This paper introduced a system for decomposing Pokémon sprites into image metrics that can be used to learn a mapping between the Pokémon's type(s) and its visual appearance. Decision trees were shown to be fairly accurate at sufficient depth, especially when combining color information with other information such as sprite size and brightness. Using an evolutionary algorithm, color palettes based on the original sprites and colors were evolved to create new Pokémon on a local or global scale that matched to or diverged from specific types, as well as to lessen imbalances between the instances of each type. Results showed that at its core the recoloring strategy is able to perform most of these tasks, creating in most cases visually coherent and appealing Pokémon assigned to new types. This initial study could be expanded with more features to learn (either based on color, on other visual metrics, or on in-game statistics) and to generate. Several directions for future work must be explored, such as the use of a more granular representation, different machine learning approaches, and the generation of more Pokémon details beyond their spites.

Acknowledgements. Pokémon images and names are copyright of Nintendo/Game Freak; no copyright infringement is intended. No monetary profit was made from this article.

References

1. von Neumann, J., Morgenstern, O.: Theory of Games and Economic Behavior. Princeton University Press, New Jersey (1944)
2. Perez-Liebana, D., Samothrakis, S., Togelius, J., Lucas, S.M., Schaul, T.: General video game AI: competition, challenges and opportunities. In: Proceedings of the AAAI Conference on Artificial Intelligence (2016)
3. Browne, C., Maire, F.: Evolutionary game design. IEEE Trans. Comput. Intell. AI Games **2**(1), 1–16 (2010)
4. Yannakakis, G.N., Togelius, J.: Experience-driven procedural content generation. IEEE Trans. Affect. Comput. **99**, 147–161 (2011)
5. Hunicke, R., Leblanc, M., Zubek, R.: MDA: a formal approach to game design and game research. In: Proceedings of the Challenges in Game AI Workshop, Nineteenth National Conference on Artificial Intelligence (2004)
6. Winters, G.J., Zhu, J.: Guiding players through structural composition patterns in 3D adventure games. In: Proceedings of the Foundations of Digital Games Conference (2014)
7. Yannakakis, G.N., Spronck, P., Loiacono, D., Andre, E.: Player modeling. In: Dagstuhl Seminar on Artificial and Computational Intelligence in Games (2013)
8. Lim, C.U., Liapis, A., Harrell, D.F.: Discovering social and aesthetic categories of avatars: a bottom-up artificial intelligence approach using image clustering. In: Proceedings of the International Joint Conference of DiGRA and FDG (2016)
9. Basri, R., Costa, L., Geiger, D., Jacobs, D.: Determining the similarity of deformable shapes. Vis. Res. **38**, 15–16 (1998)
10. Russakovsky, O., Deng, J., Su, H., Krause, J., Satheesh, S., Ma, S., Huang, Z., Karpathy, A., Khosla, A., Bernstein, M., Berg, A.C., Fei-Fei, L.: ImageNet large scale visual recognition challenge. Int. J. Comput. Vis. **115**(3), 211–252 (2015)
11. Martins, T., Correia, J., Costa, E., Machado, P.: Evotype: evolutionary type design. In: Johnson, C., Carballal, A., Correia, J. (eds.) EvoMUSART 2015. LNCS, vol. 9027, pp. 136–147. Springer, Cham (2015). https://doi.org/10.1007/978-3-319-16498-4_13
12. Lehman, J., Risi, S., Clune, J.: Creative generation of 3D objects with deep learning and innovation engines. In: Proceedings of the International Conference on Computational Creativity (2016)
13. Kao, D., Harrell, D.F.: Exigent: an automatic avatar generation system. In: Proceedings of the Foundations of Digital Games Conference (2015)
14. Liapis, A., Yannakakis, G.N., Togelius, J.: Computational game creativity. In: Proceedings of the Fifth International Conference on Computational Creativity (2014)
15. Risi, S., Lehman, J., D'Ambrosio, D.B., Hall, R., Stanley, K.O.: Combining search-based procedural content generation and social gaming in the petalz video game. In: Proceedings of the Artificial Intelligence and Interactive Digital Entertainment Conference (2012)
16. Hastings, E.J., Guha, R.K., Stanley, K.O.: Evolving content in the galactic arms race video game. In: Proceedings of the IEEE Conference on Computational Intelligence and Games (2009)
17. Liapis, A., Yannakakis, G.N., Togelius, J.: Adapting models of visual aesthetics for personalized content creation. IEEE Trans. Comput. Intell. AI Games **4**(3), 213–228 (2012)
18. Howlett, A., Colton, S., Browne, C.: Evolving pixel shaders for the prototype video game subversion. In: Proceedings of the AI and Games Symposium (AISB 2010) (2010)

19. Summerville, A., Mateas, M.: Sampling hyrule: multi-technique probabilistic level generation for action role playing games. In: Proceedings of the Foundations of Digital Games Conference (2015)
20. Beyer, H.G., Schwefel, H.P.: Evolution strategies - a comprehensive introduction. Nat. Comput. **1**(1), 3–52 (2002)

Mapping Chess Aesthetics
onto Procedurally Generated
Chess-Like Games

Jakub Kowalski[1(✉)], Antonios Liapis[2], and Lukasz Żarczyński[1]

[1] Institute of Computer Science, University of Wrocław, Wrocław, Poland
jko@cs.uni.wroc.pl, luk.zarczynski@gmail.com
[2] Institute of Digital Games, University of Malta, Msida, Malta
antonios.liapis@um.edu.mt

Abstract. Variants of chess have been generated in many forms and for several reasons, such as testbeds for artificial intelligence research in general game playing. This paper uses the visual properties of chess pieces as inspiration to generate new shapes for other chess-like games, targeting specific visual properties which allude to the pieces' in-game function. The proposed method uses similarity measures in terms of pieces' strategic role and movement in a game to identify the new pieces' closest representatives in chess. Evolution then attempts to minimize the distance from chess pieces' visual properties, resulting in new shapes which combine one or more chess pieces' visual identities. While experiments in this paper focus on two chess-like games from previous publications, the method can be used for broader generation of game visuals based on functional similarities of components to known, popular games.

Keywords: Procedural content generation · Chess variants
Digital aesthetics · Evolutionary algorithms · Simplified Boardgames

1 Introduction

For over a decade, digital games have been the domain of choice for research in computational and artificial intelligence, culminating in several handbooks on the topic [1,2]. The vast majority of the research output on this domain has been treating digital games as *systems*, focusing on their functional aspects. Specifically, research in artificial agents for playing the game usually focuses on their efficiency, using the game score attained as a benchmark of their success [3]. On the other hand, research in procedural content generation (PCG) often focuses on functional components of games, such as rules and levels, and assesses them based on solvability in the sense that the game rules allow an end-state to be attained [4] and a level's goal to be reached [5].

J. Kowalski—Supported in part by the National Science Centre, Poland under project number 2015/17/B/ST6/01893.

K. Sim and P. Kaufmann (Eds.): EvoApplications 2018, LNCS 10784, pp. 325–341, 2018.
https://doi.org/10.1007/978-3-319-77538-8_23

An example of functional concerns of game research can be found in the General Game Playing (GGP) domain for general-purpose agents [6,7]. However, recent research on General Video Game AI [3] broadens this scope towards level generation [8,9] and game rules generation [10]. This paper is inspired by early GGP research on chess-like games [11,12], approaching it using Simplified Boardgames [13]. As Pell's generator for METAGAME was able to produce game rules using randomized choices without any automatic evaluation [12], the rule generator for Simplified Boardgames uses artificial evolution combined with agent-based heuristics to ensure the strategic depth of generated games [14].

However, games are also aesthetic experiences that capture players' attention and allow for user interaction not only based on the combination of their rules or the spatial arrangement of their levels. Digital games elicit players' emotions through a combination of audio, visual and gameplay stimuli, and motivate exploration of the game's world by spreading visually stunning and unique vistas in different locations. While game art has been generated algorithmically in a number of commercial games and research projects, it is not clear how the functional components can be mapped to a specific audiovisual look and feel. As an example, the *Sonancia* system [15] generates levels and then uses the components within these levels (e.g. the presence or absence of monsters) to allocate background sounds in each room of the level. In the case of Sonancia, the mapping is made on design assumptions that the presence of monsters leads to a more tense experience; however, it is possible that such a mapping between different elements of games can be learnt [16].

Even board games, which have a more limited physical medium, use visuals to convey important gameplay affordances, e.g. the symbols in card games such as *Uno* (Mattel, 1992) or the shape, size and color of house tokens in *Monopoly* (Parker Bros., 1935). A systems-heavy board game such as chess also relies on the shape and size of its pieces to denote their importance and function: the size of the queen and king show that they are powerful pieces that should not be placed in harm's way (compared to the smaller, simpler pawn pieces).

Procedurally generated game rules thus require assets tailored to this particular game, so that they allow easy distinction between games created by the same system, and better fit to this game's style. For chess and chess-like games, multiple human-made piece shapes already exist. These pieces can be used as an *inspiration set* towards which new game pieces can be generated based on a mapping between the visual appearance and the function of chess pieces.

In this paper, we present an evolutionary-based method of generating shapes for any chess-like game, given its rules in Simplified Boardgames language. The goal for the generator is two-fold. First, the shapes evolved for one game should look similar, so that they are easily identified as parts of a whole. Second, we would like the shapes of the pieces to correspond to their role and importance in the game. Chess pieces are used as inspiration and their mapping between visual and strategic properties is used to create the visuals of pieces in generated games. This is done by finding similarities in the functional properties of chess pieces and new pieces, and targeting the visual dimensions of the closest chess pieces for evolving the shape of the new piece. Experiments in this paper focus on evolving pieces for two procedurally generated games introduced in [14,17].

2 Background Work

This section highlights relevant work on procedural content generation for games and provides a brief description of the Simplified Boardgames language.

2.1 Procedural Content Generation

Digital games have used algorithms to generate content since the early 1980s with games such as Rogue (Toy and Wichman, 1980) and ELITE (Acornsoft, 1984). Generating content procedurally has been primarily motivated within commercial game development to increase replayability with nigh-endless variations of games and to decrease development time and cost. The game industry has traditionally focused on generating levels such as the star systems of *Stellaris* (Paradox, 2016), the gameworld of *Minecraft* (Mojang, 2011) or the dungeons of *Diablo* (Blizzard, 1996). There has been a strong academic interest in procedural content generation (PCG) in the last decade, focused primarily in level generation [5,18,19]. Contrary to the carefully scripted algorithms traditionally used in commercial games, PCG research regularly uses complex artificial and computational intelligence methods such as machine learning [19], declarative programming [4] and artificial evolution [20].

While level generation has been the most popular domain for PCG in academia and in commercial games, other facets of games such as visuals, audio, and game rules have also been explored [21]. Relevant examples for this study include the evolution of rulesets for colliding objects and scoring [22] or the evolution of mechanics based on direct code modification [23]. For board games, board layouts and rules have been evolved based on a broad range of metrics in the *Ludi* system [24]. In our work, we are using the games generated by the evolutionary system described in [14] for Simplified Boardgames. The system extends and formalizes the idea of Relative Algorithm Performance Profiles (RAPP) [25] and produces fully symmetrical games with one royal piece, and an initial row of pawn-like pieces. The evaluation function uses a number of algorithms (player profiles) with various degrees of intelligence. To assess the strategic properties of a generated game, different AI algorithms are simulated against each other and results are compared with the results obtained on human-made chess-like games. Based on the RAPP assumption, we expect that all games that behave similarly to human-made games will also be good. Results show that playable and balanced games of good quality can be obtained in this fashion. However, such games' rules might not necessary be intuitive and easy to learn for human players. For this reason, additional human-readability measures and generated natural language descriptions of the game rules have been presented in [17].

Game visuals have often been evolved for different domains and with different purposes. Game shaders have been evolved towards a designer-specified prevalent color [26]. The color and trajectory of particle effects representing players' weapons have been evolved based on how often the weapon was fired compared to others [27,28]. Colorful flowers have been evolved collaboratively in a Facebook game [29] based on the principles of interactive evolution [30]. In terms of evolving shapes for use as game sprites, spaceships' outlines have been evolved towards breaking patterns found in previous evolutionary steps [31] as well as to portray specific gameplay properties visually [32]. Inspired by cognitive psychology, several fitness dimensions of shapes were defined in [33] and used to evolve symmetrical shapes of spaceships' hulls. Spaceships could be evolved based on a weighted sum of these dimensions; the weights could be adapted to a user's choice among spaceships [33] or specified by a designer to create visual styles for different alien races [34]. The visual metrics used in this paper are largely inspired by the dimensions of [33], although in this case the goal is to minimize distance with known chess shapes or combinations thereof.

2.2   Simplified Boardgames

Simplified Boardgames is the class of fairy chess-like games introduced by Björnsson [13]. The language describes turn-based, two player, zero-sum chess-like games on a rectangular board with piece movements described in regular language and independent of move history. The language can describe many of the fairy chess variants in a concise way, including games with asymmetry and position-dependent moves. The usage of finite automata for describing pieces' rules, and thus for move generation, allows fast and efficient computation of all legal moves given a board setup. However, it has some important limitations, as it cannot express actions like castling, en-passant, or promotions.

Here we follow formal specifications from [35] to provide a shortened necessary introduction. A chess-like game is played between a *black* and *white* player; the white player always moves first. During a single turn, a player has to make a move using one of their pieces, changing its position according to the specified movement rule for this piece. At any time, at most one piece can occupy a square: finishing the move on a square containing a piece (regardless of the owner) results in removing it (capturing). No piece addition is possible. After performing a move, the player gives control to the opponent.

For a given piece, the set of its legal moves is defined as the set of words described by a regular expression over an alphabet Σ containing triplets (Δx, Δy, on), where Δx and Δy are relative column/row distances, and on describes the content type of the destination square, which can be empty, occupied by an opponent piece, or occupied by an own piece.

Consider a piece and a word $w \in \Sigma^*$ that belongs to the language described by the regular expression in the movement rule for this piece. Let $w = a_1 a_2 \ldots a_k$, where each $a_i = (\Delta x_i, \Delta y_i, on_i)$, and suppose that the piece stands on a square $\langle x, y \rangle$. Then, w describes a move of the piece, which is applicable in the current board position if and only if, for every i such that $1 \leq i \leq k$, the content condition on_i is fulfilled by the content of the square $\langle x + \sum_{j=1}^{i} \Delta x_j, y + \sum_{j=1}^{i} \Delta y_j \rangle$.

The game may end in a tie, when a preset turn limit is reached. The player can win by moving a certain piece to a fixed set of squares (positional win), by capturing a fixed amount of the opponent's pieces of a certain type (capturing win), or by bringing the opponent into a state with has no legal moves. The terminal conditions may be asymmetric.

3 Methodology

The main task of our system is to read rules of an arbitrary chess-like game, and produce the shape for each piece defined in this game. We decided to ground our method on chess: the most famous boardgame in Western culture, and the game where both the rules and the shapes are commonly recognized.

This section describes our system's worflow, summarized in Fig. 1. First, the strategic and visual metrics for chess are computued; then, the strategic metrics of a generated game are computed and pieces of this new game are mapped onto chess pieces based on their similarity in strategic metrics. We use that mapping to obtain target visual scores as an evolutionary objective. Two-step evolution first generates a common base shape and then individually evolves each piece starting from this base shape towards that shapes target visual scores.

To describe this full workflow, Sect. 3.1 first describes the strategic properties used and how we compute metrics for the most important aspects of pieces' behavior. Similarly, Sect. 3.2 introduces visual metrics that capture the visual style of a piece's shape. Section 3.3 describes how we compare pieces in a new game with those of chess, and how we find a mapping for their desired visual metrics. Finally, we can evolve the shape of each piece in a new game. The proposed algorithm operates in *steps*: first, a general shape is evolved based on the average of all pieces' visual metrics; then, the general shape is evolved further to closely match each piece's target visual metrics. Section 3.4 describes the genetic encoding of a piece's shape, while details of the evolutionary algorithm and alternative approaches for choosing the final shapes are described in Sect. 3.5.

Apart from chess, experiments in this paper use two procedurally generated games as a case study: *The Legacy of Ibis* described in [14], and the game presented in [17], which we refer to as *The Weather Chess*.

3.1 Strategic Metrics

We identify several *strategic metrics* to describe a piece in terms of its role in the strategic gameplay of chess: its importance, its movement (e.g. agile, bulky), its usefulness in attack/defense, etc. This paper uses the following strategic metrics:

s_{po} The fraction of the piece occurrences in the game's initial state.
s_{ec} The fraction of piece movements that end with a capture.
s_{pw} This value is 1 if the piece can be used for a positional win, 0 otherwise.
s_{cw} This value is 1 if piece can be used for a capturing win, 0 otherwise.
s_{ba} The average ratio of the board area that can be covered by a piece from its initial position(s).

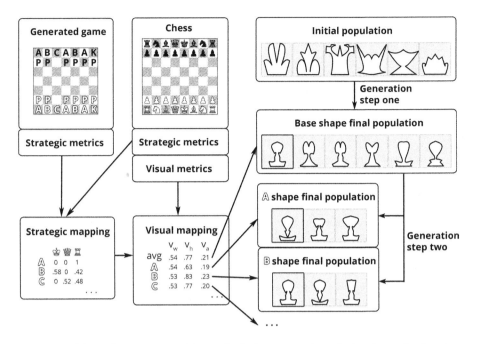

Fig. 1. Workflow of our system. After calculating strategic and visual metrics for chess and a generated game, we map pieces of this game onto chess pieces based on their strategic properties. Then, we use that mapping to obtain target visual scores as an objective. Two-step evolution first generates a common base shape and then individually evolves each piece starting from this base shape.

s_{mr} The number of moves required to reach the most distant square from its initial position(s).

s_{lm} The average number of legal moves for each reachable position on the board.

s_{sd} The average shift distance for one letter, i.e. $\sqrt{\Delta x^2 + \Delta y^2}$.

s_{dd} The average displacement distance for a word, i.e. $\sqrt{(\sum \Delta x)^2 + (\sum \Delta y)^2}$.

These measures are chosen because: s_{po} estimates the rarity of a piece; s_{ec} assesses its aggressiveness; s_{pw} and s_{cw} define a piece's importance in terms of winning the game; s_{ba}, s_{mr} and s_{lm} describe a piece's mobility; while s_{sd} and s_{dd} are indicators of the piece's movement style. Several other metrics were considered, but were omitted due to redundancies with existing metrics which would bias the similarity assessment for new games' pieces.

Table 1 lists values of strategic metrics for all considered games. When encoding chess as a Simplified Boardgame, we use a slightly modified version: there is no initial double pawn move, and —to compensate the lack of promotions— a player can win by reaching the opponent's back-rank with a pawn.

Table 1. Values of strategic metrics for each piece in considered games.

metric	Chess						The Legacy of Ibis [14]					The Weather Chess [17]					
s_{po}	0.5	0.13	0.13	0.13	0.06	0.06	0.46	0.23	0.15	0.08	0.08	0.46	0.13	0.13	0.07	0.13	0.07
s_{ec}	0.66	0.5	0.5	0.5	0.5	0.5	0	0.25	0.5	0.6	0.5	0.5	0.75	0.5	0.5	0.75	0.66
s_{pw}	1	0	0	0	0	0	1	0	0	0	0	1	0	0	0	0	0
s_{cw}	0	0	0	0	0	1	0	0	0	0	1	0	0	0	0	0	1
s_{ba}	0.55	1	1	1	1	1	0.1	0.50	0.7	0.82	1	0.13	1	1	0.13	1	0.5
s_{mr}	6	5	2	2	2	7	2	4	6	4	7	6	5.5	10	4	8	7
s_{lm}	2.48	5.25	8.75	14	22.7	6.56	1.16	3.92	2.49	3.95	3.55	1.75	4.63	2.84	2.5	4.81	3.06
s_{sd}	1.28	2.24	1.41	1	1.21	1.21	2.36	1.31	1.28	1.74	1.72	1	1.91	1.83	1.33	1.31	1.41
s_{dd}	1.28	2.24	5.66	4	4.8	1.21	2.36	2.27	1.28	2.31	1.72	1	1.91	1.83	1.33	1.31	1.41

3.2   Visual Metrics

We have defined four aspects that should be represented in visual metrics to capture the most important aspects of piece shape: piece size, style of its enclosed area (regardless of the size), style of its lines; and style of its angles. Inspired by [33,34], we use the following metrics:

v_w The ratio of the piece's width to the width of the drawing area.

v_h The ratio of the piece's height to the height of the drawing area.

v_a The ratio of the piece's area to the drawing area.

v_{ta} The ratio of the piece's top 1/3 area to the piece's area.

v_{ma} The ratio of the piece's middle 1/3 area (on the x axis) to the piece's area.

v_s The intersection to union ratio between piece's left half and the (mirrored) right half; symmetrical shapes score 1 in this metric.

v_{my} The ratio of the piece's middle half on the y axis to the piece's area.

v_{tr} The area intersecting the piece and an upward-pointing triangle shape, over the piece's area.

v_p The ratio of the piece's perimeter to double its bounding box perimeter.

v_{sl} The ratio of the length of straight lines to the piece's perimeter.

v_{sa} The ratio of sharp angles (0°–60°) to all angles between lines.

v_{ga} The ratio of gentle angles (120°–180°) to all angles between lines.

Values in all metrics are bound to [0, 1]. Table 2 lists the visual metrics for games in this paper. Values for chess were extracted from the set of shapes of Fig. 2. Values for the other games were computed using the method described in Sect. 3.3.

3.3   Mapping from General Games to Chess

As noted above, chess pieces have certain visual properties that denote their function in game. New games, on the other hand, can be evaluated only in terms of their function; finding what visuals these new pieces should have is not straightforward. In this paper, we compare the functional properties of chess

Table 2. Values of visual metrics for each piece in considered games. Values for chess are computed from the shapes in Fig. 2. Values for the generated games are obtained by our algorithm.

metric	Chess						The Legacy of Ibis [14]					The Weather Chess [17]					
v_w	0.45	0.59	0.52	0.54	0.52	0.52	0.55	0.54	0.53	0.53	0.55	0.54	0.53	0.53	0.53	0.52	0.45
v_h	0.52	0.8	0.82	0.63	0.90	0.98	0.81	0.63	0.83	0.77	0.83	0.63	0.76	0.75	0.78	0.98	0.53
v_a	0.12	0.29	0.18	0.19	0.20	0.26	0.23	0.19	0.23	0.20	0.24	0.19	0.20	0.19	0.20	0.26	0.12
v_{ta}	0.29	0.31	0.26	0.46	0.24	0.35	0.28	0.46	0.40	0.34	0.34	0.46	0.35	0.34	0.33	0.35	0.29
v_{ma}	0.28	0.31	0.29	0.18	0.29	0.25	0.30	0.18	0.22	0.24	0.26	0.18	0.23	0.25	0.24	0.25	0.29
v_s	1	0.77	1	1	1	1	0.91	1	1	1	0.94	1	1	1	1	1	1
v_{my}	0.84	0.73	0.88	0.73	0.85	0.83	0.82	0.73	0.79	0.79	0.78	0.73	0.79	0.82	0.80	0.83	0.85
v_{tr}	0.73	0.58	0.79	0.50	0.81	0.69	0.70	0.50	0.61	0.66	0.64	0.50	0.65	0.68	0.68	0.69	0.73
v_p	0.41	0.43	0.43	0.45	0.49	0.47	0.44	0.45	0.46	0.47	0.46	0.45	0.47	0.44	0.47	0.47	0.41
v_{sl}	0	0.04	0	0.29	0	0	0.02	0.29	0.12	0.14	0.08	0.29	0.15	0.11	0.12	0	0
v_{sa}	0.22	0	0.15	0	0.27	0.40	0.09	0	0.23	0.14	0.16	0	0.13	0.09	0.15	0.40	0.22
v_{ga}	0.33	0.6	0.38	0.29	0.33	0.33	0.50	0.29	0.32	0.31	0.42	0.29	0.31	0.35	0.32	0.33	0.33

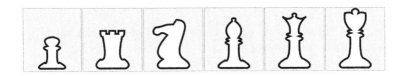

Fig. 2. The set of chess piece shapes used as a base for further computations.

pieces and new generated pieces, and approximate the visuals of these new pieces based on the visuals of their closest chess pieces. Even with this basic premise, a number of questions arise: (a) how is the functional similarity of pieces in different games with different rulesets assessed? (b) can a generated piece be similar to more than one chess pieces, and how is that handled? The following paragraphs elaborate on the decisions taken to address these questions.

A broad range of functional properties have been described both qualitatively and in terms of heuristics for calculating them in Sect. 3.1. The most straightforward way of assessing how closely a new generated piece matches another is through an Euclidean distance treating the nine strategic features as a 9-dimensional vector. Comparing pieces in this fashion ignores the fact that the pieces originate from different games, and are thus sensitive to the value ranges of the other pieces in the same game. For example, a game in which most pieces move to one or two adjacent spaces would classify all of its pieces as chess pawns or kings, ignoring the fact that some pieces may be more mobile (e.g. moving two spaces) than others (e.g. that move one space). Moreover, from a practical perspective not all strategic metrics are in the same value range (e.g. s_{mr} and s_{sd}) nor do their values deviate from one piece to the other in the same way.

To address these concerns, pieces from both games are first standardized to their z-scores, which processes a raw value x as $z = (x - \bar{x})/\sigma_x$ where $\bar{x}$ is the mean value of all pieces in the same game and σ_x is the standard deviation of those values. This standardization ensures all metrics are in the same value range and clearly denotes outliers. In this way, more mobile pieces of one game will have similar scores to more mobile pieces in the other game (compared to the average mobility of each game) and thus would be mapped closer together.

Once the distance in terms of the nine standardized strategic metrics between all pieces in the new game and all chess pieces is calculated, the closest chess piece to each new piece is identified and its distance is compared to the distance between other chess pieces and the new piece. Choosing the closest chess piece and its visuals as the target of evolution is an option, but in practice two pieces of a new game were often mapped to the same chess piece. Using all chess pieces' visuals based on a weighted sum where weights are proportional to the chess piece's similarity to the new piece is another option. In practice, however, the resulting target visual metrics were very similar for all pieces in the new game. An intermediate solution was devised instead, considering only chess pieces which are relatively close to the closest chess piece. This is done by dividing the distance between the new piece and a chess piece with the distance to the closest chess piece: the resulting metric W_i has a value range of $(0, 1]$: values close to 1 show that a chess piece is almost as similar to the new piece as the closest chess piece. Choosing an appropriate threshold, above which a piece is considered similar enough, is an ad-hoc design decision which can affect the results. Based on a preliminary sensitivity analysis (see Fig. 3), we chose to consider only pieces with a strategic distance at most 160% that of the closest chess piece ($W_i \geq 0.625$). Each visual metric for a new piece amounts to a weighted sum of visual metrics of all considered chess pieces, where the weight of chess piece i is a normalized version of W_i so that all normalized weights sum up to 1. These normalized weights for the two tested games are shown in Table 3.

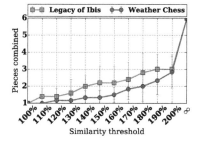 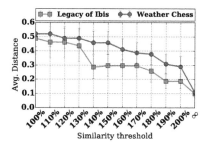

Fig. 3. Sensitivity of the chess piece mapping to different thresholds. The threshold is the highest distance ratio of the closest chess piece that is considered. Results are on average number of shapes combined and average pairwise visual distance; error bars show the 95% confidence interval for 5 shapes and 10 distances in Legacy of Ibis, and 6 shapes and 15 distances in Weather Chess. Infinity uses all chess pieces.

Table 3. Weight of chess pieces in terms of strategic similarity with pieces for the Legacy of Ibis game (left) and The Weather Chess (right).

	♙	♘	♗	♖	♕	♔
🐟	0.42	0.58				
🐍			1.00			
⚓			0.42		0.58	
🦅				0.48	0.52	
🪲	0.29			0.24	0.20	0.28

	♙	♘	♗	♖	♕	♔
☁				1.00		
☁			0.52	0.48		
☁			0.61	0.39		
☁				0.42	0.58	
☁						1.00
☀	1.00					

3.4   Representation

Generated shapes are encoded in Scalable Vector Graphics (SVG) format, which makes them directly useful for real applications. The genotype of every piece is a series of lines (encoded in an array) that may contain straight lines, quadratic Bézier curves and cubic Bézier curves. The starting point of every line (except the first) is the end point of its predecessor, so it is omitted. The drawing area has been set to 200×200 units. The first point of every shape should be placed on the lowest horizontal line. The first point is automatically connected to the last point, closing the shape and making the piece's basis. The line array is interpreted differently for symmetric and asymmetric pieces. When a piece is flagged as symmetric, we assume the array represents only the right half of the piece, while the left half is mirrored. For asymmetric pieces, its genotype explicitly contains all parts of the shape.

3.5   Evolution and Its Variants

A standard evolutionary algorithm scheme is used for evolving shapes. Tournament selection chooses $n/2$ pairs of parents to crossover from the current generation containing n individuals. Crossover produces two children, and each of them can be additionally mutated. This may produce inconsistent individuals, which are removed from the population. The next generation is created by choosing the best n shapes from the joint set of parents and children.

To encourage novelty, during selection any shapes similar to already selected shapes are omitted. Similarity is computed as a fraction of the area of intersection and the area of union of both pieces. Crossover cuts the array of parents' lines in half and joins both halves to create new shapes. If only one of the parents is symmetric, its representation is temporarily changed to asymmetric.

The mutation operator is more complex: one possibility is that the piece is converted to asymmetric. The other possibility is that one of its lines is chosen at random and one of two operations is applied: (a) the line type is modified: straight to arc, arc to double arc, double arc to straight, or a straight line to be split in half into two straight lines; (b) the line's points are transformed by a random vector (including control points of Bézier curves which can affect the shape without modifying the start and end points).

This paper proposes a two-step evolutionary algorithm: the first step evolves deeply and widely a population towards the average of all pieces' target values. All pieces' target values are averaged together on the same dimension; evolution targets similarity with those target (average) values as its fitness based on the distance in a 12-dimensional vector for the 12 metrics of Sect. 3.2. Once evolution is complete, the fittest individual is chosen and evolution is carried out in a second step for each piece individually. The initial population for these runs uses copies of the fittest individual of the first evolutionary step. Each run targets similarity with the target values of that shape specifically as its fitness, and evolves for a few generations. The fittest individual of each run in the second step is chosen for that piece. To prevent shapes from being too similar, an additional similarity check is made when choosing the best shape for each piece.

The second step can be radically simplified by choosing shapes directly from the final population of the first step described above. This makes the process slightly faster, yet reduces the likelihood that chosen pieces will be visually consistent with the desired ones. Additionally, in this case a similarity check is required to prevent the same shape from being chosen for different pieces.

The last variant evolves each piece independently from the beginning, using the similarity with that piece's target values (see Table 2) as its fitness. This method is the slowest and is likely to produce visually inconsistent shapes, but is used for comparison with the other two approaches.

4 Results

To test how the three variants of our algorithm compare, we use each of them to generate shapes for chess, The Legacy of Ibis, and The Weather Chess. In the first case, we aim to recreate the exact chess aesthetic. For the remaining two games, we create novel visuals based on our mapping method in Sect. 3.3.

In an initial exploration of the types of shapes produced by each method, we used randomized parameter sets. The first evolutionary step was run in two uniformly distributed settings: deep (200–400 generations, population size 40–100) or wide (50–200 generations, population size 200–500). For two-step evolution, the second step ran for 1–10 generations. We have used three ways to initialize the population: using copies of a triangle shape; using copies of chess pawns; using random shapes. The best shape representatives of these runs were chosen manually and presented in Fig. 4, covering most of the tested combinations of variants and initial shapes for all games.

Based on the findings of the initial exploratory phase, most parameters of the algorithms were chosen and finalized. To perform statistical comparisons between approaches, games and initial shapes, however, 20 independent evolutionary runs were performed on the same combination; their results are averaged across methods and shapes or games. All runs evolve a population of 100 individuals over a total of 100 generations; for two-step evolution, these generations

init	avg.	♙	♘	♗	♖	♕	♔	avg.	♙	♘	♗	♖	♕	♔		♙	♘	♗	♖	♕	♔
	Two-step evolution variant							One-step evolution and pick							Independent evolution variant						
△		1.06	1.07	1.08	1.09	1.03	1.06	1.11	1.06	1.07	1.05	1.06	1.04	1.07	1.06	0.54	0.06	0.45	0.55	0.52	0.59
♙		0.43	0.60	0.24	0.50	0.48	0.54	0.63	0.39	0.52	0.35	0.44	0.46	0.54	0.42	0.60	0.03	0.50	0.60	0.56	0.66
RANDOM		0.46	0.55	0.32	0.48	0.61	0.52	0.62	0.39	0.46	0.37	0.48	0.41	0.47	0.50	0.61	0.24	0.47	0.58	0.56	0.67

Exploratory results for Chess

init	avg.	𓆓	𓁢	⌐	𓅦	𝄐	avg.	𓆓	𓁢	⌐	𓅦	𝄐		𓆓	𓁢	⌐	𓅦	𝄐
	Two-step evolution variant						One-step evolution and pick						Independent evolution variant					
△		0.14	0.16	0.41	0.18	0.18	0.11	0.12	0.15	0.19	0.15	0.17	0.12	0.16	0.41	0.16	0.20	0.09
♙		0.12	0.23	0.19	0.15	0.22	0.12	0.16	0.12	0.23	0.14	0.17	0.10	0.19	0.41	0.15	0.17	0.07
RANDOM		0.12	0.18	0.33	0.15	0.14	0.14	0.30	0.24	0.24	0.19	0.18	0.20	0.16	0.46	0.16	0.17	0.11

Exploratory results for Legacy of Ibis

init	avg.	⋮	𓃻	𓃛	𓃠	⌣	☼	avg.	⋮	𓃻	𓃛	𓃠	⌣	☼		⋮	𓃻	𓃛	𓃠	⌣	☼
	Two-step evolution variant							One-step evolution and pick							Independent evolution variant						
△		0.31	0.45	0.39	0.30	0.0	0.33	0.49	0.42	1.03	1.05	1.05	1.05	1.03	1.04	1.03	0.53	0.31	0.30	0.31	0.52	0.09
♙		0.29	0.47	0.33	0.38	0.30	0.44	0.20	0.30	0.31	0.30	0.33	0.28	0.33	0.26	0.52	0.35	0.34	0.34	0.53	0.04
RANDOM		0.29	0.44	0.34	0.26	0.32	0.36	0.23	0.29	0.38	0.34	0.31	0.30	0.32	0.23	0.53	0.32	0.36	0.33	0.56	0.09

Exploratory results for The Weather Chess

Fig. 4. Example sets of evolved shapes for each game, initial shape (triangle, pawn, random) and algorithm variant. Fitness values are presented below the shapes.

were split between first and second step in several configurations, with 10, 20, or 50 generations dedicated to the second step (the first step respectively evolves for 90, 80 and 50 generations). Figure 5 shows the average values of the final chosen pieces and the 95% confidence interval. Two relevant performance metrics are tested: (a) as the objective of evolution, the Euclidean visual distance from the target values of each piece (in Table 2); (b) as an indication of the visual consistency of shapes of the same game, the average Euclidean visual distance among all pairs in the same evolved set. With 6 pieces for chess and Weather chess, and 5 pieces for Legacy of Ibis, each method had a total of 340 pieces (in 20 runs) for the same initial shape.

It is clear from Fig. 5 that each method behaves as expected: independent evolution more closely matches the desired visuals of each piece but the resulting

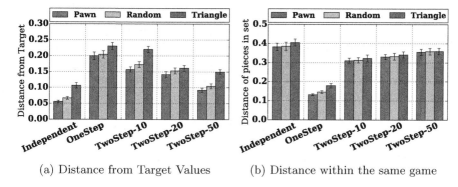

(a) Distance from Target Values   (b) Distance within the same game

Fig. 5. Sensitivity of the chess piece mapping to different thresholds. The threshold is the highest distance ratio of the closest chess piece that is considered. Results are collected from 20 runs per game, initial shape, and method; error bars show the 95% confidence interval for 340 individuals for (a) and 60 runs for (b).

pieces are very different from each other, while the opposite is true for one-step evolution where shapes are picked from a final population of average shapes. Two-step evolution finds itself in-between the two extremes, with more generations dedicated to the second step leading to shapes closer to the desired visuals. Even with a few generations for the second step, however, the divergence among pieces in the same set is much higher (often double) than that of one-step evolution.

In terms of initial shapes, clearly pawns are better starting points since they are both more complex than triangle shapes and closer to the visual features targeted by any chess variant than random shapes. Comparing across games, it is surprising that chess shapes are more challenging to evolve for (in terms of final distance to target values) than those of the two new games despite the fact that its target values are derived directly from chess shapes.

5 Discussion

This paper describes a method for evolving shapes of chess-like pieces that belong to a number of previously generated games. Our approach maps the visual aesthetics of chess pieces to their in-game function. This allows us to estimate the intended visual aesthetics of new games' pieces based on their role for this particular game. A number of processing steps allow the system to identify pieces that, while in raw values may e.g. move slower than some chess piece, they serve a similar role in a game where generally all pieces move slower, for example. Generated shapes are encoded in SVG, a popular vector graphics format, which makes them easily scalable and useful for real applications.

The defined goal in this paper is to produce sets of shapes: (a) which can be distinguished as belonging to the same game, and (b) where shapes of individual pieces intuitively correspond to their role and importance in the game.

To satisfy the first goal, we use a two-step variant of the evolutionary algorithm, as well as a variant one-step algorithm which picks pieces from a general population. However, we observed that generated piece sets may contain too similar pieces. Although our similarity tests remove the most obvious cases, many cases may be sufficiently different in terms of area coverage but are still easily mistaken by human players due to common visual details. The third algorithm variant runs evolution independently for each piece and usually produces pieces that are easier to distinguish and remember. Combined together, however, the pieces do not look like parts of the same game and can be too easily swapped with any other piece generated for other games. The balance between insufficient variability and too much variability is subjective, and results of the three algorithms often explore the limits in one or the other end of the spectrum.

The degree to which the second goal is fulfilled is more disputable. Although the chess-based grounding achieves its stated aim in some cases (e.g. often pieces needed to win the game are bigger), it is hard to unambiguously decide what style should characterize a piece given its rules. In the presented approach, the mappings to chess pieces based on strategic similarities gives results that can be justified. However, the process of evolution itself usually blurs all differences that are not close to extremes. As with the first goal, further experimentation on different similarity thresholds (e.g. in Fig. 3) can assess the tension between having too many pieces map to the same chess piece versus combining too many chess shapes in a way that makes the results indistinguishable.

This initial attempt at evolving shapes for games with procedurally generated rules focuses on making them visually pleasing and playable. While currently not all generated sets can be used immediately by players, a decent piece set can always be chosen by a human judge. Future work will analyze and improve on the strategic and visual metrics for a better mapping and a more concrete visual identity, respectively. In terms of evolution, we intend to explore using novelty search [36] —similarly to [34]— instead of the diversity preservation mechanisms used in this paper. Finally, we plan to address the problem of identifying which pieces are visibly consistent while being distinguishable. Towards that end, a deep learning approach [31] could be useful for visual similarity assessment rather than purely pixel-by-pixel operations currently used for diversity preservation.

This work, combined with past achievements in chess-like rule generation and generated natural language descriptions of such rules [14,17], can lead to a system that can generate, on demand, games together with their rule explanations and their full visuals. Playing games offered by such a system will be a human equivalent of the General Game Playing challenge.

6   Conclusion

This paper proposed a way of generating the shapes of pieces in unseen, generated games based on their functional similarities with pieces in known, popular games. Focusing on several generated chess-like games and the original chess, experiments explored whether generated shapes could achieve a consistent look (as pieces of the same game) while allowing players to distinguish between pieces for actual play. Results indicate that depending on whether pieces were evolved as a whole (for one game) or independently, the balance between these two goals can be skewed towards one or the other. This first generative attempt can be strengthened algorithmically in order to better achieve both goals at the same time. Future work could also explore the use of similar techniques for other games, including other board games or even digital games.

References

1. Shaker, N., Togelius, J., Nelson, M.J.: Procedural Content Generation in Games: A Textbook and an Overview of Current Research. Springer, Cham (2016). https://doi.org/10.1007/978-3-319-42716-4
2. Yannakakis, G.N., Togelius, J.: Artificial Intelligence and Games. Springer, New York (2018). https://doi.org/10.1007/978-1-4419-8188-2. http://gameaibook.org
3. Perez, D., Samothrakis, S., Togelius, J., Schaul, T., Lucas, S., Couëtoux, A., Lee, J., Lim, C., Thompson, T.: The 2014 general video game playing competition. IEEE Trans. Comput. Intell. AI Games 8(3), 229–243 (2015)
4. Smith, A.M., Mateas, M.: Variations forever: Flexibly generating rulesets from a sculptable design space of mini-games. In: IEEE Conference on Computational Intelligence and Games (2010)
5. Smith, G., Whitehead, J., Mateas, M.: Tanagra: reactive planning and constraint solving for mixed-initiative level design. IEEE Trans. Comput. Intell. AI Games 3(3), 201–215 (2011)
6. Genesereth, M., Love, N., Pell, B.: General game playing: overview of the AAAI competition. AI Mag. 26, 62–72 (2005)
7. Genesereth, M., Björnsson, Y.: The international general game playing competition. AI Mag. 34(2), 107–111 (2013)
8. Nielsen, T.S., Barros, G.A.B., Togelius, J., Nelson, M.J.: Towards generating arcade game rules with VGDL. In: IEEE Conference on Computational Intelligence and Games, pp. 185–192 (2015)
9. Khalifa, A., Perez, D., Lucas, S., Togelius, J.: General video game level generation. In: Genetic and Evolutionary Computation Conference, pp. 253–259 (2016)
10. Khalifa, A., Green, M., Perez, D., Togelius, J.: General video game rule generation. In: IEEE Conference on Computational Intelligence and Games (2017)
11. Pitrat, J.: Realization of a general game-playing program. In: IFIP Congress, pp. 1570–1574 (1968)
12. Pell, B.: Metagame in symmetric chess-like games. In: Heuristic Programming in Artificial Intelligence: The Third Computer Olympiad (1992)
13. Björnsson, Y.: Learning rules of simplified boardgames by observing. In: European Conference on Artificial Intelligence, FAIA, vol. 242, pp. 175–180 (2012)
14. Kowalski, J., Szykuła, M.: Evolving chess-like games using relative algorithm performance profiles. In: Squillero, G., Burelli, P. (eds.) EvoApplications 2016, Part I. LNCS, vol. 9597, pp. 574–589. Springer, Cham (2016). https://doi.org/10.1007/978-3-319-31204-0_37
15. Lopes, P., Liapis, A., Yannakakis, G.N.: Targeting horror via level and soundscape generation. In: AAAI Artificial Intelligence for Interactive Digital Entertainment Conference (2015)

16. Karavolos, D., Liapis, A., Yannakakis, G.N.: Learning the patterns of balance in a multi-player shooter game. In: FDG workshop on Procedural Content Generation in Games (2017)
17. Kowalski, J., Żarczyński, Ł., Kisielewicz, A.: Evaluating chess-like games using generated natural language descriptions. In: Winands, M.H.M., van den Herik, H.J., Kosters, W.A. (eds.) ACG 2017. LNCS, vol. 10664, pp. 127–139. Springer, Cham (2017). https://doi.org/10.1007/978-3-319-71649-7_11
18. Liapis, A., Yannakakis, G.N., Togelius, J.: Towards a generic method of evaluating game levels. In: AAAI Artificial Intelligence for Interactive Digital Entertainment Conference (2013)
19. Summerville, A.J., Mateas, M.: Sampling hyrule: multi-technique probabilistic level generation for action role playing games. In: AIIDE Workshop on Experimental AI in Games (2015)
20. Togelius, J., Yannakakis, G.N., Stanley, K.O., Browne, C.: Search-based procedural content generation: a taxonomy and survey. IEEE Trans. Comput. Intell. AI Games 3(3), 172–186 (2011)
21. Liapis, A., Yannakakis, G.N., Togelius, J.: Computational game creativity. In: International Conference on Computational Creativity (2014)
22. Togelius, J., Schmidhuber, J.: An experiment in automatic game design. In: IEEE Symposium on Computational Intelligence and Games (2008)
23. Cook, M., Colton, S., Raad, A., Gow, J.: Mechanic miner: reflection-driven game mechanic discovery and level design. In: Esparcia-Alcázar, A.I. (ed.) EvoApplications 2013. LNCS, vol. 7835, pp. 284–293. Springer, Heidelberg (2013). https://doi.org/10.1007/978-3-642-37192-9_29
24. Browne, C., Maire, F.: Evolutionary game design. IEEE Trans. Comput. Intell. AI Games 2(1), 1–16 (2010)
25. Nielsen, T.S., Barros, G.A.B., Togelius, J., Nelson, M.J.: General video game evaluation using relative algorithm performance profiles. In: Mora, A.M., Squillero, G. (eds.) EvoApplications 2015. LNCS, vol. 9028, pp. 369–380. Springer, Cham (2015). https://doi.org/10.1007/978-3-319-16549-3_30
26. Howlett, A., Colton, S., Browne, C.: Evolving pixel shaders for the prototype video game subversion. In: Proceedings of AISB 2010 (2010)
27. Hastings, E.J., Guha, R.K., Stanley, K.O.: Automatic content generation in the galactic arms race video game. IEEE Trans. Comput. Intell. AI Games 1(4), 245–263 (2009)
28. Hoover, A.K., Cachia, W., Liapis, A., Yannakakis, G.N.: AudioInSpace: exploring the creative fusion of generative audio, visuals and gameplay. In: Johnson, C., Carballal, A., Correia, J. (eds.) EvoMUSART 2015. LNCS, vol. 9027, pp. 101–112. Springer, Cham (2015). https://doi.org/10.1007/978-3-319-16498-4_10
29. Risi, S., Lehman, J., D'Ambrosio, D., Hall, R., Stanley, K.: Petalz: search-based procedural content generation for the casual gamer. IEEE Trans. Comput. Intell. Games 8(3), 244–255 (2015)
30. Takagi, H.: Interactive evolutionary computation: fusion of the capabilities of EC optimization and human evaluation. Proc. IEEE 9, 1275–1296 (2001)
31. Liapis, A., Martínez, H.P., Togelius, J., Yannakakis, G.N.: Transforming exploratory creativity with DeLeNoX. In: International Conference on Computational Creativity (2013)
32. Soule, T., Heck, S., Haynes, T.E., Wood, N., Robison, B.D.: Darwin's Demons: does evolution improve the game? In: Squillero, G., Sim, K. (eds.) EvoApplications 2017, Part I. LNCS, vol. 10199, pp. 435–451. Springer, Cham (2017). https://doi.org/10.1007/978-3-319-55849-3_29

33. Liapis, A., Yannakakis, G.N., Togelius, J.: Adapting models of visual aesthetics for personalized content creation. IEEE Trans. Comput. Intell. AI Games **4**(3), 213–228 (2012)
34. Liapis, A.: Exploring the visual styles of arcade game assets. In: Johnson, C., Ciesielski, V., Correia, J., Machado, P. (eds.) EvoMUSART 2016. LNCS, vol. 9596, pp. 92–109. Springer, Cham (2016). https://doi.org/10.1007/978-3-319-31008-4_7
35. Kowalski, J., Sutowicz, J., Szykuła, M.: Simplified Boardgames. arXiv:1606.02645 (2016). [cs.AI]
36. Lehman, J., Stanley, K.O.: Abandoning objectives: evolution through the search for novelty alone. Evol. Comput. **19**(2), 189–223 (2011)

Evolving a TORCS Modular Fuzzy Driver Using Genetic Algorithms

Mohammed Salem[1]([✉]) [iD], Antonio Miguel Mora[2], Juan Julian Merelo[3], and Pablo García-Sánchez[4]

[1] Department of Computer Sciences, University of Mascara, Mascara, Algeria
salem@univ-mascara.dz
[2] Department of Computer Sciences and Technology, ESIT,
International University of La Rioja (UNIR), Granada, Spain
antoniomiguel.mora@unir.net
[3] Department of Architecture and Computer Technology, University of Granada,
Granada, Spain
jmerelo@ugr.es
[4] Department of Computer Science, University of Cádiz, Cádiz, Spain
pablo.garciasanchez@uca.es

Abstract. This work presents an evolutionary approach to optimize the parameters of a Fuzzy-based autonomous driver for the open simulated car racing game (TORCS). Using evolutionary algorithms, we intend to optimize a modular fuzzy agent designed to determine the optimal target speed as well as the steering angle during the race. The challenge in this kind of fuzzy systems is the design of the membership functions, which is usually done through a trial and error process, but in this paper an adapted real-coded Genetic Algorithm with two different fitness functions - has been applied to find the best values for these parameters, obtaining a robust design for the TORCS controller. The evolved drivers were tested and evaluated competing against other TORCS controllers in practice mode, without rivals, and real races. The optimized fuzzy-controllers yield a very good performance, mainly in tracks that have many turning points, which are, in turn, the most difficult for any autonomous agent. Thus, this is a real enhancement of the baseline fuzzy controllers which had several difficulties to drive in this kind of circuits.

Keywords: Videogames · Fuzzy controller · TORCS
Steering control · Optimization · Genetic algorithms

1 Introduction

Since the massive interest by vehicle manufacturers of autonomous driving, it has become also a hot research topic. Autonomy needs the creation of real self-driving cars that can travel in everyday roads and streets or, for that matter, in a desert or hostile environment, but this is only a constraint; autonomous vehicles must

K. Sim and P. Kaufmann (Eds.): EvoApplications 2018, LNCS 10784, pp. 342–357, 2018.
https://doi.org/10.1007/978-3-319-77538-8_24

also optimize fuel consumption as well as car safety and, in some cases, occupant comfort [12]. Optimization in car racing games can be placed in that context, with solutions obtained there having utility beyond the game itself; this explains the popularity of car racing games challenges, which are usually performed using game simulators; for instance, The Open Racing Car Simulator (TORCS) [23] is a realistic racing simulator with a sophisticated engine used for many standalone racing competition challenges every year. This fact, combined with the ability to compare controllers, have made TORCS the most used simulator in the field of autonomous driving [5,8,11,18].

Many kinds of controllers have been used in this simulator, but one of the most efficient controllers so far are fuzzy-based ones, as they simulate in part the human reasoning when driving [14,19,20]. In this line, the authors presented previously an approach in which two specialized fuzzy controllers were combined to decide the car's steering angle and desired speed in every single point (or tick) during a race [22]. The obtained results were promising, but the performance of the autonomous driver showed some flaws in difficult tracks – those with many curves, or where 'external' factors affected the asphalt – and against the most competitive rivals.

We argue here that the major disadvantage of this approach is that the parameters of the controllers' fuzzy membership functions were defined following a trial/error process in the absence of experts to do so. Thus, in this work we consider the selection of the best values for these parameters as an optimization problem, so we have applied an evolutionary algorithm to obtain them. Concretely, we propose to apply a real-coded Genetic Algorithm (GA) [9] with this purpose. The considered approach requires, in addition to a good codification of solutions and selection of operators, the choice of an adequate cost function (fitness), due to the uncertainty and noisiness of the problem itself. So two different proposals have been studied, the first one is computed using the mean lap time and damage while the second consider also the Top speed. The genetic-fuzzy based controller has been evaluated in a practice race - without rivals - first, and then in a real race against different drivers in TORCS. The obtained results show that the enhanced controllers (one per fitness function) perform both much better than the original fuzzy controller (previously presented) in the practice race, increasing the top speed while they are not damaged, and obtaining a very good lap time. In addition, they compete very well against tough rivals, getting a high rank in the race (time close to the winner) and a very low received damage.

So, we can conclude from these results that the proposed approach successfully evolves the fuzzy controller membership parameters giving good performances in terms of damage avoidance and race time. This suggest that GAs with the proposed fitness functions are well-suited for finding the best trade-off between the two objectives of any racing controller: damage and speed.

2   State of the Art

Evolutionary algorithms have been used by several researchers in many different ways in the car racing simulator TORCS.

For instance, Loiacono et al. [3] applied a single-objective and a multi-objective real-coded GA to the automatic generation of tracks for high-end racing games while Floreano et al. [5], used a GA for tuning up a neural network which visually recognizes edges, corners and height, resembling strategies observed in simple insects which obtained results that performed equal or better than well trained human drivers tested on the same circuits.

Another application of evolutionary algorithms was to determine the optimal trajectory of a lap in a known circuit [21], but this approach suffers from the problem that the obtained trajectory in the evolving process strongly depends on the initial state of the car. In the same context, the authors in [16] tried to design a novel approach to compute the optimal racing line without any human intervention, using a GA to find the best trade-off between the minimization of two conflicting objectives: the length and the curvature of the racing line.

However, definitely, the most prolific area of application of EAs inside TORCS, has been the optimization of autonomous controllers for car driving, i.e. conducting a meta-optimization process. Thus, EAs have been applied to 'refine' the parameters which define the driver's behavior [1,11], or to improve the structure/architecture of the models [11,13], working offline, or online (during the game) [2,24].

Our approach is focused in this line, proposing the application of an offline genetic algorithm for the improvement of the parameters which determine the behavior of a controller for TORCS. We have focused on a Fuzzy-based model, as it is one of the best options for modeling human-like decisions and actions, as others authors have also used this kind of technique in the literature with good results [18]. For instance, in [8], a fuzzy rule-based car controller for a Car Racing Competition was built and tuned with co-evolutionary genetic algorithms. Two fuzzy controllers were designed (acceleration and turning angle). But this approach was applied to a simpler simulator than TORCS which is a more realistic and time-constrained simulator.

Pérez et al. presented an evolutionary fuzzy approach for TORCS in [14], where they applied EAs for improving fuzzy models to infer the acceleration and turning angle. However, the models were not so specialized as the proposed here, since their controller did not compute the target speed, which is a key factor for a competitive controller.

Onieva et al. [18] presented a parametrized modular architecture with a fuzzy system and a GA in the design of fuzzy logic controllers for steering wheel management that can reproduce human driver behavior, but it did not take the target speed into account, unlike our previous controller [22] which computed the target speed and the steer with two fuzzy sub-controllers and whose membership functions parameters were defined by trial/error process. In this paper, we propose to optimize these parameters using a real coded genetic algorithm aiming to improve the performance of the original fuzzy controller.

3   Experimental Setup

This section presents the environment to make the study (TORCS), and the previous fuzzy controller to be optimized.

3.1   The TORCS Simulator

The Open Racing Car Simulator (TORCS) [23] is an open source, modern, multi-player, modular and portable racing simulator that allows users to race against computer-controlled opponents. Its high degree of modularity and portability, together with the realistic and real-time driving simulation, make it an ideal testbed for artificial intelligence research, as it can be seen in the literature (See Sect. 2). The game offers different types of races from the practical single session to the championship.

There is a large set of sensors [15] which the car can consider during a race, such as distances to track borders, to rivals, current fuel, current gear, position in the race, speed, or damage, among others. These sensors values a re used by any TORCS driver bot to control the car by means of a set of actuators [15]: the steering wheel 'Steer', the accelerator 'accel', the brake pedal and the gearbox. Hence, a controller is a program, which runs inside TORCS, that automatically drives a car. It gets as input information about the current state of the car and its situation on the track (sensors). These collected data are used to decide actions to perform in the next simulation tick.

3.2   Fuzzy Controller

The initial proposed controller [22] has the same modular architecture as the simple driver of TORCS, however, the target speed and steering angle are computed by means of two modular and specialized fuzzy sub-controllers, which consider five position sensors. This is the controller which will be improved by means of a GA in this work. The two sub-controllers are summarized in the following paragraphs.

Fuzzy Target Speed Sub-controller
This controller aims to estimate the optimal target speed of the car, both in straight parts and curves of the track, taking into account two criteria: move as fast as possible and be safe.

This estimation is based on two general cases: if the car is in a straight line, the target speed will take a maximum value ($maxSpeed$ km/h). However, if it is close to a curve, the controller will decrease the current speed to a value included in the interval $[minSpeed, maxSpeed]$ km/h.

This fuzzy controller has an output, the speed, and three input values:

- Front = Track[9]: front distance to the track border (angle $0°$).
- M5 = max (Track[8], Track[10]): max distance to the track border in an angle of $+5°$ and $-5°$ with respect to Front.

– M10 = max (Track[7], Track[11]): max distance to track border in an angle
of +10° and −10°.

It is a Mamdani-based fuzzy system [10] with three trapezoidal Membership
Functions (MF) for every input variable. The description of these fuzzy inputs
and output are represented in Table 1.

Table 1. Fuzzy variables description.

Variable	Range	Name	MF	Low	Medium	High
Input	[0–100] m	Front	trapezoidal	[0–50]	[20–80]	[60–100]
Input	[0–100] m	M5	trapezoidal	[0–40]	[10–70]	[50–100]
Input	[0–100] m	M10	trapezoidal	[0–30]	[20–60]	[50–100]
Output	[0–200] m/s	TargetSpeed	singleton	/	/	/

The base of rules was composed modeling the behavior of a human expert
driver. Thus, this set is designed to maximize the car speed depending on the
distance to the track border. The fuzzy rules are:

```
- IF Front is High THEN TargetSpeed is TS1
- IF Front is Medium THEN TargetSpeed is TS2
- IF Front is Low and M5 is High THEN TargetSpeed is TS3
- IF Front is Low and M5 is Medium THEN TargetSpeed is TS4
- IF Front is Low and M5 is Low and M10 is High THEN TargetSpeed is TS5
- IF Front is Low and M5 is Low and M10 is Medium THEN TargetSpeed is
  TS6
- IF Front is Low and M5 is Low and M10 is Low THEN TargetSpeed is TS7
```

In addition, a crisp rule is added to obtain a maximum value of the target
speed when the three input variables are as big as possible:

```
- IF Front = MAXDISTSPEED or M5 = MAXDISTSPEED or M10 = MAXDISTSPEED THEN
  TargetSpeed = MAXSPEED
```

MAXDISTSPEED is the longest possible value for the track sensors, and
MAXSPEED is the maximal speed for the specific car. The output value is
encoded by seven singletons TS1 to TS7, being respectively: 280, 240, 220, 180,
120, 60 and 30.

Fuzzy Steering Control Sub-controller
The second fuzzy controller aims to control the steering, estimating and determining the target position of the car.

The structure of this sub-controller is similar to the speed one, but, obviously,
with the steering as output. Thus, the set of sensors considered is the same as
in the speed case (in Table 1).

Then, as general rules: if the car is in a straight line, it will set as target
position half width of the race track (central position of the lane). Whereas, if

the car is near a right curve, it will approach the path leading to the right, with a space between the car and the border of the track to avoid the loss of control. The same approach is considered if the car is near a left curve.

In order to detect the curves, the controller focuses on the sensor values (M10, M5, and Front). So, if the value on Front sensor is the longest, there is a straight road; whereas if the values of M5 and M10 with positive angles (+5 and +10) are the longest, there is right curve; and the other way round.

The base of rules has been defined again modeling the behavior of a human driver, so, for this controller:

- IF Front is High THEN steer is S1
- IF Front is Medium AND M10 is High THEN steer is S2
- IF Front is Medium AND M10 is Medium AND M5 is Medium THEN steer is S2
- IF Front is Medium AND M10 is Medium AND M5 is Low THEN steer is S3
- IF Front is Low AND M10 is High THEN steer is S3
- IF Front is Low AND M10 is Medium AND M5 is Medium THEN steer is S4
- IF Front is Low AND M10 is Medium AND M5 is Low THEN steer is S4

The values for S1 to S4 are respectively: 0, 0.25, 0.5, and 1. When M10 = Track[7] we will take negative values of the steer (steer = −steer).

These controllers were defined with our own criteria, but they could be far from being optimal, so, in the following section we apply a Genetic Algorithm for their improvement.

4   Optimizing the Fuzzy Controllers with GA

Designing an optimal fuzzy controller for TORCS racing needs a human expert to define the membership functions parameters and the rule base. This expert, even if he exists, could not provide an exact repartition of the fuzzy membership functions values over the universe of discourse.

This difficulty have led us to move towards the use of Genetic Algorithms [7] because of their global exploration characteristic in a complex environment, as this problem plots.

The proposed optimization approach aims to find the optimal parameters of the membership functions of the two sub-controllers previously introduced. The followed process is depicted in Fig. 1, in which, as it can be seen, the GA uses TORCS for the evaluation of every individual during the evolutionary process.

Indeed, the GA starts by creating the initial population with random values for the parameters in the defined range [0, 100]. The fitness of each candidate solution is computed by injecting its gene values to the parameters of the membership functions of the two fuzzy sub-controllers. The defined autonomous controller is used to drive a car in a 20 laps race in E-Track5 circuit without opponents, and the results (Top speed, Damage and Mean Lap time) are used to compute the fitness value.

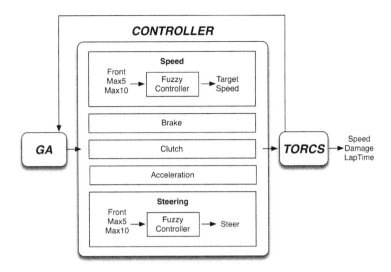

Fig. 1. Optimization of a fuzzy controller flowchart. The evaluation of an individual is performed by: putting the parameter values on the two sub-controllers, launching a race in TORCS with this configuration, obtaining the resulting values of Damage, Top Speed and mean Lap Time and using these values for the computation of the fitness of the individual.

4.1 Genetic Algorithm Settings

As previously stated, the designed fuzzy controllers have trapezoidal member-ship functions given by Eq. 1. In such a controller, fuzzy rules are applied to linguistic terms. These terms, which qualify a linguistic variable, are defined through membership functions, which, in turn, depend on a set of parameters that 'describes' their shape (and operation).

The parameters to be optimized are those of all the membership functions that constitute the fuzzy partition of the linguistic variable [25].

The input linguistic variables in our problem, *Front, Max5* and *Max10*, are represented by three trapezoidal membership functions (See Table 1).

A trapezoidal membership function in a finite universe of discourse $[a, b]$ can be defined by:

$$\mu_A(x) = \begin{cases} \frac{x-x_1}{x_2-x_1}, & x_1 \leq x \leq x_2 \\ 1, & x_2 \leq x \leq x_3 \\ \frac{x_4-x}{x_4-x_3}, & x_3 \leq x \leq x_4 \\ 0, & else \end{cases} \tag{1}$$

with:

$$x_1 \leq x_2 \leq x_3 \leq x_4 \tag{2}$$

This MF function is defined by four parameters x_1, x_2, x_3 and x_4 taking their values in the interval $[a, b]$ (See Fig. 2).

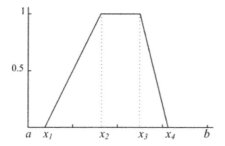

Fig. 2. Trapezoidal MFs

More generally, a fuzzy partition with n trapezoidal membership functions is defined by $2n$ variables ($a = x_1, x_2,..., x_{2n} = b$) (Eq. 4). In this case, the representation is given by the Fig. 3 with:

Fig. 3. Trapezoidal-shaped MFs coding

$$a = x_1 \leq x_2 \leq ... \leq x_{2n-1} \leq x_{2n} = b \tag{3}$$

$$\mu_{A1}(x) = \begin{cases} 1, & x_1 \leq x \leq x_2 \\ \frac{x_3-x}{x_3-x_2}, & x_2 \leq x \leq x_3 \\ 0, & x > x_3 \end{cases}$$

$$\mu_{Ai}(x) = \begin{cases} 0, & x \leq x_{2i-2} \\ \frac{x-x_{2i-2}}{x_{2i-1}-x_{2i-2}}, & x_{2i-2} \leq x \leq x_{2i-1}, n = 2, ..., i-1 \\ 1, & x_{2i-1} \leq x \leq x_{2i} \\ \frac{x_{2i+1}-x}{x_{2i+1}-x_{2i}}, & x_{2i} \leq x \leq x_{2i+1} \\ 0, & x > x_{2i+1} \end{cases} \tag{4}$$

$$\mu_{An}(x) = \begin{cases} 0, & x \leq x_{2n-2} \\ \frac{x-x_{2n-2}}{x_{2n-1}-x_{2n-2}}, & x_{2n-2} \leq x \leq x_{2n-1} \\ 1, & x > x_{2n-1} \end{cases}$$

As we have just seen, a linguistic variable is represented by a number of parameters that depend both on the number and type of used membership functions [25]. Also the choice of coding to use for these different parameters depends both on the desired precision on the values and on their range of values.

When the number of parameters is reduced and their ranges of variations are well defined, a GA with a binary coding is largely sufficient to find their optimal values. On the other hand, if the number of parameters becomes important, and their variation interval is not well known, the real coding is the most appropriate [4]. Since our work requires some precision and the variation interval of each parameter is not well known, we have considered a real coding implementation.

In that GA, every individual is a vector of 18 values/parameters, 6 per variable. Figure 4 illustrates the structure of the chromosome.

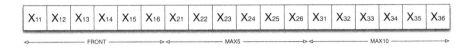

Fig. 4. Chromosome description

The initialization of the chromosomes (first population) is performed assigning random values inside a range of variation [7], in order to start from feasible values [22]. Tournament based selection has been used to elect chromosomes as parents for genetic operators, while simple arithmetic two point crossover [26] and non uniform mutation [17] have been chosen, as two of the most contrasted methods in the literature.

4.2   Fitness Definition

The fitness function for optimizing the structure of a fuzzy controller is highly dependent on the application in which the controller is involved. It is therefore not possible to give a general formulation of this function able to adapt to all the peculiarities of a problem. However, we can specify some rules to choose the best evaluation function [4].

The fuzzy controller should aim to:

- Minimize the damage of the car *damage*.
- Minimize the mean of lap time *LapTime*.
- Maximize the TopSpeed *MaxSpeed*.

From these goals, we can derive two possible fitness functions:

Fitness 1:
$$f_1 = Min\ damage + \alpha \cdot Min\ LapTime \tag{5}$$

Fitness 2:

$$f_2 = Min\ damage + \alpha \cdot Min\ LapTime + Min\beta \cdot \frac{1}{TopSpeed} \tag{6}$$

Being α and β two weighting parameters to prioritize the importance of the different objectives. To evaluate the candidate controllers during the evolutionary process, we will make each of them compete in a 20 laps practice race in a medium difficulty circuit without rivals. We have omitted the presence of opponents in order to avoid including additional uncertainty sources to the optimization process.

Then, the obtained output values *damage*, *LapTime* and *TopSpeed* are collected to compute the corresponding fitness value. As a clarification, *LapTime* is the average of the 20 laps time.

5   Results

This section is dedicated to the performance evaluation of our fuzzy-genetic controller, called *FGC*.

We will first need to choose whose tracks and cars are going to be used in the experiment among the ones TORCS provides; in our case, we have selected the E-Track5 circuit as it is a quite complex one, with multiple turns. *car1-tbr1* has been selected as the driving car [22]. According to previous experiments, this is a fair choice due to its moderate performance. This will lead our controller to be prepared to drive in the most usual conditions.

We have evaluated the FGC with the two proposed fitness functions, comparing them for racing performance. We have considered the following bots in the experiments, making 20 evolutionary runs for every one, with the configuration: Population size $= 20$, Generations $= 50$, Crossover rate $= 0.7$, Mutation rate $= 0.3$.

- **GFC1**: GA-Fuzzy controller with fitness 1 (Eq. 5).
- **GFC2**: GA-Fuzzy controller with fitness 2 (Eq. 6).
- **AD**: Fuzzy controller [22].

The coefficients α and β are chosen to be 1 and $10 * MaxSpeed$ respectively, where *MaxSpeed* is the maximum value of speed that *car1-tbr1* could take ($MaxSpeed = 300$) [22], this choice is motivated by the fact to normalize the Top speed values and make them in the same level as other fitness terms. The results of these runs are shown in Table 2. From the Table, we can see that the 3rd run has given the best fitness value for the two considered fitness functions and obtained the minimal LapTime and damage and for the second fitness, the higher TopSpeed in the track. The fact that the GA gave the minimum for two fitness functions in the same run is due to the random initialization of the start population in a favorite region of the space search so the GA has found the optimal solution, as we used the same random start population to compare the two fitness functions. The worst values are obtained by 1st Run for fitness 1 and 4th run for the second fitness, thee bad values are produced by the damage when the car was in stuck or chocked with the track corner. The second fitness has given higher Top Speed values which minimize the LapTime and makes the controller operates at higher performances. Also, implying late breaking in turns which maximize the Top Speed. Wilcoxon rank sum non-parametric test [6] is used to reject or accept the null hypothesis of equality of medians of the values of the two fitness functions for the 10 runs. The obtained p-value was $p = 0.0017$ and the test statistic is $stats = -3.1371$, this results lead to the rejection of null

Table 2. Results of 10 runs of GA with the two fitness functions. Please bear in mind that fitness follow different formula, and thus cannot be compared; LapTime and Damage should be the quantities used for comparison.

	Fitness 1				Fitness 2			
	Min fit. 1	$LapTime$	$Damage$	$TopSpeed$	Min fit. 2	$LapTime$	$Damage$	$TopSpeed$
Best	**29.44**	29.44	0	231	**39.74**	29.25	0	286
Mean	33.88	30.79	3.10	227.43	44.14	30.14	2.70	267.30
St. Dev.	5.61	1.18	4.58	32.55	6.73	0.78	5.81	22.03

hypothesis with a threshold $\alpha = 0.01$ which allows us to conclude that the two samples sets are different.

The best solution obtained with each fitness function from these runs have been considered to be tested. We represented the resulted membership functions of these two optimal individuals considering the different fitness functions in Figs. 5, 6 and 7.

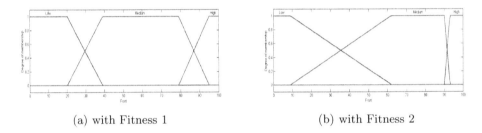

(a) with Fitness 1   (b) with Fitness 2

Fig. 5. Front input MFs with GA

The shapes of the obtained memberships are completely different from those obtained by Trial/Error in the previous work [22] where the Medium linguistic variable of the new functions has bigger range. This makes the controller very sensitive to the middle distances of the inputs, like for a real driver who considers most of the cases the car distance from the borders in that range. The other remark from the obtained membership functions is the dimension of the common range between the LOW and MEDIUM, which provide a higher diversity in the output values.

The two best genetic based fuzzy controllers obtained in the previous experiments, one per fitness function and thus named $GFC1$ and $GFC2$, are going to be tested in a practice race together with the AD fuzzy controller which we have considered as a base line. They will run each one for 20 laps in E-Track5 circuit, which was the one used during the evolution; then, they will be tested also in a practice race in E-Road, a track they had not encountered previously. The obtained results are presented in Table 3.

From the table, we can see that the fuzzy controllers optimized by the GA have given the best results, minimizing the global race time and damages

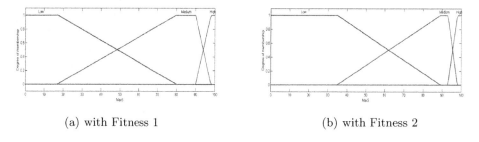

(a) with Fitness 1   (b) with Fitness 2

Fig. 6. Max5 input MFs with GA

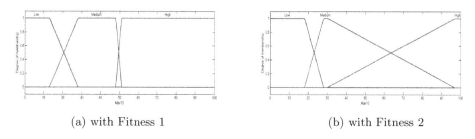

(a) with Fitness 1   (b) with Fitness 2

Fig. 7. Max10 input MFs with GA

(0 in the two GA-based fuzzy controllers), while the AD controller has finished the practice race with many damages. Testing the controllers in this E-Road, which is quite long and difficult as it can be seen by the time it takes a single

Table 3. Results of the three controllers in a 20 laps practice race

E-Track 5			
Results	AD	GFC1	GFC2
Best lap time	29:70	30:03	29:50
Top speed	209	216	216
Min speed	168	148	182
Last lap time	29:79	30:03	29:94
Damage	936	0	0
E-Road			
Results	AD	GFC1	GFC2
Best lap time	02:31:71	02:26:72	02:26:54
Top speed	206	205	208
Min speed	30	39	37
Last lap time	03:12:79	02:42:26	02:33:36
Damage	0	0	0

lap, has proved their value in the adaptation to other tracks different from the one used for 'training', that is, the optimization of the fuzzy controllers.

The GFC2 controller has run with a higher speed (considering overall Top Speed and Min Speed) than GFC1 in the two tracks. This is a positive consequence of the inclusion of the *TopSpeed* variable in the fitness computation so the GA based fuzzy controller has optimized the speed of the car due to early braking and detection of turns and their curving angles. This ability of the GA-fuzzy controller collaborates to minimize the overall race time and thus the final ranking. According to these results, GFC2 seems to be the best controller.

Comparing average lap time gives us an overall idea of which controller performs the best; however, at the end of the day in a racing game the race has to be won. That is why we have tested every fuzzy separately from the others in a real race against five standard controllers from each team integrated with TORCS. Tables 4 and 5 illustrate their performance in two 5 laps real races.

Table 4. Results of GFC1 in two real races (5 laps)

E-TRACK5	GFC1	berwin 10	bt 3	damned 2	inferno 5	tita 10
Ranking	3/6	4/6	1/6	5/6	2/6	6/6
Race time	02:29:32 +24:11	02:29:32 +1 lap	02:29:32	02:29:32 +1 lap	02:29:32 +13:67	02:29:32 +1 lap
Best lap	33:79	35:39	28:09	36:73	31:49	34:12
Max speed	199	206	233	198	229	219
Damages	0	0	0	599	7	566
CG Track2	GFC1	berwin 10	bt 3	damned 2	inferno 5	tita 10
Ranking	3/6	4/6	1/6	6/6	5/6	2/6
Race time	05:10:66 +25:43	05:10:66 +55:65	05:10:66	05:10:66 +1 lap	05:10:66 +38:44	05:10:66 +19:82
Best time	1:03:65	1:04:21	1:00:57	1:04:26	1:03:19	1:03:98
Max speed	233	236	288	200	238	229
Damage	112	376	433	988	541	890

Table 5. Results of GFC2 in two real races (5 laps)

E-TRACK5	GFC2	berwin 10	bt 3	damned 2	inferno 5	tita 10
Ranking	2/6	4/6	1/6	6/6	3/6	5/6
Race time	02:29:17 +02:45	02:29:17 +1 lap	02:29:17	02:29:17 +1 lap	02:29:17 +07:11	02:29:17 +1 lap
Best time	28:82	35:01	28:08	36:91	31:63	36:98
Max speed	218	205	243	180	227	208
Damage	0	0	249	877	0	432
CG Track2	GFC2	berwin 10	bt 3	damned 2	inferno 5	tita 10
Ranking	2/6	5/6	1/6	6/6	4/6	3/6
Race time	05:09:55 +08:43	05:09:55 +1 lap	05:09:55	05:09:55 +1 lap	05:09:55 +24:97	05:09:55 +43:93
Best time	1:02:07	1:04:09	1:01:92	1:04:94	1:04:31	1:03:01
Max speed	244	241	255	210	233	238
Damage	98	699	755	988	653	699

First of all, as it can be seen, the original controller AD has had a poor performance, getting the last position in both races. Whereas both $GFC1$ and $GFC2$ controllers showed to be more competitive. GFC2 has got an excellent second position in the track used during optimization (E-Track), and it has also got a remarkable third rank in the unknown track (E-Road). Both controllers have dealt very well for not being damaged, which even the winner, bt 3, could not avoid.

These results are a confirmation of the good optimization done by the GA and mainly when the Top Speed was considered in the fitness. The obtained results in real race with opponents from tough teams from TORCS are encouraging even the optimization process was in practice races. This good adaptation of the proposed controller in races with rivals is due to the fact the modular fuzzy controller takes into consideration the presence of rivals in the track [22]. The enhancement of that driver by the optimal values of the membership function values, allows it to detect and overtake the opponents with no damage or stuck.

6   Conclusions and Future Work

In this work, we presented a Genetic Algorithm implementation to optimize and improve AD, an existing fuzzy driver for TORCS simulator [22], which combines two sub-controllers, one to calculate the target speed and the other for the direction (steer).

In the evolutionary approach, we tested two fitness functions which use the results obtained in a race conducted by the controller being optimized. The first one considers the average lap time and the car damage; the second uses these two factors and also the top speed reached.

The fuzzy-genetic controllers obtained were compared with the original AD controller whose parameters were determined empirically. The comparison was made first without opponents and then, with several cars from the TORCS teams in realistic races.

The obtained results are very promising since the optimized controllers overcome the original in the practice races, and also they were ranked among the first ones in the evaluation races, with the minimum of damage.

Nevertheless, these results can be improved by extending the evaluation of population controllers in the Genetic algorithm to other tracks and not just one, to allow the elected controller to practice effectively in multiple tracks and in real-life situations. Moreover, we could also try to generate, optimize and tune automatically the rule base of the fuzzy controller by means of a Genetic Programming algorithm.

Acknowledgments. This work has been supported in part by: Ministerio español de Economía y Competitividad under project TIN2014-56494-C4-3-P (UGR-EPHEMECH), TIN2017-85727-C4-2-P (UGR-DeepBio) and TEC2015-68752 (also funded by FEDER).

References

1. Butz, M.V., Lönneker, T.D.: Optimized sensory-motor couplings plus strategy extensions for the TORCS car racing challenge. In: Lanzi, P.L. (ed.) Proceedings of the 2009 IEEE Symposium on Computational Intelligence and Games, CIG 2009, Milano, Italy, 7–10 September 2009, pp. 317–324. IEEE (2009)
2. Cardamone, L., Loiacono, D., Lanzi, P.L.: On-line neuroevolution applied to the open racing car simulator. In: Proceedings of the Eleventh Conference on Congress on Evolutionary Computation, CEC 2009, pp. 2622–2629. IEEE Press, Piscataway (2009)
3. Loiacono, D., Cardamone, L., Lanzi, P.L.: Automatic track generation for high-end racing games using evolutionary computation. IEEE Trans. Comput. Intell. AI Games **3**, 245–259 (2011)
4. Elsayed, S.M.M., Sarker, R., Essam, D.L.: A genetic algorithm for solving the CEC2013 competition problems on real-parameter optimization. In: IEEE Congress on Evolutionary Computation, CEC 2013, Cancun, Mexico, 21–23 June 2013, , pp. 356–360 (2013)
5. Floreano, D., Kato, T., Marocco, D., Sauser, E.: Coevolution of active vision and feature selection. Biol. Cybern. **90**, 218–228 (2004)
6. Garcia, S., Molina, D., Lozano, M., Herrera, F.: A study on the use of non-parametric tests for analyzing the evolutionary algorithms behaviour a case study on the CEC2005 special session on real parameter optimization. J. Heuristics **15**–**6**, 617–644 (2009)
7. Goldberg, D.E.: Genetic Algorithms in Search, Optimization and Machine Learning. Addison Wesley, Reading (1989)
8. Guadarrama.S, Vazquez, R.: Tuning a fuzzy racing car by coevolution. In: Genetic and Evolving Systems, GEFS 2008. IEEE, March 2008
9. Herrera, F., Lozano, M., Verdegay, J.: Automatic track generation for high-end racing games using evolutionary computation. Artif. Intell. Rev. **12**(4), 265–319 (1998)
10. Iancu, I.: A Mamdani type fuzzy logic controller, pp. 325–352. InTech (2012)
11. Kim, T.S., Na, J.C., Kim, K.J.: Optimization of an autonomous car controller using a self-adaptive evolutionary strategy. Int. J. Adv. Robot. Syst. **9**(3), 73 (2012). https://doi.org/10.5772/50848
12. Kolski, S., Ferguson, D., Stacniss, C., Siegwart, R.: Autonomous driving in dynamic environments. In: Proceedings of the Workshop on Safe Navigation in Open and Dynamic Environments at the IEEE/RSJ International Conference on Intelligent Robots and Systems (IROS), Beijing, China (2006)
13. Koutnik, J., Cuccu, G., Schmidhuber, J., Gomez, F.: Evolving large scale neural networks for vision based TORCS. In: Foundations of Digital Games. Koutnik, J.: Dipartimento tecnologie innovative Istituto Dalle Molle di studi sull'intelligenza artificiale, March 2013. http://repository.supsi.ch/id/eprint/4548
14. Liébana, D.P., Recio, G., Sáez, Y., Isasi, P.: Evolving a fuzzy controller for a car racing competition. In: Lanzi, P.L. (ed.) Proceedings of the 2009 IEEE Symposium on Computational Intelligence and Games, CIG 2009, Milano, Italy, 7–10 September 2009, pp. 263–270. IEEE (2009)
15. Loiacono, D., Cardamone, L., B, M., Lanzi, P.L.: The 2011 simulated car racing championship @ CIG-2011. TORCS News (2011). http://cig.dei.polimi.it/wpcontent/

16. Loiacono, D., Lanzi, P.L., Bardelli, A.P.: Searching for the optimal racing line using genetic algorithms. In: 2010 IEEE Proceedings of the Symposium on Computational Intelligence and Games (CIG). IEEE Press, Copenhagen (2010)
17. Neubauer, A.: A theoretical analysis of the non-uniform mutation operator for the modified genetic algorithm. In: Proceedings of the IEEE International Conference on Evolutionary Computation. IEEE Press, Indianapolis (1997)
18. Onieva, E., Alonso, J., Perez, J., Milanés, V.: Autonomous car fuzzy control modeled by iterative genetic algorithms. In: Fuzzy Systems, pp. 1615–1620 (2009)
19. Onieva, E., Pelta, D., Godoy, J., Milanés, V., Rastelli, J.: An evolutionary tuned driving system for virtual car racing games: the AUTOPIA driver. Int. J. Intell. Syst. **27**, 217–241 (2012)
20. Onieva, E., Pelta, D.A., Alonso, J., Milanés, V., Pérez, J.: A modular parametric architecture for the torcs racing engine. In: Proceedings of the 5th IEEE Symposium on Computational Intelligence and Games (CIG 2009), pp. 256–262. IEEE Press, Piscataway (2009)
21. Saez, Y., Perez, D., Sanjuan, O., Isasi, P.: Driving cars by means of genetic algorithms. In: Rudolph, G., Jansen, T., Beume, N., Lucas, S., Poloni, C. (eds.) PPSN 2008. LNCS, vol. 5199, pp. 1101–1110. Springer, Heidelberg (2008). https://doi.org/10.1007/978-3-540-87700-4_109
22. Salem, M., Mora, A.M., Merelo, J.J., García-Sánchez, P.: Driving in TORCS using modular fuzzy controllers. In: Squillero, G., Sim, K. (eds.) EvoApplications 2017. LNCS, vol. 10199, pp. 361–376. Springer, Cham (2017). https://doi.org/10.1007/978-3-319-55849-3_24
23. Sourceforge: Web TORCS, Web, November 2016. http://torcs.sourceforge.net/
24. Tan, C.H., Ang, J.H., Tan, K.C., Tay, A.: Online adaptive controller for simulated car racing. In: Proceedings of the IEEE Congress on Evolutionary Computation, CEC 2008, June 1–6, 2008, Hong Kong, China, pp. 2239–2245. IEEE (2008)
25. Thang, H.D., Garibaldi, J.M.: A novel fuzzy inferencing methodology for simulated car racing. In: FUZZ-IEEE 2008, IEEE International Conference on Fuzzy Systems, Hong Kong, China, 1–6 June 2008, Proceedings, pp. 1907–1914. IEEE (2008)
26. Varun Kumar, S.G., Panneerselvam, R.: A study of crossover operators for genetic algorithms to solve VRP and its variants and new sinusoidal motion crossover operator. Int. J. Comput. Intell. Res. **13**(7), 1717–1733 (2017)

Self-adaptive MCTS for General Video Game Playing

Chiara F. Sironi[1]([⊠]) , Jialin Liu[2] , Diego Perez-Liebana[2] ,
Raluca D. Gaina[2] , Ivan Bravi[2] , Simon M. Lucas[2] ,
and Mark H. M. Winands[1]

[1] Games and AI Group, Department of Data Science and Knowledge Engineering,
Maastricht University, Maastricht, The Netherlands
{c.sironi,m.winands}@maastrichtuniversity.nl
[2] Game AI Group, School of Electronic Engineering and Computer Science,
Queen Mary University of London, London, UK
{jialin.liu,diego.perez,r.d.gaina,i.bravi,simon.lucas}@qmul.ac.uk

Abstract. Monte-Carlo Tree Search (MCTS) has shown particular success in General Game Playing (GGP) and General Video Game Playing (GVGP) and many enhancements and variants have been developed. Recently, an on-line adaptive parameter tuning mechanism for MCTS agents has been proposed that almost achieves the same performance as off-line tuning in GGP.

In this paper we apply the same approach to GVGP and use the popular General Video Game AI (GVGAI) framework, in which the time allowed to make a decision is only 40 ms. We design three Self-Adaptive MCTS (SA-MCTS) agents that optimize on-line the parameters of a standard non-Self-Adaptive MCTS agent of GVGAI. The three agents select the parameter values using Naïve Monte-Carlo, an Evolutionary Algorithm and an N-Tuple Bandit Evolutionary Algorithm respectively, and are tested on 20 single-player games of GVGAI.

The SA-MCTS agents achieve more robust results on the tested games. With the same time setting, they perform similarly to the baseline standard MCTS agent in the games for which the baseline agent performs well, and significantly improve the win rate in the games for which the baseline agent performs poorly. As validation, we also test the performance of non-Self-Adaptive MCTS instances that use the most sampled parameter settings during the on-line tuning of each of the three SA-MCTS agents for each game. Results show that these parameter settings improve the win rate on the games *Wait for Breakfast* and *Escape* by 4 times and 150 times, respectively.

Keywords: MCTS · On-line tuning · Self-adaptive
Robust game playing · General video game playing

© Springer International Publishing AG, part of Springer Nature 2018
K. Sim and P. Kaufmann (Eds.): EvoApplications 2018, LNCS 10784, pp. 358–375, 2018.
https://doi.org/10.1007/978-3-319-77538-8_25

1   Introduction

Monte-Carlo Tree Search (MCTS) [1,2] is a simulation-based search technique that Yannakakis and Togelius [3] list among the commonly used methods in games. Browne *et al.* [4] reviewed the evolution of MCTS, its variations and their successful applications till 2012. Different techniques have been studied for enhancing the MCTS variants, such as the All Moves As First (AMAF) [5], the Rapid Action Value Estimation (RAVE) [6], Generalized RAVE (GRAVE) [7], HRAVE [8] and the Move Average Sampling Technique (MAST) [9]. Powley *et al.* introduced the ICARUS (Information Capture And ReUse Strategy) framework for describing and combining such enhancements [10].

Moreover, MCTS has been proved to be a success in many domains, including the Go game [11,12] and General (Video) Game Playing [13–15]. General Video Game Playing (GVGP) [14,15] aims at creating agents that are capable of playing any unknown video game successfully without using prior knowledge or intervention by human beings. The General Video Game AI (GVGAI) framework[1] has been implemented for this research purpose [14]. Many successful General Video Game Playing agents are MCTS-based, like YOLOBOT, the agent that won the GVGAI Single-Player Planning Championship in 2017, and *MaastCTS2* [16], the agent that won the GVGAI Single-Player Planning Championship in 2016.

One of the difficulties of GVGP and the GVGAI competition is parameter tuning for AI agents. Examples are the exploration factor and the play-out depth of MCTS-based agents, or population size, mutation probability and planning horizon for the rolling horizon evolutionary agents. A common approach is to tune the parameters off-line with some given games. Gaina *et al.* [17] varied the population size and planning horizon of a vanilla Rolling Horizon Evolutionary Algorithm (RHEA) and compared their performance on a subset of games in the GVGAI framework. Bravi *et al.* [18] used Genetic Programming (GP) to evolve game-specific Upper Confidence Bound (UCB) alternatives, each of which outperformed the MCTS using standard UCB1 (Eq. 1) on at least one of the tested games. These UCB alternatives can be used to build a portfolio of MCTS agents to achieve robust game playing. However, such off-line tuning is computationally expensive and game dependent. Tuning the parameters of a given agent off-line for a new game is therefore sometimes not possible.

Recently, Sironi and Winands [19] have proposed on-line adaptive parameter tuning for MCTS agents and almost achieved the same performance as off-line tuning in General Game Playing. Their approach is based on the idea of interleaving parameter tuning with MCTS. Before each MCTS simulation a different combination of parameter values is selected to control the search. The reward obtained by the simulation is used to update some statistics on the performance of such combination of parameter values. These statistics are then used to choose which parameter values will control the next simulations. Four allocation strategies are proposed in [19] to decide which parameter values should be evaluated for each MCTS simulation and in which order.

---

[1] http://www.gvgai.net.

In this work, we apply the same approach for tuning on-line the parameters K (the UCB exploration factor) and D (the depth limit for the search) of a standard MCTS agent, *sampleMCTS*, of the GVGAI framework. First of all we verify if the on-line tuning approach can be applied successfully to GVGP by testing the most promising among the four allocation strategies presented in [19], Naïve Monte-Carlo (NMC). Second, we want to see if the performance on GVGP of the on-line tuning mechanism can be further improved by using the principles of evolutionary algorithms. Therefore, we propose two more allocation strategies, one based on an Evolutionary Algorithm (EA) and one base on an N-tuple Bandit Evolutionary Algorithm (NTupleBanditEA). Finally, to validate the allocation strategies we evaluate the performance of the instances of *sampleMCTS* that use as fixed parameter settings the combinations of values that were used the most during game playing by each of the proposed allocation strategies.

This paper is structured as follows. Section 2 introduces the background, including GVGAI, MCTS and the on-line parameter tuning problem. Section 3 describes the approach and tuning algorithms. Section 4 presents the design of experiments and Sect. 5 analyzes the results. Finally, Sect. 6 concludes and proposes some future research.

2   Background

This section briefly introduces the General Video Game AI framework (Subsect. 2.1), the principles of Monte-Carlo Tree Search (Subsect. 2.2) and the formulation of the on-line parameter tuning problem (Subsect. 2.3).

2.1   General Video Game AI

The General Video Game AI (GVGAI) framework was initially designed and developed by the Games Intelligence Group at the University of Essex (UK) aiming at using it as a research and competition framework for studying General Video Game Playing (GVGP). The GVGAI consists of five tracks: two planning tracks (single- and two-player) where the forward model of every game is available [14,15]; the single-playing learning track where no forward model is given [20]; the level generation track [21] and rule generation track [22]. The games were defined in Video Game Description Language (VGDL) [23] and the framework was mainly written in Java. More about the tracks and competitions can be found on the GVGAI website. In this paper, we focus on a subset of the GVGAI single-player games. More about the game set is presented in Subsect. 4.1. Compared to the Atari Learning Environment (ALE) [24] framework, GVGAI has the advantage of being more extensible, meaning that it is much easier to add new games and variations of those games, and also offers two-player games which provide a greater range of challenges than single player games. ALE currently has the advantage of offering commercial games, albeit from a few decades ago.

2.2   Monte-Carlo Tree Search

MCTS is a best-first search algorithm that incrementally builds a tree representation of the search space of a problem (e.g., a game) and estimates the values of states by performing simulations [1,2]. An iteration of the MCTS consists of four phases: (i) **Selection:** starting from the root node of the tree a *selection strategy* is used to select the next actions to visit until a node is reached that is not fully expanded, i.e., at least one successor state is not visited and its corresponding node is not added to the tree yet; (ii) **Expansion:** in a node that is not fully expanded, an *expansion strategy* is used to choose one or more nodes that will be added to the tree; (iii) **Play-out:** starting from the last node added to the tree a *play-out* strategy chooses which actions to simulate until either a given depth (maximum play-out depth) or a terminal state are reached; and (iv) **Back-propagation:** at the end of the play-out, the result of the simulation is propagated back through all the nodes traversed in the tree and used to update the estimate of their value. These four phases are repeated until the search budget in terms of time or state evaluations has been exhausted. At this point, the best action in the root node is returned to be played in the real game. Different recommendation policies can be used to decide which action to return and perform, for instance, recommending the one with the highest estimated average score or the one with the highest number of visits.

Many strategies have been proposed for the different phases of MCTS. The standard *selection strategy* is UCT (Upper Confidence bounds applied to Trees) [2]. UCT sees the problem of choosing an action in a certain node of the tree as a Multi-Armed Bandit (MAB) problem and uses the UCB1 [25] sampling strategy to select the action to visit next. UCT selects in node s the action a that maximizes the following formula:

$$UCB1(s,a) = Q(s,a) + K \times \sqrt{\frac{\ln N(s)}{N(s,a)}}, \qquad (1)$$

where $Q(s,a)$ is the average result obtained from all the simulations in which action a was played in node (state) s, $N(s)$ is the number of times node s has been visited during the search and $N(s,a)$ is the number of times action a has been selected whenever node s was visited. The K constant is used to control the balance between exploitation of good actions and exploration of less visited ones.

2.3   On-line Parameter Tuning

The parameters of an AI agent can be seen as a vector of integers and doubles (boolean parameters can be handled as integers with only two legal values). The tuning of parameters is therefore a problem of searching optimal numerical vector(s) in a given parameter search space. Given the combinatorial structure of the search space, Sironi and Winands [19] considered the tuning problem as a Combinatorial Multi-Armed Bandit (CMAB) [26]. The definition of the parameter tuning problem as a CMAB is given by the following three components:

- A set of d parameters, $P = \{P_1, ..., P_d\}$, where each parameter P_i can take m_i different values $V_i = \{v_i^1, ..., v_i^{m_i}\}$.
- A reward distribution $R : V_1 \times ... \times V_d \to \mathbb{R}$ that depends on the combination of values assigned to the parameters.
- A function $L : V_1 \times ... \times V_d \to \{true, false\}$ that determines which combinations of parameter values are legal.

In this paper we use the same approach for on-line tuning that was presented in [19]. This approach consists in interleaving MCTS simulations with parameter tuning, as shown in Algorithm 1. Before each MCTS simulation the tuner $\mathcal{T}$ selects a combination of values for the parameters $\mathbf{p}$. These values are set for the parameters of the agent AI_{MCTS} that performs an MCTS simulation of the game and returns the associated reward. This reward is used by the tuner to update the statistics for the combination of parameters $\mathbf{p}$. Different allocation strategies can be used by the tuner to decide which parameter combination should be evaluated next depending on these statistics. In this paper we consider the most promising allocation strategy that was introduced in [19], Naïve Monte-Carlo (NMC), and propose two more, one based on an Evolutionary Algorithm and one based on a N-tuple bandit Evolutionary Algorithm.

Algorithm 1. On-line parameter tuning for a given MCTS agent AI_{MCTS}.

Require: G: game to be played
Require: AI_{MCTS}: an agent with parameter vector $\in \mathcal{S}_{AI_{MCTS}}$
Require: $\mathcal{T}$: tuner
1: **while** time not elapsed **do**
2:     $\mathbf{p} \leftarrow \mathcal{T}.\text{CHOOSEPARAMVALUES}()$ ▷ Select param. combination using the tuner $\mathcal{T}$
3:     $AI_{MCTS}.set(\mathbf{p})$ ▷ Set parameters for AI_{MCTS}
4:     $r \leftarrow G.simulate(AI_{MCTS})$ ▷ Perform MCTS simulation
5:     $\mathcal{T}.\text{UPDATEVALUESSTATS}(\mathbf{p}, r, ...)$ ▷ Update the statistics, defined by the tuner $\mathcal{T}$

---

3   Allocation Strategies

This section describes the three allocation strategies that are integrated to the GVGAI *sampleMCTS* agent: Naïve Monte-Carlo, Evolutionary Algorithm and N-tuple Bandit Evolutionary Algorithm. As a result, three Self-Adaptive MCTS (SA-MCTS) agents are created. The NMC strategy is the same that is presented in [19]. Among the four strategies proposed in the paper we decide to test this one for GVGAI because it was the one that had more promising results when used to tune parameters for GGP.

3.1   Naïve Monte-Carlo

Naïve Monte-Carlo (NMC) was first proposed by Ontañon [26] to be applied to Real-Time Strategy games. This approach proved suitable to deal with combinatorial search spaces, thus in [19] it was applied to the on-line parameter tuning problem, that is characterized by a combinatorial parameter space. NMC is based on the *naïve assumption*, which is the assumption that the reward associated with a combination of parameter values can be approximated by a linear combination of the rewards associated with each of the single values: $R(\mathbf{p} = \langle p_1, ..., p_d \rangle) \approx \sum_{i=1}^{d} R_i(p_i)$.

Algorithm 2 gives the pseudo-code for this strategy. NMC considers one global MAB (MAB_g) and n local MABs ($MAB_i, i = 1...d$), one for each parameter. Each arm of MAB_g corresponds to one of the legal combinations of parameter values that have been evaluated so far, while each arm in MAB_i corresponds to one of the legal values for parameter P_i. This allocation strategy alternates between an *exploration* and an *exploitation* phase. For each MCTS simulation a combination of parameter values is selected by exploration with probability ϵ_0 and by exploitation with probability $(1 - \epsilon_0)$. If exploring, the next combination to be evaluated is selected by choosing each parameter value independently from the corresponding MAB_i (note that a combination that has never been visited before can be generated, thus there is exploration of the search space).

Algorithm 2. On-line parameter tuning for a given MCTS agent AI_{MCTS} using Naïve Monte-Carlo.

Require: G: game to be played
Require: AI_{MCTS}: MCTS agent with parameter vector $\in \mathcal{S}_{AI_{MCTS}}$
Require: d: number of parameters to be tuned
Require: $\mathcal{S}$: parameter search space for AI_{MCTS}
Require: ϵ_0: probability of performing exploration
Require: π_l: policy to select a parameter value from the local MABs
Require: π_g: policy to select a parameter combination from the global MAB
1: $MAB_g \leftarrow$ create a MAB with no arms
2: **for** $i \leftarrow 1 : d$ **do**
3:     $MAB_i \leftarrow$ create a MAB for parameter P_i with one arm for each of its possible values
4: **while** time not elapsed **do**
5:     $\mathbf{p} \leftarrow$ CHOOSEPARAMVALUES($\mathcal{S}, \epsilon_0, \pi_l, \pi_g, MAB_g, MAB_1, ..., MAB_d$)
6:     $AI_{MCTS}.set(\mathbf{p})$ ▷ Set parameters for AI_{MCTS}
7:     $r \leftarrow G.simulate(AI_{MCTS})$ ▷ Perform MCTS simulation
8:     UPDATEVALUESSTATS($\mathbf{p}, r, MAB_g, MAB_1, ..., MAB_d$)
9: **function** CHOOSEPARAMVALUES($\mathcal{S}, \epsilon_0, \pi_l, \pi_g, MAB_g, MAB_1, ..., MAB_d$)
10:     $\mathbf{p} \leftarrow$ create empty combination of values
11:     **if** $RAND(0, 1) < \epsilon_0$ **then**   ▷ Exploration
12:         **for** $i \leftarrow 1 : d$ **do**
13:             $\mathbf{p}[i] \leftarrow \pi_l.$CHOOSEVALUE($\mathcal{S}, MAB_i$)
14:         $MAB_g.$ADD($\mathbf{p}$)
15:     **else**   ▷ Exploitation
16:         $\mathbf{p} \leftarrow \pi_g.$CHOOSECOMBINATION($\mathcal{S}, MAB_g$)
17:     **return** $\mathbf{p}$
18: **function** UPDATEVALUESSTATS($\mathbf{p}, r, MAB_g, MAB_1, ..., MAB_d$)
19:     $MAB_g.$UPDATEARMSTATS($\mathbf{p}, r$)
20:     **for** $i \leftarrow 1 : d$ **do**
21:         $MAB_i.$UPDATEARMSTATS($\mathbf{p}[i], r$)

If exploiting, the next combination is selected from the global MAB, MAB_g (in this case only previously seen combinations will be selected). MAB_g starts with no arms and a new arm is added whenever a new combination in generated using the local MABs. Whenever a combination of values is evaluated, the reward obtained by the corresponding MCTS simulation is used to update both the statistics associated with the global MAB and the ones associated with each of the local MABs. The SA-MCTS agent built using NMC as a tuner is denoted as SA-MCTS$_{NMC}$.

3.2   Evolutionary Algorithm

Genetic Algorithms (GA) achieve overall good performance in General Video Game Playing [17]. However, in the case of on-line parameter tuning, we aim at using a simple algorithm as tuner, making the best use of the time budget to evaluate more MCTS instances with different parameter settings or more times a good MCTS instance. A combination of parameter values is considered to be an individual, where each single parameter is a gene. A simple Evolutionary Algorithm (EA) with λ individuals has been considered for evolving on-line the parameters for an MCTS agent, where the μ elites in the previous generation are kept and $(\lambda - \mu)$ new individuals are reproduced. Each new individual is reproduced with probability p_c by uniformly random crossover between two elites selected uniformly at random, or by uniformly mutating one bit of a randomly selected elite otherwise. When evaluating a population, each individual (i.e. the corresponding parameter combination) is used to control a different MCTS simulation of the game and the outcome of the simulation is considered as the fitness of the individual. The SA-MCTS agent built using this EA as a tuner is referred to as SA-MCTS$_{EA}$.

3.3   N-Tuple Bandit Evolutionary Algorithm

The N-Tuple Bandit Evolutionary Algorithm (NTupleBanditEA) is firstly proposed by Kunanusont *et al.* [27] for automatic game parameter tuning where strong stochastic AI agents were used to evaluate the evolved games with uncertainties. Then, it was applied to the GVGAI framework for evolving game rules and parameter setting in games [28]. It makes use of all the statistics of the previously evaluated solutions and balances the exploration and exploitation between evaluating a new generated solution and re-evaluating an existed solution using UCB1. The detailed algorithm is not given in this paper due to lack of space, more can be found in [27]. We apply the NTupleBanditEA to optimizing the parameters on-line by modeling each parameter to be tuned as a 1-tuple and considering their combinations as n-tuples. For this strategy we need to specify the number of neighbors generated at one iteration, n, and the exploration factor, denoted as K_{NEA} (cf. Algorithm 3 in [27]). The SA-MCTS agent built using this NTupleBanditEA as a tuner is referred to as SA-MCTS$_{NEA}$.

4   Experimental Settings

In this section we introduce the design of the experiments, including games used as test problem, the baseline AI agent to be tuned and the tested tuners.

4.1   Games

Each of the approaches described in Sect. 3 is tested on all 5 levels of 20 games (Table 1) of the GVGAI framework. The 20 games are same as the ones used by Gaina *et al.* [17] for studying the parameters of a vanilla RHEA. Gaina *et al.* [17] uniformly randomly selected 20 games from a merged list of games exploited by Nelson [29] and Bontrager *et al.* [30] previously, on which the vanilla MCTS agent performs differently. During every game playing, an agent has 40 ms per game tick to decide an action. In all the games, there is no draw. A game terminates if the agent wins or loses the game before 2, 000 game ticks or the game is forced to terminate as a loss of the agent after 2, 000 game ticks. This is the same setting as in the GVGAI Single-Playing Planning competitions. The only difference is that if the agent exceeds the 40 ms limit per game tick it will not be disqualified and can still apply its selected move.

4.2   Tuned Agent and Parameters

We consider the single-player *sampleMCTS* agent in the GVGAI framework as the AI_{MCTS} to be tuned, the performance of which mainly relies on two parameters, the maximum play-out depth D and the UCB1 exploration factor K. The heuristic used by the *sampleMCTS* agent for evaluating a game state is defined as follows:

$$Value(GameState) = \begin{cases} score(GameState) - 10,000,000.0 & \text{if a loss,} \\ score(GameState) + 10,000,000.0 & \text{if a win,} \\ score(GameState) & \text{otherwise.} \end{cases} \quad (2)$$

Table 1. The 20 tested games. The authors of [17] have confirmed that some games have been wrongly listed as deterministic games. *Wait for Breakfast* was listed as deterministic game as it has negligible randomness (detailed in Subsect. 5.1).

Deterministic games: Bait, Camel Race, Escape, Hungry Birds, Modality	
Stochastic games	
Negligible randomness	Plaque Attack, Wait for Breakfast
Non-deterministic chasing/fleeing behaviors	Chase, Lemmings, Missile Command, Roguelike
Random NPC(s)	Butterflies, Infection, Roguelike
Very stochastic	Aliens, Chopper, Crossfire, Dig Dug, Intersection, Sea Quest, Survive Zombies

Based on this *sampleMCTS*, the SA-MCTS agents are designed. These agents tune D and K on-line considering 15 possible values for each parameter (i.e. 225 possible combinations of parameters). The same state evaluation heuristic (Eq. 2) is used by the self-adaptive agents. The SA-MCTS agents are compared to a baseline agent, the default *sampleMCTS*, with a fixed value for D and K. The parameter settings are summarized as follows:

- *sampleMCTS*: $D = 10$, $K = 1.4$ (default setting in GVGAI);
- **SA-MCTS** agents: $D \in \{1, 2, 3, 4, 5, 6, 7, 8, 9, 10, 11, 12, 13, 14, 15\}$, $K \in \{0.6, 0.7, 0.8, 0.9, 1.0, 1.1, 1.2, 1.3, 1.4, 1.5, 1.6, 1.7, 1.8, 1.9, 2.0\}$.

4.3   Tuning Strategies

Three SA-MCTS agents are considered in the experiments, one for each of the presented tuning strategies, NMC, EA and NTupleBanditEA. To distinguish them, in the tables and in subsequent sections they are denoted as SA-MCTS$_{NMC}$, SA-MCTS$_{EA}$ and SA-MCTS$_{NEA}$, respectively. The following are the settings for the tuning strategies:

- **SA-MCTS$_{NMC}$:** $\epsilon_0 = 0.75$ (i.e. select next combination using the local MABs with probability 0.75 and the global MAB with probability 0.25), $\pi_g =$ UCB1 policy with exploration factor $K_g = 0.7$, $\pi_l =$ UCB1 policy with exploration factor $K_l = 0.7$ (note that these two exploration factors are distinct from the UCB1 exploration factor to be tuned and used by the *sampleMCTS* agent).
- **SA-MCTS$_{EA}$:** population size $\lambda = 50$, elite size $\mu = 25$ (lower values for μ were tested when applying this strategy to GGP and none of them outperformed $\mu = 25$), probability of generating an individual by crossover of two parents, $p_c = 0.5$.
- **SA-MCTS$_{NEA}$:** number of neighbors generated during evolution $n = 5$ (preliminary tests showed that higher values added no benefit), $K_{NEA} = 0.7$ (exploration constant for the UCB1 formula used to compute the value for a parameter combination [27]).

5   Results and Discussion

The results of the designed SA-MCTS agents and the baseline agent are analyzed and discussed in Sect. 5.1. Section 5.2 illustrates the performance of some static agents using constant parameters, the most visited parameter combination during the on-line tuning for each game.

5.1   On-line Tuning Performance

Each of the SA-MCTS agents has been performed on the 5 levels of each of the games 500 times (100 per level), as well as the baseline *sampleMCTS* agent.

Table 2. Average win rate (%) and average game score over 5 levels of each game for the *sampleMCTS* agent and the SA-MCTS agents. The best values are in bold.

(a) Average win rate (%) over 5 levels of each game

Games	sampleMCTS	SA-MCTS$_{NMC}$	SA-MCTS$_{EA}$	SA-MCTS$_{NEA}$
Aliens	**100.0($\pm$0.00)**	99.8($\pm$0.39)	**100.0($\pm$0.00)**	99.4($\pm$0.68)
Bait	6.6($\pm$2.18)	7.0($\pm$2.24)	7.8($\pm$2.35)	**8.4($\pm$2.43)**
Butterflies	95.2($\pm$1.88)	95.0($\pm$1.91)	94.2($\pm$2.05)	**95.4($\pm$1.84)**
Camel Race	4.2($\pm$1.76)	4.6($\pm$1.84)	**6.2($\pm$2.12)**	5.2($\pm$1.95)
Chase	3.2($\pm$1.54)	7.2($\pm$2.27)	**9.2($\pm$2.54)**	7.4($\pm$2.30)
Chopper	**91.4($\pm$2.46)**	88.6($\pm$2.79)	83.2($\pm$3.28)	50.8($\pm$4.39)
Crossfire	4.2($\pm$1.76)	11.6($\pm$2.81)	11.4($\pm$2.79)	**15.6($\pm$3.18)**
Dig Dug	0.0($\pm$0.00)	0.0($\pm$0.00)	0.0($\pm$0.00)	0.0($\pm$0.00)
Escape	0.2($\pm$0.39)	4.4($\pm$1.80)	7.6($\pm$2.33)	**13.0($\pm$2.95)**
Hungry Birds	**5.4($\pm$1.98)**	2.6($\pm$1.40)	4.6($\pm$1.84)	3.8($\pm$1.68)
Infection	97.0($\pm$1.50)	95.6($\pm$1.80)	97.6($\pm$1.34)	**97.8($\pm$1.29)**
Intersection	100.0($\pm$0.00)	100.0($\pm$0.00)	100.0($\pm$0.00)	100.0($\pm$0.00)
Lemmings	0.0($\pm$0.00)	0.0($\pm$0.00)	0.0($\pm$0.00)	0.0($\pm$0.00)
Missile Command	60.4($\pm$4.29)	**60.8($\pm$4.28)**	58.0($\pm$4.33)	58.6($\pm$4.32)
Modality	27.0($\pm$3.90)	27.4($\pm$3.91)	26.0($\pm$3.85)	**28.4($\pm$3.96)**
Plaque Attack	91.8($\pm$2.41)	92.0($\pm$2.38)	**92.8($\pm$2.27)**	92.6($\pm$2.30)
Roguelike	0.0($\pm$0.00)	0.0($\pm$0.00)	0.0($\pm$0.00)	0.0($\pm$0.00)
Sea Quest	55.0($\pm$4.37)	47.8($\pm$4.38)	**55.6($\pm$4.36)**	43.2($\pm$4.35)
Survive Zombies	41.0($\pm$4.32)	41.0($\pm$4.32)	34.8($\pm$4.18)	34.8($\pm$4.18)
Wait for Breakfast	15.4($\pm$3.17)	20.4($\pm$3.54)	28.8($\pm$3.97)	**44.0($\pm$4.36)**
Avg Win%	39.9($\pm$0.96)	40.3($\pm$0.96)	**40.9($\pm$0.96)**	39.9($\pm$0.96)

(b) Average game score over 5 levels of each game. Note that in GVGAI, wining a game with low score is higher ranked than losing a game with a high score

Games	sampleMCTS	SA-MCTS$_{NMC}$	SA-MCTS$_{EA}$	SA-MCTS$_{NEA}$
Aliens	**67.8($\pm$1.27)**	64.5($\pm$1.17)	64.4($\pm$1.18)	65.6($\pm$1.23)
Bait	2.6($\pm$0.27)	4.5($\pm$0.55)	2.3($\pm$0.28)	**5.6($\pm$0.63)**
Butterflies	30.3($\pm$1.34)	30.4($\pm$1.32)	30.0($\pm$1.27)	**31.1($\pm$1.33)**
Camel Race	−0.8($\pm$0.05)	−0.8($\pm$0.05)	**−0.7($\pm$0.05)**	**−0.7($\pm$0.05)**
Chase	2.7($\pm$0.18)	3.1($\pm$0.18)	3.1($\pm$0.19)	**3.2($\pm$0.20)**
Chopper	**11.4($\pm$0.55)**	10.8($\pm$0.56)	9.7($\pm$0.65)	4.4($\pm$0.73)
Crossfire	0.1($\pm$0.09)	0.3($\pm$0.15)	0.2($\pm$0.16)	**0.4($\pm$0.18)**
Dig Dug	**11.2($\pm$0.79)**	10.1($\pm$0.83)	10.3($\pm$0.81)	9.0($\pm$0.74)
Escape	0.0($\pm$0.00)	0.0($\pm$0.02)	**0.1($\pm$0.02)**	**0.1($\pm$0.03)**
Hungry Birds	**7.4($\pm$2.09)**	3.5($\pm$1.48)	5.3($\pm$1.88)	4.4($\pm$1.72)
Infection	14.3($\pm$0.71)	13.4($\pm$0.69)	**14.5($\pm$0.75)**	14.1($\pm$0.74)
Intersection	1.0($\pm$0.0)	1.1($\pm$0.09)	**2.1($\pm$0.27)**	1.0($\pm$0.04)
Lemmings	−3.5($\pm$0.30)	−2.3($\pm$0.23)	−4.3($\pm$0.34)	**−1.4($\pm$0.16)**
Missile Command	**4.4($\pm$0.44)**	4.2($\pm$0.45)	4.0($\pm$0.46)	3.9($\pm$0.44)
Modality	0.3($\pm$0.04)	0.3($\pm$0.04)	0.3($\pm$0.04)	0.3($\pm$0.04)
Plaque Attack	46.9($\pm$1.64)	46.4($\pm$1.54)	**50.4($\pm$1.68)**	48.6($\pm$1.60)
Roguelike	**3.5($\pm$0.41)**	2.9($\pm$0.38)	3.2($\pm$0.40)	3.2($\pm$0.39)
Sea Quest	1734.6($\pm$169.97)	1575.1($\pm$163.41)	**1774.2($\pm$167.22)**	1288.1($\pm$135.44)
Survive Zombies	2.6($\pm$0.30)	**2.7($\pm$0.31)**	2.2($\pm$0.29)	2.2($\pm$0.29)
Wait for Breakfast	0.2($\pm$0.03)	0.2($\pm$0.04)	0.3($\pm$0.04)	**0.4($\pm$0.04)**
Avg Score	96.8($\pm$11.25)	88.5($\pm$10.56)	**98.6($\pm$11.26)**	74.2($\pm$8.70)

During every game playing, an agent has $40ms$ per game tick to decide an action. More about the games and settings has been presented in Subsect. 4.1. The win rate and average score for the *sampleMCTS* agent and the SA-MCTS agents on the 20 games are summarized in Tables 2a and b, respectively. In our setting, wining a game has the highest priority (Eq. 2), thus the win rate is used as the criterion for evaluating a tuner rather than the average score.

The SA-MCTS agents perform overall well on the games where the default *sampleMCTS* also performs well, except for the games of *Chopper* and *Survive Zombies*. Moreover, in some of the games that the *sampleMCTS* has poor performance, e.g. *Chase*, *Escape*, *Crossfire* and *Wait for Breakfast* (Fig. 1), the SA-MCTS agents significantly improve the win rate. These four games are detailed below.

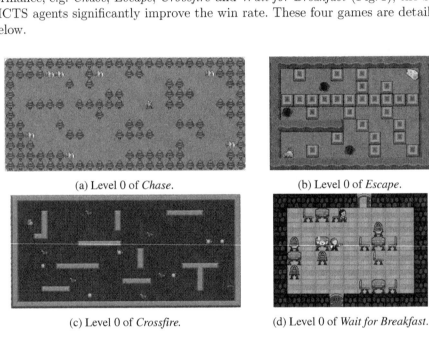

(a) Level 0 of *Chase*.   (b) Level 0 of *Escape*.

(c) Level 0 of *Crossfire*.   (d) Level 0 of *Wait for Breakfast*.

Fig. 1. Screenshots of game screen of *Chase, Escape, Crossfire* and *Wait for Breakfast*.

Chase. (Figure 1(a)) The player must chase and kill scared goats that flee from the player. A dead goat turns to a corpse immediately and the player gains 1 point as score. A goat becomes angry as soon as it finds another goat's corpse, and starts to chase the player. The player wins the game if all scared goats are dead, but it will lose one point and loses the game immediately if is caught by an angry goat. The game is very difficult as an angry goat will never turn back to a normal one, and by default the game ends with a loss of the player after running 2,000 game ticks. Thus, once a goat becomes angry, it will inevitably lead to a lost game for the player, but this negative reward is delayed until the end of the game. In our context, the game rules are not given to the agent, so the agent will not be aware of the defeat until being caught or after 2,000 game ticks. The baseline agent, *sampleMCTS* only wins 32 games out of 500, while the SA-MCTS agents win at least 72 games.

Escape. (Figure 1(b)) It is a puzzle game with wide search space and required long-term planning. The player (rat) wins the game by taking the cheese. The player's score is 1 if it wins, -1 otherwise. Sometimes, the player needs to push a block *into* a hole in order to *clear* a path to the cheese. Each of the 3 on-line tuning agents greatly improves the win rate (at least 22 times higher) compared to the baseline agent, in particular, SA-MCTS$_{NEA}$, increases the win rate from 0.2% to 13.0%. In a similar tested puzzle game *Bait*, the player needs to push a block to *fill* a hole in order to *build* a path to the cheese. Interestingly, the win rate on *Bait* is not that highly improved, though some significant improvements have been observed.

Crossfire. (Figure 1(c)) The player wins the game if it reaches the exit door without being hit by any shell and gets 5 as game score. Once the player is hit by a shell, the game ends immediately with a loss of the player and -1 as game score. The win rates achieved by the SA-MCTS agents are at least 2 times higher than the one by the baseline agent.

Wait for Breakfast. (Figure 1(d)) In this game, all tables are empty when the game starts, a waiter (NPC in black in Fig. 1(d)) serves a breakfast to the table with only one chair at a random time. The player (avatar in green in Fig. 1(d)) wins the game only if it sits on the chair on the table after the breakfast is served, otherwise (taking a wrong chair or taking the right chair before the breakfast is served), it loses the game. When the waiter serves the breakfast is defined as: at any game tick, if no breakfast is served yet, the waiter serves a breakfast with probability 0.05; the waiter serves at most one breakfast during a whole game playing. The probability of no breakfast has been served 10 game ticks after starting a game is $0.05^{10} = 9.7656e-14$. This game can be considered as a deterministic game. The win rate is significantly improved by all the 3 SA-MCTS agents, among which SA-MCTS$_{NEA}$ increases the win rate from 15.4% to 44.0%.

For reference, the average of median numbers of iterations per game tick for all tested agents are given in Table 3. Note that during one iteration of any of the agents, the forward model is called multiple times.

The most visited combination of the UCB1 exploration factor K and the maximum play-out depth D per game (over 500 runs) for each of the SA-MCTS agents are extracted and listed in Table 4. Surprisingly, the most used play-out depth is 1. The SA-MCTS agents prefers the averaged instant reward than the averaged long-term reward. A possible reason is the heuristic (Eq. 2) used by the agents. Assuming an MCTS agent with maximum play-out depth 10, even for a deterministic game, the number of possible game states after a play-out can increase at most exponentially, the reward after a play-out can vary between a large range due to the same reason. If it is a loss after a play-out, then the average reward obtained by the parameter combinations with $D = 10$ will decrease a lot due to the 10, 000, 000.0 penalty in score; if it is a win, then the average reward

Table 3. Average median number of iterations per tick for the *sampleMCTS* agent and the SA-MCTS agents. The number of forward model calls per iteration depends on the tuner and is sometimes not a constant. For space reasons, headers have been shortened as follows: SA-MCTS$_{NMC}$ = NMC, SA-MCTS$_{EA}$ = EA, SA-MCTS$_{NEA}$ = NEA.

Games	sampleMCTS	NMC	EA	NEA	Games	sampleMCTS	NMC	EA	NEA
Aliens	35.16	41.80	25.46	50.46	Infection	23.77	25.50	21.24	23.72
Bait	70.83	123.71	86.88	154.77	Intersection	35.66	46.83	68.96	39.93
Butterflies	26.97	29.54	24.01	29.32	Lemmings	22.24	36.57	69.07	62.04
Camel Race	21.88	24.55	24.55	24.55	Missile Command	39.08	43.12	52.30	43.78
Chase	29.33	37.49	36.98	45.46	Modality	96.49	104.80	108.51	103.09
Chopper	17.30	22.60	23.63	50.71	Plaque Attack	15.92	18.43	14.75	17.70
Crossfire	19.55	33.68	45.74	52.46	Roguelike	15.45	19.54	20.96	27.61
Dig Dug	14.17	20.24	25.25	34.21	Sea Quest	34.25	45.47	28.55	79.28
Escape	37.75	69.86	96.02	119.70	Survive Zombies	18.43	30.80	47.85	53.12
Hungry Birds	46.37	50.56	52.34	51.32	Wait for Breakfast	83.96	106.30	158.73	178.17

Table 4. Most visited combination of parameters per game for each of the SA-MCTS agents. Parameter combination are expressed with the format $[K, D]$. K refers to the UCB1 exploration factor and D is the maximum play-out depth.

Games	NMC	EA	NEA	Games	NMC	EA	NEA
Aliens	[1.4, 1.0]	[0.6, 15.0]	[0.6, 1.0]	Infection	[1.8, 2.0]	[0.6, 15.0]	[2.0, 15.0]
Bait	[1.1, 1.0]	[0.7, 1.0]	[0.7, 1.0]	Intersection	[1.3, 1.0]	[0.7, 1.0]	[1.2, 15.0]
Butterflies	[1.3, 3.0]	[0.6, 15.0]	[1.6, 13.0]	Lemmings	[0.6, 1.0]	[0.6, 1.0]	[0.6, 1.0]
Camel Race	[1.8, 1.0]	[2.0, 4.0]	[1.4, 14.0]	Missile Command	[0.6, 12.0]	[0.7, 1.0]	[0.8, 15.0]
Chase	[0.7, 1.0]	[0.6, 1.0]	[0.7, 1.0]	Modality	[1.1, 1.0]	[1.0, 4.0]	[0.8, 13.0]
Chopper	[0.6, 1.0]	[0.7, 1.0]	[0.8, 1.0]	Plaque Attack	[0.8, 4.0]	[0.7, 15.0]	[0.7, 15.0]
Crossfire	[0.7, 1.0]	[0.6, 1.0]	[0.7, 1.0]	Roguelike	[0.8, 1.0]	[0.6, 1.0]	[0.7, 1.0]
Dig Dug	[0.7, 1.0]	[0.7, 1.0]	[0.6, 1.0]	Sea Quest	[0.6, 1.0]	[0.6, 15.0]	[1.0, 1.0]
Escape	[1.1, 1.0]	[0.6, 1.0]	[0.6, 1.0]	Survive Zombies	[0.7, 1.0]	[0.6, 1.0]	[0.7, 1.0]
Hungry Birds	[1.4, 13.0]	[2.0, 1.0]	[1.0, 1.0]	Wait for Breakfast	[1.0, 1.0]	[1.0, 1.0]	[0.7, 1.0]

will increase thanks to the $10,000,000.0$ award in score. In the games where a SA-MCTS agent gets a very low win rate, the parameter combinations with $D = 10$ are more likely to have an overall low average reward and prefer a lower maximum play-out depth D, whereas in the games where a SA-MCTS agent gets a high win rate, the parameter combinations with higher D are favorable. For instance, in the game *Plaque Attack*, all agents achieve a win rate higher than 90%, the most visited maximum play-out depth D is 4, 15, and 15 for SA-MCTS$_{NMC}$, SA-MCTS$_{EA}$ and SA-MCTS$_{NEA}$ respectively.

Table 5. Average win rate (%) and average game score over 5 levels for the *sampleMCTS* agent with default parameter values and the *sampleMCTS* agents with the most visited combination per game by each of the SA-MCTS agents. The best values are in bold.

(a) Average win rate (%) over 5 levels for each game

Games	sampleMCTS	instance$_{NMC}$	instance$_{EA}$	instance$_{NEA}$
Aliens	**100.0(±0.00)**	68.0(±4.09)	**100.0(±0.00)**	69.6(±4.04)
Bait	**6.6(±2.18)**	4.2(±1.76)	3.6(±1.63)	3.6(±1.63)
Butterflies	95.2(±1.88)	93.0(±2.24)	**95.4(±1.84)**	95.0(±1.91)
Camel Race	4.2(±1.76)	3.8(±1.68)	**6.0(±2.08)**	4.2(±1.76)
Chase	3.2(±1.54)	6.2(±2.12)	**7.4(±2.30)**	6.2(±2.12)
Chopper	**91.4(±2.46)**	0.0(±0.00)	0.0(±0.00)	0.2(±0.39)
Crossfire	4.2(±1.76)	**9.8(±2.61)**	9.2(±2.54)	**9.8(±2.61)**
Dig Dug	0.0(±0.00)	0.0(±0.00)	0.0(±0.00)	0.0(±0.00)
Escape	0.2(±0.39)	29.4(±4.00)	**30.8(±4.05)**	**30.8(±4.05)**
Hungry Birds	5.4(±1.98)	**5.0(±1.91)**	1.4(±1.03)	2.8(±1.45)
Infection	97.0(±1.50)	97.2(±1.45)	**97.8(±1.29)**	96.6(±1.59)
Intersection	100.0(±0.00)	100.0(±0.00)	100.0(±0.00)	100.0(±0.00)
Lemmings	0.0(±0.00)	0.0(±0.00)	0.0(±0.00)	0.0(±0.00)
Missile Command	60.4(±4.29)	**64.2(±4.21)**	31.8(±4.09)	**64.2(±4.21)**
Modality	27.0(±3.90)	16.0(±3.22)	25.4(±3.82)	**27.2(±3.90)**
Plaque Attack	91.8(±2.41)	67.2(±4.12)	**96.0(±1.72)**	**96.0(±1.72)**
Roguelike	0.0(±0.00)	0.0(±0.00)	0.0(±0.00)	0.0(±0.00)
Sea Quest	55.0(±4.37)	18.2(±3.39)	**58.4(±4.32)**	18.2(±3.39)
Survive Zombies	41.0(±4.32)	28.8(±3.97)	25.4(±3.82)	28.8(±3.97)
Wait for Breakfast	15.4(±3.17)	**60.8(±4.28)**	**60.8(±4.28)**	60.2(±4.29)
Avg Win%	**39.9(±0.96)**	33.6(±0.93)	37.5(±0.95)	35.7(±0.94)

(b) Average score over 5 levels for each game. Note that in GVGAI, wining a game with low score is higher ranked than losing a game with a high score

Games	sampleMCTS	instance$_{NMC}$	instance$_{EA}$	instance$_{NEA}$
Aliens	**67.8(±1.27)**	55.9(±0.90)	64.1(±1.16)	55.8(±0.96)
Bait	2.6(±0.27)	3.0(±0.40)	**3.1(±0.41)**	**3.1(±0.41)**
Butterflies	30.3(±1.34)	**31.1(±1.30)**	30.7(±1.29)	30.8(±1.31)
Camel Race	−0.8(±0.05)	−0.8(±0.04)	**−0.7(±0.05)**	−0.8(±0.05)
Chase	2.7(±0.18)	2.7(±0.20)	**3.0(±0.20)**	2.7(±0.20)
Chopper	**11.4(±0.55)**	−10.6(±0.33)	−10.8(±0.34)	−10.8(±0.33)
Crossfire	**0.1(±0.09)**	−0.3(±0.15)	−0.3(±0.15)	−0.3(±0.15)
Dig Dug	**11.2(±0.79)**	4.9(±0.53)	4.9(±0.53)	4.9(±0.52)
Escape	0.0(±0.00)	**0.3(±0.04)**	**0.3(±0.04)**	**0.3(±0.04)**
Hungry Birds	**7.4(±2.09)**	6.7(±2.01)	2.0(±1.10)	3.0(±1.47)
Infection	**14.3(±0.71)**	12.7(±0.65)	14.0(±0.70)	12.9(±0.62)
Intersection	1.0(±0.00)	6.4(±0.64)	**6.6(±0.63)**	1.0(±0.00)
Lemmings	−3.5(±0.30)	**−0.1(±0.03)**	**−0.1(±0.03)**	**−0.1(±0.03)**
Missile Command	4.4(±0.44)	4.5(±0.44)	0.7(±0.33)	**4.6(±0.46)**
Modality	**0.3(±0.04)**	0.2(±0.03)	**0.3(±0.04)**	**0.3(±0.04)**
Plaque Attack	46.9(±1.64)	31.4(±1.36)	**52.6(±1.59)**	**52.6(±1.59)**
Roguelike	**3.5(±0.41)**	1.8(±0.28)	1.6(±0.26)	1.7(±0.29)
Sea Quest	1734.6(±169.97)	591.2(±98.53)	**1891.8(±177.09)**	583.7(±95.36)
Survive Zombies	**2.6(±0.30)**	2.0(±0.29)	1.8(±0.28)	2.0(±0.29)
Wait for Breakfast	0.2(±0.03)	**0.6(±0.04)**	**0.6(±0.04)**	**0.6(±0.04)**
Avg Score	96.8(±11.25)	37.2(±5.53)	**103.3(±11.96)**	37.4(±5.37)

5.2   On-line Tuning Validation

The most visited parameter combinations during learning are set to the *samplemMCTS* and tested on the same set of games. The parameters are fixed during game playing, so no more tuning happened. We denote these instances of *samplemMCTS* as $instance_{NMC}$, $instance_{EA}$ and $instance_{NEA}$. The average win rate and average final score for the *sampleMCTS* agent with default parameter values and the *sampleMCTS* instances, *sampleMCTS* agents with the most visited combination per game by each of the SA-MCTS agents (cf. Table 4) are presented in Table 5a and b, respectively.

In the game *Escape* (Fig. 1(b)), the win rate is significantly improved from 0.2% (baseline agent) to 30.8% by the $instance_{NEA}$ with parameters tuned by NEA, while the highest win rate of on-line tuning agents is 13.0% by *sampleMCTS$_{NEA}$* (shown in Table 2). In the game *Wait for Breakfast* (Fig. 1(d)), the win rate is significantly improved from 15.4% (baseline) to 60.8% by the $instance_{NMC}$ and $instance_{EA}$, while the highest win rate obtained by the on-line tuning agents is 44.0% by *sampleMCTS$_{NEA}$* (shown in Table 2). However, some instances with constant parameter values performed much worse than the baseline agent in some games. For instance, in the game *Aliens*, the baseline agent ($D = 10$) and $instance_{EA}$ ($D = 15$) win all the games, while $instance_{NMC}$ and $instance_{NEA}$ win $\sim$ 68% games due to the maximum play-out depth $D = 1$. The same scenarios happen in the games *Sea Quest* and *Survive Zombies*. Due to the maximum play-out depth $D = 1$, $instance_{NMC}$, $instance_{EA}$ and $instance_{NEA}$ lose more often the puzzle game *Bait* and lose almost all the 500 runs of *Chopper*. Our SA-MCTS agents are more robust than the non-SA MCTS instances with constant parameter values.

6   Conclusion and Future Work

General Video Game Playing has attracted interest from researchers during the last years. On-line tuning an agent for GVGP provides more adaptive and robust agents, however, it is rather difficult due to the real-time setting. In this paper, we have incorporated three different algorithms, Naïve Monte-Carlo, the Evolutionary Algorithm, and N-Tuple Bandit Evolutionary Algorithm, to tune on-line the *sampleMCTS* agent in the GVGAI framework and create three Self-Adaptive MCTS (SA-MCTS) agents. The SA-MCTS agents have been compared to the baseline MCTS agent, *sampleMCTS*, on 20 single-player GVGAI games. The SA-MCTS agents perform similarly to the *sampleMCTS* on the games that *sampleMCTS* performs well, and significantly improve the win rate in the games that *sampleMCTS* perform poorly. The SA-MCTS agents achieve more robust results on the tested games. Additionally, the *sampleMCTS* instances using most sampled parameter settings by each of the three SA-MCTS agents per game improve the win rate on *Wait for Breakfast* and *Escape* by 4 times and 150 times, respectively.

The approaches used in this paper and the tested tuning strategies have been a success in GVGAI, in particular the tuning strategy NMC has also obtained promising results in GGP. On-line agent tuning for GVGP is important because successful approaches can rapidly improve and specialize the general abilities of the agents, leading to better performance across a wide range of games. The research has application outside of games to any problem that has a fast simulation model and requires rapid and adaptive decision making.

This work can be extended in different directions. Applying the SA-MCTS agents for playing 2-player GVGAI games, where the time limit remains $40ms$, will be interesting. The heuristic (Eq. 2) of *sampleMCTS* is directly used as the reward for tuners. The preference of maximum play-out depth 1 encourages us to explore a better reward function for the tuners. In this paper, we focus on the discrete search space, the search space of the UCB1 exploration factor is discretized by being uniformly sampled within a range using a fixed gap, though that was just an experimental design choice: all algorithms under test can work with any selection of parameter choices. An interesting future work is applying continuous parameter tuning using Evolutionary Strategies (ES), such as the Covariance Matrix Adaptation Evolution Strategy (CMA-ES), which does not rely on the assumption of smooth problem. Another work in the future is tuning a more advanced agent possibly with more parameters to be tuned. A potentially good choice is the winner agent of the 2016 GVGAI Single-Player Planing Championship, *MaastCTS2* [16], which is also MCTS-based. There is also much work to be done in tuning the play-out policy. A particular challenge is to deal more efficiently with flat reward landscapes using methods that seek diverse points in the (game) state space in the absence of any differences in the explicit reward (e.g. Novelty Search). Tuning a non-MCTS-based agent, such as an Rolling Horizon Evolutionary Algorithm, will be interesting and challenging due to the real-time control in evaluating a population. In general, agents with more parameters to be optimized will provide a more challenging test for the sample efficiency of the tuning methods.

Acknowledgments. This work is partially funded by the Netherlands Organisation for Scientific Research (NWO) in the framework of the project GoGeneral, grant number 612.001.121, and the EPSRC IGGI Centre for Doctoral Training, grant number EP/L015846/1.

References

1. Coulom, R.: Efficient selectivity and backup operators in Monte-Carlo Tree Search. In: van den Herik, H.J., Ciancarini, P., Donkers, H.H.L.M.J. (eds.) CG 2006. LNCS, vol. 4630, pp. 72–83. Springer, Heidelberg (2007). https://doi.org/10.1007/978-3-540-75538-8_7

2. Kocsis, L., Szepesvári, C.: Bandit based Monte-Carlo planning. In: Fürnkranz, J., Scheffer, T., Spiliopoulou, M. (eds.) ECML 2006. LNCS (LNAI), vol. 4212, pp. 282–293. Springer, Heidelberg (2006). https://doi.org/10.1007/11871842_29

3. Yannakakis, G.N., Togelius, J.: Artificial Intelligence and Games. Springer (2018), http://gameaibook.org

4. Browne, C.B., Powley, E., Whitehouse, D., Lucas, S.M., Cowling, P.I., Rohlfshagen, P., Tavener, S., Perez, D., Samothrakis, S., Colton, S.: A survey of Monte Carlo tree search methods. IEEE Trans. Comput. Intell. AI Games **4**(1), 1–43 (2012)
5. Helmbold, D.P., Parker-Wood, A.: All-moves-as-first heuristics in Monte-Carlo Go. In: IC-AI, pp. 605–610 (2009)
6. Gelly, S., Silver, D.: Combining online and offline knowledge in UCT. In: Proceedings of the 24th International Conference on Machine Learning, pp. 273–280. ACM (2007)
7. Cazenave, T.: Generalized rapid action value estimation. In: Proceedings of the 24th International Joint Conference on Artificial Intelligence, pp. 754–760. AAAI Press (2015)
8. Sironi, C.F., Winands, M.H.M.: Comparison of rapid action value estimation variants for general game playing. In: 2016 IEEE Conference on Computational Intelligence and Games (CIG), pp. 309–316. IEEE (2016)
9. Finnsson, H., Björnsson, Y.: Simulation-based approach to general game playing. In: AAAI, vol. 8, pp. 259–264 (2008)
10. Powley, E.J., Cowling, P.I., Whitehouse, D.: Information capture and reuse strategies in Monte Carlo tree search, with applications to games of hidden information. Artif. Intell. **217**, 92–116 (2014)
11. Silver, D., Huang, A., Maddison, C.J., Guez, A., Sifre, L., Van Den Driessche, G., Schrittwieser, J., Antonoglou, I., Panneershelvam, V., Lanctot, M., et al.: Mastering the game of Go with deep neural networks and tree search. Nature **529**(7587), 484–489 (2016)
12. Silver, D., Schrittwieser, J., Simonyan, K., Antonoglou, I., Huang, A., Guez, A., Hubert, T., Baker, L., Lai, M., Bolton, A., et al.: Mastering the game of Go without human knowledge. Nature **550**(7676), 354–359 (2017)
13. Björnsson, Y., Finnsson, H.: CadiaPlayer: a simulation-based general game player. IEEE Trans. Comput. Intell. AI Games, **1**(1), 4–15 (2009)
14. Perez-Liebana, D., Samothrakis, S., Togelius, J., Schaul, T., Lucas, S.M., Couëtoux, A., Lee, J., Lim, C.U., Thompson, T.: The 2014 general video game playing competition. IEEE Trans. Comput. Intell. AI Games **8**(3), 229–243 (2016)
15. Gaina, R.D., Couetoux, A., Soemers, D.J.N.J., Winands, M.H.M., Vodopivec, T., Kirchgeßner, F., Liu, J., Lucas, S.M., Perez-Liebana, D.: The 2016 two-player GVGAI competition. IEEE Trans. Comput. Intell. AI Games (2017, accepted for publication)
16. Soemers, D.J.N.J., Sironi, C.F., Schuster, T., Winands, M.H.M.: Enhancements for real-time Monte-Carlo tree search in general video game playing. In: 2016 IEEE Conference on Computational Intelligence and Games (CIG), pp. 1–8. IEEE (2016)
17. Gaina, R.D., Liu, J., Lucas, S.M., Pérez-Liébana, D.: Analysis of vanilla rolling horizon evolution parameters in general video game playing. In: Squillero, G., Sim, K. (eds.) EvoApplications 2017. LNCS, vol. 10199, pp. 418–434. Springer, Cham (2017). https://doi.org/10.1007/978-3-319-55849-3_28
18. Bravi, I., Khalifa, A., Holmgård, C., Togelius, J.: Evolving game-specific UCB alternatives for general video game playing. In: Squillero, G., Sim, K. (eds.) EvoApplications 2017. LNCS, vol. 10199, pp. 393–406. Springer, Cham (2017). https://doi.org/10.1007/978-3-319-55849-3_26
19. Sironi, C.F., Winands, M.H.M.: On-line parameters tuning for Monte-Carlo tree search in general game playing. In: 6th Workshop on Computer Games (CGW) (2017)
20. Liu, J., Perez-Liebana, D., Lucas, S.M.: The single-player GVGAI learning framework - technical manual (2017)

21. Khalifa, A., Perez-Liebana, D., Lucas, S.M., Togelius, J.: General video game level generation. In: Proceedings of the 2016 on Genetic and Evolutionary Computation Conference, pp. 253–259. ACM (2016)
22. Khalifa, A., Green, M.C., Perez-Liebana, D., Togelius, J.: General video game rule generation. In: 2017 IEEE Conference on Computational Intelligence and Games (CIG), pp. 170–177. IEEE (2017)
23. Ebner, M., Levine, J., Lucas, S.M., Schaul, T., Thompson, T., Togelius, J.: Towards a video game description language. In: Dagstuhl Follow-Ups, vol. 6. Schloss Dagstuhl-Leibniz-Zentrum fuer Informatik (2013)
24. Bellemare, M.G., Naddaf, Y., Veness, J., Bowling, M.: The arcade learning environment: an evaluation platform for general agents. J. Artif. Intell. Res. (JAIR) **47**, 253–279 (2013)
25. Auer, P., Cesa-Bianchi, N., Fischer, P.: Finite-time analysis of the multiarmed bandit problem. Mach. Learn. **47**(2–3), 235–256 (2002)
26. Ontanón, S.: Combinatorial multi-armed bandits for real-time strategy games. J. Artif. Intell. Res. **58**, 665–702 (2017)
27. Kunanusont, K., Gaina, R.D., Liu, J., Perez-Liebana, D., Lucas, S.M.: The n-tuple bandit evolutionary algorithm for automatic game improvement. In: 2017 IEEE Congress on Evolutionary Computation (CEC). IEEE (2017)
28. Perez-Liebana, D., Liu, J., Lucas, S.M.: General video game AI as a tool for game design. In: Tutorial at IEEE Conference on Computational Intelligence and Games (CIG) (2017)
29. Nelson, M.J.: Investigating vanilla MCTS scaling on the GVG-AI game corpus. In: Proceedings of the 2016 IEEE Conference on Computational Intelligence and Games, pp. 403–409 (2016)
30. Bontrager, P., Khalifa, A., Mendes, A., Togelius, J.: Matching games and algorithms for general video game playing. In: Twelfth Artificial Intelligence and Interactive Digital Entertainment Conference, pp. 122–128 (2016)

Deceptive Games

Damien Anderson[1(✉)] ⓘ, Matthew Stephenson[2], Julian Togelius[3],
Christoph Salge[3], John Levine[1], and Jochen Renz[2]

[1] Computer and Information Science Department,
University of Strathclyde, Glasgow, UK
Damien.Anderson@strath.ac.uk
[2] Research School of Computer Science, Australian National University,
Canberra, Australia
[3] NYU Game Innovation Lab, Tandon School of Engineering,
New York University, New York, USA

Abstract. Deceptive games are games where the reward structure or other aspects of the game are designed to lead the agent away from a globally optimal policy. While many games are already deceptive to some extent, we designed a series of games in the Video Game Description Language (VGDL) implementing specific types of deception, classified by the cognitive biases they exploit. VGDL games can be run in the General Video Game Artificial Intelligence (GVGAI) Framework, making it possible to test a variety of existing AI agents that have been submitted to the GVGAI Competition on these deceptive games. Our results show that all tested agents are vulnerable to several kinds of deception, but that different agents have different weaknesses. This suggests that we can use deception to understand the capabilities of a game-playing algorithm, and game-playing algorithms to characterize the deception displayed by a game.

Keywords: Games · Tree search · Reinforcement learning · Deception

1 Introduction

1.1 Motivation

What makes a game difficult for an Artificial Intelligence (AI) agent? Or, more precisely, how can we design a game that is difficult for an agent, and what can we learn from doing so?

Early AI and games research focused on games with known rules and full information, such as Chess [15] or Go. The game-theoretic approaches [17] to these games, such as min-max, are constrained by high branching factors and large computational complexity. When Deep Blue surpassed the top humans in Chess [3], the game Go was still considered very hard, partly due to its much larger branching factor. Also, the design of Arimaa [14], built to be deliberately difficult for AI agents, relies heavily on an even higher branching factor than Go.

© Springer International Publishing AG, part of Springer Nature 2018
K. Sim and P. Kaufmann (Eds.): EvoApplications 2018, LNCS 10784, pp. 376–391, 2018.
https://doi.org/10.1007/978-3-319-77538-8_26

But increasing the game complexity is not the only way to make games more difficult. To demonstrate this we will here focus on old arcade games, such as Sokoban, Dig Dug or Space invaders, which can be implemented in VGDL. Part of the motivation for the development of VGDL and GVGAI was the desire to create a generic interface that would allow the same AIs to play a range of different games. GVGAI competitions have been held annually since 2013, resulting in an openly accessible corpus of games and AI agents that can play them (with varying proficiency).

VGDL games have relatively similar game complexity: the branching factor is identical (there are six possible actions) and the game state space is not too different between games because of the similar-sized levels. Yet, if we look at how well different agents do on different games we can see that complexity is not the only factor for game difficulty. Certain games seem to be very easy, while others are nearly impossible to master for all existing agents. These effects are still present if the agents are given considerably more time which could compensate for complexity [8]. Further analyses also shows that games cannot easily be ordered by difficulty, as agents based on different types of algorithms seem to have problems with different games—there is a distinct non-transitivity in performance rankings [2]. This raises the question of what makes a game difficult for a specific agent but not for others?

One way to explain this is to consider that there are several methods for constructing agents to play games. One can train a function approximator to map from a state observation to an action using reinforcement learning algorithms based on approximate dynamic programming (the temporal difference family of methods), policy gradients or artificial evolution; alternatively, and complementary, if you have a forward model of the game you can use tree search or evolution to search for action sequences that maximize some utility [20]. Additionally, there are hybrid algorithms combining elements from several of these methods, such as the very successful AlphaGo [13] system which combines supervised learning, approximate dynamic programming and Monte Carlo Tree Search.

A commonality between these game-playing methods is that they rely on rewards to guide their search and/or learning. Policies are learned to maximize the expected reward, and when a model is available, action sequences are selected for the same criterion. Fortunately, rewards are typically well-defined in games: gaining score is good, losing lives or getting hurt is bad. Indeed, one of the reasons for the popularity of games as AI testbeds is that many of them have well-defined rewards (they can also be simulated cheaply, safely and speedily). But it's not enough for there to be rewards; the rewards can be structured in different ways. For example, one of the key problems in reinforcement learning research, credit allocation, is how to assign reward to the correct action given that the reward frequently occurs long after the action was taken.

Recently, much work has gone into devising reinforcement learning algorithms that can learn to play simple arcade games, and they generally have good performance on games that have short time lags between actions and rewards. For comparison, a game such as *Montezuma's Revenge* on the Atari 2600, where there is a long time lag between actions and rewards, provides a very hard challenge for all known reinforcement learning algorithms.

It is not only a matter of the time elapsed between action and reward; rewards can be more or less helpful. The reward structure of a game can be such that taking the actions the lead to the highest rewards in the short-to-medium term leads to lower overall rewards, i.e. playing badly. For example, if you spend all your time collecting coins in *Super Mario Bros*, you will likely run out of time. This is not too unlike the situation in real life where if you optimize your eating policy for fat and sugar you are likely to achieve suboptimal global nutritional reward. Designing a reward structure that leads an AI away from the optimal policy can be seen as a form of deception, one that makes the game harder, regardless of the underlying game complexity. If we see the reward function as a heuristic function approximating the (inverse) distance from a globally optimal policy, a deceptive reward function is an *inadmissible heuristic*.

1.2   Biases, Deception and Optimization

In order to understand why certain types or agents are weak against certain kinds of deceptions it is helpful to consider different types of deception through the lens of cognitive biases. Deceptive games can be seen as exploiting a specific cognitive bias[1] of the (human or AI) player to trick them into making a suboptimal decision. Withholding or providing false information is a form of deception, and can be very effective at sabotaging a player's performance. In this paper though, we want to focus on games where the player or AI has full access to both the current game state and the rules (forward model). Is it still possible to design a game with these constraints that tricks an artificial agent? If we were facing an agent with unlimited resources, the answer would be no, as unbounded computational resources makes deception impossible: an exhaustive search that considers all possible action sequences and rates them by their fully modeled probabilistic expected outcome will find the optimal strategy. Writing down what a unbounded rational agent should do is not difficult. In reality, both humans and AI agents have bounded rationality in that they are limited in terms of computational resources, time, memory, etc.

To compensate for this, artificial intelligence techniques rely on approximations or heuristics that are easier to compute and still return a better answer than random. In a naive interpretation, this seems to violate the free lunch theorem. This is still a viable approach though if one only deals with a subset of all possible problems. These assumptions about the problems one encounters can be turned into helpful cognitive biases. In general, and in the right context, this is a viable cognitive strategy - one that has been shown to be effective for both humans and AI agents [6,16]. But reasoning based on these assumptions also makes one susceptible to deceptions - problems that violate this assumption and

---

[1] To simplify the text we talk about the game as if it has agency and intentions; in truth the intentions and agency lies with the game's designer, and all text should be understood in this regard.

are designed in a way so that the, now mistaken, assumption leads the player to a suboptimal answer. Counter-intuitively, this means that the more sophisticated an AI agent becomes, the better it is at exploiting typical properties of the environment, the more susceptible it becomes to specific deceptions based on those cognitive biases.

This phenomenon can be related to the No Free Lunch theorem for search and optimization, which implies that, given limited time, making an agent perform better on a particular class of search problems will make it perform worse on others (because over all possible search problems, all agents will perform the same) [19]. Of course, some search algorithms are in practice better than others, because many "naturally occurring" problems tend to fall in a relatively restricted class where deception is limited. Within evolutionary computation, the phenomenon of deceptive optimization problems is well-defined and relatively well-studied, and it has been claimed that the only hard optimization problems are the deceptive ones [4,18].

For humans, the list of cognitive biases is quite extensive, and subsequently, there are many different deception strategies for tricking humans. Here we focus on agent which have their own specific sets of biases. Identifying those cognitive biases via deceptive games can help us to both categorize those agents, and help us to figure out what they are good at, and on what problem they should be used. Making the link to human biases could also help us to understand the underlying assumptions humans use, enabling us to learn from human mistakes what shortcuts humans take to be more efficient than AIs.

1.3   Overview

The rest of this paper is structured as follows. We first outline some AI-specific deceptions based on our understanding of current game-playing algorithms. We present a non-exhaustive list of those, based on their assumptions and vulnerabilities. We then introduce several new VGDL games, designed to specifically deceive the existing AI algorithms. We test a range of existing agents from the GVGAI framework on our new deceptive games and discuss the results.

2   Background

2.1   Categories of Deception

By linking specific cognitive biases to types of deception we can categorize different deceptive games and try to predict which agents would perform well on them. We can also construct deceptive games aimed at exploiting a specific weakness. The following is a non-exhaustive list of possible AI biases and their associated traps, exemplified with some of the games we present here.

Greed Trap: A common problem simplification is to only consider the effect of our actions for a limited future. These greedy algorithms usually aim to maximize some immediate reward and rely on the assumption that the local reward gradient will guide them to a global maximum. One way to specifically exploit this bias (a greedy trap) is to design a game with an accumulated reward and then use some initial small reward to trick the player into an action that will make a later, larger reward unattainable. The later mentioned *DeceptiCoins* and *Sister Saviour* are examples of this. Delayed rewards, such as seen in *Invest* and *Flower*, are a subtype. In that case, an action has a positive reward that is only awarded much later. This can be used to construct a greedy trap by combining it with a smaller, more immediate reward. This also challenges algorithms that want to attach specific rewards to actions, such as reinforcement learning.

Smoothness Trap: Several AI techniques also rely on the assumption that good solutions are "close" to other good solutions. Genetic Algorithms, for example, assume a certain smoothness of the fitness landscape and MCTS algorithms outperform uninformed random tree search because they bias their exploration towards branches with more promising results. This assumption can be exploited by deliberately hiding the optimal solutions close to a many really bad solutions. In the example of *DeceptiZelda* the player has two paths to the goal. One is a direct, safe, low reward route to the exit which can be easily found. The other is a long route, passing by several deadly hazards but incurring a high reward if the successful route is found. Since many of the solutions along the dangerous part lead to losses, an agent operating with the smoothness bias might be disinclined to investigate this direction further, and would therefore not find the much better solution. This trap is different from the greedy trap, as it aims at agents that limit their evaluation not by a temporal horizon, but by only sampling a subset of all possible futures.

Generality Trap: Another way to make decision-making in games more manageable, both for humans and AI agents, is to generalize from particular situations. Rather than learning or determining how to interact with a certain object in every possible context, an AI can be more efficient by developing a generalized rule. For example, if there is a sprite that kills the avatar, avoiding that sprite as a general rule might be sensible. A generality trap can exploit this by providing a game environment in which such a rule is sensible, but for few critical exceptions. *WafterThinMints* aims to realize this, as eating mints gives the AI points unless too many are eaten. So the agent has to figure out that it should eat a lot of them, but then stop, and change its behavior towards the mints. Agents that would evaluate the gain in reward greedily might not have a problem here, but agents that try to develop sophisticated behavioral rules should be weak to this deception.

2.2 Other Deceptions

As pointed out, this list is non-exhaustive. We deliberately excluded games with hidden or noisy information. Earlier GVGAI studies have looked at the question of robustness [11], where the forward model sometimes gives false information. But this random noise is still different from a deliberate withholding of game information, or even from adding noise in a way to maximize the problems for the AI.

We should also note that most of the deceptions implemented here are focused on exploiting the reward structure given by the game to trick AIs that are optimized for actual rewards. Consider though, that recent developments in intrinsically motivated AIs have introduced ideas such as curiosity-driven AIs to play games such as *Montezuma's Revenge* [1] or *Super Mario* [9]. The internal curiosity reward enhances the AI's gameplay, by providing a gradient in a flat extrinsic reward landscape, but in itself makes the AI susceptible to deception. One could design a game that specifically punished players for exploration.

3   Experimental Setup

3.1   The GVGAI Framework

The General Video Game AI competition is a competition focused on developing AI agents that can play real-time video games; agents are tested on unseen games, to make sure that the developer of the agent cannot tailor it to a particular game [12]. All current GVGAI games are created in VGDL, which was developed particularly to make rapid and even automated game development possible [5]. The competition began with a single planning track which provided agents with a forward model to simulate future states but has since expanded to include other areas, such as a learning track, a rule generation track, and a level generation track [10].

In order to analyze the effects of game deception on GVGAI agent performance, a number of games were created (in VGDL) that implemented various types of deception in a relatively "pure" form. This section briefly explains the goal of each game and the reasons for its inclusion. In order to determine whether an agent had selected the rational path or not, requirements were set based on the agent's performance, which is detailed in this section also.

3.2   DeceptiCoins (DC)

The idea behind *DeceptiCoins* is to offer agents two options for which path to take. The first path has some immediate rewards and leads to a win condition. The second path similarly leads to a win condition but has a higher cumulative reward along its path, which is not immediately visible to a short-sighted agent. Once a path is selected by the agent, a wall closes behind them and they are no longer able to choose the alternative path.

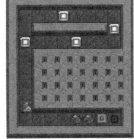

Fig. 1. The first level of DeceptiCoins   **Fig. 2.** The second level of DeceptiCoins   **Fig. 3.** The third level of DeceptiCoins

In order for the performance of an agent to be considered rational in this game, the agent must choose the path with the greatest overall reward. In Fig. 1, this rational path is achieved by taking the path to the right of the agent, as it will lead to the highest amount of score.

Two alternative levels were created for this game. These levels are similar in how the rules of the game work, but attempt to model situations where an agent may get stuck on a suboptimal path by not planning correctly. Level 2, shown in Fig. 2, adds some enemies to the game which will chase the agent. The agents need to carefully plan out their moves in order to avoid being trapped and losing the game. Level 3, shown in Fig. 3 has a simple path which leads to the win condition, and a risky path that leads to large rewards. Should the agent be too greedy and take too much reward, the enemies in the level will close off the path to the win condition and the agent will lose.

The sprites used are as follows:

– 🦊 Avatar - Represents the player/agent in the game.
– 🔲 Gold Coin - Awards a point if collected.
– 🅖 G Square - Leads to winning the game when interacted with.
– 🐟 Piranha - Enemies, if the avatar interacts with these, the game is lost.

The rational paths for level 2 and 3 are defined as reaching the win condition of the level, while also collecting a minimum amount of reward (5 for level 2 and 10 for level 3).

3.3   DeceptiZelda (DZ)

DeceptiZelda looks at the risk vs reward behavior of the GVGAI agents. As in *DeceptiCoins*, two paths are presented to the agent, with one leading to a quick victory and the other leading to a large reward, if the hazards are overcome. The hazards in this game are represented as moving enemies which must either be defeated or avoided.

Two levels for this game were created as shown in Figs. 5 and 4. The first level presents the agent with a choice of going to the right, collecting the key and

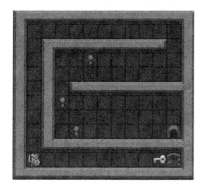

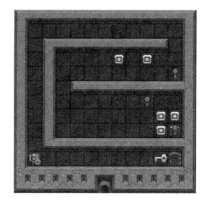

Fig. 4. The first level of Deceptizelda   **Fig. 5.** The second level of Deceptizelda

exiting the level immediately without tackling any of the enemies. The second path leading up takes the agent through a hazardous corridor where they must pass the enemies to reach the alternative goal. The second level uses the same layout but instead of offering a win condition, a lot of collectible rewards are offered to the agent, who must collect these and then return to the exit.

The sprites used are as follows:

-  Avatar: Represents the player/agent in the game.
- Spider: The enemies to overcome. If defeated awards 2 points.
- Key: Used to unlock the first exit. Awards a point if collected.
- Gold Coin: Awards a point to the agent if collected.
- Closed Door: The low value exit. Awards a point if moved into.
- Open Door: The high value exit. Awards 10 points if moved into.

The rational path for this game is defined as successfully completing the path with the most risk. In the first level, this is defined as achieving at least 10 points and winning the game. This can be done by taking the path leading up and reaching the exit beyond the enemies. The second level of *DeceptiZelda* is played on the same map, but instead of offering a higher reward win condition, a large amount of reward is available, and the agent has to then backtrack to the single exit in the level. This level can be seen in Fig. 5.

3.4   Butterflies (BF)

Butterflies is one of the original games for the GVGAI that prompted the beginning of this work. This game presents a situation where if the agent aims for the win condition too quickly, they will lower their maximum potential score for the level. The goal of the game is simple; collect all of the butterflies before they reach their cocoons, which in turn creates more butterflies. To solve the game all that is required is that every butterfly is collected. Each collected butterfly

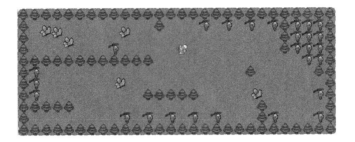

Fig. 6. The first level of Butterflies

grants a small reward to the agent. If the agent is able to defend a single cocoon and wait until all other cocoons have been spawned, there will be the maximum number of butterflies available to gain reward from. So long as the last cocoon is not touched by a butterfly, the game can still be won, but now a significantly higher score is possible. The level used is shown in Fig. 6.

The sprites used are as follows:

– 🦋 Avatar: Represents the player/agent in the game.
– 🦋 Butterfly: Awards 2 points if collected.
– 🐚 Cocoon: If a butterfly interacts with these, more butterflies are created.

The rational path for *Butterflies* is defined as any win condition with a final score over 30. This is achieved by allowing more than half of the cocoons to be spawned and then winning the level.

3.5 SisterSaviour (SS)

The concept of *SisterSaviour* was to present a moral choice to the agent. There are 3 hostages to rescue in each level, and a number of enemies guarding them, as shown in Fig. 7. It is not possible for the agent to defeat these enemies immediately. The agent is given a choice of either rescuing the hostages or killing them. If the agent chooses to rescue the hostages they receive a small reward and will be able to defeat the enemies, which grants a large point reward. On the other hand, if the agent chooses to kill the hostages, they are granted a larger reward immediately, but now lack the power to defeat the enemies and will lose the game.

The sprites used are as follows:

– 🧍 Avatar: Represents the player/agent in the game.
– 🦂 Scorpion: An enemy which chases the avatar. Immune to attacks from the avatar, unless all of the hostages have been rescued. Awards 14 points if defeated.
– 🧍 Hostage: Can be either killed, by attacking them or rescued by moving into their space. Awards 2 points if killed, and 1 point if rescued. If all are rescued then the avatar can kill the enemy.

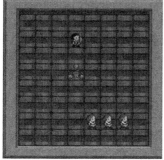

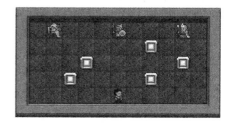

Fig. 7. The first level of SisterSaviour

Fig. 8. The first level of Invest

The rational path for *SisterSaviour* is defined as reaching a score of 20. This involves rescuing all of the hostages, by moving the avatar onto their space, and then defeating the enemy.

3.6 Invest (Inv)

Invest looks at the ability of a GVGAI agent to spend their accumulated reward, with the possibility of receiving a larger reward in the future. This game is shown in Fig. 8. The agent begins with a set number of points which need to be collected from the level, which can then be spent on investment options. This is done by moving onto one of the 3 human characters to the north of the level. Investing will deduct an amount from their current score, acting as an immediate penalty, and will trigger an event to occur at a random point in the future where the agent will receive a large score reward. Should the agent invest too much, and go into a negative score, then the game is lost, otherwise, they will eventually win. The interesting point of this game was how much reward they accumulate over the time period that they have, and would they overcome any loss adversity in order to gain higher overall rewards?

The sprites used are as follows:

-  Avatar: Represents the player/agent in the game.
- Gold Coin: Awards a point when collected.
- Green Investment: Takes 3 points when moved onto, returns 8.
- Red Investment: Takes 7 points when moved onto, returns 15.
- Blue Investment: Takes 5 points when moved onto, returns 10.

The rational path in *Invest* is defined as investing any amount of score successfully without suffering a loss.

3.7 Flower (Flow)

Flower is a game which was designed to offer small immediate rewards, and progressively larger rewards if some time is allowed to pass for the reward to grow.

As shown in Fig. 9, a single seed is available for the agent to collect, which is worth 0 points. As time passes the value of the seed increases as it grows into a full flower, from 0 up to 10. Once collected, the seed will begin to regrow, starting from 0 again. The rational solution for this game is to wait for a seed to grow into a full flower, worth 10 points, and then collecting it.

The sprites used are as follows:

- 🦸 Avatar: Represents the player/agent in the game.
- 🌱 Seed: Awards 0 points initially, but this increases up to 10.

The rational path in *Flower* is defined as achieving a score of at least 30. This can only be done by allowing the flower to grow to at least the second stage and consistently collecting at that level.

3.8   WaferThinMints (Mints)

WaferThinMints introduces the idea that gathering too much reward can lead to a loss condition. The agent has to gather resources in order to increase their reward, but if they collect too many they will die and lose the game.

Two variants of this game were created. One which includes an exit from the level, shown in Fig. 11, and one that does not, shown in Fig. 10. These variants were created in order to provide a comparison of the effect that the deception in the level has on overall agent performance.

The sprites used are as follows:

- 🦸 Avatar: Represents the player/agent in the game.
- 🧀 Cheese: Awards a point when collected. If 9 have been collected already, then the 10th will kill the avatar causing a loss.
- 🚪 Exit: Leads to a win condition when moved into.

The rational path for both versions of the game is defined as collecting a score of 9, and then either waiting for the timeout, in level 1 or exiting the game, in level 2.

4   Experiments and Results

The agents used were collected from the GVGAI competitions. Criteria for selection were the uniqueness of the algorithm used and competition ranking in the past. The hardware used for all of the experiments was a Ubuntu 14.04 desktop PC with an i7-4790 CPU and 16 GB Ram.

Each agent was run 10 times on each level of the deceptive games outlined in Sect. 3. If an agent was disqualified for any reason it was given another run to collect 10 successful results for each game and agent. In addition to comparing these performance statistics, observations were made on the choices that the agents made when faced with potentially deceptive choices. Each game's rational path is defined in Sect. 3. The results of these experiments are shown in Fig. 12.

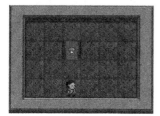

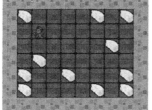

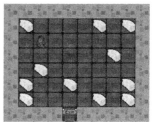

Fig. 9. The first level of Flower

Fig. 10. The first level of WaferThinMints

Fig. 11. The second level of WaferThinMints

Each game was played a total of 360 times. The totals at the bottom of the table show how many of those games were completed using the defined rational path. The results are ranked in descending order by their number of rational trials, and then the number of games where they managed to play with 100% rationality.

Noticeably from the initial results is that no single algorithm was able to solve all the games, with *DeceptiZelda* and *SisterSaviour* being particularly challenging. Furthermore, no single algorithm dominated all others in all games. For Example, IceLab, the top agent in overall results, only has 2 rational trials in *Butterflies*, compared to 9 for Greedy Search, which is in the 33rd place. In general, the results for *Butterflies* are interesting, as top agents perform poorly compared to some of the lower ranking agents.

Butterflies also has a good spread of results, with all but 4 of the algorithms being able to find the rational path at least once. While many of the algorithms are able to make some progress with the game, only 2 are able to achieve 100% rationality.

There is an interesting difference in the performance of agents between *DeceptiCoins* level 1 and 2. The agents that performed well in *Decepticoins* 1 seemed to perform significantly worse in level 2. The requirements of the levels are quite different which appears to have a significant effect on the agents. If a ranking was done with only the performance of *DeceptiCoins* level 2 then IceLab, the 1st ranked in this experiment, would be in the bottom half of the results table.

The hardest games for the agents to solve were *DeceptiZelda* levels 1 and 2, and *SisterSaviour*. *DeceptiZeldas* levels had only 4 and 13 runs solved respectively, and *SisterSaviour* having 14. These games present interesting challenges to the agents, with the rational solution requiring a combination of long-range planning and sacrificing apparent reward for the superior, long-range goal.

Another interesting case here is Mints, the only game in our set with a generalization trap. Most algorithms do well in Mints, suggesting that they do not generalize. This is to be expected, as a tree search algorithm does not in itself generalize from one state to another. But bladerunner, AtheneAI, and SJA86 completely fail at these games, even though they perform reasonably well otherwise. This suggests that they perform some kind of surrogate modeling of game states, relying on a generality assumption that this game breaks.

Agent Name	DC1	DC 2	DC 3	DZ 1	DZ 2	SS	BF	Flow	Inv	Mints 1	Mints 2	Rational
1. IceLab	10	2	10	0	0	0	2	10	10	10	10	8
2. Return42	10	1	7	0	0	2	1	10	10	10	0	8
3. MH2015	2	4	5	1	3	0	5	0	1	10	0	8
4. YoloBot	10	3	10	0	0	0	6	6	0	10	10	7
5. jaydee	9	6	9	0	0	0	1	10	0	10	3	7
6. NovTea	3	4	10	0	0	6	3	2	0	10	0	7
7. number27	0	5	4	0	1	0	4	6	3	10	0	7
8. YBCriber	10	5	10	0	0	0	0	0	10	10	10	6
9. adrienctx	0	3	4	0	0	0	1	10	0	10	10	6
10. TeamTopBug	9	5	10	0	0	0	1	10	0	10	0	6
11. Catlinux	0	7	10	0	4	0	6	7	0	10	0	6
12. muzzle	6	2	1	0	0	0	3	0	10	10	0	6
13. novelTS	1	4	10	0	0	0	3	0	4	10	0	6
14. bladerunner	10	4	8	0	3	0	1	0	10	0	0	6
15. maastCTS2	0	2	0	2	0	0	3	3	1	10	0	6
16. SJA86	1	1	0	0	1	0	9	6	0	1	0	6
17. Catlinux3	0	3	10	0	0	0	10	8	0	10	0	5
18. aStar	2	1	0	0	0	0	0	10	10	10	0	5
19. AtheneAI	10	6	0	1	0	0	10	0	10	0	0	5
20. Rooot	0	1	7	0	0	0	7	10	0	10	0	5
21. SJA862	3	0	7	0	0	0	3	0	10	10	0	5
22. roskvist	0	2	0	0	0	0	5	2	0	10	3	5
23. EvolutionStrategies	0	1	1	0	0	0	3	5	0	10	0	5
24. AlJim	0	1	0	0	0	0	9	1	5	5	0	5
25. HillClimber	2	0	0	0	0	0	7	3	1	0	1	5
26. MnMCTS	0	1	0	0	1	0	6	0	8	6	0	5
27. mrtndwrd	0	0	0	0	0	4	3	4	0	10	0	4
28. simulatedAnnealing	4	0	0	0	0	0	8	4	0	0	1	4
29. TomVodo	3	0	0	0	0	0	5	5	0	4	0	4
30. ToVo1	1	0	0	0	0	0	9	1	0	9	0	4
31. Thorbjrn	0	4	5	0	0	0	9	0	1	0	0	4
32. BFS	0	1	0	0	0	0	5	0	10	0	0	3
33. Greedy Search	10	0	0	0	0	0	9	0	0	0	0	2
34. IterativeDeepening	0	0	0	0	0	2	1	0	0	0	0	2
35. Catlinux4	0	0	0	0	0	0	0	0	10	0	0	1
36. DFS	0	0	0	0	0	0	0	0	0	0	0	0
Totals	116	79	138	4	13	14	158	133	124	235	48	

Fig. 12. The results of the first experiment

The inclusion of an accessible win condition in *Mints 2* also dramatically reduced the number of algorithms that achieved the maximum amount of score, from 26 to 8. This seems to be due to also introducing a specific greed trap that most algorithms seem to be susceptible too - namely preferring to win the game outright, over accumulating more score.

Note that, the final rankings of this experiment differ quite significantly from the official rankings on the GVGAI competition. It is important to note that a different ranking algorithm is used in the competition, which may account for some of the differences observed. Many of the agents have a vastly different level of performance in these results compared to the official rankings. First of all, IceLab and MH2015 have historically appeared low in the official rankings, with their highest ranks being 10th place. The typical high ranking algorithms in the official competition seem to have been hit a bit harder by the new set of games. Yolobot, Return42, maastCTS2, YBCriber, adrienctx and number27 tend to feature in the top 5 positions of the official rankings, and have now finished in positions 2, 4, 15, 8, 9, and 7. For them to lose their positions in this new set of games could show how the games can be constructed to alter the performance of agents [10,12].

Agent Name	Algorithm	DC 1	DC 2	DC 3	DZ 1	DZ 2	SS	BF	Flow	Inv	Mints	Mints 2	Rational
1. IceLab	Portfolio	20	3	19	0	0	0	9	20	2	20	20	8
2. Return42	Portfolio	20	3	13	0	0	4	5	20	20	20	0	8
3. MH2015	GA	2	10	10	2	3	0	11	0	6	20	0	8
4. SJA86	MCTS	1	2	0	2	1	0	17	10	16	8	0	8
5. YBCriber	Portfolio	20	9	20	0	0	0	2	0	20	20	20	7
6. YoloBot	Portfolio	20	8	20	0	0	0	12	13	0	20	20	7
7. Catlinux	GA	0	10	20	2	4	0	15	15	0	20	0	7
8. muzzle	GA	12	3	2	0	0	1	10	0	20	20	0	7
9. NovTea	Tree	8	7	20	0	0	12	9	3	0	20	0	7
10. SJA862	MinMax	8	3	13	0	0	0	8	2	20	20	0	7
11. number27	Portfolio	0	9	6	0	1	0	11	12	5	20	0	7
12. adrienctx	MCTS	0	5	10	0	0	0	7	20	0	20	20	6
13. TeamTopBug	GA	19	9	20	0	0	0	3	20	0	20	0	6
14. bladerunner	Portfolio	20	6	12	4	5	0	3	0	0	0	0	6
15. EvolutionStrategies	GA	0	1	1	0	0	0	3	8	0	20	1	6
16. HillClimber	Hill	3	0	0	0	0	0	13	6	8	1	1	6
17. aStar	A*	4	1	0	0	0	0	0	20	20	20	0	5
18. novelTS	Tree	2	5	20	0	0	0	8	0	0	20	0	5
19. TomVodo	MCTS	5	0	0	0	0	0	14	8	3	8	0	5
20. mrtndwrd	MCTS/A*	0	0	0	0	0	9	9	7	0	20	0	4
21. simulatedAnnealing	SA	8	0	0	0	0	0	14	10	0	0	1	4
22. Greedy Search	Tree	20	0	0	0	0	0	10	0	0	0	0	2
23. BFS	Best First	0	1	0	0	0	0	8	0	0	0	0	2
24. IterativeDeepening	ID	0	0	0	0	0	3	1	0	0	0	0	2
25. DFS	Depth	0	0	0	0	0	3	0	0	0	0	0	1
Total Clever		192	95	206	10	14	32	202	194	140	337	83	

Fig. 13. The results of the second experiment.

In order to look at the effect of deception on specific types of algorithms, such as genetic algorithms (GA) or Tree Search techniques, a second set of experiments were performed. A selection of algorithms were ran an additional 10 times on each of the games, and each algorithm was investigated to identify the core component of its operation. It should be noted that these classifications are simple, and an in-depth analysis of the specifics used by the algorithms might reveal some further insights. The results for these experiments are shown in Fig. 13.

These results show a number of interesting observations. First of all, for *DeceptiZelda*1 and 2 it appears that agents using a genetic algorithm perform better than most other approaches, but do poorly compared to tree search techniques at *SisterSaviour*. Portfolio search agents, which employ different algorithms for different games or situations, take the top two positions of the table and place quite highly overall compared to single algorithm solutions.

5   Discussion and Future Work

The results suggest that the types of deception presented in the games have differing effects on the performance of different algorithms. The fact that algorithms, that are more sophisticated and usually perform well in the regular competition are not on top of the rankings is also in line with our argument, that they employ sophisticated assumptions and heuristics, and are subsequently susceptible to deception. Based on the data we have now it would be possible to build a game to defeat any of the agents on the list, and it seems possible to design a specific set of games that would put any specific AI at the bottom of the table. The difficulty of a game is, therefore, a property that is, at least in part, only well defined in regards to a specific AI.

In regards to categorization, it seems there is a certain degree of similarity between groups of games and groups of AIs that perform similarly, but a more in-depth analysis would be needed to determine what exact weakness each AI has. The games in this corpus already contain, like *Mints 2*, a mixture of different deceptions. Similarly, the more sophisticated agents also employ hybrid strategies and some, like YoloBot, switch between different AI approaches based on the kind of game they detect [7]. One way to explore this further would be to use a genetic algorithm to create new VGDL games, with a fitness function rewarding a set of games that can maximally discriminate between the existing algorithms.

There are also further possibilities for deception that we did not explore here. Limiting access to the game state, or even requiring agents to actually learn how the game mechanics work open up a whole new range of deception possibilities. This would also allow us to extend this approach to other games, which might not provide the agent with a forward model, or might require the agent to deal with incomplete or noisy sensor information about the world.

Another way to deepen this approach would be to extend the metaphor about human cognitive biases. Humans have a long list of cognitive biases - most of them connected to some reasonable assumption about the world, or more specifically, typical games. By analyzing what biases humans have in this kind of games we could try to develop agents that use similar simplification assumptions to humans and thereby make better agents.

References

1. Bellemare, M., Srinivasan, S., Ostrovski, G., Schaul, T., Saxton, D., Munos, R.: Unifying count-based exploration and intrinsic motivation. In: Advances in Neural Information Processing Systems, pp. 1471–1479 (2016)
2. Bontrager, P., Khalifa, A., Mendes, A., Togelius, J.: Matching games and algorithms for general video game playing. In: Twelfth Artificial Intelligence and Interactive Digital Entertainment Conference, pp. 122–128 (2016)
3. Campbell, M., Hoane, A.J., Hsu, F.-H.: Deep blue. Artif. Intell. **134**(1–2), 57–83 (2002)
4. Deb, K., Goldberg, D.E.: Analyzing deception in trap functions

5. Ebner, M., Levine, J., Lucas, S.M., Schaul, T., Thompson, T., Togelius, J.: Towards a video game description language. In: Dagstuhl Follow-Ups, vol. 6. Schloss Dagstuhl-Leibniz-Zentrum fuer Informatik (2013)

6. Gigerenzer, G., Goldstein, D.G.: Reasoning the fast and frugal way: models of bounded rationality. Psychol. Rev. **103**(4), 650 (1996)

7. Mendes, A., Togelius, J., Nealen, A.: Hyper-heuristic general video game playing. In: 2016 IEEE Conference on Computational Intelligence and Games (CIG), pp. 1–8. IEEE (2016)

8. Nelson, M.J.: Investigating vanilla MCTS scaling on the GVG-AI game corpus. In: 2016 IEEE Conference on Computational Intelligence and Games (CIG), pp. 1–7. IEEE (2016)

9. Pathak, D., Agrawal, P., Efros, A.A., Darrell, T.: Curiosity-driven exploration by self-supervised prediction. arXiv preprint arXiv:1705.05363 (2017)

10. Perez-Liebana, D., Samothrakis, S., Togelius, J., Lucas, S.M., Schaul, T.: General video game AI: competition, challenges and opportunities. In: Thirtieth AAAI Conference on Artificial Intelligence (2016)

11. Pérez-Liébana, D., Samothrakis, S., Togelius, J., Schaul, T., Lucas, S.M.: Analyzing the robustness of general video game playing agents. In: 2016 IEEE Conference on Computational Intelligence and Games (CIG), pp. 1–8. IEEE (2016)

12. Perez-Liebana, D., Samothrakis, S., Julian, T., Schaul, T., Lucas, S.M., Couëtoux, A., Lee, J., Lim, C.-U., Thompson, T.: The 2014 general video game playing competition. IEEE Trans. Comput. Intell. AI Games **8**(3), 229–243 (2016)

13. Silver, D., Huang, A., Maddison, C.J., Guez, A., Sifre, L., Van Den Driessche, G., Schrittwieser, J., Antonoglou, I., Panneershelvam, V., Lanctot, M., Dieleman, S., Grewe, D., Nham, J., Kalchbrenner, N., Sutskever, I., Lillicrap, T., Leach, M., Kavukcuoglu, K.: Mastering the game of Go with deep neural networks and tree search. Nature **529**(7585), 484–489 (2016)

14. Syed, O., Syed, A.: Arimaa-a new game designed to be difficult for computers. ICGA J. **26**(2), 138–139 (2003)

15. Turing, A.M.: Chess. In: Bowden, B.V. (ed.) Fasther than Thought, pp. 286–295. Pitnam, London (1953)

16. Tversky, A., Kahneman, D.: Judgment under uncertainty: heuristics and biases. Science **185**(4157), 1124–1131 (1974)

17. Von Neumann, J., Morgenstern, O.: Theory of Games and Economic Behavior. Princeton University Press, Princeton (1945)

18. Whitley, L.D.: Fundamental principles of deception in genetic search. In: Foundations of Genetic Algorithms (1991)

19. David, D.H., Macready, W.G.: No free lunch theorems for optimization. IEEE Trans. Evol. Comput. **1**(1), 67–82 (1997)

20. Yannakakis, G.N., Togelius, J.: Artificial Intelligence and Games. Springer, Heidelberg (2018). http://gameaibook.org

EvoIASP

Evolution of Convolutional Highway Networks

Oliver Kramer[(✉)]

Computational Intelligence Group, Department of Computer Science,
University of Oldenburg, Oldenburg, Germany
`oliver.kramer@uni-oldenburg.de`

Abstract. Convolutional highways are based on multiple stacked convolutional layers for feature preprocessing. Like many other convolutional networks convolutional highways are parameterized by numerous hyperparameters that have to be tuned carefully. We introduce an evolutionary algorithm (EA) for optimization of the structure and tuning of hyperparameters of convolutional highways and demonstrate the potential of this optimization setting on the well-known MNIST data set. The EA employs Rechenberg's mutation rate control and a niching mechanism to overcome local optima. An experimental study shows that the EA is capable of evolving convolutional highway networks from scratch with only few evaluations but achieving competitive accuracy. Further, the EA is able to significantly improve standard network configurations.

Keywords: Deep neuroevolution · Convolutional networks · Niching
(1+1)-EA

1 Introduction

Convolutional highways [1] allow training of convolutional networks with large numbers of layers and introduce the concept of gates known from long short-term memory (LSTM) networks. Each convolutional highway layer employs two gates for the flow of information, i.e., for convolution and for passing information. This turns out to be a useful feature extraction mechanism for recognition tasks.

For novel applications the optimal convolutional highway structure and configuration of hyperparameters is unknown. The application of evolutionary optimization heuristics for finding optimal or near-optimal networks offers great potentials [2]. Due to the fact EAs are embarrassingly parallelizable, they can arbitrarily be scaled to large optimization scenarios [3]. Most early research on neuroevolution concentrated on the evolution of connections between neurons and the number of neurons in layers of multilayer perceptrons (MLPs) [4–6]. Recent developments show that EAs can foster the success of deep learning with architecture search and optimization of hyperparameters.

The objective of this paper is to show that a (1+1)-EA with Rechenberg mutation rate control and a niching mechanism is an effective method for evolving convolutional highway networks from scratch and for tuning standard network configurations.

© Springer International Publishing AG, part of Springer Nature 2018
K. Sim and P. Kaufmann (Eds.): EvoApplications 2018, LNCS 10784, pp. 395–404, 2018.
https://doi.org/10.1007/978-3-319-77538-8_27

This paper is structured as follows. In Sect. 2 we introduce convolutional highways. Related work on optimization of deep networks is discussed in Sect. 3. The optimizing EA with niching is introduced in Sect. 4 and experimentally analyzed on the MNIST data set in Sect. 5. Results are summarized in Sect. 6, where also the role of EAs in deep learning is discussed.

2   Convolutional Highways

Convolutional neural networks have been introduced by LeCun et al. [7]. They are based on convolutional layers, which consist of three parts. The first part applies filters, also known as kernels (small weight matrices), that are convolved with the input $\mathbf{x}$ by matrix multiplication. Filters move over the input volume and repeat this convolutional process. The part of the input that is convolved with the kernel is called receptive field. The result of the convolution process is written into an activation map. The higher the similarity between filter and input the larger is the corresponding activation map entry. A set of filters is applied, known as filter bank. Over the training process, which is based on backpropagation, the filter bank adapts to the features most relevant in the training data for the learning process.

The convolutional process is followed by an activation layer applying a non-linear function. For example, the activation function ReLu (rectified linear unit) turns all negative numbers to 0. The activation map is subject to a pooling process, which reduces the dimensionality, for example with the maximum value of a rectangular (max pooling), or the average (average pooling). A classic convolutional network consists of a set of such convolutional layers followed by two or more dense layers, which correspond to the original MLP layers.

Convolutional highways are based on two ideas. First, they stack multiple convolutional layers for feature preprocessing. Second, each convolutional highway layer uses two gates for the flow of information. A shared convolutional gate is based on the usual convolutional layer, which is combined with a weight matrix $\mathbf{W}_C$ computing output $C(\mathbf{x}, \mathbf{W}_C)$. A transform gate controls the amount of information that is passed through the convolutional layer with a transform matrix $\mathbf{W}_T$. The inverse, i.e., $1 - T(\mathbf{x}, \mathbf{W}_T)$ defines the amount of information of input $\mathbf{x}$ that is passed through the layer. Hence, one convolutional highway layer outputs[1]

$$\mathbf{y} = C(\mathbf{x}, \mathbf{W}_C) \cdot T(\mathbf{x}, \mathbf{W}_T) + \mathbf{x} \cdot (1 - T(\mathbf{x}, \mathbf{W}_T)). \tag{1}$$

The highway network is composed of multiple modules each consisting of k succeeding convolutional layers with decreasing kernel size followed by max pooling and normalization. The convolutional highway layers are followed by dense layers and a final softmax layer. Figure 2 in Sect. 4.4 illustrates the general network structure and its parameter space. The EA adapts the number of convolutional highway layers within each module, the number of modules and hyperparameters like kernel sizes and activation function types.

---

[1] Leaving out the bias for the sake of readability.

3   Related Work

The line of research on neuroevolution began in the nineties with numerous approaches. Most concentrated on tuning the number of neurons, fewer on evolving the connections between neurons and other structural properties of MLPs. Some early approaches are, similar to the approach presented in this paper, based on binary encodings, e.g. [4], where the bit string encodes the connection matrix between neurons. Other approaches are based on graph encodings, e.g. [5], and allow the direct representation of the neural network structure. On graph representation crossover operators are possible that allow the substitution of subgraphs.

One of the most famous contributions in this line of research is NEAT [6], which is able to evolve MLPs using techniques like augmenting topologies and niching. Its successor HyperNEAT [8] has been applied to convolutional networks. Compositional pattern-producing networks (CPPN) [9] are evolutionary approaches that assume that the general network structure is predefined, while its components are independent of each other. Fernando et al. [10] extend CPPN for autoencoders with a Lamarckian approach that inherits learned weights.

Loshchilov and Hutter [11] apply the CMA-ES to evolve the hyperparameters of convolutional networks optimizing dropout and learning rates, batch sizes, numbers of filters, and numbers of units in dense layers. Suganuma et al. [12] propose a genetic programming (GP) approach for designing convolutional networks achieving competitive results to state-of-the-art convolutional networks. Recently, Real et al. [13] invested exhaustive evolutionary search to evolve convolutional networks for image classification on CIFAR.

Recurrent networks belong to a related and also very successful branch of deep learning approaches, in particular LSTMs, which employ mechanisms like forget and input gates. Józefowicz et al. [14] presented an evolutionary architecture search for LSTM cells and their variants. While better network structures could have been evolved for special problems, there was no optimal architecture consistently outperforming the standard cell.

Recent related approaches by Bello et al. [15] and Baker et al. [16] use reinforcement learning for evolving deep convolutional networks. Reinforcement learning allows adaptation of the network during the learning process with complex interactions. An application to convolutional highways has not been introduced yet to the best of our knowledge.

Also related to evolutionary optimization of deep learning methods is the evolutionary tuning of machine learning algorithms. In particular, the evolution of machine learning pipelines with EAs has recently gained attention. The tree-based pipeline optimization tool (TPOT) by Olson et al. [17] is a successful example for a supervised learning pipeline. Also for unsupervised learning, i.e., kernel PCA pipelines [18], EAs have successfully been applied.

4   Evolutionary Approach

Evolutionary algorithms are powerful tools for blackbox optimization problems with local optima. While finding numerous successful applications, from numerical to structural optimization, EAs are grounded on a solid theoretical basis, see e.g. [19]. This section presents a variant of the (1+1)-EA that allows a fast adaptation of convolutional highways.

4.1   (1+1)-EA

For network evolution we employ a (1+1)-EA that generates a new child $\mathbf{z}' \in \mathbb{B}^N$ in binary representation with bit string length N based on a single parent $\mathbf{z}$ in one generation with bit flip mutation. If the fitness of the child is better than the fitness of its parent, it replaces its parent. The process is repeated until a termination condition is met. As we represent the phenotype of the convolutional highway as bit string, the EA makes use of bit flip mutation with probability σ. The EA uses mutation rate control and niching, see Algorithm 1.

Algorithm 1. (1+1)-EA

1: intialize $\mathbf{z} \in \mathbb{B}^n$ randomly
2: **repeat**
3:     **if** niching_mode = **true** for κ gen. **and** $f(\mathbf{z}_n) \geq f(\mathbf{z})$
4:         replace $\mathbf{z}$ with $\mathbf{z}_n$, niching_mode = **false**
5:     mutate $\mathbf{z} \rightarrow \mathbf{z}'$ with bit flip
6:     adapt σ with Rechenberg
7:     replace $\mathbf{z}$ with $\mathbf{z}'$ if $f(\mathbf{z}) \geq f(\mathbf{z}')$
8:     **else** with probability η $\mathbf{z}_n = \mathbf{z}$, replace $\mathbf{z}$ with $\mathbf{z}'$ and
9:                     count gen. with κ, niching_mode = **true**
10: **until** termination condition

4.2   Mutation Rate Control

For a flexible mutation rate during the optimization process, Rechenberg's rule is applied. It adapts the mutation rate according to the success rate of mutations during the optimization process. In case of high success rates with $g/G \geq 1/5$, i.e., with number g of successful generations in a generation window G, the mutation rate σ is increased by multiplication $\sigma' = \sigma \cdot \tau$ with $\tau > 1$. Otherwise for $g/G < 1/5$, σ is decreased with $\sigma' = \sigma/\tau$. The rule allows larger steps in case of sequently successful generations and smaller steps in case of stagnation.

4.3   Niching for (1+1)-EA

To overcome local optima, we introduce a simple niching approach for the (1+1)-EA in the following. A (1+1)-population scheme follows successful directions greedily, but might suffer from local optima. We propose the following niching mechanism. If a child is worse than its parent, it is not rejected with probability η and optimized for κ generations. The notion of an optimization process as a tree with niching optimization branches is depicted in Fig. 1. The fitness of the last child of this optimization branch replaces the last parent in the main optimization branch, if it achieves a better fitness. Otherwise, the original parent is the basis for the remaining optimization run.

Fig. 1. The niching process depicted as tree allows the (1+1)-EA to follow a worse solution with probability η in an optimization branch for κ generations. It replaces the main branch in case of improvement and jumps back if the fitness is worse.

4.4   Network Evolution

The EA optimizes the convolutional highway structure and its hyperparameters, see Fig. 2. With regard to the network structure, the EA adapts the number of highway modules $(1, 2, 4, 8)$. Within each module it further adapts the number of convolutional 2d layers $(1, 2, 4, 8)$. The numbers of neurons for the two dense layers are also optimized (from set $32, 64, 128, 256$). Further, the EA adapts hyperparameters like the kernel size of all highways $(8, 12, 16, 24)$, the kernel size of the max pooling layers $(1, 2, 3, 4)$, and the activation function types of all highways and of the dense layers. The activation functions applied are ELU with

$$x \text{ for } x > 0, \text{ and } \alpha(e^x - 1) \text{ for } x \le 0, \tag{2}$$

ReLU with $\max(x, 0)$, PReLU, which is a parametric version of ReLU, and Softsign with

$$x/(|x| + 1). \tag{3}$$

Last, the EA evolves the learning rate of the network applying *Adam* as gradient descent optimizer.

The convolutional highway network is represented as bit string **z**. It is translated to a phenotype by piecewise mappings to integers, which are used as indices for lists containing parameterizations. We use the TENSORFLOW Deep Learning Library (TFLEARN) to build a TENSORFLOW model that is executed for each fitness function evaluation. The network is trained using cross-validation. The final classifier is evaluated on the independent test set, on which the categorical cross-entropy is computed as fitness value. In total, 20 bits are used to represent a convolutional highway network resulting in a solution space size of over one million network configurations.

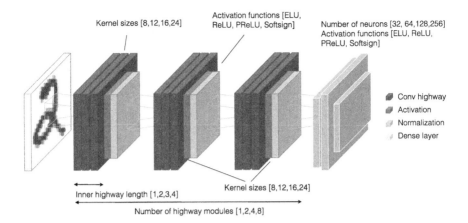

Kernel sizes [8,12,16,24]

Activation functions [ELU, ReLU, PReLU, Softsign]

Number of neurons [32, 64,128,256] Activation functions [ELU, ReLU, PReLU, Softsign]

Conv highway
Activation
Normalization
Dense layer

Inner highway length [1,2,3,4]

Kernel sizes [8,12,16,24]

Number of highway modules [1,2,4,8]

Fig. 2. The evolutionary convolutional highway network allows an adaptation of the number of highway modules, their inner module structures, and the network hyperparameters.

5   Experimental Study

In the following, we analyze the evolutionary highway networks in detail starting with the evolution from scratch. Then we compare the best evolved highway network to the original one and last demonstrate that post-optimization of the original network can further improve the classification performance.

5.1   Evolution from Scratch

The first part of our experimental study concentrates on the evolution of convolutional highways from scratch based on a completely random solution. Our experiments use the well-known image recognition data set MNIST with training set size 55,000 and test set size 10,000. The (1+1)-EA runs for 30 generations. The (1+1)-EA with Rechenberg uses the settings $G = 10$ and $\tau = 0.5$, the niching mechanism uses $\eta = 0.1$ and $\kappa = 10$. These are settings that turned out to work well on pre-experiments. Each network is trained for 5 epochs. Table 1 summarizes the parameter settings of our study.

Table 2 shows the results of the experimental study of the evolved convolutional network in terms of test set accuracy. For comparison, the accuracy of the network with original specifications (like employed in TFLEARN) is shown, see Fig. 5(a), and the median fitness of the first random initial networks. All runs are repeated 10 times. The accuracy on the test set of the final best network and the mean of the best networks of all runs are presented. The results show that the (1+1)-EA is able to evolve a competitive convolutional highway network from scratch.

The random initial networks achieve significantly worse results than the networks with recommended original setting, but the EA is able to improve the

Table 1. Parameter settings of the optimizing EA (left) and the convolutional highway network (right).

EA		Highway network	
Parameter	Setting	Parameter	Setting
init. mutation rate σ	1/N	type	conv. highway
Rechenberg G	10	epochs	5
Rechenberg τ	0.5	learning rate	evolved
niching η	0.1	gradient descent	*Adam*
niching κ	10	error/loss	categorial cross-entropy
generations	30	init.	random

Table 2. Experimental study of convolutional highway test accuracy on MNIST of the (1+1)-EA, the EA variant with Rechenberg mutation rate control, and with the niching mechanism. The best network is evolved by the (1+1)-EA with niching and achieves an accuracy of over 99%.

(1+1)-EA	Original	Median init.	Min	Mean	Std	Max
simple	0.977	0.979	0.972	0.983	0.007	0.989
Rechenberg	0.977	0.917	0.941	0.970	0.020	0.986
niching	0.977	0.973	0.986	0.989	0.001	**0.991**

networks in all cases. The (1+1)-EA with Rechenberg performs worse than the simple (1+1)-EA. But the variant with Rechenberg and niching beats both other types in best, mean, and worst results, while achieving stable performance with a small standard deviation.

Figure 3 shows the fitness development (in terms of test accuracy) of the (1+1)-EA variants optimizing the convolutional highways on MNIST. All runs show a stable convergence towards values over 0.94 accuracy level. In particular the worst initial nets can be adapted by the EA to achieve competitive performance.

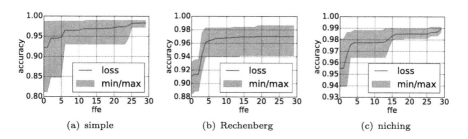

(a) simple   (b) Rechenberg   (c) niching

Fig. 3. Fitness developments of the (1+1)-EA variants evolving convolutional highways for 30 generations.

5.2   Optimization of Original Network

Now, we analyze the performance of the (1+1)-EA optimizing the original highway network configuration. Figure 4 shows the fitness development of the (1+1)-EA with Rechenberg and niching optimizing the original convolutional highway network, see Fig. 5(a) on MNIST. The experimental setting is the same like in the previous experiments. The plot shows that the EA is able to improve the original network accuracy of about 0.980 to a value of about 0.986 in average. Also the mean and worst results show significant improvements.

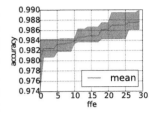

Fig. 4. (1+1)-EA optimizing the original highway network

5.3   Network Comparison

Figure 5 compares the best evolved network to the original one. The best network has been optimized with the (1+1)-EA, Rechenberg's mutation rate control, and niching. The comparison shows that the EA has evolved significantly different network structures with four highways modules.

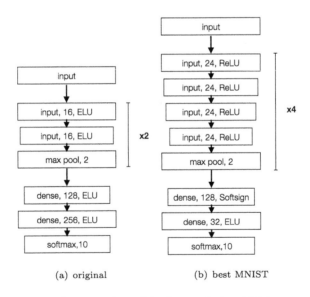

(a) original   (b) best MNIST

Fig. 5. The comparison between the original convolutional highway network and the best highway network variant evolved shows significant differences between the highway structures and parameters.

6   Conclusions

This paper demonstrates that a comparatively simple EA with mutation rate control and a niching mechanism is able to evolve convolutional highways from scratch, i.e., from random initializations. The evolved network structures are significantly different from the original networks in deep learning frameworks. The results allow the conclusion that EAs are powerful techniques for optimization of highway network structures and hyperparameters. Mutation rate control and niching are helpful to support the optimization process. Further, the EA is able to improve the original network design. The application of EAs to network learning has numerous advantages. EAs do not require gradients, prior assumptions regarding problem knowledge, or human expertise. Further, EAs are embarrassingly parallelizable, allow unexpected results, and can easily optimize two or more conflicting objectives at a time. The latter allows balancing learning error and regularization or further conflictive classifier objectives. Future work could concentrate on the application of evolutionary convolutional highways to domains like video and speech recognition. Further, an extension of the experimental analysis to large-scale data sets would enrich our results.

A   Implementation

The convolutional highway network experiments are based on PYTHON and TFLEARN, which builds upon TENSORFLOW. The EA's bit string z is mapped to list indices, which specify TFLEARN's function parameters, with a function `toInt`. The following code is an example of a convolutional layer parameterized with four values for the number `nb_filter` of filters and for the type of activation functions that are collected in the list `activation_functions`. The corresponding bits of z are coded between indices 4 to 6 and 6 to 8, respectively.

```
nb_filter = [8,12,16,24][toInt(z[4:6])]
activation_functions = ['elu', 'relu', 'PReLU', 'Softsign']
activation = activation_functions[toInt(z[6:8])]
network = highway_conv_2d(network, nb_filter, filter_size, activation)
```

References

1. Srivastava, R.K., Greff, K., Schmidhuber, J.: Highway networks. CoRR abs/1505.00387 (2015). http://arxiv.org/abs/1505.00387
2. Sipper, M., Olson, R.S., Moore, J.H.: Evolutionary computation: the next major transition of artificial intelligence? BioData Min. 10(1), 26 (2017)
3. Salimans, T., Ho, J., Chen, X., Sutskever, I.: Evolution strategies as a scalable alternative to reinforcement learning, pp. 1–12 (2017). https://arxiv.org/abs/1703.03864
4. Dasgupta, D., McGregor, D.: Designing application-specific neural networks using the structured genetic algorithm. In: International Conference on Combinations of Genetic Algorithms and Neural Networks, pp. 87–96 (1992)

5. Pujol, J.C.F., Poli, R.: Evolving the topology and the weights of neural networks using a dual representation. Appl. Intell. **8**(1), 73–84 (1998)
6. Stanley, K.O., Miikkulainen, R.: Evolving neural networks through augmenting topologies. Evol. Comput. **10**(2), 99–127 (2002)
7. Lecun, Y., Bottou, L., Bengio, Y., Haffner, P.: Gradient-based learning applied to document recognition. Proc. IEEE **86**(11), 2278–2324 (1998)
8. Stanley, K.O., D'Ambrosio, D.B., Gauci, J.: A hypercube-based encoding for evolving large-scale neural networks. Artif. Life **15**(2), 185–212 (2009)
9. Stanley, K.O.: Compositional pattern producing networks: a novel abstraction of development. Genet. Program Evolvable Mach. **8**(2), 131–162 (2007)
10. Fernando, C., Banarse, D., Reynolds, M., Besse, F., Pfau, D., Jaderberg, M., Lanctot, M., Wierstra, D.: Convolution by evolution: differentiable pattern producing networks. In: Genetic and Evolutionary Computation Conference (GECCO), pp. 109–116 (2016)
11. Loshchilov, I., Hutter, F.: CMA-ES for hyperparameter optimization of deep neural networks. In: International Conference on Learning Representations (ICLR) Workshop, pp. 513–520 (2016)
12. Suganuma, M., Shirakawa, S., Nagao, T.: A genetic programming approach to designing convolutional neural network architectures. In: Genetic and Evolutionary Computation Conference (GECCO), pp. 497–504 (2017)
13. Real, E., Moore, S., Selle, A., Saxena, S., Suematsu, Y.L., Tan, J., Le, Q.V., Kurakin, A.: Large-scale evolution of image classifiers. In: International Conference on Machine Learning (ICML), pp. 2902–2911 (2017)
14. Józefowicz, R., Zaremba, W., Sutskever, I.: An empirical exploration of recurrent network architectures. In: International Conference on Machine Learning (ICML), pp. 2342–2350 (2015)
15. Bello, I., Zoph, B., Vasudevan, V., Le, Q.V.: Neural optimizer search with reinforcement learning. In: International Conference on Machine Learning (ICML), pp. 459–468 (2017)
16. Baker, B., Gupta, O., Naik, N., Raskar, R.: Designing neural network architectures using reinforcement learning. In: International Conference on Learning Representations (ICLR) (2017). https://arxiv.org/abs/1611.02167
17. Olson, R.S., Bartley, N., Urbanowicz, R.J., Moore, J.H.: Evaluation of a tree-based pipeline optimization tool for automating data science. In: Genetic and Evolutionary Computation Conference (GECCO), pp. 485–492 (2016)
18. Kramer, O.: Evolving kernel PCA pipelines with evolution strategies. In: Kern-Isberner, G., Fürnkranz, J., Thimm, M. (eds.) KI 2017. LNCS (LNAI), vol. 10505, pp. 170–177. Springer, Cham (2017). https://doi.org/10.1007/978-3-319-67190-1_13
19. Neumann, F., Witt, C.: Bioinspired Computation in Combinatorial Optimization. NCS. Springer, Heidelberg (2010). https://doi.org/10.1007/978-3-642-16544-3

Adapting Bagging and Boosting to Learning Classifier Systems

Yi Liu[✉], Will N. Browne, and Bing Xue

Victoria University of Wellington, Wellington 6014, New Zealand
liuyi4@myvuw.ac.nz, {Will.Browne,bing.xue}@ecs.vuw.ac.nz

Abstract. Learning Classifier Systems (LCSs) have demonstrated their classification capability by employing a population of polymorphic rules in addressing numerous benchmark problems. However, although the produced solution is often accurate, the alternative ways to represent the data in a single population obscure the underlying patterns of a problem. Moreover, once a population is dominated by over-general rules, the system will sink into the local optimal trap. To grant a problem's patterns more transparency, the redundant rules and optimal rules need to be distinguished. Therefore, the bagging method is introduced to LCSs with the aim to reduce the variance associated with redundant rules. A novel rule reduction method is proposed to reduce the rules' polymorphism in a problem. This is tested with complex binary problems with typical epistatic, over-lapping niches, niche-imbalance, and specific-addiction properties at various scales. The results show the successful highlighting of the patterns for all the tested problems, which have been addressed successfully. Moreover, by combining the boosting method with LCSs, the hybrid system could adjust previously defective solutions such that they now represent the correct classification of data.

Keywords: Learning classifier systems · Multiple domain learning
Ensemble learning

1 Introduction

Learning classifier systems (LCSs) [1] are a family of rule-based evolutionary computation techniques that are capable of discovering a given task's underlying pattern that links features (input) to targets (output). This is achieved by interacting with the initially unknown task environment to generate a population of *'condition-action'* heuristics (rules). LCSs are competent to provide solutions in domains revealing epistasis (e.g. the importance of one feature depends on the value of another), non-linear feature interaction and heterogeneity (e.g. different attribute combinations producing the same class) [2]. The transparent nature of the rule format enables humans to interrogate the discovered knowledge.

Accuracy-based LCS (XCS) [3] is the most popular LCS formulation, which employs accuracy-based fitness to explore and exploit a problem. XCSs are

© Springer International Publishing AG, part of Springer Nature 2018
K. Sim and P. Kaufmann (Eds.): EvoApplications 2018, LNCS 10784, pp. 405–420, 2018.
https://doi.org/10.1007/978-3-319-77538-8_28

reinforcement-learning based, which guarantees their capability to address both single-step problems and multi-step problems [4]. XCSs have demonstrated their ability by successfully addressing massive benchmark problems including classification, regression, sequence labeling and sequential decision making [5].

In XCSs, when exploring, a population is established by covering a problem's observed states with each available action, whilst evolution is guided according to the expected payoffs from an environment. This evolutionary process enables XCSs to successfully construct a complete action map for the majority of the presented tasks, and therewith, a maximally accurate population with maximally general rules. However, such populations are commonly associated with an enormous amount of redundant information, which obscures the important patterns within a problem. Additionally, the population can become stuck in local optima if over-general rules (generalization-addiction) or over-specific rules (accuracy-addiction) dominate a population.

Recently, a novel rule reduction method has been introduced, termed EECC (Elite selection, Experience assessment, Consistency assessment, Correctness partition) and Attribute-search, with the aim to detect a problem's underlying pattern [6]. Unlike the classic rule compression methods [7], that merely investigate individuals in a population and simply pursue prediction accuracy, such as Wilson's CRA and CRA2 [8–10], this new proposed method investigates individuals in multiple populations and focuses on reducing rules' polymorphism. The EECC method has been tested on four 6-bit famous benchmark problems including Multiplexer, Carry, Majority-on, and Even-parity. The results show success highlighting the patterns for all the tasks. However, the EECC & Attribute search is merely at the human-guided level and could be considered as an umbrella for four individual rule reduction methods. This is because the parameters in EECC need to be hand tuned in advance. Moreover, the architecture used in attribute-search for each different domain needs to be adjusted. Meanwhile, EECC & Attribute search has not been tested on any medium sized binary task, i.e. search spaces beyond enumeration in a practical time frame.

The aim of this work is to develop the EECC & Attribute search methods such that human set up is no longer required for each problem type. The methods' ability to detect automatically the optimal rules for four benchmark problems that scale from 3-bit to 37-bit will be tested. Another objective is for the underlying patterns of a problem to be made apparent. As the proposed rule reduction method is based on multiple populations, the bagging method is introduced to generate multiple individuals. The boosting method is also assimilated to assist LCSs to avoid the local optima problem.

2   Background

Learning Classifier System. Traditionally, an LCS represents a Michigan approach rule-based agent, which incorporates evolutionary computing and Q-learning [11] to solve a given task by interacting with an unknown environment. An XCS evolves a population of rules, where each rule consists of a fixed length condition. Environmental features are encoded, e.g. in a ternary alphabet $0,1,\#$, and one of a set of plausible actions.

Seven parameters are also introduced to assist the evolutionary process. The *numerosity* indicates the number of duplicates of a rule, *experience* relates to a rule's training time, *prediction* is a recency weighted sum of the environmental rewards gained, prediction *error* shows by how much this prediction is incorrect, *accuracy* is a function of this error, *fitness* shows a rule's potential performance based on the previous parameters and *action set size* shows a rule's approximate niche size [5].

Bagging and Boosting. The core idea behind bagging (bootstrap aggregating) [12] and boosting [13] is to use a classification algorithm to create a general set of models, then construct a new model by integrating the generated ones in order to improve performance. During the bagging process, all the models randomly observe the global problem domain. Therefore, for these models, they have similar bias and variance but weak correlation. When reconstructing a solution based on these models the variance should decrease. In boosting, the main hypothesis is to minimise the loss function by greedy search. Therefore, the bias should decrease. However, as the models correlate with each other the variance problem cannot be remitted.

Original Intelligence System. For the sake of seeking mutual collaboration between multiple LCSs and their outcome agents, Original Intelligence System (OIS) [14] emerged recently, as it approaches the task of learning multiple problems in an ensemble manner. In OIS, tasks can be done by many LCSs in parallel. Subsequently, the LCSs' produced rules go through a rule reduction method to generate a highly compacted and precise agent. Eventually, the final product will become a part of OIS in order to recognise any newly presented environment in an interactive manner. OIS is different to the GALE system [15] for individual problems as OIS seeks continuous learning using multiple agents for multiple problems.

Benchmark Problems. Four problems are included, firstly, a typically highly non-linear problem, **Multiplexer**, which contains multi-modality, heterogeneity and epistasis properties [2]. Then, two niche imbalance problems are introduced, which are **Carry** and **Majority-on** [16]. Investigating these problems evaluate our novel method's ability in avoiding the creation of over-general rules and in selecting the optimal number of rules to express a problem's global patterns. Lastly, **Even-parity** [17] is tested to investigate the method's ability to select the correct specific rules among a population of incorrect general rules. This is necessary as a ternary alphabet based LCS cannot form any useful general rules for this problem domain.

3   The Proposed Method

The core hypothesis behind Ockham's razor is "Entities are not to be multiplied without necessity" [18]. This theory inspires an alternative way to handle the rule compaction problem, where it is hypothesised that rules can be compacted under macro view rather than micro view. The previous rule reduction methods focus on interrogating individual rule's performance in a population, despite how individuals interact with each other. Moreover, sampling all rules from a single population results in a substantial risk of being misguided by the variance in the ways the correct rules population can be formulated (termed polymorphism). This may explain why although LCSs are competent to generate optimal rules for the addressed problem, the previous rule reduction methods find it difficult to compact a population to its optimal state, i.e. just containing one set of only optimal rules.

3.1   Bagging in LCS

To avoid the variances in rule populations, the samples for rule reduction are selected from a group of populations instead of a single one. To combine the bagging method with OIS the populations from the multiple XCSs in OIS act as weak classifiers in the bagging method. The random sampling of environments in OIS guarantees that the XCSs observe the target's states stochastically. The final generated populations will be sent to a novel rule reduction method, termed Razor Cluster Razor (RCR), to reconstruct one highly compacted and accurate population (Fig. 1).

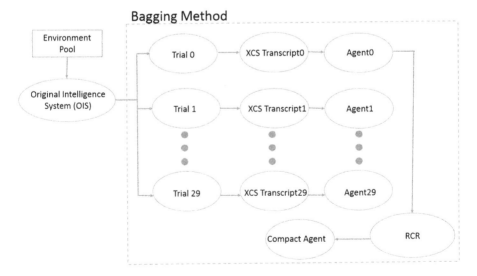

Fig. 1. The graph for the bagging process. The Original Intelligence System (OIS) [14] forms the base of the bagging methods (an agent is the output from an XCS, which consists of a population of rules).

3.2 Rule Reduction Method Razor Cluster Razor

RCR is a triphasic rule reduction method, which aims to reduce rules' polymorphism in a problem. The three-phases of RCR are *razors in micro*, *rules cluster*, and *razors in macro*, which are processed in sequence. Razors seek to simplify as much as possible, but no simpler. Razors in micro aims to remove the poor performance rules in each individual population. Subsequently, the remaining rules in all populations will be gathered together to be clustered according to number of attributes kept in each individual, where this process is termed as rules cluster. Finally, for the sake of reducing rules' polymorphism in the clustered set, the razors in macro is introduced (Fig. 2).

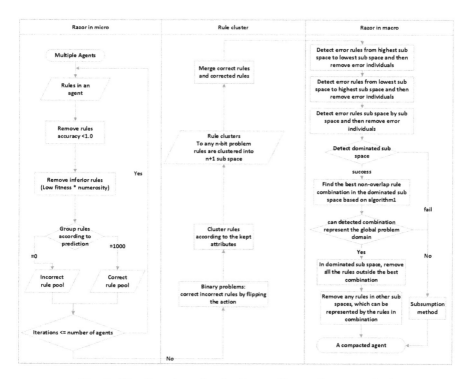

Fig. 2. The flow chart for the Razor Cluster Razor method

Razors in Micro. The size of an XCS population is larger than the real demand to enable the search of the problem space by considering multiple competing hypotheses at the same time. As a result, XCSs cannot guarantee all the generated classifiers are most suited to address the task. In certain domains, the majority of rules are not good at representing the task. Moreover, a few rules may even make a negative contribution. Hence, this pre-processing phrase is employed to select the superior individuals in a population.

In general, a superior rule needs to be trained adequately, so that it can produce consistent prediction and make an outstanding contribution to represent the observed data. Any rule that does not meet the above requirements is deleted. The whole process is split into three sections: firstly, remove all the rules that are not maximally accurate. Secondly, the product of fitness and numerosity is employed as an indicator to estimate how important a rule is to address the task. Subsequently, a derivation method is introduced to approximately distinguish superior rules from inferior rules, where the inferior ones will be removed from the population. Thirdly, all the surviving rules will be classified into two groups according to whether the rule's prediction is the maximum or minimum known value.

In razors in micro, accuracy is employed as a criteria to measure whether a rule has been trained adequately. In an XCS, when a rule's prediction error is lower than the epsilon zero, ϵ_0, (the threshold for measuring whether a rule is correct), the value of accuracy will be set as the maximum. Otherwise the accuracy is associated with a very scaled amount of the maximum. Therefore, when a rule's accuracy is maximum it indicates that the XCS admits this rule has trained appropriately, so there is no need to revisit the experience parameter.

The last step in *razors in micro* is to split the selected rules into two groups and put them into related rule pools according to whether their prediction is the minimum or maximum. All the rules with maximum prediction are sent to the correct rule pool, since these rules can continue to make correct predictions, the remaining rules are categorized as the incorrect group, so will be placed into the incorrect rule pool.

Rule Cluster. The rule cluster method is responsible to cluster the previously selected rules into relevant sub-search spaces. This method consists of two steps: firstly, in binary classification problems, flipping a completely incorrect rule's action could make it become a completely correct rule, so all the rules' actions in the incorrect rule pool are flipped. These transformed rules are merged into the correct rule pool. Secondly, all the rules will be clustered into a corresponding sub-space based on the generality of their kept attributes. Incidentally, during this process, all identical rules will be merged into one macroclassifier by merging their learnt parameters. Thus, the OIS retains the learnt knowledge properties from all these subsumed rules.

In XCSs, when the ternary alphabet is employed to represent the condition, an XCS's global search space for an N-bit binary problem can be split into $N + 1$ sub-search spaces according to the number of kept attributes i.e. for a 6-bit prbolem, there will be seven sub-spaces ranging from the bottom (i.e. no specified bits, e.g. *######:1*) to the top (i.e. seven specified bits, e.g. *101110:1*). Taken together, all the sub-spaces are capable of representing the global problem domain. Hence, for any N-bit boolean problem, a search space can be quantified by summing the number of the available rules in each sub-search space. Equation (1) displays this process, where N_{ac} is the number of the unique actions and N_{at} means the number of the attributes in a single condition C.

$$N_{ucr} = N_{ac} * \sum_{N_{at}=0}^{n} (C_n^{N_{at}} * 2^{N_{at}}) \tag{1}$$

Razors in Macro. Razors in macro is devoted to detecting the most stable combination of rules to represent the task among the selected rules from the previous phases. As each XCS generates various solutions, defective rules are unavoidable, which need to be removed. During the evaluation process each rule will be associated with a new parameter named error indicator. This records the sum of the numerosity of rules that conflict with the tested rule, i.e. when two rules have overlap in search space but different action. At the beginning of each step (see below), the value of the error indicator will return to zero.

To achieve the goal, this method is split into two steps. In the first step, the error detection iterates from the bottom cluster to the top cluster in terms of number of specified attributes. A rule will be compared with all the other rules that are in a higher sub-space. For any rule where its error indicator surpasses its numerosity then this rule will be removed. Next the iteration order is reversed. A rule is compared with all its companions that are in a lower sub-space. As above, all the detected erroneous rules will be removed. Then the rules will be interrogated by the alternative rules in the same cluster to discover the redundant candidates.

In the second step, all the remaining redundant rules need to be removed. After the previous process, if the optimal set exists, any over-general rule will have been removed, since to any over-general rule, it must conflict with at least one optimal rule. All remaining redundant rules will be over-specific, thus, a subsumption method is sufficient to achieve this objective (in subsumption, if a rule is covered by a more general version that is accurate, then it will be removed). However, for the rules assembled in one sub-search space, non-over-general rules may still be redundant rules. The easiest way to judge whether a problem domain has a dominated sub-space is, in each sub-space, sum all the pertinent rules' numerosity. If one sub-space's numerosity value is much higher than that of others, then it indicates that this problem domain has a dominated sub-space, e.g. in the tested Multiplexer problems, the dominant sub-space occupied almost 80% of the total numerosity amongst all the rules.

If a problem domain is determined to have a dominant sub-space, then it is necessary to find the best non-overlapping rule combination in the dominant sub-space as displayed in Algorithm 1. However, in some problem domains, even if a dominated sub-space exists, all the redundant rules may still be over-specific rules, e.g. 7-bit Majority-on problem. Thus, the detected combination of best rules will be interrogated by its represented problem space. If it cannot represent the global problem domain on test instances, then rollback is actived. Otherwise, all the rules outside the detected best combination will be evaluated. If any rules can be represented by the individuals in the best detected combination, then they will be removed (since the overlap between them eliminates this combination of best rules). Therefore, it is possible to detect whether a rule in a lower sub-space can be expressed by the detected combination.

Algorithm 1. Find the best non-overlap combination of classifiers from the best sub-space

---

begin
> **Input**: $S \leftarrow$ a set of classifier n rules;
> **Output**: $BestSubset \leftarrow$ a subset of classifiers;
> $BestSubset \leftarrow$ an empty classifier set;
> $MaximumNumerosity \leftarrow 0$;
> Rank the n rules in S in a descending order, according to their numerosity values;
> **foreach** $s \in S$ **do**
> > $S_{temp} \leftarrow S$;
> > $Subset \leftarrow$ an empty rule set;
> > Add s to $Subset$; // every rule has a chance to be a priority rule to be returned
> > Remove s from S_{temp};
> > **foreach** $s' \in S_{temp}$ **do**
> > > **if** s' *does not have overlap with any rule in* $Subset$ **then**
> > > > Add s' to $Subset$;
> >
> > $TotalNumerosity \leftarrow$ calculate the total Numerosity of rules in $Subset$;
> > **if** $TotalNumerosity > MaximumNumerosity$ **then**
> > > Update $MaximumNumerosity \leftarrow TotalNumerosity$;
> > > Update $BestSubset \leftarrow Subset$;
>
> Return $BestSubset$;

3.3 Boosting in LCSs

The most general, accurate rules are the targets, which ternary based XCSs pursue, to represent Boolean problem domains. In certain domains, which exhibit epistasis, this generalisation strategy is effective. Whereas in other domains, which exhibit the over-lapping property, this strategy becomes a learning obstacle as it leads the XCSs into local optimal traps. To overcome this deficiency, boosting is introduced to XCSs.

In the boosting process, firstly, all the rules in the RCR produced agent are clustered into their corresponding sub-spaces. Then all the sub-spaces are tested one by one through evaluating their accuracy based on all the matched instances from the target problem domain. For any sub-spaces that are not empty during the evaluating process, if any error occurs it will be marked as *contains error rules*. Otherwise, the sub-space will be marked as *completely correct*. Any *completely correct* sub-space before the first erroneous sub-space will be selected and then introduced to the training process as a barrier. During the XCS based training process only the instances that cannot be matched by the barrier will be involved. Eventually, a new agent is generated based on the observed local data, whilst a refined RCR agent will also be created based on rules in the selected sub-spaces. The prediction task is fulfilled via two agents' cooperation. The prediction priority is given to the refined RCR agent, i.e. the newly trained agent is defaulted to in order to generate actions for the states that cannot be matched by the refined RCR agent.

4   Results

For all the domains, 30 adequately trained agents are involved in RCR to implement the compaction process. Table 1 shows how RCR improved LCSs' performance by keeping the highest accuracy, whilst reducing the number of introduced rules as much as possible. In all the tasks that LCS can address successfully, the RCR compaction worked to obtain the optimally compact population, i.e. agent.

For the problems where LCS failed to reach 100% performance, the vanilla RCR also failed. However, by introducing boosting to the LCS, the hybrid system assisted LCS to solve Carry problems to a scale beyond previous LCS set-ups. However, this strategy does not affect the Majority-on domains, since no optimal rule exists in the LCS generated agents. As a result RCR cannot detect the optimal rule set with boosting.

Table 1. RCR results vs. LCS results in involved number of rules and accuracy. In the 12-bit Carry result, in the *RCR_Rules* column, the first figure represents the number of RCR compacted rules, whist the second figure represents the number of rules introduced by boosting the result.

Problem Domains	Original Rules	RCR_Rules	Original Accuracy	RCR_Accuracy
6-bit Even-parity	[848, 1324]	64	[98.2%, 100%]	100%
11-bit Even-parity	[3606, 3691]	2048	[92.4%, 97.6%]	100%
6-bit Multiplexer	[170, 222]	8	[100%, 100%]	100%
11-bit Multiplexer	[198, 240]	16	[100%, 100%]	100%
20-bit Multiplexer	[4117, 4394]	32	[100%, 100%]	100%
37-bit Multiplexer	[6816, 6937]	64	[100%, 100%]	100%
6-bit Majority-on	[144, 222]	35	[100%, 100%]	100%
7-bit Majority-on	[531, 617]	70	[100%, 100%]	100%
12-bit Majority-on	[9749, 10224]	0	[98.5%, 99.1%]	0%
6-bit Carry	[101, 149]	18	[100%, 100%]	100%
8-bit Carry	[486, 612]	38	[100%, 100%]	100%
12-bit Carry	[934, 1052]	[14 + 119, 14 + 136]	[98.3%, 98.7%]	100%

4.1   GP Results vs. LCS Results

To place the performance of the novel LCS in context it is compared with a standard Genetic Programming (GP) approach on the binary problems. For the sake of fairness both GP's and LCS's population is capped at 500 (trees and rules respectively). Moreover, both systems are permitted to observe the whole problem domain. The whole training process involved 30 generations of each dataset for GP and 1920 individual data instances (iterations) for LCS (1 GP generation is equal to 64 iterations).

In general, GP addressed the 6-bit Even-parity but LCS did not. The reason is that LCS needs a population of around 3000 rules for this task, but only 500 is provided. Both systems achieve maximum accuracy for the Multiplexer problem, but LCS's result is more stable than GP's as shown in Table 2. For the Carry and Majority-on domains, the LCS tests are mainly successful, but the majority of GP test fail. The reason is that in these two domains, unlike in the Multiplexer and Even-parity domains, the function sets are only basic functions without human intervention in their selection. These results indicated GPs' performance heavily depends on the selected function set (see training process shown in Fig. 4).

Generally, LCS's and GP's performance on 6-bit binary problems are similar. However, when the problem scales, the LCS's performance surpasses GP significantly, as shown in Fig. 4. Based on the 11-bit Multiplexer problem, LCS spends around 20000 iterations to successfully address the task, whereas GP fails after 15 generations (on 11-bit problems one generation is equivalent to 2048 iterations). As well as scaling performance, LCS rules are interpretable as shown in Fig. 3 and Table 3, with the output from GP and LCS for the 6-bit Multiplexer problem. By analyzing the LCS's outputs it is possible to observe the importance of each attribute, but in GPs' output, due to the rich representation, this important information is obscured.

Table 2. GP vs. LCS in accuracy interval and average accuracy in 30 runs

ProblemDomains	GP_Interval	GP_Average	LCS_Interval	LCS_Average
6-bit Multiplexer	[87.5%, 100%]	98.7%	[96.8%, 100%]	99.53%
6-bit Even-parity	[73.4%, 100%]	91.2%	[79.5%, 98.2%]	91.1%
6-bit Carry	[93.8%, 100%]	96.5%	[92.4%, 100%]	99.1%
6-bit Majority-on	[92.2%, 98.4%]	95%	[95.9%, 100%]	98.5%

4.2   Attribute Importance

The attribute intervals following the sub-space clustering in RCR generated classifiers are showed in Fig. 5 for the 30 agents of each problem. Essentially, for a given attribute level, this shows how likely a given attribute is to be specified. This clearly visualises the different underlying patterns in each problem domain. Moreover, by implementing this method to the same domain with various scales (length of the condition), the hidden patterns that influence the attributes at a specific scale can be detected.

The RCR successfully addressed the **Multiplexer** problem from 6-bits to 37-bits, for all the results, the attribute intervals limited to one sub-space. Moreover, although the data bits' attribute importance is decreased while the problem scales, all the address bits' attribute importance is kept at 1.0.

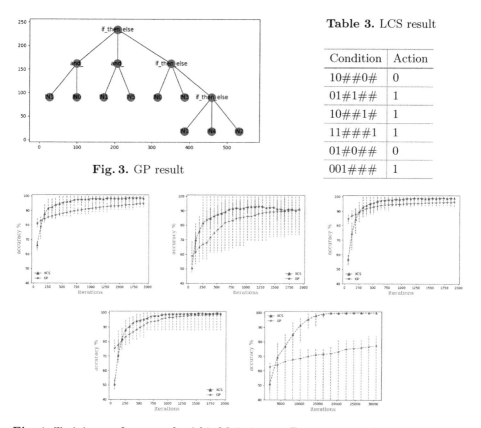

Fig. 3. GP result

Table 3. LCS result

Condition	Action
10##0#	0
01#1##	1
10##1#	1
11###1	1
01#0##	0
001###	1

Fig. 4. Training performance for 6-bit Majority-on, Even-parity, and Carry problems, where the second line shows 6 and 11-bit Multiplexer problems.

The attribute interval for 3 + 3-bit **Carry** is limited to [2, 4] and for 4 + 4-bit is limited to [2, 5], one interesting finding is that while the problems' increased by 2 bits, only one additional sub-space is introduced. Moreover, the result shows that the problem should be split into two parts. Incidentally, standard LCSs cannot solve any Carry problem that exceeds 5 + 5, the performance will become stuck at around 98% accuracy as important rules cannot be found by the LCS trained agent. However, by introducing boosting the system does achieve 100% accuracy.

The result for the **Majority-on** problem reflects the relationship between the length of conditions and attributes. As in the 6-bit domain the attribute interval across two sub-spaces, i.e. [3, 4]. However, when the problem becomes odd, it only uses one sub-space, i.e. [4].

The **Even-parity** results show that the sub-space is limited to a maximum of one. This phenomenon indicates that all the attributes are important for making decisions as all the attributes need to be specified.

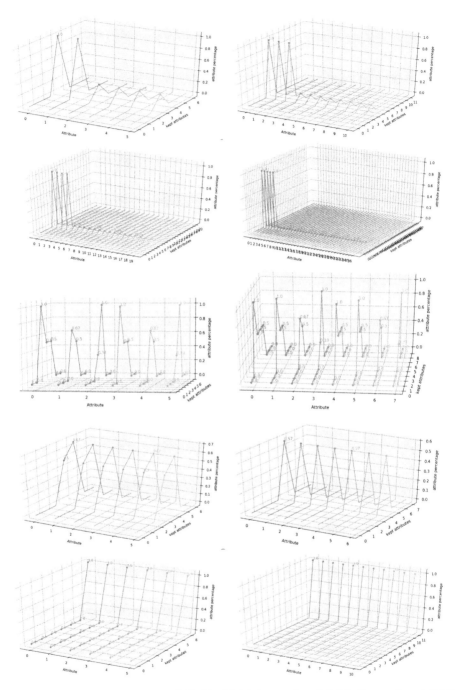

Fig. 5. Results for 6, 11, 20, and 37 bit Multiplexer; 6 and 8 bit Carry; 6 and 7 bit majority; 6 and 11 bit Even-parity problems (left to right, top to bottom).

5 Discussion

Single Rule Selected Method. The rate for calculating the boundary between superior rules and inferior rules in the novel rule selection method is associated with 0.3 and the performance is displayed in Table 4 and Fig. 6, which is interrogated through True positive rate (TPR) and False negative rate (FNR) among four tested 6-bit benchmark problems. TPR is equal to the number of selected optimal rules divided by the number of selected rules. Whilst, the FNR is measured by the number of unselected optimal rules divided by the number of unselected rules. The red points and blue triangles indicate the false positive and true negative respectively of individuals. Meanwhile, the green stars and cubes display false negative optimal rules and true positive optimal rules, respectively.

The results explain why the rule reduction method is based on multiple populations instead of one, as in problems such as the Multiplexer and Even-parity it is possible to detect all the optimal rules in a single population, but in problems such as Majority-on and Carry, fewer optimal rules are close to the cluster of the non-optimal rules. This makes it difficult to distinguish these important candidates in such a farrago. The strategy of selecting candidates among multiple populations can effectively prevent losing the optimal rules' diversity, which is caused by the variance in a single population.

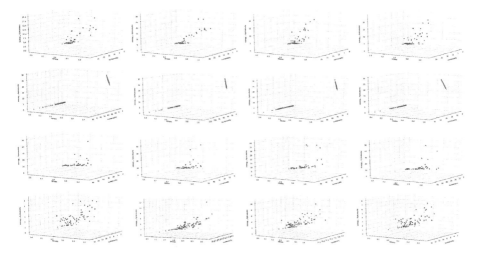

Fig. 6. Distribution of rule niches, first row Multiplexer; second row Even-parity; third row Carry; last row Majority-on. X axis: fitness; Y axis: numerosity; Z axis: their product. Green cube TP, green star FN, red FP, blue TN.

Rules' Polymorphism. Rule polymorphism means that different rule combinations represent the same knowledge. The main difference between rules' polymorphism and rules' diversity is the background philosophy. In rules' diversity each produced solution is considered as an individual. Therefore, when seeking a good performance solution, all the produced combinations are compared with each other to elect the best. However, in rules' polymorphism, all the produced solution are treated equality. An analogy is that H_2O can have a morphology of ice, water or steam, where only one morphology is likely suitable to a given task. Thus, when trying to detect the optimal solution, the goal is altered to detect the most stable morphism for a task. Hence, all the involved combinations are interrogated as an entirety. As a result, the hidden commonality for a task can be detected.

Indeed, XCSs often generates various solutions for a task. Furthermore, it is quite hard to identify two equivalent solution sets even for some simple tasks, such as a 6-bit Multiplexer problem. However, when analyzing XCS produced solutions in detail a uniqueness dominated rule set is discovered among all the observed samples.

Generally, rules in an XCS produced solution can be categorized into four groups: in the first group, all the rules do not participate in the prediction process. Therefore, these rules are meaningless to represent a problem. The second group refers to the rules that are not important to solve a task nor making a negative contribution, such as over-specific rules or over-general rules. The third group, all the members are correct rules, but these rules are not unreplaceable - not all the problem domains contain this group. The last group is the optimal group, which means all the rules in this group are essential rules to represent a data set. Moreover, this rule set is unique. For all the tested benchmark problems in this paper, when a produced rule combination reaches the maximum accuracy the complete fourth group is detected. However, for any less rule combination the observed area of the fourth group depends on the problem domain as showing in Table 1.

Table 4. Results of the novel method

$Problem Domains$	$TP\_Interval$	$TP\_Average$	$FN\_Interval$	$FN\_Average$
6-bit Multiplexer	[33.33%, 53.57%]	45.83%	[0%, 1.68%]	0.67%
6-bit Even-parity	[100%, 100%]	100%	[0.37%, 0.74%]	0.59%
6-bit Carry	[100%, 100%]	100%	[3.77%, 10.64%]	5.74%
6-bit Majority-on	[98.11%, 100%]	99.27%	[12.96%, 16.96%]	15.49%

6   Conclusions

The overall aim to develop the LCS technique to avoid rule polymorphism without the need for post-processing compaction algorithms or human set up for each problem type was successful. Results showed that for non-overlapping niche problems, such as the Multiplexer problem, the introduced bagging method could detect and visualise the optimal rule population. The novel boosting-like method enabled the LCS to avoid local-optima even in overlapping problem domains, such as the Carry problem. 100% classification performance could be reached, which compares favourably with the benchmark GP approach. This was despite individual LCSs not reaching this performance level, thus the novel methods represent a major contribution to the field.

Further work is required to implement this approach in real-valued problems. An analogy to generality sub-spaces is required. Therefore, we are keen to see whether the same phenomenon will happen in rich alphabet based LCS, such as XCSCFA [19] or XCSCFC [20]. It is plausible that the number of functions and terminals will help guide the sub-space structure.

References

1. Urbanowicz, R.J., Moore, J.H.: Learning classifier systems: a complete introduction, review, and roadmap. J. Artif. Evol. Appl. **2009**, 1 (2009)
2. Iqbal, M., Naqvi, S.S., Browne, W.N., Hollitt, C., Zhang, M.: Salient object detection using learning classifier systems that compute action mappings. In: Proceedings of the 2014 Annual Conference on Genetic and Evolutionary Computation, pp. 525–532. ACM (2014)
3. Wilson, S.W.: Classifier fitness based on accuracy. Evol. Comput. **3**(2), 149–175 (1995)
4. Urbanowicz, R.J., Moore, J.H.: Exstracs 2.0: description and evaluation of a scalable learning classifier system. Evol. Intel. **8**(2–3), 89–116 (2015)
5. Urbanowicz, R.J., Browne, W.N.: Introduction to Learning Classifier Systems. Springer, Heidelberg (2017). https://doi.org/10.1007/978-3-662-55007-6
6. Liu, Y., Xue, B., Browne, W.N.: Visualisation and optimisation of learning classifier systems for multiple domain learning. In: Shi, Y., et al. (eds.) SEAL 2017. LNCS, vol. 10593, pp. 448–461. Springer, Cham (2017). https://doi.org/10.1007/978-3-319-68759-9_37
7. Nakata, M., Lanzi, P.L., Takadama, P.: Rule reduction by selection strategy in XCS with adaptive action map. Evol. Intel. **8**(2–3), 71–87 (2015)
8. Dixon, P.W., Corne, D.W., Oates, M.J.: Encouraging compact rulesets from XCS for enhanced data mining. In: Bull, L. (ed.) Applications of Learning Classifier Systems, pp. 92–109. Springer, Heidelberg (2004). https://doi.org/10.1007/978-3-540-39925-4_4
9. Dixon, P.W., Corne, D.W., Oates, M.J.: A ruleset reduction algorithm for the XCS learning classifier system. In: Lanzi, P.L., Stolzmann, W., Wilson, S.W. (eds.) IWLCS 2002. LNCS (LNAI), vol. 2661, pp. 20–29. Springer, Heidelberg (2003). https://doi.org/10.1007/978-3-540-40029-5_2
10. Shi, L., Shi, Y., Gao, Y.: Clustering with XCS and agglomerative rule merging. In: Corchado, E., Yin, H. (eds.) IDEAL 2009. LNCS, vol. 5788, pp. 242–250. Springer, Heidelberg (2009). https://doi.org/10.1007/978-3-642-04394-9_30
11. Watkins, C.J.C.H., Dayan, P.: Q-learning. Mach. Learn. **8**(3–4), 279–292 (1992)
12. Breiman, L.: Bagging predictors. Mach. Learn. **24**(2), 123–140 (1996)
13. Freund, Y., Schapire, R.E.: A desicion-theoretic generalization of on-line learning and an application to boosting. In: Vitányi, P. (ed.) EuroCOLT 1995. LNCS, vol. 904, pp. 23–37. Springer, Heidelberg (1995). https://doi.org/10.1007/3-540-59119-2_166

14. Liu, Y., Iqbal, M., Alvarez, I., Browne, W.N.: Integration of code-fragment based learning classifier systems for multiple domain perception and learning. In: 2016 IEEE Congress on Evolutionary Computation (CEC), pp. 2177–2184. IEEE (2016)
15. Bernadó, E., Llorà, X., Garrell, J.M.: XCS and GALE: a comparative study of two learning classifier systems on data mining. In: Lanzi, P.L., Stolzmann, W., Wilson, S.W. (eds.) IWLCS 2001. LNCS (LNAI), vol. 2321, pp. 115–132. Springer, Heidelberg (2002). https://doi.org/10.1007/3-540-48104-4_8
16. Bull, L., Bernadó-Mansilla, E., Holmes, J.: Learning Classifier Systems in Data Mining, vol. 125. Springer, Heidelberg (2008). https://doi.org/10.1007/978-3-540-78979-6
17. Gathercole, C., Ross, P.: Tackling the boolean even n parity problem with genetic programming and limited-error fitness. Genet. Program. **97**, 119–127 (1997)
18. Iacca, G., Neri, F., Mininno, E., Ong, Y.-S., Lim, M.-H.: Ockham's Razor in memetic computing: three stage optimal memetic exploration. Inf. Sci. **188**, 17–43 (2012)
19. Iqbal, M., Browne, W.N., Zhang, M.: Learning overlapping natured and niche imbalance boolean problems using XCS classifier systems. In: IEEE Congress on Evolutionary Computation (CEC), pp. 1818–1825 (2013)
20. Alvarez, I.M., Browne, W.N., Zhang, M.: Reusing learned functionality to address complex boolean functions. In: Dick, G., et al. (eds.) SEAL 2014. LNCS, vol. 8886, pp. 383–394. Springer, Cham (2014). https://doi.org/10.1007/978-3-319-13563-2_33

An Automatic Feature Extraction Approach to Image Classification Using Genetic Programming

Ying Bi[$\boxtimes$], Bing Xue, and Mengjie Zhang

Evolutionary Computation Research Group,
School of Engineering and Computer Science,
Victoria University of Wellington, Wellington 6140, New Zealand
{Ying.Bi,Bing.Xue,Mengjie.Zhang}@ecs.vuw.ac.nz

Abstract. Feature extraction is an essential process for image data dimensionality reduction and classification. However, feature extraction is very difficult and often requires human intervention. Genetic Programming (GP) can achieve automatic feature extraction and image classification but the majority of existing methods extract low-level features from raw images without any image-related operations. Furthermore, the work on the combination of image-related operators/descriptors in GP for feature extraction and image classification is limited. This paper proposes a multi-layer GP approach (MLGP) to performing automatic high-level feature extraction and classification. A new program structure, a new function set including a number of image operators/descriptors and two region detectors, and a new terminal set are designed in this approach. The performance of the proposed method is examined on six different data sets of varying difficulty and compared with five GP based methods and 42 traditional image classification methods. Experimental results show that the proposed method achieves better or comparable performance than these baseline methods. Further analysis on the example programs evolved by the proposed MLGP method reveals the good interpretability of MLGP and gives insight into how this method can effectively extract high-level features for image classification.

Keywords: Genetic Programming · Image classification
Feature extraction · Image analysis

1 Introduction

Image classification is an important task in computer vision and pattern recognition with a wide range of applications such as image database annotation, image retrieval and video annotation [1]. Image classification can be defined as categorising an image into different predefined groups based on the content of the image. Although a number of techniques have been proposed to find solutions to this task [1], image classification is still an open issue due to the large variations in images, which needs further investigation.

© Springer International Publishing AG, part of Springer Nature 2018
K. Sim and P. Kaufmann (Eds.): EvoApplications 2018, LNCS 10784, pp. 421–438, 2018.
https://doi.org/10.1007/978-3-319-77538-8_29

Feature extraction is a key component of image classification. It can reduce the high dimensionality of the image data. The presences of stable and representative image features have positive effects on the performance of the classification system. A number of approaches such as the Grey-Level Co-occurrence Matrix (GLCM) [2], Local Binary Patterns (LBP) [3], Histogram of Orientated Gradients (HOG) [4], and Scale Invariant Feature Transform (SIFT) [5] are designed to extract features from the whole image or keypoints. However, it is very difficult to design an effective feature extraction method among these methods when dealing with a specific tasks. Generally, image domain experts and human intervention are required for image feature extraction, which needs cost and time to find [6].

Evolutionary computation (EC) techniques have a big potential to find the best solution from a set of solutions through a number of iterations/generations for a particular problem without domain knowledge and human intervention. Among the EC techniques, Genetic Programming (GP) is the most widely used technique on image analysis [7]. In the past decade, GP has been successfully applied to image classification, feature extraction, image segmentation, object detection, image registration and so on [8,9]. The flexible representation and the good ability of handling different data types allow GP to easily perform a particular image task by using image-related operators in its function set. For example, GP can evolve effective edge detectors based on Gaussian-based filters [10]. However, the existing work on using image-related operators/descriptors in GP for feature extraction and image classification is limited. Therefore, this work attempts to develop a GP approach to feature extraction and image classification which can benefit from the prior designed image-related operators/descriptors.

In [11–14], GP has been successfully applied to achieve automatic region detection, feature extraction, feature construction, and image classification simultaneously. However, there are a variety of image operators such as Gaussian filter, Histogram Equalisation, Sobel edge detector, Laplacian, which are more advanced for facilitating feature extraction than the simple pixel statistic feature extraction approaches in [11,12]. These operators can reduce noise, increase contrast or detect edges of an image, which are helpful for improving the quality of image data or finding more distinctive features such as edges from an image. The existing HOG and LBP image descriptors also have good ability for describing specific image features including shape and texture. Rather than only using HOG in [14], employing a set of image operators/descriptors in GP allows it to evolve high-level image features according to the data set it is trained on.

1.1   Goals

The overall goal of this paper is to develop a GP approach to achieving automatic region detection and feature extraction for effective image classification. This approach aims at integrating a set of image-related operators/descriptors in GP to detect more informative high-level image features for image classification. To achieve this, we propose a new MLGP approach, where a new program representation is designed, a set of operators including image operators and region detectors, and a new terminal set are developed. The new method will be examined and compared with five other GP-based methods and 42 non-GP methods on six different image data sets of varying difficulty. Specifically, the overall goal can be divided into the following four objectives.

(1) Develop a new program representation in GP which can integrate region detection, feature extraction, feature construction, and classification to a single solution/tree;
(2) Develop a new function set and a new terminal set which allow GP to benefit from the combination of image-related operators/descriptors and produce high-level features with the potential of achieving good classification performance;
(3) Investigate whether the proposed method can outperform the other five GP methods and 42 non-GP methods; and
(4) Analyse the example trees with high performance to understand how the high-level features are extracted from the detected regions and further be constructed for effective classification.

2 Related Work

Zhang and Ciesielski [15] proposed a domain independent image feature extraction method (simplified as FeEx in this paper) and employed GP to evolve classifiers based on these features for object detection. The evolved classifier was used for classifying pixels into object or non-object groups. Compared to neural networks, the GP method achieved better detection rate and false alarm rate. Nandi *et al.* [16] introduced GP for classifying breast mass into the benign and malignant categories based on the selected texture features. The GP approach has shown promising results in classification. However, this approach requires domain experts to identify regions of interest and to extract image features. The other similar work on medical image classification can be found in [17,18]. Human intervention and domain experts are required to extract image features when using GP to evolve classifiers. The performance of the GP method on image classification highly relies on these extracted features.

Al-Sahaf *et al.* [6] proposed a GP approach to automatically evolving texture descriptor for texture image classification with a small number of training instances. A number of conventional classification methods such as Nearest Neighbour (1NN) were employed to perform classification based on the extracted features. A dynamic GP method was proposed in [8], where a flexible length of feature vector is synthesised for texture classification. Experimental results have shown that this method outperformed the previous method where a fixed length of feature vector is extracted. However, these two GP descriptors were inspired by the LBP descriptor and are originally proposed for describing the texture feature, which might not perform well on the other image data.

Atkins *et al.* [13] proposed a multi-tier GP approach (simplified as 3TGP in this paper) to achieving automatic image feature extraction and classification. There are three tiers, i.e. an image filtering tier, an aggregation tier and a classification tier designed in this method, where each tier targets a subtask. The image filtering tier is used for evolving several general filters such as max, mean and min to perform convolution operations to the input image. The aggregation tier is employed for detecting square regions and extracting domain independent features namely pixel statistics from these regions. However, the method performs image filtering before region detection, which might not be efficient.

Later, Al-Sahaf et al. [11] proposed a two-tier GP (2TGP) approach for image feature extraction and classification using raw images as input. The representation of 3TGP was simplified in 2TGP where only the aggregation tier and the classification tier are employed. Two variants of 2TGP are proposed in [12] to detect more flexible regions and to extract features from these regions.

The features extracted by the 3TGP and 2TGP methods from detected regions are pixel statistics, which are relatively simple. To address this problem, Lenson et al. [14] designed a GP-HoG method based on the framework of 2TGP. This method designed the advanced feature descriptor HOG as a function in GP to extract high-level HOG histogram features from the detected regions. The GP-HoG method demonstrated a good example to integrate the HOG descriptor in GP to achieve high-level feature extraction and showed promising results in image classification. However, only using the HOG descriptor might not be efficient for GP to deal with complex image classification tasks such as texture image or scene image classification.

3   The Proposed Method

This section presents the proposed MLGP method in detail, including the GP program structure, the function set, the terminal set, and the fitness function.

3.1   Program Structure

To achieve automatic region detection, feature extraction, feature construction, and classification simultaneously, a multi-layer program structure is designed

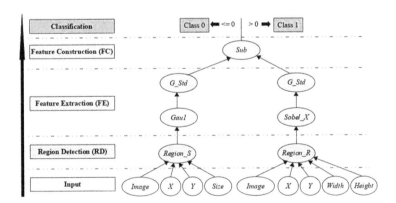

Fig. 1. An example of the program structure.

in the MLGP method. Figure 1 gives an example program to show how the multiple layers are constructed in a single program tree. There are five layers in the example program, i.e. Input, Region Detection, Feature Extraction, Feature Construction, and Classification, where each layer is shown in a different colour in Fig. 1.

The first (bottom) layer is **Input**, where images and constant parameters are feed from this layer to the GP method. The second layer is **Region Detection (RD)**, where prominent regions in an image are identified. The third layer is **Feature Extraction (FE)**, where several image operators are applied to deal with the detected regions such as using Gaussian smooth filter to reduce noise or using Sobel to detect edge features. Benefiting from these image operators, important and good features are expected to be detected and extracted. The fourth layer is **Feature Construction (FC)**, where extracted features are further constructed to a new high-level feature. The final (top) layer is **Classification**, in which a class label is assigned to the input image according to the value of the new feature and the predetermined threshold.

The program structure of the proposed MLGP method is constructed according to the five layers in a bottom-up manner, as shown in Fig. 1. It is a tree-based representation, where operators consist of the internal nodes and terminals consist of the leaf nodes. To deal with different tasks at each layer, a set of operators and terminals are employed. As the example program tree shown in Fig. 1, there are operators i.e. *Region_S, Gau1, G_Std, Sub, Region_R, Sobel_X* and terminals i.e. *Image, X, Y, Size, Width, Height*. More details about the operators and terminals can be seen in Sect. 3.2.

3.2   Functions and Terminals

(1) Terminals for the Input layer: There are four types of terminals for this layer, which represent the input image and the constant parameters of the proposed GP method. They are **Image, X, Y, Size, Width**, and **Height**. The *Image* terminal represents the input grey-scale image, which is a 2-D array with image pixel values in range [0, 1] (the raw image is normalised by dividing 255). The *X* and *Y* terminals are the coordinates of the top left point of a detected region in the input image. They are integers in range [0, Image Width] or [0, Image Height]. The terminals *Size, Width* and *Heigh* mean the width and height of a square/rectangle region. They are between [20, 70] as the image sizes of our data sets are 128×128 or 40×100. In the MLGP method, the values of *X, Y, Size, Width,* and *Height* are randomly generated initially and evolved during evolutionary process.

(2) Operators for the RD layer: There are two operators **Region_S** and **Region_R** are used for this layer. These two operators can detect a square/rectangle region at an appropriate position in an image with a suitable size by taking arguments from the Input layer as inputs. The *Region_S* operator detects a square region, which requires four arguments, including *Image, X, Y,* and *Size*. The *Region_R* operator detects a rectangle region, which needs five arguments, including *X, Y, Size, Width,* and *Height*. Notice that if there is an area in the detected region beyond the input image, only the area inside the input image is used as the detected region.

Table 1. Operators for the FE layer

Operator	Input	Output	Description
G_Std	A region	A number	The standard deviation of a region
Hist_Eq	A region	A region	Histogram Equalisation
Gau1	A region	A region	Gaussian smooth filter with $\sigma = 1$
Gau11	A region	A region	The first derivatives of Gaussian filter with $\sigma = 1$
GauXY	A region	A region	Gradient magnitude using Gaussian derivatives with $\sigma = 1$
Lap	A region	A region	Laplacian filter
Sobel_X	A region	A region	Sobel filter along X axis
Sobel_Y	A region	A region	Sobel filter along Y axis
LoG1	A region	A region	Laplacian of Gaussian filter with $\sigma = 1$
LoG2	A region	A region	Laplacian of Gaussian filter with $\sigma = 2$
LBP	A region	A region	Uniform LBP descriptor
HOG	A region	A region	HOG descriptor

(3) Operators for the FE layer: There are one designed operator and 11 image-related operators used for this layer, as listed in Table 1. The 11 image-related operators are used for dealing with regions detected by the RD layer. These operators include one histogram equalisation operator, eight image filters and two image descriptors. The *Hist_Eq* operator is designed to increase contrast and equalize the histogram of an image. The *Gau1, Gau11, GauXY, Lap, Sobel_X, Sobel_Y, LoG1,* and *LoG2* filters perform convolution operations on an image. The *Gau1* operator is used for reducing noise, and the remain filters are used for edge detection, flat detection or shape detection. In all these filters, the size are set to 3×3 as it is the commonly used. Two well-known image descriptors *LBP* [19] and *HOG* [4] are used in the function set for describing important shape and texture information of an image. In the *LBP* operator, the number neighbours is set to 8 and the radius is set to 1.5. In the *HOG* operator, the number of orientations is 9, the block size is 3×3 and the cell size is 8×8.

Another important operator for this layer is *G_Std*, which calculates the standard deviation of an image/region. This operator must be selected in each program tree, which means only the standard deviation value is finally extracted from the detected/processed region. The standard deviation is a good measure for quantifying the variation of pixel values in an image/region. It is invariant to the pixel location changes. It should be pointed out that all the image operators and the orders among these operators are automatically evolved during GP evolutionary process. Hence, these operators allow GP to find good combinations of them to identify the difference of the standard deviation values of the images/regions from different classes and to extract good features.

(4) Operators for the FC layer: There is one arithmetic function used for this layer. It is *Sub(−)*, which takes two floating-point numbers as input and returns a floating-point number. One of its child nodes is the *G_Std* operator. Due to the standard deviation is always positive, only the *Sub* operator is employed in this

layer in order to reduce the search space and allow the final program output to be possible or negative.

(5) *Operators for the Classification layer*: The operation for this layer is that if the output from the FC layer is positive, the class label for the input image is 1 (class 1), otherwise the class label is 0 (class 2).

3.3   The Fitness Function

In the MLGP method, the fitness function (F) is the classification accuracy, which is straightforward and commonly used for binary image classification. The formula is shown by Eq. (1).

$$F = Classification\ Accuracy = \frac{TP + TN}{TOTAL} \times 100\% \tag{1}$$

where TP is the total number of True Positives, TN is the total number of True Negatives, and $TOTAL$ is the total number of classified images in the data set. TP represents the positive samples correctly classified into the positive class, and TN means the negative samples correctly categorised into the negative class. The proposed MLGP method is employed to evolve programs which can maximize the fitness function, i.e. classification accuracy.

4   Experiment Design

4.1   Datasets

To evaluate the performance of the proposed method, six different data sets are used in the experiments. These selected data sets represent six typical image classification tasks, including **COIL-20** [20] as object classification, **UIUC** [21] as car detection, **JAFFE** [22] as facial expression classification, **SCENE** [23] as scene classification, **TEXTURE** [24] as texture classification, and **BIRDS** [25] as fine-grained image classification. As the proposed method aims at dealing with binary image classification, each data set (except for UIUC) is formed by selecting two classes from the original data set. The difficulties of these data sets are various due to different variations such as scale, illumination, rotation in images. The majority

Fig. 2. Example images from COIL-20, JAFFE, SCENE, TEXTURE, and BIRDS.

data sets (except for BIRDS) are original gray-scale image data sets as this paper focuses on gray-scale image. The colour images in BIRDS are converted to gray-scale images.

In the experiments, each image data set is spilt into the training set, the validation set and the test set, having 50%, 25%, 25% images respectively. In JAFFE, the number of images in each set is the same due to the total number of images is small. The original images of the JAFFE, SCENE, TEXTURE, and BIRD data sets are resized to 128×128 with high quality in order to maintain the image size consistent of each data set and to reduce the dimensionality of image data. Details of the data sets are listed in Table 2. Several resized and transformed example images from each data set are shown in Figs. 2 and 3.

Fig. 3. Example images from UIUC.

Table 2. Data set properties

Name	Size	Classes	Training set	Validation set	Test set
COIL-20	128×128	*Obj20*	36	18	18
		Obj10	36	18	18
UIUC	100×40	*Cars*	275	110	165
		Non-cars	250	100	150
JAFFE	128×128	*Happy*	10	10	10
		Surprised	10	10	10
SCENE	128×128	*Highway*	130	65	65
		Streets	146	73	73
TEXTURE	128×128	*Cork*	216	103	113
		Brown bread	216	108	108
BIRDS	128×128	*Pelagic Cormorant*	30	15	15
		Red Faced Cormorant	26	13	13

4.2   Baseline Methods

In order to examine the performance of the proposed method, five GP-based methods and 42 non-GP methods are implemented as baseline methods in the experiments. The five GP-based methods are 3TGP [13], 2TGP [11], FeEx+GP [15], Hist+GP, and uLBP+GP. The Hist+GP method uses 64 histogram features as input and the uLBP+GP method utilises 59 uniform LBP histogram features as input, where GP is used as a classification method. The 42 non-GP methods are based on seven commonly used machine learning classification methods and six existing image feature extraction methods. In each method, image features are extracted by a commonly used feature extraction method and then feed to a classification method to learn a classifier/classifiers. The six image feature extraction methods are FeEx [15], Histogram, GLCM [26], HOG [4], LBP [3], and ulBP [19], and details are shown in Table 3. The seven classification methods include 1NN, Gaussian Naive Bayes (NB), Decision Tree (DT), Multilayer Perception (MLP), Adaptive Boosting (AdaBoost), Random Forest (RF), Support Vector Machine (SVM with Radial Basis Function (RBF)). The implementation of these methods are based on the well-known *scikit-learn* [27] Python package. In the MLP method, the number of neurons in the hidden layer is set to 50 [28], the activation function is the logistic sigmoid function, and the learning rate is adaptive. The non-linear kernel RBF is employed in SVM as it is commonly used. For all these non-GP methods, the training instances include the training set and the validation set used in the GP approaches, while the test set keeps the same.

Table 3. Image feature extraction methods

Methods	Description
FeEx	20 domain independent features [15]
Histogram	256 histogram features based on the pixel intensities of the gray-scale image
GLCM	24 GLCM features. Four different orientations are used and the contrast, dissimilarity, homogeneity, energy, correlation and ASM are extracted from each GLCM
HOG	HOG features. Using the HOG method to extract features. In HOG, the orientation is set to 9, the pixels in each cell is set to 32×32 (12×12 for UIUC), and the cells in each block is set to 3×3
LBP	256 LBP histogram features. In LBP, the number of neighbour is set to 8 and the radius is set to 1.5
ulBP	59 uniform LBP histogram features

4.3   Parameter Settings

All the GP methods are implemented in Python based on the *DEAP (Distributed Evolutionary Algorithm in Python)* [29] package. Parameter settings in all the GP methods are the same as listed in Table 4. On each data set, each algorithm has been run 30 times independently with different random seeds.

In the evolutionary process, each individual is evaluated at each generation on the training set. To avoid overfitting, the best individual on the training set is evaluated on the validation set. After 50 generations, the best individual on the validation set is tested on the test set to evaluate the performance of the method. Notice that this process is conducted in all the GP methods rather than only in the proposed method.

Table 4. GP run time parameters

Parameter	Value	Parameter	Value
Generations	50	Crossover rate	0.8
Population size	1024	Mutation rate	0.19
Selection type	Tournament	Elitism rate	0.01
Tournament size	7	Tree-depth	2–6

5   Results and Discussions

All the experimental results of GP methods are shown in Table 5 and that of non-GP methods are listed in Table 6. The Student's t-test with a 5% significance level is employed to compare the proposed method with a GP or non-GP method. In Tables 5 and 6, the "+" indicates that the proposed method is significantly better than the corresponding method, the "–" indicates the proposed method performs significantly worse than the corresponding method, and the "=" indicates that the proposed method performs similar to the corresponding method.

5.1   Compared with GP Methods

Table 5 shows the test results in terms of maximum, mean and standard deviation of classification accuracies obtained by the MLGP method and the other five GP methods on the six data sets in 30 runs. The first COIL-20 data set is easy so that all the GP methods obtain 100% maximum accuracy. There is no significant improvement over the other GP methods on this data set. On UIUC and JAFFE, the MLGP method obtains significantly better or similar performance compared to the other GP methods. On JAFFE, the MLGP method obtains 100% maximum classification accuracy and 91.67% mean classification accuracy, which achieves nearly 9% increase to the 82.83% maximum mean classification accuracy obtained by the 2TGP method. On SCENE and TEXTURE, the proposed MLGP method achieves significantly better performance than the 2TGP, 3TGP, FeEx+GP and Hist+GP methods. Compared to these four GP methods, the MLGP method has a 7% and 3% increase in the mean classification accuracy on SCENE and TEXTURE. However, the uLBP+GP method outperforms the MLGP method significantly on these two data sets. Images in these two data sets contain a large amount of texture information, which can be captured well by the uniform LBP histogram features in the uLBP+GP method. The proposed MLGP method extracts features from the detected regions while the uLBP+GP method uses uniform LBP histogram features from the overall image, which might further improve its performance. On the final BIRDS data set, the proposed MLGP method achieves significantly better or comparable performances than the other GP methods.

Table 5. Classification accuracy (%) of all the GP methods on the six data sets

	Max	Mean ± St.D.	Max	Mean ± St.D.	Max	Mean ± St.D.
	COIL-20		**UIUC**		**JAFFE**	
MLGP	100.0	99.91 ± 0.5	92.38	89.47 ± 2.06	100.0	91.67 ± 6.50
2TGP	100.0	100.0 ± 0.0=	90.48	86.55 ± 2.89+	95.00	82.83 ± 8.53+
3TGP	100.0	100.0 ± 0.0=	93.02	88.42 ± 2.42=	100.0	82.67 ± 9.20+
FeEx+GP	100.0	100.0 ± 0.0=	88.25	81.76 ± 2.56+	90.00	70.67 ± 13.59+
Hist+GP	100.0	99.91 ± 0.50=	65.71	60.81 ± 2.08+	75.00	52.17 ± 9.28+
uLBP+GP	100.0	99.81 ± 0.69=	85.71	81.51 ± 2.22+	65.00	53.83 ± 6.01+
	SCENE		**TEXTURE**		**BIRDS**	
MLGP	92.75	90.97 ± 1.40	97.74	90.23 ± 3.48	71.43	61.67 ± 6.45
2TGP	86.23	81.33 ± 2.12+	81.90	75.60 ± 3.87+	67.86	51.79 ± 7.70+
3TGP	88.41	82.56 ± 2.19+	88.24	82.68 ± 4.18+	71.43	56.19 ± 5.75+
FeEx+GP	86.96	83.16 ± 2.37+	88.69	83.65 ± 2.36+	64.29	54.64 ± 5.77+
Hist+GP	86.96	83.29 ± 1.65+	94.57	87.36 ± 3.86+	78.57	51.67 ± 9.53+
uLBP+GP	96.38	92.85 ± 1.92−	97.29	92.37 ± 2.77−	71.43	60.36 ± 7.57=

In total, the proposed MLGP method achieves significantly better performance in 21 cases and comparable performance in 7 cases of out of the total 30 cases. In summary, the proposed MLGP method achieves significantly better or comparable performance on these six different image classification tasks compared to the other GP methods.

5.2 Compared with Non-GP Methods

Table 6 lists all the test results of the total 42 non-GP methods on the six data sets. On COIL-20, the proposed method achieves similarly or significantly better results than the non-GP methods. On UIUC, the MLGP method gains significantly better results than all the classification methods with the FeEx, Histogram, GLCM, LBP, uLBP features. In total, the MLGP method obtains 39 "+" and 3 "−" on this data set. On JAFFE, the MLGP method obtains 100% maximum accuracy and 91.67% mean accuracy, which achieves better or comparable performance in 40 cases out of the 42 cases. On SCENE, the MLGP method significantly outperforms all the classification methods with the FeEx and Histogram features. But this method is significantly worse than the classification methods with the other four features in some cases. The results on TEXTURE also show a similar pattern. In total, the proposed MLGP method outperforms the non-GP methods in 25 cases out of 42 cases on both SCENE and TEXTURE, and is significant worse than these methods in 13 cases on the SCENE data set and in 10 cases on the TEXTURE data set. On the most difficult BIRDS data set, the proposed MLGP method achieves comparable or significantly better results than the classification methods with the FeEx, Histogram, GLCM, and HOG features. But the classification methods with

Table 6. Classification accuracy (%) of 42 non-GP methods on the six data sets

	1NN	NB	DT	MLP	AdaBoost	RF	SVM-RDF
COIL-20		(MLGP 100/99.91 ± 0.5)					
FeEX	100.0=	100.0=	97.22+	100.0=	97.22+	100.0=	97.22+
Histogram	100.0=	100.0=	100.0=	100.0=	100.0=	100.0=	50.00+
GLCM	100.0=	100.0=	100.0=	80.56+	100.0=	100.0=	50.00+
HOG	100.0=	100.0=	100.0=	100.0=	100.0=	100.0=	100.0=
LBP	100.0=	100.0=	100.0=	100.0=	100.0=	100.0=	52.78+
uLBP	100.0=	100.0=	97.22+	100.0=	97.22+	100.0=	50.00+
UIUC		(MLGP 92.38/89.47 ± 2.06)					
FeEX	83.49+	87.62+	83.49+	77.78+	86.67+	86.67+	77.14+
Histogram	55.87+	66.03+	62.22+	60.95+	65.08+	67.94+	52.38+
GLCM	84.13+	79.68+	85.40+	61.90+	86.98+	86.67+	52.38+
HOG	92.06-	64.76+	86.98+	68.89+	97.14-	92.38-	66.98+
LBP	85.71+	85.40+	79.37+	86.35+	88.25+	84.76+	52.38+
uLBP	86.67+	85.08+	82.22+	83.17+	86.98+	87.62+	52.38+
JAFFE		(MLGP 100.0/91.67 ± 6.5)					
FeEX	90.00=	55.00+	80.00+	50.00+	85.00+	75.00+	50.00+
Histogram	90.00=	55.00+	60.00+	90.00=	60.00+	45.00+	90.00=
GLCM	65.00+	60.00+	80.00+	50.00+	75.00+	70.00+	50.00+
HOG	100.0-	100.0-	90.00=	50.00+	90.00=	90.00=	90.00=
LBP	75.00+	65.00+	70.00+	80.00+	55.00+	60.00+	50.00+
uLBP	75.00+	65.00+	35.00+	45.00+	65.00+	85.00+	75.00+
SCENE		(MLGP 92.75/90.97 ± 1.4)					
FeEX	88.41+	85.51+	80.43+	80.43+	86.23+	86.23+	79.71+
Histogram	79.71+	81.16+	81.88+	82.61+	85.51+	87.68+	52.90+
GLCM	92.03-	88.41+	89.86+	91.30=	91.30=	93.48-	52.90+
HOG	94.93-	87.68+	89.13+	89.86+	92.75-	92.03-	90.58=
LBP	89.86+	94.20+	94.20-	87.68+	96.38-	94.93-	52.90+
uLBP	89.86+	94.20-	95.65-	90.58=	96.38-	94.93-	52.90+
TEXTURE		(MLGP 97.74/90.23 ± 3.48)					
FeEX	90.50=	84.16+	87.33+	51.13+	90.50=	90.50=	78.28+
Histogram	93.21-	85.97+	91.86-	90.95+	95.93-	94.12-	48.87+
GLCM	83.71+	72.40+	94.57-	47.06+	96.38-	92.31-	48.87+
HOG	81.90+	52.04+	74.21+	52.04+	76.02+	78.73+	52.04+
LBP	98.19-	83.26+	87.78+	93.67+	91.40=	88.69+	48.87+
uLBP	96.83-	86.88+	85.07+	85.52+	90.05=	90.05=	48.87+
BIRDS		(MLGP 71.43/61.67 ± 6.45)					
FeEX	57.14+	53.57+	46.43+	53.57+	64.29-	46.43+	53.57+
Histogram	53.57+	50.00+	53.57+	50.00+	53.57+	53.57+	53.57+
GLCM	53.57+	53.57+	60.71=	60.71=	53.57+	53.57+	53.57+
HOG	57.14+	60.71=	57.14+	57.14+	64.29-	53.57+	57.14+
LBP	71.43-	71.43-	57.14+	64.29-	75.00-	78.57-	53.57+
uLBP	78.57-	75.00-	57.14+	75.00-	71.43-	78.57-	53.57+

the uLBP and LBP features achieves significantly better results than the MLGP method in the majority cases, which indicates that images in the BIRDS data set also contain much texture information and the global features is very important for the difficult fine-grained classification task.

The methods that achieve significantly better results than the proposed MLGP method in some cases are mainly AdaBoost and Random Forest, which are boosting and ensemble classifiers, while the proposed MLGP method only uses a single evolved program. In addition, compared with the non-GP methods that learn classifiers from a set of image features which are global features extracted from the whole image, the proposed method only use a single constructed feature from smaller regions for classification based on the predefined threshold. The comparison to the non-GP methods is actually not entirely fair for the proposed method. Even in these cases, the proposed method still obtains better or comparable performance compared to the non-GP methods.

The results also confirm that the performance of these non-GP methods highly rely on the feature extraction method and the classification method for dealing with different image classification tasks. For example, the HOG features with 1NN achieves better results on the JAFFE and TEXTURE data sets, but obtains worse results on the SCENE and BIRDS data sets. Even the boosting and ensemble classification methods perform better than the others in most cases, the simplest 1NN with particular features such as LBP or uLBP performs much better than using the other classification methods with the same features on the TEXTURE data set. These results reveal that the feature extraction method and the classification method must be carefully selected and suited when dealing with image classification tasks. Oppositely, the proposed MLGP method can obtain promising results in image classification without such considerations.

6 Further Analysis

This section analyses two example programs evolved by the MLGP method to show the good interpretability and understandability of the proposed method. These two example programs evolved on COIL-20 and JAFFE will give more insight into how they achieve good classification performance.

6.1 Example Program on the COIL-20 Data Set

As the COIL-20 data set is very easy, the majority programs evolved by MLGP in 30 runs can achieve perfect classification performance. To show the good interpretability and understandability, a simplest program is selected for analysis, as shown in Fig. 4. This program achieves 100% classification accuracy on training, validation and test sets. Figure 4 gives the example program, the example image from different classes, and the outputs of each nodes of the example program. In the figure, the red colour represents the outputs/regions of the *Obj10* class, and the green colour indicates that of the *Obj20* class.

This program identifies two rectangle regions with different sizes at different positions in an input image. The size of the left identified region (the left side of program in Fig. 4) is actually 60 × 57 as the size of the image is 128 × 128. This region captures the differences of the partial objects from different classes. The size of the right detected region (the right side of program in Fig. 4) is 43 × 48. This region finds the distinctive difference among two classes by capturing an area from the top right side of an image. In this region, the *Obj10* class shows more white colour of the lid of the Vaseline product, while the *Obj20* class contains more black colour. The *G_Std* operator calculates the standard deviation value of each detected region in this program. In terms of the standard deviation value, the *Obj10* is smaller than the *Obj20* in the left region, but it is bigger than the *Obj20* in the right region. Hence, the difference is constructed by the *Sub* operator for classification.

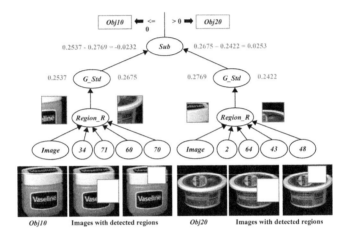

Fig. 4. An example program evolved by the MLGP method on the COIL-20 data set. (Color figure online)

6.2   Example Program on the JAFFE Data Set

Figure 5 demonstrates an example program evolved by the MLGP method on the JAFFE data set. This program achieves 95% classification accuracy on the training set, 80% accuracy on the validation set, and 100% accuracy on the test set. This program detects two different rectangle regions of an image. The left detected region with a size of 22 × 28 is smaller than the right region with a size of 46 × 31. The left region captures an area between the two eyes/eyebrows in a face image. The *Happy* and *Surprised* classes do not show significant difference in the left region. The *Hist_Eq* and *Lap* operators are evolved to deal with the left region, where the first one increases the contrast of the region, and the second operator detects the flat area and the area with edges. The difference of the two classes in the left region is enhanced by the two operators as we can see from the

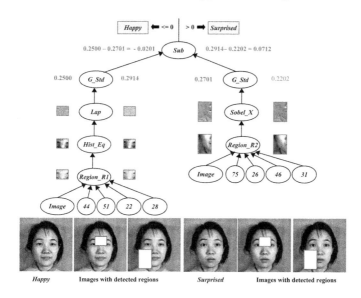

Fig. 5. An example program evolved by the MLGP method on the JAFFE data set.

left side of Fig. 5. The right detected region detects the lower left side of an face where the partial shape of the face is included. The *Sobel_X* operator is evolved to detect the edges along the horizontal direction. By these evolved operators, more features such as edges are detected and the differences of the standard deviation values between two classes are enhanced. The two standard deviation values of two detected regions are constructed by the *Sub* operator further for classification. This example program describes a relationship between two regions by using a set of operators, which achieves perfect classification performance on the test set of the JAFFE data set.

7 Conclusions

This paper proposed an MLGP approach to achieving automatic region detection, high-level feature extraction, feature construction, and image classification simultaneously. A novel program structure and a new function set were designed in the MLGP method, which well combined the prior image domain common sense knowledge and the flexible representation of GP. The performance of MLGP was examined on six image data sets of varying difficulty and was compared to other five GP methods and 42 non-GP methods. The experimental results shown that the MLGP method achieved significantly better or comparable results than the other five GP methods. Compared with the 42 non-GP methods where traditional feature extraction and classification methods are used, the MLGP method achieved more stable and better performance. The proposed MLGP method could automatically adjust to different image tasks and find good solutions due to the utilisation of prior general domain knowledge. Besides the good performance on classification, the further analysis on the evolved programs illustrated the good interpretability and understandability of the MLGP method. The MLGP method evolved very simple programs but with very high or perfect classification accuracy. The analysis of evolved programs shown that important and prominent high-level image features could be extracted and constructed by MLGP from the automatically detected regions for classification.

In this paper, only one high-level feature is constructed by MLGP for image classification, which might not be efficient. To address this problem, the features extracted by the FC layer of MLGP will be further investigated. A conventional classification method will be used for image classification based on these features to investigate whether the classification performance can be further improved on these data sets.

References

1. Pinz, A.: Object categorization. Found. Trends Comput. Graph. Vis. **1**(4), 255–353 (2005)
2. Haralick, R.M., Shanmugam, K., et al.: Textural features for image classification. IEEE Trans. Syst. Man Cybern. **6**, 610–621 (1973)
3. Ojala, T., Pietikainen, M., Harwood, D.: Performance evaluation of texture measures with classification based on kullback discrimination of distributions. In: Proceedings of the 12th IAPR International Conference on Pattern Recognition, vol. 1, pp. 582–585. IEEE (1994)
4. Dalal, N., Triggs, B.: Histograms of oriented gradients for human detection. In: IEEE Computer Society Conference on Computer Vision and Pattern Recognition, vol. 1, pp. 886–893. IEEE (2005)
5. Lowe, D.G.: Distinctive image features from scale-invariant keypoints. Int. J. Comput. Vis. **60**(2), 91–110 (2004)
6. Al-Sahaf, H., Al-Sahaf, A., Xue, B., Johnston, M., Zhang, M.: Automatically evolving rotation-invariant texture image descriptors by genetic programming. IEEE Trans. Evol. Comput. **21**(1), 83–101 (2017)
7. Xue, B., Zhang, M.: Evolutionary feature manipulation in data mining/big data. ACM SIGEVOlution **10**(1), 4–11 (2017)
8. Al-Sahaf, H., Zhang, M., Al-Sahaf, A., Johnston, M.: Keypoints detection and feature extraction: a dynamic genetic programming approach for evolving rotation-invariant texture image descriptors. IEEE Trans. Evol. Comput. (2017). https://doi.org/10.1109/TEVC.2017.2685639
9. Bi, Y., Zhang, M., Xue, B.: An automatic region detection and processing approach in genetic programming for binary image classification. In: The 32nd International Conference Image and Vision Computing New Zealand (IVCNZ 2017), pp. 1–6. IEEE (2017)
10. Fu, W., Johnston, M., Zhang, M.: Genetic programming for edge detection: a Gaussian-based approach. Soft Comput. **20**(3), 1231–1248 (2016)
11. Al-Sahaf, H., Song, A., Neshatian, K., Zhang, M.: Extracting image features for classification by two-tier genetic programming. In: 2012 IEEE Congress on Evolutionary Computation, pp. 1–8. IEEE (2012). https://doi.org/10.1109/CEC.2012.6256412

12. Al-Sahaf, H., Song, A., Neshatian, K., Zhang, M.: Two-tier genetic programming: towards raw pixel-based image classification. Expert Syst. Appl. **39**(16), 12291–12301 (2012)
13. Atkins, D., Neshatian, K., Zhang, M.: A domain independent genetic programming approach to automatic feature extraction for image classification. In: 2011 IEEE Congress on Evolutionary Computation, pp. 238–245. IEEE (2011)
14. Lensen, A., Al-Sahaf, H., Zhang, M., Xue, B.: Genetic programming for region detection, feature extraction, feature construction and classification in image data. In: Heywood, M.I., McDermott, J., Castelli, M., Costa, E., Sim, K. (eds.) EuroGP 2016. LNCS, vol. 9594, pp. 51–67. Springer, Cham (2016). https://doi.org/10.1007/978-3-319-30668-1_4
15. Zhang, M., Ciesielski, V.: Genetic programming for multiple class object detection. In: Foo, N. (ed.) AI 1999. LNCS (LNAI), vol. 1747, pp. 180–192. Springer, Heidelberg (1999). https://doi.org/10.1007/3-540-46695-9_16
16. Nandi, R., Nandi, A.K., Rangayyan, R.M., Scutt, D.: Classification of breast masses in mammograms using genetic programming and feature selection. Med. Biol. Eng. Compu. **44**(8), 683–694 (2006)
17. Ain, Q.U., Xue, B., Al-Sahaf, H., Zhang, M.: Genetic programming for skin cancer detection in dermoscopic images. In: 2017 IEEE Congress on Evolutionary Computation, pp. 2420–2427. IEEE (2017)
18. Ryan, C., Fitzgerald, J., Krawiec, K., Medernach, D.: Image classification with genetic programming: building a stage 1 computer aided detector for breast cancer. In: Gandomi, A.H., Alavi, A.H., Ryan, C. (eds.) Handbook of Genetic Programming Applications, pp. 245–287. Springer, Cham (2015). https://doi.org/10.1007/978-3-319-20883-1_10
19. Ojala, T., Pietikainen, M., Maenpaa, T.: Multiresolution gray-scale and rotation invariant texture classification with local binary patterns. IEEE Trans. Pattern Anal. Mach. Intell. **24**(7), 971–987 (2002)
20. Nene, S.A., Nayar, S.K., Murase, H., et al.: Columbia object image library (coil-20). Technical report, Columbia University (1996)
21. Agarwal, S., Awan, A., Roth, D.: Learning to detect objects in images via a sparse, part-based representation. IEEE Trans. Pattern. Anal. Mach. Intell. **26**(11), 1475–1490 (2004)
22. Lyons, M., Akamatsu, S., Kamachi, M., Gyoba, J.: Coding facial expressions with Gabor wavelets. In: The Third IEEE International Conference on Automatic Face and Gesture Recognition, pp. 200–205. IEEE (1998)
23. Fei-Fei, L., Perona, P.: A Bayesian hierarchical model for learning natural scene categories. In: IEEE Computer Society Conference on Computer Vision and Pattern Recognition, vol. 2, pp. 524–531. IEEE (2005)
24. Mallikarjuna, P., Targhi, A.T., Fritz, M., Hayman, E., Caputo, B., Eklundh, J.O.: The KTH-TIPS2 database. Computational Vision and Active Perception Laboratory (CVAP), Stockholm, Sweden (2006). http://www.nada.kth.se/cvap/databases/kth-tips
25. Welinder, P., Branson, S., Mita, T., Wah, C., Schroff, F., Belongie, S., Perona, P.: Caltech-UCSD Birds 200. Technical report CNS-TR-2010-001, California Institute of Technology (2010)
26. Haralick, R.M.: Statistical and structural approaches to texture. Proc. IEEE **67**(5), 786–804 (1979)

27. Pedregosa, F., Varoquaux, G., Gramfort, A., Michel, V., Thirion, B., Grisel, O., Blondel, M., Prettenhofer, P., Weiss, R., Dubourg, V., Vanderplas, J., Passos, A., Cournapeau, D., Brucher, M., Perrot, M., Duchesnay, E.: Scikit-learn: machine learning in Python. J. Mach. Learn. Res. **12**, 2825–2830 (2011)
28. Khotanzad, A., Lu, J.H.: Classification of invariant image representations using a neural network. IEEE Trans. Acoust., Speech, Signal Process. **38**(6), 1028–1038 (1990)
29. Fortin, F.A., De Rainville, F.M., Gardner, M.A., Parizeau, M., Gagné, C.: DEAP: evolutionary algorithms made easy. J. Mach. Learn. Res. **13**, 2171–2175 (2012)

Improving Evolutionary Algorithm Performance for Feature Selection in High-Dimensional Data

N. Cilia, C. De Stefano, F. Fontanella$^{(\boxtimes)}$, and A. Scotto di Freca

Dipartimento di Ingegneria Elettrica e dell'Informazione (DIEI),
Università di Cassino e del Lazio meridionale,
Via G. Di Biasio, 43, 03043 Cassino, FR, Italy
{nicoledalia.cilia,destefano,fontanella,a.scotto}@unicas.it

Abstract. In classification and clustering problems, selecting a subset of discriminative features is a challenging problem, especially when hundreds or thousands of features are involved. In this framework, Evolutionary Computation (EC) techniques have received a growing scientific interest in the last years, because they are able to explore large search spaces without requiring any a priori knowledge or assumption on the considered domain. Following this line of thought, we developed a novel strategy to improve the performance of EC-based algorithms for feature selection. The proposed strategy requires to rank the whole set of available features according to a univariate evaluation function; then the search space represented by the first M ranked features is searched using an evolutionary algorithm for finding feature subsets with high discriminative power. Results of comparisons demonstrated the effectiveness of the proposed approach in improving the performance obtainable with three effective and widely used EC-based algorithm for feature selection in high dimensional data problems, namely Ant Colony Optimization (ACO), Particle Swarm Optimization (PSO) and Artificial Bees Colony (ABC).

Keywords: Feature selection · High-dimensional data
Evolutionary algorithms · Feature ranking

1 Introduction

Real-world machine learning applications often involve a large number of features. However, not all the available features are essential since many of them are redundant or even irrelevant, and may reduce the performance of any classification algorithm. Feature selection techniques aim to solve this problem by selecting only a small subset of relevant features from the original set of features. By removing irrelevant and redundant features, feature selection can alleviate the curse of the dimensionality problem by reducing the dimensionality of the data, speeding up the learning process, simplifying the learnt model, and increasing

© Springer International Publishing AG, part of Springer Nature 2018
K. Sim and P. Kaufmann (Eds.): EvoApplications 2018, LNCS 10784, pp. 439–454, 2018.
https://doi.org/10.1007/978-3-319-77538-8_30

the performance [1]. Finally, the computational cost of the classification operations depends on the number of features actually used. Then, reducing this number results in a significant reduction of the cost.

The feature selection problem consists in selecting the subset of them from the whole set of available features, providing the most discriminative power. The choice of a good feature subset is crucial since if the selected features do not contain enough information to discriminate patterns belonging to different classes, the performances may be unsatisfactory, regardless of the effectiveness of the classification system employed. Moreover, irrelevant and noisy features unnecessarily enlarge the search space, increasing both the time and the complexity of the learning process.

Feature selection algorithms usually imply the definition of an evaluation function and of a search procedure. Evaluation functions can be divided into two broad classes *filter* and *wrapper* [1] Wrapper approaches use a classification algorithm as an evaluation function. The goodness of a given subset is measured in terms of classification performance; this leads to high computational costs when a large number of evaluations is required, especially when large datasets are involved. Filter evaluation functions, instead, are independent of any classification algorithm and, in most cases, are computationally less expensive and more general than wrapper algorithms.

As concerns the search strategies, given a measure, the optimal subset can be found by exhaustively evaluating all the possible solutions. Unfortunately, the exhaustive search is impracticable in most situations, because the total number of possible solutions is 2^N, for a dataset with N features. For this reason, many search techniques have been applied to feature selection, such as complete search, greedy search and heuristic search [1,2]. Since these algorithms do not take into account complex interactions among the features, most of these methods suffer from stagnation in local optima and/or high computational cost.

Evolutionary computation (EC) techniques have recently received much attention from the feature selection community as they are well-known for their global search ability [3–6]. Moreover, EC techniques do not need domain knowledge and do not make any assumptions about the search space, such as whether it is linearly or non-linearly separable, and differentiable. Most of the EC-based approaches for feature evaluation use wrapper evaluation functions [2]. For these approaches different classification algorithms have been adopted, among them: decision tree (DT), Support Vector Machines (SVMs), K-Nearest Neighbor (KNN) and Artificial Neural Networks (ANNs) [7,8]. As mentioned above, wrapper evaluation functions lead to high computational costs since their computational complexity is determined by the number of samples actually used for training the classifier. As a consequence, such approaches are not well suited to deal with problems involving a huge number of instances and features.

Also filter fitness functions have been used; the approach presented in [9] uses an information theory-based evaluation function, while in [10] the authors adopt a consistency measure. Moreover, in [11,12] the authors present a filter fitness function that extends the Fisher's linear discriminant.

Recently, in order to reduce the search space size for high-dimensional data, different strategies have been adopted for EC-based algorithms [13–17]. In [14], the search space reduction for the GA is performed by using different filter approaches. The information provided by these approaches is used to build a part of the individuals making up the initial population. Then, individuals are evaluated by means of a neural network-based wrapper function. The approach has been tested on a credit assessment risk problem involving just 33 features. In [13] the authors present a genetic programming (GP) approach for feature selection of high dimensional mass spectrometry data, on binary classification problems. In this GP-based approach the available features are first ranked, according to the information gain univariate measure, then the top 50 features are included in the terminal set of the GP algorithm. This number is fixed a priori and the authors does not justify the choice of this value. When dealing with high-dimensional data, this choice implies the exclusion of many features that are weakly relevant to the target concept by itself, but could significantly improve the classification accuracy if used together with some complementary features. Finally, in [15] the authors present a new GA-based approach for feature selection which uses three different ranking algorithms for reducing the search space for the GA, which uses an SVM-based wrapper as fitness function. However, in this case, the GA algorithm is used in a very limited way because the search space is reduced to only 12 features.

In this paper, we present a novel strategy for improving the performance of EC-based algorithms for feature selection. The proposed strategy first ranks the whole set of available features according to a univariate evaluation function, then a given number of ranked features is given as input to the EC-based algorithm chosen for feature selection. The block diagram of the proposed system is shown in Fig. 1. The proposed system is based on the hypothesis that the reduced search space provided to the EC algorithm still contains most of the good and near-optimal solutions. In practice, the filtering performed by the feature ranking step does not discard those features that performs well only when used in combination with other ones; this allows the EC algorithm to focus its search on these good areas.

It is worth noticing that, differently from previously proposed approaches, we do not make any assumption on the number of ranked features to provide to the EC algorithm. In our strategy this value (we will denote it as M in the rest of the paper) is not fixed a priori for all datasets. In fact, for each data set a range of values is tested according to the total number of available features. We propose to choose this range of values in an exponential way.

As univariate measure for the preliminary feature ranking, we used the Chi-square measure introduced in [18]. As fitness function for the EC-based algorithms we used the Correlation-based Feature Selection function (CFS) [19]. This is a filter function that evaluates the merit of a subset by considering both the correlation between the class labels and the single features, and the inter-correlation among the selected features.

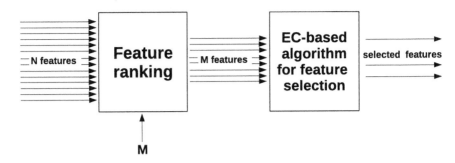

Fig. 1. The block diagram of the proposed strategy.

The effectiveness of the proposed approach has been tested on six different datasets publicly available, whose total number of features ranges from 600 to about 18000. We assessed the effectiveness of our strategy on the following algorithms: Ant Colony Optimization (ACO), Particle Swarm Optimization (PSO) and Artificial Bees Colony (ABC). Two sets of experiments have been performed. In the former, the results obtained by using the proposed strategy were compared with those of the related standard EC approaches. In the latter, our results were compared with three well-known approaches for feature selection. The experimental results confirmed the effectiveness of our approach in improving the performance of the three EC-based algorithms taken into account, both in terms of recognition rate and number of selected features.

The remainder of the paper is organized as follows: in Sect. 2 the feature evaluation functions are described, Sect. 3 illustrates the EC–based approaches for feature selection taken into account to evaluate the proposed strategy. In Sect. 4 the experimental results are detailed. Finally, Sect. 5 is devoted to the conclusions.

2   Feature Evaluation

Feature evaluation functions can also be broadly divided into two classes, namely *univariate* measures and *multivariate* measures. In the following, the univariate measure adopted to preliminarily rank the available features and the subset evaluation criterion used as fitness function of the EC algorithm are detailed.

2.1   Univariate Measures

Univariate measures evaluate the effectiveness of each single feature in discriminating samples belonging to different classes and are used to rank the available features. Once the features have been evaluated, the subset search procedure is straightforward: the features are ranked according to their merit and the best M features are selected, where the value of M must be chosen by the user [20]. For our approach, we used the Chi-square univariate measure [18]. This measure estimates feature merit by using a discretization algorithm: if a feature can be discretized to a single value, it has not discriminative power and it can safely be discarded. The discretization algorithm adopts a supervised heuristic method based on the χ^2 statistic. The range of values for each feature is initially discretized by considering a certain number of intervals (heuristically determined). Then, the χ^2 statistic is used to determine if the relative frequencies of the classes in adjacent intervals are similar enough to justify the merging of such intervals. The formula for computing the χ^2 value for two adjacent intervals is the following:

$$\chi^2 = \sum_{i=1}^{2} \sum_{j=1}^{C} \frac{(A_{ij} - E_{ij})^2}{E_{ij}} \tag{1}$$

where C is the number of classes, A_{ij} is the instance number of the j-th class in the i-th interval and E_{ij} is the expected frequency of A_{ij} given by the formula: $E_{ij} = R_i C_j / N_T$ where R_i is the number of instances in the i-th interval and C_j and N_T are the instance number of the j-th class and the total number of instances, respectively, in both intervals.

The extent of the merging process is controlled by a threshold, whose value represent the maximum admissible difference among the occurrence frequencies of the samples in adjacent intervals. The value of this threshold has been heuristically set during preliminary experiments.

2.2   Subset Evaluation

As fitness function we chose a filter one, called CFS (Correlation-based Feature Selection) [19], which uses a correlation based heuristic to evaluate feature subset quality. Given two features X and Y, their correlation r_{XY} is computed as follows[1]:

$$r_{XY} = 2.0 \cdot \frac{H(X) + H(Y) - H(X,Y)}{H(X) + H(Y)} \tag{2}$$

where the symbol H denotes the entropy function. The function r_{XY} takes into account the usefulness of the single features for predicting class labels along with the level of inter-correlation among them. The idea behind this approach is that good subsets contain features highly correlated with the class and uncorrelated with each other.

Given a feature selection problem in which the patterns are represented by means of a set Y of N features, the CFS function computes the merit of the generic subset $X \subseteq Y$, made of k features, as follows:

$$f_{CFS}(X) = \frac{k \cdot \overline{r_{cf}}}{\sqrt{k + k \cdot (k-1) \cdot \overline{r_{ff}}}} \tag{3}$$

where $\overline{r_{cf}}$ is the average feature-class correlation, and $\overline{r_{ff}}$ is the average feature-feature correlation. Note that the numerator estimates the discriminative power

---

[1] Note that the same holds also for the feature-class correlation.

of the features in X, whereas the denominator assesses the redundancy among them. The CFS function allows irrelevant and redundant features to be discarded. The former because they are poor in discriminating the different classes at the hand; the latter because they are highly correlated with one or more of the other features. In contrast to previously presented approaches [14,21], this fitness function is able to automatically find the number of features and does not need the setting of any parameter.

Finally, given a dataset $\mathcal{D}$ to estimate the quantities in (2) and a feature subset X to be evaluated, the computation of $f_{CFS}(X)$ $(X \subseteq Y)$ can be made very fast. In fact, before starting the search procedure (the EC algorithm in our case), the correlation vector V_{cf}, containing N elements, and the $N \times N$ symmetric correlation matrix M_{ff} can be computed. The i-th element of V_{cf} contains the value of the correlation between the i-th feature and the class, whereas the element $M_{ff}[i, j]$ represents the correlation between the i-th and the j-th feature. Once the values of V_{cf} and M_{ff} have been computed, given a subset X containing k features, the computation of $f_{CFS}(X)$ only requires $2k$ memory accesses.

3   Evolutionary Algorithms for Feature Selection

As mentioned in the Introduction, Evolutionary Computation techniques proved very effective as a methodology for solving optimization problems whose search space are discontinuous and very complex. In the following subsections, the three EC methods for feature selection taken into account to test the proposed strategy are detailed.

3.1   Artificial Bee Colony (ABC)

Artificial bee colony (ABC) mimics the foraging behaviors of a honey bee colony [22], where the food sources and their nectar amounts represent probable solutions and their corresponding fitness values, respectively. In the ABC algorithms there are three types of bees, which behave as follows. *Employed* bees search exploiting the food sources explored before and share this information with the *onlooker* bees. The onlooker bees, instead, make a decision on the selection of food source to be exploited with the help of the information gained by the employed bees. Finally, *Scout* bees are responsible for searching new food sources; the search of these bees can be guided by internal rules or even possible external clues. The basic implementation of ABC consists of four phases:

1. *Initializazion.* N_s food sources $x = (x_{i1}, \ldots, x_{iD})$, $i \in (1, \ldots, N_s)$ are randomly initialized, where D is the dimensionality of the search space.
2. *Employed bee phase.* For each food source (solution) an employed bee tries to find a richer one (better solution) modifying its current position, by applying a mutation operator. If the new solution found has a fitness value better than the old one, then the employed bee replaces the old source with the new one.

3. *Onlooker bee phase.* After getting the information concerning the fitness value and positions of food sources from employed bees, each onlooker bee selects a food source by using the roulette-wheel scheme.
4. *Scout bee phase.* Once a food source has been modified for N_L trials without producing a better solution, it is considered *exhausted* and it is replaced by a new randomly generated solution.

In the ABC algorithm for solving feature selection problem, food sources are binary strings and the mutation operator can be easily implemented by randomly flipping the bit of the food source.

3.2   Artificial Colony Optimization (ACO)

In the ACO metaheuristics, artificial ants probabilistically build a solution by iteratively adding solution components to partial solutions by using: (i) heuristic information about the problem at hand (ii) (artificial) pheromone trails which represent the information previously acquired by the ants in their search experience.

The problem representation is a graph where the nodes represent the points that the ants can visit and the edges are the link between points. Links are unidirectional and there are no cycles. At the beginning of the algorithm every ant is located at a different graph node and it will construct a solution moving on the graph until the stop condition is met.

The main steps of the algorithm are the following:

1. *Initialisation.* All the pheromone variables are initialized to a value τ_0 which represents an algorithm parameter.
2. *Solution construction.* Each of the N_a ants constructs a solution by hopping from node i to node j according to a probabilistic decision rule, which is a function of the pheromone trail τ and the heuristic information value ν.
3. *Pheromone update.* Pheromone trails are updated according to the quality of the solutions found.

The whole set of available features is represented by a fully connected graph, where each node represents a feature and a solution is represented by a path on the graph.

3.3   Particle Swarm Optimization (PSO)

PSO is an EC technique inspired by social behaviors such as bird flocking and fish schooling. In the PSO approach each solution is represented as a particle in the swarm. The i–th particle has a position in the search space, which is represented by a vector $x = (x_{i1}, \ldots, x_{iD})$, where D is the dimensionality of the search space. PSO particles move in the search space to seek for good solutions. Therefore, the i–th particle has a velocity, which is represented as $v = (v_{i1}, \ldots, v_{iD})$. Each particle updates its position and velocity according to its own experience and that of its neighbors. The best previous position of the particle is recorded as the

Table 1. The datasets used in the experiments.

Datasets	Attributes	Samples	Classes
Arcene	10000	100	2
Breast	17816	286	2
Cnae	856	1080	9
GCM	16063	190	14
Micro	1300	571	20
Ovarian	2190	216	2

personal best p_{best}, and the best position obtained by the population thus far is called g_{best}. Based on p_{best} and g_{best}, PSO searches for the optimal solutions by updating the velocity and the position of the i–th particle according to the following equations:

$$x_{ij}^{t+1} = x_{ij}^t + v_{ij}^{t+1} \quad j \in (1, \dots, D)$$

$$v_{ij}^{t+1} = \omega * v_{ij}^t + c_1 * r_1 * (p_{ij} - x_{ij}^t) + c_2 * r_2 * (p_{gj} - x_{ij}^t) \quad j \in (1, \dots, D)$$

where t represents the t–th iteration of the evolutionary process and j the j–th dimension of the search space; ω is the inertia weight and it controls the impact of the previous velocities on the current velocity; c_1 and c_2 are acceleration constants, while r_1 and r_2 are random values uniformly distributed in $[0, 1]$; p_{ij} and p_{gj} denote the elements of p_{best} and g_{best} in j–th dimension, respectively. The velocity is limited by a predefined maximum velocity v_{max}. The algorithm stops when a predefined criterion is met, which could be a good fitness value or a predefined maximum number of iterations.

In the PSO approach feature selection solutions (subsets) can be represented by using a threshold value θ: the value x_{ij} of the i–th particle is compared with the θ; if $x_{ij} > \theta$ then the j–th is selected for that particle.

4   Experimental Results

We tested the proposed approach on high-dimensional data. For each dataset, a set of values for parameter M (see Fig. 1) was tested. For each value of M, 30 runs were performed. At the end of every run, the feature subset encoded by the individual with the best fitness, was used to build a Decision Tree classifier (DT in the following), trained by using the C4.5 algorithm. The classification performances of the classifiers built have been obtained by using the 10-fold cross-validation approach. The results reported in the following have been obtained averaging the performance of the 30 DTs built.

The proposed approach was tested on the following, publicly available, datasets: *Arcene, Breast, Cnae, Isolet, Micromass* and *Ovarian*. The characteristics of the datasets are summarized in Table 1. They present different characteristics as regards the number of attributes, the number of classes (two or multiple classes problems) and the number of samples.

In order to test the effectiveness of our strategy, we performed two sets of comparisons. In the first set, we compared the results achieved by the proposed strategy with those obtained by the basic versions of the three algorithms taken into account, which searches on the whole set of available features. In the second set, instead, our results were compared with three state-of-the-art feature selection methods: sequential floating forward selection [23], Fast Correlation-Based Filter [24] and the Minimum Redundancy and Maximum Relevance [25].

To statistically validate the obtained results, we performed the non-parametric Wilcoxon rank-sum test ($\alpha = 0.05$) over the 30 runs performed.

Both sets of experiments are described in the following subsections.

4.1   First Set of Comparisons

The purposes of the first set of experiments were: (i) to investigate how the value of parameter M affects the performance of the presented strategy; (ii) to assess whether the proposed approach improves the performance of the EC-based algorithms for feature selection considered; (iii) comparing the performances of the three EC algorithms for feature selection taken into account.

As concerns the value of M, since the number of attributes of the datasets taken into account differs widely, for each dataset these values were chosen considering its dimensionality. In order to cover a wide range of values, but avoiding testing too many values, we chose these values in an exponential way. For all the datasets, except Breast, we used five values. For example, for Ovarian (2190 features) we tested the following values: $\{50, 100, 200, 500, 1000\}$, while for Arcene the set of values of M tested was: $\{100, 200, 500, 1000, 2000\}$. Table 2 reports the obtained results in terms of average recognition rate (RR) and average number of features (NF). The abbreviations *-RNK and *-ALL denote the EC algorithms modified according to the proposed strategy and the standard version EC algorithms, respectively. The recognition rates in bold highlight the best result. In the case that two or more results do not present statistically significant differences, the result achieved with the minimum number of features was considered.

From the table it can be seen that in most of the cases our strategy improves the performance of the EC-algorithms, both in terms of recognition rate and number of selected features. Only for Isolet do the recognition rate performances of the compared approaches not present statistically significant differences. Most probably, this is due to the fact that this dataset contains a relatively low number of features, which allow the EC-algorithms to find good solutions, even in the search space made of the whole set of available features. As concerns the other datasets, for Arcene, the proposed strategy strongly improve the recognition rate, by using a few dozen features; these results were obtained considering up to the first 500 ranked features. As for the Breast dataset, at the most 200 features are needed to get the best RR performance; it is worth noting that in this case the number of features was reduced from thousands to few dozens. The performances on the dataset Cnae were improved by considering no more than 200 features out of the 856 available features; our approach strongly improves the performance of the ABC algorithm, especially in terms of recognition rate; nonetheless, also for PSO and ACO the improvements are significant. As regards Micromass, the ABC algorithm performs worse than PSO and ACO and was able to find the best subset by using the first 200 ranked features; it is worth noting that, in this case, both PSO and ACO selected a number of features slightly less than those selected by searching the whole set features, i.e. 1300. In this case, our strategy proved able to include all the features needed to improve the recognition rate performance, discarding only those features that are deceptive for DT learning. Finally, for the Ovarian dataset, our method improves the performance of the three algorithms by significantly increasing the recognition rate and strongly reducing the number of selected features; for the three algorithms these results were achieved by searching in the search space made of the first 50 ranked features.

By comparing the results of the three basic versions of the EC algorithms, searching on the whole search space, it can be seen that ABC performs a bit worse than ACO and PSO in terms of RR, and selecting in most cases the larger subset. As concerns ACO and PSO, they obtain similar results, both in terms of RR and NF.

As for the results of the EC algorithms modified according to our strategy, it can be seen that in most cases the best RR values are achieved by using the same or similar values of M. This seems to confirm the robustness of the proposed approach. In terms of RR, PSO and ACO achieved very similar results, whereas, also in this case ABC performed worse, at least on some datasets. In terms of NF, if we consider the number of selected features with respect to the M features given in input, ABC selects on average more features (42%), while ACO and PSO select 25% and 30% of the input features, respectively.

4.2   Second Set of Comparisons

In order to test the effectiveness of the proposed strategy, we compared the achieved results with those obtained by the following three state-of-the-art algorithms for feature selection:

- *Sequential Forward Floating Search.* This strategy searches the solution space by using a greedy hill-climbing technique. It starts with the empty set of features and, at each step, selects the best feature according to the subset evaluation function. The algorithm also verifies the possibility of improvement of the criterion if a feature is excluded. In this case, the worst feature, according to the evaluation function, is excluded from the set. We used an improved version of this algorithm, presented in [23]. It will be denoted as *SFFS* in the following.
- *Fast Correlation-Based Filter.* This algorithm uses the concept of "predominant correlation" to select good features that are strongly relevant to the class concept and are not redundant. In order to identify non-linear correlations the adopted measure is based on the well-known information-theoretical concept of entropy, which measure the uncertainty of a random variable. The algorithm consists essentially of two steps: in the first step the features are ranked

Table 2. Comparison results between the EC algorithms modified according to our approach (*-RNK) and their basic versions, which take as input the whole set of available features.

Dataset	M	ABC				ACO				PSO			
		ABC-RNK		ABC		ACO-RNK		ACO		PSO-RNK		PSO	
		RR	NF	RR	NF	RR	NF	NF	NF	RR	NF	RR	NF
Arcene	100	84.15	29.45	75.5	2301.05	82.25	12.6	73.65	1173	81.83	8.66	71.6	1026
	200	**85.15**	**61.6**			84.65	12.5			**86**	**16.0**		
	500	84	156.3			**87.3**	**34.5**			**87.35**	**57.6**		
	1000	82.5	262.7			81.35	122.7			81.6	173.9		
	2000	78.85	514.6			80.5	456.2			80.7	271.0		
Breast	100	**85.54**	**42.8**	82.90	4844.5	85.27	34.0	82.88	2215	**85.33**	**33.9**	82.02	1423
	200	85.24	85.1			**86.06**	**47.6**			85.17	51.1		
	500	83.86	187.4			84.17	105.5			83.91	148.1		
	1000	84.17	385.3			84.80	253.4			84.66	299.8		
	2000	84.05	757.2			83.88	669.6			83.93	684.9		
	5000	82.01	1316.1			83.65	1539.1			83.56	686.7		
Cnae	20	72.06	14.4	71.19	203.7	74.63	15.0	79.48	58	74.52	15.0	80.54	55.5
	50	**81.66**	**29.3**			82.24	26.0			82.18	26.0		
	100	**83.12**	**52.4**			83.27	28.7			83.32	28.0		
	200	71.53	57.1			**85.06**	**37.1**			**84.87**	**36.0**		
	400	68.77	99.3			84.73	53.4			84.36	40.4		
Isolet	20	56.69	11	**81.81**	**253.9**	56.8	11	**82.69**	**278**	56.63	11	**82.64**	**281.2**
	50	76.06	33.9			76.28	33.85			75.99	34.85		
	100	78.25	52.95			78.31	50.9			78.32	50.35		
	200	**81.06**	**82.5**			81.53	79.4			81.53	78.8		
	300	81.42	139.15			**82.4**	**134.85**			**82.06**	**136.15**		
Micromass	20	62.67	13.50	73.23	334.20	63.45	14.00	75.50	176	63.75	14.00	74.64	154
	50	68.94	29.45			69.79	27.00			69.61	27.00		
	100	73.17	51.80			75.62	41.50			75.52	42.10		
	200	**76.28**	**98.65**			78.71	70.40			78.87	70.40		
	500	73.32	129.15			**80.27**	**140.25**			**80.12**	**131.45**		
Ovarian	50	**90.18**	**20.25**	83.58	603.70	**90.37**	**13.00**	85.69	313	**91.08**	**13.00**	85.99	271
	100	88.17	36.40			90.30	18.05			89.89	16.54		
	200	87.70	68.45			88.68	28.85			89.37	25.78		
	500	85.34	163.80			87.93	88.85			88.49	64.89		
	1000	84.99	303.9			87.03	191.6			87.4	135.6		

according to their correlation to the class; in the second step, the ordered list is further processed to remove redundant features. It will be denoted as *FCBF* in the following.

– *minimum Redundancy Maximum Relevance.* This approach finds the best feature subset, of fixed size, made up of the features that are highly correlated with the class concept (max. relevance) and minimally correlated each other (minimum redundancy). As correlation measure this approach uses the mutual information criterion for the discrete variables and the F-test for the continuous ones. Further details of the algorithm can be found in [25]. It will be denoted as *mRMR* in the following.

Since the above methods are deterministic, they generated a single feature subset. In order to perform a fair comparison with the proposed approach, for each

Table 3. Comparison results for the ABC algorithm.

Dataset	ABC-RNK			FCBF		mRMR		SFFS	
	M	RR	NF	RR	NF	RR	NF	RR	NF
Arcene	200	**85.15**	**11.2**	80.05	39	83.15	33	**86.15**	**38**
Breast	100	85.54	31.5	**86.95**	**215**	85.17	34	75.81	62
Cnae	100	**83.12**	**29.4**	79.81	29	**83.27**	**38**	80.86	28
Isolet	300	**81.06**	**253.9**	77.33	40	79.6	125	80.61	54
Micro	200	**76.28**	**74.60**	74.99	59	63.09	160	**75.81**	**62**
Ovarian	50	**90.18**	**12.80**	88.42	18	74.25	13	**89.56**	**20**

dataset, 30 DT's have been learned by using the 10-fold cross-validation technique, with different initial seeds. The results reported in the following have been obtained averaging the performance of the 30 DT's learned and are shown in Tables 3, 4 and 5. For each dataset, the recognition rate in bold highlight the best result, according to the Wilcoxon test. In the case that two or more results do not present statistically significant differences, the corresponding values are in bold.

From Table 3 it can be noted that the RNK-ABC algorithm obtains the best results for five out of the six datasets taken into account; as for Isolet, RNK-ABC achieves a result that is statistically better than the second best one (SFFS); moreover, on the Breast dataset, RNK-ABC obtains the second best result (1.41% less in RR with respect to FCBF), but using far fewer features (31.5 instead of 215). From Table 4 it can be observed that the RNK-ACO algorithm obtains best results on all datasets; in particular, for three datasets (Cnae, Isolet and Micromass) RNK-ACO results present statistically significant differences with the second best ones. Finally, Table 5 shows that the RNK-PSO, so as RNK-ABC, obtains best results on all datasets except Breast. Moreover, for four datasets (Cnae, Isolet, Micromass and Ovarian) RNK-PSO results present statistically significant differences with the second best ones.

Table 4. Comparison results for the ACO algorithm.

Dataset	ACO-RNK			FCBF		mRMR		SFFS	
	M	RR	NF	RR	NF	RR	NF	RR	NF
Arcene	500	**87.3**	**17.8**	80.05	39	83.15	33	**86.15**	**38**
Breast	200	**86.06**	**47.80**	**86.95**	**215**	85.17	34	75.81	62
Cnae	100	**85.06**	**28.70**	79.81	29	83.27	38	80.86	28
Isolet	300	**82.4**	**278**	77.33	40	79.6	125	80.61	54
Micro	500	**80.27**	**104.50**	74.99	59	63.09	160	75.81	62
Ovarian	50	**90.37**	**13.00**	88.42	18	74.25	13	**89.56**	**20**

Table 5. Comparison results for the PSO algorithm.

Dataset	PSO-RNK			FCBF·		mRMR		SFFS	
	M	RR	NF	RR	NF	RR	NF	RR	NF
Arcene	500	**87.35**	**17.9**	80.05	39	83.15	33	**86.15**	**38**
Breast	100	85.33	34.0	**86.95**	215	85.17	34	75.81	62
Cnae	200	**84.87**	**32.9**	79.81	29	83.27	38	80.86	28
Isolet	300	**82.06**	120.15	77.33	40	79.6	125	80.61	54
Micro	500	**80.12**	**104.65**	74.99	59	63.09	160	75.81	62
Ovarian	50	**91.08**	**13**	88.42	18	74.25	13	89.56	20

As concerns the results of the algorithms considered for the comparison, it is worth noticing that they obtain the best results, in terms of RR, only in few cases. In particular, SFFS obtained the best RR only for the Arcene dataset, but without any statistically significant difference with respect to any of the EC-based algorithms, and selecting twice the number of features than the EC algorithms; SFFS was also able to obtain the second best RR for three datasets (Isolet, Micromass and Ovarian). As regards the MRMR algorithm, it only achieved one second best result (on Cnae). Finally, the FCBF approach obtained the best RR on the Breast dataset, but without any statistically significant difference with respect to RNK-ACO and found a subset four times larger.

The above results confirm the assumptions underlying our strategy: (i) a feature ranking algorithm can be used to "preselect" a number of features among the whole set of available features; (ii) the search space consisting of the subsets made of these selected features contains most of the good and near-optimal solutions (subsets); (iii) different values of M must be tested, in order to find the value which allows most of the useful features to be considered.

In practice, the filtering performed by the feature ranking makes easier the task of searching for good solutions and this filtering is crucial in improving the performance of any EC-based algorithm for feature selection when thousands of features are involved.

5   Conclusions

We presented a novel strategy for improving the performance of EC-based algorithms for feature selection. The proposed strategy consists of two steps. The first uses a feature ranking-based approach that reduces the search space made of the whole set of available features. This reduction is performed by discarding the features that, according to the univariate measure employed, are less useful for discriminating among the different classes at hand. In the second step, a given number M of ranked features are provided as input to the EC-based algorithm.

The effectiveness of the proposed system was tested on high-dimensional datasets. As regards the EC-based algorithms for feature selection we took into account the following ones: Artificial Bee Colony (ABC), Ant Colony Optimization (ACO) and Particle Swarm Optimization (PSO). The achieved results was compared with those of three state-of-the-art feature selection algorithms: Sequential Forward Floating Search (SFFS), Fast Correlation-Based Filter (FCBF) and minimum Redundancy Maximum Relevance (mRMR). Experimental results confirmed that the proposed strategy: (i) allows EC-based algorithms to improve their performance on feature selection problems; (ii) achieves results that in most cases are better than those of the algorithms taken into account for the comparison.

Future works will investigate different feature evaluation functions, both filter and wrapper. Moreover, system performance will be evaluated also for different classification schemes.

References

1. Dash, M., Liu, H.: Feature selection for classification. Intell. Data Anal. **1**(1–4), 131–156 (1997)
2. Xue, B., Zhang, M., Browne, W.N., Yao, X.: A survey on evolutionary computation approaches to feature selection. IEEE Trans. Evol. Comput. **20**(4), 606–626 (2016)
3. Bevilacqua, V., Mastronardi, G., Piscopo, G.: Evolutionary approach to inverse planning in coplanar radiotherapy. Image Vis. Comput. **25**(2), 196–203 (2007). Soft Computing in Image Analysis
4. Menolascina, F., Tommasi, S., Paradiso, A., Cortellino, M., Bevilacqua, V., Mastronardi, G.: Novel data mining techniques in acgh based breast cancer subtypes profiling: the biological perspective. In: 2007 IEEE Symposium on Computational Intelligence and Bioinformatics and Computational Biology, pp. 9–16, April 2007
5. Menolascina, F., Bellomo, D., Maiwald, T., Bevilacqua, V., Ciminelli, C., Paradiso, A., Tommasi, S.: Developing optimal input design strategies in cancer systems biology with applications to microfluidic device engineering. BMC Bioinform. **10**(12) (2009)
6. Bevilacqua, V., Brunetti, A., Triggiani, M., Magaletti, D., Telegrafo, M., Moschetta, M.: An optimized feed-forward artificial neural network topology to support radiologists in breast lesions classification. In: Proceedings of the 2016 on Genetic and Evolutionary Computation Conference Companion, GECCO 2016 Companion, pp. 1385–1392. ACM, New York (2016). https://doi.org/10.1145/2908961.2931733
7. Manimala, K., Selvi, K., Ahila, R.: Hybrid soft computing techniques for feature selection and parameter optimization in power quality data mining. Appl. Soft Comput. **11**(8), 5485–5497 (2011)
8. Xue, B., Zhang, M., Browne, W.N.: Particle swarm optimization for feature selection in classification: a multi-objective approach. IEEE Trans. Cybern. **43**(6), 1656–1671 (2013)
9. Spolaôr, N., Lorena, A.C., Lee, H.D.: Multi-objective genetic algorithm evaluation in feature selection. In: Takahashi, R.H.C., Deb, K., Wanner, E.F., Greco, S. (eds.) EMO 2011. LNCS, vol. 6576, pp. 462–476. Springer, Heidelberg (2011). https://doi.org/10.1007/978-3-642-19893-9_32

10. Lanzi, P.: Fast feature selection with genetic algorithms: a filter approach. In: IEEE International Conference on Evolutionary Computation, pp. 537–540, April 1997
11. Cordella, L.P., De Stefano, C., Fontanella, F., Marrocco, C., Scotto di Freca, A.: Combining single class features for improving performance of a two stage classifier. In: 20th International Conference on Pattern Recognition (ICPR 2010), pp. 4352–4355. IEEE Computer Society (2010)
12. De Stefano, C., Fontanella, F., Marrocco, C.: A GA-based feature selection algorithm for remote sensing images. In: Giacobini, M., et al. (eds.) EvoWorkshops 2008. LNCS, vol. 4974, pp. 285–294. Springer, Heidelberg (2008). https://doi.org/10.1007/978-3-540-78761-7_29
13. Ahmed, S., Zhang, M., Peng, L.: Feature selection and classification of high dimensional mass spectrometry data: a genetic programming approach. In: Vanneschi, L., Bush, W.S., Giacobini, M. (eds.) EvoBIO 2013. LNCS, vol. 7833, pp. 43–55. Springer, Heidelberg (2013). https://doi.org/10.1007/978-3-642-37189-9_5
14. Oreski, S., Oreski, G.: Genetic algorithm-based heuristic for feature selection in credit risk assessment. Expert Syst. Appl. **41**(4, Part 2), 2052–2064 (2014)
15. Tan, F., Fu, X., Zhang, Y., Bourgeois, A.G.: A genetic algorithm-based method for feature subset selection. Soft. Comput. **12**(2), 111–120 (2007)
16. Ugolotti, R., Mesejo, P., Zongaro, S., Bardoni, B., Berto, G., Bianchi, F., Molineris, I., Giacobini, M., Cagnoni, S., Cunto, F.D.: Visual search of neuropil-enriched rnas from brain in situ hybridization data through the image analysis pipeline hippoatesc. PLOS ONE **8**(9) (2013)
17. De Stefano, C., Fontanella, F., Scotto di Freca, A.: Feature selection in high dimensional data by a filter-based genetic algorithm. In: Squillero, G., Sim, K. (eds.) EvoApplications 2017. LNCS, vol. 10199, pp. 506–521. Springer, Cham (2017). https://doi.org/10.1007/978-3-319-55849-3_33
18. Liu, H., Setiono, R.: Chi2: Feature selection and discretization of numeric attributes. In: ICTAI, pp. 88–91. IEEE Computer Society, Washington, DC (1995)
19. Hall, M.A.: Correlation-based feature selection for discrete and numeric class machine learning. In: Proceedings of the Seventeenth International Conference on Machine Learning, pp. 359–366. Morgan Kaufmann Publishers Inc., San Francisco (2000)
20. De Stefano, C., Fontanella, F., Maniaci, M., Scotto di Freca, A.: A method for scribe distinction in medieval manuscripts using page layout features. In: Maino, G., Foresti, G.L. (eds.) ICIAP 2011. LNCS, vol. 6978, pp. 393–402. Springer, Heidelberg (2011). https://doi.org/10.1007/978-3-642-24085-0_41
21. Huang, J., Cai, Y., Xu, X.: A hybrid genetic algorithm for feature selection wrapper based on mutual information. Pattern Recogn. Lett. **28**(13), 1825–1844 (2007)
22. Karaboga, D.: An idea based on Honey Bee Swarm for Numerical Optimization. Technical report TR06, Erciyes University, October 2005
23. Gütlein, M., Frank, E., Hall, M., Karwath, A.: Large scale attribute selection using wrappers. In: Proceedings of the IEEE Symposium on Computational Intelligence and Data Mining (CIDM 2009) (2009)
24. Yu, L., Liu, H.: Feature selection for high-dimensional data: a fast correlation-based filter solution. In: Proceedings of the Twentieth International Conference on International Conference on Machine Learning, ICML 2003, pp. 856–863. AAAI Press (2003)
25. Peng, H., Long, F., Ding, C.: Feature selection based on mutual information criteria of max-dependency, max-relevance, and min-redundancy. IEEE Trans. Patt. Anal. Mach. Intell. **27**(8), 1226–1238 (2005)

26. Babiloni, C., Triggiani, A.I., Lizio, R., Cordone, S., Tattoli, G., Bevilacqua, V., Soricelli, A., Ferri, R., Nobili, F., Gesualdo, L., Millán-Calenti, J.C., Buján, A., Tortelli, R., Cardinali, V., Barulli, M.R., Giannini, A., Spagnolo, P., Armenise, S., Buenza, G., Scianatico, G., Logroscino, G., Frisoni, G.B., del Percio, C.: Classification of single normal and alzheimer's disease individuals from cortical sources of resting state eeg rhythms. Front. Neurosci. **10**, 47 (2016)
27. Bria, A., Marrocco, C., Molinara, M., Tortorella, F.: An effective learning strategy for cascaded object detection. Inf. Sci. **340**, 17–26 (2016)
28. Marrocco, C., Molinara, M., Tortorella, F.: On linear combinations of dichotomizers for maximizing the area under the ROC curve. IEEE Trans. Syst. Man Cybern. Part B (Cybernetics) **41**(3), 610–620 (2011)
29. Marrocco, C., Tortorella, F.: Exploiting coding theory for classification: an ldpc-based strategy for multiclass-to-binary decomposition. Inf. Sci. **357**, 88–107 (2016)
30. Ricamato, M.T., Marrocco, C., Tortorella, F.: MCS-based balancing techniques for skewed classes: an empirical comparison. In: IEEE 19th International Conference on Pattern Recognition, ICPR 2008, pp. 1–4 (2008)

CGP4Matlab - A Cartesian Genetic Programming MATLAB Toolbox for Audio and Image Processing

Rolando Miragaia[1]([✉]), Gustavo Reis[1], Francisco Fernandéz[2],
Tiago Inácio[1,2], and Carlos Grilo[1]

[1] School of Technology and Management, Computer Science and Communications
Research Centre, Polytechnic Institute of Leiria, Leiria, Portugal
{rolando.miragaia,gustavo.reis,tiago.inacio,carlos.grilo}@ipleiria.pt
[2] University of Extremadura, Badajoz, Spain
fcofdez@unex.es

Abstract. This paper presents and describes CGP4Matlab, a powerful toolbox that allows to run Cartesian Genetic Programming within
MATLAB. This toolbox is particularly suited for signal processing and
image processing problems. The implementation of CGP4Matlab, which
can be freely downloaded, is described. Some encouraging results on the
problem of pitch estimation of musical piano notes achieved using this
toolbox are also presented. Pitch estimation of audio signals is a very
hard problem with still no generic and robust solution found. Due to the
highly flexibility of CGP4Matlab, we managed to apply a new cartesian
genetic programming based approach to the problem of pitch estimation.
The obtained results are comparable with the state of the art algorithms.

Keywords: Cartesian genetic programming · MATLAB toolbox
Pitch estimation

1 Introduction

Cartesian Genetic Programming (CGP) has already demonstrated its capabilities on synthesizing complex functions, extracting main features from images
and performing image segmentation [1].

Although there are a number of public domain genetic algorithm and genetic
programming toolboxes for MATLAB, there are no toolboxes for cartesian
genetic programming. CGP4Matlab was developed as a contribution to the
community, providing a free toolbox that can be used and extended by other
researchers, allowing them to benefit from MATLAB's great mathematical
potential on audio and image processing. Also, with this toolbox, researchers
that already work with genetic programming in MATLAB are now able to try
the cartesian version of genetic programming.

CGP4Matalb toolbox is generic and flexible enough to be applied in any
kind of audio or image processing problems. It is completely free and available

© Springer International Publishing AG, part of Springer Nature 2018
K. Sim and P. Kaufmann (Eds.): EvoApplications 2018, LNCS 10784, pp. 455–471, 2018.
https://doi.org/10.1007/978-3-319-77538-8_31

for download at https://github.com/tiagoinacio/CGP4Matlab. This toolbox has already been useful on solving some simple problems such as linear regression, and also on addressing the problem pitch estimation of piano music [2].

The next section describes the cartesian genetic programming process. Section 3 describes the CGP4Matlab architecture and its implementation. In Sect. 4, we describe a new approach to the picth estimation problem using our toolbox and show our experimental results. Finally, Sect. 5 presents our conclusions.

2   Cartesian Genetic Programming

Genetic Programming is a type of evolutionary algorithm based on Darwin's theory of evolution, where in each generation (iteration) exists a population of possible solutions (candidate solutions) to the problem, which are referred as individuals. During each iteration, all the individuals are evaluated by an evaluation function, often referred to as fitness function. After the evaluation, individuals are submitted to a process of selection, where the best are preferably chosen. Those individuals can be recombined and suffer mutations. The resulting individuals will constitute the next population in the new generation. **Cartesian Genetic Programming** (CGP) grew out of the work of Miller et al. [3], as a method of evolving digital circuits. However, the term "Cartesian Genetic Programming" appeared two years later in [4]. According to Miller [4], CGP is more efficient than standard GP methods in learning Boolean functions.

CGP is *Cartesian* because it encodes programs as a two-dimensional grid of nodes that are addressed in the *Cartesian* coordinate system (see Sect. 2.2). In its classic form, it uses a very simple integer based genetic representation of a program in the form of a directed graph instead of a tree. Graphs are very useful program representations, more general than trees.

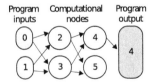

Fig. 1. Overall strucuture of a CGP program. Program inputs and computational nodes are numbered sequentially. The program outputs can link to any computational node or program input.

2.1   Programs

CGP programs have three major components: program inputs, computational nodes and program outputs. **Computational nodes** are structures organized and composed by input connections and a function. The input connections of a node have their origin in any program input or other precedent nodes. The function is among the ones previously defined in a look-up table and it takes as arguments the values received through the node's inputs. The node itself is indexed by an integer value so that it can be referenced by other node input connections. The computational nodes, organized in a two-dimensional grid of nodes, are numbered sequentially and linked directly between them in a feed-forward manner (see Fig. 1). A program can have several inputs, named **program inputs**. **Program outputs** are indexes that link to some nodes. For example, if the program's output is the number 4, the result of the program is the value computed by node 4's function (see Fig. 1). Program inputs and nodes are referenced by sequential numbers. The idea is best explained with a simple example. In Fig. 1 we can see that the program has two inputs, four nodes and one output.

2.2   Genotype

The genotype is the codification of a program as it is used and manipulated by the CGP algorithm. It describes what are the programs inputs, computational nodes, program outputs and how they are connected together. In general, it is a list of genes where each gene is an integer. As we have seen earlier, program inputs and nodes are referenced by their index. Since a node is a structure with input connections and a function, each node has multiple genes (see Fig. 2). The genetic structure that encodes a node first references the function value and then the values of the node's connections sources. In Fig. 2, the list of genes to encode the node are: 2 3 4.

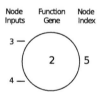

Fig. 2. Example of a node that has two connection genes: node 3 and node 4. It computes the function number 2 in the function-set. The node is referenced by the number 5.

Each node has a function gene which is an address in a look-up table of functions. Usually, all functions have as many inputs as the maximum function arity and unused connections are ignored. This introduces an additional redundancy into the genome. In the example of Fig. 2, the node 5 has nodes 3 and 4 has inputs and it applies the function number 2 defined previously. If function 2 represents a sum, node 5 would compute the following:

$$y = c_1 + c_2, \tag{1}$$

where c_1 is the value coming through the first connection and c_2 is the value coming through the second connection. If $c_1 = 2$ and $c_2 = 1$, the value of node 5 would be $2 + 1 = 3$ (see Fig. 3).

Node 5 = 2 + 1 = 3.

Fig. 3. The result of node 5 will be $2 + 1 = 3$.

There are a few number of parameters that we need to define in order to encode a CGP program. The number of program inputs is given by ni and the number of program outputs is given by no. Given that nodes are organized in a tabular way, the number of columns is given by nc and the number of rows by nr. For example, the program in Fig. 4 has the following attributes: $ni = 3$, $no = 1$, $nc = 3$, $nr = 1$ and the genotype is the following list of integers: 512 303 102 and 4. Knowing that $ni = 3$, the genotype encodes the first node at index 3, since the first three indexes represent the program inputs and the first index is 0. The first node in the genotype, node 3, computes function 5, and its connections are the program input 1 and program input 2. Node 4 computes function 3, and its connections are the program input 0 and the value of node 3. The output of that program is the value of node 4. We point that there are no program outputs nor nodes whose input connections reference node 5. This means that this node cannot influence the program output.

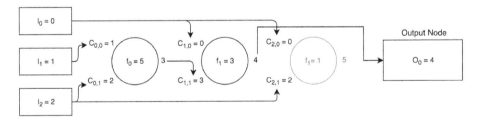

Fig. 4. CGP graph, where $ni = 3$ and $no = 1$. The grid has $nc = 3$ (columns) and $nr = 1$ (row).

Table 1, enumerates a few parameters of the program illustrated in the above figure.

There are some allelic constrains, that the genotype must respect. The alleles (values) of function genes f_i must take valid address values in the look-up table

Table 1. Parameters of the program illustrated in Fig. 4

Parameter	Value
Number of inputs (ni)	3
Number of outputs (no)	1
Number of rows (nr)	1
Number of columns (nc)	3
Inputs (i_i)	0,1,2
Functions (f_i)	5,3,1
Outputs (O_i)	4
Genotype	512 303 102 4
Phenotype	512 303 4

of primitive functions. Let nf represent the number of allowed functions. Then f_i must obey to the following range:

$$0 \le f_i < nf. \tag{2}$$

There is another parameter called **levels-back** l, which determines how many previous columns of nodes may connect to a node in the current column. When $nr = 1$ and $l = nc$, any node can have input connections coming from any program input and any node on its left, which allows unrestricted connectivity. However, if $nr > 1$, nodes cannot connect to other nodes in the same column. Then, having a node in column j, and $j \ge l$, node connections, C_{ij}, must obey to the following range:

$$ni + (j - l)nr \le C_{ij} \le ni + j \times nr. \tag{3}$$

If $j < l$, then the following condition must be met:

$$0 \le C_{ij} \le ni + j \times nr. \tag{4}$$

Program output genes O_i can connect to any node or program input:

$$0 \le O_i < ni + Ln, \tag{5}$$

where Ln is the number of nodes in the genotype, computed by the following:

$$Ln = nr \times nc. \tag{6}$$

This representation is very simple, flexible and convenient for many problems.

2.3 Genotype-Phenotype

One of the key characteristics of CGP is the genotype-phenotype mapping. The genotype is of fixed-length but the phenotype is not, due to the fact that the genotype can have inactive genes. Thus, they are redundant because they cannot influence the programs output. The corresponding genes are called **non-coding genes** or **inactive genes**. This means that we can have a phenotype different from the genotype because non-coding genes are not expressed in the phenotype, that is, the program that will run in practice.

The output or outputs of the CGP are nodes that point to other nodes (connection genes) and so on. Decoding the program is recursive in nature and works from the program output genes first. To decode the program outputs, the active nodes should be identified. The process begins by looking at which nodes are directly connected to the output genes. Then, these nodes are examined to find out which nodes are directly linked to them. Since non-coding genes are not addressed, they present little computational overhead.

2.4   Algorithm

The evolutionary strategy widely used for CGP is a special case of the strategy $\mu + \lambda$ [5] where $\mu = 1$ (Algorithm 1). This means that, in this special case, the population size is always one. At each iteration (generation), λ new offspring are generated from the current one through mutation. Then, the best among the current individual and the offspring becomes the current individual in the next iteration. An offspring can become the current individual in the next iteration when it has the same fitness as the current individual and there is no other individual with a better fitness.

Algorithm 1. Algorithm $((1 + \lambda) EA)$

1: $t \leftarrow 0$;
2: Set current individual I_0 as the best of λ individuals created randomly;
3: **while** a stop condition is not fulfilled, **do**
4:     **for** i = 1 to λ **do**
5:         Create a copy x_i of current individual I_t;
6:         Mutate each gene of x_i with probability p;
7:     **end for**
8:     Set new current individual I_{t+1} as the best of $I_t \cup \{x_1, \dots, x_\lambda\}$;
9:     $t \leftarrow t + 1$;
10: **end while**

---

3   Cartesian Genetic Programming Toolbox

For the first step of our research on applying cartesian genetic programming to sound processing, we decided to create a MATLAB Toolbox for audio processing. The idea was to have a highly flexible toolbox, configurable throughout parameters and function callbacks, so that, we could move and focus on the problem of Pitch Estimation by applying and configuring the same toolbox to our particular case.

The CGP4Maltab's architecture will be introduced throughout this section. Then, each component will be explained in detail.

3.1 Architecture

The CGP Toolbox is very simple to use and allows to quickly encode a problem. The structure of classic CGP is reproduced in the toolbox. One of the main goals was to have a generic toolbox that could help us to encode from smaller to bigger problems. With that in mind, a few design decisions were made that will be explained next. All the combinations of rows and columns are possible, considering that $nr > 0$ and $nc > 0$. The allelic constrains are generated dynamically, depending on the cartesian representation of the nodes. *Levels-back* was also taken into consideration. Additionally, the toolbox is prepared to use parameters in the genotype. There are no limits for the number of parameters. The fitness function is any function provided by the user. The toolbox is prepared to receive one or more program inputs of any types and values. The number of program outputs can be one or more, in order to address different problem requirements. The function-set is also provided by the user and the look-up table is automatically generated. Furthermore, there is a system of callbacks which is discussed later. The Evolutionary Algorithm (EA) used is the $1 + \lambda$, referred previously in Sect. 2.4. The goal is to have a toolbox as generic as possible, so a few parameters for the evolutionary process were chosen to be configurable.

The number of **offspring** (λ) is defined by the user. This is useful because there can be some problems that require a small number of offspring and others that require a bigger number of offspring. The **mutation rate** (p) is also configurable. This is the mutation probability for each gene. The maximum number of **runs**, mr, and maximum number of **generations**, mg, are also required parameters. Finally, the last parameter is the maximum or minimum **fitness**, f, for a solution to be considered valid, depending if we want to maximize or minimize the fitness function. The EA needs to know when a candidate solution can be considered as a valid solution for the problem, in order to stop the evolutionary process.

The toolbox is divided into several components (see Fig. 5). Each one has its purpose and special role. The first one is the **CGP** component. It exposes all the functionality to encode an application built on top of the toolbox. This component communicates with the **EA** and **Structure** components. The Structure is just an helper, which stores the positions of the genes according to the type of gene (connection, function, program output and parameter). The EA component is responsible for initializing the runs in the evolutionary algorithm. It starts with a certain number of **Offspring**, created by the **Genotype** component which, in turn, is composed by the **Connection**, **Functions**, **Ouputs** and **Fitness** components. **Run** is connected to the **Generation** component, by executing it multiple times. In each generation, **Mutation** can occur, which will change the genotypes (using the Connection, Functions, Outputs and Fitness

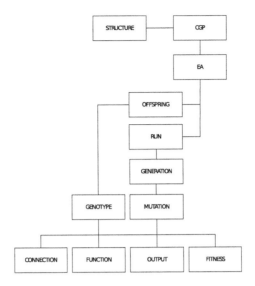

Fig. 5. Components that are part of the toolbox.

components). Figure 5 shows the overall structure of the toolbox's components. Each component will be addressed in detail next.

3.2 Classes

The toolbox was built using Object Oriented Programming methodology of MATLAB (version R2016a). All the *classes* that compose the toolbox will be introduced throughout this section. For some classes, a detailed explanation of the most relevant properties and methods is also presented.

CGP: The *CGP* class provides access to an API that lists all the features needed to encode a program. It is the *core* of the toolbox and its primary component. The *CGP* class lets the user add the program inputs, provide the fitness function, add parameters and define the function-set. The constructor takes a configuration object. This object will contain all the configuration necessary for the CGP and for the EA.

For the CGP, the parameters are divided into: number of rows, number of columns, number of levels back and number of program outputs. Since some CGP approaches assume that the output node is the last node of the graph, this option was also taken into consideration. So, if we pass the value *last* to the *output_type*, the last node of the genotype will be considered the program output. This option only works when the number of program outputs is set to 1, otherwise it will be ignored. Having these parameters configurable, the user has total control of the grid layout of the generated program (genotype).

For the EA, the parameters are: maximum number of generations, maximum number of runs, number of offspring, mutation rate, the fitness threshold and the fitness operator. The fitness threshold is the limit for which a candidate solution is considered a valid solution to the problem. This allows the evolutionary process to stop or skip to the next run. In some kind of problems, the goal is to minimize an error rate, where 0 would be the best value for the fitness. Also, there are other problems where the goal is to maximize the fitness function. The *fitness_solution* property covers that necessity. However, the operator to use in the comparison between fitness values also needs to be configurable, because the optimization of those values is different. The fitness operator, O, is the operator to use when comparing the new fitness candidate solution with the parent's fitness, and can take the following values: '>', '<', '>='and '<='. For example, consider the parent's fitness as f_0 and an offspring fitness as f_1: if $O =$ '>', $f_0 = 0.5$ and $f_1 = 0.6$, then the offspring will replace the parent in the new generation; if $O =$ '<', $f_0 = 0.5$ and $f_1 = 0.6$, the parent will remain as it has the best fitness. This operator is also used for checking if a solution is a valid solution for the given problem. Therefore, it is also used for comparison between a solution's fitness and the *fitness_solution* value, also configurable. Table 2 describes every possible field for the configuration.

Table 2. Configuration table with the fields that the structure should have, the type of value and the description of each one.

Key	Type	Description
rows	double	number of rows
columns	double	number of columns
levels_back	double	number of levels-back
outputs	double	number of outputs
output_type	string	set the program output as the last node (last, random)
runs	double	number of runs
generations	double	number of generations
offspring	double	number of offspring
mutation	double	probability of mutation
fitness_solution	double	fitness for a solution to be considered valid
fitness_operator	string	fitness operator $(>,<,>=$ or $<=)$

At the time of instantiaton, the *CGP* class verifies if all the required settings were passed in the configuration object. This class also exposes the functionally of adding program inputs. Each problem requires a specific set of program input or inputs. Some may require one integer as input, others may require an array, or even a complex type of object. To address this abstraction, the input provided for the CGP toolbox is of type **struct** (structure). Each field in the structure is a program input. Therefore, the program inputs can be of any type: integers, strings, structs, arrays, matrix, etc. The number of fields present in the structure indicates the number of inputs that the toolbox needs to set in the genotype, which is dynamically set: there is no need to specify how many program inputs the programs will have.

The fitness function is passed by callback (function pointer) to the program.

The toolbox reads the function set from a specific directory provided by the user. This directory should have all the functions that could be used in the genotype. All the functions should receive as many inputs as the maximum function arity. This is a requirement for the program to work. Besides the maximum function arity, if the user added parameters to the genotype, these should also be passed to each function. This method iterates through all the MATLAB files in the directory passed as argument, and it creates a function handle for each one.

Some specific signal processing functions might require special arguments like ranges or constants to be executed (e.g.: a low pass filter needs to know which percentage of the original signal will be attenuated). Those parameters might need to evolve through time, because their best values for the contribution to the solution of the problem is unknown beforehand. The genotype can encode those parameters and add them to the evolutionary process. Parameters should have integer or double values. Each parameter is encoded by a structure with a name, a callback function for the initialization of the parameter value, and another callback function for mutating the value. The initialization and mutation functions should return an integer or a double. The mutation function should also accept an argument, that is the value of the current parameter to mutate. When running the algorithm, there are a number of events from the evolutionary process that can be useful to handle, for running additional scripts or simply to add some kind of report. In order to have that range of possibilities, the user is able to pass optional callbacks, each of which, will fire at the following events: the configuration has been set, a fittest solution is achieved after a run, a fittest solution is achieved in a generation, a new solution is created, a new generation starts, a new run starts and a genotype is mutated. After adding all the program inputs, fitness function, parameters and callbacks, the configuration callback is fired, with a few useful parameters about the configuration of the program.

Structure: There are several components that need to know how many genes are in the genotype, or if a specific gene is a function-gene or a connection gene. Instead of having to determine those properties multiple times and at different stages, this information is only computed once, in this class. The *Structure* class serves as an helper throughout the entire evolutionary process. The main goal is to classify each gene *a priori*, according to its type: connection, paremeter, program output or function. For example, if we have 3 genes per computational node and our genotype starts at number 1 (MATLAB does not accept zero-based vectors), we know in advance that gene 1 represents a function and genes 2 and 3 both correspond to connections. Since this class is responsible for defining the type of genes, it needs to know a few parameters, such as: the number of genes, the number of genes per node, the connection genes per node, the number of computational nodes and the number of parameters.

EA: The *EA* class is responsible for starting the evolutionary process. It iterates for the maximum number of runs, defined in the configuration of the CGP, storing the fittest candidate solution of each one.

If the callback *Run Ended* is provided, it will be fired after each run, with a few parameters, such as the genes of the fittest solution and their fitness.

Run: The *Run* class is responsible for initializing a run. First, it generates a few candidate solutions. Then, it will start the evolutionary loop over the generations. The class stores the best candidate solution, while evaluating if a solution for the problem was found.

The *Run* class contains two callback events. The *Fittest Solution* occurs when a candidate solution has better fitness than the previous stored solution. The *Generation Ended* occurs each time a new generation ends.

Generations: The *Generation* class is responsible for initializing a new generation. It starts with the previous fittest candidate solution (parent), and generates a few mutated versions, according to the configuration provided. If the λ chosen in the configuration phase is 4, it will generate four mutated versions of the parent solution. All the new genotypes are evaluated, and the fittest solution is stored.

The *Generation* class contains two callback events: *New Solution In Generation* and *Fittest Solution Of Generation*. The first, occurs every time a new solution is generated. The last one, occurs each time a new solution is generated and has a better fitness than the parent.

Offspring: The *Offspring* class is responsible for the initialization of a specific number of offspring, previously defined, at random, before iterating through the generations. It initializes randomly different genotypes which are then evaluated. The fittest solution is stored and used as the parent solution, for the generation loop initialization.

Genotype: The *Genotype* class is responsible for the creation of a genotype, restricted to the configuration provided: number of columns, number of rows, number of program inputs, parameters, and so on. First, the function genes are added to the genotype. Then, the connection genes are randomly generated, as well as the parameters and program outputs. After the genotype is created, the active nodes are recursively found by analyzing the program outputs. For each output, the connection nodes are retrieved and stored in an array. For each of those, their connections are also saved in that array, and so on. This process stops when there are no more nodes to analyze. Lastly, the fitness of this new candidate solution is computed.

Connection: The *Connection* class is responsible for generating a random and valid connection for a specific node. It receives the connection gene index as argument. The class first finds which node belongs the connection gene. This is done by subtracting the number of program inputs from the gene index and dividing that value by the number of genes per node. Then, it finds all the possible connections for that node. This is achieved by recursively iterating through the previous nodes, taking into account that nodes in the same row cannot be connected between each other, and also taking into account the number of levels-back. Lastly, it randomly pick one connection from the possible connections.

Functions: The *Functions* class is responsible for randomly generating the function genes for the genotypes. It takes into account the number of functions present in the function-set, to be able to generate valid function genes. It can generate one function gene at a time or multiple function genes. This is useful, because we find where all the function-genes are positionated in the genotype, and call this class once, which returns function genes to all those positions. If we have 10 nodes, we have to generate 10 function-genes in the genotype. If our function-set is composed by 5 functions, this class generates 10 random values between 1 and 5, each corresponding to a function-gene mapped to one of the functions in the function-set.

Output: The *Output* class is responsible for generating a valid program output. Depending on the settings provided initially, this class can pick the last node to be the program output, or randomly pick any program input or computational node in the genotype.

Fitness: The *Fitness* class is responsible for calling the fitness callback provided in the configuration phase. A few properties are passed to that callback, such as the genes in the genotype, active nodes, function-set, program inputs and others. It has a validation of the type returned by the function, which should return an integer or double value. The returned value, is stored and used as the fitness of that particular candidate solution.

Mutation: The *Mutation* class receives a genotype and iterates over its genes. All the genes have the same mutation probability. For a gene being mutated, we first find what type of gene it is: connection, function, parameter or program output. If it is a program output, the *Output* class is used. If it is a connection gene, the *Connection* class is used. If it is a function gene, the *Functions* class is used. Recall that when we add parameters to the CGP, we must provide an initialization function and a mutation function. If it is a parameter gene, the mutation function provided is called.

After iterating all genes, the active nodes are found again, and the fitness is recalculated. If the *Genotype Mutated* callback is provided, it will be called, having as arguments the genes before the mutation, the genes after the mutation and the index of the mutated genes.

4 Using CGP Approach to Pitch Estimation on Piano Notes

As mentioned before, the CG4Matlab toolbox has already proven to be useful during our first approach on addressing the pitch estimation problem [2]. However, to better demonstrate the capabilities of the developed toolbox, we decided to extend our previous work and propose a new approach. The problem of Pitch estimation on sound signals, also known as F0 detection, is a very important task of Automatic Music Transcription.

Music transcription is a very difficult problem from both musical and computational points of view: although there has been much research devoted to it, it still remains an unsolved problem. Over the years, there has been a lot of research on Pitch Estimation [6–10]. However, to the best of our knowledge, there are no Cartesian Genetic Programming approaches for addressing this problem.

In our CGP approach to Pitch Estimation, we have multiple inputs and we have only one row of graph nodes, one output (the result of the corresponding classifier), and *levels-back* = *nc*. To perform pitch detection using CGP, we developed a system where some important decisions and tasks were made besides the CGP. We had to define what kind of inputs to use from the original piano audio signal, through a preprocessing task. We also had to develop a process to reach a binary output in order to perform our fitness function.

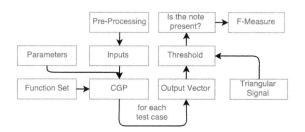

Fig. 6. System architecture.

The block diagram of our proposed system is much more than a simple CGP process and is depicted in Fig. 6. Our goal is to train 61 classifiers, each one corresponding to one pitch or piano note: from C1 to C6. To train one classifier, we first start with a set of learning cases: a group of audio signals corresponding to the pitch that we want to identify and a group of audio signals without that pitch. Those audio signals are pre-processed in order to extract some important features that will be used as program inputs like, for example, the magnitude spectrum. The computational nodes in the genotype have two connection inputs, one function and two parameters. Each program is an evolved mathematical function, which is applied to each of the learning cases. The output of that function is compared to a triangular signal, where a threshold is applied, for binary classification. After the binary classification of all learning cases, the fitness function is applied.

The polyphonic audio signals of the piano notes were extracted from the MAPS database [11]. This is a huge data-set with multiple piano samples, chords and melodies in wave format.

4.1 Experiments and Results

Table 3 shows the values of the configurable parameters for our system. The evolutionary process consisted of 30 runs with 5000 generations each, using 50 positive and 50 negative cases for each musical note. The number of computational nodes is 100. The classifiers were evaluated using the F-measure.

Table 3. List of parameters used in the experiments.

Parameter	Value
Frame size	4096
Fitness threshold	0.5
Positive test cases	50
Negative test cases	50
Outputs	1
Rows	1
Columns	100
Levels back	100
Offspring	4
Mutation probability	5%
Runs	30
Generations	5000

After the training process, each classifier was tested with a different test set. Each test set consisted in 144 negative notes (48×3) and 5 positive notes, comprising a total of 149 piano sound samples. Table 4 shows our results. We made a more complete set of tests then the preliminary results, and we trained and tested 61 different classifiers. These results are very encouraging, since for almost all notes we achieved a classifier with F-Measure values greater than 70%.

The graph depicted in Fig. 7 shows, besides F-measure, the error rate in percentage for the data-set test with 96ms frames. Our pitch estimator using cartesian genetic programming reaches the mean error rate of 6%. When compared to the state of the art, these are very encouraging results. According to Emiya [12], the three main monophonic pitch estimators are: Parametric F0 estimator, the Non-parametric F0 estimator and the YIN estimator [13] and those estimators have mean error rates of 2.4%, 3.0% and 11.0% respectively. Our CGP approach to F0 estimation reaches the mean error rate of 6%.

Table 4. Test results for 61 classifiers

classifier	tp	tn	fp	fn	f-measure	classifier	tp	tn	fp	fn	f-measure	classifier	tp	tn	fp	fn	f-measure
24	5	138	6	0	0.63	44	5	112	32	0	0.24	64	5	138	6	0	0.63
25	5	127	17	0	0.37	45	5	135	9	0	0.53	65	5	141	3	0	0.77
26	5	127	17	0	0.37	46	3	138	6	2	0.43	66	5	139	5	0	0.67
27	5	127	17	0	0.37	47	4	119	25	1	0.24	67	5	141	3	0	0.77
28	5	127	17	0	0.37	48	5	135	9	0	0.53	68	5	141	3	0	0.77
29	5	124	20	0	0.33	49	5	136	8	0	0.55	69	5	141	3	0	0.77
30	4	122	22	1	0.26	50	5	140	4	0	0.71	70	5	142	2	0	0.83
31	5	108	36	0	0.22	51	5	127	17	0	0.37	71	5	142	2	0	0.83
32	5	132	12	0	0.46	52	5	138	6	0	0.63	72	5	142	2	0	0.83
33	4	138	6	1	0.53	53	5	142	2	0	0.83	73	5	144	3	0	0.77
34	5	111	33	0	0.23	54	5	128	16	0	0.39	74	5	146	1	0	0.91
35	5	139	5	0	0.66	55	5	138	6	0	0.63	75	5	142	5	0	0.66
36	5	140	4	0	0.71	56	5	128	16	0	0.39	76	5	142	5	0	0.66
37	5	121	23	0	0.30	57	5	139	5	0	0.67	77	5	146	1	0	0.91
38	5	140	4	0	0.71	58	5	139	5	0	0.67	78	5	143	4	0	0.71
39	5	113	31	0	0.24	59	5	137	7	0	0.59	79	5	144	3	0	0.77
40	4	130	14	1	0.35	60	5	142	2	0	0.83	80	5	143	4	0	0.71
41	4	138	6	1	0.53	61	4	142	2	1	0.73	81	5	147	0	0	1
42	4	124	20	1	0.28	62	4	144	0	1	0.88	82	5	147	0	0	1
43	4	138	6	1	0.53	63	4	144	0	1	0.88	83	5	146	1	0	0.91
												84	5	145	2	0	0.83

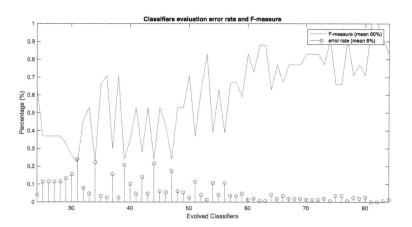

Fig. 7. Graph with 61 classifiers evaluation results in error rate and F-measure.

5   Conclusion

This paper presented the CGP4Matlab toolbox. This toolbox is generic and flexible enough to be applied to any kind of signal or image processing problems. Its internal architecture and modules were also presented and discussed.

A cartesian genetic programming strategy for addressing the pitch recognition of piano notes was also presented using our toolbox. The obtained results show the feasibility of our approach. Also, the results accomplished with the CGP technique are in line with the most popular algorithms for pitch recognition on piano notes.

Planning ahead, we aim to continue our research on addressing of polyphonic pitch estimation using cartesian genetic programming with our toolbox.

Acknowledgements. The authors would like to thank Spanish Ministry of Economy, Industry and Competitiveness and European Regional Development Fund (FEDER) under projects TIN2014-56494-C4-4-P (Ephemec) and TIN2017-85727-C4-4-P (Deep-Bio); Junta de Extremadura FEDER, projects GR15068, GRU10029 IB16035 Regional Government of Extremadura, Consejería of Economy and Infrastructure, FEDER.

References

1. Harding, S., Leitner, J., Schmidhuber, J.: Cartesian genetic programming for image processing. In: Genetic Programming Theory and Practice X, pp. 31–44. Springer, New York (2013). https://doi.org/10.1007/978-1-4614-6846-2_3
2. Inácio, T., Miragaia, R., Reis, G., Grilo, C., Fernandéz, F.: Cartesian genetic programming applied to pitch estimation of piano notes. In: 2016 IEEE Symposium Series on Computational Intelligence (SSCI), pp. 1–7. IEEE (2016)
3. Miller, J., Thomson, P., Fogarty, T.: Designing electronic circuits using evolutionary algorithms. arithmetic circuits: a case study 219 (1997). http://citeseerx.ist.psu.edu/viewdoc/summary?doi=10.1.1.27.7671
4. Miller, J.F.: An empirical study of the efficiency of learning boolean functions using a cartesian genetic programming approach. In: Proceedings of the 1st Annual Conference on Genetic and Evolutionary Computation GECCO1999, vol. 2, pp. 1135–1142. Morgan Kaufmann Publishers Inc., San Francisco (1999). http://dl.acm.org/citation.cfm?id=2934046.2934074
5. Hansen, N., Arnold, D.V., Auger, A.: Evolution Strategies, pp. 871–898. Springer, Berlin (2015). https://doi.org/10.1007/978-3-662-43505-2_44
6. Yeh, C., Roebel, A., Rodet, X.: Multiple fundamental frequency estimation and polyphony inference of polyphonic music signals. Trans. Audio Speech Lang. Proc. **18**(6), 1116–1126 (2010). https://doi.org/10.1109/TASL.2009.2030006
7. Klapuri, A.P.: Multiple fundamental frequency estimation based on harmonicity and spectral smoothness. IEEE Trans. Speech Audio Process. **11**(6), 804–816 (2003)
8. Reis, G., Fernandéz de Vega, F., Ferreira, A.: Audio analysis and synthesis-automatic transcription of polyphonic piano music using genetic algorithms, adaptive spectral envelope modeling, and dynamic noise level estimation. IEEE Trans. Audio Speech Lang. Process. **20**(8), 2313 (2012)

9. Marolt, M.: A connectionist approach to automatic transcription of polyphonic piano music. IEEE Trans. Multimedia **6**(3), 439–449 (2004)
10. Mueller, M., Wiering, F. (eds.): An efficient temporally-constrained probabilistic model for multiple-instrument music transcription. In: ISMIR, Malaga, Spain (October 2015)
11. Emiya, V., Bertin, N., David, B., Badeau, R.: Maps-a piano database for multipitch estimation and automatic transcription of music (2010)
12. Emiya, V., David, B., Badeau, R.: A parametric method for pitch estimation of piano tones. In: 2007 IEEE International Conference on Acoustics, Speech and Signal Processing-ICASSP 2007, vol. 1, pp. 1–249. IEEE (2007)
13. De Cheveigné, A., Kawahara, H.: Yin, a fundamental frequency estimator for speech and music. J. Acoust. Soc. Am. **111**(4), 1917–1930 (2002)

Can the Relevance Index be Used
to Evolve Relevant Feature Sets?

Laura Sani[1], Riccardo Pecori[1,2], Emilio Vicari[3], Michele Amoretti[1],
Monica Mordonini[1], and Stefano Cagnoni[1(✉)]

[1] Dipartimento di Ingegneria e Architettura, Università di Parma, Parma, Italy
stefano.cagnoni@unipr.it
[2] SMARTEST Research Centre, eCampus University, Novedrate (CO), Italy
[3] Camlin Italy, Parma, Italy

Abstract. The Relevance Index (RI) is an information theory-based
measure that was originally defined to detect groups of functionally similar neurons, based on their dynamic behavior. More in general, considering the dynamical analysis of a generic complex system, the larger the
RI value associated with a subset of variables, the more those variables
are strongly correlated with one another and independent from the other
variables describing the system status. We describe some early experiments to evaluate whether such an index can be used to extract relevant
feature subsets in binary pattern classification problems. In particular,
we used a PSO variant to efficiently explore the RI search space, whose
size equals the number of possible variable subsets (in this case 2^{104}) and
find the most relevant and discriminating feature subsets with respect
to pattern representation. We then turned such relevant subsets into a
new smaller set of richer features, whose values depend on the values
of the binary features they include. The paper reports some exploratory
results we obtained in a simple character recognition task, comparing
the performance of RI-based feature extraction and selection with other
classical feature selection/extraction approaches.

Keywords: Feature selection · Feature extraction
Information theory · Relevance Index

1 Introduction

Modeling complex systems by detecting their main functional components is a
research topic which impacts and interacts with a number of disciplines. Thus,
it is not surprising that Villani et al. [1] have used a method based on information theory, originally designed to model the interactions between subsets of
neurons [2] to describe the behavior of complex systems. Such a method detects
subsets of variables which show a strong integration among one another, while
being only loosely correlated with the others. The method assesses such a property by computing a score, termed Relevance Index or $RI(X)$, X being a subset
of the variable set describing the status of a system.

© Springer International Publishing AG, part of Springer Nature 2018
K. Sim and P. Kaufmann (Eds.): EvoApplications 2018, LNCS 10784, pp. 472–479, 2018.
https://doi.org/10.1007/978-3-319-77538-8_32

Intuitively, the property measured by the RI seems not to be very different from the properties, namely relevance and non-redundancy, exhibited by the most discriminating feature sets describing patterns of interest in classification tasks. This paper is a first attempt at confirming this conjecture, by applying an evolutionary approach, detecting high-RI variable subsets to a simple binary character classification problem. After all, the literature reports several examples in which evolutionary algorithms and information theory-derived criteria are the main components of effective feature-selection approaches [3].

In particular, we have applied the K-means Particle Swarm Optimization (PSO) algorithm [4] to the exploration of the huge space of all possible feature subsets[1], looking for the subsets with the highest Relevance Index. Such subsets have then been transformed into a new representation, where the new features are obtained by considering each subset as a single discrete integer variable. Finally, we have compared the results obtained by applying the same configuration of a reference classifier to the original data and to the new representation, to gain some insights in support of the hypothesis that the latter is more effective and/or compact with respect to the original one.

1.1 The Relevance Index

The RI can be used to analyze several classes of dynamical systems described by multiple variables, by identifying variable subsets that behave in a somehow coordinated way. In short, this means that the variables belonging to such subsets are *correlated* with one another much more than with the other variables not belonging to the subset. These subsets can be used to describe the whole system organization. This is why they are termed *relevant subsets* (RSs).

The RI is a measure based on Shannon's entropy, usually based on observational data, where probabilities are estimated as the relative frequencies of the values observed for each variable. The RI can be defined starting from the concept of joint entropy for a pair of variables $H(X, Y)$, defined as follows:

$$H(X,Y) = -\sum_x \sum_y p(x,y) \ log_2 \ p(x,y) \tag{1}$$

as an extension of Shannon's entropy for a single variable which can be naturally further extended to sets of k elements.

For a system U including n random variables $X_1, X_2, ..., X_n$ of which S_k is a subset composed of $k < n$ variables, the RI of S_k is defined as:

$$RI(S_k) = \frac{I(S_k)}{MI(S_k; U \backslash S_k)}, \tag{2}$$

where I is the integration (multi-information), which measures the mutual dependence among the k elements in S_k, and MI is the mutual information, which measures the mutual dependence between subset S_k and the remaining part of the system $U \backslash S_k$.

---

[1] Of size 2^N for patterns described by N features.

The integration is defined as

$$I(S_k) = \sum_{s \in S_k} H(s) - H(S_k) \tag{3}$$

The mutual information $MI(S_k; U \backslash S_k)$ is defined as

$$MI(S_k; U \backslash S_k) = H(S_k) + H(U \backslash S_k) - H(S_k, U \backslash S_k) \tag{4}$$

For details about how to compute entropy, integration and mutual information for sets of variables, we refer the reader to [5].

The RI is undefined if $MI(S_k; U \backslash S_k) = 0$. However, a vanishing MI is a sign of separation of the subset under examination from the rest of the system, which suggests that the subset should be studied separately.

Since the RI scales with the subset size, a normalization method is required to compare RI values of subsets of different sizes, which can also measure, at least approximately, the statistical significance of the differences of the RI. For these reasons, a statistical significance index was introduced [2]:

$$T_c(S_k) = \frac{RI(S_k) - \langle RI_h \rangle}{\sigma(RI_h)} = \frac{\nu RI - \nu \langle RI_h \rangle}{\nu \sigma(RI_h)} \tag{5}$$

where $\langle RI_h \rangle$ and $\sigma(RI_h)$ are, respectively, the average and the standard deviation of the RI of a sample of subsets of size k extracted from a reference *homogeneous* system U_h, and $\nu = \langle MI_h \rangle / \langle I_h \rangle$ is its normalization constant. The homogeneous system corresponding to the one under observation is an ideal system, sharing with it the dimension and the marginal distributions while showing constant correlation among its variables.

The subsets can thus be ranked according to their T_c: the higher the T_c, the higher the correlation degree between the variables within the subset and the lower the interaction with the variables outside the subset. The most relevant sets, characterized by the highest T_c values, are referred to as *Candidate Relevant Sets* (CRSs). In fact, the properly called *Relevant Subsets* (RSs) are CRSs that do not include (or are not included in) other CRSs with higher T_c values. More details can be found in [1,6].

2   GPU/PSO-Based Fast Computation of Relevant Sets

K-means PSO uses the K-means clustering algorithm [7] as a niching technique to maintain diversity among the particles and allow the swarm to explore and converge onto many peaks in parallel. In particular, at regular intervals, the K-means clustering algorithm is applied to the swarm to reorganize it into sub-swarms whose elements are close to one another in the search space. The standard PSO algorithm is then independently applied to each sub-swarm thus identified.

Therefore, K-means PSO requires two additional parameters with respect to standard PSO: the number C of PSO cycles between two clustering steps, and the number nc of clusters by which each K-means run is initialized.

When applying PSO to searching CRSs, each particle i of the swarm represents a CRS as a binary string P_i of size N, where N is the number of variables that describe the system. The value of P_i is defined as follows:

$$P_i(j) = \begin{cases} 1 \text{ if variable } j \text{ is included in the CRS} \\ 0 \text{ otherwise} \end{cases} \tag{6}$$

where $j \in [1, N]$. Since the search space is $\mathcal{R}^N$, the binary vector P_i derives from the corresponding coordinates $p_r^i \in \mathcal{R}^N$ of particle i as follows:

$$P_i(j) = \begin{cases} 1 \text{ if } p_r^i(j) \geq 0 \\ 0 \text{ otherwise} \end{cases} \tag{7}$$

Thus, all steps of the algorithm, e.g., position and velocity update, use the floating-point vectors p_r^i, except the computation of the fitness function $f(P_i) = T_c(P_i^*)$, P_i^* being the CRS represented by P_i.

The fitness function is implemented through a CUDA C [8] kernel that computes in parallel the fitness values of large blocks of particles. The kernel is described in details in a recent paper [6]. Position and velocity updates have been parallelized as well.

A buffer has been introduced to store the highest-T_c subsets found during the run, and their corresponding fitness (T_c) values. Thus, at the end of the run, the best CRSs are not only the ones represented by the last swarm, but the best ones found during the whole search process.

3 A Case Study: Binary Digit Classification

The dataset used in our experiments, downloadable at ftp://ftp.ce.unipr.it/pub/cagnoni/license_plate/, was collected by Società Autostrade SpA at highway toll booths. It includes 6024 patterns representing the ten digits from 0 to 9, roughly uniformly distributed among the ten classes under consideration. The patterns have a size of 13×8 pixels, and have been trivially binarized pixelwise using a threshold of 0.5 (considering pixel values normalized between 0 and 1). This resulted in strings of 104 binary features.

In [9] the authors showed that K-means PSO is able to match the results of an exhaustive search almost perfectly for problem dimensions up to 30 variables, in fractions of the time required by the former. For larger-size problems, the results tend to be more variable, i.e., K-means PSO cannot detect all RSs in each run. However, for the application we are considering, this is less penalizing than for modeling problems, in which missing even a single component of the complex system being analyzed may totally invalidate the results.

The experiments aimed at answering the following questions:

- *(Pre-processing)* How should one organize data to detect the relevant sets?
- *(Feature extraction)* How can one build new variables from the relevant sets detected?
- *(Feature selection)* How should one select the new variables?

3.1   Computing the Relevant Sets

When the RI is used to detect subsystems of a complex system, the analysis cannot be based but on the values of the system status. When feature selection for classification is the goal, as in this case, most often a labeled data set is available. The question, then, is whether one should approach the problem as a plain filter approach, without taking the class information into account, or otherwise, opt for a "supervised" approach.

The former option would imply extracting RSs from all patterns in the dataset at the same time, regardless of the class to which they belong. Conversely, in the latter case, the RI computation would be repeated, class-wise, for each subset of patterns representing a certain digit.

The filter approach would have the obvious advantage of being universally applicable while unifying classical data clustering approaches with the search for RSs. However, such an approach would have the drawback of highlighting correlations among feature sets, which may, in turn, be totally uncorrelated with the labels. This problem, to a certain extent, would be similar to the presence of a non-discriminating component, common to most data, when performing Principal Component Analysis.

However, there is also a low-level technicality, which, finally, forced us to opt for the supervised approach. What can usually be observed, in fact, is that feature sets that include the same RS tend to have RI values that are often almost equally high. Therefore, if two feature sets that are relevant have significantly different RI values, in a virtual ranking of all possible subsets, the distance between their rankings may be in the order of thousands.

When GPU are used, the advantages of the fine-grained parallel processing allowed by graphic processors can be more than (negatively) compensated by the slow GPU/CPU communication, if processing is data-intensive and requires frequent data exchanges between the two processors. Because of this, to maximize computation speed, one needs to keep all candidate relevant sets in memory (at least, up to the quantity of free available GPU memory) while computing the RI. Therefore, within the first few thousands of most relevant subsets that such a constraint allows one to keep in memory, in an extreme case, we could find only the most relevant set and all other thousands of groups that include it or differ from it just by a few elements. Moreover, the consideration that relevant feature sets that recur in different classes tend to have a higher RI value, despite their poor discrimination power, clarifies why we finally had no better option but the supervised approach.

We ran 100, 000 iterations of PSO for each digit set, with a swarm size of 300 and 15 seeds for the K-means algorithm, executed at intervals of 500 iterations.

The experimental results confirmed that, while with the filter approach we could hardly detect a handful of sets having an independent stem within the first 10, 000 sets, we could easily detect a few dozens of independent sets using the supervised approach, keeping, in each run, only the best 3, 000 RSs in memory.

3.2   Feature Extraction

After detecting the relevant sets for each class, one needs to transform them into a single variable, to remove redundancy and, possibly, reinforce their impact onto classification accuracy.

In these preliminary experiments, we have done so in the simplest and possibly most natural way, by directly turning each relevant set into a single binary string whose bits are the original binary variables belonging to the sets, and whose value is the decoding of the variable as an unsigned integer.

This choice, theoretically, has two main drawbacks. The first one is the sparse mapping of binary strings into integer values, which is such that strings, having a Hamming distance equal to one, may not preserve their neighbor relationships when converted into integers. The other problem is the different scale of the new variables, which obviously depend on the size of the subset they represent. Both problems have rather straightforward solutions, consisting, on the one hand, of using Gray coding, while, on the other hand, of normalizing the values within the same range. In our experiments, however, we observed that the accuracies obtained with and without such a preprocessing were virtually the same. This is probably related with the discrete nature of such variables, which makes them substantially equivalent to nominal variables whose ordering is irrelevant, even if one uses classifiers which require numeric inputs.

3.3   Feature Selection

The main goal of the experiments we have performed was to compare the results obtained using the new features, with respect to using the original data.

The main problem with the supervised approach is that, for each class, the obtained RI values are normalized with respect to a different homogeneous system, and therefore, despite having similar ranges, they are not rigorously comparable. Moreover, as explained above, even when retaining the best few thousands RSs extracted by the RI method, most RSs can be referred to a common "ancestor", i.e., the largest-RI RS which is included in them or includes them. Therefore, it is sometimes very hard to identify "independent" sets of variables within such a huge number of nearly-identical or nearly-equivalent sets, even resorting to filtering out all related sets, according to the above-mentioned criterion, except the one having the largest RI.

In the end, this has prompted us, in this preliminary phase, to choose the relevant sets manually. In doing so, as a first step, we tried to be not too selective, and retained a rather large number of sets, almost comparable to the size of the patterns in the original datasets (79 vs. 104 features), selecting, for each class, the sets whose RI was within 10% of the best RI for each class, with a minimum of five sets per class.

A first qualitative assessment of the reasonability of the selected feature sets was done by checking where the pixels selected as relevant features were located. As expected, the features selected by the RI method appear to have been extracted from the regions of the patterns which are most visually distinctive for each class.

We then used the Weka [10] implementation of the Random Forest classifier (with the "default" settings of 100 random trees, each using $log_2(n_{features}) + 1$ random features) and 10-fold cross-validation on the license-plate dataset to classify the original and the transformed data. The results obtained by the two full sets of features are virtually equivalent, with slightly better accuracy obtained on the original data set (an average of 99.08% vs. 98.93% over five runs, with negligible standard deviations, possibly due to the rather large size of the dataset with respect to pattern variability).

In a subsequent experiment, we pooled together all features, new and original, and applied to the resulting 183-feature set the Weka implementation of the CfsSubsetEval feature selector with Genetic Search (population size=200; crossover rate: 0.6; mutation rate: 0.033; 200,000 generations) to see which features would be selected. Two independent runs of the genetic selector resulted in two sets of 50 and 53 features, respectively, with virtually the same proportion of original and new features: 27/23 and 28/25, respectively. These ratios seem to speak slightly in favor of the new features, since these two ratios are closer to 1 than the ratio between the number of features in the two sets. Incidentally, the best results we obtained using the features thus selected were just slightly worse than those obtained with the full set of features: 98.77%.

When Weka InfoGainAttributeEval was used to select the attributes, we noticed that, among the new variables, it tended to privilege features corresponding to larger sets. This is intuitively reasonable, since variables assuming more possible values may correspond to higher entropy "dynamics" with respect to "less complex" variables. Following this hint, we selected, among the new features, the 20 features which corresponded to sets of four or more original features.

After such a rather dramatic reduction of the representation size, we still obtained a reasonably good result (97.74%). However, what looks interesting, is that these features perform better (or much better) than the following feature sets:

1. The first 20 Principal Components derived from the original data (97.54%)
2. Full binary digits rescaled at 6×4 resolution (97.34%)
3. The 20 best original features according to the InfoGainAttributeEval filter (93.47%)

4   Conclusions and Future Work

Answering the title question with a clear "Yes" would be probably over-optimistic, at the present stage of the research. However, the results seem to support the idea that feature extractors/selectors may be built using the RI as a criterion.

Among the many questions that remain open, the definition of some more sophisticated ways of building new variables from the feature subsets extracted by the *RI* method is of primary importance. Possibly, an evolutionary approach such as Genetic Programming could be the key to optimizing their use.

A further topic of interest could be the assessment of the effect of a synthetic extension of the data set, e.g., the introduction of new patterns obtained by slightly shifting or distorting the original data, on both the computation of the *RI* and on the final classification quality.

Of even more general interest could be an extension of this approach to continuous feature representations. This, however, would require also a generalization (or, possibly, just a different implementation) of the *RI* method.

Acknowledgments. The authors would like to thank Andrea Roli, Marco Villani, and Roberto Serra for their collaboration, discussions on the topic, and sincere friendship, and Gianluigi Silvestri for implementing K-means PSO in CUDA.

The work of Michele Amoretti was supported by the University of Parma Research Fund - FIL 2016 - Project "NEXTALGO: Efficient Algorithms for Next-Generation Distributed Systems".

References

1. Villani, M., Filisetti, A., Benedettini, S., Roli, A., Lane, D., Serra, R.: The detection of intermediate level emergent structures and patterns. In: Liò, P., Miglino, O., Nicosia, G., Nolfi, S., Pavone, M. (eds.) Proceedings of ECAL2013, the 12th European Conference on Artificial Life. MIT Press (2013)
2. Tononi, G., McIntosh, A., Russel, D., Edelman, G.: Functional clustering: identifying strongly interactive brain regions in neuroimaging data. Neuroimage **7**, 133–149 (1998)
3. Xue, B., Zhang, M., Browne, W., Yao, X.: A survey on evolutionary computation approaches to feature selection. IEEE Trans. Evol. Comput. **20**(4), 606–626 (2016)
4. Passaro, A., Starita, A.: Particle swarm optimization for multimodal functions: a clustering approach. J. Artif. Evol. Appl. **2008**, 8 (2008)
5. Cover, T., Thomas, J.: Element of Information Theory, 2nd edn. Wiley, Hoboken (2006)
6. Vicari, E., Amoretti, M., Sani, L., Mordonini, M., Pecori, R., Roli, A., Villani, M., Cagnoni, S., Serra, R.: GPU-based parallel search of relevant variable sets in complex systems. In: Rossi, F., Piotto, S., Concilio, S. (eds.) WIVACE 2016. CCIS, vol. 708, pp. 14–25. Springer, Cham (2017). https://doi.org/10.1007/978-3-319-57711-1_2
7. Mac Queen, J.: Some methods for classification and analysis of multivariate observations. In: Proceedings of the Fifth Berkeley Symposium on Mathematical Statistics and Probability, vol. 1, pp. 281–297 (1967)
8. CUDA Toolkit. http://developer.nvidia.com/cuda-toolkit. Accessed 19 Jan 2018
9. Silvestri, G., Sani, L., Amoretti, M., Pecori, R., Vicari, E., Mordonini, M., Cagnoni, S.: Searching relevant variable subsets in complex systems using K-means PSO. In: Roli, A., Slanzi, D., Villani, M. (eds.) Advances in Artificial Life and Evolutionary Computation: 12th Italian Workshop. Springer (2018, in press)
10. Bouckaert, R.R., Frank, E., Hall, M., Kirkby, R., Reutemann, P., Seewald, A., Scuse, D.: WEKA manual for version 3-7-8. University of Waikato, NZ (2013)

Towards Evolutionary Super-Resolution

Michal Kawulok[1,2]([✉]) [ID], Pawel Benecki[1,2], Daniel Kostrzewa[1,2] [ID],
and Lukasz Skonieczny[1]

[1] Future Processing, Gliwice, Poland
{mkawulok,pbenecki,dkostrzewa,lskonieczny}@future-processing.com
[2] Silesian University of Technology, Gliwice, Poland
{michal.kawulok,pawel.benecki,daniel.kostrzewa}@polsl.pl

Abstract. Super-resolution reconstruction (SRR) allows for producing
a high-resolution (HR) image from a set of low-resolution (LR) observations. The majority of existing methods require tuning a number of hyper-parameters which control the reconstruction process and configure the
imaging model that is supposed to reflect the relation between high and
low resolution. In this paper, we demonstrate that the reconstruction process is very sensitive to the actual relation between LR and HR images,
and we argue that this is a substantial obstacle in deploying SRR in practice. We propose to search the hyper-parameter space using a genetic algorithm (GA), thus adapting to the actual relation between LR and HR,
which has not been reported in the literature so far. The results of our
extensive experimental study clearly indicate that our GA improves the
capacities of SRR. Importantly, the GA converges to different values of
the hyper-parameters depending on the applied degradation procedure,
which is confirmed using statistical tests.

Keywords: Genetic algorithm · Image processing · Super-resolution

1 Introduction

Computer vision systems require certain spatial resolution of the input images for
proper operation, which is often difficult to provide or it is subject to a number of
trade-offs, ranging from image acquisition costs to accessibility and safety. This
motivated the researchers to develop algorithms that allow for reconstructing a
high resolution (HR) image from a series of images of lower spatial resolution
(LR)—this process is known as *super-resolution reconstruction* (SRR). Although
SRR has gained considerable attention over the years, the capacities of the state-of-the-art methods are very often insufficient for real-world scenarios.

1.1 Related Work

SRR has been applied to a variety of computer vision fields, including remote
sensing [1], medical imaging [2,3], microscopy imaging [4], facial image analysis [3], or document image processing [5]. The reconstruction can be executed
(i) given a single image [6], including processing hyper-spectral data [7], or
(ii) from a sequence of images acquired with some shifts in the spatial domain [8].

© Springer International Publishing AG, part of Springer Nature 2018
K. Sim and P. Kaufmann (Eds.): EvoApplications 2018, LNCS 10784, pp. 480–496, 2018.
https://doi.org/10.1007/978-3-319-77538-8_33

Single-Image SRR. The majority of works on enhancing the resolution from a single image employ a form of example-based learning [9]—the reconstruction consists in matching image patches between LR and HR images (this can also be done within a single image based on self exemplars [10]). This allows for achieving visually plausible results, but may easily lead to introducing some artifacts.

Recently, deep convolutional neural networks (CNNs) were used to model the mapping from LR to HR by learning prior knowledge from LR-HR image pairs. In [11], a super-resolution CNN (SRCNN) of a relatively simple architecture was shown to outperform the state-of-the-art methods. In [12], SRCNN was successfully trained with Sentinel-2 satellite images. Also, much deeper architectures were exploited, relying on fast residual training [13]. An interesting observation was done by Efrat et al. [14], who investigated the sensitivity of SRR algorithms to the assumed blur model and demonstrated that accurate estimation of the blur model is instrumental to achieving good reconstruction result.

SRR from Multiple Images. This direction, addressed in the research reported here, usually employs a parametrized imaging model (IM) that simulates the process of degrading a hypothetical HR image into a set of N observed LR ones—$I^{(L)} = \left\{ \mathcal{I}_i^{(l)} : i \in [1..N] \right\}$. In general, such models include image warping, blurring, downsampling and finally contamination with the noise [15].

The reconstruction is an ill-posed problem, which is usually solved by employing the Bayesian framework or gradient-based techniques with some regularization imposed to provide spatial smoothness of the reconstructed HR image ($\mathcal{I}'^{(h)}$). Regularization [16] translates a *maximum likelihood* (ML) problem into *maximum a posteriori* (MAP) estimation. In one of the earliest approaches, SRR was performed relying on image registration (hence reducing the IM to subpixel shifts) using iterative back-projection (IBP) [17]. A hierarchical subpixel displacement estimation was combined with the Bayesian reconstruction in the gradient projection algorithm (GPA) [18]. If a video sequence is processed, then the motion blur is also incorporated into the IM [19]. Another fairly popular optimization technique applied here is the projection onto convex sets (POCS) [20], which consists in updating the high-resolution target image iteratively based on the error measured between $\mathcal{I}^{(l)}$ and $\mathcal{I}'^{(l)}$—a downsampled version of reconstructed $\mathcal{I}'^{(h)}$, degraded using the assumed IM. Fast and robust super-resolution (FRSR) based on ML estimation coupled with simplified regularization was proposed in [21]—importantly, the error is measured in the HR coordinates, thus avoiding the expensive scaling operation. Among other methods, adaptive Wiener filter [22] and random Markov fields [23] were used to specify the IM. Recently, multiple-image SRR for satellite images was proceeded using adaptive detail enhancement (SR-ADE) [1]—this employs bilateral filter to decompose the input images and amplify the high-frequency detail information.

Evolutionary techniques were exploited for SRR in [24]—the subpixel registration parameters are determined with a genetic algorithm (GA). Here, the regularization is ensured by imposing certain constraints on the genetic operators (especially mutation). Also, particle swarm optimization (PSO) [25], simulated annealing [26] and differential evolution [27] were exploited to reconstruct an HR image given an assumed IM. Importantly, while the SRR process may determine some image-specific IM parameters, both the model, as well as the process itself, are controlled with a set of *hyper-parameters* that are common for all LR images, and the problem of their optimization has not been given much attention.

Evaluation of SRR Outcome. A commonly adopted way to evaluate the outcome of SRR is to degrade an HR image $\mathcal{I}^{(h)}$ using an IM defined on a theoretical basis to obtain the set $\boldsymbol{I}^{(L)}$ [21]. Subsequently, SRR is employed to reconstruct $\mathcal{I}'^{(h)}$ from $\boldsymbol{I}^{(L)}$, and its quality is assessed based on the similarity between $\mathcal{I}'^{(h)}$ and $\mathcal{I}^{(h)}$, measured with peak signal-to-noise ratio (PSNR) or structural similarity index (SSIM) [28,29]. Such a scenario makes it possible to evaluate the optimization process, but it does not verify whether the assumed IM is appropriate [30]. The latter is often done only qualitatively—SRR is performed for camera-captured images and the outcome is subject to visual inspection.

1.2 Contribution

It can be seen from Sect. 1.1 that the problem of selecting IMs and tuning their hyper-parameters has not been deeply studied in the literature and it remains an open issue. Although there were some attempts to estimate the blur kernel for single-image SRR [14], this was not considered for IMs assumed in multiple-image SRR.

Our contribution is doublefold: (i) we introduce a genetic algorithm (GA) to optimize the hyper-parameters that control the SRR process, including the IM, and (ii) we demonstrate the importance of adapting these hyper-parameters to the actual IM. In the research reported here, we focus on a well-established FRSR algorithm [21], whose hyper-parameters ($\mathcal{H}$) are optimized by evolving a population of individuals. To validate our new algorithm (GA-FRSR), we consider nine different degradation models to generate the pairs of training ($\boldsymbol{T}$) and test ($\boldsymbol{\Psi}$) sets, each of which contains artificially degraded LR images $\boldsymbol{I}^{(L)}$ associated with an HR ground-truth image $\mathcal{I}^{(h)}$. In addition to that, we use real satellite images captured within Sentinel-2 (LR images) and SPOT (HR images) missions. We demonstrate that for each of them, GA-FRSR converges to significantly different values of the hyper-parameters, and that the results obtained for $\boldsymbol{\Psi}$ are highly dependent on which variant of $\boldsymbol{T}$ was used for optimization. Overall, we show that FRSR is very sensitive to the IM and that the proposed GA is capable of adapting this SRR method both to the IM used to degrade the HR images, and to the real-world satellite images. Importantly, our GA is thought to be highly generic, hence it may be applied to optimize the hyper-parameters of other SRR methods as well.

1.3 Paper Structure

In Sect. 2, we outline the imaging model commonly assumed in multiple-image SRR and we explain the details of the FRSR algorithm, along with presenting the hyper-parameters that we optimize. Our GA is demonstrated and discussed in Sect. 3 and the experimental study is reported in Sect. 4. Finally, in Sect. 5, we conclude the paper and we outline the future research pathways.

2 SRR from Multiple Images

Generic Imaging Model. The existing multiple-image SRR methods are based on a premise that any observed LR image $\mathcal{I}^{(l)}$ can be obtained from a hypothetic image of higher resolution $\mathcal{I}'^{(h)}$ by applying the following generic degradation model [31]:

$$\mathcal{I}_i^{(l)} = \boldsymbol{D}_i \boldsymbol{B}_i \boldsymbol{W}_i \mathcal{I}'^{(h)} + n_i, \tag{1}$$

where $\boldsymbol{W}$ is the warp matrix (including translation and rotation), $\boldsymbol{B}$ is the blur matrix, $\boldsymbol{D}$ downscales the image, and n stands for the additive noise. Importantly, if the observed images are captured by the same sensor, it may be assumed that $\boldsymbol{B}$ and $\boldsymbol{D}$ are common for all the images in the series (thus, they do not depend on i). Hence, the differences among the observed images are resulting from translations and rotations, as well as from the additive noise.

A super-resolved image is found based on *maximum a posteriori* (MAP) theory as a solution ($\mathcal{X}$) of the minimization problem:

$$\mathcal{I}'^{(h)} = \arg\min_{\mathcal{X}} \sum_{i=1}^{N} \rho\left(\mathcal{I}_i^{(l)}, \boldsymbol{D}\boldsymbol{B}\boldsymbol{W}_i\mathcal{X}\right) + \lambda U(\mathcal{X}), \tag{2}$$

where $\rho(\cdot)$ is the dissimilarity between images and $U(\cdot)$ is the regularization term. The existing SRR methods differ in the way the degradation matrices and regularization terms are defined, as well as they adopt various optimization strategies.

The Reconstruction Process. In the research reported here, we exploit the well-established FRSR method [21]. The dissimilarity ρ is measured based on the L_1 norm, $\boldsymbol{B}$ matrix implements the Gaussian blur (controlled with the kernel width σ), and for regularization, the total variation method [32] is combined with a bilateral filter:

$$U(\mathcal{X}) = \sum_{l=-P}^{P} \sum_{m=-P}^{P} \alpha^{|m|+|l|} \left\| \mathcal{X} - \boldsymbol{S}_y^m \boldsymbol{S}_x^l \mathcal{X} \right\|_1, \tag{3}$$

where $\boldsymbol{S}_x^l$ and $\boldsymbol{S}_y^m$ shift an image by l and m pixels in horizontal and vertical direction, respectively, $0 < \alpha < 1$ is a parameter of spatial decay, and P is a natural number, usually not greater than 3. The reconstructed image is obtained by minimizing the term (2), which is done with the iterative steepest gradient descent. Importantly, the reconstruction error is computed in the HR domain—an initial HR image ($\mathcal{X}_0$) is obtained from the co-registered LR inputs (which can be either averaged or combined with median shift-and-add technique). The update step $\Delta \mathcal{X} = \mathcal{X}_{n+1} - \mathcal{X}_n$ is obtained as

$$\Delta \mathcal{X} = -\beta \left[\boldsymbol{B}^T \boldsymbol{A}^T \mathrm{sgn}(\boldsymbol{A}\boldsymbol{B}\mathcal{X}_n - \boldsymbol{A}\mathcal{X}_0) + \lambda \sum_{l,m} \alpha^{|m|+|l|} \boldsymbol{S}' \mathrm{sgn}(\mathcal{X}_n - \boldsymbol{S}_y^m \boldsymbol{S}_x^l \mathcal{X}_n) \right], \quad (4)$$

where $\boldsymbol{S}' = \mathbb{1} - \boldsymbol{S}_y^{-m} \boldsymbol{S}_x^{-l}$, and $\boldsymbol{A}$ is a diagonal matrix with the values equal to the square root of the number of the LR measurements that contributed to each element of $\mathcal{X}_0$. Overall, the SRR process is controlled with (i) Gaussian kernel width σ in $\boldsymbol{B}$, (ii) P used in the regularization (3), and (iii) the remaining hyper-parameters related to the optimization process (4), namely: α, β and λ. In addition to that, the technique to initialize $\mathcal{X}_0$ is relevant—here, we control it with $F_{sa} \in \{0,1\}$ (median shift-and-add is realized for $F_{sa} = 1$, and the averaging otherwise). It is worth noting that in [21], FRSR is applied to several images, for each of which different values of the hyper-parameters were reported. The parameters specific to every single presented image $\mathcal{I}_i^{(l)} \in \boldsymbol{I}^{(L)}$ are concerned with the $\boldsymbol{W}_i$ matrix (hence with $\mathcal{X}_0$ and $\boldsymbol{A}$ in (4)), and they are determined by subpixel registration of the images within each $\boldsymbol{I}^{(L)}$.

3   Genetic Algorithm to Optimize SRR

Existing SRR algorithms are controlled with a number of hyper-parameters, which severely influence the quality of the reconstructed image, and the problem of their tuning has been paid little attention in the literature so far. In this work, we introduce a new GA for optimizing such hyper-parameters and we apply it to the FRSR method, outlined earlier in Sect. 2. Our goal is to find optimal values of the hyper-parameters $\mathcal{H} = [\alpha, \beta, \lambda, \sigma, P, F_{sa}]$ given a training set $\boldsymbol{T}$ which contains pairs of an HR image associated with a set of LR images.

3.1   Outline of GA-FRSR

The pseudocode of the proposed algorithm is presented in Algorithm 1. A population $\mathcal{P}$ of N_P individuals is initialized (line 1)—a chromosome of each individual $p = \{p^{(1)}, p^{(2)}, ..., p^{(K)}\}$ defines the values of K hyper-parameters which control the SRR process (the values $p^{(i)}$ are initialized randomly within an allowed range specific to each hyper-parameter). Subsequently, each individual in $\mathcal{P}$ is considered for mutation with the probability P_m and the selected individuals ($\mathcal{P}_M$) are excluded from the individuals selected for crossover ($\mathcal{P}_C$) (lines 3–4). The individuals in $\mathcal{P}_C$ are paired and crossed over to create an offspring population $\mathcal{P}'_C$ of the same size as $\mathcal{P}_C$, hence $\#\mathcal{P}_C = \#\mathcal{P}'_C$. During crossover (line 5) of two individuals p_a and p_b, the values of the continuous-domain parameters (i.e., α, β, λ, σ) of the child p_{a+b} are drawn randomly from the range $\left[\min(p_a^{(i)}, p_b^{(i)}); \max(p_a^{(i)}, p_b^{(i)}) \right]$ and for the discrete-domain parameters (here, P and F_{sa}), the new value is copied from p_a or p_b with equal probability. For

Algorithm 1. A GA for optimizing the SRR hyper-parameters (GA-FRSR).

1: Initialize population $\mathcal{P} = \{p_i\}$ of size N_P;
2: **repeat**
3:     $\mathcal{P}_M \leftarrow$ SELECTFORMUTATION($\mathcal{P}$, P_m);
4:     $\mathcal{P}_C \leftarrow \mathcal{P} \setminus \mathcal{P}_M$;
5:     $\mathcal{P}'_C \leftarrow$ CROSSOVER($\mathcal{P}_C$);
6:     $\mathcal{P}'_M \leftarrow$ MUTATE($\mathcal{P}_M$);
7:     $\mathcal{P}' \leftarrow \mathcal{P} \cup \mathcal{P}'_M \cup \mathcal{P}'_C$;
8:     **for all** $\{p_i\} \in \mathcal{P}'$ **do**
9:         $\eta(p_i) \leftarrow$ FITNESS(p_i);
10:    **end for**
11:    $\mathcal{P} \leftarrow$ SELECT($\mathcal{P}'$, N_P);
12:    $p_B \leftarrow \arg\max_{p_i \in \mathcal{P}}\{\eta(p_i)\}$;
13:    **if** REGENERATECONDITION **then**
14:        $\mathcal{P}' \leftarrow$ REGENERATE($N_P - 1$);
15:        $\mathcal{P} \leftarrow \mathcal{P}' \cup p_B$;
16:    **end if**
17: **until** STOPCONDITION;
18: **return** (p_B);

---

each individual selected for mutation, one value in the chromosome is selected and modified within the range $\left[0.75 \cdot p^{(i)}; 1.25 \cdot p^{(i)}\right]$ for a continuous domain and within the entire domain for the discrete values (line 6). The existing population $\mathcal{P}$ is appended with the mutated individuals $\mathcal{P}'_M$ and those created during the crossover ($\mathcal{P}'_C$)—this creates a new population $\mathcal{P}'$ (line 7). Fitness η of each new solution is retrieved (this is explained later in Sect. 3.2) to select the N_P fittest individuals (line 11). If the average fitness of the population does not grow in three subsequent generations, then the population is regenerated, preserving the best individual (line 13). After three regenerations, the stop condition is met (line 17), and the best solution p_B is returned (line 18) which configures FRSR (or potentially another SRR method).

3.2 Computing the Fitness

The process to retrieve the fitness η of an individual p_i is illustrated in Fig. 1. Basically, this requires a training set $\boldsymbol{T}$ of M HR images, each of which is coupled with a set of LR counterparts $\boldsymbol{I}^{(L)}$, presenting the same scene or region.

To evaluate the fitness η of an individual p_i, the hyper-parameters defined by its chromosome are used to configure the SRR algorithm, which is run to process each $\boldsymbol{I}^{(L)}$ and reconstruct a high-resolution image $\mathcal{I}'^{(h)}$. Quality of the reconstruction is assessed based on the similarity between $\mathcal{I}'^{(h)}$ and $\mathcal{I}^{(h)}$, measured with SSIM (however other metrics may be used for this purpose as well). The final fitness $\eta(p_i)$ is obtained as the mean of the M similarity scores—basically, the better the values of $\mathcal{H}$ are, the more similar is the reconstructed image to the ground truth, and this similarity is expected to increase during the evolutionary optimization.

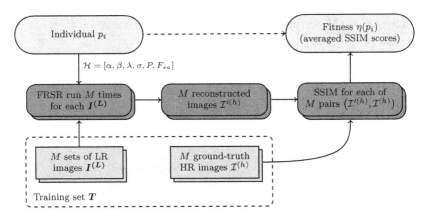

Fig. 1. The process of computing the fitness $\eta(p_i)$ of an individual p_i.

4 Experimental Validation

4.1 Experimental Setup

We validated our method using two categories of satellite images: (i) SPOT images, artificially degraded using different IMs and (ii) real HR and LR images (SPOT and Sentinel-2, respectively) presenting the same Earth region, captured at different native resolution. We decided to use satellite images for validation because of two reasons—first, this is a very important direction of potential SRR applications, and second, the challenges the satellite images induce for SRR are concerned mainly with the IM, while their registration is relatively easy, as it is limited to the displacements without any warping. Also, their quality is usually high, hence they can be used without any additional pre-processing.

For artificially-generated LR images, we used nine degradation scenarios defined in Table 1. Basically, the original HR images are optionally blurred using a Gaussian kernel of the width $\sigma_B \in \{1.0, 2.0\}$ and downscaled by a factor of 2 in each dimension. Finally, the noise is added, either Gaussian with standard deviation $\sigma_N = 5.0$ and the mean value $\mu = 128$ (for 256 levels of brightness), or with the salt-and-pepper noise (here, the probability of turning the pixel value is 0.025 in each direction). For artificial images, the training set T covers 5 scenes, each of which contains 4 LR images of size 50×50 pixels (the HR images are of size 100×100 pixels). The test set Ψ contains the same number of images (unseen during training), degraded using the same procedure. The image dimensions may appear small, but we have not observed substantial differences in the scores when using larger dimensions or including more images in T and Ψ. So as to reduce the optimization time, we rely on these rather small images in the T and Ψ sets, as we found them sufficient to validate our concept. Examples of HR and LR images degraded using different variants are demonstrated in Fig. 2.

In the case of the real satellite images (termed rs), we prepared SPOT images of size 317×317 and 211×211 pixels as HR ground-truth data, each of which

Table 1. Different variants of the degradation procedure applied to the T.

Operation ↓	b^0n^0	b^0n^g	b^0n^{sp}	b^an^0	b^an^g	b^an^{sp}	b^bn^0	b^bn^g	b^bn^{sp}
Blurring (σ_B)	—	—	—	1.0	1.0	1.0	2.0	2.0	2.0
Gaussian noise	—	Yes	—	—	Yes	—	—	Yes	—
Salt-and-pepper noise	—	—	Yes	—	—	Yes	—	—	Yes

is associated with 5 LR images of size 75×75 and 50×50 pixels, respectively, captured by Sentinel-2. Both T and Ψ are composed of 10 scenes. An example of such a scene is presented in Fig. 3a. It is worth noting that these images are visually very dissimilar due to image sensor differences. Hence even for good reconstruction, the simple metrics (such as SSIM) may remain rather low.

The values of the hyper-parameters were initialized in the following ranges, set based on the results reported in [21]: $\alpha \in (0;1)$, $\beta \in (0;100)$, $\lambda \in (0;1)$, $\sigma \in (0;20)$, $P \in \{1,2,3\}$, and $F_{sa} \in \{0,1\}$. GA-FRSR was tested with population size $N_P = 10$ and mutation probability $P_m = 0.2$. As our GA is a randomized technique, each test was repeated 30 times for each configuration. In addition to the stop condition explained earlier in Sect. 3, we interrupt every optimization after reaching a time limit of $\tau = 1500$ s, which corresponds to ca. 40 generations. We implemented all the algorithms in C++ (using OpenCV library) and we ran the experiments on an Intel Xeon 3.2 GHz computer with 16 GB RAM.

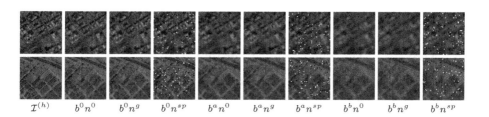

$\mathcal{I}^{(h)}$ b^0n^0 b^0n^g b^0n^{sp} b^an^0 b^an^g b^an^{sp} b^bn^0 b^bn^g b^bn^{sp}

Fig. 2. Examples of the images from the T set with different degradation variants.

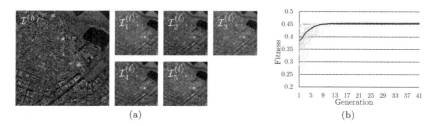

(a)   (b)

Fig. 3. An example of real satellite images used to train GA-FRSR (a) and the maximum fitness in subsequent generations (the black line shows the averaged score) (b).

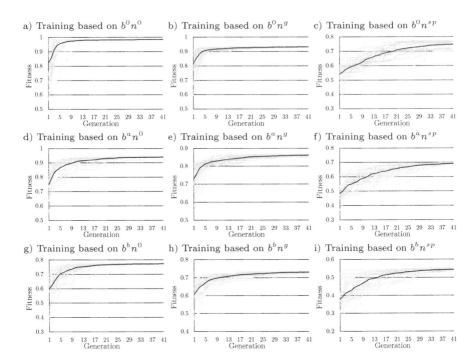

Fig. 4. Maximum fitness value obtained in subsequent generations (each run is shown as a gray line, and the black line shows the average across all the runs).

4.2 Analysis of the Evolutionary Optimization

In Fig. 3b, the fitness growth for T composed of the rs images is presented (the gray lines show the maximum fitness in particular runs, while the black line shows the averaged score). The fitness growth for different variants of T depending on the degradation procedure applied, is illustrated in Fig. 4. It can be seen from these plots that in most cases our GA converges well, although for the salt-and-pepper noise, the time limit occurred to be too rigorous, as the process converges much slower in these cases, especially for $b^0 n^{sp}$.

The hyper-parameter values returned by the best solution in each training scenario are reported in Table 2 (we report the mean score and standard deviation across all the runs). As there are three values possible for P, we present the average percentage of each value across all the runs in each variant. The F_{sa} flag was set on after running the process for the artificially-degraded images in most of the runs, while it was usually off for rs. For the continuous hyper-parameters, we verified if their values are significantly different for each pair of the training variants. Our null hypothesis saying that "using different variants of T for computing the fitness in GA-FRSR leads to obtaining the same values of the hyper-parameter", was verified employing the Mann-Whitney U-test [33]. The results, reported in Table 3, show that for many pairs, one or two hyper-parameters were not statistically different, however for only six pairs there were

Table 2. Optimized values of $\mathcal{H}$ for different variants of T.

Train ↓	α	β	λ	σ	$P=1$	$P=2$	$P=3$
$b^0 n^0$	$.29 \pm .29$	0.21 ± 0.35	$.21 \pm .28$	4.18 ± 5.61	37.5%	18.8%	43.8%
$b^0 n^g$	$.48 \pm .21$	2.15 ± 1.12	$.57 \pm .28$	2.33 ± 1.15	30.0%	23.3%	46.7%
$b^0 n^{sp}$	$.50 \pm .16$	12.26 ± 2.68	$.72 \pm .25$	2.02 ± 0.43	23.3%	26.7%	50.0%
$b^a n^0$	$.10 \pm .21$	3.92 ± 0.72	$.27 \pm .32$	2.13 ± 1.04	36.7%	30.0%	33.3%
$b^a n^g$	$.34 \pm .18$	7.13 ± 2.13	$.37 \pm .28$	2.50 ± 0.86	26.7%	13.3%	60.0%
$b^a n^{sp}$	$.55 \pm .18$	11.23 ± 1.71	$.88 \pm .13$	2.27 ± 0.27	46.7%	16.7%	36.7%
$b^b n^0$	$.10 \pm .17$	5.45 ± 0.85	$.26 \pm .32$	3.21 ± 0.97	46.7%	6.7%	46.7%
$b^b n^g$	$.23 \pm .16$	14.72 ± 1.62	$.31 \pm .21$	3.79 ± 1.18	3.3%	20.0%	76.7%
$b^b n^{sp}$	$.59 \pm .21$	10.40 ± 2.18	$.84 \pm .16$	3.75 ± 0.44	51.7%	0.0%	48.3%
rs	$.50 \pm .31$	1.59 ± 2.78	$.44 \pm .29$	5.84 ± 6.01	33.3%	20.0%	46.7%

Table 3. Statistical significance of the differences between the optimized values of the hyper-parameters (considering α, β, λ and σ) obtained after training using different T's. The table shows which parameters were not significantly different ($p > 0.05$) between the particular configurations relying on the Mann-Whitney U-test. The cases, when more than two hyper-parameters were not different, are marked as gray.

Train ↓→	b^0n^0	b^0n^g	b^0n^{sp}	b^an^0	b^an^g	b^an^{sp}	b^bn^0	b^bn^g	b^bn^{sp}	rs
b^0n^0	—	σ	σ	α,λ,σ	α,λ,σ	σ	α,λ,σ	α,λ,σ	σ	λ,σ
b^0n^g		—	α,σ	λ,σ	σ	α,σ			σ	α,β,λ
b^0n^{sp}			—	σ		α,β		α,λ		α
b^an^0				—	λ,σ	σ	α,λ	λ		λ
b^an^g					—	σ	λ	λ		λ,σ
b^an^{sp}						—	α	α,β,λ		α
b^bn^0							—	α,λ	σ	λ,σ
b^bn^g								—	σ	σ
b^bn^{sp}									—	α,σ

three hyper-parameters for which the null hypothesis cannot be rejected (marked as gray in Table 3), and for every pair there was at least one hyper-parameter significantly different. This indicates that depending on the degradation model, there are different optimal values of the hyper-parameters.

4.3 Quantitative Analysis

In Table 4, we report the SSIM scores obtained for different variants of T and Ψ. Importantly, we performed the cross checks to verify the GA-FRSR performance for all the variants of Ψ, when the $\mathcal{H}$'s were optimized using different variants of T. The corresponding T and Ψ are highlighted with gray color in the table, and the best average, minimum and maximum score for each test variant are marked as bold (the correspondence between T and Ψ means that the two sets contain different images, but degraded in the same way). It can be seen that in most of the cases, the best scores were obtained when $\mathcal{H}$'s are optimized using images degraded in the same way, hence the $\mathcal{H}$'s are adapted to a particular IM that models the relation between low and high resolution (importantly, this cannot be perceived as overfitting, as T and Ψ contain different images). Furthermore, it is worth noting that the rs test set containing real LR images is also quite sensitive

Table 4. SSIM scores obtained for T (i.e., the fitness η) and for the different variants of the test set Ψ (average, minimum and maximum scores in 30 runs are reported for each variant).

GA-FRSR Train ↓		η	$b^0 n^0$	$b^0 n^g$	$b^0 n^{sp}$	$b^a n^0$	$b^a n^g$	$b^a n^{sp}$	$b^b n^0$	$b^b n^g$	$b^b n^{sp}$	rs
$b^0 n^0$	avg	.984	**.977**	.870	.477	.865	.759	.406	.653	.562	.330	.355
	min	.983	**.976**	.842	.417	.862	.734	.381	.652	.535	.304	.323
	max	.987	**.980**	.876	.486	.886	.764	.415	.669	.567	.341	.386
$b^0 n^g$	avg	.932	.948	**.919**	.572	.860	.820	.491	.676	.636	.401	.412
	min	.928	.926	**.911**	.491	.801	.798	.419	.639	.617	.255	.384
	max	.935	.962	**.925**	.633	.892	.840	.550	.707	.654	.439	.439
$b^0 n^{sp}$	avg	.747	.828	.817	**.754**	.733	.742	.650	.591	.570	.516	.384
	min	.702	.757	.766	**.691**	.663	.673	.613	.525	.498	.487	.344
	max	.774	.910	.865	**.787**	.848	.809	.673	.665	.631	.534	.421
$b^a n^0$	avg	.940	.949	.850	.512	**.933**	.782	.454	.709	.564	.353	.356
	min	.936	.931	.834	.496	**.929**	.769	.430	.700	.551	.328	.331
	max	.945	.962	.863	.609	**.937**	.802	.542	.716	.589	.420	.391
$b^a n^g$	avg	.862	.927	.901	.595	.885	**.844**	.533	.690	.661	.427	.408
	min	.851	.853	.849	.516	.834	**.815**	.458	.658	.631	.360	.381
	max	.868	.961	.924	.647	.902	**.854**	.578	.716	.684	.460	.432
$b^a n^{sp}$	avg	.691	.839	.815	**.761**	.766	.755	**.674**	.599	.572	.526	.387
	min	.683	.786	.767	**.730**	.691	.714	**.660**	.553	.540	.497	.350
	max	.698	.901	.859	.780	.829	.789	**.683**	.637	.595	.539	.414
$b^b n^0$	avg	.773	.941	.865	.560	.883	.794	.499	**.746**	.625	.425	.365
	min	.770	.929	.855	.508	.872	.785	.458	**.743**	.603	.386	.324
	max	.777	.955	.873	.589	.901	.802	.529	**.749**	.635	.443	.394
$b^b n^g$	avg	.730	.862	.854	.565	.813	.806	.516	.692	**.697**	.435	.371
	min	.720	.841	.837	.497	.781	.776	.449	.671	**.690**	.375	.337
	max	.734	.884	.875	.596	.839	.825	.543	.704	**.700**	.457	.406
$b^b n^{sp}$	avg	.544	.749	.748	.673	.723	.715	.628	.615	.604	**.535**	.376
	min	.523	.662	.658	.628	.636	.637	.591	.566	.552	**.505**	.355
	max	.554	.814	.808	.730	.785	.769	.660	.657	.665	**.550**	.410
rs	avg	.455	.842	.841	.564	.752	.735	.484	.598	.589	.392	.418
	min	.453	.803	.804	.548	.725	.709	.464	.566	.576	.366	.405
	max	.459	.864	.857	.608	.797	.765	.538	.669	.622	.444	**.446**
Other SRR algorithms												
GPA [18]			.937	.902	.412	.788	.779	.332	.583	.586	.240	.404
IBP [17]			.911	.897	.581	.836	.810	.490	.614	.610	.370	**.424**
SR-ADE [1]			.848	.836	.649	.755	.744	.560	.603	.593	.452	.388

to the T used for training, and the best scores were obtained when GA-FRSR was trained also with the real rs images (obviously different than those used for testing), hence our GA succeeded in adapting $\mathcal{H}$ to the actual relation between Sentinel-2 (LR) and SPOT (HR) images. It can be seen that other SRR methods deliver comparable scores for rs images, but they are also very sensitive to the actual degradation model. The IBP method [17] offers better reconstruction than the average GA-FRSR performance, however the best performing variant of GA-FRSR is still better. Overall, this indicates that high sensitivity of the reconstruction process is the common problem of SRR methods and confirms that determining their optimal values is not a trivial task.

Table 5. The level of statistical significance according to the two-tailed Wilcoxon test between the scores obtained for the real satellite images after training with different variants of T (the scores are presented in the last column of Table 4). The cases with non-significant differences ($p > 0.05$) are marked as gray.

Train ↓→	b^0n^0	b^0n^g	b^0n^{sp}	b^an^0	b^an^g	b^an^{sp}	b^bn^0	b^bn^g	b^bn^{sp}	rs
b^0n^0	—	< .001	< .001	> .2	< .001	< .001	< .05	< .001	< .001	< .001
b^0n^g		—	< .001	< .001	> .1	< .001	< .001	< .001	< .001	< .05
b^0n^{sp}			—	< .001	< .001	> .2	< .001	< .05	> .1	< .001
b^an^0				—	< .001	< .001	> .1	< .005	< .001	< .001
b^an^g					—	< .001	< .001	< .001	< .001	< .005
b^an^{sp}						—	< .001	< .005	< .02	< .001
b^bn^0							—	> .1	> .05	< .001
b^bn^g								—	> .2	< .001
b^bn^{sp}									—	< .001

We employed the two-tailed Wilcoxon test to verify the level of statistical difference between the results obtained for the rs images in $\boldsymbol{\Psi}$ when trained with different variants of T (the scores presented in the rightmost column in Table 4), and the results are reported in Table 5. The null hypothesis saying that "using different variants of T leads to obtaining the scores of the same quality for the rs set" can be safely rejected when comparing the training based on rs images against the training from the artificially-degraded ones (the rs column in

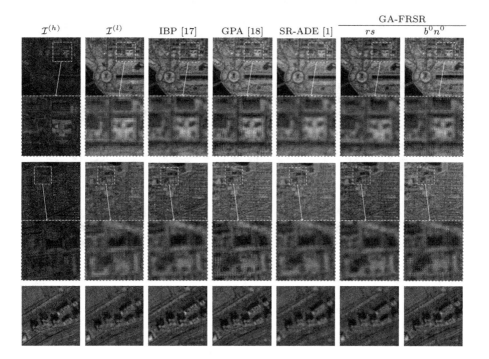

Fig. 5. Examples of the reconstruction outcome for the real satellite images (upper and middle row) and an artificially degraded image (b^0n^0 variant) (bottom row).

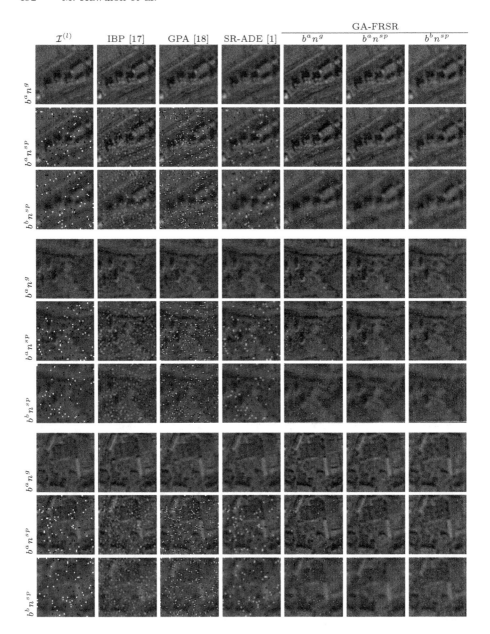

Fig. 6. Examples of the reconstruction outcome for the artificially-degraded images.

Table 5). Among the latter, the $b^0 n^g$ degradation model reflects the real relation the best, but still the scores are statistically different here (at $p < 0.05$).

4.4   Qualitative Analysis

In Fig. 5, we present the reconstruction outcome obtained using different SRR methods, including GA-FRSR trained with two different variants of T (rs and b^0n^0). It can be seen that some methods introduce artifacts to the reconstructed image, including GA-FRSR trained with b^0n^0 images (the results are much better when GA-FRSR is trained with rs images). In the bottom row, the reconstruction outcomes of artificially-degraded images (with the b^0n^0 model applied) are illustrated, and it can be seen that GA-FRSR performs definitely better when trained with the images degraded using the same model (b^0n^0). On the other hand, when FRSR is trained with $\mathcal{H}$ optimized for rs, the outcome is similar to that obtained with SR-ADE [1].

In Fig. 6, we present more examples of artificially-degraded images reconstructed with GA-FRSR optimized using the corresponding variants of T. It can be noticed that for FRSR the best reconstruction is achieved when the hyper-parameters are adapted to a given IM. Other methods, as well as GA-FRSR (b^an^g) do not cope well with the salt-and-pepper noise (in particular, GPA amplifies the noise).

5   Conclusions and Future Work

In this paper, we introduced a new approach to optimizing hyper-parameters that control the process of super-resolution reconstruction. We demonstrated that our GA is capable of improving the performance of the well-established FRSR method. The results of our extensive experimental study indicate high sensitiveness of FRSR, as well as of other SRR algorithms to the actual imaging model employed to obtain the LR observations (this holds regardless of whether the imaging process is natural or simulated). This is an important observation, given that most of the algorithms for SRR are reported to be validated using artificially-degraded images, and they may not reflect the realistic conditions.

Although in this paper we presented a thorough method to optimize the hyper-parameters of the FRSR algorithm, the general shape of the imaging model was not subject to the optimization. While this may be important when bridging the gap between the SRR performance for real and artificially-degraded images, our intention is to add more degrees of freedom to the imaging model to allow for its full evolution. This may also require improving the optimization process, possibly using evolution strategy operators [34], as well as other techniques, such as PSO, known for its effectiveness in optimizing hyper-parameters [35]. Nevertheless, the research presented here is an important step towards developing such evolutionary imaging models for super-resolution reconstruction. Evolving the imaging models that reflect the real-world conditions may also help generate large amounts of artificial, yet realistic data that can be used for training deep neural networks that are already widely applied to single-image SRR.

The study reported in this paper has also revealed some problems that must be addressed in the future, especially when applying the proposed strategy to the real-world scenarios. Evaluation of the SRR outcome requires realistic benchmark datasets that would encompass a variety of real-world relations between low and high resolution. This in turn brings the necessity of more advanced image similarity metrics, as the images captured using different sensors at different resolution are visually quite dissimilar, especially for the satellite images. Robust quantitative evaluation is instrumental, when the computed image similarity scores are exploited in the evolutionary process to determine the fitness.

Acknowledgments. The reported work is a part of the SISPARE project run by Future Processing and funded by European Space Agency. The authors were partially supported by Institute of Informatics funds no. BK-230/RAu2/2017 (MK) and BKM-509/RAu2/2017 (DK).

References

1. Zhu, H., Song, W., Tan, H., Wang, J., Jia, D.: Super resolution reconstruction based on adaptive detail enhancement for ZY-3 satellite images. In: Proceedings ISPRS Congress, pp. 213–217 (2016)
2. Yang, F., Chen, Y., Wang, R., Zhang, Q.: Super-resolution microwave imaging: time-domain tomography using highly accurate evolutionary optimization method. In: Proceedings EuCAP, pp. 1–4. IEEE (2015)
3. Jiang, J., Hu, R., Wang, Z., Han, Z.: Face super-resolution via multilayer locality-constrained iterative neighbor embedding and intermediate dictionary learning. IEEE Trans. Image Process. **23**(10), 4220–4231 (2014)
4. Lukinavičius, G., Umezawa, K., Olivier, N., Honigmann, A., Yang, G., Plass, T., Mueller, V., Reymond, L., Corrêa Jr., I.R., Luo, Z.G., et al.: A near-infrared fluorophore for live-cell super-resolution microscopy of cellular proteins. Nature Chem. **5**(2), 132–139 (2013)
5. Capel, D., Zisserman, A.: Super-resolution enhancement of text image sequences. In: Proceedings IEEE ICPR, vol. 1, pp. 600–605
6. Demirel, H., Anbarjafari, G.: Discrete wavelet transform-based satellite image resolution enhancement. IEEE Trans. Geosci. Remote Sens. **49**(6), 1997–2004 (2011)
7. Qian, S.E., Chen, G.: Enhancing spatial resolution of hyperspectral imagery using sensor's intrinsic keystone distortion. IEEE Trans. Geosci. Remote Sens. **50**(12), 5033–5048 (2012)
8. Li, L., Zhang, Y., Tian, Q.: Multi-face location on embedded dsp image processing system. In: Proceedings CISP, vol. 4, pp. 124–128 (2008)
9. Timofte, R., De Smet, V., Van Gool, L.: A+: adjusted anchored neighborhood regression for fast super-resolution. In: Cremers, D., Reid, I., Saito, H., Yang, M.-H. (eds.) ACCV 2014. LNCS, vol. 9006, pp. 111–126. Springer, Cham (2015). https://doi.org/10.1007/978-3-319-16817-3_8
10. Huang, J.B., Singh, A., Ahuja, N.: Single image super-resolution from transformed self-exemplars. In: Proceedings IEEE CVPR, pp. 5197–5206 (2015)
11. Dong, C., Loy, C.C., He, K., Tang, X.: Image super-resolution using deep convolutional networks. IEEE Trans. Pattern Anal. Mach. Intell. **38**(2), 295–307 (2016)
12. Liebel, L., Körner, M.: Single-image super resolution for multispectral remote sensing data using convolutional neural networks. In: Proceedings ISPRS Congress, pp. 883–890 (2016)

13. Kim, J., Kwon Lee, J., Mu Lee, K.: Accurate image super-resolution using very deep convolutional networks. In: Proceedings IEEE CVPR, pp. 1646–1654 (2016)
14. Efrat, N., Glasner, D., Apartsin, A., Nadler, B., Levin, A.: Accurate blur models vs. image priors in single image super-resolution. In: Proceedings IEEE ICCV, pp. 2832–2839 (2013)
15. Nasrollahi, K., Moeslund, T.B.: Super-resolution: a comprehensive survey. Mach. Vis. Appl. 25(6), 1423–1468 (2014)
16. Panagiotopoulou, A., Anastassopoulos, V.: Super-resolution image reconstruction techniques: trade-offs between the data-fidelity and regularization terms. Inf. Fusion 13(3), 185–195 (2012)
17. Irani, M., Peleg, S.: Improving resolution by image registration. CVGIP. Graph. Mod. Image Process. 53(3), 231–239 (1991)
18. Schultz, R.R., Stevenson, R.L.: Extraction of high-resolution frames from video sequences. IEEE Trans. Image Process. 5(6), 996–1011 (1996)
19. Wang, Y., Fevig, R., Schultz, R.R.: Super-resolution mosaicking of UAV surveillance video. In: Proceedings IEEE ICIP, pp. 345–348. IEEE (2008)
20. Akgun, T., Altunbasak, Y., Mersereau, R.M.: Super-resolution reconstruction of hyperspectral images. IEEE Trans. Image Process. 14(11), 1860–1875 (2005)
21. Farsiu, S., Robinson, M.D., Elad, M., Milanfar, P.: Fast and robust multiframe super resolution. IEEE Trans. Image Process. 13(10), 1327–1344 (2004)
22. Hardie, R.: A fast image super-resolution algorithm using an adaptive wiener filter. IEEE Trans. Image Process. 16(12), 2953–2964 (2007)
23. Li, F., Jia, X., Fraser, D.: Universal HMT based super resolution for remote sensing images. In: Proceedings IEEE ICIP, pp. 333–336 (2008)
24. Ahrens, B.: Genetic algorithm optimization of superresolution parameters. In: Proceedings GECCO, pp. 2083–2088. ACM (2005)
25. Cheng, M.H., Hwang, K.S., Jeng, J.H., Lin, N.W.: PSO-based fusion method for video super-resolution. J. Sign. Proces. Syst. 73(1), 25–42 (2013)
26. Wu, B., Li, C., Zhan, X.: Integrating spatial structure in super-resolution mapping of hyper-spectral image. Procedia Eng. 29, 1957–1962 (2012)
27. Zhong, Y., Zhang, L.: Remote sensing image subpixel mapping based on adaptive differential evolution. IEEE Trans. Syst. Man Cybern. Part B (Cybernetics) 42(5), 1306–1329 (2012)
28. Wang, Z., Bovik, A.C., Sheikh, H.R., Simoncelli, E.P.: Image quality assessment: from error visibility to structural similarity. IEEE Trans. Image Proces. 13, 600–612 (2004)
29. Kawulok, M., Smolka, B.: Texture-adaptive image colorization framework. EURASIP J. Adv. Sign. Proces. 2011(99) (2011)
30. Kawulok, M., Benecki, P., Nalepa, J., Kostrzewa, D., Skonieczny, L.: Towards robust evaluation of super-resolution satellite image reconstruction. In: ACIIDS 2018, Part I. LNAI, vol. 10751. Springer, Cham (2018)
31. Yue, L., Shen, H., Li, J., Yuan, Q., Zhang, H., Zhang, L.: Image super-resolution: the techniques, applications, and future. Sig. Process. 128, 389–408 (2016)
32. Rudin, L.I., Osher, S., Fatemi, E.: Nonlinear total variation based noise removal algorithms. Phys. D 60(1–4), 259–268 (1992)
33. Arcuri, A., Briand, L.: A practical guide for using statistical tests to assess randomized algorithms in software engineering. In: Proceedings ICSE, pp. 1–10. IEEE (2011)

34. Fister, I., Fister, I.: On the mutation operators in evolution strategies. In: Fister, I., Fister Jr., I. (eds.) Adaptation and Hybridization in Computational Intelligence. ALO, vol. 18, pp. 69–89. Springer, Cham (2015). https://doi.org/10.1007/978-3-319-14400-9_3
35. Lorenzo, P.R., Nalepa, J., Kawulok, M., Ramos, L.S., Pastor, J.R.: Particle swarm optimization for hyper-parameter selection in deep neural networks. In: Proceedings GECCO, pp. 481–488. ACM, New York (2017)

Evolvable Deep Features

Jakub Nalepa[1,2](✉) ⓘ, Grzegorz Mrukwa[1], and Michal Kawulok[1] ⓘ

[1] Silesian University of Technology, Gliwice, Poland
{jakub.nalepa,grzegorz.mrukwa,michal.kawulok}@polsl.pl
[2] Future Processing, Gliwice, Poland

Abstract. Feature extraction is the first step in building real-life classification engines—it aims at elaborating features to characterize objects that are to be labeled by a trained model. Time-consuming feature extraction requires domain expertise to effectively design features. Deep neural networks (DNNs) appeared as a remedy in this context—their shallow layers perform representation learning, being an automated discovery of various-level features that robustly represent objects. However, the representations that are being learnt are still extremely difficult to interpret, and DNNs are prone to memorizing small datasets. In this paper, we introduce evolvable deep features (EDFs)—a DNN is used to extract automatic features that undergo genetic feature selection. Such evolved features are fed into a supervised learner. The experiments, backed up with statistical tests, performed on multi- and binary-class sets showed that our approach automatically learns object representations, greatly reduces the number of features without deteriorating the performance of trained models, and can even boost their classification performance.

Keywords: Deep learning · Genetic algorithm · Feature selection

1 Introduction

Applying machine-learning techniques requires designing extractors which elaborate features that effectively describe underlying real-life entities. Feature engineering, being a fairly challenging and expensive process, involves exploiting domain knowledge to create meaningful features that can make machine learning algorithms work. Both quality and quantity of features are very important and influence the behaviour of predictive models. Although automated feature extraction techniques, with DNNs being their famous example, are continuously gaining attention, deep models are still difficult to interpret, automatically extracted deep features are really numerous and therefore hard to analyze and understand. Also, DNNs are prone to overfitting, especially in the case of small datasets. Currently, an interesting research pathway encompasses automatic extraction of deep features using DNNs, and using them to train supervised learners. In this paper, we build on this idea and introduce *evolvable deep*

© Springer International Publishing AG, part of Springer Nature 2018
K. Sim and P. Kaufmann (Eds.): EvoApplications 2018, LNCS 10784, pp. 497–505, 2018.
https://doi.org/10.1007/978-3-319-77538-8_34

features (EDFs) which are elaborated with DNNs and are subjected to evolutionary feature selection. EDFs are later used to train a classifier. This pipeline allows for reducing the number of deep features (hence making them easier to analyze and process), making the learning and classification faster, and it is flexible in a sense that any supervised classifier can be easily applied to EDFs.

1.1   Related Work

Feature selection is aimed at finding the most relevant features out of these extracted from the raw data [1]. Not only does it allow for creating simpler models, which helps understand the data, but it also improves the prediction performance, if some redundant, incorrect or noisy features are eliminated. There are three major categories of feature selection [2], depending on the data labeling: (i) *supervised* methods for fully-labeled data, (ii) *unsupervised* [3–5], if no labels are available, and (iii) *semi-supervised* [1] for partially-labeled data. Also, the approaches towards selecting the features are classified considering the data processing stage, as (i) *filter*, (ii) *wrapper* [3,6], and (iii) *embedded* [7]. The filter methods consist in ranking the features based on their intrinsic properties, or quantifying the goodness of feature subsets (by investigating their properties) prior to learning a model. In contrast to that, the wrapper techniques select the features to maximize the performance of data classification or clustering. This can be achieved using evolutionary methods, such as particle swarm optimization [8] or genetic and memetic algorithms (GAs and MAs) [9]. In the embedded approaches, the selection is often a part of the training, and the relations between features, along with those between features and labels are analyzed.

DNNs [10] allow for learning features alongside the classification rules, which is in contrast to the earlier pattern recognition frameworks based on hand-crafted features. In DNNs, features are extracted by the initial (e.g., convolutional and pooling) layers and they are processed by fully-connected layers to classify the data (or achieve other analysis goals). The purpose of the pooling layers is to select the features, but this task can also be fulfilled relying on conventional feature selection methods. The *deep features* extracted with DNNs [11] can be selected using well-established methods and classified by supervised learners. Poria et al. [12] proposed to use a deep convolutional neural net to extract visual features, which are selected using two approaches: cyclic correlation feature subset selection or principal component analysis, and classified with support vector machines (SVMs). In [13], the forward-backward greedy algorithm was exploited to select the deep features for face verification. Nezhad et al. [14] analyzed the demographic data for assessing the health risk factors. The features extracted using stacked autoencoders are selected with random forests and they are subject to supervised learning. A different research direction is to exploit deep architectures, especially deep belief networks, for selecting the features, in particular in genomics [15] and remote sensing [16]. Finally, Kowaliw et al. proposed an evolutionary deep feature extractor which exploits genetic programming [17].

Overall, although there are many approaches and techniques for selecting features, they have not been widely exploited in deep learning yet. In the reported cases [12–14], feature selection was achieved relying on relatively simple methods and evolutionary computation was not employed for this task at all. Selecting the deep features may be extremely important, if the deep feature extraction layers of DNNs are to be topped with another classifier of high computational complexity of training (e.g., an SVM). Moreover, well-established and thoroughly researched approaches towards feature selection could complement the pooling layers and improve the performance of known DNNs.

1.2   Contribution

The contribution presented in this paper is multi-fold. We introduce EDFs—automatically extracted deep features which undergo genetic evolution in search of the most valuable and discriminative features, that are later fed into a training procedure of a supervised classifier. The following insights can be learned from our experiments performed for binary and multi-class datasets and coupled with sensitivity analysis together with statistical tests:

– Evolutionary selection of deep features allows for reducing the number of features and improving the classification performance of a trained model.
– EDFs can be successfully applied to any underlying deep convolutional architecture and they do not require any fine-tuning.
– Training a supervised classifier on EDFs is significantly faster than training a deep classification model.

1.3   Paper Structure

The remaining part of this paper is structured as follows. Evolvable deep features are introduced in Sect. 2. Section 3 presents our experimental study alongside the discussion on the obtained results. Section 4 concludes the paper.

2   Evolvable Deep Features

In our EDF classification framework, deep features are extracted in the first step using a feature-extraction part of any DNN architecture, and then they are being genetically evolved in search of a subset of the most important deep features (see the flowchart of the entire process visualized in Fig. 1; in light red we render the steps of feature extraction and learning a classifier, whereas in light violet we present those steps which are concerned with the evolution of deep features).

Once $\mathcal{F}$ deep features are extracted, an initial population of *candidate solutions* is randomly generated (using the binomial distribution and a fill-up rate ζ, specifying the number of features that are initially enabled in a candidate solution). Each candidate solution p_i, where $i = \{1, 2, \ldots, N\}$, is a binary vector of a length $\mathcal{F}$ which encodes features that are selected as important or *active* (1's) or discarded or *inactive* (0's). In the course of evolution, N pairs of parental solutions are retrieved for *crossover* using the roulette-wheel selection scheme

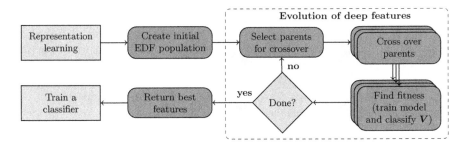

Fig. 1. Flowchart of an evolvable deep features-based classification engine. The operations that are inherently parallelizable are rendered as stacked steps. (Color figure online)

(the probability of a candidate solution being selected as a parent is proportional to its *fitness*, being a classification performance of a supervised learner over the validation set V trained with a training set T). Parental solutions are recombined using the *uniform crossover* with a random number of crossover points (at least one). Importantly, the number of active features $\mathcal{F}'$ in offspring solutions may be different from the number of active features in parents. Therefore, $\mathcal{F}'$ can be adaptively increased (for challenging datasets) or decreased (for easier ones). Children are subject to *mutation*—each entry in a child solution is flipped with a fixed probability $\mathcal{P}_m$. Finally, we apply elitism, thus a subset of N_b best-performing candidate solutions always survive.

The evolution of deep features may be terminated once: (i) a classifier of an acceptable performance have been elaborated (taking into account its performance over V), (ii) the maximum number of generations $G_{\max}$ have been processed, (iii) the time limit elapsed, or (iv) there is no search progress, and the best candidate solutions cannot be further improved. Eventually, the best candidate solution is returned and a final classifier is learned using T with a subset of $\mathcal{F}'$ active features encoded within this individual (the last step in Fig. 1), and it is evaluated using the test set Ψ (unseen while evolving deep features).

3   Experimental Validation

Our GA for evolving EDFs was implemented in `Python` with an extensive usage of `numpy`. For training DNNs (for both deep features extraction and classification), we used `Keras`[1] with the `Tensorflow` backend[2]. The experiments were executed on an Intel Xeon E5-2670 2.30 GHz (hyper-threaded) machine with 256 GB of RAM equipped with NVIDIA Tesla K80 GPU 24 GB DDR5.

In this paper, we focused on two datasets—one benchmark (MNIST), and one real-life (ECU) dataset (concerning a skin segmentation task). MNIST is a dataset of handwritten digits encompassing 70,000 grayscale images (28×28

---

[1] Available at: https://keras.io/ (last access: November 7, 2017).
[2] Available at: https://www.tensorflow.org/ (last access: November 7, 2017).

Fig. 2. Example MNIST training (first row) and test (second row) images.

pixels) divided into 10 classes, with approximately 7,000 images per class (see example MNIST images rendered in Fig. 2). This dataset is randomly split into T of 55,000 images, V of $10,000$ images (the validation set is used for evaluating fitness during the evolution of deep features), and Ψ of $5,000$ images. Note that the patch size (for DNNs) equals the image size in MNIST.

Fig. 3. Example ECU images (first row) with ground-truth skin masks (second row).

ECU dataset contains 4,000 color images (with the corresponding ground-truth masks), and the task is to segment regions presenting human skin (Fig. 3). We divided this set randomly into T (2,400 images), V (800), and Ψ (800). For each ECU image, we extract 50 random patches of size 32×32.

3.1 Experiment 1: Sensitivity Analysis (MNIST)

In this experiment, we focused on getting insights into EDFs executed in various configurations (specifically, with various population sizes $N = \{10, 20, 50\}$ and fill-up rates $\zeta = \{0.1, 0.25, 0.5\}$). For each setup, we report the accuracy obtained for both V and Ψ over MNIST. In Fig. 4, we present a DNN exploited in this experiment—its feature extraction part is rendered in light violet, whereas the classification (being a standard fully-connected neural net)—in light red (we compare the accuracy of the EDF-based classifier with this DNN too). The following parameters were tuned experimentally and kept unchanged: $\mathcal{P}_m = 0.1$, $N_b = \lceil 0.3 \cdot N \rceil$, and $G_{max} = 40$ (populations are fairly small to decrease the convergence time of our GA and enhance its exploitation capabilities). The feature extractor (here we extract $\mathcal{F} = 64$ in total) was being learned in 2,000 epochs with 100 random images per batch, and the network during the evolution was being trained in 200 epochs. Each configuration was executed only *once*.

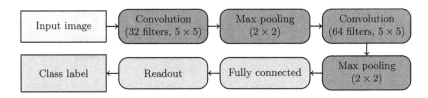

Fig. 4. DNN used for extracting deep features and classifying MNIST.

The results (best and averaged across candidate solutions in the final populations) obtained using our EDF-based classifier for various population sizes and fill-up rates are gathered in Table 1. The classifiers trained with significantly smaller numbers of features (approx. 50% of all extracted deep features) retrieve consistently high accuracy for both V and Ψ, therefore can generalize well. The differences between variants with different N's are *not* statistically important (Wilcoxon test at $p < 0.01$)—smaller populations should be preferred in practice due to smaller computation burden. The DNN presented in Fig. 4 elaborated the accuracy of 0.992 for V and 0.990 for Ψ (its training took 840 s), and its classification was instant as well (less than 0.001 s per example). Hence, our EDF-based technique—even executed only once—drastically decreased the number of active features without affecting the classification accuracy (the difference is only 0.006, e.g., for $N = 20$ and $\zeta = 0.25$). Although EDFs offer $\approx 25\times$ faster training of the classifier, evolution is an additional overhead here (processing one generation of $N = 10$ individuals takes approx. 30 s using N GPUs).

Table 1. Accuracy of EDF-based classifier, number of active features $\mathcal{F}'$, alongside classification time of one example τ_c and training times τ_{tr} (in sec.) for MNIST.

ζ	$Acc_{max}(V/\Psi)$	$Acc_{avg}(V/\Psi)$	$\mathcal{F}'(\%)$	$\mathcal{F}'_{max}$	$\mathcal{F}'_{avg}$	$\mathcal{F}'_{min}$	τ_c	τ_{tr}
Population size: $N = 10$								
0.1	0.976/0.980	0.967/0.968	51.1	38	32.7	28	<0.001	30.02
0.25	0.986/0.978	0.972/0.969	51.6	45	33	24	<0.001	37.76
0.5	0.978/0.976	0.966/0.967	53.1	40	34	27	<0.001	30.01
Population size: $N = 20$								
0.1	0.984/0.974	0.967/0.966	55.3	43	35.4	27	<0.001	35.46
0.25	0.982/0.984	0.967/0.969	51.5	40	32.9	27	<0.001	32.55
0.5	0.982/0.984	0.970/0.965	50.2	42	32.1	26	<0.001	30.03
Population size: $N = 50$								
0.1	0.984/0.986	0.968/0.967	53.1	43	34	26	<0.001	36.16
0.25	0.984/0.982	0.967/0.965	52.2	43	33.4	23	<0.001	32.42
0.5	0.990/0.982	0.969/0.967	52.3	43	33.5	25	<0.001	33.40

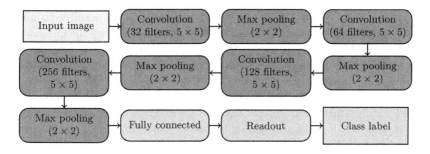

Fig. 5. DNN used for extracting deep features and classifying ECU.

3.2   Experiment 2: Applying EDFs for Skin Segmentation (ECU)

In this experiment, we tackled a real-life binary-class problem of skin segmentation using a DNN and our EDF learner (executed 20× with the same GA parameters as discussed in the previous experiment, whereas $\mathcal{F} = 256$ and $\zeta = 0.5$). We
report not only accuracy of these classifiers for V and Ψ, but also DICE, given as
$D = 2 \cdot |A \cap B|/(|A| + |B|)$ (an overlap metric commonly used to assess the quality of segmentation), where A and B are two segmented images, i.e., using our
algorithm and manually by a human (the latter constituting the ground-truth
segmentation). Training a DNN (Fig. 5) took 630 s (classification of a single patch
consumes 0.005 s) and DICE for Ψ was 0.443 with accuracy equal to 0.796. The
accuracy of this DNN was slightly higher compared with our classifier (Table 2),
but EDF model outperformed DNN in DICE (it is a far more important metric
for this task). Thus, EDFs allowed for building a higher-quality classifier using
less than 50% of all extracted deep features.

Table 2. Classification accuracy and DICE of EDF-based classifier, number of active
features $\mathcal{F}'$, alongside classification τ_c and training times τ_{tr} (in seconds) for ECU.

D_{max}	D_{avg}	Acc_{max}	Acc_{avg}	$\mathcal{F}'(\%)$	$\mathcal{F}'_{max}$	$\mathcal{F}'_{avg}$	$\mathcal{F}'_{min}$	τ_c	τ_{tr}
0.626	0.435	0.774	0.677	45.8	157	117.4	26	0.096	20.43

4   Conclusions and Outlook

In this paper, we presented a new technique for building supervised classifiers
exploiting evolvable deep features. Such features are automatically extracted
from input images using initial layers of DNNs, and they undergo evolutionary
feature selection in search of an adequate (representative) subset of all features.
A training set with pruned features is finally pushed into a training procedure
of any supervised learner. Our experiments, coupled with sensitivity analysis

and statistical tests showed that—by the use of EDFs—it is possible to notably reduce the number of automatic deep features without lowering the classification performance of the model (or even improving it for the skin segmentation task).

Our current research is focused on designing evolvable deep neural networks (especially deep convolutional networks), in which both feature-extraction and classification topologies evolve in time. Also, we strive for designing hands-free technique for building EDF-based classification engines which will couple automated training set, feature and hyperparameter selection. These approaches will be applied in real-life scenarios, especially in the medical imaging field.

Acknowledgments. JN was supported by the Polish National Centre for Research and Development under the Innomed grant POIR.01.02.00-00-0030/15. JN and MK were supported by the National Science Centre, Poland, under Research Grant No. DEC-2017/25/B/ST6/00474.

References

1. Sheikhpour, R., Sarram, M.A., Gharaghani, S., Chahooki, M.A.Z.: A survey on semi-supervised feature selection methods. Pattern Recogn. **64**, 141–158 (2017)
2. Chandrashekar, G., Sahin, F.: A survey on feature selection methods. Comput. Electr. Eng. **40**(1), 16–28 (2014)
3. Dy, J.G., Brodley, C.E.: Feature selection for unsupervised learning. J. Mach. Learn. Res. **5**, 845–889 (2004)
4. Wang, X., Zhang, X., Zeng, Z., Wu, Q., Zhang, J.: Unsupervised spectral feature selection with l 1-norm graph. Neurocomputing **200**, 47–54 (2016)
5. Shi, H., Li, Y., Han, Y., Hu, Q.: Cluster structure preserving unsupervised feature selection for multi-view tasks. Neurocomputing **175**, 686–697 (2016)
6. Nakariyakul, S., Casasent, D.P.: An improvement on floating search algorithms for feature subset selection. Pattern Recogn. **42**(9), 1932–1940 (2009)
7. Chakravarty, K., Das, D., Sinha, A., Konar, A.: Feature selection by differential evolution algorithm - a case study in personnel identification. In: Proceedings of IEEE CEC, pp. 892–899 (2013)
8. Alba, E., Garcia-Nieto, J., Jourdan, L., Talbi, E.G.: Gene selection in cancer classification using PSO/SVM and GA/SVM hybrid algorithms. In: Proceedings of IEEE CEC, pp. 284–290 (2007)
9. Lee, J., Kim, D.W.: Memetic feature selection algorithm for multi-label classification. Inf. Sci. **293**, 80–96 (2015)
10. Goodfellow, I., Bengio, Y., Courville, A.: Deep Learning. MIT Press, Cambridge (2016)
11. Zhou, B., Lapedriza, A., Xiao, J., Torralba, A., Oliva, A.: Learning deep features for scene recognition using places database. In: Proceedings of NIPS, pp. 487–495 (2014)
12. Poria, S., Cambria, E., Gelbukh, A.: Deep convolutional neural network textual features and multiple kernel learning for utterance-level multimodal sentiment analysis. In: Proceedings of EMNLP, pp. 2539–2544 (2015)
13. Sun, Y., Chen, Y., Wang, X., Tang, X.: Deep learning face representation by joint identification-verification. In: Proceedings of NIPS, pp. 1988–1996 (2014)

14. Nezhad, M.Z., Zhu, D., Li, X., Yang, K., Levy, P.: Safs: a deep feature selection approach for precision medicine. In: Proceedings of IEEE BIBM, pp. 501–506. IEEE (2016)
15. Li, Y., Chen, C.Y., Wasserman, W.W.: Deep feature selection: theory and application to identify enhancers and promoters. J. Comput. Biol. **23**(5), 322–336 (2016)
16. Zou, Q., Ni, L., Zhang, T., Wang, Q.: Deep learning based feature selection for remote sensing scene classification. IEEE Geosci. Remote Sens. Lett. **12**(11), 2321–2325 (2015)
17. Kowaliw, T., Banzhaf, W., Doursat, R.: Networks of transform-based evolvable features for object recognition. In: Proceedings of GECCO, USA, pp. 1077–1084. ACM (2013)

Estimation of the 3D Pose of an Object Using Correlation Filters and CMA-ES

Juan Carlos Dibene[1], Kenia Picos[2], Victor H. Díaz-Ramírez[3], and Leonardo Trujillo[1(✉)]

[1] Instituto Tecnológico de Tijuana, Tijuana, B.C., Mexico
juan.carlos.dibene.simental@gmail.com,
leonardo.trujillo@tectijuana.edu.mx
[2] Universidad Rey Juan Carlos, C. Tulián S/N, 28933 Madrid, Spain
kenia.picos@urjc.es
[3] Instituto Politécnico Nacional – CITEDI, Tijuana, B.C., Mexico
vdiazr@ipn.mx

Abstract. Object recognition is a widely studied problem in computer vision. Template matching with correlation filters is one of the most accurate strategies for target recognition. However, it is computationally expensive, particularly when there is no restriction in the pose of the object of interest and an exhaustive search is implemented. This work proposes the use of a Covariance Matrix Adaptation Evolution Strategy (CMA-ES) for post-processing template matched filters. The proposed strategy searches for the best template matching guided by the discrimination capability of a correlation-based filter, considering a vast set of filters. CMA-ES is used to find the best match and determine the correct pose or orientation parameters of a target object. The proposed method demonstrates that CMA-ES is effective for multidimensional problems in a huge search space, which makes it a suitable candidate for target recognition in unconstrained applications. Experimental results show high efficiency in terms of the number of function evaluations and locating the correct pose parameters based on the DC measure.

Keywords: CMA-ES · Correlation filters · Pose estimation

1 Introduction

Template matched filters are used for solving a wide variety of pattern recognition problems. These filters can be defined by a combination of several training templates chosen by a designer in an ad hoc manner [1]. The performance of these filters highly depend on a proper selection of the image templates used to define the filter. The design of an optimal filter requires selecting the proper subset of templates from a vast search space of feasible training templates (views of the target), which can be posed as a combinatorial optimization problem [1]. These kind of problems can be approached using Evolutionary Algorithms.

© Springer International Publishing AG, part of Springer Nature 2018
K. Sim and P. Kaufmann (Eds.): EvoApplications 2018, LNCS 10784, pp. 506–520, 2018.
https://doi.org/10.1007/978-3-319-77538-8_35

Evolutionary algorithms (EA) [2] are methods inspired by Darwinian evolution, based on the idea of optimizing systems through the imitation of nature and applying the so called genetic operators, such as selection, mutation and recombination. An interesting feature of these algorithms is that they are quite versatile. They can be applied with relatively minor changes and without problem specific knowledge. A downside is that they cannot guarantee finding an optimal solution if one exists, but most methods cannot guarantee this in difficult global optimization tasks.

Evolution Strategies (ES) [3] are one of the many classes of EA. The usual goal of an ES is to optimize some objective or quality function(s) $F(\mathbf{x})$ with respect to a set of decision variables $\mathbf{x} = (x_1, x_2, ..., x_n)$. A peculiarity of ES is the presence of endogenous strategy parameters. These are used to control certain statistical properties of the genetic operators. Endogenous strategy parameters can be tuned during the evolution process and are needed in self-adaptive ES.

In this work, we use the Covariance Matrix Adaptation Evolution Strategy (CMA-ES) [4] to determine the orientation of a target object in a scene. Given a single image of the scene, the Euler angles describing the orientation of the target are estimated using CMA-ES as a black-box optimization procedure in conjunction with correlation filters.

This paper is organized as follows. Section 2 presents previous work on which this paper is based. Section 3 describes the proposed approach for this problem. Section 4 presents the experiments performed and the obtained results. Finally, Sect. 5 outlines the conclusions and future work.

2 Background

In [5], an algorithm is presented to solve the problem of 3D object recognition and pose tracking for monocular images. The proposal assumes that the input images contain an object of interest placed over a background and may be degraded by additive noise, geometrical distortions and partial occlusions.

The input scene $f(x, y)$ is denoted by the following signal model [6]

$$f(x, y) = t(x - x_0, y - y_0) + b(x, y)\bar{w}(x - x_0, y - y_0) + n(x, y) \qquad (1)$$

where $t(x, y)$ is the target to be recognized located at (x_0, y_0), with a cluttered background $b(x, y)$ and additive noise $n(x, y)$. The area that the target occupies in the space, namely support region, is given by

$$w(x, y) = \begin{cases} 1, & t(x - x_0, y - y_0) \\ 0, & \text{elsewhere.} \end{cases} \qquad (2)$$

The term $\bar{w}(x, y)$ represents the inverse support region of the target, which is computed as $\bar{w}(x, y) = 1 - w(x, y)$. From the input scene given in Eq. 1, we can model a matched filter as a linear system. The correlation between the input scene $f(x, y)$ and an optimum filter $h(x, y)$ can be performed as $c(x, y) = f(x, y) \otimes h(x, y)$. A template matched filter can be synthesized by optimization of several performance measures [7,8]. One of the most used criteria for model a robust filter through image conditions is signal-to-noise ratio (SNR), which is given by the relationship of the expected value of the correlation produced by the target $t(x, y)$ located at (x_0, y_0), and the variance of the output correlation peak. This can be notated as follows:

$$SNR = \frac{|E\{c(x_0, y_0)\}|^2}{Var\{c(x, y)\}} \tag{3}$$

A generalized matched filter (GMF) is an optimal filter for producing a high correlation value in terms of SNR [9]. The frequency response of the filter is given by [10]

$$H^*(\mu, \nu) = \frac{2\pi(T(\mu, \nu) + m_b W_b(\mu, \nu) + m_t W_t(\mu, \nu))}{|W_b(\mu, \nu)|^2 * N_b^0(\mu, \nu) + |W_t(\mu, \nu)|^2 * N_t(\mu, \nu)}, \tag{4}$$

where (μ, ν) denotes coordinates in frequency domain. $T(\mu, \nu)$, $W_t(\mu, \nu)$ and $W_b(\mu, \nu)$ are the Fourier transforms of the functions $t(x, y)$, $w(x, y)$ and $\bar{w}(x, y)$, respectively. The terms m_t and m_b represent the mean value of $t(x, y)$ and the mean value of the background image $b(x, y)$, respectively. The terms $N_b(\mu, \nu)$ and $N_t(\mu, \nu)$ are the spectral density functions of the zero-mean background, and zero-mean additive noise, respectively.

The purpose of using the GMF correlation filter in the frequency domain is to improve target recognition in terms of location errors for noisy environments, which is important for accurate estimation. The frequency response of the GMF filter is a suitable approach for the case of non-stationary noise, such as a cluttered background, where statistical parameters of the noise are space-variant. In this way, the filter is locally adapted to these parameters estimated in spatially homogeneous areas of the input scene.

Pose estimation is performed using template matching with a bank of correlation filters, which considers several possible poses of the object. The templates are generated from a 3D model of the object of interest using computer graphics techniques. Each template i contains a unique pose of the object in the 2D image space. The 2D pose parameters are given by the position, orientation and scale of the object $\alpha_i = [x_i, y_i, \phi_{x_i}, \phi_{y_i}, \phi_{z_i}, s_i]$, where: x_i, y_i is the position of the object in the image; $\phi_{x_i}, \phi_{y_i}, \phi_{z_i}$ is the orientation of the object in the 3D space; and s_i is the scale of the object in the image.

An initial estimation of the pose parameters, $\hat{\alpha}$, for the object in the input image is obtained by finding the best matching template in the bank. The Discrimination Capability (DC) metric is used to determine the matching accuracy between the current view of the target in the scene and the filter. The DC can be formally defined as follows:

$$DC = 1 - \frac{|c^b|^2}{|c^t|^2}, \tag{5}$$

where c^t is the maximum correlation value of the plane in the object area; and c^b is the maximum peak in the background area. A DC value close to unity means that the filter is able to detect the object of interest, whereas a value close to zero means that the filter failed to detect the object.

The algorithm of [5] has shown high efficiency in estimating the 3D pose of an object from monocular images [5], and exhibits a higher performance when noise is present and the object of interest is partially occluded, compared to existing algorithms in the literature. Because there are many possible views of the object within the scene, generating all of the possible templates is not feasible for practical applications. Therefore, the task is posed as a search problem. Given that the 3D pose of an object varies with multiple degrees of freedom, the search space is huge. This work seeks to evaluate the performance of [5] when using an optimization procedure based on the CMA-ES algorithm.

2.1 CMA-ES

The CMA-ES [4,11,12] is a stochastic method for real-parameter optimization of non-linear, non-convex functions. Search points are generated by sampling a multivariate normal distribution.

$$x_k^{(g+1)} \sim m^{(g)} + \sigma^{(g)}\mathcal{N}(0, C^{(g)}), \tag{6}$$

where $\sim$ denotes a symetric distribution; $\mathcal{N}(0, C^{(g)})$ is a multivariate normal distribution with zero mean and covariance matrix $C^{(g)}$; $x_k^{(g+1)} \in \mathbb{R}^n$, denotes the k-th search point from generation $g+1$; $m^{(g)} \in \mathbb{R}^n$, represents the mean value of the search distribution in the algorithm's generation g. This value represents the best fitted solution; $\sigma^{(g)} \in \mathbb{R}_{>0}$, is the overall standard deviation, step-size, at generation g; $C^{(g)} \in \mathbb{R}^{n \times n}$, is the covariance matrix at generation g. Determines the shape of the distribution ellipsoid; $\lambda \geq 2$, represents the population size.

Iteratively, $m^{(g)}$, $\sigma^{(g)}$ and $C^{(g)}$ are updated to guide the search to more likely regions to contain better solutions. The CMA-ES requires few parameters to operate when compared to other evolutionary algorithms. An initial solution m^0 and step-size σ^0 are required. Optionally, λ may be modified to alter the characteristics of the search. The values m^0, σ^0 and λ are chosen according to the objective function. On ill-conditioned, non-separable problems, CMA-ES can improve the performance by orders of magnitude without decreased performance on simple problems [12]. Furthermore, it is highly competitive on a considerable number of test functions and has been successfully applied to many real world problems [4]. In [13], Hansen describes a modification of the CMA-ES for the application to mixed-integer problems. Integer variables with small variation undergo an additional integer mutation and are disregarded in the global update of $\sigma^{(g)}$ to prevent random fluctuations of $\sigma^{(g)}$. This mutation is also used for updating $m^{(g)}$. This variant is used in the present work.

3   Proposed Approach

The goal is to estimate the orientation parameters of the target object in the 3D space from a given input image. Two different cases are considered: with 2 pose

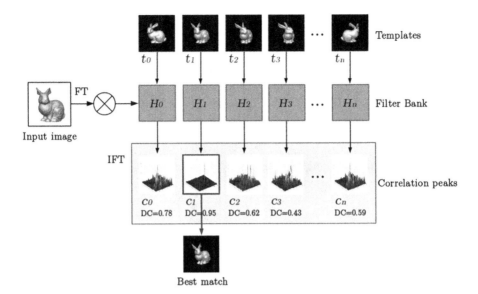

Fig. 1. Template matched filtering procedure for target recognition.

parameters (2D case) and 3 parameters (3D case). When using 2 pose parameters (2D case), we consider that the orientation of the object is only described by two angles: ϕ_X and ϕ_Y (ϕ_z is always zero). With 3 parameters (3D case), the orientation is fully described by all the angles: ϕ_X, ϕ_Y and ϕ_Z.

To estimate the orientation angles in both cases the input image is compared with many templates of the target in a specific orientation. These templates are computer-generated views of the target for which the orientation angles are known. The orientation angles are obtained by finding the template producing the highest DC value. The domain for each orientation angle is discretized, in order to obtain an integer problem.

The above task is posed as a black-box optimization problem. The search space contains all of the templates and the only information available is the matching accuracy of a template, which is given by the DC metric. We define an objective function which takes for inputs the estimated orientation angles and outputs a DC value that measures the matching accuracy. Note that the best matching template is the one whose DC value is closest to one (global optimum).

Figure 1 shows a sample procedure of template matched filters used for target recognition. First, an input image is given to the system, which we assume is composed of a target with unknown three-dimensional parameters. Second, a set of synthetic templates are generated for different 3D parameters. From a digital model, variations of orientation angles are computed for several configurations of the target. Here, we assume that the target is placed at the origin, where $x_0 = 0$ and $y_0 = 0$, from Eq. (1), with an uncluttered background $b(x, y)$ with intensity levels equal to unity. Third, a filter is computed in frequency domain using a priori known statistical parameters for each synthetic template. The filter set is calculated with the help of Eq. (4). Fourth, the correlation operation is performed between the input image and the current filter as $c(x, y) = f(x, y) \otimes h_i(x, y)$, where $h_i(x, y) = IFT\{H_i(\mu, \nu), i = 0, 1, 2, ..., N\}$ with IFT denoting the inverse Fourier transform, and the symbol $\otimes$ denotes linear correlation. This operation produces a correlation peak, which determines the accuracy of the match. Fifth, the quality of each filter is evaluated with the help of Eq. (5), where $DC_{best} = max\{DC_0, DC_1, DC_2, ..., DC_N\}$. Sixth, as shown in Fig. 1, the best match is determined by the maximum value of the overall DC evaluations.

CMA-ES is used to perform the search for the global optimum, which is to find the orientation angles that maximize the DC value of the objective function. Although CMA-ES is designed for continuous problems, a few modifications can make it suitable for mixed-integer problems.

4   Experiments

We test the proposed approach on two test cases: the 2 parameters case, where the target object changes its pose with respect to two angles (ϕ_X and ϕ_Y) and the 3 parameters case which considers all three orientation angles (ϕ_X, ϕ_Y and ϕ_Z). In the experiments we use a standard 3D model[1], which contains 35947 vertices, about 725×10^3 triangles. For both test cases a set of image templates of the object in different orientations was created, with examples shown in Fig. 2 for the 2 parameters case and Fig. 3 for the 3 parameters case.

To test the algorithm, each one of the templates was used as a possible target. The expected result is the orientation angles corresponding to the target template. Because CMA-ES is a stochastic algorithm, several runs using the same inputs were performed. It is of interest to determine the success rate of the algorithm (i.e., the number of runs where the global optimum was found), the number of function evaluations required to find the global optimum and the orientation error. For this, we process offline data of the DC evaluations from a vast number of filters. The orientation error (OE) is calculated using

$$OE = \sqrt{OE_X^2 + OE_Y^2 + OE_Z^2}, \tag{7}$$

where $OE_u = |\phi_u - \hat{\phi}_u|$ is the error in direction u, with ϕ_u the ground truth angle and $\hat{\phi}_u$ the angle estimated by CMA-ES.

4.1   Test Case with 2 Parameters

For the 2 parameter case, the templates consider ϕ_X in the range of 0° to 44° and ϕ_Y in the range of 0° to 358°, both angles in increments of 2°. This gives a total of 4140 images. For each image, 30 runs were performed resulting in a total of 124200 runs. During preliminary experiments, it was observed that using a torus

---

[1] http://graphics.stanford.edu/data/3Dscanrep.

Fig. 2. A small sample of the rendered templates for the 2 parameters case. For the upper left $\phi_X = 0°$, $\phi_Y = 0°$ and $\phi_Z = 0°$. Upper right $\phi_X = 0°$, $\phi_Y = 180°$ and $\phi_Z = 0°$. Bottom left $\phi_X = 44°$, $\phi_Y = 0°$ and $\phi_Z = 0°$. Bottom right $\phi_X = 44°$, $\phi_Y = 180°$ and $\phi_Z = 0°$.

Table 1. Results obtained on the 2 parameters test case.

Percentage of runs with global optimum found	87.7%		
	Mean	Median	Std. Dev.
Function evaluations required to find the global optimum	149	123	116
Orientation error (global optimum not found)	55.9°	24.4°	56.0°
Orientation error (all runs)	8.5°	0.0°	26.6°

grid in orientation space for the angles resulted in finding the optimal solution more often and with fewer function evaluations. CMA-ES was configured with a population size $\lambda = 6$ and a maximum of 1000 function evaluations. The starting point is $[\phi_X = 22°, \phi_Y = 180°]$ the center of the search space. However, similar results are obtained when the starting point is selected randomly. A summary of the results is presented in Table 1.

To illustrate the search performed by CMA-ES, Fig. 4 shows the convergence plots for all 30 runs when setting the image with orientation angles $[\phi_X = 0°, \phi_Y = 0°]$ as the target. It can be observed that in some of the runs the algorithm stagnates before reaching the global optimum. This could be due to the flatness of the search space for this problem. Figure 5 shows the complete fitness landscape for this problem based on the DC measure, showing that it is quite flat, making the search a difficult endeavor. Moreover, although for this problem instance it is expected that the global optimum will be at $[\phi_X = 0°, \phi_Y = 0°]$ it actually is at $[\phi_X = 6°, \phi_Y = 352°]$ $(OE = 10°)$. In other words, the DC measure produces a deceptive landscape, where the global optimum is not located at the true correct match. In fact such is the case for other problem instances (orientation angles), in total 1776 out of 4140.

Fig. 3. A small sample of the rendered templates for the 3 parameters case. For the upper left $\phi_X = 0°$, $\phi_Y = 0°$ and $\phi_Z = -20°$. Upper right $\phi_X = 0°$, $\phi_Y = 180°$ and $\phi_Z = -20°$. Bottom left $\phi_X = 44°$, $\phi_Y = 0°$ and $\phi_Z = -20°$. Bottom right $\phi_X = 44°$, $\phi_Y = 180°$ and $\phi_Z = -20°$.

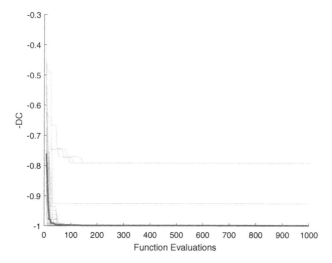

Fig. 4. Convergence plot for the 2 parameters case for 30 runs, shown in green, of the $[\phi_X = 0°, \phi_Y = 0°]$ problem. Median shown in red. (Color figure online)

The median of the orientation error for all 4140 problems is shown in Fig. 6. It can be observed that for a few of the test cases the error is very high. The number of failed runs, out of 30, for each test case is shown in Fig. 7. There is a correspondence between the orientation error and the number of failed runs. A run is considered failed if the DC value found by CMA-ES is less than the DC value of the true orientation of the target. In an attempt to understand the reason behind the high failure rate of some of the test cases, we observe the fitness landscape of those two with the highest median orientation error.

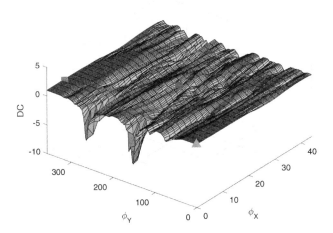

Fig. 5. Fitness landscape for the $[\phi_X = 0°, \phi_Y = 0°]$ problem. Starting point is the center $[\phi_X = 22°, \phi_Y = 180°]$ (circle). The true global optimum should be located at $[\phi_X = 0°, \phi_Y = 0°]$ (triangle) but the global optimum located based on the DC measure is at $[\phi_X = 6°, \phi_Y = 352°]$ (square). Although they might appear to be very far from each other, they are actually quite close, $OE = 10°$.

Median OE

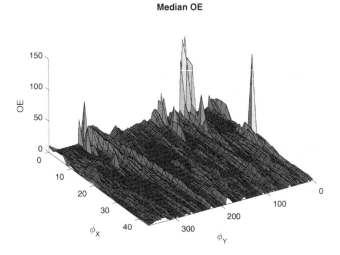

Fig. 6. Median orientation error for all 4140 test cases with 30 runs.

In Fig. 8 the fitness landscape for the $[\phi_X = 18°, \phi_Y = 4°]$ problem is presented. This is the one with the highest median orientation error. We observe that the high orientation error may be, for the most part, due to the ruggedness of the landscape, and, to a lesser extent, to the mismatch between the global optimum of the landscape ($[\phi_X = 26°, \phi_Y = 358°]$) and the true orientation of the

Failed runs for each problem

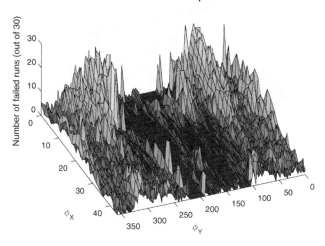

Fig. 7. Failed runs for all 4140 test cases with 30 runs.

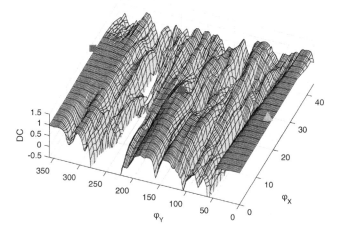

Fig. 8. Fitness landscape for the $[\phi_X = 18°, \phi_Y = 4°]$ problem. Starting point is the center $[\phi_X = 22°, \phi_Y = 180°]$ (circle). The true global optimum should be located at $[\phi_X = 18°, \phi_Y = 4°]$ (triangle) but the global optimum located based on the standard DC measure is at $[\phi_X = 26°, \phi_Y = 358°]$ (square). $OE = 10°$. For ease of viewing the DC axis has been clipped to $[-0.5, 1.5]$.

target $([\phi_X = 18°, \phi_Y = 4°])$. Also note that the region near the global optimum is very flat. In Fig. 9 the fitness landscape of the $[\phi_X = 0°, \phi_Y = 62°]$ problem is shown. This is the one with the second highest median orientation error. Similar characteristics to those of the $[\phi_X = 18°, \phi_Y = 4°]$ problem are observed. For comparison, we show the fitness landscape of a problem with median orientation

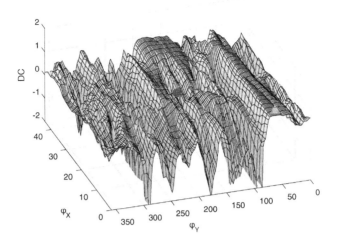

Fig. 9. Fitness landscape for the $[\phi_X = 0°, \phi_Y = 62°]$ problem. Starting point is the center $[\phi_X = 22°, \phi_Y = 180°]$ (circle). Both the true global optimum and the global optimum located based on the DC measure are at $[\phi_X = 0°, \phi_Y = 62°]$ (triangle, square). For ease of viewing the DC axis has been clipped to $[-2, 2]$.

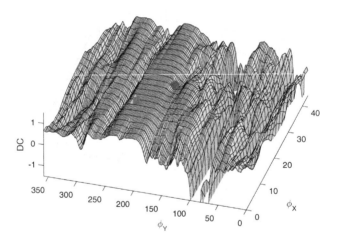

Fig. 10. Fitness landscape for the $[\phi_X = 12°, \phi_Y = 226°]$ problem. Starting point is the center $[\phi_X = 22°, \phi_Y = 180°]$ (circle). The true global optimum should be located at $[\phi_X = 12°, \phi_Y = 226°]$ (triangle) but the global optimum located based on the DC measure is at $[\phi_X = 12°, \phi_Y = 224°]$ (square). $OE = 2°$. For ease of viewing the DC axis has been clipped to $[-1, 1]$.

error of zero. The selected problem for this purpose is $[\phi_X = 12°, \phi_Y = 226°]$ and its fitness landscape is shown in Fig. 10, posing an easier search.

Table 2. Results obtained on the 3 parameters test case.

Percentage of runs with global optimum found	92.2%		
	Mean	Median	Std. Dev.
Function evaluations required to find the global optimum	206	122	688
Orientation error (global optimum not found)	7.1°	4.0°	7.2°
Orientation error (all runs)	0.8°	0.0°	2.8°

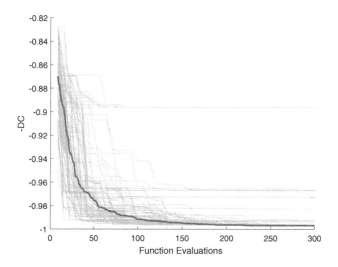

Fig. 11. Convergence plot for the 3D case for 100 runs, shown in green, of the $[\phi_X = -20°, \phi_Y = 50°, \phi_Z = -20°]$ problem. Median shown in red. (Color figure online)

4.2 Test Case with 3 Parameters

For the 3 parameters case, we consider ϕ_x in the range of $-20°$ to $18°$, ϕ_y in the range $20°$ to $58°$ and ϕ_z in the range of $-20°$ to $18°$ in steps of $2°$, for a total of 8000 templates. However, given the size of the search space, only 60 target templates were randomly generated and tested. For each of the 60 tested templates, 100 runs were performed, resulting in 6000 runs total.

CMA-ES was configured with a population size $\lambda = 7$ and a maximum of 300 function evaluations. The starting point is $[\phi_X = 0°, \phi_Y = 40°, \phi_Z = 0°]$. A summary of the results is presented in Table 2. The convergence plot for 100 runs of a problem instance where the target is located at $[\phi_X = -20°, \phi_Y = 50°, \phi_Z = -20°]$ is shown in Fig. 11.

These results show, in fact, very good performance relative to what was assumed to be the simpler 2 parameter case. Notice that the percentage of global optimums found and the orientation error of the solutions found is actually less in this case, as also summarized in Figs. 12 and 13. This might be due to the relatively small sample set drawn, instead of an exhaustive evaluation of all

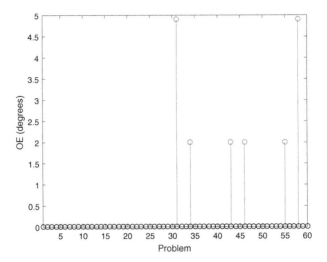

Fig. 12. Median of orientation error for all 60 problems with 100 runs.

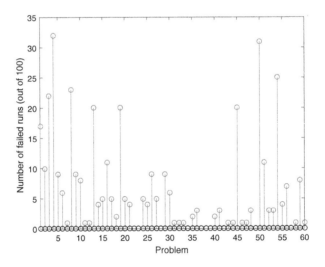

Fig. 13. Number of failed runs for all 60 problems with 100 runs.

the search space, as was done in the previous experiments. However, we also can hypothesize that considering all 3 pose parameters of the object actually helps the DC measure to differentiate between the true and deceptive optima. Nonetheless, one encouraging result is that the number of function evaluations continues to be quite low in this increased search space, with the median and mean values practically the same. However, the standard variation does increase, with at least a few cases requiring much longer searches to find the optima.

5   Conclusions

Determining the presence, location and pose of an object in a 3D scene is one of the most important computer vision tasks. One approach to solve this task is to use template matching algorithms, such as correlation filters. However, when the pose of an object is unknown, determining the best match filter can be a computationally expensive problem. In this work, we proposed a CMA-ES algorithm to search for the best pose parameters (orientation angles) of an object in a 3D scene. In other words, finding the three-dimensional pose parameters of a rigid target object from an input scene is posed as a black-box search problem. The algorithm searches in a large and multi-modal space with many plateaus, where fitness s given by the discrimination capability of the filter.

This algorithm shows high efficiency in terms of convergence, finding the maximum DC value in almost all experiments, considering both a simple case where only 2 parameters are determined, and a more complex case where all 3 pose parameters must be found. When the algorithm does not find the true pose parameters of the target it is not due to the search process, but to the failure of the DC measure, where the optimum value is actually located in a deceptive optima in the search space. Future work will consider the development and use of an evaluation metric that provides a better guide for an automatic search process for template matching. Moreover, the efficiency and robustness of the proposal will be tested on synthetic and real-life scenes with more challenging image conditions, such as additive noise, cluttered environments, and partial occlusions of the target.

In closing, the accuracy of the experimental results demonstrates that CMA-ES is suitable for target recognition in a large and multi-modal search space. The proposed methodology yields good estimation in terms of the found orientation parameters, particularly when the DC measure correctly assigns the highest peek to the true pose parameters of the object.

Acknowledgments. This work was funded by CONACYT (Mexico) project FC-2015-2/944 *Aprendizaje Evolutivo a Gran Escala*. First author was supported by CONACYT scholarship No. 605992.

References

1. Diaz-Ramirez, V.H., Cuevas, A., Kober, V., Trujillo, L., Awwal, A.: Pattern recognition with composite correlation filters designed with multi-objective combinatorial optimization. Opt. Commun. **338**, 77–89 (2015). http://www.sciencedirect.com/science/article/pii/S0030401814009547
2. Beyer, H.G.: The Theory of Evolution Strategies. Springer, Heidelberg (2013)
3. Beyer, H.G., Schwefel, H.P.: Evolution strategies-a comprehensive introduction. Nat. Comput. **1**(1), 3–52 (2002)
4. Hansen, N.: The CMA Evolution Strategy: A Tutorial. ArXiv e-prints, April 2016
5. Picos, K., Diaz-Ramirez, V.H., Kober, V., Montemayor, A.S., Pantrigo, J.J.: Accurate three-dimensional pose recognition from monocular images using template matched filtering. Opt. Eng. **55**(6), 063102 (2016)

6. Diaz-Ramirez, V.H., Picos, K., Kober, V.: Target tracking in nonuniform illumination conditions using locally adaptive correlation filters. Opt. Commun. **323**, 32–43 (2014)
7. Kumar, B.V.K.V., Hassebrook, L.: Performance measures for correlation filters. Appl. Opt. **29**(20), 2997–3006 (1990)
8. Kerekes, R., Vijaya-Kumar, B.: Correlation filters with controlled scale response. IEEE Trans. Image Process. **15**(7), 1794–1802 (2006)
9. Kober, V., Campos, J.: Accuracy of location measurement of a noisy target in a nonoverlapping background. J. Opt. Soc. Am. A **13**(8), 1653–1666 (1996)
10. Javidi, B., Wang, J.: Design of filters to detect a noisy target in nonoverlapping background noise. J. Opt. Soc. Am. A **11**, 2604–2612 (1994)
11. Auger, A., Hansen, N.: Tutorial CMA-ES: evolution strategies and covariance matrix adaptation
12. Hansen, N.: The CMA Evolution Strategy: A Comparing Review, pp. 75–102. Springer, Heidelberg (2006). https://doi.org/10.1007/3-540-32494-1_4
13. Hansen, N.: A CMA-ES for Mixed-Integer Nonlinear Optimization. Research Report RR-7751, INRIA, October 2011. https://hal.inria.fr/inria-00629689

EvoINDUSTRY

Evaluating the Performance of an Evolutionary Tool for Exploring Solution Fronts

Neil B. Urquhart[✉]

School of Computing, Edinburgh Napier University, 10 Colinton Road,
Edinburgh EH10 5DT, UK
n.urquhart@napier.ac.uk

Abstract. Evofilter is an evolutionary algorithm based tool for searching through large non-dominated fronts in order to find a subset of solutions that are of interest to the user. EvoFilter is designed to take the output of existing Multi Objective Evolutionary Algorithms and act as a decision support tool for users. Currently EvoFilter is available for all to use on-line [1]. This paper evaluates the performance of EvoFilter by creating a large number of randomised filter specifications which are then applied using EvoFilter and a simple filter to a range of non-dominated fronts created by a portfolio of Multi Objective Genetic Algorithms (MOGAs). The results show that EvoFilter is capable of finding sets of solutions that meet the users' requirements more closely than those found using the simple filter. EvoFilter increases performance on some objectives by including relevant solutions event if these solutions slightly lessen performance on other objectives. The filter discussed in this paper may be accessed at [1].

Keywords: Visualisation · Multi-objective
Optimisation · Scheduling

1 Introduction and Motivation

Real-world optimisation problems are often multi-objective, with objectives that may conflict and may have differing priorities in the view of the end user. Such objectives could include minimising financial costs, CO_2 produced, distance travelled or resources (e.g. staff or vehicles) required. In such cases a common approach is to utilise a multi-objective genetic algorithm (MOGA) which produces a non-dominated front of solutions. Such a front of solutions can have many advantages from a user perspective, the front might allow the user to examine a range of solutions, exploring what is possible both in terms of extreme solutions, which optimise one objective to the maximum or compromise solutions which optimise a number of constraints as best possible. There exists a final decision to be carried out by the user when selecting the solution from within the front,

© Springer International Publishing AG, part of Springer Nature 2018
K. Sim and P. Kaufmann (Eds.): EvoApplications 2018, LNCS 10784, pp. 523–537, 2018.
https://doi.org/10.1007/978-3-319-77538-8_36

there may be no single solution which is ideal in all aspects. This level of political decision making is difficult to incorporate into the problem formulation and so must be undertaken by planners, with domain expertise, based on factors such as political and legislative pressure, public opinion, financial constraints or corporate policies. For example, if environmental impact conflicts with staff cost, then there exists a level of political decision making required in order to determine which objectives should be prioritised.

The non-dominated front may be large, sizes of over 200 items are not uncommon, in such cases the decision for the user becomes more complex. If the problem has only two dimensions then the front may be plotted as a curve against two axes which gives the user a visualisation which can help them choose. But, with greater than two dimensions, visualisation becomes more complex, one option is to use Parallel Coordinates [2]. which allow visualisation of many dimensions. When using Parallel Coordinates the plot may become crowded when too many solutions are plotted, thus for larger fronts it becomes difficult for the user to make a choice.

In this paper we seek to evaluate the EA based filter, known as *EvoFilter* in order to assess its usefulness alongside a more traditional filtering technique. This evaluation is necessary, should we wish to advocate the use of EvoFilter which is available as an on-line tool [1] for anyone to make use of. As in [3] we use a multi-objective Workforce Scheduling and Routing Problem (WSRP) to test the filter. The WSRP is a useful problem to test the filter on as it has multiple objectives, some of which are conflicting, and when solved using a MOGA produces non-dominated fronts in a range of sizes.

2   Previous Work

A survey of a priori and post priori methods of supporting decision makers faced with a Pareto front of solutions to choose from is presented in [4], the authors use a multi-objective evolutionary algorithm to solve a multi-objective control problem, the output of which is a non-dominated front of potential solutions. Methods of decision support include self-organising maps and subtractive clustering, fuzzy scoring and data envelopment analysis (all post priori approaches) and a guided multi-objective genetic algorithm (a priori). The authors suggest that the post priori approach of subtractive clustering, fuzzy scoring and data envelopment analysis is the most promising approach of those examined.

The EvoFilter algorithm was previously described in [1], it attempts to filter a non-dominated front to just those solutions that are of interest to the user. The user can specify this areas of interest in terms of the *range* of solutions of interest on a particular axis and by specifying the minimum difference between solutions, of interest to the user. The input to the algorithm is an existing non-dominated front, and the output, a smaller front that meets the users' specifications, selected by an Evolutionary Algorithm. A similar approach of reducing the size of the non-dominated front after creation is described in [5], but the approach taken is to partition the front into clusters, using techniques such as k-means, and then select one solution to represent each cluster in a reduced size of front. Cluster analysis is also undertaken by the authors of [6].

The authors of [7] take the approach of generating a smaller front, rather than searching through an existing front, using a method known as the Smart Normal Constraint (SNC) method which generates a reduced size Pareto set, by directing the search to areas of interest.

The concept of using filters to filter out redundant solutions from a Pareto front is introduced in [8] where a two stage process is used to filter solutions from an existing Pareto front. The first stage known as the global filter, removes any non-Pareto solutions, the second stage reduces the size of the front by removing any solutions that do not meet a pre-defined trade-off requirement. The combination of the two filters results in a small front whose members exhibit the maximum amount of trade-off between objectives. Earlier work with filters includes [9] where the filter is incorporated within an evolutionary algorithm.

The Workforce Scheduling and Routing Problem (WSRP) has been extensively investigated, although similar to vehicle routing problems, the focus of the WSRP is on individuals rather than vehicles. For a comprehensive introduction to the WSRP and an overview of the latest developments, the reader is directed towards [10–12]. A number of previous researchers have examined the scheduling and routing of workforces, including home care scheduling [13], security personnel scheduling [14] and technician scheduling [15]. A attempt to model the WSRP as a bi/multi-objective problem can be found in [11], the authors use cost and patient convenience as the twin objectives. The solution cost is the travel cost and staff overtime costs, patient convenience is defined as to whether the member of staff allocated is preferred, moderately preferred or not preferred, with penalties allocated as appropriate. The results presented show a strong relationship between convenience and cost; the more convenient a solution the higher the cost is likely to be.

3 Methodology

3.1 The Workforce Scheduling and Routing Problem

In order to evaluate EvoFilter we apply it to a multi-objective Workforce Scheduling and Routing Problem (WSRP) as previously described in [3]. A set of clients each require a visit, each visit has a specific location (within greater London), a duration and a time window, within which the visit must commence. Each visit must be allocated to an employee, who will undertake the visit, each employee is allocated a set of visits which comprise a days work. An employee may be set to travel by public transport or by motor car, which will determine the times taken to travel between visits and the CO_2 produced.

The output from a portfolio of Multi-Objective Evolutionary Algorithms (MOEAs), are merged to produce a set of non-dominated solutions. Each of the MOEAs within the portfolio uses a problem representation based on a grand tour permutation of visits and travel modes between visits. When constructing a solution each visit is added to the solution in the permutation order, initially, there will be no employees within the solution so the first visit is added as the initial visit of a new employee, the travel mode for that employee being determined by this visit. Each subsequent visit i is then considered, being added to the first employee that can feasibly undertake the visit using the travel mode from their previous visit. If the visit cannot be added to any of the existing employees, a new employee is created and the visit is added to that employee. In this manner a feasible solution is constructed from the problem representation. When a solution has been built, its internal costs, CO_2 emission and impact on traffic may be calculated.

Within our problem we have the following dimensions (each of which may or may not be used as objectives):

1. Total Cost (£)
2. Staff Cost (£)
3. Travel Cost (£)
4. Staff required
5. CO_2
6. Car use

Note that items 1–4 are internal costs to the organisation providing the service, items 5 and 6 are external costs.

We utilise a portfolio of algorithms to produce non-dominated fronts, the algorithms in the portfolio are based upon NSGA-II [16,17], SEAMO [18] and SPEA2 [19], see [3] for a full description. It is useful to be able to visualise a Pareto front in order to determine the range of the objectives covered and the trade-offs available. For a 2-dimensional problem the front can be plotted by allocating each dimension to the X and Y coordinates, but for dimensions greater than two, plotting becomes problematic. When considering problems with a more than 2 dimensions than 2 a parallel coordinate plot [2] allows fronts to be visualised and the relationships between the solutions objectives to be explored. Within a parallel coordinates plot a vertical axis is created for each dimension, each solution being represented by a poly-line intersecting each axis at the point appropriate for that solution.

3.2   The EvoFilter Algorithm

The EvoFiler algorithm is used to select a subset of solutions from a nondominated front based on a specification set by the user (Fig. 1). EvoFilter has been incorporated with a web based tool [1] (see Fig. 2) which allows the user to specify the ranges within each axis that interest them and to specify a minimum distance on each axis which should separate solutions. The source code for the algorithm is available on line [20]. Selecting a range on an axis is analogous to the practice of "brushing" [2] which allows the user to specify sections of one or more axes in order to select only those poly-lines that pass through the specified sections.

EvoFilter is based upon an evolutionary algorithm, the representation being a binary string, one bit for each member of the Pareto front, a 1 signifies that

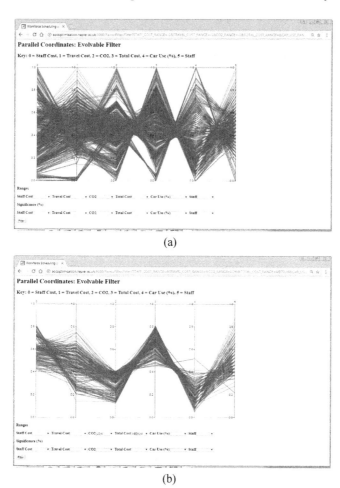

(a)

(b)

Fig. 1. EvoFilter is incorporated within a web tool, which may be used to open a front of solutions and find sets of solutions of interest to the user. (a) shows a large 6 dimensional front loaded from a .CSV file. We apply a simple range filter to the CO_2 and Total cost dimensions in (b).

the solution is filtered a 0 signifies that the solution is to be left in. We use a population size of 20, creating one child using uniform crossover and a random bit flip mutation in each generation, see Algorithm 1 and Table 1.

The fitness function examines each item within the front and adds penalties as follows:

1. Any solution not filtered on an axis that is out of range add a penalty of the difference between the item value and the closest range limit
2. Any solution that is filtered, but lies within a range then add a fixed penalty of 0.01

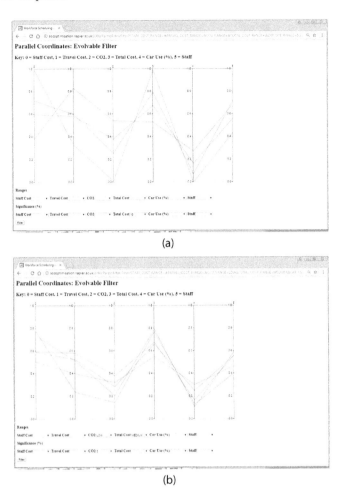

Fig. 2. EvoFilter can filter by difference, (a) shows the effect of placing a requirement of a minimum of 10% difference on the Total Cost axis. A combination of minimum difference and range filtering may be seen in (b).

3. Any pair of solutions on an axis that are closer together than the specified criteria add a penalty based on the actual difference, less the minimum specified

   The first two items penalise solutions which are unfiltered outside of the specified range on an axis and solutions that are filtered which lie within the specified ranges. Items 1 and 3 allocate penalties which increase depending on the severity of the issue. The algorithm has been implemented in Java (and is contained within a Java Servlet) can undertake 400,000 evaluations in approx. 10 s, allowing a fast response to the user, who may set and adjust the criteria interactively.

Algorithm 1. EvoFilter

---

1 randomise_population();
2 **while** *evals<MAX_EVALS* **do**
3 | parent1 = tournament();
4 | parent2 = tournament();
5 | **if** *rnd()* <*RECOMBINATION_PRESSURE* **then**
6 | | child = new Individual(parent1,parent2);
7 | **else**
8 | |_ child = parent1.clone();

9 | **if** *rnd()* <*MUTATION_PRESSURE* **then**
10 | |_ mutate(child);

11 | evaluate(child);
12 | rip = replacementTournament();
13 | **if** *rip.finCost()* >*child.finCost()* **then**
14 | | population.remove(rip);
15 | |_ population.add(child);

16 return findBest();

Table 1. Parameters used within the evolutionary algorithm

Parameter	Value
Population size	20
Recombination pressure	0.5
Mutation pressure	0.5
Selection tournament size	2
Replacement tournament size	2

3.3 Experimental Methodology

In order to assess the performance of the evolutionary filter we generate random filter specifications and then compare the front produced by the evolutionary filter, with the front produced using a simple filter and the original unfiltered front. In total 75,000 random filter specifications were generated, random specifications were used to simulate the web based environment where a user may pick any combination of range filter and minimum difference filter across the problem dimensions. When generating a random filter specification we first randomly select a non-dominated front to which the filter will be applied, 10 fronts generated by a MOGA (described in Sect. 3.1) were used, the specifications are given in Table 2. Three types of random filter specifications were generated; those with only range filters, those with only minimum difference filters and those with a mixture of both types.

The algorithm has been implemented in Java (and is contained within a Java Servlet) can undertake 400,000 evaluations in approx. 10 s, allowing a fast response to the user, who may set an adjust the criteria interactively.

The range filters were applied randomly to dimensions with a probability of 0.3, if a dimension is selected then the upper and lower bounds of the range are selected randomly in the range 0–1 (in 0.1 increments). A minimum difference filter was applied to a dimension with a probability of 0.2, the minimum difference is selected randomly from the values 0.01, 0.05, 0.1, 0.15 and 0.2.

The simple filter operates as follows:

- For each axis with a range filter specified, any individual solution not within the range is filtered out.
- For each axis with a minimum distance filter, each solution X_i is considered in turn, and compared against every other remaining solution X_j, if the distance between X_i and X_j is less than the minimum specified then X_j is filtered out.

Table 2. The non-dominated fronts used within the experiment.

Problem instance	Optimisation criterion	Front size
offset-r00	CO2 TotalCost CarUse	867
offset-8	CO2 TotalCost CarUse	495
lon-1	CO2 TotalCost CarUse	338
blon-1	CO2 TotalCost CarUse	225
cluster-4	CO2 TotalCost	132
blon-2	CO2 TotalCost	91
offset-1	CO2 TotalCost	53
blon-1	CO2 TravelCost	21
offset-8	CO2 TravelCost	7

4   Results

We simulate the actions of a user, by creating 75,000 filter specifications, each of which represents a possible interaction with EvoFilter via the web interface. Our results are based on comparing the results produced for each specification

To simulate the range of possible user interactions with the filter 75,000 filter specifications were generated (see Sect. 3.3). Within these filter specifications there will be a number which specify a filter which eliminates all of the solutions in a front. Table 3 shows the number of instances in which a front was produced after filtering, the first thing that we note is that fronts are only produced in less than 50% of cases. We note that from a users' perspective there is a significant chance that their filter will not produce any solutions, but fast run time of EvoFilter allows them to adjust and re-filter rapidly. More significant are the

5% of cases where EvoFilter can find some results, but simple filter cannot. Such cases suggest that EvoFilter can find some members of the front which closely match the filter, but fall out width the filter in a minor way, but which may still be of interest to the user. Ultimately, it is the domain expertise of the user that will evaluate the usefulness of a particular solution in context (Fig. 3).

Table 3. The number of filter specifications which resulted in a front with more than 0 members.

Filter specifications	75000	
Simple filter	31558	42.08%
EvoFilter	35443	47.26%

It is useful to get some idea of the reduction in front size that occurs during the filtering process, Table 4 gives the average sizes of fronts before and after the application of a filter. On average EvoFilter results in a front that is only 14% of the size of the original, which is smaller than that produced by Simplefilter. As might be expected filters than include elements of both range and difference filtering are the most strict and result in the largest % reduction in front size, least effective are those filters that only reduce the minimum difference between members of the front. We can investigate the front sizes further by examining how, for each filter specification type, the size of the fronts resulting from each of the filter compares, see Table 5. Overall, when all filter specifications are considered, we note that approximately equal numbers (37%) are have a larger front produced by the EvoFilter or the Simple Filter, with 25% having an equal size for both filters. If we only consider those filter specifications which have a mixture of range and minima difference filters we note that in the majority of cases (70%) the EvoFilter finds a smaller front that the front found by the Simple-filter.

Table 4. The size of front produced (for instances where a front is produced by the filter). The column marked all shows for all instances where a front was found. The results are further broken down by filter type.

	All		Both filters		Range only		Diff only	
	Absolute	%	Absolute	%	Absolute	%	Absolute	%
Original front	237.99		297.67		328.84		216.76	
Simple filter	54.71	22.99	19.06	6.40%	39.78	12.10%	60.54	27.93%
Evofilter	34.75	14.60	30.46	10.23%	49.90	15.18%	32.51	15.00%

The size of front produced by the filters may vary, but it is the content of the front that determines its usefulness to the end user. Ideally a filter is

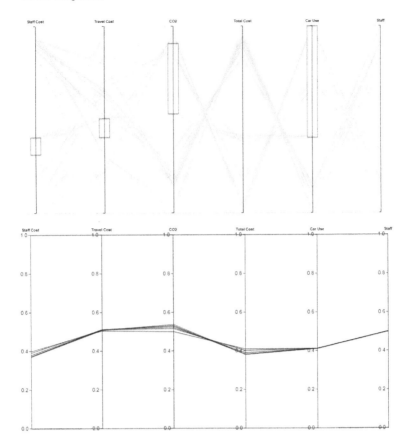

Fig. 3. The upper plot shows the parallel coordinates plot for a non-dominated front (comprising 91 examples). The boxes on the axis denote a set of filter criterion. In this case we note that a simple filter does not return any solutions, as there are no solutions that intersect all of the areas of interest. The lower plot shows the output from EvoFilter, which has found a small set of solutions which although not an exact match are close enough to be of interest to the user. Plots produced by http://www. parallelcoordinates.de/

required that allows the smallest number of solutions required to give the user reasonable choice within the bounds of the filter specification. Traditionally, non-dominated fronts have been compared using the Hyper Volume metric, which measures the area contained behind a non-dominated front. Table 6 shows the average Hypervolumes produced in the experiment. It is worth noting that both filters (EvoFilter and Simple Filter) reduce the Hypervolume by 50%, whilst the filters themselves have broadly similar averages. This suggests that although the fronts are considerably reduced in scope from the original, by filtering the fronts output by the filter are largely the same in scope, regardless of the filter used.

Table 5. A comparison of front sizes produced by each type of filter.

	All		Both		Range		Diff	
Total > 0	31282		2246		4304		24732	
EvoFilter > Simple filter	11851	37.88%	27	1.20%	70	1.63%	11754	47.53%
EvoFilter == Simple filter	7670	24.52%	661	29.43%	1227	28.51%	5782	23.38%
EvoFilter < Simple filter	11761	37.60%	1558	69.37%	3007	69.87%	7196	29.10%

Table 6. Average Hypervolume produced within the experiment.

	Original front	Simple filter	Evol filter
All	6.948	3.536	3.567
Both	8.412	2.639	3.182
RangeOnly	8.669	3.036	3.361
DiffOnly	6.516	3.704	3.637

Although there is difference in size between the fronts produced by the two filtering techniques, what is more important from a users' perspective, examining the difference in the solution space covered by the filtered front. A metric known as range error may be calculated for each dimension of the front as shown in Algorithm 2.

Algorithm 2. CalcRangeError

---

1 **foreach** *dimension* d **do**
2   **if** $dMax_d > fMax_d$ **then**
3      $rangeErr_d = (dimMax_d - fMax_d)$
4   **if** $dMin_d < fMin_d$ **then**
5      $rangeErr_d += (fMin_d - dimMin_d)$

The range error records any dimensions upon which there are solutions that are outside of the filter range, the further outside the filter the larger the error. Table 7 records the average range errors found in the experiment. We note that the Simple Filter always produced a range error of 0 as it filters out any individual which is outside of the range in any dimension. We note large error values with no filter in place, and very small values when using the EvoFilter. The range error tells us that EvoFilter sometimes allows an individual that has some dimensions that are out of range, but this does not show any advantage in using the EvoFilter. EvoFilter is only of any benefit if the errors recoded in Table 7 are counterbalanced by benefits. One major benefit is a greater range of solutions within a filtered dimension, allowing greater choice to the user. Table 8 examines the range Δ of solutions on dimensions that have a range filter. For each filter specification, we compare the fronts produced on thee basis:

- Δ **EvoFilter** > Δ **Simple-filter** True if the difference between the maximum and minimum values plotted on the axis for EvoFilter is greater than that for Simple Filter.
- Δ **EvoFilter within the Filter Specification** True if the maximum and minimum values plotted on the axis after using EvoFilter are within the range specified by the filter specification.
- Δ **EvoFilter** > Δ **Simple-filter AND** Δ **EvoFilter is within the Filter Specification** True, if both of the above two conditions are true.

It is the last condition that is of interest to us, that suggests a situation where, on a given axis the EvoFilter has found a set of solutions that offer a wider choice than the Simple-filter, but without violating the range set out in the filter specification. Table 8 shows the number of instances (fronts) where the above three conditions hold true and the number of individual axis as well. We note that when filtering on both minimum difference and range over 50% of instances have at least one axis where EvoFilter outperforms the Simple-filter. We note that the advantages shown in Table 8 should be used to offset the errors shown in Table 7.

Table 7. Average range error

	Original front	Simple filter	Evol filter
All	23.38	0.00	0.03
Both	97.48	0.00	0.08
RangeOnly	119.08	0.00	0.15

Table 8. A comparison as to how the range of data points present after filtering compares with the spread requested by the filter. Criterion A = **EvoFilter** Δ > simple Δ, Criterion B = **EvoFilter** Δ **within range**. Criterion C = **EvoFilter** Δ **within range and** > **simple**

Examples		Criterion A			Criterion B			Criterion C		
		Axis	Fronts		Axis	Fronts		Axis	Fronts	
All	31282	60146	16545	52.89%	13073	5913	18.90%	5967	3392	10.84%
Both filters	2246	7869	1580	70.35%	4847	2080	92.61%	2513	1304	58.06%
Range only	4304	13713	1580	36.71%	8221	3834	89.08%	3454	2088	48.51%
Diff only	24732	38564	11959	48.35%	0	0	0.00%	0	0	0.00%

As well as comparing performance on the basis of range filtering, it is also useful to examine performance on the basis of minimum difference filtering. An error value may be calculated for each axis to be subject to minimum difference filtration. To calculate the error the distance between each item on the axis is calculated, if the distance is < than the minimum distance specified the error is deemed to be the $min_dist - actual_dist$ such errors are summed across the entire front. The results of calculating these errors can be seen in Table 9. We note that when only filtering on minimum difference 68% of instances show a lesser error from EvoFilter than from Simple-filter.

Table 9. Average min difference errors.

	Original	SimpleFilter	EvoFilter	Evo diff err. < Simple diff err.	%
All	26.59	3.88	3.64	17054	54.52
Both filters	21.52	0.73	1.19	74	3.29
Range only	6.00	1.07	1.28	53	1.23
Diff only	30.63	4.65	4.27	16927	68.44

5 Conclusions and Future Work

The experiment conducted uses randomly generated filter specifications to simulate users undertaking filtering using the on-line tool [1], we note that only just under half of these situations does EvoFilter find a result (Table 3). When dealing with real-world problems there will be a number of cases where solutions simply do not exist - for instance as a general rule within the WSRP problem examined solutions with low CO_2 and low financial cost are rare. In such cases it is usually better to let the user know that no solutions that meet their requirements exist, rather than attempting to find the nearest matches which are too far removed from the users' request to be of use. We do note that EvoFilter can find solutions in 5% cases where the simple filter cannot (see Table 3). The knowledge that there is a 50% chance that a users' first set of requirements will not return any solutions, makes the fast runtime of EvoFilter all the more necessary, so that the user may refine their requirements over a number of iterations.

We note that EvoFilter is at its most useful when filtering by range (also known as *brushing* in Parallel Coordinates literature), and that Table 8 shows that EvoFilter can find sets of solutions which, although braking user constraints on range on some axis can result in other axis having a greater spread of solutions within range. The primary advantage of EvoFilter is the ability to include solutions which cause a slight breach of the users' requirements on one axis, but compensate for that by increasing performance on another axis.

It is hoped to encourage use of the EvoFilter tool, in conjunction with a number of real-world problems. The file format used to upload fronts could be modified to include more information, including phenotype information, this would allow the user to also specify features within the phenotype that are desirable. and could be included in the filtering criterion. Currently we only search through non-dominated fronts, but these do not represent the entire final population of most MOGAs, we could increase the search space to include other, dominated, solutions, on the basis that they might be a good match for user criterion.

References

1. Urquhart, N.: Evolutionary decision support for multi-objective problems (2017). http://socoptimisation.napier.ac.uk:8080/ParetoFilter/main.jsp
2. Inselberg, A.: Parallel Coordinates: Visual Multidimensional Geometry and its Applications. Springer, New York (2009). https://doi.org/10.1007/978-0-387-68628-8
3. Urquhart, N., Hart, E.: Creating optimised employee travel plans. In: Proceedings of the 11th edition of the International Conference on Evolutionary and Deterministic Methods for Design, Optimization and Control with Applications to Industrial and Societal Problems (2015)
4. Zio, E., Bazzo, R.: Computational intelligence systems in industrial engineering. In: A Comparison of Methods for Selecting Preferred Solutions in Multiobjective Decision Making. Atlantis Computational Intelligence Systems, vol. 6. Atlantis Press (2012)
5. Cheikh, M., Jarboui, B., Loukil, T., Siarry, P.: A method for selecting pareto optimal solutions inmultiobjective optimization. J. Inform. Math. Sci. **2**(1), 51–62 (2010)
6. Chaudhari, P.M., Dharaskar, R., Thakare, V.M.: Computing the most significant solution from pareto front obtained in multi-objective evolutionary. Int. J. Adv. Comput. Sci. Appl. (IJACSA) **1**(4), 63–68 (2010)
7. Hancock, B.J., Mattson, C.A.: The smart normal constraint method for directly generating a smart Pareto set. Struct. Multi. Optim. **48**(4), 763–775 (2013). https://doi.org/10.1007/s00158-013-0925-6
8. Mattson, C.A., Mullur, A.A., Messac, A.: Smart Pareto filter: obtaining a minimal representation of multiobjective design space. Eng. Optim. **36**(6), 721–740 (2004). https://doi.org/10.1080/0305215042000274942
9. Cheng, F.Y., Li, D.: Genetic algorithm development for multiobjective optimization of structures. AIAA J. **36**(6), 1105–1112 (1998). https://doi.org/10.2514/2.488
10. Castillo-Salazar, J.A., Landa-Silva, D., Qu, R.: Workforce scheduling and routing problems: literature survey and computational study. Ann. Oper. Res. **239**(1), 39–67 (2016). https://doi.org/10.1007/s10479-014-1687-2
11. Braekers, K., Hartl, R.F., Parragh, S.N., Tricoire, F.: A bi-objective home care scheduling problem: analyzing the trade-off between costs and client inconvenience. Eur. J. Oper. Res. **248**(2), 428–443 (2016). http://www.sciencedirect.com/science/article/pii/S037722171500661X
12. Hiermann, G., Prandtstetter, M., Rendl, A., Puchinger, J., Raidl, G.R.: Metaheuristics for solving a multimodal home-healthcare scheduling problem. Central Eur. J. Oper. Res. **23**(1), 89–113 (2015). https://doi.org/10.1007/s10100-013-0305-8
13. Rasmussen, M., Justesen, T., Dohn, A., Larsen, J.: The Home Care Crew Scheduling Problem: Preference-Based Visit Clustering and Temporal Dependencies. DTU Management (2010)

14. Misir, M., Smet, P., Verbeeck, K., Berghe, G.V.: Security personnel routing and rostering: a hyper-heuristic approach. In: Proceedings of the 3rd International Conference on Applied Operational Research, ICAOR 2011 (2011)
15. Nissen, V., Gunther, M.: Application of particle swarm optimization to the British telecom workforce scheduling problem. In: Proceedings of the 9th International Conference on the Practice and Theory of Automated Timetabling (PATAT 2012), Son, Norway (2012)
16. Deb, K., Pratap, A., Agarwal, S., Meyarivan, T.: A fast elitist multi-objective genetic algorithm: NSGA-II. IEEE Trans. Evol. Comput. **6**, 182–197 (2000)
17. Seshadri, A.: NSGA-II: a multi-objective optimization algorithm. Matlab Central File Exchange (2006)
18. Valenzuela, C.: A simple evolutionary algorithm for multi-objective optimization (SEAMO). In: 2002 Congress on Proceedings of the Conference on Evolutionary Computation, 2002 (CEC 2002), vol. 1, pp. 717–722, May 2002
19. Zitzler, E., Laumanns, M., Thiele, L.: Spea 2: improving the strength Pareto evolutionary algorithm for multiobjective optimization. In: Evolutionary Methods for Design, Optimisation, and Control, pp. 95–100. CIMNE (2002)
20. Urquhart, N.: Evofilter source code, January 2018. https://github.com/NeilUrquhart/EvoFilter

A Classifier to Identify Soft Skills in a Researcher Textual Description

Antonia Azzini[1](✉), Andrea Galimberti[2], Stefania Marrara[1], and Eva Ratti[1]

[1] Consorzio C2T, via Nuova Valassina 50, 20158 Carate Brianza, MB, Italy
{antonia.azzini,stefania.marrara,eva.ratti}@consorzioc2t.it
[2] University of Milano Bicocca, Piazza dell'Ateneo Nuovo, 1, 20126 Milano, Italy
andrea.galimberti1@unimib.it

Abstract. Find Your Doctor (FYD) aims at becoming the first Job-placement agency in Italy dedicated to PhDs who are undergoing the transition outside Academia. To support the FYD Human Resources team we started a research project aimed at extracting, from texts (questionnaires) provided by a person telling his/her experience, a set of well defined soft skills. The final aim of the project is to produce a list of researchers ranked w.r.t. their degree of soft skills ownership. In the context of this project, this paper presents an approach employing machine learning techniques aimed at classifying the researchers questionnaires w.r.t. a pre-defined soft skills taxonomy. This paper also presents some preliminary results obtained in the "communication" area of the taxonomy, which are promising and worth of further research in this direction.

Keywords: Text classification · Machine learning
Evolutionary approach

1 Introduction

In the last few years there have been several debates about what types of occupations PhD graduates find after the end of their studies. Several recent studies, mostly commissioned by the European Union, confirm that most of the PhDs, who graduate across Europe, are not going to find long-term occupation in the Academia, but will eventually migrate towards both private and public companies and organizations.

However, while in some countries the value of a PhD is widely recognized and several support programs do exist to guide and optimize the transition of Doctors outside the academic research, other states, especially in the Mediterranean area, are far less accustomed to exploit this professional background.

In 2014, a first attempt in Italy to systematically tackle this issue was the *Find Your Doctor* project, by the not-for-profit consortium of companies C2T-Consortium for Technology Transfer. Find Your Doctor (FYD) has been recently formalised as an innovative Start-Up.

© Springer International Publishing AG, part of Springer Nature 2018
K. Sim and P. Kaufmann (Eds.): EvoApplications 2018, LNCS 10784, pp. 538–546, 2018.
https://doi.org/10.1007/978-3-319-77538-8_37

Within FYD we developed a job-matching semi-automatic tool based on a particular approach: we start with a questionnaire of open questions, a semi-structured interview that leads the candidate to reason on a given number of macro-skills usually considered important by employers, such as communication, relation, rigor, ability to face uncertainty and more. These are commonly referred to as *soft skills* or *transversal skills*.

By the analysis of the text interview we infer the set of soft skills that characterize a researcher. Each questionnaire response is thus associated to a set of univocally defined labels: a hidden vocabulary that can be used for both the analysis of the job requirements and that of the candidates profile, matching the two based on some shared metric purged by interpretation asymmetries on the two sides. This set of skills has been formalized in a taxonomy as described in Sect. 4. The aim of our approach is to build a decision-support, pre-filtering tool able to shift the focus from the ability of a person to tell his/her experience with the proper words to the content of his/her expertise, in terms of transversal skills, providing as output a list of candidates ranked w.r.t. their degree of ownership of each skill in the taxonomy. Once this list is provided by the system, the employer will always have the chance to dig deeper in the candidates profile, CV and narratives to further elaborate above the software suggestions. In the context of this project, this paper presents an approach based on machine learning techniques aimed at classifying the researchers questionnaires w.r.t. our pre-defined soft skills taxonomy. The approach evaluates sentence by sentence the questionnaire of the candidate, by classifying each sentence w.r.t. the taxonomy. The set of soft skills identified evaluating the whole questionnaire represents the profile of the researcher. Then it is possible to provide ranked lists of researchers ordered by one or more skills.

The remaining of the paper is organized as follows. After an initial presentation in Sect. 2 of some of the most relevant approaches already presented in the literature, Sect. 3 discusses the background related to the algorithms usually applied during a preprocessing analysis. The taxonomy of the researcher's soft skills are then reported in Sect. 4, while the approach is described in Sect. 5. The preliminary results of our ongoing research are summarized in Sect. 6. Conclusions and final remarks are reported in Sect. 7.

2   Related Work

The automatic extraction of meaningful information from unstructured texts has been mainly devoted to identify the most suitable candidate for an open position from a set of applicants or to help a job seeker in identifying the most suitable open positions. For example, the work described in [1] extracts information from unstructured resumes through the use of probabilistic information extraction techniques.

Extracting knowledge with text classification has proven to give good results for many real-life web-based data such as, for instance, those gathered by institutional scientific information platforms [2] in many different research areas such as opinion spam detection [3] and sentiment analysis [4].

Machine learning and text mining approaches are very popular techniques that have been successfully applied in many fields, text classification included. In the literature the survey [5] is a good starting point to review the main approaches that use the machine learning paradigm to classify texts. Such works describe the different phases of text classification as document indexing, classifier definition and results evaluation, while another brief survey is presented in [6].

In text classification handling different attributes of the dataset, and tuning different types of parameters that have to be set in the preprocessing phase are important issues. For this reason several works propose the use of filter, parameters and features optimization algorithms, based also on the evolutionary paradigm. Aghdam and colleagues present an approach based on the application of Ant Colony Optimization (ACO) algorithms for the feature selection problem [7]. Bali and colleague present, a combining ACO and GA-based approach for the text document classification [8], while a Genetic Programming (GP) is applied in [9] in order to learn term-weighting schema designed. Moreover, in the feature's optimization task, studies consider the extension of the feature space beyond conventional features representation as carried out in [10].

3 Text Preprocessing

In the design phase of a text classifier, one of the most critical issues regards the definition of the best formal representation suitable as input to a machine learning system. Moreover, the formal representation considerably affect the quality of the classification [11]. The literature provides several techniques used to create the formal representation of a document, as for instance Bag of Words (BoW) or Word2Vec[1]. Most techniques include pre-filtering steps as *Word parsing and tokenization, Stop-words removal, Lemmatization and stemming*, and *Term selection/feature extraction.*

Tokenization. Given a character sequence or a defined document unit, this task breaks it up into pieces, called *tokens* (words/phrases), by also removing useless characters such as punctuation. *Stop Words removal:* less meaningful words such as auxiliary verbs, conjunctions and articles can be removed without losing information in the text [12]. *Stemming* reduces the size of the initial feature set, and removes words misspelled or with the same stem. *Lemmatization* considers the morphological analysis of the words, i.e. grouping together the various inflected forms of a word so they can be analyzed as a single item. The approach presented in this paper adopts Word2Vec, which includes all the previous described steps.

The aim of *feature-selection* methods is the reduction of the dimensionality of the dataset by removing features that are considered irrelevant for the classification. The literature provides several tools[2] able to handle attribute selection filters. Generally these filters allow to choose an attribute evaluation method and a search strategy. Standard methods usually work by choosing attributes

---

[1] Introduction to Information Retrieval https://nlp.stanford.edu/IR-book/.
[2] See for instance: https://weka.waikato.ac.nz/explorer.

that are highly correlated with the class attribute while having a low correlation with other attributes. In our approach we used an evolutionary based approach to optimize the feature selection phase, as detailed in Sect. 5.

4   A Taxonomy of the Researcher's Soft Skills

In the last years literature there have been a strong interest in new techniques for recognizing, evaluating and in case enhancing soft skills in employees. In fact, *transferable skills* enhance people future employability, adaptability and occupational mobility. Released in late September 2011, a timely report for the European Commission is entitled Transferability of Skills across Economic Sectors[3]. In FYD we focus on the issue of employing researchers in companies, and therefore on identifying the skills, both hard and soft, that can be transferred from the Academy experience. There is a lack of consistent theory for defining and classifying various skills, and there is no generally accepted transferable skills taxonomy. The European project team thus decided to distinguish three categories of skills on the basis of previous analysis: (1) soft skills; (2) generic hard skills; (3) specific hard skills. Specific hard skills are characterized by their lower level of transferability, whereas soft skills and generic hard skills are skills with high transferability across sectors and occupations and can be identified as transversal skills. Focusing on researchers our attention was centered on capturing the soft skills within transversal skills that support innovation activity. Having these skills, which can be transferred from one context to another, is a good basis for accumulation of specific skills required by a given job expected in managing a robust innovation pipeline and portfolio to deliver new growth opportunities. Inspired by this work, our approach classifies the researcher soft skills into 6 categories: *carefulness*, i.e., the candidate is careful to look at or consider every part of something to make certain it is correct or safe; *creativity*, i.e., the ability to produce original and unusual ideas, or to make something new or imaginative; *unexpected/emergency* i.e., the ability to deal in an effective way with something that happens suddenly or expectantly and needs fast action in order to avoid harmful results; *uncertainty*, i.e., the ability to deal with a situation in which something is not known, or with something that is not known or certain; *communication*, i.e., the ability to communicate with people; and *networking*, i.e., the process of meeting and talking to a lot of people, esp. in order to get information that can help you.

Each skill category is divided into several classes, each class representing a particular soft skill. For instance, the *communication* category contains the following skills: *effectiveness*, i.e., the candidate must be able to transfer meaningful information in a way clear and easy for the receiver; *dissemination*, i.e., the candidate must be able to transfer technical information in a peer-to-peer context; *teaching*, i.e., teaching experience in Academy or school; *operative communication* i.e., the candidate must be careful in transferring operative informations,

---

[3] http://ec.europa.eu/social/main.jsp?catId=738&langId=en&pubId=6070&type=2 &furtherPubs=no.

for instance mails flow; *verbal communication* i.e., the candidate must be at ease and effective in public talking; *written communication* i.e., the candidate must be at effective and clear when writing documents; *internationality*, i.e., the ability to communicate in an international context; *self-learning*, i.e., the ability to transform a communication task in a learning experience; and *fair measure*, i.e., the ability to find the right equilibrium between talking and listening. A detailed description of the taxonomy is available in [13].

5   The Approach

Figure 1 depicts the system architecture and the data pipeline. The *Paragraph identification* module analyses the questionnaire answer (called "experience pill" or simply "pill") by dividing its text into paragraphs (based on punctuation). The *Preprocessing* module performs the text preprocessing activities as detailed in Sect. 3. Then, the *Feature Selection* module finds the optimal set of features to be input to the machine learning classifier.

The feature selection task is based on the evolutionary paradigm where a population of solutions (in this case the tokens acquired after the preprocessing phase) is repeatedly evaluated and updated, by replacing some attributes with new potentially better ones. In particular, the individual ranking values of the final trained model provide a measure for the importance of the features in the classification task, representing then the individual performances of the evolving population.

In our approach, an initial set of tokens defines the training sample obtained by the preprocessing phase. These tokens constitute the initial population of features. In this approach the feature ranking values coming from the feature selection filters provide a measure for the importance of the features in the classification task and will be used as the "fitness" measure for determining features in the evolving population. First of all, an initial pool of features is produced by parsing the training sample for all basic words. These words constitute the initial population. Then the feature set will be iterated through the evaluation, analysis and reproduction process. During the iteration, the feature pool is used to train a classifier which provides an evaluation for the performance of the individual features. The set will be iterated through the Fitness Evaluation, Selection and Replacement blocks. The iteration will be stopped when some criteria is reached, according to the conditions explained into the Fitness Evaluation block.

Fitness Evaluation: the fitness of each feature is calculated according the feature rank obtained from the application of one of the feature selection filter. After the evaluation, the results are analyzed. The evolutionary process is stopped accordingly one of these conditions: (1) the evaluation returns the maximum value that performance can reach. (2) No new best value was given in past n iteration. We set n as 500. (3) No new attribute is found in the last iteration.

Selection: a threshold th is used to select the best n features of the entire population (in this work is set to 0.25).

Replacement: unlike the usual reproduction process in an evolutionary algorithm, no feature is generated based on genes cross-overs and mutations, since, due to the usual sparseness of words in relation to documents samples, a random generation of attributes could be ineffective. The eliminated tokens are replaced by applying the *Attribute Selection Filters* of well known Machine Leaning Tools[4] and replacing them with the new ones with a better ranking value. Such a new population is then considered again into the Fitness Evaluation block. The final overall performances are calculated over the test set. The outcomes of the classification step are then stored in a database, ready to be used to create the soft skills researcher's profile.

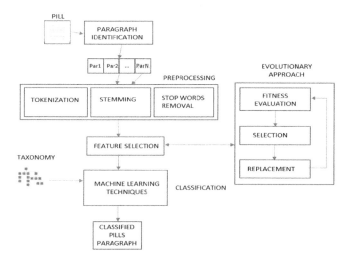

Fig. 1. Architecture representation.

6 Preliminary Experiments and Evaluations

A benchmark dataset was prepared by analyzing about 600 questionnaires gathered by the Find Your Doctor (FYD) HR team, by dividing each questionnaire answer in sentences, and by labeling each sentence with the most appropriate soft skill. This analysis step gathered around 15,000 labeled sentences. Unfortunately not all the soft skills categories detailed in the taxonomy were populated enough to perform a classifier training task. The most populated category was "communication" with around 5000 sentences randomly partitioned in the 9 soft skills belonging to this area, and stating the classes of the ML classifiers. For this reason we decided to perform a preliminary evaluation only on this area, with the aim to assess the benefits of using machine learning in this context.

---

[4] https://www.cs.waikato.ac.nz/ml/weka/.

The benchmark creation activity is currently an ongoing work, with the aim to complete the labeling of all questionnaires available now in the FYD collection. In this first prototype 5 different machine learning techniques (see Table 1) have been selected and applied for a comparative evaluation in the task of soft skills classification.

During these preliminary experiments in the "communication" area, only six out of 9 soft skills had enough instances to perform the training phase of the classifiers. These soft skills were, respectively *effectiveness*, *dissemination*, *teaching*, *written communication*, *verbal communication* and *internationality*, for a total of 4389 sentences.

The labeled sentences were randomly partitioned into training and test sets. In particular, the 75% of the overall dataset was randomly selected and devoted to the training phase, while the remaining 25% to the test (the *Percentage Split* experiments set). The first part of Table 1 shows these preliminary results. The effectiveness of the considered classifiers was evaluated based on the measures of precision, recall [11], and accuracy.

Table 1. Preliminary results.

Classifier	Percentage Split 75% Train - 25% Test			10 Fold Cross Validation		
	Precision 0–1	Recall 0–1	Accuracy %	Precision 0–1	Recall 0–1	Accuracy %
Naive Bayes	0.808	0.723	72.3343	0.7713	0.698	69.7624
K-Nearest Neighbor						
K=1	0.638	0.628	62.8212	0.599	0.595	59.5392
K=5	0.683	0.654	65.4179	0.683	0.658	65.8027
K=9	0.742	0.666	66.5706	0.721	0.669	66.8826
Support Vector Machine	0.731	0.726	**72.6225**	0.721	0.717	**71.7163**
Decision Tree	0.746	0.741	74.0638	0.705	0.706	70.5544
Random Forest	0.694	0.674	67.4352	0.648	0.635	63.4989

In order to validate the performances obtained over the *Percentage Split* experiments, a second set of experiments was performed applying the *10 Fold Cross Validation* approach over the same dataset. The results are reported in Table 1.

From the first set of experiments carried out in this work the best results were obtained by using the Support Vector Machine. In this approach SVM allows to obtain outperforming combinations of the text features previously optimized by the evolutionary iterative blocks. Such interesting results (even if they are still not satisfactory) were reached for both the two experimental sessions, and they were validated by the 10 Fold Cross Validation.

The Naive Bayes approach also obtained interesting results over the dataset, even if they appear performing only for the Percentage Split experiments, while not for the validating phase. Similar results were obtained by the Decision Tree: while it can reach the best results for the first phase, the same performance is not reached in the validating one, since the accuracy decreases becoming lower than that obtained by using SVM. The KNN classifier uses the distance-based measures to perform the classification, based on the concept of similarity among the instances of the dataset. Together with Random Forest they were the two kinds of classifiers that were not able to reach interesting results in these first experimental session.

7   Conclusion and Future Work

The approach presented in this paper aims at evaluating, sentence by sentence, the questionnaire answers of researchers, and classifying each sentence w.r.t. a pre-defined taxonomy. The feature selection task was challenging due to the dimension of the initial feature set and the solution adopted an evolutionary approach. This preliminary results obtained in the "communication" area of the taxonomy confirmed that a SVM classifier is the best choice in this context, with promising results that are worth of further research in this direction. Future work involves several tasks: (1) extending the benchmark by analyzing and labeling the entire dataset composed by 2000 questionnaires, (2) defining a proper formal representation of the user profiles based on the soft skills identified by the SVM classifier, and (3) building a HR support tool able to search the profiles collection and provide lists of researchers ranked on the basis of one or more soft skills.

References

1. Singh, A., Rose, C., Visweswariah, K., Chenthamarakshan, V., Kambhatla, N.: Prospect: a system for screening candidates for recruitment. In: Proceedings of the 19th ACM International Conference on Information and Knowledge Management, pp. 659–668. ACM (2010)
2. Koperwas, J., Skonieczny, Ł., Kozłowski, M., Andruszkiewicz, P., Rybiński, H., Struk, W.: Intelligent information processing for building university knowledge base. J. Intell. Inf. Syst., 1–23 (2016)
3. Jindal, N., Liu, B.: Opinion spam and analysis. In: Proceedings of the 2008 International Conference on Web Search and Data Mining, pp. 219–230. ACM (2008)
4. Bifet, A., Frank, E.: Sentiment knowledge discovery in twitter streaming data. In: Pfahringer, B., Holmes, G., Hoffmann, A. (eds.) DS 2010. LNCS (LNAI), vol. 6332, pp. 1–15. Springer, Heidelberg (2010). https://doi.org/10.1007/978-3-642-16184-1_1
5. Sebastiani, F.: Machine learning in automated text categorization. ACM Comput. Surv. 34(1), 1–47 (2002)
6. Allahyari, M., Pouriyeh, S.A., Assefi, M., Safaei, S., Trippe, E.D., Gutierrez, J.B., Kochut, K.: A brief survey of text mining: classification, clustering and extraction techniques. CoRR abs/1707.02919 (2017)
7. Hosseinzadeh Aghdam, M., Ghasem-Aghaee, N., Ehsan Basiri, M.: Text feature selection using ant colony optimization. Expert Syst. Appl. Int. J. 36, 6843–6853 (2009)

8. Bali, M., Gore, D.: Text document classification using ant colony optimization and genetic algorithm. Int. J. Innov. Res. Comput. Commun. Eng. **3**(12), 12551–12558 (2015)

9. Garcia, M., Escalante, H.J., Montes, M., Morales, A., Morales, E.: Towards the automated generation of term-weighting schemes for text categorization. In: Proceedings of the Companion Publication of the 2014 Annual Conference on Genetic and Evolutionary Computation, GECCO Comp 2014, pp. 1459–1460. ACM, New York (2014)

10. Wong, A.K.S., Lee, J.W.T.: An evolutionary approach for discovering effective composite features for text categorization. In: 2007 IEEE International Conference on Systems, Man and Cybernetics, pp. 3045–3050. IEEE, October 2007

11. Boselli, R., Cesarini, M., Marrara, S., Mercorio, F., Mezzanzanica, M., Pasi, G., Viviani, M.: Wolmis: a labor market intelligence system for classifying web job vacancies. J. Intell. Inf. Syst. (2017)

12. Ikonomakis, E., Kotsiantis, S., Tampakas, V.: Text classification using machine learning techniques **4**, 966–974 (2005)

13. Azzini, A., Galimberti, A., Marrara, S., Ratti, E.: A taxonomy of researchers soft skills. Internal report, ConsorzioC2T (2017)

Toward the Online Visualisation of Algorithm Performance for Parameter Selection

David J. Walker[1]([✉]) and Matthew J. Craven[2]

[1] University of Exeter, Exeter, UK
D.J.Walker@exeter.ac.uk
[2] University of Plymouth, Plymouth, UK
matthew.craven@plymouth.ac.uk

Abstract. A visualisation method is presented that is intended to assist evolutionary algorithm users with the parametrisation of their algorithms. The visualisation method presents the convergence and diversity properties such that different parametrisations can be easily compared, and poor performing parameter sets can be easily identified and discarded. The efficacy of the visualisation is presented using a set of benchmark optimisation problems from the literature, as well as a benchmark water distribution network design problem. Results show that it is possible to observe the different performance caused by different parametrisations. Future work discusses the potential of this visualisation within an online tool that will enable a user to discard poor parametrisations as they execute to free up resources for better ones.

Keywords: Visualisation · Multi-objective · Optimisation
Water distribution network design

1 Introduction

Visualisation remains an open problem within evolutionary computation (EC). Recently, considerable effort has been expended in investigating methods for visualising sets of solutions, with the aim of presenting the final set of generated solutions to a decision maker so that one can be selected for implementation. The visualisation of algorithm performance lags somewhat behind. Such visualisation is an important avenue of research, as useful visualisations of algorithm operation can help to reveal the inner workings of an evolutionary algorithm (EA), which to a non-expert are a black box. By exposing the operation of an EA to a non-expert user, the uptake of evolutionary computation by industry will be increased.

This paper presents a new visualisation that is intended to assist an algorithm user when parametrising their algorithms. All varieties of EA require a range of parameters to be set. Most, including genetic algorithms (GAs), differential evolution (DE) and particle swarm optimisation (PSO) are extremely sensitive to their parameters being set correctly, with a poor set of parameters

© Springer International Publishing AG, part of Springer Nature 2018
K. Sim and P. Kaufmann (Eds.): EvoApplications 2018, LNCS 10784, pp. 547–560, 2018.
https://doi.org/10.1007/978-3-319-77538-8_38

resulting in a poor set of solutions. The EC literature contains a range of ways of characterising performance; in this work, multi-objective problems are considered, and algorithm performance is characterised in terms of convergence to the true Pareto front and population diversity. Both of these aspects are revealed through the proposed visualisation, and a "good" parametrisation requires both good convergence and population diversity.

The visualisation is demonstrated on well-known continuous test problems from the literature (the DTLZ problem suite [1]). Problems are selected that will demonstrate the algorithm's performance on a range of problem characteristics. As well as these problems, an industrial benchmark problem is demonstrated – the water distribution network design problem. This is a combinatoric problem, and represents a class of problem that are commonly optimised using EAs. The paper is structured as follows: a brief survey of relevant visualisation approaches is presented in Sect. 2 before the proposed visualisation is introduced in Sect. 3. The experimental framework is discussed and the visualisation method demonstrated in Sect. 4, before its results are discussed in Sect. 5. The final section serves as a conclusion to the paper, as well as containing as discussion of future work.

2   Background

2.1   Multi-objective Optimisation

This paper is concerned with continuous and discrete multi-objective optimisation problems. In both cases, consider a solution $\mathbf{x}$, wherein x_p is one of P decision variables. Solution quality is determined with a set of M objective functions f_m, forming an objective vector $\mathbf{y}$:

$$\mathbf{y} = (f_1(\mathbf{x}), \ldots, f_M(\mathbf{x})) . \tag{1}$$

Relative solution quality is assessed using *dominance*, such that given two solutions $\mathbf{x}_i$ is superior to $\mathbf{x}_j$ if it dominates $\mathbf{x}_j$. This is the case if it is no worse than $\mathbf{x}_j$ on all objectives and better on at least one (assuming a minimisation problem, without loss of generality):

$$\mathbf{y}_i \prec \mathbf{y}_j \iff \forall m(y_{im} \leq y_{jm}) \wedge \exists m(y_{im} < y_{jm}). \tag{2}$$

If neither of two solutions dominate the other then they are called *mutually non-dominating*. If a solution has no dominating solutions, it is said to be *non-dominated*. The optimal set of solutions are called the Pareto set, which map to the Pareto front in objective space. This is the mutually non-dominated set of non-dominated feasible solutions, and represents the best possible trade-off between the problem objectives. In order to produce a suitable estimate of the Pareto front, the job of a multi-objective EA (MOEA) is to converge to a point close to the Pareto front, and cover the front's full extent.

2.2   Visualisation of Evolution

Of the visualisation work within EC, a considerable amount is focused on displaying populations of solutions (e.g., [2,3]). In particular, many-objective optimisation (wherein problems comprise four or more objectives) pose a particular challenge for visualisation [3], as human decision makers can only comprehend three or fewer spatial dimensions. Many-objective problems are not considered herein, however current ongoing work is considering how they can be incorporated into the proposed framework.

Fewer publications consider visualising the process of evolution itself. An example that is directly relevant to this work is proposed in [4], which uses a visualisation method to assess the stability of parameters for an EA used to solve a single-objective cryptology problem. They define metrics over the parameter space[1] and perturb parameters to show the effect of moving them around within a small neighbourhood. One of the first examples of visualisation work within the EC field was [5], which proposed a set of standard tools for visualising solutions, populations, and algorithm characteristics such as convergence. A similar system was proposed by [6], which allowed a user to view the propagation of genetic material throughout the execution of an EA (they optimised the 0/1 Knapsack problem). Elsewhere, an example of a tool that seeks to visualise the evolution process is GAVEL [7], which presents maps of populations of solutions in terms of the genetic operators used to generate them. Other aspects of the tool show the rate at which solutions are generated, as well as fitness information. A visualisation developed for water distribution network (WDN) design was proposed by [8] in which a visualisation of a single solution (a single WDN) is coloured according to the frequency that each decision variable (an individual pipe diameter) within the solution is perturbed. Within the realm of genetic programming there have been various examples of visualising the ancestry of solutions (e.g., [9]).

3   Visualising Stability Within Multi-objective EAs

The method proposed herein visualises the stability of an algorithm's parameters by showing how important properties of a MOEA (such as convergence to the Pareto front and diversity within the population) change over time for given parametrisations of algorithms.

Figure 1 shows a schematic describing the construction of the visualisation. The plot itself is circular, and is designed to contain information about multiple executions of an EA. Each point within the visualisation represents a single solution within an algorithm's population for a single generation, and has three degrees of freedom: its angle from the origin, distance from the centre of the plot, and its colour; each of these is used to convey an aspect of algorithm performance. The choice of characteristic these variables are used to show is up to the user to

---

[1] Herein the term *parameter* is used to refer to algorithm parameters; *decision variable* is used to refer to an aspect of a solution's design, to avoid confusion.

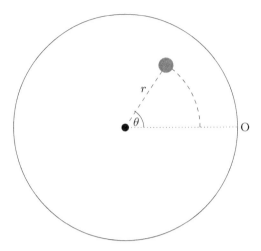

Fig. 1. A schematic showing the placement of a solution within the visualisation.

decide. Two important aspects of the execution of a MOEA are convergence, to ensure that the algorithm generates solutions that are close to the true Pareto front, and diversity, to ensure that the search population is properly explored. This work utilises two well-known measures from the evolutionary computation literature to illustrate both characteristics across a set of algorithms optimising benchmark test problems.

To show convergence, the hypervolume indicator [10] is employed. This provides a measure of dominated space between the current search population and a reference point; in this work, the hypervolume of individual solutions is considered. A reference point is computed by taking the maximum value for each objective seen at any point in the optimisation process. As the population converges, the distance from this reference point increases. Hypervolume is used to determine the angle θ by multiplying the hypervolume value (lying between 0 and 1 as a proportion of the space that could be dominated) by 2π. At the beginning of an optimisation run, when working with randomly generated solutions, points are typically scattered across the extent of the circle. As more optimal solutions are generated, and the algorithm converges towards the true Pareto front, this angle decreases and the population tend to be clustered around the origin (shown by a dotted line and the label "O" in Fig. 1).

Diversity is evaluated using the crowding distance. Crowding distance provides a measure of the proximity of the nearest solution in each objective, and is well-known for its use in the selection operator of NSGA-II [11]. It is important to note the flexibility of the proposed method. In this work, hypervolume and crowding distance have been used as well-known measures of convergence and diversity that do not require *a priori* knowledge about the true Pareto front (which is known for the continuous test problems tested later, but not for the industrial benchmark problem also demonstrated). These indicators can be easily substituted for any measure required – for example, an indicator of decision space diversity, or measures indicating (for example) velocities within a particle swarm optimiser. These are aspects of ongoing work, which are not discussed further in this paper.

4 Experimental Setup

In order to demonstrate the potential of the proposed method, continuous test problems from the multi-objective literature are considered, before an industrial benchmark is evaluated.

4.1 Continuous Test Problems

Three benchmark multi-objective problems from the literature are optimised with three variants of a basic MOEA, and the various algorithm performances are visualised. The test problems employed are a 2-objective DTLZ1 and a 3-objective DTLZ2 [1], both of which have different problem characteristics. Both are real-valued, with legal parameters in the range (0,1). To facilitate an easier analysis of the visualisations, the MOEA works with a population size of 10. DTLZ1 is known to be a harder problem than DTLZ2; as such, the optimiser executes for 5,000 generations, while DTLZ2 is optimised for 500 generations.

Three algorithms are selected for their different optimisation behaviours; all three variants follow the same basic arrangement. The algorithm begins by initialising a random search population, which is evaluated under the problem objective functions. An elite archive, in which the current approximation to the Pareto front will be stored, is initialised. The archive is passive, in that it does not participate in the evolutionary process. At each generation, a child population is generated by applying crossover and mutation operators, and is evaluated under the objectives. The archive is updated, so that any newly dominated solutions are removed, and any members of the child population that are not dominated by members of the archive are added to it. Finally, elitist selection is applied to the combined parent and child populations to select the parent population for the next generation. The specific operators used to obtain specific optimisation behaviours are now discussed.

In the first EA, single-point crossover is used to combine two candidate parent solutions chosen at random. A child solution is created by joining the decision variables prior to the crossover point on one of the parents with the decision variables following the crossover point on the other. The child is then mutated using an additive Gaussian mutation, and evaluated. To demonstrate different parametrisations of the algorithm, the standard deviation of the Gaussian distribution from which the additive mutation is drawn is chosen randomly in the range (0,1). The selection operator performs non-dominated sorting on the combined parent and child populations. As solutions are added to the new parent population, if the current non-dominated front contains more solutions than are needed to fill the population then the number required are selected from that front at random. This algorithm provides good convergence to the Pareto front, and is able to cover its full extent, so providing an example of an optimiser with good performance.

The second EA operates largely in the same way as the first. It generates solutions using the crossover and mutation operators described above, and uses the archive in the same way. The difference is in the choice of selection operator; *average rank* [12] is used to determined which solutions are carried forward into the next generation. Average rank is a method proposed to deal with many-objective optimisation problems, where non-dominated sorting is unable to provide sufficient selection pressure to properly optimise [13]. It is formalised as follows:

$$\bar{r}_i = \frac{1}{M} \sum_{m=1}^{M} r_{im}, \tag{3}$$

where r_{im} is the rank of the i-th solution when ranked according to the m-th objective. Having ranked the population, the top N solutions from the combined parent and child populations are retained. On its own, average rank is able to provide extremely good convergence to the Pareto front, but this is at the expense of the diversity. The resulting approximation to the Pareto front is clustered around the extremes of the front, where the lowest objective values, and therefore the best ranks, are to be found. This is used herein as an example of an optimiser suffering from premature convergence.

The final algorithm is a random search of the feasible space, and is used to highlight an example of poor convergence. Rather than retaining the fittest solutions, a population of N solutions is chosen uniformly at random from the $2N$-member combination of the parent and child populations.

4.2   Water Distribution Network Design

In addition to the continuous test problems demonstrated in the previous section, the algorithm is used to optimise a benchmark water distribution network (WDN) design problem from the field of hydroinformatics. This problem is discrete, requiring the identification of a set of pipe diameters that will form the optimal WDN. The problem is multi-objective, with a candidate network evaluated both in terms of its cost and its hydraulic properties.

The New York Tunnels problem [14] comprises 21 nodes connected by 20 pipes. The correct diameter for each pipe must be identified, from one of 16 possibilities. Hence, the feasible search space is of size $20^{16} \approx 6.55 \times 10^{20}$. The problem objectives are formulated as follows:

$$f_1 = \sum_{k=1}^{K} \left(1.1 d_k^{1.24} \times l_k\right), \tag{4}$$

$$f_2 = \sum_{n=1}^{N} \left(\left(\hat{h}_n - h_n\right) > 0\right). \tag{5}$$

The diameter of the k-th pipe is given by d_k, while l_k represents that pipe's length. The *head deficit* for node n is specified by h_n, and $\hat{h}_n$ is the target head deficit for that node.

Whereas the continuous problems are optimised with fifty parametrisations of an additive Gaussian mutation, this problem must be optimised with combinatoric perturbations. The crossover portion of the MOEA is retained, and the mutation operator is swapped with one of five different heuristics:

- **Change by one size:** a randomly chosen pipe's diameter is replaced with the next largest or smallest available diameter (also known as *creep mutation*).
- **Shuffle:** a randomly selected block of diameters is randomly reordered.
- **Ruin & recreate:** the solution is replaced with an entirely new chromosome.
- **Change pipe:** a randomly chosen pipe's diameter is replaced with a randomly chosen available pipe.
- **Swap:** two randomly chosen pipe diameters are swapped.

As before, the algorithm operates with a population of 10 solutions and runs for 5,000 generations.

5 Results

5.1 DTLZ2

The first set of visualisation, shown in Fig. 2, demonstrates the optimisation of DTLZ2. The figure presents a grid of nine visualisations. Each row shows a different algorithm's optimisation progress: the top row shows the Pareto sorting-based algorithm; the second row is average rank, and the bottom row shows the random selection strategy. In each case, the left-hand column shows the population after selection in the first generation; the middle column shows generation 20 and the right-hand column shows the final search population. Each visualisation shows the ten solutions comprising a population for each of the fifty algorithm parametrisations.

The ideal situation is shown by the top row, presenting results for the Pareto sorting approach. As can be seen, the solutions have progressed around the arc of the visualisation, and are clustered around the zero angle line. This indicates that most of the populations have converged to a good approximation of the Pareto front, as their hypervolume is close to the optimal observed value. Some of the populations have not quite converged. The final population is repeated in Fig. 3, which shows this in more detail. Six of the parametrisations have been highlighted – those shown in blue have converged, and those shown in red have not. Recalling that the distance from the centre of the visualisation represents the standard deviation of the additive Gaussian mutation applied to the chosen parameter, this is intuitively correct. Small Gaussian mutations are known to provide better convergence than larger ones, which cause behaviour closer to a random walk through the space. Returning to Fig. 2, the diversity within the population is also good. As can be seen, the colours of the points representing

(a) Gen 0   (b) Gen 20   (c) Gen 499

(d) Gen 0   (e) Gen 20   (f) Gen 499

(g) Gen 0   (h) Gen 20   (i) Gen 499

Fig. 2. Visualisations of DTLZ2. The top row shows the populations generated by using the basic GA; the middle row shows corresponding results for the average rank optimiser, and the bottom row for the random solution generation algorithm. Colour indicates crowding distance – a low crowding distance is shown in blue, high distances are in red. (Color figure online)

Generation 499

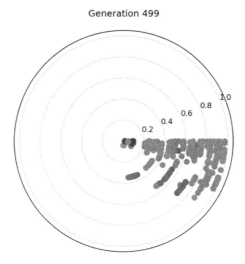

Fig. 3. The final set of populations for the algorithm using Pareto sorting to optimise DTLZ2. The blue group show better convergence than the red group. (Color figure online)

solutions are a mixture of light blues and oranges. This indicates a mixture of solutions with medium crowding distances, and suggests that the algorithms have not suffered from a loss of diversity (which would be shown by exclusively small crowding distances – blue solutions, in the visualisations).

The bottom two rows show less satisfactory behaviour of the optimisers. The middle row shows a set of results for an optimiser using average rank. At first glance, the optimiser has performed well; the solutions are very well converged to the true Pareto front. In fact, they are closer to the optimal set of solutions than those generated using Pareto sorting. Unfortunately, this convergence is premature, and is at the expense of the diversity within the population. As can be seen, the solutions are generally dark blue, indicating a low crowding distance. The effect of this can be seen in the example Pareto front shown in Fig. 4, which shows two final estimated Pareto fronts from the last generation of the average rank optimiser. In both cases, the solutions (shown with black crosses) are generally clustered around the edges and corners of the true Pareto front (samples of which are shown with grey dots). Though these solutions are very close to the front (with a few exceptions, which are too close to minimising one of the objectives that they are extremely difficult to dominate) they do not properly cover the front. A large proportion of the true Pareto front is unexplored by the optimiser, and the resulting solution set does not properly describe the trade-off between objectives. The final row has the opposite problem: optimised using a random selection operator, there is very little selection pressure to drive the population to the Pareto front. As a result, the populations do not converge, as shown by the large spread of solutions that have not reached the zero angle line. The populations have, however, retained their diversity. As was the case with the Pareto sorting example, solutions are coloured between blue and orange.

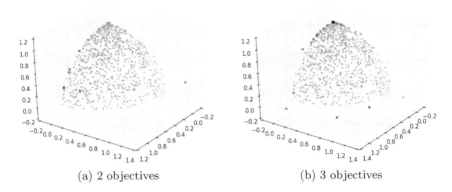

(a) 2 objectives   (b) 3 objectives

Fig. 4. Exemplar Pareto front approximations for DTLZ2 obtained using average rank selection. Black crosses show the generated solutions; grey dots are samples from the true Pareto front. The optimiser has clearly preferred the corners of the front, with some poor solutions remaining in the archive from early generations.

5.2   DTLZ1

Figure 5 presents two snapshots from the execution of DTLZ1 using the Pareto sorting optimiser (generations 33 and 96). As can be seen, by this early stage in the optimisation process the algorithm has already made substantial progress in converging toward the true Pareto front – the solutions are all in the bottom section of the visualisation. What is interesting in these visualisations is that it is possible to observe the algorithm dealing with the deceptive fronts present in the test problem. These are locally optimal regions of the search space on which the algorithm becomes stuck, and as can be seen this is occurring during these two generations. Whereas for DTLZ2, smaller mutations were causing more rapid convergence than larger ones, here, the opposite is true. Larger mutation values are causing those populations to converge faster than their slower counterparts, which are struggling to generate mutations strong enough to escape the deceptive fronts on which they have become trapped. Though they will eventually escape, it will take longer with smaller mutations. That said, as the populations reach the true Pareto front, smaller mutations will induce the desired exploitative behaviour that will cover the entire front.

5.3   Water Distribution Network Design

Figures 6 and 7 present the results for the WDN design problem. Figure 7 shows the different mutation heuristics used to solve the problem, each of which is shown on its own ring within the visualisation. The left-hand plot shows the initial generation, with a random spread of solutions in the top portion of the visualisation. The second plot shows generation 20, and the populations are moving into the lower portion of the visualisation, indicating that they are starting to converge. By the final plot, three of the five heuristics have mostly converged.

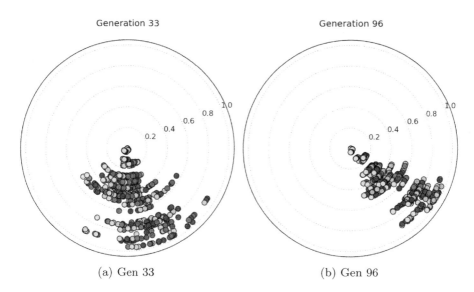

(a) Gen 33   (b) Gen 96

Fig. 5. Two snapshots of the Pareto sorting MOEA optimising DTLZ1. The left-hand visualisation shows the population during generation 33, while the right-hand shows generation 96. Those optimisers with larger standard deviations are advancing faster than those generating smaller mutations, as the optimiser is temporarily stuck on deceptive fronts. This can be seen by the outer cluster of solutions being further around the circle than the inner cluster, in both cases. Eventually, all populations converge over time to the true front. Again, colour indicates diversity.

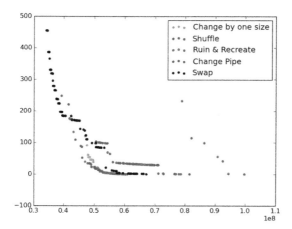

Fig. 6. The estimated Pareto fronts generated by the optimisers for the New York Tunnels problem.

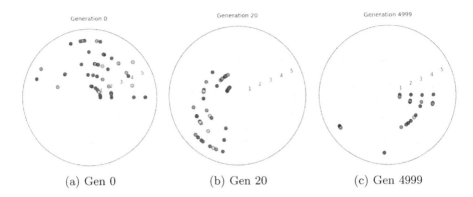

(a) Gen 0   (b) Gen 20   (c) Gen 4999

Fig. 7. Visualisations of algorithm performance. Each ring represents a different perturbation heuristic. 1: change by one size; 2: change pipe; 3: ruin and recreate; 4: shuffle; 5: swap. Position indicates convergence while diversity is shown according to the solution colour.

These include the change by one size heuristic and the change pipe heuristic, which are known to work well on such problems [15]. Neither the ruin and recreate heuristic or the swap heuristic have converged. This is intuitively correct, as the ruin and recreate heuristic does not learn from one generation to the next, and the swap heuristic is incapable of introducing novel genetic material. This is confirmed by the Pareto front approximation generated in each case, and shown in Fig. 6 (neither front has converged toward the knee identified by the other heuristics). That said, from observing the colouring in Fig. 7, the swap heuristic has the most diverse population. The effect of this is to generate a more extensive Pareto front approximation, again, as shown in Fig. 6.

6   Conclusions

This paper has presented a visualisation tool designed to address the issue of identifying good parametrisations of EAs. By allowing algorithm users to directly compare the effect of different parametrisations on the ability of the algorithm to converge and retain population diversity, it is possible for a user to select a good parameter scheme without requiring an indepth understanding of how their specific algorithm operates on their given problem. The properties shown here demonstrate convergence in terms of the hypervolume of solutions at a specific generation, which increases as the population converges toward the Pareto front, and the crowding distance of the population, which in the presence of a loss of diversity will decrease. This work showed the potential for using these characteristics to understand algorithm operation; however the flexibility of the proposed method allows for any indicator of algorithm performance to be represented. As well as demonstrating the work on continuous test problems, an industrial benchmark problem – optimising the design of water distribution networks – was demonstrated.

Having demonstrated the efficacy of the basic method, there are various aspects of future work. While it has effectively visualised GA performance, current work is evaluating its use for other types of algorithms. Two examples are differential evolution (DE) and particle swarm optimisation (PSO), the performance of both of which is highly dependent on their chosen parameters. In addition, the current version of the visualisation somewhat neglects the multi-objective nature of the problems demonstrated. A useful addition to the visualisation would include information about the current approximation to the Pareto front, and the trade-off between objectives, and work is also continuing to study how this can best be incorporated into the visualisation. As discussed earlier, a prominent difficulty with this is the extension of the tool to the many-objective problem arena. Two aspects of this are difficult; in the first, representing many-objective problems is known to be difficult, and though methods have been proposed, any method would have to be incorporated into the framework proposed herein (or something like it). In the second, this work has relied on the hypervolume as a measure of convergence to the true Pareto front. Hypervolume calculations are too expensive to compute for even modestly large numbers of objectives. Current work is investigating the use of Monte Carlo sampling to avoid having to compute the exact hypervolume (as used in the HypE algorithm [16]), as well as identifying that can be used in its place. An important aspect of this is finding indicators that do not require knowledge of the true Pareto front, so that the method can be used with industrial problems.

The ultimate aim of this tool is to use it online, so that the progress of the optimiser can be seen as the algorithms are running. That way, the user can identify which parametrisations are not producing usable solutions, and they can be halted to direct their resources to more productive instances. This represents a considerable step forward from the current position of the method, and will require the use of high performance computing to facilitate the processing needed to produce the visualisations in real time. It will, however, result in an extremely valuable way of benchmarking algorithm parametrisations that is likely to be of great use to industrial practitioners.

References

1. Deb, K., Thiele, L., Laumanns, M., Zitzler, E.: Scalable multi-objective optimization test problems. In: Proceedings of IEEE Congress on Evolutionary Computation, vol. 1, pp. 825–830, May 2002
2. Bhattacharjee, K.S., Singh, H.K., Ryan, M., Ray, T.: Bridging the gap: many-objective optimization and informed decision-making. IEEE Trans. Evol. Comput. **21**(5), 813–820 (2017)
3. Walker, D.J., Everson, R.M., Fieldsend, J.E.: Visualising mutually non-dominating solution sets in many-objective optimization. IEEE Trans. Evol. Comput. **17**(2), 165–184 (2013)
4. Craven, M.J., Jimbo, H.C.: EA stability visualization: perturbations, metrics and performance. In: Proceedings of Visualisation in Genetic and Evolutionary Computation (VizGEC 2014), Held at GECCO 2014 (2014)

5. Polheim, H.: Visualization of evolutionary algorithms - set of standard techniques and multidimensional visualization. In: Proceedings of Genetic and Evolutionary Computation Conference (GECCO 1999), pp. 533–540 (1999)
6. Kerren, A., Egger, T.: EAVis: a visualisation tool for evolutionary algorithms. In: Proceedings of 2005 IEEE Symposium on Visual Languages and Human-Centric Computing, pp. 299–301 (2005)
7. Hart, E., Ross, P.: GAVEL - a new tool for genetic algorithm visualization. IEEE Trans. Evol. Comput. 5(4), 335–348 (2001)
8. Keedwell, E., Johns, M., Savić, D.: Spatial and temporal visualisation of evolutionary algorithm decisions in water distribution network optimisation. In: GECCO Companion 2015 Proceedings of Visualisation in Genetic and Evolutionary Computation (VizGEC 2015) Held at GECCO 2015, pp. 941–948 (2015)
9. Burlacu, B., Affenzeller, M., Kommenda, M., Winkler, S., Kronberger, G.: Visualization of genetic lineages and inheritance information in genetic programming. In: GECCO Companion 2013 Proceedings of Visualisation in Genetic and Evolutionary Computation (VizGEC 2013) Held at GECCO 2013, pp. 1351–1358 (2013)
10. Fleischer, M.: The measure of Pareto optima applications to multi-objective metaheuristics. In: Fonseca, C.M., Fleming, P.J., Zitzler, E., Thiele, L., Deb, K. (eds.) EMO 2003. LNCS, vol. 2632, pp. 519–533. Springer, Heidelberg (2003). https://doi.org/10.1007/3-540-36970-8_37
11. Deb, K., Pratap, A., Agarwal, S., Meyarivan, T.: A fast and elitist multiobjective genetic algorithm: NSGA-II. IEEE Trans. Evol. Comput. 6(2), 182–197 (2002)
12. Bentley, P.J., Wakefield, J.P.: Finding acceptable solutions in the Pareto-optimal range using multiobjective genetic algorithms. In: Chawdhry, P.K., Roy, R., Pant, R.K. (eds.) Soft Computing in Engineering Design and Manufacturing, pp. 231–240. Springer, London (1998). https://doi.org/10.1007/978-1-4471-0427-8_25
13. Garza-Fabre, M., Toscano-Pulido, G., Coello, C.: Two novel approaches for many-objective optimization. In: Proceedings of the IEEE Congress on Evolutionary Computation, pp. 4480–4487, July 2010
14. Schaake, J., Lai, D.: Linear programming and dynamic programming application to water distribution network design. Technical report. MIT (1969)
15. Walker, D.J., Keedwell, E., Savić, D.: Multi-objective optimisation of a water distribution network with a sequence-based selection hyper-heuristic. In: Proceedings of Computing and Control in the Water Industry (CCWI 2016) (2016)
16. Bader, J., Zitzler, E.: HypE: an algorithm for fast hypervolume-based many-objective optimization. Evol. Comput. 19(1), 45–76 (2011)

Integrating Evolution Strategies into Genetic Algorithms with Fuzzy Inference Evaluation to Solve a Steelmaking and Continuous Casting Scheduling Problem

Eduardo Salazar$^{(\boxtimes)}$

Universidad de Concepción, Concepción, Chile
esalazar@udec.cl

Abstract. This contribution presents a metaheuristic approach that integrates evolution strategies into genetic algorithms using a fuzzy rule based inference system to evaluate schedules in a generalized steelmaking and continuous casting production system. The genetic algorithm controls the job sequences assigned to the machines while the setting of jobs initial processing dates at the converter are optimize by means of evolution strategies. The fuzzy inference system gives an overall evaluation of the schedule quality by controlling discontinuities and transit times with different degrees of acceptance throughout the evolution process. This approach integrates an embedded search procedure to overcome one of the weaknesses of metaheuristic scheduling methods of setting initial dates for task processing and is especially suited for highly nonlinear objective functions as in this case. A general structure of the steelmaking and continuous casting production system is consider with an arbitrary number of machines at each stage, with production of several steel grades and types (e.g. slabs and billets). Technological constraints such as continuous casting between jobs (batches) and in process time of liquid steel are included. For illustration purposes, a real sized problem is solve.

Keywords: Integration of metaheuristics · Genetic algorithm
Evolution strategies · Fuzzy inference · Steel continuous casting

1 Introduction

1.1 A Steelmaking and Continuous Casting Scheduling Problem (SCCSP)

The multistage batch production system considered in this paper is a generalization of one of the most important production subsystem of an integrated steel plant. The steel production process, including steel making and continuous casting (SCC) is usually the bottleneck in steel production [1], because its production capacity is generally lower than that of hot and cold rolling stages. Therefore, effective planning and scheduling at the steel making stages is of great importance to improve the complete production system [2].

© Springer International Publishing AG, part of Springer Nature 2018
K. Sim and P. Kaufmann (Eds.): EvoApplications 2018, LNCS 10784, pp. 561–577, 2018.
https://doi.org/10.1007/978-3-319-77538-8_39

In the steel making process, the casting stage is critical, because a certain number of jobs (charges) cast continuously on the corresponding casting machine. Any interruption at this stage causes a setup of the machine (casting machine setups are very costly) and may generate scrap from the jobs of liquid steel coming out of the converter, so that coordination at the steel making stages (i.e. between converter and casting machine) is crucial for the plant efficiency.

This paper deals with the scheduling problem of the steelmaking and continuous casting stages within an integrated steel manufacturing plant (see Fig. 1). The complete planning and scheduling process of the SCC phase consists of determining the cast sequences and its schedules to run continuously on the casting machines, based on customer requirements.

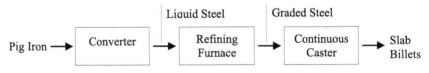

Fig. 1. Steelmaking and continuous casting.

In most cases, one assume that jobs begin processing at all machines as soon as possible. This approach can be valid in almost all of the scheduling problems, but not so in the steelmaking and continuous casting production system (see Fig. 2).

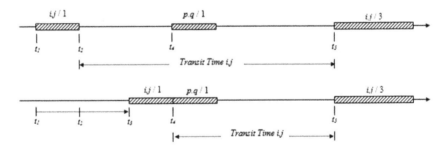

Fig. 2. Job start time at the converter.

In the first diagram of Fig. 2, job $i.j$ (j-th job of production order i) starts at the converter (stage 1) as soon as possible at t_1 (with ending at time t_2) and at the casting machine (stage 3) in t_5, so its transit time is $T_{ij} = t_5 - t_2$. This transit time may be too large so that maximum allowable transit time exceeded. This situation can be avoided if start time at the converter of job $i.j$ is delayed to time t_3 (with ending at time t_4), so the transit time for job $i.j$ is now $T_{ij} = t_5 - t_4$ which is clearly less than the first one. However, delaying a job at the converter in order to meet transit time constraints is limited by the start time of the subsequent job. In Fig. 2, the start time at stage 1 of job $i.j$ cannot be delayed beyond time t_3, because its ending time cannot be later than the start time of job $p.q$ on the same converter.

The question whether job $p.q$ can also be delayed is connected with the slack time of job $p.q$. It is crucial for obtaining good quality schedules to determine how much time a job must or can be delayed at the converter, taken into account the start times of the following jobs on the same converter.

The scheduling problem is defined as the determination of the sequence in which the jobs are to be processed at the converter so that the continuity constraints and the transit times (in process time) constraints are met. The main problem is to decide when and in which order to process the jobs at the converter, to meet the continuity constraints at the casting machines for all production orders (or at least, to meet these constraints to a high degree). Figure 3 shows a general configuration for the SCC system considered in this paper, a three stages system with an arbitrary number of converters and refining furnaces at stage 1 and 2 respectively and an arbitrary number of types of casting machines (e.g. slabs, billets, etc.) with an arbitrary number of machines within a type at stage 3. Without loss of generality, it is possible to include more than one intermediate stages [3].

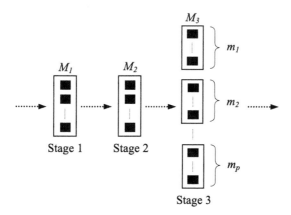

Fig. 3. General structure of the SCC system [3].

The SCC production planning and scheduling problems are recognized as one of the most difficult industrial planning and scheduling problems (Tang and Wang 2008) [2]. Unlike for other manufacturing systems, the SCCSP must consider special process constraints, products are processed and handled in charges of liquid material at high temperatures and then transformed into solid pieces, under extremely strict requirements on material flow continuity and flow times.

Several approaches have been applied to solve this problem, from mathematical programming and related optimization techniques have been developed by [1, 3–9], and combining mathematical programming with heuristics [10]. Meta-heuristic procedures are developed by [3, 11, 12]. The re-scheduling and dynamic scheduling problem are addressed by [13–15]. Managing schedule disturbances is called as repair actions which can be applied in a static way once a schedule is generated and before execution [3] or dynamically (re-scheduling) once the schedule is in execution.

2   Metaheuristic Approach for the SCCSP

The hybrid metaheuristic approach for the SCCSP addressed [3] is a *genetic algorithm* with objective **function** that controls *discontinuities* and *transit times* by means of a *fuzzy rule inference system*, which is hybridize with an *evolution strategy* algorithm to optimize processing start times at converters.

The input to the scheduling problem is the set Ω of N production orders that we assume to be given by a short term planning system: $\Omega = \{1, ..., N\}$. These production orders are pre assigned in a given order to casting machines (there is possible that these machines can be of different type). The jobs within a production order must be processed continuously on the same casting machine; between consecutive orders on a given casting machines normally setup times exist.

2.1   Genetic Algorithm

The main decision using genetic algorithms is how to model the structure of population individuals, called *chromosome*. The chromosome represents a feasible solution, it is the solution itself or it is a structure from which a unique solution is derived. Normally in production scheduling problems, an individual is a representation of jobs (e.g. a permutation of jobs) with their characteristics. So, in a scheduling problem one individual represents a feasible schedule of the problem under study.

The chromosome of the genetic algorithm is defined as a sequence of n jobs ($n = n_1 + n_2 + ... + n_N$), i.e. the number of genes of the chromosome is n, which represent the total number of jobs to be processed. The genes are associated with the casting machine in which the corresponding job must be processed. The genes (jobs) associated with a production order that is to be produced on casting machine 1 are set to 1, and those genes (jobs) associated with a production order that is to be produced on casting machine 2 are set to 2, and so on.

The order of jobs in the chromosome operates as a *dispatching rule* at the converters, i.e., the order in which the jobs initiate their processing is given by the order stated on the chromosome (jobs are assigned to a machine as soon as possible when the machine becomes available).

The example shown in Table 1 considers a set of 5 production orders ($N = 5$ and $\Omega = \{1, 2, 3, 4, 5\}$) with $n_1 = 5$, $n_2 = 4$, $n_3 = 4$, $n_4 = 3$ and $n_5 = 6$ jobs that must be processed in a system with 3 casting machines.

Production orders 1 and 2 must be processed on casting machine 1, production orders 3 and 4 must be processed on casting machine 2, and production order 5 must be processed on casting machine 3.

Table 1. Example of production orders for chromosome illustration.

Order i	1	2	3	4	5
n_i	5	4	4	3	6
p	1	1	2	2	3

The number of genes the chromosome will have is $n = 22$, with 9 times the value 1, 7 times the value 2 and 6 times the value 3. An individual (instance with specific values on each gene of the chromosome) is shown in Fig. 4, which shows the relation between gene value and jobs position in the sequence of production orders 1, 2 and 5.

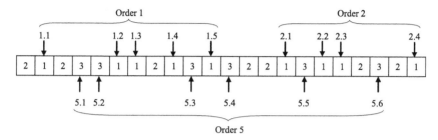

Fig. 4. Structure of the chromosome.

Crossover Operator. The crossover operator is one adapted in the sense of the OX operator, which generates two children by interchanging information of two parents. A randomly determined cut position determines a first and a second part of each parent. The children are generated by selecting the first part of one parent and preserving the relative order of elements from the other parent.

Mutation Operator. Three (classical) mutation operators are proposed to be used in this application. The *exchange or swap* mutation operator, the *shift* mutation operator and the *inversion* mutation operator.

Schedule Quality. The objective function considers two main objectives of the scheduling problem under study, to meet the continuity constraints and to avoid too large jobs transit times (see Sect. 4).

Start Time Determination. Assuming d the average time delay per job (this can be calculated if one assume that all jobs initiate processing as soon as possible at converters) the initial delay at the converter for each job will be generated randomly from the uniform distribution in the interval $[0, 2d]$. The chromosome will now be associated with an array of the same dimension of random numbers, so that the corresponding job of gene k in the chromosome will have a delay equal to the value of position k in the array of delays (see Fig. 5).

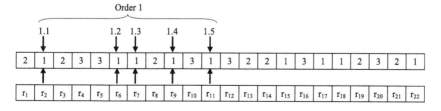

Fig. 5. Individual for the evolution strategy.

In Fig. 5 the connection between job delay and job is made through the chromosome. The first 1 in the chromosome is the first job processed on casting machine 1, which correspond to job 1.1 (see Fig. 3). Since this job is associated with gene 2, a delay of r_2 time units is determined for job 1.1 at stage 1; for jobs 1.2, 1.3, 1.4 and 1.5 delays of r_6, r_7, r_9 and r_{11} time units are respectively determined.

3 Evolution Strategies to Optimize Initial Processing Times

One of the weaknesses of most metaheuristics applied to scheduling problems is the job starting time setting. In most cases, the assumption that jobs begin processing at all machines as soon as possible is made. This approach is not valid in this case where casting continuity requirements and limited job transit times between the processing finish time at the converter and processing start time at the casting machine are mandatory.

There is not much literature on applications of metaheuristics in scheduling problems with specific job start times determination [16], and the approach to be used seems to be highly problem dependent.

3.1 Evolution Strategies

As in all population based optimization procedures, the individuals of the populations in Evolution Strategies are solutions (or representations from which a unique solution is obtained) of the problem. A fitness function (a measure of the quality of the corresponding solution) evaluates the individuals. The evolution of populations is done by *recombining* and *mutating* individuals and they usually used an elitist replacement.

The evolution strategies performs the optimization by modeling the evolution of populations in a similar way as genetic algorithms does, recombining and mutating the individuals, but the construction of the population across the evolution process is different. They enlarge the population of a generation and then apply a selection process taking the best members up to the original population size [17].

3.2 Optimization of Start Times

Once the start times are determined, an optimization process based on evolution strategies to optimize start times is considered. The proposed $(\mu + \lambda)$ – ES evolution strategy approach used to optimize the delay times before a job begins processing at converter takes the chromosome definition as an array of random delay times. Figure 6 shows the chromosome structure with n (total number of jobs) random numbers generated from the $[0, 2 \cdot d]$ interval for the $(\mu + \lambda)$ – ES optimization process.

r_1	r_2	r_3	...	r_j	...	r_n

Fig. 6. Chromosome structure for the $(\mu + \lambda)$ – ES individuals.

The *evolution strategies metaphor* performs the optimization by modeling the evolution process of populations in a similar way as the genetic algorithms do, recombining and mutating the individuals of the population, but the construction of the population across the evolution process is different. The $(\mu + \lambda) - ES$ evolution strategy constructs a population of μ individuals, in each generation the population is increased by λ individuals according to the evolution strategies metaphor, and then the population is reduced to the best μ individuals from the $(\mu + \lambda)$ sized transition population. The initial population (P_0) is generated randomly, i.e., for each of the μ individuals the n genes are randomly generated from the $[0, 2 \cdot d]$ interval. Because the embedding of the evolution strategy algorithm into the genetic algorithm, its objective function is taken from the genetic algorithm.

Genetic Operators for the Evolution Strategy. The proposed recombination (crossover) operator is one of the classical operators proposed for evolution strategies. The operator produces one offspring (child) by taking randomly the genetic information of one of two parents. With equal probability (0.5) the offspring takes the information of parent 1 or parent 2, i.e. based on a random binary vector, gene i is taken from parent 1 if and only if position i of the binary vector has the value 1, otherwise the offspring takes the information from parent 2. The recombination of $r_1 = (r_{11}, r_{12}, ..., r_{1n})$ and $r_2 = (r_{21}, r_{22}, ..., r_{2n})$ results in $r = (r_1, r_2, ..., r_n)$, where $r_j = v_j r_{1j} + (1 - v_j) r_{2j}$ with $v_j \in \{0, 1\}$ with equal propability.

For example, consider the parent p_1 and p_2, whose genes was generated from the interval $[0, 60]$ and assume that the binary vector $v = 1\ 0\ 1\ 1\ 0\ 1\ 0\ 1$ was randomly generated: $p_1 = \mathbf{23}\ 52\ \mathbf{40}\ \mathbf{31}\ 7\ \mathbf{28}\ 43\ \mathbf{17}$ and $p_2 = 42\ \mathbf{39}\ 53\ 12\ \mathbf{19}\ 5\ \mathbf{27}\ 58$. The offspring (child) c takes the information of first position from p_1 (position 1 of vector v has the value 1), the information of second position from p_2 (position 2 of vector v has the value 0) and so on to becomes: $c = 23\ 39\ 40\ 31\ 19\ 28\ 27\ 17$.

The selected mutation operator is the classical mutation operator proposed for the evolution strategies. The mutation operator randomly changes the value of each gene by adding a randomly generated perturbation (positive or negative): the n – dimensional individuals $r = (r_1, r_2, ..., r_n)$ are mutated in the form $r^{t+1} \leftarrow r^t + \varepsilon$ where $\varepsilon \sim U(-\sigma, \sigma)$ with $\sigma = (\sigma_1, \sigma_2, ..., \sigma_n)$ is a vector of independent uniformly distributed random variables. The setting of the mutation step (σ_j) is crucial for the optimization process because the lower the mutation step the higher the number of iterations needed, and the higher the mutation step the lower the precision of the approximation to the optimum.

The random variation $\varepsilon \sim N(0, \sigma^2)$ of the individuals in the original definition of the *evolution strategies* is normally distributed. In this application the random variation (perturbation) for each delay time is considered uniformly distributed in the $[-\sigma, \sigma]$ interval, where σ represents the maximal perturbation step that can be applied to a given start time.

For example, consider the parent $p: = 23\ 52\ 40\ 31\ 7\ 28\ 43\ 17$. Assuming that the perturbation vector: $[1\text{-}3\ 0\ 5\ \text{-}1\ 3\text{-}4\ 2]$ is generated randomly from the $[-5, 5]$ interval the offspring (children) c results: $c = 24\ 49\ 40\ 36\ 6\ 31\ 39\ 19$.

3.3   Integration of the Evolution Strategy into the Genetic Algorithm

In the evaluation step of the genetic algorithm, for each individual of the population an optimization process is performed to determine the best possible delays, i.e., the evolution *strategy* optimization process searches for the combination of delay times for optimum objective function values, keeping the sequence of jobs from the individual of the genetic algorithm population fixed. Figure 7 shows the integration of the optimization process of the evolution strategy into the genetic algorithm. For each individual x_{it} of the t-th population P_t of the genetic algorithm, the evolution strategy performs an optimization process. For a fixed individual x_{it}, i.e., a fixed jobs sequences and machine assignments, the evolution strategy searches for the best delay times at converters. This means that at the end of this search process, the individual x_{it} has got delay times for the jobs at stage 1 with the best value of the objective function of the scheduling problem founded.

GA population $P_t = \{ x_{it} / i = 1, \dots, Np \} / t = 1, \dots, N_g$

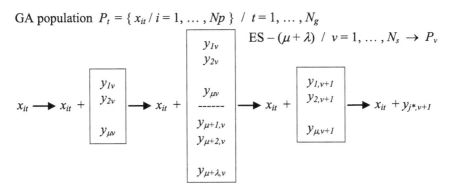

Fig. 7. Integration of the $(\mu + \lambda) - ES$ into the genetic algorithm.

Figure 6 shows how in each generation t (of a total of N_g generations) of the genetic algorithm, each individual x_{it} of the population P_t is optimized by the evolution strategy algorithm running over N_s generations. At each generation v of the evolution strategy, the incoming population P_{v-1} of size μ is enlarged by λ individuals using pair wise recombination followed by mutation and subsequently reduced to its size selecting the best μ individuals.

The optimized timing determined by the evolution strategy is now available for the fitness evaluation performed by the genetic algorithm. Furthermore, when the genetic algorithm produces its final optimization results these results are already associated with an optimized timing.

On one hand, one expects that the integration of the evolution strategy into the optimization process of the genetic algorithm to produce better solutions, on the other hand, more computational effort is required. Therefore, a tradeoff between solution quality and computational effort must be made. Since the evolution strategy has to be run for every individual of the population of the genetic algorithm the effort for each of these runs must be restricted by evaluating only a small population over a small number of generations.

4   Schedule Quality Evaluation by Means of Fuzzy Inference

4.1   Continuity Evaluation

Discontinuities occur when in a sequence of jobs that belong to the same production order a casting machine schedule shows at least one pair of jobs where the start time of one job is strictly greater than the finish time of the previous job on a casting machine. Figure 8 shows some cases that can occur.

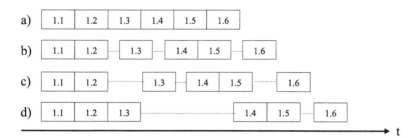

Fig. 8.   Continuity of sequences at the casting machine.

In case (a) of Fig. 8 the proposed schedule shows no discontinuities, i.e. this is the ideal case, while case (b) shows three low discontinuities, which probably can be absorbed during execution of the production program. Case (c) however, also presents three discontinuities but it is not clear whether the first and third discontinuity can be absorbed during execution. Finally, case (d) shows a sequence with two discontinuities, the first of them is clearly a discontinuity that cannot be compensated during execution of the production program. It is clear that the schedule evaluation of Fig. 8, based on the continuity characteristic will go from case (a) with a perfect evaluation, through case (d) with the worst evaluation.

Schedules such as case (a) in Fig. 8 must correspond with the maximum degree to any concept of *good continuity*. Case (d) must correspond with a very low degree (maybe the lowest) of any concept of *good continuity*. The evaluation of cases (b) and (c) in Fig. 7 must be somewhere between the evaluation of cases (a) and (d), but with better evaluation for case (b) than for case (c). It is also important to note, that trying to "average" in some way the discontinuities in case (d) maybe not a good decision. Once a large discontinuity appears, it is clear that it will be not feasible to produce the whole sequence in this way.

Let p_{ijm} be the processing time of job $i.j$ at the casting machine, the absolute discontinuity prior to begin the process of job $i.j$ at this stage is $[x_{ijm} - (x_{i,j-1,m} + p_{i,j-1,m})]$, where x_{ijm} is the casting start time of job $i.j$. Then the discontinuity is defined as the fraction between the absolute discontinuity and the process time of job $j-1$ at the casting machine, i.e., $D_{ij} = [x_{ijm} - (x_{i,j-1,m} + p_{i,J-1,m})]/p_{i,j-1,m}$. If $D_{ij} = 0$ no discontinuity between job $j-1$ and job j of production order i exist; if $D_{ij} > 0$ one must distinguish the cases when D_{ij} take values in a neigborhood of 0, i.e., $D_{ij} \in (0, c]$, or when D_{ij} take values far away from 0, i.e., $D_{ij} \in (c, \infty)$. In the first case, the discontinuity can be regarded as a not so strong discontinuity, and in the second case as strong to very strong discontinuity. Note that $D_{i1} = 0$ for all $i = 1, \ldots, N$, because in any production order the first job does not have discontinuity.

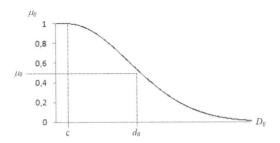

Fig. 9. Membership function of fuzzy set "good job continuity".

Let D_{ij} be the discontinuity of job $i.j$ associated to the universe of a *fuzzy set "good job continuity"* defined through a Gaussian membership function of the form $\mu_{ij}(x) = e^{-k\,(x-c)^2}$ for $x \in [c, \infty)$ and $\mu_{ij}(x) = 1$ for $x \in [0, c]$, where k is a constant that must be adjusted. The constant c establishes the interval in which discontinuities are considered as *"good job continuity"* with degree 1, and the constant k establishes the relationship between the value of a discontinuity d_0 and it desired degree μ_0 given by the user (see Fig. 9).

The continuity associated with a global measure of schedule continuity is defined as the variable *Continuity* = $min\{\mu_{ij} / i = 1, \ldots, N; j(i) = 2, \ldots, n_i \}$, i.e. the evaluation of the schedule based on continuities is equal to the worst membership degree of *"good job continuity"* of all jobs.

The linguistic variable *Continuity* represents the degree to which the continuity constraints are met: *low*, *medium* and *high*, where $\mu_{Continuity}$ represents the membership function of the terms of the linguistic variable *Continuity* (see Fig. 10).

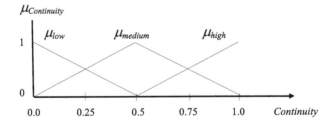

Fig. 10. Linguistic variable continuity.

4.2   Transit Time Evaluation

Let T_{ij} be the transit time, i.e., the time interval between finish time at the converter and start time at the casting machine of job $i.j$. Let T_{min} be the minimal possible transit time of job $i.j$, i.e. the sum of processing and transfer times out from converter to casting. The difference $Slack_{ij} = T_{ij} - T_{min}$ represents the slack time of job $i.j$ and the lower this difference is, the more it is associated with a *"good job transit time"*. If $T_{ij} = T_{min}$ then job $i.j$ has no unnecessary waits which is apparently the ideal case. Since not every transit time above the minimum transit time is equally bad, values of $T_{ij} > T_{min}$ must distinguish cases when T_{ij} take values in a neigborhood of T_{min}, i.e., $T_{ij} \in (T_{min}, c]$, or when T_{ij} take values far away from T_{min}, i.e., $T_{ij} \in (c, \infty)$. In the first case, transit times can be accepted as relatively good transit times, and in the second case transit times can be considered as increasingly bad transit times.

The membership function for the fuzzy set *"good job transit time"* is defined by a Gaussian membership function of the form $\mu_{ij}(x) = e^{-k\ (x-c)^2}$ for $x \in [c, \infty)$ and $\mu_{ij}(x) = 1$ for $x \in [0, c]$, where k is a constant to be adjusted. The constant c defines the interval in which transit times are considered *good (ideal) transit times* values with membership degree 1 to the concept of *"good job transit time"*, and the constant k establishes the relationship between the value of a transit time value T_0 and it desired degree μ_0 given by the user (see Fig. 11).

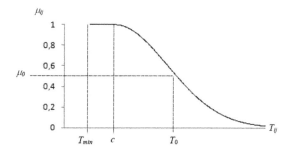

Fig. 11. Membership function of fuzzy set "good job transit time".

The transit time associated with a global measure is defined as the variable $Transit = min\{\mu_{ij}/i = 1, ..., N; j(i) = 1, ..., n_i\}$, i.e. the evaluation of the schedule based on transit times is equal to the worst degree of *good transit time* of any job.

The linguistic variable *Transit* represents the degree to which the transit constraints are met: *low*, *medium* and *high*, where $\mu_{Transit}$ represents the membership function of the terms of the linguistic variable *Transit* showed in Fig. 12.

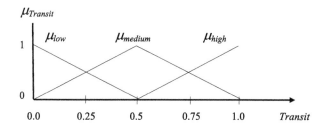

Fig. 12. Linguistic variable Transit.

4.3   Schedule Quality Evaluation

The linguistic variable *Schedule* represents the quality of the evaluated schedule: *low*, *medium* and *high*. Figure 13 shows the membership function of the terms for this variable, where $\mu_{Schedule}$ represents the membership function of the terms of the linguistic variable *Schedule*. Good, middle and bad schedule qualities are associated to, respectively, values near 1, 0.5 and 0.

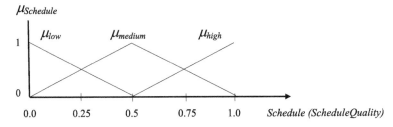

Fig. 13. Linguistic variable Schedule.

The Inference Process. The inference process is defined as *if – then* rules [18] taking into account all possible combinations of the three terms of the linguistic variables *Continuity* and *Transit* modeled with the *min (and)* operator as aggregation in the *if* statement of the rule and with the *max (or)* operator as aggregation in the *then* statements. The inference process is summarized in Table 2.

Table 2. Inference process for schedule evaluation.

		Transit		
		low	medium	high
	low	low	low	medium
Continuity	medium	low	medium	medium
	high	medium	medium	high

The fuzzy sets of the terms of the linguistic variables *Continuity*, *Transit* and *Schedule* are modeled as triangular fuzzy sets, widely used in automatic control [19]. The way in which the genetic algorithm evaluates using the proposed fuzzy inference system in his optimization process, is automatic without human intervention.

Due to its computational efficiency and the ability to generate the extreme values of the response (principally the value *Schedule* = 1.0) the classical and widely used center of maxima (CoM) method is selected for the *defuzzyfication* process. Figure 14 shows the complete response surface of the inference process for linguistic variable *Schedule* (*Schedule Quality*).

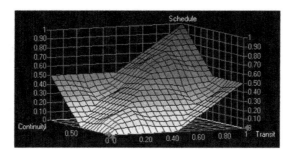

Fig. 14. Response surface for schedule (schedule quality) (with *fuzzy*TECH v5.7)

5 Results with a Real Size Problem

The whole approach is illustrated on a SCCSP of real size (similar to [1, 4–7, 20]), with two converters, three refining furnaces at stage 2 and two types of casting machines each with one machine. Table 3 shows the details of the production orders, which are processed beginning with production order 1 on casting machine 1 (type 1) and beginning with the production order 4 on casting machine 2 (type 2).

Table 3. Description of production orders.

Order	n_i	p	Setup	p_{ij1}	p_{ij2}	p_{ij3}
1	14	1	0	45	30	65
2	6	1	90	45	30	95
3	8	1	60	45	30	85
4	5	2	0	45	30	50
5	5	2	60	45	30	50
6	8	2	60	45	30	60
7	6	2	60	45	30	50
8	9	2	60	45	30	55

Transfer times between converter and furnaces and between furnaces and casting machines are assumed to be 25 and 5 min respectively. The maximum allowed transit time is assumed to be the same for all jobs (MT = 180 min). Therefore, the minimum possible transit time for any job is Tmin = 60 min.

Only discontinuities equal to 0 are regarded as ideal, i.e., only they belong to the concept of "*good job continuity*" with degree 1 ($c = 0$). To define the slope of the membership function we select the discontinuity $d_0 = 0.5$ to be associated with degree 0.5 to the concept "*good job continuity*" ($\mu_0 = 0.5$ and $d_0 = 0.5$). A value of $D_{ij} = 0.5$ means that a discontinuity of half (total) previous job processing time is considered to be medium. Of course, in a real situation such a discontinuity will not be desirable, but this parameter setting is due to algorithmic reasons, it is needed to drive the search process in the early phase of the genetic algorithm when all solutions are more or less of bad quality and not acceptable in practice.

Transit times between 60 and 90 min belong to the concept "*good job transit time*" with degree 1, i.e., transit times of up to 30 min more than the minimum transit time are considered as ideal transit times, higher transit times are associated with degrees lower than 1. A transit time equal to the maximum allowable transit time of 180 min is associated with a degree of 0.5 ($c = 90$, $\mu_0 = 0.5$ and $T_0 = 180$). Although solutions with more than 180 min of transit time are not allowed in the real situation they are not excluded from the search process. Again, this parameter setting is done for algorithmic purposes to assure a deep search process of the implemented genetic algorithm.

The *genetic algorithm* used following parameter values: $N_p = 80$ (population size), $p_c = 0.8$ (crossover probability), $p_m = 0.05$ (mutation probability) and $N_g = 120$ (number of generations). Initial delays are generated from the interval [0, 60] ($d \sim 30$) and the *makespan* lower bound is $C_{LB} = 2415$ which means that the production of the planned orders covers a time horizon of at least 40 h (approximately two days with 3 production shifts of 8 h per day). The *evolution strategy* used following parameter values: $\mu = 20$ ($\lambda = \mu$), $N_e = 30$ (number of generations) and $\sigma = 3$.

Tables 4 and 5 shows the five best solutions found. The best value of the objective function (see Table 4) is *Schedule* = 0.900480, with individual evaluations of the linguistic variables *Continuity* of $\mu_{Continuity} = 0.925875$ and *Transit* of $\mu_{Transit} = 0.900480$ obtained in generation 103. The *makespan* value results $C_{max} = 2425$ min. The value of $\mu_{Continuity} = 0.925875 < 1$ indicates that some discontinuities exist, but all of them are very close to 0. The maximum discontinuity is *MaxDisc* = 0.166667 (16.67% of the previous job casting time with absolute value of *aDisc* = 10 min) and there are 4 discontinuities (*nDisc* = 4).

Concerning the transit times (see Table 5), the value of $\mu_{Transit} = 0.900480 > 0.5$ indicates that no job has transit time over the maximum allowed transit time (*MT* = 180), and all of them are very close to the upper threshold for ideal transit time of 90 min. The maximum observed transit time is 125 min, far from the maximum allowed (*MT* = 180) min. Therefore, no job with transit time over the maximum allowed exists, with 57.38% of the jobs with ideal transit times less or equal than 90 min and 36.07% of the jobs have transit times between 90 and 120 min.

Table 4. Best solutions (objective and continuity).

Solution	t	Schedule	C_{max}	$\mu_{Continuity}$	$\mu_{Transit}$	maxDisc	aDisc	nDisc
1	103	0.900480	2425	0.925875	0.900480	0.166667	10	4
2	83	0.895025	2432	0.895025	0.895025	0.200000	11	9
3	117	0.895025	2443	0.911021	0.895025	0.183333	11	10
4	118	0.889451	2460	0.895025	0.889451	0.200000	13	11
5	118	0.889451	2444	0.915043	0.889451	0.178947	17	10

Table 5. Best solutions (transit).

Solution	[60–90]	(90–120]	(120–180]	maxT	T_{avg}
1	35/57.38%	22/36.07%	4/6.56%	125	88.97
2	40/65.57%	18/29.51%	3/4.92%	126	83.51
3	38/62.30%	18/29.51%	5/8.20%	126	82.52
4	34/55.74%	20/32.79%	7/11.48%	127	87.05
5	35/57.38%	19/31.15%	7/11.48%	127	86.30

Figure 15 shows graphically the evolution of the fitness function *Schedule* and the evolution of the population quality measured as the average of schedule evaluation, through the generations. These curves are in agreement with the expected evolution of fitness functions and population quality in genetic algorithms.

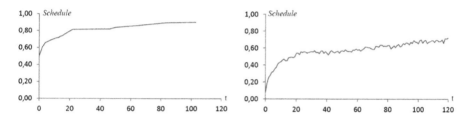

Fig. 15. Evolution of best schedule value and population quality.

The complete schedule (not presented here) obtained with the algorithm leads to a global assessment of the schedule quality. The best solution does not strictly satisfy all constraints since there are four discontinuities, but these discontinuities can be leveled out during production execution or one can delaying the cast start of some production orders; also during the cast of jobs it is possible to slow down the casting speed slightly eliminating this discontinuities.

The hybridized genetic algorithm with embedded evolution strategies and fuzzy inference system was programmed in C/C++ programming language and run on an Intel Core i7 – 3667U CPU, 2.0 GHz computer with 8 GB RAM (64 bits Windows 10 Pro). The illustrated problem was solved in approximately 5 min CPU time.

6 Conclusions

A hybridized metaheuristic approach to solve the SCCSP is presented. A *genetic algorithm* controls the job assignment to the machines embedded with an *evolution strategy algorithm* to optimize the jobs start times at the converter overcoming the weaknesses of metaheuristic procedures in the determination of task processing start times, especially well suited with complex nonlinear objective functions.

A *fuzzy inference system* evaluates the individuals (schedules) giving an overall assessment of the schedule quality, by controlling discontinuities and transit times throughout the generations.

The evaluation takes into account that discontinuities and transit times beyond the maximum allowed may exist, but to different degrees of acceptance. The algorithm always deliver a set of best solutions in an adequate amount of time. These solutions may be unfeasible but gives the user the flexibility to select the most suitable schedule and to repair it.

References

1. Tang, L., Luh, P., Liu, J., Fang, L.: Steel-making process scheduling using Lagrangian relaxation. Int. J. Prod. Res. **40**(1), 55–70 (2002). https://doi.org/10.1080/00207540110073000
2. Tang, L., Wang, G.: Decision Support system for the batching problems of steelmaking and continuous-casting production. Omega Int. J. Manag. Sci. **36**, 976–991 (2008). https://doi.org/10.1016/j.omega.2007.11.002
3. Salazar, E.: Scheduling Multi-Stage Batch Production Systems with Continuity Constraints – The Steelmaking and Continuous Casting System. Dissertation, RWTH Aachen (2013)
4. Tang, L., Liu, J., Rong, A., Yang, Z.: A mathematical programming model for scheduling steelmaking-continuous casting production. Europ. J. Oper. Res. **120**, 423–435 (2000). https://doi.org/10.1016/S0377-2217(99)00041-7
5. Harjunkoski, I., Grossmann, I.: A decomposition approach for the scheduling of a steel plant production. Comput. Chem. Eng. **25**, 1647–1660 (2001). https://doi.org/10.1016/S0098-1354(01)00729-3
6. Pacciarelli, D., Pranzo, M.: Production scheduling in a steelmaking – continuous casting plant. Comput. Chem. Eng. **28**, 2823–2835 (2004). https://doi.org/10.1016/j.compchemeng.2004.08.031
7. Bellabdaoui, A., Teghem, J.: A mixed-integer linear programming model for the continuous casting planning. Int. J. Prod. Econ. **104**, 260–270 (2006). https://doi.org/10.1016/j.ijpe.2004.10.016
8. Tang, L., Liu, G.: A mathematical programming model and solution for scheduling production orders in Shangai Baoshan Iron and Steel Complex. Eur. J. Oper. Res. **182**, 1453–1468 (2007). https://doi.org/10.1016/j.ejor.2006.09.090
9. Sbihi, A., Bellabdaoui, A., Teghem, J.: Solving mixed-integer linear program with times setup for the steel-continuous casting planning and scheduling problem. Int. J. Prod. Res. **52**(24), 7276–7296 (2014). https://doi.org/10.1080/00207543.2014.919421
10. Missbauer, H., Hauber, W., Stadler, W.: A scheduling system for the steelmaking-continuous casting process – a case study from the steel-making industry. Int. J. Prod. Res. **47**(15), 4147–4172 (2009). https://doi.org/10.1080/00207540801950136
11. Ferretti, I., Zanoni, S., Zavanella, L.: Production – inventory scheduling using ant system metaheuristic. Int. J. Prod. Econ. **104**, 317–326 (2006). https://doi.org/10.1016/j.ijpe.2005.01.008
12. Atighehchian, A., Bijari, M., Tarkesh, H.: A novel hybrid algorithm for scheduling steel-making continuous casting production. Comput. Oper. Res. **36**, 2450–2461 (2009). https://doi.org/10.1016/j.cor.2008.10.010
13. Roy, R., Adesola, B.A., Thornton, S.: Development of a knowledge model for managing schedule disturbance in steel-making. Int. J. Prod. Res. **42**(18), 3975–3994 (2004). https://doi.org/10.1080/00207540410001716453

14. Hou, D.-L., Li, T.-K.: Analysis of random disturbances on shop floor in modern steel production dynamic environment. Procedia Eng. **29**, 663–667 (2012). https://doi.org/10. 1016/j.proeng.2012.01.020
15. Long, J., Zheng, Z., Gao, X.: Dynamic scheduling in steelmaking-continuous casting production for continuous caster breakdown. Int. J. Prod. Res. **55**(11), 3197–3216 (2017). https://doi.org/10.1080/00207543.2016.1268277
16. Abido, M.A., Elazouni, A.M.: Precedence-preserving GAs operators for scheduling problems with activities start times encoding. J. Comput. Civil Eng., 345–356 (2010). https://doi.org/10.1061/(asce)cp.1943-5487.0000039
17. Michalewicz, Z.: Genetic Algorithms + Data Structures = Evolution Programs., 3rd edn. Springer, Heidelberg (1999)
18. Zimmermann, H.-J.: Fuzzy Set Theory – and Applications, 4th edn. Kluwer, Boston (2001)
19. Ross, T.J.: Fuzzy Logic with Engineering Applications, 2nd edn. Wiley, Chichester (2004)
20. Salazar, E.: Sistema de Programación Acerías – Coladas Continuas/CSH. Informe Técnico - IIT/Facultad de Ingeniería, Universidad de Concepón, Chile (2001)

Automatic Generation of Constructive Heuristics for Multiple Types of Combinatorial Optimisation Problems with Grammatical Evolution and Geometric Graphs

Christopher Stone$^{(\boxtimes)}$, Emma Hart, and Ben Paechter

Edinburgh Napier University, Edinburgh, UK
{c.stone,e.hart,b.paechter}@napier.ac.uk

Abstract. In many industrial problem domains, when faced with a combinatorial optimisation problem, a "good enough, quick enough" solution to a problem is often required. Simple heuristics often suffice in this case. However, for many domains, a simple heuristic may not be available, and designing one can require considerable expertise. Noting that a wide variety of problems can be represented as graphs, we describe a system for the automatic generation of constructive heuristics in the form of Python programs by mean of grammatical evolution. The system can be applied seamlessly to different graph-based problem domains, only requiring modification of the fitness function. We demonstrate its effectiveness by generating heuristics for the Travelling Salesman and Multi-Dimensional Knapsack problems. The system is shown to be better or comparable to human-designed heuristics in each domain. The generated heuristics can be used 'out-of-the-box' to provide a solution, or to augment existing hyper-heuristic algorithms with new low-level heuristics.

Keywords: Combinatorial optimisation · Grammatical evolution
Generative hyper-heuristics · Combinatorial geometry

1 Introduction

Combinatorial optimisation (CO) is an extremely active area of research with wide-ranging applications that span from computer science and mathematics to a wide-range of industrially relevant domains such as logistics, biomedical research, scheduling and finance [1].

In order to attempt to find optimal solutions to CO problems, a great deal of research within the bio-inspired meta-heuristic community has focused on developing algorithms that are customised to specific problem domains; this generally involves exploiting unique features of the problem [2], using a specialised representation and tailoring operators to fit the domain. While this is a

© Springer International Publishing AG, part of Springer Nature 2018
K. Sim and P. Kaufmann (Eds.): EvoApplications 2018, LNCS 10784, pp. 578–593, 2018.
https://doi.org/10.1007/978-3-319-77538-8_40

very effective approach, it narrows the applicability of the developed tool and requires considerable expertise on the part of the developer. In response to this, the field of hyper-heuristics has developed rapidly since around 2000 [3], focusing on using 'heuristics to choose heuristics'. The motivation underlying this is the wish to raise the level of generality at which search methodologies can operate, making them more widely applicable and easier to implement. In a typical hyper-heuristic approach, a number of low-level domain-specific heuristics are separated from a high-level selection algorithm by a domain-barrier. The idea is that the user simply needs to replace the low-level heuristics in order to use the method in a different domain. Although this clearly results in greater generality, the methods rely on a suitable set of low-level heuristics. In some domains, such heuristics may not be available, and even if there are existing heuristics, a hyper-heuristic method can often be improved by the addition of new low-level heuristics.

In this paper, we describe an approach for the automatic generation of low-level constructive heuristics. The method can be applied to a wide range of different problem domains, changing only the fitness function. In contrast to classical GP based hyper-heuristic approaches, the same grammar can be used in multiple domains, without requiring a change of terminal or function nodes. The only caveat to this is that the problem's solutions must be able to be represented as a *graph*, i.e. a mathematical structure formed by vertices and edges connecting the vertices. This encompasses a wide spectrum of CO domains, and in fact, various forms of graph theory have been used in the context of combinatorics to model problems in a formal manner. For instance, travelling salesman problems naturally fit planar graphs forming an Hamiltonian path in which the goal is to minimize the total length of all the edges [4]. Scheduling problems can easily be transformed into graph colouring problems, e.g. Nurse-Scheduling [5], Exam Timetabling [6], Job Shop Scheduling [7], Aircraft scheduling, and TV program scheduling [8].

In our approach, problems are treated as geometric objects of arbitrary dimensions encoded as graphs. The items of a problem become vertices that will then be ordered, connected or selected by a heuristic. We generate *constructive* heuristics in the form of Python programs using grammatical evolution [9]. Constructive heuristics are commonly used to rapidly provide a solution in time-critical systems, to initialise solutions for more complex solvers, or in hyper-heuristics as ruin-recreate operators [3]. The grammar used to evolve the programs is exclusively composed of geometric properties and functions that are problem independent. We do not implement problem-specific components, only graph-manipulation techniques. For example we do not provide heuristics that prefer shorter edges in the solution graph of a TSP problem. The system is required to learn that (for example) a suitable heuristic should choose points in the proximity of other points and form short connections while in other instances heuristics should chose points that are further away from each other. We address two questions:

– To what extent is it possible to develop a single generic grammar to produce constructive heuristics for multiple problem domains, assuming those domains are represented as a graph?
– To what extent can the grammar be used to evolve (a) reusable and (b) disposable heuristics in multiple domains?

We evaluate our system in two domains: Travelling Salesman Problem and Multidimensional Knapsack Problem. The system is first trained using synthesised random instances, and then evaluated on well-known benchmarks in each domain. We then compare this to generating a heuristic in response to a single problem instance from each domain. We show that human-competitive results can be obtained in each case, and that the heuristic generator is de-facto cross-domain in the sense that the system can create heuristics for instances of the travelling salesman problem and for the multidimensional knapsack problem. As might be expected, disposable (i.e. instance specific) heuristics outperform reusable ones. However, the reusable heuristics are competitive with human heuristics in the majority of examples tested.

2   Background

Designing any iterative meta-heuristic or hyper-heuristic algorithm needs an encoding (representation) of a solution. This is a central design problem in the development of an algorithm and plays a major role in the efficiency and effectiveness of an algorithm [10]. But while the importance of choosing an appropriate representation is already recognised, we are still far from a complete theory of representations [11]. Many representations can be used to describe a given problem, but all representations must be *complete*, which means that all solutions associated with the problem must be represented in some way by the chosen encoding. Secondly it should be *efficient*. It is important that the move operator that manipulates the solution should be able to do so with minimal time and space complexity [10,12]. At this time there is a wealth of different algorithms that translate the encoded sequence of symbols into a specific metaphorical container, e.g. chromosomes [13], particles [14], or ant's paths [15]. Symbols themselves can be represented as bits, integers, real-values or strings. While these metaphors help in understanding the mechanism of the underlying algorithms, each problem requires a specific translation that takes the elements and variables of an acceptable solution and turns them into one of these containers. In many cases the actual implementation of the solution is identical for a given problem regardless of the semantic chosen to name it. This often obscures the relationship between the different algorithms. As mentioned above, this is a critical element for the success of an algorithm and while literature that provides recommendations on how to approach the problem exists [16,17] it's not always easy to achieve it [18,19]. Furthermore, even if an "appropriate representation" can be defined, then customised operators are then required to obtain high-quality results, and it can often be difficult to abstract generalised principles from successful approaches.

We note that a *graph* is a general structure that can be used to represent a large number of combinatorial domains and therefore represents a reasonably 'general' representation. A graph $G = (V, E)$ consists of a set of objects $V = v_1$, v_2, ...,v_n called vertices and a set of objects $E = e_1$, e_2,...,e_n called edges which are a subset of V. Any object that involves points and connections between them may be called a graph. Configuration of nodes and connections occur in a great diversity of applications. They may represent physical networks, such as electrical circuits, roadways, or organic molecules [20]. They are also used in representing less tangible interactions such as ecosystems, sociological relationships, databases, or in the flow of control in a computer program [21]. Various forms of graph theory have been used in the context of combinatorics to model problems in a formal manner. As noted in the introduction, TSP and scheduling problems naturally form graphs. Graph theoretical approaches have been used to provide insight and basis for models in the area of Operational Research [22]. In [23] Wagner and Neshat measure and manage supply chain vulnerabilities using graph modelling. Graph based descriptions are used in the catalogue of global constraints in an effort to accelerate and improve the areas of constraint programming and related operation research activities [24]. In industrial engineering, graphs are used to model the production planning and control, and assist with the design of the layout of physical facilities [25]. Finally, Graph Theory is used as an abstraction tool in many successful industrial applications, where efficiency is a vital element, such as: Google's page rank [26], Amazon and Netflix recommendation system [27], Drug Discovery [28], General Electric's power distribution system [29] and GSM mobile phone network frequency assignment [30]. While there might be other "generic" representations, this is a first step towards systems in which solvers and problems can be represented in the same way.

The question of constructing more generally applicable solvers is tackled by the *Hyper-heuristics* field, that addresses the issue through creating general purpose solvers that operate on domain-specific low-level heuristics [31]. Unlike meta-heuristic approaches, where the solver navigates the space of possible solutions, hyper-heuristics search in the space of possible heuristics that may be suitable for solving a problem. This can be understood as the idea of looking for good algorithms that can solve a problem instead of looking directly for solutions of the problem [32]. The term *Hyper-Heuristics* covers a variety of methods, classified along two axes according to [3] as *Selection* methodologies or *Generation* methodologies. The latter focus on generating novel low-level heuristics from components of existing heuristics and themselves can be further classified as *constructive* or *pertubative*. The former construct a solution from scratch by adding one element at time and are the focus of our investigation. Typical methods to generate constructive heuristics include Genetic Programming (GP) [33] and Grammatical Evolution (GE) [9]. GP constructs trees that, for example, output a number representing an item priority, e.g. for vehicle routing [34], job-shop scheduling [35], TSP [36]. GE is a form of grammar based genetic programming developed for the automatic generation of programs. Differently from GP, it does not apply the evolutionary process directly to a program but on a variable length genome. A mapping process then turns the genome into a program by following grammar rules specified using Backus Naur Form [9]. This approach ensures the creation of syntactically correct programs that then are executed and their fitness function evaluated. GE has already been applied to construct heuristics for the capacitated vehicle routing problem and for the bin packing problem [37].

3   Methodology

The goal of the paper is to develop a generic heuristic generator that generates heuristics for problems that can be represented as a graph. We choose two domains to illustrate this. The first domain is the NP-hard symmetric TSP which is often formulated as a graph theory problem where given a complete weighted graph the problem is to find the Hamiltonian Cycle with the lowest weight. The second is the Multi-Dimensional Knapsack problem. This is a variant of the standard knapsack problem which often arises in resource allocation [38]. In a simple knapsack, a set of n items each with a weight w_i and value v_i have to be packed in a container of weight capacity W. It is usually formulated as:

Maximise

$$\sum_{i=1}^{n} v_i x_i$$

subject to

$$\sum_{i=1}^{n} w_i x_i < W$$

with $x_i \in \{0,1\}$ and x_i is a boolean vector that describes if the i_{th} object is in the knapsack. In the Multi-Dimensional version, multiple constraints exist and the weights w_i of the object and the capacity W of the knapsack are substituted by a vector of constraints $\overline{w_i}$ and $\overline{W}$. Grammatical Evolution is used to evolve Python programs representing constructive heuristics. We evaluate the system in two ways. First, in terms of its ability to generate *reusable* heuristics, i.e. evolve a heuristic using a training set and apply to an unseen set of problem instances. Secondly, we generate *disposable* heuristics, i.e. a single heuristic is evolved in response to a single instance. In each domain, a set of standard benchmarks is chosen for testing. A separate set of instances for training are synthesised at random.

3.1   Representation

In the proposed system we encode all the properties of the problems into a graph embedded in some arbitrary space. Whenever possible, we convert properties into some spatial concept to which we can associate some arbitrary metric. In the case of the Travelling Salesman Problem, the cities to visit can be trivially encoded as vertices in 2-D Euclidean space. For the knapsack problem we use one vertex for each object, and one vertex for the knapsack. The properties of the vertex can be interpreted as coordinates that determine the location of the vertices in some constraint-profit space. A geometric interpretation of the problem can be intuitively described as follows: when an object is chosen (connected to the knapsack vertex) the knapsack is moved toward the constraints origin. The amount of the motion is equal to the values of the object's vector in constraint space and in the opposite direction in the profit space. The configuration of objects connected to the knapsack that move the knapsack the furthest in profit space without the knapsack crossing the origin in any of its constraint dimensions is the best configuration.

In both cases we construct a solution by ranking candidate vertices and composing a *partial permutation*, defined as a sequence without repetition of the first k vertices taken from a set of n vertices. With $k = n$ in the case of solutions of the travelling salesman problem (equivalent to a classical permutation) and $k < n$ for the knapsack problem. The ranking of the vertices is given by the heuristic generated with grammatical evolution.

3.2 Constructive Heuristics Without Domain Barrier Using GE

Grammatical Evolution is a population based approach to construct sequences of symbols by exploring the space of codon values. The codons are used to chose the production rules, and the possible expansions within one production rule, in a given grammar. The production rules are then used to produce the symbols in the defined language. In our case the language described by the grammar is a subset of the programming language Python. Our implementation builds on top of the Python implementation of Fenton et al. [39]. Their implementation proved to be accessible, straightforward to reuse and is the most recent version of GE. A more detailed description of the algorithm can be found in [39]. The code is also open-source and available on *github*[1]. Implementation specific details are as follows:

Genome. Fenton's implementation uses a linear genome representation that is encoded as a list of integers (codons). Codons are responsible for selecting the symbols in production rules with more than one possible product (branches). The mapping between the genotype and the phenotype is actuated by the use of the modulus operator on the value of the codon, i.e. *Selected node* $= c$ mod n, where c is the integer value of the codon to be mapped and n is the number of options available in the specific production rule.

Mutation. An integer flip at the level of the codons is used. One of the codons that has been used for the phenotype is changed each iteration and substituted with a completely new codon.

Crossover. Variable one-point crossover, where the crossing point between 2 individuals is chosen randomly.

Replacement. Generational replacement strategy with elitism 1, i.e. one genome is guaranteed to stay in the pool on the next generation.

---

[1] https://github.com/PonyGE/PonyGE2.

The heuristics, which are functions, created using grammatical evolution are then used as part of a system for the creation of solutions. Each heuristic assigns a rank or "preference value" to the vertices of a graph. Heuristics are queried by the *rankVertex(v,h)* method in Algorithm 1 where v is the current vertex to be scored and h is the heuristic function that will provide the ranking. As explained in Algorithm 1, the system starts with a set of vertices u yet to be ranked, a set of vertices c that will form the solution chain and a specific heuristic h. In order to construct the solution chain, each unranked vertex is ranked according to the heuristic under consideration; the best ranked vertex is added to the chain. The chain is then used to construct the actual solution: the quality of the solution determines the fitness of the heuristic h. Note this is a very straight forward, greedy approach. This could be improved in future by using more nuanced methods when choosing the vertices after they have been ranked or by ranking only a small subset of the vertices each iteration.

The main difference between solutions of the TSP and the MKP is in how the chain ordered by the heuristic is interpreted in order to construct the solution. In the case of a TSP solution, each successive vertex of the chain is used to describe *the next city to visit*. In the case of MKP, each successive vertex of the chain is used to describe *the next item to be placed in the knapsack*. As shown in Fig. 1 our graphical interpretation of the MKP is different from the classical 0/1 approach that defines which items should be placed in the knapsack. However it is still very intuitive and easy to interpret.

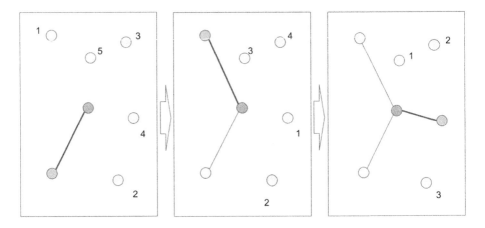

Fig. 1. Constructing a solution for the MKP. Blue node is the knapsack. Green node is the last appended vertex (Color figure online)

3.3   Grammar

The specified grammar is the heart of any Grammatical Evolution approach. Nodes of the grammar can be whole heuristics, mathematical operations, raw numbers and even elements of other grammars. The grammar is typically defined

Algorithm 1. Construct solution chain

$u \leftarrow$ unchosen vertices
$c \leftarrow$ solution chain
$h \leftarrow$ heuristic
while $u > 0$ **do**
    for *each* v in u **do** {Rank unchosen vertices}
        $f_h(v) \leftarrow rankVertex(v, h)$
    end for
    $v^* \leftarrow min(sort(u))$
    $c \leftarrow c + v^*$
    $u \leftarrow u - v^*$
end while
Return c

---

using Backus-Naur Form (BNF), a notation used to express grammars in the form of production rules. Similar to the mechanics used in Genetic Programming, BNF consists of terminal nodes and non-terminal nodes. Terminal nodes are symbols that can appear in the final language and do not have any child nodes. Terminal nodes are also known as leaf nodes, external nodes or outer nodes in other common applications. Non-terminal nodes are nodes that can be expanded into one or more nodes (either terminal or non-terminal). Non-terminal nodes are also known as branch nodes, internal nodes or parent nodes. In BNF notation non-terminal nodes are surrounded by <> brackets. Production rules consist of instructions on how to substitute (or expand) non-terminal nodes, starting from a specifically define non-terminal node, until all the nodes are terminal nodes. Production rules offer the possibility to substitute one non-terminal node with more than one possible choice. The different substitution choices are delimited by the symbol "|". This is a key element of the notation: in Grammatical Evolution the codons of the genome specify exactly which choice should be made on each branch. In the grammar we have specified, the terminal nodes are pieces of python programs that can be composed to create an evaluable python program which can become one of our heuristic ranking functions.

Here, we restrict ourselves to using only basic arithmetic operations and geometric properties of the given graph (either given or derived). One of the goals is to produce a system that is independent from the specific problems we are going to solve, yet reducible to concrete or abstract spacial concepts. This includes, measuring distances over a metric space, counting (vertices), measuring areas, measuring angles, arithmetic operation and basic trigonometry operations. Within the grammar there are a number of terminal nodes that are custom functions and properties that the generator can access:

- *distance(vertex, metric)* returns the distance between the last chosen vertex and the currently evaluated vertex over a specified metric.
- *euclidean* selects the euclidean distance as a metric.
- *cosine distance* selects the cosine similarity as a metric.

- *kd-leg-angle(vertex)* returns the angle that would be formed by connecting the currently evaluated vertex to the previously chosen vertex.
- *estimated graph complexity* returns the difference between the total number of vertices and the number of vertices in the convex hull constructed around the graph. We do not give the program the actual vertices of the hull as this would count as a heuristic and facilitate excessively the algorithm.
- *hull area* returns the area of the convex hull constructed around the graph.
- *longest edge* returns the highest value in the distance matrix.
- *v0* is an optional vertex that can be used as a reference. In the TSP solvers it is used to store the starting point of the tour. In the MKP solvers it is used for the knapsack.
- *chain delta vectorsum* returns the vectorial sum of the vectorial differences of each pair of vertices in the order in which they are in the chain.
- *distance to v0* returns the distances between the currently evaluated vertex and the reference vertex using a specified metric.
- *vec_max* returns the highest value of the given vector.
- *vec_min* returns the smallest value of the given vector.
- *elements_sum* returns the sum over all elements of a vector.

The grammar used to generate heuristics for both TSP and MKP can be seen in Fig. 2 (the rules are the same for both problems and all rules are used).

```
<exp> → <exp><arithmetic_op><exp> |
        protected_division(<exp>,<exp>) |
        root(<exp>) |
        log(<exp>) |
        <c><c>.<c><c> |
        <trig> |
        <graph_function> |
        <info> |
        <constant>
<c> →   0 | 1 | 2 | 3 | 4 | 5 | 6 | 7 | 8 | 9
<arithmetic_op> → + | * | -
<trig> → sine(<exp>) |
        cosine(<exp>) |
        tangent(<exp>)
```

```
<graph_function> → distance(vertex, <metric>) |
        kd_angle_leg(vertex) |
        estimated_graph_complexity |
        hull_area
        longest_edge |
        distance_to_v0(vertex, <metric>) |
        vec_max(<vector>) |
        vec_min(<vector>) |
        elements_sum(<vector>)
<vector> → v0_difference(vertex) |
        chain_delta_vectorsum |
        v0
<metric> → euclidean | cosine distance
<constant> → π | ε
<info>    → chain_length | vertices_num
```

Fig. 2. Complete grammar

4   Experimental Setup

The first experiment generates *reusable* heuristics. A training set is synthesised for each domain. For TSP, a set of cities are generated using a uniform-random distribution. Each instance has 50 cities. For MKP, instances have 20 objects with 10 constraints each. 10 instances are generated for each domain. A uniform random distribution is used to generate the object constraints and normal distributions for the profits of the objects and the constraints of the knapsack. The exact parameters of the synthesisers can be found in Tables 1 and 3. The chosen parameters are not the result of a fine tuning process, but are for the most part default values and in part chosen in such a way to produce outputs within a reasonable time-frame. We generate 10 problems for each problem domain. For MKP, the mean profit of a single object is proportional to the total constraints of the objects and the size of each knapsack is large enough to accommodate, on average, half of the objects in the problem instance. This is to ensure that there are no cases in which it is possible to fit either all the objects in the knapsack or no objects at all, which would make the instance useless for training purposes. As in all learning algorithms, the quality of the training set is important. However, here, we aim to simply give the generator minimal examples of the type of problem it might expect to solve, assuming we have no *a priori* information regarding the specific distributions of points that might be found in future problems. For both the TSP and MKP instances, the fitness of a heuristic on the training set is calculated as the *median* fitness returned from the set of training instances.

For each domain, the best heuristic found is applied to a set of benchmark instances: for TSP. We use 9 instances from TSPlib benchmark [40]; for MKP, 7 instances of the mdknap1 benchmark from the OR-library[2] are used. In the case of the TSP instances, due to the fact that there is a difference of more than 2 orders of magnitude between the synthesised instances and the test problem, we normalise the coordinate of the data to the range 0–100. For TSP, we compare against two human-designed heuristics, *nearest-neighbour(NN)* and *insertion* based on the minimum spanning tree *(MST)* [41]. These heuristics are always applied starting from the same initial city and hence provide deterministic results. For MKP, we compare our generated heuristics against a greedy *depth first search* algorithm [42].

The second experiment generates *disposable* heuristics, i.e. one per instance. For each instance we run GE for 200 iterations with a population of 100 to produce a single heuristic for the specific instance. Both experiments are repeated 20 times and we account for best, median and worse cases for each scenario. The experiments are run on "n1-standard-1" instances of Google Compute Engine. The instances have 1 virtual CPU using 2.3 GHz Intel Xeon E5 v3 (Haswell Architecture) and 3.75 GB of Ram. Scenarios that are run multiple times for statistical validation use multiple independent virtual machines (Table 2).

---

[2] http://people.brunel.ac.uk/mastjjb/jeb/info.html.

Table 1. Resuable heuristics

Parameter	Value
Number of generations	100
Population	100
Mutation	int flip
Crossover Prob.	0.80
Crossover type	one point
Max initial tree	10
Max tree depth	17
Replacement	generational
Tournament size	2

Table 2. Disposable heuristics

Parameter	Value
Generations	200
Population	100
Mutation	int flip
Crossover Prob.	0.80
Crossover type	one point
Max initial tree	10
Max tree depth	17
Replacement	generational
Tournament size	2

Table 3. Parameters of the problem synthesiser

Parameter	Value
Number of cities	50
Cities distribution type	Uniform
Cities distribution range	0–100
Number of objects	20
Number of constraints	10
Object constraints distribution	Uniform
Object constraints range	0–100
Object profit distribution	Normal
Object profit mean	Sum of constraints
Object profit deviation	15
Knapsack constraints distribution	Normal
Knapsack constraints mean	500
Knapsack constraints deviation	100

5   Results and Analysis

Reusable Heuristics: The results in Table 5 and Fig. 3 show a comparison of the best, worse and median fitness of the evolved heuristics on each problem of the TSP benchmark. These are compared to the deterministic values obtained from a single run of the human heuristic. It can be seen that in 5 out of 9 instances the median performance of the evolved heuristics is better than both the simple human heuristics. In all 9 instances at least one evolved heuristic is better than both the human heuristics. From Table 4, we can see that the best evolved heuristics for the MKP outperform the greedy (deterministic) heuristic in 4 out of 7 instances, where in 2 cases the global optima is reached by the best heuristics. The worst performing evolved heuristics are still better than the greedy heuristic in 3 out of 7 instances. The median profit reached by the evolved heuristics appears better in some instances but a statistical analysis using the Wilcoxon rank test highlighted that they are not significantly better and should be considered on par with the human heuristics.

Table 4. Reusable heuristics: multidimensional knapsack problem

Instance	Optima	Worst rand	Median rand	Best rand	Worst greedy	Median greedy	Best greedy	Worst our-H	Median our-H	Best our-H
mknap1-1	3800	100	1700	3100	1200	2700	3800	**1800**	3300	**3800**
mknap1-2	8706.1	1482.1	5059	8687.5	4340.7	6504.8	8650.1	4212.4	7059.8	**8706.1**
mknap1-3	4015	985	2235	2860	1895	3325	3765	**2390**	2480	3725
mknap1-4	6120	1320	3240	5820	2460	3525	5390	**2480**	3020	**5640**
mknap1-5	12400	3770	7770	10340	7590	8990	11550	6855	8150	10510
mknap1-6	10618	4286	6566	9770	7400	8032	10345	7238	7641	9352
mknap1-7	16537	5661	9509	12769	8770	12363	15330	8335	10887	**15668**

Disposable Heuristics: The results in Table 6 show the best and median fitness obtained by evolving a single heuristic per instance. The generator constructs a heuristic that finds the global optima on the simplest instance (oliver30). It reaches fitness within 15% of the global optima in 8 out of 9 instances.

The results in Table 7 show the best and median fitness reached by the generator directly used on each problem of the MKP benchmark. Here, the global optima is found on 3 out of 7 instances, even in the worst run. In 4 out of 7 instances, the global optima is reached by the median performing generator. In one instance the global optima is missed by only 0.24%. Finally the very worst result of all 140 runs on the MKP benchmark is only 3.57% away from the global optima which happens in the hardest instance.

Table 5. Reusable heuristics: TSP

Instance name	Optima	NN	MST	Rand	H-Median	H-Best	H-Worse
att48	10628	43000	43956	162098	**40602**	**36750**	*46396*
berlin52	7542	8868	10404	30290	9196	**8452**	*10515*
ch130	6110	7575	8277	46099	**7501**	**6942**	*8469*
eil101	629	826	846	3434	**803**	**736**	897
eil51	426	521	605	1635	547	**451**	*620*
eil76	538	700	739	2494	**652**	**603**	678
KroA100	21282	26506	27921	171940	26914	**25603**	*32683*
KroB100	22141	29264	28804	170564	30182	**26064**	*32213*
oliver30	423	464	513	1379	474	**449**	499
rd100	7910	10733	11855	55064	**9863**	**9260**	11338

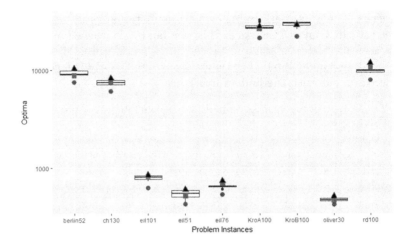

Fig. 3. Reusable Heuristics (TSP): optima (green circles), nearest neighbour (blue squares) and minimum spanning trees (red triangles) (Color figure online)

Table 6. Disposable heuristics (TSP)

Instance name	Optima	Best	Median
berlin52	7542	8212.09	8972.69
ch130	6110	6781.6	7171.57
eil101	629	724.62	775.47
eil51	426	474.19	509.86
eil76	538	592.08	638.08
KroA100	21282	23866.88	26858.24
KroB100	22141	25019.18	27959.35
oliver30	423	**423**	442.56
rd100	7910	8796.43	9369.94

Table 7. Disposable heuristics (MKP)

Instance name	Optima	Best	Median
mknap1-1	3800	**3800**	**3800**
mknap1-2	8706.1	**8706.1**	**8706.1**
mknap1-3	4015	**4015**	**4015**
mknap1-4	6120	**6120**	**6120**
mknap1-5	12400	12370	12355
mknap1-6	10618	10532	10462
mknap1-7	16537	16260	16022.5

6   Conclusion

In this paper, we proposed a representation based on geometric graphs and partial permutations with a method to automatically generate constructive low-level heuristics that are applicable to instances of both the Travelling Salesman Problem and the Multidimensional Knapsack Problem. We have shown that the proposed grammar and representation, operated by Grammatical Evolution, can be used to develop both reusable and disposable heuristics using very few simple examples. The generator can thus be considered "cross-domain". It represents a first step towards developing a generic heuristic generator that can be used across multiple domains with very little modification. The system can be extended to new domains as long as the problem is formulated in such a way to allow the construction of a graph (solution) one edge at a time. The generated heuristics can be used off-the-shelf, or could be combined into a hyper-heuristic framework to provide greater search potential. The same grammar could be further used to generate local-search heuristics to improve constructed solutions. Many improvements are possible including expanding the components of the grammar that currently uses only a fraction of the possible geometric information derivable from a graph, and extensive tuning of the parameters of the approach.

Finally, note that from an industry perspective, it is pertinent to consider the *cost* of generating a new heuristic method to solve a new problem. Evolving a population of heuristics for the TSP, of which only the best is used (but more could be exported and reused), with the chosen provider takes approximately 1.5 h (on average) at a cost of $0.034 per hour: this is $0.051 per run. A statistically validated experiment over 20 runs costs $1.02. Evolving a population of heuristics for the MKP takes only 0.5 h (on average) with a cost per single run of $0.0017 and final cost of approximately $0.34 for a statistically validated experiment.

Code

Together with the paper we provide the source code used to run all the experiments: https://github.com/Stone-2018/Geo-GE-Evostar2018. Furthermore we provide a virtual machine complete with OS (Ubuntu14.04) libraries (Anaconda, Ponyge2) and code of the system and experiments ready for launch. The download links can be found inside the git repository.

References

1. Korte, B., Vygen, J.: Combinatorial Optimization, vol. 21. Springer, Heidelberg (2012). https://doi.org/10.1007/978-3-642-24488-9
2. Rothlauf, F., Goldberg, D.E.: Representations for Genetic and Evolutionary Algorithms. Physica-Verlag, Heidelberg (2002)
3. Burke, E.K., Hyde, M., Kendall, G., Ochoa, G., Özcan, E., Woodward, J.R.: A classification of hyper-heuristic approaches. In: Gendreau, M., Potvin, J.Y. (eds.) Handbook of Metaheuristics. ISOR, vol. 149, pp. 449–468. Springer, Boston (2010). https://doi.org/10.1007/978-1-4419-1665-5_15
4. Biggs, N., Lloyd, E.K., Wilson, R.J.: Graph Theory 1736–1936. Clarendon Press, Oxford (1976)
5. Goodman, M.D., Dowsland, K.A., Thompson, J.M.: A grasp-knapsack hybrid for a nurse-scheduling problem. J. Heuristics **15**(4), 351–379 (2007)
6. Sabar, N., Ayob, M., Qu, R., Kendall, G.: A Graph Coloring Constructive Hyper-Heuristic for Examination Timetabling Problems, cs.nott.ac.uk. http://www.cs.nott.ac.uk/~pszrq/files/APIN11.pdf

7. Kouider, A., Haddadene, H.A., Ourari, S., Oulamara, A.: Mixed integer linear programs and tabu search approach to solve mixed graph coloring for unit-time job shop scheduling. In: 2015 IEEE International Conference on Automation Science and Engineering (CASE), pp. 1177–1181. IEEE, August 2015
8. Pal, M., Pal, A.: Scheduling algorithm to select k optimal programme slots in television channels: a graph theoretic approach, p. 25, May 2014. http://arxiv.org/abs/1405.2199
9. O'Neil, M., Ryan, C.: Grammatical Evolution. In: Grammatical Evolution, pp. 33–47. Springer, Boston (2003). https://doi.org/10.1007/978-1-4615-0447-4_4
10. Talbi, E.G.: Metaheuristics: From Design to Implementation, vol. 74. John Wiley & Sons, Hoboken (2009)
11. Rothlauf, F.: Representations for genetic and evolutionary algorithms. Springer, Heidelberg (2006). https://doi.org/10.1007/3-540-32444-5
12. Gendreau, M., Potvin, J.Y. (eds.): Handbook of Metaheuristics. International Series in Operations Research & Management Science, vol. 146. Springer, Boston (2010). https://doi.org/10.1007/978-1-4419-1665-5
13. Holland, J.: Genetic algorithms. Sci. Am. (1992). http://www.geos.ed.ac.uk/~mscgis/12-13/s1100074/Holland.pdf
14. Kennedy, J.: Particle swarm optimization. In: Encyclopedia of Machine Learning (2011)
15. Dorigo, M., Birattari, M., Stutzle, T.: Ant colony optimization. IEEE Comput. Intell. Mag. 1(4), 28–39 (2006). http://ieeexplore.ieee.org/lpdocs/epic03/wrapper.htm?arnumber=4129846
16. Hertz, A., Widmer, M.: Guidelines for the use of meta-heuristics in combinatorial optimization. Eur. J. Oper. Res. (2003). http://www.sciencedirect.com/science/article/pii/S0377221702008238
17. Talbi, E.: Metaheuristics: From Design to Implementation (2009)
18. Liepins, G.E., Vose, M.D.: Representational issues in genetic optimization. J. Exp. Theor. Artif. Intell. 2(2), 101–115 (1990)
19. O'Neill, M., Vanneschi, L., Gustafson, S., Banzhaf, W.: Open issues in genetic programming. Genet. Program. Evolvable Mach. 11(3–4), 339–363 (2010)
20. Foulds, L.R.: Graph Theory Applications. Springer Science & Business Media, Berlin (2012)
21. Gross, J.L., Yellen, J.: Graph Theory and its Applications. CRC Press, Boca Raton (2005)
22. Gross, J., Yellen, J., Zhang, P.: Handbook of Graph Theory (2013). http://wmich.pure.elsevier.com/en/publications/handbook-of-graph-theory-2
23. Wagner, S.M., Neshat, N.: Assessing the vulnerability of supply chains using graph theory. Int. J. Prod. Econ. 126(1), 121–129 (2010)
24. Beldiceanu, N., Carlsson, M., Rampon, J.X.: Global Constraint Catalog (2005). https://hal.archives-ouvertes.fr/hal-00485396/
25. Seppänen, J., Moore, J.M.: Facilities planning with graph theory. Manag. Sci. 17(4), B-242–B-253 (1970). http://pubsonline.informs.org/doi/abs/10.1287/mnsc.17.4.B242
26. Page, L., Brin, S., Motwani, R., Winograd, T.: The PageRank citation ranking: bringing order to the web (1999). http://ilpubs.stanford.edu:8090/422
27. Bogers, T.: Movie recommendation using random walks over the contextual graph. In: Proceedings of the 2nd International Workshop on Context-Aware (2010). http://ids.csom.umn.edu/faculty/gedas/cars2010/bogers-cars-2010.pdf
28. Amigó, J., Gálvez, J., Villar, V.: A review on molecular topology: applying graph theory to drug discovery and design. Naturwissenschaften 96(7), 749–761 (2009)

29. Elgerd, O., Happ, H.: Electric energy systems theory: an introduction. IEEE Trans. Syst. Man Cybern. (1972)
30. Gamst, A.: Application of graph theoretical methods to GSM radio network planning. In: Circuits and Systems, 1991, IEEE International (1991)
31. Burke, E.K., Gendreau, M., Hyde, M., Kendall, G., Ochoa, G., Özcan, E., Qu, R.: Hyper-heuristics: a survey of the state of the art. J. Oper. Res. Soc. **64**(12), 1695–1724 (2013)
32. Pappa, G., Ochoa, G., Hyde, M., Freitas, A.: Contrasting meta-learning and hyper-heuristic research: the role of evolutionary algorithms. Genet. Program. Evolvable Mach. **15**(1), 3–35 (2014). http://link.springer.com/article/10.1007/s10710-013-9186-9
33. Koza, J.: Genetic programming: on the programming of computers by means of natural selection (1992)
34. Sim, K., Hart, E.: A combined generative and selective hyper-heuristic for the vehicle routing problem. In: Proceedings of the 2016 on Genetic and Evolutionary Computation Conference, pp. 1093–1100. ACM (2016)
35. Hart, E., Sim, K.: A hyper-heuristic ensemble method for static job-shop scheduling. Evol. Comput. **24**(4), 609–635 (2016)
36. Keller, R.E., Poli, R.: Linear genetic programming of parsimonious metaheuristics. In: 2007 IEEE Congress on Evolutionary Computation, pp. 4508–4515. IEEE, September 2007. http://ieeexplore.ieee.org/document/4425062/
37. Sabar, N.R., Ayob, M., Kendall, G., Qu, R.: Grammatical evolution hyper-heuristic for combinatorial optimization problems. IEEE Trans. Evol. Comput. **17**(6), 840–861 (2013)
38. Kellerer, H., Pferschy, U., Pisinger, D.: Introduction to NP-completeness of knapsack problems. In: Knapsack Problems, pp. 483–493. Springer, Heidelberg (2004). https://doi.org/10.1007/978-3-540-24777-7_16
39. Fenton, M., McDermott, J., Fagan, D., Forstenlechner, S., Hemberg, E., O'Neill, M.: PonyGE2. In: Proceedings of the Genetic and Evolutionary Computation Conference Companion on - GECCO 2017, pp. 1194–1201. ACM Press, New York, March 2017. https://doi.org/10.1145/3067695.3082469
40. Reinelt, G.: TSPLIBA traveling salesman problem library. ORSA J. Comput. **3**(4), 376–384 (1991). http://pubsonline.informs.org/doi/abs/10.1287/ijoc.3.4.376
41. Prim, R.C.: Shortest connection networks and some generalizations. Bell Labs Tech. J. **36**(6), 1389–1401 (1957)
42. Knuth, D.E.: The Art of Computer Programming: Sorting and Searching, vol. 3. Pearson Education, Upper Saddle River (1998)

EvoKNOW

Rotation Invariance and Rotated Problems: An Experimental Study on Differential Evolution

Fabio Caraffini[(✉)] and Ferrante Neri

School of Computer Science and Informatics, De Montfort University, Leicester, UK
{fabio.caraffini,fneri}@dmu.ac.uk

Abstract. This paper presents an experimental study on the efficacy of a rotation-invariant Differential Evolution (based on current-to-rand mutation) on a benchmark of test problems in its non-rotated and rotated version. Numerical results show that standard Differential Evolution outperforms rotation-invariant Differential Evolution on the benchmark under consideration for both non-rotated and rotated problems. In other words, the rotation-invariant Differential Evolution does not seem to be more efficient than its standard counterpart to address rotated problems. According to our interpretation, these experimental results show that rotated problems are simply different problems with respect to the non-rotated problems. Furthermore, rotation-invariant Differential Evolution is characterised by its moving operator: it generates an offspring by perturbing all the design variables of a candidate solution at the same time. This logic does not appear to guarantee a better performance on rotated problems.

Keywords: Differential Evolution · Rotational invariant algorithms
Separability · Epistasis · Continuous optimisation

1 Introduction

Modern real-world applications often impose the solution of complex optimisation problems. These problems can be rarely tackled by exact methods since they do not have the hypotheses for their application (see [1]). Thus, general purpose solvers, aka metaheuristics, are a popular alternative to search for an approximate solution to the optimisation problems.

The totality of metaheuristics are not founded on a solid rigorous foundation and thus are not guaranteed to work. Only a small portion of the existing metaheuristics are designed on the basis of a mathematically sound justification, see e.g. [2,3]. For this reason, a rigorous experimentalism plays a fundamental role in metaheuristic optimisation, see [4]. The performance of algorithms gets statistically compared in order to assess the suitability of an algorithm to address a certain problem. Researchers in computer science proposed some test problems, i.e. some artificially built mathematical functions, to be used to test the viability

© Springer International Publishing AG, part of Springer Nature 2018
K. Sim and P. Kaufmann (Eds.): EvoApplications 2018, LNCS 10784, pp. 597–614, 2018.
https://doi.org/10.1007/978-3-319-77538-8_41

of newly proposed algorithms and compare them, in a fair manner, to already existing metaheuristics. An early list of objective functions was proposed in [5] but only a decade later standardised test problems have become a benchmark for testing the performance of optimisation metaheuristics. A famous example of benchmark for numerical optimisation problems has been proposed in [6]. Other more modern benchmarks have been proposed [7,8]. Some benchmarks focus on specific classes of problems such as scalable/large scale problems [9].

When the function landscape possesses a symmetry or when the perturbation of single variables allows easy improvements (this is the case for functions composed of sums, or product of functions applied to each variable separately), an approximate solution of the test problem may be easily achieved by a naive or relatively simple algorithm. Real-world problems can be completely unpredictable since they may be connected to a simulator or an actual experiment [10]. Thus, the problem's rotation is one of the recurring countermeasures that computer scientists have introduced with the intention of making the promising gradient directions hard to find and the overall problem harder to solve. In all the benchmarks since [6], the rotation is achieved by a matrix-vector multiplication where the matrix is a rotation/perturbation matrix and the vector is the candidate solution.

In the same years when rotated test problems became increasingly popular, computer scientists who design algorithms proposed implementation that supposedly solve problems in both cases without and with rotation. In the present article, we will refer to algorithms belonging to this class as *rotation-invariant* algorithms.

Although many algorithms implicitly address potential rotation of the function by detecting and following the direction of the gradient, see e.g. [2], this paper will focus on those studies that explicitly state that algorithms contain a rotation-invariant component. Moreover, this paper focuses on Differential Evolution (DE) frameworks, see e.g. [11,12].

An early version of rotation-invariant DE was proposed in [13] in the context of mechanical engineering design by means of a rotation-invariant mutation. In [14] the Gram-Schmidt orthogonalisation is integrated into the mutation operator. In [15] a rotation-invariant crossover is proposed within a DE framework to address rotated problems. In [16] an adaptive DE with multiple mutations including the rotation-invariant mutation proposed in [13] is presented to solve a diverse benchmark composed of both non-rotated and rotated problems.

The present paper proposes a study on the performance of rotation-invariant DE on a list of problems belonging to a modern benchmark. For each test function, both the non-rotated and rotated versions are considered. The standard DE, with both binomial and exponential crossover [11], and the rotation-invariant mutation present in [13,16] has been tested for all the problems involved in this study.

The remainder of the paper is organised in the following way. Section 2 introduces the notation and briefly outlines what a rotated problem is. Section 3 briefly presents DE and its rotation-invariant versions. Section 4 describes the experiments and displays the results of this study. Section 5 gives the conclusion of this work.

2   Rotated Optimisation Problems

Without a loss of generality, we will refer to the minimization problem of an objective function (a.k.a. fitness) $f(\mathbf{x})$, where the candidate solution $\mathbf{x}$ is a vector of n design variables (or genes) $x_1, x_2, \ldots, x_n$ in an n-dimensional decision space $\mathbf{D}$. Thus, the optimization problem considered in this paper consists of the detection of that solution $\mathbf{x}^* \in \mathbf{D}$ such that $f(\mathbf{x}^*) < f(\mathbf{x})$, and this is valid $\forall \mathbf{x} \in \mathbf{D}$. Array variables are highlighted in bold face throughout this paper.

Rotation is a geometric concept which has a clear meaning in two and three dimensions. Furthermore, while the rotation of an object in the space always has a meaning, the rotation of a function (a fitness landscape) may lead to something that is not a function. Besides this fact, in the n-dimensional case, the rotation of an object (so is the rotation of a fitness landscape) does not have a geometric meaning. However, in algebra, an n-dimensional rotation is interpreted as an extension of the rotation operation of a point through a matrix, see [17].

In other words, if $\mathbf{x}$ is an n-dimensional vector, its rotated vector is

$$\mathbf{x^{rot}} = \mathbf{Qx}$$

where $\mathbf{Q}$ is a rotation matrix. The rotation matrix $\mathbf{Q}$ is an orthogonal matrix, i.e. $\mathbf{Q^T} = \mathbf{Q^{-1}}$, or

$$\mathbf{QQ^T} = \mathbf{Q^TQ} = \mathbf{I}$$

where $\mathbf{Q^T}$ and $\mathbf{Q^{-1}}$ are the transposed and the inverse of the matrix $\mathbf{Q}$, respectively and $\mathbf{I}$ is the identity matrix [17]. From simple linear algebra considerations, we can observe that the determinant $\det(\mathbf{Q})$ is either equal to 1 or to -1, thus, the rotation matrix $\mathbf{Q}$ is non-singular.

In this sense, the rotation of a point/vector in the n-dimensional space can be interpreted as a special case of change of basis. However, since the optimisation process occurs on a static domain $\mathbf{D}$ and thus on a static reference system, the operation $\mathbf{Qx}$ is in practice a systematic replacement of the candidate solution.

In order to clarify the functioning of the rotated problems in modern benchmarks, let us consider a test problem, for example the popular Rastrigin function in n dimensions [6]:

$$f_{Rastr}(\mathbf{x}) = a \cdot n + \sum_{i=1}^{n} \left(x_i^2 + a \cdot \cos\left(2\pi x_i\right) \right)$$

with $a = 10$. The optimisation problem consists of minimising f_{Rastr} in $\mathbf{D} = [-5.12, 5.12]^n$.

The rotated Rastrigin function as in [6, 18, 19] does not mean that the fitness landscape is directly rotated. The rotated Rastrigin function is simulated by systematically perturbing the position of a candidate solution by means of the linear transformation $\mathbf{Qx}$.

For the sake of clarity, every time the objective function of the rotated Rastrigin has to be calculated for the candidate solution $\mathbf{x}$, the two steps in Algorithm 1 are applied [18,19].

Algorithm 1. Calculation of the rotated Rastrigin fitness value

1: input $\mathbf{x}$
2: $\mathbf{x^{rot}} = \mathbf{Qx}$
3: $y = f_{Rastr}\left(\mathbf{x^{rot}}\right)$
4: output y

The same two-step procedure is applied for all rotated problems.

3 Rotation-Invariant Differential Evolution

Differential Evolution (DE) is a popular population-based metaheuristic, see [11,20], based on the perturbation of candidate solution and the selection of the most promising ones. An updated survey on the topic is reported in [21]. DE algorithms work with a population of N_p candidate solutions:

$$\mathbf{x^1}, \mathbf{x^2}, \ldots, \mathbf{x^i}, \ldots, \mathbf{x^{N_P}}.$$

The algorithmic cyclically performs a set of operations. During each cycle, here indicated as generation, each candidate solution $\mathbf{x^i}$ is perturbed by means of a first mechanism, called *mutation* and a second perturbation mechanism called *crossover*. The perturbed individual, namely offspring, is indicated with $\mathbf{x_{off}}$. The fitness of the offspring is then calculated and compared with that of $\mathbf{x^i}$. The result of the comparison is recorded but no replacement occurs before the end of the generation. At the end of the generation each $\mathbf{x^i}$ outperformed by its corresponding offspring $\mathbf{x_{off}}$ is replaced by it.

Algorithm 2 describes the general DE structure.

Over the past twenty years a wealth of DE variants have been proposed, see e.g. [22]. These variants can include various adaptive mechanism e.g. [23–25], multiple crossovers/mutations e.g. [26], and hybridisation at various levels with other algorithms e.g. [27].

The list of all the proposed DE variants is extensive. One of the reasons why so many DE variants have been proposed is that the DE framework is originally a flexible framework that can use several mutation and crossover variants, see [28,29].

The original and most famous mutation scheme is the so called DE/rand/1. This mutation perturbs the individual $\mathbf{x^i}$ without using it directly. The DE/rand/1 mutation randomly samples three candidate solutions from the population: $\mathbf{x^r}$, $\mathbf{x^s}$, and $\mathbf{x^t}$, respectively. Then, the provisional offspring $\mathbf{x'_{off}}$ is calculated by means of the following formula

$$DE/rand/1 : \mathbf{x'_{off}} = \mathbf{x^t} + F\left(\mathbf{x^r} - \mathbf{x^s}\right)$$

Algorithm 2. General Differential Evolution Framework

1: Generate an initial population of Np individuals
2: Calculate the fitness of each solution in population Np
3: **while** termination condition is not met **do**
4:    **for** each $\mathbf{x}^i$ in Np **do**
5:       Generate provisional offspring $\mathbf{x}'_{\text{off}}$ by mutation
6:       Generate offspring $\mathbf{x}_{\text{off}}$ by crossover
7:       Calculate the fitness of $\mathbf{x}_{\text{off}}$
8:       Make a note whether $\mathbf{x}^i$ or $\mathbf{x}_{\text{off}}$ has a better performance
9:    **end for**
10:   **for** each $\mathbf{x}^i$ in Np **do**
11:      Perform all the replacements by choosing the best between parent and offspring
12:   **end for**
13: **end while**

where the scale factor F is a parameter to be set (usually $F > 0$ and $F < 1$ [30,31]). The DE crossover consists of generating the offspring solution $\mathbf{x}_{\text{off}}$ by combining the design variables of $\mathbf{x}'_{\text{off}}$ and those of $\mathbf{x}^i$.

Two popular crossover strategies have been considered in this study (DE frameworks either employ the first or the second). The first, the binomial crossover, consists of the following steps. A design variable index j_{rand} is randomly selected. The corresponding design variable in $\mathbf{x}'_{\text{off}}$ is selected and copied in $\mathbf{x}_{\text{off}}$. For all the other variables, a random number is generated by means of uniform distribution $\mathcal{U}(0,1)$. If this number is equal or less than a parameter Cr (chosen between 0 and 1), the corresponding design variable is copied from $\mathbf{x}'_{\text{off}}$ to $\mathbf{x}_{\text{off}}$. If the generated number is greater than the parameter Cr, the corresponding design variable is copied from $\mathbf{x}_i$ to $\mathbf{x}_{\text{off}}$.
The pseudocode of the binomial crossover is shown in Algorithm 3.

Algorithm 3. Binomial Crossover Between $\mathbf{x}^i$ and $\mathbf{x}^{\text{off}'}$

1: generate an integer random index j_{rand}
2: $x^{off}_{j_{rand}} = x^{off'}_{j_{rand}}$
3: **for** $j = 1 : n$, $j \neq j_{rand}$ **do**
4:   generate a random value h from a uniform distribution $\mathcal{U}(0,1)$
5:   **if** $h \leq Cr$ **then**
6:     $x^{off}_j = x^{off'}_j$
7:   **else**
8:     $x^{off}_j = x^i_j$
9:   **end if**
10: **end for**

The second, the exponential crossover consists of the following steps. Also in this case, the design variable index j_{rand} is randomly selected and the corresponding design variable in $\mathbf{x}'_{\text{off}}$ is selected and copied in $\mathbf{x}_{\text{off}}$. Then, contiguous design variables are copied, one by one, from the provisional offspring $\mathbf{x}'_{\text{off}}$ to the final offspring $\mathbf{x}_{\text{off}}$ until a random number is less than the crossover probability Cr.

Algorithm 4. Exponential Crossover Between $\mathbf{x}^i$ and $\mathbf{x}^{\text{off}'}$

1: $\mathbf{x}^{\text{off}} = \mathbf{x}^i$
2: generate an integer random index j_{rand}
3: $x^{off}_{j_{rand}} = x^{off'}_{j_{rand}}$
4: generate a random value h from a uniform distribution $\mathcal{U}(0,1)$
5: $j = j_{rand} + 1$
6: $k = 1$
7: **while** $h \leq Cr$ AND $k < n$ **do**
8:     $x^{off}_j = x^{off'}_j$
9:     **if** $j == n$ **then**
10:         $j = 1$
11:     **end if**
12:     $k = k + 1$
13:     generate a random value h from a uniform distribution $\mathcal{U}(0,1)$
14: **end while**

The two version of DE with binomial and exponential crossover are indicated with DE/rand/1/bin and DE/rand/1/exp, respectively.

The rotation-invariant DE, studied in this article and here indicated with rotDE is a DE implementation which does not apply either of the crossovers but integrates it within a mutation, namely current-to-rand mutation, see [13, 32]. The resulting algorithm, namely DE/current-to-rand/1 applies the following moving operator in order to generate $\mathbf{x}^{\text{off}}$ from a candidate solution $\mathbf{x}^i$

$$DE/current-to-rand/1 : \mathbf{x}^{\text{off}} = \mathbf{x}^i + K\left(\mathbf{x}^t - \mathbf{x}^i\right) + K \cdot F\left(\mathbf{x}^r - \mathbf{x}^s\right)$$

where $\mathbf{x}^r$, $\mathbf{x}^s$, and $\mathbf{x}^t$ are three candidate solutions randomly sampled from the population (exactly like in the case of DE/rand/1). The parameter K, namely combination coefficient, is randomly sampled from a uniform distribution $\mathcal{U}(0,1)$ at each offspring calculation. The parameter F is a constant to be set in algorithm design phase and plays the same role as the scale factor in DE/rand/1 mutation.

Thus the rotation-invariant version of DE (rotDE) according to the implementation in [13,32] is displayed in Algorithm 5.

Let us consider the rotation-invariant mutation DE/current-to-rand and analyse its working principle and difference with respect to the standard DE/rand/1/bin and DE/rand/1/exp.

The DE/rand/1 mutation is essentially a weighted sum of three randomly selected candidate solutions. Thus, the provisional offspring $\mathbf{x}'_{\text{off}}$ is a solution generated by means of a random direction and has no relation with a potential rotation. In other words, there is no reason to conjecture that this mutation

Algorithm 5. Rotation-Invariant Differential Evolution [13, 32]

1: Generate an initial population of Np individuals
2: Calculate the fitness of each solution in population Np
3: **while** termination condition is not met **do**
4:    **for** each $\mathbf{x}^i$ in Np **do**
5:        Sample the random number K from $\mathcal{U}(0, 1)$
6:        Generate the offspring $\mathbf{x_{off}}$ by mutation
           DE/current-to-rand: $\mathbf{x^{off}} = \mathbf{x}^i + K\left(\mathbf{x^t} - \mathbf{x}^i\right) + K \cdot F\left(\mathbf{x^r} - \mathbf{x^s}\right)$
7:        Calculate the fitness of $\mathbf{x_{off}}$
8:        Make a note whether $\mathbf{x}^i$ or $\mathbf{x_{off}}$ has a better performance
9:    **end for**
10:    **for** each $\mathbf{x}^i$ in Np **do**
11:        Perform all the replacements by choosing the best between parent and off-spring
12:    **end for**
13: **end while**

would work better or worse in case of rotated functions. In this sense, as observed in [15], the basic DE/rand/1 mutation is rotation-invariant. According to our interpretation it would be more exact to state that the DE/rand/1 mutation is "rotation-independent" (the provisional offspring does not depend on rotation).

On the other hand, both the crossovers, binomial and exponential, generate $\mathbf{x_{off}}$ by combining the design variables of $\mathbf{x'_{off}}$ with those of $\mathbf{x_i}$. Thus, regardless of the result of the survivor selection, some of the design variables of $\mathbf{x_i}$ will

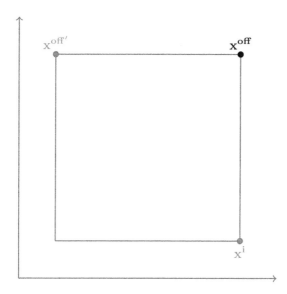

Fig. 1. Standard DE offspring generation

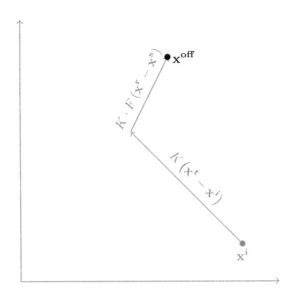

Fig. 2. DE/current-to-rand/1 offspring generation

be transferred over the following generation. Fig. 1 schematically illustrates the functioning of the standard DE algorithm.

If the objective function can be easily optimised by maintaining some of the variables constant and perturbing the others, then a standard DE/rand/1/bin or DE/rand/1/exp would display a good performance. However, if the same problem were rotated then the performance of standard DE would be highly deteriorated.

The DE/current-to-rand/1 in rotDE attempts to overcome this limitation of the standard DE by integrating the crossover into the mutation as a linear combination. More specifically, the DE/current-to-rand/1 generates the offspring $\mathbf{x}^{\text{off}}$ by adding a randomised vector (which is the linear combination of two randomised vectors by means of randomised scalars) to the candidate solution $\mathbf{x}^i$. A graphical representation of DE/current-to-rand/1 is shown in Fig. 2.

By reproducing the same reasoning used for the standard DE mutation, since this moving operator simply adds a random vector to $\mathbf{x}^i$ to generate $\mathbf{x}^{\text{off}}$, the offspring generation by DE/current-to-rand/1 is independent on a possible rotation. In this sense we can conclude that DE/current-to-rand/1 is a rotation-invariant operator.

4   Experimental Results

In order to test the performance of rotDE on non-rotated and rotated problems, the following benchmark has been designed.

We have considered a modern testbed composed of non-rotated and rotated problems, i.e. the CEC2014 testbed [18]. It is worth mentioning that the subsequent testbed, i.e. the CEC2015 [19], makes use only of some of the objective functions of the CEC2014, which is then more comprehensive.

For all the problems in CEC2014, two versions have been considered, the non-rotated and rotated versions, respectively. The non-rotated version can be easily obtained by removing the instruction $\mathbf{x}^{rot} = \mathbf{Qx}$, see Algorithm 1. Conversely, a rotated version has been generated by adding the instruction $\mathbf{x}^{rot} = \mathbf{Qx}$. Since in the original testbed, f_8 and f_9 are already the Rastrigin functions in the non-rotated and rotated version, respectively, f_8 is in the non-rotated testbed and f_9 in the rotated version. The same logic has been applied to f_{10} and f_{11}, i.e. non-rotated and rotated Schwefel function.

Thus, out of the 30 test problems we have derived 56 test problems, 28 being non-rotated and 28 being rotated. In order to report an extensive study which allows us to draw convincing conclusions, the 56 problems under considerations have been repeated for multiple levels of dimensionality: 10, 20, 30, 50, 100. In total, 280 test problems have been considered in this study.

In order to address these 280 test problems, DE/rand/1/bin, DE/rand/1/exp, and rotDE (using the DE/current-to-rand) have been run. Each experiment (each run) has been performed with a budget of $5000 \times n$ where n is the problem dimensionality.

For each test problem and each algorithm 30 independent runs have been performed. All the results in this study are presented in the form of average value (over 30 runs) $\pm$ standard deviation. Furthermore, to strengthen the statistical significance of the experiments, the two-tailed Rank-sum Wilcoxon's test [33] with confidence level 0.95 has been performed with rotDE average performance as the reference. A "$+$" sign indicates that rotDE significantly outperforms the standard DE. A "$-$" sign indicates that rotDE is significantly outperformed by the standard DE competitor. An "$=$" sign indicates that neither of the algorithms in the pair-wise comparison significantly outperforms the other one, i.e. the two algorithms perform comparably well.

Furthermore, the results have been grouped into two sets, non-rotated and rotated problems, respectively. For each set of results, the statistical significance of the results has been further studied by applying the Holm-Bonferroni procedure, see [34] so that a ranking of the algorithms involved could be established and a summary of the results presented.

Each algorithm in this study has been run with a population size of $N_p = 10$ candidate solutions. In order to guarantee a fair comparison, the same scale factor, $F = 0.4$, has been used for all the algorithms in this study. Regarding the crossover rate, both DE/rand/1/bin and DE/rand/1/exp use $Cr = 0.3$.

Experimental results for non-rotated problems in 10, 50, and 100 dimensions are displayed in Tables 1, 2, and 3, respectively. The best results are highlighted in bold face.

Numerical results show that for non-rotated problems rotDE never achieves the best performance. As displayed, rotDE never outperforms neither of the standard DE algorithms for the entire testbed. Apart from isolated cases in low dimensions DE/rand/1/exp appears to have the best performance for the non-

Table 1. Average error ± standard deviation and Wilcoxon's test (reference: rotDE) for rotDE against DE/rand/1/bin and DE/rand/1/exp on non-rotated CEC2014 [18] in 10 dimensions.

	rotDE	DE/rand/1/bin		DE/rand/1/exp	
f_1	$2.17e+08 \pm 3.92e+08$	$1.73e+06 \pm 3.72e+06$	–	**2.71e − 01 ± 8.13e − 01**	–
f_2	$4.51e+09 \pm 1.78e+09$	$1.55e+08 \pm 3.07e+08$	–	**0.00e + 00 ± 0.00e + 00**	–
f_3	$3.09e+04 \pm 4.83e+04$	$9.12e+02 \pm 9.20e+02$	–	**9.66e − 01 ± 2.89e + 00**	–
f_4	$2.50e+03 \pm 1.78e+03$	$5.12e+01 \pm 6.81e+01$	–	**1.42e + 01 ± 4.23e + 01**	–
f_5	$2.03e+01 \pm 7.29e-02$	$1.54e+01 \pm 7.22e+00$	–	**8.93e + 00 ± 8.59e + 00**	–
f_6	$9.67e+00 \pm 9.20e-01$	$4.65e-01 \pm 5.97e-01$	–	**1.65e − 03 ± 4.94e − 03**	–
f_7	$1.29e+02 \pm 4.73e+01$	$6.61e+00 \pm 7.80e+00$	–	**9.51e − 03 ± 1.04e − 02**	–
f_{8-9}	$5.83e+01 \pm 1.01e+01$	$9.68e+00 \pm 5.02e+00$	–	**2.03e + 00 ± 1.66e + 00**	–
f_{10-11}	$1.25e+03 \pm 2.09e+02$	$7.13e+01 \pm 3.79e+01$	–	**6.25e + 00 ± 6.11e + 00**	–
f_{12}	$6.81e-01 \pm 2.30e-01$	$1.53e-02 \pm 9.16e-03$	–	**5.32e − 04 ± 1.04e − 03**	–
f_{13}	$4.05e+00 \pm 8.99e-01$	**1.73e − 01 ± 6.46e − 02**	–	$1.91e-01 \pm 2.63e-02$	–
f_{14}	$5.16e+01 \pm 1.90e+01$	**1.61e − 01 ± 7.13e − 02**	–	$2.19e-01 \pm 3.48e-02$	–
f_{15}	$1.65e+04 \pm 2.62e+04$	$1.27e+01 \pm 2.93e+01$	–	**1.86e − 01 ± 1.28e − 01**	–
f_{16}	$3.51e+00 \pm 3.29e-01$	$3.97e-01 \pm 1.79e-01$	–	**1.42e − 01 ± 1.85e − 01**	–
f_{17}	$5.92e+05 \pm 8.91e+05$	**7.03e + 02 ± 1.15e + 03**	–	$4.92e+03 \pm 1.48e+04$	–
f_{18}	$3.11e+07 \pm 3.99e+07$	$4.03e+04 \pm 1.20e+05$	–	**1.10e + 00 ± 1.18e + 00**	–
f_{19}	$3.07e+01 \pm 1.95e+01$	$3.10e+00 \pm 1.50e+00$	–	**8.68e − 02 ± 5.86e − 02**	–
f_{20}	$1.13e+07 \pm 3.08e+07$	**1.23e + 01 ± 9.33e + 00**	–	$2.10e+07 \pm 6.30e+07$	–
f_{21}	$3.12e+06 \pm 6.73e+06$	$1.94e+02 \pm 2.37e+02$	–	**2.14e + 00 ± 5.17e + 00**	–
f_{22}	$2.36e+02 \pm 1.46e+02$	$3.86e+01 \pm 4.65e+01$	–	**4.03e + 00 ± 7.04e + 00**	–
f_{23}	$4.98e+02 \pm 1.29e+02$	$3.21e+02 \pm 7.15e+00$	–	**3.17e + 02 ± 3.39e + 00**	–
f_{24}	$2.06e+02 \pm 2.43e+01$	$1.15e+02 \pm 9.21e+00$	–	**1.09e + 02 ± 3.71e + 00**	–
f_{25}	$2.05e+02 \pm 3.28e+00$	$1.93e+02 \pm 1.02e+01$	–	**1.42e + 02 ± 4.51e + 00**	–
f_{26}	$1.37e+02 \pm 4.48e+01$	$1.00e+02 \pm 4.94e-01$	–	**1.00e + 02 ± 7.46e − 02**	–
f_{27}	$4.70e+02 \pm 7.39e+01$	$3.85e+02 \pm 4.14e+01$	–	**2.54e + 02 ± 1.01e + 02**	–
f_{28}	$1.23e+03 \pm 2.44e+02$	$4.91e+02 \pm 2.57e+01$	–	**4.43e + 02 ± 1.81e + 01**	–
f_{29}	$7.41e+05 \pm 1.53e+06$	$6.52e+02 \pm 7.88e+02$	–	**3.39e + 02 ± 1.57e + 02**	–
f_{30}	$1.39e+05 \pm 9.47e+04$	**6.02e + 02 ± 5.32e + 02**	–	$8.27e+02 \pm 1.96e+02$	–

rotated CEC 2014 test. This result could be explained by the fact that these non-rotated problems can be more efficiently tackled by an exploitative strategy, i.e. a crossover, since some design variables are perturbed while the others are inherited from $\mathbf{x}^i$ to $\mathbf{x}^{off}$. This explanation is intuitive for the base problems which are mostly constructed as the sum of contributions. The same straightforward explanation can be given for the hybrid functions. Since hybrid functions are weighted sums of base functions, the properties of the base functions are transferred by the linear transformation to the hybrid functions.

The same straightforward interpretation cannot be reproduced for composition functions. A composition function is still a weighted sum but each weight is a function itself, see [18]. For example, the function f_{23} can be written as

Table 2. Average error ± standard deviation and Wilcoxon's test (reference: rotDE) for rotDE against DE/rand/1/bin and DE/rand/1/exp on non-rotated CEC2014 [18] in 50 dimensions.

	rotDE	DE/rand/1/bin		DE/rand/1/exp	
f_1	$3.35e+09 \pm 1.01e+09$	$2.02e+08 \pm 1.08e+08$	−	$\mathbf{5.50e+06 \pm 1.64e+07}$	−
f_2	$1.18e+11 \pm 1.10e+10$	$2.01e+10 \pm 7.36e+09$	−	$\mathbf{6.61e+06 \pm 1.98e+07}$	−
f_3	$1.35e+05 \pm 4.05e+04$	$2.86e+04 \pm 9.27e+03$	−	$\mathbf{5.32e+01 \pm 1.59e+02}$	−
f_4	$3.14e+04 \pm 7.06e+03$	$4.05e+03 \pm 2.28e+03$	−	$\mathbf{2.15e+01 \pm 2.58e+01}$	−
f_5	$2.11e+01 \pm 2.67e-02$	$2.03e+01 \pm 1.30e-01$	−	$\mathbf{1.92e+01 \pm 1.18e+00}$	−
f_6	$7.19e+01 \pm 2.57e+00$	$2.25e+01 \pm 2.37e+00$	−	$\mathbf{3.21e-02 \pm 6.89e-02}$	−
f_7	$1.07e+03 \pm 1.25e+02$	$2.08e+02 \pm 5.46e+01$	−	$\mathbf{4.87e-02 \pm 6.74e-02}$	−
f_{8-9}	$5.93e+02 \pm 3.87e+01$	$1.60e+02 \pm 2.93e+01$	−	$\mathbf{7.82e+00 \pm 3.21e+00}$	−
f_{10-11}	$1.37e+04 \pm 6.16e+02$	$2.96e+03 \pm 6.42e+02$	−	$\mathbf{3.33e+01 \pm 7.09e+01}$	−
f_{12}	$2.60e+00 \pm 6.04e-01$	$1.25e-02 \pm 2.47e-03$	−	$\mathbf{1.48e-04 \pm 1.09e-04}$	−
f_{13}	$7.25e+00 \pm 4.80e-01$	$2.84e+00 \pm 9.23e-01$	−	$\mathbf{3.68e-01 \pm 5.34e-02}$	−
f_{14}	$3.29e+02 \pm 3.02e+01$	$6.69e+01 \pm 1.37e+01$	−	$\mathbf{3.28e-01 \pm 2.63e-02}$	−
f_{15}	$2.79e+06 \pm 1.52e+06$	$4.39e+05 \pm 5.46e+05$	−	$\mathbf{5.87e+00 \pm 1.04e+01}$	−
f_{16}	$2.23e+01 \pm 3.65e-01$	$1.33e+01 \pm 2.38e+00$	−	$\mathbf{7.43e-01 \pm 1.43e-01}$	−
f_{17}	$8.08e+08 \pm 5.07e+08$	$1.11e+07 \pm 1.78e+07$	−	$\mathbf{6.82e+01 \pm 1.03e+02}$	−
f_{18}	$2.54e+10 \pm 6.21e+09$	$1.81e+09 \pm 2.42e+09$	−	$\mathbf{3.74e+00 \pm 1.93e+00}$	−
f_{19}	$3.06e+03 \pm 1.16e+03$	$2.46e+02 \pm 9.84e+01$	−	$\mathbf{1.84e+00 \pm 2.75e+00}$	−
f_{20}	$6.82e+05 \pm 6.18e+05$	$4.45e+04 \pm 6.17e+04$	−	$\mathbf{4.61e+00 \pm 2.16e+00}$	−
f_{21}	$5.00e+08 \pm 3.38e+08$	$3.50e+06 \pm 4.56e+06$	−	$\mathbf{4.38e+01 \pm 5.56e+01}$	−
f_{22}	$5.21e+05 \pm 3.76e+05$	$5.68e+03 \pm 9.59e+03$	−	$\mathbf{3.62e+01 \pm 3.90e+01}$	−
f_{23}	$1.98e+03 \pm 7.72e+02$	$5.29e+02 \pm 1.12e+02$	−	$\mathbf{3.29e+02 \pm 5.11e+00}$	−
f_{24}	$5.57e+02 \pm 4.57e+01$	$3.64e+02 \pm 2.00e+01$	−	$\mathbf{2.84e+02 \pm 3.63e+00}$	−
f_{25}	$3.43e+02 \pm 4.89e+01$	$2.31e+02 \pm 7.39e+00$	−	$\mathbf{2.08e+02 \pm 3.49e-01}$	−
f_{26}	$3.28e+02 \pm 8.65e+01$	$1.79e+02 \pm 4.95e+01$	−	$\mathbf{1.00e+02 \pm 5.88e-02}$	−
f_{27}	$2.86e+03 \pm 3.33e+02$	$9.42e+02 \pm 8.97e+01$	−	$\mathbf{3.26e+02 \pm 3.09e+01}$	−
f_{28}	$1.25e+04 \pm 1.78e+03$	$2.42e+03 \pm 3.49e+02$	−	$\mathbf{1.38e+03 \pm 7.19e+01}$	−
f_{29}	$1.88e+09 \pm 3.48e+08$	$1.58e+07 \pm 1.06e+07$	−	$\mathbf{1.44e+04 \pm 1.55e+04}$	−
f_{30}	$5.21e+07 \pm 2.79e+07$	$1.39e+05 \pm 1.13e+05$	−	$\mathbf{2.74e+04 \pm 2.07e+04}$	−

$$f_{23}(\mathbf{x}) = w_1 g_1(\mathbf{x}) f_4(\mathbf{x}) + w_2 g_2(\mathbf{x}) f_2(\mathbf{x}) + w_3 g_3(\mathbf{x}) f_3(\mathbf{x}) + {}$$
$$+ w_4 g_4(\mathbf{x}) f_2(\mathbf{x}) + w_5 g_5(\mathbf{x}) f_3(\mathbf{x})$$

w_i for $i = 1, \ldots 5$ are constant weights and $g_i(\mathbf{x})$ for $i = 1, \ldots 5$ are weights that depend on the candidate solution $\mathbf{x}$.

In other words, composition functions do not maintain the same properties of the base functions composing them. However, numerical results clearly indicate that the inheritance/crossover logic seems beneficial in these cases too.

Tables 4, 5, and 6 show the experimental results for rotated problems in 10, 50, and 100 dimensions.

Table 3. Average error ± standard deviation and Wilcoxon's test (reference: rotDE) for rotDE against DE/rand/1/bin and DE/rand/1/exp on non-rotated CEC2014 [18] in 100 dimensions.

	rotDE	DE/rand/1/bin		DE/rand/1/exp	
f_1	$1.44e + 10 \pm 4.29e + 09$	$1.02e + 09 \pm 3.12e + 08$	−	$\mathbf{4.27e + 04 \pm 1.24e + 05}$	−
f_2	$2.38e + 11 \pm 1.07e + 10$	$7.28e + 10 \pm 1.11e + 10$	−	$\mathbf{6.77e + 06 \pm 1.51e + 07}$	−
f_3	$3.25e + 05 \pm 1.28e + 05$	$1.06e + 05 \pm 1.71e + 04$	−	$\mathbf{1.54e + 00 \pm 2.98e + 00}$	−
f_4	$7.31e + 04 \pm 6.92e + 03$	$1.81e + 04 \pm 6.52e + 03$	−	$\mathbf{3.56e + 01 \pm 3.28e + 01}$	−
f_5	$2.13e + 01 \pm 3.48e - 02$	$2.04e + 01 \pm 6.54e - 02$	−	$\mathbf{1.95e + 01 \pm 5.69e - 01}$	−
f_6	$1.58e + 02 \pm 3.21e + 00$	$6.92e + 01 \pm 3.45e + 00$	−	$\mathbf{4.96e - 02 \pm 1.37e - 01}$	−
f_7	$2.36e + 03 \pm 1.25e + 02$	$7.28e + 02 \pm 1.23e + 02$	−	$\mathbf{2.08e + 00 \pm 6.15e + 00}$	−
f_{8-9}	$1.42e + 03 \pm 6.56e + 01$	$5.03e + 02 \pm 4.88e + 01$	−	$\mathbf{1.85e + 01 \pm 4.05e + 00}$	−
f_{10-11}	$3.12e + 04 \pm 4.82e + 02$	$1.05e + 04 \pm 1.51e + 03$	−	$\mathbf{1.56e + 02 \pm 1.40e + 02}$	−
f_{12}	$3.31e + 00 \pm 3.27e - 01$	$2.54e - 02 \pm 9.40e - 03$	−	$\mathbf{5.69e - 05 \pm 4.10e - 05}$	−
f_{13}	$7.94e + 00 \pm 2.63e - 01$	$4.94e + 00 \pm 4.38e - 01$	−	$\mathbf{4.34e - 01 \pm 2.75e - 02}$	−
f_{14}	$7.01e + 02 \pm 7.38e + 01$	$2.38e + 02 \pm 4.97e + 01$	−	$\mathbf{3.40e - 01 \pm 1.84e - 02}$	−
f_{15}	$1.23e + 07 \pm 8.70e + 06$	$4.46e + 06 \pm 2.45e + 06$	−	$\mathbf{2.40e + 02 \pm 7.07e + 02}$	−
f_{16}	$4.64e + 01 \pm 3.83e - 01$	$3.32e + 01 \pm 1.74e + 00$	−	$\mathbf{1.84e + 00 \pm 3.15e - 01}$	−
f_{17}	$5.04e + 09 \pm 1.59e + 09$	$1.11e + 08 \pm 8.13e + 07$	−	$\mathbf{2.66e + 04 \pm 7.93e + 04}$	−
f_{18}	$5.03e + 10 \pm 1.14e + 10$	$5.84e + 09 \pm 2.45e + 09$	−	$\mathbf{3.08e + 07 \pm 9.24e + 07}$	−
f_{19}	$9.79e + 03 \pm 2.18e + 03$	$9.79e + 02 \pm 3.44e + 02$	−	$\mathbf{9.36e + 00 \pm 2.21e + 01}$	−
f_{20}	$5.18e + 07 \pm 1.43e + 08$	$1.10e + 05 \pm 1.31e + 05$	−	$\mathbf{8.51e + 00 \pm 3.58e + 00}$	−
f_{21}	$1.80e + 09 \pm 9.56e + 08$	$8.00e + 07 \pm 1.01e + 08$	−	$\mathbf{3.10e + 01 \pm 7.01e + 01}$	−
f_{22}	$2.88e + 05 \pm 2.47e + 05$	$4.28e + 03 \pm 5.42e + 03$	−	$\mathbf{3.96e + 01 \pm 3.34e + 01}$	−
f_{23}	$3.64e + 03 \pm 4.50e + 02$	$1.17e + 03 \pm 2.31e + 02$	−	$\mathbf{3.91e + 02 \pm 3.29e + 01}$	−
f_{24}	$1.06e + 03 \pm 1.31e + 02$	$5.93e + 02 \pm 1.97e + 01$	−	$\mathbf{3.72e + 02 \pm 4.31e + 00}$	−
f_{25}	$5.64e + 02 \pm 1.02e + 02$	$3.23e + 02 \pm 1.76e + 01$	−	$\mathbf{2.15e + 02 \pm 5.05e - 01}$	−
f_{26}	$4.44e + 02 \pm 9.86e + 01$	$2.60e + 02 \pm 4.00e + 01$	−	$\mathbf{1.01e + 02 \pm 4.03e - 02}$	−
f_{27}	$5.67e + 03 \pm 5.56e + 02$	$2.43e + 03 \pm 2.46e + 02$	−	$\mathbf{3.14e + 02 \pm 2.04e + 01}$	−
f_{28}	$2.95e + 04 \pm 2.18e + 03$	$7.56e + 03 \pm 5.78e + 02$	−	$\mathbf{2.41e + 03 \pm 1.24e + 02}$	−
f_{29}	$5.84e + 09 \pm 1.18e + 09$	$2.62e + 08 \pm 1.10e + 08$	−	$\mathbf{9.28e + 04 \pm 1.26e + 05}$	−
f_{30}	$1.58e + 08 \pm 4.30e + 07$	$1.69e + 06 \pm 1.03e + 06$	−	$\mathbf{3.79e + 04 \pm 1.46e + 04}$	−

Experimental results on rotated problems show that, on isolated cases, more specifically once in 10 dimensions, twice in 50 and 100 dimensions rotDE outperformed DE/rand/1/bin while in one case in 10 dimensions and in one case in 100 dimensions, rotDE and DE/rand/1/bin achieve comparable results. In the remaining cases the standard DE/rand/1/bin outperformed rotDE.

The comparison of rotDE and DE/rand/1/exp shows that rotDE is significantly outperformed on all the rotated problems. At first, this outcome can appear unexpected since we are observing that a rotation-invariant algorithm displays, on a rotated benchmark, a significantly worse performance than a standard and rotation-variant algorithm.

Table 4. Average error ± standard deviation and Wilcoxon's test (reference: rotDE) for rotDE against DE/rand/1/bin and DE/rand/1/exp on rotated CEC2014 [18] in 10 dimensions.

	rotDE	DE/rand/1/bin		DE/rand/1/exp	
f_1	$4.72e+08 \pm 5.25e+08$	$7.64e+06 \pm 9.29e+06$	−	$3.77e+05 \pm 8.81e+05$	−
f_2	$7.88e+09 \pm 3.94e+09$	$2.20e+08 \pm 3.34e+08$	−	$7.04e+05 \pm 2.56e+06$	−
f_3	$2.26e+04 \pm 9.44e+03$	$6.06e+03 \pm 8.84e+03$	−	$1.51e+02 \pm 5.33e+02$	−
f_4	$3.07e+03 \pm 2.14e+03$	$5.09e+01 \pm 2.72e+01$	−	$3.07e+00 \pm 8.66e+00$	−
f_5	$2.03e+01 \pm 8.87e-02$	$2.03e+01 \pm 9.39e-02$	+	$1.81e+01 \pm 4.88e+00$	−
f_6	$9.65e+00 \pm 1.39e+00$	$2.16e+00 \pm 1.24e+00$	−	$4.08e-01 \pm 4.81e-01$	−
f_7	$2.23e+02 \pm 7.69e+01$	$8.15e+00 \pm 1.51e+01$	−	$2.75e-02 \pm 2.27e-02$	−
f_{8-9}	$6.38e+01 \pm 1.49e+01$	$1.17e+01 \pm 6.60e+00$	−	$6.42e+00 \pm 2.27e+00$	−
f_{10-11}	$1.37e+03 \pm 2.95e+02$	$3.10e+02 \pm 2.54e+02$	−	$2.52e+02 \pm 1.25e+02$	−
f_{12}	$6.68e-01 \pm 1.94e-01$	$7.17e-01 \pm 3.70e-01$	=	$2.29e-01 \pm 6.71e-02$	−
f_{13}	$4.97e+00 \pm 1.42e+00$	$5.28e-01 \pm 9.57e-01$	−	$1.79e-01 \pm 5.18e-02$	−
f_{14}	$4.29e+01 \pm 1.43e+01$	$1.09e+00 \pm 2.25e+00$	−	$2.42e-01 \pm 6.70e-02$	−
f_{15}	$1.78e+04 \pm 2.58e+04$	$4.19e+00 \pm 5.06e+00$	−	$1.19e+00 \pm 1.31e+00$	−
f_{16}	$3.63e+00 \pm 2.32e-01$	$\mathbf{1.67e+00 \pm 6.52e-01}$	−	$2.06e+00 \pm 2.52e-01$	−
f_{17}	$1.31e+06 \pm 1.39e+06$	$1.73e+05 \pm 3.25e+05$	−	$1.55e+05 \pm 2.14e+05$	−
f_{18}	$2.78e+07 \pm 9.05e+07$	$5.46e+03 \pm 6.62e+03$	−	$2.06e+03 \pm 4.92e+03$	−
f_{19}	$6.54e+01 \pm 7.47e+01$	$2.72e+00 \pm 3.76e+00$	−	$5.58e-01 \pm 3.72e-01$	−
f_{20}	$2.75e+04 \pm 3.99e+04$	$3.29e+03 \pm 5.73e+03$	−	$8.36e+02 \pm 1.16e+03$	−
f_{21}	$1.97e+07 \pm 9.44e+07$	$3.97e+05 \pm 2.00e+06$	−	$2.97e+03 \pm 5.01e+03$	−
f_{22}	$1.96e+02 \pm 9.65e+01$	$3.86e+01 \pm 4.19e+01$	−	$1.32e+01 \pm 3.15e+01$	−
f_{23}	$5.99e+02 \pm 2.40e+02$	$3.37e+02 \pm 8.96e+00$	−	$3.29e+02 \pm 1.93e+01$	−
f_{24}	$2.16e+02 \pm 2.05e+01$	$1.43e+02 \pm 3.43e+01$	−	$1.21e+02 \pm 7.32e+00$	-
f_{25}	$2.04e+02 \pm 3.88e+00$	$1.93e+02 \pm 2.09e+01$	−	$1.49e+02 \pm 2.06e+01$	−
f_{26}	$1.47e+02 \pm 4.72e+01$	$\mathbf{1.00e+02 \pm 2.67e-01}$	−	$1.04e+02 \pm 1.79e+01$	−
f_{27}	$5.97e+02 \pm 1.88e+02$	$\mathbf{2.99e+02 \pm 1.37e+02}$	−	$3.03e+02 \pm 1.34e+02$	−
f_{28}	$1.43e+03 \pm 3.10e+02$	$4.87e+02 \pm 6.04e+01$	−	$4.03e+02 \pm 3.35e+01$	−
f_{29}	$3.45e+07 \pm 4.21e+07$	$8.50e+04 \pm 4.47e+05$	−	$3.67e+02 \pm 7.56e+01$	−
f_{30}	$1.33e+05 \pm 3.02e+05$	$9.34e+02 \pm 3.11e+02$	−	$7.04e+02 \pm 1.88e+02$	−

However, if the meaning of rotated problems and rotation-invariant problems were better analysed this result would come less surprising. If we consider again the mechanism to generate rotated problems [18] we can observe that the matrix rotation perturbs the fitness calculation and does not really perform a fitness landscape rotation. Furthermore, rotDE, albeit rotation-invariant, does not take the rotation of the problem into account: all the algorithms in this study perform a "blind" stochastic sampling of points followed by a replacement mechanism. In other words, from the perspective of the algorithm, there are no rotated and non-rotated problem, there are only black-box problems.

The actual difference between the standard DE implementations and rotDE is in the strategy that generates the trial candidate solutions. As represented in

Table 5. Average error ± standard deviation and Wilcoxon's test (reference: rotDE) for rotDE against DE/rand/1/bin and DE/rand/1/exp on rotated CEC2014 [18] in 50 dimensions.

	rotDE	DE/rand/1/bin		DE/rand/1/exp	
f_1	$8.23e + 09 \pm 3.08e + 09$	$2.50e + 08 \pm 1.58e + 08$	−	$1.92e + 07 \pm 4.78e + 06$	−
f_2	$1.93e + 11 \pm 2.29e + 10$	$3.15e + 10 \pm 8.00e + 09$	−	$4.12e + 07 \pm 1.31e + 08$	−
f_3	$2.12e + 05 \pm 9.87e + 04$	$6.66e + 04 \pm 1.68e + 04$	−	$1.33e + 04 \pm 6.43e + 03$	−
f_4	$6.05e + 04 \pm 1.62e + 04$	$4.40e + 03 \pm 2.47e + 03$	−	$8.09e + 01 \pm 2.00e + 01$	−
f_5	$2.11e + 01 \pm 5.17e - 02$	$2.12e + 01 \pm 3.39e - 02$	+	$2.03e + 01 \pm 2.63e - 02$	−
f_6	$7.36e + 01 \pm 3.03e + 00$	$3.41e + 01 \pm 3.37e + 00$	−	$2.96e + 01 \pm 2.78e + 00$	−
f_7	$1.82e + 03 \pm 2.46e + 02$	$3.11e + 02 \pm 1.02e + 02$	−	$3.40e - 01 \pm 5.04e - 01$	−
f_{8-9}	$7.98e + 02 \pm 7.28e + 01$	$2.55e + 02 \pm 3.80e + 01$	−	$1.24e + 02 \pm 1.94e + 01$	−
f_{10-11}	$1.35e + 04 \pm 6.50e + 02$	$1.27e + 04 \pm 5.91e + 02$	−	$4.18e + 03 \pm 3.37e + 02$	−
f_{12}	$2.56e + 00 \pm 3.79e - 01$	$3.44e + 00 \pm 3.38e - 01$	+	$2.31e - 01 \pm 3.17e - 02$	−
f_{13}	$9.40e + 00 \pm 8.59e - 01$	$3.80e + 00 \pm 7.31e - 01$	−	$4.47e - 01 \pm 4.30e - 02$	−
f_{14}	$4.71e + 02 \pm 7.36e + 01$	$8.21e + 01 \pm 2.41e + 01$	−	$3.40e - 01 \pm 3.04e - 02$	−
f_{15}	$2.38e + 07 \pm 2.25e + 07$	$1.07e + 05 \pm 1.12e + 05$	−	$1.55e + 01 \pm 2.94e + 00$	−
f_{16}	$2.24e + 01 \pm 3.35e - 01$	$2.14e + 01 \pm 5.38e - 01$	−	$1.76e + 01 \pm 6.54e - 01$	−
f_{17}	$9.21e + 08 \pm 3.93e + 08$	$1.45e + 07 \pm 1.27e + 07$	−	$6.35e + 06 \pm 2.16e + 06$	−
f_{18}	$2.73e + 10 \pm 5.99e + 09$	$8.67e + 08 \pm 7.78e + 08$	−	$4.90e + 04 \pm 2.55e + 05$	−
f_{19}	$4.00e + 03 \pm 1.33e + 03$	$2.06e + 02 \pm 8.59e + 01$	−	$2.70e + 01 \pm 1.27e + 01$	−
f_{20}	$9.38e + 06 \pm 4.61e + 07$	$3.12e + 04 \pm 1.38e + 04$	−	$4.48e + 04 \pm 1.52e + 04$	−
f_{21}	$3.03e + 08 \pm 2.92e + 08$	$4.86e + 06 \pm 5.72e + 06$	−	$4.09e + 06 \pm 1.37e + 06$	−
f_{22}	$8.22e + 05 \pm 9.86e + 05$	$1.05e + 03 \pm 4.01e + 02$	−	$9.07e + 02 \pm 2.09e + 02$	−
f_{23}	$2.16e + 03 \pm 5.40e + 02$	$5.45e + 02 \pm 1.05e + 02$	−	$3.58e + 02 \pm 2.20e + 01$	−
f_{24}	$5.71e + 02 \pm 8.36e + 01$	$3.62e + 02 \pm 1.65e + 01$	−	$2.74e + 02 \pm 2.72e + 00$	−
f_{25}	$3.95e + 02 \pm 7.68e + 01$	$2.49e + 02 \pm 1.20e + 01$	−	$2.17e + 02 \pm 2.00e + 00$	−
f_{26}	$3.42e + 02 \pm 6.34e + 01$	$1.99e + 02 \pm 2.61e + 01$	−	$1.04e + 02 \pm 1.81e + 01$	−
f_{27}	$3.15e + 03 \pm 4.54e + 02$	$1.35e + 03 \pm 6.17e + 01$	−	$1.12e + 03 \pm 1.29e + 02$	−
f_{28}	$1.53e + 04 \pm 2.15e + 03$	$3.12e + 03 \pm 5.90e + 02$	−	$1.66e + 03 \pm 1.19e + 02$	−
f_{29}	$2.85e + 09 \pm 8.02e + 08$	$3.51e + 07 \pm 2.45e + 07$	−	$8.23e + 04 \pm 2.72e + 05$	−
f_{30}	$5.85e + 07 \pm 2.57e + 07$	$5.57e + 05 \pm 6.02e + 05$	−	$1.42e + 04 \pm 1.00e + 04$	−

Figs. 1 and 2, the main difference between the strategies is that while the standard DE always retains some (a few) design variables, rotDE perturbs a solution by adding a vector to it and thus changes all its design variables. According to our interpretation, although the latter strategy is theoretically connected with the concept of rotation, it does not necessarily help to solve rotated problems. We are not advocating here that it is always better to retain some of the design variables. However, this seems to be a clear indication for the benchmark under consideration.

As a final observation, we remind that the crossover rate Cr has been set equal to 0.3. For the exponential crossover, this means that one design variable is surely copied from x^i to x^{off}, a second design variable has a 30% of chance of

Table 6. Average error $\pm$ standard deviation and Wilcoxon's test (reference: rotDE) for rotDE against DE/rand/1/bin and DE/rand/1/exp on rotated CEC2014 [18] in 100 dimensions.

	rotDE	DE/rand/1/bin		DE/rand/1/exp	
f_1	$1.28e+10 \pm 2.52e+09$	$8.88e+08 \pm 2.85e+08$	$-$	$9.10e+07 \pm 1.92e+07$	$-$
f_2	$3.69e+11 \pm 2.28e+10$	$1.27e+11 \pm 2.66e+10$	$-$	$5.78e+07 \pm 1.31e+08$	$-$
f_3	$6.64e+05 \pm 1.15e+06$	$1.92e+05 \pm 2.61e+04$	$-$	$2.73e+04 \pm 7.25e+03$	$-$
f_4	$1.34e+05 \pm 2.96e+04$	$1.75e+04 \pm 5.63e+03$	$-$	$2.02e+02 \pm 2.97e+01$	$-$
f_5	$2.13e+01 \pm 3.14e-02$	$2.13e+01 \pm 2.53e-02$	$+$	$2.05e+01 \pm 2.25e-02$	$-$
f_6	$1.63e+02 \pm 4.14e+00$	$9.45e+01 \pm 4.97e+00$	$-$	$7.72e+01 \pm 2.75e+00$	$-$
f_7	$3.75e+03 \pm 3.01e+02$	$1.15e+03 \pm 2.37e+02$	$-$	$9.69e-01 \pm 9.74e-01$	$-$
f_{8-9}	$1.69e+03 \pm 1.08e+02$	$7.75e+02 \pm 8.09e+01$	$-$	$4.09e+02 \pm 4.13e+01$	$-$
f_{10-11}	$3.09e+04 \pm 8.72e+02$	$3.00e+04 \pm 4.65e+02$	$-$	$1.09e+04 \pm 9.55e+02$	$-$
f_{12}	$3.28e+00 \pm 3.24e-01$	$4.13e+00 \pm 2.75e-01$	$+$	$3.47e-01 \pm 3.87e-02$	$-$
f_{13}	$1.05e+01 \pm 6.46e-01$	$5.60e+00 \pm 5.33e-01$	$-$	$4.38e-01 \pm 4.09e-02$	$-$
f_{14}	$1.08e+03 \pm 1.00e+02$	$3.51e+02 \pm 8.16e+01$	$-$	$3.56e-01 \pm 2.13e-02$	$-$
f_{15}	$8.74e+07 \pm 4.52e+07$	$1.06e+06 \pm 6.87e+05$	$-$	$4.89e+01 \pm 6.44e+00$	$-$
f_{16}	$4.63e+01 \pm 5.13e-01$	$4.62e+01 \pm 3.00e-01$	$=$	$3.97e+01 \pm 4.75e-01$	$-$
f_{17}	$2.74e+09 \pm 7.60e+08$	$1.00e+08 \pm 4.23e+07$	$-$	$2.06e+07 \pm 4.91e+06$	$-$
f_{18}	$5.22e+10 \pm 8.72e+09$	$5.59e+09 \pm 2.59e+09$	$-$	$5.54e+04 \pm 2.77e+05$	$-$
f_{19}	$1.38e+04 \pm 3.91e+03$	$8.67e+02 \pm 2.59e+02$	$-$	$8.04e+01 \pm 1.62e+01$	$-$
f_{20}	$5.43e+06 \pm 1.03e+07$	$1.05e+05 \pm 3.97e+04$	$-$	$1.16e+05 \pm 3.00e+04$	$-$
f_{21}	$7.51e+08 \pm 3.25e+08$	$4.13e+07 \pm 2.56e+07$	$-$	$1.45e+07 \pm 3.45e+06$	$-$
f_{22}	$5.06e+05 \pm 3.60e+05$	$2.94e+03 \pm 8.27e+02$	$-$	$2.11e+03 \pm 3.09e+02$	$-$
f_{23}	$3.44e+03 \pm 6.14e+02$	$1.09e+03 \pm 2.04e+02$	$-$	$3.85e+02 \pm 2.53e+01$	$-$
f_{24}	$1.13e+03 \pm 1.09e+02$	$6.69e+02 \pm 4.05e+01$	$-$	$3.80e+02 \pm 4.21e+00$	$-$
f_{25}	$6.49e+02 \pm 1.16e+02$	$3.81e+02 \pm 2.36e+01$	$-$	$2.57e+02 \pm 4.48e+00$	$-$
f_{26}	$5.05e+02 \pm 1.11e+02$	$2.46e+02 \pm 1.60e+01$	$-$	$1.77e+02 \pm 4.62e+01$	$-$
f_{27}	$7.83e+03 \pm 1.96e+03$	$2.90e+03 \pm 1.32e+02$	$-$	$2.20e+03 \pm 3.27e+02$	$-$
f_{28}	$3.61e+04 \pm 3.15e+03$	$9.15e+03 \pm 9.35e+02$	$-$	$4.24e+03 \pm 6.63e+02$	$-$
f_{29}	$8.02e+09 \pm 1.50e+09$	$2.79e+08 \pm 8.83e+07$	$-$	$4.79e+05 \pm 7.57e+05$	$-$
f_{30}	$5.54e+08 \pm 2.57e+08$	$4.12e+06 \pm 2.41e+06$	$-$	$4.64e+04 \pm 1.03e+04$	$-$

being inherited, and a third one has less 10% of chance of being inherited. The following variables have an exponential decreasing probability of being inherited. Thus, it is safe to say that for experiments in 100 dimensions, on average, rarely more than 3% of the design variables are inherited from x^i to x^{off}. It interesting to see how this apparently minor action can lead to a major difference in performance regardless the problem rotation.

The results have been ranked by applying the Holm-Bonferroni procedure [34]. The summary of the collated results related to the 140 non-rotated problems and 140 rotated problems are listed in Table 7. The statistical test clearly confirms that rotDE is significantly outperformed by the standard DE algorithms on both versions of CEC2014 benchmark.

Table 7. Holm-Bonferroni procedure on non-rotated (reference: rotDE, Rank = 1.01e+00) and rotated (reference: rotDE, Rank = 1.06e+00) CEC2014 [18] for 10, 20, 30, 50, and 100 dimensions

Non-rotated problems

j	Algorithm	Rank	z_j	p_j	δ/j	Hypothesis
1	DE/rand/1/exp	2.95e + 00	2.30e + 01	1.00e + 00	5.00e−02	Accepted
2	DE/rand/1/bin	2.04e + 00	1.23e + 01	1.00e + 00	2.50e−02	Accepted

Rotated Problems

j	Algorithm	Rank	z_j	p_j	δ/j	Hypothesis
1	DE/ran/1/exp	2.95e+00	2.24e+01	1.00e+00	5.00e-02	Accepted
2	DE/rand/1/bin	1.99e+00	1.11e+01	1.00e+00	2.50e-02	Accepted

5 Conclusion

This experimental study presents a summary of an extensive computational comparison between two standard DE implementations, i.e. DE/rand/1/bin and DE/rand/1/exp, and a classical rotation-invariant version of DE endowed with DE/current-t-rand/1 mutation, here referred to as rotDE.

Numerical results performed on a modern testbed show that the standard DE implementations appear to consistently outperform its rotation-invariant counterpart on both non-rotated and rotated problems. Since the main difference among the algorithms is that DE/rand/1/bin and DE/rand/1/exp, unlike DE/current-t-rand/1, transfer some (possibly very few) design variables to the offspring, we conclude that this transfer could be beneficial, regardless of the problem rotation. Furthermore, rotation invariance, in the sense of DE/current-to-rand/1 mutation, does not seem to help to solve rotated problems.

References

1. Michalewicz, Z., Fogel, D.B.: How to Solve It: Modern Heuristics. Springer, Heidelberg (1999). https://doi.org/10.1007/978-3-662-07807-5
2. Hansen, N., Ostermeier, A.: Completely derandomized self-adaptation in evolution strategies. Evol. Comput. **9**(2), 159–195 (2001)
3. Caraffini, F., Neri, F., Iacca, G.: Large scale problems in practice: the effect of dimensionality on the interaction among variables. In: Squillero, G., Sim, K. (eds.) EvoApplications 2017. LNCS, vol. 10199, pp. 636–652. Springer, Cham (2017). https://doi.org/10.1007/978-3-319-55849-3_41
4. Garcia, S., Fernandez, A., Luengo, J., Herrera, F.: A study of statistical techniques and performance measures for genetics-based machine learning: accuracy and interpretability. Soft. Comput. **13**(10), 959–977 (2008)
5. Bäck, T.: Evolutionary Algorithms in Theory and Practice: Evolution Strategies, Evolutionary Programming, Genetic Algorithms. Oxford University Press, Oxford (1996)

6. Suganthan, P.N., Hansen, N., Liang, J.J., Deb, K., Chen, Y.P., Auger, A., Tiwari, S.: Problem definitions and evaluation criteria for the CEC 2005 special session on real-parameter optimization. Technical report 2005005, Nanyang Technological University and KanGAL, Singapore and IIT Kanpur, India (2005)
7. Hansen, N., Auger, A., Finck, S., Ros, R., et al.: Real-parameter black-box optimization benchmarking 2010: noiseless functions definitions. Technical report, RR-6829, INRIA (2010)
8. Liang, J.J., Qu, B.Y., Suganthan, P.N., Hernáindez-Díaz, A.G.: Problem definitions and evaluation criteria for the CEC 2013 special session on real-parameter optimization. Technical report, 201212, Zhengzhou University and Nanyang Technological University, Zhengzhou China and Singapore (2013)
9. Lozano, M., Molina, D., Herrera, F.: Editorial scalability of evolutionary algorithms and other metaheuristics for large-scale continuous optimization problems. Soft. Comput. 15(11), 2085–2087 (2011)
10. Caponio, A., Cascella, G.L., Neri, F., Salvatore, N., Sumner, M.: A fast adaptive memetic algorithm for on-line and off-line control design of PMSM drives. IEEE Trans. Syst. Man Cybern. part B 37(1), 28–41 (2007)
11. Neri, F., Tirronen, V.: Recent advances in differential evolution: a review and experimental analysis. Artif. Intell. Rev. 33(1–2), 61–106 (2010)
12. Poikolainen, I., Neri, F., Caraffini, F.: Cluster-based population initialization for differential evolution frameworks. Inf. Sci. 297(Supplement C), 216–235 (2015)
13. Lampinen, J., Zelinka, I.: Mechanical engineering design optimization by differential evolution. In: Corne, D., Dorigo, M., Glover, F. (eds.) New Ideas in Optimization, pp. 127–146. McGraw-Hill (1999)
14. Takahama, T., Sakai, S.: Solving nonlinear optimization problems by differential evolution with a rotation-invariant crossover operation using Gram-Schmidt process. In: Proceedings of the World Congress on Nature and Biologically Inspired Computing, pp. 533–540 (2010)
15. Anik, T.A., Noman, A.S.M., Ahmed, S.: Preserving rotation invariant properties in differential evolution algorithm. In: 2013 2nd International Conference on Advances in Electrical Engineering (ICAEE), pp. 235–240 (2013)
16. Bujok, P., Tvrdík, J., Poláková, R.: Differential evolution with rotation-invariant mutation and competing-strategies adaptation. In: 2014 IEEE Congress on Evolutionary Computation (CEC), pp. 2253–2258, July 2014
17. Neri, F.: Linear Algebra for Computational Sciences and Engineering. Springer, Cham (2016). https://doi.org/10.1007/978-3-319-40341-0
18. Liang, J., Qu, B., Suganthan, P.: Problem definitions and evaluation criteria for the CEC 2014 special session and competition on single objective real-parameter numerical optimization. Technical report, Computational Intelligence Laboratory, Zhengzhou University, Zhengzhou China and Technical Report, Nanyang Technological University, Singapore (2013)
19. Liang, J., Qu, B., Suganthan, P., Chen, Q.: Problem definitions and evaluation criteria for the CEC 2015 competition on learning-based real-parameter single objective optimization. Technical report, Computational Intelligence Laboratory, Zhengzhou University, Zhengzhou China and Technical Report, Nanyang Technological University, Singapore (2014)
20. Das, S., Suganthan, P.: Differential evolution: a survey of the state-of-the-art. IEEE Trans. Evol. Comput. 15(1), 4–31 (2011)
21. Das, S., Mullick, S.S., Suganthan, P.: Recent advances in differential evolution - an updated survey. Swarm Evol. Comput. 27(Supplement C), 1–30 (2016)

22. Suganthan, P.N.: Differential evolution algorithm: recent advances. In: Dediu, A.-H., Martín-Vide, C., Truthe, B. (eds.) TPNC 2012. LNCS, vol. 7505, pp. 30–46. Springer, Heidelberg (2012). https://doi.org/10.1007/978-3-642-33860-1_4

23. Tirronen, V., Neri, F.: Differential evolution with fitness diversity self-adaptation. In: Chiong, R. (ed.) Nature-Inspired Algorithms for Optimisation. SCI, vol. 193, pp. 199–234. Springer, Heidelberg (2009). https://doi.org/10.1007/978-3-642-00267-0_7

24. Zhao, S.Z., Suganthan, P.N., Das, S.: Self-adaptive differential evolution with multi-trajectory search for large-scale optimization. Soft Comput. **15**(11), 2175–2185 (2011)

25. Suganthan, P.N., Das, S., Mukherjee, S., Chatterjee, S.: Adaptation methods in differential evolution: A review. In: 20th International Conference on Soft Computing MENDEL (2014)

26. Qin, A.K., Huang, V.L., Suganthan, P.N.: Differential evolution algorithm with strategy adaptation for global numerical optimization. IEEE Trans. Evol. Comput. **13**(2), 398–417 (2009)

27. Iacca, G., Caraffini, F., Neri, F.: Multi-strategy coevolving aging particle optimization. Int. J. Neural Syst. **24**(01), 1450008 (2014)

28. Storn, R., Price, K.: Differential evolution - a simple and efficient adaptive scheme for global optimization over continuous spaces. TR-95-012 (1995)

29. Storn, R., Price, K.: Differential evolution - a simple and efficient adaptive scheme for global optimization over continuous spaces. J. Glob. Optim. **11**(TR–95–012), 341–359 (1997)

30. Zaharie, D.: Critical values for control parameters of differential evolution algorithm. In: Matusek, R., Osmera, P. (eds.) Proceedings of 8th International Mendel Conference on Soft Computing, pp. 62–67 (2002)

31. Weber, M., Neri, F., Tirronen, V.: A study on scale factor in distributed differential evolution. Inf. Sci. **181**(12), 2488–2511 (2011)

32. Price, K.: An introduction to differential evolution. In: Corne, D., Dorigo, M., Glover, F., Dasgupta, D., Moscato, P., Poli, R., Price, K.V. (eds.) New Ideas in Optimization, pp. 79–108. McGraw-Hill (1999)

33. Wilcoxon, F.: Individual comparisons by ranking methods. Biometrics Bull. **1**(6), 80–83 (1945)

34. Holm, S.: A simple sequentially rejective multiple test procedure. Scand. J. Stat. **6**(2), 65–70 (1979)

EvoNUM

Multi-strategy Differential Evolution

Anil Yaman[1(✉)] ⓘ, Giovanni Iacca[2] ⓘ, Matt Coler[3], George Fletcher[1],
and Mykola Pechenizkiy[1]

[1] Eindhoven University of Technology, Eindhoven, The Netherlands
{a.yaman,g.h.l.fletcher,m.pechenizkiy}@tue.nl
[2] RWTH Aachen University, Aachen, Germany
giovanni.iacca@gmail.com
[3] University of Groningen/Campus Fryslân, Leeuwarden, The Netherlands
m.coler@rug.nl

Abstract. We propose the Multi-strategy Differential Evolution (MsDE) algorithm to construct and maintain a self-adaptive ensemble of search strategies while solving an optimization problem. The ensemble of strategies is represented as agents that interact with the candidate solutions to improve their fitness. In the proposed algorithm, the performance of each agent is measured so that successful strategies are promoted within the ensemble. We propose two performance measures, and show their effectiveness in selecting successful strategies. We then present three population adaptation mechanisms, based on sampling, clone-best and clone-multiple adaptation schemes. The MsDE with different performance measures and population adaptation schemes is tested on the CEC2013 benchmark functions and compared with basic DE and with Self-Adaptive DE (SaDE). Our results show that MsDE is capable of efficiently adapting the strategies and parameters of DE and providing competitive results with respect to the state-of-the-art.

Keywords: Continuous optimization · Differential evolution
Parameter control · Strategy adaptation

1 Introduction

Evolutionary algorithms (EAs) are meta-heuristic search algorithms that operate on a population of candidate solutions. Biologically inspired evolutionary operators -namely selection, mutation and crossover- are used to manipulate iteratively the candidate solutions to improve their fitness [1]. Among EAs, Differential Evolution (DE) has been shown to be an efficient method for several optimization problems [2]. Various kinds of strategies have been suggested in the literature for improving upon basic DE [3,4]: these strategies typically adapt, according to some logics, the mutation scale factor (F) and crossover rate (CR) [5]. Such strategies significantly influence the behavior of DE as they alter the balance between exploration and exploitation [6].

© Springer International Publishing AG, part of Springer Nature 2018
K. Sim and P. Kaufmann (Eds.): EvoApplications 2018, LNCS 10784, pp. 617–633, 2018.
https://doi.org/10.1007/978-3-319-77538-8_42

An appropriate strategy and parameter setting of an algorithm is the best or near-best of all possible settings. Finding an appropriate strategy and parameter setting is an optimization problem that is as hard as finding the solution to the problem [7–9]. Eiben *et al.* categorized the parameters setting problem into two main categories, parameter tuning and parameter control [7]:

1. *Parameter tuning* aims to find the appropriate parameter settings offline, before an evolutionary run. The parameter tuning process can be performed by trial and error, from studies in the literature [10,11], or by using settings of similar problems [12].
2. *Parameter control* on the other hand, aims to adjust the parameter settings during an evolutionary process because the goodness of a parameter setting varies depending on the state of the search [6]. *Deterministic, adaptive* and *self-adaptive* methods have been proposed for the parameter control task [7].

We propose here a Multi-strategy Differential Evolution (MsDE) approach to self-adapt strategies and their parameters in DE during an evolutionary process. Most of the self-adaptive parameter control approaches aim to adapt algorithm parameters by including them within the genotype of the individuals and inheriting with the successful individuals during an evolutionary run. In MsDE, distinct from the inheritance based methods, an ensemble of search strategies are employed to operate on, and co-evolve with the candidate solutions. The strategies are referred as agents to distinguish them from the candidate solutions, and underline their function. The agent-based representation of the strategies provides the flexibility to apply a wide range of population adaptation mechanisms. In this work, we present three population adaptation schemes (sampling-based, clone-best and clone-multiple), to show how various self-adaptive agent-based approaches perform on the CEC2013 benchmark functions. Notably, the approach we propose here can be easily extended to any evolutionary algorithm to adapt their operators and parameters.

The rest of the paper is organized as follows: in Sect. 2, we provide the related work, where we discuss the basic DE algorithm and some strategy and parameter adaptation mechanisms proposed in the literature for DE; in Sect. 3, we describe our algorithm, MsDE, and present the three mechanisms for population adaptation; in Sect. 4, we present our test results, with the different population adaptation schemes, on the CEC2013 benchmark functions; finally, in Sect. 5 we provide the conclusions of this work.

2   Related Work

The DE algorithm is a population-based search algorithm proposed for continuous optimization [2]. A candidate solution set $\{x_1, x_2, \ldots, x_{NP}\}$ with a population size of NP is represented as D-dimensional real-valued vectors $x_i \in \mathbb{R}^D, i = 1, 2, \ldots, NP$. In the initialization phase of the algorithm, the candidate solutions are randomly sampled within the domain boundaries of each dimension $j = 1, 2, \ldots, D$.

The algorithm employs a strategy composed of a mutation, crossover, and selection operators with their specified parameters. For each generation g, a candidate solution x_i^g, called *target vector*, is selected $\forall i \in \{1, 2, \ldots, NP\}$. The mutation, crossover and selection operators are then applied to generate a *trial vector* u_i^g, and replace the target vector. The *mutation operator* generates a *mutant vector* v_i^g by perturbing the target vector x_i^g using the scaled differences of several distinct individuals selected randomly from the population. The *crossover operator* generates a trial vector u_i^g by performing recombination between the target vector and the mutant vector. The *selection operator* replaces the target vector x_i^g in the population with the trial vector u_i^g if the fitness value of u_i^g is better than or equal to x_i^g. This process is iteratively executed until a stopping criteria is met.

The **mutation operator** is controlled by the parameter *scale factor* (F) that is used to adjust the magnitude of the perturbation. There are various mutation operators suggested in the literature [3,4]. Four types of mutation strategies, referred as *"DE/rand/1"*, *"DE/rand/2"*, *"DE/rand-to-best/2"*, and *"DE/current-to-rand/1"* are provided in Eqs. (1), (2), (3), and (4), respectively, see [5].

$$v_i^g = x_{r_1}^g + F \cdot (x_{r_2}^g - x_{r_3}^g) \tag{1}$$

$$v_i^g = x_{r_1}^g + F \cdot (x_{r_2}^g - x_{r_3}^g) + F \cdot (x_{r_4}^g - x_{r_5}^g) \tag{2}$$

$$v_i^g = x_i^g + F \cdot (x_{best}^g - x_i^g) + F \cdot (x_{r_1}^g - x_{r_2}^g) + F \cdot (x_{r_3}^g - x_{r_4}^g) \tag{3}$$

$$v_i^g = x_i^g + K \cdot (x_{r_1}^g - x_i^g) + F \cdot (x_{r_2}^g - x_{r_3}^g) \tag{4}$$

where r_1, r_2, r_3, r_4, and r_5 are mutually exclusive integers different from i, and selected randomly from the range $[1, NP]$; the parameter K is a random number uniformly sampled in $(0, 1]$; x_i^g is the target vector; x_{best}^g is the best individual at generation g in terms of fitness.

The **crossover operator** is used to recombine the target vector and the mutant vector with a certain rate, CR, to generate a trial vector u_i^g. The *binomial (uniform) crossover* operator is given in (5). There are several more existing crossover operators such as the *exponential crossover* [13].

$$u_{i,j}^g = \begin{cases} v_{i,j}^g, & \text{if } rand([0,1)) \leq CR \text{ or } j = randi([1, D]); \\ x_{i,j}^g, & \text{otherwise.} \end{cases} \tag{5}$$

where j is an integer within the range $[1, D)$, functions $rand()$ and $randi()$ return a real and an integer value uniformly sampled from a defined range, respectively. The notation $x_{i,j}^g$ refers to the jth dimension of ith vector in the population at generation g.

If the value of the trial vector along the jth dimension exceeds the boundaries defined as x_j^{min} and x_j^{max}, it is randomly and uniformly sampled within the domain boundary range [5], using a toroidal boundary condition [14].

The **selection operator** determines whether or not the trial vector is kept for the next generation $g + 1$. If the fitness value of the trial vector is better

than or equal to the target vector, then the target vector is replaced by the trial
vector as it is shown in Eq. (6), which assumes a minimization problem:

$$x_i^{(g+1)} = \begin{cases} u_i^g, & \text{if } f(u_i^g) < f(x_i^g); \\ x_i^g, & \text{otherwise.} \end{cases} \tag{6}$$

The selection phase can be performed synchronously or asynchronously. In
synchronous selection, the selected trial vectors are stored in a temporary set,
and replaced with target vectors after the selection process of all individuals is
complete. In asynchronous selection, a selected trial vector is replaced directly
with the target vector without waiting the selection procedure for all individuals.
Asynchronous selection makes it possible to use a newly generated trial vector
in the trial vector generation process of all the remaining target vectors within
the same generation.

2.1 Strategy and Parameter Control in DE

In this section, we highlight the recent developments in strategy and parameter
control for DE. Modern variants of DE aim to employ adaptive mechanisms to
adjust the algorithm's parameters during an evolutionary run, or across different problems. Strategy and parameter control in DE can be examined in two
broad classes: *both strategy and parameter* control, and *only parameter* control
[3], where the parameters involved are F and CR. There are also methods for
adapting the population size NP, see e.g. [15]; however, in this work we limit
our scope to the methods for adapting the strategies, and the parameters F and
CR. In the following we briefly describe four of the main DE variants falling in
this category, namely EPSDE, SaDE, JADE and jDE.

In the Ensemble of Parameters and mutation Strategies Differential Evolution (EPSDE), mutation strategy and parameter pools are used [16–18]. Each
individual in the candidate solution population is assigned with a strategy and
a parameter setting from these pools. The strategies and their parameters are
inherited from the target to trial vectors as long as they are successful in generating a better trial vector. Otherwise, the strategy and parameters that are
associated with the target vector are reinitialized by either randomly sampling
from their respective pools, or assigning a strategy and its parameters from the
set where successful strategies and parameters are stored.

Self-adaptive differential evolution (SaDE) uses only two mutation strategies,
namely *"DE/rand/1/bin"* and *"DE/rand-to-best/1"*, and adapts the parameters
F and CR [19]. The strategies and parameters are selected for their properties of
generating diverse individuals and faster convergence rate respectively. For each
generation, a mutation strategy is randomly selected based on its probability of
generating a trial vector successfully. The success probability of the two mutation
strategies is initialized uniformly and updated after each generation, based on
the number of individuals generated successfully. The scale factor F is randomly
sampled, for each individual, from the normal distribution with mean 0.5 and
standard deviation 0.3. The parameter CR is initialized for each individual from

a normal distribution with mean 0.5 and standard deviation 0.1. The strategy pool of the SaDE has been later extended by Qin *et al.* [5].

The JADE algorithm introduces a new mutation strategy called "DE/current-to-pbest" with optional archive, and controls the parameters F and CR [20]. The optional archive keeps track of recently explored worse solutions, to provide additional information for the progression of the search. At each generation, the crossover rate CR_i is independently initialized from a normal distribution. The mean of the normal distribution μ_{CR} is initialized as 0.5 in for the first generation, and updated based on the mean of the CR_i of the trial vectors that are generated successfully. The mutation factor F_i is generated and updated in similar fashion by using a Cauchy distribution.

Finally, in jDE [21] the mutation and crossover parameters F and CR are attached to the genotype of the individuals in the population. The algorithm is based on the idea that the parameters that survive with the individuals are likely to produce successful trial vectors; thus, the parameters of the target vectors are propagated to the successive trial vectors in the next generations.

3 Multi-strategy Differential Evolution (MsDE)

The MsDE aims to self-adapt the strategy types (mutation and crossover operators) and their parameters (F and CR) used in DE while solving the optimization problem. It employs an ensemble of strategies with certain parameter settings, and applies population adaptation schemes to construct and maintain the ensemble strategy set. Different from the established ensemble methods in the literature, the MsDE considers the strategies as agents that interact with the candidate solution set. The agent-based representation of the strategies provides the basis for an easy application of population adaptation approaches.

The pseudocode of MsDE (assuming an asynchronous population, see below) is provided in Algorithm 1. The algorithm takes NP (number of solutions) and m (number of strategies) as parameters. In addition, there are two thresholds we refer to as performance and maturation thresholds, τ and δ, for determining the performance of a strategy and limiting the test phase of a strategy. The performance threshold τ is an adaptive threshold based on the average value of all the performances in the strategy ensemble. The maturation threshold δ is typically a small integer (e.g. 5) used to control how many algorithm iterations should be invested for the testing phase of new strategies.

The candidate solution set X consisting of NP D-dimensional real-valued vectors $x_i \in \mathbb{R}^D$ that represent a solution to the problem. The initial candidate solutions are randomly sampled in the domain range for each dimension. The population size NP is chosen during the initialization phase, and remains fixed throughout the run.

The ensemble strategy set Σ consists of m strategies $\sigma_1, \sigma_2, \ldots, \sigma_m \in \Sigma$. Each σ_j defines a kind of mutation and crossover operator, with specified parameters F and CR. In the initialization phase, each strategy is initialized by selecting a random mutation strategy with a type of crossover operator from a predefined

---

Algorithm 1. Asynchronous MsDE

1: **procedure** MsDE(NP, m)
2:     $g \leftarrow 0$ ▷ generation count
3:     initialize X ▷ randomly initialize NP solutions
4:     $\forall \sigma_j \in \Sigma, j = 1, 2, \ldots, m; \sigma_j \leftarrow InitializeRandomStrategy()$ ▷ see Alg. 2
5:     $F \leftarrow evaluate(X)$
6:     **while** termination criterion is not satisfied **do**
7:         $\tau \leftarrow mean(P_\Sigma)$ ▷ τ is the average performance of the strategies
8:         **for each** $\sigma \in \Sigma$ **do**
9:             $targetVector \leftarrow randSelect(X)$ ▷ randomly select a target vector
10:            $mutantVector \leftarrow \sigma.mutate(targetVector)$
11:            $trialVector \leftarrow \sigma.crossover(targetVector, mutantVector)$
12:            $\sigma.totalActivation \leftarrow \sigma.totalActivation + 1$
13:            $F_{trial} \leftarrow evaluate(trialVector)$
14:            **if** $F_{trial} < F_{target}$ **then**   ▷ selection operator (assuming minimization)
15:                $targetVector \leftarrow trialVector$
16:                $F_{target} \leftarrow F_{trial}$
17:                $\sigma.successfulActivation \leftarrow \sigma.successfulActivation + 1$
18:            **end if**
19:            $P_{\sigma_j} \leftarrow evaluate(\sigma)$ ▷ performance of a strategy
20:            **if** $P_{\sigma_j} < \tau$ and $\sigma.totalActivation > \delta$ **then**
21:                reinitialize σ
22:            **end if**
23:        **end for**
24:        $g \leftarrow g + 1$
25:    **end while**
26: **end procedure**

---

set of strategies S, of size l. The parameters F and CR are randomly sampled from a uniform distribution in $(0, 1.2]$ and $[0, 1]$, respectively. The upper limit of the scale factor is set to 1.2 because of the works that report the effective range for F between $(0, 1.2]$ [16]. The initialization procedure is illustrated in Algorithm 2.

Algorithm 2. Initialize random strategy

1: **function** InitializeRandomStrategy()
2:     $randomIndex \leftarrow randi[1, l]$
3:     $\sigma_{random}.type \leftarrow S[randomIndex]$
4:     $\sigma_{random}.F \leftarrow rand(0, 1.2]$
5:     $\sigma_{random}.CR \leftarrow rand[0, 1]$
6:     **return** σ_{random}
7: **end function**

The main loop of MsDE repeats until a stopping criteria is reached. In each iteration, each strategy agent σ_j is executed $\forall j \in (1, 2, \ldots, m)$, such that: first, a target vector x_i from X is randomly selected; secondly, the mutation and crossover operators are applied to generate a trial vector u_i; finally, the selection operator is applied to replace the target vector with the trial vector if its fitness value is better or equal. The selection operator can be *synchronous* or *asynchronous* as discussed in Sect. 2.

The MsDE calculates a performance measure within the function $evaluate(\sigma)$ to evaluate each strategy. Based on this performance measure, the strategies are classified as successful or unsuccessful. To solve the problem efficiently, firstly successful or unsuccessful strategies should be identified as quickly as possible; and secondly, the number of successful strategies in the population should be maximized, or, vice versa, the number of unsuccessful strategies should be minimized. We discuss these two aspects in the following sections.

Identifying Successful Strategies. Constructing and maintaining a successful set of strategies is crucial for the performance of the algorithm. The self-adaptive mechanism for ensemble construction and maintenance should be capable of managing the trade-off of exploring and exploiting successful strategies efficiently and adaptively. We use a performance measure to asses the quality of a strategy. We propose two measures P_1 and P_2 with different properties. The performance measure P_1, given in Eq. (7), measures the ratio between the number of strategy activations that led to a successful action and the total number of strategy activations:

$$P_1 = \frac{\sigma_j.successfulActivation}{\sigma_j.totalActivation} \tag{7}$$

where $\sigma_j.successfulActivation$ is the number of activations in which a strategy σ_j produced a trial vector with better fitness than the target vector, and $\sigma_j.totalActivation$ is the number of total activations.

As we will demonstrate in Sect. 4, a strategy selection criterion based on P_1 is likely to facilitate fast convergence; the drawback is a high probability of getting stuck onto a local optimum if the function is multimodal. This is because the strategies that are exploitative are more likely to score higher on P_1 than the exploratory strategies because small exploitative increments on the solutions are more likely to yield better solutions. To prevent the domination of exploitative strategies in the ensemble, the performance measure should be improved to promote also exploratory strategies. We measure the exploratory value of a strategy by its capability to produce diverse individuals with better fitness values. Such performance evaluation criteria would also encourage the diversity in the population; thus, it may be less susceptible to early convergence.

Methods used in multi-objective optimization, such as non-dominated sorting, can be used to select the strategies that have diverse trial vectors generation rate and high ratio of success [22]. On the other hand, these methods can increase the complexity of the algorithm. Thus, to avoid further complexity, we provide a performance measure P_2 for a single selection criterion to combine these two aspects implicitly in Eq. (8), where we calculate the average differences between target and trial vectors for the last γ activations in which the trial generation was successful.

$$P_2 = \begin{cases} \dfrac{1}{\sum_{a=TA_{\sigma_j}-\gamma+1}^{TA_{\sigma_j}} \psi_{\sigma_j}^{(a)}} \cdot \sum_{a=TA_{\sigma_j}-\gamma+1}^{TA_{\sigma_j}} \Delta_{\sigma_j}^a \cdot \psi_{\sigma_j}^{(a)}, & \text{if } TA_{\sigma_j} \geq \gamma; \\ \dfrac{1}{\sum_{a=1}^{TA_{\sigma_j}} \psi_{\sigma_j}^{(a)}} \cdot \sum_{a=1}^{TA_{\sigma_j}} \Delta_{\sigma_j}^a \cdot \psi_{\sigma_j}^{(a)}, & \text{otherwise.} \end{cases} \tag{8}$$

$$\Delta_{\sigma_j}^{(a)} = \sum_{d=1}^{D} | x_{i,d}^{(a)} - u_{i,d}^{(a)} | \tag{9}$$

$$\psi_{\sigma_j}^{(a)} = \begin{cases} 1, & \text{if } f(x_i^{(a)}) < f(u_i^{(a)}); \\ 0, & \text{otherwise.} \end{cases} \tag{10}$$

where $\Delta_{\sigma_j}^{(a)}$, defined by the distance metric given in Eq. (9), is the sum of the absolute differences along each dimension between target and trial vectors, and TA_{σ_j} represents $\sigma_j.totalActivation$. The parameter γ is introduced into this measure to sum only the differences in the most recent history of activations, to have a self-adaptive property. If γ is a large number then the measure may promote exploratory strategies that may have a few successful activations with large diversity.

Maximizing the Number of Successful Strategies. For an efficient search, the strategies that are classified as successful should be kept in the ensemble as long as they remain successful. To identify the performance of a strategy, strategies are tested for a certain time. The testing phase consumes resources, namely function evaluations (FEs). Since the strategies activated during the testing phase may not be necessarily good, the resources consumed in this phase should be minimized.

To distinguish the successful and unsuccessful strategies, the average performance values of all strategies τ is used. If the performance value of a strategy $P_{\sigma_j} < \tau$, then it is considered to be unsuccessful. To collect necessary evidence on the performance of a strategy, a *maturation threshold* δ is used such that if a strategy does not exceed δ then it is neither classified as successful nor unsuccessful.

3.1   Strategy Population Adaptation Schemes

We propose three mechanisms for strategy population adaptation: sampling-based, clone-best, and clone-multiple population adaptation schemes. These population adaptation schemes provide the logic for initiating new strategies into the ensemble, and removing existing strategies from the ensemble. The population adaptation methods are implemented in Line 21 of Algorithm 1.

Sampling-Based Population Adaptation. The sampling-based adaptation scheme initiates new strategies based on random sampling. The sampling function given in Algorithm 2 is used to reinitialize a mature unsuccessful strategy.

Clone-Best Population Adaptation. The clone-best adaptation scheme implements a clonal reproduction mechanism to replace unsuccessful strategies. The clone-best scheme is inspired by the clonal selection principle of the immune system theory [23,24]. The main idea is to replace an unsuccessful strategy with a clone of the best performing strategy with a small perturbation.

Algorithm 3. Strategy reinitialization by clone-best

1: **function** Clone(σ_j^g)
2:     **if** $rand(0,1) < \phi$ **then**
3:         **if** $rand(0,1) < \eta$ **then**
4:             $\sigma_{clone}^g.type \leftarrow S[randomIndex]$
5:         **else**
6:             $\sigma_{clone}^g.type \leftarrow \sigma_j^g.type$
7:         **end if**
8:         $\sigma_{clone}^g.F \leftarrow \sigma_j^g.F + \eta \cdot \mathcal{N}(0,1)$
9:         $\sigma_{clone}^g.CR \leftarrow \sigma_j^g.CR + \eta \cdot \mathcal{N}(0,1)$
10:    **else**
11:        $\sigma_{clone} \leftarrow InitializeRandomStrategy()$
12:    **end if**
13:    **return** σ_{clone}
14: **end function**

Algorithm 3 shows the function that is used to clone a strategy. In clone-best, the function takes σ_{best}^g as an argument, where σ_{best}^g is the best strategy in the current generation g. With probability ϕ, the *type*, (F and CR) of an unsuccessful strategy is replaced by the *type* (F, and CR) of the best strategy in the ensemble, with a small perturbation with scale factor $\eta \in (0,1]$. In our experiments, we use $\eta = 0.1$. If the parameter boundaries are exceeded, they are reinitialized by a value close to the boundaries. If $rand(0,1) \geq \phi$ the strategy is reinitialized using the uniform sampling scheme given in Algorithm 2.

Clone-Multiple Population Adaptation. The clone-multiple adaptation is an extension of the clone-best adaptation where m successful strategies are kept in a separate set referred to as memory strategies (Σ). If the limit of Σ is not exceeded, the scheme aims to find more successful strategies to add to Σ by going through the *cloning*, *selection*, *maturation* and *promotion* phases. These phases are described below:

1. *Clonal expansion:* n best strategies from Σ are selected and assigned into the best strategy set B. Each strategy in B is cloned (with a small perturbation) proportional to their performance. The higher the performance of a

strategy, the higher the number of clones generated. Algorithm 3, without ϕ parameter (or $\phi = 1$), is used for generating each clone for each $\sigma_j^g \in B$. Generated clones are added to a temporary candidate clone set T.

2. **Clonal selection:** h ($h \leq n$) candidate clones from T are selected based on their similarity to the strategies in B; and $v(v \leq h)$ strategies are generated randomly. The selected and randomly generated individuals are then added to the clone set C, that has size $h + v$. The similarity-based clone selection and the random strategy generation criteria are executed as follows:
    - h individuals are selected as follows: for each $\sigma_i \in T, i = 1, 2, \ldots, size(T)$ and $sigma_j \in B, j = 1, 2, \ldots, n$, $d_{\sigma_i} = \sum_{j=1}^n dist(\sigma_i, \sigma_j)$ is calculated. The h candidate clones with smallest d_{σ_i} are added to the clone set C. The $dist(\sigma_i, \sigma_j)$ computes the Euclidean distance between the parameters (F and CR) of σ_i and σ_j;
    - v random strategies are generated using Algorithm 2.
3. **Maturation:** each strategy in C is tested for δ FEs.
4. **Promotion:** strategies in C that are successful (i.e., that satisfy the performance threshold) are added to the memory set Σ. The same classification criterion for finding unsuccessful/successful strategies is used for finding successful strategies in C.

The logic behind the clone-multiple population adaptation scheme is such that it reduces the trial and error of newly generated strategies, by cloning successful strategies that are kept in a separate set. It also aims to find strategies that are likely to perform well by making a similarity-based selection. Mutations during the cloning phase allow for exploration of different strategies with different parameter settings.

4   Experimental Setup and Results

In this section, we present our experimental results on the CEC2013 benchmark functions [25]. The objective of our experiments is threefold. First, we show the effect of the two strategy performance measures P_1 and P_2 proposed in Sect. 3 on MsDE, with three population adaptation schemes. Second, we illustrate how the strategy adaptation dynamics compare between the sampling, clone-best and clone-multiple based population adaptation schemes during an evolutionary run. Finally, we compare the MsDE with basic DE and SaDE.

The types of the strategies and parameters of the algorithms are the same for all the experiments, unless otherwise specified. We employ four types of DE strategies referred to as *"DE/rand/1/bin"*, *"DE/rand/2/bin"*, *"DE/rand-to-best/2/bin"*, and *"DE/current-to-rand/1"*. The suffix *"bin"* refers to the binomial crossover. Note that *"DE/current-to-rand/1"* does not include a crossover operator. These strategies are selected on the basis of previous comparisons performed in the literature; furthermore, they are also used in SaDE [5]. Asynchronous selection is used for the selection operator.

All the experiments were performed using $NP = 100$ candidate solutions and $m = 50$ strategies. The algorithms were run for at most $5000 \times D$ function evaluations (FEs), where D is the dimension of the problem. If the error between the best solution found and the global optimum is less than or equal to $1e-8$, we terminate the algorithm. Each algorithm was executed for 25 independent runs; the mean and standard deviation of minimum error $f(x_{best}) - f(x^*)$ achieved are presented.

The three strategy adaptation schemes (sampling-based, clone-best and clone-multiple) are referred to as $MsDE\text{-}Sam$, $MsDE\text{-}CB$, and $MsDE\text{-}CM$, respectively. For MsDE-CB, the probability for cloning the best strategy ϕ is set to 0.7. For MsDE-CM, the number of selected best strategies n is set to 10, the max number of clones per strategy is set to 10 for the best strategy and reduced by 1 per each lower ranked strategy, the number of similar selected strategies is set to $h = 7$, and the number of randomly initialized strategies is set to $v = 3$; thus the number of strategies adds up to a total number of 10. For all algorithms, the maturation threshold and the history threshold γ are set to 5 FEs and 10 activations, respectively.

Comparing the Performance Measures. In Table 1, we compare the two different performance measures P_1 and P_2 for each kind of population adaptation scheme on the CEC2013 functions in 10 dimensions. The suffixes "$-P_1$" and "$-P_2$" indicate the performance measure used with a specific kind of population adaptation scheme. The best results for each performance measure for each algorithm setting is highlighted in bold. The results that do not have significant difference were not highlighted. The global best result for each function is marked by the symbol "*".

We observed that all three population adaptation schemes perform significantly better using P_2 on almost all benchmark functions. Since P_1 promotes the strategies based solely on the ratio of producing successful trial vectors, it is likely to promote exploitative strategies that can cause early convergence, or stalling the progress with small improvements. Performance measure P_2, on the other hand, promotes strategies that can produce diverse trial vectors successfully. The rest of the experiments are performed using P_2.

Strategy Ensemble Adaptation Dynamics. Next, we examine how the strategies adapt over time. In Fig. 1, we provide the results on f_2 (first column) and f_6 (second column) in 30 dimensions.

Each sub-figure in Fig. 1 shows how the distribution of strategies changes during an evolutionary run. Each line in the figures represents the number of strategies of a given type in the strategy population, at a given generation. Only the strategies that are mature and above the success threshold are counted. We observe that in MsDE-Sam (a) and (d), there is a baseline pool of random strategies that explores new strategies. The ratio of these pool is about %30 of the whole population. In MsDE-CB (b) and (e), this ratio is about %20; and in MsDE-CM (c) and (f), we observe that the random strategy pool is almost nonexistent, and there is usually one type of strategy that is dominant at each time. MsDE-Sam scheme constantly explores different strategies by keeping a

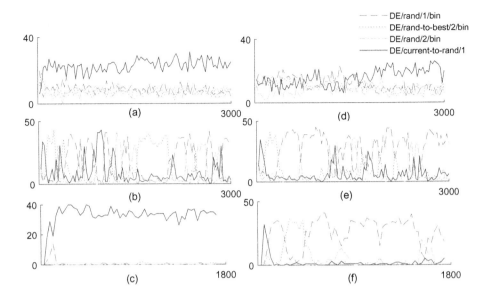

Fig. 1. The distribution of strategies in the strategy population during an evolutionary run. The first and second columns show the results for f_2 and f_6 in 30 dimensions, while the rows show the results of MsDE-Sam, MsDE-CB, and MsDE-CM, respectively.

small set of random strategies which can consume resources (number of function evaluations). On the other hand, MsDE-CB and MsDE-CM aims to exploit already found successful strategies by reintroducing them into the ensemble by reproduction.

Comparing with Other Algorithms. Finally, we test MsDE-Sam, MsDE-CB, MsDE-CM, basic DE and SaDE [5] on the CEC2013 benchmark functions in 30 dimensions. The parameters F and CR of the basic DE set are as 0.5 and 0.3 respectively. The results are given in Table 2. The global best result for each function is highlighted in bold.

To assess the statistical significance of the results, we perform the Wilcoxon rank-sum test [26] based on the results provided in Table 2. The Wilcoxon rank-sum test is a non-parametric test that does not assume normality condition [14,26]. It is a pairwise test that aims to detect the significant difference between two different means that are the results of two algorithms. We reject the null-hypothesis, that is the behavior of the two algorithms are the same, if the p-value is smaller than $\alpha = 0.05$. We compare the MsDE-CM with the other algorithms using the best function error values of 25 independent runs for each benchmark function. The results are given in Table 2 next to the columns of the specified algorithms (except MsDE-CM, which is taken as the reference algorithm), where "=", "+" and "−" indicate no significant difference, significant difference in favor of MsDE-CM, and significant difference in favor of the specified algorithm.

Table 1. The experiment results with performance measures P_1 and P_2 on the CEC2013 benchmark problems in 10 dimensions.

f_i	MsDE-Sam-P_1	MsDE-Sam-P_2	MsDE-CB-P_1	MsDE-CB-P_2	MsDE-CM-P_1	MsDE-CM-P_2
f_1	8.47E-09 ± 1.92E-09	8.74E-09 ± 1.15E-09	9.04E-09 ± 1.31E-04	8.52E-09 ± 1.63E-09	8.49E-09 ± 2.31E-02	8.77E-09 ± 5.37E-09
f_2	1.27E+03 ± 4.20E+03	8.37E+02 ± 3.20E+03	1.79E+05 ± 3.34E+05	9.42E-09 ± 3.52E-05*	1.00E+05 ± 3.50E+06	8.16E-09 ± 1.15E-06*
f_3	5.77E+05 ± 1.03E+07	2.08E+01 ± 3.99E+05	1.72E+07 ± 4.99E+08	4.95E-03 ± 1.28E+00*	3.44E+07 ± 1.06E+09	1.62E-01 ± 1.25E+00
f_4	8.19E-03 ± 9.28E-01	2.51E-03 ± 5.32E-02	5.45E+02 ± 4.52E+03	8.83E-01 ± 1.31E-09*	5.36E-01 ± 6.69E+03	8.66E-09 ± 9.76E-09*
f_5	9.27E-09 ± 1.07E-09	8.65E-09 ± 1.11E-09	9.70E-09 ± 7.56E-02	9.50E-09 ± 6.92E-08	9.02E-09 ± 8.79E-02	8.97E-09 ± 1.16E-07
f_6	9.53E-09 ± 4.97E+00*	9.81E+00 ± 4.81E+00	1.01E+01 ± 8.31E+00	8.06E+00 ± 3.67E+00	9.82E+00 ± 2.66E+01	8.67E-09 ± 2.72E+00*
f_7	1.63E+01 ± 1.61E+01	1.53E+00 ± 8.36E+00	6.13E+01 ± 2.80E+01	2.04E+01 ± 1.21E+01	3.13E+01 ± 4.49E+01	1.21E-03 ± 5.52E-02*
f_8	2.04E+01 ± 7.74E-02	2.04E+01 ± 9.58E-02	2.04E+01 ± 8.67E-02	3.44E+00 ± 7.08E-02	2.04E+01 ± 1.22E-01	2.04E+01 ± 9.15E-02*
f_9	3.78E+00 ± 1.27E+00	2.92E+00 ± 9.42E-01	6.60E+00 ± 1.39E+00	4.43E-02 ± 1.28E+00*	7.41E+00 ± 1.70E+00	1.96E+00 ± 1.20E+00
f_{10}	2.78E-01 ± 2.71E-01	1.40E-01 ± 6.72E-02	8.89E-01 ± 2.73E+00	1.99E+00 ± 4.68E-02	8.82E-01 ± 1.62E+01	5.88E-08 ± 2.99E-02*
f_{11}	2.98E+00 ± 3.52E+00	9.34E-09 ± 6.47E-01*	1.39E+01 ± 1.14E+01	1.09E+01 ± 2.36E+00	6.59E+00 ± 1.41E+01	9.15E-09 ± 4.97E-01*
f_{12}	1.59E+01 ± 8.37E+00	1.09E+01 ± 5.33E+00	3.28E+01 ± 1.79E+01	2.44E+01 ± 5.04E+00	1.88E+01 ± 1.73E+01	3.98E+00 ± 2.58E+00*
f_{13}	2.65E+01 ± 9.99E+00	1.58E+01 ± 7.46E+00	4.66E+01 ± 2.75E+01	4.33E+01 ± 1.09E+01	3.57E+01 ± 2.52E+01	5.05E+00 ± 5.09E+00*
f_{14}	1.51E+01 ± 3.80E+01	3.54E+00 ± 6.96E+00	6.17E+01 ± 1.91E+02	7.68E+02 ± 1.08E+02	6.48E+01 ± 2.53E+02	3.12E-01 ± 3.86E+00*
f_{15}	7.96E+02 ± 2.53E+02	7.02E+02 ± 2.74E+02	8.19E+02 ± 3.41E+02	4.24E-02 ± 2.11E+02*	9.42E+02 ± 4.02E+02	7.83E+02 ± 2.65E+02
f_{16}	9.49E-01 ± 3.27E-01	1.07E+00 ± 3.00E-01	4.91E-01 ± 2.11E-01*	1.22E+01 ± 5.89E-01	1.07E+00 ± 4.45E-01	1.08E+00 ± 6.94E-01
f_{17}	1.04E+01 ± 3.64E+00	1.02E+01 ± 9.64E-02*	3.15E+01 ± 1.31E+01	1.98E+01 ± 1.21E+01	1.44E+01 ± 6.61E+00	1.03E+01 ± 6.07E-01
f_{18}	2.09E+01 ± 4.75E+00*	2.14E+01 ± 5.71E+00	4.02E+01 ± 1.97E+01	7.42E-01 ± 4.09E+00*	3.04E+01 ± 1.32E+01	1.60E+01 ± 2.63E+00
f_{19}	6.00E-01 ± 2.52E-01	3.68E-01 ± 1.39E-01*	1.45E+00 ± 1.28E+00	3.30E+00 ± 2.30E-01	1.02E+00 ± 6.46E-01	5.13E-01 ± 1.70E-01
f_{20}	2.43E+00 ± 5.81E-01	2.78E+00 ± 5.05E-01	3.89E+00 ± 5.17E-01	4.00E+02 ± 6.05E-01	3.55E+00 ± 6.30E-01	2.40E+00 ± 5.13E-01*
f_{21}	4.00E+02 ± 6.28E+01	4.00E+02 ± 5.54E+01	4.00E+02 ± 2.31E-01	8.44E+01 ± 2.32E-13*	4.00E+02 ± 8.73E+01	4.00E+02 ± 7.08E+01
f_{22}	7.54E+01 ± 8.53E+01	3.12E+02 ± 7.26E+01*	1.68E+02 ± 2.35E+02	9.33E+02 ± 1.69E+02	3.20E+02 ± 2.79E+02	4.99E+01 ± 5.09E+01
f_{23}	9.89E+02 ± 3.11E+01	8.33E+02 ± 2.40E+02	7.92E+02 ± 3.28E+02	2.06E+02 ± 2.66E+02*	1.21E+03 ± 3.45E+02	8.67E+02 ± 3.07E+02
f_{24}	2.12E+02 ± 2.64E+01	2.09E+02 ± 2.56E+01	2.21E+02 ± 2.49E+01	2.00E+02 ± 2.06E+01	2.18E+02 ± 3.52E+01	2.00E+02 ± 1.62E+01*
f_{25}	2.11E+02 ± 2.18E+01	2.02E+02 ± 2.28E+01	2.20E+02 ± 2.17E+01	1.19E+02 ± 1.74E+01*	2.18E+02 ± 1.98E+01	2.00E+02 ± 1.78E+01
f_{26}	1.56E+02 ± 4.10E+01	2.00E+02 ± 3.88E+01	1.32E+02 ± 3.65E+01	3.00E+02 ± 3.21E+01	1.51E+02 ± 3.54E+01	1.06E+02 ± 2.67E+01*
f_{27}	4.00E+02 ± 8.74E+01	3.00E+02 ± 7.35E+01	4.58E+02 ± 9.41E+01	3.00E+02 ± 2.76E+01*	4.41E+02 ± 1.09E+02	3.00E+02 ± 2.00E+01
f_{28}	3.00E+02 ± 1.43E+02	3.00E+02 ± 6.63E+01*	3.00E+02 ± 2.15E+01*	3.00E+02 ± 9.80E+01	3.00E+02 ± 1.86E+02*	3.00E+02 ± 4.00E+01

Table 2. The experiment results of the selected algorithms on the CEC2013 benchmark problems in 30 dimensions.

f_i	MsDE-Sam	MsDE-CB		MsDE-CM		DE		SaDE	
f_1	9.56E-09 ± 7.88E-10	9.26E-09 ± 9.58E-10	=	9.54E-09 ± 6.05E-10	=	9.24E-09 ± 5.51E-10	=	9.14E-09 ± 1.14E-09	=
f_2	1.40E+05 ± 1.32E+05	1.71E+05 ± 1.15E+05	=	**1.19E+05 ± 1.91E+05**	=	2.21E+08 ± 4.53E+07	+	1.76E+05 ± 1.45E+05	+
f_3	1.15E+05 ± 4.06E+06	6.01E+06 ± 1.37E+07	+	**8.60E+04 ± 1.59E+06**	+	1.56E+09 ± 8.56E+08	+	1.43E+05 ± 1.72E+06	+
f_4	**1.22E+01 ± 3.63E+01**	1.73E+02 ± 3.74E+02	-	4.40E+01 ± 6.08E+01	+	1.16E+05 ± 1.64E+04	+	3.52E+03 ± 2.42E+03	+
f_5	9.58E-09 ± 4.97E-10	9.64E-09 ± 7.46E-10	=	9.71E-09 ± 3.71E-10	+	9.58E-09 ± 5.56E-10	=	9.60E-09 ± 6.51E-10	=
f_6	9.67E+00 ± 5.07E+00	9.41E+00 ± 6.67E+00	=	**9.17E+00 ± 1.72E+01**	+	2.63E+01 ± 3.33E-01	+	1.22E+01 ± 1.25E+01	+
f_7	1.46E+01 ± 1.03E+01	7.23E+01 ± 1.64E+01	-	2.87E+01 ± 1.40E+01	+	1.46E+02 ± 1.48E+01	+	**1.22E+01 ± 6.62E+00**	-
f_8	**2.10E+01 ± 6.72E-02**	2.10E+01 ± 4.33E-02	-	2.10E+01 ± 6.37E-02	-	2.10E+01 ± 5.53E-02	-	2.10E+01 ± 5.50E-02	-
f_9	**1.73E+01 ± 3.08E+00**	2.72E+01 ± 4.73E+00	+	2.24E+01 ± 5.74E+00	+	3.94E+01 ± 1.14E+00	+	1.91E+01 ± 2.32E+00	+
f_{10}	3.45E-02 ± 2.64E-02	5.17E-02 ± 3.94E-02	=	**3.45E-02 ± 2.56E-02**	=	1.27E+02 ± 3.62E+01	+	4.93E-02 ± 4.01E-02	=
f_{11}	8.95E+00 ± 4.54E+00	2.98E+01 ± 1.16E+01	+	1.69E+01 ± 8.36E+01	+	6.83E+01 ± 5.55E+00	+	**1.81E-05 ± 5.57E+00**	-
f_{12}	4.58E+01 ± 9.63E+00	7.16E+01 ± 2.25E+01	+	**3.18E+01 ± 8.87E+00**	+	2.03E+02 ± 1.06E+01	+	3.48E+01 ± 6.34E+00	+
f_{13}	8.77E+01 ± 2.31E+01	1.54E+02 ± 4.15E+01	+	**6.86E+01 ± 2.37E+01**	+	2.10E+02 ± 1.50E+01	+	6.94E+01 ± 2.64E+01	=
f_{14}	**2.90E+01 ± 3.26E+01**	9.99E+02 ± 4.87E+02	+	6.11E+01 ± 1.25E+02	=	3.93E+03 ± 2.33E+02	+	1.81E+03 ± 6.37E+02	+
f_{15}	6.41E+03 ± 1.15E+03	3.63E+03 ± 5.78E+02	+	3.68E+03 ± 1.49E+03	=	7.78E+03 ± 3.10E+02	+	**3.42E+03 ± 5.60E+02**	=
f_{16}	2.59E+00 ± 2.30E-01	**2.03E-01 ± 8.17E-01**	+	2.33E+00 ± 9.58E-01	-	2.71E+00 ± 3.02E-01	+	2.51E+00 ± 3.66E-01	=
f_{17}	**3.34E+01 ± 1.61E+00**	6.01E+01 ± 1.11E+01	-	3.57E+01 ± 4.18E+00	+	1.00E+02 ± 6.01E+00	+	5.80E+01 ± 9.32E+00	+
f_{18}	1.70E+02 ± 4.10E+01	8.28E+01 ± 1.76E+01	+	**5.15E+01 ± 3.82E+01**	+	2.32E+02 ± 1.05E+01	+	5.55E+01 ± 1.15E+01	+
f_{19}	2.70E+00 ± 1.04E+00	4.95E+00 ± 2.64E+00	+	**2.40E+00 ± 5.24E-01**	+	1.10E+01 ± 6.77E-01	+	2.75E+00 ± 9.47E-01	+
f_{20}	1.14E+01 ± 5.08E-01	1.18E+01 ± 1.34E+00	+	**1.03E+01 ± 1.12E+00**	=	1.37E+01 ± 1.71E-01	+	1.04E+01 ± 7.84E-01	=
f_{21}	**3.00E+02 ± 8.32E+01**	3.00E+02 ± 8.77E+01	=	3.00E+02 ± 8.04E+01	=	3.00E+02 ± 4.26E+01	+	3.00E+02 ± 6.78E+01	+
f_{22}	**1.40E+02 ± 5.62E+01**	1.29E+03 ± 5.41E+02	+	1.66E+02 ± 2.01E+02	+	4.55E+03 ± 3.33E+02	+	1.47E+03 ± 7.88E+02	+
f_{23}	6.67E+03 ± 1.24E+03	4.52E+03 ± 7.48E+02	+	3.97E+03 ± 1.14E+03	=	8.04E+03 ± 2.95E+02	+	**3.60E+03 ± 6.42E+02**	=
f_{24}	2.19E+02 ± 6.43E+00	2.40E+02 ± 1.11E+01	=	2.16E+02 ± 7.23E+00	+	3.01E+02 ± 2.62E+00	+	**2.09E+02 ± 3.28E+00**	-
f_{25}	**2.69E+02 ± 8.14E+00**	2.92E+02 ± 1.11E+01	=	2.80E+02 ± 3.02E+01	+	3.02E+02 ± 2.63E+00	+	2.73E+02 ± 6.39E+00	+
f_{26}	2.00E+02 ± 3.58E-03	2.00E+02 ± 7.16E-03	=	**2.00E+02 ± 8.89E-03**	=	2.79E+02 ± 3.73E-01	+	2.00E+02 ± 9.65E-03	=
f_{27}	4.94E+02 ± 6.56E+01	8.49E+02 ± 1.27E+02	+	5.28E+02 ± 1.03E+02	+	1.32E+03 ± 1.91E+01	+	**4.56E+02 ± 7.11E+01**	-
f_{28}	**3.00E+02 ± 4.14E-13**	3.00E+02 ± 1.04E-10	-	3.00E+02 ± 1.02E-07	-	3.00E+02 ± 1.66E-08	+	3.00E+02 ± 1.87E-09	-

The results show that MsDE-CM is significantly better than basic DE and MsDE-CB, and on average better than SaDE and MsDE-Sam.

5 Conclusions

In this work, we propose the Multi-strategy Differential Evolution (MsDE) algorithm to construct and maintain an ensemble set of strategies with various parameters. MsDE is capable of self-adapting the type of strategy and its parameters F and CR. Different from the alternative approaches, MsDE represents the ensemble strategy population as agents that interact with the candidate solutions. The performance of the strategies is measured by a performance measure which is used to self-adapt the ensemble population.

We propose two performance measures, and compare their efficiency in constructing an ensemble of successful strategies. Our results show that favoring strategies that can produce diverse trial vectors successfully yields better than favoring them based solely on their ratio of producing successful trial vectors.

We propose three approaches for self-adapting the strategy population. The simplest approach is based on random sampling where new strategies are randomly introduced into, and the ones that do not satisfy a performance criterion are removed from the ensemble. Other two approaches use clonal selection mechanism to proliferate successful strategies in the ensemble. While, four different types of strategies with their continuous F and CR parameters are aimed to be optimized, the sampling based approach requires only a parameter for ensemble size, and a threshold for defining a successful strategy based on its performance metric. The clonal selection based algorithms introduce an additional parameter for perturbing strategies. In this work, we used asynchronous selection operator. Asynchronous selection can speed up the convergence and decrease the population diversity. We would like to examine the effect of synchronous/asynchronous update in the future work.

We compare the MsDE with basic DE and the SaDE algorithm with different combinations strategy performance measure and population adaptation schemes. Overall, our results show that the MsDE provides better results on CEC2013 benchmark functions. In future works, we will try to extend the MsDE approach to other evolutionary algorithms.

 Acknowledgments. We would like to thank Dr. Samaneh Khoshrou from Eindhoven University of Technology for the informative discussion. This project has received funding from the European Union's Horizon 2020 research and innovation programme under grant agreement No 665347.

References

1. Goldberg, D.E.: Genetic algorithms in search, optimization, and machine learning (1989)
2. Storn, R., Price, K.: Differential evolution-a simple and efficient heuristic for global optimization over continuous spaces. J. Global Optim. **11**(4), 341–359 (1997)
3. Das, S., Mullick, S.S., Suganthan, P.N.: Recent advances in differential evolution-an updated survey. Swarm Evol. Comput. **27**, 1–30 (2016)
4. Neri, F., Tirronen, V.: Recent advances in differential evolution: a survey and experimental analysis. Artif. Intell. Rev. **33**(1–2), 61–106 (2010)
5. Qin, A.K., Huang, V.L., Suganthan, P.N.: Differential evolution algorithm with strategy adaptation for global numerical optimization. IEEE Trans. Evol. Comput. **13**(2), 398–417 (2009)
6. Črepinšek, M., Liu, S.H., Mernik, M.: Exploration and exploitation in evolutionary algorithms: a survey. ACM Comput. Surv. (CSUR) **45**(3), 35 (2013)
7. Eiben, Á.E., Hinterding, R., Michalewicz, Z.: Parameter control in evolutionary algorithms. IEEE Trans. Evol. Comput. **3**(2), 124–141 (1999)
8. Karafotias, G., Hoogendoorn, M., Eiben, Á.E.: Parameter control in evolutionary algorithms: trends and challenges. IEEE Trans. Evol. Comput. **19**(2), 167–187 (2015)
9. Kramer, O.: Self-adaptive Heuristics for Evolutionary Computation, vol. 147. Springer, Heidelberg (2008)
10. De Jong, K.A.: Analysis of the behavior of a class of genetic adaptive systems. Ph.D. thesis (1975)
11. Yaman, A., Hallawa, A., Coler, M., Iacca, G.: Presenting the ECO: evolutionary computation ontology. In: Squillero, G., Sim, K. (eds.) EvoApplications 2017. LNCS, vol. 10199, pp. 603–619. Springer, Cham (2017). https://doi.org/10.1007/978-3-319-55849-3_39
12. Hallawa, A., Yaman, A., Iacca, G., Ascheid, G.: A framework for knowledge integrated evolutionary algorithms. In: Squillero, G., Sim, K. (eds.) EvoApplications 2017. LNCS, vol. 10199, pp. 653–669. Springer, Cham (2017). https://doi.org/10.1007/978-3-319-55849-3_42
13. Price, K., Storn, R.M., Lampinen, J.A.: Differential Evolution: A Practical Approach to Global Optimization. Springer Science & Business Media, Heidelberg (2006)
14. Iacca, G., Caraffini, F., Neri, F.: Multi-strategy coevolving aging particle optimization. Int. J. Neural Syst. **24**(01), 1450008 (2014)
15. Iacca, G., Mallipeddi, R., Mininno, E., Neri, F., Suganthan, P.N.: Super-fit and population size reduction in compact differential evolution. In: 2011 IEEE Workshop on Memetic Computing (MC), pp. 1–8, April 2011
16. Mallipeddi, R., Suganthan, P.N., Pan, Q.K., Tasgetiren, M.F.: Differential evolution algorithm with ensemble of parameters and mutation strategies. Appl. Soft Comput. **11**(2), 1679–1696 (2011)
17. Mallipeddi, R., Iacca, G., Suganthan, P.N., Neri, F., Mininno, E.: Ensemble strategies in compact differential evolution. In: 2011 IEEE Congress of Evolutionary Computation (CEC), pp. 1972–1977, June 2011
18. Iacca, G., Neri, F., Caraffini, F., Suganthan, P.N.: A differential evolution framework with ensemble of parameters and strategies and pool of local search algorithms. In: Esparcia-Alcázar, A.I., Mora, A.M. (eds.) EvoApplications 2014. LNCS, vol. 8602, pp. 615–626. Springer, Heidelberg (2014). https://doi.org/10.1007/978-3-662-45523-4_50

19. Qin, A.K., Suganthan, P.N.: Self-adaptive differential evolution algorithm for numerical optimization. In: The 2005 IEEE Congress on Evolutionary Computation, vol. 2, pp. 1785–1791. IEEE (2005)
20. Zhang, J., Sanderson, A.C.: JADE: adaptive differential evolution with optional external archive. IEEE Trans. Evol. Comput. **13**(5), 945–958 (2009)
21. Brest, J., Greiner, S., Boskovic, B., Mernik, M., Zumer, V.: Self-adapting control parameters in differential evolution: a comparative study on numerical benchmark problems. IEEE Trans. Evol. Comput. **10**(6), 646–657 (2006)
22. Deb, K., Pratap, A., Agarwal, S., Meyarivan, T.: A fast and elitist multiobjective genetic algorithm: NSGA-II. IEEE Trans. Evol. Comput. **6**(2), 182–197 (2002)
23. De Castro, L.N., Von Zuben, F.J.: Learning and optimization using the clonal selection principle. IEEE Trans. Evol. Comput. **6**(3), 239–251 (2002)
24. De Castro, L.N.: Fundamentals of Natural Computing: Basic Concepts, Algorithms, and Applications. CRC Press (2006)
25. Liang, J., Qu, B., Suganthan, P., Hernández-Díaz, A.G.: Problem definitions and evaluation criteria for the CEC 2013 special session on real-parameter optimization. Computational Intelligence Laboratory, Zhengzhou University, Zhengzhou, China and Nanyang Technological University, Singapore, Technical Report 201212, 3–18 (2013)
26. Wilcoxon, F.: Individual comparisons by ranking methods. Biometrics Bull. **1**(6), 80–83 (1945)

A Generic Framework for Incorporating Constraint Handling Techniques into Multi-Objective Evolutionary Algorithms

Hiroaki Fukumoto[(⊠)] and Akira Oyama

Institute of Space and Astronautical Science, Japan Aerospace Exploration Agency, Sagamihara 252-5210, Japan
fukumoto@flab.isas.jaxa.jp

Abstract. A generic framework for incorporating constraint handling techniques (CHTs) into multi-objective evolutionary algorithms (MOEAs) is proposed to resolve the differences between MOEAs from algorithmic and implementation perspective with respect to the incorporation of CHTs. To verify the effectiveness of the proposed framework, the performances of the combined algorithms of five CHTs and four MOEAs on eight constrained multi-objective optimization problems are investigated with the proposed framework. The experimental results show that the outperforming CHT can vary by constrained multi-objective optimization problems, as far as examined in this study.

Keywords: Constraint handling techniques
Constrained multi-objective optimization problems
Multi-objective evolutionary algorithms

1 Introduction

Most real-world optimization problems involve multiple objectives and constraints. The problems with such multiple objectives and constraints, which are so-called constrained multi-objective optimization problems, can be formulated as follows without loss of generality:

$$\begin{aligned}
\text{minimize} \quad & f_i(\boldsymbol{x}), i \in \{1, ..., M\} \\
\text{subject to} \quad & g_i(\boldsymbol{x}) \geq 0, i \in \{1, ..., p\} \\
& h_i(\boldsymbol{x}) = 0, i \in \{p+1, ..., N\}
\end{aligned} \tag{1}$$

where $\boldsymbol{f} : \mathbb{S} \to \mathbb{R}^M$ is an objective function vector which consists of M objective functions, and $\mathbb{R}^M$ is the objective function space. $\boldsymbol{x} = (x_1, ..., x_D)^{\mathrm{T}}$ is a D-dimensional solution vector, and $\mathbb{S} = \Pi_{j=1}^{D}[x_j^{min}, x_j^{max}]$ is the bound-constrained search space, where $x_j^{min} \leq x_j \leq x_j^{max}$ for each $j \in \{1, ..., D\}$. A solution who

K. Sim and P. Kaufmann (Eds.): EvoApplications 2018, LNCS 10784, pp. 634–649, 2018.
https://doi.org/10.1007/978-3-319-77538-8_43

satisfies all the constraint functions is called a feasible solution, otherwise is called a infeasible solution.

For two feasible solutions x^1, x^2, we say that x^1 dominates x^2 and denote $x^1 \prec x^2$ if and only if $f_i(x^1) \leq f_i(x^2)$ for all $i \in \{1, ..., M\}$ and $f_i(x^1) < f_i(x^2)$ for at least one index i. For a feasible solution x^*, x^* is called a Pareto optimal solution if there exists no feasible solution x such that $x \prec x^*$. The set of all x^* is called a Pareto optimal solution Set (PS), and the set of all $f(x^*)$ is called a Pareto Frontier (PF).

Over the past decades, multi-objective evolutionary algorithms (MOEAs) have been regarded as promising approaches for solving multi-objective optimization problems [1]. Since MOEAs are population based optimization approaches, a set of non-dominated feasible solutions can be obtained in a single run. Although a lot of time and effort have been made to develop evolutionary algorithms, much of the studies have been on single-objective optimization problems with and without constraints and multi-objective optimization problems without constraints [2]. It is resent that the research focus had started moving onto constrained multi-objective optimization problems: MOEAs in whose original article an incorporation of constraint handling technique (CHT) is introduced can be found more frequently in recent literatures (for example, NSGA-III [3], I-DBEA [4], MOEA/DD [5], and RVEA [6]). Here, constrained multi-objective optimization problem is specially denoted as CMOEA in this paper.

Many of CHTs have been developed for constrained single-objective optimization problems while there are few CHTs that have been developed for constrained multi-objective optimization problems [2]. The few CHT for constrained multi-objective optimization problems, however, are embedded into each MOEA and none of these literatures discusses about applicability of the proposed CHT to other MOEAs. From the point of view of the versatility of CHTs, on the other hand, CHTs that are not embedded into any specific MOEAs are appreciated [7–9]. With the versatility of CHTs, we do not need to develop an effective CHT each time new MOEA is developed. Mezura-Montes assumes in his review paper [2], that the reason why there are few literatures on CHTs for constrained multi-objective optimization problems is that CHTs developed for constrained single-objective optimization problems can be easily coupled to MOEAs. If it were truly easy, then most of CHTs for constrained single-objective optimization problems can be applied to MOEAs and it can be said to be versatile. However, we can find only some literatures that incorporate CHTs developed for constrained single-objective optimization problems into some MOEAs, and we cannot find any comprehensive study for CMOEAs to the best of the authors' survey. We suppose that the reason of this is either one of the followings: the incorporation of CHTs for constrained single-objective optimization problems into MOEAs is more difficult than expected, or versatile CMOEAs are not so desired. However, as for our research group, we have a certain demand for versatile CHTs in order to find out the most effective strategy of CHTs as a first step for developing further effective CHTs for constrained multi-objective optimization problems in actual industrial design realm. In addition, we have noticed that some modifications need to be implemented so as to incorporate CHTs for constrained single-objective optimization problems into MOEAs.

In this context, we propose an generic framework for incorporating CHTs into MOEAs. With this proposed framework, many of existing CHTs can be treated as a module of MOEA framework. Here, the incorporated MOEAs can be classified into any of the categories: dominance-based, decomposition-based, or indicator-based.

2 Constraint Handling Techniques

2.1 CHTs Developed for Solving Constrained Single-Objective Optimization Problems

CHTs for constrained single-objective optimization problems can be roughly classified into four categories, penalty, repair, separatist, and hybrid approaches [10].

Penalty approach [11] is one of the most frequently used techniques among the four categories [12]. In this approach, a constrained single-objective optimization problem is transformed into an unconstrained single-objective optimization problem by adding a certain value to the objective function based on the amount of constraint violation so that the infeasible solutions get less preferred. The key of this approach lies in how to determine the penalty factor, which defines the balance between the objective function and the measure of constraint violation [13]. The measure of constraint violation (often denoted as CV or ϕ) can be anything related the degree of constraint violation and its definition varies by CHTs. Among recent penalty approaches, the self-adaptive penalty method (SP) proposed by Tessema et al. [14] is a representative one (denoted as T&Y after the authors' name). This method balances between the objective function and the measure of constraint violation in a self-adaptive manner.

Repair approach [15] converts infeasible solutions to feasible ones. This approach is suitable for the problems in which the way for repairing infeasible solutions to feasible ones is known and easy. However, this approach is completely problem-dependent and is off-topic of this paper.

The separatist approach handles objective function and constraints separately. Deb et al. proposed the superiority of feasible solutions [16], whose basic idea was subsequently extended to a most popular CHT for constrained multi-objective optimization problems as introduced later. Epsilon constraint handling method [17] introduces a relaxation factor ϵ to the superiority of feasible solutions. With the ϵ factor, pairwise comparison of solutions x^1 and x^2 are modified as follows:

$$(f(x^1), CV(x^1)) <_\epsilon (f(x^2), CV(x^2))$$

$$\Updownarrow$$

$$\begin{cases} f(x^1) < f(x^2), & \text{if } CV(x^1), CV(x^2) \leq \epsilon \\ f(x^1) < f(x^2), & \text{if } CV(x^1) = CV(x^2) \\ CV(x^1) < CV(x^2), & \text{otherwise.} \end{cases} \tag{2}$$

If $\epsilon = 0$, the ϵ-level comparison is equivalent to the superiority of feasible solutions and if $\epsilon = \infty$ the ϵ-level comparison is equivalent the ordinary comparisons $<$ and $\le$ between function values. Usually, the ϵ value is controlled in a dynamic or adaptive way.

Other representative CHTs in the separatist approach are multi-objective-based approaches [18], co-evolutionary-based approaches [19], and rank-based approaches [20]. Recently, a novel and competitive CHT in this category, called multiple constraint ranking (MCR) [9], is published. MCR is one of the rank-based CHTs, in which the fitness function of the solutions are calculated using the rank rather than directly using fitness function. In MCR, the fitness function is calculated by summing up the rank based on the objective function, the rank based on the measure of each constraint's violation, and the rank based on the number of violating constraints. This approach is tested on four sets of experiments against five CHTs including SP and showed outstanding performance [9].

Hybrid approach uses several CHTs together. For example, Lagrangian multipliers [21] and Fuzzy logic [22] are classified in this category.

2.2 CHTs Developed for Solving Constrained Multi-Objective Optimization Problems

CHTs for constrained multi-objective optimization problems can also be classified with the same way with these for constrained single-objective optimization problems.

Jan et al. applied penalty approach for constrained multi-objective optimization problems to MOEA/D [23]. This CMOEA incorporates adaptive penalty into the objective functions or the Tchebycheff aggregation function (i.e. fitness function). As this CMOEA does, there are two ways to incorporate penalty-approached CHTs for constrained single-objective optimization problems into MOEAs. One is applying penalty term to the objective functions and the other is to the fitness function. The results from CMOEA/D-DE-ATP show that the incorporation into the objective functions performs better than that into the fitness function.

Many of CHTs for constrained multi-objective optimization problems can be categorized in separatist approach. The constraint-domination principle (CDP) [24], which is a most commonly used CHT, is categorized in this approach. CDP is an extension of the Deb's superiority of feasible solutions. Similarly, the ϵ-level comparison is also extended for constrained multi-objective optimization problems [25]. In the ϵ-level comparison in constrained multi-objective optimization problems, $f(\boldsymbol{x}^1) < f(\boldsymbol{x}^2)$ in the Eq. (2) is replaced with $\boldsymbol{x}^1 \prec \boldsymbol{x}^2$, where $\prec$ is the usual domination principle. CDP can be regarded as a special case of the ϵ-level comparison with $\epsilon = 0$. Note that CDP is developed earlier and used more commonly than the ϵ-level comparison while the ϵ-level comparison demonstrates its very competitive performance on other CHTs including CDP. NSGA-III, RVEA, and MOEA/DD employ CDP or CDP-equivalent CHTs and I-DBEA employs the ϵ-level comparison in their original articles.

Infeasibility driven evolutionary algorithm (IDEA) [26] is an example of multi-objective-based approaches and of CHT-embedded CMOEAs. IDEA transforms a constrained multi-objective optimization problem to an unconstrained multi-objective optimization problem by treating the constraint violation measure as an additional objective.

3   Incorporation of Constraint Handling Techniques into Multi-Objective Evolutionary Algorithms

3.1   Current Situations

Generally, MOEAs can be roughly classified into three categories. They are dominance-based, decomposition-based, and indicator based MOEAs. We pick NSGA-II [24], MOEA/D [27], and IBEA [28] as representative MOEAs in each respective category for example. Figure 1 depicts general algorithm flow from the calculation of the objective functions to the final indicator used in the selection. These MOEAs convert the objective functions to rank or fitness first. Then the rank or fitness is used in the environmental selection: the selection is performed by populaionwise rank comparison, pairwise fitness comparison, and simple maximum fitness finding, respectively for NSGA-II, MOEA/D, and IBEA. The important differences with regard to CHT are, the final indicator is rank or fitness, the comparison is conducted in populationwise or pairwise way, and the environmental selection is based on rank or fitness.

As seen in Fig. 1 and the subsequent figure, CHTs in different categories or approach take effect in different phases. In this study, we classify CHTs based on the phase where CHTs work, for the sake of actual use or implementation. Penalty approach CHTs can be applied to MOEAs in two different ways: penalty term can be applied to the objective functions or the fitness function. Here, objective-type CHT is not depicted in Fig. 1 because it has no difference between the MOEAs. Rank-based CHTs such as MCR literally work on the rank. IDEA changes the number of objectives by treating the measure of constraint violation as an additional objective function and it may be regarded as affecting on the problem itself. CDP and $i\epsilon$ modifies the pairwise comparator. Here, stochastic ranking [20] works as a comparator and so is classified into the comparator-type CHT with this method of classification.

Here, it seems that there is a general tendency as for existing CMOEAs. For dominance-based MOEAs, CDP (i.e. comparator-type CHT) is frequently used and the reason is easily assumed that domination principle is inherently compatible with ranking. Note that the pairwise comparison like CDP is an element of populationwise ranking. On the other hand, the fitness-type CHTs are not so often used for dominance-based MOEAs. For decomposition-based MOEAs, both of the fitness-type and comparator-type CHTs are commonly used. As aforementioned, decomposition-based MOEAs perform pairwise fitness comparison in the environmental selection and so both of these two types of CHTs can be implemented without any difficulty. As shown here, MOEAs have some incompatibilities with certain types of CHTs. Here, with regard to indicator-based MOEAs, there is rare work for indicator-based CMOEAs. This would be because that indicator-based MOEAs themselves attracting less popularity compared with MOEAs in the other two categories, irrespective to CHT.

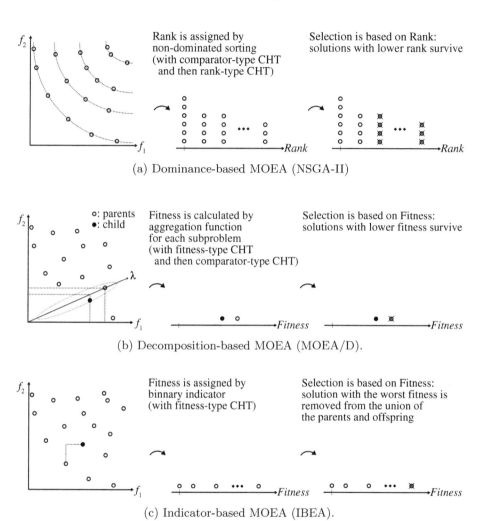

(a) Dominance-based MOEA (NSGA-II)

(b) Decomposition-based MOEA (MOEA/D).

(c) Indicator-based MOEA (IBEA).

Fig. 1. Conversion from objective function to the final indicator in three different types of MOEA

3.2   Proposed Framework

The proposed framework aims to resolve the differences between the MOEAs from algorithmic and implementation perspective for CHT incorporation. The proposed framework is illustrated in Fig. 2 and formulated in Algorithm 1.

In Algorithm 1, the conversion from the objective functions to the fitness function is written with $M_F : \mathbb{R}^M \to \mathbb{R}$ and the modification of the fitness function and the rank by CHTs are written with $C_F : \mathbb{R} \to \mathbb{R}$ and $C_R : \mathbb{R} \to \mathbb{R}$, respectively.

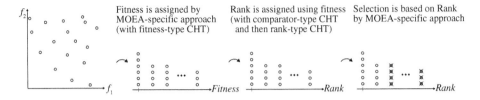

Fig. 2. Conversion from objective function to the final indicator in the proposed framework

---

Algorithm 1. Proposed framework: conversion from the objective functions to the rank

---

Input   : A set of solutions S and their objective functions
Output: A ranked set of solutions S
1 //Calcluate fitness of y by MOEA-specific approach with fitness-type CHT
2 **foreach** *solution* $y \in S$ **do**
3 | $Fitness(y) \leftarrow C_F(M_F(\boldsymbol{f}(y)))$;
4 **end**
5 //Rank solutions with comparator-type CHT and then modify the rank by rank-type CHT
6 Rank solutions based on their fitness with comparator-type CHT ;
7 **foreach** *solution* $y \in S$ **do**
8 | $Rank(y) \leftarrow C_R(Rank(y))$;
9 **end**

First, the conversion from the objective functions to the fitness function is performed by MOEA-specific approach (lines 2–4 of Algorithm 1). For example, in NSGA-II, the result of the non-dominated sorting is regarded as a fitness assignment and the rank is stored as a fitness in an actual implementation. Note that the fitness function is usually one dimensional, CHTs for constrained single-objective optimization problems can be applied as they are, only by replacing the objective function with the fitness function in the original formulation. Then the solutions are ranked based on their fitness function with comparator-type CHTs (line 6 of Algorithm 1). Rank-type CHT such as MCR are applied after the ranking (lines 7–9 of Algorithm 1). Finally, the environmental selection is performed based on the solutions' rank instead of fitness function.

The key of this framework is twofold. One is to force to track the flow of conversion, the first conversion from the objective functions to the fitness function and then the conversion from the fitness function to the rank. The other is to force to compare the solutions using the rank in the selection. By making

MOEAs pass through both the fitness function and the rank, this framework enables the incorporation of at least comparator-type, objective-type, fitness-type, and rank-type CHTs into MOEAs. This framework also helps us to implement new hybrid CHTs, which hybridize CHTs work in different phases, and also the actual hybridizing operation is extremely easy: just turning on some flags to activate the CHTs in different phases at a time.

Note that the original algorithms of MOEAs are not changed by employing this framework because of the equivalence of the comparison using the fitness function itself ($Fitness(\boldsymbol{x})$) and rank based on the fitness function ($Rank(Fitness(\boldsymbol{x}))$), and the comparison using the rank $Rank(\boldsymbol{x})$ and the rank based on the rank ($Rank(Rank(\boldsymbol{x}))$). With regard to MOEAs with two or more preferences such as NSGA-II (pareto-dominance and crowding distance) and CHEETAH [29] (chebyshev relation and additive ϵ indicator), this framework should be applied so that the original mechanisms of these MOEAs are kept unchanged.

As for the computational complexity, the additional operation brought by this framework is the ranking based on the fitness function and the additional complexity is $O(KlogK)$, where K is the population size.

4   Experimental Setting

To verify the effectiveness of the proposed framework and to investigate the effectiveness of each MOEA and CHT, some CMOEAs are tested on eight constrained multi-objective optimization problems. The details of constrained multi-objective optimization problems, MOEAs, and CHTs are described in the following subsections.

4.1   Constrained Multi-Objective Optimization Problems

We have tested CMOEAs with two groups of benchmark constrained multi-objective optimization problems. The first is the artificially designed problems, and the other is the engineering constrained optimization problems.

We employed the constrained DTLZ (C-DTLZ) problems proposed by Jain and Deb [3] as the first group problems. In C-DTLZ problems, the number of objectives of the problems can be set to an arbitrary number, and so they have frequently been used in recent comparative studies [3,5,6,30].

The other group consists of three engineering constrained optimization problems. The three problems are the car side impact problem (CSI) [3], the ship parametric design problem (SPD) [31], and the water problem (WTR) [32]. These engineering constrained optimization problems are derived from the real-world design problems and are considered to have more practical characteristics than the artificial constrained multi-objective optimization problems.

The number of objectives M is set as 2, 3, and 5 for each C-DTLZ problem instance. The number of constraints N is the same as M for C-DTLZ problems. For CSI, SPD, and WTR, (M, N) is $(3, 10)$, $(3, 9)$, and $(5, 7)$, respectively.

In this study, the population size is set as 100, 91, 210 for the C-DTLZ group problems respectively with $M = 2$, 3, and 5, and 153 and 210 for the engineering constrained problems respectively with $M = 3$ and 5. The stopping criterion is set by the number of generations rather than the number of function evaluations. The cases with $M = 2, 3$, and 5 stop respectively until 500, 500, and 600 generations and each case is run for 31 times independently with different initial population. These values are determined mainly referring to Jain's experiments [3].

4.2   MOEAs

To investigate the performances of MOEAs in different categories, we employed three MOEAs: NSGA-III [33], MOEA/D-STM [34], and IBEA$_{\epsilon+}$ [28] (IBEA with additive ϵ indicator) as representatives of dominance-based, decomposition-based, and indicator based MOEA. Here, in order to omit unrelated effects from the results, we have chosen the MOEAs with generational scheme with the same population and offspring size. MOEA/D-STM is employed because this is one of the few MOEA/D variants with generational scheme. For the above reason, the dynamic resource allocation (DRA) function of MOEA/D-STM is disabled in this study. The details of the MOEAs are listed as follows:

1. Mutation: The polynomial mutation [35] is employed for all the MOEAs. The probability p_m is set as $1/D$ and the distribution index η_m is set as 20.
2. Crossover: The simulated binary crossover (SBX) [35] is employed for all the MOEAs. The probability p_c is set as 1.0 and the distribution index η_c is set as 20 and 30 for the MOEA/D-STM and the other MOEAs, respectively.
3. Parameter for reference/weight vectors: The number of weight or reference vectors used by NSGA-III and MOEA/D-STM is set the same with the population size. The vectors are generated using Das and Dennis's systematic approach [36].
4. Specific parameters in MOEA/D-STM: The neighbor size T is set as 20 and the probability used to select in the neighborhood δ is set as 0.9. The Tchebycheff approach is adopted as the aggregation method.
5. Specific parameters in IBEA$_{\epsilon+}$: The scaling factor κ is set as 0.02.

4.3   CHTs

Two classical and two state-of-the-art CHTs are employed in this study. The former ones are CDP and T&Y, and the latter ones are the improved ϵ-level comparison [25] (iϵ) and MCR. iϵ incorporated into MOEA/D showed the best performance among eight other CMOEAs including IDEA and NSGA-II with CDP. In this study, two versions of T&Y are employed: one replaces the objective function with the i-th objective function and the fitness function with modified objective functions. The other replaces the objective function with the fitness function and the fitness function with modified fitness function. The former is denoted as T&Y-O, the latter is T&Y-F. Note that T&-O is similar to the modification by Woldesenbet et al. [37].

Only the $i\epsilon$ has user-defined parameters and the parameters are set as follows: $\alpha = 0.8$, $T_c = 0.8G_{\text{final}}$, $cp = 2$, $\tau = 0.1$, and $\theta = 0.2NI$, where G_{final} is the maximum generation and NI is the number of infeasible solutions in the initial population.

4.4 Performance Metric

In this study, the hypervolume indicator [38] is used as the performance indicator. In advance of calculating hypervolume indicator, the objective values of all non-dominated feasible solutions are normalized using the ideal and nadir point. The ideal and nadir point are experimentally estimated by using all solutions obtained through all the calculations. Then hypervolume indicator is calculated using the reference point of $(1.1, \ldots, 1.1)^T$.

In this study, the performance of CMOEAs is evaluated with the unbounded external archive [39], in which all non-dominated feasible solutions found during the entire search process are stored, rather than with the final population, considering that there are some issues around the traditional performance evaluation using the final population, as pointed by Tanabe et al. [40].

To investigate the significance of each CHT, we use the average performance score (APS) [41]. Suppose that n algorithms $\{A_1, ..., A_n\}$ are tested on a benchmark problem for multiple independent runs. For each $i \in \{1, ..., n\}$ and $j \in \{1, ..., n\}\backslash i$, let $\delta_{i,j} = 1$ if A_j significantly outperforms A_i and $\delta_{i,j} = 0$ otherwise. To test the significance, Wilcoxon rank-sum test with $p < 0.05$ is used. Based on $\delta_{i,j}$, for each algorithm A_i the performance score $P(A_i)$ is determined as $\sum_{j \in \{1,...,n\}\backslash i} \delta_{i,j}$. Here, in this study, the "algorithm" is each CHT with a MOEA (A_i and A_j correspond respectively to C_i incorporated into M_l and C_j incorporated into M_l for an incorporating MOEA M_l). Then the performance score of each CHT $APS(C_i)$ is calculated as follows:

$$APS(C_i) = \frac{1}{L} \sum_{l \in \{1,...,L\}} P(C_i \text{ incorporated into } M_l), \qquad (3)$$

where L is the number of MOEAs. Note that this $P(C_i)$ is calculated against a problem. APS indicates how many other CHTs are better than the corresponding CHT and the smaller APS value the better the CHT in the problem. In addition to APS against each problem, average APSs are calculated on some subsets of benchmark problems.

5 Experimental Results

The mean and standard deviation values of hypervolume indicator of each MOEA and CHT is listed in Tables 1 and 2. Due to lack of space, only the results with $M = 5$ are listed for C-DTLZ problems. First of all, with regard to MOEA, the best performing MOEA varies by constrained multi-objective optimization problems, but in general MOEA/D-STM performs well on more constrained multi-objective optimization problems than the other two MOEAs. Despite of its unpopularity, $IBEA_{\epsilon+}$ shows its competitive performance with state-of-the-art popular MOEAs on some constrained multi-objective optimization problems.

As for CHT, it is interesting that without-CHT (denoted as w/o-CHT) show the best performance in some constrained multi-objective optimization problems, and some CHTs can perform worse than w/o-CHT on not a few constrained multi-objective optimization problems. Especially, C1-DTLZ3 problem can be solved efficiently only without employing any CHT. However, in general, it seems that no single CHT outperforms on every constrained multi-objective optimization problem as far as examined in this study.

Table 1. Mean and standard deviation of hypervolume indicator for C-DTLZ problems with $M = 5$. Each CHT is tested its significance by Wilcoxon's rank-sum test with 0.05 significance level against CDP. † and ‡ denotes that the performance of the corresponding CHT is significantly worse or better than that of CDP, respectively. The best mean on each constrained multi-objective optimization problem with same MOEA is highlighted in boldface. They have the same meanings in another table

		w/o-CHT	CDP	i_ϵ	T&Y-O	T&Y-F	MCR
C1-DTLZ1	NSGA-III	1.574E+00	1.580E+00	**1.583E+00**	1.581E+00	1.581E+00	1.579E+00
		(2.355E-02)	(1.169E-02)	(9.294E-03)	(1.271E-02)	(1.011E-02)	(1.420E-02)
	MOEA/D-STM	**1.591E+00**‡	1.588E+00	1.591E+00	1.535E+00†	1.588E+00	1.588E+00
		(3.383E-03)	(6.124E-03)	(2.630E-03)	(5.352E-02)	(5.998E-03)	(5.048E-03)
	$IBEA_{\epsilon+}$	1.568E+00	1.509E+00	1.564E+00	1.321E+00†	**1.576E+00**‡	1.464E+00
		(1.068E-02)	(1.305E-01)	(1.828E-02)	(1.871E-01)	(3.892E-03)	(1.587E-01)
C1-DTLZ3	NSGA-III	**1.373E+00**‡	0.000E+00	0.000E+00	0.000E+00	0.000E+00	0.000E+00
		(1.487E-02)	(0.000E+00)	(0.000E+00)	(0.000E+00)	(0.000E+00)	(0.000E+00)
	MOEA/D-STM	**1.375E+00**‡	0.000E+00	0.000E+00	0.000E+00	4.329E-02	4.337E-02
		(6.340E-03)	(0.000E+00)	(0.000E+00)	(0.000E+00)	(2.371E-01)	(2.375E-01)
	$IBEA_{\epsilon+}$	**7.741E-01**‡	0.000E+00	9.698E-02	0.000E+00	0.000E+00	0.000E+00
		(1.216E-01)	(0.000E+00)	(2.551E-01)	(0.000E+00)	(0.000E+00)	(0.000E+00)
C2-DTLZ2	NSGA-III	1.280E+00†	**1.301E+00**	1.301E+00	1.300E+00†	1.301E+00	1.301E+00
		(1.187E-03)	(1.439E-02)	(1.256E-03)	(9.356E-04)	(1.105E-03)	(1.053E-03)
	MOEA/D-STM	**1.275E+00**‡	1.241E+00	1.260E+00‡	1.233E+00†	1.240E+00	1.240E+00
		(3.679E-03)	(7.883E-03)	(4.484E-03)	(1.043E-02)	(9.295E-03)	(6.608E-03)
	$IBEA_{\epsilon+}$	1.288E+00†	1.315E+00	1.312E+00†	1.310E+00†	**1.321E+00**‡	1.315E+00
		(9.526E-04)	(6.755E-04)	(8.206E-04)	(8.485E-04)	(7.955E-04)	(9.835E-04)
C3-DTLZ1	NSGA-III	1.605E+00†	1.607E+00	1.607E+00	**1.608E+00**†	1.607E+00	1.607E+00
		(5.379E-04)	(1.580E-03)	(1.580E-03)	(1.985E-04)	(1.580E-03)	(1.580E-03)
	MOEA/D-STM	1.600E+00†	1.607E+00	1.607E+00	1.603E+00†	1.607E+00	**1.607E+00**‡
		(1.929E-03)	(8.123E-04)	(8.123E-04)	(2.059E-03)	(8.250E-04)	(7.437E-04)
	$IBEA_{\epsilon+}$	1.532E+00†	1.583E+00	1.581E+00†	**1.603E+00**‡	1.566E+00†	1.583E+00
		(1.612E-02)	(3.708E-03)	(4.120E-03)	(5.421E-03)	(1.913E-02)	(3.708E-03)
C3-DTLZ4	NSGA-III	1.516E+00†	1.573E+00	1.573E+00	**1.574E+00**‡	1.573E+00	1.573E+00
		(6.131E-02)	(2.857E-04)	(3.161E-04)	(7.092E-05)	(6.882E-04)	(3.190E-04)
	MOEA/D-STM	1.483E+00†	1.573E+00	1.573E+00	**1.573E+00**	1.573E+00	1.573E+00
		(3.372E-02)	(7.324E-04)	(4.219E-04)	(5.680E-04)	(4.418E-04)	(7.974E-04)
	$IBEA_{\epsilon+}$	1.482E+00†	**1.572E+00**	1.571E+00	1.570E+00†	1.546E+00†	1.572E+00
		(3.918E-02)	(3.767E-04)	(1.882E-03)	(1.140E-02)	(3.296E-02)	(8.115E-04)

Table 2. Mean and standard deviation of hypervolume indicator for engineering constrained optimization problems

		w/o-CHT	CDP	iϵ	T&Y-O	T&Y-F	MCR
CSI	NSGA-III	8.803E-01†	8.871E-01	8.875E-01	**8.883E-01**‡	8.870E-01	8.872E-01
		(8.403E-04)	(1.348E-03)	(1.490E-03)	(1.269E-03)	(1.569E-03)	(1.377E-03)
	MOEA/D-STM	8.863E-01†	8.950E-01	8.945E-01†	8.935E-01†	**8.950E-01**	8.950E-01
		(7.367E-04)	(2.143E-04)	(4.239E-04)	(4.394E-04)	(2.107E-04)	(2.617E-04)
	IBEA$_{\epsilon+}$	8.643E-01†	**8.796E-01**	8.714E-01†	8.755E-01†	7.897E-01†	8.771E-01
		(1.137E-02)	(6.956E-03)	(1.005E-02)	(6.897E-03)	(6.938E-02)	(7.137E-03)
SPD	NSGA-III	6.412E-01†	8.370E-01	8.376E-01	**8.833E-01**‡	8.071E-01†	8.381E-01
		(3.932E-02)	(1.621E-02)	(1.666E-02)	(2.630E-03)	(1.593E-02)	(1.712E-02)
	MOEA/D-STM	6.451E-01†	8.918E-01	8.875E-01†	**8.936E-01**‡	8.927E-01	8.921E-01
		(3.770E-02)	(2.464E-03)	(1.440E-02)	(6.177E-04)	(2.682E-03)	(9.896E-04)
	IBEA$_{\epsilon+}$	6.404E-01†	8.729E-01	8.624E-01†	**8.843E-01**‡	7.796E-01†	8.664E-01
		(3.744E-02)	(1.605E-02)	(1.778E-02)	(3.108E-03)	(2.298E-02)	(2.307E-02)
WTR	NSGA-III	1.089E+00†	1.092E+00	1.092E+00	**1.092E+00**‡	1.092E+00	1.092E+00
		(3.453E-04)	(7.145E-05)	(5.872E-05)	(7.131E-05)	(6.976E-05)	(5.663E-05)
	MOEA/D-STM	1.069E+00†	1.077E+00	1.077E+00	1.077E+00	**1.083E+00**‡	1.076E+00
		(2.363E-03)	(1.552E-03)	(1.414E-03)	(1.152E-03)	(1.426E-03)	(1.701E-03)
	IBEA$_{\epsilon+}$	1.085E+00†	1.092E+00	1.091E+00†	1.074E+00†	1.070E+00†	**1.092E+00**
		(2.999E-03)	(4.901E-04)	(6.561E-04)	(6.810E-04)	(1.581E-02)	(3.543E-04)

To discuss the significance of each CHT statistically, Fig. 3 shows the APS for each constrained multi-objective optimization problem. It seems that there is no outstanding CHT that performs the best across benchmark problems here again. However, some trends can be observed when the focus is on details: for example, T&Y-O shows its poor performance on C1-DTLZ1 and C1-DTLZ3 problems irrespective to M and T&Y-F shows its poor performance on C3-DTLZ4 irrespective to M and thee engineering constrained optimization problems. Without-CHT shows a clear and the most largest trend across the constrained multi-objective optimization problems than other CHTs: it performs well on some constrained multi-objective optimization problems whereas it performs the worst on other problems.

Based on the results of w/o-CHT, constrained multi-objective optimization problems are divided into two in the following analysis: the problems where w/o-CHT can perform well (denoted as "easier" problems), and there where cannot ("more difficult" problems). Specifically, the "easier" problems here comprise C1-

Table 3. Average performance score calculated on different sets of benchmark problems

	w/o CHT	CDP	iϵ	T&Y-O	T&Y-F	MCR
All tested problems	2.67	**0.91**	1.13	1.59	1.41	**0.91**
"Easier" problems	**0.22**	0.94	0.78	1.89	0.67	0.94
"More difficult" problems	3.89	**0.89**	1.31	1.44	1.78	**0.89**

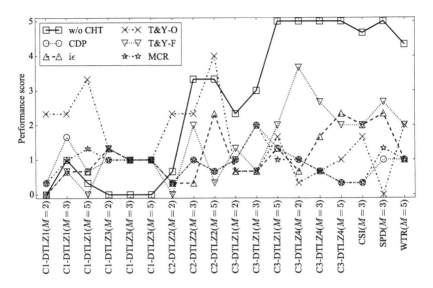

Fig. 3. Average performance score for all benchmark problems (lower is better)

DTLZ1 and C1-DTLZ3 problems, and the "more difficult" problems comprise the other tested problems. More clear statistical results are found in Table 3. Note that the reasons why w/o-CHT can perform well on these C-DTLZ problems were already discussed by Tanabe et al. [40].

In Table 3, the values of averaged APS calculated on all the tested problems, the "easier" problems, and the "more difficult" problems are presented. First, the averaged APS on all the problems shows that CDP and MCR show the best performances followed by iϵ. When the average is calculated on "easier" problems, the best CHT turns to w/o-CHT, followed by T&Y-F and iϵ. On "more difficult" problems, however, CDP and MCR win the first place followed by T&Y-O. Here, CDP and MCR show relatively stable performances across the problems and show higher performances as the complexity of problem increases (increasing M in "more difficult" C-DTLZ problems), as also shown in Fig. 3.

6   Conclusion

We have proposed a generic framework for incorporating CHTs into MOEAs. The proposed framework resolves the differences between different types of MOEAs with regard to incorporation of CHT by forcing two conversions: conversion from the objective functions to the fitness function and that from the fitness function to the rank. With the proposed framework, CHTs for constrained single-objective optimization problems can be easily incorporated into MOEAs regardless of its type: dominance-based, decomposition-based, or indicator-based.

Performances of CMOEAs, each of these is a combination of CHTs and MOEAs, are investigated with the proposed framework. First of all, one of the results is that it became possible to investigate the effectiveness of arbitrary combination of MOEAs and CHTs with the proposed framework. The experimental results show that there is no single CHT outperforms on every constrained multi-objective optimization problem in general, as far as examined here. The current comprehensive study reveals that the performance of CHTs is highly dependent on constrained multi-objective optimization problems and it is suggested that we have to take care of the problems on which the performance of CMOEAs are examined. To develop further effective CHTs for constrained multi-objective optimization problems in actual industrial design, further investigations on the effective mechanisms to handle constraints should be held on more wide kinds of constrained multi-objective optimization problems, with the proposed framework.

Acknowledgements. This work was supported by MEXT Development of Innovative Design and Production Processes that Lead the Way for the Manufacturing Industry in the Near Future through Priority Issue on Post-K computer.

References

1. Li, B., Li, J., Tang, K., Yao, X.: Many-objective evolutionary algorithms: a survey. ACM Comput. Surv. **48**(1), 13 (2015)
2. Mezura-Montes, E., Coello Coello, C.A.: Constraint-handling in nature-inspired numerical optimization: past, present and future. Swarm Evol. Comput. **1**(4), 173–194 (2011)
3. Jain, H., Deb, K.: An evolutionary many-objective optimization algorithm using reference-point based nondominated sorting approach, Part II: handling constraints and extending to an adaptive approach. IEEE TEVC **18**(4), 602–622 (2014)
4. Asafuddoula, M., Ray, T., Sarker, R.A.: A decomposition-based evolutionary algorithm for many objective optimization. IEEE TEVC **19**(3), 445–460 (2015)
5. Li, K., Deb, K., Zhang, Q., Kwong, S.: An evolutionary many-objective optimization algorithm based on dominance and decomposition. IEEE TEVC **19**(5), 694–716 (2015)
6. Cheng, R., Jin, Y., Olhofer, M., Sendhoff, B.: A reference vector guided evolutionary algorithm for many-objective optimization. IEEE TEVC **20**(5), 773–791 (2016)
7. Mallipeddi, R., Suganthan, P.N.: Ensemble of constraint handling techniques. IEEE TEVC **14**(4), 561–579 (2010)
8. Rodrigues, M.D.C., de Lima, B.S.L.P., Guimarães, S.: Balanced ranking method for constrained optimization problems using evolutionary algorithms. Inf. Sci. **327**(C), 71–90 (2016)
9. de Paula Garcia, R., de Lima, B.S.L.P., de Castro Lemonge, A.C., Jacob, B.P.: A rank-based constraint handling technique for engineering design optimization problems solved by genetic algorithms. Comput. Struct. **187**(Supplement), 77–87 (2017)
10. Jordehi, A.R.: A review on constraint handling strategies in particle swarm optimisation. Neural Comput. Appl. **26**(6), 1265–1275 (2015)
11. Courant, R.: Variational methods for the solution of problems of equilibrium and vibrations. Bull. Amer. Math. Soc. **49**(1), 1–23 (1943)

12. Homaifar, A., Lai, S.H., Qi, X.: Constrained optimization via genetic algorithm. Simulation **62**(4), 242–254 (1994)
13. Coello Coello, C.A.: Theoretical and numerical constraint-handling techniques used with evolutionary algorithms: a survey of the state of the art. Comput. Methods Appl. Mech. Eng. **191**(11), 1245–1287 (2002)
14. Tessema, B., Yen, G.G.: A self adaptive penalty function based algorithm for constrained optimization. In: IEEE CEC, pp. 246–253 (2006)
15. Xiao, J., Michalewicz, Z., Zhang, L., Trojanowski, K.: Adaptive evolutionary planner/navigator for mobile robots. IEEE TEVC **1**, 18–28 (1997)
16. Deb, K.: An efficient constraint handling method for genetic algorithms. Comput. Methods Appl. Mech. Eng. **186**(2), 311–338 (2000)
17. Takahama, T., Sakai, S.: Constrained optimization by the ε constrained differential evolution with gradient-based mutation and feasible elites. In: IEEE CEC, pp. 246–253 (2006)
18. Mezura-Montes, E., Coello Coello, C.A., Tun-Morales, E.I.: Simple feasibility rules and differential evolution for constrained optimization. In: Monroy, R., Arroyo-Figueroa, G., Sucar, L.E., Sossa, H. (eds.) MICAI 2004. LNCS (LNAI), vol. 2972, pp. 707–716. Springer, Heidelberg (2004). https://doi.org/10.1007/978-3-540-24694-7_73
19. Paredis, J.: Co-evolutionary constraint satisfaction. In: Davidor, Y., Schwefel, H.-P., Männer, R. (eds.) PPSN 1994. LNCS, vol. 866, pp. 46–55. Springer, Heidelberg (1994). https://doi.org/10.1007/3-540-58484-6_249
20. Runarsson, T.P., Yao, X.: Stochastic ranking for constrained evolutionary optimization. IEEE TEVC **4**(3), 284–294 (2000)
21. Adeli, H., Cheng, N.T.: Augmented lagrangian genetic algorithm for structural optimization. J. Aerosp. Eng. **7**, 104–118 (1994)
22. Le, T.V.: A fuzzy evolutionary approach to solving constraint problems. In: IEEE CEC, vol. 1, pp. 317–319 (1995)
23. Jan, M.A., Tairan, N.M., Khanum, R.A., Mashwani, W.K.: A new threshold based penalty function embedded MOEA/D. Int. J. Adv. Comput. Sci. Appl. **7**(2), 645–655 (2016)
24. Deb, K., Agrawal, S., Pratap, A., Meyarivan, T.: A fast and elitist multiobjective genetic algorithm: NSGA-II. IEEE TEVC **6**(2), 182–197 (2002)
25. Fan, Z., Li, H., Wei, C., Li, W., Huang, H., Cai, X., Cai, Z.: An improved epsilon constraint handling method embedded in MOEA/D for constrained multi-objective optimization problems. In: 2016 IEEE Symposium Series on Computational Intelligence (SSCI), pp. 1–8 (2016)
26. Singh, H.K., Ray, T., Sarker, R.A.: Optimum oil production planning using infeasibility driven evolutionary algorithm. Evol. Comput. **21**(1), 65–82 (2013)
27. Zhang, Q., Li, H.: MOEA/D: a multiobjective evolutionary algorithm based on decomposition. IEEE TEVC **11**(6), 712–731 (2007)
28. Zitzler, E., Künzli, S.: Indicator-based selection in multiobjective search. In: Yao, X., Burke, E.K., Lozano, J.A., Smith, J., Merelo-Guervós, J.J., Bullinaria, J.A., Rowe, J.E., Tiňo, P., Kabán, A., Schwefel, H.-P. (eds.) PPSN 2004. LNCS, vol. 3242, pp. 832–842. Springer, Heidelberg (2004). https://doi.org/10.1007/978-3-540-30217-9_84
29. Jaimes, A.L., Oyama, A., Fujii, K.: A ranking method based on two preference criteria: Chebyshev function and $\in$-indicator. In: IEEE CEC, pp. 2827–2834 (2015)
30. Chugh, T., Sindhya, K., Miettinen, K., Hakanen, J., Jin, Y.: On constraint handling in surrogate-assisted evolutionarymany-objective optimization. In: PPSN, pp. 214–224 (2016)

31. Parsons, M.G., Scott, R.L.: Formulation of multicriterion design optimization problems for solution with scalar numerical optimization methods. J. Ship Res. **48**(1), 61–76 (2004)
32. Ray, T., Tai, K., Seow, C.: An evolutionary algorithm for multiobjective optimization. Eng. Opt. **33**(3), 399–424 (2001)
33. Deb, K., Jain, H.: An evolutionary many-objective optimization algorithm using reference-point-based nondominated sorting approach, part I: solving problems with box constraints. IEEE TEVC **18**(4), 577–601 (2014)
34. Li, K., Zhang, Q., Kwong, S., Li, M., Wang, R.: Stable matching-based selection in evolutionary multiobjective optimization. IEEE TEVC **18**(6), 909–923 (2014)
35. Deb, K., Agrawal, R.B.: Simulated binary crossover for continuous search space. Complex Syst. **9**(2), 115–148 (1994)
36. Das, I., Dennis, J.E.: Normal-boundary intersection: a new method for generating the pareto surface in nonlinear multicriteria optimization problems. SIAM J. Optim. **8**(3), 631–657 (1998)
37. Woldesenbet, Y.G., Yen, G.G., Tessema, B.G.: Constraint Handling in multiobjective evolutionary optimization. IEEE TEVC **13**(3), 514–525 (2009)
38. Zitzler, E., Thiele, L., Laumanns, M., Fonseca, C.M., da Fonseca, V.G.: Performance assessment of multiobjective optimizers: an analysis and review. IEEE TEVC **7**(2), 117–132 (2003)
39. Krause, O., Glasmachers, T., Hansen, N., Igel, C.: Unbounded population MO-CMA-ES for the BI-objective BBOB test suite, pp. 1177–1184. Association for Computing Machinery (2016)
40. Tanabe, R., Ishibuchi, H., Oyama, A.: Benchmarking multi- and many-objective evolutionary algorithms under two optimization scenarios. IEEE Access **5**, 19597–19619 (2017)
41. Bader, J., Zitzler, E.: HypE: an algorithm for fast hypervolume-based many-objective optimization. Evol. Comput. **19**(1), 45–76 (2011)

EvoPAR

A CPU-GPU Parallel Ant Colony Optimization Solver for the Vehicle Routing Problem

Antón Rey[✉], Manuel Prieto, J. I. Gómez, Christian Tenllado, and J. Ignacio Hidalgo

Departamento de Arquitectura de Computadores y Automática,
Facultad de Informática, Universidad Complutense de Madrid,
Prof. J. G. Santesmases, 9, 28040 Madrid, Spain
{anrey,mpmatias,jigomez,tenllado,hidalgo}@ucm.es

Abstract. This paper exposes a new hybrid approach based on Ant Colony Optimization heuristics, Route First-Cluster Second methods and Local search procedures, combined to generate high quality solutions for the Vehicle Routing Problem. This method uses the parallel computing power of modern general purpose GPUs and multicore CPUs, outperforming current ACO-based VRP solvers and showing to be a competitive approach compared to other high performing metaheuristic solvers.

Keywords: ACO · VRP · Parallel · Metaheuristic · GPU

1 Introduction

The basic definition of the Vehicle Routing Problem (VRP) asks for finding the optimal set of routes to be traversed by a fleet of vehicles in order to serve a set of customers. The VRP is one of the most studied and important combinatorial optimization problem even in its basic formulation. Its relevance relies on its applicability in logistic problems, since this situation arises naturally in most manufacturing or delivery companies. Multiple VRP variants are defined to model additional sets of constraints such as customer time windows or different capacity limitations for each vehicle. In this work we target the *Capacitated* VRP, in which all vehicles have the same capacity, although our approach can be generalized to other variants. In this case, any VRP feasible solution satisfies tree basic constraints: (1) all the customer nodes must be visited exactly once, (2) the aggregated demand of the customers visited by a vehicle must not exceed its capacity, and (3) every vehicle must start and end at a specific node, usually called the depot node.

Dantzig and Ramser introduced the problem and proposed the first algorithm to solve it in 1959. Since then, hundreds of exact and approximate algorithmic

K. Sim and P. Kaufmann (Eds.): EvoApplications 2018, LNCS 10784, pp. 653–667, 2018.
https://doi.org/10.1007/978-3-319-77538-8_44

approaches were developed. However, due to its NP-hard nature, the most efficient exact approaches hardly solves an instance with few hundred customers in an acceptable amount of time. Nevertheless, approximate approaches based on modern metaheuristics currently belong to the best performing solving methods, both in terms of quality of the solutions and computation time. The work of Blum and Roli [1] exposes a review of the role that metaheuristic approaches play in general combinatorial optimization problems. In particular, they highlight the importance of developing methods able to maintain a proper balance between the intensification and diversification components during the search: in order to find high quality solutions, a metaheuristic must explore efficiently the solution space via diversification mechanisms, while focusing at the same time on those promising regions through intensification techniques. Specifically, nature-inspired metaheuristics such as genetic-, evolutionary- and swarm-based algorithms among others, have proven to be excellent approaches in many combinatorial optimization problems. Hybridization between different approaches and integration of some metaheuristics with other traditional methods also proved to be useful in certain scenarios.

However, it is noteworthy that both approximate and exact methods demands a significant computational effort, since a typically vast solution space has to be efficiently explored. For this reason, the aid of parallel computing resources plays an important role in order to find high quality solutions in a short time.

In this context, we review some of the best performing VRP solvers. The work of [2] combines a Genetic algorithm approach with neighborhood-based metaheuristics reinforced with several specific diversification techniques. [3] exposes an intrinsically parallel algorithm based on the execution of multiple tabu searches in parallel that cooperate and maintain a dynamic balance in diversification and intensification. In the thesis of Groer [4] it is exposed another hybrid parallel approach and given an extensive overview of both parallel and serial methods. The works in [5] and [6] hybridize a GRASP approach with both iterative and evolutionary-based local search methods. Subramanian exposes in [7] an extensive study about both exact and heuristic methods, while also presenting a highly competitive approach based on the Iterated Local Search metaheuristic that uses a Variable Neighbourhood Descent, capable of handling several VRP variants.

This paper exposes a hybrid metaheuristic based on the Max Min Ant System (MMAS) [8] method derived from Ant Colony Optimization (ACO) approaches and some deterministic methods designed to build and optimize VRP solutions constructed from Traveling Salesman Problem (TSP) routes related to the VRP problem. In this approach, we show that the MMAS, originally designed for the TSP, is capable of generating through the usual operations of ACO algorithms the source of stochasticity needed to explore efficiently –but indirectly– the search space of the Vehicle Routing Problem.

From the implementation perspective, our approach exploits different levels of parallelism. A set of TSP routes is constructed in parallel by an ACO algorithm implemented in GPU, in which every ant builds a single TSP route exploiting a lower level of parallelism. Next, a CPU thread builds a complete VRP solution from each TSP route, using a Route First-Cluster Second (RFCS) algorithm [9]. Next, each CPU thread improves its VRP solution by applying Local search (LS) procedures based on inter- and intra-route optimizations.

Summarizing our contributions, we present a new parallelization strategy for the Ant Colony Optimization to the Traveling Salesman Problem, a new metaheuristic for the Vehicle Routing Problem, and we expose the parallelization of the whole algorithm through a heterogeneous CPU-GPU implementation.

2 Method

We propose a new approach for the Capacitated Vehicle Routing Problem based on Ant Colony Optimization [8] framework integrated with a Route First-Cluster Second method [9] and followed by specific inter-route based on λ-interchanges [10] and intra-route k-opt intensification mechanisms.

Given a set of locations, the TSP asks for finding the least cost route that visits each location exactly once. Any route that satisfies this criteria but it is not necessarily optimal is referred as a *TSP route* or *TSP solution*. Similarly, a feasible set of vehicle routes that satisfies the constraints of a VRP instance will be referred as a *VRP solution*. Note that any TSP route can be regarded as a VRP solution in which just a single vehicle with enough capacity to serve all customers is available. Similarly, taking into account the corresponding VRP constraints, a given TSP route can be partitioned into a set of subroutes to form a feasible VRP solution. Specifically, the VRP solution is built from a least cost path calculated on a transformed graph that depends on the VRP constraints, as it is explained in Sect. 2.2. On top of these ideas, we designed an iterative process meant to find a TSP tour whose RFCS split and consequent Local search optimizations yields the optimal VRP solution. Similar methods were already implemented by [5,6]. They both used a GRASP instead of our ACO method to generate the TSP routes to split and applied different local search techniques in the post-optimization stage. They showed that it was a promising alternative among the best performing VRP and some of its variants. In our case, the process of generating TSP tours is made by an Ant Colony Optimization algorithm. First, the ACO algorithm generates a set of TSP routes that are split independently in a set of subroutes to form an intermediate set of VRP solutions. Once all VRP solutions are improved, the arcs that belong to the best found solution or the best solution at current iteration will be more desirable for the ants to be chosen at the next step. Next, we expose the main stages of our method.

2.1 Ant Colony Optimization Overview

The first stage of the iterative process implements Ant Colony Optimization techniques and it is the only source of stochasticity of the whole method.

The ACO algorithms construct routes in a graph, imitating the half-erratic/half-guided movement of natural ants. The basic stages of a simple ACO algorithm are exposed in Algorithm 1.

Algorithm 1. General ACO algorithm for the Traveling Salesman Problem

Initialize pheromone trails.
while Stop condition is not met **do**
   Every ant builds a TSP route favoring arcs with high amount of pheromone.
   Compute the costs of each TSP route.
   Add pheromone on those arcs belonging to the best route.
   Evaporate pheromone on all arcs.
end while

Each route is constructed starting from a node and adding neighboring nodes sequentially. Being in a node i, the probability of choosing a certain node j in i's neighborhood N_i is given by:

$$p_{ij} = \frac{(\tau_{ij})^\alpha (\eta_{ij})^\beta}{\sum_{l \in N_i} (\tau_{il})^\alpha (\eta_{il})^\beta} \; if \; j \in N_i,$$

where η_{ij} represents the *heuristic information* (usually set as the inverse of the distance from the node i to the node j), and τ_{ij} represents the *amount of pheromone* on the arc ij. The greater the pheromone and heuristic information values associated to an ij arc, the more likely is that node j will be chosen after node i is visited. α and β are parameters that quantify the relative importance of the pheromone information versus the heuristic information.

The following stage of an ACO algorithm comprises the pheromone update of the arcs. First, the amount of pheromone evaporation of a given arc that links the nodes i y j is set by the rule

$$\tau_{ij} \leftarrow (1 - \rho)\tau_{ij}, \; \forall(i,j),$$

which depends on an evaporation rate parameter ρ ($0 < \rho < 1$). Moreover, given a set of arcs $(i, j \in K)$ belonging to a certain route K with positive cost C, the amount of pheromone added on them is defined by:

$$\tau_{ij} \leftarrow \tau_{ij} + 1/C, \; \forall(i,j) \in K.$$

Among the ACO methods for the TSP solving, the one which exhibits the best balance between exploration and exploitation is the Max-Min Ant System (MMAS) [8], which introduces four main modifications respect to the most basic Ant System (AS). First, it exploits the best routes found: only those arcs belonging to the best route found either at (A) current iteration or (B) the best found route, get their pheromone increased, thus increasing the probability of being chosen in next iterations. The first option (A) makes the ants explore the solution space (exploration phase), while the second option forces all ants to concentrate the exploration in a neighborhood of a given solution (exploitation phase). It is suggested [8] that the exploration phase has to be done at the beginning of the convergence process while the exploitation phase has to be activated once a given number of iterations is reached. This transition is suggested to be smooth, for instance by increasing the frequency in which the pheromone of the best-so-far solution is added.

Stagnation Control. Nevertheless, with these simple mechanisms the convergence may get interrupted due to solution stagnation, in which all ants will eventually follow the same route, due to an excessive pheromone growing on those arcs belonging to a suboptimal route. To counteract this effect, a second modification keeps the pheromone amount within a range $[\tau_{min}, \tau_{max}]$. At the beginning of the algorithm all arcs are initialized to the upper bound, so that the algorithm can explore the search space in a diversified manner. Finally, the pheromone trails are reinitialized again to the upper bound if any stagnation condition is met or when a certain number of iterations is reached.

We want to highlight that we do not need to modify the normal MMAS design in the TSP route construction stage. We can explore the VRP solution space just using the mentioned ACO TSP parameters in the same way. We only added one ad-hoc condition to force a pheromone reset when stagnation is detected, happening when the VRP solutions are not sufficiently diversified. This situation arises either when all arcs of the graph have the minimum amount of pheromone –except the ones that belong to the best known solution–, or when a certain number of iterations is reached without improvement. For these cases, pheromone of all arcs with τ_{min} pheromone is raised to 95%τ_{max} so these arcs are more likely to be chosen again in the next iteration. Doing this we make the iterative process to *jump* outside a local suboptimal solution while still keeping memory of the best found solutions –as their arcs pheromone is kept at τ_{max}–.

2.2   Splitting Procedure via Route First-Cluster Second Method

As mentioned, a TSP route can be divided with the RFCS [9] splitting procedure in an optimal way, so the attractiveness of the method lies in the exploration of a *simpler* TSP solution space.

The method works as follows. Assigning a particular direction to the TSP route, letting the index $i + a$ be the ath node visited after the node i (assigning 0 to the depot node), and being d_{ij} the components of the distance matrix, another matrix c_{ij} is built following the rules:

- c_{ij} = Distance traveled by a vehicle following the route $(i + 1, i + 2, ..., j)$ if the route $(0, i + 1, i + 2, ..., j, 0)$ is feasible $(i < j)$, or
- $c_{ij} = \infty$ If the same route is infeasible.

Namely, if the aggregated customer demands in route $(0, i+1, i+2, ..., j, 0)$ can be satisfied by a single vehicle, then

$$c_{ij} = d_{0(i+1)} + \sum_{k=i+1}^{j-1} d_{k(k+1)}.$$

Considering first an homogeneous fleet where all vehicles have the same capacity, if we compute the least cost path from node 0 to node N in the graph defined by the arc costs c_{ij}, we would have computed an optimal split of the initial directed tour. If the least cost path calculated has m arcs, this path would correspond to a VRP solution with m vehicles. Contrary, if no route from 0 to N exists, then the problem is infeasible.

Note that setting a maximum length per route L_{max}, and thus solving a Distance Constrained VRP (DCVRP), would simply require to add the following condition:

- $c_{ij} = \infty$ if the length of the route $(0, i+1, i+2, ..., j, 0)$ is greater than L_{max}.

Note that it can also be easily generalized to the heterogeneous fleet case, which would imply the resolution of a Resource Constrained Shortest Path Problem. Other VRP constraints can be modeled similarly, which illustrate the versatility of this method for solving other VRP variants.

2.3   Local Search Optimizations

After splitting a TSP route, every VRP solution is improved independently via inter-route optimizations based on λ-interchanges [10]. These interchanges apply *shift* and *swap* operations between groups of nodes assigned to a pair of vehicles.

Algorithm 2. Pseudocode for a given λ-interchange operator.

for every VRP solution **do**
    for every subroute r_A **do**
        for every subroute r_B **do**
            if $r_A \neq r_B$ **then**
                Loop over r_A and r_B nodes and evaluate all possible shift/swap movements.
                Make the movement that leads to the best improvement.
            end if
        end for
    end for
end for

Shift movements comprise movements of blocks of nodes: a $shift(\lambda, 0)$ subroutine moves λ adjacent nodes from route A to route B. Swap movements involve swapping of nodes: a $swap(\lambda, \mu)$ movement interchanges λ adjacent nodes of route A with μ adjacent nodes of route B. The larger the arguments of both shift and swap procedures, the better the potential improvements, while also implying more computational load. The implementation of the first two simplest shifts ($\lambda = 1, 2$) and the three simplest swaps $((\lambda, \mu) = (1, 1), (2, 1), (2, 2))$ was enough to achieve good performance while keeping the computational load not too high. This stage not only helps to achieve best cost solutions, but it also helps in minimizing the number of vehicles. After these inter-route improvements, an intra-route improvement stage is made by applying the well known 2-opt or 3-opt procedures to every vehicle route, which finds the best interchanges between two or three arcs, respectively. k-opt operators with $k > 3$ are rarely considered because their typical improvements do not worth their increase in computational complexity. Instead, 2-opt and 3-opt operators implementing the usual speed-up techniques provided a good balance between solution improvement and processing time.

2.4 LKH Intialization

Before starting the iterative process, a pheromone initialization is done from an optimal or near optimal solution of the TSP associated to the VRP graph. The TSP solver by Helsgaun [11] (*LKH*) provides optimal or high quality TSP solutions for problems up to several thousands of nodes in a very short time. By setting extra pheromone on those arcs belonging to this TSP route found by the LKH solver, we get good VRP solutions to start with, which speeds up the convergence process of the algorithm.

   Finally, it can be noticed that the whole iterative process involves a considerable computational load specially if many ants are run. As a matter of fact, this method is population-based: its good convergence behavior depends on handling a population with several number of members/ant/VRP solutions. From the computational perspective, although the RFCS stage is relatively lightweight, the following stages running local search optimizations imply remarkable computing demands. For this reason, the use of the parallel processing is highly desirable. In Sect. 3 it is shown that the TSP route construction motivates the use of the general purpose GPUs while the VRP-specific stages can be targeted via CPU threads.

3 Parallel Implementation

In this section we describe the parallel implementation of the two main stages performed at each iteration. The source code under MIT license can be found in https://github.com/aarv87/aco-rfcs-vrp.

3.1 ACO on GPU for TSP Routes

Fortunately, the Max-Min Ant System (MMAS) is the ACO variant with best convergence to optimum for the TSP and also the best candidate for implementation on GPU. A number of m blocks of GPU threads is assigned to perform the computation associated to m ants. Specifically, the ant decision process can be parallelized in a way such that every GPU thread computes the probability p_{ij} of visiting every candidate node j when the ant is in node i: a $O(nn)$ task is parallelized being nn the number of candidate nodes or nearest neighbors. Once all the probabilities of the nn nodes are calculated, the ant may choose one candidate using the standard roulette algorithm; however this is not well suited for a parallel GPU implementation. Instead, the GPU-specific *All-In-Roulette* approach exposed in [12] was implemented. Moreover, in the MMAS approach only those arcs belonging to a single route are the ones where the pheromone is increased. Thus the pheromone addition on $n-1$ independent arcs of the n-nodes route can be distributed over $n-1$ parallel GPU threads straightforwardly.

GPU data is arranged as matrices whose sizes depend on the number of nodes n of the problem instance, the number of nearest neighbors considered nn and the number of ants m.

- Distance matrix: $[n \times n]$
  distance[i][j] represents the distance or cost from node i to node j.
- Pheromone matrix: $[n \times nn]$
  pheromone[i][j] stores the amount of pheromone of the arc that connects node i with node j.
- Probability matrix:$[n \times nn]$
  prob[i][j] represents the probability of choosing the node j being at node i. It is computed from the pheromone and distance matrices, and α, β parameters.
- Taboo matrix: $[m \times n]$
  taboo[i][j] equals 0 if the ant i has visited node j and 1 if not.
- Solutions matrix: $[m \times (n+1)]$
  traveled[i][j] stores for each ant i the index of the node visited in the jth place of its route. Since the routes are closed, traveled[i][1] = traveled[i][n+1] $\forall i$.
- Random matrix: $[m \times nn]$
  dice[i][j] stores random numbers uniformly distributed in $(0,1]$.

The main idea in the GPU parallelization relies on mapping every matrix row into each block i of threads, in such a way that its threads get mapped in an aligned way to its columns, thus facilitating high throughput transfers from/to GPU memory. If a certain matrix has C columns, in general every thread j of the block i reads or writes every element $j + b \times nTpB$, being b a loop variable $\in [0, C/nTpB]$.

In the route construction stage, every block of threads is responsible for constructing every solution. Supposing the ant i is located at node traveled[i][k], the calculation of each total probability element TP[i][j] is made in parallel by:

TP[i][j] $\leftarrow$ taboo[i][j]*dice[i][j]*prob[traveled[i][k]][j],

where each thread j of the block i performs the computation for the candidate j of the current node traveled[i][k]. Once all the total probabilities of all candidate nodes are computed, `traveled` matrix is updated with the next node j^* to be visited, by doing a parallel reduction over the corresponding i-row elements of the TP matrix to get the maximum element:

`traveled[i][k+1]` $\leftarrow j^*$.

Analogously, once all routes are constructed, each block with index i is responsible for the total distance computation of its route i making the corresponding parallel reduction in on-chip shared memory. In this case, aligned thread-to-element initial reads of **distance** matrix elements will not be satisfied in general. However, some locality could be exploited if the proximity of nodes in the graph is correlated with the proximity in their index number.

For the update of **pheromone** and **prob** matrices, every thread j is straightforwardly mapped to every arc $(j, j+1)$ without the need of any synchronization.

3.2 RFCS + Local Search on CPU Threads for VRP Solutions

For each TSP route, a CPU thread performs a RFCS split and consequent Local search optimizations on it. CPU threads are synchronized at the end of this stage before selecting the best VRP solution. Note that VRP solutions might be different in size, so the duration in their Local search stage can be very different among each other, making some threads to wait for others to finish.

4 Experimental Results

In this section we first expose metrics for scalability to evaluate the parallel performance in both CPU and GPU stages, running sequential executions as references, and show the impact of these stages in the overall time to solution. Secondly, we run our solver on a set of well-known VRP instances to compare the solving performance of our approach against ACO-based solvers (Tables 1 and 2) and against some of the best performing solvers (Tables 3 and 4) –values in bold correspond to optimal solutions–.

4.1 CPU and GPU Scalability and Relative Computation Times

First we expose in Fig. 1 the scalability of the RFCS + LS stage, where VRP solutions are constructed and refined via RFCS and local search methods by each thread (see Sect. 3.2). For each problem we run 5 executions for different number of threads: 4, 8 and 16 threads executions were run on a CPU with 2×4 cores, mapping explicitly each thread to a single processor for the 4 and 8 cases and enabling Simultaneous Multithreading (SMT) for the 16 threads case. This was done analogously on the 2×6 CPU machine, enabling the SMT thread scheduling for the 24 threads case. We calculated the speed-up dividing the sequential time by the parallel time measured when running 100 iterations.

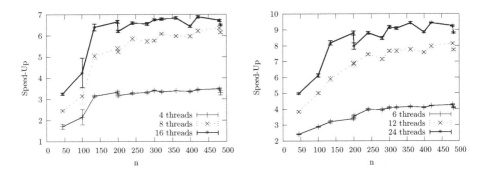

Fig. 1. CPU Speed-Up results for (left) 4, 8 and 16 threads/VRP solutions in 2 × 4 CPU Intel Xeon X5570 *Nehalem* @ 2.93Ghz and (right) for 6, 12 and 24 threads/VRP solutions in 2 × 6 CPU Intel Xeon E5645 *Westmere* @2.40GH.

It is worth noting that every thread constructs and optimizes independently its own VRP solution from a diversified set of TSP routes, so the VRP solutions may be very different among them. This fact implies that the optimizations done in the subsequent λ-interchanges and 3-opt operations may take very different times depending on the VRP solution, which causes load imbalance among threads, thus making some of them to wait for others to finish.

Note that the higher the number of nodes, the greater is the speed-up obtained until saturation at around 200 nodes. A reasonable good ratio between the number of threads and the speed-up is seen when a single thread is assigned to each physical core –i.e. SMT disabled–, noticing that speed-up practically doubles from 4 to 8 threads (Fig. 1 left) and from 6 to 12 threads (Fig. 1 right).

Secondly, we show how the speed-up of the ACO stage increases with the number of nodes of the problem. Note that in this analysis the number of vehicles does not play any role, since the ACO stage constructs TSP routes considering only the location of the nodes in the graph. Similarly, our GPU parallel implementation of the ACO-MMAS method was compared with the sequential version of Dorigo and Stutzle ([8]). Both computation times were measured using the same set of parameters that are relevant on the computation times, taking into account only the main five ACO stages: (1) initialization, (2) solution construction, (3) cost calculation, (4) best solution checking and (5) pheromone updating. In the parallel executions, the number of ants equals the number of blocks of threads, and the number of candidates during the solution construction defines the number of threads per block, as explained in Sect. 3.1.

A linear behavior of the speed-up factor with the size of the problem can be observed in Fig. 2. In fact, a saturation plateau in the speed-up was not reached for the instance sizes tested, suggesting that the GPU resources are not fully utilized for this set of instances.

Third, we compare how the relative computation times of both stages ACO-GPU and RFCS-CPU depend on the size of the problem, both in the sequential and parallel cases. In Fig. 3 it can be seen that VRP stage dominates the

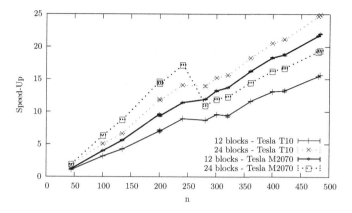

Fig. 2. Speed-Up results for the ACO stage in which TSP routes are constructed, comparing sequential implementation and single GPU implementation.

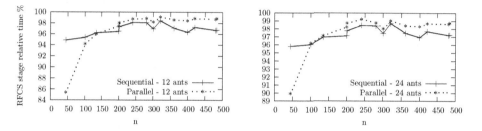

Fig. 3. Relative times of the sequential and parallel RFCS + LS stage, generating 12 and 24 VRP solutions per iteration.

computation –specifically, the Local search computation dominates the RFCS split–. In fact, the relative computation time of the CPU stage grows rapidly with the size of the problem in the parallel implementation, while it remains approximately stable around 96% of the total time in the sequential implementation. It should be noticed that the LKH initialization stage has not been taken into account because of its negligible impact in the overall time to solution for the instances studied.

4.2 Convergence to Optimum

In this section we study the convergence behavior of our algorithm in terms of the average quality for Christofides [6] and Golden [13] instances. Measurements of convergence time are also exposed but they should not be used for comparing the different solvers, since each one is tested on different hardware. First, we compare our method with the best ACO-based VRP solvers in Tables 1 and 2, showing that it provides the best average convergence among all of them. In Tables 3 and 4 our method is compared with some of the best performing VRP solvers,

Table 1. Comparison of ACO-RFCS with best ACO-based VRP solvers in Christofides [6] instances.

	BKS	[14]	[15]	[16]	[17]	ACO-RFCS
C1	524.61	528.90	**524.61**	526.65	–	**524.61**
C2	835.26	–	840.61	850.27	–	836.87
C3	826.14	865.65	828.21	849.32	–	828.55
C4	1028.42	1123.28	1037.57	1051.90	1049.80	1030.70
C5	1291.29	–	1306.91	1351.54	1334.73	1306.09
C6	555.43	–	**555.43**	562.53	–	**555.43**
C7	909.68	–	917.50	923.07	–	910.30
C8	865.94	–	**865.94**	877.59	–	866.74
C9	1162.55	–	1173.94	1182.97	–	1166.46
C10	1395.85	–	1415.53	1453.92	–	1405.54
C11	1042.11	–	1043.46	1044.64	–	**1042.11**
C12	819.56	–	**819.56**	843.93	–	**819.56**
C13	1541.14	–	1546.84	1553.75	–	1544.43
C14	866.36	–	**866.36**	867.62	–	**866.36**
Avg. gap (%)		4.94	0.48	1.87	2.72	0.23

Table 2. Comparison of ACO-RFCS with best ACO-based VRP solvers in Golden [13] instances.

	BKS	[15]	[17]	ACO-RFCS
D241-10k	5623.47	5690.67	-	5718.68
D321-10k	8404.61	8476.64	-	8628.88
D401-10k	11036.22	11117.89	-	11188.68
D481-12k	13590.00	13755.32	-	13662.62
D201-05k	6460.98	**6460.98**	-	**6460.98**
D281-08k	8400.33	8412.90	-	8412.90
D361-09k	10102.70	10209.86	-	10229.94
D441-11k	11635.30	11867.81	-	11910.28
E256-14k	579.71	590.14	-	586.64
E324-16k	735.66	752.76	-	749.28
E400-18k	912.03	942.01	-	928.34
E484-19k	1101.50	1144.33	-	1126.11
E253-27k	857.19	873.84	-	862.31
E321-30k	1080.55	1097.86	-	1085.02
E397-34k	1337.87	1367.29	-	1354.17
E481-38k	1611.56	1654.55	-	1640.69
E241-22k	707.76	711.11	-	709.83
E301-28k	995.13	1010.64	1034.02	1011.13
E361-33k	1365.60	1379.38	1414.3	1372.73
E421-41k	1817.89	1840.46	1890.96	1840.93
Avg. gap (%)		1.56	3.83	1.24

Table 3. Comparison of ACO-RFCS with best VRP metaheuristics in Christofides [6] instances. Average time in seconds.

		[5]		[4]	[2]		[7]		ACO-RFCS		
	BKS	Av.cost	Av.t	Av. cost	Av. cost	Av.t	Av. cost	Av.t	Best cost	Av.cost	Av.t
C1	524.61	**524.61**	0.06	**524.61**	**524.61**	177.60	**524.61**	2.11	**524.61**	**524.61**	1.65
C2	835.26	**835.26**	15.01	**835.26**	**835.26**	298.80	835.73	5.49	**835.26**	836.87	118.80
C3	826.14	**826.14**	3.19	**826.14**	**826.14**	379.80	826.33	12.87	**826.14**	828.55	290.69
C4	1028.42	1029.48	44.84	**1028.42**	**1028.42**	639.00	1032.16	39.75	1029.56	1030.70	414.71
C5	1291.29	1294.09	11.85	1291.45	1291.74	1171.20	1305.43	92.25	1297.95	1306.09	986.51
C6	555.43	**555.43**	0.14	**555.43**	**555.43**	196.80	556.84	1.43	**555.43**	**555.43**	1.90
C7	909.68	**909.68**	5.18	**909.68**	**909.68**	353.40	910.70	6.24	**909.68**	910.30	334.75
C8	865.94	**865.94**	0.32	**865.94**	**865.94**	400.80	866.07	10.21	**865.94**	866.74	22.01
C9	1162.55	**1162.55**	6.58	1162.99	**1162.55**	720.00	1167.78	31.65	**1162.55**	1166.46	329.47
C10	1395.85	1401.46	25.57	1398.52	1397.70	1985.40	1411.50	69.40	1401.55	1405.54	1000.91
C11	1042.11	**1042.11**	0.64	**1042.11**	**1042.11**	399.00	**1042.11**	23.58	**1042.11**	**1042.11**	11.59
C12	819.56	**819.56**	0.17	**819.56**	**819.56**	303.60	**819.56**	7.69	**819.56**	**819.56**	2.86
C13	1541.14	1545.43	9.25	1542.86	1542.86	759.00	1544.57	18.61	1542.86	1544.43	1069.71
C14	866.37	**866.37**	0.27	**866.37**	**866.37**	409.80	**866.37**	8.54	**866.37**	**866.37**	3.17
	Av.gap(%)	0.07		0.03	0.02		0.27		0.08	0.23	

Table 4. Comparison of ACO-RFCS with VRP metaheuristics in Golden [13] instances. Average time in seconds.

	[5]		[3]		[2]		[7]		ACO-RFCS		
BKS	Av.cost	Av.t	Av.cost	Av.t	Av.cost	Av.t	Av.cost	Av.time	Best cost	Av.cost	Av.t
5623.47	5644.52	3.97	5623.65	22.05	5625.10	66.90	5711.19	2.53	5646.58	5718.68	6.68
8404.61	8447.92	1.55	8434.78	34.22	8419.25	103.91	8480.62	7.37	8623.48	8628.88	21.64
11036.22	**11036.22**	6.42	**11036.22**	44.64	**11036.22**	116.43	11076.20	15.90	**11036.22**	11188.68	4.06
13590.00	13624.52	5.83	13620.30	60.87	13624.52	175.22	13665.85	28.38	13624.50	13662.62	10.52
6460.98	**6460.98**	1.05	**6460.98**	15.83	**6460.98**	13.25	**6460.98**	1.88	**6460.98**	**6460.98**	0.16
8400.33	8412.90	1.41	8404.06	26.76	8412.90	41.95	8412.90	5.55	8412.90	8412.90	0.77
10102.70	10195.59	7.72	10134.93	39.01	10134.90	108.49	10228.80	11.35	10195.60	10229.94	13.90
11635.30	11643.90	4.97	11635.34	54.61	**11635.30**	152.42	11842.80	21.54	11828.80	11910.28	23.97
579.71	586.23	1.31	580.04	19.43	581.08	51.69	589.54	4.34	584.93	586.64	39.51
735.66	744.36	7.30	737.16	28.82	738.92	104.02	749.16	9.98	744.85	749.28	41.91
912.03	922.40	4.55	912.72	41.33	914.37	131.23	928.23	20.51	925.01	928.34	47.90
1101.50	1116.12	29.11	1103.20	58.29	1105.97	196.52	1121.24	49.50	1124.37	1126.11	43.80
857.19	862.32	2.14	858.57	18.06	859.08	25.56	865.64	2.85	860.16	862.31	37.87
1080.55	1089.35	9.12	**1080.55**	25.08	1081.99	43.35	1092.07	5.74	1081.31	1085.02	20.43
1337.87	1352.39	10.22	1340.13	36.33	1341.95	109.14	1354.24	13.07	1349.84	1354.17	50.82
1611.56	1634.27	21.05	1614.73	48.14	1616.92	174.70	1635.62	20.79	1634.74	1640.69	52.41
707.76	708.85	1.03	707.80	16.39	707.84	28.98	709.21	2.95	708.99	709.83	29.34
995.13	1002.15	2.93	998.90	25.01	996.95	40.83	1003.13	8.16	1007.46	1011.13	39.79
1365.60	1371.67	17.98	1366.12	32.60	1366.39	81.49	1376.01	11.86	1368.21	1372.73	39.88
1817.89	1830.98	5.77	1819.76	41.93	1819.75	88.31	1836.06	21.91	1834.91	1840.93	53.10
Av. gap (%)	0.65		0.12		0.18		1.06		0.85	1.24	

exposing average behaviors for all approaches and also best-case behavior for our ACO-RFCS solver. The experimental results are not definitive, but we can affirm that the proposed method gives comparable results in terms of average quality and excellent results in the best cases.

5 Conclusions

In this paper we have presented a hybrid parallel implementation of a VRP iterative solver composed of two stages. The first stage applies Ant Colony Optimization MMAS method to generate TSP routes in the GPU. The second stage is run by CPU threads and applies the Route First-Cluster Second method to split each TSP route into a VRP solution, which is subsequently optimized via inter- and intra-route Local search procedures. The convergence is guided by making the arcs belonging to the best found VRP solutions more likely to be chosen in the TSP route generation of the next iteration. We have provided metrics for parallel scalability and shown that on average our solver is able to find high quality solutions on two sets of VRP instances. As future work, convergence time is expected to be improved by (1) exploiting concurrent execution capabilities in some GPU devices and (2) managing a concurrent pool of VRP solutions. With these improvements CPU-GPU synchronization is relaxed and idle times in CPU threads are expected to be greatly reduced.

Acknowledgements. This work has been supported by the EU (FEDER) and the Spanish MINECO, under grants TIN2014-54806-R, TIN2015-65277-R and BES-2016-076806.

References

1. Blum, C., Roli, A.: Metaheuristics in combinatorial optimization: overview and conceptual comparison. ACM Comput. Surv. (CSUR) **35**(3), 268–308 (2003)
2. Vidal, T., Crainic, T., Gendreau, M., Lahrichi, N., Rei, W.: A hybrid genetic algorithm for multidepot and periodic vehicle routing problems. Oper. Res. **60**(3), 611–624 (2012)
3. Jin, J., Crainic, T., Lokketangen, A.: A Cooperative Parallel Metaheuristic for the Capacitated Vehicle Routing Problem (2012)
4. Groer, C.: Parallel and serial algorithms for vehicle routing problems. In: ProQuest (2008)
5. Prins, C.: A grasp × evolutionary local search hybrid for the vehicle routing problem. In: Pereira, F.B., Tavares, J. (eds.) Bio-inspired Algorithms for the Vehicle Routing Problem, Studies in Computational Intelligence, vol. 161, pp. 35–53. Springer, Heidelberg (2009). https://doi.org/10.1007/978-3-540-85152-3_2
6. Christophe, D., Philippe, L., Prodhon, C., et al.: A GRASPxELS with Depth First Search Split Procedure for the HVRP (2012)
7. Subramanian, A.: Heuristic, Exact and Hybrid Approaches for Vehicle Routing Problems. Ph.D. thesis, Universidade Federal Fluminense, Niterói, Brazil (2012)
8. Dorigo, M., Birattari, M., Stutzle, T.: Ant colony optimization. IEEE Comput. Intell. Mag. **1**(4), 28–39 (2006)

9. Beasley, J.: Route first–cluster second methods for vehicle routing. Omega **11**(4), 403–408 (1983)
10. Osman, I.: Metastrategy simulated annealing and tabu search algorithms for the vehicle routing problem. Ann. Oper. Res. **41**(4), 421–451 (1993)
11. Helsgaun, K.: An effective implementation of the lin-kernighan traveling salesman heuristic. Eur. J. Oper. Res. **126**(1), 106–130 (2000)
12. Guohua, F.: Parallel ant colony optimization algorithm with GPU-acceleration based on all-in-roulette selection. Comput. Digital Eng. **5**, 007 (2011)
13. Golden, Bruce L., Wasil, Edward A., Kelly, James P., Chao, I-Ming: The impact of metaheuristics on solving the vehicle routing problem: algorithms, problem sets, and computational results. In: Crainic, Teodor Gabriel, Laporte, Gilbert (eds.) Fleet Management and Logistics. CRT, pp. 33–56. Springer, Boston, MA (1998). https://doi.org/10.1007/978-1-4615-5755-5_2
14. Bell, J., McMullen, P.: Ant colony optimization techniques for the vehicle routing problem. Adv. Eng. Inform. **18**(1), 41–48 (2004)
15. Reimann, M., Doerner, K., Hartl, R.: D-ants: savings based ants divide and conquer the vehicle routing problem. Comput. Oper. Res. **31**(4), 563–591 (2004)
16. Chen, C., Ting, C.: An improved ant colony system algorithm for the vehicle routing problem. J. Chin. Inst. Ind. Eng. **23**(2), 115–126 (2006)
17. Lucka, M., Piecka, S.: Ant colony optimizer with application to the vehicle routing problem. J. Appl. Math. **4** (2011)

EvoROBOT

Evolving Artificial Neural Networks for Multi-objective Tasks

Steven Künzel[(✉)] and Silja Meyer-Nieberg

Universität der Bundeswehr München, Werner-Heisenberg-Weg 39,
85577 Neubiberg, Germany
{steven.kuenzel,silja.meyer-nieberg}@unibw.de

Abstract. Neuroevolution represents a growing research field in Artificial and Computational Intelligence. The adjustment of the network weights and the topology is usually based on a single performance criterion. Approaches that allow to consider several – potentially conflicting – criteria are only rarely taken into account.

This paper develops a novel combination of the NeuroEvolution of Augmenting Topologies (NEAT) algorithm with modern indicator-based evolutionary multi-objective algorithms, which enables the evolution of artificial neural networks for multi-objective tasks including a large number of objectives. Several combinations of evolutionary multi-objective algorithms and NEAT are introduced and discussed. The focus lies on variants with modern indicator-based selection since these are considered as efficient methods for higher dimensional tasks. This paper presents the first combination of these algorithms and NEAT. The experimental analysis shows that the novel algorithms are very promising for multi-objective Neuroevolution.

Keywords: Neuroevolution · Evolutionary algorithms
Multi-objective · NEAT

1 Introduction

Reinforcement Learning (RL) is an important subdiscipline of Artificial Intelligence. It represents a very active field in research [1] as well as in practical applications. Artificial neural networks, or short neural networks, are often applied in the context of Reinforcement Learning. They act as controllers for the agents or robots. Here, Neuroevolution plays an important role since it allows to learn the structure and the weights of neural networks, see e.g. [2]. In many cases, however, the intended behaviour does not only depend on a single criterion, e.g. to balance two poles on a cart, but on multiple criteria, e.g. to balance two poles on a cart *and* to use as little energy as possible. Most real world problems are based on multiple (possibly) conflicting objectives, which makes it necessary to develop neural networks that consider *all* objectives, to make an algorithm applicable for practical issues. Today's quasi-standard in Neuroevolution, Stanley's NeuroEvolution of

© Springer International Publishing AG, part of Springer Nature 2018
K. Sim and P. Kaufmann (Eds.): EvoApplications 2018, LNCS 10784, pp. 671–686, 2018.
https://doi.org/10.1007/978-3-319-77538-8_45

Augmenting topologies (NEAT) is able to evolve neural networks that are adapted to only a single criterion of behaviour [2], which makes it not applicable for multi-objective tasks without further knowledge and abstraction of the problem.

Research regarding this topic is sparse: Only a few papers could be identified. Schrum and Miikkulainen [3] were the first to consider a combination of neural networks and evolutionary multi-objective algorithms: They used NEAT and NSGA-II[1] for multi-objective Neuroevolution. Their algorithm uses a not fully featured NEAT that operates with a modified version of NSGA-II [3]. In addition Schrum and Miikkulainen [5] introduced the Modular Multiobjective NEAT (MM-NEAT) which evolves modular neural networks (each module describes a behaviour) using NSGA-II and NEAT. The MM-NEAT uses all features of NEAT's framework in combination with the procedure of NSGA-II [5]. Van Willigen et al. [6] introduced the NEAT-PS, a combination of NEAT and SPEA2. The Pareto Strength approach used in NEAT-PS computes a single fitness value for all fitness functions and each individual. This makes it easy to apply in the environment of the original NEAT [6].

We were unable to find approaches that consider the more recent evolutionary multi-objective algorithms, which make use of quality indicators as the Hypervolume which allows a good approximation of the Pareto front combined with a sufficient spread of the solutions even for many objectives.

In the first part of this paper, Sect. 2, we provide the foundations of multi-objective optimization and evolutionary algorithms, additionally we give a brief overview of the NEAT algorithm. In the second part, we introduce a novel extension of NEAT, called mNEAT, which is potentially able to evolve neural networks for high-dimensional multi-objective tasks (Sect. 3). Furthermore, we present and investigate novel combinations of NEAT and the SMS-EMOA/R2-EMOA for the first time (Sect. 4). In Sect. 5 we define a multi-objective version of the Double Pole Balancing problem and provide an experimental analysis of the new algorithms. Finally, we give a summary and an outlook on future work in Sect. 6.

2 Foundations

This paper considers multi-objective optimization problems (MOPs) consisting of K objectives $f_k : \mathbb{R}^N \to \mathbb{R}$ which have to be optimized although they may be possibly conflicting [7, p. 8]. The term *optimization* may stand for the maximization or minimization of an objective function. In this paper, we focus on *minimization problems*. MOPs are hard to solve, because in many cases the K different objectives are conflicting. Here, evolutionary algorithms (EAs) are often applied. They were developed to address tasks for which, for example, no efficient algorithm is known or can be developed due to time constraints. Due to the evolutionary approach, which mimics natural evolution, EAs have a broad applicability with a relatively easy problem-specific adaptation. The field of evolutionary algorithms is also referred to as *Evolutionary Computing* [8, p. 14].

---

[1] An algorithm which addresses multi-objective optimization problems. See [4] for a detailed description of the NSGA-II.

2.1 Quality Indicators

To determine the quality of a solution in a MOP, multiple dimensions need to be considered. Therefore, we introduce the Pareto Dominance:

Definition 1 (Pareto Dominance). [7, p. 11] *A decision vector $u = (u_1, \ldots, u_n)$ dominates another decision vector $v = (v_1, \ldots, v_n)$, read as $u \prec v$, iff $\forall k \in \{1, \ldots, K\} : f_k(u) \leq f_k(v) \wedge \exists k \in \{1, \ldots, K\} : f_k(u) < f_k(v)$.*

The goal in MOPs is to identify the set of non-dominated solutions. The concept of Pareto Dominance represents a partial order. Therefore, decision vectors may exist that are not comparable. To make the solutions of a set A comparable in this case, quality indicators are necessary. They are defined as follows:

Definition 2 (Quality Indicator). [7, p. 251] *Let A be a vector of H sets $A_1, \ldots, A_H$. An H-ary quality indicator is a function $\mathcal{I} : \Omega^H \to \mathbb{R}$, which assigns the vector $A = (A_1, \ldots, A_H)$ a real value $\mathcal{I}(A_1, \ldots, A_H)$.*

We state a set A has a higher quality than another set B, if A at least weakly dominates B.[2] If a quality indicator $\mathcal{I}$ assigns a value $\mathcal{I}(A) \geq \mathcal{I}(B)$ under the condition that $A \preceq B$ (and vice versa), $\mathcal{I}$ is called *Pareto Compliant* [7, p. 253].

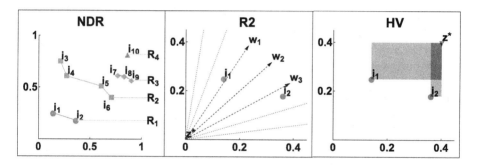

Fig. 1. Example for the quality indicators Nondominated Ranking (left), R2-Indicator (center) and Hypervolume (right). Consider a two-dimensional MOP and a set A consisting of ten individuals i_1 to i_{10}. The R2-Indicator and the Hypervolume do only focus on i_1 and i_2 in this example. The reference point is denoted by z^*.

In the following, we provide a brief overview of three important quality indicators in the context of this paper. Figure 1 gives an example for a set $A = \{i_1, \ldots, i_{10}\}$ for each of the following quality indicators:

Nondominated Ranking. The Nondominated Ranking [4] orders the solutions of a set A using the Pareto Dominance. Therefore all solutions are assigned into ranks R_1 to R_H. Let $1 \leq i < j \leq H$ then $\forall b \in R_j \exists a \in R_i : a \prec b$. Solutions of

---

[2] See [7, Table 5.2, p. 244] for an overview of the dominance relations.

equal rank are incomparable with respect to Pareto Dominance. In Fig. 1 the individuals i_1 and i_2, which dominate all remaining individuals, are assigned to R_1. The individuals i_3 to i_6, which are dominated by i_1 and i_2 each, but dominate the individuals i_7 to i_{10}, are assigned to R_2 and so on.

R2-Indicator. The R2-Indicator is based on the standard weighted Tchebycheff utility function, where z is a solution, z^* an (ideal) reference point and $\lambda = \{\lambda_1, \ldots, \lambda_K\} \in \Lambda$ is a weight vector [9]:

$$u(z) = - \max_{i \in \{1, \ldots, K\}} \{\lambda_i |z_i^* - z_i|\} \tag{1}$$

Λ is a set of (usually) uniformly distributed weight vectors over the weight space [10]. The R2-Indicator returns the averaged sum of the minimum distances for all $a \in A$ in any dimension for each weight vector $\lambda \in \Lambda$:

$$R2(A) = R2(A, \Lambda, z^*) = \frac{1}{|\Lambda|} \sum_{\lambda \in \Lambda} \min_{a \in A} \left\{ \max_{i \in \{1, \ldots, k\}} \{\lambda_i |z_i^* - a_i|\} \right\} \tag{2}$$

A lower R2 value means that the set's solutions are located closer to the reference point. The contribution of a single solution $a \in A$ to the R2 value is computed by $R2(A \setminus \{a\}) - R2(A)$ [10]. In Fig. 1 there are three weight vectors $w_1 = \left(\frac{3}{8}, \frac{5}{8}\right)$, $w_2 = \left(\frac{1}{2}, \frac{1}{2}\right)$ and $w_3 = \left(\frac{5}{8}, \frac{3}{8}\right)$. Each assigns a certain importance to each dimension. For each weight vector, the individual's contribution is increased, which is nearest to the reference point z^* with respect to the vector's weights. The following individuals are selected: i_1 for w_2 and i_2 for w_1 and w_3. In the above case, considering only i_1 and i_2 their total R2 contribution is 0.062 respectively 0.007. Thus i_1 is evaluated as better than i_2 concerning the R2-indicator.

Hypervolume. The Hypervolume (HV) defines the volume of the objective space that is covered by the solutions of a set A and a reference point z^*. The Hypervolume is defined as follows:

$$HV(A) = HV(A, z^*) = \left\{ \bigcup_{a \in A} vol(a, z^*) \right\} \tag{3}$$

where $vol(a, z^*)$ denotes the volume of the space bounded between a and z^* [7, p. 260]. The larger the value of $HV(A)$ the more space is covered by A, hence the solutions in A are closer to the ideal point (in case that z^* is the nadir point, e.g. $z^* = (1, \ldots, 1)$ for normalized minimization problems) [11]. The contribution of a single solution $a \in A$ to the HV value (the space that is *only* covered by a) is computed by $HV(A) - HV(A \setminus \{a\})$ [12]. In Fig. 1 the area, dominated exclusively by i_1 or i_2 is shaded in light gray. The dark gray area is dominated by both individuals. In this example it is obvious that the area exclusively dominated by i_1 is larger than i_2's area, therefore i_1 is to prefer over i_2 with respect to the dominated Hypervolume.

2.2 Evolutionary Multi-objective Algorithms

To address MOPs, evolutionary multi-objective algorithms (EMOAs) can be used. The class of EMOAs is also referred to as multi-objective evolutionary algorithms, short MOEAs. Well-known examples include the NSGA-II [4] and the SMS-EMOA [13]. Additionally, Trautmann et al. [14] introduced the R2-EMOA. We have selected the SMS- and the R2-EMOA for further investigations, because both have been shown to have a high performance while they do only require the user to set the population size μ. The SMS-EMOA is able to deal with an arbitrary large number of fitness functions K and uses two criteria for sorting a population's individuals: first all individuals are sorted into ranks using fast nondominated sorting of the NSGA-II [4]. If the (worst) rank R_H contains more than one individual, the Hypervolume contribution of each individual in R_H is computed to make these individuals comparable (survivor selection). Note that there exist different variants of SMS-EMOA using the Dominance count as primary selection criterion [13]. The R2-EMOA works similar to SMS-EMOA, the only difference is that the R2-EMOA relies on the R2-Indicator as the secondary criterion instead of the Hypervolume [14].

As already stated, both, the R2-EMOA and the SMS-EMOA will be considered to derive multi-objective variants of the NEAT approach. But first, the next section provides the details of the original method.

2.3 NeuroEvolution of Augmenting Topologies

The NeuroEvolution of Augmenting Topologies algorithm (NEAT) was introduced in [2]. It addresses the evolution of neural networks for performing single objective tasks. Therefore it depends on a node based encoding, where neural networks are described by a list of links, which each contains information about the connected nodes (or neurons) [2, p. 34f.]. NEAT relies on three basic principles:

Historical Markings. For the crossover of two networks, their structure has to be considered. NEAT addresses this by tracking each structural mutation (new link or neuron) with an Innovation ID. If a mutation occurs twice or more, it is always assigned the same Innovation ID. Thereby two networks can be combined without any structural analysis, the equal parts of two networks can be determined by their Innovation IDs, likewise their unequal parts [2, pp. 36–38].

Speciation. To protect innovation, NEAT sorts the networks of a population into niches of similar networks, called species. Thus networks do only have to compete against the other members of their species, and may evolve a competitive structure. Additionally it keeps the genomes as small as possible: As long as the fitness of smaller networks is comparable to the fitness of other, larger networks, the smaller networks remain in the population and thus are not unnecessarily replaced by larger networks [2, pp. 38–40].

Complexification. Every network in NEAT starts with the same minimal topology: each input neuron is directly connected to every output neuron (with random link weights), there are no hidden neurons, only an optional bias neuron. By structural mutation the networks grow incrementally and only well performing ones will survive. Thereby NEAT needs to search a minimal number of weight dimensions and is able to find well performing networks very quickly, additionally this prevents the networks' structures from growing unnecessarily large [2, p. 40f.].

NEAT is a powerful algorithm which is able to outperform other algorithms for evolving neural networks like Cellular Encoding [15], Symbiotic Adaptive Neuroevolution [16] and Enforced Subpopulations [17] in several experiments [2, pp. 44–49]. As it has been shown, NEAT is capable to evolve neural networks for single objective tasks, but how can Neuroevolution be used to address multi-objective problems?

3   Multi-Objective NEAT: A First Approach

In the real world, there exist many tasks that are suitable to be controlled by neural networks, but depend on more than one criterion. The NEAT approach allows to evolve neural networks considering a single objective, but for problems with more than one, NEAT has to fall back to using a weighted fitness function (scalarisation). The drawback of weighted fitness functions is that the user has to determine the weights a-priori and thus needs to know the importance of each goal *before* optimization [8, p. 196]. To avoid this and other disadvantages of scalarisation, we introduce a novel multi-objective version of NEAT, called Multi-Objective NEAT (mNEAT) as the foundation of our research. The mNEAT is an indicator-based algorithm and utilizes the R2-Indicator for quality assessment. Its main procedures are described in the following.

3.1   Procedure of mNEAT

The novel approach starts with an initially random population $\mathcal{P}_t$ (for time $t = 0$) consisting of μ minimal networks. The mNEAT is based on speciation. Here, the user defines the target number of species and mNEAT automatically adjusts the speciation threshold (the maximum difference of two networks of same species) according to the networks' difference. This step is executed at the beginning of every epoch. Note that mNEAT provides a general selection and sorting procedure, that is, the outer loop of an EMOA. It assumes that the neural networks in the population ($p \in \mathcal{P}_t$) have been evaluated and assigned a fitness $f(p) = (f_1(p), \ldots, f_K(p))$ before each epoch.

The networks in $\mathcal{P}_t$ are sorted depending on their R2 contribution with respect to the population $\mathcal{P}_t$. All networks are assigned to the corresponding species s, which results in a set of species S. Already existing network-to-species mappings are removed in advance. The first network assigned to a species is chosen as its representative. After speciation, the fitness $f(s) = (f_1(s), \ldots, f_K(s))$ of each species $s \in S$ is computed (determined by the species' members' fitness): The approach uses fitness sharing to keep species as small as possible and to maximize the diversity otherwise. Therefore, the species' fitness is computed by $\forall k \in \{1, \ldots, K\} : f_k(s) = \sum_{p \in s} f_k(p)$. When used for minimization problems, large species are assigned a comparatively large fitness with respect to smaller species. A large species has only then the chance to compete with smaller species if it contains much better networks than the smaller species. In a maximization problem, the fitness could be exponentiated with -1 for example in order to penalize larger species. The species' fitness is normalized between 0 and 1 for each fitness function, which makes the fitness functions comparable to each other. Finally the R2 contribution of each species $s \in S$ with respect to S is computed: The number of solutions, offspring(s), the species s is allowed to create, is proportional to its R2 contribution:

$$\text{offspring}(s) = \frac{R2(s, S, \Lambda, z^*)}{\sum_{t \in S} R2(t, S, \Lambda, z^*)} \left(\mu - |S| \right). \tag{4}$$

Every epoch $\mu - |S|$ offspring networks are created by crossover and mutation. Each species internally performs parent selection by using Stochastic Universal Sampling[3]. The mNEAT approach employs the variation operators that were defined in NEAT [2]. All newly created networks enter the next generation's population $\mathcal{P}_{t+1}$. Additionally, the representative (i.e., best network) of each species $s \in S$ will be part of $\mathcal{P}_{t+1}$. All other networks are discarded.

3.2 Variations of mNEAT

First experiments with mNEAT have shown that it is able to find good solutions fast but that the final Pareto front is typically only sparsely populated by good solutions because many of these are discarded during evolution. To improve the performance of mNEAT, we introduced and investigated several variations: (1) an *archive* of best individuals [7, p. 14], (2) using a *steady state* population model [8, p. 80] and (3) *reducing the replacement rate* in each epoch (not discarding all networks, except the species' leaders, but preserving a part of the other (mutated) networks for the next generation).

Our initial idea of the cooperation of these variations was as follows: The **archive** (Variation 1) records the progress of the algorithm and keeps a list of the best networks that have been found during the optimization. This allows the

---

[3] Stochastic Universal Sampling (SUS) behaves similar to the Roulette Wheel Selection (RWS), where each individual gets assigned a hole on a one-armed roulette wheel, the hole's size depends on the individual's fitness compared to all individuals' fitness. The roulette wheel is spun once and an individual is selected then. SUS uses an equally-spaced λ-armed roulette wheel to select λ different individuals at once instead of spinning the wheel λ times. The better an individual's fitness, the better it's chance to be selected as parent [8, p. 84]. Every individual (even the worst of the population) has a nonzero chance of being selected [8, p. 81f.]. The advantage of SUS over RWS is that a set of λ unique individuals can be selected at once. Using RWS for selecting $\lambda > 1$ individuals would require λ executions and a mechanism to avoid the same individual being selected twice.

mNEAT to explore arbitrary new networks without losing the progress already made. Using a **steady state** population model (Variation 2) results in always taking over the best networks of $\mathcal{P}_t$ and the offspring into $\mathcal{P}_{t+1}$. Without this variation mNEAT would only keep the species' representatives and discard any other networks. By Variation 2, the mNEAT does not discard promising networks any more, only because their fitness is not at its maximum at timestep t due to lack of evolution. Finally, the **reduction of the replacement rate** (Variation 3) allows younger networks to evolve and maximize their fitness. By doing so, less networks are newly generated but more existing networks are mutated. Thus *exploitation* plays a bigger role instead of a pronounced utilization of *exploration* [8, p. 41f.]. Preliminary experiments (Multi-objective Double Pole Balancing experiment with all eight possible combinations of these variations) have shown that the Variations 2 and 3 do only have a small influence on the algorithm's performance. Using mNEAT only with Variation 1 (archive) provides the best results with respect to the Pareto front. This behaviour is caused by the archive, which always saves the best known solutions and returns these as the finally known Pareto Front. Due to space restrictions we do not provide details concerning the experiment and its results in this paper. In future work further variations of the mNEAT will be investigated to create an even better performing algorithm.

4   NEAT as the Foundation of Evolutionary Multi-objective Algorithms

We already provided a brief description of the two efficient evolutionary multi-objective algorithms *SMS-EMOA* and *R2-EMOA* with indicator-based selection. Since these algorithms are capable of optimizing solutions in multiple dimensions simultaneously, they should be suitable for adapting the behaviour of neural networks. As both algorithms are designed as general frameworks and not specifically to work with neural networks, we introduce the following extensions, similar to Schrum and Miikkulainen [3,5] and van Willigen et al. [6]:

For giving SMS- and R2-EMOA the ability to evolve neural networks, we base them on the framework that NEAT provides: We use the same genetic encoding of neural networks, the Innovation IDs and variation (crossover and mutation) operators of NEAT and implement those for an SMS- and R2-EMOA. Following this approach, we combine the power and efficiency of SMS-EMOA and R2-EMOA for multi-objective optimization and NEAT for evolving neural networks. This results in an algorithm Multi-Objective NEAT-Indicator Based, short mNEAT-IB that is capable of evolving neural networks for multi-objective tasks quite efficiently using different components for selection. Beside the selection mechanisms used in R2-EMOA and SMS-EMOA, we apply and investigate two indicator (only) based as selection components. Table 1 gives an overview over these variations and additionally provides information about their computationally complexities.

Table 1. Variations of the mNEAT-IB using different combinations of sorting criteria. K denotes the number of objectives and μ the population size. Λ defines the set of weight vectors used for the R2-indicator. The computational complexities are based on the following values: NDR: $O\left(K\mu^2\right)$ [4], HV (contribution of individual): $O\left(\mu \log \mu + \mu^{\frac{K}{2}+1}\right)$ [11], R2 (contribution of individual): $O\left(K\mu |\Lambda|\right)$ [18].

	Sorting		Computational complexity	
Variation	Primary	Secondary	Minimum	Maximum
1	NDR	HV	$O\left(K\mu^2\right)$	$O\left(K\mu^2 + \mu \log \mu + \mu^{\frac{K}{2}+1}\right)$
2	NDR	R2	$O\left(K\mu^2\right)$	$O\left(K\mu^2 + K\mu |\Lambda|\right)$
3	HV			$O\left(\mu \log \mu + \mu^{\frac{K}{2}+1}\right)$
4	R2			$O\left(K\mu |\Lambda|\right)$

In the following, we provide the details of the novel neuroevolutionary approach: The mNEAT-IB creates an initial population of μ minimal networks (with randomized weights). The population is sorted by the first and, optionally second sorting criterion. Then λ (instead of strictly one like in SMS-EMOA [13]) new networks are created by using NEAT's variation operators which then are added to $\mathcal{P}_t$. The parameter λ needs to be defined by the user. A large number of offspring λ may lead to a faster convergence of the population towards the Pareto front. However, this may cause the algorithm to miss potentially good networks by replacing them too quickly. For giving younger networks a chance to evolve, mNEAT-IB provides a small fitness-boost to younger networks, while it slightly penalizes the fitness of elder ones. The 2λ parents for crossover are selected using Stochastic Universal Sampling from the sorted population $\mathcal{P}_t$. The resulting intermediate population has a size of $\mu + \lambda$ and has to be reduced by λ networks. Because the λ new networks require fitness values before the reduction, the epoch ends here and the new networks are evaluated. At the beginning of the next epoch the population $\mathcal{P}_t$ is sorted as described above. The worst λ networks are removed from $\mathcal{P}_t$ which decreases its size to μ. The remainder are already sorted and the mNEAT-IB continues with the selection of 2λ parents for the next generation. The algorithm terminates if the stopping criterion is met.

Due to the exponential growth of the Hypervolume-computation's runtime, the R2-indicator is to be preferred for a larger number of objectives $(K \geq 4)$. Its runtime heavily depends on the number of weight vectors applied. Here, Brockhoff et al. [10] discuss the optimal number of weight vectors for $K = 2$. Further investigations are necessary to give a suggestion for the case $K > 2$. We use a default of 100 weight vectors for our experiments described in Sect. 5.

5   Experimental Analysis

To compare the performance of our novel algorithms and variations, we conducted a series of experiments using a variant of the Double Pole Balancing problem. This section provides the experimental set-up and discusses the experimental findings. First we introduce a multi-objective version of the Double Pole Balancing problem before we describe the design of the experiments. The last part of the section summarizes and discusses the results.

5.1   A Multi-objective Double Pole Balancing Problem

The Double Pole Balancing problem describes the following task: Given a **cart** c with mass c_m ($= 1\,\mathrm{kg}$) on which two **poles** p_1 and p_2 are mounted using a hinge. Each pole p has a length p_l ($= 1\,\mathrm{m}/0.1\,\mathrm{m}$) and a mass p_m ($= 0.1\,\mathrm{kg}\,/\,0.01\,\mathrm{kg}$). At time $t = 0$ both poles are poised, inclined in angles p_{1_α} ($= 0°$) and p_{2_α} ($= 1°$). Left by themselves, the two poles would fall to the left or right side over the time t. If one or both poles' inclination exceeds a given maximum angle γ ($= 36°$), the experiment has failed and the time t is stopped. The cart is positioned at the centre of a track with length L ($= 4.8\,\mathrm{m}$). The experiment's target is to keep the two poles balanced by moving the cart to left or right without leaving the track for a given amount of time T ($= 10.000$ units). The cart is controlled by a neural network which has to be evolved using our proposed algorithms. The networks consider the following input parameters: The position c_{pos} and velocity c_v of the cart and the angles and rates of fall of the poles p_1 and p_2. The networks' output is a value which determines the force that affects the cart (direction and strength) in the next timestep. The Double Pole Balancing problem was used by Stanley [2] for comparing the performance of the single-criterion NEAT to other neuroevolutionary algorithms and ablations of the original NEAT. It is an enhanced version of the Pole Balancing problem [16] which became too simple to solve for modern algorithms to be a measure for comparison [2]. The Double Pole Balancing problem is typically used to evaluate the performance of algorithms for Reinforcement Learning.

We transform this problem into a multi-objective optimization problem using the following fitness functions: **(1)** The first fitness function f_1 describes how long the controller x is capable of keeping the poles p_1 and p_2 balanced. **(2)** Additionally the number of directional changes (per time unit) r of the cart c is counted. The reason is that for each change of direction the cart has to be slowed down to $c_v = 0$ and then be accelerated in the other direction – this consumes much more energy than the movement with constant speed [19]. This results in the number of directional changes being proportional to the energy consumption of the cart. **(3)** Finally the cart's position c_{pos} relative to the centre of the track $L/2$ is considered. Therefore the average distance per timestep f_3 is computed – a larger value of f_3 means a greater distance that is covered by the cart and that results in a higher energy consumption. Additionally this leads to a lower distance to one end of the track, which increases the probability of the cart to leave the track. We introduced f_3 due to the fact that a controller can achieve a good fitness value for f_2 with the following behaviour: If the controller moves the cart from the very left to the very right end of the track continuously, the cart executes very few directional changes but always travels a distance of nearly L between each. This would increase the energy consumption and makes f_3 necessary.

The three fitness functions read as follows, where the parameter c_{pos_t} describes the position of the cart on the track at time t:

$$
\begin{aligned}
f_1(x) &= T - t & \forall x \in \Omega : 0 \le f_1(x) \le T \\
f_2(x) &= \tfrac{r}{t} & \forall x \in \Omega : 0 \le f_2(x) \le 1 \\
f_3(x) &= \tfrac{1}{t}\sum_1^t \left| \tfrac{L}{2} - c_{pos_t} \right| & \forall x \in \Omega : 0 \le f_3(x) \le \tfrac{L}{2}
\end{aligned}
\tag{5}
$$

5.2 Experiments and Statistical Analysis

All algorithms under consideration have control parameters that strongly influence the performance. Therefore, we first conducted preliminary experiments with a meta-EA in order to identify suitable parameter settings. The best were investigated more closely in the context of the analysis described in this paper. Due to space restrictions we do not show the configurations in this paper, but will offer these in a technical report. We conduct two different types of experiments which are repeated 120 times each:

Average Number of Evaluations. In this experiment we test an algorithm's ability to find a solution of predefined minimum fitness within a given amount of maximum evaluated networks. For each repetition, we record the number of evaluations needed to find an individual of desired fitness. At the end of the experiment, we compare the average number of evaluations and the success rate of each algorithm. Finally, we investigate the algorithms' results for statistically significant differences.

Mean Fitness. The second experiment tests an algorithm's ability to find a "good" Pareto front. Therefore each algorithm will be executed for a predefined number of evaluated networks with the final Pareto front (last generation or archive) being stored. All solutions of all Fronts are combined (one Pareto front per repetition) and used to compute the following quality indicators: ϵ, *Spacing, generational Distance, Inverted generational Distance, Inverted generational Distance Plus* and *Hypervolume*. This gives us the ability to evaluate the quality of the Pareto fronts that have been found by the algorithms. We show the averaged results of each algorithm for each performance measure and finally analyse the results for statistically significant differences.

For the statistical comparison of the algorithms (with the predefined configuration) we use the procedure described by Calvo and Santafé [20] using the R-library *scmamp*[4]. First we determine if there is a statistically significant difference between any two algorithms (Friedman-Test [21]). If a difference has been ascertained we determine the pairwise difference between the algorithms (Friedman Aligned Ranks test [22]). The determined p-values are adjusted (Shaffer's algorithm [23]) and then evaluated.

---

[4] R-library for comparing algorithms: https://cran.r-project.org/web/packages/scmamp/index.html.

Average Number of Evaluations. Table 2 shows the results of the Double Pole Balancing experiment with velocities. We investigate the average number of evaluated networks until an algorithm found a network x^* for which $f_1(x^*) = 0$, $f_2(x^*) \leq \frac{1}{20}$ and $f_3(x^*) \leq \frac{1}{5}$. This calls for a neural network that balances the poles of the cart for at least T timesteps and performs a change of direction at most every 20th timestep. Additionally it is not allowed to stay away from the centre of the track more than 20 cm on average. We were looking for a safe and energy-efficient controller for the cart.

Table 2. Number of evaluated networks until the algorithm found a network of the desired fitness in the Double Pole Balancing experiment with velocities (Average Number of Evaluations) averaged over 120 repetitions. A repetition was not successful, if no network x^* has been found within 25,000 evaluated networks.

Algorithm	Variation	Mean	$+-$	Success rate
mNEAT	Original	10,789	7,497	0.86
	Archive	10,733	7,870	0.85
mNEAT-IB	NDR + HV	14,150	8,295	0.7
	NDR + R2	9,946	7,836	0.85
	HV	11,180	9,537	0.72
	R2	8,272	6,050	0.92

The results in Table 2 show that the mNEAT was able to find a suitable network x^* in 85% of all repetitions. Note that the mNEAT (without variation) and the mNEAT with archive behave identical in this type of experiment[5] – this can be observed in both variants' results, which are nearly equal in this experiment. The mNEAT-IB (R2) shows the best results with respect to number of evaluations (8,272) and success rate (92%). On the other hand the mNEAT-IB (NDR + HV) evaluated 14,150 networks until it found a network x^* and thus performed worst (even statistically significant for $\alpha = 0.05$). It has to be investigated whether the quality indicators in mNEAT-IB (NDR + HV) are not suitable for evolving neural networks or this variation has not been configured properly by the meta-EA. To summarize, all algorithms were capable of finding an energy efficient controller for the cart in at least 70% of all repetitions with a maximal number of 25,000 evaluations. Most of the algorithms even exceeded a success rate of 85%.

---

[5] The only difference between the original mNEAT and the mNEAT with archive is that the latter saves the best solutions ever found in an archive. Because the archive is only kept as a "second population" and finally returned as Pareto front, there is no difference in both variants' behaviour in the Average Number of Evaluations experiment.

Table 3. Quality indicator values of the algorithms and variations using the previously determined parameter settings for the Double Pole Balancing experiment with velocities (Mean Fitness). (first row = mean value, second row = standard deviation)

Algorithm	Variation	ϵ	S	GD	IGD	IGD+	HV
mNEAT	Original	0.843	0.992	0.065	0.032	0.621	0.147
		0.297	0.092	0.004	0.006	0.233	0.299
	Archive	0.073	1.144	0.03	0.018	0.036	0.927
		0.2	0.136	0.009	0.004	0.144	0.204
mNEAT-IB	NDR + HV	0.59	1.018	0.083	0.031	0.437	0.408
		0.474	0.08	0.032	0.008	0.352	0.474
	NDR + R2	0.159	1.067	0.065	0.023	0.113	0.84
		0.351	0.11	0.023	0.006	0.261	0.351
	HV	0.477	1.024	0.086	0.029	0.352	0.522
		0.483	0.085	0.033	0.008	0.359	0.484
	R2	0.053	1.145	0.019	0.019	0.036	0.946
		0.211	0.128	0.01	0.004	0.156	0.211

Mean Fitness. The results of the Double Pole Balancing experiment with velocities (Mean Fitness) are shown in Table 3. We examined the commonly used quality indicators ϵ (smallest amount ϵ that is necessary to translate one set A into another set B) [24,25], *Spacing* (short S – the spread of the solutions of a set A), *generational Distance* (short GD – the average distance from a set A to the Pareto front) [25], *Inverted generational Distance* (short IGD – the average distance from the Pareto front to a set A, Pareto Noncompliant), *Inverted generational Distance Plus* (short IGD+ – the average distance from the Pareto front to a set A, weakly Pareto Compliant) [26] and *Hypervolume* [24,25]. See [7, pp. 256–262] for more details on ϵ, S, GD and [26] for IGD and IGD+. The Hypervolume (HV) has been described in Sect. 2.1.

Table 3 shows that the mNEAT-IB (R2) achieves the best results in ϵ, GD, IGD+ (beside mNEAT (Archive)) and HV and second best in IGD. The mNEAT (Archive) performs best with respect to IGD and IGD+ and second best regarding ϵ, GD and HV. To summarize the findings: All examined quality indicators, except Spacing, are dominated by mNEAT-IB (R2) and mNEAT (Archive). Concerning Spacing, the original mNEAT performs best, followed by mNEAT-IB (NDR + HV), while these results are still not good at all: The solutions are concentrated around the most promising areas of the objective space and not spread equidistantly. The mNEAT performs worst regarding all quality indicators, except Spacing (where the mNEAT-IB (R2) gives the worst results) and GD (where the mNEAT-IB (HV) is worst). With respect to the quality indicators shown in Table 3, we find that the mNEAT-IB (NDR + R2), the mNEAT-IB (R2) and the mNEAT (Archive) show statistically significant better results than the mNEAT-IB (NDR + HV), the mNEAT-IB (HV) and the mNEAT in many cases. This would indicate that this group were to be preferred for further investigations. In contrast, mNEAT shows best results in Spacing, which could be caused by mNEAT's behaviour to replace large parts of the population by new individuals. We assume that mNEAT rather explores the objective space instead of exploiting promising areas. It has to be investigated whether the differences that have been observed between the algorithms and variations concerning the quality indicators depend on the selected parameter settings or the problem instance, therefore further experiments will be carried out in future research.

6   Conclusions and Future Work

This paper focused on multi-objective Neuroevolution. We followed two main research directions both based on the well-known neuroevolutionary approach NEAT which was designed for single-objective tasks. The first focused on developing multi-objective variants of NEAT itself. Here, we introduced a novel indicator-based algorithm. The second direction considered the combination of efficient evolutionary multi-objective algorithms developed for a large number of objectives and NEAT. In this case, the multi-objective algorithms provide the framework into which the main principles of NEAT are integrated. We derived and tested four different variants. This is the first approach which uses these modern multi-objective algorithms with indicator-based selection in the context of Neuroevolution: Previous research utilized the SPEA2 with the original NEAT (Pareto Strength approach is mapping K objectives into a single objective, making it applicable to NEAT without any modifications) or the NSGA-II which is not considered as performant when the number of objectives is relatively large.

All in all this paper is intended as a proof of concept showing that our algorithms are suitable to address multi-objective Neuroevolution. The first experimental results are very promising. Our experimental analysis shows that the novel algorithms are capable of finding an energy efficient cart controller for a multi-objective version of the well-known Double Pole Balancing problem within very few evaluations. Concerning the *Mean Fitness* experiment which addresses the quality of the final Pareto front, we find that all algorithms are capable of evolving good controllers within a predefined number of maximum evaluations. However, statistically significant differences between the algorithms exist. The research will be continued in several directions. First of all, we are currently investigating more difficult variants of the Pole Balancing problem.

Despite the promising first results, further experiments on truly high - dimensional MOPs are necessary to test the algorithms ability of optimizing more than three fitness functions. Currently we are investigating the **FighTing Game AI** Competition [27], for which we apply our algorithms to create neural networks as controllers for an AI player (with four and five objectives). Preliminary results show that our algorithms are capable of beating already established AI opponents after very few evaluations.

To gain more insights concerning the algorithms' behaviour, especially with respect to robustness, we have to compare a larger number of different configurations in future research. For exploring [8, p. 41f.] the search space of parameter configurations, we will follow the guidelines provided by the design and analysis of simulation experiments (DASE) [28]. Additionally the newly proposed algorithms have to be compared to other existing algorithms like NEAT-PS or MM-NEAT to assess their performance in comparison to these. In the future, further areas as for example computer games or maze navigation will be considered in order to investigate the range of applicability of our algorithms. This will provide insights regarding the question whether one and then which of the novel algorithms/variations emerges as preferable in the area of Reinforcement Learning. Additionally, further variations of the algorithms should be investigated to create an even more powerful algorithm for multiobjective Neuroevolution. Another interesting aspect to investigate is in how far the parameters of the algorithms can be automatically configured by the algorithms during execution. Reducing the number of parameters that have to be predefined by the user reduces the complexity of the search space (for parameter configurations) and on the other hand increases the usability of the algorithms. Therefore, it represents an important point of future research.

References

1. Sutton, R.S., Barto, A.G.: Reinforcement Learning: An Introduction, vol. 1. MIT press, Cambridge (1998)
2. Stanley, K.O.: Efficient evolution of neural networks through complexification. Ph.D. thesis, Department of Computer Sciences, The University of Texas at Austin (2004)
3. Schrum, J., Miikkulainen, R.: Constructing complex NPC behavior via multiobjective neuroevolution. AIIDE **8**, 108–113 (2008)
4. Deb, K., Pratap, A., Agarwal, S., Meyarivan, T.: A fast and elitist multiobjective genetic algorithm: NSGA-II. IEEE Trans. Evol. Comput. **6**(2), 182–197 (2002)
5. Schrum, J., Miikkulainen, R.: Discovering multimodal behavior in Ms. Pac-Man through evolution of modular neural networks. IEEE Trans. Comput. Intell. AI Games **8**(1), 67–81 (2016)
6. van Willigen, W., Haasdijk, E., Kester, L.: Fast, comfortable or economical: evolving platooning strategies with many objectives. In: 16th International IEEE Conference on Intelligent Transportation Systems-(ITSC), 2013, pp. 1448–1455 (2013)
7. Coello, C.A.C., Lamont, G.B., van Veldhuizen, D.A., et al.: Evolutionary Algorithms for Solving Multi-objective Problems, vol. 5. Springer, US (2007). https://doi.org/10.1007/978-0-387-36797-2
8. Eiben, A.E., Smith, J.E.: Introduction to Evolutionary Computing. NCS. Springer, Heidelberg (2015). https://doi.org/10.1007/978-3-662-44874-8
9. Hansen, M.P., Jaszkiewicz, A.: Evaluating the Quality of Approximations to the Non-dominated Set. Department of Mathematical Modelling, Technical Universityof Denmark, IMM (1998)
10. Brockhoff, D., Wagner, T., Trautmann, H.: On the properties of the R2 indicator. In: Proceedings of the 14th Annual Conference on Genetic and Evolutionary Computation, pp. 465–472 (2012)
11. Beume, N., Rudolph, G.: Faster S-metric calculation by considering dominated hypervolume as Klee's measure problem. In: Kovalerchuk, B. (ed.) Proceedings of the Second IASTED International Conference on Computational Intelligence, 20–22 November 2006, pp. 233–238. IASTED/ACTA Press, San Francisco (2006)

12. Emmerich, M., Beume, N., Naujoks, B.: An EMO algorithm using the hypervolume measure as selection criterion. In: Coello Coello, C.A., Hernández Aguirre, A., Zitzler, E. (eds.) EMO 2005. LNCS, vol. 3410, pp. 62–76. Springer, Heidelberg (2005). https://doi.org/10.1007/978-3-540-31880-4_5
13. Beume, N., Naujoks, B., Emmerich, M.: SMS-EMOA: multiobjective selection based on dominated hypervolume. Eur. J. Oper. Res. **181**(3), 1653–1669 (2007)
14. Trautmann, H., Wagner, T., Brockhoff, D.: R2-EMOA: focused multiobjective search using R2-indicator-based selection. In: Nicosia, G., Pardalos, P. (eds.) LION 2013. LNCS, vol. 7997, pp. 70–74. Springer, Heidelberg (2013). https://doi.org/10.1007/978-3-642-44973-4_8
15. Gruau, F.: Cellular encoding as a graph grammar. In: IEE Colloquium on Grammatical Inference: Theory, Applications and Alternatives, pp. 17/1–1710 (1993)
16. Moriarty, D.E., Mikkulainen, R.: Efficient reinforcement learning through symbiotic evolution. Mach. Learn. **22**(1–3), 11–32 (1996)
17. Gomez, F.J., Miikkulainen, R.: Solving non-markovian control tasks with neuroevolution. In: IJCAI, vol. 99, pp. 1356–1361 (1999)
18. Diaz-Manriquez, A., Toscano-Pulido, G., Coello, C.A.C., Landa-Becerra, R.: A ranking method based on the R2 indicator for many-objective optimization. In: IEEE Congress on Evolutionary Computation (CEC), 2013, pp. 1523–1530. IEEE, Piscataway (2013)
19. Gamow, G., Cleveland, J.M., Freeman, I.M.: Physics: foundations and frontiers. Am. J. Phys. **29**(1), 60 (1961)
20. Calvo, B., Santafé, G.: Statistical Assessment of the Differences (2018). https://cran.r-project.org/web/packages/scmamp/vignettes/Statistical_assessment_of_the_differences.html
21. Friedman, M.: The use of ranks to avoid the assumption of normality implicit in the analysis of variance. J. Am. Stat. Assoc. **32**(200), 675–701 (1937)
22. García, S., Fernández, A., Luengo, J., Herrera, F.: Advanced nonparametric tests for multiple comparisons in the design of experiments in computational intelligence and data mining: experimental analysis of power. Inf. Sci. **180**(10), 2044–2064 (2010)
23. Shaffer, J.P.: Modified sequentially rejective multiple test procedures. J. Am. Stat. Assoc. **81**(395), 826–831 (1986)
24. Fonseca, C.M., Knowles, J.D., Thiele, L., Zitzler, E.: A tutorial on the performance assessment of stochastic multiobjective optimizers. In: Third International Conference on Evolutionary Multi-Criterion Optimization (EMO 2005), vol. 216, p. 240 (2005)
25. Zitzler, E., Thiele, L., Laumanns, M., Fonseca, C.M., Da Fonseca, V.G.: Performance assessment of multiobjective optimizers: an analysis and review. IEEE Trans. Evol. Comput. **7**(2), 117–132 (2003)
26. Ishibuchi, H., Masuda, H., Nojima, Y.: A study on performance evaluation ability of a modified inverted generational distance indicator. In: Proceedings of the 2015 Annual Conference on Genetic and Evolutionary Computation, pp. 695–702 (2015)
27. Lu, F., Yamamoto, K., Nomura, L.H., Mizuno, S., Lee, Y., Thawonmas, R.: Fighting game artificial intelligence competition platform. In: IEEE 2nd Global Conference on Consumer Electronics (GCCE), 2013, pp. 320–323 (2013)
28. Kleijnen, J.P.C.: Design and Analysis of Simulation Experiments, vol. 20. Springer, US (2008). https://doi.org/10.1007/978-0-387-71813-2

Revolve: A Versatile Simulator for Online Robot Evolution

Elte Hupkes[1,2], Milan Jelisavcic[1(✉)] ⓘ, and A. E. Eiben[1]

[1] Vrije Universiteit Amsterdam,
De Boelelaan 1105, 1081 HV Amsterdam, The Netherlands
{m.j.jelisavcic,a.e.eiben}@vu.nl
[2] University of Amsterdam,
Science Park 904, 1098 XH Amsterdam, The Netherlands

Abstract. Developing robotic systems that can evolve in real-time and real-space is a long term objective with technological as well as algorithmic milestones on the road. Technological prerequisites include advanced 3D-printing, automated assembly, and robust sensors and actuators. The necessary evolutionary mechanisms need not wait for these, they can be developed and investigated in simulations. In this paper, we present a system to simulate *online* evolution of *constructible* robots, where (1) the population members (robots) concurrently exist and evolve their morphologies and controllers, (2) all robots can be physically constructed. Experiments with this simulator provide us with insights into differences of using online and offline evolutionary setups.

Keywords: Evolutionary algorithms · Reality gap · Online learning
Offline learning · Modular robots

1 Introduction

The motivation for this paper comes from the vision of the Evolution of Things described by Eiben and Smith [1]. In particular, the interest is in physical robots that "can evolve in real time and real space" [2]. The ultimate system of our interest consists of robots with evolvable bodies and brains that 'live and work' concurrently in the same physical environment. However, the current technology lacks essential components to this end, in particular, the mechanisms that enable that robots to reproduce, i.e., 'have children'. This technology is being developed, but in the meanwhile, simulators can be of great value as they allow us to study various system setups and generate scientific insights as well as know-how regarding the working of physically evolving robotic systems.

Looking into existing work on evolvable morphologies we can note a large variety of approaches. Yet, there are two important limitations shared by most of them. First, evolution is executed in an offline fashion, that is, through a (centralised) evolutionary algorithm that runs the standard EA loop and only calls the simulator to establish the fitness of a new genotype. Such fitness evaluations typically happen in isolation: the phenotype, i.e., the robot, that belongs

© Springer International Publishing AG, part of Springer Nature 2018
K. Sim and P. Kaufmann (Eds.): EvoApplications 2018, LNCS 10784, pp. 687–702, 2018.
https://doi.org/10.1007/978-3-319-77538-8_46

to the given genotype is placed and evaluated in an environment without other robots present. This is in contrast to our vision with genuinely embodied online evolution, where all population members concurrently operate in the same environment. An important question is whether the differences between online and offline evolution are purely procedural or do the two types of systems exhibit different behaviour. To answer this question experimentally we would need a simulator that can be configured for both types of evolution keeping all other system properties identical.

Second, the robots in most of the existing simulations are not constructible. Certainly, this is not limiting for fundamental studies but the long-term goal of constructing a system of physical robots that can evolve in real time and real space implies a need for a simulator with a hi-fidelity model of real robots with an evolvable morphology.

In summary, current systems and the investigations performed with them suffer from either or both of these limitations and are less realistic that we would prefer. To this end, we present a new simulator with a unique combination of features that supports experimental research that cannot be done with existing systems. In particular,

1. All robots are physically constructible by assembling off-the-shelf components (e.g., servo motors, LED lights) and 3D-printed body parts.
2. Robots have evolvable morphologies and controllers. Both the physical and the mental makeup are encoded by genotypes that can be mutated and recombined. The phenotype space and the corresponding genetic code is based on RoboGen [3].
3. Evolution is carried out in an online, embodied fashion. Robots populate an environment simultaneously and selection and reproduction are determined by the (inter)actions of the robots and the environment. Thus, evolution is induced 'from inside', robots are not just isolated candidate solutions in some traditional genetic algorithm.

An important feature of this simulator is that it can be used in a traditional offline mode as well. Thus, it allows us to answer the research question: what are the main differences between online and offline evolution and how do these affect the dynamics of the evolving robot population? For this purpose, we specify three scenarios, one with offline evolution, one with online evolution, and a combined form and compare the emerging dynamics.

The rest of this paper is organised as follows. In Sect. 2 we briefly review the most relevant existing works. The details of the Revolve simulator are presented in Sect. 3. Section 4 describes the robots, followed by the outlines of the evolutionary system in Sect. 5 and the three scenarios in Sect. 6. The experimental results are presented in Sect. 7.

2   Related Work

Current technology limitations confine studies on evolving morphologies to software simulations. Although works based purely on simulation fall outside the present overview, the classic experiments of Sims deserve to be mentioned [4]. This system works through a traditional EA that evaluates virtual creatures one by one in a simulator, assessed by different locomotion skills, such as walking, hopping, swimming, and for the task of fighting over a block in between two organisms.[1] The virtual organisms are modular, consisting of blocks of different sizes which are connected through actuators driven by neural network controllers. A couple of other papers follow a similar approach: they evolve artificial organisms and their control structures in simulation using evolutionary algorithms [5–7]. These creatures are not very realistic, they cannot be directly manufactured in real hardware. The evolutionary systems are not natural either (centralised, offline), but the papers demonstrate the concept of morphology evolution.

The work of Auerbach and Bongard is especially interesting because it casts morphological evolution in a broader context of the body-mind-environment trichotomy [5]. In particular, they study the relation between morphological, neural, and environmental complexity in an evolutionary system. They use a simple and a complex environment and evolve robots that comprise triangular meshes and are driven by neural controllers. Comparing the evolution of morphological complexity in different environments they find that "When no cost was placed on morphological complexity, no significant difference in morphological complexities between the two sets of robots evolved. However, when the robots were evolved in both environments again, and a cost was placed on complexity, robots in the simple environment were simpler than the robots evolved in the complex environment" (quote from [8]).

An interesting cluster of papers gets closer to reality by using simulations for evolving morphologies and constructing the end result. Lipson and Pollak used an EA and a simulator to evolve robotic organisms that consisted of bars and actuators (but no sensors) driven by a neural net for the task of locomoting over an infinite horizontal plane [9].

Perhaps the most interesting work in this cluster of papers is the recently developed RoboGen system [3]. RoboGen works with modular robots encoded by artificial genomes that specify the morphology and the controller of a robot, a simulator that can simulate the behaviour of one single robot in a given environment, and a classic evolutionary algorithm that calls the simulator for each fitness evaluation. The system is used to evolve robots in simulation and the evolved robots can be easily constructed by 3D-printing and manually assembling their components. RoboGen was not meant and is not being used for physical robot evolution, but it could be the starting point for such a system after a number of extensions (e.g., crossover for both morphologies and controllers).

2.1 Reality Gap

A notorious problem in evolutionary robotics is the *reality gap* first mentioned by Jakobi et al. [10], referring to the behavioural differences between simulated sys-

---

[1] http://www.karlsims.com/evolved-virtual-creatures.html.

tems and their real physical counterparts. While a simplification, rounding and numerical instability lead to differences whenever computer models are involved, this effect is amplified in evolutionary systems. The reason for this is that evolution, as previously noted, will often solve its set challenges with unexpected solutions. While this is generally a favourable property, it also means that the process may eventually 'exploit' whatever modelling errors or instabilities are present, arriving at a solution that is valid only in the context of the simulation. Aside from careful calibration of the behaviour of the simulator, the simplest and therefore most commonly used approach to counter this problem is to add noise to a virtual robot's sensors and actuators. While straightforward, this greatly increases the number of sensory representations of otherwise similar or identical states, slowing down the evolutionary process. More complicated approaches may involve alternating fitness evaluations between simulation and reality [11–14], but this is infeasible when simulating entire artificial ecosystems. Crossing the reality gap is by no means a solved problem and as always one should be cautious drawing definitive conclusions from a model.

3   The Simulator

The main design decision when conceiving Revolve was a choice between either (a) building on top of a dynamics engine directly, (b) modifying the code of an existing research project or (c) using a simulation platform. Out of these (b) and (c) are more viable options because they take away a large part of the bootstrapping process, and in addition, ensure improvements and fixes to the underlying infrastructure regardless of the development of the toolkit. The important factor for making the final decision was the ability of any of the possible options to integrate C++ libraries into its environment. The importance of using these native libraries lays behind the idea to recreate all simulated robots in hardware with Raspberry Pi as a controller.

Investigations were performed with the NASA Tensegrity and RoboGen source codes [3,15], running benchmarks and trying to realise simple artificial ecosystems using the existing code base. There was a particular focus on RoboGen as an attractive candidate for a proof of concept, given that its robot body space is easily constructed using 3D printing, and is subject to an ongoing real-life calibration process. During the setup of simple scenarios, however, it was found that the RoboGen software suite was too much tailored to its serial, offline evolution to be conveniently re-factored to the new use case. In addition, all code would have to be written in the C++ language, which provides high performance at the expense of being verbose and sometimes tedious to develop. While the choice for the RoboGen body space as a proof of concept remained, the decision was made to build the Revolve Toolkit on top of a general purpose simulation platform instead. The decision was made based on the fact that it appeared to be much easier to develop a simulation platform for a specific need on top of a flexible system than to modify any of existing solutions.

Out of the considered simulation platforms (Webots[2], MORSE[3], V-REP[4], Gazebo[5]), only Webots was discarded beforehand because it is a commercial and closed-source platform, and constraints in Webots limited the number of individuals that could be simulated, regardless of performance. MORSE appeared to be a suitable candidate but lacked the ability for high-performance C++ integration that Gazebo and V-REP provided, as well as the lack a choice of physics engines. A comparative analysis of the last two remaining platforms was conducted [16], ruling in favour of V-REP by a slight margin. However, a much older version (2.2) of Gazebo was used than was available, even at the time the paper was written. Additionally, the methodology compares CPU usage rather than simulation work performed over time. Considering all points, the bottom line is that V-REP and Gazebo are very similar platforms in terms of features. The eventual choice for Gazebo is motivated by its non-commercial nature, its large online community and the XML format it uses to describe models, which simplifies creating dynamic robot morphologies from external applications. That being said, V-REP would likely also have been very suitable as a platform. While Revolve has been written with Gazebo in mind, large parts are simulator agnostic and could potentially be used for creating a similar platform for use with V-REP. Following paragraphs will describe system parts in details.

Revolve. [6]The **R**obot **Evolve** toolkit is a set of Python and C++ libraries created to aid in setting up simulation experiments involving robots with evolvable bodies and/or minds. It builds on top of Gazebo, complementing this simulator with a set of tools that aim to provide a convenient way to set up such experiments. Revolve's philosophy is to make the development of simulation scenarios as easy as possible while maintaining the performance required to simulate large and complex environments. In general this means that performance critical parts (e.g. robot controllers and parts relating to physics simulation) are written in the C++ language, which is highly performant but can be tedious to write, whereas less performance-focused parts (such as world management and the specification of robots) are written in the slower yet more development-friendly Python language. The bulk of the logic of a simulation setup commonly falls in the latter category, which means the experimenter will be able to implement most things quickly in a convenient language.

Gazebo. An open source, multi-platform robotic simulation package that is available free of charge. It provides both physics simulation and visualisation of rigid body robotic structures and their environments. Abstraction wrappers are provided for several well-established physics simulation engines: The Open Dynamics Engine (ODE), Bullet Physics, SimBody, the Dynamic Animation and Robotics Toolkit (DART), Having these abstractions available means that the

---

[2] https://www.cyberbotics.com/.
[3] https://www.openrobots.org/wiki/morse.
[4] http://www.v-rep.eu/.
[5] http://gazebosim.org/.
[6] http://www.github.com/ci-group/revolve.

same simulation can, in theory, be run using any of these physics engines by changing a single parameter - the caveat being that subtle differences between these engines often require additional parameter tuning to get a stable simulation.

In order to describe robots and environments, Gazebo uses the Simulation Description Format (SDF)[7], which allows an end user to specify anything from the texture of the terrain to the physical and visual properties of robots in an XML-based format. Because XML can be cumbersome to write for human beings, the sdf-builder[8] Python package was developed concurrently with Revolve to provide a thin, structured wrapper over this format that aids with positioning and alignment of geometries, and calculation of their physical properties.

What makes Gazebo particularly useful is the means by which it allows programmatic access to observing and modifying the simulation. It provides two main interfaces to do this and Revolve makes use of both:

- **A messaging API.** Gazebo comes bundled with a publisher/subscriber messaging system, in which any component can subscribe to and/or publish on so-called topics. Many aspects of the system can be controlled using these messages, which are specified in Google's *Protocol Buffers* (Protobuf) format. Because this communication happens over TCP sockets, access to this interface is quite straightforward in most programming languages.
- **The plugin infrastructure.** It is possible to load shared libraries as a plugin for several types of Gazebo components, providing programmatic access to the simulation using Gazebo's C++ API. As an example, one can specify a certain piece of compiled C++ code to be loaded with every robot that is inserted into the world.

Revolve Libraries. At the heart of Revolve lie a set of general purpose tools, which can be roughly separated into Python components and Gazebo C++ plug-in components. A certain layering is present in the provided tools, ranging from anything from closely related to the specification to more practical tools that can be used to quickly implement an actual experiment.

Revolve Angle. Alongside the modules to create a wide variety of experimental setups described in the previous sections, Revolve includes a more opinionated module called revolve.angle, implementing a specific subset of all possible experimental setups. Its function is twofold, in that (a) it allows for setting up any experiment matching these setup descriptions rapidly, and (b) it serves as an example of how to use Revolve. It implements the following functionality: (a) a genome including both a robot's body and brain, (b) a conversion from this genome to a usable SDF robot, (c) evolutionary operators functioning on this genome: crossover and mutation, and (d) the entire RoboGen body space is included as Revolve components, though its use is optional and other body parts may just as well be used with the genome.

---

[7] http://sdformat.org/.
[8] https://github.com/ci-group/sdf-builder.

Gazebo plugins. In order to actually control a robot in simulation, Gazebo has to be told what sensor values to read, what joints to control, etc. While it is possible in principle to provide most of these functionalities through the messaging API, when it comes to controlling a robot the code is closely related to the simulation, runs often and is, therefore, more apt to be considered as a high-performance aspect to be written in C++. Revolve supplies a base *robot controller* plugin to deal with this aspect of the simulation setup. When the SDF contents of a robot are produced for simulation, a reference to this plugin is included alongside information about its sensors, actuators and brain. Gazebo supports many types of sensors, all of which are accessed in a different fashion. Revolve wraps around a number of often used sensors and unifies them in a generic interface passed to the robot controller. The same holds for actuators, which control the joints of robots in the simulation. Rather than having to specify the forces that operate on these joints, Revolve allows setting either a position or velocity target which, combined with a predefined maximum torque, resembles the interface of a real-world servo motor.

In addition to the robot controller, Revolve also includes a *world controller* plugin, which should be included with each loaded simulation world. While using this plugin is not strictly necessary, it includes some convenient functionality to insert robots into the world, keep track of their position and remove them. Overall, Revolve system is a simulation toolkit designed specifically for the purpose to study embodied co-evolution, specifically described in [2]. However, having in mind that it is based on highly flexible Gazebo simulator, it can be also used for a research related to specific parts of the system, e.g.individual learning, group learning, island model evolution.

4   The Robots

The robot design in our system is based on the RoboGen framework[9]. RoboGen robots are designed to be evolvable and easily manufacturable from a pre-defined set of 3D printable components (some of which are parametrisable) coupled with off the shelf electronic elements. The following paragraphs describe the possible components in detail.

The Phenotype of Morphologies. The robots used in this work are built out of seven possible component types, which can connect to each other at specified attachment slots.

1. Each RoboGen robot contains at a minimum a **core component** that houses a battery and a microcontroller, with an onboard 6-dimensional inertial measurement unit (IMU) composed of an accelerometer and a gyroscope. This component has four attachment slots: apart from the top and bottom faces, it is possible to attach other components to every side. It is slightly larger than other components so it could contain any needed electronics if the robot would be recreated in real-space.

---

[9] http://robogen.org.

2. The **fixed brick** has the smaller dimensions than the core component, and it does not contain any electronics or sensors. In addition, other components can be attached to its four faces.
3. The **parametric bar joint** is a connection element with parametrised length and connection angle. It has two attachment slots, one at either end.
4. The **active hinge** is a simple hinge joint powered by a servo motor. Each active hinge adds one actuated degree of freedom to the robot: this DOF is controlled by a single value per time step, which defines a desired angular position between −45 and 45 degrees. Like the parametric bar joint, it has two attachment slots.
5. The **passive hinge** is similar to the active hinge, but as the name suggests the passive hinge is not powered by a servo but rather can move freely. It, therefore, adds one un-actuated DOF to the robot. It also has two attachment slots.
6. The **touch sensor**, which contains two binary inputs. Each input represents whether or not one half of the sensor is in contact with another object. Like the light sensor, the touch sensor has a single attachment slot.

Each of these components is defined by two-part model: a detailed mesh suitable for visualisation and 3D-printing and a set of geometric primitives that define the components' mass distribution and a contact surface. As described above, each model also defines the number and placement of possible attachment slots, as well as the **inputs** (sensors) and **outputs** (motors) contained within it. Each input i is defined as a single numerical value. If a sensor outputs more than one value (as is this case with the IMU and the touch sensor) then this results in multiple defined inputs. Similarly, each output o is defined by a single value.

The Phenotype of Controllers. Each robot is controlled by a neural network that receives inputs from the robot's sensors and provides output to the robot's actuators. In this way, there is a one-to-one correspondence between a morphology's inputs and its controller's input neurons as well as between a morphology's outputs and its controller's output neurons. The neural network can also contain hidden units.

The neurons in the hidden and output layers of a robot's neural network may have one of three activation functions. The first two–linear and sigmoid–are common neural network activations whose parameter set consists of bias and gain values. The third possible type is an oscillator neuron, whose value depends not on its input values but rather is a sinusoid depending only on the current time. The three parameters for this neuron type are the oscillator's period, phase offset and amplitude. This neuron type was added to accommodate the needs of simplifying the experiment while still producing proper locomotion patterns.

The Genotype of Morphologies. Robots are genetically encoded by a tree-based representation where each node represents one building block of the robot and edges between nodes represent physical connections between pieces. Each node contains information about the type of the component it represents, its name, orientation, possible parametric values, and its colour. The colour parameter is included to allow handily tracking of which body parts originate from which parent. Each edge also defines which of the parent node's available attachment slots the child will attach to.

Construction of a robot from this representation begins with the root node, defined to always represent the requisite core component. The robot body is then constructed by traversing the tree edges and attaching the components represented by child nodes to the current component at the specified slot positions and orientations.

The Genotype of Controllers. The tree representation describing a robot's morphology also describes its controller. Based on a unique identifier and a type of each module, input and output neurons are defined. Subsequently, neurons in a hidden layer are added and connections between layers. The detailed description of how genotypes of morphologies and controllers are recombined are described in Sect. 5.2.

5   Evolutionary System

5.1   System Architecture: The Triangle of Life

The proverbial Cycle of Life revolves around birth and so does a system of self-reproducing robots. To capture the relevant components of such a robotic life cycle we need a loop that does not run from birth to death, but from conception (being conceived) to conception (conceiving one or more children). A conceptual framework for such an ecosystem in which physical robots actually reproduce was proposed in [2].

This framework, called the Triangle of Life, represents an overall system architecture with three main components or stages. This system is generic, the only significant assumption we maintain is the genotype-phenotype dichotomy. That is, we presume that the robotic organisms as observed 'in the wild' are the phenotypes encoded by their genotypes. As part of this assumption, we postulate that reproduction takes place at the genotypic level. This means that the evolutionary operator's mutation and crossover are applied to the genotypes (to the code) and not to the phenotypes (to the robotic organisms). The first stage in the ToL is the creation of a new robotic organism in a so-called Production Center [19]. This stage starts with a new piece of genetic code that is created by mutating or recombining existing pieces of code (of the robot parents) and ends with the delivery of a new robot. The second stage takes place in a Training Center; it starts when the morphogenesis of a new robot organism is completed and ends when this organism acquires the skills necessary for living in the given world and becomes capable of conceiving offspring. The third stage in the Triangle is the period of maturity. It starts when the organism in question becomes fertile and leads to a new Triangle when this organism conceives a child, i.e., produces a new genome through recombination and/or mutation.

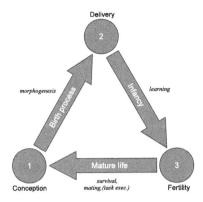

Fig. 1. Robotic life cycle captured as a triangle after [2]. The pivotal moments that span the triangle are: (1) Conception: A new genome is activated, construction of new robot starts. (2) Delivery: Construction of the new robot is completed. (3) Fertility: The robot becomes ready to conceive offspring.

Figure 1 exhibits the stages of the Triangle of Life. Similarly to the general EA scheme that does not specify the representation of candidate solutions, the ToL does not make assumptions regarding the makeup of the robots.

5.2   Evolutionary Operators

Two parent robots can produce offspring through several reproduction operators on their genotype trees. This section discusses these operations in the order in which they are applied to create a child robot c from parents a and b. In the first step, a node a_c from a is randomly chosen to be the crossover point. A random node b_c from b is chosen to replace this node, with the condition that doing so would not violate the restrictions as given in Table 1. If no such node is available, evolution fails at this point and no offspring are produced. If such a node is found, c_1 is created by duplicating a and replacing the subtree specified by a_c with the subtree b_c. With probability $p_{swap\_subtree}$, a random node s_1 is chosen from c_3. Another random node s_2 is chosen provided it has no ancestral relationship with s_1 (i.e. it is not a parent or child of this node). If no such node is available the step is again skipped, otherwise s_1 and s_2 are swapped in c_3 to produce c_4. Again in order to keep robot complexity roughly the same, a new part is added with a probability proportional to the number of parts that are expected to have been removed by subtree removal, minus the number of parts expected to have been added by subtree duplication. The new part is randomly generated by both hidden neurons, neural connections and all parameters, and attached to a random free slot on the tree to produce the final robot c. Again, this step is skipped if adding a part would violate restrictions.

In general, selection operators in an EA do not depend on the given representation and reproduction operators. Hence, the experimenter is free to use any standard mechanism without application-specific adjustments. For online evolution, this is slightly different. The main difference is the lack of synchronisation between birth and death events. In an offline evolutionary process, these are synchronised and the population size is typically kept constant. In online evolution birth and death events are triggered independently by (local) circumstances and the populations can grow or shrink depending on the actual numbers. The specific mechanism we use here is discussed in the next section.

6 Experimental Setup

The purpose of the experiments is to compare online and offline evolution in a ToL-based system of robots with evolvable morphologies. By design, we will perform pure evolutionary experiments without learning in the Infancy stage. Thus, the controllers of the robots will not change during their lifetime and the fertility test in node 3 of Fig. 1 is void: all individuals become mature/fertile 15 s after birth, which is 3 s insertion time for when the robot is dropped into the arena followed by 12 s evaluation time.

All experiments share a set of values for previously specified parameters, which are specified in Table 1 and each run is repeated 30 times.

Table 1. Parameter values shared across all experiments

Parameter	Description	Value
$|\mathcal{R}|_{max}$	Maximum number of nodes	30
$|\mathcal{R}|_{min}$	Minimum number of nodes	3
o_{max}	Maximum number of outputs	10
i_{max}	Maximum number of inputs	10
h_{max}	Maximum number of hidden neurons	10
μ_{parts}	Mean of randomly generated parts $\mathcal{N}(\mu_{parts}, \sigma^2_{parts})$	12
σ_{parts}	Standard deviation of randomly generated parts	5
$p_{remove\ subtree}$	Probability of removing subtree	0.05
$p_{duplicate\ subtree}$	Probability of duplicating subtree	0.1
$p_{swap\ subtree}$	Probability of swaping subtree	0.05
$p_{remove\ hidden\ neuron}$	Probability of removing hidden neuron	0.05
$p_{remove\ neural\ connection}$	Probability of removing neural connection	0.05

We consider three different experimental scenarios. The first two are offline scenarios in which individuals are evaluated in isolation and a population consists of distinguishable generations. What differentiates these two scenarios is the parent selection method: in the first scenario 15 new individuals are produced before further selection takes place, whereas in the second scenario selection happens after each newly born robot. This method of parent selection is more akin to the online scenario in which robots coexist in the environment and are continuously evaluated and selected.

The fitness function of a robot ρ is the same in all of these scenarios and reads

$$f(\rho) = v + 5s, \tag{1}$$

where v is the length of the path the robot has travelled over the last $12\,\mathrm{s}$ and s is the straight distance that the robot has covered the point where it was $12\,\mathrm{s}$ ago and the point where it is now (i.e. the length of a straight line between that point and the current point).

The following table summarises the three simulation scenarios.

	Scenario 1	Scenario 2	Scenario 3
Scenario type	Offline		Online
Environment	Infinite flat plane		
Evaluation	One robot at a time for $12\,\mathrm{s}$		All active robots simultaneously and continuously in $12\,\mathrm{s}$ time frame
Population size	Constant at 15 robots per generation		8 to 30 robots[a]
Selection scheme	$(15 + 15)$[b]	$(15 + 1)$[c]	A new robot every $15\,\mathrm{s}$
Parent selection	4-tournament selection		
Survivor selection	Select the 15 fittest individuals		Robots with a fitness greater than a 70% of the population mean.[d]
Birth location	On the ground at the origin		Random position within a radius of $2\,\mathrm{m}$ from the origin
Stop criterion	After 3000 births[e]		

[a]See 'Survivor selection'.
[b]Each generation of 15 robots produces 15 children before moving on to survivor selection.
[c]Each generation of 15 robots produces 1 child before moving on to survivor selection.
[d]A minimum of 8 robots is maintained to ensure variation and prevent extinction. If the population reaches 30 individuals without any individuals matching the death criterion, the 70% least fit robots in the population are killed regardless of their fitness to prevent a simulation stall.
[e]In scenario 1, 200 generations of 15 individuals.

Preceding the runs with these scenarios we have conducted two baseline experiments, disabling reproduction and selection, respectively. The first one makes use of the fitness selection to determine which individuals survive while disabling reproduction, thereby showing the speed at which a population would increase its fitness if a selection is made out of an increasing random population. The second baseline experiment, on the other hand, uses completely random survivor selection, while enabling reproduction. Looking at the obtained fitness values in these experiments serves as a simple sanity check to confirm that evolution is really working, cf. Fig. 2(b).

7   Experimental Results

The fitness values of a final population are defined by the last generation of robots in the offline experiments and all alive, mature robots in the online experiment. These results are shown in Fig. 2b.

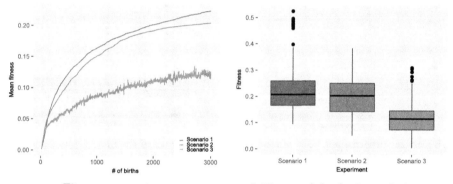

a Fitness progressions.   b Fitness of the final populations.

Fig. 2. Fitness values observed in each scenario aggregated over all 30 runs. The plots in Fig. 2a use the number of born individuals on a time scale because it is uniform across all scenarios. Error bars are omitted for clarity. Note that the experimental setups guarantee a monotonically increasing function for the offline experiments, whereas the non-constant fitness values in the online experiment lead to fluctuations.

The three experiments with both selection and reproduction show a significantly higher fitness than the baseline experiments, indicating that indeed we have evolution at work in the system. Between offline scenarios 1 and 2, only a slight difference in fitness is observed, with a more noticeable difference in fitness variation. Scenario 3 shows a significantly lower fitness. We hypothesise that this is caused by the fundamentally different ways of evaluating robots. In scenarios 1 and 2 each (newborn) robot is evaluated once, while in scenario 3 robots undergo continuous evaluation. This reduces the possible artefacts of getting lucky during the first and only evaluation. In other words, scenarios 1 and 2 allow for survival base on an optimistic estimate of a robots fitness, while scenario 3 works with more realistic fitness values.

Further to analysis, we are also interested in diversity to provide an adequate picture. To provide an adequate picture, a heuristic measure is applied to quantify the genetic diversity within robot populations at each time point. This measure applies a Tree Edit Distance (TED) algorithm as described by Zhang and Sasha [17] to the genetic trees of pairs of robots that are part of the same population. The algorithm is applied to the following cost rules:

- Removing a node, adding a node or changing a node to a different type has a cost of 1.
- Attaching a node to a different parent slot has a cost of 1.

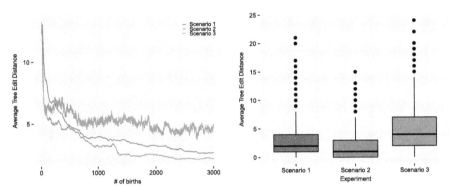

a. Diversity progression over number of births. Error bars are omitted for clarity.

b. Diversity of the final populations.

Fig. 3. Genetic diversity in robot populations using Tree Edit Distance averaged over all runs.

Note that differences between neural network contributions between nodes are ignored in this measure because they are harder to quantify. The outcome of the algorithm is included for both the final populations cf. Fig. 3b and as a progression during the experiments cf. Fig. 3a. This shows an initial rapid decline of diversity in all scenarios, possibly as a result of 'bad genes' being eliminated. Diversity decline then slows down, although it decreases faster in scenario 2 than in scenario 1. This makes sense as the populations that scenario 2 uses for reproduction are very similar for each birth, which is expected to decrease variation. The same can be said about scenario 3, but the same effect cannot be observed there, meaning something is keeping diversity relatively high here.

8   Discussion and Conclusions

As shown in this paper, Revolve has proven its merit a a research tool, but there are of course several possible improvements. First, the scenarios of Sect. 6 could be extended by making the controllers evolvable and/or adding learning capabilities to the robots. This will facilitate research into Lamarckian evolution, where we already have nice initial results [21]. Adding a dedicated Production Center, as in our previous work [18], is also a logical extension. In the meanwhile, adding obstacles and different types of ground surfaces will make the system more realistic. Hereby the software and hardware-based system development will be more aligned [19,20].

Something to be wary of in this context is the 'bootstrapping problem', a term used to describe the failure of a system to evolve into interesting dynamics simply because there are no dynamics, to begin with. Robot learning could be developed and integrated into Revolve as a potential solution to this problem. This would enable robots to make more rapid and efficient use of any sensors they have, which is expected to have an impact on the influence of robot interactions and the environment in which they operate. Varying environmental properties is also an interesting line of research, in conjunction with for instance evaluating the robustness and adaptability of robots and robot populations.

The significance of this study is twofold. First, we presented a simulator for studying online evolution of realistic robot morphologies and controllers. Second, using this simulator we established that online and offline evolution are indeed different. This implies that the current practice of relying on offline evolution within evolutionary robotics has inherent limitations. To develop evolutionary mechanisms towards the long term goal of real-world robot evolution we recommend to use simulators that can handle online evolutionary systems.

Acknowledgement. The choice of modular robots used for this research is based on the design of Josh Aurebach's RoboGen project—a flexible and scalable modular robot design.

References

1. Eiben, A., Smith, J.: From evolutionary computation to the evolution of things. Nature **521**(7553), 476–482 (2015)
2. Eiben, A., Bredeche, N., Hoogendoorn, M., Stradner, J., Timmis, J., Tyrrell, A., Winfield, A.: The triangle of life: evolving robots in real-time and real-space. In: Liò, P., Miglino, O., Nicosia, G., Nolfi, S., Pavone, M. (eds.) Advances in Artificial Life, ECAL 2013, pp. 1056–1063. MIT Press, Cambridge (2013)
3. Auerbach, J., Aydin, D., Maesani, A., Kornatowski, P., Cieslewski, T., Heitz, G., Fernando, P., Loshchilov, I., Daler, L., Floreano, D.: RoboGen: robot generation through artificial evolution. In: Artificial Life 14: Proceedings of the Fourteenth International Conference on the Synthesis and Simulation of Living Systems, pp. 136–137. The MIT Press, New York, July 2014. http://mitpress.mit.edu/sites/default/files/titles/content/alife14/978-0-262-32621-6-ch022.pdf
4. Sims, K.: Evolving 3D morphology and behavior by competition. Artif. Life **1**(4), 353–372 (1994)
5. Auerbach, J.E., Bongard, J.C.: Environmental influence on the evolution of morphological complexity in machines. PLoS Comput. Biol. **10**(1), e1003399 (2014)
6. Bongard, J.C., Pfeifer, R.: Evolving complete agents using artificial ontogeny. In: Hara, F., Pfeifer, R. (eds.) Morpho-functional Machines: The New Species, pp. 237–258. Springer, Tokyo (2003)

7. Komosinski, M.: The Framsticks system: versatile simulator of 3D agents and their evolution. Kybernetes **32**(1/2), 156–173 (2003)
8. Bongard, J., Lipson, H.: Evolved machines shed light on robustness and resilience. Proc. IEEE **102**(5), 899–914 (2014)
9. Lipson, H., Pollack, J.B.: Automatic Design and manufacture of robotic lifeforms. Nature **406**(6799), 974–978 (2000)
10. Jakobi, N., Husbands, P., Harvey, I.: Noise and the reality gap: the use of simulation in evolutionary robotics. In: Morán, F., Moreno, A., Merelo, J.J., Chacón, P. (eds.) ECAL 1995. LNCS, vol. 929, pp. 704–720. Springer, Heidelberg (1995). https://doi.org/10.1007/3-540-59496-5_337
11. Koos, S., Mouret, J.B., Doncieux, S.: The transferability approach: crossing the reality gap in evolutionary robotics. IEEE Trans. Evol. Comput. **17**(1), 122–145 (2013)
12. Bongard, J., Zykov, V., Lipson, H.: Resilient machines through continuous self-modeling. Science **314**(5802), 1118–1121 (2006)
13. Eiben, A.E., Smith, J.E.: Evolutionary Robotics. Introduction to Evolutionary Computing. In: NCS, pp. 245–258. Springer, Heidelberg (2015). https://doi.org/10.1007/978-3-662-44874-8_17
14. Cully, A., Clune, J., Tarapore, D., Mouret, J.B.: Robots that can adapt like animals. Nature **521**(7553), 503–507 (2015). http://www.nature.com/articles/nature14422
15. Caluwaerts, K., Despraz, J., Işçen, A., Sabelhaus, A.P., Bruce, J., Schrauwen, B., SunSpiral, V.: Design and control of compliant tensegrity robots through simulation and hardware validation. J. Roy. Soc. Interface **11**(98), 20140520 (2014)
16. Nogueira, L.: Comparative analysis between Gazebo and V-REP robotic simulators. Seminario Interno de Cognicao Artificial-SICA **2014**, 5 (2014)
17. Zhang, K., Shasha, D.: Simple fast algorithms for the editing distance between trees and related problems. SIAM J. Comput. **18**(6), 1245–1262 (1989)
18. Weel, B., Crosato, E., Heinerman, J., Haasdijk, E., Eiben, A.E.: A robotic ecosystem with evolvable minds and bodies. In: 2014 IEEE International Conference on Evolvable Systems, pp. 165–172 (2014)
19. Jelisavcic, M., De Carlo, M., Hupkes, E., Eustratiadis, P., Orlowski, J., Haasdijk, E., Auerbach, J.E., Eiben, A.E.: Real-world evolution of robot morphologies: a proof of concept. Artif. Life **23**(2), 206–235 (2017). pMID: 28513201
20. Jelisavcic, M., De Carlo, M., Haasdijk, E., Eiben, A.E.: Improving RL power for on-line evolution of gaits in modular robots. In: 2016 IEEE Symposium Series on Computational Intelligence (SSCI), pp. 1–8. IEEE (2016)
21. Jelisavcic, M., Kiesel, R., Glette, K., Haasdijk, E., Eiben, A.E.: Analysis of Lamarckian evolution in morphologically evolving robots. In: Proceedings of the European Conference on Artificial Life 2017, ECAL 2017, pp. 214–221. MIT Press, September 2017

Search Space Analysis of Evolvable Robot Morphologies

Karine Miras[1](✉), Evert Haasdijk[1], Kyrre Glette[2], and A. E. Eiben[1]

[1] Vrije Universiteit Amsterdam, Amsterdam, The Netherlands
{k.s.m.a.dasilvamirasdearaujo,e.haasdijk,a.e.eiben}@vu.nl
[2] University of Oslo, Oslo, Norway
kyrrehg@ifi.uio.no

Abstract. We present a study on morphological traits of evolved modular robots. We note that the evolutionary search space –the set of obtainable morphologies– depends on the given representation and reproduction operators and we propose a framework to assess morphological traits in this search space regardless of a specific environment and/or task. To this end, we present eight quantifiable morphological descriptors and a generic novelty search algorithm to produce a diverse set of morphologies for any given representation. With this machinery, we perform a comparison between a direct encoding and a generative encoding. The results demonstrate that our framework permits to find a very diverse set of bodies, allowing a morphological diversity investigation. Furthermore, the analysis showed that despite the high levels of diversity, a bias to certain traits in the population was detected. Surprisingly, the two encoding methods showed no significant difference in the diversity levels of the evolved morphologies or their morphological traits.

Keywords: Modular robots · Evolutionary Robotics · Morphology
Generative encoding · Novelty search

1 Introduction

Evolutionary Robotics (ER) [1–4] is a field that "aims to apply evolutionary computation techniques to evolve the overall design or controllers, or both, for real and simulated autonomous robots" [3]. Traditionally, the emphasis lies on evolving controllers for fixed robot bodies, but there is a growing interest in evolving the morphologies as well [5–9]. For instance, a generic architecture for a system of embodied on-line evolution of robots in real time and real space was proposed in [10]. However, the current technology of rapid prototyping (3D-printing) and automated assembly is a limiting factor, and studies in simulations remain important.

In this paper we address the issue of morphological diversity in an evolutionary robotic system. In general, there are three essential factors that determine the course of evolution in such a system, (1) the encoding, including the phenotypes

© Springer International Publishing AG, part of Springer Nature 2018
K. Sim and P. Kaufmann (Eds.): EvoApplications 2018, LNCS 10784, pp. 703–718, 2018.
https://doi.org/10.1007/978-3-319-77538-8_47

(the set of possible morphologies), the genotypes (the syntactical representation of these phenotypes), and the mapping from genotypes to phenotypes, (2) the reproduction operators that generate new genotypes from existing ones, and (3) the selection operators that depend on the environment and the task at hand. For the sake of this study we distinguish the search space and the application space of an evolutionary robotic system. The search space consists of the encoding and the reproduction operators, while the application space is formed by the environment and the given task. Besides the impact of the environment [11], clearly, the properties of the search space also have a paramount impact of what evolution can achieve. The main research question we address here is: How to investigate the effect of the search space on the set of evolvable morphologies? This question will be broken down into two subquestions:

Q1: How to quantify and measure morphological properties?
Q2: How to isolate the effects of the encoding and the reproduction from the effects of selection?

The measures and the methodology we propose to answer these questions will be applied to compare a direct encoding and an indirect encoding scheme for the morphological space we work with in our research programme towards physically evolvable modular robots.

2   Morphology Space and Morphological Descriptors

Our robot bodies are composed of modules[1] as shown in Fig. 1, based on Robo-Gen [12]. For this study, the bodies are flat, constructed in 2D, i.e., the modules do not permit attachment on the top or bottom slots, only the lateral ones. Each module type is represented by a letter in the genotype and by a colored block in the visualized phenotype (color indicating the type of block), and any module can be attached to any other through its attachment slots. An arrow inside the block points to the parent module to which the module is attached.

For quantitatively assessing a given modular body we designed and utilized eight morphological descriptors. The maximum number of modules in a robot is limited to m_{max}. Given an m_{max}, each descriptor can assume a discrete number of values, and the calculation for these numbers can be found in the accompanying documentation[2]. Each morphological descriptor was normalized to a range between 0 and 1, as explained below.

Branching. This descriptor captures how the attachments of the modules are grouped together in the body, and envisions to measure whether the components of the body are more spread or agglomerated. It is defined with Eq. (1):

$$B = \begin{cases} \frac{b}{b_{max}}, & \text{if } m >= 5 \\ 0 & \text{otherwise} \end{cases} \tag{1}$$

---

[1] http://robogen.org/docs/robot-body-parts/.
[2] https://tinyurl.com/y9s8ssuc.

(a) modules   (b) simulated robot

Fig. 1. (a) Modules of robots: core-component C holds a controller board; brick B is a cubic module; active hinge A is a joint moved by a servo motor. C and B have attachment slots on its four lateral faces, and A has attachment slots on its two opposite lateral faces; (b) example of a simulated robot.

where m is the total number of modules in the body, b the number of modules that are attached on all four faces, and $b_{max} = \lfloor (m-2)/3 \rfloor$ – the maximum possible number of modules that can be attached on four faces in a body of m modules. See Fig. 2 for a few illustrative examples.

(a) Branching: 0   (b) Branching: 1   (c) Branching:0.5

Fig. 2. Morphology (a) has no module with its four faces attached, (b) has one module with its four faces attached, which is the maximum possible given the size of the body, and (c) has one module with its four faces attached, but could have two, if using the modules indicated by pink arrows to be attached to the one indicated by the orange arrow. (Color figure online)

Limbs. This describes the number of extremities of a body:

$$L = \begin{cases} \frac{l}{l_{max}}, & \text{if } l_{max} > 0 \\ 0 & \text{otherwise} \end{cases}$$

$$l_{max} = \begin{cases} 2 * \lfloor \frac{(m-6)}{3} \rfloor + (m-6) \pmod 3 + 4, & \text{if } m >= 6 \\ m - 1 & \text{otherwise} \end{cases}$$

(2)

where m is the total number of modules in the body, l the number of modules which have only one face attached to another module (except for the core-component) and l_{max} is the maximum amount of modules with one face attached that a body with m modules could have, if containing the same amount of modules arranged in a different way (Fig. 3).

Length of Limbs. Describes how extensive the limbs of the body are and is defined with Eq. (3):

$$E = \begin{cases} \frac{e}{e_{max}}, & \text{if } m >= 3 \\ 0 & \text{otherwise} \end{cases}$$

(3)

(a) Limbs: 0.5      (b) Limbs: 1

Fig. 3. Morphology (a) has four modules that could be extremities (considering the limit determined by the size of the body), but only the two indicated by green arrows are; (b) has the maximum number of extremities it could have. (Color figure online)

where m is the total number of modules of the body, e is the number of modules which have two of its faces attached to other modules (except for the core-component), and $e_{max} = m - 2$ – the maximum amount of modules that a body with m modules could have with two of its faces attached to other modules, if containing the same amount of modules arranged in a different way[3] (Fig. 4).

(a) Length of limbs: 0.67      (b) Length of limbs: 1

Fig. 4. While in morphology (b) the maximum possible quantity of modules was used as the extension of a limb, in (a), the module indicated by an orange arrow was used as an extra limb. (Color figure online)

Coverage. Describes how full is the rectangular envelope around the body. The greater this number, the less empty space there is between neighbor modules. It is defined as Eq. (4):

$$C = \frac{m}{m_{area}} \tag{4}$$

where m is the total number of modules of the body, and $m_{area} = m_l * m_w$ – the supported number of modules in the area of the body, with m_l being the number of modules that would fit in a column as long as the length of the body, and m_w the number of modules that would fit in a row as long as the width of the body (Fig. 5).

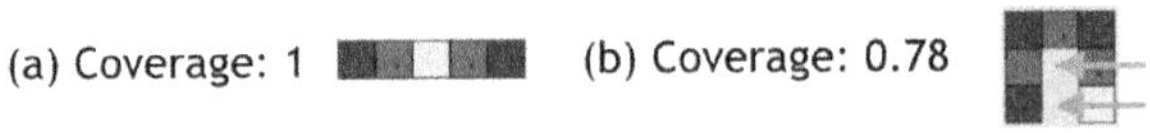

(a) Coverage: 1   ▪▪▪▫▪▪▪   (b) Coverage: 0.78

Fig. 5. While in morphology (a) all the area created by the body contains modules, in (b), there is space for two more modules.

---

[3] The types of modules would not have to be necessarily the same, as long as the body had the same amount of modules.

Joints. This describes how movable the body is and is defined with Eq. (5):

$$J = \begin{cases} \frac{j}{j_{max}}, & \text{if } m >= 3 \\ 0 & \text{otherwise} \end{cases} \tag{5}$$

where m is the total number of modules of the body, j is the number of effective joints, i.e., joints which have both of its opposite faces attached to the core-component or a brick, and $j_{max} = \lfloor (m - 1)/2 \rfloor$ – the maximum amount of modules with two opposite faces attached that a body with m modules could have, in an optimal arrangement (Fig. 6).

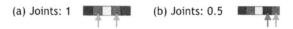

(a) Joints: 1   (b) Joints: 0.5

Fig. 6. Although both morphologies have two joints, in (b) the second joint is not effective, and would be only if the module indicated by the green arrow was switched with the one indicated by the orange arrow. (Color figure online)

Proportion. This describes the 2D ratio of the body and is defined with Eq. (6):

$$P = \frac{p_s}{p_l} \tag{6}$$

where p_s is the shortest side of the body, and p_l is the longest side, after measuring both dimensions of length and width of the body (Fig. 7).

(a) Proportion: 0.2   (b) Proportion: 1

Fig. 7. Morphology (a) is disproportional and (b) is proportional.

Symmetry. This describes the reflexive symmetry of the body with Eq. (7):

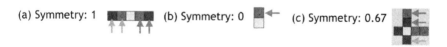

(a) Symmetry: 1   (b) Symmetry: 0   (c) Symmetry: 0.67

Fig. 8. Morphology (a) has the modules indicated by green arrows horizontally reflected by the modules indicated by orange arrows; (b) has no modules reflected; (c) has the module indicated by the orange arrow vertically reflected by the modules indicated by the green arrow, but no reflection for the module indicated by the pink arrow. (Color figure online)

$$Z = \max_{z_v z_h} \tag{7}$$

where $z_h = o_h/q_h$ – is the horizontal symmetry, and $z_v = o_v/q_v$ – the vertical symmetry. For calculating each of these symmetry values, a referential center for the body is defined as the core-component. For both horizontal h and vertical v axes, a spine is determined as a line dividing the body into two parts according to the center and this axis. Each value is the number o of modules that have a mirrored module on the other side of the spine (each match of modules accounts for two), divided by the total number q of compared modules. The spine is not accounted in the comparison (Fig. 8).

Size. This describes the extent of the body in terms of number of modules and is defined with Eq. (8):

$$S = \frac{m}{m_{max}} \tag{8}$$

where m is the total number of modules in the body and m_{max} the maximum number of modules permitted in any body (Fig. 9).

(a) Size: 0.25   (b) Size: 0.15

Fig. 9. Morphology (a) is bigger than (b). Example for $m_{max} = 20$.

3   Exploring the Space of Morphologies

In the foregoing we have introduced eight morphological descriptors that can be used to analyze any given set of robotic morphologies. For instance, they can be measured and plotted during the evolutionary search process and/or applied to assess the final population from a morphological perspective. In this section we demonstrate how they can be used to compare two different representations. To this end, we present a generic methodology for sampling the search space (specified by the encoding and the reproduction operators) independently from the application space (defined by the environment and the task).

The main idea is to create a set of sample morphologies through a *generate-and-test* search process where the *generate* step uses the actual reproduction operators, but the *test* step is based on morphological properties, not influenced by its behavior. The code of our method and the experiments can be found on GitHub[4].

For these experiments the size of the morphologies, m_{max}, was limited to 100 modules regardless of the genotype size. Thus, in the body construction phase, after reaching the limit size, extra modules in the genotype were ignored and not included in the phenotype. Additionally, modules which would overlap with other modules were not included in the body. Any morphology generated via crossover or mutation was allowed to lose any part of its genome, except for the mandatory and unique core-component.

---

[4] https://tinyurl.com/yc364pfe.

3.1 Encodings

Generative Encoding: Our generative encoding represents the genotype of a robot with a Lindenmayer-System (L-System) [9,13], which is a grammatical parallel rewriting system. The grammar of an L-System is defined as a tuple $G = (V, w, P)$, where

- V, the alphabet, is a set of symbols containing replaceable and non-replaceable elements
- w, the axiom, is a symbol from which the system starts
- P is a set of production rules for the replaceable symbols

In our design, the symbols of the grammar represent the modules of a robotic body and the commands to assemble them together. The system starts as a simple string of elements and grows to a more complex string iteratively during the rewriting, which performs substitutions of elements through production rules according to a grammar. The alphabet is formed by three letters and two groups of commands as shown in Table 1. For every letter, there is a production rule that might contain any letter or command, and this rule takes place in the rewriting phase to replace its correspondent letter by all of its elements. This representation functions as a developmental process for the genome. Initially, the genome is turned into a single-component structure, the axiom, as the first stage of the L-System. The axiom in this L-System is C (the core-component), and the rewriting process, i.e., development of the genome, iteratively goes on substituting each letter for the items of its production rule. The rewriting results in a string of symbols that straightforwardly maps onto a morphology.

Table 1. Alphabet

Symbol	Type	Function
C	module	core-component
B	module	brick
A	module	joint
addr	command	adds the next module to the right of the current one
addl	command	adds the next module to the left of the current one
addf	command	adds the next module to the front of the current one
mover	command	moves the reference to the module to the right of the current
movel	command	moves the reference to the module to the left of the current
movef	command	moves the reference to the module in front of the current
moveb	command	moves the reference to the module behind the current

The decoding of a simple genome is illustrated in Fig. 10a. The genome starts with the axiom C, and for 2 iterations the rewriting rules are performed using the production rules for the replacements. During this construction, a turtle reference

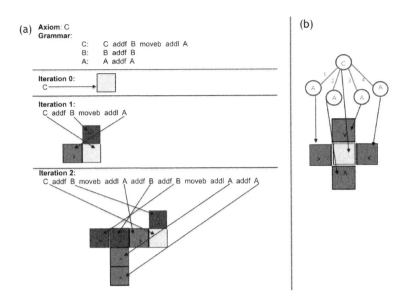

Fig. 10. Encoding methods: (a) generative encoding and (b) direct encoding.

is kept for the parser to be localized in the phenotype, which starts at the bottom of the core-component. The turtle reference is updated according to the direction of the new addition movement made. If the current module is a joint, any addition command attaches the new module to the front of it. If all left, front, and right faces of the core-component were occupied, any command of attachment would place a new module to its back. After the replacements, it is possible that some commands end up without a letter in front of it, and in this case the command is a violation and is ignored. Additionally, it is possible that a new module might be supposed to be added in a position where there is a module already. This also generates a violation, and the module is ignored. These violations, which result in ignoring elements of the genotype, can be thought of as non-expressed genes.

Direct Encoding: The direct encoding (Fig. 10b) uses a tree-based structure as proposed in [12], and it uses the same modules as the generative encoding. The genotype is composed with one symbol in the tree directly representing each part of the phenotype, and thus, there is a direct genotype-phenotype mapping.

3.2 Sampling Algorithm

Our algorithm to generate the set of morphology samples is, in fact, evolutionary. However, selection is based on robot structure, not on robot behavior. We use Novelty Search [14] to maximize the morphological diversity of the sample and to cover a large part of the search space, i.e., find as many different types of morphologies as possible. The corresponding fitness measure is based on the distance of an individual from the others in a multidimensional space defined by the eight morphological descriptors proposed above. The novelty of an individual x is calculated as the average distance to its k-nearest neighbors, where $k = 15$ and the distance is the Euclidean distance [15] using the morphological descriptors. The set of neighbors for the comparison is formed by the current population, plus an archive, to which every new individual has a 5% probability of being added. The individuals added to the archive remain in it until the end.

Using this novelty objective our evolutionary sampling algorithm was run with a population size of $\mu = 500$ for 100 generations. In each generation pairs of parents were selected by binary tournament selection, $\lambda = 250$ offspring were created, and survivors to remain in the population were selected from the set of parents and offspring by 2-tournament selection again. The experiments with each of the two encoding methods were repeated 10 times.

Reproduction Operators for the Generative Encoding. The initial random population was created by adding from 1 to 3 random triples of elements to each production rule in the grammar of a genome. A triple was formed by one addition command, one letter and one movement command (Fig. 11a). Crossover of two parents generated one new individual by choosing the production rules randomly from the parents (Fig. 11b). The mutation had 10% of chance of being performed, by choosing a random production rule and applying one of the actions: delete one element in a random position, add one random element in a random position or swap two elements at random positions (Fig. 11c). An exception is made for the production rule of C, which always contains C as its first element, and C cannot be included again, ensuring that a robot has one unique core-component.

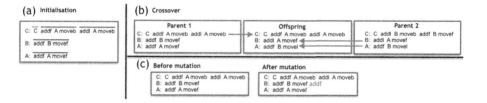

Fig. 11. GE operators.

Reproduction Operators for the Direct Encoding. The population was initialized randomly, by adding between 2 and 10 modules to each genome. Crossover was implemented by swapping random subtrees between parents as is standard practice for tree-based genomes (for instance, in Genetic Programming, [16]). Mutations were performed having 10% of chance of applying one of the following the operators: removing a subtree, duplicating a subtree, swapping subtrees, inserting a node or removing a node.

4   Results and Discussion

To analyze the morphologies obtained by our evolutionary sampling we use the eight morphological descriptors. The full results are available on Drive[5].

4.1   Individual Morphological Descriptors

In Fig. 12 we see that the search keeps finding new values for all morphological descriptors along the generations. Regarding the distributions of the descriptors, as depicted by Fig. 13, for all of them, the distribution of the values is not uniform, there being a concentration of phenotypes in some values, happening consistently for all runs with both encoding methods. To compare the encoding methods, the descriptors were divided into bins and the frequencies were calculated for the results with both encodings. Table 2 shows correlations for the descriptors ($p < 0.001$), indicating that the concentrations (high frequencies of phenotypes) occur in the same values for both encoding methods. This seems to indicate that there are common regions of attraction, i.e., morphological traits that are more likely to occur, independent of the encoding. Nevertheless, there are other encoding methods in the literature [7,17], for which we do not know if this result would persist.

Table 2. Pearson correlations between the distributions of the descriptors using the two encoding methods. M1 = Branching, M2 = Limbs, M3 = Length of Limbs, M4 = Coverage, M5 = Joints, M6 = Proportion, M7 = Symmetry, and M8 = Size.

M1	M2	M3	M4	M5	M6	M7	M8
0.98	0.95	0.89	0.99	0.98	0.99	0.90	0.98

Some of the concentrations can be explained taking the nature of our system into consideration, such as Branching, Joints, and Symmetry with concentrations in the value 0. This outcome makes sense, because they measure constrained aspects of a morphology. For instance, not all morphologies possess symmetry, while any morphology has a size. The stronger a morphological constraint may be, the harder it may also be for the evolution to find such cases. Coverage, Length of Limbs and Proportion have a concentration in 1, and it is not clear why this happens. By the concentrations of Limbs in 0.5 and Length of Limbs in 1, we see that leg length wins in the tradeoff with the number of limbs.

---

[5] https://tinyurl.com/ybpcvdqp.

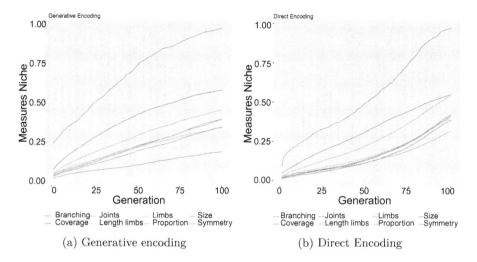

(a) Generative encoding   (b) Direct Encoding

Fig. 12. The proportion (average of the runs) of the values discovered for the descriptors, considering the number of all the possible values that the descriptors can assume.

4.2 Multidimensional Diversity

To observe the progress of the search for morphological diversity, we define a new measure called Morphological Niche (MN). MN is the number of cubes in the morphological space filled with at least one phenotype, accumulated along the evolutionary run. The grid of cubes was constructed having its dimensions composed of our eight morphological descriptors, each divided into 100 bins of size 0.01 (100^8 cubes in total). Each new phenotype was attributed to its suitable cube, given its morphological descriptors. If the cube had not been filled by any phenotype yet, it accumulated one more point in the MN, otherwise, the number of phenotypes concentrated in that same cube was incremented. In Fig. 14a we see the progression of the MN along the generations, where the values are the averages of the runs. Both methods start with similar values, and the GE surpasses the DE along the generations, but converges to similar values again in the end, presenting no statistically significant difference for the averages of the final MN values. The standard deviations grow along the generations, maybe indicating that the more diverse the population, the more unpredictable the level of diversity of the next generation might be. For both methods, all the MN curves keep on growing linearly along the generations and present growth trend (Mann-Kendall Trend Test $p < 0.001$), suggesting that a longer search will continue to discover new cubes. Notably, the progressive discovery of new cubes may be due not only to the discovery of new values for the individual descriptors, as also to combinations of different discovered values.

As a next step, for each encoding method, we evaluated the density of each point in the multidimensional morphological space, i.e., how many phenotypes found during the search fit the same cube, considering the phenotypes of all

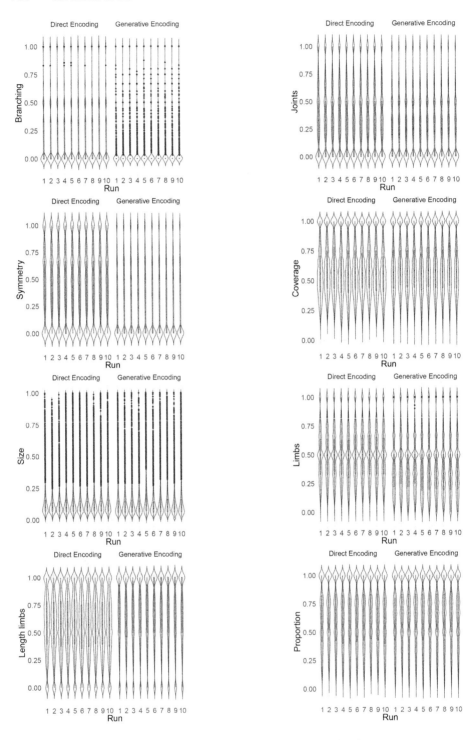

Fig. 13. Violin plots showing the distributions of the descriptors.

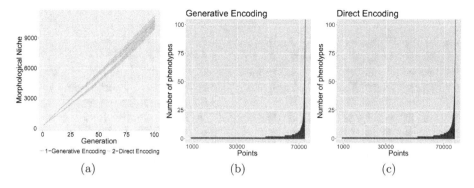

Fig. 14. (a) Progression of the Morphological Niche along the generations; (b) and (c) Quantity of phenotypes fit in each discovered point of the morphological space over all runs (the graphs were scaled).

runs (Fig. 14b and c). For both encoding methods, we see that occurrences of phenotypes in the same cube of the morphological space are concentrated. The frequencies of phenotypes in the cubes for the individual runs were correlated with each other, showing a significant relation, with Pearson strengths ranging from 0.72 to 0.92 ($p < 0.01$) for all pairs of cases. This shows that for both encoding mechanisms, there is a tendency in discovering certain types of morphologies.

Furthermore, we compared the encoding methods, considering the frequencies of phenotypes in the cubes discovered by them, verifying that there is also correlation (Pearson 0.81, $p < 0.01$). This implies that some types of morphologies are more likely to be found, i.e., there seems to be a bias in morphological traits even without regarding the robot behaviors. Figure 15 shows the most common morphologies, ranked in order from left to right, of each of the runs with both encoding methods. The most common bodies are very similar in all runs, for both encoding methods. These bodies are composed of few modules, mostly from one to four, having frequently one or two limbs, using the extra modules to make limbs a little longer.

This observation could be interesting when analyzing morphological traits of genuinely evolved populations, where robot behavior is taken into account. For instance, one might wonder if the evolved morphological traits are due to the given environment and the nature of the task being performed, or they simply occur because they are more likely to be generated within the used design space. The random initialization and mutations that the system performs could have a tendency to generate some specific types of morphologies, and being aware about it would help one to understand the results of the experiments better.

On the other hand, despite this bias, the morphological diversity of the population is vast, according to the previously mentioned results regarding the MN and values of the descriptors. Figure 16 shows a sample with ten very diverse morphologies found after one evolutionary run.

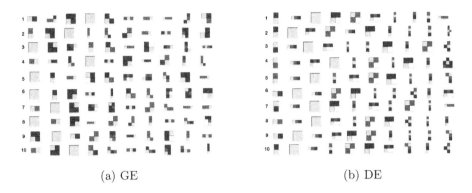

(a) GE   (b) DE

Fig. 15. For 10 different runs, the most common discovered morphologies. From left to right, the most common to the least common.

Fig. 16. Sample of diverse morphologies found after one evolutionary run.

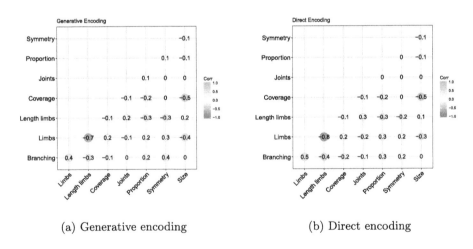

(a) Generative encoding   (b) Direct encoding

Fig. 17. Correlations between descriptors

4.3 Relations Between Morphological Descriptors

The correlations between the morphological descriptors are shown in Figs. 17a and b. The data show that most descriptors are not correlated, indicating that morphologies with a wide range of combinations of the values are possible. The exceptions are cases for which the nature of the descriptors is competitive, not permitting some combinations of values. For instance, Limbs and Length of Limbs are negatively correlated because the longer the limbs are, the less there are modules available for new limbs. Size and Coverage are also correlated, as the more modules a body has, there is a higher chance of the extents forming a large rectangular envelope which is hard to fill, thus giving a low coverage score.

5   Conclusion and Further Work

This paper presented a framework for assessing the space of possible morphologies within a system of evolving modular robots. The main question was: How to study the properties of (and possible biases in) the search space as defined by the representation and the reproduction operators? To this end we defined eight morphological descriptors and an evolutionary algorithm that sampled the space of possible robots by considering only morphological properties and disregarding behavior. We used Novelty Search and conducted two sets of experiments, each one based on a different representation. The first encoding method was a benchmark direct encoding and the second method was an L-System-based representation, proposed for the purpose of this study.

Our results showed that it is possible to assess morphological diversity utilizing the proposed framework. The resulting morphologies with both encoding methods display a wide range of values for all descriptors. However, we did not observe significant differences in the achieved morphological diversity using each encoding. Furthermore, despite the high diversity achieved, with both methods there are morphological traits that are more commonly found. This indicates that in the utilized design space, a search process is more likely to find some types of morphologies than others. Being aware of such tendencies within a design space could help understand issues related to the morphological traits of evolved populations of robots.

As further work we will add a locomotion task to the fitness of the robots and analyze the impact it will have on the morphological features of the population.

Acknowledgements. This project has received funding from the European Unions Horizon 2020 research and innovation programme under grant agreement No. 665347.

References

1. Nolfi, S., Floreano, D.: Evolutionary Robotics: The Biology, Intelligence, and Technology of Self-organizing Machines. MIT Press, Cambridge (2000)
2. Bongard, J.C.: Evolutionary robotics. Commun. ACM **56**(8), 74–83 (2013)

3. Vargas, P., Paolo, E.D., Harvey, I., Husbands, P. (eds.): The Horizons of Evolutionary Robotics. MIT Press, Cambridge (2014)
4. Doncieux, S., Bredeche, N., Mouret, J.B., Eiben, A.: Evolutionary robotics: what, why, and where to. Front. Robot. AI **2**(4) (2015)
5. Sims, K.: Evolving 3D morphology and behavior by competition. Artif. Life **1**(4), 353–372 (1994)
6. Hornby, G.S., Pollack, J.B.: Evolving L-systems to generate virtual creatures. Comput. Graph. **25**(6), 1041–1048 (2001)
7. Samuelsen, E., Glette, K., Torresen, J.: A hox gene inspired generative approach to evolving robot morphology. In: Proceedings of the 15th Annual Conference on Genetic and Evolutionary Computation, pp. 751–758. ACM (2013)
8. Corucci, F., Calisti, M., Hauser, H., Laschi, C.: Novelty-based evolutionary design of morphing underwater robots. In: Proceedings of the 2015 Annual Conference on Genetic and Evolutionary Computation, pp. 145–152. ACM (2015)
9. Veenstra, F., Faina, A., Risi, S., Stoy, K.: Evolution and morphogenesis of simulated modular robots: a comparison between a direct and generative encoding. In: Squillero, G., Sim, K. (eds.) EvoApplications 2017. LNCS, vol. 10199, pp. 870–885. Springer, Cham (2017). https://doi.org/10.1007/978-3-319-55849-3_56
10. Eiben, A., Bredeche, N., Hoogendoorn, M., Stradner, J., Timmis, J., Tyrrell, A., Winfield, A., et al.: The triangle of life: evolving robots in real-time and real-space. Adv. Artif. Life ECAL **2013**, 1056–1063 (2013)
11. Auerbach, J.E., Bongard, J.C.: Environmental influence on the evolution of morphological complexity in machines. PLoS Comput. Biol. **10**(1), e1003399 (2014)
12. Auerbach, J., Aydin, D., Maesani, A., Kornatowski, P., Cieslewski, T., Heitz, G., Fernando, P., Loshchilov, I., Daler, L., Floreano, D.: Robogen: robot generation through artificial evolution. In: Artificial Life 14: Proceedings of the Fourteenth International Conference on the Synthesis and Simulation of Living Systems, pp. 136–137. The MIT Press (2014)
13. Jacob, C.: Genetic L-system programming. In: Davidor, Y., Schwefel, H.-P., Manner, R. (eds.) Parallel Problem Solving from NaturePPSN III, pp. 333–343. Springer, Heidelberg (1994)
14. Lehman, J., Stanley, K.O.: Abandoning objectives: evolution through the search for novelty alone. Evol. Comput. **19**(2), 189–223 (2011)
15. Lehman, J., Stanley, K.O.: Exploiting open-endedness to solve problems through the search for novelty. In: ALIFE, pp. 329–336 (2008)
16. Koza, J.R.: Genetic Programming: On The Programming of Computers by Means of Natural Selection, vol. 1. MIT Press, Cambridge (1992)
17. Stanley, K.O., D'Ambrosio, D.B., Gauci, J.: A hypercube-based encoding for evolving large-scale neural networks. Artif. Life **15**(2), 185–212 (2009)

Combining MAP-Elites and Incremental Evolution to Generate Gaits for a Mammalian Quadruped Robot

Jørgen Nordmoen[✉], Kai Olav Ellefsen, and Kyrre Glette

Department of Informatics, University of Oslo,
P.O. Box 1080, Blindern, 0316 Oslo, Norway
jorgehn@ifi.uio.no

Abstract. Four-legged mammals are capable of showing a great variety of movement patterns, ranging from a simple walk to more complex movement such as trots and gallops. Imbuing this diversity to quadruped robots is of interest in order to improve both mobility and reach. Within the field of Evolutionary Robotics, Quality Diversity techniques have shown a remarkable ability to produce not only effective, but also highly diverse solutions. When applying this approach to four-legged robots an initial problem is to create viable movement patterns that do not fall. This difficulty stems from the challenging fitness gradient due to the mammalian morphology. In this paper we propose a solution to overcome this problem by implementing incremental evolution within the Quality Diversity framework. This allows us to evolve controllers that become more complex while at the same time utilizing the diversity produced by Quality Diversity. We show that our approach is able to generate high fitness solutions early in the search process, keep these solutions and perform a more open-ended search towards the end of evolution.

Keywords: MAP-Elites · Incremental evolution · Quadruped
Gait generation · Movement primitives

1 Introduction

Legged robots have a high degree of mobility and can reach many places that are outside the reach of wheeled robots [1,2]. This mobility enables legged robots to aid in many difficult situations and also work in environments optimized for human locomotion. However, designing a controller for a legged robot is a difficult challenge. Legged robots have many degrees of freedom and often require tight coordination to keep the body in balance. Manually designing such controllers is often time-consuming and as such *machine learning* is often seen as a promising alternative to generate the controller [3].

The field of Evolutionary Robotics (ER) takes inspiration from natural evolution to automatically create controllers for a large range of robots [4]. A recent development in ER is to let the algorithms explore both diverse and high-quality

© Springer International Publishing AG, part of Springer Nature 2018
K. Sim and P. Kaufmann (Eds.): EvoApplications 2018, LNCS 10784, pp. 719–733, 2018.
https://doi.org/10.1007/978-3-319-77538-8_48

solutions. This class of algorithms are called Quality Diversity (QD) [5–8]. One interesting aspect of QD algorithms is their ability to produce a range of behaviors that can be utilized as a repertoire for subsequent selection [9–11]. These behavioral repertoires are especially interesting when utilized as a method to develop movement primitives that can later be operated by a higher-level controller [10]. By generating these primitives, higher-level abstractions can be created to facilitate re-use and sharing of controllers for different robots.

Four-legged, or *quadruped*, robots with legs underneath the body, pose a challenge for the control algorithm. Because the legs have to move out from under the robot, the center of gravity is shifted in such a way that the whole platform can become unstable [12,13]. This instability makes it difficult to detect the gradient of the fitness function and often impedes the discovery of initial solutions. This is in contrast to other morphologies, such as the spider configuration in the Quadratot [14], where the legs are positioned on the side of the body.

The difficulty in discovering the initial solutions is described as the *bootstrap problem* in ER [4,15,16]. The bootstrap problem occurs when the initial population is difficult to generate and is of poor quality. In complex search spaces this often occurs because initial individuals are not able to complete the task. In the context of quadruped gait generation, the bootstrap problem occurs because any gait must have a high degree of coordination between all four legs. With many degrees of freedom in each leg, coordination becomes increasingly unlikely requiring several beneficial changes to occur together for the motion to become synchronized. Since many ER algorithms typically initialize the search randomly, the problem becomes even greater, because evolution might use many evaluations in unproductive regions of the search space [15].

In this paper we propose to combine Multi-dimensional Archive of Phenotypic Elites (MAP-Elites) [7,8] with incremental evolution. Our contribution is two-fold, firstly we show that it is possible to use MAP-Elites to generate a diverse set of high-quality movement primitives for the difficult quadruped morphology. Secondly, we study the effect of incremental controller complexification within the MAP-Elites framework.

2   Background

This section will review background material on gait generation and incremental evolution before describing QD. A special focus will be given to MAP-Elites, one of the more popular QD algorithms, as well as the basis for our algorithm.

2.1   Gait Generation

Generating gaits has a long history within machine learning and ER. Some early examples of generating gaits can be found in [1,17,18]. A very successful example of gait generation in ER is the work of [3] which used an Evolutionary Algorithm (EA) to optimize the gait of the Sony AIBO robot, the result of which ended up in the commercial release of the robot.

In recent years a large body of research has focused on the control structure, and learning of such structures, in order to produce a gait. One such approach is using Artificial Neural Networks (ANNs) to produce the control signals for the legs [19]. By using EAs, optimizing network weights, parameters and even whole structures has been shown effective at creating controllers for legged robots [20,21].

As hardware improves, real-world evolution–evaluating the fitness of a real robot instead of a simulated version–has also been applied to the problem of gait generation. This approach avoids the reality gap problem and can produce good results [14,22]. However, this approach is difficult to apply to mammalian morphologies and open-ended evolution of the control structure has not been demonstrated [23].

Since its introduction, QD has been used extensively to generate gaits. One example is [24] which compared different control structures within the QD framework, they showed that QD can be used with many different control structures, but noted that the effectiveness of QD can depend on the control structure.

2.2 Incremental Evolution

The bootstrap problem is one of the fundamental problems within ER [16,25]. The problem arises when the fitness function is not able to guide the set of randomly generated initial solutions to improve [15]. One solution to the bootstrap problem is incremental evolution [15]. Incremental evolution starts by decomposing the goal into smaller sub-tasks that evolution is able to solve individually. When the desired fitness is reached in a sub-task, the task is either updated to the next sub-task or the task is made more complex. To benefit from the previous solution special care is taken when the task is decomposed so that the previous solution is a component to solve the next sub-task. Once all sub-tasks have been solved the tasks can be combined into the goal task. Alternatively, if controller complexification is used the problem can be considered solved when the controller is complex enough to solve the goal.

In their seminal paper on incremental evolution Gomez [15] used task decomposition to evolve a neural network in a predator-prey scenario. Similar task decomposition has been used to evolve gait and navigation controller for a 6-legged robot [26], evolving control for soccer players [27] and cooperative phototaxis with hole avoidance [28]. Other forms of incremental evolution has also been show to be effective. Bongard [29] showed that changing the morphology over both the 'lifetime' and during evolution increases performance and robustness of the robot's controller. Bongard [30] also demonstrated that combining environmental and morphological incremental evolution is not only possible, but yields better performance than either version alone. Mouret [31] identified some of the challenges with incremental evolution, such as the difficulty in specifying how a task should be decomposed. Their innovative solution of task decomposition with a multi-objective EA was able to overcome some of these problems, however, incremental evolution still requires careful consideration in its implementation.

2.3 Quality Diversity

A recent advance in ER is the use of QD algorithms to overcome some of the fundamental problems within the field. This new class of algorithms eschews some of the traditional focus on fitness alone and instead concentrates on the behavior of the system [5,32]. These algorithms have shown a remarkable ability to solve problems that before were considered too complex [6,11,33].

QD algorithms like MAP-Elites [8] separates the behavior, of the system in question, from the fitness. This separation allows QD algorithms to search for interesting differences in behavior rather than solely focusing on fitness. The separation of behavior and fitness makes QD different from a Multi-Objective Evolutionary Algorithm (MOEA) since lower performing solutions are kept as long as they are behaviorally different from what has already been encountered. That is, even though a solution is not on the Pareto front it could still be included if it is behaviorally different from other solutions. The advantage of this diversity is that the search is less likely to be stuck in local optima, and for high performing solutions to be built on top of similar, lower performing solutions [7].

A recent development within QD [10] showed that it was possible to create control primitives by pairing MAP-Elites with an ANN to create control abstractions for a simulated vehicle. This work built on the strengths of QD to discover a diverse set of high quality control primitives that could be paired with higher-level control abstractions. The ANN was used to select control primitives and was shown to be able to transition between different vehicle control modes enabling the authors to abstract the underlying vehicle dynamics from the high-level ANN control system. The work demonstrated the strength of using these higher-level abstractions in creating complex controllers for unknown robots possibly enabling new robots to be more easily developed and tested.

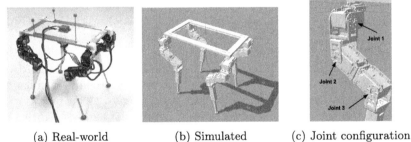

(a) Real-world   (b) Simulated   (c) Joint configuration

Fig. 1. The quadruped robot used in this paper.

3 Approach

This paper combines MAP-Elites with incremental complexification to evolve a set of controllers for a four-legged quadruped robot. The robot (Fig. 1) was developed as an experimental platform to perform real-world evolution *in hardware* [23]. Each leg has three degrees of freedom as shown in Fig. 1c, for a total of twelve degrees of freedom, with each joint controlled by an internal PID-controller. In order to run our experiments the robot was simulated using Gazebo version 7.8.1[1] with ODE[2] in conjunction with Robot Operating System (ROS)[3]. In addition, we used the *SFERESv2* framework [34] with its default MAP-Elites implementation[4]. To understand how incremental evolution is integrated with MAP-Elites we will introduce the gait controller and explain how this controller can be complexified.

3.1 Gait Controller

To create a 'complexifying', or 'upgrading', gait controller we started by parameterizing a simple quadruped walk, where the parameters are *amplitude, phase, duty cycle, offset* and *gait period* for each joint. These parameters describe a continuous first-order spline which represents the commanded angle of a joint[5]. Complexification is performed by locking, not allowing evolution to mutate, selected parameters to default values and later unlocking these same parameters, this is illustrated in Fig. 2 for a simple four valued genome. The parameterization makes it trivial to do non-destructive upgrades, retaining the phenotypic expression, which is important when integrating with MAP-Elites since individuals in the population are not re-evaluated. In the experiments all individuals in the population are upgraded at the same time to ensure that mutations are allowed to happen for the newly unlocked parameters. The parameters used for the different experiments are explained in Sect. 3.3.

	Joint 1		Joint 2	
	Amplitude	Phase	Amplitude	Phase
2 Parameters	0.0	0.0	X	Y
4 Parameters	0.0	0.0	X	Y

Fig. 2. Parameter upgrade for two simple joints. The full configuration is parameterized by four values, two values for each joint. In the first scenario two of the values are locked, marked in red, and two are unlocked. To upgrade the configuration, we copy the two values, X and Y, and unlock the two remaining parameters. The figure illustrate how two different configurations can behave identically, but the '4 Parameter' configuration has the possibility to exhibit new behavior as it can actuate 'Joint 1'.

---

[1] http://gazebosim.org/.
[2] http://www.ode.org/.
[3] http://ros.org.
[4] Source code: https://folk.uio.no/jorgehn/dyret_map_gaits-0.1.0.zip.
[5] For further details see the source code.

3.2   Evolutionary Setup

The shared MAP-Elites parameters can be found in Table 1. Each individual is simulated for 10 s and an evaluation ends if the individual falls over. The fitness of each individual is

$$
fitness(n) = \begin{cases} T_i & \text{if the robot fell over} \\ T_i + stability(n) & \text{otherwise} \end{cases} \tag{1}
$$

where T_i is the time the individual was upright, and $stability$ is defined as

$$
stability(n) = \begin{cases} C - SM(\omega_x, \omega_y) & \text{if } SM(\omega_x, \omega_y) < C \\ 0 & \text{otherwise} \end{cases} \tag{2}
$$

where SM is the Squared Magnitude of the x and y components of the body angular momentum over the evaluation period and C is a constant allowing for maximization of SM. This fitness function ensures that MAP-Elites is able to progress even if none of the individuals are able to walk the full evaluation time. By using SM of the angular momentum MAP-Elites optimizes the stability in each grid cell, where less angular momentum is interpreted as a more stable gait. This was chosen to increase viability of the gait and matches the MAP-Elites notion of optimizing fitness while letting behavior characteristics explore the behavior space.

The behavior characteristics used in the simulation are inspired by [10] and are designed to support higher-level control abstractions. The behavior characteristics are average turn rate defined as

$$
\frac{1}{N} \sum_{i=2}^{N} \frac{(\psi_i - \psi_{i-1})}{(t_i - t_{i-1})} \tag{3}
$$

and average velocity defined as

$$
\frac{1}{N} \sum_{i=1}^{N} \overline{v}_i \tag{4}
$$

for x and y dimensions respectively, where N is the number of samples *before* the robot fell, ψ is the yaw in radians, t_i is the time of sample i and $\overline{v}$ is the velocity of the robot. The behavior characteristics drive the search to explore a variety of velocities and turn rates while fitness optimizes for stability of each behavior.

3.3   Experimental Setup

To investigate if incremental evolution can supplement MAP-Elites we tested four different configurations of the gait controller. For the experiments in this paper, *phase, duty cycle* and *offset* are kept static in all configurations. For each leg the phase parameter is kept identical for all joints set to 0.00, 0.75, 0.50 and

Table 1. MAP-Elites simulation parameters.

Evaluations	*30 000*
	Generations: 300
	Batch size: 100
Initial population	1000
Evaluation time	10 s
Recombination	None
Mutation	Type: Gaussian
	σ: 0.2
	Probability: 1.0
Behavior characteristics	Dimensions: 2
	X-axis: turn rate
	Y-axis: Average speed

0.25 for the front left, front right, back left and back right leg respectively where the value is a percentage of the total gait period. The duty cycle is set to 0.25 and the offset for each joint is set to the resting pose of the robot. This increases the probability of discovering viable gaits while still allowing enough freedom to differentiate the four configurations. The four configurations are described below. The setup consists of three base-configurations which function as reference implementation and are compared to our incremental configuration.

Simple. To ensure that the gait controller is capable of producing viable gaits the first configuration tested restricts almost all parameters of the gait. In this configuration most parameters are set to best practices and only a few parameters are evolved. The evolved parameters are as follows, see Fig. 1c,

– First parameter describes amplitude of Joint 1.
– Second parameter describes amplitude of Joint 2.
– Third parameter describes amplitude of Joint 3.

These parameters are then replicated for each leg and movement is ensured by different phases between the legs.

Medium. The next configuration tested relaxes a few more restrictions and allows the amplitude of each joint in the left and right legs to be evolved separately. The parameters evolved are

– The first three (1–3) parameters describe the amplitude of the joints in the two left legs.
– The next three (4–6) parameters describe the amplitude of the joints in the two right legs.

This configuration has the potential to explore more gaits along the X axis compared to the *simple* configuration, due to the decoupling between the left and right side of the robot. Since the left and right side can have independent amplitudes, the gait pattern has the potential to create behaviors more suited to turning. However, the increase in number of parameters also requires more coordination.

Complex. In this configuration each leg has independent amplitude control of all joints, giving 12 parameters to optimize. This configuration is the least restrictive of the base-configurations, which could lead to more diverse gaits with better performance. The expressiveness could also be a hindrance as the number of parameters that must be coordinated is larger.

Incremental Controller. The incremental controller is a combination of the above configurations. During evolution this configuration will start with the 'Simple' configuration and will change, first, to the 'Medium' and then lastly to the 'Complex' configuration. This controller tests if incremental evolution can be combined with MAP-Elites to produce diverse, high performing solutions. The gait is incrementally upgraded at static points during the evolution, fixed to $\frac{1}{3}$ of the total evaluations for each sub-configuration.

In the results we have also added a configuration called *Incremental 2* which also performs incremental evolution, but instead of starting with 'Simple' starts in the 'Medium' configuration and *Incremental 3* which starts with 'Simple' and upgrades to 'Complex'. Both of these configurations incrementally complexify after $\frac{1}{2}$ of the total evaluations have been performed. These configurations are included to gain insight into the effect of upgrading and how upgrading is affected by the initial configuration.

4   Experimental Results

To compare the different configurations and to understand how incremental evolution performs within the MAP-Elites framework we ran each configuration with 15 repetitions and used the metrics described in [7] to analyze the results. These metrics, *reliability*, the average fitness for all cells in the map, *coverage*, the percentage of filled cells, and *precision*, the average fitness of filled cells, give an overview of the state in the map. Since we are evolving gait primitives we are interested in both a diverse set of solutions (large coverage) and high performance (high precision). Reliability then becomes the product of these two objectives and gives a summary of the performance.

In the results we annotate the three incremental configurations, described in Sect. 3.3, as 'Incr', 'Incr 2' and 'Incr 3' respectively, see Fig. 4. Note also that even though fitness is evaluated even if the solution fell these solutions are not included in the results presented below, the individuals are removed before any calculations take place. In other words, the results only considers gait controllers that were able to walk the full simulation time without falling over. For the results below all fitness values have been normalized by subtracting T_i and dividing by the constant C.

To further illustrate the results, we have plotted the resulting map, in Fig. 3, from a few select generations for representative runs of each configuration. These maps give a good overview of the distinction between precision and coverage. From the maps it is clear to see that 'Incremental' and 'Simple' find higher performing solutions while 'Complex' is better able to explore the search space.

4.1 Precision

Figure 4 shows the average fitness for the filled cells for each of the configurations tested throughout evolution. For the static configurations the precision slowly increases over the generations. Most improvement is seen in the 'Complex' configuration while 'Simple' and 'Medium' start higher and have little to no increase over the course of evolution. For the incremental configurations the plots look quite different and actually decrease towards the end of the evolutionary run. The large difference in precision seen for the static configurations is likely due to the relative difference in difficulty of finding good solutions. For the 'Simple' configuration the parameters require very little coordination which seems to result in higher precision. This is also very evident from the initial random population where the difference in precision should be directly correlated to the difficulty in randomly generating a functioning gait. Analyzing the box plot for generation 300, in Fig. 4 top right, the results show very little spread and most of the variation is in the 'Complex' configuration.

4.2 Coverage

Figure 4, middle row, shows the number of filled cells over all generations and a box plot of the last generation. From the generational plot it is clear that the 'Complex' configuration is best able to explore the search space. The two other static configurations achieve significantly less coverage, which is expected considering the limitations in the number of parameters and resulting gaits. For the incremental configurations we clearly see that more parameters open up more possibilities as each configuration quickly explores more of the search space after each upgrade, generation 100, 200 for 'Incremental' and 150 for the two-other incremental configurations.

It is also interesting to note that the initial coverage for all configurations is about the same, but the coverage quickly diverges in subsequent generations. The box plots also show that the difference is significant between several of the configurations for the final generation.

4.3 Reliability

To get an overall impression of the performance of the tested configurations we can combine precision and coverage into reliability as seen in Fig. 4. Reliability is defined as the average fitness of all cells divided by the number of cells,

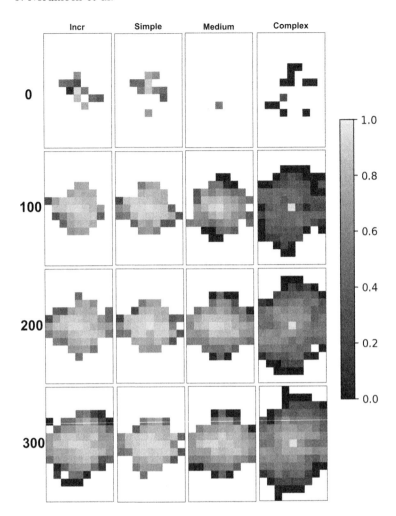

Fig. 3. Illustration of evolved maps for generation, 0, 100, 200 and 300. The X and Y axis represent the behavior dimensions while the color represents fitness where bright yellow is higher fitness. For the 'Incremental' configuration the upgrade happens at generation 100 and 200. The figure illustrates the distinction between precision and coverage, where 'Complex' spans a much wider area with lower performing solutions while 'Simple' has fewer solutions with higher fitness. (Color figure online)

empty cells are given a fitness of zero. From the generational figure it seems that 'Complex' performs better than the two other static configurations although the difference is not statistically significant. The three incremental configurations show different growths throughout evolution, but by the end of the run start to converge to the same performance.

All of the incremental configurations show large increases in reliability after upgrading, which is correlated with the increase in coverage, as noted in the

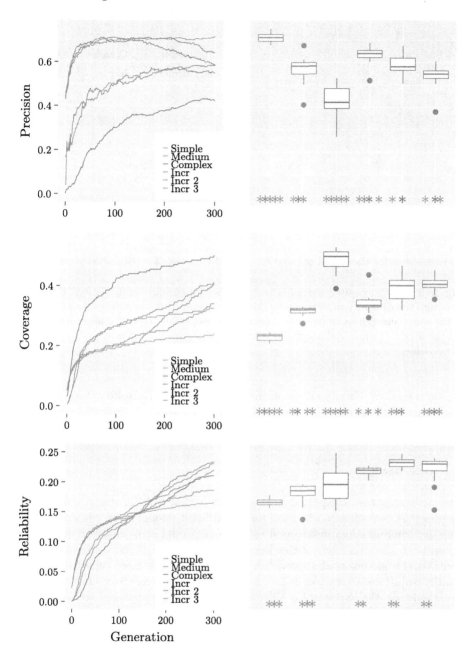

Fig. 4. The plots show precision, coverage and reliability. The median is plotted over all generations, left, and a box plot is shown for the last generation on the right. The box plots also show the result of a pairwise Wilcoxon Rank Sum test, adjusted using Holm's method, where an *asterisk* corresponds to a significant difference at the $p < 0.001$ level.

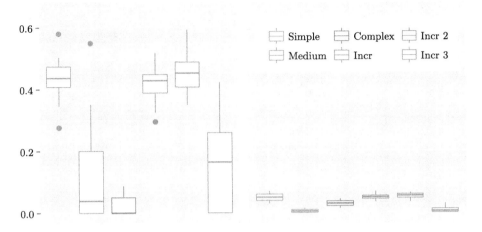

(a) Precision for the initial population.   (b) Coverage for the initial population

Fig. 5. These figures show precision and coverage for the initial population. The figures illustrate the difficulty in discovering the initial population depending on the 'freedom' of the controller. This can be seen as coverage is essentially equal for all configurations, yet the fitness of the initial populations are very different, as illustrated by the difference in precision.

previous section. These configurations also have higher reliability throughout the beginning of the evolution compared to the 'Complex' configuration correlated with the large difference in precision.

5   Discussion

The main hypothesis explored in this paper is that MAP-Elites combined with incremental evolution can be used for the difficult task of generating gait primitives for a mammalian quadruped robot. The results show that the quality and quantity of the primitives varies between the different static configurations. In contrast the incremental approach is able to develop a large repertoire of high quality solutions that span a larger area in the search space. It can also be observed that the variance for all three incremental approaches are much lower than for the best static configuration, as seen in Fig. 4, this could indicate that the incremental configurations are more consistently finding diverse and high fitness solutions. From manual inspection of the gaits produced, all configurations are able to discover satisfying controllers that exhibit desired behavior[6].

From the precision plot in Fig. 4, it can be seen that complexity is related to fitness, as more complex configurations achieve lower precision scores. The lower precision can be attributed to the difficulty in coordinating the joints. To further

---

[6] For videos see: https://folk.uio.no/jorgehn/map_gaits/.

explore this we plot the initial population in Fig. 5. Even though the difference in coverage is low the difference in precision is large.

Because of the limitations imposed on the 'Simple' and 'Medium' configurations they are not able to gain the same coverage as the 'Complex' configuration. This can be attributed to the forced coordination imposed on these configurations. These results are interesting because they illustrate the difficulty in designing an algorithm to overcome the bootstrap problem. By restricting the configurations they are able to more quickly discover high performing solutions, as evident in their precision Fig. 4, but are not able to produce the same range of behaviors as the 'Complex' configuration. We can see that in the reliability that the incremental configurations seem to be able to get the benefit of both–however, because of the limited number of evaluations in this paper–they are not able to completely surpass the 'Complex' configuration.

The incremental approach is able to generate higher fitness controllers as well as explore more of the search space, as seen in the results Fig. 4. This is because it is able to keep the high precision from before the upgrade, and also explore the new behavior space after the upgrade. The improvement is evident in each of the three incremental approaches and is a result of the increase in coverage.

6   Conclusion and Future Work

We have investigated how incremental evolution can be combined with MAP-Elites to create movement primitives for quadruped robots. In the experiments we compared several gait parameterizations of different levels of complexity with a controller that is able to incrementally complexify. The results show that MAP-Elites was able to create viable controllers, and–when combined with incremental evolution–also produced a diverse set of solutions with high fitness. This indicates that for more open-ended controllers incremental complexification could be a promising approach for introducing some guidance into the search.

This paper also shows that evolving movement primitives for mammalian quadruped robots is possible and a large repertoire of gait patterns can be evolved. By showing that movement primitives are achievable with such a difficult morphology, we open the possibility to apply the technique to a large group of robots so far not explored with Quality Diversity techniques.

A natural next step for this research is to verify that the evolved gait primitives are able to function in the real-world. An extension to this work could also explore performing the complexification adaptively as a means to achieve faster convergence.

Acknowledgments. Supported by The Research Council of Norway as a part of the Engineering Predictability with Embodied Cognition (EPEC) project, under grant agreement 240862.

References

1. Wettergreen, D., Thorpe, C.: Gait generation for legged robots. In: IEEE International Conference on Intelligent Robots and Systems (1992)
2. Bares, J.E., Whittaker, W.L.: Configuration of autonomous walkers for extreme terrain. Int. J. Robot. Res. **12**(6), 535–559 (1993)
3. Hornby, G.S., Takamura, S., Yokono, J., Hanagata, O., Yamamoto, T., Fujita, M.: Evolving robust gaits with AIBO. In: IEEE International Conference on Robotics and Automation, Proceedings, ICRA2000, vol. 3, pp. 3040–3045. IEEE (2000)
4. Doncieux, S., Bredeche, N., Mouret, J.B., Eiben, A.E.G.: Evolutionary robotics: what, why, and where to. Front. Robot. AI **2**, 4 (2015)
5. Pugh, J.K., Soros, L.B., Stanley, K.O.: Quality diversity: a new frontier for evolutionary computation. Front. Robot. AI **3**, 40 (2016)
6. Lehman, J., Stanley, K.O.: Exploiting open-endedness to solve problems through the search for novelty. In: ALIFE, pp. 329–336 (2008)
7. Mouret, J.B., Clune, J.: Illuminating search spaces by mapping elites. arXiv preprint arXiv:1504.04909 (2015)
8. Cully, A., Clune, J., Tarapore, D., Mouret, J.B.: Robots that can adapt like animals. Nature **521**(7553), 503–507 (2015)
9. Cully, A., Mouret, J.B.: Behavioral repertoire learning in robotics. In: Proceedings of the 15th Annual Conference on Genetic and Evolutionary Computation, pp. 175–182. ACM (2013)
10. Duarte, M., Gomes, J., Oliveira, S.M., Christensen, A.L.: EvoRBC: evolutionary repertoire-based control for robots with arbitrary locomotion complexity. In: Proceedings of the 18th Annual Conference on Genetic and Evolutionary Computation. ACM (2016)
11. Cully, A., Mouret, J.B.: Evolving a behavioral repertoire for a walking robot. Evol. Comput. **24**(1), 59–88 (2016)
12. Van de Panne, M., Lamouret, A.: Guided optimization for balanced locomotion. In: Terzopoulos, D., Thalmann, D. (eds.) Computer Animation and Simulation 1995, pp. 165–177. Springer, Vienna (1995). https://doi.org/10.1007/978-3-7091-9435-5_13
13. de Santos, P.G., Garcia, E., Estremera, J.: Quadrupedal locomotion: an introduction to the control of four-legged robots. Springer, London (2007). https://doi.org/10.1007/1-84628-307-8
14. Yosinski, J., Clune, J., Hidalgo, D., Nguyen, S., Zagal, J., Lipson, H.: Evolving robot gaits in hardware: the HyperNEAT generative encoding vs. parameter optimization. In: Proceedings of the 20th European Conference on Artificial Life, pp. 890–897 (2011)
15. Gomez, F., Miikkulainen, R.: Incremental evolution of complex general behavior. Adapt. Behav. **5**(3–4), 317–342 (1997)
16. Silva, F., Duarte, M., Correia, L., Oliveira, S.M., Christensen, A.L.: Open issues in evolutionary robotics. Evol. Comput. **24**(2), 205–236 (2016)
17. Brooks, R.A.: A robot that walks; emergent behaviors from a carefully evolved network. Neural Comput. **1**(2), 253–262 (1989)
18. Mataric, M., Cliff, D.: Challenges in evolving controllers for physical robots. Robot. Autonom. Syst. **19**(1), 67–83 (1996)
19. Billard, A., Ijspeert, A.J.: Biologically inspired neural controllers for motor control in a quadruped robot. In: Proceedings of the IEEE-INNS-ENNS International Joint Conference on Neural Networks, IJCNN 2000, vol. 6, pp. 637–641. IEEE (2000)

20. Clune, J., Beckmann, B.E., Ofria, C., Pennock, R.T.: Evolving coordinated quadruped gaits with the HyperNEAT generative encoding. In: 2009 IEEE Congress on Evolutionary Computation, pp. 2764–2771. IEEE (2009)
21. Lee, S., Yosinski, J., Glette, K., Lipson, H., Clune, J.: Evolving gaits for physical robots with the HyperNEAT generative encoding: the benefits of simulation. In: Esparcia-Alcázar, A.I. (ed.) EvoApplications 2013. LNCS, vol. 7835, pp. 540–549. Springer, Heidelberg (2013). https://doi.org/10.1007/978-3-642-37192-9_54
22. Zykov, V., Bongard, J., Lipson, H.: Evolving dynamic gaits on a physical robot. In: Proceedings of Genetic and Evolutionary Computation Conference, Late Breaking Paper, GECCO, vol. 4 (2004)
23. Nygaard, T.F., Tørresen, J., Glette, K.: Multi-objective evolution of fast and stable gaits on a physical quadruped robotic platform. In: 2016 IEEE Symposium Series on Computational Intelligence (SSCI) (2016)
24. Tarapore, D., Clune, J., Cully, A., Mouret, J.B.: How do different encodings influence the performance of the MAP-Elites algorithm? In: Genetic and Evolutionary Computation Conference (2016)
25. Mouret, J.B., Doncieux, S.: Overcoming the bootstrap problem in evolutionary robotics using behavioral diversity. In: 2009 IEEE Congress on Evolutionary Computation, pp. 1161–1168. IEEE (2009)
26. Filliat, D., Kodjabachian, J., Meyer, J.A., et al.: Incremental evolution of neural controllers for navigation in a 6-legged robot. In: Proceedings of the Fourth International Symposium on Artificial Life and Robots, pp. 753–760 (1999)
27. Whiteson, S., Kohl, N., Miikkulainen, R., Stone, P.: Evolving soccer keepaway players through task decomposition. Mach. Learn. **59**(1), 5–30 (2005)
28. Christensen, A.L., Dorigo, M.: Incremental evolution of robot controllers for a highly integrated task. In: Nolfi, S., Baldassarre, G., Calabretta, R., Hallam, J.C.T., Marocco, D., Meyer, J.-A., Miglino, O., Parisi, D. (eds.) SAB 2006. LNCS (LNAI), vol. 4095, pp. 473–484. Springer, Heidelberg (2006). https://doi.org/10.1007/11840541_39
29. Bongard, J.: Morphological change in machines accelerates the evolution of robust behavior. Proc. Nat. Acad. Sci. **108**(4), 1234–1239 (2011)
30. Bongard, J.: Morphological and environmental scaffolding synergize when evolving robot controllers: artificial life/robotics/evolvable hardware. In: Proceedings of the 13th Annual Conference on Genetic and Evolutionary Computation, pp. 179–186. ACM (2011)
31. Mouret, J.-B., Doncieux, S.: Incremental evolution of animats' behaviors as a multi-objective optimization. In: Asada, M., Hallam, J.C.T., Meyer, J.-A., Tani, J. (eds.) SAB 2008. LNCS (LNAI), vol. 5040, pp. 210–219. Springer, Heidelberg (2008). https://doi.org/10.1007/978-3-540-69134-1_21
32. Auerbach, J.E., Iacca, G., Floreano, D.: Gaining insight into quality diversity. In: Proceedings of the 2016 on Genetic and Evolutionary Computation Conference Companion, pp. 1061–1064. ACM (2016)
33. Lehman, J., Stanley, K.O.: Evolving a diversity of virtual creatures through novelty search and local competition. In: Proceedings of the 13th Annual Conference on Genetic and Evolutionary Computation, pp. 211–218. ACM (2011)
34. Mouret, J.B., Doncieux, S.: SFERESv2: evolvin' in the multi-core world. In: Proceedings of Congress on Evolutionary Computation (CEC), pp. 4079–4086 (2010)

Evolving a Repertoire of Controllers for a Multi-function Swarm

Sondre A. Engebråten[1,2](✉), Jonas Moen[1,2], Oleg Yakimenko[3],
and Kyrre Glette[1,2]

[1] Norwegian Defence Research Establishment,
P.O. Box 25, 2027 Kjeller, Norway
Sondre.Engebraten@ffi.no
[2] University of Oslo, P.O. Box 1080, 0316 Oslo, Blindern, Norway
[3] Naval Postgraduate School, 1 University Circle,
Monterey, CA 93943, USA

Abstract. Automated design of swarm behaviors with a top-down approach is a challenging research question that has not yet been fully
addressed in the robotic swarm literature. This paper seeks to explore
the possibility of using an evolutionary algorithm to evolve, rather than
hand code, a wide repertoire of behavior primitives enabling more effective control of a large group or swarm of unmanned systems. We use
the MAP-elites algorithm to generate a repertoire of controllers with
varying abilities and behaviors allowing the swarm to adapt to user-
defined preferences by selection of a new appropriate controller. To test
the proposed method we examine two example applications: perimeter
surveillance and network creation. Perimeter surveillance require agents
to explore, while network creation requires them to disperse without losing connectivity. These are distinct application that have drastically different requirements on agent behavior, and are a good benchmark for our
swarm controller optimization framework. We show a performance comparison between a simple weighted controller and a parametric controller.
Evolving controllers allows for specifying desired behaviors top-down, in
terms of objectives to solve, rather than bottom-up.

Keywords: Swarm UAVs · MAP-elites · Evolutionary robotics
Multi-function

1 Introduction

In a robotic swarm system, a large number of agents interact in order to conduct
missions and solve specific tasks. Some swarm systems require collaboration, as a
single agent will not be able to complete the task alone [1]. Other swarm systems
might consider agents with competing interests or goals [2]. Yet, others might
consider how heterogeneous teams of agents can collaborate in order to make
use of the strengths of each agent [3].

© Springer International Publishing AG, part of Springer Nature 2018
K. Sim and P. Kaufmann (Eds.): EvoApplications 2018, LNCS 10784, pp. 734–749, 2018.
https://doi.org/10.1007/978-3-319-77538-8_49

For swarm systems it is common that the most interesting part of the behavior happens on a macro level, i.e. considering the swarm as one single system. For example; is the swarm, as a whole, able to solve the given task? Is the swarm able to optimize agent use for efficiency? This is different from a micro level, considering the individual behavior of each agent or platform. Swarm behaviors require some form of rules or controller for each individual agent. This can be a neural network [4], or a set of rules [5], or even a hybrid of the two [6].

An unsolved problem in the swarm literature is the top-down design of swarm behaviors or controllers, or automatic controller synthesis. This is a problem, as the high-level behavior is very dependent on the low level behavior, but the relation is not easily predictable. Evolutionary robotics attempts to address this issue by evolving controllers, rather than designing them by hand [7]. We propose to expand on this idea by evolving not just a single controller, but a set of controllers for controlling a swarm. Previous works have evolved sets or repertoires of controllers for robotics application [8], but these have been focused on single robot application. We propose to expand this to swarms of robots, in order to generate a varied set of primitives for swarm control.

We are also investigating the potential to tackle multiple tasks or application simultaneously. Imagine a swarm, not limited to a singular task, but solving multiple tasks such as perimeter surveillance and communication network. This could be approached from a resource or task allocation perspective [9], but this paper chooses to view this as a problem of generating a suitable controller with an internal notion of priority between the tasks. This is related to multi-modal learning, multi-task learning and multi-function learning. All of these attempt to solve multiple tasks at once, but with slight variations. For example, in multi-modal behavior learning [10,11], the challenge is to evolve a game-playing agent for multiple sequential tasks. The agent has to learn both how to solve the individual tasks and when to change from one behavior to another in order to succeed. This is significantly more challenging, as it also requires handling potentially conflicting knowledge in the controller. Further, this can also be related to the challenge of learning two related, but potentially conflicting tasks. For this approach, modularity in the controller has been shown to improve performance [12]. In this paper the authors propose to explore whether it is possible to evolve controllers for multi-functional robotic swarms where the tasks are not sequential, but rather concurrent goals that all have to be satisfied at the same time.

Two applications will be considered in this paper: perimeter surveillance and network creation. The task of perimeter surveillance has been explored in previous work [13], and so has the use of swarms to maintain communication networks [14]. The challenge is now to consider both of them at once. Both perimeter surveillance and network creation have their own specific requirements in terms of movement and behavior. As such, it is expected that it will be hard for a single controller to perform well on both tasks.

For this paper, on the evolution of multi-function swarms, we propose two controller types: a weight-based controller and a parametric controller. The weight based controller is, as the name suggests, a simple weighting of input components or forces. A simple weighting of input forces is similar to the motor schema [15]. The parametric controller has a more complicated and powerful controller description, capable of describing a wider array of controller behaviors. Our controllers were inspired by the use of artificial potential fields and artificial physics [16]. Artificial potential fields have previously been employed in collision avoidance [17–19]. Using artificial potential fields for collision avoidance can be viewed as a problem of weighting a number of independent forces from objects of potential collision risk. Essentially, this becomes a weighted forces problem where the net force from all the potential collision risks should point in a collision-free direction. In many cases this works well, assuming the environment is not too cluttered or the collision risks too many. For the controllers examined in this paper, we propose a similar approach, using several contributions from interesting objects and weighting these to provide a controller for a robotic swarm. In essence, each application provides some input to the controller and have certain requirements on the behavior or movement of the platform for optimal performance. Concurrently handling requirements from multiple applications is a challenging problem - one not yet fully explored in the literature.

Using a single controller for multiple tasks could allow for development of more complex behaviors. A hand-coded strategy may be able to solve either of the given tasks alone, but describing how to handle complex interaction between the tasks and the requirements that each task brings to the behavior may be too hard for conventional methods. For this reason, we chose to explore the option of evolving controllers using the MAP-elites algorithm [8,20]. It is also important to realize that this is different from the work on hybrid controllers, as we chose to approach the controller design as a single monolithic problem rather than trying to solve it through decomposition [6,21,22]. Using MAP-elites will lessen the need for bootstrapping or incremental evolution, which is often required in evolutionary robotics [23,24].

Both the weighted and parametric swarm controllers are optimized on the tasks of perimeter surveillance and communication network creation, using MAP-elites to generate a large repertoire of possible solution candidates. This is related to multi-objective optimization where, rather than a single best solution, a good approximation of a Pareto front is sought. The advantage of this approach is that not only one, but many interesting solutions may be examined. This may also provide a better insight into the problem and contributing factors to the generated solutions by illuminating the search space [20]. Both the weighted and parametric swarm controllers can be considered direct controller architectures, which have been shown to have higher performance than indirect encodings [25].

2   Simulator Setup and Swarm Model

Each platform or agent is modeled as a point mass with independent limits on acceleration and velocity. This makes it possible to simulate a wide variety of platform types including non-holonomic ground and aerial vehicles. While modeling platforms as a point mass is a major simplification, compared to real-world dynamics, it is suitable for these experiments. Here, we wish to examine the dynamics of the swarm as a whole, and the high-level behaviors generated. We are less interested in the exact motion of individual agents; as such, this is a viable model for the swarm. The bounds on acceleration and velocity for these experiments are $1\,\mathrm{m/s^2}$ and $10\,\mathrm{m/s}$ respectively. The agents operate in a $1000 \times 1000\,\mathrm{m}$ area. Each platform is controlled by setting a velocity setpoint $\mathbf{v}_{sp}$, this can be considered the outer control loop. The goal of the inner-loop controller is to change the acceleration to match the velocity setpoint, i.e. minimize the norm $||\mathbf{v} - \mathbf{v}_{sp}||$. This is done by a simple proportional controller. The cascaded control architecture allows setting a position setpoint as well, which is then be transferred to a velocity setpoint. For interaction between platforms or agents we assume that each agent is able to localize itself in a global and shared coordinate frame. Our controller require the agents to be able to communicate their position to neighbors. This effectively gives each agent accurate direction and heading to neighboring agents within communication range.

The details can be found in the full source code available online[1].

3 Velocity Setpoint Controllers

Our two proposed velocity setpoint controllers receive 4 inputs, from which a single controller output is generated. The controller inputs are:

1. Direction and distance to closest neighbor
2. Direction and distance to second closest neighbor
3. Direction and distance to third closest neighbor
4. Direction to the least-visited neighboring field (square)

To find the least visited square surrounding the agent, a histogram over visits to each area is collected amongst the agents. This is based on a Moore neighborhood model, i.e. least of the eight surrounding squares. If two or more squares have the same visitation count, one is chosen at random. The current implementation uses a shared blackboard structure, but in principle, there is nothing that requires this information to be globally known to all agents. A local history of visitations could be used in place of this structure.

The 4 controller inputs are coded as a difference vector $\mathbf{F}_i$ ($i = 1, 2, 3, 4$), or relative vector to the agent's current position. For example; if the input is directly returned as the output, the net result is that the agent moves towards the neighboring agent or the least visited field surrounding it. This is different from other similar works, where sensors are directional, covering a slice of the agents total view.

Each of the inputs are weighted - a process which vary depending on the type of controller, and accumulated/summed to generate a single output direction. This direction can also be is the velocity setpoint for the agent. As such, the weights directly influence the speed of the agent at any given time.

---

[1] https://github.com/ForsvaretsForskningsinstitutt/Paper-towards-multi-function-swarm.

3.1   Weighted Controllers

Using the forces defined in Sect. 3, a simple controller could be generated by defining the controller output as a weighted sum of the inputs. This is inspired by artificial potential fields [17–19]. This allows the generation of a varied set of behaviors such as clustering, avoidance, gather all, and more. This requires a single weight parameter for each given force resulting in a total of 4 parameters for a single controller.

$$\mathbf{v}_{sp} = \frac{1}{4} \sum_{i}^{N} \frac{\mathbf{F}_i}{||\mathbf{F}_i||} * w_i \tag{1}$$

$\mathbf{F}_i$ is a relative vector between the agent and the sensed object or the force direction. w_i is the weight for a given force vector. $\mathbf{v}_{sp}$ is the combined controller output, given all the input forces, which is fed to the inner-loop controller. As can be seen from Eq. 1, this controller does not use the distance-part of the input, and relies solely on the input directions. As such, the weights w_i directly influences the velocity of an agent at any given time.

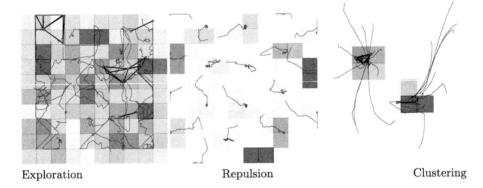

Exploration   Repulsion   Clustering

Fig. 1. Example of hand designed controllers using the weighted controller structure. Darker squares have been more frequently visited. From left to right, exploration, repulsion and clustering type behavior. Based on manual manipulation of the weight controller, it is hard to get the right tradeoffs to get controllers balancing these traits. Videos of these behaviors can be found at https://www.youtube.com/playlist?list=PL18bqX3rX5tQN2HKdHSCna8ysbX9lUeSM

The weighted controller is able to define simple behaviors such as attraction and repulsion. Hand coded examples of this can be seen in Fig. 1. The weights used to generate these behaviors are [−0.5,0,0,1] for exploration, [−1,0,0,0] for repulsion and [0,0,1,0] for clustering. The first three of the weights are used to weigh the contribution from the three nearest neighbors, in order of distance. The final weight is used to specify the attraction or repulsion towards the least frequently visited square of the eight that surrounds the agent. The exploration controller with weights $[-0.5, 0, 0, 1]$ attempts to move towards the least visited area, while keeping the closest neighbor agent away.

3.2   Parametric Controllers

A potential issue with a simple weighted controller is the inability to describe a behavior keeping a given distance from another agent. This type of behavior might be very useful, e.g. when robots are to created and maintain a stationary grid. To address this problem we propose to use a parametric function instead of a simple weight.

$$g_i(d_i) = -t_i * 2 * (d_i - c_i) * e^{-(d_i - c_i)^2/\sigma_i^2} \tag{2}$$

$$a_i(d_i) = k_i * \left(\frac{2}{1 + e^{-(d_i - c_i)/\sigma_i}} - 1 \right) \tag{3}$$

$$w_{p,i}(d_i) = a_i(d_i) + g_i(d_i) \tag{4}$$

$$\mathbf{v}_{sp} = \frac{1}{4} \sum_i^4 \frac{\mathbf{F}_i}{||\mathbf{F}_i||} * w_p(d_i) \tag{5}$$

The parametric weight function $w_{p,i}(d_i)$ consists of two components, $a_i(d_i)$ and $g_i(d_i)$. This function gives a weight that depends on the distance d_i to the sensed object. In other words, the contribution of the force to the velocity of the agent can be made to vary with the distance to the sensed object. $a_i(d_i)$ is responsible for static repulsion/attraction forces, while $g_i(d_i)$ account for distance holding at a predefined distance. Figure 2 is an example plot of $w_p(d_i)$.

$g_i(d_i)$ or the gravity well enables holding a distance c_i to an object. This is based on a normal distribution with a mean of c_i. The outputs to the platform consists of a velocity setpoint, rather than a position setpoint; as such we use the derivative of the normal distribution as part of our parametric function. In order to approach a distance and stop, we need a function with a variable zero crossing point, which is accomplished through c_i. In addition, the parameters σ_i and t_i allow for the adjustment of the width or range of the force, and the strength of the force respectively. t_i allows for both repulsive and attractive behaviors around center c_i by inverting the sign of the function.

$a_i(d_i)$ contributes a fixed attractive or repulsive force across a greater area. This allows for pure attraction or repulsion behaviors, which can be useful for collision avoidance or exploration. This component is based on a Sigmoid activation function and exhibits a jump from $-k_i$ to k_i around the center-point c_i. The transition between the two values is smooth, which is important for stability once the agent is close to the center point c_i.

Together, $a_i(d_i)$ and $g_i(d_i)$ make the weight $w_{p,i}(d_i)$ for a given input i in the parametric controller - we call this the Sigmoid-well function (Fig. 2). It consists of two parts; a Sigmoid for general attraction/repulsion from objects and a gravity well component $g_i(d_i)$ for keeping a given distance. This function combines the weights from the simple controller, through the scaling of the Sigmoid

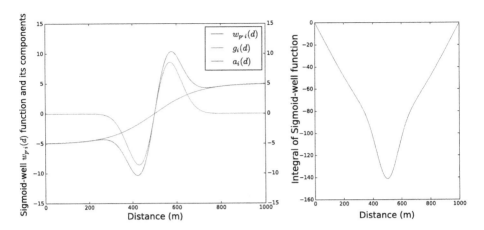

Fig. 2. The Sigmoid-well function (Eq. 4) is shown in the left part of the figure. The green line represents the Sigmoid component $a_i(d_i)$. The red line is the gravity well component $g_i(d_i)$. Added together they form the blue line: the Sigmoid-well function $w_{p,i}(d_i)$. The right part of the figure depicts the integral of the Sigmoid-well function $w_{p,i}(d_i)$, which has a clear strong attraction (minimum) around a center $c_i = 500.0$ The remaining parameters are $t_i = -0.1$, $k_i = 5.0$ and $\sigma_i = 100.0$. (Color figure online)

function (parameter k_i) and the ability to describe hold at a distance c_i through a gravity well component. Furthermore, it is easily optimizable and described by 4 real-coded values for each force contribution, or 16 for our complete controller with 4 input forces. Figure 2 show the individual contributions given distance, and the combined resulting weighting $w_{p,i}(d_i)$.

Table 1. Parameters for hand coded parametric example controllers

	k_i	c_i	σ_i	t_i
Exploration	$[-2,0,0,3]$	$[150,150,150,1000]$	$[100, 100, 100, 100]$	$[0,0,0,0]$
Combination	$[-2,1,0,3]$	$[150,150,150,1000]$	$[100, 100, 100, 100]$	$[-0.1,-0.1,-0.1,0]$
Network	$[-1,1,0,0]$	$[150,150,150,1000]$	$[100, 100, 100, 100]$	$[-0.1,-0.1,-0.1,0]$

This controller allows for defining a "hold at a distance" behavior (Fig. 3). Parameters for controllers in Fig. 3, can be seen in Table 1. Both the network focused behavior and the controller featuring a combination of network and exploration focus exhibit clear lattice structure. This is made possible by the parametric controller architecture. Onwards we consider k_i, t_i, c_i and σ_i as vectors **k**, **t**, **c** and $\boldsymbol{\sigma}$ - each a vector of 4 real-coded values.

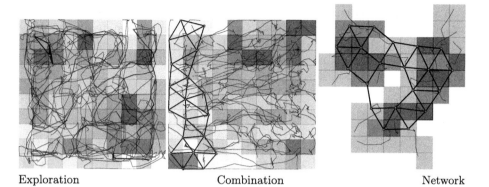

Exploration   Combination   Network

Fig. 3. Example hand designed controllers using the parametric controller structure. From left to right are examples of exploration focus (left), combination of exploration and network creation (middle) and a controller that results in a static network (right). Videos of these behaviors can be found at https://www.youtube.com/playlist? list=PL18bqX3rX5tQN2HKdHSCna8ysbX9lUeSM

4 Methods

4.1 Fitness and Characteristics

For these experiments, two behavioral characteristics were used: exploration median and network coverage. First, exploration median is calculated by accumulating all distinct visitations to each square/bin in the area during the simulation. Then the median across all the bins in the search area is calculated. The median is normalized for agent count, speed and size of the grid. This gives a measure that is independent of the number of agents and the simulator setup. This can also be considered a percentage of the maximal median possible to achieve, given a number of agents.

The second metric, network coverage, is calculated by first finding the largest group of connected agents. In this context, connectivity is defined by a simple range test, which for these experiments was defined as within a fixed range of 200 m. The behaviors adapt to this distance through the evolution of the controller, as such the controllers evolved are specific to this connectivity distance. Once the largest set of connected agents is determined, the area their communication radius cover is used as a characteristic dimension. This number is also normalized for the greatest possible coverage a swarm of agents can achieve. Since some of the agents will cover overlapping areas, the maximum area possible to cover is scaled by a factor of 0.5.

Finally, fitness is a metric related to the movement or energy use for the swarm as a whole. Fitness is defined as:

$$\text{fitness} = \frac{2}{1+b} \tag{6}$$

Where b is proportional to an average agent's speed during a simulation run. Without loss of generality, this quantity can be approximated deterministically based on the parameters for the controller. Specifically, for the weighted controller b is the norm of the weight vector ($||\mathbf{w}||$), and for the parametric controller b is the sum of norm t_i and norm k_i ($||\mathbf{k}|| + ||\mathbf{t}||$).

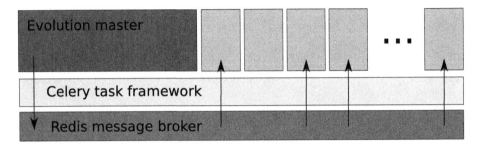

Fig. 4. Overview of our evolutionary framework in Python using Celery and Redis message broker. The evolution master generates the candidate controllers to be tested and maintains the repertoire of controllers, and the worker threads evaluate candidate solutions and return a log of the experiment for review by the master.

4.2   MAP-elites

Both controllers are defined as a finite sequence of real-coded values. For the weighted controller, a vector of 4 real-coded values is used. For the parametric controller, a vector of 16 real-coded values is used. MAP-elites uses only a mutation operator for permutation of individuals; this is implemented as an additive Gaussian variation with mean of 0 for all parameters. The standard deviation of the Gaussian mutation is 10.0 for the weighted controller, and the weights are clamped between -100.0 and 100.0.

For the parametric controller, the real-coded genome has a different interpretation. We have 16 real-coded values. For each input force there is a scaling weight for the Sigmoid function (k_i), scaling weight for the gravity well strength (t_i), center distance for the gravity well (c_i) and spread or range for the gravity well (σ_i). These form the vectors $\mathbf{k}$, $\mathbf{t}$, $\mathbf{c}$ and $\boldsymbol{\sigma}$ - each a vector of 4 real-coded values. The range and mutation used for the individual elements of these vectors can be found in Table 2.

This research utilizes a parallel version of MAP-elites. The original MAP-elites algorithm specifies that, at each iteration a single individual is selected, mutated, evaluated and then placed back in the appropriate cell. The parallel version is similar, but works on a batch of individuals, selecting 200 individuals at a time, mutating, evaluating and placing them back in their cells. Each individual in the repertoire is one potential controller. The controller is evaluated by simulating a swarm, where each agent is controlled by the given controller. Our experiments use an initial population (generated randomly) of 200 individuals and up to 200 generations or batches of 200 individuals per experiment.

Table 2. Range and mutation parameters for the parametric controller

Param	Min	Max	Mut. std. dev.
k	−100	100	10.0
t	−1.0	1.0	0.1
c	100.0	1000.0	100.0
σ	0.0	100.0	10.0

This evaluates some 40200 possible solutions. We run our experiments using task parallelism, this is briefly outlined in Fig. 4.

5   Results

5.1   Weighted Controller Experiments

Preliminary experiments used only a single simulation per controller; which was insufficient and caused significant noise in the final repertoire. For this reason we simulate each controller five times, varying the starting positions and random seed, in order to get a better estimate of the controller performance. Figure 5 shows the resulting repertoire after 1, 10, 100 and 200 epochs (batches of evaluations). In this figure, the resultant exploration-median values are placed in 10 bins (shown along the vertical axis), and network-coverage values - in 100 bins (shown along the horizontal axis). Bins for which MAP-elites found a controller has a gradient color from white to dark blue, where dark blue indicates a high fitness value. Bins for which no solution was found are black.

Some of the evolved behaviors from the evolution are shown in Fig. 6. Evolved behaviors that explore a lot, without providing a large network coverage, typically cluster most or all the agents into groups that traverse the area. This can be seen in the left part of the figure. Behaviors that are more balanced between the applications, keep the agents further apart while exploring a small part of their surroundings. The controllers with the greatest network coverage accomplish this by standing still and balancing clustering and repulsion. It should be noted that this latter swarm behavior poses quite a challenge for the weighted controller, as there is no explicit support for holding a distance to another agent.

5.2   Parametric Controller Experiments

The result for the same set of experiment for the parametric controller are shown in Fig. 7. Compared to Fig. 5 there is less noise (almost none) and a more clearly defined structure to this repertoire. This is due to the fact that the parametric controller is more reliable and consistent, compared to the weighted controller.

Similar to Fig. 6, Fig. 8 shows some examples of parametric controllers generated by our approach. These are more structured, compared to the weighted controllers and feature partial lattice patterns. It is important to note that the

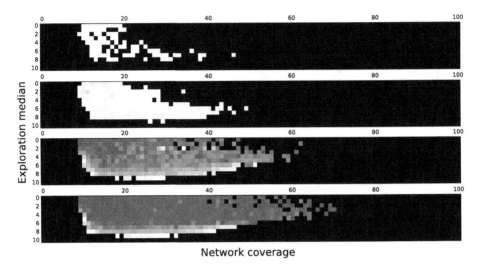

Network coverage

Fig. 5. Evolving a weighted controller. Figure shows epoch 1, 10, 100 and 200 with 5 evaluations per controller

controller has no incentive to generate stable or highly structured behaviors. A less direct encoding might allow for more structured behaviors - this is an area with potential for future improvement.

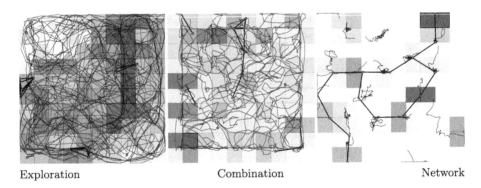

Exploration   Combination   Network

Fig. 6. Example evolved controllers using the weighted controller structure. From left to right it is possible to see: an exploration focused controller, a combination of exploration and network focused controller, and a pure network focused controller. Notice the difference in coverage and the links between the individual agents. Videos of these behaviors can be found at https://www.youtube.com/playlist?list=PL18bqX3rX5tQN2HKdHSCna8ysbX9lUeSM

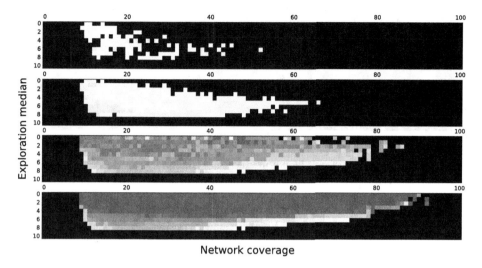

Fig. 7. Evolving parametric controllers. Figure shows epoch 1, 10, 100 and 200 with 5 evaluations per controller.

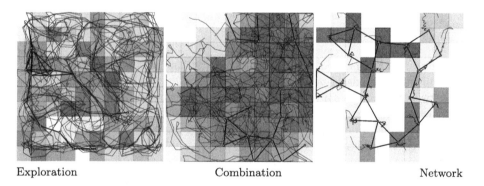

Exploration   Combination   Network

Fig. 8. Example evolved controllers using the parametric controller structure. From left to right, controllers were selected based on exploration performance, a combination of exploration and network performance, and solely large network coverage. Videos of these behaviors can be found at https://www.youtube.com/playlist?list=PL18bqX3rX5tQN2HKdHSCna8ysbX9lUeSM.

6   Discussion

6.1   Comparison Weighted and Parametric

When comparing the result from the weighted and parametric controller it is clear that the weighted controller is inferior to the parametric controller. This is highlighted in Fig. 9, which shows the difference between the repertoire from the parametric controller, after subtracting all the bins that the weighted controller

also found solutions for. The difference is also documented in Table 3, where the
number of unique solutions to each controller type is shown.

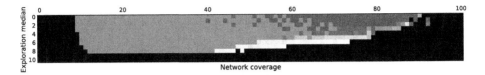

Fig. 9. The difference between the parametric controller and weighted controller repertoires at final epoch. Grey bins indicate where both controllers have a solution.

Table 3. Comparison between the weighted and parametric controller. The unique
column are solutions found with one controller type but not the other. Relative average
fitness % is the average fitness achieved, compared to the best fitness found across all
experiments.

	Solutions	Fill %	Unique	Fitness %
Weighted	429	38.6	14	96.7
Parametric	608	54.7	193	89.3

The results for the weighted controller suggest that this representation is not
powerful enough to describe a controller that is good at both the exploration and
the networking at the same time (Fig. 5). While it successfully manages to fill
up 38.6% of the characteristics space, it is unable to do very well on the task of
creating a stable communication network. As mentioned earlier, creating a stable
network requires the ability to keep a given distance to neighboring agents, this
is challenging for the weighted controllers as the description does not explicitly
allow for hold-distance type primitive and the only way to achieve this is to make
use of the boundary of the simulation area. As such, the problem with creating
a stable network is exaggerated in cases where there are too few agents to cover
the entire area of operations. This was the case for all the experiments described
previously.

In order to extend this architecture, we propose to use a different weight, or
more precisely: a different non-scalar parametric weight function. This allows for
controllers with the ability to hold a distance, effectively enabling the application
of communication network maintenance. The parametric controller manages to
fill 54.7% of the characteristic space, which is a 41.7% improvement over the
weighted controller. From the results, it is also possible to see signs of another
issue with the weighted controller approach. Compared to the weighted controller, the MAP or repertoire generated with the parametric controller is much
more consistent in terms of fill. This is connected to the MAP-elites algorithm
itself, the evaluation of the individuals, as well as the lack of an explicit hold distance primitive. Fitness and behavioral characteristics are evaluated post-test,

based on the log for the given test. For instance, the networking characteristic considers two snapshots from the simulation; one at the end of the test and one in the middle of the test. By calculating the networking characteristic based on just these two snapshots, the metric may be susceptible to noise. In addition, we are simulating these agents, and initial conditions such as initial position, speed or even just random seed may vary. This shows an interesting challenge with the MAP-elites algorithm.

The MAP-elites algorithm is highly elitist. Within a characteristic bin, the only solution that will survive or be kept, is the best performing solution, according to fitness. Similarly, if a solution is found for an empty bin, this solution is kept, always. While these two traits may be beneficial for exploring or illuminating the search landscape, they are also detrimental to determining the exact shape of this landscape given noisy measurements. In essence, any and all variance in the fitness or characteristic function will be amplified by the MAP-elites algorithm. This is an issue that is not yet fully addressed. We introduced multiple tests for each controller in order to reduce the variation in test results. However, this comes at a cost in terms of time and processing power. Further, this may not fully solve the problem.

Consider two swarm controllers: one is unreliable, with a large spread in performance with a mean of μ. The other, a controller with a lesser spread, and with a mean of $\mu + 1$. Comparing the two, we would prefer a controller with lesser spread and a higher/better mean. However, as the MAP-elites algorithm is greedy it may very well choose the worse solution, with the higher spread and lesser mean. The worse solution only has to get lucky once, in order to beat the better and more reliable controller. A similar issue can be seen with an elitist genetic algorithm. However, we believe that this is a lesser concern for a genetic algorithm, as the population gives lesser performing solutions a chance while the MAP or repertoire does not. This suggests that care should be taken in order to avoid noise in the evaluation of candidate solutions, if the resulting repertoire is to be as accurate as possible.

7   Conclusion and Future Work

We have shown that it is possible to automatically synthesize swarm controllers for a multi-function swarm system. Our experiments showcase the ability of the proposed framework to generate a large variety of controllers that can allow for finely tuned optimized behaviors for any requirements presented by a human operator. The behaviors evolved could also be used as swarm primitives with a different type of high level controller choosing the appropriate controller for the task. Evolution was done in a top-down approach, where only the skeleton of the controllers was specified, and the goals for the swarm as a whole. This also presents a contribution towards the issue of automatically generating low-level controllers from high level goals or requirements.

A focus of this study was to allow for further expansion through testing on real-world unmanned aerial vehicles by making sure that the controller inputs and outputs use only local information and are compatible with current state-of-the-art unmanned aerial vehicles. As such, a natural starting point for future work would be to conduct real-world tests on a robotics swarm platform.

It would also be possible to expand the presented framework to optimize more complex controller architectures. For instance, instead of a simple weighted sum or parametric function, a neural network could be used. With a more complex controller structure it could also be possible to include more complex tasks; for instance tasks that require sequential actions, or tasks that require agents to segment into smaller groups for optimal performance.

We would also like to conduct a more thorough investigations into the effects of noise on the MAP-elites algorithm as this poses some interesting challenges for divergent evolution.

References

1. Gross, R., Dorigo, M.: Towards group transport by swarms of robots. Int. J. Bio-Inspired Comput. **1**(1–2), 1–13 (2009)
2. Mitri, S., Floreano, D., Keller, L.: The evolution of information suppression in communicating robots with conflicting interests. Proc. Natl. Acad. Sci. **106**(37), 15786–15790 (2009)
3. Ducatelle, F., Di Caro, G.A., Gambardella, L.M.: Cooperative self-organization in a heterogeneous swarm robotic system. In: Proceedings of the 12th Annual Conference on Genetic and Evolutionary Computation, pp. 87–94. ACM (2010)
4. Duarte, M., Costa, V., Gomes, J., Rodrigues, T., Silva, F., Oliveira, S.M., Christensen, A.L.: Evolution of collective behaviors for a real swarm of aquatic surface robots. PLoS ONE **11**(3), e0151834 (2016)
5. Krupke, D., Ernestus, M., Hemmer, M., Fekete, S.P.: Distributed cohesive control for robot swarms: maintaining good connectivity in the presence of exterior forces. In: 2015 IEEE/RSJ International Conference on Intelligent Robots and Systems (IROS), pp. 413–420. IEEE (2015)
6. Duarte, M., Oliveira, S.M., Christensen, A.L.: Hybrid control for large swarms of aquatic drones. In: Proceedings of the 14th International Conference on the Synthesis & Simulation of Living Systems, pp. 785–792. MIT Press, Cambridge (2014)
7. Nolfi, S., Bongard, J.C., Husbands, P., Floreano, D.: Evolutionary Robotics (2016)
8. Cully, A., Clune, J., Tarapore, D., Mouret, J.B.: Robots that can adapt like animals. Nature **521**(7553), 503–507 (2015)
9. Berman, S., Halász, Á., Hsieh, M.A., Kumar, V.: Optimized stochastic policies for task allocation in swarms of robots. IEEE Trans. Rob. **25**(4), 927–937 (2009)
10. Schrum, J., Miikkulainen, R.: Evolving multimodal networks for multitask games. IEEE Trans. Comput. Intell. AI Games **4**(2), 94–111 (2012)
11. Schrum, J., Miikkulainen, R.: Evolving multimodal behavior with modular neural networks in Ms. Pac-Man. In: Proceedings of the 2014 Annual Conference on Genetic and Evolutionary Computation, pp. 325–332. ACM (2014)
12. Ellefsen, K.O., Mouret, J.B., Clune, J.: Neural modularity helps organisms evolve to learn new skills without forgetting old skills. PLoS Comput. Biol. **11**(4), e1004128 (2015)

13. Basilico, N., Carpin, S.: Deploying teams of heterogeneous UAVs in cooperative two-level surveillance missions. In: 2015 IEEE/RSJ International Conference on Intelligent Robots and Systems (IROS), pp. 610–615. IEEE (2015)
14. Hauert, S., Zufferey, J.C., Floreano, D.: Evolved swarming without positioning information: an application in aerial communication relay. Auton. Robots **26**(1), 21–32 (2009)
15. Balch, T., Arkin, R.C.: Behavior-based formation control for multirobot teams. IEEE Trans. Robot. Autom. **14**(6), 926–939 (1998)
16. Spears, W.M., Spears, D.F., Heil, R., Kerr, W., Hettiarachchi, S.: An overview of physicomimetics. In: Şahin, E., Spears, W.M. (eds.) SR 2004. LNCS, vol. 3342, pp. 84–97. Springer, Heidelberg (2005). https://doi.org/10.1007/978-3-540-30552-1_8
17. Vadakkepat, P., Tan, K.C., Ming-Liang, W.: Evolutionary artificial potential fields and their application in real time robot path planning. In: Proceedings of the 2000 Congress on Evolutionary Computation, vol. 1, pp. 256–263. IEEE (2000)
18. Park, M.G., Jeon, J.H., Lee, M.C.: Obstacle avoidance for mobile robots using artificial potential field approach with simulated annealing. In: Proceedings of the IEEE International Symposium on Industrial Electronics, ISIE 2001, vol. 3, pp. 1530–1535. IEEE (2001)
19. Lee, M.C., Park, M.G.: Artificial potential field based path planning for mobile robots using a virtual obstacle concept. In: Proceedings of 2003 IEEE/ASME International Conference on Advanced Intelligent Mechatronics, AIM 2003, vol. 2, pp. 735–740. IEEE (2003)
20. Mouret, J.B., Clune, J.: Illuminating search spaces by mapping elites. arXiv preprint arXiv:1504.04909 (2015)
21. Duarte, M., Oliveira, S., Christensen, A.L.: Hierarchical evolution of robotic controllers for complex tasks. In: 2012 IEEE International Conference on Development and Learning and Epigenetic Robotics (ICDL), pp. 1–6. IEEE (2012)
22. Duarte, M., Oliveira, S.M., Christensen, A.L.: Evolution of hybrid robotic controllers for complex tasks. J. Intell. Robot. Syst. **78**(3–4), 463 (2015)
23. Uchibe, E., Asada, M.: Incremental coevolution with competitive and cooperative tasks in a multirobot environment. Proc. IEEE **94**(7), 1412–1424 (2006)
24. Mouret, J.B., Doncieux, S.: Incremental evolution of animats behaviors as a multi-objective optimization. From Anim. Animats **10**, 210–219 (2008)
25. Tarapore, D., Clune, J., Cully, A., Mouret, J.B.: How do different encodings influence the performance of the map-elites algorithm? In: Genetic and Evolutionary Computation Conference (2016)

HyperNTM: Evolving Scalable Neural Turing Machines Through HyperNEAT

Jakob Merrild, Mikkel Angaju Rasmussen, and Sebastian Risi$^{(\boxtimes)}$

IT University of Copenhagen, Copenhagen, Denmark
{jmer,mang,sebr}@itu.dk

Abstract. Recent developments in memory-augmented neural networks allowed sequential problems requiring long-term memory to be solved, which were intractable for traditional neural networks. However, current approaches still struggle to scale to large memory sizes and sequence lengths. In this paper we show how access to an external memory component can be encoded geometrically through a novel HyperNEAT-based Neural Turing Machine (*HyperNTM*). The indirect HyperNEAT encoding allows for training on small memory vectors in a bit vector copy task and then applying the knowledge gained from such training to speed up training on larger size memory vectors. Additionally, we demonstrate that in some instances, networks trained to copy nine bit vectors can be scaled to sizes of 1,000 *without further training*. While the task in this paper is simple, the HyperNTM approach could now allow memory-augmented neural networks to scale to problems requiring large memory vectors and sequence lengths.

Keywords: Neural Turing Machine · HyperNEAT · Neuroevolution
Indirect encoding

1 Introduction

Memory-augmented neural networks are a recent improvement on artificial neural networks (ANNs) that allows them to solve complex sequential tasks requiring long-term memory [1–3]. Here we are particularly interested in Neural Turing Machines (NTM) [3], which augment networks with an external memory tape to store and retrieve information from during execution. This improvement also enabled ANNs to learn simple algorithms such as copying, sorting and planning [2].

However, scaling to large memory sizes and sequence length is still challenging. Additionally, current algorithms have difficulties *extrapolating* information learned on smaller problem sizes to larger once, thereby bootstrapping from it. For example, in the copy task introduced by Graves et al. [3] the goal is to store and later recall a sequence of bit vectors of a specific size. It would be desirable that a network trained on a certain bit vector size (e.g. eight bits) would be

© Springer International Publishing AG, part of Springer Nature 2018
K. Sim and P. Kaufmann (Eds.): EvoApplications 2018, LNCS 10784, pp. 750–766, 2018.
https://doi.org/10.1007/978-3-319-77538-8_50

able to scale to larger bit vector sizes without further training. However, current machine learning approaches often cannot transfer such knowledge.

Recently, Greve et al. [4] introduced an *evolvable* version of the NTM (ENTM), which allowed networks to be trained through neuroevolution instead of the gradient descent-based training of the original NTM. This combination offered some unique advantages. First, in addition to the network's weights, the optimal neural architecture can be learned at the same time. Second, a hard memory attention mechanism is directly supported and the complete memory does not need to be accessed each time step. Third, a growing and theoretically infinite memory is now possible. Additionally, in contrast to the original NTM, the evolved networks were able to perfectly scale to very long sequence lengths. However, because it employed a direct genetic encoding (NEAT [5]), which means that every parameter of the network is described separately in its genotype, the approach had problems scaling to copy tasks with vectors of more than eight bits.

To overcome this challenge, in this paper we present an indirectly encoded version of the ENTM based on the Hypercube-based NeuroEvolution of Augmenting Topologies (HyperNEAT) method [6]. In HyperNEAT the weights of a neural network are generated as a function of its geometry through an indirect encoding called compositional pattern producing networks (CPPNs), which can compactly encode patterns with regularities such as symmetry, repetition, and repetition with variation [7]. Neurons are placed at certain locations in space, allowing evolution to exploit topography (as opposed to just topology) and correlating the geometry of sensors with the geometry of the brain. This geometry appears to be a critical facet of natural brains [8] but lacks in most ANNs. HyperNEAT allowed large ANNs with regularities in connectivity to evolve for high-dimensional problems [6,9].

In the approach introduced in this paper, called *HyperNTM*, an evolved neural network generates the weights of a main model, *including how it connects to the external memory component*. We show that because HyperNEAT can learn the geometry of how the ANN should be connected to the external memory, it is possible to train a CPPN on a small bit vector size and then scale it to larger bit vector sizes *without further training*.

While the task in this paper is simple it shows – for the first time – that access to an external memory can be indirectly encoded, an insight that could now also directly benefit indirectly encoded HyperNetworks trained through gradient descent [10]. Additionally, an exciting future opportunity is to combine our HyperNTM approach with recent advances in evolutionary strategies [11] and genetic programming [12], to solve complex problems requiring large external memory components.

2   Background

This section reviews NEAT, HyperNEAT, and Evolvable Neural Turing Machines, which are foundational to the approach introduced in this paper.

2.1   Neuroevolution of Augmenting Topologies (NEAT)

The HyperNEAT method that enables learning from geometry in this paper is an extension of the NEAT algorithm that evolves ANNs through a *direct* encoding [5,13]. It starts with a population of simple neural networks and then *complexifies* them over generations by adding new nodes and connections through mutation. By evolving networks in this way, the topology of the network does not need to be known a priori; NEAT searches through increasingly complex networks to find a suitable level of complexity.

The important feature of NEAT for the purpose of this paper is that it evolves *both* the network's topology and weights. Because it starts simply and gradually adds complexity, it tends to find a solution network close to the minimal necessary size. The next section reviews the HyperNEAT extension to NEAT that is itself extended in this paper.

2.2   HyperNEAT

In direct encodings like NEAT, each part of the solution's representation maps to a single piece of structure in the final solution [14]. The significant disadvantage of this approach is that even when different parts of the solution are similar, they must be encoded and therefore discovered separately. Thus this paper employs an *indirect* encoding instead, which means that the description of the solution is compressed such that information can be reused. Indirect encodings are powerful because they allow solutions to be represented as a *pattern* of parameters, rather than requiring each parameter to be represented individually [15–18]. HyperNEAT, reviewed in this section, is an indirect encoding extension of NEAT that is proven in a number of challenging domains that require discovering regularities [6,16,19]. For a full description of HyperNEAT see Gauci and Stanley [16].

In HyperNEAT, NEAT is altered to evolve an indirect encoding called *compositional pattern producing networks* (CPPNs [7]) *instead* of ANNs. CPPNs, which are also networks, are designed to encode *compositions of functions*, wherein each function in the composition loosely corresponds to a useful regularity.

The appeal of this encoding is that it allows spatial patterns to be represented as networks of simple functions (i.e. CPPNs), which means that NEAT can evolve CPPNs just like ANNs. CPPNs are similar to ANNs, but they rely on more than one activation function (each representing a common regularity) and are an abstraction of biological development rather than of brains. The indirect CPPN encoding can compactly encode patterns with regularities such as symmetry, repetition, and repetition with variation [7]. For example, simply by including a Gaussian function, which is symmetric, the output pattern can become symmetric. A periodic function such as sine creates segmentation through repetition. Most importantly, *repetition with variation* (e.g. such as the fingers of the human hand) is easily discovered by combining regular coordinate frames (e.g. sine and Gaussian) with irregular ones (e.g. the asymmetric x-axis).

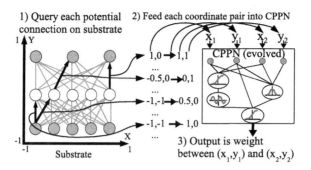

Fig. 1. Hypercube-based Geometric Connectivity Pattern Interpretation. A collection of nodes, called the *substrate*, is assigned coordinates that range from −1 to 1 in all dimensions. (1) Every potential connection in the substrate is queried to determine its presence and weight; the dark directed lines in the substrate depicted in the figure represent a sample of connections that are queried. (2) Internally, the CPPN (which is evolved) is a graph that determines which activation functions are connected. As in an ANN, the connections are weighted such that the output of a function is multiplied by the weight of its outgoing connection. For each query, the CPPN takes as input the positions of the two endpoints and (3) outputs the weight of the connection between them. Thus, CPPNs can produce regular patterns of connections in space.

The potential for CPPNs to represent patterns with motifs reminiscent of patterns in natural organisms has been demonstrated in several studies [7, 20–22].

The main idea in HyperNEAT is that CPPNs can naturally encode *connectivity patterns* [6, 16]. That way, NEAT can evolve CPPNs that represent large-scale ANNs with their own symmetries and regularities. Formally, CPPNs are *functions* of geometry (i.e. locations in space) that output connectivity patterns whose nodes are situated in n dimensions, where n is the number of dimensions in a Cartesian space. Consider a CPPN that takes four inputs labeled x_1, y_1, x_2, and y_2; this point in four-dimensional space *also* denotes the connection between the two-dimensional points (x_1, y_1) and (x_2, y_2), and the output of the CPPN for that input thereby represents the weight of that connection (Fig. 1). By querying every possible connection among a pre-chosen set of points in this manner, a CPPN can produce an ANN, wherein each queried point is a neuron position. Because the connections are produced by a function of their endpoints, the final structure is produced with *knowledge* of its geometry.

In the original HyperNEAT, the experimenter defines both the location and role (i.e. hidden, input, or output) of each such node (more advanced Hyper-NEAT variations can infer the position of hidden nodes from the weight pattern generated by the CPPN [21, 23]). As a rule of thumb, nodes are placed on the substrate to reflect the geometry of the task [6, 19]. That way, the connectivity of the substrate is a function of the task structure. How to integrate this setup with an ANN that has an external memory component is an open question, which this paper tries to address.

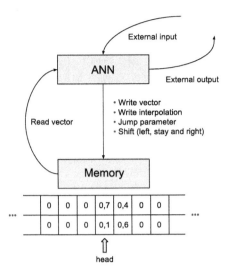

Fig. 2. Evolvable Neural Turing Machines. Shown is the activation flow between the ANN and its external memory. Extra ANN outputs determine the vector to be written to memory and the movement of the read and write heads. The ANN receives the content of the current memory location as input at the beginning of the next time-step. In addition to the NTM specific inputs and outputs, the ANN also has domain dependent inputs and outputs.

2.3   Neural Turing Machines

The recently introduced Neural Turing Machine (NTM) is a neural network coupled with an external memory component [2,3]. The neural network controller determines what is written to and read from the memory tape. At each time step, the ANN emits a number of different signals, including a data vector and various control inputs. These signals allow the NTM to focus its read and write heads on different parts of the external memory. The write heads modify the tapes content and the information from the read heads is used as input to the ANN during the next time step. At the same time, the ANN receive input from its environment and can interact with it through its outputs.

While the original NTM was trained through gradient descent, the recently introduced evolvable variant (ENTM) uses NEAT to learn the topology and weights of the ANN controller [4] (Fig. 2). That way the topology of the network does not have to be defined a priori (as is the case in the original NTM setup) and the network can grow in response to the complexity of the task. As demonstrated by Greve et al., the ENTM often finds compact network topologies to solve a particular task, thereby avoiding searching through unnecessarily high-dimensional spaces. Additionally, the ENTM was able to solve a complex continual learning problem [24]. Because the network does not have to be differentiable, it can use hard attention and shift mechanisms, allowing it to generalize perfectly to longer sequences in a copy task. Additionally, a dynamic, theoretically unlimited tape size is now possible.

The ENTM has a single combined read/write head. The network emits a write vector w of size M, a write interpolation control input i, a content jump control input j, and three shift control inputs s_l, s_0, and s_r (left shift, no shift, right shift). The size of the write vector determines the size of each memory location on the tape. The write interpolation component allows blending between the write vector and the current tape values at the write position, where $M_h(t)$ is the content of the tape at the current head location h, at time step t, i_t is the write interpolation, and w_t is the write vector at time step t: $M_h(t) = M_h(t-1) \cdot (1 - i_t) + w_t \cdot i_t$.

The content jump determines if the head should be moved to the location in memory that most closely resembles the write vector. A content jump is performed if the value of the control input exceeds 0.5. The similarity between write vector w and memory vector m is determined by:

$$s(w, m) = \frac{\sum_{i=1}^{M} |w_i - m_i|}{M}.$$

At each time step t, the following actions are performed in order: (1) Record the write vector w_t to the current head position h, interpolated with the existing content according to the write interpolation i_t. (2) If the content jump control input j_t is greater than 0.5, move the head to location on the tape most similar to the write vector w_t. (3) Shift the head one position left or right on the tape, or stay at the current location, according to the shift control inputs s_l, s_0, and s_r. (4) Read and return the memory values at the new head position to the ANN controller.

3   Approach: Hyper Neural Turing Machine (HyperNTM)

In the novel HyperNTM approach introduced in this paper, the CPPN does not only determine the connections between the task related ANN inputs and outputs but also how the information coming from the memory is integrated into the network and how information is written back to memory. Because Hyper-NEAT can learn the geometry of a task it should be able to learn the geometric pattern of the weights connecting the external memory component to the neural network.

In this paper the HyperNTM approach is applied to the copy task, which was first introduced by Graves et al. [3]. In the copy task the network is asked to store and later recall a sequence of random bit vectors. At the start of the task the network receives a special input, which denotes the start of the input phase. Afterwards, the network receives the sequence of bit vectors, one at a time. Once the full sequence has been presented to the network, it receives another special input, signaling the end of the input phase and the start of the output phase. For any subsequent time steps the network does not receive any external input.

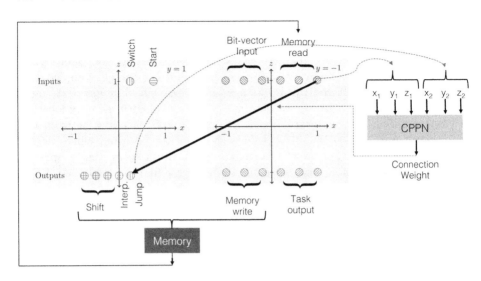

Fig. 3. In the HyperNTM approach the CPPN does not only determine the connectivity between the task related inputs and outputs but also how information is written/read from memory. This figure depicts the HyperNTM substrate for the copy task. All inputs are in $z = 1$ and all outputs in $z = -1$. The plane on the left shows all nodes with $y = 1$, which are the start/switch inputs and the TM controls. Notably the x-coordinate is the same for the switch input and the jump control output. The plane on the right shows the nodes in $y = -1$, which are the bit vector and memory vector input and outputs. Bit vector input nodes share x-coordinates with memory vector write nodes, while memory vector read nodes share x-coordinates with bit vector output nodes. The potential connections between all pairs of inputs and outputs are queried for by the CPPN. The dark line shows an example of such a potential connection that connects an input in the $y = -1$ plane with an output in the $y = 1$ plane.

In summary, the network has the following inputs. *Start:* An input that is activated when the storing of bit vectors should begin. *Switch:* An input that is activated when the recitation of the stored sequence should start. *Bit vector input:* The bit vector that should be stored in memory. *Memory read input:* The memory vector at the current position in memory. The network has the following outputs. *Bit vector output:* The bit vector that the network outputs to the environment. During the input phase this output is ignored. *Memory write output:* The memory vector that should be written to memory. *TM controls:* TM specific control outputs: Jump, interpolation, and three shift controls (left, stay, and right).

3.1   Copy Task Substrate

The HyperNEAT substrate for the copy task is shown in Fig. 3. The substrate is designed such that the bit vector input nodes share x-coordinates with the memory vector write nodes and vice versa with memory vector read nodes and bit vector output nodes. Furthermore, the switch input shares its x-coordinate with the jump output, thus encouraging the network to jump in memory when it should start reciting. In this paper, the size of the memory vector equals the bit vector size. Furthermore, none of the substrates contain hidden nodes as it has been shown previously that it is possible to solve the copy task without any hidden nodes [25].

Following Verbancsics and Stanley [26], in addition to the CPPN output that determines the weights of each connection, each CPPN has an additional step-function output, called the *link-expression output* (LEO), which determines if a connection should be expressed. Potential connections are queried for each input on layers $y = 1$ and $y = -1$ to each output on layers $y = 1$ and $y = -1$. The CPPN has an additional output that determines the bias values for each node in the substrate. These values are determined through node-centric CPPN queries (i.e. both source and target neuron positions xyz are set to the location of the node whose bias should be determined).

3.2   Scaling

A particularly intriguing property of HyperNEAT is the fact that, because it is able to capture the particular domain geometry, the number of inputs and outputs in the substrate can theoretically be scaled without further training [27–29].

In this paper the substrate reflects the domain geometry of the copy tasks (Fig. 3), which means the number of inputs and outputs on the $y = -1$ layer can be scaled dependent on the size of the copy task bit vector. Networks that can store larger bit vectors can be generated without further evolution by requerying the same CPPN at higher-resolutions (Fig. 8). When rescaled, neurons are uniformly distributed in the x interval $[-1.0, -0.2]$ for bit vector inputs and memory write vector and in the interval $[0.2, 1.0]$ for the memory read vector and bit vector output.

4   Experiments

A total of three different approaches are evaluated on bit-sizes of 1, 3, 5, and 9. **HyperNTM**, a NTM based on HyperNEAT, is compared to one evolved by **NEAT**, and a **Seeded HyperNTM** treatment that starts evolution with a manually designed CPPN seed that encourages locality on both the x- and y-coordinates (Fig. 7a). A similar locality seed has been shown useful in Hyper-NEAT to encourage the evolution of modular networks [26]. This locality seed is then later adjusted by evolution (e.g. by adding/removing nodes and connections and changing their weights).

The fitness function follows the one in the original ENTM paper [4]. During training the network is given a sequence of random bit vectors with sequence lengths between 1 and 10, which it then has to recite. The network is tested on a total of 50 random sequences. Fitness is determined by comparing the bit vectors recited by the network to those given to it during the input phase; for every bit vector the network is given a score based on how close the output from the network corresponds to the target vector. If the two bit vectors have a match m of at least 25%, fitness is increased by: $f = \frac{|m-0.25|}{0.75}$, otherwise the network is not awarded for that specific bit vector. The fitness for a complete sequence is the sum of the fitness values for each bit vector normalized to the length of the sequence. Thus final fitness scores are in the interval $[0, 1]$ and reward the network for gradually getting closer to the solution, but do not actively reward the network for using the memory to store the presented sequence.

4.1 Experimental Parameters

For the NEAT experiments, offspring proportions are 50% sexual (crossover) and 50% asexual (mutation). We use 98.8% synapse weight mutation probability, 9% synapse addition probability, and 5% synapse removal probability. Because previous results [4] have demonstrated that the task can be solved without any hidden nodes, node addition probability is set to a relatively low value of 0.05%.

The code is build on a modified version of SharpNEAT v2.2.0.0[1], which is an implementation of NEAT and HyperNEAT made in C# by Colin Green. Our code is available from: https://github.com/kalanzai/ENTM_CSharpPort. This NEAT implementation uses a complexity regulation strategy for the evolutionary process, which has proven to be quite impactful on our results. A threshold defines how complex the networks in the population can be (here defined as the number of genes in the genome and set to 10 in our experiments), before the algorithm switches to a simplifying phase, where it gradually reduces complexity.

For the HyperNTM experiments the following parameters are used. Elitism proportion is 2%. Offspring generation proportions are 50% sexual (crossover) and 50% asexual (mutation). CPPN connection weights have a 98.8% probability of being changed, a 1% change of connection addition, and 0.1% change of node addition and node deletion. The activation functions available to new neurons in the CPPN are Linear, Gaussian, Sigmoid, and Sine, each with a 25% probability of being added.

Parameters for both NEAT and HyperNEAT have been tuned through prior experimentation. Both methods run with a population size of 500 for a maximum of 10,000 generations or until a solution is found.

5   Results

Figure 4a shows the mean champion fitness over $10,000$ generations for each of the different approaches and bit vector sizes. While NEAT performs best on smaller bit vectors, as the size of the vector grows to 9 bits, the seeded HyperNTM variant outperforms both NEAT and non-seeded HyperNTM. The numbers of solutions found (i.e. networks that reach a training score ≥ 0.999) for

---

[1] http://sharpneat.sourceforge.net/.

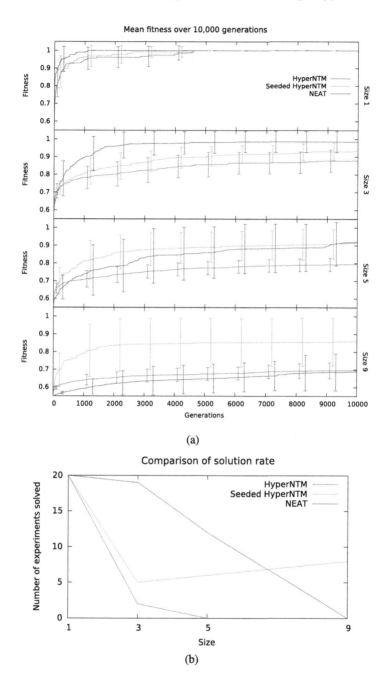

Fig. 4. (a) Shown are mean champion fitness for the different treatments and bit sizes, averaged over 20 independent evolutionary runs. Error bars show one standard deviation. The number of solutions found by each configuration for the four different bit vector sizes are shown in (b).

Comparison of final fitness

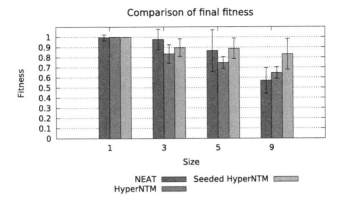

Fig. 5. The mean testing performance of the champion networks from the last generation. In contrast to NEAT, the seeded HyperNTM approach is able to better maintain performance with an increase in bit vector size. Error bars show one standard deviation.

the different bit vector sizes are shown in Fig. 4b. For bit size 1 all approaches solve the problem equally well. However, as the size of the bit vector is increased the HyperNTM configuration with the locality seed performs best and is the only method able to find any solutions for size 9.

Testing Performance. To determine how well the champions from the last generation generalize, they were tested on 100 random bit vector sequences with sequence lengths varying randomly from 1 to 10 (Fig. 5). With 1 and 5 bit vectors there is no statistical difference between either treatment (following a two-tailed Mann-Whitney U test). On size 3, NEAT performs significantly better than the seeded HyperNTM ($p < .0001$). Finally, seeded HyperNTM performs significantly better than NEAT on size 9 ($p < .00001$). The main conclusions are that (1) while NEAT performs best on smaller bit vectors it degrades rapidly

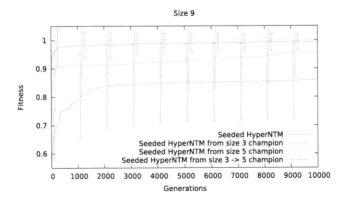

Fig. 6. Comparison of training performance on bit size 9 with the locality seed and with champion seeds from smaller sizes.

Table 1. Training and Generalization. Shown are the number of solutions (#sol) that were able to solve sequences of up to length 10 during training, together with the average number of generations it took to find those solutions (gens) and standard deviation (sd). The number of those solutions that generalize (#gen) to sequences of length 100 during testing are also shown.

	Size	#sol.	#gen	gens.	sd.
Seeded	1	20	20	1055.8	1147.4
HyperNTM	3	5	5	4454.8	3395.8
	5	6	5	2695.5	2666.5
	9	8	5	1523.25	2004.1
HyperNTM	1	20	20	1481.45	1670.8
	3	2	2	4395.5	388.2
	5	0	0	N/A	N/A
	9	0	0	N/A	N/A
NEAT	1	20	19	281	336.3
	3	19	19	2140.5	1594.4
	5	12	11	3213.4	2254.2
	9	0	0	N/A	N/A

with increased bit sizes, and (2) the seeded HyperNTM variant is able to scale to larger sizes while maintaining performance better.

Generalizing to longer sequences. We also tested how many of the solutions, which were trained on sequences of up to length 10, generalize to sequences of length 100. The training and generalization results are summarized in Table 1, which shows the number of solutions for each of the three approaches, the average number of generations it took to find a solution, and how many of those solutions generalized to sequences of length 100. For all three methods, most solutions generalize perfectly to sequences that are longer than the sequences encountered during training.

5.1 Transfer Learning

To test the scalability of the Seeded HyperNTM solutions, champion genomes from runs which found a solution for a given size were used as a seed for evolutionary runs of higher sizes. The specific runs and which seeds were used can be seen in Table 2.

Because the number of solutions found varied between the different sizes (see Table 1), the scaling experiments were not run exactly 20 times. Instead, the number of runs was the smallest number above or equal to 20 which allowed for each champion to be seeded an equal number of times, e.g. if there were 6 solutions 24 runs were made; 4 runs with the champion from each solution. Figure 6 shows a comparison of HyperNTM seeded with the locality seed and

Table 2. Transfer Learning. Seeds $X \to Y$ refer to champions from a run of size Y which were seeded with a champion from a run of size X. Networks evolved under these treatments were then tested on larger bit vector sizes without further training.

Seed	Size	#sol	#general	gens.	sd.
3	5	12/20	6	434.1	574.6
3	9	16/20	2	1150.3	2935.9
5	9	23/24	11	58.9	129.2
3→5	9	23/24	8	588	1992
5	17	18/20	12	258.9	301.3
9	17	24/24	12	89.3	235.9
5→9	17	20/20	17	36.25	47.5
9	33	23/24	17	94	217
9→17	33	24/24	19	456.5	2002.4

seeded with champion genomes of smaller sizes on the size 9 problem. HyperNTM yielded significantly better results when seeded with size 5 and 3→5 champions compared to starting with the locality seed ($p < .001$), but not when seeded with the champion from size 3 ($p > 0.05$).

5.2 Scaling Without Further Training

The champions from runs which found a solution were tested for scaling to larger bit vector sizes without further evolutionary training (i.e. new input and output nodes are created and queried by the CPPN but no evolutionary optimization is performed; see copy task substrate Sect. 3.1). Each genome was tested on 50 sequences of 100 random bit vectors of size 1,000. Some of the champions found using only the LEO size 9 configuration scaled perfectly to a bit-size of 1,000 without further training, as seen in Table 3. The main results is that it is possible to find CPPNs that perfectly scale to any size. The fact that evolution with HyperNEAT performs significantly better when seeded with a champion genome which solved a smaller size of the problem, together with the fact that evolution sometimes finds solutions which scale without further training, demonstrates that the HyperNTM approach can be used to scale the dimensionality of the bit vector in the copy task domain.

5.3 Solution Example

Here we take a closer look at one of the champion genomes (trained on bit vector size 9), which was able to scale perfectly to the size 1,000 problem (Table 3). Figure 7 shows a visualization of the champion genome, as well as the locality seed from which it was evolved. The champion genome does resemble the seed but also evolved several additional connections that are necessary to solve the problem.

Table 3. Scaling using LEO without further evolution.

Size	# of champions	# which scaled to 1000
9	8	2
9 → 17	24	7[†]

[†]6 of these can be traced back to the 2 champions from size 9 which scaled perfectly.

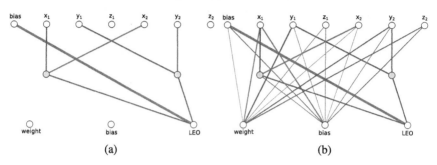

(a)   (b)

Fig. 7. (a) The manually designed CPPN seed that is used to promote locality on the x and y axes. (b) A champion trained on the size 9 problem, which was able to scale without further evolution to size 1,000. Blue connections have a positive weight, while red connections have a negative weight. (Color figure online)

Figure 8 shows two ANNs for different bit vector sizes generated by the same CPPN, which is shown in Fig. 7. It can be seen that for non-bias connections to be expressed, the source and destination nodes have to be located in the same position on both the x position and y layer in the substrate. These results suggest that the locality encouraging seed works as intended.

To further demonstrate the scalability of this evolved CPPN, memory usage for bit vector sizes of 9 and 17 are shown in Fig. 9. Both generated NTMs solve the task perfectly, continually performing a left shift while writing the given

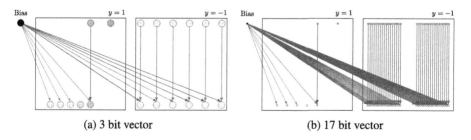

(a) 3 bit vector   (b) 17 bit vector

Fig. 8. Networks produced by the champion CPPN (Fig. 7b) for bit sizes 3 (a) and 17 (b). The CPPN discovered a connectivity pattern that only expresses non-bias connections in which the source and destination nodes are located in the same position on both the x position and y layer in the substrate.

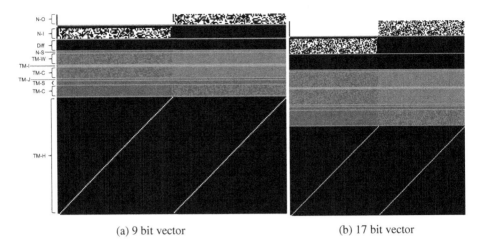

(a) 9 bit vector   (b) 17 bit vector

Fig. 9. Recordings of the activities for bit sizes 9 (a) and 17 (b) networks. Both networks are produced by the same CPPN. The different rows show the activity of the network and the state of the memory over time. After the input sequence is given to the network it has to recite the sequence of random binary vectors. In more detail, row **N-O** shows the output produced by the ANN. **N-I** is the bit vector input to the network. **Dif** is the difference in produced and expected output (i.e. how well the network recited the sequence given to it); here the section is black since the network reproduces the sequences perfectly. **TM-W** is the write vector, and **TM-I** write interpolation. **TM-C** shows the content of the tape at the current head position after write. **TM-J** is the content jump input, **TM-S** the three shift values, and **TM-R** the read vector. **TM-H** shows the current head position that the TM is focused on when writing (left) and reading (right).

input to memory. When reaching the delimiter input that signals the start of the recall phase, the networks perform a content-jump to the original position and continue shifting left while reading from the memory, reciting the correct sequence through the network's outputs.

6   Conclusion

This paper showed that the indirect encoding HyperNEAT makes it feasible to train ENTMs with large memory vectors for a simple copy task, which would otherwise be infeasible to train with an direct encoding such as NEAT. Furthermore, starting with a CPPN seed that encourages locality, it was possible to train solutions to the copy task that perfectly scale with the size of the bit vectors which should be memorized, without any further training. Lastly, we demonstrated that even solutions which do not scale perfectly can be used to shorten the number of generations needed to evolve a solution for bit vectors of larger sizes. In the future it will be interesting to apply the approach to more complex and less regular domains, in which the geometry of the connectivity pattern to discover is more complex. Additionally, combining the presented approach with recent advances in evolutionary strategies [11] and genetic programming [12], which have been shown to allow evolution to scale to problems with extremely high-dimensionality is a promising next step.

References

1. Sukhbaatar, S., Weston, J., Fergus, R., et al.: End-to-end memory networks. In: Advances in Neural Information Processing Systems, pp. 2440–2448 (2015)
2. Graves, A., Wayne, G., Reynolds, M., Harley, T., Danihelka, I., Grabska-Barwińska, A., Colmenarejo, S.G., Grefenstette, E., Ramalho, T., Agapiou, J., et al.: Hybrid computing using a neural network with dynamic external memory. Nature **538**(7626), 471–476 (2016)
3. Graves, A., Wayne, G., Danihelka, I.: Neural turing machines. CoRR abs/1410.5401 (2014), http://arxiv.org/abs/1410.5401
4. Greve, R.B., Jacobsen, E.J., Risi, S.: Evolving neural turing machines for reward-based learning. In: Proceedings of the Genetic and Evolutionary Computation Conference 2016, GECCO 2016, pp. 117–124. ACM, New York (2016), https://doi.org/10.1145/2908812.2908930
5. Stanley, K.O., Miikkulainen, R.: Evolving neural networks through augmenting topologies. Evol. Comput. **10**(2), 99–127 (2002)
6. Stanley, K.O., D'Ambrosio, D.B., Gauci, J.: A hypercube-based encoding for evolving large-scale neural networks. Artif. Life **15**(2), 185–212 (2009)
7. Stanley, K.O.: Compositional pattern producing networks: a novel abstraction of development. Genet. Program. Evolvable Mach. **8**(2), 131–162 (2007)
8. Sporns, O.: Network analysis, complexity, and brain function. Complexity **8**(1), 56–60 (2002)
9. Clune, J., Stanley, K.O., Pennock, R.T., Ofria, C.: On the performance of indirect encoding across the continuum of regularity. IEEE Trans. Evol. Comput. **15**(3), 346–367 (2011)
10. Ha, D., Dai, A., Le, Q.V.: Hypernetworks. arxiv preprint. arXiv preprint arXiv:1609.09106 (2016)
11. Salimans, T., Ho, J., Chen, X., Sutskever, I.: Evolution strategies as a scalable alternative to reinforcement learning. arXiv preprint arXiv:1703.03864 (2017)
12. Such, F.P., Madhavan, V., Conti, E., Lehman, J., Stanley, K.O., Clune, J.: Deep neuroevolution: genetic algorithms are a competitive alternative for training deep neural networks for reinforcement learning. arXiv preprint arXiv:1712.06567 (2017)
13. Stanley, K.O., Miikkulainen, R.: Competitive coevolution through evolutionary complexification. J. Artif. Int. Res. **21**(1), 63–100 (2004), http://dl.acm.org/citation.cfm?id=1622467.1622471
14. Floreano, D., Dürr, P., Mattiussi, C.: Neuroevolution: from architectures to learning. Evol. Intel. **1**(1), 47–62 (2008)
15. Bongard, J.C.: Evolving modular genetic regulatory networks. In: Proceedings of the 2002 Congress on Evolutionary Computation (2002)
16. Gauci, J., Stanley, K.O.: Indirect encoding of neural networks for scalable go. In: Schaefer, R., Cotta, C., Kołodziej, J., Rudolph, G. (eds.) PPSN 2010. LNCS, vol. 6238, pp. 354–363. Springer, Heidelberg (2010). https://doi.org/10.1007/978-3-642-15844-5_36

17. Hornby, G.S., Pollack, J.B.: Creating high-level components with a generative representation for body-brain evolution. Artif. Life **8**(3), 223–246 (2002)
18. Stanley, K.O., Miikkulainen, R.: A taxonomy for artificial embryogeny. Artif. Life **9**(2), 93–130 (2003)
19. Clune, J., Beckmann, B.E., Ofria, C., Pennock, R.T.: Evolving coordinated quadruped gaits with the HyperNEAT generative encoding. In: Proceedings of the IEEE Congress on Evolutionary Computation (CEC-2009) Special Session on Evolutionary Robotics. IEEE Press, Piscataway (2009)
20. Secretan, J., Beato, N., D'Ambrosio, D.B., Rodriguez, A., Campbell, A., Stanley, K.O.: Picbreeder: evolving pictures collaboratively online. In: CHI 2008: Proceedings of the Twenty-Sixth Annual SIGCHI Conference on Human Factors in Computing Systems, pp. 1759–1768. ACM, New York (2008)
21. Risi, S., Stanley, K.O.: A unified approach to evolving plasticity and neural geometry. In: The 2012 International Joint Conference on Neural Networks (IJCNN), pp. 1–8. IEEE (2012)
22. Cellucci, D., MacCurdy, R., Lipson, H., Risi, S.: 1D printing of recyclable robots. IEEE Robot. Autom. Lett. **2**(4), 1964–1971 (2017)
23. Risi, S., Stanley, K.O.: An enhanced hypercube-based encoding for evolving the placement, density, and connectivity of neurons. Artif. Life **18**(4), 331–363 (2012)
24. Lüders, B., Schläger, M., Korach, A., Risi, S.: Continual and one-shot learning through neural networks with dynamic external memory. In: Squillero, G., Sim, K. (eds.) EvoApplications 2017. LNCS, vol. 10199, pp. 886–901. Springer, Cham (2017). https://doi.org/10.1007/978-3-319-55849-3_57
25. Greve, R.B., Jacobsen, E.J., Risi, S.: Evolving neural turing machines for reward-based learning. In: Proceedings of the 2016 on Genetic and Evolutionary Computation Conference, pp. 117–124. ACM (2016)
26. Verbancsics, P., Stanley, K.O.: Constraining connectivity to encourage modularity in hyperneat. In: Proceedings of the 13th Annual Conference on Genetic and Evolutionary Computation, GECCO 2011, pp. 1483–1490. ACM, New York (2011). https://doi.org/10.1145/2001576.2001776
27. D'Ambrosio, D.B., Lehman, J., Risi, S., Stanley, K.O.: Evolving policy geometry for scalable multiagent learning. In: Proceedings of the 9th International Conference on Autonomous Agents and Multiagent Systems, vol. 1, pp. 731–738. International Foundation for Autonomous Agents and Multiagent Systems (2010)
28. Gauci, J., Stanley, K.O.: Autonomous evolution of topographic regularities in artificial neural networks. Neural Comput. **22**(7), 1860–1898 (2010)
29. Woolley, B.G., Stanley, K.O.: Evolving a single scalable controller for an octopus arm with a variable number of segments. In: Schaefer, R., Cotta, C., Kołodziej, J., Rudolph, G. (eds.) PPSN 2010. LNCS, vol. 6239, pp. 270–279. Springer, Heidelberg (2010). https://doi.org/10.1007/978-3-642-15871-1_28

EvoSET

Investigating the Evolvability of Web Page Load Time

Brendan Cody-Kenny[1]([✉]), Umberto Manganiello[2], John Farrelly[2],
Adrian Ronayne[2], Eoghan Considine[2], Thomas McGuire[2],
and Michael O'Neill[1]

[1] Natural Computing Research and Applications Group (NCRA),
Michael Smurfit Graduate Business School, University College Dublin,
Dublin, Ireland
{Brendan.Cody-Kenny,M.ONeill}@ucd.ie
[2] Fidelity Investments, Dublin, Ireland
{Umberto.Manganiello,John.Farrelly,Adrian.Ronayne,
Eoghan.Considine,Thomas.McGuire}@fmr.com

Abstract. Client-side Javascript execution environments (browsers)
allow anonymous functions and event-based programming concepts such
as callbacks. We investigate whether a mutate-and-test approach can be
used to optimise web page load time in these environments. First, we characterise a web page load issue in a benchmark web page and derive performance metrics from page load event traces. We parse Javascript source
code to an AST and make changes to method calls which appear in a web
page load event trace. We present an operator based solely on code deletion
and evaluate an existing "community-contributed" performance optimising code transform. By exploring Javascript code changes and exploiting
combinations of non-destructive changes, we can optimise page load time
by 41% in our benchmark web page.

Keywords: Javascript · Performance · Web applications
Genetic Programming · Search-based software engineering

1 Introduction

Performance characteristics vary across browsers where improvements in one
version may degrade performance in another [1]. Performance characteristics
also change frequently as a Javascript engine is subject to re-design. As a result,
performance tuning is a never-ending task. Javascript developers optimise code
for Javascript engines while Javascript engine developers optimise for how the
engine will likely be used.

While a range of work has looked at mutation-based performance [2,3] and
energy improvement [4], no work we are aware of has inspected source code
mutation for page load time in the browser. Related work has looked at web
service component selection [5], though this targets components which are a
higher level granularity of software unit.

© Springer International Publishing AG, part of Springer Nature 2018
K. Sim and P. Kaufmann (Eds.): EvoApplications 2018, LNCS 10784, pp. 769–777, 2018.
https://doi.org/10.1007/978-3-319-77538-8_51

In this paper we investigate the base mechanisms needed for a Genetic Programming (GP) code improvement system: fitness measures and operators. We trace page load for a simple benchmark web app and calculate (i) time, (ii) number of events, and (iii) the largest depth of event chains found in the trace. We inspect two operators, one which deletes statements and expressions containing method names found in the trace, and another which transforms loops to more optimal versions. To validate these mechanisms, we apply each operator iteratively to all source code locations where they are applicable using a greedy search loop. After applying an operator, if the web page appears as expected, we keep the source code mutation.

Our code deletion operator was able to reduce (i) page load time by 41%, (ii) total events by 30% and (iii) event depth by 26%. While these results are encouraging they are relevant only to our benchmark application, which contains much redundancy by design.

We cover related work in the following section, with Sect. 3 providing the experimental setup, the target web application is described in Sect. 4. We then outline the observations arising from the experiments in Sect. 5 before drawing conclusions and suggesting directions for future work (Sect. 6).

2   Related Work

Previous work on performance improvement has focused on run-time [2,3] and energy improvement [4]. Program performance improvements frequently result from code deletion [6], motivating us to initially investigate a deletion operator. Repeatedly applying deletion produces a sub-program similar to one which could be found using program slicing techniques [7,8]. Designing operators for performance improvement is an open problem, though it has been proposed that new operators may be derived by mining existing code and code generated during GP runs [9]. Program transforms are also written and released by developers in the spirit of making useful transforms reusable [10], adding another potential source of operators.

Exhaustive mutation has been used to find how robust program functionality is to source code change. Mutating small programs with fine-grained operators in a relatively statically typed language such as Java appears to result in relatively low mutational robustness of 30% [3], while larger programs in C++ appear to have high mutational robustness of up to 89% [11,12] and 68% in more recent work [13]. As mutational robustness varies depending on the software under evolution, we currently have relatively few data points to draw comparisons.

When using search algorithms on large programs it is important to focus operators to reduce search space size [6,14]. More targeted mutation operators perform program transforms which are highly likely to impact performance while leaving functionality unchanged. For example, multiple different list implementations which have the same interface can be evaluated [15].

3   Experimental Setup

We gather performance measures based on (i) page load time, (ii) number of events during this time as well as (iii) the depth of event chains. We investigate two operators, one written by the authors which deletes code based on method names and one which has been made available as a community contribution. The search loop used simply keeps a code change if the page does not show any error.

3.1   Metrics for Web Page Load

We are mainly interested in improving **page load time** for a web app. We gather traces of the web app loading via chrome browser's devtools functionality[1] (with caching disabled) using a client for NodeJS[2]. Page load traces list events which can be used to build a call graph for the entire page load process. The elapsed time for all events to complete and the depth of call sequences can be calculated from a page trace. We take the time between the first and last event recorded in the browser to give load time.

We sum browser **events** as a pseudo-measure of performance, which is subject to less variation than time-based measures. The number of events in total gives us an idea of how much work is being performed by the browser. We also take a measure of the most deeply nested sequence of event calls, which gives us a rough idea of how interdependent events are. Our intuition is that time can elapse while this call graph is traversed even though more computation could be performed during the same elapsed time if dependent method calls could be rearranged.

We assume we are beginning with an "oracle" web app which is considered **correct**. During page load, we check what elements have been loaded onto the page, and the page is only considered fully loaded when a string appears as part of the Document Object Model (DOM) for the page. We sum the number of pixels by which screenshots differ and use this as our only measure of functional correctness[3] (as this is the only functionality our benchmark provides). We compare two oracle screenshots to get a measure of acceptable variation while still considering the web app correct. We use a multiple of this acceptable pixel variability measure to get a threshold value, above which the page is considered incorrect, that is, too different to be considered the same as the original. Subsequent screenshots taken of web app variants are compared with the original oracle screenshot.

A screenshot captures the final state of the page after it has been loaded. The screenshot does not capture anything about the underlying state of the web page or the structure of the web page Document Object Model (DOM). As a result, using screenshots to measure correctness relaxes the constraints on what

---

[1] https://developer.chrome.com/devtools.
[2] https://github.com/cyrus-and/chrome-remote-interface.
[3] http://www.imagemagick.org/Usage/compare/#statistics.

is considered correct and frees the evolutionary search process to make changes which affect the underlying structure of the web page HTML. A screenshot only tells us if the page loaded as expected or not, and does not give us any gradient or measure of subsequent page functionality. A screenshot gives no way of telling apart a completely disfunctional page load from a partially functional version of the app. Some functionality is better than none, and Evolutionary algorithms rely on this gradient. In future work the HTML state could additionally be used to give partial functionality gradient.

3.2 Operators

We investigate the use of two operators, one which was developed by the authors of this paper, and the other, which was developed and made freely available by open source contributors. Both operators build an Abstract Syntax Tree (AST) of Javascript source files which are searched, manipulated and written back to a file.

Deletion Operator. The simplest way to reduce page load time is to reduce the amount of computation done. To inspect this, we delete portions of the web app source code. Deleting code gives us some indication of the mutational robustness of the software we are targeting. If any portion of the code can be deleted without affecting the correctness of the resulting web page, then we can say that there is some level of redundancy in the code. Claims of robustness can only be made within the context of the operators and test cases used. If the correctness tests (pixel differences between screenshots) do not capture important features or functionality of the web app, then deletion may find performance improvements which turn out to have an undesirable effect on functionality.

A page load trace contains method calls but also which Javascript file the method calls were made from. We use this information to find where methods are called and defined within the Javascript source. We should also note that deletion is distinct from dead code removal. Only method names which appear in the page load trace are considered for deletion. As these methods appear in the trace, we know they have been executed and would not be removed by dead code removal.

Loop Optimiser. The "loop optimiser" operator has made freely available[4] as a "community" contribution to the Babel project[5]. This source code transform is intended to improve the performance of loops. A potential issue with this type of operator is that it is not well tested[6]. While community written program transforms can contain useful improvements, they are not written or tested with the same rigour that might be found in, for example, the transforms performed by a compiler.

---

[4] https://github.com/vihanb/babel-plugin-loop-optimizer.
[5] https://babeljs.io/.
[6] The version we used was specifically marked as experimental.

Similar community efforts to produce code transforms gives the Evolutionary Computation community a potential source of operators. Though an operator may perform a beneficial transform in most contexts, a developer will still need to test and validate the effect this transform has on their code. A potential impediment to the uptake of these transforms is that we do not have a high level of assurance that these transforms are rigorously semantics preserving. For languages that are dynamically typed, it is more difficult to ensure new transforms preserve semantics. If program transforms are to be crowd-sourced to some extent, we may end up with a scenario where the proliferation of transforms becomes an issue in itself for a developer as time is required to choose, apply and validate transforms. This motivates a Genetic Programming mutate-and-test approach to the application of community operators.

3.3   Search Loop

The search loop iterates through a list of file names from the web app and applies an operator to each one. When applying deletion, the loop iterates through a list of method names and associated files. Method names and files are extracted from a page load trace and used to focus operators on statements and expressions which contain the method name. For each file, each mention of a method name in the AST is found. From each element in the AST which contains the method name, the parent statement or expression is deleted. The app is then loaded over HTTP via the chrome browser which captures a trace of the page load and a screenshot. Tracing will timeout after twice the time the oracle page load takes (3 s). Runtime and event counts are extracted from the trace (used in post-analysis only) and the screenshot is compared with the oracle screenshot to give correctness values. If the page is considered correct, the mutation is kept, otherwise the mutation is discarded and the next operator application is made. To be clear, the performance metrics are not used to guide the search process. The only metric which determines whether a change is kept, is whether the page loads as expected. The performance metrics are not used directly as part of the search loop but are used for post-analysis. When all possible operator applications have been made, we compare the most recent patch, which contains the culmination of all code changes, to the original. By virtue of the operator we inspect, if the page loads correctly after many deletions, we can perform more in-depth performance bench-marking to quantify the performance improvement found.

4   Web Application

In this paper we use an Angular2 web app which is written in typescript and is compiled to Javascript[7] It is this generated Javascript that we target for optimisation. The app is designed to contain redundancy and as an exemplar app

---

[7] Full web app code: https://github.com/mlaval/optimize-angular-app.

with performance issues. The functionality provided by the app is to load a paragraph on the screen and display page load time[8]. Page load takes under two seconds even though the resulting page would be far more effectively delivered as static HTML, instead of being loaded via Angular2 functionality. Any optimisations found will show a clearly measurable improvement in runtime as well as being easy to understand and validate. In this scenario, Angular is far too heavyweight a solution for the resulting web page state. While this appears an easy optimisation target, it is however a challenging benchmark problem for an evolutionary approach and an excellent initial problem on which to validate our approach. The challenge lies in disentangling the extensive sequence of method calls which ultimately produce a static page of text. The oracle web application triggers over 5000 events to a depth of 242 nested method calls. Although Angular is designed to deliver more complex functionality, the increased level of abstraction nonetheless makes it difficult to understand interactions between many layers of sometimes anonymous and interleaved method calls for this simple app. Our hope is that an evolutionary algorithm utilising a range of operators which can reduce the dependencies and redundancies in this benchmark application will also be able to reduce other "real world" web applications in terms of load time.

5   Results

Figure 1 shows 100 repeated measurements of page load time for the original web app and an optimised version of the web app which was derived by the exhaustive application of the **deletion operator**. Each sequence of traces shows roughly

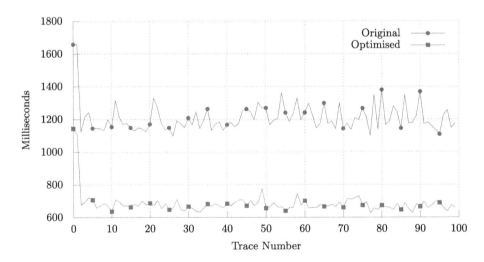

Fig. 1. Trace of original and optimised web app versions

---

[8] Demo: https://mlaval.github.io/optimize-angular-app/dev.

the same pattern, though they appear offset by roughly 500 ms. We notice that there is a warm-up factor when traces are repeatedly gathered on the same page as initial page load time measures are high in the first couple of traces when compared to the relatively stable measures gathered subsequently.

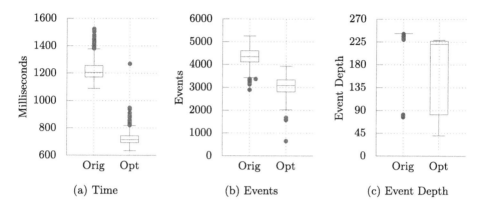

(a) Time   (b) Events   (c) Event Depth

Fig. 2. Average Metrics (1000 samples) for original (orig) and optimised (opt) versions of the web app

Figure 2 shows average values for time, number of events and largest event depth from 1000 samples taken after browser warm-up. On average, there is a 41% saving in page load time. 30% less events occurred and event depth was 26% lower. Variance in measures was roughly the same except for event depth which varied significantly in the optimised version of the app. This may indicate that there are reduced dependencies in this version of the app which leave the browser more freedom in when and how events are triggered. Although a saving of 500 ms is a lot in terms of page load time, the mean page load time for the optimised version of the app was still 720 ms. Given that the final rendered page is mostly static and the page is loading from the local machine we should be able to achieve far lower load times with additional operators and further refinements of our approach leaving us ample room for future improvement on this benchmark problem.

22% of deletions had no effect on functionality as measured and we can say that the benchmark app we used is relatively robust to deletions. This is an interesting result as we expected removing code which appears in the load trace to be more destructive. 8966 lines were deleted out of a total of 17022 (52%).

Method names found in traces of the app appear 982 times in the app source code. For this particular benchmark app, as method calls were deleted, other method calls would appear in the trace. This is due to the redundancy contained in this benchmark application.

We found one iteration of our search loop, which performs parsing, AST traversal, file writing, page load over HTTPS, trace call tree building, call tree traversal and source code diffing took between 7 and 13 s. We feel this is not prohibitive for evolution in the browser, especially given that it is likely to be reduced on further refinement of our approach.

We used the **Loop Optimiser** transform in our search loop but unfortunately no performance improvements were found. During experimentation we also applied the loop optimiser to all Javascript files in the web app and found that it resulted in a page that did not load. The existence and availability of such experimental operators justify a search-based approach which can discover what operators are applicable where.

For GI research, these results reiterate the question as to what is the best way to go about operator design. We could have a wide range of specific operators which are only applicable to certain code patterns (loop optimisation), or have a few very general operators (delete, clone, replace) which are unlikely to leave a program in a fully functional state and only rarely improve performance.

Limitations. The main limitation of this work is that the benchmark app is very simple and contains a lot of redundancy by design. As a result, the findings give little indication as to how generalisable the approach is. When considering more real-world applications of this approach we feel it is unlikely that they will contain the same level of redundancy or be so cleanly structured that deleting lines of code will improve performance while leaving functionality similarly unaffected. Additionally, though comparing screenshots is enough to detect a "correct" page load for our benchmark app, a web app which provides user functionality would need extensive additional testing.

6   Conclusion

We find that improvement of browser-based Javascript using iterative mutation and testing is possible. We reduce a benchmark app to only what code is necessary to provide the desired functionality, saving 41% in runtime. We may compare code changes against those derived through program slicing techniques [8] and investigate if they produce similar performance improvements. Finding performance improvements further to a minimal code "slice" will likely require more inventive operators. What operators to use is a pertinent open question. We highlight that community contributed code transforms may make ideal candidate operators for search-based approaches. Our findings also give a good base for expanding the work toward more complex "real world" applications with more detailed measures of functionality (e.g. HTML diff or navigation testing) and performance (e.g. user interface jitter).

Acknowledgements. This research is based upon works supported by Science Foundation Ireland under grant 13/IA/1850 and 13/RC/2094 which is co-funded under the European Regional Development Fund through the Southern & Eastern Regional Operational Programme to Lero - the Irish Software Research Centre (www.lero.ie).

References

1. Selakovic, M., Pradel, M.: Performance issues and optimizations in Javascript: an empirical study. In: International Conference on Software Engineering (ICSE) (2016)
2. Langdon, W.B.: Performance of genetic programming optimised Bowtie2 on genome comparison and analytic testing (GCAT) benchmarks. BioData Min. **8**(1) (2015)
3. Cody-Kenny, B., Galván-López, E., Barrett, S.: LocoGP: improving performance by genetic programming java source code. In: Proceedings of the Genetic and Evolutionary Computation Conference Companion (GECCO) (2015)
4. Bokhari, M.A., Bruce, B.R., Alexander, B., Wagner, M.: Deep parameter optimisation on android smartphones for energy minimisation. In: Proceedings of the Genetic and Evolutionary Computation Conference Companion (GECCO), Berlin (2017)
5. Chang, W.C., Wu, C.S., Chang, C.: Optimizing dynamic web service component composition by using evolutionary algorithms. In: International Conference on Web Intelligence, WIC (2005)
6. Langdon, W.B.: Which is faster: Bowtie2 GP Bowtie> Bowtie2> BWA. In: Proceedings of the Genetic and Evolutionary Computation Conference Companion (GECCO) (2013)
7. Binkley, D., Harman, M.: A survey of empirical results on program slicing. Adv. Comput. **62** (2004)
8. Ye, J., Zhang, C., Ma, L., Yu, H., Zhao, J.: Efficient and precise dynamic slicing for client-side javascript programs. In: International Conference on Software Analysis, Evolution, and Reengineering (SANER), vol. 1 (2016)
9. Petke, J.: New Operators for non-functional genetic improvement. In: Proceedings of the Genetic and Evolutionary Computation Conference Companion (GECCO) (2017)
10. Various: jscodeshift (2017), https://github.com/facebook/jscodeshift
11. Langdon, W.B., Petke, J.: Software is not fragile. In: Parrend, P., Bourgine, P., Collet, P. (eds.) First Complex Systems Digital Campus World E-Conference 2015. SPC, pp. 203–211. Springer, Cham (2017). https://doi.org/10.1007/978-3-319-45901-1_24
12. Schulte, E., Fry, Z.P., Fast, E., Weimer, W., Forrest, S.: Software mutational robustness. Genetic Programming and Evolvable Machines (GPEM) (2014)
13. Langdon, W.: Evolving better RNAfold C source code. bioRxiv (2017)
14. Forrest, S., Nguyen, T., Weimer, W., Goues, C.L.: A genetic programming approach to automated software repair. In: Genetic and Evolutionary Computation Conference (GECCO) (2009)
15. Basios, M., Li, L., Wu, F., Kanthan, L., Barr, E.T.: Optimising darwinian data structures on Google guava. In: Menzies, T., Petke, J. (eds.) SSBSE 2017. LNCS, vol. 10452, pp. 161–167. Springer, Cham (2017). https://doi.org/10.1007/978-3-319-66299-2_14

Late Acceptance Hill Climbing for Constrained Covering Arrays

Mosab Bazargani(✉)📷, John H. Drake📷, and Edmund K. Burke

Operational Research Group,
School of Electronic Engineering and Computer Science,
Queen Mary University of London, London E1 4FZ, UK
{m.bazargani,j.drake,e.burke}@qmul.ac.uk

Abstract. The Late Acceptance Hill-Climbing (LAHC) algorithm is a one-point search meta-heuristic with a single parameter. Like Simulated Annealing (SA) it sometimes accepts worsening moves, however it is far more simple and does not require complex parameter setting. In this paper we study an application of LAHC to the Combinatorial Interaction Testing (CIT) problem. CIT is a cost-effective black-box sampling technique for discovering interaction faults in highly configurable systems. There are several techniques for CIT; one of the most established and well-known is Covering Arrays by Simulated Annealing (CASA). CASA is a layered search framework using SA in its most inner layer. Here we replace SA in CASA with LAHC, proposing a modified framework, Covering Arrays by Late Acceptance (CALA). Our experimental evaluation demonstrates that LAHC yields better or equal quality solutions compared to SA for all but one of the 35 benchmark instances tested.

Keywords: Late Acceptance Hill-Climbing
Constrained Combinatorial Interaction Testing
Constrained Covering Arrays · Simulated Annealing

1 Introduction

Late Acceptance Hill-Climbing (LAHC) is a one-point randomised search algorithm. It was introduced relatively recently by Burke and Bykov [1,2], and shown to be competitive (and often superior) to other algorithms of its kind [3,4]. The major advantage, when compared with other one-point randomised search algorithms that accept worsening moves, is the simplicity of use. Unlike Simulated Annealing (SA) [5], Threshold Accepting (TA) [6], and Great Deluge Algorithm (GDA) [7], it does not require a cooling schedule. Rather than focusing on short-term improvement when deciding whether to accept a solution, LAHC attempts to promote a trend of improvement during the search, comparing the quality of the current solution to that of a candidate solution generated a number of steps before. In this paper we study an application of LAHC to a well-known Search Based Software Engineering (SBSE) problem, Combinatorial Interaction Testing (CIT).

© Springer International Publishing AG, part of Springer Nature 2018
K. Sim and P. Kaufmann (Eds.): EvoApplications 2018, LNCS 10784, pp. 778–793, 2018.
https://doi.org/10.1007/978-3-319-77538-8_52

Rather than producing an entire application from scratch, modern software development often produces components of related products, where some components are integrated from existing applications. This provides reusable components that help developers to produce new products more quickly, offering a wider choice of features to both developers and users. As a result, newly produced software are highly-configurable systems, which can add or remove features from the core set of software functionality in a flexible manner. Such highly-configurable systems are more difficult to validate than traditional software with comparable scale and complexity. These systems raise the issue of interaction faults, since faults in a system may be triggered by interactions between features of different components. In the literature, it has been shown that it is generally impractical to test all possible configurations by validating one combination in a single run of a system [8]. Instead of doing so, testers need a technique to judiciously sample some combinations for validating the system. Empirical studies suggest that combinations of relatively few features actually cause triggering failures [8]. This finding has significant implications for testing, since testing combinations of all parameters is no longer required. This technique is known as Combinatorial Interaction Testing (CIT).

Different types of heuristic and meta-heuristic approaches have been proposed to solve the CIT problem. Among them, one of the most well-known frameworks is Covering Arrays by Simulated Annealing (CASA) introduced by Garvin et al. [9]. CASA is a three-nested-layer search framework using SA in its most inner layer. In this paper, we present a set of experiments using LAHC within CASA, introducing a modified framework we call Covering Arrays by Late Acceptance (CALA). Our experimental evaluation demonstrates that the CALA framework, except in one problem instance out of 35 instances, is able to generate either better or equal solutions than CASA.

The rest of this paper is organised as follows. In the next section, we present background material and related work. Section 3 briefly explains the three-layer search framework of CASA and presents the proposed modified framework, CALA. The benchmarks used, experimental settings and results are given in Sect. 4. The paper ends with a summary and conclusion of this work.

2 Background

In this section we first introduce the LAHC algorithm that we replace SA with in the CASA framework, providing a detailed description of LAHC and its advantages compared to SA. Thereafter we explain the Constrained CIT problem and notations typically used in the literature to represent it, giving a simple example. We finish this section with an overview of existing heuristic and meta-heuristic approaches to the CIT problem.

2.1 Late Acceptance Hill-Climbing

As mentioned above, Late Acceptance Hill-Climbing is a one-point randomised search algorithm which is able to accept non-improving moves introduced by

Burke and Bykov [1]. The LAHC algorithm uses a list to *memorize* quality values of previous solutions. LAHC relies on a single parameter, the *history length* (L_h), whose effect appears to be well understood. Instead of comparing a candidate solution with the current solution of the immediate previous iteration (i.e., how a traditional hillclimber, or a $(1+1)$ Evolutionary Algorithm works), LAHC compares that candidate solution with a solution which was current several iterations before; more precisely L_h iterations before. By setting $L_h = 1$, LAHC behaves as a traditional hillclimber. Burke and Bykov showed that there is a trade-off between the history length of LAHC on one hand, and the execution time and solution quality on the other. Specifically, the longer the history length is, the longer it takes to reach a good quality solution; but at the same time a better solution quality can be expected at the end of search process.

Aside from its simplicity, another advantage of LAHC is that its history list only contains the cost function (fitness) values of solutions, not the solutions themselves. This contrasts with other search algorithms that use information gathered from previously visited solutions, such as Tabu Search [10]. This feature of the LAHC algorithm makes it a memory-affordable algorithm, particularly when finding a high quality solution requires more exploration of the search space and subsequently a longer length history list. The pseudocode of the final version of LAHC based on the work of Burke and Bykov [2] is reproduced in Algorithm 1.

Algorithm 1. Late Acceptance Hill-Climbing (LAHC).

Input : The history length, L_h.
Output: A solution to a given problem.

1 Produce an initial solution s // Usually at random
2 Calculate its cost function value $C(s)$
3 **forall the** $k \in \{0 \ \dots \ L_h - 1\}$ **do**
4 $\quad \lfloor \ f_k = C(s)$
5 $I = 0$ // Iteration counter
6 **do until** *stopping criterion is satisfied*
7 $\quad$ Construct a candidate solution s^*
8 $\quad$ Calculate its cost function value $C(s^*)$
9 $\quad v = I \bmod L_h$ // Virtual beginning
10 $\quad$ **if** $C(s^*) < f_v$ **or** $C(s^*) \le C(s)$ **then**
11 $\quad \quad \lfloor \ s = s^*$ // Accept candidate
12 $\quad$ **else**
13 $\quad \quad \lfloor \ s = s$ // Reject candidate
14 $\quad$ **if** $C(s) < f_v$ **then**
15 $\quad \quad \lfloor \ f_v = C(s)$ // Update the fitness array
16 $\quad \lfloor \ I = I + 1;$
17 **return** s

The algorithm uses a randomly generated solution as an initial solution. Thereafter, it initialises all the L_h elements of the history list with the quality value of the initial solution (lines 3-4 of Algorithm 1). During a search, the current solution is replaced by a newly generated candidate solution in one of the two following cases; 1) if it is not worse than the current solution of the immediate previous iteration (Simulated Annealing also does this), 2) if it is better than that solution which was current L_h iterations before. This is shown in lines 10-13 of Algorithm 1. The history list of LAHC is only updated with values of better quality solutions, so worse values would not be recorded in the history list (lines 14-15 of Algorithm 1). The algorithm halts when the given stopping criterion is met.

The pseudocode presented in the original paper of LAHC [2] used a specific stopping criterion. It stops when the number of consecutive non-improving iterations reaches two percent of the total number of iterations, and in order to avoid early termination, this kicks in when at least 100,000 iterations have been executed. One should note that these two parameters used in the original paper are not LAHC parameters, but parameters of the stopping criterion. Thus, any other stopping criterion can be used within the LAHC algorithm, e.g., elapsed time or number of iterations.

LAHC has been applied as a move acceptance mechanism within methods solving a wide variety of problem domains. Burke and Bykov [2] originally demonstrated its effectiveness using the classic travelling salesman problem and exam timetabling benchmarks. Their work on exam timetabling was extended by Özcan et al. [11], who used Late Acceptance as a move acceptance mechanism in selection hyper-heuristics. Jackson et al. [12] also used LAHC within selection hyper-heuristics, in the context of cross-domain search over six benchmark problem domains. Other application areas also include lock scheduling [13], high-school timetabling [14], vehicle routing [4], and the multidimensional knapsack problem [15].

2.2 Constrained Combinatorial Interaction Testing Problem

In the literature, a t-way interaction test suite covers a set of t combinatorial features and is known as the strength of combinatorial interaction testing. The central problem of CIT is to construct Covering Arrays (CA) with a minimum number of rows. A CA contains N rows with k columns, where each column represents a feature of the system. Each column can only contain valid values of the corresponding feature. In CA, for any choice of t columns, all combinations of t features (all sets of t-way interactions) should appear in at least one row. Consequently, the t-way interactions are said to be covered. The aim is to cover all possible sets of t-way interactions in a minimum number of rows N. In the literature, the notation of covering arrays is typically presented as $CA(t, v_1^{k_1} v_2^{k_2} \ldots v_m^{k_m})$, where t is the strength of the array, the sum of $k_1, k_2 \ldots k_m$, is the number of features, and v_i denotes the number of values that each of the k_i feature(s) can take.

The finding of empirical studies reveal that most failures are triggered by interaction between only two features (2-way) of a system, and that no failure was recorded to be triggered with t greater than 6 features (6-way) [8,16]. Most real-world systems also have constraints, where some values of different features cannot appear together. CAs supporting constraints are referred to as Constrained Covering Arrays (CCA) [17]. In this context, the goal of the combinatorial interaction problem is to find a minimum number of rows that cover all valid t-way combinations of features' values of a system, also known as tuples, with respect to its constraints. The presence of constraints in CIT is a major impediment to building an optimised CCA [9,18].

CIT has proven to be useful when testing software product lines, operating systems, development environments, and many other systems that are typically governed by a large configuration, parameters, and feature spaces [16].

2.3   Heuristic Approaches to the CIT Problem

Heuristic search methods have been successfully applied to the constrained CIT problem to construct CCA. More often than not those methods use an off-the-shelf satisfiability (SAT) solver to check whether or not the constructed rows of a CCA satisfy the constraints. In the literature, heuristic techniques devoted to CCA can be classified into two categories [16], one-test-at-a-time (e.g. [19]) and in-parameter-order (e.g. [20]).

A number of different meta-heuristic methods have been proposed for constructing and improving CCAs. Many of these methods first construct a valid CCA with N rows for a CIT problem instance, using one of the one-test-at-a-time methods. They then iteratively reduce the number of arrays of the initial CCA, using a meta-heuristic search algorithm to make the new CCA feasible with respect to the given constraints [21]. This process continues until a given stopping criterion is met, such as a particular number of iterations or a given time budget. The most well-established software application among this kind of frameworks is the Covering Arrays by Simulated Annealing (CASA) [9] tool. CASA is based on a nested three-layer search framework. An outer search layer, resembling binary search, selects a target value for N, with an inner layer based on SA used to attempt to cover all tuples within a CCA of that size. As CASA is the basis for much of our experimentation in this paper, it is discussed in detail in Sect. 3.

In addition to CASA, two other frameworks of this nature have recently shown promising results for the CIT. Lin et al. presented a 'Two-mode meta-heuristic framework for Constrained Covering Arrays' (TCA) [22], which uses a mixture of random walk and Tabu Search. In each iteration of TCA, one uncovered valid t-tuple is inserted into a randomly selected array (row) modifying only one cell. The modification only happens if that cell has not been changed during the last T iterations (where T is the length of tabu tenure). More recently, Galiner et al. proposed Covering Array by Tabu Search (CATS) [18]. Unlike other methods that are restricted to feasible areas of the search space, CATS extends the search process to allow infeasible solutions, using an objective function that balances between the number of constraint violations and the number of uncovered valid tuples. Like TCA, it also puts restrictions on modifying a recently changed cell in a CCA for a number of iterations based on the length of the tabu tenure.

There has recently also been work applying hyper-heuristics to the CIT problem. Jia et al. [23] reported that their hyper-heuristic approach outperforms CASA, employing a Simulated Annealing-based hyper-heuristic and six low-level heuristics. Zamli et al. [24] proposed a high-level hyper-heuristic (HHH) to tackle CIT, using Tabu Search as a high-level meta-heuristic operating over four different low-level meta-heuristics.

Although here we have provided a review of some of the best-known methods for combinatorial interaction testing, we refer the interested reader to the following recent surveys on the topic [16,25] for a detailed review of these and other approaches.

3   Covering Arrays by Late Acceptance (CALA)

In 2003, Cohen et al. [26] first introduced a two-layer framework for the constrained CIT problem, based on an outer search layer, and an inner search layer. The proposed framework works iteratively, performing outer search and inner search in each iteration. The outer search, resembling binary search, decides a target value for the size of CCA (N) to search for, within a particular range. The inner search layer, aided by SA, then attempts to fit all valid t-way interactions within a covering array of that size. Using a covering array initialised by AETG [19], a simple mutation operator then generates a new solution, with SA used to decide whether to accept the new solution. The mutation operator replaces the value of a randomly chosen feature from a random row of a CCA with another valid value for that feature. If the inner search fails, the outer search decreases the upper bound on the range of current CCA sizes to the current CCA size and defines a target value for N within the new range. In the case that the inner layer is successful, the lower bound on the range of CCA sizes is increased to the current CCA size and again another value for N is taken from the new range.

Extending this existing framework, Garvin et al. [9,27] introduced the three-layer Covering Array by Simulated Annealing (CASA) framework. The features of this three-layer search algorithm for the constrained CIT problem are shown in Fig. 1. The three layers are referred to as *outermost search, binary search*, and *inner search*. Binary search and inner search are called iteratively in a similar manner to the previous version, to build a CCA. Once binary search is terminated it sends the constructed CCA to the outermost-search layer. Then that layer will again call binary search for further search. The outermost search halts the search process once the binary search in cooperation with inner search cannot find a smaller size CCA.

The three-layer search starts from the outermost-search layer with a given problem, lower and upper bounds on the range of CCA sizes, and inner iteration

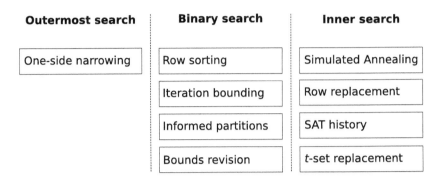

Fig. 1. Features of each layer of the three-layer search framework of CASA.

limit (IIL). The IIL is the stopping criterion for SA-based inner-search layer below. This layer is complementary to the binary-search layer. The binary search supposes that the inner search can determine whether or not it is possible to generate a CCA for a given size N. Based on the result that binary search receives from the inner-search layer, it eliminates a range of sizes of N and will never again revisit that range. As the inner search uses a stochastic algorithm, it cannot assure that finding a CCA of that size is possible. As a result, following the termination of the binary-search layer, the outermost-search layer does *one-side narrowing* of the range of CCA sizes (N) from the upper bound, and then calls the binary-search layer again. This way the soundness of using binary search is somehow guaranteed, as it has a chance of revisiting those ranges that were eliminated earlier in the previous call of the binary-search layer.

The binary-search layer has four features, namely *row sorting, iteration bounding, informed partitioned,* and *bounds revision*. This layer receives three parameters from the outermost-search layer, i.e., upper and lower bounds as well as IIL. Based on the feedback it receives from the inner-search layer, it modifies IIL (iteration bounding) and the upper and lower bounds (bounds revision). Iteration bounding doubles the inner iteration limit under certain conditions. The binary-search layer estimates the best choice for the next value of N, based on the number of iterations taken to find a feasible CCA for the current N value (informed partitions). When the inner-search layer successfully finds a feasible solution for a given N, some rows of the current solution will need to be removed as the next value of N will be smaller. When doing so, the binary-search layer keeps the rows containing less frequent t-sets for the next call of the inner-search layer, as they are more difficult to make than t-sets that are already duplicated multiple times within a solution.

The inner-search layer receives a CCA from the binary-search layer. If it receives a valid CCA, it immediately returns to the binary-search layer and receives a smaller CCA. Once it receives an invalid CCA, it attempts to transform it into a valid CCA. The inner-search layer uses three different strategies to modify and create rows, using SA to decide whether to accept newly generated solutions. In each iteration, it writes a missing t-set to a randomly chosen row (*t-set replacement*). It then sends the modified row to a SAT solver to check feasibility. It accepts the modified row if it is feasible, otherwise it tries again to modify a randomly chosen row with a *t*-set replacement strategy. If for 32 consecutive attempts it fails to make a feasible *t*-set replacement, then row replacement is performed. The *row replacement* strategy randomly picks a row and replaces it with a entirely new generated row. Before using the newly generated row, it will be sent to a SAT solver to ensure it is feasible. If it is not feasible, values of that row will keep being perturbed until it becomes a feasible solution. During this process, the algorithm remembers infeasible values that are rejected and does not try them again (*SAT history*).

SA accepts worsening moves with probability $p = \exp((C - C^*)/T)$, with C and C^* denoting the cost function values of current and candidate solutions, respectively, and T is the temperature. In CASA, the cost function is the number of non-covered tuples. The starting temperature is 0.5, and is updated in each iteration using a cooling rate of 0.0001% [9]. SA halts once it finds a CCA for a given number of rows N, or when it exceeds the inner iteration limit (IIL) as defined by the binary-search layer.

3.1 Proposed Modifications

In this work we study the use of LAHC in the context of the constrained CIT problem. To provide a fair comparison between SA and LAHC, we use the CASA framework as the basis of our work. We replace SA in that framework with the LAHC search technique, calling this modified approach Covering Arrays by Late Acceptance (CALA). Note that the three-layer CASA framework was designed and tested specifically using SA. Replacing SA in CASA with LAHC will provide us an insight whether or not LAHC is an effective alternative to SA within this framework.

To implement CALA we added the history list of LAHC to the inner-search layer. Each time that the inner-search layer is called, the list will be initialised with the number of non-covered tuples in the CCA received from the binary-search layer. CALA modifies the current solution using the same strategies as CASA. The initial length of the history list is set to 32, since very small history lengths are not that effective [28]. We double the length of the history list whenever the maximum number of iterations are doubled by iteration bounding. The idea behind doubling the maximum number of iterations (IIL) is that the inner-search requires more time to find a CCA. Building on this notion, the idea behind doubling the length of history list is to allow LAHC to accept a greater number of worsening moves, in order explore the search space more widely.

To provide a simple baseline for comparison, we also replaced SA with standard Hill-Climbing (HC) and a non-deterministic naïve move acceptance (naïve) [29]. The results of HC will provide evidence as to whether accepting worsening moves is necessary to improve performance in the three-layer search framework of CASA. This has not been reported in the literature so far. The non-deterministic naïve move acceptance accepts all improving moves, and worsening solutions with a given fixed probability. This will give some indication as to whether it is the presence of non-improving moves that improves performance, or the adaptive mechanism that controls such moves that is required.

4   Experimentation

This section describes the experiments performed to evaluate the performance of LAHC within the three-layer search framework of CASA. Since the presence of constraints increases the difficulty of constructing an optimised CCA and better reflects problems found in the real world, we performed all our experiments on constrained problem instances. We use two well-known benchmark suites:

- **[Real-2]** [17] contains five constrained 2-way real problem instances. Apache is a web server application, Bugzilla is a web-based bug tracking system, GCC is a compiler system from the GNU project, Spin-S and Spin-V are two components for model simulation and model verification.
- **[Syn-C2]** [9] contains 30 constrained 2-way problem instances. This benchmark suite was randomly generated, based on the structure of the five real-world problem instances in [Real-2].

To implement the modifications outlined in Sect. 3.1 above, we used the freely available C++ code of CASA from http://cse.unl.edu/citportal/. In our experiments, we applied four different acceptance methods to each problem instance using eight different inner iteration limit (IIL) of 256, 512, 1024, 2048, 4096, 8192, 16384, and 32768. For each IIL, 100 independent runs were executed. In the case of non-deterministic naïve move acceptance experiments, for each IIL, we used 9 different probabilities for accepting worsening moves, i.e., 10%, 20%, ..., 90%. In this case, 100 independent runs were executed for each probability.

4.1   Experimental Results

Here we present and analyse the results obtained using four different acceptance methods within the CASA framework. We report the best results as is the practice in the CIT literature [18,27]. For each instance, results are obtained from 100 independent runs of 8 different inner iteration limits per algorithm.

Table 1 compares the best results obtained using SA, LAHC, HC and the best of the nine variants of naïve hill climbing, from the eight IIL values tested for each. The first column lists the name of each problem instance. The first five problem instances are real problem instances from the [Real-2] benchmark, and the remaining 30 instances are the synthetic problem instances from the [Syn-C2] benchmark. The number of unconstrained and constrained parameters of these problem instances are presented in the second and third columns respectively. Figure 2 presents box plots for a selection of instances, showing the performance of methods over all 100 runs for those instances.

Despite the fact that CASA was designed and tuned to use SA, LAHC performs very well in general in terms of CCA size as shown in Table 1. CALA

Table 1. Best solutions (size of CCA, N) produced by CASA, CALA, Hill-Climbing (HC) and non-deterministic naïve move acceptance implemented within the three-layer search framework of CASA over 100 independent runs.

Name	Model	Constraints	CASA	CALA	HC	naïve
Apache	$2^{158}3^84^45^16^1$	$2^33^14^25^1$	**30**	**30**	31	33
Bugzilla	$2^{49}3^14^2$	2^43^1	**16**	**16**	**16**	**16**
GCC	$2^{189}3^{10}$	$2^{37}3^3$	18	**16**	19	18
SPIN-S	$2^{13}4^5$	2^{13}	**19**	**19**	**19**	20
SPIN-V	$2^{42}3^24^{11}$	$2^{47}3^2$	33	**32**	34	37
1	$2^{86}3^34^15^56^2$	$2^{20}3^34^1$	37	**36**	39	46
2	$2^{86}3^34^35^16^1$	$2^{19}3^3$	**30**	**30**	**30**	31
3	$2^{27}4^2$	2^93^1	**18**	**18**	**18**	**18**
4	$2^{51}3^44^25^1$	$2^{15}3^2$	**20**	**20**	**20**	**20**
5	$2^{155}3^74^35^56^4$	$2^{32}3^64^1$	44	**43**	48	56
6	$2^{73}4^36^1$	$2^{26}3^4$	**24**	**24**	**24**	**24**
7	$2^{29}3^1$	$2^{13}3^2$	**9**	**9**	**9**	**9**
8	$2^{109}3^24^25^36^3$	$2^{32}3^44^1$	38	**37**	42	48
9	$2^{57}3^14^15^16^1$	$2^{30}3^7$	**20**	**20**	**20**	**20**
10	$2^{130}3^64^55^26^4$	$2^{40}3^7$	41	**38**	45	53
11	$2^{84}3^44^25^26^4$	$2^{28}3^4$	40	**39**	43	51
12	$2^{136}3^44^35^16^3$	$2^{23}3^4$	**36**	**36**	41	45
13	$2^{124}3^44^15^26^2$	$2^{22}3^4$	**36**	**36**	**36**	37
14	$2^{81}3^54^36^3$	$2^{13}3^2$	**36**	**36**	38	40
15	$2^{50}3^44^15^26^1$	$2^{20}3^2$	**30**	**30**	**30**	31
16	$2^{81}3^34^26^1$	$2^{30}3^4$	**24**	**24**	**24**	**24**
17	$2^{128}3^34^25^16^3$	$2^{25}3^4$	**36**	**36**	40	44
18	$2^{127}3^24^45^66^2$	$2^{23}3^44^1$	40	**38**	43	50
19	$2^{172}3^94^95^36^4$	$2^{38}3^5$	45	**42**	48	57
20	$2^{138}3^44^55^46^7$	$2^{42}3^6$	**51**	**51**	53	66
21	$2^{76}3^34^25^16^3$	$2^{40}3^6$	**36**	**36**	37	39
22	$2^{72}3^44^16^2$	$2^{31}3^4$	**36**	**36**	**36**	**36**
23	$2^{25}3^16^1$	$2^{13}3^2$	**12**	**12**	**12**	**12**
24	$2^{110}3^25^36^4$	$2^{25}3^4$	40	**39**	43	51
25	$2^{118}3^64^25^26^6$	$2^{23}3^34^1$	46	**45**	49	59
26	$2^{87}3^14^35^4$	$2^{28}3^4$	29	**27**	31	35
27	$2^{55}3^24^25^16^2$	$2^{17}3^3$	**36**	**36**	**36**	**36**
28	$2^{167}3^{16}4^25^36^6$	$2^{31}3^6$	49	**47**	51	62
29	$2^{134}3^75^3$	$2^{19}3^3$	26	**25**	28	30
30	$2^{73}3^34^3$	$2^{20}3^2$	**16**	17	19	18

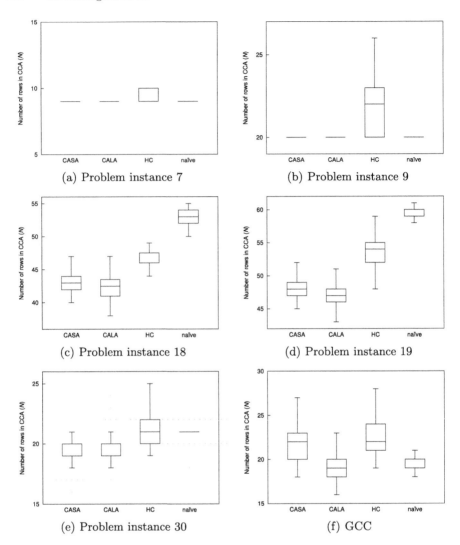

Fig. 2. Sizes of CCA obtained over 100 independent runs for 6 different problem instances. In (e) we also show the statistical outliers. In problem instance 30 only in one run —a statistical outlier— CASA reports a smaller CCA than CALA.

is able to outperform CASA in terms of CCA size obtained in 14 of the 35 problem instances tested, matching the performance of CASA in another 20 problem instances. CASA yields a better result than CALA in only one problem instance, instance 30 of [Syn-C2]. However, Fig. 2(e) shows that there is little difference in performance between CASA and CALA on that problem instance. Interestingly simple HC is able to find the same results as CASA and CALA in 14 problem instances (2 of [Real-2] and 12 of [Syn-C2]), suggesting that an advanced high-level search method is not required for all instances. Despite this, inferior performance in the remaining instances indicates that accepting worsening moves during the search is required to find very high-quality CCA. Of the 14 instances that HC achieved the same results that were reported by CASA and CALA, simple naïve acceptance was also able to obtain the same results for 10 of them. This highlights two things. Firstly, for those 14 instances where naïve acceptance matches CASA and CALA, it might be that performance is determined by other parts of the framework than the inner-search layer that are not varied within our experiments. Secondly, if it is the case that accepting non-improving moves is necessary for good performance, as we have supposed based on the performance of HC, clearly an intelligent mechanism to manage such moves is required.

Although Table 1 and Fig. 2 provide an overview of the performance of each acceptance method, due to the nature of the termination criteria of the CASA framework the computational effort to generate these results can differ. Table 2 reports the number of function evaluations executed (FE) and inner iteration limit (IIL) used by the the acceptance methods which obtain the results given in Table 1. The probability that was used by the non-deterministic naïve move acceptance to obtain the best results for each instance is also reported (p_n). Note that in Table 2, we give the results with the smallest size CCA executing the smallest number of FEs. Thus, in a few cases, it is possible that a smaller IIL is able to generate the same 'best' size CCA, however the IIL of the acceptance criterion using the smallest number of FEs is given. Figure 3 shows the average of the 35 best CCAs found by each acceptance method, for each of the eight IIL values tested.

Here we observe that increasing the IIL when using SA is not leading to improved performance, with the majority of best results using a limit of 256 iterations. Although we tested the iteration limit for CASA at eight different levels (from 256 through to 32768, improvement in solution quality was only observed in a handful of cases. This is in contrast to CALA, where a higher iteration limit can lead to improved performance. Note that in general a higher iteration limit corresponds to a longer list length, which has previously shown to improve the performance of LAHC in other problem domains. This trend is clearly visible in Fig. 3, where we plot best sizes of CCA using eight different levels of IIL averaged over all 35 problem instances. For ten of the eleven problem instances that CASA and CALA report the same solution quality from the same IIL, it is also worth highlighting that CALA usually performs fewer FEs on average than CASA (i.e. [Syn-C2] instances 2, 3, 4, 6, 9, 15, 16, 22, 23, 27). For HC, most of the best solutions reported have an inner iteration limit (IIL) of 256, the smallest iteration limit used. This is perhaps to be expected, since HC does not have a strategy to escape from local optimum and can quickly arrive at sub-optimal solutions.

For the naïve approach, the best results are almost always obtained with $p_n = 0.1$, i.e. worsening moves are accepted 10% of the time. Again this might be expected, as increasing the value of p_n simply leads the search to behave as a random walk. What is not shown in Table 2 are the cases where other values

Table 2. Average function evaluations (FE) and inner iteration limit (IIL), used by acceptance methods obtaining the best results for each instance over 100 independent runs. p_n reports the probability that was used by the best-performing non-deterministic naïve move acceptance.

Name	CASA		CALA		HC		naïve		
	FE	IIL	FE	IIL	FE	IIL	FE	IIL	p_n
Apache	12428	256	42984	1024	21318	1024	3217527	32768	0.1
Bugzilla	6906	256	5014	256	3042	256	14601	256	0.2
GCC	23966	256	170960	4096	19933	256	47475	256	0.1
SPIN-S	31709	256	28599	256	5609	256	263872	8192	0.1
SPIN-V	85587	1024	249668	4096	440130	8192	652949	2048	0.1
1	271544	256	705174	2048	93010	4096	387637	2048	0.1
2	12800	256	9515	256	7497	512	135987	1024	0.1
3	3971	256	2530	256	2550	256	2914	256	0.1
4	18606	256	7382	256	96610	8192	125470	2048	0.1
5	337674	2048	1725605	32768	211295	4096	1446352	8192	0.1
6	9279	256	9138	256	3868	256	321926	4096	0.1
7	2239	256	3723	256	2302	256	5494	256	0.1
8	262800	256	276528	4096	48474	2048	720739	2048	0.1
9	10502	256	9009	256	8851	256	24964	256	0.1
10	1773201	16384	728932	8192	14899	256	341910	1024	0.1
11	299857	256	408347	8192	18350	512	83994	256	0.1
12	78917	256	134122	512	83982	4096	166717	256	0.1
13	25669	512	14098	256	7728	512	97738	512	0.1
14	44803	256	56625	2048	303042	16384	2115549	16384	0.1
15	19422	256	6979	256	162134	8192	349896	4096	0.1
16	8815	256	8445	256	3632	256	53157	512	0.1
17	183186	512	150178	2048	21319	1024	393618	2048	0.1
18	204717	256	921257	16384	223842	8192	692631	4096	0.1
19	215703	512	1418309	32768	825576	32768	2126520	16384	0.1
20	990948	512	1826568	32768	1369898	32768	569307	1024	0.1
21	44435	256	26059	512	33339	2048	95927	512	0.1
22	5836	256	3431	256	2818	256	21103	256	0.2
23	9171	256	7767	256	6068	256	12667	256	0.5
24	572118	2048	516839	8192	622386	32768	1468696	8192	0.1
25	600257	512	1685187	32768	27570	256	1971717	8192	0.1
26	67397	256	212219	4096	10488	512	46200	256	0.1
27	11015	256	7809	256	4698	256	39820	256	0.1
28	525787	256	2672647	32768	133453	4096	1817860	8192	0.1
29	104441	2048	59401	256	378675	16384	123522	256	0.1
30	488065	16384	26133	1024	11888	512	38258	512	0.1

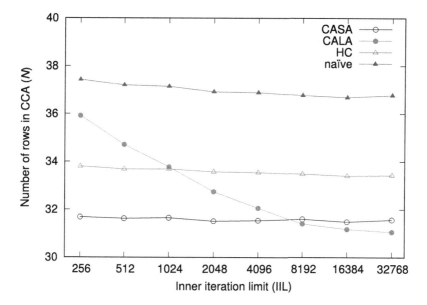

Fig. 3. Best sizes of CCA using eight different levels of IIL averaged over all 35 problem instances.

of p_n achieve the same best CCA size, albeit using a greater number of FEs. As mentioned above, it appears that some instances are easier to solve than others within the overall CASA framework. For a number of instances (Bugzilla and [Syn-C2] instances 3, 4, 6, 7, 9, 16, 22, 23 and 27) the same best CCA size is found using all four acceptance methods. Figures 2(a) and (b) show two of these instances. In the case of instance 3 and 23 from [Syn-C2], the same best results are obtained by all inner iteration limits (256, ..., 32768) of all naïve probabilities (10%, ..., 90%). As discussed above, it seems that in the case of these instances the search process is driven by other mechanisms within the framework.

5   Summary and Conclusion

In this paper we studied the application of Late Acceptance Hill Climbing (LAHC) to the constrained CIT problem using the well-established CASA framework. CASA was specifically designed and tuned to use Simulated Annealing. In the proposed modified framework, CALA, Simulated Annealing is replaced within CASA by Late Acceptance. LAHC is a local search method that is easy to implement and only has one parameter. Using the structure of the CASA framework, this parameter is set and controlled automatically, in a deterministic manner throughout the search process. Although CASA was originally designed and tuned to use Simulated Annealing, LAHC shows good performance compared to Simulated Annealing in the CASA framework. In 14 of the 35 benchmark problem instances tested CALA outperforms CASA, with CASA only outperforming CALA in one instance. Our experimental results also showed that some of the problem instances in the [Real-2] and [Syn-C2] benchmark suites can be solved using any acceptance mechanism within CASA, with even a naïve approach accepting worsening solutions 90% of the time able to find the same best results reported by CALA and CASA. Future work will focus on attempting to further improve the performance of the framework, through other features of the framework such as the mutation operator used, and the upper and lower bound control (bounds revision) within the binary search layer.

References

1. Burke, E.K., Bykov, Y.: A late acceptance strategy in hill-climbing for examination timetabling problems. In: Proceedings of the 7th International Conference on the Practice and Theory of Automated Timetabling (PATAT 2008) (2008)
2. Burke, E.K., Bykov, Y.: The late acceptance hill-climbing heuristic. Eur. J. Oper. Res. **258**(1), 70–78 (2017)
3. Franzin, A., Stützle, T.: Comparison of acceptance criteria in randomized local searches. In: 13th Biennal International Conference on Artificial Evolution, pp. 24–37 (2017)
4. Swan, J., Drake, J.H., Özcan, E., Goulding, J., Woodward, J.R.: A comparison of acceptance criteria for the daily car-pooling problem. In: Gelenbe, E., Lent, R. (eds.) Computer and Information Sciences III, pp. 477–483. Springer, London (2012). https://doi.org/10.1007/978-1-4471-4594-3_49
5. Kirkpatrick, S., Gelatt, C.D., Vecchi, M.P.: Optimization by simulated annealing. Science **220**(4598), 671–680 (1983)
6. Dueck, G., Scheuer, T.: Threshold accepting: a general purpose optimization algorithm appearing superior to simulated annealing. J. Comput. Phys. **90**(1), 161–175 (1990)
7. Dueck, G.: New optimization heuristics: the great deluge algorithm and the record-to-record travel. J. Comput. Phys. **104**(1), 86–92 (1993)
8. Kuhn, D.R., Wallace, D.R., Gallo, A.M.: Software fault interactions and implications for software testing. IEEE Trans. Software Eng. **30**(6), 418–421 (2004)
9. Garvin, B.J., Cohen, M.B., Dwyer, M.B.: Evaluating improvements to a metaheuristic search for constrained interaction testing. Empirical Software Eng. **16**(1), 61–102 (2011)
10. Glover, F.: Tabu search-Part I. ORSA J. Comput. **1**(3), 190–206 (1989)
11. Ozcan, E., Bykov, Y., Birben, M., Burke, E.K.: Examination timetabling using late acceptance hyper-heuristics. In: IEEE Congress on Evolutionary Computation, (CEC 2009), pp. 997–1004. IEEE (2009)
12. Jackson, W.G., Ozcan, E., Drake, J.H.: Late acceptance-based selection hyper-heuristics for cross-domain heuristic search. In: 13th UK Workshop on Computational Intelligence (UKCI 2013), pp. 228–235. IEEE (2013)
13. Verstichel, J., Berghe, G.V.: A late acceptance algorithm for the lock scheduling problem. In: In: Voß, S., Pahl, J., Schwarze, S. (eds.) Logistik Management, pp. 457–478. Springer, Heidelberg (2009). https://doi.org/10.1007/978-3-7908-2362-2_23
14. Fonseca, G.H., Santos, H.G., Carrano, E.G.: Late acceptance hill-climbing for high school timetabling. J. Sched. **19**(4), 453–465 (2016)

15. Drake, J.H., Özcan, E., Burke, E.K.: A case study of controlling crossover in a selection hyper-heuristic framework using the multidimensional knapsack problem. Evol. Comput. **24**(1), 113–141 (2016)

16. Nie, C., Leung, H.: A survey of combinatorial testing. ACM Comput. Surv. **43**(2), 11:1–11:29 (2011)

17. Cohen, M.B., Dwyer, M.B., Shi, J.: Constructing interaction test suites for highly-configurable systems in the presence of constraints: A greedy approach. IEEE Trans. Software Eng. **34**(5), 633–650 (2008)

18. Galinier, P., Kpodjedo, S., Antoniol, G.: A penalty-based tabu search for constrained covering arrays. In: Proceedings of the Genetic and Evolutionary Computation Conference, (GECCO 2017), pp. 1288–1294. ACM (2017)

19. Cohen, D.M., Dalal, S.R., Kajla, A., Patton, G.C.: The automatic efficient test generator (AETG) system. In: 5th International Symposium on Software Reliability Engineering, (ISSRE 1994), pp. 303–309. IEEE (1994)

20. Yu, L., Lei, Y., Borazjany, M.N., Kacker, R., Kuhn, D.R.: An efficient algorithm for constraint handling in combinatorial test generation. In: Sixth IEEE International Conference on Software Testing, Verification and Validation, ICST 2013, pp. 242–251. IEEE Computer Society (2013)

21. Bryce, R.C., Colbourn, C.J.: One-test-at-a-time heuristic search for interaction test suites. In: Proceedings of the 9th Annual Conference on Genetic and Evolutionary Computation (GECCO 2007), pp. 1082–1089. ACM (2007)

22. Lin, J., Luo, C., Cai, S., Su, K., Hao, D., Zhang, L.: TCA: an efficient two-mode meta-heuristic algorithm for combinatorial test generation (T). In: 30th IEEE/ACM International Conference on Automated Software Engineering, ASE 2015, pp. 494–505. IEEE Computer Society (2015)

23. Jia, Y., Cohen, M.B., Harman, M., Petke, J.: Learning combinatorial interaction test generation strategies using hyperheuristic search. In: 37th IEEE International Conference on Software Engineering, ICSE 2015, vol. 1, pp. 540–550 (2015)

24. Zamli, K.Z., Alkazemi, B.Y., Kendall, G.: A tabu search hyper-heuristic strategy for t-way test suite generation. Appl. Soft Comput. **44**, 57–74 (2016)

25. Khalsa, S.K., Labiche, Y.: An orchestrated survey of available algorithms and tools for combinatorial testing. In: 25th IEEE International Symposium on Software Reliability Engineering, (ISSRE 2014), pp. 323–334. IEEE Computer Society (2014)

26. Cohen, M.B., Colbourn, C.J., Ling, A.C.H.: Augmenting simulated annealing to build interaction test suites. In: 14th International Symposium on Software Reliability Engineering (ISSRE 2003), pp. 394–405. IEEE Computer Society (2003)

27. Garvin, B.J., Cohen, M.B., Dwyer, M.B.: An improved meta-heuristic search for constrained interaction testing. In: 2009 1st International Symposium on Search Based Software Engineering, pp. 13–22 (2009)

28. Bazargani, M., Lobo, F.G.: Parameter-less late acceptance hill-climbing. In: Proceedings of the Genetic and Evolutionary Computation Conference, GECCO 2017, Berlin, Germany, July 15–19 2017, pp. 219–226. ACM (2017)

29. Burke, E.K., Curtois, T., Hyde, M.R., Kendall, G., Ochoa, G., Petrovic, S., Rodríguez, J.A.V., Gendreau, M.: Iterated local search vs. hyper-heuristics: towards general-purpose search algorithms. In: Proceedings of the IEEE Congress on Evolutionary Computation (CEC 2010), pp. 1–8 (2010)

Search-Based Temporal Testing
in an Embedded Multicore Platform

Komsan Srivisut[1]([✉])[iD], John A. Clark[2][iD], and Richard F. Paige[1][iD]

[1] Department of Computer Science, University of York, York YO10 5GH, UK
{ks1077,richard.paige}@york.ac.uk
[2] Department of Computer Science, University of Sheffield, Sheffield S1 4DP, UK
john.clark@sheffield.ac.uk

Abstract. Multicore processors have now become the norm. However, for many embedded real-time systems their use introduces challenges in verification as their shared components are potential channels for interference. Of particular interest is the determination for each task of its worst case (longest) execution time (WCET). In this paper, we investigate the effectiveness of a variety of metaheuristic search algorithms for dynamically finding extreme execution times of tasks executing on a multicore processor. Over finite search spaces, these are shown to perform considerably better than randomly generated test inputs and the work reveals significant performance differences between the various algorithms.

Keywords: Genetic algorithms · Hill climbing · Multicore
Simulated annealing · Temporal testing

1 Introduction

Timing issues are crucially important in many real-time embedded systems, especially safety-critical systems, since violations of timing constraints may be damaging [1]. The correctness of system function relies not only on logical correctness but also on temporal correctness [2,3]. Accordingly, timing analysis is typically performed to verify the behaviour of real-time systems [4]; it is used to show that stringent timing constraints are satisfied by determining the worst-case execution time (WCET) of each task [5]. However, since the execution time of a task varies, it is infeasible to determine the *exact* WCET. Furthermore, in most cases, the state space is too large to exhaustively explore all possible executions [5]. As a result, either an upper bound or conservative estimate of the WCET is used for safety assurance instead [4,5].

There are three main techniques for determining WCET: static, dynamic and hybrid [4]. For static analysis approaches, an *upper bound* on the execution times of a task is commonly computed from a control-flow analysis in combination with an abstract model of the hardware architecture [5]. Static approaches require neither knowledge of the input nor execution of the actual application [5].

© Springer International Publishing AG, part of Springer Nature 2018
K. Sim and P. Kaufmann (Eds.): EvoApplications 2018, LNCS 10784, pp. 794–809, 2018.
https://doi.org/10.1007/978-3-319-77538-8_53

The results from these analysis techniques provide overestimates of the WCETs in many cases, i.e. they give conservative upper bounds [5]. For a path through a task a bound can, for example, be derived as the sum of the worst case bounds for components executed along that path. A bound for executing an if-then-else statement can be taken as the greater of the bounds for executing each alternative path etc.

Dynamic approaches verify the temporal performance of a task by running that task with a set of inputs on real hardware or a processor simulator and using the resulting information to provide an *estimate* of the WCET [5]. Compared to static analysis, these measurement-based methods are simpler to implement on new target processors because there is no need to model the processor behaviour [5], which may prove difficult due to Intellectual Property Right (IPR). A lower bound from dynamic approach can be used in combination with an upper bound from static analysis to form a confidence interval, so that the WCET can be guaranteed to fall within this interval [6]. There have also been a number of attempts to combine the dynamic approaches with static analysis—so-called hybrid methods [4].

The measurement-based approaches are also known as *temporal testing* [2, 7], which primarily aims to find test inputs that will cause the system to violate performance timing requirements [2]. There are several ways to carry out temporal testing of embedded real-time systems, including constrained random-based, stress-based, search-based and mutation-based approaches [2]. The latter two approaches appear to be more effective in identifying temporal failures in embedded or complex systems [2]. In this paper, search-based temporal testing is the main focus.

In terms of hardware, most of the today's processors are multicore. The move towards multicore platforms raises numerous challenges to the real-time system community since *interference*, which is an unintended interaction between threads on shared resources in multicore [8], prevents execution times being composable, predictable or even deterministic [9]. These qualities are the main ones expected from platforms for time-critical computing and are also dictated by the safety standards, such as DO-178 for avionics systems [9].

Interference increases the difficulty of verifying the embedded systems, especially their temporal qualities. In particular, the additional non-functional dependencies introduced by interference might not only lead to common-cause failures but also could make overloads unpredictable, which implies additional delays possibly violating the timing constraints of a system [9].

This paper presents the results of an investigation into the effectiveness of applying metaheuristics on temporal testing of a task running on an embedded multicore environment. The contributions of this paper are:

- Empirical evidence to demonstrate that metaheuristic search approaches are effective ways of reaching extreme execution times of numerical functions running on an embedded multicore system.
- Empirical evidence to show that shared resources within a multicore environment genuinely impact on the temporal behaviour.

The structure of the remainder of this paper is as follows. Section 2 reviews relevant research work on search-based temporal testing. Section 3 outlines the software under test (SUT) examples whose extreme temporal behaviour is sought. Section 4 provides the detail on how experiments are carried out. The results from our experiments are presented and discussed in Sect. 5. Finally, Sect. 6 summarises the paper and presents future research directions.

2   Related Work

Metaheuristic algorithms are widely recognised as effective approaches for many hard optimisation problems [10]. Afzal et al. [11] systematically reviewed existing work during the time frame of 1997 to 2007 on search-based testing for non-functional system properties. Their work shows that genetic algorithms (GAs) [12,13] have been primarily applied to the problem domain of temporal testing, excepting Tracey's work [14], where simulated annealing (SA) was employed.

Overall, almost all of those studies aimed to search for input situations that produce very long execution times (or WCETs), e.g. [12,14,15]; some of them further included finding temporal test inputs for very short execution times, e.g. [16–18]. In addition, some research attempted to improve the performance of evolutionary testing by using particular strategies, such as the incorporation of cluster analysis [19], the use of multiple sub-populations (each using different strategy) [3], a prediction model for evolutionary testability [16,20], and the use of high structural coverage test data as seeds and search space reduction [18]. The effectiveness of a search-based temporal testing was compared with other timing analysis techniques [11]; none of those works considered comparing the effectiveness of the metaheuristics themselves. In this paper, a number of metaheuristics are empirically investigated to determine how effective each metaheuristic algorithm is in finding test cases to exhibit the longest (or at least extreme) execution times of a task running on an embedded multicore platform.

The fitness or cost function of temporal testing, in general, is the execution time, which is measured either by a system clock or in terms of processor cycles [11]. The measurement in terms of processor cycles is dependent on the compiler and optimiser used, and the processor cycles differ for each platform [11]. This paper measures the execution time by the system clock in nanoseconds (ns).

An analysis of the search-based software engineering (SBSE) repository [21] shows that there have been a few recent studies on applying search-based approaches to verify temporal constraints that explicitly addressed the issue of interference introduced by multicore platforms. Bate and Khan [22] investigated the effectiveness of GA in estimating WCET of software running on a modern processor, i.e. the ARM processor simulated on the SimpleScalar architecture [23]. Besides using the execution time as a fitness function alone, a number of program characteristics (e.g. loop iterations) and hardware features (e.g. branch prediction misses, data cache misses and instruction cache misses), which affect the WCET, were examined to support and guide the search to find the WCET; the approach is called a multi-criteria heuristic function [24]. The results showed that, in several cases, the multi-criteria fitness functions performed worse than a single criterion of execution time [22].

There is no rule of thumb on how to choose a particular search approach for a particular (or instance of a) problem [25]. A metaheuristic approach can be successful in providing a 'sufficiently' good solution only when it is able to balance exploration and exploitation over such problem space [10]. In this research, therefore, several metaheuristic algorithms are assessed on their ability to find temporal test inputs for a task running on an embedded multicore platform. The metaheuristic techniques include stochastic hill climbing (HC) [7,26], steepest ascent hill climbing (SHC) [27], SA [7,27] and GA [7].

3   Software Under Test

For the experiments presented in this paper, the problem domain of temporal testing is separated into two problem instances: (1) verifying the temporal behaviour of a single-threaded (or sequential) routine, and (2) verifying the temporal behaviour of a multi-threaded (or parallel) routine. We choose to address single-threaded use of multicore since this approach is actually considered a feasible proposition for some critical environments: although it clearly does away with many of the advantages of multicore, it also reduces complexity, which is a major criterion in safety-critical systems.

Numeric functions are used in this paper as benchmarks because they are widely used in applications to perform basic calculations and as elements of more complex mathematical computations. Such functions are provided in scientific libraries, including the GNU Scientific Library (GSL) [28] for C language, and Apache Commons Mathematics Library (Commons Math) [29] for Java.

GSL[1] [28] is free software provided by the GNU operating system. All GSL functions are thread-safe, so they can be used in multi-threaded programs [28]; albeit they are implemented in a single-threaded procedure. A GSL's function for finding roots of general polynomial equation in the form of $a_0 + a_1 x + a_2 x^2 + \ldots + a_{n-1} x^{n-1} = 0$, where the coefficient of the highest order term must be non-zero, is chosen for the single-threaded study because it allows us to explore the temporal behaviour with varying numbers of integer inputs (for polynomials of differing degrees).

Sorting algorithms are also used for the multi-threaded study. Although these are not inherently complex routines, remains a vital part of computation [31]. The parallel sorting routines used in this paper are written in POSIX threads (pthreads) API [32], and include: bubble sort [33], shell sort [34], quicksort [34] and merge sort [35]. These sorting routines were implemented using different parallel algorithm designs. Each routine allows a varied number of threads. For instance, the bubble sort was implemented in a parallel manner by using a data decomposition design on the odd-even transposition sort algorithm [31]. A concurrent design of shell sort is to sort an entire h-partition of data before going to

---

[1] The GSL used in this paper is version 2.1, while the current one is version 2.4 (released on 19 June 2017 [30]).

the next h-partition [31]. Two divide-and-conquer algorithms, i.e. quicksort and merge sort, were implemented with fixed partitions: two threads for the former and three threads for the latter.

4   Experiments

4.1   Preparation

A FreeScale QorIQ P4080 processor (P4080) [36] was used as a primary embedded multicore platform in this study owing to a wide variety of applications of the P4080 in industrial real-time embedded systems [37]. In terms of a supporting toolkit, the Java-based Evolutionary Computation Research System (ECJ) was utilised as it is one of the most popular evolutionary computation toolkits [38], is extensible, has a clear descriptive manual and also has strong community support. Version 23 was used since it was the latest release available at the time this study was conducted. As a result, the $(\mu+\lambda)$–evolution strategy (ES) feature was adapted and modified for the experiments of the single-state approaches[2]. Particularly, a simple HC and SA could be considered as the degenerate cases, i.e. $(1 + 1)$–ES [27].

In this research, a test case for temporal testing was given as a sequence of values (or an integer vector) between $-32,768$ and $32,767$, which equals to a 2-byte signed integer data's range in C programming language. The sizes of such the test inputs (or a genome size) were 5, 7, 9 and 11 for polynomial root finding, and were 100 and 200 for sort algorithms. We decided to expand the number of input arguments to the hundreds since it is adequate enough—not too small, not too big—to be executed by a parallel sorting routine. The rest of the parameter settings of metaheuristic algorithms are listed in Tables 1 and 2.

Table 1. Parameter settings for metaheuristic search algorithms

Parameter	Algorithm		
	HC	SA	GA
Generations	10,099	10,099	101
Population size	2	2	100
μ	1	1	-
λ	1	1	-
Crossover probability (P_c)	-	-	0.5
Mutation probability (P_m)	0.1	0.1	0.05
Tournament size	-	-	2
Elitism	-	-	0.1
Evaluations	10,100	10,100	10,100

---

[2] Single-state methods have recently been included in ECJ version 25.

Table 2. Parameter settings for steepest ascent hill climbing

Parameter	Input size					
	5	7	9	11	100	200
Generations	1,011	723	562	460	52	27
Population size	2	2	2	2	2	2
μ	1	1	1	1	1	1
λ	10	14	18	22	200	400
δ	50	50	50	50	50	50
P_m	0.1	0.1	0.1	0.1	0.1	0.1
Evaluations	10,102	10,110	10,100	10,100	10,202	10,402

In particular, as illustrated in Table 1, for GA, the population size was defined at 100 individuals over 100 generations (plus the initial generation). The mutation probability (P_m) and crossover probability (P_c) were given at 0.05 and 0.5, respectively. A selection was set at a default tournament size of two [27] and the number of elite members was defined at ten per cent of the population size.

In addition, the time spent running each metaheuristic algorithm, was controlled by specifying the parameters of such algorithms so that they would take almost the same number of evaluations. Accordingly, the total number of evaluations for the GA (which is 10,100) was used as our desired number of fitness evaluations. Therefore, the number of generations for HC and SA were given at 10,099. Specifically, their initial generation evaluates two initial individuals of the population, and only the newly generated individual will be evaluated once for the remaining generations. Furthermore, a common mutator for a vector individual was used to generate a candidate solution. Hence, the P_m was set at 0.1 to produce the new solution which is *randomly slightly different* from the current one.

For SA the geometric reduction cooling function [39], $T_{k+1} = \alpha T_k$, was used since it is the most common scheme used in the SA literature and is normally used as a baseline for comparison with more elaborate schemes [40]. The parameters were as follows: the initial temperature $T_0 = 1,000$ and cooling rate $\alpha = 0.99$. In fact, the value of α is typically in the range of $0.9 \leq \alpha \leq 0.99$ [40]. Since the number of iterations for SA is high, we, therefore, chose 0.99 as the α value for the moderately slow cooling rate.

For SHC, neighbours of an individual were defined as a set of candidate solutions, where only one position within a vector of each candidate is slightly different—either by adding or subtracting a value within a position with a fixed delta value (δ) from the current one. This requires an implementation of a spacial breeding pipeline for ECJ to generate a set of neighbours in correspond to the definition mentioned above. Since a number of neighbours (or λ) are double the length of the current solution (or genome size), the number of generations and λ for SHC are varied, as shown in Table 2.

4.2   Method

The empirical work is divided into two experiments as previously indicated in Sect. 3. For a single-threaded polynomial root finder, each metaheuristic algorithm was executed ten times with each problem input size. For multi-threaded sorting routines, each metaheuristic algorithm was executed with each problem input size of each sorting function and with a given number of threads for ten trials. In order to assess the effectiveness of the metaheuristics, random search (RS), which is used as a baseline for comparison, also executed in the same way, i.e. running it for ten trials, each of which was given a random seed with the same numbers of evaluations (10,100).

Moreover, to obtain a more precise fitness value of each test case, rather than using a benchmark's execution time from a single run, each test case is given to repeatedly run with the benchmark for 100 times and then a *median* of these runs is used to represent the benchmark's fitness function. The median is used because it is not affected by extremely large or small values. Although this approach is undoubtedly computationally intensive, it is a good way of eliminating noise from the collected data. For proof of concept, we simply need a reliable cost function. Thus, such the median of a significant number of repeated measurements suffices. Other measures are not precluded.

Furthermore, since the tasks naturally take very small amounts of time for computation, their execution times are therefore captured in ns by using function clock_gettime with a clock source CLOCK_MONOTONIC[3] in order to get more precise and accurate timing. Also, this clock source is not affected by changes in the system time-of-day clock.

5   Results and Discussions

5.1   Single-Threaded Routine

The overall results for polynomial solver are illustrated in Fig. 1. Each bar chart shows the differences between the initial and the final (best) fitness values gained from ten trials of each metaheuristic algorithm on stressing the GLS's polynomial routine with a different number of input arguments, i.e. 5, 7, 9 and 11, respectively. Particularly, an initial fitness is represented by a darker bar, whereas the best fitness is represented by a lighter bar. On the tip of each lighter bar, a percentage improvement is given.

Figure 2 shows a box-and-whisker plot, where each box depicts a distribution of the best fitness values obtained from ten trials of each metaheuristic approach to stress the polynomial solver with a particular number of input arguments. In particular, the bottom and top of the box are the first and third quartiles, and the band inside the box is the median. Also, the box's whiskers indicate variability outside the upper and lower quartiles, such as extreme fitness values.

---

[3] The time from another clock source, namely CLOCK_REALTIME, may leap forward or even backward after a time adjustment.

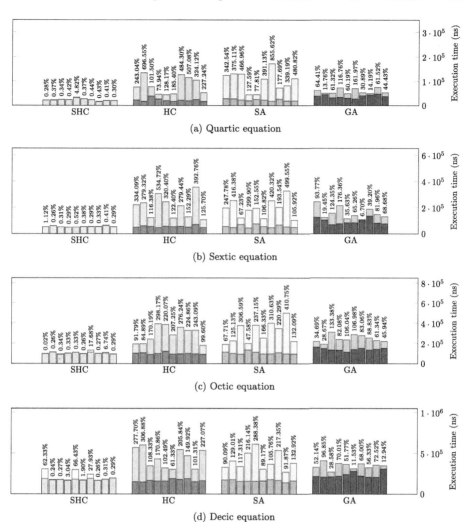

Fig. 1. Results of each algorithm on the quartic, sextic, octic and decic equations (5, 7, 9 and 11 coefficients, respectively) for 10 trials

The most extreme execution time among ten trials of each algorithm on each particular input size is given in Table 3. In each problem input size, the best performer is highlighted in blue, while the worst is highlighted in red. According to Fig. 1, there was a very small improvement on finding temporal test inputs that maximise the execution time from SHC. Only a few trials clearly gave an improvement, such as the first and fifth trials of the problem size of 11, as shown in Fig. 1(d). SHC seems to have difficulty escaping local optima. Besides, GA regularly started its initial fitness with a higher value compared with those single-solution based techniques as it gets more chance to select the

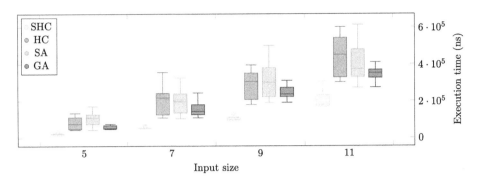

Fig. 2. Distribution of execution times for each metaheuristic approach across 10 trials on the polynomial equation formed $a_0 + a_1x + a_2x^2 + \ldots + a_{n-1}x^{n-1} = 0$

best candidate solution from its population. On the other hand, although HC and SA began the search process with a low fitness value, both of them delivered more desirable fitness value at the end.

In addition, Fig. 2 shows that the final fitness values among ten trials of SHC were very low and close to each other in almost all cases, except for the problem input size of 11, where there were slightly varied between the trials and the extreme values appeared. On the contrary, the distributions of best fitness values among ten trials from HC and SA fluctuated wildly, but overall they performed very well and extremely impressive values presented in all cases. Although GA was largely capable of stressing the polynomial solver and gave better results than SHC, it was inferior to HC and SA in all the cases.

Table 3 shows that the longest execution time among ten trials of RS was worse than the ones of SA and HC in all the cases, but better than the ones of GA in problem input sizes of 9 and 11. SHC was the worst in all cases. SA substantially outperformed other techniques, except the problem input size of 7, where HC was superior. The test cases that produced such the extreme execution times of the polynomial solver (the blue ones in Table 3) are listed in Table 4. These test cases were verified by executing each of them for 100 times and their

Table 3. A comparison of best fitness value of each algorithm over different sizes of test inputs on polynomial equations

	Input size			
Algorithm	**5**	**7**	**9**	**11**
SHC	33,980	64,984	131,467	307,227
HC	134,449	355,198	394,979	600,362
SA	171,629.5	326,249	500,971	612,587.5
GA	75,917	243,980	311,219	410,202
RS	66,978	204,990	317,108	558,421.5

execution times are summarised in Table 5. The verification confirmed that the metaheuristics are able to effectively seek values of the coefficients that maximise the execution time of the polynomial root-finding routine.

5.2 Multi-threaded Routines

We present only a distribution of the best fitness values gained from ten trials of each metaheuristic approach on stressing each sorting routine with different problem input sizes and numbers of threads (as depicted in Fig. 3), together with the most extreme execution time among trials (as given in Table 6).

With regard to Fig. 3, the ability of each metaheuristic algorithm to search for the sequences of values that maximise the execution time was divergent among the sorting routines. For bubble sort, particularly, the final fitness values of HC, SA and GA were approximately constant over different numbers of threads, whereas the fitness values of SHC were varied and lower than other techniques, as illustrated in Fig. 3(a) and (b). For shell sort and quicksort, HC, SA and GA performed almost the same in terms of stability as in bubble sort, as presented in Fig. 3(c) to (e), respectively. However, there were some variations in some cases, such as HC and SA in the problem size of 200 with 2 threads in shell sort (Fig. 3(c)), and HC and SA in the problem size of 200 in quicksort (Fig. 3(e)). SHC performed worse on seeking the temporal test inputs in both bubble sort and shell sort but was exceptionally better than SA and GA on average in the case of merge sort with the input arguments of 200 as shown in Fig. 3(f). Also, it was able to seek the sequences of 100 values that escalate the execution time of merge sort to be higher than those of GA.

Table 4. The best values of coefficients

Input size	Values of coefficients
5	21,508; 15,894; −22,267; −20,437 and 17,985
7	3,797; −24,011; 28,203; 26,154; −31,873; −6,095 and 2,622
9	26,880; 2,291; 23,227; 8,105; −12,774; 4,007; −29,306; −8,575 and 20,905
11	−15,999; 18,598; 1,673; −23,003; −29,935; −10,917; 6,219; 6,246; 19,083; 8,416 and −16,062

Figure 3(a) to (d) additionally show that the execution time was approximately double-increased when the numbers of threaded increased. It can be interpreted that shared component resources on a multicore platform may cause interference and consequently impact the execution time of a task running on such the environment.

According to Table 6, either HC, SA or GA was predominantly capable of seeking temporal test inputs that produce the longest execution time. Broadly, SHC and RS fell behind that of the other techniques. However, for merge sort,

Table 5. Execution times of the best values of coefficients

Input size	N	Mean	Mdn	SD	Min.	Max.
5	100	171,600	170,900	3,483	170,920	203,340
7	100	355,300	354,400	4,466	354,360	390,360
9	100	500,300	499,300	3,682	499,320	532,180
11	100	612,200	611,200	4,395	611,180	653,280

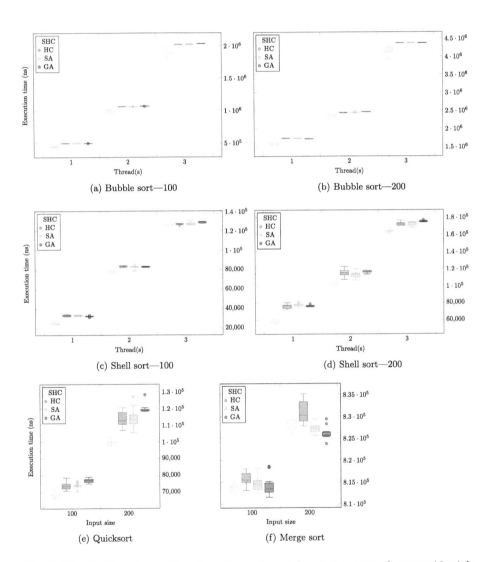

(a) Bubble sort—100

(b) Bubble sort—200

(c) Shell sort—100

(d) Shell sort—200

(e) Quicksort

(f) Merge sort

Fig. 3. Distribution of execution times for each metaheuristic approach across 10 trials on sorting algorithms

RS surpassed HC and SA on the problem input size of 100, and SA was the worst of the problem input size of 200.

Overall, there was not much difference among these four metaheuristics in the ability to search for temporal test inputs that maximise the execution time of the sortings due to the infinite search space sizes of both problem sizes.

Table 6. A comparison of best fitness value of each algorithm over different threads on sorting algorithms

(a) Bubble sort

Algo	100			200		
	1 thread	2 threads	3 threads	1 thread	2 threads	3 threads
SHC	455,695.5	1,021,941.5	2,011,617	1,625,372.5	2,412,950	4,269,500
HC	498,359.5	1,065,114	2,024,320	1,740,700	2,447,100	4,380,680
SA	497,770.5	1,065,540.5	2,031,089.5	1,741,974.5	2,452,520.5	4,384,920
GA	496,420.5	1,069,218.5	2,037,010	1,721,700.5	2,464,131	4,373,701.5
RS	474,795.5	1,057,870	2,015,250	1,649,699	2,431,220	4,346,010

(b) Shell sort

Algo	100			200		
	1 thread	2 threads	3 threads	1 thread	2 threads	3 threads
SHC	26,841	79,450	128,172	60,743	106,100	166,040
HC	34,279	84,639	127,417.5	80,300	122,254.5	175,816
SA	34,002	84,455.5	129,860	80,779	119,858	174,062.5
GA	33,256	83,689	129,299.5	78,858	117,566	176,276.5
RS	28,481	79,988	123,396.5	64,197	105,420	166,087.5

(c) Quicksort

Algo	100	200
SHC	71,375	102,942.5
HC	78,612.5	120,340.5
SA	76,774.5	126,864.5
GA	78,974	128,062
RS	70,744	106,664.5

(d) Merge sort

Algo	100	200
SHC	815,440.5	830,370.5
HC	818,020	835,110
SA	818,071	826,947
GA	818,599	829,366.5
RS	818,444.5	827,390

6   Conclusion and Future Work

This paper investigated the ability of metaheuristic algorithms, i.e. HC, SHC, SA and GA, to seek temporal test inputs that maximise the execution time of a task running on a multicore platform. The study was separated into two major empirical experiments based on a task running on an embedded multicore platform: sequential and parallel routines. The first experiment was to stress the single-threaded GSL's polynomial root-finding routine with a various number of input arguments (i.e. 5, 7, 9 and 11, respectively), which were generated by metaheuristics. The results indicated that two single-point metaheuristics, i.e. HC and SA, surpassed the population-based metaheuristic, i.e. GA, for seeking values of the coefficients that maximise the polynomial root finder's execution time. On the other hand, SHC and RS were the worst and the second-worst performers, respectively. This could be interpreted that SHC was probably too exploitative, while was RS probably too explorative in finding the optimal temporal test cases on the finite search spaces of the polynomial root-finding routine. The second experiment was to stress the multi-threaded sorting routines with a number of input arguments (i.e. 100 and 200, respectively). For these cases of infinite search spaces of sorting routines, GA was largely found to perform best in several cases, and followed by HC and SA, respectively. However, in some cases, either SHC or RS outperformed at least one-third of above-mentioned techniques (i.e. HC, SA and GA). It could be pointed out that, with the same number of evaluations for each metaheuristic algorithm to search for optimal temporal test inputs over the infinite search space of a sorting routine, there was no explicit outstanding approach.

Beside the inestimable search space, it is possible that extreme execution times may be concentrated in small partitions of the input space; this makes the search more difficult. It would be beneficial if we could reduce the input domain sampled to increase the chances of inputs with extreme times being sampled. Also, there may be a dependency between arguments so that extreme times are incurred, for example, when both arguments are large or when both are small. Future work will examine an approach that allows the restriction to a subset of the input domain and which also allows the sampling distribution for an argument to depend on the sampled values of earlier arguments.

Acknowledgements. Komsan Srivisut's work is sponsored by the Royal Thai Government. John A. Clark is sponsored by the Engineering and Physical Sciences Research Council (EPSRC) under the Dynamic Adaptive Automated Software Engineering (DAASE) project EP/J017515/1. The authors would also like to thank Nathan Burles (also sponsored by DAASE) for his contribution to the development of execution infrastructure on the P4080.

References

1. Burns, A., McDermid, J.A.: Real-time safety-critical systems: analysis and synthesis. Softw. Eng. J. **9**(6), 267–281 (1994)
2. Engel, A.: Verification, Validation and Testing of Engineered Systems. Wiley Series in Systems Engineering and Management, 2nd edn. John Wiley & Sons, Hoboken (2010)
3. Pohlheim, H., Wegener, J.: Testing the temporal behavior of real-time software modules using extended evolutionary algorithms. In: Proceedings of the 1st Annual Conference on Genetic and Evolutionary Computation - vol. 2, GECCO 1999, p. 1795. Morgan Kaufmann Publishers Inc., San Francisco (1999)

4. Graydon, P., Bate, I.: Realistic safety cases for the timing of systems. Comput. J. **57**(5), 759–774 (2014)
5. Wilhelm, R., Engblom, J., Ermedahl, A., Holsti, N., Thesing, S., Whalley, D., Bernat, G., Ferdinand, C., Heckmann, R., Mitra, T., Mueller, F., Puaut, I., Puschner, P., Staschulat, J., Stenström, P.: The worst-case execution-time problem - overview of methods and survey of tools. ACM Trans. Embed. Comput. Syst. **7**(3), 36:1–36:53 (2008). http://doi.acm.org/10.1145/1347375.1347389
6. Tracey, N., Clark, J., McDermid, J., Mander, K.: A search-based automated test-data generation framework for safety-critical systems. In: Henderson, P. (ed.) Systems Engineering for Business Process Change: New Directions, pp. 174–213. Springer, New York (2002). https://doi.org/10.1007/978-1-4471-0135-2_12. http://dl.acm.org/citation.cfm?id=763012.763025
7. McMinn, P.: Search-based software testing: past, present and future. In: Proceedings of the 2011 IEEE Fourth International Conference on Software Testing, Verification and Validation Workshops, ICSTW 2011, pp. 153–163. IEEE Computer Society, Washington (2011). http://dx.doi.org/10.1109/ICSTW.2011.100
8. Poulding, S., Clark, J.A.: The problems with multi-core: Challenges for the critical systems community. Technical report, Department of Computer Science, University of York, York, United Kingdom (2012). version 0.1
9. Saidi, S., Ernst, R., Uhrig, S., Theiling, H., de Dinechin, B.D.: The shift to multi-cores in real-time and safety-critical systems. In: 2015 International Conference on Hardware/Software Codesign and System Synthesis (CODES+ISSS), pp. 220–229, October 2015
10. Boussad, I., Lepagnot, J., Siarry, P.: A survey on optimization metaheuristics. Inf. Sci. **237**, 82–117 (2013). http://www.sciencedirect.com/science/article/pii/S0020025513001588
11. Afzal, W., Torkar, R., Feldt, R.: A systematic review of search-based testing for non-functional system properties. Inf. Softw. Technol. **51**(6), 957–976 (2009). http://www.sciencedirect.com/science/article/pii/S0950584908001833
12. Wegener, J., Grimm, K., Grochtmann, M., Sthamer, H., Jones, B.: Systematic testing of real-time systems. In: 4th International Conference on Software Testing Analysis and Review (EuroSTAR 1996) (1996)
13. Wegener, J., Sthamer, H., Jones, B.F., Eyres, D.E.: Testing real-time systems using genetic algorithms. Softw. Qual. J. **6**(2), 127–135 (1997). https://doi.org/10.1023/A:1018551716639
14. Tracey, N., Clark, J.A., Mander, K.: The way forward for unifying dynamic test-case generation: The optimisation-based approach. In: Proceedings of the IFIP International Workshop on Dependable Computing and Its Applications (DCIA), York (1998)
15. Alander, J.T., Mantere, T., Moghadampour, G., Matila, J.: Searching protection relay response time extremes using genetic algorithm-software quality by optimization. In: 1997 Fourth International Conference on Advances in Power System Control, Operation and Management, APSCOM-1997, (Conf. Publ. No. 450), vol. 1, pp. 95–99, November 1997
16. Gross, H.G., Jones, B.F., Eyres, D.E.: Structural performance measure of evolutionary testing applied to worst-case timing of real-time systems. IEE Proc. Softw. **147**(2), 25–30 (2000)
17. Wegener, J., Mueller, F.: A comparison of static analysis and evolutionary testing for the verification of timing constraints. Real-Time Syst. **21**(3), 241–268 (2001). https://doi.org/10.1023/A:1011132221066

18. Tlili, M., Wappler, S., Sthamer, H.: Improving evolutionary real-time testing. In: Proceedings of the 8th Annual Conference on Genetic and Evolutionary Computation, GECCO 2006, pp. 1917–1924. ACM, New York (2006). http://doi.acm.org/10.1145/1143997.1144316

19. O'Sullivan, M., Vössner, S., Wegener, J.: Testing temporal correctness of real-time systems-a new approach using genetic algorithms and cluster analysis. In: Proceedings of the 6th European Conference on Software Testing, Analysis and Review (EuroSTAR 1998), Munich, Germany (1998)

20. Groß, H.G.: A prediction system for dynamic optimisation-based execution time analysis. In: Proceedings of the First International Workshop on Software Engineering using Metaheuristic Innovative Algorithms (SEMINAL), ISCE 2001, Toronto, Canada (2001)

21. Harman, M., Jia, Y., Zhang, Y.: Achievements, open problems and challenges for search based software testing. In: 2015 IEEE 8th International Conference on Software Testing, Verification and Validation (ICST), pp. 1–12, April 2015

22. Bate, I., Khan, U.: Wcet analysis of modern processors using multi-criteria optimisation. Empirical Softw. Eng. 16(1), 5–28 (2011). https://doi.org/10.1007/s10664-010-9133-9

23. Burger, D., Austin, T.M.: The simplescalar tool set, version 2.0. SIGARCH Comput. Archit. News. 25(3), 13–25 (1997). http://doi.acm.org/10.1145/268806.268810

24. Khan, U., Bate, I.: WCET analysis of modern processors using multi-criteria optimisation. In: 2009 1st International Symposium on Search Based Software Engineering, pp. 103–112, May 2009

25. Burke, E.K., Gendreau, M., Hyde, M., Kendall, G., Ochoa, G., Özcan, E., Qu, R.: Hyper-heuristics: a survey of the state of the art. J. Oper. Res. Soc. 64(12), 1695–1724 (2013). https://doi.org/10.1057/jors.2013.71

26. Talbi, E.G.: Metaheuristics: From Design to Implementation. Wiley Publishing, Hoboken (2009)

27. Luke, S.: Essentials of Metaheuristics, 2nd edn. Lulu (2013). http://cs.gmu.edu/~sean/book/metaheuristics/

28. Galassi, M., Davies, J., Theiler, J., Gough, B., Jungman, G., Alken, P., Booth, M., Rossi, F., Ulerich, R.: GNU Scientific Library Reference Manual, 3rd edn. Network Theory Limited, UK (2015). The GSL Team

29. The Apache Software Foundation: Commons math: The apache commons mathematics library (2016). http://commons.apache.org/proper/commons-math/. Accessed 29 Mar 2017

30. Free Software Foundation Inc: Gsl - gnu scientific library (2017). https://www.gnu.org/software/gsl/. Accessed 21 Oct 2017

31. Breshears, C.: The Art of Concurrency: A Thread Monkey's Guide to Writing Parallel Applications. O'Reilly Media Inc., Sebastopol (2009)

32. IEEE: Standard for information technology-portable operating system interface (posix(r)) base specifications, issue 7. IEEE Std 1003.1, 2016 Edition (incorporates IEEE Std 1003.1-2008, IEEE Std 1003.1-2008/Cor 1–2013, and IEEE Std 1003.1-2008/Cor 2–2016), pp. 1–3957, September 2016

33. Sparger, J.: COSC 462 - Parallel Programming, Department of Electrical Engineering & Computer Science at the University of Tennessee, Knoxville. http://web.eecs.utk.edu/~jsparger/cosc462/pp/parallelProject3/. Accessed 09 Sept 2017

34. Weems, B.: CSE 4351: Parallel Processing, Department of Computer Science and Engineering at the University of Texas, Arlington. http://ranger.uta.edu/~weems/NOTES4351/cse4351.html. Accessed 09 Sept 2017

35. Stough, J.: Strategies for Introducing Parallelism with Python, Department of Computer Science at Washington and Lee University, Lexington. http://home. wlu.edu/~stoughj/SC13/. Accessed 09 Sept 2017

36. Freescale semiconductor: P4080 Development System User's Guide. Technical report (2011)

37. Levy, M., Conte, T.M.: Embedded multicore processors and systems. IEEE Micro **29**(3), 7–9 (2009)

38. White, D.R.: Software review: the ECJ toolkit. Genetic Program. Evol. Mach. **13**(1), 65–67 (2012). http://dx.doi.org/10.1007/s10710-011-9148-z

39. Kirkpatrick, S., Gelatt, C.D., Vecchi, M.P.: Optimization by simulated annealing. Science **220**(4598), 671–680 (1983). http://science.sciencemag.org/content/220/4598/671

40. Abramson, D., Krishnamoorthy, M., Dang, H.: Simulated annealing cooling schedules for the school timetabling problem. Asia Pac. J. Oper. Res. **16** (1998)

EvoSTOC

Robust Evolutionary Optimization Based on Coevolution

Steffen Limmer$^{(\boxtimes)}$ and Tobias Rodemann

Honda Research Institute Europe GmbH,
63073 Offenbach am Main, Germany
{steffen.limmer,tobias.rodemann}@honda-ri.de

Abstract. A way to deal with uncertainties in the fitness function of an optimization problem is robust optimization, which optimizes the expected value of the fitness. In the context of evolutionary optimization, it is a common practice to compute the expected value of the fitness approximately with the help of Monte-Carlo simulation. This approach requires a lot of evaluations of the fitness function in order to evaluate an individual and thus it can be very compute-intensive.

In the present paper, we propose a coevolution-based approach for the robust optimization of problems with a fitness function basically depending on discrete random variables, which conditionally depend on the decision variables. Experiments on three benchmark functions show that the approach yields a good trade-off between the number of required fitness function evaluations and the quality of the results.

Keywords: Robust optimization · Coevolution
Particle swarm optimization · Evolutionary optimization

1 Introduction

For many real-world optimization tasks, the exact fitness of a vector $\boldsymbol{x}$ of decision variables is not known at the time of optimization, because the fitness function $f(\boldsymbol{x}, \boldsymbol{\alpha})$ does not only depend on the decision variables, but additionally on certain parameters $\boldsymbol{\alpha}$, whose values are not exactly known.

This problem arises, for example, often in the domain of design optimization, where design parameters of a certain product are optimized with respect to a given objective function f. Due to a limited precision of the manufacturing process, often the design parameters can be realized only to a certain degree of accuracy. In this case, the fitness of given design parameters $\boldsymbol{x}$ is actually not $f(\boldsymbol{x})$, but $f(\boldsymbol{x} + \boldsymbol{\alpha})$ with random disturbances $\boldsymbol{\alpha}$ underlying a certain probability distribution.

Another example of an optimization, where the exact fitness is often not known, is the optimization of a scheduling or control plan, like the plan for the operation of certain components of a microgrid. Here, the quality of a given

© Springer International Publishing AG, part of Springer Nature 2018
K. Sim and P. Kaufmann (Eds.): EvoApplications 2018, LNCS 10784, pp. 813–831, 2018.
https://doi.org/10.1007/978-3-319-77538-8_54

plan x often depends on future environmental or operational conditions α, like the future energy demand in a microgrid, which cannot be predicted with 100% accuracy.

A common way to deal with this problem is *robust optimization* [1,2], which searches for a solution $x*$ that is as robust as possible regarding the uncertainties in the parameters α by optimizing the expected fitness

$$\mathbb{E}(f(x,\alpha)) = \int_{-\infty}^{\infty} f(x,\alpha) \cdot p(\alpha)\, d\alpha, \qquad (1)$$

where $p(\alpha)$ is the probability distribution of α. A popular approach for robust optimization with evolutionary algorithms (EAs) is to approximate the expected fitness with the help of Monte-Carlo simulation: In order to evaluate a vector x of decision variables, κ samples $\alpha_1, \dots, \alpha_\kappa$ are drawn from $p(\alpha)$ and the mean of the corresponding fitness values is used as fitness value for x:

$$F(x) := \frac{1}{\kappa} \sum_{i=1}^{\kappa} f(x,\alpha_i). \qquad (2)$$

There are many examples of robust evolutionary optimization using this approach [3–8]. Its advantages are that it is easy to use, that it can be applied for arbitrary probability distributions of the parameters α and that it does not require any information about properties of the function f, like its derivatives. But a disadvantage is that it requires a lot of evaluations of f, what makes it very compute-intensive.

Different approaches for accelerating the Monte-Carlo simulation can be found in the literature. For example, Loughlin and Ranjithan [9] propose to use Latin hypercube sampling (LHS) [10] instead of random sampling in order to reduce the number of required samples. Branke [11] suggests reducing the number of samples by using more samples for the evaluation of seemingly good individuals than for the evaluation of seemingly bad ones. Additionally, he suggests estimating the expected fitness of an individual by using information about the fitness of neighboring individuals. Aizawa and Wa [12] propose to use only a small number of samples for evaluations in the initial generations and to gradually increase the number of samples during the optimization. Like for conventional evolutionary optimization, the use of surrogate models is another option to speed up robust evolutionary optimization. Lee and Park [13] construct a kriging based surrogate model for f and use this model instead of f for the approximation of the expected fitness according to Eq. (2). Paenke *et al.* [14] describe the construction of a surrogate model for F. Thus, this model can be used as a surrogate for the complete Monte-Carlo simulation.

In the present paper, we propose an approach based on coevolution for the robust optimization of problems with a fitness function that is basically a function in discrete random variables, which conditionally depend on the decision variables. The proposed approach might not be as accurate as Monte-Carlo simulation according Eq. (2), but experiments show that it yields a good trade-off between the number of required fitness function evaluations and the quality of the optimization results. Furthermore, the approach can be used for the fast computation of a good initial population for robust optimization with full Monte-Carlo simulation.

The rest of the paper is organized as follows: In the next section, the problem is described more in detail. Section 3 outlines the proposed approach for solving the problem as well as the conventional approach and a further approach that is based on an approximation of the expected fitness, which is only very rough. These three approaches are evaluated in numerical experiments, which are described and discussed in Sect. 4. Finally, Sect. 5 summarizes the work and its findings and provides an outlook on future work.

2 Problem Description

Before the assumed problem is described in general terms, a real-world example of a problem of the assumed type is given: The robust optimization of prices for products or services offered to N customers $c_1, \ldots, c_N$. Here, a decision variable x_i is a vector $(p_i^1, \ldots, p_i^K)$ of K prices for K products offered to customer c_i. Each customer can select exactly one of the offered products/prices or can alternatively decline all offers. The choice of a customer c_i is reflected by a random variable Y_i. Although the choices of the customers can be controlled to a certain degree by the selection of the prices, the exact choices are usually not known before the customers make their decisions. The costs associated with the delivery of the chosen products or services are computed over a function $g(\boldsymbol{Y})$. This might require the optimal scheduling of resources used for the provisioning of the products/services (e.g. with the help of linear programming), which is a compute-intensive task. A function $h(\boldsymbol{Y}, \boldsymbol{x})$ reflects the amount of money, the customers pay for the chosen products/services given the prices $\boldsymbol{x}$. The goal is the optimization of the prices with respect to the maximization of the profit $f(\boldsymbol{x}, \boldsymbol{Y}) = h(\boldsymbol{Y}, \boldsymbol{x}) - g(\boldsymbol{Y})$ robust to the uncertainties in the choices of the customers.

In the following, we assume the general problem of optimizing a vector $\boldsymbol{x} = (x_1, \ldots, x_N)$ of N decision variables. Each decision variable x_i is associated with a discrete random variable Y_i, which can take a small number K of values $y_i^1, \ldots, y_i^K$. Further, it is assumed that Y_i conditionally depends on x_i and that the probability distribution $p(Y_i|x_i)$ is known for each $i = 1, \ldots, N$. The fitness function is of the form

$$f(\boldsymbol{x}, \boldsymbol{Y}) = m(g(\boldsymbol{Y}), h(\boldsymbol{Y}, \boldsymbol{x})) \tag{3}$$

with $\boldsymbol{Y} = (Y_1, \ldots, Y_N)$. It is assumed that the function g is non-separable and compute-intensive, that m is a linear function and that h and m are computationally inexpensive. Thus, the fitness is a linear combination of a function that only depends on the random variables and a function that can also depend on the decision variables. Note that a special case of (3) is a fitness function that only depends on g and thus only on the random variables:

$$f(\boldsymbol{x}, \boldsymbol{Y}) = g(\boldsymbol{Y}). \tag{4}$$

The goal is to find a solution $\boldsymbol{x}*$ that minimizes/maximizes f robust to the uncertainties in the random variables $\boldsymbol{Y}$. Since g is assumed to be compute-intensive, only a small budget of evaluations of g is allowed.

3 Approaches for Solving the Problem

As outlined in Sect. 1, a problem like described in the previous section is commonly solved by minimizing[1] the expected fitness

$$F(\boldsymbol{x}) = \mathbb{E}(f(\boldsymbol{x}, \boldsymbol{Y})|\boldsymbol{x}). \tag{5}$$

According to Eq. (3) and under consideration that m is linear, the expected fitness can be computed as

$$F(\boldsymbol{x}) = m(\mathbb{E}(g(\boldsymbol{Y})|\boldsymbol{x}), \mathbb{E}(h(\boldsymbol{Y}, \boldsymbol{x})|\boldsymbol{x})). \tag{6}$$

The expected value of g, given the decision variables $\boldsymbol{x}$, can be computed as

$$\mathbb{E}(g(\boldsymbol{Y})|\boldsymbol{x}) = \sum_{(i_1,\ldots,i_N)\in\{1,\ldots,K\}^N} g(y_1^{i_1},\ldots,y_N^{i_N}) \cdot P(\boldsymbol{Y} = (y_1^{i_1},\ldots,y_N^{i_N})|\boldsymbol{x}), \tag{7}$$

where $P(\boldsymbol{Y} = (y_1^{i_1},\ldots,y_N^{i_N})|\boldsymbol{x})$ is the probability for $\boldsymbol{Y} = (y_1^{i_1},\ldots,y_N^{i_N})$, given the decision variables $\boldsymbol{x}$. The computation of the expected value of g for a given $\boldsymbol{x}$ according (7) requires K^N evaluations of g. Since g is assumed to be compute-intensive, this is very time consuming and the runtime grows exponentially in the number N of decision variables.

In the case that g is a separable function, the runtime can be significantly reduced. Like described in Sect. 2, we assume g to be non-separable. But for the sake of completeness, the following subsection addresses the special case of a separable g.

3.1 The Special Case of a Separable Function g

If g is an additively separable function, i.e. $g(Y_1,\ldots,Y_N)$ can be computed as $g_1(Y_1) + \cdots + g_N(Y_N)$ with certain functions $g_1,\ldots,g_N$, the expected value of g for a given $\boldsymbol{x}$ can be computed as the sum of the expected values of the functions $g_1,\ldots,g_N$:

$$\mathbb{E}(g(\boldsymbol{Y})|\boldsymbol{x}) = \sum_{i_1=1}^{K} g_1(y_1^{i_1})P(Y_1 = y_1^{i_1}|\boldsymbol{x}) + \cdots + \sum_{i_N=1}^{K} g_N(y_N^{i_N})P(Y_N = y_N^{i_N}|\boldsymbol{x}). \tag{8}$$

---

[1] In the rest of the paper, we assume that the optimization problem at hand is a minimization problem.

Thus, the computation of the expected value requires only $N \cdot K$ evaluations of g. For multiplicatively separable functions g, $\mathbb{E}(g(\mathbf{Y})|\mathbf{x})$ can be computed analogously as a product of N sums. Since g does not depend on the decision variables, the $N \cdot K$ function values of g in Eq. (8) can be computed offline before the actual optimization and can be reused in each evaluation of a vector $\mathbf{x}$ of decision variables. Thus, only $N \cdot K$ evaluations of g are required for the total optimization.

In the context of optimization, there exists the following definition of separability [15]: A function $f \colon S^N \to \mathbb{R}$ is separable, if and only if for all $k \in \{1, \ldots, N\}$ the following implication holds:

$$f(x_1, \ldots, x_k, \ldots, x_N) < f(x_1, \ldots, x_k', \ldots, x_N)$$
$$\to f(z_1, \ldots, x_k, \ldots, z_N) < f(z_1, \ldots, x_k', \ldots, z_N), \forall z_i \in S, 1 \leq i \leq N, i \neq k. \quad (9)$$

Note that additively separable functions represent a special case of this type of separable functions, but a multiplicatively separable function does not necessarily fulfill implication (9). A function that is separable according to the previous definition, can be optimized by optimizing each decision variable individually. If the fitness function depends only on the function g (see Eq. (4)) and g is separable, it is not necessary to compute the expected value of g in order to minimize the expected fitness. Instead, from (9) it follows that each decision variable x_i, $i = 1, \ldots, N$, can be optimized separately while assuming that the other decision variables x_j, $j \neq i$ equal an arbitrary constant, like 1, resulting in the following fitness function for the optimization of an individual decision variable x_i:

$$F'(x_i) = \mathbb{E}(g(1, \ldots, 1, Y_i, 1, \ldots, 1)|x_i)$$
$$= \sum_{j=1}^{K} g(1, \ldots, 1, y_i^j, 1, \ldots, 1) \cdot P(Y_i = y_i^j | x_i). \quad (10)$$

Again, the K function values of g required in (10) can be computed offline and thus, for the optimization of the N decision variables, only $N \cdot K$ evaluations of g are required.

3.2   The Conventional Approach

In general, the analytical computation of the expected value of g requires K^N evaluations of g according Eq. (7). Typically, the computation is accelerated by computing an approximation of the expected value over Monte-Carlo simulation as shown in Algorithm 1. In the following, this approach is denoted as the *conventional approach*.

With a sufficiently large number κ of samples, this approach will yield a good approximation of the true expected value. Using n times more samples, reduces the variance of the results of the Monte-Carlo simulation by a factor of $\sqrt{n}$. But a fitness evaluation of an individual requires a lot of evaluations of g if κ is chosen large.

Algorithm 1. Computation of the fitness of decision variables x over the conventional approach.

$fit \leftarrow 0$
for $s = 1, \ldots, \kappa$ **do**
$\quad Y_s \leftarrow$ sample from distribution $p(Y|x)$
$\quad fit \leftarrow fit + m(g(Y_s), h(Y_s, x))$
end for
return $\frac{fit}{\kappa}$

3.3   The Lazy Approach

An approach that requires only one evaluation of g for the computation of the fitness of an individual is to approximate the expected value $\mathbb{E}(g(Y)|x)$ of the function in the random variables as the function value $g(\mathbb{E}(Y|x))$ in the expected value of the random variables.[2] In this case, the Monte-Carlo sampling is done only on the random variables and not on their function values, as shown in Algorithm 2. We denote this approach in the following as *lazy approach*. The expected value $\mathbb{E}(h(Y, x)|x)$ of the function h might be computed analogously to the conventional approach, since h is assumed to be not compute-intensive.

Algorithm 2. Approximation of $\mathbb{E}(g(Y)|x)$ in the lazy approach.

$Y_{exp} \leftarrow 0$
for $s = 1, \ldots, \kappa$ **do**
$\quad Y_s \leftarrow$ sample from distribution $p(Y|x)$
$\quad Y_{exp} \leftarrow Y_{exp} + Y_s$
end for
return $g(\frac{Y_{exp}}{\kappa})$

For most functions g, $\mathbb{E}(g(Y)|x) \neq g(\mathbb{E}(Y|x))$ holds. Thus, generally the lazy approach can provide only a very rough approximation of the expected value of g. This may guide the optimization in the wrong direction, leading to a suboptimal solution of low robustness.

3.4   The Proposed Approach Based on Coevolution

As discussed in the previous two subsections, the conventional approach usually requires a high number of evaluations of g in order to find a good solution, while the lazy approach is likely to converge to a solution of low robustness. We propose an approach that combines the conventional and the lazy approach with the objective of achieving a reasonable trade-off between compute-intensity and quality of the optimization results. Unlike the conventional and the lazy approach,

---

[2] Since Y is assumed to be discrete, g might be undefined for $\mathbb{E}(Y|x)$. In this case, the most probable value of Y given x can be used instead of the expected value.

the proposed approach does not only affect the way, individuals are evaluated, but also the control flow of the optimization. The approach employs coevolution analogous to the cooperative coevolutionary genetic algorithm proposed by Potter and De Jong [16]. Hence, we call it in the following *coevolution-based approach*.

The approach decomposes the N decision variables $x = (x_1, \ldots, x_N)$ in $\frac{N}{G}$ groups $x_1, \ldots, x_{\frac{N}{G}}$ of G decision variables, each. This yields $\frac{N}{G}$ corresponding groups $Y_1, \ldots, Y_{\frac{N}{G}}$ of random variables. Each decision variable group is optimized one after another, what is repeated for C cycles like illustrated in Fig. 1a.

In the optimization of a group x_i, the currently best values x_j^*, $j \neq i$ for the other groups are used for the evaluation of a candidate solution. After the optimization, the currently best value x_i^* for the i-th group is replaced by the optimization result.

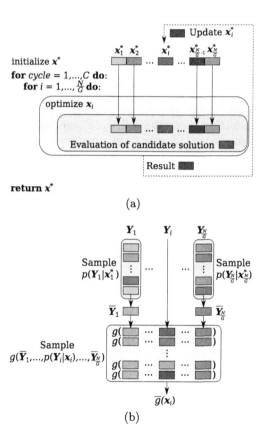

(a)

(b)

Fig. 1. Working principle of the coevolution-based approach: (a) Coevolution of multiple groups of decision variables. (b) Approximation of the expected value $\mathbb{E}(g(Y_1, \ldots, Y_{\frac{N}{G}})|x_1^*, \ldots, x_i, \ldots, x_{\frac{N}{G}}^*)$ for the evaluation of a group x_i of decision variables.

In the evaluation of a group x_i of decision variables, the expected fitness according Eq. (6) is approximated for $x = (x_1^*, \ldots, x_i, \ldots, x_{\frac{N}{G}}^*)$. The approximation of $\mathbb{E}(h(Y, x)|x)$ is done over the conventional approach. The expected value of g given x is approximated like illustrated in Fig. 1b. The random variables Y_j associated with all groups x_j, $j \neq i$ are sampled from $p(Y_j, x_j^*)$ in order to approximate the expected values $\mathbb{E}(Y_j|x_j^*)$ of the random variables and these approximations are used together with samples of Y_i given x_i for the approximation of the expected value of g. Thus, group x_i is evaluated with the following fitness function:

$$F_i(x_i) = m(\mathbb{E}(g(\mathbb{E}(Y_1|x_1^*), \ldots, Y_i, \ldots, \mathbb{E}(Y_{\frac{N}{G}}|x_{\frac{N}{G}}^*))|x_i), \mathbb{E}(h(Y, x)|x)), \quad (11)$$

where the expected values are approximated over Monte-Carlo simulation.

Since the currently best variables x_j^*, $j \neq i$ are fixed during an optimization of x_i, the approximations $\overline{Y}_j$ of the expected values $\mathbb{E}(Y_j|x_j^*)$ can be precomputed before the optimization and can be used for the evaluations of different candidate solutions. This allows to precompute $g(\overline{Y}_1, \ldots, Y_i, \ldots, \overline{Y}_{\frac{N}{G}})$ for all possible values of Y_i according Algorithm 3 and to use the precomputed values in the Monte-Carlo simulation for the fitness evaluation of a candidate solution. This requires K^G evaluations of g per optimization of a group, independent of the number of actual fitness evaluations during the optimization. The total coevolutionary optimization according to Fig. 1a requires $C \cdot \frac{N}{G} \cdot K^G$ evaluations of g. Thus, with a group size G of only 1 and only one cycle in the optimization, $N \cdot K$ evaluations of g are required.

Although the fitness (11) is only a rough approximation of the expected fitness (6), the approximation should be in general better than that used in the lazy approach and compared to the conventional approach, less evaluations of g are required as long as C and G are not chosen too high.

Algorithm 3. Precomputation of $\overline{Y}_j = \mathbb{E}(Y_j|x_j^*)$ and of $g(\overline{Y}_1, \ldots, Y_i, \ldots, \overline{Y}_{\frac{N}{G}})$ for the optimization of a group x_i of decision variables with associated random variables $Y_i = (Y_{i_1}, \ldots, Y_{i_G})$.

$g\_vals = \emptyset$
$\overline{Y}_j \leftarrow 0$ for $j = 1, \ldots, \frac{N}{G}$, $j \neq i$
for $j = 1, \ldots, \frac{N}{G}$, $j \neq i$ **do**
    for $s = 1, \ldots, \kappa$ **do**
        $\overline{Y}_j \leftarrow \overline{Y}_j +$ sample from distribution $p(Y_j|x_j^*)$
    end for
    $\overline{Y}_j \leftarrow \frac{\overline{Y}_j}{\kappa}$
end for
for all $(k_1, \ldots, k_G) \in \{1, \ldots, K\}^G$ **do**
    $g_{k_1, \ldots, k_G} \leftarrow g(\overline{Y}_1, \ldots, (y_{i_1}^{k_1}, \ldots, y_{i_G}^{k_G}), \ldots, \overline{Y}_{\frac{N}{G}})$
    $g\_vals = g\_vals \cup \{g_{k_1, \ldots, k_G}\}$
end for
return g_vals

In experiments we compared the coevolution-based approach with the conventional and the lazy approach. This is discussed in the next section.

4 Numerical Experiments

4.1 Experimental Setup

The different approaches described in Sect. 3 are compared on the following benchmark problem: The K possible values $y_i^1, \ldots, y_i^K$ of the random variable Y_i associated with decision variable x_i, $i = 1, \ldots, N$, are chosen normally distributed with a mean of 0 and a standard deviation of 15. Additionally, for each random variable Y_i, helper variables $U_1^i, \ldots, U_K^i$ are chosen randomly as follows:

$$U_j^i = \mathcal{N}(20, \sigma_U^2) - (j - 1), \text{ for } j = 1, \ldots, K, \tag{12}$$

and Y_i is set to y_i^k, if and only if U_k^i is the helper variable with the smallest distance to the decision variable x_i:

$$Y_i = y_i^k \leftrightarrow |x_i - U_k^i| \leq |x_i - U_j^i|, \text{ for all } j = 1, \ldots, K. \tag{13}$$

The exact values of the helper variables and thus, the values of the random variables for a given vector $\boldsymbol{x}$ of decision variables are not known to the optimization. Only the distribution of the helper variables as well as all possible values of the random variables are known to the optimization.

In the experiments we restrict ourselves to the case that the fitness function only depends on the random variables (Eq. 4). We evaluated the different approaches for robust optimization on the three different fitness functions given in Table 1. All of them are non-separable (i.e., implication (9) does not hold).

Table 1. Benchmark functions used in the experiments.

Function name	Function
Scaled Schwefel 1.2	$g_1(Y_1, \ldots, Y_N) = \left(\sum_{i=1}^{N} (\sum_{j=1}^{i} Y_j)^2 \right) / 100$
Cubed Maximum	$g_2(Y_1, \ldots, Y_N) = \max(|Y_1|, \ldots, |Y_N|)^3$
Scaled Rosenbrock	$g_3(Y_1, \ldots, Y_N) = \sum_{i=1}^{N-1} \left[100(Y_{i+1} - Y_i^2)^2 + (1 - Y_i)^2 \right] / 100N$

For the actual optimization, Particle Swarm Optimization (PSO) [17] is used. We also tested CMA-ES (Covariance Matrix Adaptation Evolution Strategy) [18], but did not observe significant differences in the results compared to PSO. The update of the velocity $\boldsymbol{v}$ of a particle in order to update its position $\boldsymbol{x}$ is done as follows:

$$\boldsymbol{v}_{n+1} = w \cdot \boldsymbol{v}_n + c_1 \cdot u_1 \cdot (\boldsymbol{x}_{best} - \boldsymbol{x}_n) + c_2 \cdot u_2 \cdot (\boldsymbol{x}_{g\_best} - \boldsymbol{x}_n), \tag{14}$$

with random u_1 and u_2 uniformly distributed chosen from $[0,1]$, $c_1 = c_2 = 2.05$ and $w = \frac{2}{|2-c-\sqrt{c^2-4c}|}$ with $c = c_1 + c_2$. x_{best} is the so far best position of the particle and x_{g_best} is the so far best position of the complete population.

For the lazy and the coevolution-based approach, the population size is set to 20. For the conventional approach a population size of 10 is chosen, which yielded the best results in initial experiments. The number of generations per cycle of the coevolution-based approach is set to 500 and the number of Monte-Carlo samples per fitness evaluation (the lower part in Fig. 1b) is also set to 500. The number κ of samples for the computation of the expected values of the random variables in the lazy and the coevolution-based approach (see Algorithms 2 and 3) is set to 1000. The grouping of the decision variables in the coevolution-based approach is done randomly and is changed in each cycle.

4.2   Experimental Results

The three approaches are evaluated on the three benchmark functions in Table 1 with 10, 20, 50 and 100 decision variables. The optimizations are executed with different values for the number g_{max} of allowed evaluations of the fitness function. These values correspond to different settings of the group size G and the number C of cycles in the coevolution-based approach. In the experiments, the standard deviation σ_U of the helper variables is set to 0.5 and the number K of possible values per random variable is set to 5. The conventional approach is executed with different values (5, 10, 50 and 100) for the number κ of Monte-Carlo samples. For each setting, 100 optimization trials with different seeds for the random initialization of the helper variables and of the possible values of the random variables are executed. At the end of each trial, the helper variables initialized at the beginning of a trial are used to evaluate the decision variables yielded by the optimization.

The Tables 2, 3, 4 and 5 show the medians of the results of the 100 trials with the different approaches on the Schwefel No. 1.2 function g_1 for 10, 20, 50 and 100 decision variables, respectively. In the tables, $conv_\kappa$ stands for the conventional approach with κ Monte-Carlo samples, $coevo$ stands for the coevolution-based approach and $lazy$ for the lazy approach.

The superscripts indicate whether the results of an approach are significantly better than the results of another approach, according to the two-sided Wilcoxon rank sum test with a significance level of 0.05. For example, a 1 means significant better results than with the first approach in the table (conventional approach with $\kappa = 5$). A "-" in the table indicates that the number g_{max} of allowed evaluations of the fitness function is too low to execute at least one generation of the optimization.

With 10 and 20 decision variables, the proposed coevolution-based approach yielded the best results for 10 of the 12 settings. With 50 and 100 variables, it is even more superior compared to the other evaluated approaches. With 10 decision variables, the conventional approach is significantly better than the lazy approach for $g_{max} \geq 6250$. This is not the case for higher numbers of decision variables.

Table 2. Medians of 100 optimization trials with the different approaches on benchmark function g_1 (Schwefel No. 1.2) with 10 decision variables. The superscripts indicate whether an approach performed significantly better compared to another approach (according to two-sided Wilcoxon rank-sum test with a significance level of 0.05).

G	C	g_{max}	$conv_5$	$conv_{10}$	$conv_{50}$	$conv_{100}$	coevo	lazy
1	1	50	35.73	-	-	-	**16.60**[1]	25.05[1]
1	2	100	30.54	35.73	-	-	**13.84**[1,2,6]	25.24[2]
1	4	200	25.91	31.69	-	-	**13.07**[1,2,6]	19.56[1,2]
1	8	400	21.58	22.68	-	-	**12.78**[1,2]	18.48
2	1	125	31.71	34.66	-	-	**17.07**[1,2]	21.13[1,2]
2	2	250	24.44	24.09	-	-	**14.04**[1,2]	20.28
2	4	500	20.75[3]	22.96[3]	35.39	-	**11.94**[1,2,3,6]	18.62[3]
2	8	1000	16.28[3,4]	17.90[3,4]	24.49	34.03	**10.77**[1,2,3,4,6]	20.69[4]
5	1	6250	11.55[3,4,6]	12.37[4]	15.21	16.88	**10.82**[3,4,6]	16.30
5	2	12500	**10.07**[6]	12.02[6]	13.40	13.10	10.56[3,4,6]	18.72
5	4	25000	**9.73**	11.79[6]	10.81	12.15	10.22[6]	16.52
5	8	50000	10.54	12.11[6]	10.36[6]	10.85[6]	**10.00**[6]	18.77

Table 3. Results on g_1 analogous to Table 2 with 20 decision variables.

G	C	g_{max}	$conv_5$	$conv_{10}$	$conv_{50}$	$conv_{100}$	coevo	lazy
1	1	100	134.71	145.52	-	-	**72.18**[1,2]	77.15[1,2]
1	2	200	120.15	139.53	-	-	**57.11**[1,2,6]	78.34[1,2]
1	4	400	99.87	96.75	-	-	**52.32**[1,2,6]	67.00[1,2]
1	8	800	79.74[3]	89.08[3]	134.33	-	**51.31**[1,2,3,6]	86.19[3]
2	1	250	120.63	102.17	-	-	**61.57**[1,2]	74.63[1,2]
2	2	500	89.33[3]	97.64[3]	145.52	-	**42.46**[1,2,3,6]	73.87[3]
2	4	1000	82.73[3,4]	79.84[3,4]	118.37[4]	136.61	**40.69**[1,2,3,4,6]	72.40[3,4]
2	8	2000	59.04[3,4]	75.54[4]	80.95	99.65	**31.99**[1,2,3,4,6]	71.03[3,4]
5	1	12500	49.69	**45.03**[4]	50.72	61.07	45.70	56.83
5	2	25000	50.18	**37.97**[1,4]	45.42	48.27	38.42	50.16
5	4	50000	42.47	40.48	35.32	42.67	**34.60**[1,4]	48.13
5	8	100000	44.77	39.09	33.19	42.50	**27.68**[1,4,6]	43.08

The experimental results on the Cubed Maximum function g_2 are shown in the Tables 6, 7, 8 and 9. Again, in most cases the coevolution-based approach yielded the best results. But it can be seen that the results do not improve with an increasing group size. With a group size of 1 and 8 cycles, the coevolution-based approach yielded better results than the other approaches with a g_{max} corresponding to a group size of 5 and 8 cycles for all considered numbers of

Table 4. Results on g_1 analogous to Table 2 with 50 decision variables.

G	C	g_{max}	$conv_5$	$conv_{10}$	$conv_{50}$	$conv_{100}$	coevo	lazy
1	1	250	705.93	754.01	-	-	**326.68**[1,2,6]	675.99
1	2	500	675.42[2,3]	825.89	782.23	-	**329.83**[1,2,3,6]	539.26[2,3]
1	4	1000	600.76[4]	571.68[4]	661.59[4]	923.60	**294.05**[1,2,3,4,6]	441.36[1,3,4]
1	8	2000	427.66[3,4]	508.02[4]	567.20[4]	747.29	**262.38**[1,2,3,4,6]	356.26[1,2,3,4]
2	1	625	652.42[3]	680.87	780.59	-	**407.45**[1,2,3,6]	552.25[3]
2	2	1250	572.30[4]	552.51[4]	647.36	898.28	**275.49**[1,2,3,4,6]	418.28[1,2,3,4]
2	4	2500	390.34[4]	592.61[4]	554.56[4]	721.24	**253.68**[1,2,3,4,6]	310.17[2,3,4]
2	8	5000	422.12[4]	515.12	528.57	557.56	**194.30**[1,2,3,4,6]	342.74[2,3,4]
5	1	31250	332.09	305.71	355.56	354.41	**244.02**[3,4]	271.80[4]
5	2	62500	255.99	288.86	333.69	317.69	**220.16**[3,4]	234.56
5	4	125000	222.08	255.69	276.04	238.07	**220.95**	304.01
5	8	250000	237.04	247.01	231.36	217.12	**164.68**[1,2,3,4,6]	245.84

Table 5. Results on g_1 analogous to Table 2 with 100 decision variables.

G	C	g_{max}	$conv_5$	$conv_{10}$	$conv_{50}$	$conv_{100}$	coevo	lazy
1	1	500	2507.85[3]	3014.68[3]	3841.61	-	1681.57[1,2,3]	**1643.98**[1,2,3]
1	2	1000	2432.49[3,4]	2192.03[3,4]	3617.54	4322.18	**1302.16**[1,2,3,4]	1663.43[1,2,3,4]
1	4	2000	2336.02[4]	2444.14[4]	2971.89	3326.27	**1077.93**[1,2,3,4,6]	1574.03[1,2,3,4]
1	8	4000	2057.88[4]	2179.68	2451.37	2795.51	**963.33**[1,2,3,4,6]	1281.49[1,2,3,4]
2	1	1250	2320.20[3,4]	2192.03[3,4]	3355.35	3662.65	**1216.28**[1,2,3,4]	1663.43[1,2,3,4]
2	2	2500	2387.29[4]	2477.34	2439.90	3219.95	**900.02**[1,2,3,4,6]	1557.61[1,2,3,4]
2	4	5000	1912.52[4]	1693.14[4]	2702.69	2704.55	**714.14**[1,2,3,4,6]	1201.97[1,2,3,4]
2	8	10000	2119.62	1720.91[4]	2037.06	2197.62	**584.07**[1,2,3,4,6]	1265.38[1,2,3,4]
5	1	62500	1440.20	1309.60	1219.28	1347.65	**1130.05**	1232.24
5	2	125000	1404.63	1217.75	1171.65	1029.05	**907.52**[1,2,3,4]	1170.57
5	4	250000	1169.78	1080.15	1032.91	1067.33	**666.39**[1,2,3,4]	1064.13
5	8	500000	973.41	935.23	1121.89	869.31	**532.67**[1,2,3,4]	851.56[3]

decision variables. With an increasing number of variables, the conventional approach becomes more and more superior to the lazy approach.

Tables 10, 11, 12 and 13 show the results on the Rosenbrock function. It can be seen that the coevolution-based approach yields the best results for all settings. With 20, 50 and 100 decision variables, it is significantly better than all other approaches for all considered values of g_{max}. Interestingly, the results do not improve with an increasing group size or an increasing number of cycles. This indicates that the Rosenbrock function is well suited for the separate optimization of the individual decision variables, although it is non-separable.

Table 6. Medians of 100 optimization trials with the different approaches on benchmark function g_2 (Cubed Maximum) with 10 decision variables. The superscripts indicate whether an approach performed significantly better compared to another approach (according to two-sided Wilcoxon rank-sum test with a significance level of 0.05).

G	C	g_{max}	$conv_5$	$conv_{10}$	$conv_{50}$	$conv_{100}$	$coevo$	$lazy$
1	1	50	13817	-	-	-	$\mathbf{5425}^1$	7044^1
1	2	100	8173^2	13044	-	-	$\mathbf{3210}^{1,2,6}$	7283^2
1	4	200	6289^2	8324	-	-	$\mathbf{2389}^{1,2,6}$	6046^2
1	8	400	5687	6500	-	-	$\mathbf{2389}^{1,2,6}$	6362
2	1	125	7608^2	11052	-	-	$\mathbf{4857}^{1,2}$	6937^2
2	2	250	6289	7421	-	-	$\mathbf{3163}^{1,2,6}$	6723
2	4	500	5426^3	6500^3	13044	-	$\mathbf{2440}^{1,2,3,6}$	6636^3
2	8	1000	$4169^{3,4}$	$5376^{3,4}$	9168^4	13044	$\mathbf{2484}^{1,2,3,4,6}$	$5626^{3,4}$
5	1	6250	$\mathbf{2890}^{3,4,5,6}$	$3263^{3,4,6}$	5280	6411	4648^4	5746
5	2	12500	$3329^{4,6}$	$2997^{4,6}$	$3939^{4,6}$	5241	$\mathbf{2991}^{3,4,6}$	7154
5	4	25000	3390^6	2997^6	3198^6	3844^6	$\mathbf{2799}^{4,6}$	6977
5	8	50000	3329^6	2860^6	2908^6	3313^6	$\mathbf{2799}^6$	6504

Table 7. Results on g_2 analogous to Table 6 with 20 decision variables.

G	C	g_{max}	$conv_5$	$conv_{10}$	$conv_{50}$	$conv_{100}$	$coevo$	$lazy$
1	1	100	17682	20521	-	-	$\mathbf{9871}^{1,2,6}$	$14257^{1,2}$
1	2	200	15167	18059	-	-	$\mathbf{6303}^{1,2,6}$	14199^2
1	4	400	10644^2	15092	-	-	$\mathbf{4148}^{1,2,6}$	13574
1	8	800	8983^3	11192^3	18960	-	$\mathbf{4227}^{1,2,3,6}$	10146^3
2	1	250	13817	17105	-	-	$\mathbf{9716}^{1,2,6}$	14109^2
2	2	500	$9808^{2,3}$	13109^3	20390	-	$\mathbf{6303}^{1,2,3,6}$	12075^3
2	4	1000	$8636^{2,3,4}$	$10949^{3,4}$	16918^4	19809	$\mathbf{4227}^{1,2,3,4,6}$	$11531^{3,4}$
2	8	2000	$7530^{3,4}$	$7587^{3,4}$	13527^4	16490	$\mathbf{4227}^{1,2,3,4,6}$	$8868^{3,4}$
5	1	12500	$6763^{4,5}$	$\mathbf{6693}^{4,5,6}$	$7544^{4,5}$	9269	9845	10862
5	2	25000	6411^6	6384^6	6411^6	7680	$\mathbf{5839}^{4,6}$	10073
5	4	50000	6411^6	6539^6	5821^6	6220^6	$\mathbf{4178}^{1,2,3,4,6}$	11235
5	8	100000	6929^6	6290^6	$5807^{1,6}$	$5733^{1,6}$	$\mathbf{4178}^{1,2,3,4,6}$	12946

In a further experiment, we investigated the impact of the standard deviation σ_U of the distribution of the helper variables on the optimization results and executed the optimizations with different values for σ_U. With an increasing σ_U, the uncertainty increases. Table 14 shows the median results of 100 optimization trials on benchmark function g_1 with 20 decision variables executed with a group size of $G = 2$ and with $C = 8$ cycles and a corresponding g_{max}

Table 8. Results on g_2 analogous to Table 6 with 50 decision variables.

G	C	g_{max}	$conv_5$	$conv_{10}$	$conv_{50}$	$conv_{100}$	coevo	lazy
1	1	250	27436	30258	-	-	**20482**^{1,2,6}	26887
1	2	500	23945^3	23593^3	35884	-	**12896**^{1,2,3,6}	25945^3
1	4	1000	19622^{3,4,6}	20854^{3,4,6}	30020^4	35884	**7340**^{1,2,3,4,6}	23794^{3,4}
1	8	2000	17646^{3,4,6}	17291^{3,4,6}	23579^4	30866	**7199**^{1,2,3,4,6}	22659^4
2	1	625	22778^3	23224^3	35884	-	**20187**^{2,3}	23307^3
2	2	1250	19262^{3,4,6}	19524^{3,4,6}	28100^4	35884	**13031**^{1,2,3,4,6}	23682^{3,4}
2	4	2500	16042^{3,4,6}	16868^{3,4,6}	22565^4	26548	**7304**^{1,2,3,4,6}	21822^4
2	8	5000	15382^{3,4,6}	14335^{3,4,6}	19642^4	23811	**7260**^{1,2,3,4,6}	21245^4
5	1	31250	12343^{4,5,6}	**11575**^{4,5,6}	12335^{4,5,6}	15640^5	19152	18980
5	2	62500	11950	**11605**^{6}	12153^6	13238^6	11634^{4,6}	18300
5	4	125000	11950^6	11575^6	11421^6	11917^6	**7428**^{1,2,3,4,6}	18247
5	8	250000	11961	11495^6	11237^6	11498^6	**7160**^{1,2,3,4,6}	17738

Table 9. Results on g_2 analogous to Table 6 with 100 decision variables.

G	C	g_{max}	$conv_5$	$conv_{10}$	$conv_{50}$	$conv_{100}$	coevo	lazy
1	1	500	32419^{2,3,6}	36690^3	54329	-	**31159**^{2,3,6}	39621^3
1	2	1000	31353^{3,4,6}	32777^{3,4}	45533^4	54006	**18258**^{1,2,3,4,6}	37695^{3,4}
1	4	2000	25868^{2,3,4,6}	27504^{3,4,6}	39369^4	45940	**11158**^{1,2,3,4,6}	33938^4
1	8	4000	23801^{3,4,6}	24153^{3,4,6}	32101^4	37976	**10811**^{1,2,3,4,6}	33003^4
2	1	1250	**27794**^{2,3,4,6}	32661^{3,4}	43599^4	50762	31159^{3,4,6}	37624^{3,4}
2	2	2500	24673^{3,4,6}	25772^{3,4,6}	37185^4	40577	**18683**^{1,2,3,4,6}	33513^4
2	4	5000	22889^{3,4,6}	23684^{3,4,6}	31152^4	35774	**11294**^{1,2,3,4,6}	32508
2	8	10000	20412^{3,4,6}	21163^{3,4,6}	27660^{4,6}	31840	**11278**^{1,2,3,4,6}	33098
5	1	62500	18372^{4,5,6}	**18163**^{4,5,6}	19750^{5,6}	21410^{5,6}	31520	27921^5
5	2	125000	18198^6	**17828**^{4,6}	19530^6	19673^6	18843^6	24101
5	4	250000	18403^6	17720^6	19298^6	18499^6	**11385**^{1,2,3,4,6}	23739
5	8	500000	18339^6	17962^6	19152^6	18383^6	**10811**^{1,2,3,4,6}	23739

of 2000 for different values of σ_U. The number K of possible values per random variable is again set to 5. For all considered values of σ_U, the coevolution-based approach yields the best results. But with an increasing σ_U, the results with the different approaches become more and more similar because the quality of the optimization results becomes more and more random due to an increasing uncertainty. The results on the benchmark functions g_2 and g_3 are not shown because they are similar to those on g_1.

In a final experiment, we evaluated the different approaches for different numbers K of possible values per random variable. Again, the optimizations

Table 10. Medians of 100 optimization trials with the different approaches on benchmark function g_3 (Rosenbrock) with 10 decision variables. The superscripts indicate whether an approach performed significantly better compared to another approach (according to two-sided Wilcoxon rank-sum test with a significance level of 0.05).

G	C	g_{max}	$conv_5$	$conv_{10}$	$conv_{50}$	$conv_{100}$	$coevo$	$lazy$
1	1	50	57256	-	-	-	$\mathbf{4818}^{1,6}$	30652^1
1	2	100	32068^2	46138	-	-	$\mathbf{4684}^{1,2,6}$	$20554^{1,2}$
1	4	200	21377	26245	-	-	$\mathbf{4684}^{1,2,6}$	18364^2
1	8	400	18300	26135	-	-	$\mathbf{4684}^{1,2,6}$	18100
2	1	125	30100	39979	-	-	$\mathbf{5137}^{1,2,6}$	$18492^{1,2}$
2	2	250	20488^2	27624	-	-	$\mathbf{4818}^{1,2,6}$	18212^2
2	4	500	15647^3	21396^3	47510	-	$\mathbf{4818}^{1,2,3,6}$	15999^3
2	8	1000	$11630^{3,4}$	$13549^{3,4}$	31299^4	46590	$\mathbf{4846}^{1,2,3,4,6}$	$14000^{3,4}$
5	1	6250	$8019^{3,4}$	$6736^{3,4,6}$	12410^4	17922	$\mathbf{5234}^{1,3,4,6}$	12605
5	2	12500	$7060^{4,6}$	$6832^{3,4,6}$	10510^4	14437	$\mathbf{4818}^{3,4,6}$	13174
5	4	25000	6913^6	6889^6	8016^6	9759^6	$\mathbf{5060}^{3,4,6}$	13513
5	8	50000	8392^6	6168^6	$5697^{1,6}$	6702^6	$\mathbf{5067}^{1,6}$	18181

Table 11. Results on g_3 analogous to Table 10 with 20 decision variables.

G	C	g_{max}	$conv_5$	$conv_{10}$	$conv_{50}$	$conv_{100}$	$coevo$	$lazy$
1	1	100	57784^2	75051	-	-	$\mathbf{6908}^{1,2,6}$	$30752^{1,2}$
1	2	200	43596^2	55369	-	-	$\mathbf{6982}^{1,2,6}$	$22469^{1,2}$
1	4	400	32469^2	40201	-	-	$\mathbf{7026}^{1,2,6}$	$21306^{1,2}$
1	8	800	24902^3	29510^3	60345	-	$\mathbf{7026}^{1,2,3,6}$	$19921^{1,2,3}$
2	1	250	40389^2	52267	-	-	$\mathbf{6943}^{1,2,6}$	$20310^{1,2}$
2	2	500	28443^3	34056^3	69687	-	$\mathbf{6982}^{1,2,3,6}$	$20231^{1,2,3}$
2	4	1000	$23606^{3,4}$	$25749^{3,4}$	53045^4	68999	$\mathbf{7026}^{1,2,3,4,6}$	$18019^{1,2,3,4}$
2	8	2000	$15279^{3,4}$	$20317^{3,4}$	40388^4	51314	$\mathbf{7024}^{1,2,3,4,6}$	$19157^{3,4}$
5	1	12500	13401^4	12336^4	16939^4	19943	$\mathbf{7131}^{1,2,3,4,6}$	19907
5	2	25000	13881	12014^6	13936^6	15450	$\mathbf{7088}^{1,2,3,4,6}$	21131
5	4	50000	12601^6	10956^6	11245^6	11784^6	$\mathbf{7082}^{1,2,3,4,6}$	22700
5	8	100000	13488^6	11331^6	10316^6	$10446^{1,6}$	$\mathbf{7111}^{1,2,3,4,6}$	22610

were executed with 20 decision variables, a group size of $G = 2$ with $C = 8$ cycles and corresponding values for g_{max}. The results on benchmark function g_1 are shown in Table 15. For $K > 2$, the results with the coevolution-based approach are significantly better than the results with the other approaches. Again, the results on g_2 and g_3 are not shown, because they are similar to those on g_1.

Table 12. Results on g_3 analogous to Table 10 with 50 decision variables.

G	C	g_{max}	$conv_5$	$conv_{10}$	$conv_{50}$	$conv_{100}$	$coevo$	$lazy$
1	1	250	64888	75595	-	-	$\mathbf{8409}^{1,2,6}$	$48225^{1,2}$
1	2	500	51861^3	61087^3	100546	-	$\mathbf{8389}^{1,2,3,6}$	$40756^{1,2,3}$
1	4	1000	$43120^{2,3,4}$	$48826^{3,4}$	80348^4	103644	$\mathbf{8389}^{1,2,3,4,6}$	$34539^{1,2,3,4}$
1	8	2000	$34328^{2,3,4}$	$38838^{3,4}$	64652^4	76346	$\mathbf{8389}^{1,2,3,4,6}$	$30280^{1,2,3,4}$
2	1	625	$46592^{2,3}$	57531^3	92147	-	$\mathbf{8505}^{1,2,3,6}$	$36261^{1,2,3}$
2	2	1250	$39092^{2,3,4}$	$45377^{3,4}$	74919^4	95448	$\mathbf{8412}^{1,2,3,4,6}$	$34546^{2,3,4}$
2	4	2500	$32853^{3,4}$	$36845^{3,4}$	60446^4	71424	$\mathbf{8387}^{1,2,3,4,6}$	$30469^{2,3,4}$
2	8	5000	$27736^{3,4}$	$29926^{3,4}$	49395^4	59516	$\mathbf{8387}^{1,2,3,4,6}$	$23774^{2,3,4}$
5	1	31250	$20502^{3,4}$	$21629^{3,4}$	26046^4	32472	$\mathbf{8588}^{1,2,3,4,6}$	$20865^{3,4}$
5	2	62500	19175^4	$19734^{3,4}$	22280	25708	$\mathbf{8741}^{1,2,3,4,6}$	22259
5	4	125000	19048	18543	19955	21010	$\mathbf{8915}^{1,2,3,4,6}$	21349
5	8	250000	18399	18993	17705^6	18626	$\mathbf{8915}^{1,2,3,4,6}$	21029

Table 13. Results on g_3 analogous to Table 10 with 100 decision variables.

G	C	g_{max}	$conv_5$	$conv_{10}$	$conv_{50}$	$conv_{100}$	$coevo$	$lazy$
1	1	500	$72617^{2,3}$	84144^3	113734	-	$\mathbf{9332}^{1,2,3,6}$	$52837^{1,2,3}$
1	2	1000	$61254^{2,3,4}$	$71151^{3,4}$	102737^4	114470	$\mathbf{9222}^{1,2,3,4,6}$	$47996^{1,2,3,4}$
1	4	2000	$51946^{2,3,4}$	$62341^{3,4}$	86136^4	102519	$\mathbf{9222}^{1,2,3,4,6}$	$42478^{1,2,3,4}$
1	8	4000	$44142^{2,3,4}$	$51299^{3,4}$	72186^4	84957	$\mathbf{9222}^{1,2,3,4,6}$	$39415^{2,3,4}$
2	1	1250	$60493^{2,3,4}$	$67511^{3,4}$	98498^4	109598	$\mathbf{9336}^{1,2,3,4,6}$	$46690^{1,2,3,4}$
2	2	2500	$51326^{2,3,4}$	$55208^{3,4}$	82215^4	98302	$\mathbf{9221}^{1,2,3,4,6}$	$42038^{1,2,3,4}$
2	4	5000	$42615^{2,3,4}$	$48619^{3,4}$	67437^4	79279	$\mathbf{9221}^{1,2,3,4,6}$	$38793^{2,3,4}$
2	8	10000	$35346^{3,4}$	$39242^{3,4}$	58246^4	66962	$\mathbf{9229}^{1,2,3,4,6}$	$35067^{3,4}$
5	1	62500	$29190^{3,4}$	$27686^{3,4}$	36627^4	40393	$\mathbf{9271}^{1,2,3,4,6}$	$28983^{3,4}$
5	2	125000	28773^4	$26938^{3,4}$	31241^4	36239	$\mathbf{9139}^{1,2,3,4,6}$	29264^4
5	4	250000	27716	25926^4	29269	30209	$\mathbf{9128}^{1,2,3,4,6}$	28556
5	8	500000	28626	27393	26740	27725	$\mathbf{9128}^{1,2,3,4,6}$	28001

5 Summary and Outlook

In the present work, we proposed a coevolution-based approach for the robust optimization of problems with a fitness function basically depending on discrete random variables, which conditionally depend on the decision variables. Numerical experiments have shown that it is able to outperform the conventional approach based on full Monte-Carlo simulation and the "lazy" approach with a very rough approximation of the expected fitness on common benchmark functions. The proposed approach is particularly beneficial if the number

Table 14. Medians of 100 optimization trials with the different approaches on benchmark function g_1 (Schwefel No. 1.2) with 20 decision variables, a group size of $G = 2$ and $C = 8$ cycles ($g_{max} = 2000$) with different values for the standard deviation σ_U of the distribution of the helper variables. Superscripts indicate statistical significance according to two-sided Wilcoxon rank-sum test with a significance level of 0.05.

σ_U	$conv_5$	$conv_{10}$	$conv_{50}$	$conv_{100}$	$coevo$	$lazy$
0.2	20.25[2,3,4]	27.26[3,4]	48.38[4]	63.64	**10.16**[1,2,3,4,6]	19.21[2,3,4]
0.5	59.04[3,4]	75.54[4]	80.95	99.65	**31.99**[1,2,3,4,6]	71.03[3,4]
1.0	164.40	148.94	133.12	185.66	**95.38**[1,2,3,4,6]	122.88[4]
1.5	203.40	209.99	176.33	214.98	**104.66**[1,2,3,4,6]	151.50[1,2,4]
2.0	268.21	235.65	307.91	231.79	**135.79**[1,2,3,4,6]	189.08[1,3,4]
2.5	266.46	288.74	226.92	259.04	**147.34**[1,2,3,4]	196.42[2,4]
3.0	221.03	204.39	236.11	250.26	**159.37**[3,4]	186.70[4]
3.5	229.43	239.08	259.02	341.83	**189.84**[1,3,4]	222.13[4]
4.0	378.14	287.21	276.47	331.84	**181.13**[1,2,3,4]	204.46[1,2,3,4]
4.5	293.08	314.05	283.23	325.91	**172.27**[1,2,3,4]	209.03[1,2,3,4]
5.0	293.93	213.36[1,3,4]	296.96	305.57	**207.02**[1,3,4]	226.13[1,3,4]

Table 15. Medians of 100 optimization trials with the different approaches on benchmark function g_1 (Schwefel No. 1.2) with 20 decision variables, a group size of $G = 2$ and $C = 8$ cycles with different numbers K of possible values per random variable. Superscripts indicate statistical significance according to two-sided Wilcoxon rank-sum test with a significance level of 0.05.

K	g_{max}	$conv_5$	$conv_{10}$	$conv_{50}$	$conv_{100}$	$coevo$	$lazy$
2	320	72.70[2]	97.43	-	-	**52.54**[1,2]	56.92[1,2]
3	720	70.35[3]	71.77[3]	127.19	-	**38.59**[1,2,3,6]	59.92[3]
4	1280	8.50[3,4]	78.67[3,4]	111.87[4]	165.43	**37.38**[1,2,3,4,6]	50.52[1,2,3,4]
5	2000	59.04[3,4]	75.54[4]	80.95	99.65	**31.99**[1,2,3,4,6]	71.03[3,4]
6	2880	63.72[4]	64.93[3,4]	84.82	106.23	**26.35**[1,2,3,4,6]	66.47[3,4]
7	3920	55.56[3,4]	51.15[3,4]	79.24	79.67	**29.65**[1,2,3,4,6]	61.98[3,4]
8	5120	52.27[3,4]	51.33[3,4]	77.08	76.96	**28.43**[1,2,3,4,6]	74.75
9	6480	52.07[3,4]	49.83[4]	71.03[4]	95.62	**35.53**[1,2,3,4,6]	46.42[3,4]
10	8000	54.45[4]	47.94[4]	53.67[4]	70.94	**26.26**[1,2,3,4,6]	51.47[4]
11	9680	40.38[3,4]	52.05[3,4]	64.63	68.21	**26.55**[1,2,3,4,6]	68.56
12	11520	45.63[3,4,6]	56.30[4]	62.46	76.54	**25.78**[1,2,3,4,6]	75.23
13	13520	50.08[4]	40.76[3,4]	55.83[4]	79.62	**23.65**[1,2,3,4,6]	59.87[4]
14	15680	40.49[3,4]	43.42[4]	56.55	61.28	**18.73**[1,2,3,4,6]	50.64
15	18000	53.33[4]	48.11[4]	47.30[4]	65.21	**24.71**[1,2,3,4,6]	60.03

of allowed evaluations of the function in the random variables is small. With an increasing amount of uncertainty or an increasing number of possible values of the discrete random variables, the proposed approach is still highly competitive with the other evaluated approaches.

In a next step, we plan to evaluate the approach on a real-world problem, more precisely, the optimization of dynamic prices for the charging of electric vehicles at public charging stations. Furthermore, we plan to investigate the effect of more advances strategies for the grouping of the decision variables, like delta grouping [19], and acceleration techniques, like described in Sect. 1, on the performance of the proposed approach.

References

1. Jin, Y., Branke, J.: Evolutionary optimization in uncertain environments - a survey. IEEE Trans. Evol. Comp. **9**(3), 303–317 (2005)
2. Beyer, H.G., Sendhoff, B.: Robust optimization - a comprehensive survey. Comput. Methods Appl. Mech. Eng. **196**(33), 3190–3218 (2007)
3. Leon, V.J., Wu, S.D., Storer, R.H.: Robustness measures and robust scheduling for job shops. IIE Trans. **26**(5), 32–43 (1994)
4. Wiesmann, D., Hammel, U., Bäck, T.: Robust design of multilayer optical coatings by means of evolutionary algorithms. IEEE Trans. Evol. Comp. **2**(4), 162–167 (1998)
5. Hacker, S., Lewis, K.: Robust design through the use of a hybrid genetic algorithm. In: Proceedings of 28th Design Automation Conference, pp. 703–712. The American Society of Mechanical Engineers (2002)
6. Singh, A., Minsker, B.: Uncertainty based multi-objective optimization of groundwater remediation at the umatilla chemical depot. In: Proceedings of World Water and Environmetal Resources Congress, pp. 3589–3598 (2004)
7. Wang, H., Kim, N., Kim, Y.J.: Safety envelope for load tolerance and its application to fatigue reliability design. J. Mech. Des. **128**(4), 919–927 (2006)
8. Kavakeb, S., Nguyen, T.T., Yang, Z., Jenkinson, I.: Identifying the robust number of intelligent autonomous vehicles in container terminals. In: Esparcia-Alcázar, A.I., Mora, A.M. (eds.) EvoApplications 2014. LNCS, vol. 8602, pp. 829–840. Springer, Heidelberg (2014). https://doi.org/10.1007/978-3-662-45523-4_67
9. Loughlin, D.H., Ranjithan, S.R.: Chance-constrained genetic algorithms. In: Proceedings of GECCO 1999, pp. 369–376. Morgan Kaufmann Publishers Inc., San Francisco (1999)
10. McKay, M.D., Beckman, R.J., Conover, W.J.: A comparison of three methods for selecting values of input variables in the analysis of output from a computer code. Technometrics **21**(2), 239–245 (1979)
11. Branke, J.: Creating robust solutions by means of evolutionary algorithms. In: Eiben, A.E., Bäck, T., Schoenauer, M., Schwefel, H.-P. (eds.) PPSN 1998. LNCS, vol. 1498, pp. 119–128. Springer, Heidelberg (1998). https://doi.org/10.1007/BFb0056855
12. Aizawa, A.N., Wah, B.W.: Dynamic control of genetic algorithms in a noisy environment. In: Proceedings of 5th International Conference on Genetic Algorithms, pp. 48–55. Morgan Kaufmann Publishers Inc., San Francisco (1993)

13. Lee, K.H., Park, G.J.: A global robust optimization using kriging based approximation model. JSME Int. J. Ser. Mech. Syst. Mach. Elem. Manuf. **49**(3), 779–788 (2006)
14. Paenke, I., Branke, J., Jin, Y.: Efficient search for robust solutions by means of evolutionary algorithms and fitness approximation. IEEE Trans. Evol. Comp. **10**(4), 405–420 (2006)
15. Yang, Z., Tang, K., Yao, X.: Large scale evolutionary optimization using cooperative coevolution. Inf. Sci. **178**(15), 2985–2999 (2008)
16. Potter, M.A., De Jong, K.A.: A cooperative coevolutionary approach to function optimization. In: Davidor, Y., Schwefel, H.-P., Männer, R. (eds.) PPSN 1994. LNCS, vol. 866, pp. 249–257. Springer, Heidelberg (1994). https://doi.org/10.1007/3-540-58484-6_269
17. Kennedy, J., Eberhart, R.: Particle swarm optimization. In: Proceedings of IEEE Conference on Neural Networks, vol. 4, pp. 1942–1948 (1995)
18. Hansen, N., Ostermeier, A.: Completely derandomized self-adaptation in evolution strategies. Evol. Comput. **9**(2), 159–195 (2001)
19. Omidvar, M.N., Li, X., Yao, X.: Cooperative co-evolution with delta grouping for large scale non-separable function optimization. In: Proceedings of IEEE CEC, pp. 1762–1769 (2010)

On the Use of Repair Methods
in Differential Evolution for Dynamic
Constrained Optimization

Maria-Yaneli Ameca-Alducin$^{(\boxtimes)}$, Maryam Hasani-Shoreh, and Frank Neumann

Optimisation and Logistics, School of Computer Science,
The University of Adelaide, Adelaide, SA 5005, Australia
{maria-yaneli.ameca-alducin,maryam.hasanishoreh,
frank.neumann}@adelaide.edu.au

Abstract. Dynamic constrained optimization problems have received increasing attention in recent years. We study differential evolution which is one of the high performing class of algorithms for constrained continuous optimization in the context of dynamic constrained optimization. The focus of our investigations are repair methods which are crucial when dealing with dynamic constrained problems. Examining recently introduced benchmarks for dynamic constrained continuous optimization, we analyze different repair methods with respect to the obtained offline error and the success rate in dependence of the severity of the dynamic change. Our analysis points out the benefits and drawbacks of the different repair methods and gives guidance to its applicability in dependence on the dynamic changes of the objective function and constraints.

Keywords: Repair methods · Dynamic constrained optimization
Constraint-handling techniques · Differential evolution

1 Introduction

Differential evolution (DE) is known as one of the most competitive, reliable and versatile evolutionary algorithm for optimization on the continuous spaces [1]. DE has shown successful results in a variety of ranges of optimization problems including multi-objective [2], multi-modal [3], large-scale [4], expensive [5], constrained [6] and dynamic optimization problems [7,8]. Among these, constrained optimization problems have a great importance, since in the real world problems, most of the optimization problems have inequality and/or equality constraints. Constrained optimization problems are usually harder to tackle than unconstrained ones, and evolutionary algorithms require a constrained handling technique to deal with the constraints. A review of the different constraint handling techniques can be found in [9].

Another area that have attracted researcher's attention in recent years is dynamic optimization and DE has been regarded as a high performing algorithm in this area [7,10,11]. Considering constraints and dynamism simultaneously (known as dynamic constrained optimization problems: DCOPs) has been

© Springer International Publishing AG, part of Springer Nature 2018
K. Sim and P. Kaufmann (Eds.): EvoApplications 2018, LNCS 10784, pp. 832–847, 2018.
https://doi.org/10.1007/978-3-319-77538-8_55

even more challenging for an algorithm, as it will be harder to track the global optimum solution when the constraints or the objective function change over-time. The algorithms that solve these kind of problems need to incorporate some mechanisms to deal with the changes in the environment. Different mechanisms have been proposed in the literature on DCOPs including change detection (re-evaluation of solutions, and decreasing the quality of solutions) [12], introducing diversity (increase the mutation) [13], maintaining diversity (adding random solutions called random immigrants) [14], memory-based approaches [15], and the population-based approaches [16].

In order to handle the constraints in these problems, different constraint han-dling techniques have been applied including penalty functions [13,17], feasibility rules [8], and repair methods [7,11,18]. The last technique has not only been suit-able to deal with the constraints, but also has been able to improve the algorithm performance when has been used in dynamic environments. The reason is because this technique is not only choosing between the solutions in the selection, but also moves the solution toward the feasible region by the repair operator. Indeed, the main idea of a repair method is to convert infeasible solutions into feasible ones. Based on the competitive results that these methods have shown, we carry out investigations on the behaviour of these repair methods for DCOPs.

Based on the literature on the current repair methods applied in DCOPs, four types of repair methods including (i) reference-based repair [19], (ii) offspring-repair [7,20], (iii) mutant-repair [11,21] and (iv) gradient-based repair [18] have been distinguished. (i) uses reference solutions in order to convert an infeasible solution to a feasible one. In (ii) the repair method is similar to (i), the only difference between these two methods is that choosing the feasible reference solution in (i) is completely random, while in (ii) the nearest feasible reference solution is selected. (iii) is a repair method which does not require feasible solu-tions to operate, and is inspired by the differential mutation operator. (iv) is based on gradient information derived from the constraint set to systematically repair infeasible solutions.

Our main focus is to investigate the specifications of each of these methods on a recent benchmark set for DCOPs [19] when applying DE. For the compari-son of the effectiveness of each method, the offline error [19] and two newly pro-posed measures are used. The analysis shows that the gradient-based method out-performs other repair methods based on almost of the measures. However, this method can not be used like a black-box, since it should be known if the constraints have derivative. On the contrary, based on offline error, the worst method seem to be mutant repair method, but this method repairs the solutions very fast after only a few tries. Although, these small number of tries for repairing a solution in this method is mostly because in this benchmark, most of the problems have a huge feasible area. Finally, based on the analysis, the benefits and drawbacks of each method are pointed out and directions for future work are given.

The rest of this paper is organized as follows. In Sect. 2, we define our notion of dynamic constrained optimization problems and provide an introduction into differential evolution together with the different repair methods investigated in this paper. In Sect. 3, the experimental investigations regarding the effectiveness of repair methods with respect to different performance measures are described and the experimental results are divided in offline error analysis and success rate analysis and are presented in Sect. 4 and Sect. 5 respectively. Finally, we finish with some conclusions and directions for future work.

2   Preliminaries

In this section, first we define the problem statement for DCOPs, then we give a brief description of DE algorithm and the mechanism that we have added to it in order to deal with the changes in the environment (called dynamic DE) and finally we present different repair methods that have been applied.

2.1   Problem Statement

A dynamic constrained optimization problem (DCOP) is an optimization problem where the objective function and/or the constraints can change over time [19,22]. Formally, a DCOP can be defined as follows.
Find $\boldsymbol{x}$, at each time t, which:

$$\min_{\boldsymbol{x} \in F_t \subseteq [L,U]} f(\boldsymbol{x}, t) \tag{1}$$

where $f : S \to \mathbb{R}$ is a single objective function, $\boldsymbol{x} \in \mathbb{R}^D$ is a solution vector and $t \in N^+$ is the current time,

$$[L, U] = \{\boldsymbol{x} = (x_1, x_2, ..., x_D) \mid L_i \leq x_i \leq U_i, i = 1 \ldots D\} \tag{2}$$

is called the search space (S), where L_i and U_i are the lower and upper boundaries of the ith variable,
subject to:

$$F_t = \{\boldsymbol{x} \mid \boldsymbol{x} \in [L, U], g_i(\boldsymbol{x}, t) \leq 0, i = 1, \ldots, m, \\ h_j(\boldsymbol{x}, t) = 0, j = 1, \ldots, p\} \tag{3}$$

is called the feasible region at time t, where m is the number of inequality constraints and p is the number of equality constraints at time t.
$\forall \boldsymbol{x} \in F_t$ if there exists a solution $\boldsymbol{x}^* \in F_t$ such that $f(\boldsymbol{x}^*, t) \leq f(\boldsymbol{x}, t)$, then $\boldsymbol{x}^*$ is called a feasible optimal solution and $f(\boldsymbol{x}^*, t)$ is called the feasible optima value at time t. The objective function and the constrains can be linear or nonlinear.

2.2   Dynamic Differential Evolution

Differential evolution (DE) was first introduced in [23] as a stochastic search algorithm that is simple, reliable and fast. Each vector $\boldsymbol{x}_{i,G}$ in the current population (called at the moment of the reproduction as target vector) generates one trial vector $u_{i,G}$ by using a mutant vector $v_{i,G}$. The mutant vector is created applying $v_{i,G} = x_{r0,G} + F(x_{r1,G} - x_{r2,G})$, where $x_{r0,G}$, $x_{r1,G}$, and $x_{r2,G}$ are vectors chosen at random from the current population ($r0 \neq r1 \neq r2 \neq i$); $x_{r0,G}$ is known as the base vector and $x_{r1,G}$, and $x_{r2,G}$ are the difference vectors and $F > 0$ is a parameter called scale factor. Then the trial vector is created by the recombination of the target vector and mutant vector using a probability crossover $CR \in [0, 1]$.

In this paper DE/rand/1/bin variant is adopted [24], where "rand" indicates how the base vector is chosen (at random in our case), "1" represents how many vector differences (vector pairs) will contribute in differential mutation, and "bin" is the type of crossover (binomial in our case).

In a DCOP an important task is to verify that the solutions' information is correct during the search process. Because when a new change occurs in the environment, the values of the objective function and/or the constraints may change. For this reason a change detection mechanism is required to detect the changes in the objective function and/or the constraints [11,12]. A general overview of DDE algorithm is presented in Algorithm 1.

Algorithm 1. Dynamic differential evolution (DDE)

1: Create and evaluate a randomly initial population $x_{i,G} \forall i, i = 1, \ldots, NP$
2: **for** $G \leftarrow 1$ to MAX_GEN **do**
3:   **for** $i \leftarrow 1$ to NP **do**
4:     Change detection mechanism ($x_{i,G}$)
5:     Randomly select $r0 \neq r1 \neq r2 \neq i$
6:     $J_{rand} = randint[1, D]$
7:     **for** $j \leftarrow 1$ to D **do**
8:       **if** $rand_j \leq CR$ Or $j = J_{rand}$ **then**
9:         $u_{i,j,G} = x_{r1,j,G} + F(x_{r2,j,G} - x_{r3,j,G})$
10:       **else**
11:         $u_{i,j,G} = x_{i,j,G}$
12:       **end if**
13:     **end for**
14:     **if** $u_{i,j,G}$ is infeasible **then**
15:       Use the repair method
16:     **end if**
17:     **if** $f(u_{i,G}) \leq f(x_{i,G})$ **then**
18:       $x_{i,G+1} = u_{i,G}$
19:     **else**
20:       $x_{i,G+1} = x_{i,G}$
21:     **end if**
22:   **end for**
23: **end for**

2.3   Repair Methods

Repair methods have shown competitive results compared to other constraint handling methods in constrained optimization. The main idea of a repair method is to use a transformation process to convert an infeasible solution into a feasible one. Although, there is no need for special operators or any modifications of the fitness function in this method like other constraint handling methods, in some repair methods, reference feasible solutions are required [7,19,20,25]. However, the repair methods presented in [11,18] does not require feasible reference solutions. Repair methods used in dynamic constrained optimization problems have had an important role in the algorithm's recovery after a change since they help to move the infeasible solutions toward feasible region. Basically on the related literature of dynamic constrained optimization problems, there have been four repair methods utilized for constraint handling as follows.

Reference-based repair method: This method was originally proposed in [25], and [19] utilized this method with a simple genetic algorithm for solving DCOPs. In this method, firstly, a reference feasible population (R) is created. If an individual of the search population (S) is infeasible, a new individual is generated on the straight line joining the infeasible solution and a randomly chosen member of R. This process will continue until the infeasible solution is repaired or a repair limit (RL = 100) attempts are computed. If the new feasible solution has better fitness value, it will be replaced by the selected reference individual. An overview of this method used for our investigations is presented in Algorithm 2, however the boldface part is only used for offspring-repair method.

Offspring-repair method: This method was applied in DCOPs in [7,20]. In this method, a reference feasible population (R) is generated. For any infeasible solution of the search population (S), a new individual is generated on the straight line joining the infeasible solution and the nearest member of the reference population R based on Euclidean distance. This process will continue until the infeasible solution is repaired or a repair limit (RL = 100) attempts are computed. If the new feasible solution has better fitness value, it will be replaced by the selected reference individual. This method is similar to the reference-based repair method [19]. The only difference is in the process of selecting the reference solution. An overview of this method is presented in Algorithm 2.

Mutant-repair method: The mutant-repair method (see Algorithm 3) is based on the differential mutation operator, and does not require reference solutions [11]. For each infeasible solution, three new and temporal solutions are generated at random and a differential mutation operator similar to the one used in DE is applied. This repair method is applied until the infeasible solution is repaired or a specific number of unsuccessful trials to obtain a feasible solution have been carried out (RL).

Gradient-based repair method: The gradient-based repair method (see Algorithm 4) was first applied into a simple GA [26] to handle constraints in a static optimization problem and in [18] was applied for solving DCOPs. In this method,

---

Algorithm 2. Reference-based and offspring-repair methods

Require: $u_{i,G}$ {trial vector}

$counter = 0$

2: **while** $u_{i,G}$ is infeasible and $counter \leq$ RL **do**

Select the reference individual $r \in R$ based on:

4: $\begin{cases} \text{Randomly} & <\text{reference-based}> \\ \text{Min distance between } u_{i,G} \text{ and } r & <\text{offspring}> \end{cases}$

6: Create random number $a = U[0,1]$

Create a new individual in the segment between $u_{i,G}$ ($s \in S$) and r

8: $u_{i,G} = a * r + (1 - a) * u_{i,G}$

if $u_{i,G}$ is infeasible **then**

10: go to step 2

else

12: Update reference population if the repaired solution has better fitness value than R

end if

14: $counter = counter + 1$

end while

16: Return $u_{i,G}$

Algorithm 3. Mutant-repair method

Require: $u_{i,G}$ {trial vector}

$counter = 0$

2: **while** $u_{i,G}$ is infeasible and $counter \leq$ RL **do**

Generate three random vectors ($u_{r0,G}$, $u_{r1,G}$ and $u_{r2,G}$)

4: $u_{i,G} = u_{r0,G} + F(u_{r1,G} - u_{r2,G})$

$counter = counter + 1$

6: **end while**

Return $u_{i,G}$

---

the gradient information of the constraints are utilized to repair the infeasible solutions [26]. For this purpose the gradient of the constraints based on the solution vector (that represent the rate of change of constraints based on each variable) will be calculated. At the next step the constraint violations are calculated and based on this amount and the vector of gradient, the solutions will move toward the feasible region with the proportional quantity. The constraints that are non-violated are not considered in these calculations. In this method the main idea is to only change the effective variables over the constraints that have a violation. More detail about this method can be found in [18].

3 Experimental Investigations

In this section, the utilized test problems, the performance measures and the experimental setup are presented.

Algorithm 4. Gradient-based repair method

Require: $u_{i,G}$ {trial vector}

  $counter = 0$

2: **while** $u_{i,G}$ is infeasible and $counter \leq$ RL **do**

  Calculate the constraint violation

4:   Calculate the amount of solution movement $\Delta u_{i,G}$ based on the current constraint violation and the gradient information

  $u_{i,G} = u_{i,G} + \Delta u_{i,G}$

6:   $counter = counter + 1$

  end while

8: Return $u_{i,G}$

3.1 Test Problems and Performance Measures

The chosen benchmark problem originally has 18 functions [19], however in this work, 10 functions among them were used for the experiments. The reason for this selection was that part of these functions were not constrained and part of them did not have derivative for the constraints and could not be applied in Gradient-based method. The test problems in this benchmark consist a variety of characteristics like (i) disconnected feasible regions (1–3), (ii) the global optima at the constraints' boundary or switchable between disconnected regions, or (iii) the different shape and percentage of feasible area. In the experiments, for the objective function, only medium severity is considered ($k = 0.5$), while different change severities are considered for the constraints ($S = 10, 20$ and 50). Based on the definition of the constrains in this benchmark [19], $S = 10$ represents for large severity, $S = 20$ for medium severity and $S = 50$ for the small severity of changes on the constraints. The frequency of change (f_c) is considered equal to 1000 evaluations (only in the objective function). Worth to mention that, in the repair methods, the constraints evaluations are not considered as extra evaluations when using for DCOPs [21]. More details on the benchmark can be found in [19].

For the purpose of comparing the effectiveness of each repair method, the following performance measures were used:

Offline error (off_e) [27]: This measurement is equal to the average of the sum of errors in each generation divided by the total number of generations. The zero value of offline error indicates a perfect performance [22]. This measure is defined as:

$$off\_e = \frac{1}{G_{max}} \sum_{G=1}^{G_{max}} e(G) \tag{4}$$

where G_{max} is the number of generations computed by the algorithm and $e(G)$ denotes the error in the current iteration G (see 5):

$$e(G) = |f(x^*, t) - f(x_{best,G}, t)| \tag{5}$$

where $f(\boldsymbol{x}^*, t)$ is the feasible global optima[1] at current time t, and $f(\boldsymbol{x}_{best,G}, t)$ represent the best solution (feasible or infeasible) found so far at generation G at current time t.

Success rate: This measure is calculated such that considers how many of the infeasible solutions were successful to be repaired after 100 iterations. For each infeasible solution, a repair is needed and at the end of repair iteration (Maximum 100 tries), if the solution is feasible a counter is increased. In another words, it is considered a success if before achieving to the maximum number of allowed iterations for repair (100 in our case) a solution is feasible. The total number of these successful repaired solutions (s) divided by the total number of solutions that need repair (n_T) is equal to success rate percentage. Based on this, the repair methods with success rate values equals to 100%, are able to convert all the solutions.

$$s_r = \frac{s}{n_T} \tag{6}$$

Required number of iterations: In order to distinguish the difference between the number of evaluations that each method consumes for repairing the solution, a measurement is defined called as required number of iterations (rn_i). In this way, it is possible to compare the efficiency of each repair method. The range of values of this measure is $\in (1 - 100)$. The more efficient method uses lower number of evaluations in order to repair an infeasible solution. The final amount for this measurement value is the average between the number of tries taken to convert each infeasible solution into feasible one.

3.2 Experimental Setup

The experimental results are divided as (i) offline error analysis and (ii) success rate and required number of iterations. In these experiments we investigate the behaviour of different repair methods in DDE algorithm based on the previous defined measures. In the analysis, the effects of different severities on the constraints are considered for these ten test problems. We do not bring the results for changes of frequency since it does not have any effect in the behaviour of the repair methods.

The configurations for the experiments are as follows. The number of runs in the experiments are 50, and number of considered times for dynamic perspective of the test algorithm is $5/k$ ($k = 0.5$). Parameters relating to DDE algorithm are as follows: DE variant is DE/rand/1/bin, population size is 20, scaling factor (F) is a random number $\in [0.2, 0.8]$, and crossover probability is 0.2. In the experiments, four repair methods including Reference-based, Offspring, Mutant and Gradient-based as explained in Sect. 2.3 have been applied for handling the constraint in DDE algorithm.

---

[1] This global optima is an approximation, which is the best solution found by DE in 50 runs for the current time.

Table 1. Average and standard deviation of offline error values obtained by all the repairs methods with $k = 0.5$, $S = 10$, 20 and 50, and $f_c = 1000$. Best results are remarked in boldface.

Algorithms	$S = 10$				
	G24_1	G24_f	G24_2	G24_3	G24_3b
Reference	0.07(±0.029)	0.029(±0.022)	0.394(±0.212)	0.041(±0.025)	0.058(±0.027)
Offspring	0.07(±0.053)	0.036(±0.036)	0.451(±0.317)	0.068(±0.056)	0.073(±0.048)
Mutant	0.271(±0.051)	0.095(±0.048)	0.29(±0.021)	0.159(±0.031)	0.193(±0.041)
Gradient	**0.043(±0.028)**	**0.004(±0.003)**	**0.259(±0.012)**	**0.01(±0.004)**	**0.033(±0.015)**
	G24_3f	G24_4	G24_5	G24_7	G24_8b
Reference	0.007(±0.004)	0.071(±0.035)	0.071(±0.024)	0.12(±0.088)	0.105(±0.062)
Offspring	0.04(±0.083)	0.067(±0.031)	0.089(±0.035)	0.253(±0.128)	0.114(±0.056)
Mutant	0.046(±0.019)	0.187(±0.045)	0.126(±0.021)	0.208(±0.034)	0.338(±0.048)
Gradient	**0.002(±0.003)**	**0.032(±0.013)**	**0.024(±0.007)**	**0.021(±0.008)**	**0.031(±0.009)**

Algorithms	$S = 20$				
	G24_1	G24_f	G24_2	G24_3	G24_3b
Reference	0.078(±0.042)	0.026(±0.019)	0.406(±0.328)	0.02(±0.009)	0.06(±0.036)
Offspring	0.086(±0.061)	0.03(±0.025)	0.416(±0.321)	0.039(±0.033)	0.035(±0.023)
Mutant	0.246(±0.047)	0.1(±0.05)	0.296(±0.02)	0.156(±0.033)	0.207(±0.031)
Gradient	**0.048(±0.026)**	**0.004(±0.004)**	**0.258(±0.009)**	**0.004(±0.002)**	**0.035(±0.017)**
	G24_3f	G24_4	G24_5	G24_7	G24_8b
Reference	0.008(±0.005)	0.06(±0.032)	0.075(±0.033)	0.107(±0.045)	0.108(±0.041)
Offspring	0.023(±0.029)	0.043(±0.038)	0.092(±0.048)	0.213(±0.075)	0.12(±0.069)
Mutant	0.05(±0.019)	0.218(±0.033)	0.132(±0.024)	0.267(±0.039)	0.333(±0.044)
Gradient	**0.002(±0.002)**	**0.033(±0.015)**	**0.029(±0.013)**	**0.021(±0.009)**	**0.033(±0.008)**

Algorithms	$S = 50$				
	G24_1	G24_f	G24_2	G24_3	G24_3b
Reference	0.069(±0.031)	0.031(±0.024)	0.371(±0.232)	0.011(±0.005)	0.045(±0.025)
Offspring	0.06(±0.032)	0.039(±0.037)	0.39(±0.187)	0.037(±0.069)	0.029(±0.025)
Mutant	0.26(±0.051)	0.1(±0.047)	0.298(±0.023)	0.1(±0.023)	0.161(±0.024)
Gradient	**0.043(±0.018)**	**0.003(±0.003)**	**0.257(±0.01)**	**0.002(±0.002)**	**0.027(±0.011)**
	G24_3f	G24_4	G24_5	G24_7	G24_8b
Reference	0.008(±0.009)	0.053(±0.042)	0.062(±0.018)	0.084(±0.024)	0.096(±0.041)
Offspring	0.03(±0.049)	0.038(±0.046)	0.08(±0.032)	0.2(±0.078)	0.111(±0.065)
Mutant	0.046(±0.018)	0.162(±0.022)	0.145(±0.025)	0.289(±0.037)	0.351(±0.04)
Gradient	**0.003(±0.003)**	**0.026(±0.011)**	**0.033(±0.012)**	**0.026(±0.011)**	**0.031(±0.007)**

4   Offline Error Analysis

The results obtained for the four repair methods using offline error are summarized in Table 1. Furthermore, for the statistical validation, the 95%-confidence Kruskal-Wallis (KW) test and the Bergmann-Hommels post-hoc test, as suggested in [28] are presented (see Table 2). Non-parametric tests were adopted because the samples of runs did not fit to a normal distribution based on the Kolmogorov-Smirnov test. Based on the results, for the constraint's change severity $S = 10$, the gradient-based repair outperformed almost all of the other methods in nine test problems (G24_f, G24_2, G24_3, G24_3b, G24_3f, G24_4, G24_5, G24_7 and G24_8b) except one test problem (G24_1) that in which offspring-repair has similar performance. For this severity, reference-based repair and offspring-repair performed almost the same for nine test problems (G24_1, G24_f, G24_2, G24_3, G24_3b, G24_3f, G24_4, G24_5 and G24_8b) except one test

Table 2. Statistical tests on the offline error values in Table 1. "$X^{(-)}$" means that the corresponding algorithm outperformed algorithm X. "$X^{(+)}$" means that the corresponding algorithm was dominated by algorithm X. If algorithm X does not appear in column Y means no significant differences between X and Y.

Functions	$S = 10$			
	Reference(1)	Offspring(2)	Mutant(3)	Gradient(4)
G24_1 (44.2%)	$3^{(-)}$ and $4^{(+)}$	$3^{(-)}$	$1^{(+)}, 2^{(+)}$ and $4^{(+)}$	$1^{(-)}$ and $3^{(-)}$
G24_f (44.2%)	$3^{(-)}$ and $4^{(+)}$	$3^{(-)}$ and $4^{(+)}$	$1^{(+)}, 2^{(+)}$ and $4^{(+)}$	$1^{(-)}, 2^{(-)}$ and $3^{(-)}$
G24_2 (44.2%)	$4^{(+)}$	$4^{(+)}$	$4^{(+)}$	$1^{(-)}, 2^{(-)}$ and $3^{(-)}$
G24_3 (7.1-49.21%)	$3^{(-)}$ and $4^{(+)}$	$3^{(-)}$ and $4^{(+)}$	$1^{(+)}, 2^{(+)}$ and $4^{(+)}$	$1^{(-)}, 2^{(-)}$ and $3^{(-)}$
G24_3b (7.1-49.21%)	$3^{(-)}$ and $4^{(+)}$	$3^{(-)}$ and $4^{(+)}$	$1^{(+)}, 2^{(+)}$ and $4^{(+)}$	$1^{(-)}, 2^{(-)}$ and $3^{(-)}$
G24_3f (7.1%)	$3^{(-)}$ and $4^{(+)}$	$3^{(-)}$ and $4^{(+)}$	$1^{(+)}, 2^{(+)}$ and $4^{(+)}$	$1^{(-)}, 2^{(-)}$ and $3^{(-)}$
G24_4 (0-44.2%)	$3^{(-)}$ and $4^{(+)}$	$3^{(-)}$ and $4^{(+)}$	$1^{(+)}, 2^{(+)}$ and $4^{(+)}$	$1^{(-)}, 2^{(-)}$ and $3^{(-)}$
G24_5 (0-44.2%)	$3^{(-)}$ and $4^{(+)}$	$3^{(-)}$ and $4^{(+)}$	$1^{(+)}, 2^{(+)}$ and $4^{(+)}$	$1^{(-)}, 2^{(-)}$ and $3^{(-)}$
G24_7 (0-44.2%)	$2^{(-)}, 3^{(-)}$ and $4^{(+)}$	$1^{(+)}$ and $4^{(+)}$	$1^{(+)}$ and $4^{(+)}$	$1^{(-)}, 2^{(-)}$ and $3^{(-)}$
G24_8b (44.2%)	$3^{(-)}$ and $4^{(+)}$	$3^{(-)}$ and $4^{(+)}$	$1^{(+)}, 2^{(+)}$ and $4^{(+)}$	$1^{(-)}, 2^{(-)}$ and $3^{(-)}$
	$S = 20$			
	Reference(1)	Offspring(2)	Mutant(3)	Gradient(4)
G24_1 (44.2%)	$3^{(-)}$ and $4^{(+)}$	$3^{(-)}$ and $4^{(+)}$	$1^{(+)}, 2^{(+)}$ and $4^{(+)}$	$1^{(-)}, 2^{(-)}$ and $3^{(-)}$
G24_f (44.2%)	$3^{(-)}$ and $4^{(+)}$	$3^{(-)}$ and $4^{(+)}$	$1^{(+)}, 2^{(+)}$ and $4^{(+)}$	$1^{(-)}, 2^{(-)}$ and $3^{(-)}$
G24_2 (44.2%)	$4^{(+)}$		$4^{(+)}$	$1^{(-)}$ and $3^{(-)}$
G24_3 (7.1-49.21%)	$3^{(-)}$ and $4^{(+)}$	$3^{(-)}$ and $4^{(+)}$	$1^{(+)}, 2^{(+)}$ and $4^{(+)}$	$1^{(-)}, 2^{(-)}$ and $3^{(-)}$
G24_3b (7.1-49.21%)	$2^{(+)}, 3^{(-)}$ and $4^{(+)}$	$1^{(-)}$ and $3^{(-)}$	$1^{(+)}, 2^{(+)}$ and $4^{(+)}$	$1^{(-)}$ and $3^{(-)}$
G24_3f (7.1%)	$3^{(-)}$ and $4^{(+)}$	$3^{(-)}$ and $4^{(+)}$	$1^{(+)}, 2^{(+)}$ and $4^{(+)}$	$1^{(-)}, 2^{(-)}$ and $3^{(-)}$
G24_4 (4.75-44.2%)	$2^{(+)}, 3^{(-)}$ and $4^{(+)}$	$1^{(-)}$ and $3^{(-)}$	$1^{(+)}, 2^{(+)}$ and $4^{(+)}$	$1^{(-)}$ and $3^{(-)}$
G24_5 (4.75-44.2%)	$3^{(-)}$ and $4^{(+)}$	$3^{(-)}$ and $4^{(+)}$	$1^{(+)}, 2^{(+)}$ and $4^{(+)}$	$1^{(-)}, 2^{(-)}$ and $3^{(-)}$
G24_7 (4.75-44.2%)	$2^{(-)}, 3^{(-)}$ and $4^{(+)}$	$1^{(+)}$ and $4^{(+)}$	$1^{(+)}$ and $4^{(+)}$	$1^{(-)}, 2^{(-)}$ and $3^{(-)}$
G24_8b (44.2%)	$3^{(-)}$ and $4^{(+)}$	$3^{(-)}$ and $4^{(+)}$	$1^{(+)}, 2^{(+)}$ and $4^{(+)}$	$1^{(-)}, 2^{(-)}$ and $3^{(-)}$
	$S = 50$			
	Reference(1)	Offspring(2)	Mutant(3)	Gradient(4)
G24_1 (44.2%)	$3^{(-)}$ and $4^{(+)}$	$3^{(-)}$	$1^{(+)}, 2^{(+)}$ and $4^{(+)}$	$1^{(-)}$ and $3^{(-)}$
G24_f (44.2%)	$3^{(-)}$ and $4^{(+)}$	$3^{(-)}$ and $4^{(+)}$	$1^{(+)}, 2^{(+)}$ and $4^{(+)}$	$1^{(-)}, 2^{(-)}$ and $3^{(-)}$
G24_2 (44.2%)	$3^{(+)}$		$1^{(+)}$ and $4^{(+)}$	$3^{(-)}$
G24_3 (7.1-18.63%)	$3^{(-)}$ and $4^{(+)}$	$3^{(-)}$ and $4^{(+)}$	$1^{(+)}, 2^{(+)}$ and $4^{(+)}$	$1^{(-)}, 2^{(-)}$ and $3^{(-)}$
G24_3b (7.1-18.63%)	$2^{(+)}, 3^{(-)}$ and $4^{(+)}$	$1^{(-)}$ and $3^{(-)}$	$1^{(+)}, 2^{(+)}$ and $4^{(+)}$	$1^{(-)}$ and $3^{(-)}$
G24_3f (7.1%)	$3^{(-)}$ and $4^{(+)}$	$3^{(-)}$ and $4^{(+)}$	$1^{(+)}, 2^{(+)}$ and $4^{(+)}$	$1^{(-)}, 2^{(-)}$ and $3^{(-)}$
G24_4 (28.9-44.2%)	$2^{(+)}, 3^{(-)}$ and $4^{(+)}$	$1^{(-)}$ and $3^{(-)}$	$1^{(+)}, 2^{(+)}$ and $4^{(+)}$	$1^{(-)}$ and $3^{(-)}$
G24_5 (28.9-44.2%)	$3^{(-)}$ and $4^{(+)}$	$3^{(-)}$ and $4^{(+)}$	$1^{(+)}, 2^{(+)}$ and $4^{(+)}$	$1^{(-)}, 2^{(-)}$ and $3^{(-)}$
G24_7 (28.9-44.2%)	$2^{(-)}, 3^{(-)}$ and $4^{(+)}$	$1^{(+)}, 3^{(-)}$ and $4^{(+)}$	$1^{(+)}, 2^{(+)}$ and $4^{(+)}$	$1^{(-)}, 2^{(-)}$ and $3^{(-)}$
G24_8b (44.2%)	$3^{(-)}$ and $4^{(+)}$	$3^{(-)}$ and $4^{(+)}$	$1^{(+)}, 2^{(+)}$ and $4^{(+)}$	$1^{(-)}, 2^{(-)}$ and $3^{(-)}$

problem (G24_7) where reference-based repair outperformed offspring-repair. As Table 2 illustrates, mutant-repair is the worst between all the methods for eight test problems (G24_1, G24_f, G24_3, G24_3b, G24_3f, G24_4, G24_5 and G24_8b) except two test problems in which has similar results with reference-based repair (G24_2) and offspring-repair (G24_2 and G24_7).

For the constraint's change severity $S = 20$, the gradient-repair excelled almost all the other methods in seven test problems (G24_1, G24_f, G24_3, G24_3f, G24_5, G24_7 and G24_8b) with exceptions including G24_2, G24_3b and G24_4, that in which offspring-repair had similar performance. For this change severity, reference-based repair and offspring-repair performed almost the same for seven test problems (G24_1, G24_f, G24_2, G24_3, G24_3f, G24_5 and G24_8b) except three test problems (G24_3b, G24_4 and G24_7). For these three problems, while in two test problems (G24_3b and G24_4) offspring-repair had better results, in one test problem (G24_7) reference-based repair outperformed the offspring-repair. Mutant-repair had the worst results between all the methods for eight test problems (G24_1, G24_f, G24_3, G24_3b, G24_3f, G24_4, G24_5 and G24_8b) except two test problems in which had similar results with reference-based repair (G24_2) and offspring-repair (G24_2 and G24_7).

For the constraint's change severity $S = 50$, the gradient-repair excelled the other methods in six test problems (G24_f, G24_3, G24_3f, G24_5, G24_7 and G24_8b) with exceptions of having similar performance with offspring-repair (G24_1, G24_2, G24_3b and G24_4) and reference-based repair (G24_2). For this change severity, reference-based repair and offspring-repair performed almost the same for seven test problems (G24_1, G24_f, G24_2, G24_3, G24_3f, G24_5 and G24_8b) except three test problems (G24_3b, G24_4 and G24_7). For these three problems, while in two test problems (G24_3b and G24_4) offspring-repair had better results, in one test problem (G24_7) reference-based repair outperformed the offspring-repair. Mutant-repair had the worst results between all the methods for nine test problems (G24_1, G24_f, G24_3, G24_3b, G24_3f, G24_4, G24_5, G24_7 and G24_8b) except one test problem (G24_2) in which showed similar results with offspring-repair.

Gradient-repair for all severities outperformed other methods, because in this work, all of the test problems have the global optimum on the constraints' boundaries, and since this method moves slowly toward the feasible area its less probable that loses the information of global optima in the boundaries by crossing it. Although, this method cannot be applied for the functions that do not have derivative for their constraints. For this reason, the four functions G24_6a, G24_6b, G24_6c and G24_6d (that are functions inside this set of benchmark), were not used in our experiments. Therefore, for this method an understanding about the behaviour of the constraints is specifically needed. Changes in severity do not decrease the performance of this method. Even if for severity $S = 50$, it outperformed other methods in less test problems, this is because offspring-repair performance increased for some test problems for this severity. Similar behaviour in reference-based repair and offspring-repair based on offline error for all the severities is due to the similar procedure (uniform crossover in GA) that they use for repairing the infeasible solutions. The only difference is the way that they choose the reference solution.

5   Analysis of Success Rate and Required Number of Iterations for Repairing Solutions

Regardless of severity the total number of infeasible solutions (n_T) that needed repair for different functions were in the range between 1882 and 2981. The n_T values were increased for the functions that had dynamic constraints like G24_3, G24_3b, G24_4, G24_5 and G24_7. The reason is because, when the constraints

Table 3. Average and standard deviation of: (i) Success rate(s_r), (ii) required number of iterations (rn_i) for each of the repairs methods with $k = 0.5$, $S = 10$, 20 and 50, and $f_c = 1000$. Best results are remarked in boldface.

Functions	Success rate(s_r)				Required number of iterations(rn_i)			
	Reference	Offspring	Mutant	Gradient	Reference	Offspring	Mutant	Gradient
			$S = 10$					
G24_1	99.95(±0.08)	99.94(±0.08)	**100.00(±0.00)**	99.72(±0.15)	67.98(±7.99)	79.78(±4.33)	**2.26(±0.03)**	4.30(±0.24)
G24_f	99.97(±0.05)	99.97(±0.05)	**100.00(±0.00)**	99.71(±0.17)	64.77(±8.41)	74.95(±8.33)	**2.26(±0.03)**	3.96(±0.23)
G24_2	99.99(±0.02)	99.96(±0.08)	**100.00(±0.00)**	99.78(±0.18)	51.20(±10.65)	70.18(±5.94)	**2.26(±0.04)**	3.80(±0.26)
G24_3	99.98(±0.04)	99.96(±0.06)	**99.98(±0.02)**	95.19(±1.73)	60.35(±7.92)	70.91(±6.07)	**4.74(±0.13)**	8.03(±1.64)
G24_3b	99.97(±0.07)	99.97(±0.06)	**99.99(±0.03)**	95.96(±1.38)	66.51(±7.95)	71.81(±7.50)	**4.74(±0.11)**	7.60(±1.30)
G24_3f	99.88(±0.11)	99.85(±0.12)	**99.94(±0.05)**	93.33(±2.21)	84.66(±3.47)	89.90(±3.49)	14.04(±0.25)	**10.26(±2.10)**
G24_4	99.98(±0.04)	99.94(±0.07)	**99.99(±0.02)**	95.45(±1.75)	62.23(±9.58)	72.54(±6.27)	**4.77(±0.15)**	8.05(±1.66)
G24_5	**95.76(±3.55)**	74.16(±11.24)	71.44(±0.69)	74.31(±1.90)	47.28(±6.52)	72.00(±3.66)	38.09(±0.74)	**28.79(±1.78)**
G24_7	**92.79(±6.18)**	75.81(±9.57)	72.40(±0.66)	75.55(±2.06)	63.57(±6.47)	73.20(±4.76)	37.30(±0.73)	**27.44(±1.97)**
G24_8b	99.97(±0.06)	99.95(±0.06)	**100.00(±0.00)**	99.75(±0.13)	63.29(±6.01)	69.54(±6.26)	**2.26(±0.03)**	3.94(±0.19)
			$S = 20$					
G24_1	99.97(±0.05)	99.94(±0.08)	**100.00(±0.00)**	99.75(±0.11)	66.87(±7.25)	78.58(±5.85)	**2.25(±0.04)**	4.22(±0.24)
G24_f	99.98(±0.04)	99.97(±0.07)	**100.00(±0.00)**	99.67(±0.19)	65.19(±8.69)	76.88(±6.91)	**2.26(±0.04)**	4.02(±0.26)
G24_2	99.97(±0.05)	99.95(±0.10)	**100.00(±0.00)**	99.83(±0.11)	50.61(±10.83)	69.63(±6.42)	**2.26(±0.03)**	3.75(±0.22)
G24_3	99.96(±0.07)	99.93(±0.09)	**100.00(±0.01)**	92.37(±2.48)	69.44(±5.67)	74.51(±4.81)	**6.11(±0.14)**	11.09(±2.37)
G24_3b	99.96(±0.07)	99.89(±0.11)	**100.00(±0.01)**	92.12(±2.83)	71.79(±6.88)	79.61(±3.70)	**6.08(±0.14)**	11.60(±2.68)
G24_3f	99.90(±0.11)	99.84(±0.13)	**99.94(±0.04)**	92.96(±2.17)	85.00(±3.61)	90.97(±2.55)	14.12(±0.23)	**10.63(±2.04)**
G24_4	99.96(±0.07)	99.89(±0.10)	**99.99(±0.02)**	92.54(±2.23)	72.50(±6.14)	79.75(±3.84)	**6.12(±0.12)**	11.22(±2.11)
G24_5	97.47(±1.84)	82.19(±9.70)	**100.00(±0.00)**	92.46(±2.64)	39.24(±11.07)	69.08(±4.56)	**4.96(±0.11)**	10.85(±2.53)
G24_7	96.09(±1.84)	86.39(±5.93)	**100.00(±0.00)**	93.03(±2.25)	56.24(±6.08)	69.03(±4.75)	**4.90(±0.11)**	10.41(±2.17)
G24_8b	99.97(±0.05)	99.95(±0.07)	**100.00(±0.00)**	99.70(±0.20)	61.55(±5.67)	68.86(±7.18)	**2.27(±0.04)**	3.95(±0.26)
			$S = 50$					
G24_1	99.97(±0.05)	99.91(±0.10)	**100.00(±0.00)**	99.70(±0.15)	68.09(±8.06)	78.75(±4.43)	**2.26(±0.04)**	4.28(±0.23)
G24_f	99.97(±0.05)	99.95(±0.07)	**100.00(±0.00)**	99.69(±0.15)	64.98(±10.06)	74.94(±7.47)	**2.26(±0.04)**	4.02(±0.27)
G24_2	99.99(±0.02)	99.93(±0.11)	**100.00(±0.00)**	99.84(±0.08)	50.01(±10.05)	69.64(±5.59)	**2.27(±0.04)**	3.76(±0.17)
G24_3	99.92(±0.09)	99.89(±0.13)	**99.99(±0.01)**	92.90(±2.42)	75.99(±4.35)	80.88(±4.04)	**8.63(±0.15)**	10.62(±2.31)
G24_3b	99.92(±0.10)	99.86(±0.12)	**99.99(±0.02)**	93.04(±2.19)	77.14(±5.02)	83.60(±2.87)	**8.63(±0.18)**	10.82(±2.12)
G24_3f	99.91(±0.09)	99.84(±0.11)	**99.95(±0.04)**	93.18(±2.16)	84.12(±3.39)	90.11(±3.96)	14.01(±0.25)	**10.40(±2.08)**
G24_4	99.90(±0.10)	99.85(±0.13)	**99.99(±0.02)**	93.36(±2.01)	78.17(±4.62)	84.28(±2.89)	**8.66(±0.15)**	10.51(±1.91)
G24_5	97.64(±1.30)	86.30(±8.46)	**100.00(±0.00)**	91.57(±3.13)	40.28(±9.01)	66.52(±6.61)	**2.83(±0.05)**	11.66(±2.99)
G24_7	96.88(±1.65)	89.71(±6.01)	**100.00(±0.00)**	93.04(±2.82)	55.12(±6.69)	66.17(±5.68)	**2.82(±0.04)**	10.38(±2.70)
G24_8b	99.97(±0.06)	99.97(±0.07)	**100.00(±0.00)**	99.77(±0.16)	63.97(±7.20)	71.18(±6.15)	**2.27(±0.03)**	3.89(±0.24)

are changing, it is more probable that some feasible solutions be converted to infeasible ones after a change occurs.

The results for the success rate (s_r) and required number of iterations (nr_i) measures are presented in Table 3. Regarding to these results, some general observations can be concluded. The number of required iterations (nr_i), was the smallest for mutant-repair with a range between 2 to 8 and in second place is gradient-repair with the range between 4 to 10. An exception of this trend was seen in the function G24_3f in all the severities, and functions G24_5 and G24_7 for the severity $S = 10$, which gradient-repair excelled mutant-repair since the percentage of feasible area in these cases were small (see Table 2 for the feasibility percentages). Overall, in mutant-repair method since the process of producing a feasible solution is completely random and in this applied benchmark functions, the percentage of feasible area is huge, so this method achieved to feasible solutions after a few tries. In another words, this method is roughly dependent to the percentage of the feasible area. As mentioned before, the second smallest values for this measure was for gradient-based method; but in this case the reason was based on this method's wise selection and the fact that it only moves in the direction and with the amount of satisfying the constraint violations.

The worse results for this measure belonged to offspring-repair with an average number of required iterations ranging from 66 to 91 and reference-based repair with a range from 47 to 85. Compared to offspring-repair, reference-based repair required lower number of iterations, and this was because offspring-repair's step sizes are smaller and for this reason it needed more iterations to convert the infeasible solution to a feasible one. Other drawback in these two methods is that a number of evaluations is needed to produce feasible reference population. This can be expensive in high computational complex problems [5].

Generally based on considering all the measures, offspring and reference-based repair methods in most functions had similar behaviours. This is mostly because, the process of converting the infeasible solutions to feasible ones are approximately the same in these methods, and the only difference is the way that they choose the feasible reference solution. They do not loose the information of infeasible solution completely, as they use this individual to move in the direction of one of the feasible solutions (this is more evident in offspring as it uses the nearest reference feasible solution).

As regards to the third measure (success rate), although mutant-repair has the best values, but this is because in this set of benchmark, most of the functions

Table 4. Main features of each repair method

Method	Advantages	Disadvantages
Reference	(i) Maintain infeasible solution information, (ii) increase diversity	(i) Random behavior (ii) high number of required iterations and (iii) reference solutions needed
Offspring	(i) Maintain infeasible solution information	(i) High number of required iterations and (ii) roughly random behavior
Mutant	(i) High success rate, (ii) low iterations needed, (iii) no reference solution needed, (iv) increase diversity	(i) Not a good performance (offline error) (ii) loose the information and (iii) random behavior
Gradient	(i) Prominent performance when the optimal solution is in the boundaries of the feasible area, (ii) good performance (offline error), (iii) no reference solution needed, (iv) maintain infeasible solution information and (v) low iterations needed	(i) Knowledge about the characteristic of constraints needed and (ii) only can be applied when the constraints have derivate

has a huge percentage of feasible area. For this reason reaching to a feasible solution randomly after a few tries is easily possible based on this method. Obviously, for the cases of small percentage of feasible area, this method's efficiency will decrease. This was the case for the functions G24_5 and G24_7; as can be seen from Table 1, the values for this measure dropped drastically for this method as the percentage of feasible area is small for some time periods in these two functions. Reference-based and offspring were on the second place based on the values of this measure and the results of these two methods are roughly similar. Although, gradient-based method seemed to have worse results based on this measure, the differences between these values and the values for other methods were not significant. Moreover, practically, there is no need to convert all the infeasible solutions. In Table 4 a review of the advantages and disadvantages of each method is presented.

6   Conclusion and Future Work

In this paper, an investigation on different current repair methods in DCOPs were carried out. For the comparison, three different measures called: offline error, success rate and average number of required iterations for repairing the infeasible individuals, for each method were used. The results showed regardless of the change severities, in most cases gradient-based method outperformed the other methods based on offline error. This method especially performs much better than the other methods for the problems that have the optimal solution in the boundaries of the feasible area. Indeed, this method, moves very small steps and will not lose the optimal solution in the boundaries. Although, this method can not be applied for the functions that do not have derivative of the constraints. For the other measurement criteria, the number of required repair for mutant repair was the smallest and the second rank was for gradient-based method. Finally, based on the success rate, all of the repair methods were able to repair most of the infeasible solutions; such good performance was based on the fact that the feasible region of the main static test problem (G24) [29], occupy around 79% of the whole search space [11]. For future work, a combination of different repair methods can be investigated in order to make the most of each method. In addition, other constraint handling methods like ϵ-constrained, stochastic ranking and multi objective concepts that have not been applied in DCOPs can be applied and compared as well.

Acknowledgement. This work has been supported through Australian Research Council (ARC) grants DP140103400 and DP160102401.

References

1. Das, S., Mullick, S.S., Suganthan, P.N.: Recent advances in differential evolution – an updated survey. Swarm Evol. Comput. **27**, 1–30 (2016). http://www.sciencedirect.com/science/article/pii/S2210650216000146
2. Rakshit, P., Konar, A., Das, S., Jain, L.C., Nagar, A.K.: Uncertainty management in differential evolution induced multiobjective optimization in presence of measurement noise. IEEE Trans. Syst. Man. Cybern. Syst. **44**(7), 922–937 (2014)
3. Basak, A., Das, S., Tan, K.C.: Multimodal optimization using a biobjective differential evolution algorithm enhanced with mean distance-based selection. IEEE Trans. Evol. Comput. **17**(5), 666–685 (2013)
4. Omidvar, M.N., Li, X., Mei, Y., Yao, X.: Cooperative co-evolution with differential grouping for large scale optimization. IEEE Trans. Evol. Comput. **18**(3), 378–393 (2014)
5. Elsayed, S.M., Ray, T., Sarker, R.A.: A surrogate-assisted differential evolution algorithm with dynamic parameters selection for solving expensive optimization problems. In: 2014 IEEE Congress on Evolutionary Computation (CEC), pp. 1062–1068. IEEE (2014)
6. Bu, C., Luo, W., Zhu, T.: Differential evolution with a species-based repair strategy for constrained optimization. In: 2014 IEEE Congress on Evolutionary Computation (CEC), pp. 967–974. IEEE (2014)
7. Pal, K., Saha, C., Das, S.: Differential evolution and offspring repair method based dynamic constrained optimization. In: Panigrahi, B.K., Suganthan, P.N., Das, S., Dash, S.S. (eds.) SEMCCO 2013. LNCS, vol. 8297, pp. 298–309. Springer, Cham (2013). https://doi.org/10.1007/978-3-319-03753-0_27
8. Ameca-Alducin, M.Y., Mezura-Montes, E., Cruz-Ramirez, N.: Differential evolution with combined variants for dynamic constrained optimization. In: 2014 IEEE Congress on Evolutionary Computation (CEC), pp. 975–982, July 2014
9. Mezura-Montes, E., Coello, C.A.C.: Constraint-handling in nature-inspired numerical optimization: past, present and future. Swarm Evol. Comput. **1**(4), 173–194 (2011)
10. Eita, M.A., Shoukry, A.A.: Constrained dynamic differential evolution using a novel hybrid constraint handling technique. In: 2014 IEEE International Conference on Systems, Man and Cybernetics (SMC), pp. 2421–2426. IEEE (2014)
11. Ameca-Alducin, M.Y., Mezura-Montes, E., Cruz-Ramírez, N.: A repair method for differential evolution with combined variants to solve dynamic constrained optimization problems. In: Proceedings of the 2015 on Genetic and Evolutionary Computation Conference, GECCO 2015, ACM, New York, NY, USA, pp. 241–248 (2015). https://doi.org/10.1145/2739480.2754786
12. Richter, H.: Detecting change in dynamic fitness landscapes. In: IEEE Congress on Evolutionary Computation, CEC 2009, pp. 1613–1620 (2009)
13. Cobb, H.: An investigation into the use of hypermutation as an adaptive operator in genetic algorithms having continuous, time-dependent nonstationary environments. Technical report, Naval Research Lab, Washington DC (1990)
14. Tins, R., Yang, S.: A self-organizing random immigrants genetic algorithm for dynamic optimization problems. Genet. Program. Evol. Mach. **8**(3), 255–286 (2007). https://doi.org/10.1007/s10710-007-9024-z
15. Richter, H., Yang, S.: Memory based on abstraction for dynamic fitness functions. In: Giacobini, M., et al. (eds.) EvoWorkshops 2008. LNCS, vol. 4974, pp. 596–605. Springer, Heidelberg (2008). https://doi.org/10.1007/978-3-540-78761-7_65

16. Li, C., Nguyen, T.T., Yang, M., Yang, S., Zeng, S.: Multi-population methods in unconstrained continuous dynamic environments: the challenges. Inf. Sci. **296**, 95–118 (2015)
17. Grefenstette, J.: Genetic algorithms for changing environments. In: Parallel Problem Solving from Nature 2, pp. 137–144. Elsevier (1992)
18. Bu, C., Luo, W., Yue, L.: Continuous dynamic constrained optimization with ensemble of locating and tracking feasible regions strategies. IEEE Trans. Evol. Comput. **PP**(99), 1 (2016)
19. Nguyen, T., Yao, X.: Continuous dynamic constrained optimization: the challenges. IEEE Trans. Evol. Comput. **16**(6), 769–786 (2012)
20. Pal, K., Saha, C., Das, S., Coello-Coello, C.: Dynamic constrained optimization with offspring repair based gravitational search algorithm. In: 2013 IEEE Congress on Evolutionary Computation (CEC), pp. 2414–2421 (2013)
21. Ameca-Alducin, M.Y., Mezura-Montes, E., Cruz-Ramírez, N.: Differential evolution with combined variants plus a repair method to solve dynamic constrained optimization problems: a comparative study. Soft Computing, pp. 1–30 (2016)
22. Nguyen, T., Yang, S., Branke, J.: Evolutionary dynamic optimization: a survey of the state of the art. Swarm Evol. Comput. **6**, 1–24 (2012). http://www.sciencedirect.com/science/article/pii/S2210650212000363
23. Price, K., Storn, R., Lampinen, J.: Differential evolution a practical approach to global optimization, Natural Computing. Springer-Verlag, Heidelberg (2005). http://www.springer.com/west/home/computer/foundations?SGWID=4-156-22-32104365-0&teaserId=68063&CENTER_ID=69103
24. Mezura-Montes, E., Miranda-Varela, M.E., del Carmen Gómez-Ramón, R.: Differential evolution in constrained numerical optimization: an empirical study. Inf. Sci. **180**(22), 4223–4262 (2010)
25. Michalewicz, Z., Nazhiyath, G.: Genocop III: a co-evolutionary algorithm fornumerical optimization problems with nonlinear constraints. In: IEEE International Conference on Evolutionary Computation, vol. 2, pp. 647–651, November 1995
26. Chootinan, P., Chen, A.: Constraint handling in genetic algorithms using a gradient-based repair method. Comput. Oper. Res. **33**(8), 2263–2281 (2006). http://www.sciencedirect.com/science/article/pii/S030505480500050X
27. Branke, J., Schmeck, H.: Designing evolutionary algorithms for dynamic optimization problems. In: Ghosh, A., Tsutsui, S. (eds.) Advances in Evolutionary Computing. Natural Computing Series, pp. 239–262. Springer, Heidelberg (2003). https://doi.org/10.1007/978-3-642-18965-4_9
28. Derrac, J., García, S., Molina, D., Herrera, F.: A practical tutorial on the use of nonparametric statistical tests as a methodology for comparing evolutionary and swarm intelligence algorithms. Swarm Evol. Comput. **1**(1), 3–18 (2011). http://www.sciencedirect.com/science/article/pii/S2210650211000034
29. Liang, J.J., Runarsson, T., Mezura-Montes, E., Clerc, M., Suganthan, P., Coello Coello, C.A., Deb, K.: Problem definitions and evaluation criteria for the CEC 2006 special session on constrained real-parameter optimization. Technical report, Nanyang Technological University, Singapore, Singapure, December 2005

Prediction with Recurrent Neural Networks in Evolutionary Dynamic Optimization

Almuth Meier(✉) and Oliver Kramer

Computational Intelligence Group, Department of Computing Science,
University of Oldenburg, Oldenburg, Germany
{almuth.meier,oliver.kramer}@uni-oldenburg.de

Abstract. Evolutionary algorithms (EAs) are a good choice to solve dynamic optimization problems. Objective functions changing over time are challenging because after a change the EA has to adapt its population to find the new optimum. Prediction techniques that estimate the position of the next optimum can be incorporated into the EA. After a change, the predicted optimum can be employed to move the EA's population to a promising region of the solution space in order to accelerate convergence and improve accuracy in tracking the optimum. In this paper we introduce a recurrent neural network-based prediction approach. In an experimental study on the Moving Peaks Benchmark and dynamic variants of the Sphere, Rosenbrock, and Rastrigin functions we compare it to an autoregressive prediction approach and an EA without prediction. The results show the competitiveness of our approach and its suitability especially for repeated optima.

Keywords: Dynamic optimization · Prediction · Time series
Recurrent neural network

1 Introduction

In dynamic optimization, objective functions $f(x,t) \rightarrow r$ are considered that assign a time-dependent reward $r \in \mathbb{R}$ to a solution candidate $x \in \mathbb{R}^d$, where d is the dimensionality of the solution space and t represents the time. In the context of evolutionary optimization the objective function is called *fitness function* and the reward *fitness*. In case of constrained optimization, the constraints restricting the solution space can vary as well. The time point when a change occurs is called *change step* and the time interval between two changes *change period* [1]. The goal in dynamic optimization is to find for every change period the solution x which achieves the best reward, i.e., the minimum reward in case of minimization problems.

The way in which objective functions change can be described by *when* a change occurs and *how* the function changes [2]. Changes can occur more or

© Springer International Publishing AG, part of Springer Nature 2018
K. Sim and P. Kaufmann (Eds.): EvoApplications 2018, LNCS 10784, pp. 848–863, 2018.
https://doi.org/10.1007/978-3-319-77538-8_56

less often, e.g., in every generation or after a longer time interval. The length of the time interval between two changes can be fixed or varying in a patterned or random manner. The modification of the optimum itself can be described by the extent of the change, i.e., whether the new optimum is near to the old one or far away. The extent of the change can follow some probability distribution, can be random or periodic, i.e., previous optima re-appear later. Unless the optimum changes randomly, prediction models can learn where the optimum will move.

In this paper we propose a new prediction approach that employs a recurrent neural network which turns out to be excellent in other domains. First, we explain how EAs can be adapted to deal with dynamic problems and how a prediction model can be incorporated into an EA (Sect. 2). In Sect. 3 we propose our new prediction approach. Then we describe the settings of our experimental study (Sect. 4) and present the results (Sect. 5). A summary concludes the paper in Sect. 6.

2 Related Work

2.1 Extensions of EAs for Dynamic Problems

The simplest approach to solve dynamic optimization problems is to treat each change period as a static problem and run an optimization algorithm separately in each period. In contrast, dynamic optimization algorithms assume dependencies between change periods. They are executed once and adapt to changes during their runtime [3]. An overview of existing dynamic optimization approaches can be found in [4,5]. Among them, EAs are the most used ones [4,5].

Different extensions of evolutionary algorithms have been developed in order to deal with dynamic problems. The general problem when an EA dedicated for static optimization is applied to solve a dynamic problem is, that when it was running during a time without objective function changes, it may be converged to a solution so that the whole population is placed very near to this solution. If the objective function changes partly in such a way that somewhere else in the solution space a new, better optimum appears, the EA will hardly ever find this better solution but get stuck in the previously found local optimum. Therefore, different approaches have been investigated to make EAs suitable for dynamic problems. Based on the overviews of Cruz et al. [5] and Nguyen et al. [3], we describe some of them in the following.

A strategy to overcome getting stuck in a former local optimum is to *maintain diversity*. In each generation some random solutions (*immigrants*) are inserted into the population so that other regions of the solution space can be explored as well. Another approach is to actively *detect a change* in order to adapt the algorithm behavior afterwards. A change can be detected for example by re-evaluating individuals. If their fitness values in the current time step differ from those in the former time step, the fitness function has changed. After a change has been detected, *introducing diversity* by adding random individuals into the population could be a strategy to support the EA in discovering the new optimum. Furthermore, the EA can employ *memory* that stores good solutions found during previous generations. Individuals from the memory could replace individuals of the population in later generations, if they have a better fitness. This might be helpful especially if the changes are cyclic. Additionally, approaches have been introduced that *predict the next optimum* after a change has been detected by the EA. Inserting this prediction as solution into the population, the EA starts with a population containing an individual that is located maybe somewhere near to the real optimum. This approach works best if the changes are not completely random but follow a defined pattern.

2.2   Prediction-Based Optimization

In order to accurately estimate the optimum of the next change period, prediction models require information about former optimum positions. If the EA stores for each change period i the best solution found ($\mathbf{x}_i \in \mathbb{R}^d$), these data form a time series $(\mathbf{x}_0, \ldots, \mathbf{x}_{t-2}, \mathbf{x}_{t-1})$ for that the next step $\mathbf{x}_t$ is unknown. Thus, approaches from the time series prediction domain can be applied to predict the optimum $\mathbf{x}_t$ of the next change period t. They are supposed to yield best benefit for problems where the optimum position changes in a patterned manner. If it moves completely random within the solution space, random re-initialization of the population after a change might have the same effect.

The original evolutionary algorithm needs only few modifications to integrate a prediction model. Algorithm 1 shows pseudocode for a prediction-based EA. At the beginning of every generation it has to check whether the objective function has been changed. If a change has been detected (the EA detects not necessarily all changes) the best solution found during the last change period is stored. This one and solutions stemming from previous periods are used to train the prediction model and estimate the next optimum position. Then, the population is adapted by using the prediction. This can be done for example by introducing solutions that are initialized near the predicted optimum. Afterwards, the EA is continued in well known manner by producing offspring individuals and selecting the best ones for the next generation.

Algorithm 1. $(\mu+\lambda)$-EA with prediction

1: $\mathbf{P} \leftarrow$ initialize population with μ random individuals
2: $\mathbf{O} \leftarrow [\ ]$ # list of found optima
3: **while** g in generations **do**
4:     # detect change
5:     **if** change detected **then**
6:         $\mathbf{O}$.append(best($\mathbf{P}$))
7:         $\hat{o} \leftarrow$ predict_next_optimum($\mathbf{O}$) # employs prediction model
8:         $\mathbf{P} \leftarrow$ adapt_population($\hat{o}$)
9:     # create λ offspring individuals by recombination and mutation
10:    $\mathbf{P} \leftarrow$ select best μ offspring individuals

---

For prediction, different approaches have been investigated. Several of them are summarized in [2,3]. Some approaches aim at estimating *when* the next change will occur, e.g. [6], others investigate the prediction of *where* the next optimum will be, e.g., the approach presented by Rossi et al. [7] that uses a Kalman filter. Hatzakis and Wallace [8] suggest in their work to apply an autoregressive model for prediction of the optimum. In the following we will describe the autoregressive model since we compare our predictor to such a model in the experimental study.

An autoregressive model (AR) is a stochastic time series prediction model. Like linear regression it contains linear combinations. In the d-variate case an AR of order p estimates the value of variable $\mathbf{y} \in \mathbb{R}^d$ for time step t with

$$\mathbf{y}_t = \mathbf{c} + \sum_{i=1}^{p} \boldsymbol{\Phi}_i \mathbf{y}_{t-i} + \boldsymbol{\epsilon}_t, \quad \boldsymbol{\epsilon}_t = noise(\mathbf{C}), \tag{1}$$

where $\mathbf{y}, \mathbf{c}, \boldsymbol{\epsilon} \in \mathbb{R}^d$ and $\boldsymbol{\Phi}_i \in \mathbb{R}^{d \times d}$ [9]. Variable $\mathbf{y}_i$ is the observation of variable $\mathbf{y}$ at time step i, $\boldsymbol{\Phi}_i$ defines how much $\mathbf{y}_t$ depends on $\mathbf{y}_{t-i}$ and $\mathbf{c}$ is a vector of constants. The noise parameters in $\boldsymbol{\epsilon}_t$ are uncorrelated, have mean zero and the covariance matrix $\mathbf{C} \in \mathbb{R}^{d \times d}$ [10]. Hyndman and Athanasopoulos [9] state that AR models are able to deal with various different types of dependencies in the time series. The parameters $\mathbf{c}$, $\boldsymbol{\Phi}$ and $\mathbf{C}$ of the AR model can be determined by the least squares method.

3   Recurrent Neural Networks

In our approach we employ a recurrent neural network (RNN) as prediction model. RNNs are a type of artificial neural networks (ANNs) that are well suited for time series prediction because they use memory that enables learning from previous observations. In contrast to feed-forward ANNs, where the output of a neuron is passed to the next layer (Fig. 1), in RNNs the output of a neuron can serve as additional input for itself (Fig. 2). If $\mathbf{x}_t \in \mathbb{R}^d$ is the input of a neuron with a backward connection to itself and the function it computes on the input is denoted by f, the output of the neuron is $f(\mathbf{x}_t, f(\mathbf{x}_{t-1}, f(\mathbf{x}_{t-2}, \ldots)))$, see [11]. Variable $\mathbf{x}_t$ represents the observation of $\mathbf{x}$ at time t, while $\mathbf{x}_{t-1}$ has been observed at the former time step. Backward connections are advantageous if dependencies of the observed variables between different time steps exist. The number of previous observations that the RNN should learn from have to be specified by the user. The training procedure of RNNs is an adapted backpropagation approach called *backpropagation through time*. A detailed description can be found in [11]. In addition to the simple RNN approach explained here, other types of recurrence exist. For example long short-term memory (LSTM) [12] is an approach that has a more complex memory in order to solve the vanishing gradient problem.

For our prediction model we employ a simple RNN approach instead of a LSTM because in our application we are faced with very few training data (dozens till hundreds) whereas LSTMs require due to their larger complexity more training data to fit the parameters well. Because of this, we employ a rather small network with only two layers. The first one comprises 20 neurons each with the tanh activation function. The second layer is the output layer and therefore consists of one neuron with linear activation function. It returns the d-dimensional estimation of the optimum for the next change period.

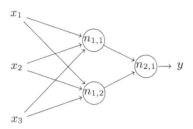

Fig. 1. Feed-forward ANN   **Fig. 2.** Recurrent ANN

4   Experimental Setup

4.1   Algorithms

We compare three different algorithms: an EA without prediction, denoted by noPred in the following sections, an EA with an autoregressive prediction model (autoPred) and an EA with our new RNN-based prediction (rnnPred). We implement the RNN with the Keras[1] library for ANNs in PYTHON. The first layer is realized by the SimpleRNN type of Keras, the second one with the Dense type. For the autoregressive model we employ the PYTHON package statsmodels.[2]

EA Framework. For all three approaches we employ the EA framework presented in Algorithm 1. The *change detection* is realized by re-evaluating half of the population and additional random solutions somewhere in the solution space. The *optimum prediction* uses either an ARR or a RNN prediction model or is not employed in case of noPred. The prediction models are trained the first time when 50 training samples have been collected. In further course of optimization, the models are trained at the beginning of every new change period with the new found optimum. The population is *adapted* by inserting a specified number of additional random immigrants into the population. In case of rnnPred and ARR half of the immigrants are the predicted optimum and neighbors obtained by adding noise to the optimum. The mutation strength of the EA is controlled by the Rechenberg 1/5th rule [13]. After a change is detected, we set it to its initial value so that the EA can better explore the solution space.

---

[1] https://keras.io/.
[2] http://www.statsmodels.org/0.6.1/vector_ar.html.

Parameter Settings. The EA framework employs a population of size $\mu = 50$ and generates $\lambda = 100$ offspring individuals in each of the *#generations* = 6000 generations. The mutation strength is initialized with $\sigma = 1.0$. The fitness function changes every *len* = 20 generations. After a change occurred, *#immigrants* = μ immigrants are incorporated into the population. The prediction models use *#steps* = 7 previous optima to estimate the next one. These parameter settings are the same for all experiments unless otherwise stated.

4.2   Benchmarks

We employ four different benchmark functions: dynamic variants of the Sphere, Rosenbrock and Rastrigin functions and the well known Moving Peaks Benchmark (MPB) [14]. The Sphere function is a simple convex function with one global and no local optimum. Rosenbrock is a non-convex function with one global optimum and, in high dimensions, one single local optimum [15]. Also Rastrigin is non-convex: Its shape resembles the Sphere function but has many local optima. We make these functions dynamic by moving the whole function linearly or sine-like within the solution space. The linear movement is realized by adding an offset, that is increased every change, to all dimensions. The sine-like movement is applied to the first two dimensions. The overall fitness level is not modified, only the position of the function changes within the space. Sphere, Rosenbrock and Rastrigin are minimization problems, the optimum fitness for every change is zero.

The MPB function comprises a specified number of peaks with different heights, widths and positions that are modified randomly over time. Therefore, it is possible that the optimum position suddenly jumps from one peak to another when the height of a different peak becomes larger. Thus, the optimum fitness may change among change periods. Since we consider minimization problems, we invert the MPB by multiplying the fitness function with -1.

4.3   Experiments

The experimental study comprises five groups of experiments that deal with different characteristics of optimization problems. Each group comprises several experiments that are repeated 20 times. In the following, we motivate the five groups of experiments and present their parameter settings.

Group 1 (SRR). The experiments of this group concern the Sphere, Rastrigin and Rosenbrock (SRR) benchmark functions. The goal is to examine whether linear or sine movement has different effects to **noPred**, **rnnPred** and **autoPred**, and whether the dimensionality of the functions plays a role. Therefore, we perform one experiment for each combination of the parameter values of the dimensionality $dim \in [2, 5, 10, 20, 50, 100]$ and the movement type $mov \in [linear, sine]$.

Group 2 (MPB-Random). In this experiments we investigate the case where the optimum movement does not follow a pattern but is random. We apply the MPB benchmark and use the settings proposed in [14]: initial peak width (0.1), initial peak height (50.0), height severity (7), width severity (0.1) and parameter s (0.6). We employ ten peaks and initialize their positions randomly within the range $[0, 100]$. For each dimension $dim \in [2, 5, 10, 20, 50, 100]$ we execute one experiment.

Group 3 (MPB-Noisy). Again the MPB benchmark is applied, but now we restrict the movements of the peak positions to be linear with noise. Among the experiments we increase the noise in order to examine to which extent randomization does affect the prediction. The settings for the MPB benchmark are the same as for group MPB-Random but we introduce an additional parameter $noise$ that represents the standard deviation for the Gaussian distribution computing the noise. Among the experiments we vary the strength of the noise $noise \in [0.0, 0.1, 1.0, 10]$ and the problem dimensionality $dim \in [2, 20]$.

Group 4 (Ros-Length). In the forth group of experiments, we modify the change frequency, i.e., the number of generations lying between two changes. We apply the Rosenbrock function with sine-like optimum movement and investigate different settings for the dimensionality $dim \in [2, 20, 50]$ and the length of the change periods $len \in [5, 10, 20, 40, 60]$. The longer the change periods the more generations are required to collect enough training data. Therefore, we initialize the number of generations with $\#generations = len \cdot 300$ so that in each experiment the overall number of training data is 300.

Group 5 (SRR-Neurons). The goal of this group is to test whether the usage of more neurons for the RNN of our `rnnPred` approach has an effect. We employ the Sphere, Rosenbrock and Rastrigin functions with sine-like optimum movement and $dim \in [2, 5, 10, 20, 50, 100]$. We set the number of neurons depending on the problem dimensionality with $\#neurons = \lceil 1.3 \cdot dim \rceil$.

4.4   Performance Measures

Measures that quantify the quality of algorithms for dynamic optimization problems often are distinguished into optimality- and behavior-based measures [3]. The optimality-based measures investigate how well the optimum is tracked, whereas the behavior-based ones quantify more abstract criteria like population diversity or convergence speed. In the work of Nguyen et al. [3] and Ben-Romdhane et al. [4] different metrics are surveyed. We employ four of those measures and additionally develop a new one. In the following we describe these measures based on [3]. For a discussion about the advantages and disadvantages of the metrics, see [3].

Best of Generation ($\overline{\text{BOG}}$). The $\overline{\text{BOG}}$ requires for each run j of an experiment per generation i the best fitness value achieved (BOG_{ij}). These values are averaged over all r runs and afterwards averaged over the g generations leading to a scalar value per experiment and algorithm:

$$\overline{\text{BOG}} = \frac{1}{g} \sum_{i=1}^{g} \left(\frac{1}{r} \sum_{j=1}^{r} \text{BOG}_{ij} \right). \tag{2}$$

Since we deal with minimization problems, $\overline{\text{BOG}}$ should be as small as possible. The exact optimum $\overline{\text{BOG}}$ depends on the problem.

Normalized $\overline{\text{BOG}}$ (norm$\overline{\text{BOG}}$). In order to obtain a measure that enables the comparison of algorithms regarding different problems, norm$\overline{\text{BOG}}$ has been proposed. The computation of norm$\overline{\text{BOG}}$ results in one value for each of a tested algorithms:

$$\text{norm}\overline{\text{BOG}}(i) = \frac{1}{p} \sum_{j=1}^{p} \frac{|e_{max}(j) - e_{i,j}|}{|e_{max}(j) - e_{min}(j)|}, \quad \forall i \in \{1, \dots, a\}. \tag{3}$$

The symbols $e_{max}(j)$ and $e_{min}(j)$ signify the largest and smallest error, respectively, any of the a tested algorithms has achieved on problem j. The error algorithm i achieved on problem j is described by $e_{i,j}$ and p denotes the number of test problems. Different error measures can be applied; we employ $\overline{\text{BOG}}$. Since norm$\overline{\text{BOG}}$ is a relative performance measure, its value lies within range $[0, 1]$. One is the best and zero the worst value.

Best Error Before Change (BEBC). In contrast to $\overline{\text{BOG}}$ which takes into account the performance in all generations, BEBC only measures how well an algorithm was able to find the global optimum before the next change occurs:

$$\text{BEBC} = \frac{1}{c} \sum_{i=1}^{c} |e_{best}(i)|, \tag{4}$$

where c is the number of changes, and $e_{best}(i)$ is the difference between the global optimum for change i and the best fitness the algorithm has found for that change. In the best case, the global optimum is found in each change resulting in a BEBC of zero. In the worst case, the BEBC can become arbitrary large.

Absolute Recovery Rate (ARR). While the former performance measures are fitness-based ones, this and the following measure are behavior-based. They measure the algorithms' convergence properties. The author proposing ARR states that it measures "how quick it is for an algorithm to start converging to

the global optimum before the next change happens" [1, p. 116]. It is computed
as follows:

$$\text{ARR} = \frac{1}{c} \sum_{i=1}^{c} \frac{\sum_{j=1}^{g(i)} |f_{best}(i,j) - f_{best}(i,1)|}{g(i)|f^*(i) - f_{best}(i,1)|}, \tag{5}$$

where c is the number of changes and $g(i)$ signifies the number of generations for
change i. The symbol $f^*(i)$ represents the global best fitness for change period i,
while $f_{best}(i,1)$ and $f_{best}(i,j)$ describe the best found fitness in the first and jth
generation of change period i, respectively. We adapted ARR by using unsigned
differences instead of signed ones. This is necessary in case the fitness function
can become negative. ARR ranges from zero (worst case) to one (best case).

Relative Convergence Speed (RCS). The ARR is designed so that it measures how fast an algorithm can get *far away* from its *first solution*, i.e., the best
found fitness in the first generation after a change. Due to this, algorithms that
start with a very poor solution may achieve a better ARR than those starting
with a better solution. We illustrate this with an example. Assuming the best
fitness values found by algorithm A during one change period are $[9, 6, 6, 0]$, those
of algorithm B are $[4, 3, 3, 0]$ and zero is the global optimum fitness. Then, A has
ARR 0.42 and B has ARR 0.36. Thus, A outperforms B although B in every but
the last generation achieves a better fitness than A.

To overcome this unexpected behavior, we propose a new measure called
RCS that takes into account how fast an algorithm finds solutions *near to* the
global optimum.

$$\text{RCS} = \frac{1}{c} \sum_{i=1}^{c} \frac{\sum_{j=1}^{g(i)} j \cdot |f_{best}(i,j) - f^*(i)|}{\sum_{j=1}^{g(i)} j \cdot |f_{worst}(i) - f^*(i)|}. \tag{6}$$

The symbols c, $g(i)$, $f_{best}(i,j)$ and $f^*(i)$ are the same as defined for ARR,
$f_{worst}(i)$ represents the best fitness for change period i found by the worst algorithm. There exist four main differences to the definition of the ARR. (1) As
motivated above, we employ the difference between $f_{best}(i,j)$ and $f^*(i)$ instead
of the difference to $f_{best}(i,1)$ in order to measure how near a solution is to the
optimum. (2) In order to scale this difference into the range $[0,1]$ it is divided by
the difference between the global optimum and the best fitness of the worst algorithm. By this, RCS measures the convergence speed of the algorithms relative
to the worst one. If instead the difference $f_{best}(i,1) - f^*(i)$ like in ARR would be
incorporated, the RCS would exhibit behavior similar to ARR in cases like the
above presented example, but with inverted range. (3) The difference terms are
weighted with the generation number within a change in order to reward early
good fitness values and penalize high fitness values at the and of change periods.
(4) In contrast to ARR, the best value for RCS is zero and the worst is one.

5   Experimental Results

To obtain an overall impression of the algorithms' quality we first have a look at the norm$\overline{\text{BOG}}$. We compute it using the results of all experiments but those of group SRR-Neurons as they are conducted only for rnnPred. The norm$\overline{\text{BOG}}$ results in 0.85 for rnnPred, 0.79 for autoPred and 0.06 for noPred. The usage of predictors therefore clearly outperforms the EA without prediction. In the following sections, we examine the different groups of experiments separately. Notice, that the result tables (e.g. Fig. 3) contain abbreviated names (e.g. "no" instead of noPred). The best values are highlighted bold. Due to rounding the differences between values sometimes are not visible in this paper.

5.1   Group SRR

All experiments of this group figure out the complexity of problems with a high dimensionality. In all experiments the algorithms show deteriorating $\overline{\text{BOG}}$ and BEBC values the larger the dimensionality gets (Figs. 3, 4, 7, 8, 9 and 10). The best possible $\overline{\text{BOG}}$ is zero in all except the MPB-based experiments. In addition, the differences among the algorithms decrease with increasing dimensionality. These findings are caused by the curse of dimensionality: The more dimensions the more difficult becomes the exploration of the search space.

Furthermore, common to all experiments is that in all cases EAs with prediction outperform noPred regarding $\overline{\text{BOG}}$ and BEBC. Another observation regarding $\overline{\text{BOG}}$ and BEBC results for Sphere, Rosenbrock and Rastrigin is that autoPred often outperforms rnnPred when the optimum is moved linearly, especially for the Sphere function. But for the more complex Rosenbrock and Rastrigin functions, rnnPred often is better than autoPred in case of a 5-, 10- or 20-dimensional linear moved problem. When the optimum is moved sine-like, rnnPred almost always has better results than autoPred, except for the 100-dimensional Sphere and Rastrigin functions. These observations emphasize the strengths of RNNs for optimization problems where the optimum movement follows a periodic pattern.

For the Sphere function, we include the results for the convergence measures ARR (Fig. 5) and RCS (Fig. 6); the results for the other functions are omitted because of limited space. Regarding ARR, noPred always is best except for three cases with sine-like movement. Whereas for the RCS measure noPred is outperformed by rnnPred and autoPred: autoPred is always best in case of linear movement and noPred converges best in sinus-like moved environments, except for the 100 dimensions. These contrary results are due to the measures' design (see discussion in Sect. 4.4). noPred has good ARR values probably because after a change it starts with a rather worse population than rnnPred and autoPred, since it has no information about the next optimum. Therefore noPred may have much more potential to quickly achieve large fitness improvements than rnnPred and autoPred. The results for RCS are consistent to the observations made for $\overline{\text{BOG}}$ and BEBC: rnnPred converges faster for sine-like and autoPred for linear moved functions.

mov	dim	no	rnn	auto
linear	2	0.21	0.09	**0.08**
linear	5	3.12	2.04	**1.71**
linear	10	15.16	10.73	**9.35**
linear	20	61.97	44.52	**39.89**
linear	50	384.65	270.22	**226.45**
linear	100	1,642.40	1,186.55	**791.27**
sine	2	1.80	**0.44**	0.67
sine	5	9.75	**4.93**	6.01
sine	10	25.28	**16.35**	21.24
sine	20	72.48	**55.73**	64.39
sine	50	345.60	**294.23**	308.14
sine	100	1,002.77	940.85	**929.48**

Fig. 3. $\overline{\text{BOG}}$ (Sphere, SRR)

mov	dim	no	rnn	auto
linear	2	0.00	0.00	**0.00**
linear	5	0.01	0.01	**0.01**
linear	10	0.50	0.36	**0.31**
linear	20	7.51	5.25	**4.66**
linear	50	125.05	85.86	**69.01**
linear	100	843.55	618.12	**376.59**
sine	2	0.00	**0.00**	0.00
sine	5	0.03	**0.02**	0.02
sine	10	0.72	**0.48**	0.62
sine	20	8.62	**6.31**	7.50
sine	50	126.20	**101.30**	108.16
sine	100	534.37	489.12	**482.72**

Fig. 4. BEBC (Sphere, SRR)

mov	dim	no	rnn	auto
linear	2	**0.92**	0.89	0.19
linear	5	**0.88**	0.85	0.30
linear	10	**0.79**	0.76	0.25
linear	20	**0.65**	0.63	0.19
linear	50	**0.47**	0.43	0.13
linear	100	**0.35**	0.29	0.12
sine	2	**0.92**	0.89	0.90
sine	5	**0.89**	0.85	0.87
sine	10	**0.81**	0.79	0.80
sine	20	0.67	**0.69**	0.68
sine	50	0.44	**0.47**	0.46
sine	100	0.29	**0.32**	0.31

Fig. 5. ARR (Sphere, SRR)

mov	dim	no	rnn	auto
linear	2	0.01	0.01	**0.00**
linear	5	0.03	0.01	**0.01**
linear	10	0.09	0.03	**0.01**
linear	20	0.20	0.07	**0.03**
linear	50	0.39	0.16	**0.07**
linear	100	0.54	0.31	**0.09**
sine	2	0.01	**0.01**	0.01
sine	5	0.03	**0.02**	0.02
sine	10	0.07	**0.04**	0.06
sine	20	0.18	**0.11**	0.14
sine	50	0.42	**0.29**	0.32
sine	100	0.60	0.50	**0.48**

Fig. 6. RCS (Sphere, SRR)

mov	dim	no	rnn	auto
linear	2	4.14E+00	2.34E+00	**2.21E+00**
linear	5	3.49E+04	3.46E+04	**3.45E+04**
linear	10	9.24E+05	**9.22E+05**	9.28E+05
linear	20	7.40E+06	7.39E+06	**7.39E+06**
linear	50	5.89E+07	5.83E+07	**5.83E+07**
linear	100	2.36E+08	2.26E+08	**2.20E+08**
sine	2	9.05E+01	**1.66E+01**	1.93E+01
sine	5	5.54E+04	**2.92E+04**	3.25E+04
sine	10	1.00E+06	**9.63E+05**	9.79E+05
sine	20	8.40E+06	**8.34E+06**	8.36E+06
sine	50	6.13E+07	**6.12E+07**	6.12E+07
sine	100	2.28E+08	**2.28E+08**	2.28E+08

Fig. 7. $\overline{\text{BOG}}$ (Rosenbrock, SRR)

mov	dim	no	rnn	auto
linear	2	1.60E-02	1.22E-02	**6.63E-03**
linear	5	7.84E+00	7.20E+00	**6.16E+00**
linear	10	9.75E+02	**9.54E+02**	3.24E+03
linear	20	1.11E+05	**1.11E+05**	1.11E+05
linear	50	7.60E+06	**7.42E+06**	7.41E+06
linear	100	7.57E+07	7.03E+07	**6.61E+07**
sine	2	8.57E-02	**3.11E-02**	4.25E-02
sine	5	1.67E+01	**1.13E+01**	1.26E+01
sine	10	1.04E+03	**9.70E+02**	9.97E+02
sine	20	1.44E+05	**1.43E+05**	1.43E+05
sine	50	8.07E+06	**8.06E+06**	8.06E+06
sine	100	6.67E+07	**6.66E+07**	6.66E+07

Fig. 8. BEBC (Rosenbrock, SRR)

mov	dim	no	rnn	auto
linear	2	5.92	2.89	**1.31**
linear	5	54.56	**38.11**	47.43
linear	10	216.57	**162.80**	184.36
linear	20	723.31	**609.14**	625.35
linear	50	3,538.31	3,445.67	**3,440.82**
linear	100	12,036.34	10,095.03	**7,242.92**
sine	2	5.29	**2.47**	3.46
sine	5	43.48	**23.42**	35.99
sine	10	191.40	**107.26**	165.88
sine	20	887.95	**600.14**	628.03
sine	50	4,868.04	**2,692.28**	2,706.65
sine	100	16,944.10	12,981.28	**8,636.41**

Fig. 9. $\overline{BOG}$ (Rastrigin, SRR)

mov	dim	no	rnn	auto
linear	2	4.42	2.06	**0.93**
linear	5	40.46	**27.22**	35.52
linear	10	162.04	**117.32**	138.73
linear	20	549.23	**463.62**	474.89
linear	50	2,850.39	2,856.81	**2,788.17**
linear	100	10,168.79	8,637.22	**5,998.13**
sine	2	0.48	**0.22**	0.41
sine	5	21.48	**10.79**	17.39
sine	10	137.59	**75.44**	124.06
sine	20	816.36	**537.36**	555.43
sine	50	4,669.82	**2,518.82**	2,536.05
sine	100	16,506.73	12,562.96	**8,248.04**

Fig. 10. BEBC (Rastrigin, SRR)

5.2 Group MPB-Random

The MPB-Random experiments are characterized by randomly changing peak heights, widths and positions. Thus, the optimal $\overline{BOG}$ varies among the settings and therefore is added into the result tables. The results show that noPred outperforms the prediction-based EAs in the 2- and 5-dimensional case regarding all four quality measures (Figs. 11, 12, 13 and 14). For the other dimensions rnnPred or autoPred are best but the differences between the three algorithms are very marginal. The prediction-based approaches perform poor in these settings since the changes are random but prediction especially makes sense when the changes follow a pattern that can be learned.

An explanation for the better performance of noPred for small dimensions may be that after a change the prediction-based approaches initialize a part of their population near to the predicted optimum. Due to the random changes, this prediction probably is very poor. Instead, noPred initializes that population part randomly somewhere in the solution space. Therefore it has more diversity within the population and can find more easily a better solution. A reason why this difference between the approaches cannot be observed in higher dimensions may be the curse of dimensionality: many more, and not only few more, random individuals are required to adequately explore the solution space.

dim	no	rnn	auto	expected
2	**-143.51**	-123.12	-126.18	-169.99
5	**-107.39**	-102.31	-102.01	-204.61
10	-56.05	**-56.45**	-56.35	-134.12
20	-51.87	**-52.12**	-52.11	-161.23
50	-58.34	-58.55	**-58.60**	-204.72
100	-63.06	-63.33	**-63.47**	-149.77

Fig. 11. $\overline{BOG}$ (MPB-Random)

dim	no	rnn	auto
2	**26.56**	47.27	44.38
5	**92.47**	98.51	98.51
10	71.53	**71.51**	71.51
20	101.14	**101.07**	101.07
50	136.31	136.19	**136.14**
100	77.01	76.76	**76.66**

Fig. 12. BEBC (MPB-Random)

dim	no	rnn	auto
2	**0.85**	0.72	0.65
5	**0.35**	0.31	0.32
10	0.27	**0.26**	0.27
20	**0.14**	0.15	0.15
50	0.10	0.10	**0.10**
100	0.12	0.12	**0.12**

Fig. 13. ARR (MPB-Random)

dim	no	rnn	auto
2	**0.51**	0.69	0.67
5	**0.62**	0.64	0.65
10	0.69	**0.69**	0.69
20	0.82	**0.81**	0.81
50	0.86	0.86	**0.86**
100	0.83	0.83	**0.83**

Fig. 14. RCS (MPB-Random)

5.3   Group MPB-Noisy

Considering BEBC (Fig. 16), it can be observed that `noPred` outperforms the prediction-based approaches (`autoPred` is better than `rnnPred`) in the 2-dimensional setting but for 20 dimensions both predictors are better than `noPred`. The results for $\overline{\text{BOG}}$ (Fig. 15) are similar. These findings are akin to the observations made in the MPB-Random experiments and can be justified by the same explanation.

In addition, it can be observed that in the MPB-Noisy experiments the results differ much more among the approaches than in the MPB-Random settings. Especially regarding BEBC the performance differences between `noPred` and the prediction approaches are larger than in MPB-Random. A reason for this is that in MPB-Noisy the peaks basically follow a linear movement. Though the relationship is disturbed to some extent by the noise, the predictors seem to be able to learn the pattern.

Furthermore, it is interesting that in the 2-dimensional case $\overline{\text{BOG}}$ and BEBC become better with increasing noise but then become worse for noise 10. In the 20-dimensional case both measures improve only for very small noise (0.1) and deteriorate for higher noise. The measures of convergence speed show no clear relationship to the strength of noise and therefore are not included due to space restrictions.

dim	noise	no	rnn	auto	expected
2	0	-137.61	-138.06	**-141.11**	-177.42
2	0.1	**-143.00**	-138.81	-142.13	-177.42
2	1	**-157.50**	-156.87	-155.90	-177.42
2	10	-125.34	**-127.40**	-126.56	-177.42
20	0	-16.41	-42.21	**-91.99**	-225.32
20	0.1	-20.07	-48.87	**-95.52**	-225.32
20	1	-10.77	-13.00	**-14.61**	-225.32
20	10	-0.62	-0.67	**-0.68**	-225.32

Fig. 15. $\overline{\text{BOG}}$ (MPB-Noisy)

dim	noise	no	rnn	auto
2	0	**34.46**	37.23	35.74
2	0.1	**28.84**	36.47	34.43
2	1	**10.95**	15.79	16.96
2	10	**21.31**	24.57	25.44
20	0	182.69	149.87	**130.52**
20	0.1	173.08	134.41	**111.09**
20	1	195.31	190.44	**187.04**
20	10	223.25	223.09	**223.06**

Fig. 16. BEBC (MPB-Noisy)

5.4   Group Ros-Length

In general, both $\overline{BOG}$ (Fig. 17) and BEBC (Fig. 18) are improving with decreasing change frequency. This is because the EA has more generations per change period to explore the solution space and may converge to a better solution. Another observation is, that rnnPred always was the best on the sine-moved Rosenbrock function in the SRR experiments and even in the Ros-Length settings is outperformed only one time. This shows that rnnPred is able to cope with fast and slow changes.

It is interesting that the prediction-based approaches in these settings always outperform noPred although, especially in case of very frequent changes, the training data for the prediction models probably are rather poor since the EA has very few generations to converge. For these experiments, the convergence results do not vary much among the algorithms and are therefore not shown here.

dim	len	no	rnn	auto
2	5	1.35E+02	**5.28E+01**	5.39E+01
2	10	9.81E+01	**2.30E+01**	2.63E+01
2	20	9.50E+01	**1.74E+01**	1.94E+01
2	40	5.45E+01	**1.14E+01**	1.26E+01
2	60	3.52E+01	**6.61E+00**	7.61E+00
20	5	3.56E+07	**3.43E+07**	3.46E+07
20	10	1.64E+07	**1.62E+07**	1.62E+07
20	20	8.23E+06	**8.17E+06**	8.19E+06
20	40	3.82E+06	**3.79E+06**	3.80E+06
20	60	2.68E+06	**2.66E+06**	2.66E+06
50	5	2.68E+08	2.65E+08	**2.65E+08**
50	10	1.23E+08	**1.23E+08**	1.23E+08
50	20	6.03E+07	**6.02E+07**	6.02E+07
50	40	3.01E+07	**3.01E+07**	3.01E+07
50	60	1.99E+07	**1.98E+07**	1.98E+07

Fig. 17. $\overline{BOG}$ (Ros-Length)

dim	len	no	rnn	auto
2	5	1.44E+01	**7.47E+00**	7.67E+00
2	10	4.17E+00	**1.13E+00**	1.44E+00
2	20	5.44E-02	**3.14E-02**	3.87E-02
2	40	1.99E-03	**1.24E-03**	1.63E-03
2	60	1.29E-04	**1.13E-04**	5.92E-04
20	5	1.86E+07	**1.79E+07**	1.80E+07
20	10	2.93E+06	**2.89E+06**	2.91E+06
20	20	1.46E+05	**1.45E+05**	1.45E+05
20	40	6.50E+02	**6.25E+02**	6.41E+02
20	60	6.58E+01	**6.08E+01**	6.26E+01
50	5	1.89E+08	1.87E+08	**1.87E+08**
50	10	5.30E+07	**5.28E+07**	5.28E+07
50	20	7.92E+06	**7.91E+06**	7.91E+06
50	40	2.62E+05	**2.61E+05**	2.61E+05
50	60	1.11E+04	**1.11E+04**	1.11E+04

Fig. 18. BEBC (Ros-Length)

5.5   Group SRR-Neurons

Figures 19 and 20 present the results for these experiments. The bold highlighting signifies results that are better than the corresponding ones in the SRR experiments. In the settings with two, five and ten dimensions, rnnPred achieves worse results compared to the corresponding experiments of the SRR settings where more neurons are employed. However, in case of 20, 50 and 100 dimensions, where more neurons are used in the SRR-Neurons settings, rnnPred becomes better and even outperforms autoPred. The reason for this is that RNNs with a complexer architecture, i.e., many neurons and layers, often can better learn difficult relationships than RNNs with simpler architectures. These experiments show that there is some potential to optimize our prediction model in order to improve the results.

dim	sphere	rosenbrock	rastrigin
2	0.66	2.56E+01	3.31
5	5.33	4.39E+04	24.29
10	16.69	1.16E+06	115.36
20	**54.91**	**8.02E+06**	**571.28**
50	**290.41**	**5.79E+07**	**2,292.96**
100	**911.16**	**2.16E+08**	**11,184.85**

dim	sphere	rosenbrock	rastrigin
2	0.00	6.11E-02	0.31
5	0.02	1.31E+01	11.05
10	0.57	1.08E+03	82.14
20	6.77	**1.37E+05**	**507.79**
50	**98.46**	**7.93E+06**	**2,123.86**
100	**473.62**	**6.05E+07**	**10,763.60**

Fig. 19. $\overline{\text{BOG}}$ (SRR-Neurons)   **Fig. 20.** BEBC (SRR-Neurons)

6   Summary

In this paper we presented a new approach to predict the position of the next optimum of a dynamically changing fitness function. We designed a recurrent neural network to serve as prediction model and trained it during the optimization with new optima found by the EA. In the experimental study, our approach showed competitiveness to an existing prediction approach (autoPred) that employs an autoregressive model.

Based on the results of the experimental study we can conclude that our new approach (rnnPred) works well for objective functions where the optimum movement follows a recurrent pattern but also yields good results for other movement patterns. It could be observed that rnnPred is able to cope with different change frequencies as well as for different problem dimensionalities. In case of noisy optimum movements it did not perform best but nevertheless yields results competitive to those of autoPred. Furthermore it turned out that our prediction model can easily be improved by incorporating more neurons into the architecture. Then it would be able to yield even better results for high-dimensional problems. In general, the prediction-based EAs performed better than the EA without predictor. Only in 2-dimensional experiments with random optimum movement noPred was able to achieve better results.

Further work may investigate the improvement of the network architecture of our prediction model by dynamically adapting it to the problem type.

Acknowledgments. This research is funded by the German Research Foundation through the Research Training Group SCARE – System Correctness under Adverse Conditions (DFG-GRK 1765), www.scare.uni-oldenburg.de.

References

1. Nguyen, T.T.: Continuous dynamic optimization using evolutionary algorithms. Ph.D. thesis, University of Birmingham (2011). http://etheses.bham.ac.uk/1296/
2. Simões, A., Costa, E.: Prediction in evolutionary algorithms for dynamic environments. Soft Comput. **18**(8), 1471–1497 (2014). https://doi.org/10.1007/s00500-013-1154-z
3. Nguyen, T.T., Yang, S., Branke, J.: Evolutionary dynamic optimization: a survey of the state of the art. Swarm Evol. Comput. **6**, 1–24 (2012)

4. Ben-Romdhane, H., Alba, E., Krichen, S.: Best practices in measuring algorithm performance for dynamic optimization problems. Soft Comput. **17**(6), 1005–1017 (2013). https://doi.org/10.1007/s00500-013-0989-7
5. Cruz, C., González, J.R., Pelta, D.A.: Optimization in dynamic environments: a survey on problems, methods and measures. Soft. Comput. **15**(7), 1427–1448 (2011). https://doi.org/10.1007/s00500-010-0681-0
6. Simões, A., Costa, E.: Improving prediction in evolutionary algorithms for dynamic environments. In: Genetic and Evolutionary Computation Conference (GECCO), pp. 875–882 (2009)
7. Rossi, C., Abderrahim, M., Díaz, J.C.: Tracking moving optima using kalman-based predictions. Evol. Comput. **16**(1), 1–30 (2008)
8. Hatzakis, I., Wallace, D.: Dynamic multi-objective optimization with evolutionary algorithms: a forward-looking approach. In: Genetic and Evolutionary Computation Conference (GECCO), pp. 1201–1208 (2006). http://doi.acm.org/10.1145/1143997.1144187
9. Hyndman, R.J., Athanasopoulos, G.: Forecasting: principles and practice. OTexts: Melbourne, Australia (2013). http://otexts.org/fpp/. Accessed 04 Nov 2017
10. Neumaier, A., Schneider, T.: Estimation of parameters and eigenmodes of multivariate autoregressive models. ACM Trans. Math. Softw. (TOMS) **27**(1), 27–57 (2001)
11. Rojas, R.: Neural Networks: A Systematic Introduction. Springer, Heidelberg (1996). https://doi.org/10.1007/978-3-642-61068-4
12. Hochreiter, S., Schmidhuber, J.: Long short-term memory. Neural Comput. **9**(8), 1735–1780 (1997). https://doi.org/10.1162/neco.1997.9.8.1735
13. Beyer, H.G., Schwefel, H.P.: Evolution strategies – a comprehensive introduction. Nat. Comput. **1**(1), 3–52 (2002)
14. Branke, J.: Memory enhanced evolutionary algorithms for changing optimization problems. In: Congress on Evolutionary Computation (CEC), pp. 1875–1882 (1999)
15. Kramer, O.: Machine Learning for Evolution Strategies. Springer, Heidelberg (2016). https://doi.org/10.1007/978-3-319-33383-0

A Multi-objective Time-Linkage Approach for Dynamic Optimization Problems with Previous-Solution Displacement Restriction

Danial Yazdani[1(✉)], Trung Thanh Nguyen[1], Juergen Branke[2], and Jin Wang[1]

[1] Department of Maritime and Mechanical Engineering,
Liverpool Logistics, Offshore and Marine Research Institute,
Liverpool John Moores University, Liverpool, UK
danial.yazdani@gmail.com,
{T.T.Nguyen,J.Wang}@ljmu.ac.uk
[2] Warwich Business School, University of Warwick, Coventry, UK
Juergen.Branke@wbs.ac.uk

Abstract. Dynamic optimization problems (DOPs) are problems that change over time and many real-world problems are classified as DOPs. However, most of investigations in this domain are focused on tracking moving optima (TMO) without considering any other objectives which creates a gap between real-world problems and academic research in this area. One of the important optimization objectives in many real-world problems is previous-solution displacement restriction (PSDR) in which successive solutions should not be much different. PSDRs can be categorized as a multi-objective problem in which the first objective is optimality and the second one is minimizing the displacement of consecutive solutions which also can represents switching cost. Moreover, PSDRs are counted as dynamic time-linkage problems (DTPs) because the current chosen solution by the optimizer will change the next search space. In this paper, we propose a new hybrid method based on particle swarm optimization (PSO) for PSDRs based on their characteristics. The experiments are done on moving peaks benchmark (MPB) and the performance of the proposed algorithm alongside two comparison ones are investigated on it.

Keywords: Dynamic multi-objective optimization problems
Dynamic time-linkage optimization problems · Dynamic optimization problems
Particle swarm optimization

1 Introduction

Many real-world problems are dynamic and changing over time. Most of previous research in the dynamic optimization problem (DOP) area focus on tracking moving optima (TMO) and researchers rarely have considered any other objective in the problems. There are different optimization objectives which one of the important ones is previous-solution displacement restriction (PSDR) [1]. In PSDRs, the algorithm

© Springer International Publishing AG, part of Springer Nature 2018
K. Sim and P. Kaufmann (Eds.): EvoApplications 2018, LNCS 10784, pp. 864–878, 2018.
https://doi.org/10.1007/978-3-319-77538-8_57

needs to find a new solution after an environmental change that is not much different from the previous one. For example, in the aircraft taking-off/landing scheduling problem [2], we can see this type of objective alongside with the optimality objective [1]. Moreover, displacement between consecutive solutions can be seen as the switching cost (SC) in many problems [3] which needs to be minimized as the second objective. In fact, changing solutions in real-world problems is costly. Therefore, larger changes have more cost and needs more resources such as time and energy. As a result, when the optimization algorithm's decision maker needs to choose the next solution after environmental changes, the displacement/SC to the new solution must be considered alongside with its optimality objective's fitness value.

Moreover, PSDRs are dynamic time-linkage problems [4], because choosing a solution for the current environment will change the next environment's search space of the displacement/SC objective. In fact, when a solution is chosen for an environment, all the feasible solutions will be evaluated based on their distance from it in terms of displacement/SC.

In this paper, a new hybrid method based on particle swarm optimization (PSO) [5] is proposed for PSDRs. The proposed algorithm that we call it PSDR-hPSO is designed based on a multi-swarm PSO (mPSO) that is responsible to find and track peaks based on the optimality objective and a single-swarm PSO (sPSO) whose task is to find the optimum solution according to both of optimality and displacement/SC objectives. After each environmental change, a new decision maker chooses a peak according to the fitness values of peaks in present and some of their characteristics which can be used to anticipate the future displacement/SC value. Then, sPSO uses the location information from the decision maker in order to accelerate the optimization process and improve the performance.

The remainder of this paper is structured as follows: in the Sect. 2, problem definitions are presented. A brief literature review is provided in Sect. 3. The proposed algorithm is introduced in Sect. 4. The experimental settings, results and analysis are shown in the 5th section. Finally, this paper is concluded in the last section.

2   Problem Definition

A DOP is usually represented as (1):

$$F(\vec{x}) = f(\vec{x}, \vec{\alpha}(t))$$ (1)

where f is the objective function, $\vec{x}$ is a design variable vector, $\alpha(t)$ is environmental parameters which change over time continually or discretely and t is the time index with $t \in [0, T_{end}]$ where T_{end} is the problem life cycle. In this research, like most of previous studies in the DOP domain, we investigate DOPs with $\alpha(t)$ that changes discretely. In this type of DOP, the environmental parameters change over time with stationary periods between changes. As a result, for a DOP with N number of environmental changes, we have a sequence of N static environments that can be shown by Eq. 2:

$$\left[f\left(\vec{x}, \vec{\alpha_1}\right), f\left(\vec{x}, \vec{\alpha_2}\right), \ldots, f\left(\vec{x}, \vec{\alpha_N}\right) \right]$$ (2)

where $\vec{\alpha_i}$ is the environmental parameters in the ith environment. In this paper, we assume that choosing solution for each environment is possible and the system is capable of tolerating frequent changes in solutions. Therefore, for PSDR in this paper, the optimization algorithm needs to choose a new solution for each environment based on both optimality and displacement/SC objectives.

Since PSDR has two conflicting objectives which need to be optimized concurrently, it can be categorized as dynamic multi-objective optimization problem (DMOOP) [6]. In DMOOP, algorithms need to find a set of solutions close to the true Pareto-optimal front (POF) for each environment [7]. A DMOOP with m objectives can be defined as follows:

$$F(\vec{x}) = \left\{ f_1(\vec{x}, \vec{\alpha}(t)), f_2\left(\vec{x}, \vec{\beta}(t)\right), \ldots, f_m(\vec{x}, \vec{\gamma}(t)) \right\} \tag{3}$$

where F is the objective function, f_i is the ith objective, $\vec{x}$ is a design variable vector, $\vec{\alpha}(t)$, $\vec{\beta}(t)$ and $\vec{\gamma}(t)$ are environmental parameters of different objectives which are changing over time and t is the time index. DMOOPs are classified into different groups based on the POF and Pareto-optimal set (POS) conditions over time [7]. The PSDR that we consider in this paper is classified in the group in which both POF and POS change over time. However, even if the optimization algorithm finds a set of solutions close to POF for each environment, its decision maker needs to choose a solution from them. As a result, for solving PSDR, we do not need to find a set of solutions and the algorithm needs to search for the preferred solution from POS of each environment. One of the best ways to solve a DMOOP in this situation is to convert the problem defined by Eq. 3 to a weighted-sum optimization problem [8]:

$$F_{w1,w2,\ldots,wm}(\vec{x}, t) = w_1 f_1(\vec{x}, \vec{\alpha}(t)) + w_2 f_2\left(\vec{x}, \vec{\beta}(t)\right) + \ldots + w_m f_m(\vec{x}, \vec{\gamma}(t)) \tag{4}$$

where w_i is the constant value which is multiplied to the fitness value of the ith objective function. By converting a MDOOP to a weighted-sum optimization problem as Eq. 4, by setting the w values, we choose one of the solutions in POS as the optimum solution for each environment.

As mentioned in Sect. 1, PSDRs have the time-linkage feature. Time-linkage property refers to that any solution chosen by the optimizer in the current environment could change the future problem space [9]. In dynamic time-linkage optimization problems (DTP), the optimizer should consider both of the present and future *i.e.* it needs to predict the future behavior of the environment based on the chosen solution.

3 Related Methods

PSDRs are counted as DMOOPs, DTPs and DOPs. As a result, we provide a brief literature review on related works in this section. The PSDR-hPSO algorithm is benefiting from a multi-swarm PSO for locating and tracking peaks in the optimality objective search space. Performing TMO using multi-swarm methods for DOPs is popular among researchers [9, 10]. In this methods, there are at least two swarms which each of them has its own tasks such as handling a separate area of the search space, tracking a peak or finding uncovered peaks. It is worth mentioning that these sub-swarms can communicate with each other to perform an effective search process. Multi-swarm methods need to follow two points: First, they need to assign different tasks to different sub-swarms such as finding peaks and tracking them; second, they need to split the sub-swarms suitably to avoid overlapping sub-swarms, covering important parts of the search space and maintaining diversity [12].

In [13], an algorithm called Self Organizing Scouts (SOS) was proposed which utilized a big sub-population for exploration and a number of small sub-populations for tracking changes of peaks that have already been identified. This strategy has also been proposed with other meta-heuristic methods such as PSO [14, 15] and artificial fish swarm algorithm [16, 17].

In [18], a population was used for performing global search, and after discovering an optimum, the population was divided into two sub-populations. The first and second sub-populations were responsible for tracking optimum changes and conducting global search, respectively. In [19] a speciation-based PSO approach was proposed for optimization in dynamic environments. In [20], a method based on clustering was proposed for developing sub-populations, and in [21], this method has been improved, in which some simplifications, *e.g.* eliminating the learning procedure, and reducing the number of phases for clustering from two phases to only one phase was made. In [22], a method called sPSO was proposed in which every cluster was divided into two. The first cluster was responsible for exploitation and the second one was in charge of exploration.

In [12], two multi-swarm methods, called MQSO and MCPSO, were proposed. In the former one, quantum particles and in the latter one, charged particles were used to generate diversity. In MQSO, quantum particles appear at random positions, uniformly distributed around the swarm's global best. In MCPSO, some or all of the particles in each swarm have a 'charge'. The number of sub-swarms in these techniques was fixed and pre-determined. In these methods, algorithms used an anti-convergence method to search for possible better peaks. In addition, in these algorithms, a new mechanism called exclusion is used to avoid over-crowding.

In [23], an approach for enhancing MQSO was proposed by adapting the number of sub-swarms, which was called AMQSO. AMQSO starts with one sub-swarm and a new sub-swarm would be created if all previous sub-swarms are converged. This method has significantly improved the performance of the algorithm.

Li et al. [24] proposed a method to adapt the number of populations based on statistical data on how many populations have found new peaks. If this number is large, more populations will be introduced and vice versa. Additionally, a new heuristic clustering, a population hibernation scheme, a population exclusion scheme, a peak hiding method and two movement methods (to track peaks and avoid stagnant) were proposed.

A PSO with two types of sub-swarms called finder-tracker multi-swarm PSO was proposed in [25]. The finder swarm searches for possible uncovered peaks. When it converges to a peak, it creates a new tracker swarm to track the peak. An exclusion mechanism re-initializes the finder swarm if it converges to a peak that already has a tracker swarm on it. In addition, a mechanism to schedule tracker swarms called sleeping-awakening was proposed. It allocates more computational resource to more promising swarms. Furthermore, a new method for re-diversification of tracker swarms (after a change) was proposed. The method re-initializes all particles randomly around *Gbest* [5] and their velocity vector is randomly set based on the peak's shift severity.

In many dynamic real-world problems, the solution chosen by the optimizer can influence how the problem would be in the future, which is called time-linkage by Bosman [26, 27]. Nguyen [1] showed that a large share of real-world DOPs has the feature of time-linkage. For solving online DTPs, Bosman pointed out that the optimizer needs to consider the feature of time-linkage, and for evaluating a solution, take its future influence into account alongside its current fitness value [26], and the method of "optimizing both the present and the future" is suggested to solve DTPs, instead of the traditional method of "optimizing only the present" [28]. A prediction method EA + predictor [26], was proposed in which the method made decision according to both the current and the predicted fitness. This method was improved in [28] in order to enhance the performance in situations that prediction is unreliable.

In [7], a baseline algorithm for DMOOPs as well as some test problems were suggested. The use of evolutionary multi-objective optimization methods in DOPs were investigated in [29]. The first objective was the original single dynamic objective and the second objective was an artificial objective to promote diversity. In [30], a PSO algorithm for tracking the varying POS and POF obtained at each environment was developed in which a hyper rectangle search was used for predicting the optimal solutions of the next environment. additionally, a new crossover operator was designed for handling constraints. [31] follows the same goals as [30]. The proposed PSO in [31] used a new points selection strategy for initializing swarm at each environment. Moreover, a local search operator was proposed to improve the exploitation. In [32], authors proposed three memory-based strategies including explicit memory, Local-search memory and hybrid memory for multi-objective evolutionary algorithms in DOPs. Authors showed how to appropriately organize and effectively reuse the changed POS information in order to improve performance and accelerate optimization process after environmental changes.

Displacement/SC was considered as an objective in multi-objective problems before [3, 33, 34] but none of them consider its time-linkage feature. In [33], Displacement/SC was investigated as optimization of adaptation. A multi-objective problem was defined which considered the cost of the adaptation and the optimality while the adaptation takes place. In [34], the need for rapid, low-cost changes in a design, in response to changes in performance requirements, within multi-objective problems, was investigated. An algorithm called ROOT/SC [3] was designed for robust optimization over time (ROOT) [35]. This algorithm was designed based on the multi-objective PSO proposed in [36] in which the first objective was to maximize the survival time metric [37] and the second one was to maximize the Euclidian distance between successive robust solutions.

4   Proposed Hybrid Method for PSDR

PSDRs are counted as dynamic multi-objective and time-linkage problems. Consequently, the proposed algorithm needs to address all of the necessary requirements of DOPs, MOOPs and DTPs.

4.1 Addressing Dynamic Optimization Problems' Requirements

One of the best ways to tackle DOPs is using multi-swarm methods [10, 11]. The proposed algorithm is equipped with a multi-swarm whose responsibility is to locate and track peaks. We use the mPSO proposed in [25] inside our proposed algorithm because it is easy to understand and competitive. However, for making it simpler, we disable the exploiter particles and sleeping-awakening mechanisms from it.

mPSO in the proposed algorithm has two main responsibilities: (1) tracking peaks; (2) gathering some information about each peak. For the first task, mPSO acts in the actual problem space without considering the displacement objective. For the second task, each sub-swarm stores the difference between *Gbest* fitness values at the end of each successive pair of environments inside its own database. The average of these values indicates the peak's height variance.

The exclusion mechanism [12] does not allow more than one sub-swarm cover a same peak. In the standard version of this mechanism, the swarm with lower *Gbest* fitness is re-initialized. In the mPSO, when the distance between two sub-swarms' *Gbest* position is less than a threshold r_{excl}, we keep the older swarm which has the bigger database and remove the younger one. Additionally, if the younger's *Gbest* is better, then we copy its *Gbest* information to the older one. In this paper, r_{excl} is calculated based on the one in [23].

4.2 Addressing Multi-objective Problems' Requirements

Alongside with the above mentioned single-objective mPSO, we have the sPSO which has one swarm and works on both PSDR objectives. Since we have to pick a solution for each environment, there is no need to find POS. To handle the multi-objective and find the suitable solution among the POS, we combine the objectives into a weighted sum of objectives [8] as Eq. 4. In this paper, we use the maximizing optimality objective which makes the fitness function of sPSO as follows:

$$\text{Maximize} : F(\vec{x}, t) = f(\vec{x}, t) - \left(w \times DC(\vec{x}, \vec{X}_{t-1}) \right) \tag{5}$$

where $f(\vec{x}, t)$ is the optimality fitness function, $\vec{X}_{t-1}$ is the chosen solution for the previous environment, w is the weight of the displacement cost (DC) function. The DC function calculates the Euclidian distance between the previous chosen solution and a new design variable vector as follows:

$$\text{Minimize} : DC(\vec{x}, \vec{X}_{t-1}) = \left\| \vec{x} - \vec{X}_{t-1} \right\| \tag{6}$$

The w parameter in Eq. 5, control the importance of the displacement cost in the optimization. Therefore, lower values of w result in finding solutions with better optimality and its higher values lead to find solutions that are closer to $\vec{X}_{t-1}$. As a result, with setting of w, we can choose a preferred solution from the POS. Moreover, we can control the ratio of both objectives in problems that naturally the ratio between the two objectives' fitness values are very large or very small. For example, the fitness values of the first objective can vary between 1000 and 2000 while the maximum displacement is less than two.

4.3   Addressing Dynamic Time-Linkage Problems' Requirements

For better performance, the proposed algorithm needs to consider the future environments alongside with the current one. In most of the previous works on DTPs [26–28], a predictor method like Autoregression was used. However, some of the DTPs can be predictor-deceptive [9] and some other can be too random to be predicted with a reasonable error. In this paper, we are working on problems with several peaks whose width, height and location change randomly over time. In such problems, using predictors cannot help the algorithm and even can deteriorate the performance, because this type of problems are too random and there is no pattern in the dynamic. As a result, the prediction involves with high error rate. In these circumstances, if the algorithm considers only the current environment, the performance would be better than considering future by high error rate in prediction.

To tackle this challenge, we propose a new decision maker based on the gathered information by mPSO's sub-swarms. After each environmental change, mPSO reacts to change in order to update memory, increasing diversity and updating database. Additionally, it sends the calculated height variances to the decision maker alongside the *Gbest* information of all sub-swarms. Then, the decision maker chooses one of the peaks as follows:

$$CP : \operatorname{argmax}_{i=1}^{SN} \left(\left[f\left(\overrightarrow{G_i}, t \right) - \left(w \times DC\left(\overrightarrow{G_i}, \overrightarrow{X}_{t-1} \right) \right) \right] + \frac{1}{B} \sum_{k=1}^{B} \left(f\left(\overrightarrow{G_k}, t \right) - HV_k - \left(w \times DC\left(\overrightarrow{G_i}, \overrightarrow{G_k} \right) \right) \right) \right) \quad (7)$$

where CP is the chosen peak, SN is the number of sub-swarms, HV_k is the calculated height variance by the kth sub-swarm, $\overrightarrow{G_k}$ is the kth sub-swarm's *Gbest* position, and B is the number of better peaks based on the $f\left(\overrightarrow{G_k}, t \right) - HV_k$ *i.e.* based on the worst expected fitness values for k^{th} sub-swarm in the next environment. In Eq. 7, in the first part *i.e.* $\left[f\left(\overrightarrow{G_i}, t \right) - \left(w \times DC\left(\overrightarrow{G_i}, \overrightarrow{X}_{t-1} \right) \right) \right]$, the decision maker considers the current fitness value of peaks and the displacement cost from $\overrightarrow{X}_{t-1}$ to it. Therefore, it tries to maximize the combined objective by Eq. 5 for the current environment. In the second part, the decision maker tries to take the future of peaks into account by considering average displacement cost from them to the B best peaks.

By Eq. 7, we try to choose a peak that is closer to other good peaks. If we need to move the solution to another peak after environmental changes, we endure a lower displacement cost. Therefore, the decision maker aims for choosing reliable peaks which alongside with good current situation, they provide a better future combined objective values. After choosing most reliable peak by Eq. 7, the $Gbest_{CP}$ is sent to the sPSO.

sPSO initializes its particles around the $Gbest_{CP}$ inside a cloud with radius of r_{cloud}. Therefore, sPSO starts optimizing the combined objective by Eq. 5, according to the location determined by the decision maker. The initialization with the controlled diversity by the r_{cloud} decrease the chance of moving particles to further regions such as other peaks. In fact, it is possible to have other regions with better fitness in the current environment, however, the decision maker in Eq. 7 tries to choose a peak by taking the future displacement cost into account. As a result, the chosen peak may not be the best peak in the current environment but it is a better option based on current and future considerations. Pseudo code of the PSDR-hPSO is shown in Algorithm 1.

Algorithm 1. PSDR-hPSO
1:      Initialize Finder_swarm of mPSO
2:      repeat:
3:       If an environment change is detected then
4:        Update memory
5:        Increase diversity
6:        Update database
7:        Calculate Height variance
8:        Choose a peak by Equation(9)
9:        Send the information to sPSO
10:      End if
11:      Execute an iteration of PSO on *Finder_swarm* [25]
12:      If the *Finder_swarm* is converged then
13:        Create a new *Tracker_swarm*
14:        Re-initialize *Finder_swarm*
15:      End if
16:      Execute an iteration of sPSO
17:      Execute exclusion mechanism
18:      Update r_{excl} if number of tracker swarm is changed
19:      until stopping criterion is met

5 Experiments

5.1 Benchmark Problems

The Moving Peaks Benchmark (MPB) [38] is the most popular benchmark in the DOP field. The standard baseline function of MPB is as follows:

$$F_t(\vec{x}) = max_{i=1}^{i=p}\left\{H_t^i - W_t^i \times \left\|\vec{x} - \vec{C}_t^i\right\|\right\} \tag{8}$$

where p is the number of peaks, $\vec{x}$ is a solution in the problem space, and H_t^i, W_t^i and $\vec{C}_t^i$ are the height, width and center of the ith peak in the tth environment, respectively. In the modified version of MPB (mMPB) [39, 40] that we use in this paper, each peak has its own height and width severities. The height, width and center of a peak change from one environment to the next one as follows:

$$H_{t+1}^i = H_t^i + HeigthSeverity^i \times N(0,1) \tag{9}$$

$$W_{t+1}^i = W_t^i + WidthSeverity^i \times N(0,1) \tag{10}$$

$$\vec{C}_{t+1}^i = \vec{C}_t^i + \left(ShiftSeverity \times \frac{(1-\lambda) \times \vec{r} + \lambda \times \vec{V}_t^i}{\|(1-\lambda) \times \vec{r} + \lambda \times \vec{V}_t^i\|} \right) \qquad (11)$$

where $N(0,1)$ represents a random number drawn from a Gaussian distribution with mean 0 and variance 1, $r \in [-0.5, 0.5]$ is a vector of random numbers with uniform distribution and λ is the correlation coefficient. The rest of mMPB's parameters and their values are shown in Table 1. The bold values in Table 1 are default parameter values of mMPB in this paper.

Table 1. Parameter settings of mMPBR (default values are in bold)

Parameter	Value(S)
Number of peaks, p	10, **20**, 50
Evaluations between changes, f	1000, 2500, **5000** evaluations
Shift severity, S	**1**, 2, 5
Height severity, HS	Randomized in [1, 10]
Width severity, WS	Randomized in [0.1,1]
Peaks' shape	Cone
Number of dimensions, D	5
Correlation coefficient, λ	0
Peaks' location range	[0, 100]
Peaks' height	[30, 70]
Peaks' width	[1, 12]
Number of environments	100

5.2   Performance Indicator

In this paper, for measuring the performance of the algorithms, we use Eq. 12:

$$AF = \frac{1}{N-1} \sum_{t=2}^{N} \left(f\left(\vec{X}_t, \vec{\alpha}(t)\right) - w \times DC\left(\vec{X}_t, \vec{X}_{t-1}\right) \right) \qquad (12)$$

where AF is average fitness of chosen solutions for all environments and $\vec{X}_t$ is the chosen solution for the tth environment.

5.3   Compared Algorithms and Parameter Settings

We compaire our proposed algorithm with two TMO algorithms on mPSO. The first one chooses the best solution according to optimality in each environment (we call it optimality TMO (oTMO)) so it does not consider the displacement objective. The second method uses Eq. 5 as fitness function (we call it combined objective TMO (cTMO)).

PSDR-hPSO, oTMO and cTMO use a simplified version of the FTMPSO [25] in which the exploiter particle and sleeping awakening mechanisms are disabled. We assume that all algorithms are informed about environmental changes. The parameter setting of them is shown in Table 2. There are two sets of parameters: those with a reference number and those without. The former have the default values as in their original papers. The latter have their values obtained by several sensitivity analyses. spSO in PSDR-hPSO is working based on [41], c1 = c2 = 2.05, χ is 0.729843788 and the population size is 10. For the PSDR-hPSO, the value of B in Eq. 7, is set to half of the sub-swarm number. r_{cloud} for initializing spSO is equal to the shift severity of peaks which is learned by averaging the Euclidian distances between *Gbest* positions at the end of successive environments. All experiments are done with different values of w *i.e.* 0.5,1 and 2. Experimental results are obtained by performing 30 independent runs and the best results based on Wilcoxon rank sum test with significance level of 0.05 are set in bold in each table.

Table 2. Parameter setting of mPSO, oTMO and cTMO.

Parameters	Initial value
c1, c2	2.05 [41]
χ	0.729843788 [41]
Trackers' Population Size	5 [25]
Finder's Population Size	10 [25]
P	1 [25]
Q	1 [25]
Conv_limit	1 [25]
K	10
$excl_{factor}$	0.1
Stop criterion	Max number of function evaluations

5.4   Experimental Results

Table 3 shows the obtained results by PSDR-hPSO, oTMO and cTMO on mMPB with different number of peaks p = 10, 20 and 50 (all other mMPB parameters have default values). The results show that the performance of the PSDR-hPSO is better than of oTMO and cTMO in all test instances in Table 3. By increasing number of peaks, due to increasing the density of peaks in the landscape, the performance of all methods increased noticeably. Indeed, by increasing peak density, the displacement cost by Eq. 6 would be decreased because the average distance between peaks is smaller. On the other hand, when the average distance between peaks is larger, the displacement cost is higher which leads to have lower performance.

In all the test instances in Table 3, with increasing w, the performance decreases significantly. In fact, by increasing w, the influence of displacements cost in the combined fitness function by Eq. 5 increased which leads to have larger changes in the problem space made by this fitness function. This issue affects the performance of the cTMO and PSDR-hPSO directly because both of them use Eq. 5. Moreover, although oTMO acts independently from the displacement objective, but it is affected by the value of w because the performance of algorithms is calculated by Eq. 12 that takes the average displacement cost between successive solutions into account. Higher values of w increase the distance between the optimum by the optimality objective and the optimum by the Eq. 5 that deteriorates the results of oTMO.

The obtained results by cTMO are better than of oTMO in Table 3. The reason is that cTMO uses Eq. 5 as objective function and consider displacement cost in the optimization. Moreover, PSDR-hPSO's performance is better than of cTMO in all test instances. The first reason is that in PSDR-hPSO, the mPSO acts based on the optimality objective. As a result, its tracker-swarms are able to track peaks easier than cTMO's tracker-swarms which need to tolerate larger changes in peaks especially when the w is larger. In fact, displacement cost can enlarge the relocation distance of peaks after environmental changes.

The second reason which is the most important one is that the PSDR-hPSO's decision maker in Eq. 7 considers the future of the search space alongside with the current one. As discussed before, PSDRs are classified as problems with time-linkage feature. Therefore, PSDR-hPSO's performance which consider both of present and future is better than of cTMO which acts based on "optimizing only the present".

Table 3. Results obtained by Eq. 12 (and standard error) on test instances with different number of peaks p (all other mMPB parameters have default values).

Algorithm	$p = 10$			$p = 20$			$p = 50$		
	$w = 0.5$	$w = 1$	$w = 2$	$w = 0.5$	$w = 1$	$w = 2$	$w = 0.5$	$w = 1$	$w = 2$
oTMO	52.67	50.38	48.48	55.28	51.33	49.55	57.12	51.61	51.59
	(0.97)	(0.97)	(1.02)	(0.67)	(1.02)	(1.25)	(0.79)	(1.00)	(0.96)
cTMO	54.74	50.88	49.11	56.47	53.28	50.44	57.57	54.22	51.89
	(0.75)	(1.04)	(1.42)	(0.95)	(1.16)	(1.21)	(0.57)	(1.08)	(1.11)
PSDR-hPSO	**55.78**	**51.13**	**49.75**	**59.27**	**55.03**	**53.98**	**60.53**	**55.82**	**54.31**
	(0.76)	**(1.48)**	**(2.04)**	**(0.45)**	**(0.67)**	**(0.87)**	**(0.56)**	**(0.68)**	**(0.92)**

Figure 1 shows the time-linkage property of the PSDR clearly. In this figure, a MPB with 5 peaks of equal height and width is shown in the sub-figure (I). Other sub-figures are made by Eq. 5 with $w = 1$ and when we choose one of the peak centers as the current solution (the chosen peak center is illustrated by a red filled circle). According to Eq. 5, when we choose a peak center as solution, all the feasible solutions' fitness values in the search space are affected by their distance to it. Therefore, choosing a solution has influence on the future environments. It is worth mentioning that PSDR-hPSO will not choose the peak in sub-figure (V) because this peak is far away from other peaks, so the average displacement cost between it and the B best peaks in Eq. 9 is high which deteriorate its chance to be chosen. Therefore, the algorithm avoids the high displacement cost in the future.

The results of algorithms on mMPB with different shift severities are reported in Table 4. Similar to the result of Table 3, PSDR-hPSO outperformed cTMO and oTMO algorithms in all test instances. By increasing shift severities, the performance algorithms is deteriorated. Higher shift severities increase the displacement cost in the circumstances that a peak is chosen for more than one successive environments.

Furthermore, peaks relocate with larger steps which makes the tracking task harder for tracker swarms.

Table 5 indicates the performance of algorithms on mMPB with different change frequencies. Again, the best results in all problem instances belong to PSDR-hPSO. Lower values of f means higher change frequencies. In such a situation, there is insufficient time for algorithms to do a good search because the environments change more rapidly, which leads to have worse performance. In mMPB with $f = 1000$, we can see exceptionally the obtained results by oTMO is better than of cTMO. As mentioned before, the displacement causes an additional step size to the shift severity of peaks when Eq. 5 is used as the objective function. Thus, in higher change frequencies and with larger relocating of peaks after each environmental change, cTMO has a harder job for tracking peaks which deteriorate its performance. On the other hand, mPSO in PSDR-hPSO uses the optimality objective function and as a result, it is not involved with this issue.

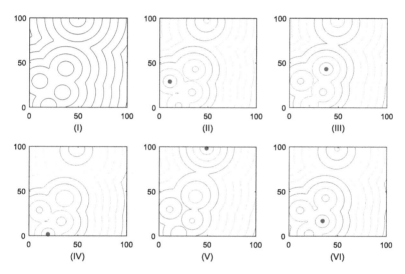

Fig. 1. Time-linkage property of the PSDR by choosing different peak centers as the current solution.

Table 4. Results obtained by Eq. 12 (and standard error) on test instances with different shift severities S (all other mMPB parameters have default values).

Algorithm	$S = 1$			$S = 2$			$S = 5$		
	w = 0.5	w = 1	w = 2	w = 0.5	w = 1	w = 2	w = 0.5	w = 1	w = 2
oTMO	55.28	51.33	49.55	54.29	49.34	48.05	53.53	48.42	43.91
	(0.67)	(1.02)	(1.25)	(0.59)	(1.04)	(0.95)	(0.80)	(1.19)	(0.96)
cTMO	56.47	53.28	50.44	55.62	51.34	49.18	54.64	50.22	46.31
	(0.95)	(1.16)	(1.21)	(0.87)	(1.03)	(1.09)	(0.82)	(1.35)	(1.04)
PSDR-hPSO	**59.27**	**55.03**	**53.98**	**58.00**	**54.43**	**49.96**	**57.67**	**51.85**	**47.97**
	(0.45)	**(0.67)**	**(0.87)**	**(0.42)**	**(0.82)**	**(1.16)**	**(0.56)**	**(1.03)**	**(1.12)**

Table 5. Results obtained by Eq. 12 (and standard error) on test instances with different change frequencies f (all other mMPB parameters have default values).

Algorithm	$f = 1000$			$f = 2500$			$f = 5000$		
	w = 0.5	w = 1	w = 2	w = 0.5	w = 1	w = 2	w = 0.5	w = 1	w = 2
oTMO	53.31	49.39	46.51	54.45	50.69	48.16	55.28	51.33	49.55
	(0.75)	(1.13)	(1.26)	(1.43)	(1.49)	(1.13)	(0.67)	(1.02)	(1.25)
cTMO	51.66	48.63	46.43	55.13	51.40	49.38	56.47	53.28	50.44
	(1.11)	(0.92)	(1.23)	(1.06)	(1.39)	(1.16)	(0.95)	(1.16)	(1.21)
PSDR-hPSO	**55.71**	**52.55**	**47.14**	**57.73**	**54.48**	**51.92**	**59.27**	**55.03**	**53.98**
	(0.57)	**(0.94)**	**(1.40)**	**(0.70)**	**(0.97)**	**(1.95)**	**(0.45)**	**(0.67)**	**(0.87)**

6   Conclusion

In this paper, dynamic optimization problems with previous-solution displacement restriction were investigated and a novel multi-objective and time-linkage based method was proposed. The proposed method utilizes a multi-swarm PSO for tracking peaks in the optimality objective search space. A new decision maker was designed which uses the information gathered by sub-swarms of multi-swarm PSO in order to choose a peak. The information transferred to the decision maker consists of location, fitness value and height variance of peaks. The proposed decision maker chooses a peak based on the current environment's peaks fitness values, their worst expected fitness values for the next environment, their distance to a pre-defined number of better peaks and also the future displacement cost for changing solutions. After each environmental change, the information of the chosen peak is sent to a single swarm PSO which works on the combined objectives *i.e.* optimality and displacement cost and is responsible for finding a solution for each environment. The single swarm PSO initializes its particles around the received peak location from the decision maker. The experimental results showed that the proposed algorithm outperformed other tested methods which only focus on optimizing the present environment.

Acknowledgments. This work was supported by a Dean's Scholarship by the Faculty of Engineering and Technology, LJMU, a Newton Institutional Links grant no. 172734213, funded by the UK BEIS and delivered by the British Council, and a NRCP grant no. NRCP1617-6-125 delivered by the Royal Academy of Engineering.

References

1. Nguyen, T.T.: Continuous dynamic optimisation using evolutionary algorithms. Ph.D. thesis, University of Birmingham (2011)
2. Atkin, J.A.D., Burke, E.K., Greenwood, J.S., Reeson, D.: On-line decision support for take-off runway scheduling with uncertain taxi times at London Heathrow airport. J. Sched. **11**(5), 323–346 (2008)
3. Huang, Y., Ding, Y., Hao, K., Jin, Y.: A multi-objective approach to robust optimization over time considering switching cost. Inf. Sci. **394–395**, 183–197 (2017)

4. Nguyen, T.T., Yao, X.: Dynamic time-linkage problems revisited. In: Giacobini, M., Brabazon, A., Cagnoni, S., Di Caro, G.A., Ekárt, A., Esparcia-Alcázar, A.I., Farooq, M., Fink, A., Machado, P. (eds.) EvoWorkshops 2009. LNCS, vol. 5484, pp. 735–744. Springer, Heidelberg (2009). https://doi.org/10.1007/978-3-642-01129-0_83

5. Kennedy, J., Eberhart, R.C.: Particle swarm optimization. In: IEEE International Conference on Neural Networks, vol. 4, pp. 1942–1948 (1995)

6. Bui, L.T., Branke, J., Abbass, H.A.: Multiobjective optimization for dynamic environments. In: IEEE Congress on Evolutionary Computation, pp. 2349–2356 (2005)

7. Farina, M., Deb, K., Amato, P.: Dynamic multiobjective optimization problems: test cases, approximations, and applications. IEEE Trans. Evol. Comput. **8**(5), 425–442 (2004)

8. Chankong, V., Haimes, Y.Y.: Multiobjective Decision Making Theory and Methodology. Noth-Holland, New York (1983)

9. Nguyen, T.T., Yang, Z., Bonsall, S.: Dynamic time-linkage problems - the challenges. In: IEEE RIVF International Conference on Computing and Communication Technologies, Research, Innovation, and Vision for the Future (2012)

10. Nguyen, T.T., Yang, S., Branke, J.: Evolutionary dynamic optimization: a survey of the state of the art. Swarm Evol. Comput. **6**, 1–24 (2012)

11. Mavrovouniotis, M., Li, C., Yang, S.: A survey of swarm intelligence for dynamic optimization: algorithms and applications. Swarm Evol. Comput. **33**, 1–17 (2017)

12. Blackwell, T., Branke, J.: Multiswarms, exclusion, and anti-convergence in dynamic environments. IEEE Trans. Evol. Comput. **10**(4), 459–472 (2006)

13. Branke, J., Kaussler, T., Smidt, C., Schmeck, H.: A multi-population approach to dynamic optimization problems. In: Parmee, I.C. (eds.) Evolutionary Design and Manufacture, pp. 299–307. Springer, London (2000). https://doi.org/10.1007/978-1-4471-0519-0_24

14. Yazdani, D., Nasiri, B., Azizi, R., Sepas-Moghaddam, A., Meybodi, M.R.: Optimization in dynamic environments utilizing a novel method based on particle swarm optimization. Int. J. Artif. Intell. **11**, 170–192 (2013)

15. Li, C., Yang, S.: Fast multi–swarm optimization for dynamic optimization problems. In: Proceedings of 4th International Conference on Natural Computation, pp. 624–628 (2008)

16. Yazdani, D., Sepas-Moghaddam, A., Dehban, A., Horta, N.: A novel approach for optimization in dynamic environments based on modified artificial fish swarm algorithm. Int. J. Comput. Intell. Appl. **15**(2), 1650010 (2016)

17. Yazdani, D., Nasiri, B., Sepas-Moghaddam, A., Meybodi, M.R., Akbarzadeh-Totonchi, M. R.: mNAFSA: a novel approach for optimization in dynamic environments with global changes. Swarm Evol. Comput. **18**, 38–53 (2014)

18. Ursem, R.K.: Multinational GAs: multimodal optimization techniques in dynamic environments. In: Proceedings of the Genetic and Evolutionary Computation Conference, pp. 19–26 (2000)

19. Parrott, D., Li, X.: Locating and tracking multiple dynamic optima by a particle swarm model using speciation. IEEE Trans. Evol. Comput. **10**(4), 440–458 (2006)

20. Li, C., Yang, S.: A clustering particle swarm optimizer for dynamic optimization. In: Proceedings of IEEE Congress on Evolutionary Computation, pp. 439–446 (2009)

21. Yang, S., Li, C.: A clustering particle swarm optimizer for locating and tracking multiple optima in dynamic environments. IEEE Trans. Evol. Comput. **14**(6), 959–974 (2010)

22. Du, W., Li, B.: Multi–strategy ensemble particle swarm optimization for dynamic optimization. Inf. Sci. **178**, 3096–3109 (2008)

23. Blackwell, T., Branke, J., Li, X.: Particle swarms for dynamic optimization problems. Swarm Intelligence: Introduction and Applications, pp. 193–217 (2008)

24. Li, C., Nguyen, T.T., Yang, M., Mavrovouniotis, M., Yang, S.: An adaptive multi-population framework for locating and tracking multiple optima. IEEE Trans. Evol. Comput. **20**(5), 590–605 (2016)
25. Yazdani, D., Nasiri, B., Sepas-Moghaddam, A., Meybodi, M.R.: A novel multi-swarm algorithm for optimization in dynamic environments based on particle swarm optimization. Appl. Soft Comput. **13**(4), 2144–2158 (2013)
26. Bosman, P.A.N.: Learning, anticipation and time-deception in evolutionary online dynamic optimization. In: Proceedings of the 7th Annual Workshop on Genetic and Evolutionary Computation, pp. 39–47. ACM (2005)
27. Bosman, P.A.N.: Learning and anticipation in online dynamic optimization. In: Yang, S., Ong, Y.S., Jin, Y. (eds.) Evolutionary Computation in Dynamic and Uncertain Environments. Studies in Computational Intelligence, vol. 51, pp. 129–152. Springer, Heidelberg (2007). https://doi.org/10.1007/978-3-540-49774-5_6
28. Bu, C., Luo, W., Zhu, T., Yue, L.: Solving online dynamic time-linkage problems under unreliable prediction. Appl. Soft Comput. **56**, 702–716 (2017)
29. Bui, L.T., Abbass, H.A., Branke, J.: Multiobjective optimization for dynamic environments. In: Proceedings of IEEE Congress on Evolutionary Computation, pp. 2349–2356 (2005)
30. Wei, J., Wang, Y.: Hyper rectangle search based particle swarm algorithm for dynamic constrained multi-objective optimization problems. In: Proceedings of IEEE Congress on Evolutionary Computation, pp. 1–8 (2012)
31. Wei, J., Jia, L.: A novel particle swarm optimization algorithm with local search for dynamic constrained multi-objective optimization problems. In: Proceedings of IEEE Congress on Evolutionary Computation, pp. 2436–2443 (2013)
32. Wang, Y., Li, B.: Investigation of memory-based multi-objective optimization evolutionary algorithm in dynamic environment. In: Proceedings of IEEE Congress on Evolutionary Computation, pp. 630–637 (2009)
33. Salomon, S., Avigad, G., Fleming, P.J., Purshouse, Robin C.: Optimization of adaptation - a multi-objective approach for optimizing changes to design parameters. In: Purshouse, R.C., Fleming, P.J., Fonseca, C.M., Greco, S., Shaw, J. (eds.) EMO 2013. LNCS, vol. 7811, pp. 21–35. Springer, Heidelberg (2013). https://doi.org/10.1007/978-3-642-37140-0_6
34. Avigad, G., Eisenstadt, E., Schuetze, O.: Handling changes of performance requirements in multi-objective problems. J. Eng. Des. **23**(8), 597–617 (2012)
35. Yu, X., Jin, Y., Tang, K., Yao, X.: Robust optimization over time – a new perspective on dynamic. In: Proceedings of IEEE Congress on Evolutionary Computation, pp. 1–6 (2010)
36. Coello, C.A., Pulido, G.T., Lechuga, M.S.: Handling multiple objectives with particle swarm optimization. IEEE Trans. Cybern. **8**(3), 256–279 (2004)
37. Fu, H., Sendhoff, B., Tang, K., Yao, X.: Robust optimization over time: problem difficulties and benchmark problems. IEEE Trans. Evol. Comput. **19**(5), 731–745 (2015)
38. Branke, J.: Memory enhanced evolutionary algorithms for changing optimization problems. In: Proceedings of IEEE Congress on Evolutionary Computation, pp. 1875–1882 (1999)
39. Jin, Y., Tang, K., Yu, X., Sendhoff, B., Yao, X.: A framework for finding robust optimal solutions over time. Memetic Comput. **5**(1), 3–18 (2013)
40. Yazdani, D., Nguyen, T.T., Branke, J., Wang, J.: A New multi-swarm particle swarm optimization for robust optimization over time. In: Squillero, G., Sim, K. (eds.) EvoApplications 2017. LNCS, vol. 10200, pp. 99–109. Springer, Cham (2017). https://doi.org/10.1007/978-3-319-55792-2_7
41. Eberhart, R.C., Shi, Y.: Comparing inertia weights and constriction factors in particle swarm optimization. In: Proceedings of IEEE Congress on Evolutionary Computation, pp. 84–88 (2001)

A Type Detection Based Dynamic
Multi-objective Evolutionary Algorithm

Shaaban Sahmoud and Haluk Rahmi Topcuoglu[(⊠)]

Computer Engineering Department, Marmara University, 34722 Istanbul, Turkey
ssahmoud@marun.edu.tr, haluk@marmara.edu.tr

Abstract. Characterization of dynamism is an important issue for utilizing or tailoring of several dynamic multi-objective evolutionary algorithms (DMOEAs). One such characterization is the change detection, which is based on proposing explicit schemes to detect the points in time when a change occurs. Additionally, detecting severity of change and incorporating with the DMOEAs is another attempt of characterization, where there is only a few related works presented in the literature. In this paper, we propose a type-detection mechanism for dynamic multi-objective optimization problems, which is one of the first attempts that investigate the significance of type detection on the performance of DMOEAs. Additionally, a hybrid technique is proposed which incorporates our type detection mechanism with a given DOMEA. We present an empirical evaluation by using seven test problems from all four types and five performance metrics, which clearly validate the motivation of type detection as well as significance of our hybrid technique.

Keywords: Dynamic Multi-objective Optimization Problems
Non-dominated Sorting Genetic Algorithm (NSGA-II) · Type detection
Dynamic Multi-objective Evolutionary Algorithms

1 Introduction

There are many real world multi-objective optimization problems which are dynamic in nature, where the dynamism is usually in the form of changes in objective(s), constraints or in parameters of the problem [1]. Those problems are called Dynamic Multi-objective Optimization Problems (DMOP), where there are various examples from different domains including network routing [2], scheduling problems [3], management systems [4], control [5], and power systems [6]. The Dynamic Multiobjective Optimization Evolutionary Algorithms (DMOEA) that are utilized to solve DMOPs receive increasing attention in the community of soft computing. Due to the existence of dynamism in DMOPs, solving such problems is more challenging than solving static MOPs since the evolutionary algorithms should handle the conflicting objectives and the changes in time.

Both of stationary and dynamic multi-objective evolutionary algorithms evolve a set of candidate solutions called population to find the set of optimal solutions. This set of candidate solutions is called Pareto Optimal Set (POS) in decision space and Pareto Optimal Front (POF) in objective space of the problem. To find the POS and POF of

© Springer International Publishing AG, part of Springer Nature 2018
K. Sim and P. Kaufmann (Eds.): EvoApplications 2018, LNCS 10784, pp. 879–893, 2018.
https://doi.org/10.1007/978-3-319-77538-8_58

the considered problem, an efficient sorting strategy is needed to compare between the population solutions. One of the most common one is the non-dominated sorting algorithm [8]. In this algorithm, the solutions are ranked based on the number of other solutions in the population that dominate the considered solution. The best solutions or non-dominated set are the set of solutions that are not dominated by any other solutions in the population.

In literature, there are many evolutionary algorithms that have been proposed to solve the static multi-objective optimization problems such as NSGA-II [8], SPEA-II [9], MOEA/D [10] and MOPSO [11, 12]. However, those static MOE algorithms are not capable of efficiently deal with DMOPs since those algorithms usually lose their diversity during the evolving process. Recalling existing DMOEAs, it can be observed that most of them are adapted from the stationary multi-objective evolutionary algorithms after that a specific dynamism handling mechanism is added to deal with new changes.

Characterization of dynamism is also important for tailoring DMOEAs to improve their performance. Detecting the points in time where a change occurs in the landscape is a critical issue for some of the DMOEAs presented in the literature, where a recent study validates incorporating change detection schemes with a selected DMOEA, based on the empirical evaluation [7]. Additionally, detecting the severity of change and providing an adaptive response mechanism based on an adaptive diversity introduction method [13] and an adaptive population management method [14] are proposed in the literature. The type of change based on Farina's classification [15] is another important characteristic of dynamism. In other words, the type of change tells us exactly if the change affects the POS and/or the POF of the optimization problem.

In this paper, we first present the importance of detecting the type of change by investigating the impact of the DMOP's type on different MOEAs by using empirical evaluation. Then, we propose a novel type detection mechanism for DMOPs. To the best of our knowledge, this is the first attempt that introduces an algorithm to detect the type of DMOPs. The results clearly validate that our proposed type detection method is very efficient; and it can detect the changes accurately without any additional computational cost. In addition, an adaptive hybrid type-based DMOEA is proposed by incorporating the new type detection mechanism into NSGA-II algorithm.

The rest of this paper is organized as follows. Section 2 presents a brief background on DMOEAs, related test problems and performance metrics considered in our experiments. In Sect. 3, the motivation of type detection is demonstrated empirically. Section 4 presents our proposed type detection mechanism. Then, a hybrid type-detection based on a DMOEA is proposed in Sect. 5. Finally Sect. 6 concludes this paper.

2 Dynamic Multi-objective Optimization

A dynamic multi-objective optimization problem (DMOP) is defined as an optimization problem that has two or more objectives functions with at least two objectives are in conflict with each other where the objective(s), the constraints, the input variables and/or parameters of the problem may change in time [1]. Formally, a DMOP can be defined as:

$$min/\max F(x, t) = \{f1(x, t), f2(x, t), f3(x, t) \ldots fM(x, t)\}$$
$$where\ h_i(x, t) = 0\ for\ i = 1 \ldots K\ and$$
$$g_j(x, t) > 0\ for\ j = 1 \ldots L$$

There are many classifications presented in literature to classify the DMOPs where the classification within the Farina's paper is the most common one [15]. Farina divides the DMOPs into four types based on the place of dynamism as described below:

- Type 1: The POS of the problem changes over time where the POF remains without change.
- Type 2: Both the POF and POS of the problem change over time.
- Type 3: The POF changes over time while the POS remains stationary.
- Type 4: No change occurs in both the POF and POS.

According to this classification, when a change occurs in the environment at least the POS, POF or both of them may change as described in first three types where the POS and POF remain static in the fourth type. Therefore, after each change in the environment, the new POS and/or the new POF of the DMOP should be tracked q before the next change occurrence.

2.1 Dynamic Multiobjective Evolutionary Algorithms

In literature there are many evolutionary algorithms have been proposed to solve DMOPs, where most of these algorithms are developed by adapting the static MOEAs through adding dynamism handling mechanisms. One of the most popular approaches is randomly reinitializing a predefined percentage of population solutions after each environmental change as in DNSGA-II-A algorithm [6]. If the change cannot be detected in the environment then the Random Immigrant (RI) algorithm [16] is the best choice since it randomly reinitializes a set of solutions in each generation without the need of change detection mechanism. Another common approach to handle the dynamism in environments is the adaptation of mutation parameters [17]. Whenever a change is detected in the landscape, the mutation can be increased to a high value for some generations and then its old value is assigned again as in hyper mutation algorithms [18]. In other algorithms, the mutation is employed in different way to quickly track the new POS and the new POF, for example DNSGA-II-B [6] algorithm a predefined percent of solutions are replaced with mutated current solutions after each environmental change.

Because of the good performance of memory based algorithms [19] in dealing with dynamic problems that have periodical changes, a number of memory based algorithms have been proposed to solve DMOPs such as MNSGA-II [20]. Recently, a number of algorithms that depend on estimating the new POS by using the history of previous POS values have been proposed to solve DMOPs [21, 22]. There are multi-population algorithms that use Particle Swarm Optimization (PSO) in order to solve DMOPs.

Helbig and Engelbrecht present DVEPSO algorithm [23], which was extended from multi-swarm PSO-based algorithm, called the vector evaluated particle swarm optimization (VEPSO) algorithm. Another multi-population approach is the Dynamic Competitive-Cooperative Coevolutionary Algorithm (dCOEA) that combines the competitive and cooperative techniques of Coevolutionary algorithms together to solve the MOPs and DMOPs [24]. It uses stochastic competitors and a temporal memory to track the Pareto front in dynamic environments.

2.2   DMOP Test Problems

Since the increasing attentions received on dynamic multiobjective optimization in the community of evolutionary computation, recently several simple and challenging benchmark test suites have been proposed to assess the performance of DMOE algorithms. Existing test suits for DMOE algorithms include FDA test suit [15], the scalable SJY framework [25], dMOP test problems [24] and time-varying T test problems [26]. In this study, seven test problems selected from different test suits are considered for the empirical evaluation of the DMOEAs (see Table 1).

Table 1. The properties of selected DMO test problems.

Test problem	Type	POF shape
FDA1	Type 1	Convex and static
FDA4	Type 1	Concave and static
FDA5	Type 2	Concave and dynamic
dMOP2	Type 2	Convex and dynamic
SJY4	Type 3	Concave and Convex
dMOP2	Type 3	Convex and dynamic
SJY5	Type 4	Concave and static

The time instance t that involved in the selected problems is defined as show in the following equation:

$$t = \frac{1}{n_t} * \left\lfloor \frac{\tau}{\tau_t} \right\rfloor$$

Where n_t represents the change severity, τ is the iteration counter and τ_t is the change frequency of the dynamic problem.

2.3   DMOP Performance Metrics

To investigate the performance of DMOE algorithms, one or more performance metrics should be adopted to measure the convergence and distribution of resulted solutions. In this study five widely used performance metrics given below are used in our comparative study.

1. *The Mean Inverted Generational Distance (mIGD)* [10]. This metric can measure both the convergence and distribution of solutions. It is designed based on the IGD metric for static MOEAs.
2. *The Mean Inverted Generational Distance Before Change (mIGDB) metric* [20]. This metric is an extension of the mIGD metrics with concentrating on the final obtained population just before next change. It can also measure both the convergence and distribution of solutions.
3. *Schott's Spacing (SS)* [25]. This metric is developed to measure the distribution of the discovered solutions without taking the conversion of solutions into account.
4. *Maximum Spread (MS)* [25]. As SS metrics, this metric measures the distribution extent of the final population on the True POF.
5. *Hyper Volume Ratio (HVR)* [27]. This metric is designed based on the well known stationary MOEAs metric which is Hyper Volume (HV) [28]. It can measure both the convergence and distribution of solutions as in mIGD metric.

3 Motivation of Type Detection for DMOPs

Although there are a large number of evolutionary algorithms that have been developed to solve DMOPs, the related work on characterization of dynamism is limited. Detecting the changes and detecting the change severity are two examples for characterizing dynamism in a DMOP. Characterization of dynamism can be used to adapt algorithms to improve their performance. Change detection and detection of change severity are incorporated with the DMOEAs by updating algorithm specific parameters or adding new schemes [7, 13, 14].

The type of the DMOPs is an important factor that may affects the shape and the behavior of the DMOPs. According to Farina et al. [15], there are four types of DMOPs which are different with respect to the place of change: *either in the POS or in the POF or in both of them*. Therefore, type detection provides information regarding the shape of the change and its impact on the POS and the POF of current population. In this section, we study the impact of types on the performance of the DMOEAs.

In order to evaluate the impact of problem type on the performance of DMOEAs, four dynamic multi-objective test instances that cover the four types are selected from Table 1. To ensure the fairness of experiments and to concentrate only on the effect of the problem type on the performance, five DMOEAs that are extended from the NSGA-II algorithm are utilized in the experiments. Unifying the base algorithm of the selected DMOEAs is required in order to enable us measuring the efficiency of each handling mechanism for each problem type. The five algorithms are the Random Immigrant algorithm (DNSGA-II-RI) [16], the memory based algorithm (MNSGA-II) [20], the hyper-mutation algorithm (DNSGA-II-HM) [18], DNSGA-II-A [6] and DNSGA-II-B [6].

The values of parameters used in the NSGA-II algorithm are same for all compared algorithms. The population size is selected to be 100 where the probability of crossover and mutation is equal to 0.7 and $1/n$ respectively (where n is the variables number in the problem). The real-valued encoding is used in variable representation and the number of variables is equal to 10 for all algorithms. Two values for the frequency of change are used, which are 10 and 20 generations; and the severity of change n_t is fixed on high value which is equal to 10.

For both the DNSGA-II-A and the DNSGA-II-B algorithms, 10% of the populations are replaced after each environmental change. The memory size of MNSGA-II algorithm is 100 and the memory is updated in every 10 generations. For the DNSGA-II-RI algorithm, 20% of the populations are replaced in each generation regardless of change detection. The mutation of DNSGA-II-HM algorithm is increased to 0.5 after the change is detected for only one generation; or otherwise the normal mutation value remains $1/n$ as mentioned before.

The following four tables (Tables 2, 3, 4 and 5) show the results of solving four DMOPs by using five performance metrics given in Sect. 2.3. The presented values are the average and the standard deviation of 30 independent runs for each test instance. In order to clarify the difference between the performances of tested algorithms, the Wilcoxon ranksum test [29] is performed at the 0.05 significance level for each test case. A "+" sign in the following tables indicates that the best algorithm that marked with bold line significantly outperforms the other algorithms with "+" signs in the same row. In case of more than one algorithm provide best results, they are given in bold.

Table 2. Performance of Algorithms for FDA1 test problem (Type 1).

Metrics	τ_t	DNSGA-II-RI	DNSGA-II-A	DNSGA-II-B	DNSGA-II-HM	MSNGA-II
mIGD	10	0.1031 (1.18E-04) +	**0.0701 (5.43E-05)**	**0.0699 (6.54E-05)**	0.0716 (3.87E-04)	0.0714 (3.51E-04)
	20	0.0580 (4.87E-05) +	**0.0386 (1.11E-05)**	**0.0384 (1.85E-05)**	0.0438 (1.89E-04) +	0.0409 (6.82E-05) +
mIGDB	10	0.0533 (5.48E-05) +	**0.0337 (4.14E-05)**	**0.0336 (3.04E-05)**	0.0506 (3.55E-04) +	0.0513 (3.60E-04) +
	20	0.0213 (1.09E-05) +	**0.0115 (3.38E-06)**	**0.0115 (5.24E-06)**	0.0291 (1.59E-04) +	0.0265 (4.78E-05) +
SS	10	0.0369 (2.72E-04) +	**0.0148 (1.28E-05)**	**0.0146 (2.57E-06)**	0.0522 (1.41E-03) +	0.0505 (3.51E-04) +
	20	0.0377 (2.62E-04) +	**0.0101 (5.49E-06)**	**0.0099 (3.72E-07)**	0.0702 (3.17E-03) +	0.0731 (2.22E-03) +
MS	10	0.9899 (1.18E-05)	**0.9909 (1.53E-05)**	**0.9913 (9.97E-06)**	0.9856 (1.30E-04)	0.9863 (1.75E-04)
	20	0.9908 (6.56E-06)	**0.9940 (3.68E-06)**	**0.9942 (2.88E-06)**	0.9867 (1.33E-04)	0.9872 (6.62E-05)
HVR	10	0.8489 (1.59E-04) +	**0.8937 (8.07E-05)**	**0.8936 (9.78E-05)**	0.8928 (6.09E-04)	0.8919 (6.09E-04)
	20	0.9174 (6.89E-05) +	**0.9447 (1.76E-05)**	**0.9449 (2.89E-05)**	0.9357 (2.32E-04)	0.9402 (1.54E-04)

Table 2 show the performance evaluation of algorithms on FDA1 test problem, which is in Type 1. The DNSGA-II-A and DNSGA-II-B are the best two algorithms since both of them outperform the other algorithms for 9 and 10 cases out of 10, cases respectively. The third best algorithm is the DNSGA-II-HM which gets accepted results for the three metrics. The MNSGA-II algorithm also performs better than other algorithms in some cases where the DNSGA-II-Rim fails in satisfying good results for any test case.

Performance comparison of algorithms on Type 2 problem is given in Table 3. The results definitely ensure the efficiency of DNSGA-II-A algorithm when both the POF and the POS change, where it outperforms the other algorithms for 9 out of 10 cases. The second best algorithm is the DNSGA-II-B which gets the best results for 5 instance cases. It is observed that the efficiency of DNSGA-II-B is decreased in Type 2 test instance because it includes higher change level than Type 1 problems. Unlike Type 1 results, the DNSGA-II-HM gets very weak performance in Type 2 test instances. The DNSGA-II-Rim algorithm gives worse results as in Type 1 test instances.

Table 3. Performance of Algorithms for FDA5 test problem (Type 2).

Metrics	τ_t	DNSGA-II-RI	DNSGA-II-A	DNSGA-II-B	DNSGA-II-HM	MSNGA-II
mIGD	10	0.1351 (1.54E-04) +	**0.1141 (9.40E-05)**	0.1419 (2.28E-04) +	0.4411 (2.66E-03) +	0.4457 (1.92E-03) +
	20	0.0824 (3.21E-05)	**0.0672 (4.73E-05)**	0.0711 (1.56E-04)	0.5056 (9.83E-04) +	0.4895 (6.61E-04) +
mIGDB	10	0.0671 (4.62E-05) +	**0.0547 (3.28E-05)**	0.0694 (9.52E-05) +	0.4229 (2.76E-03) +	0.4291 (1.93E-03) +
	20	0.0287 (1.19E-05) +	**0.0209 (1.82E-05)**	0.0227 (5.72E-05)	0.4913 (1.01E-03) +	0.4749 (6.28E-04) +
SS	10	0.0349 (7.43E-06) +	**0.0243 (2.69E-06)**	**0.0243 (1.76E-06)**	0.0616 (2.70E-03) +	0.0800 (3.00E-03) +
	20	0.0285 (5.87E-06) +	0.0181 (1.13E-06)	**0.0174 (7.36E-07)**	0.1052 (3.94E-03) +	0.0815 (2.63E-03) +
MS	10	**1.0000 (0.00E00)**	**1.0000 (0.00E00)**	**1.0000 (0.00E00)**	0.9843 (8.36E-04)	0.9803 (8.58E-04)
	20	**1.0000 (1.11E-10)**	**1.0000 (0.00E00)**	**1.0000 (0.00E00)**	0.9694 (1.57E-03) +	0.9720 (1.18E-03) +
HVR	10	0.9365 (1.18E-04)	**0.9500 (1.45E-04)**	0.9106 (3.81E-04) +	0.6241 (1.89E-04) +	0.6256 (2.54E-04) +
	20	0.9916 (1.30E-05)	**1.0048 (2.61E-05)**	**1.0015 (8.28E-05)**	0.6668 (4.12E-05) +	0.6686 (1.23E-05) +

Table 4. Performance of Algorithms for dMOP1 test problem (Type 3).

Metrics	τ_t	DNSGA-II-RI	DNSGA-II-A	DNSGA-II-B	DNSGA-II-HM	MSNGA-II
mIGD	10	0.3287 (2.76E-02) +	0.3116 (5.27E-03) +	0.3012 (1.74E-02)	**0.2879 (5.03E-03)**	0.3137 (5.97E-03) +
	20	0.1951 (2.52E-02) +	0.1925 (2.62E-02) +	**0.1614 (1.57E-02)**	0.1968 (1.50E-02) +	0.1981 (2.84E-03) +
mIGDB	10	0.1715 (2.52E-02) +	0.1444 (2.62E-03) +	0.1497 (1.40E-02) +	**0.1323 (2.93E-03)**	0.1531 (3.16E-03) +
	20	0.0948 (2.31E-02) +	0.0927 (2.81E-02) +	**0.0716 (1.47E-02)**	0.0979 (1.35E-02) +	0.1001 (2.33E-03) +
SS	10	0.0616 (1.99E-03) +	0.0441 (1.67E-04) +	0.0400 (9.12E-05) +	**0.0386 (1.14E-04)**	0.0416 (1.28E-04) +
	20	0.0272 (1.18E-04) +	0.0291 (2.00E-04) +	0.0233 (6.29E-05)	0.0240 (7.26E-05)	**0.0230 (2.82E-05)**
MS	10	0.9348 (3.81E-03) +	0.9438 (4.13E-04) +	0.9459 (2.32E-03) +	**0.9604 (4.83E-04)**	0.9504 (5.51E-04)
	20	0.9562 (3.78E-03)	0.9588 (4.67E-03)	0.9684 (2.43E-03)	**0.9688 (2.45E-03)**	**0.9688 (4.32E-04)**
HVR	10	0.7739 (2.11E-02) +	0.7902 (1.96E-03) +	0.7928 (1.21E-02) +	**0.8660 (2.72E-03)**	0.8367 (2.45E-03)
	20	0.8568 (2.18E-02) +	0.8671 (2.60E-02) +	0.8913 (1.40E-02) +	**0.9535 (1.69E-02)**	0.9486 (2.93E-03)

The results of Type 3 test instance are completely different than the results of previous problems (see Table 4). Specifically, the DNSGA-II-A and DNSGA-II-B which are the best two algorithms based on Type 1 and Type 2 results are the worst algorithms. One exception is for the DNSGA-II-B algorithm which gives good results when the frequency of change is high. For the dMOP1 problem, the best results are provided by the DNSGA-II-HM algorithm, which is the best one for 7 out of 10 cases. In addition, the MNSGA-II algorithm is the second best algorithm. It is also important to note that DNSGA-II-HM algorithm performs better for low frequency of changes than the high frequency values.

The performance results of the SJY5 test (an example Type 4 test) is given in Table 8. The DNSGA-II-HM algorithm is also the best algorithm here by obtaining the best results in 7 cases out of 10. The MNSGA-II and DNSGA-II-A algorithms have slightly good performance in this test instance since both of them got the best results in two cases. The performance of DNSGA-II-B and DNSGA-II-RI algorithms is worse than the others.

Based on the given results, it is observed that the results of Type 1 and Type 2 test instances are very similar; and the results of Type 3 and Type 4 tests are also near to each other. For Type 1 and Type 2, the best two algorithms are DNSGA-II-A and DNSGA-II-B respectively, where these two algorithms got the worst results for Type 3 and Type 4 test instances. On the other hand, DNSGA-II-HM and MNSGA-II are the best two algorithms respectively on Type 3 and Type 4 test instances but they could not satisfy good results in the Type 1 and Type 2 test instances. For a DMOP which is in either Type 1 or Type 2, the POS of the problem is updated after each environmental change which makes it better to search for completely new solutions; it is exactly what DNSGA-II-A algorithm performs. On the contrary, when a change occurs in Type 3 or Type 4 test instances, the POS remains the same; therefore, maintaining the current obtained solutions and enhancing the results by finding solutions around them are more preferable, as the DNSGA-II-HM and the MNSGA-II algorithms perform. Moreover, introducing completely new random solutions for Type 3 and Type 4 test instances can degrade the performance of the algorithms, which is consistent with the worse results of the DNSGA-II-A on dMOP1 and SJY5 test instances.

Table 5. Performance of Algorithms for SJY5 test problem (Type 4).

Metrics	τ_t	DNSGA-II-RI	DNSGA-II-A	DNSGA-II-B	DNSGA-II-HM	MSNGA-II
mIGD	10	0.0392 (6.09E-05) +	0.0409 (1.13E-04) +	0.0397 (7.70E-05) +	**0.0362 (7.55E-05)**	0.0393 (1.00E-04)
	20	0.0224 (2.88E-05)	0.0216 (1.52E-05)	0.0221 (1.53E-05) +	**0.0215 (2.50E-05)**	0.0237 (4.05E-05) +
mIGDB	10	0.0281 (6.11E-05) +	0.0294 (1.02E-04) +	0.0286 (7.20E-05) +	**0.0260 (7.27E-05)**	0.0283 (9.23E-05) +
	20	0.0120 (1.98E-05) +	**0.0105 (9.54E-06)**	0.0114 (1.32E-05)	0.0117 (1.83E-05)	0.0131 (3.98E-05) +
SS	10	0.0067 (1.27E-07)	0.0066 (1.59E-07)	0.0066 (1.53E-07)	0.0066 (2.02E-07)	0.0066 (4.77E-07)
	20	0.0062 (5.74E-08)	0.0061 (2.57E-08)	0.0061 (4.12E-08)	**0.0060 (1.82E-08)**	**0.0060 (4.77E-08)**
MS	10	0.9984 (1.58E-06)	0.9977 (6.78E-06)	0.9981 (2.72E-06)	**0.9986 (2.09E-06)**	0.9982 (3.66E-06)
	20	0.9989 (1.23E-06)	0.9990 (1.38E-06)	0.9992 (1.04E-06)	0.9991 (9.14E-07)	**0.9994 (4.88E-07)**
HVR	10	0.9164 (3.48E-04)	0.9116 (7.75E-04)	0.9130 (5.30E-04)	**0.9215 (5.31E-04)**	0.9149 (7.34E-04)
	20	0.9569 (2.03E-04)	**0.9595 (1.10E-04)**	0.9576 (1.17E-04)	0.9590 (1.83E-04)	0.9538 (2.87E-04)

4   A New Type Detection Strategy for DMOPs

Although the problem types of synthetic or test instance presented in the literature are known priori, the situation is different for the real-world DMOPs. In addition to lack of knowledge on type detection, there may be real world problems with mixed types which can change between different types during the run [30]. Therefore, it becomes important to develop a mechanism that can detect the type of DMOPs efficiently.

In this section, we propose a type detection mechanism which divides the changes of DMOPs into two types: (a) the change that causes variation in POS, (b) the change that does not make variation in POS of the DMOP. If the POS of the problem is changed this means that we are dealing with Type 1 and Type 2 DMOPs; if the POS remains without variation this indicates that the considered DMOP is either in Type 3 or in Type 4.

Our proposed type detection mechanism is based on the difference in the number of non-dominated solutions before and after a change. If the considered DMOP is Type 1 or Type 2, then the POS after the change will be different than the POS before the change; which makes many solutions in the population transfer from *non-dominated solutions* to *dominated solutions*. This situation definitely decreases the number of non-dominated solutions after each environmental change.

On the other hand, if the considered DMOP is Type 3 or Type 4 then the POS will be the same after and before the change; which means that the number of non-dominated solutions in the population will approximately be the same before and after the change. In order to detect if there is a change in the POS, the proposed mechanism computes the difference between the number of non-dominated solutions before and after the change. If this difference is high, then the tested problem is considered as Type 1 or Type 2; whereas if the difference is low (or close to zero), then the tested problem is considered as Type 3 or Type 4 (see Fig. 1).

```
begin
    Prev_Num_NonD_Sols = 0  // Number of non-dominated solutions in the previous population
    Curr_Num_NonD_Sols = 0    // Number of non-dominated solutions in the current population
    InitializeRandomSensors(S) // initialize randomly S sensors     .
    While termination condition not satisfied do
    ...
        ReevaluateSensors(S) // reevaluate the sensors
        ChangeHappened= Difference_Sensor_Values(S) // if there is any change in sensors; true or false
        If ChangeHappened Then  // if change is detected
                Curr_Num_NonD_Sols = Num_NonD_Sols_from_NSGAII()
                Diff = Prev_Num_NonD_Sols - Curr_Num_NonD_Sols
                If (Diff / Population_Size) > λ Then
                    // The POS of problem changed (Type 1 or Type 2)
                Else
                    // The POS of problem did not change (Type 3 or Type 4)
                end
        end
        Prev_Num_NonD_Sols = Prev_Num_NonD_Sols
    end  // while end
end  // Program end
```

Fig. 1. The steps of the proposed type detection mechanism.

In this algorithm, change detection mechanism is performed by randomly selecting a fixed number of sensors from any part of the fitness landscape once at the beginning of the execution, which are periodically reevaluated and compared with their previous values for determining a change [7].

The λ symbol is a threshold value that is used to distinguish between the two detected states (see Fig. 1). In order to determine the best value of λ, a set of experiments is conducted. The performance of our type detection mechanism is measured using true positive rate (TPR), which is equal to the percentage of the total number of changes that are correctly identified. Figure 2 shows the average TPR values of seven DMOPs by varying λ with different values, when our type detection mechanism is used. According to results of Fig. 2, when λ value increases, the detection rate (which is TPR value) for Type 1 and Type 2 problems decreases, while the detection rate for Type 3 and Type 4 problems increases. It is noted that the maximum TPR value (marked by continuous line in Fig. 2) is occurred when λ is equal to 5%. Therefore, in this study a value of 5% is used for setting λ, which means that if more than 5% of the population solutions transfer from non-dominated state to dominated state, then the change is considered as Type 1 or Type 2.

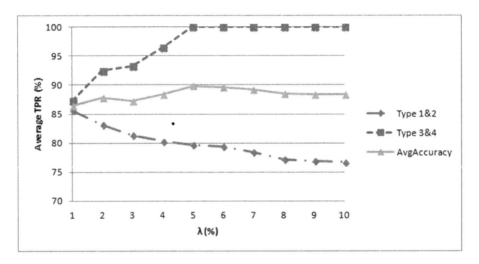

Fig. 2. The impact of the threshold λ on the proposed type detection mechanism.

The performance of the proposed type detection mechanism is tested with a new experiment using seven DMOPs with two different change frequency values (see Table 6). For each test instance, the average of 100 runs is computed using TPR. The results of Table 6 show that the proposed algorithm can accurately detect Type 3 and Type 4 test problems. On the other hand, Type 1 and Type 2 problems can be detected with approximately 70% accuracy. It is also important to note that the proposed mechanism works better for the cases with slow change frequency values (i.e., $\tau_t = 20$) than the cases with high change frequency values ($\tau_t = 10$).

Table 6. Average TPR values of the type detection mechanism for different test instances

Type	Problem	$\tau_t = 10$	$\tau_t = 20$
Type 1	FDA4	63.75	83.75
	FDA1	76.25	88.75
Type 2	FDA5	77.50	91.25
	dMOP2	68.75	87.50
Type 3	SJY4	100.00	100.00
	dMOP1	100.00	100.00
Type 4	SJY5	100.00	100.00

5 Incorporating Type Detection Mechanism

In this section, we propose a *hybridized solution* by incorporating our type detection mechanism presented in Sect. 4 and a new response mechanism with the well-known NSGA-II algorithm. In our response mechanism, if the detected type for a given test problem is Type 1 or Type 2, 10% of solutions are replaced with random generated solutions. On the other hand, if the detected type is Type 3 or Type 4, the mutation parameter is increased to a high value for only one generation. It is expected that the new hybrid DMOEA performs well for all problem types, since it benefits from the best two mechanisms of the DMOEAs (see results of Sect. 3).

Table 7. Mean and standard deviation of the three metrics when $n_t = 10$ and $\tau_t = 10$.

Problems	Metrics	DNSGA-II-RI	DNSGA-II-A	DNSGA-II-B	DNSGA-II-HM	MNSGA-II	Hybrid Algorithm
FDA1	mIGD	0.103 (1.2E-04) +	**0.068 (5.4E-05)**	**0.068 (6.5E-05)**	0.072 (3.8E-04)	0.071 (3.5E-04)	0.070 (4.9E-05)
	mIGDB	0.053 (5.5E-05) +	**0.033 (4.1E-05)**	0.033 (3.0E-05)	0.057 (3.5E-04) +	0.051 (3.6E-04) +	**0.033 (3.2E-05)**
	HVR	0.849 (1.6E-04) +	0.891 (8.1E-05)	**0.894 (9.8E-05)**	0.893 (6.1E-04)	0.892 (6.1E-04)	0.891 (8.1E-05)
FDA5	mIGD	0.135 (1.5E-04) +	**0.114 (9.4E-05)**	0.142 (2.3E-04) +	0.441 (2.7E-03) +	0.446 (1.9E-03) +	0.117 (1.7E-05)
	mIGDB	0.067 (4.6E-05) +	**0.055 (3.3E-05)**	0.069 (9.5E-05) +	0.423 (2.8E-03) +	0.429 (1.9E-03) +	**0.055 (6.3E-05)**
	HVR	0.937 (1.2E-04) +	**0.950 (1.4E-04)**	0.911 (3.8E-04) +	0.624 (1.9E-04) +	0.621 (2.5E-04) +	**0.950 (2.8E-04)**
dMOP1	mIGD	0.329 (2.8E-02) +	0.312 (5.3E-03) +	0.301 (1.7E-02)	0.288 (5.0E-03)	0.314 (5.9E-03) +	**0.276 (6.1E-03)**
	mIGDB	0.172 (2.5E-02) +	0.144 (2.6E-03) +	0.150 (1.4E-02) +	0.132 (2.9E-03)	0.153 (3.2E-03) +	**0.122 (2.4E-03)**
	HVR	0.774 (2.1E-02) +	0.790 (6.2E-03) +	0.793 (1.2E-02) +	**0.866 (2.7E-03)**	0.837 (2.4E-03)	0.836 (2.7E-03)
SJY5	mIGD	0.039 (6.1E-05) +	0.041 (1.1E-04) +	0.040 (7.7E-05) +	**0.036 (7.5E-05)**	0.039 (1.0E-04)	**0.036 (1.1E-05)**
	mIGDB	0.028 (6.1E-05) +	0.029 (1.0E-04) +	0.029 (7.2E-05) +	**0.026 (7.2E-05)**	0.028 (9.2E-05) +	**0.026 (1.0E-05)**
	HVR	0.916 (3.5E-04) +	0.912 (7.7E-04)	0.913 (5.3E-04)	**0.922 (5.3E-04)**	0.915 (7.3E-04)	**0.920 (7.0E-04)**

In order to evaluate the impact of our incorporation mechanism, an empirical study by using the experiments given in Sect. 3 is repeated with the same parameters and algorithms, where three performance metrics and four DMO test instances are considered. The test problems are determined by selecting one from each DMOP type, which are FDA1, FDA5, dMOP1 and SJY5. Two different frequency of change (τ_t) values are used, which are 10 and 20. To investigate the performance of algorithms in different severity levels, two different change severity values (n_t) are considered, which are 10 and 20. As in the tables given at Sect. 3, Wilcoxon ranksum test is performed at the 0.05 significance level for each test case given in Tables 7, 8 and 9; where a "+"

sign indicates that the best algorithm that marked with bold line significantly outperforms the other algorithms with "+" signs in the same row.

The average and standard deviation of 30 runs of each experiment instance are given in Tables 7, 8 and 9. The presented results in Table 7 show that our proposed hybridization algorithm performs good for all test instances considered; and it gets the best results in 8 out of 12 cases. Although the DNSGA-II-A and DNSGA-II-HM algorithms provide acceptable performance for some of the cases presented. As an example, the DNSGA-II-A algorithm gets the highest performance on FDA1 and FDA5 problems, but it is significantly outperformed on five cases of the dMOP1 and the SJY5 test problems.

Table 8. Mean and standard deviation of three metrics when $n_t = 10$ and $\tau_t = 20$.

Problems	Metrics	DNSGA-II-RI	DNSGA-II-A	DNSGA-II-B	DNSGA-II-HM	MNSGA-II	Hybrid Algorithm
FDA1	mIGD	0.058 (4.8E-05)+	0.039 (1.1E-05)	**0.038 (1.8E-05)**	0.044 (1.8E-04)+	0.041 (6.2E-05)+	**0.038 (1.2E-05)**
	mIGDB	0.021 (1.1E-05)+	0.012 (3.3E-06)	0.012 (5.2E-06)	0.029 (1.5E-04)+	0.026 (4.7E-05)+	**0.011 (3.5E-06)**
	HVR	0.917 (6.8E-05)+	**0.944 (1.7E-05)**	**0.944 (2.8E-05)**	0.935 (2.3E-04)	0.940 (1.5E-04)	0.943 (1.7E-05)
FDA5	mIGD	0.082 (3.2E-05)	**0.067 (4.7E-05)**	0.071 (1.5E-04)	0.505 (9.8E-04)+	0.489 (6.6E-04)+	**0.067 (4.4E-05)**
	mIGDB	0.029 (1.1E-05)+	**0.021 (1.8E-05)**	0.023 (5.7E-05)	0.491 (1.0E-03)+	0.475 (6.8E-04)+	**0.021 (1.3E-05)**
	HVR	0.992 (1.0E-05)	**1.004 (2.6E-05)**	1.003 (8.2E-05)	0.666 (4.1E-05)+	0.668 (1.2E-05)+	1.003 (2.4E-05)
dMOP1	mIGD	0.022 (2.8E-05)	0.022 (1.5E-05)	0.022 (1.5E-05)+	**0.021 (2.5E-05)**	0.023 (4.0E-05)+	0.021 (2.2E-05)
	mIGDB	0.012 (1.9E-05)+	**0.010 (9.4E-06)**	0.011 (1.3E-05)	0.012 (1.8E-05)	0.013 (3.9E-05)+	0.011 (1.8E-05)
	HVR	0.957 (2.0E-04)	**0.959 (1.1E-04)**	0.957 (1.7E-04)	0.958 (1.8E-04)	0.953 (2.8E-04)	**0.959 (1.8E-04)**
SJY5	mIGD	0.195 (2.5E-02)+	0.192 (2.6E-02)+	**0.161 (1.5E-02)**	0.196 (1.5E-02)+	0.198 (2.8E-03)+	0.196 (1.5E-02)+
	mIGDB	0.095 (2.3E-02)+	0.092 (2.8E-02)+	**0.081 (1.4E-02)**	0.097 (1.3E-02)+	0.100 (2.3E-03)+	0.097 (1.3E-02)+
	HVR	0.857 (2.1E-02)+	0.867 (2.6E-02)+	0.891 (1.4E-02)+	**0.953 (1.6E-02)**	0.948 (2.9E-03)	**0.953 (1.6E-02)**

Table 9. Mean and standard deviation of three metrics when $n_t = 20$ and $\tau_t = 10$.

Problems	Metrics	DNSGA-II-RI	DNSGA-II-A	DNSGA-II-B	DNSGA-II-HM	MNSGA-II	Hybrid Algorithm
FDA1	mIGD	0.086 (1.5E-04)+	**0.053 (4.2E-05)**	0.055 (2.8E-05)+	0.055 (1.1E-04)+	**0.053 (1.1E-04)**	**0.053 (4.1E-05)**
	mIGDB	0.046 (4.6E-05)+	0.028 (3.01E-05)	**0.027 (2.1E-05)**	0.032 (1.0E-04)+	0.031 (9.5E-05)+	0.028 (3.0E-05)
	HVR	0.877 (1.8E-04)+	**0.964 (5.6E-05)**	0.962 (3.6E-05)	0.962 (1.4E-04)	0.924 (1.7E-04)	**0.964 (5.5E-05)**
FDA5	mIGD	0.239 (1.4E-04)	**0.229 (5.0E-05)**	0.232 (7.7E-05)	0.457 (6.2E-04)+	0.458 (5.5E-04)+	**0.229 (5.2E-05)**
	mIGDB	**0.234 (9.1E-05)**	**0.234 (2.4E-05)**	0.236 (3.3E-05)	0.436 (5.8E-03)+	0.435 (6.8E-04)+	**0.234 (2.4E-05)**
	HVR	0.612 (2.1E04)	**0.707 (2.6E-05)**	0.705 (2.2E-05)	0.654 (9.2E-05)	0.613 (5.45E04)	**0.707 (2.4E-05)**
dMOP1	mIGD	0.328 (1.6E-03)	0.322 (1.6E-02)	0.329 (1.8E-02)	**0.317 (1.5E-02)**	0.340 (1.3E-02)+	**0.317 (1.1E-02)**
	mIGDB	0.323 (1.3E-04)+	**0.160 (1.3E-02)**	0.165 (1.47E-02)	**0.160 (1.2E-02)**	0.179 (7.9E-03)	**0.160 (1.2E-02)**
	HVR	0.829 (9.5E-04)+	0.875 (3.8E-03)+	0.873 (4.2E-03)+	**0.891 (3.6E-03)**	0.843 (6.7E-03)+	**0.891 (3.2E-03)**
SJY5	mIGD	0.07 (4.8E-05)+	0.038 (1.3E-04)	**0.037 (9.5E-05)**	0.037 (1.1E-04)	0.041 (9.17E-05)	0.037 (1.1E-04)
	mIGDB	0.067 (2.4E-05)+	0.027 (1.2E-04)	**0.026 (8.3E-05)**	0.026 (1.0E-04)	0.030 (7.8E-05)	0.026 (1.0E-04)
	HVR	**0.995 (2.4E-04)**	0.980 (8.5E-05)	0.981 (4.0E-05)	0.980 (6.9E-05)	0.909 (5.4E-04)+	0.984 (2.5E-04)

Tables 8 shows the results of the six DMOEAs when higher value of change frequency is considered, $\tau_t = 20$. As in previous experiment, our proposed hybrid algorithm is significantly superior to other algorithms for 8 out of 12 cases. The proposed algorithm gains better performance for high τ_t values for Type 1 and Type 2 test problems, whereas its performance slightly decreases for Type 3 and Type 4. One reason of this result is that when the change occurs slowly, the DMOEAs have enough time to find the new POF, which provided other algorithms such as DNSGA-II-B performs equally with the proposed algorithm.

Table 9 presents the results of the 6 algorithms for a different change severity, i.e., when $n_t = 20$. As in the previous tables, the proposed hybrid algorithm significantly outperforms all other 5 algorithms, where it reaches best results 10 out of 12 cases. The results presented in the last three tables significantly validate effectiveness, diversity ability and convergence ability of our type-base hybridization algorithm. It is also observed that there is only two "+" signs (out of 36 cases) at the last column of the three tables; since, our hybridized solution is the only algorithm that is not significantly outperformed by any other algorithm for majority of test cases.

6   Conclusion

In this paper, we present a type detection scheme for dynamic multi-objective optimization problems (DMOPs). The main idea is to detect the type if there is a change in the POS as in Type 1 and Type 2, or not as in Type 3 and 4. The comparative results that run out on different types of problems significantly ensure that there is a benefit for detecting the problem type.

Furthermore, a new hybrid type detection-based evolutionary algorithm is introduced by incorporating the proposed type detection mechanism. The results clearly show that the presented type detection mechanism is very efficient and the proposed hybrid type-based DMOE algorithm perform well on different types of DMOP. One of the future works is to combine severity detection and type detection mechanisms together in DMOEAs by investigating the performance of the combined approach.

References

1. Yang, S., Yao, X.: Evolutionary Computation for Dynamic Optimization Problems. Springer, Berlin (2013)
2. Constantinou, D.: Ant colony optimisation algorithms for solving multiobjective power-aware metrics for mobile ad hoc networks. Ph.D. dissertation, University of Pretoria (2011)
3. Chen, C.L., Lee, W.C.: Multi-objective optimization of multiechelon supply chain networks with uncertain product demands and prices. Comput. Chem. Eng. 28(6), 1131–1144 (2004)
4. Palaniappan, S., Zein-Sabatto, S., Sekmen, A.: Dynamic multiobjective optimization of war resource allocation using adaptive genetic algorithms. In: 2001 Proceedings of IEEE SoutheastCon, pp. 160–165. IEEE (2001)
5. Hamalainen, R.P., Mantysaari, J.: Dynamic multi-objective heating optimization. Eur. J. Oper. Res. 142(1), 1–15 (2002)
6. Deb, K., Rao, N.U.B., Karthik, S.: Dynamic multi-objective optimization and decision-making using modified NSGA-II: a case study on hydro-thermal power scheduling. In: Obayashi, S., Deb, K., Poloni, C., Hiroyasu, T., Murata, T. (eds.) EMO 2007. LNCS, vol. 4403, pp. 803–817. Springer, Heidelberg (2007). https://doi.org/10.1007/978-3-540-70928-2_60

7. Sahmoud, S., Topcuoglu, H.R.: Sensor-based change detection schemes for dynamic multi-objective optimization problems. In: 2016 IEEE Symposium Series Computational Intelligence (SSCI), pp. 1–8 (2016)
8. Deb, K., Pratap, A., Agarwal, S., Meyarivan, T.: A fast and elitist multiobjective genetic algorithm: NSGA-II. IEEE Trans. Evol. Comput. **6**(2), 182–197 (2002)
9. Zitzler, E., Thiele, L.: Multiobjective evolutionary algorithms: a comparative case study and the strength Pareto approach. IEEE Trans. Evol. Comput. **3**(4), 257–271 (1999)
10. Zhang, Q., Li, H.: MOEA/D: a multiobjective evolutionary algorithm based on decomposition. IEEE Trans. Evol. Comput. **11**(6), 712–731 (2007)
11. Hu, X., Eberhart, R.C.: Multiobjective optimization using dynamic neighborhood particle swarm optimization. In: Proceedings of IEEE Congress on Evolutionary Computation, Honolulu, pp. 1677–1681 (2002)
12. Zhang, L.B., Zhou, C.G., Liu, X.H., Ma, Z.Q., Ma, M., Liang, Y.C.: Solving multi objective problems using particle swarm optimization. In: Proceedings of IEEE Congress on Evolutionary Computation, Canberra, Australia, pp. 2400–2405 (2003)
13. Liu, M., Zheng, J., Wang, J., Liu, Y., Jiang, L.: An adaptive diversity introduction method for dynamic evolutionary multiobjective optimization. In: 2014 IEEE Congress on Evolutionary Computation (CEC), pp. 3160–3167. IEEE (2014)
14. Azzouz, R., Bechikh, S., Said, L.B.: A dynamic multi-objective evolutionary algorithm using a change severity-based adaptive population management strategy. Soft Comput. **21**(4), 885–906 (2017)
15. Farina, M., Deb, K., Amato, P.: Dynamic multiobjective optimization problems: test cases, approximations, and applications. IEEE Trans. Evol. Comput. **8**(5), 425–442 (2004)
16. Grefenstette, J.: Genetic algorithms for changing environments. In: Proceedings of International Conference on Parallel Problem Solving from Nature, pp. 137–144 (1992)
17. Cobb, H.: An Investigation into the use of hyper-mutation as an adaptive operator in genetic algorithms having continuous, time-dependent non-stationary environments. Technical report, Naval Research Laboratory (1990)
18. Vavak, F., Jukes, K., Fogarty, T.: Adaptive combustion balancing in multiple burner boiler using a genetic algorithm with variable range of local search. In: Proceedings of 7th International Conference on Genetic Algorithms, pp. 719–726 (1997)
19. Branke, J.: Memory enhanced evolutionary algorithms for changing optimization problems. In: Congress on Evolutionary Computation CEC 1999, vol. 3, pp. 1875–1882 (1999)
20. Sahmoud, S., Topcuoglu, H.R.: A memory-based NSGA-II algorithm for dynamic multi-objective optimization problems. In: Squillero, G., Burelli, P. (eds.) EvoApplications 2016. LNCS, vol. 9598, pp. 296–310. Springer, Cham (2016). https://doi.org/10.1007/978-3-319-31153-1_20
21. Zhou, A., Jin, Y., Zhang, Q., Sendhoff, B., Tsang, E.: Prediction-based population re-initialization for evolutionary dynamic multi-objective optimization. In: Obayashi, S., Deb, K., Poloni, C., Hiroyasu, T., Murata, T. (eds.) EMO 2007. LNCS, vol. 4403, pp. 832–846. Springer, Heidelberg (2007). https://doi.org/10.1007/978-3-540-70928-2_62
22. Muruganantham, A., Zhao, Y., Gee, S.B., Qiu, X., Tan, K.: Dynamic multiobjective optimization using evolutionary algorithm with Kalman filter. In: 17th Asia Pacific Symposium on IES 2013, vol. 24, pp. 66–75 (2013)
23. Greeff, M., Engelbrecht, A.P.: Solving dynamic multi-objective problems with vector evaluated particle swarm optimisation. In: IEEE Congress on Evolutionary Computation, CEC 2008, (IEEE World Congress on Computational Intelligence), pp. 2917–2924 (2008)
24. Goh, C., Tan, K.: A competitive-cooperative coevolutionary paradigm for dynamic multiobjective optimization. IEEE Trans. Evol. Comput. **13**(1), 103–127 (2009)

25. Jiang, S., Yang, S.: A framework of scalable dynamic test problems for dynamic multi-objective optimization. In: CIDUE, pp. 32–39 (2014)

26. Huang, L., Suh, I.H., Abraham, A.: Dynamic multi-objective optimization based on membrane computing for control of time-varying unstable plants. Information Sciences, **181**(11), 2370–2391 (2011)

27. Li, X., Branke, J., Blackwell, T.: Particle swarm with speciation and adaptation in a dynamic environment. In: Proceedings of the 8th Annual Conference on Genetic and Evolutionary Computation, pp. 51–58. ACM (2006)

28. Zitzler, E., Deb, K., Thiele, L.: Comparison of multiobjective evolutionary algorithms: empirical results. Evol. Comput. **8**(2), 173–195 (2000)

29. Wilcoxon, F.: Individual comparisons by ranking methods. Biometrics Bull. **1**(6), 80–83 (1945)

30. Jiang, S., Yang, S.: Evolutionary dynamic multiobjective optimization: benchmarks and algorithm comparisons. IEEE Trans. Cybern. **46**, 2862–2873 (2016)

General

Cardnutri: A Software of Weekly Menus Nutritional Elaboration for Scholar Feeding Applying Evolutionary Computation

Rafaela P. C. Moreira[1(✉)] ⓘ, Elizabeth F. Wanner[2] ⓘ, Flávio V. C. Martins[3] ⓘ, and João F. M. Sarubbi[3] ⓘ

[1] Programa de Pós-Graduação em Modelagem Matemática e Computacional, CEFET, MG, Belo Horizonte, Brazil
rafapcmor@gmail.com
[2] ALICE Group - EAS, Aston University, Birmingham, UK
e.wanner@aston.ac.uk
[3] Departamento de Computação, CEFET, MG, Belo Horizonte, Brazil
flaviocruzeiro@decom.cefetmg.br, joaosarubbi@gmail.com

Abstract. This paper aims to present and evaluate a software that uses an evolutionary strategy to design weekly nutritional menus for School Feeding. The software ensures the nutritional needs of students and also minimizes the total cost of the menu. We based our nutritional needs on the Brazilian National School Feeding Programme (PNAE). This program takes into account: (i) the age of the student; (ii) some preparations issues as color, consistency and, variety; and also (iii) the maximum amount to be paid per meal. Our software generates, in less than five minutes, a set of menus, and the nutritionist can choose the menu that suits his/her best. We evaluate our algorithm using the Weighted-Sum approach, and our results show that the obtained 5-days menus using the proposed methodology not only comply with the restrictions imposed by the authorities but also produce inexpensive and healthy menus. We also appraise the software itself using an opinion pool among nine nutritionists. The professionals considered our software above expectations.

Keywords: Evolutionary computation · Food technology
Public health informatics · Menu Planning · School feeding

1 Introduction

Society has always been concerned about feeding since an inadequate nutrition is responsible for the growth and health problems in human beings. With the new technologies' development, not only the food production has grown but also has the industrial food accessibility. An inadequate nutrition with a combination of high levels of sugar and fat presented in the industrialized food can also lead to obesity or overweight.

© Springer International Publishing AG, part of Springer Nature 2018
K. Sim and P. Kaufmann (Eds.): EvoApplications 2018, LNCS 10784, pp. 897–913, 2018.
https://doi.org/10.1007/978-3-319-77538-8_59

Food is an essential condition for life maintenance. However, it has to be ingested in a proper quantity and variety. Overall functional consequences of a malnourished individual are enormous: impairment in growth, intellectual performance and in women reproductive capacity, to name a few.

The eating guide for the Brazilian population [1] presents a broad definition of healthy eating: *"An adequate and healthy eating is a fundamental human right that guarantees access to an eating practice appropriate to the biological and social aspects of the individual and which must comply with special dietary needs. It must be referenced by social eating habits, gender, race, and ethnicity; it must be accessible from a physical and financial point of view; it must have a balance between quantity and quality while ensuring the principles of variety, balance, moderation and taste"*.

The practice of healthy eating has become important since childhood, at which stage eating habits are formed, so the family and school environment contribute to the knowledge of new foods.

In this way, this diet must supply energy, macronutrients, and micronutrients intake levels enough to meet the daily nutrient requirements of students.

In Brazil, there is a program that regulates the school feeding, called the Brazilian National School Feeding Programme (PNAE) [2]. This program aimed to attend children in darycare, preschool, elementary school, middle school and high school.

This program assures that there is a nutritionist responsible for the elaboration of the school menu in the executing entities was required. The goal was to provide a balanced diet to the students, improving the quality of the PNAE, since this activity was carried out by the school cooks. The nutritionist is responsible for school meals, preparation of the menu as well as monitoring the production of meals in schools.

The general purpose of Menu Planning is to achieve balanced and economical meals to satisfy a set of simultaneous requirements. The problem aims to find the best combination of items that meet the stipulated goals and requirements [3].

In this work, we present CardNutri, a software that uses a evolutionary strategy to design weekly nutritional menus for School Feeding. The software considers two fundamental aspects: (i) the cost that must be reduced and, (ii) the student's daily nutritional needs that must be achieved. Desirable properties such as: nutritional reference according to the age range provided by PNAE, variety, harmony of the culinary preparations and a financial cost limit for each type of meal are inserted in the problem as requirements constraints. The software uses a multiobjective approach considering the two aspects: (i) cost; and, (ii) nutritional reference.

The contributions of this work are twofold. First, a set of 5-day menus is obtained using the Weighted-Sum approach. The results show that the menus not only comply with the restrictions imposed by the Brazilian authorities but also are healthy and inexpensive menus. Secondly, the software is evaluated using an opinion pool among nine nutritionists to assess the usability and adequability issues. The professionals consider the software very useful and above expectations.

This paper is organized as follows: Sect. 2 presents related works. Section 3 presents the problem definition. Section 4 describes the applied algorithm. Section 5 shows the developed application. Section 6 describes the results. And, finally, Sect. 7 concludes the work.

2   Related Works

Since 1964, computer-aid techniques have been used to solve the Menu Planning Problem (MPP). The work of Balintfy [3] used Linear Programming (LP) techniques to construct the first menu planner, to find the minimum cost and to comply with the daily nutritional needs with a desired degree of variety, taking into account color and consistency requirements for a specific number of days. The proposed algorithm was applied in a hospital and was able to reduce up to 30% of the menu cost.

Kahraman and Seven [4] formulated a bi-objective diet problem and solved it applying the Linear Scalarization approach using a mono-objective Genetic Algorithm. The objectives were: to minimize the cost and to maximize the rating, according to the user's preference.

The Departments of Nutrition and Computer Science at the University of Sonora in Mexico, in 2007, developed a computer system *PlaDiet*, aiming to calculate individual meals, attending all the nutritional requirements established by a professional. A non-linear integer programming model was constructed, using Genetic Algorithms to solve it. The program allows to choose the type of meals (lunch, dinner, and intermediates), making available, in seconds, diets for any caloric need within 28 days [5].

In 2012, other software, Pro-Diet [6], proposes the prescription of menus and diet formulation, to meet the principles of healthy eating, taking into account the colors and meals variety, the combination of flavors, the texture and the provision of all nutrients. The software also used a Genetic Algorithm and can generate menus in seconds, which could, manually, take hours.

A model of Menu Planning for secondary schools in Malaysia using Integer Programming was proposed by Suliad and Ismail [7]. The aim was to maximize the variety of nutrient and to minimize the cost.

It is worthwhile to notice that our work differs from the others available in the literature. In the first place, the main goal is to produce a set of collective menus ensuring that some requirements are followed, such as color, variety, harmony. Furthermore, the menus need to be healthy and under a threshold value. In the second place, and not least important, a simple and easy-to-use software is presented. The software has some additional features making it very appealing for the nutritionists and reducing considerably the time spent in the Menu Planning.

3   Problem Definition

In this Section, we introduce the basic concepts to understand the problem and how model the MPP. We want to create a 5-day menu to meet the nutritional needs of full-time 4 to 5-year old students according to the nutritional reference of the PNAE.

Students in a full-time school day must get not less than three meals representing at least 70% of their daily nutritional needs. Table 1 shows the recommended values for 70% of daily nutritional needs (DNN) for preschool students [2]. In this table, CHO refers to carbohydrates, PTN to proteins and LIP to lipids. Other references can be found in [2]. These references were based to Food and Agriculture Organization of United Nations (FAO) [8].

Table 1. Reference values for energy, macro and micro nutrients for preschool (4 to 5 years) - 70% DNN

Energy	CHO	PTN	LIP	Fibers	Minerals (mg)			
(Kcal)	(g)	(g)	(g)	(g)	Ca	Fe	Mg	Zn
950.00	154.40	29.70	23.80	17.50	560.00	7.00	91.00	3.50

In this work, each day is composed of three meals: (i) breakfast; (ii) lunch; and, (iii) afternoon snack. Each meal has some preparations, according to its type. The breakfast is composed of three preparations: (i) bread or other cereal; (ii) milk or derivatives; and, (iii) fruit. The lunch is composed of seven preparations: (i) rice; (ii) beans; (iii) entree; (iv) side dish; (v) main dish; (vi) dessert: fruit or other; and, (vii) juice. The snack is composed of three preparations: (i) bread or other cereal; (ii) drink (milk or derivatives or juice); and, (iii) fruit.

We defined two objective functions and there is a set of constraints to be met. The first objective function aims to minimize the nutritional error, thus meeting the nutritional needs value. This function, based on the work proposed by [6], calculates the absolute difference of the sum of the nutrients and the sum of established reference. In this work, we use the established reference by PNAE. The second objective function aims to minimize the menu cost.

The principle of PNAE is to promote healthy and adequate school meals in accordance to the age group, among other characteristics. Given this, in this work, some constraints are adopted for the PNAE principles to be attended: (i) color; (ii) consistency, and (iii) variety. We also implemented other constraints: (i) cost limit for each meal for each student; (ii) nutritional error limit. The color, consistency, and variety constraints are related to the nutritional error function and, the cost limit constraint is related to the cost function. The constraints of the problem are described below:

- **Color:** A diversified meal in color ensures a balanced and nutrient-rich dietary. For this work, four predominant colors were defined: (i) yellow;

(ii) red; (iii) green; and, (iv) brown. This constraint is checked only for lunch and for the following types of preparations: (i) entree; (ii) side dish; (iii) dessert; and, (iv) drink, as directed by [6]. To ensure this color diversification, the number of repetition of the same color in a given meal should be less than or equal to 2.

- **Consistency**: A good texture transmits confidence in the quality and acceptability of food. The consistency is classified into 2 categories: (i) liquid/pasty; and, (ii) semi-solid/solid. It is not allowed to have more than one type of preparations classified as liquid/pasty in the lunch. The preparations checked are: (i) beans; (ii) side dish; and, (iii) main dish.

- **Variety**: The food variety is indispensable for all vital nutrients that can be supplied. To ensure that meals are varied, we checked the number of repeated preparations. We analyzed the replicates for: (i) same-day meals; and, (ii) meals on different days. For the same day, in the breakfast and snack meals, we checked the following preparations: (i) fruit; (ii) drink; and, (iii) cereal. For different days, in the lunch meal, we checked the following preparations: (i) entree; (ii) side dish; and, (iii) main dish.

- **Cost limit**: The Government transfers one value per school day for each student according to the school level. Thus, the cost of the menu has to be less than the pre-defined cost.

- **Nutritional Error limit**: Each day, each student has a nutritional needs according to their age group. The nutritional error constraint assures that no student will have a nutritional needs deviating from the ones presented in Table 1.

Although the MPP has a combinatorial nature, it is not modeled as such, because the variables are continuous. The problem is classified as bi-objective minimization problem and is given by:

$$
\begin{aligned}
&\text{Minimize } \mathcal{F}_1 = \text{nutritional error}\\
&\text{Minimize } \mathcal{F}_2 = \text{cost}\\
&\text{s.a:}
\begin{cases}
\text{Color Constraint}\\
\text{Consistency Constraint}\\
\text{Variety Constraint}\\
\text{Cost Limit Constraint}\\
\text{Nutritional Error Limit Constraint}
\end{cases}
\end{aligned} \tag{1}
$$

As said previously, the objective function $\mathcal{F}_1$ determines how close the nutritional value is from the reference value and objective function $\mathcal{F}_2$ determines the cost of the menu.

Figure 1 represents a possible solution representing a menu. Each menu is defined for some days, and for each day, we have meals that are composed by preparations. The meals and preparations are represented by lists (Fig. 1(a)). In the integer representation (Fig. 1(b)), each type of meal receives a number: (i) Breakfast (1), (ii) Lunch (2); and, (iii) Snack (3). The preparations are also represented by numbers and these numbers refer to the position of the list according to the type of preparation. Consider the last position of the list 1 that corresponds to breakfast in Fig. 1(b), the number 11 refers to index of a list of fruits with eleven options. In this case, this index represents a pear (Fig. 1(c)). For each type of preparation there is a list with several preparations.

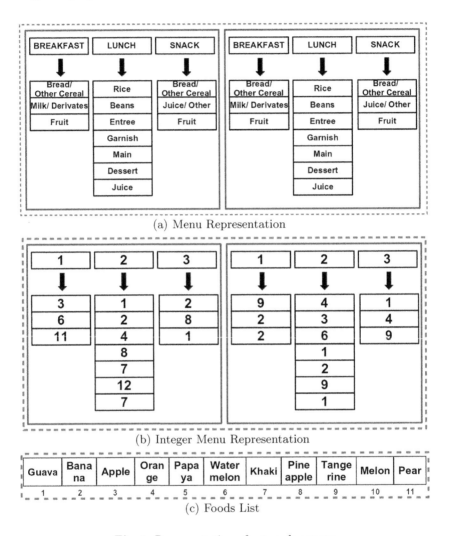

(a) Menu Representation

(b) Integer Menu Representation

(c) Foods List

Fig. 1. Representation of a two-day menu

4   Algorithm

The Menu Planning Problem (MPP) is characterized as a bi-objective problem. The problem is transformed into a mono-objective problem through a weighted-sum method and Genetic Algorithms are used to solve the problem. The weighted sum method is used not only to provide multiple solution points by varying the weights consistently, but also to provide a single solution point that reflects a priori preferences incorporated by the user.

The mono-objective problem can then be defined by Eq. 2:

$$min_{x\in\mathcal{F}_x} \sum_{i=1}^{q} \lambda_i f_i(x) \tag{2}$$

in which λ_i, $i = 1, \cdots, q$ represents the weights for each objective function, $\sum_{i=1}^{q} \lambda_i = 1, \lambda_i \geq 0$, $\mathcal{F}_x$ is the feasible set for the problem and q is the number of objective functions ($f_i(x)$).

To solve the MPP, we implemented a Genetic Algorithm. The initial population of our algorithm is generated randomly. Depending on the type of meal, we generated random values between zero and the size of the list belonging to that type. For example, since breakfast consists of a bread/other cereal, a fruit, and a drink, three random values are generated according to the size of each list. These values represent the position in the corresponding list. Then the content of that position is added to the breakfast list. In the same way, it happens with other types of meal.

The genetic operators, selection, crossover, and mutation, are defined as follows:

- **Selection**: the selection is a tournament selection in which two random individuals are chosen and, the one with the best function value is selected.
- **Crossover**: the crossover is performed within each type of meal, according to Fig. 2. Considering the crossover of breakfast and snack, the cutoff point ranges from one to three and, lunch, the cutoff points ranges from one to seven. Thus new individuals are generated preserving the genetic inheritance of its parents.
- **Mutation**: the mutation chooses a random day of the menu, and for each meal of this specific day, also chooses randomly a preparation to be changed by another one of the same type (Fig. 3). At each generation, every individual has a chance to mutate according to a mutation rate and the preparation only be exchanged for another of the same type. For example, one fruit can only be exchanged for another fruit. Thus, in a menu, 3 exchanges can be performed.

The constraints are handling via a penalization approach. The penalties for color, consistency and variety are added to the nutritional error. Color and consistency constraints are modeled by a linear function. The variety constraint is modeled by a quadratic function. The cost limit penalty is added to the cost function.

5 Application - CardNutri

Unlike the systems presented in Sect. 2, CardNutri was developed with the purpose of assisting the nutritionist responsible for the elaboration of school menus.

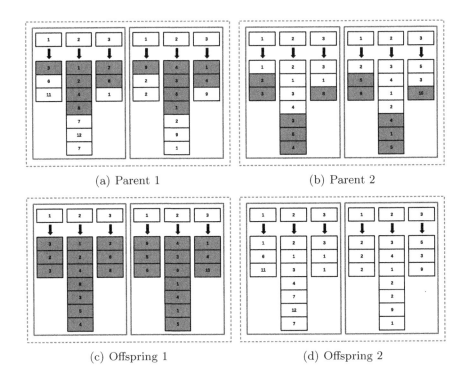

(a) Parent 1   (b) Parent 2

(c) Offspring 1   (d) Offspring 2

Fig. 2. Example of crossover: Offspring 1 gets from parent 1 preparations from the first preparation of each meal to the cut-off points (1, 4 and 2) and the cut-off points to the end of parent 2. Offspring 2 gets preparations from parent 2 of the first preparation of each meal to the cut-off points (1, 4 and 2) and the cut-off points to the end of parent 1.

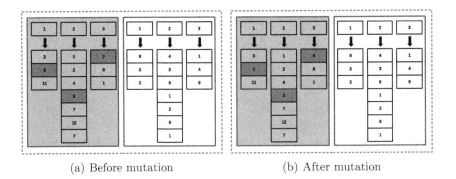

(a) Before mutation   (b) After mutation

Fig. 3. Example of a mutation that exchanges, in the breakfast, the preparation 6 by 1 of the milk or derivates; In the lunch, the mutation exchanges the preparation 8 by 3 of the side dish; In the snack meal, preparation 2 is exchanged by 5 of the bread/other cereal on the first day of a 2-day menu.

Its objective is to elaborate collective menus minimizing the total cost and attending to the daily nutritional needs of the students, respecting the nutritional reference according to the age range provided by PNAE, variety, harmony of the culinary preparations and a financial cost limit for each type of meal.

The following tools were used to develop the system:

- Java: object-oriented interpreted programming language that has a set application programming interface (API).
- NetBeans: a free integrated development environment for the development of software in several languages, for example Java.
- API Swing: graphic library responsible for graphical system interfaces, it draws necessary components.
- MySQL: database manager system that uses the SQL language (Structured Query Language), is compatible with several programming languages.
- JFreeChart: graphics library that supports formats such as: PDF, EPS, PNG, JPEG and others.

The software works with three main bases: ingredients, culinary preparations and nutritional references. The structure of each basis and its characteristics will be presented below:

- **Ingredients**: items of culinary preparations. To fill this basis, the Brazilian Table of Food Composition - TACO [9], elaborated by the Nucleus of Studies and Research in Food, was adopted. It consists of 597 foods, with nutritional values for every 100 grams. As this table does not contain all the existing ingredients, CardNutri allows you to register more ingredients. The PNAE recommends that the acquisition of some food products from smallholder or family farms. The values of the products belonging to Family Agriculture were taken from the Pricing Table Practiced in the PAA - Food Procurement Program of Minas Gerais - Year 2016, of the National Supply Company - CONAB [10] and the not-listed product values were taken from the online Supermarket VipFácil [11].

  Characteristics: Name; Price (R$) $(BRL - R\$1.00 \approx USD - \$0.31)$; Nutrients: (i) Energy (kcal), (ii) Proteins (g), (iii) Carbohydrates (g), (iv) Lipids (g), (v) Fibers (g), (vi) Minerals: Calcium (mg), Iron (mg), Zinc (mg) and Magnesium (mg); Group belonging to: 1. Cereals and derivatives, 2. Vegetables, Vegetables and Derivatives, 3. Fruit and Derivatives, 4. Fats and Oils, 5. Fish and seafood, 6. Meat and dairy products, 7. Milk and Derivatives, 8. Beverages, 9. Eggs and Derivatives, 10. Sugar products, 11. Miscellaneous, 12. Other processed products, 13. Ready-to-eat food, 14. Legumes and Derivatives, 15. Nuts and seeds.
- **Culinary Preparations**: individual culinary preparations. These were taken from the "School Food Menu" of Minas Gerais [12] and Goiás [13].

  Characteristics: Name; Type: 1. Primary side dish: (i) Rice, (ii) Beans; 2. Entree, 3. Second Side dish, 4. Main dish, 5. Dessert: (i) fruits, (ii) Other 6.

Drink: (i) Juice, (ii) Other; 7. Bread/other Cereal ; Color: (i) yellow, (ii) red, (iii) green, (iv) brown; Consistency: (i) Liquid/pasty, (ii) Semi-solid/solid; Ingredients.

– **Nutritional References**: The references were taken from Resolution 26/2013 [2]. The percentage of daily nutritional needs (NND) is: 20% that equals a meal for urban schools and 30% that is equivalent to a meal for indigenous or quilombola schools and 70% for a full-time school day.

Characteristics: Age: (i) 7 to 11 months, (ii) 1 to 3 years, (iii) 4 to 5 years, (iv) 6 to 10 years, (v) 11 to 15 years, (vi) 16 to 18 years, (vii) 19 a 30 years and (viii) 31 to 60 years; Percentage: (i) 20%, (ii) 30%, (iii) 70% and (iv) 100%; Nutrients: (i) Energy (kcal), (ii) Proteins (g), (iii), Carbohydrates (g), (iv) Lipids (g), (v) Fibers (g), (vi) Minerals: Calcium (mg), Iron (mg), Zinc (mg) and Magnesium (mg).

For generating the menu, it is necessary to inform: the types of meals: 1. Breakfast: composed of a fruit, a drink (milk or derivatives) and a bread (or other cereals); 2. Lunch: (i) Primary Side Dish: rice and beans, (ii) Entree: salad, (iii) Second Side Dish: vegetable or pasta, (iv) Main Dish: meat, (v) Dessert: pudding or fruit, (vi) Drink: juice or milk and derivatives; 3. Snack: has the same attributes of breakfast, including juice as a drink; maximum value for each type of meal; the nutritional reference to be reached and the number of days. Subsequently, all the obtained menus and its characteristics are presented. The system makes it possible to save the menus in a database as well as exporting it in pdf format.

5.1   Graphical Interface

The CardNutri interface is simple and user-friendly. It allows: register, change and deletes: ingredients, culinary preparations and nutritional references; generate menu; consult meals and menus; generate reports (pdf format): ingredients, culinary preparations, nutritional references, meals and menus; view system information; exit.

Figures 4, 5 and 6 show the registration, alteration and exclusion screens of ingredients, culinary preparation and nutritional references. Through the "Search" button it is possible to consult all the registered items. Figure 7 illustrates the menu generation screen. It is necessary to define what types of meals and the maximum value to be paid for each of these types, the nutritional reference to be reached and the number of days, in this case corresponding to a weekly menu. The "Advanced" button corresponds to the essential settings for the technique to be applied. Observe that it is not mandatory to fill the field in since the settings are pre-defined. However, tt can be modified when needed.

Figure 8 shows the menu elaborated by the system. In this screen, you can see the number of menus generated, their composition, value and nutritional error. The graphic shows the Pareto curve of the menus found, making it easier for

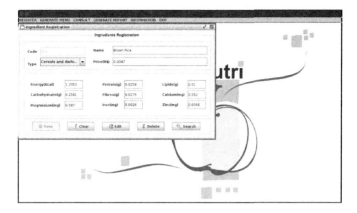

Fig. 4. Registration, alteration and exclusion of ingredients

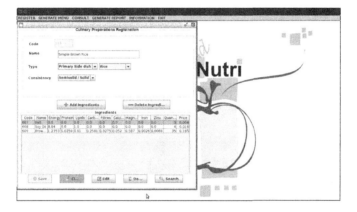

Fig. 5. Registration, alteration and exclusion of culinary preparation

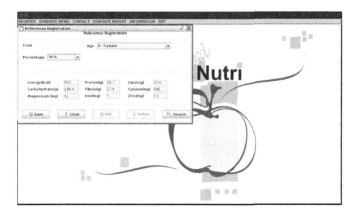

Fig. 6. Registration, alteration and exclusion of nutritional reference

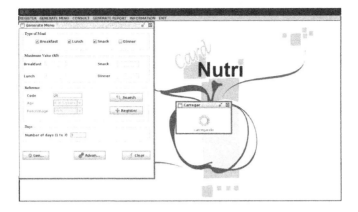

Fig. 7. Menu generation screen

the nutritionist to choose one. When you click on a point on the graphic, the corresponding weekly menu appears on the screen. The "File" menu allows you to save, and export it in a pdf format, the current menu or all menus.

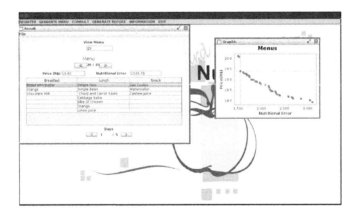

Fig. 8. Menu screen elaborated by the system

6   Results

In this Section we evaluate the CardNutri usability and adequability of the menus.

6.1   Solutions Evaluation

The multiobjective optimization is characterized by returning a set of efficient solutions (Pareto set) representing a trade-off between the objective functions and, after that, by allowing the user to choose among the solutions, the one that best suit her/him.

The problem is solved via the Weighted-Sum method. The weight is discretized in the interval [0 1], with a step of 0.1. It is an user parameter and can be easily modified. For each weight, the GA is executed 30 times. After all GA runs, the solutions are combined and a non-dominated procedure is applied to obtain the final non-dominated set of the solutions.

The parameters for GA are: 100 individuals in the population, 1000 iterations, crossover rate equal to 0.8, mutation rate equal to 0.05, three meals daily in 5 days on the week. The limit values of the meals are fixed at: breakfast: R\$ 2.00, lunch: R\$ 4.00 and snack: R\$ 2.00. The age group considered was 4 to 5 years, equivalent to the full-time preschool ($BRL - R\$1.00 \approx USD - \$0.31$).

Figure 9 shows the combined Pareto front composed of 10 different menus. Analysing this figure, it is possible to see that the algorithm found solutions with nutritional error varying, approximately, from 0.23 and 1.55 and total cost varying from R\$ 18.91 to R\$ 25.32. The range of these values complies with the pre-defined nutritional error limit and the financial cost limit. It is also worthwhile to mention that the maximum value to be paid for a 5-day menu is R\$ 40.00 and the 5-day menu with the highest cost (R\$ 25.32) represents only 63% of that value. Considering the nutritional value for a 5-day menu, the sum of all nutrients is, according to the reference, 4434.50 and the menu which is further away from the reference has a nutritional value of 4434.76, deviating only 0.006% from that.

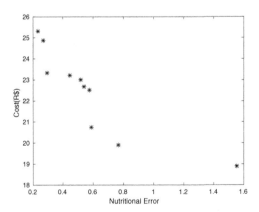

Fig. 9. Combined Pareto front of menus

It can not be said that the entire set of solutions was generated. However, despite deficiencies with respect to depicting the Pareto optimal set, the results show that the obtained 5-days menus using the proposed methodology not only comply with the restrictions imposed by the authorities but also produce inexpensive and healthy menus.

Table 2. A 5-day Menu generated by CardNutri with the respective values of nutrients

Meal	Day 1	Day 2	Day 3	Day 4	Day 5
Breakfast	Carrot Cake	Nutritive Cake	Banana Cake	Bread with butter	Nutritive Cake
	Khaki	Banana	Pineapple	Melon	Pineapple
	Fruit Vitamin	Avocado Vitamin	Avocado Vitamin	Chocolate Milk	Avocado Vitamin
Lunch	Greek Rice with Chicken	Rice with Broccoli and Chicken	Simple Rice	Rice with Scrambled Eggs	Simple Rice
	Simple Bean	Simple Bean	Liquid Bean	Simple Bean	Simple Bean
	Braised okra	Lettuce, Potato and Carrot Salad	Watercress Salad	Chard and Carrot Salad	Beet and Carrot
	Cabbage baba	Pumpkin Cream with Green Corn	Bean soup	Potato and Carrot Creamy Soup	Polenta à Bolognese
	Meatballs In Sauce	Meat quibe	Chicken Stew	Quibe Oven	Pork steak
	Tangerina	Papaya	Caramelized Banana	Apple	Papaya
	Grape Juice	Cashew Juice	Grape Juice	Cashew Juice	Mango Juice
Snack	Banana Cake	Banana Cake	Sweet Cookie	Salt Cracker	Bread with tuna fish
	Papaya	Papaya	Orange	Pineapple	Apple
	Cashew Juice	Grape Juice	Grape Juice	Caramelized Milk	Grape Juice
PTN	31.2209	37.9207	28.9064	35.1206	41.3195
LIP	33.2137	26.3383	26.5924	25.3378	34.3969
CHO	202.2888	194.1018	176.7098	161.5024	196.8131
Fiber	22.3358	20.0105	20.5028	15.7667	20.3768
Calcium	379.6543	379.8265	395.1736	459.4696	368.8871
Magnesium	209.0066	217.3593	226.2965	177.8565	213.5767
Iron	5.2033	5.8563	8.0195	6.1787	5.742
Zinc	4.4691	5.1635	4.3459	5.3078	5.8109
Nutrients sum	887.3925	886.5769	886.5469	886.5401	886.923
Cost (R$) 18.91					

6.2 Software Evaluation

CardNutri was evaluated by nine nutritionists with experience in school feeding, through a questionnaire based on the proposed Technology Acceptance Model (TAM) [14]. Participants had to use the system by performing a task list developed to help answer the questionnaire. The questionnaire contains 20 positive statements grouped into five categories: Perceived Facility, refering to the degree to which a user believes that using the system will not involve effort; Perceived Utility, refering to the degree to which a user believes that using the system will improve performance; External Variables, refering to system characteristics and training; Attitude in Relation, refering to the user's feeling of being favorable or not in relation to the use of the system; Behavioral Intention of Use, representinf the strength of intention to use the system in the future.

The questionnaire uses the five-point Likert Scale [15], which is a type of psychometric scale, where the user specifies the level of agreement or

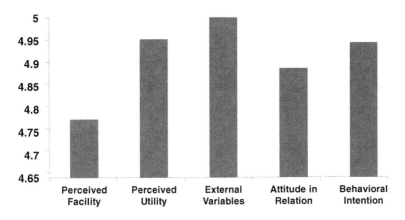

Fig. 10. Means of evaluation questionnaire categories.

disagreement, from a statement. Each point on the scale is represented by a value in parentheses. As the affirmations are positive, the point "I fully agree" has the highest value. The levels used were: I fully disagree (1), partially disagree (2), neither agree nor I disagree (3), partially agree (4), I fully agree (5). Another technique used was Thinking Aloud [16], a strategy of thinking out loud. Participants need to express their opinions and suggestions during the evaluation or while performing some task [14].

Figure 10 shows the average value for each category evaluated. The Figure shows that the Perceived Facility had the lowest average value (4.78). It is explained by the fact that some of the participants believe that there is a mental effort in the interaction with the system, mainly at the beginning. However, it is easy to use. Regarding Perceived Utility (average value = 4.95), the system adds value to the work of the participants, increasing their performance, efficiency and productivity. Regarding the External Variables (average value = 5.0), they agreed that they had a good training and the explanation was clear. Regarding Attitude in Relation (average value = 4.89), it would be very good to use the system instead of the manual method currently in use. And finally, on Behavioral Intention (average value = 4.94), if they had access to the system, they would intend to use it.

Through the Thinking Aloud technique, all the nine nutritionists have agreed that the system reached the proposed goal of automatically developing nutritious and inexpensive menus. Despite the high rating given by nutritionists, they suggested that the system should have the option of changing a preparation after the menu has been elaborated, adding home measures, recipes, and other nutritional reference tables and calculating the value of Energy (kcal) through the macronutrients.

7   Conclusions

This paper presented the system of Elaboration of Nutritional Menu for School Feeding - CardNutri, developed to assist nutritionists in the automatic elaboration of menus. The goal was to plan menus automatically, in a fast and diversified manner, with low cost while satisfying the requirements established by the government via the Brazilian School Eating Programme (PNAE) guidelines. The menus were generated via a Genetic Algorithm and with the results obtained it was possible to conclude that the proposed objectives were reached and the restrictions established by the government were respected. CardNutri was evaluated by nutritionists with experience in school feeding, through a questionnaire based on the proposed Technology Acceptance Model. In general, results showed that the system was well-accepted and some suggestions to improve the usability were given. As future work, the nutrient-rating function to take into account the minimum and maximum macronutrient limits defined by FAO/WHO can be used to improve the results and to apply a multiobjective algorithm such as NSGA-II and compare the two approaches.

Acknowledgements. This work was partially funded by CEFET-MG, CNPq, FAPEMIG and CAPES.

References

1. Brazil: Food Guide for the Brazilian population, 2 edn. Ministry of Health, Secretariat of Health Care, Department of Basic Attention, Brazilia, Brazil (2014)
2. Brazil: Ministry of education. National fund for the development of education (FNDE) PNAE: School feeding (2017). http://www.fnde.gov.br/index.php/programas/pnae
3. Balintfy, J.: Menu planning by computer. Comun. ACM **7**(4), 255–259 (1964)
4. Kahraman, A., Seven, H.A.: Healthy daily meal planner. In: Genetic and Evolutionary Computation Conference - Undergraduate Student Workshop (GECCO 2005 UGWS), pp. 25–29 (2005)
5. Flores, P., Cota, M.G., Ramírez, D., Jiménez, I.J., Raygoza, J.A., Morales, L.C., Galaviz, S., Espinoza, A., Orozco, M.E.: Pladiet: Un sistema de cómputo para el diseño de dietas individualizas utilizando algoritmos genéticos (2007)
6. Gomes, F.R.: Pro-diet: Automatic generator of personalized menus based on Genetic Algorithm. Masters dissertation, Federal University of Uberlândia, Uberlândia (2012)
7. Sufahani, S., Ismail, Z.: A new menu planning model for malaysian secondary schools using optimization approach. Appl. Math. Sci. **8**(151), 7511–7518 (2014)
8. United Nations: Food and agriculture organization of the united nations (2017). http://www.fao.org/home/en/
9. NEPA: Nucleus of studies and researches in food. Brazilian table of food composition, Taco (2011). http://www.unicamp.br/nepa/taco/tabela.php?ativo=tabela
10. CONAB: National supply company (2017). http://www.conab.gov.br/
11. VIPFACIL: Bh online supermarket (2017). https://www.vipfacil.com.br/
12. Brazil: State Secretary of Minas Gerais, 1st edn. School Meals menus (2014)

13. Brazil: State Secretary of Goiás, 1st edn. School Meals menus (2014)
14. Davis, F.D.: Perceived usefulness, perceived ease of use, and user acceptance of information technology. MIS Q. **13**(3), 319–340 (1989)
15. Likert, R.: A Technique for the Measurement of Attitudes. No. No 136–165 in a Technique for the Measurement of Attitudes, publisher not identified (1932)
16. Lewis, C.: Using the "Thinking Aloud" Method in Cognitive Interface Design. Research report, IBM T.J. Watson Research Center (1982)

Author Index

Printed in the United States
By Bookmasters